PRICE

ANTIQUES AND COLLECTIBLES

PRICE GUIDE TO

ANTIQUES AND COLLECTIBLES

SEVENTEENTH EDITION

RINKER ENTERPRISES, INC.

HOUSE OF COLLECTIBLES
THE BALLANTINE PUBLISHING GROUP • NEW YORK

Sale of this book without a front cover may be unauthorized. If this book is coverless, it may have been reported to the publisher as "unsold or destroyed" and neither the author nor the publisher may have received payment for it.

Important Notice. All of the information, including valuations, in this book has been compiled from the most reliable sources, and every effort has been made to eliminate errors and questionable data. Nevertheless, the possibility of error, in a work of such immense scope, always exists. The publisher will not be held responsible for losses that may occur in the purchase, sale, or other transaction of items because of information contained herein. Readers who feel they have discovered errors are invited to write and inform us, so they may be corrected in subsequent editions. Those seeking further information on the topics covered in this book are advised to refer to the complete line of Official Price Guides published by the House of Collectibles.

Copyright ©1999 by Rinker Enterprises, Inc.

All rights reserved under International and Pan–American Copyright Conventions

HC House of Collectibles and colophon are trademarks of Random House, Inc.

Published by: House of Collectibles
The Ballantine Publishing Group
201 East 50th Street
New York, New York 10022

Distributed by The Ballantine Publishing Group, a division of Random House, Inc., New York, and simultaneously in Canada by Random House of Canada Limited, Toronto.

www.randomhouse.com/BB/

Manufactured in the United States of America

ISSN: 1050–6144

ISBN: 0–676–60178–2

Seventeenth Edition: April 1999
10 9 8 7 6 5 4 3 2 1

CONTENTS

Introduction

The antiques market is divided into three basic parts: (1) antiques, objects made before 1945, (2) collectibles, objects made between 1945 and the late 1970s, and (3) desirables, objects made between the late 1970s and the present. Antiques and collectibles have a stable secondary market. Desirables have a speculative secondary market. *The Official Price Guide to Antiques and Collectibles, 17th Edition,* provides coverage for all three segments.

This is a general price guide. It provides a sampling of objects commonly found in the antiques marketplace. A few highly desirable, scarce items are included in most category listings to show the high end.

Obviously, it is impossible in a general price guide to list every object available in a collecting category. Hopefully, this book provides you with sufficient comparable objects to value the one you own. If it does not, the category introductions usually include information on select reference books, periodicals, and collectors' clubs where you can find more detailed information.

The Official Price Guide to Antiques and Collectibles is a field guide, a place to find basic information and a reference source as to where to turn to next.

The antiques market is experiencing a major transition as it prepares to enter the 21st century. A new breed of young collectors, more me focused than past focused, the Internet, and a trendy market are three contributing factors. Traditionalist collectors watch with dismay as their favorite collecting categories stabilize or decline in value and with disgust as contemporary desirables such as Beanie Babies capture the public's imagination.

There will be a strong, vibrant antiques and collectibles market in the 21st century. However, it will be a different market in terms of what and how objects are collected. There are exciting times ahead. There is every reason to believe the changes that are occurring and coming will be positive.

While the computer will never replace traditional printed price guides such as this one, it continues to have an exponential impact on the antiques and collectibles field. Check out these auction (www.auctionuniverse.com and www.ebay.com), direct sale (www.antiqnet.com, www.collectoronline.com, www.csmonline.com, and www.tias.com), and periodical and specialty sites (www.mainantiquedigest.com and www.rinker.com). Look for this list to triple or quadruple by the time the next edition of this book is published.

Finally, remember that the real joy of collecting is not found in the financial value of objects but the pleasure that comes from owning, living with, and enjoying the object.

COLLECTING TIPS

Condition is everything. The difference between very good and near mint can be the difference between $100 and $1000 or more!

Be a tough grader. Overgrading is a common mistake. If an item needs restoration, know what that will cost before you buy. Also remember that a restored antique is generally worth much less than an unrestored piece in pristine condition.

Just because something is scarce doesn't mean it is valuable. In today's trendy market, desirability is a major value key.

Do your homework! The information age has created an explosion of material on all subjects and topics. Taking advantage of a public library's book search service is well worth the time. Antiques and collectibles reference books are often expensive, but a $50 book can often save you from many $100 mistakes.

Learning the ordinary teaches about the extraordinary. Most pieces are far more common than people realize.

What goes up often comes down. Record prices are reported. A market that is slowly ebbing away is rarely reported.

Always ask the seller to provide a guarantee of authenticity. Get it in writing. If you do not ask for a guarantee, you had better know what you are buying.

AUCTION BUYING TIPS

Always thoroughly examine every piece before you bid on it. If you have not examined it, DO NOT BID.

Always set a dollar limit for yourself before you start bidding. Do not let auction frenzy drive your bidding, and do not forget to calculate in the buyer's penalty (premium).

Make certain the auctioneer sees your bidding. If you bid with just the nod of a head, the auctioneer may be selling to the person in front of you.

And yes, if your nose itches, you can scratch it without buying a fifteen–foot chandelier; just do not stare the auctioneer in the eye while you're doing it.

BUYING VERSUS SELLING PRICES

A dealer must make his profit to stay in business, and many businesses are expensive to run. The difference between a dealer's buying price and his selling price must cover the rent, the car, and everything else. Hence, the selling price of an item may be only a fraction of the price tagged in the window (or quoted in this guide!), especially for inexpensive items.

AUCTION SELLING TIPS

Choose your auction house by the service they offer, not the estimate they quote. You cannot deposit an estimate in the bank.

Do not be greedy. An item with a high estimate and/or a reserve scares away potential buyers. Once an item has failed to sell (or "bought in"), it is harder to sell the next time.

When evaluating the contract you are asked to sign, consider these points: (1) what is the condition?, (2) who pays for photographs?, (3) who pays for insurance?, (4) what is the reserve (or minimum price) set at?, and (4) when is payment made?

PRICES

The prices in this book represent the average price that an informed buyer will pay a knowledgeable and specialized dealer for these items.

The antiques and collectibles market is not the stock market. Prices do not tick up and down on a daily basis.

Collecting is not the same as investing. If the value of your collection increases with time and rising markets, consider it a bonus. Most collections do not make money; they consume it.

SPOTTING PROBLEM PIECES

The ever–increasing availability of cheap labor and expensive machines has resulted in the production of countless fakes in all fields. Most dealers are honest, but many honest dealers get fooled. To beware, you need to be aware. Here are a few tips:

1. If it looks new, assume it is new.
2. Assume every object is bad. Make it prove to you that it is period.
3. Beware of bargains. They deserve a very careful second and third look.
4. Learn the styles of the times. Many fakes give themselves away because they just don't "feel right."
5. Learn to recognize tool marks and which tools were used when.
6. Visit museum gift shops and other places where high quality reproductions are sold.
7. Subscribe to *Antique & Collectors Reproduction News* (Box 71174, Des Moines, IA 50325). It is a great monthly report on fakes and reproductions.

USING THIS GUIDE

Sections are laid out by category. The term "sight" preceding a measurement refers to visible image size. Abbreviations are used throughout. Some that appear most often are:

Amer. – American
attrib. – attributed
bkgd. – background
c. – circa
C – century
circ. – circular
dec. – decoration or decorated
dia. – diameter
ea. – each
emb. – embossed
ft/ftd. – feet or footed
h – height or high
j. – jewels
k – karat
l – length
mah. – mahogany
mkd. – marked
orig. – original
pr. – pair
pt. – pint
ptd. – painted
rect. – rectangular
qt. – quart
sq. – square
uph. – upholstered
w – width
w/ – with
wo/ – without

COLLECTING–RELATED PUBLICATIONS

Hundred of periodicals on antiques and collectibles exist, some for specialized areas. Rinker Enterprises recommends the following general and regional periodicals:

U.S. Publications

Antique Gazette, 6949 Charlotte Pike, Suite 106, Nashville, TN 37209; (800) 660-6143; Fax: (800) 660-6143.

Antique Journal, 1684 Decoto Road, Suite 166, Union City, CA 94587; (510) 791-8592; Fax: (510) 523-5262.

Antique Review, PO Box 538, Worthington, OH 43085; (614) 885-9757; Fax: (614) 885-9762.

The Antique Shoppe, PO Box 2175, Keystone Heights, FL 32656; (352) 475-1679.

The Antique Trader Weekly, PO Box 1050, Dubuque, IA 52004-1050; (800) 334-7165; Fax: (800) 531-0880.

Antique Trader's Collector Magazine & Price Guide, PO Box 1050, Dubuque, IA 52004-1050; (800) 334-7165.

The Antique Traveler, PO Box 656, 109 East Broad Street, Mineola, TX 75773; (903) 569-2487; Fax: (903) 569-9080.

Antique Week (Central and Eastern Editions), 27 North Jefferson Street, PO Box 90, Knightstown, IN 46148; (800) 876-5133; Fax: (800) 695-8153.

Antiques & Collectables, 500 Fensler, Suite 205, PO Box 12589, El Cajon, CA 92022; (619) 593-2930; Fax: (619) 447-7187.

Antiques & Collecting Magazine, 1006 South Michigan Avenue, Chicago, IL 60605; (800) 762-7576; Fax: (312) 939-0053.

Antiques and the Arts Weekly, The Bee Publishing Company, PO Box 5503, Newtown, CT 06470-5503; (203) 426-8036; Fax: (203) 426-1394.

Arizona Antique News, PO Box 26536, Phoenix, AZ 85068; (602) 943-9137.

Arts & Antiques, 3 East 54th Street, New York, NY 10022-3108; (800) 274-7594.

Collectors' Eye, Woodside Avenue, Suite 300, Northport, NY 11768; (516) 261-4100; Fax: (516) 261-9684.

Collectors Journal, 1800 West D Street, PO Box 601, Vinton, IA 52349-0601; (319) 472-4763; Fax: (816) 474-1427.

Cotton & Quail Antique Trail, 205 East Washington Street, PO Box 326, Monticello, FL 32345; (800) 757-7755; Fax: (850) 997-3090.

Collectors News, 506 Second Street, PO Box 156, Grundy Center, IA 50638; (800) 352-8039; Fax: (319) 824-3414.

Great Lakes Trader, 132 South Putnam Street, Williamston, MI 48895; (800) 785-6367; Fax: (517) 655-5380.

The Magazine Antiques, 575 Broadwar, New York, NY 10012; (800) 925-8059; Fax: (212) 941-2897.

Maine Antique Digest, 911 Main Street, PO Box 1429; Waldoboro, ME 04572; (207) 832-4888; Fax: (207) 832-7341.

MassBay Antiques, 2 Washington Street, PO Box 192, Ipswich, MA 01938; (508) 777-7070.

The MidAtlantic Antiques Magazine, Henderson Newspapers, Inc., 304 South Chestnut Street, PO Box 908, Henderson, NC 27536; (919) 492-4001; Fax: (919) 430-0125.

New England Antiques Journal, 4 Church Street, PO Box 120, Ware, MA 01082; (800) 432-3505; Fax: (413) 967-6009.

New York City's Antique News, PO Box 2054, New York, NY 10159-2054; (212) 725-0344; Fax: (212) 532-7294.

Old Stuff, VBM Printers, Inc., 336 North Davis, PO Box 1084, McMinnville, OR 97128; (503) 434-5386; Fax: (503) 472-2601.

The Old Times, PO Box 340, Maple Lake, MN 55358; (800) 539-1810; Fax: (320) 963-6499.

Renninger's Antique Guide, PO Box 495, Lafayette Hill, PA 19444; (610) 828-4614; Fax: (610) 834-1599.

Southern Antiques, PO Drawer 1107, Decatur, GA 30031; (888) 800-4997; Fax: (404) 286-9727.

Treasure Chest, PO Box 245, North Scituate, RI 02857-0245; (800) 557-9662; Fax: (401) 647-0051.

20th Century Folk Art News, 5967 Blackberry Lane, Buford, GA 30518; (770) 932-1000; Fax: (770) 932-0506.

Unravel the Gavel, 9 Hurricane Road, #1, Belmont, NH 03220; (603) 524-4281.

Warman's Today's Collector, Krause Publications, 700 East State Street, Iola, WI 54990; (800) 258-0929; Fax: (715) 445-4087.

West Coast Peddler, PO Box 5134, Whittier, CA 90607; (562) 698-1718; Fax: (562) 698-1500.

Yesteryear, PO Box 2, Princeton, WI 54968; (920) 787-4808; Fax: (920) 787-7381.

Foreign Publications

Antique Showcase, Trojan Publishing Corp., 103 Lakeshore Road, Suite 202, St. Catherine, Ontario, Canada L2N 2T6; (905) 646-0995.

Antique Trade Gazette, 17 Whitcomb Street, London WC2H 7PL, England.

Antiques and Collectibles Trader, PO Box 38095, 550 Eglinton Avenue West, Toronto, Ontario, Canada M5N 3A8; (416) 410-7620.

Carter's Homes, Antiques & Collectables, Carter's Promotions Pty. Ltd., Locked Bag 3, Terrey Hills, NSW 2084, Australia; Tel: (02) 9450 0011; Fax: (02) 945-2532.

The Upper Canadian, PO Box 653, Smiths Falls, Ontario, Canada K7A 4T6; (613) 283-1168; Fax: (613) 283-1345.

Advertising Memorabilia

It's too early to quote prices on Joe Camel advertising items, but our prediction is that the infamous purveyor of Camel cigarettes will stalk future collectibles sales for many years.

The diversity of advertising is astounding. Collectors can concentrate on eras, products, companies, signs, tins, trade cards, watches, premiums, dolls, figural displays, toys, etc. In recent years interest has increased in post-World War II advertising. Adding these collectors to the pre-war collectors creates a huge and growing market. The prices listed below are for items in excellent or better condition. Although some wear is expected on older items it should not be substantial or interfere with the visual appeal of the item. Condition for newer items is near mint. The other section in this book that contains advertising and promotional material is Toys and Playthings. For further reading see *Hake's Guide to Advertising Collectibles,* Ted Hake, Wallace Homestead, Radnor, PA, 1992; *Advertising Character Collectibles,* Warren Dotz, Collector Books, Paducah, KY, 1993, 1997 value update; and *Huxford's Collectible Advertising, 4th Edition,* Sharon and Bob Huxford, Collector Books, Paducah, KY, 1994.

	LOW	HIGH
7-Up Topper and Bottle, "Top O' the Mornin!"	$24	$30
Admiration Cigar Sign, tin, easel back, lady looking in mirror, 7.5" x 5.75"	250	325
Allen A Silk Stockings Postcard, 5.5" x 3.25"	10	12
Allied Mills Sign, diecut porcelain, grain bag shape, 23" x 24.5"	300	350
American Fireworks Distributing Co. Catalog, 26 pp, 1932, 8.25" x 10.5"	150	175
American League Cigar Box Label	10	12
American National Bank Li'l Abner Bank, "Can of Coins," 1953, 4.75" h	100	125
Amoco American Oil Company Blotter, "Looks Good for '48," 5.5" x 2.75"	20	25
Amoco Blotter, "Uncle Sam, You Come First," Santa, artist J.W. Wilkinson, 5.5" x 2.75"	20	25
Ansco Film Sign, diecut tin, 2-sided, film box shape, 10" x 24"	100	150
Apple Jacks Clicker	10	15
Armstrong Carriage Paperweight, glass, round, horse-drawn carriage, 3" dia	175	225
A.T.A. Nelson Co. Paperweight, glass, rect., naked woman behind leather hide, 2.5" x 4"	130	160
Atlantic Hi-Arc Blotter, "For Driving Power," 6" x 3"	20	25
Batchelder & Lincoln Company Calendar, "A Good Catch," full pad, 1908, 21.25" x 14.75"	125	175
Beech Nut Valentine Card	25	30
Big Wolf Cigar Box Label	5	8
Bill Dugan 5¢ Cigar Sign, cardboard, Dugan portrait, framed, 14.5" dia	300	350
Bleriot Cigar Box Label	20	25
Blue-Jay Corn Plasters Display, cardboard, 2 drawers, 2 hobos walking along railroad tracks, 1903, 6.5" x 9.25" x 10.25"	100	150
Bonnie Ladd Sundial Shoes Clicker	38	42
Borden's Milk Truck, 1940s, 9" l	300	500
Boston Herald Tip Tray, 3.5" dia	75	125
Bromo Seltzer Tip Tray, 1930s	60	90
Brotherhood Overalls Pocket Mirror, celluloid, 2" dia	200	275
Brown's Jumbo Bread Sign, diecut tin, circus elephant, 12.75" x 15"	300	350
Brown's Oyl for Fords Sign, tin, 13.5" x 20"	575	625
Brown's Shoes Sign, emb. tin over cardboard	175	200
Buffalo Pitts Calendar, Indian and buffalo, 1922	320	430
Buick Authorized Service Sign, round, blue and white, 42" dia	150	200
Bull Dog Malt Liquor Decal, 1940s, 7" sq	8	10
Bull Durham Bullfighters Sign, cardboard, 1920s, 14" x 22"	500	800

	LOW	HIGH
Bunny Bread Sign, red and white emb. tin, 1940s, 3.5" x 28"	60	90
Burma Shave Signs, wooden, 1930s, 10" x 3.5", set of 3	300	530
Buster Brown Bread Sign, emb. tin, Buster and Tige, 19.75" x 27.75"	200	250
Buster Brown Hosiery Clicker	35	40
Buster Brown Shoes Pocket Mirror, celluloid, "The little girl on the other side should wear Buster Brown Shoes," 1.75" dia	150	200
Cadillac Official Service Sign, rect., blue, white, 30" x 40"	300	400
Camel Cigarettes Ashtray, round, tin, logo in center, 1950s, 3.5" dia	8	12
Camel Cigarettes Booklet "Know Your Nerves," 1934, 3" x 4"	10	17
Camel Cigarettes Calendar, 1963	18	22
Campbell Kids Silverware, 3-piece set, 1940s	35	45
Campbell Kids Chef Rubber Squeeze Doll, 1950, 7" h	60	90
Canada Dry Bottle Cardboard Cutout Sign, c1940s, 40" x 11"	20	50
Canadian Club Sign, for a ceiling fan, round, 1930s, 7" dia	30	45
Cap'N Frosty Clicker	12	15
Carnation Milk Tip Tray, 1930s	45	75
Carter's Union Suits Sign, tin, young man wearing union suit, framed, 10.75" x 6.75"	175	200
Castles Ice Cream Clicker	20	30
Cavalier Cigarettes Pack Holder, plastic	20	25
Ceresota Flour Match Safe, boy slicing bread, 1915, 5.5" h	200	300
Chandlers Shoes Bill Clip	25	30
Charlie the Tuna Telephone, 1980s, 10" h	60	80
Cherry Smash Porcelain Syrup Dispenser, 1910, 16" h	800	1400
Chevrolet Clicker, "Click with Nicky"	18	24
Chevrolet Clock, electric, neon, 19" dia	500	600
Chevrolet Motor Cars Calendar, 1920, 14.5" h	300	500
Chevrolet Super Service Sign, round, yellow, blue, and white, 42" dia	600	750
Chiclets Gum Display Box, glass top, w/ orig scalloped spoon, 8" x 10"	100	150
Chief Rabban Cigar Box Label	12	15
Chivas Regal Ashtray, Wade China, triangular, 1950s, 11.5" l	8	12
Chrysler Plymouth Service Sign, round, yellow, red, and blue, 42" dia	400	500
City Club Crushed Cubes Tobacco Upright Pocket Tin, 1935, 4.5" h	175	225
Clanky Chocolate Syrup Container, 1965, 10" h	25	35
Cleo Cola Clicker	45	50
Colonel Sanders Plastic Nodder, 1965, 7" h	50	70
Columbia Bicycles Trade Card, cyclists at night, 1910	15	25
Columbia Oil Gas Sign, Central Oil Gas Stove Co., metal, c1891, 10.5" x 11"	150	175
Converse Athletic Shoes Blotter, 5.75" x 3.25"	15	18
Country Gentleman Cigar Cutter, emb., 3" h	125	175
Crackle Puppet, 1984, 4" h	8	12
Crest Sparkly Telephone, 1980s, 11" h	20	30
Crosley Sales & Service Sign, round, white and red, 42" dia	400	450
Crown Millinery Adv, 1920s	6	8
Crown Premium Motor Oil Bank, 2.5" dia, 2.75" h	20	30
Dad's Root Beer Sign, emb. tin, oversized soda bottle, 29" x 13.5"	125	150
Dairy Queen Whistle, plastic cone	12	18
Dandy Bread Door Handle, metal, loaf and slices, 1940s, 3" x 13"	50	70
De Laval Cream Separator Figural Match Holder, 1915, 6.5" h	120	180
De Soto Auto Banner, red, gold, and black fringed silk, 1951, 38" x 66"	500	900
Diamond Beverages Sign, porcelain, 13.75" x 41.75"	150	175
Diamond Dye Cabinet, "The Governess," emb. tin front w/ children playing in park, 1906, 23" x 30" x 9"	400	500
Diamond T Trucks Brochure, fold out, 6 pp, 1928, 11" x 8.5"	50	60

	LOW	HIGH
Diana, Schmidt & Co. Cigar Box Label, 21 Bowery, NY	50	60
Dino the Dinosaur Green Plastic Bank (Sinclair), 1965, 4" l	18	22
Dino the Dinosaur Inflatable Toy, 1965, 12" h	20	30
Dino the Dinosaur Soap, orig. box, 1964, 3.5" l	8	12
Dixon "Best" Pencils Blotter, 3.25" x 6"	15	18
Dobbins' Soap, 6 Trade Cards, Shakespeare's "Six Ages of Man"	20	25
Dodge Plymouth Service Sign, round, blue and white, 42" dia	400	500
Donald Duck Cola Sign, diecut cardboard, easel back, 26" x 22"	150	175
Donnelly Machine Co. Paperweight, glass, rect., scalloped edge, factory scene, 3" x 4.5"	150	175
Draffen's Grand Gorge Blotter, "You Can Tell At A Glance When It's Custom Tailored," 9.5" x 4"	12	15
Drake's Yodels Clicker	18	22
Dref's Gout and Rheumatism Pills Tin, 2" dia	15	20
Dref's Mandrake Compound Liver Pills Tin, 2" dia	15	20
Dr. Jayne's Expectorant Poster, 1895, 13.5" x 29"	500	800
Dr. Mile's Remedies Calendar, girl and boy, 1908	300	500
Dr. Pepper Bottle Opener, cast iron, 1930s	20	30
Dr. Pepper Poster, "Frosty Man, Frosty!," 1957, 25" x 15"	75	85
Dr. Pepper Tin Sign, red and white, 1950s, 6" x 18"	60	80
Dr. Swett's Pocket Mirror, cellulloid, product image, 3" dia	325	375
Dutch Boy Canvas Back Sign, familiar Dutch Boy, 12" x 24"	230	250
Dutch Boy Cardboard Sign, "wet paint" picture of boy, 1930s, 6" x 9"	80	140
Dutch Boy Statue, composition, 36" h	150	200
Edward F. Heidenreich & Sons Leather Supplies Blotter, Elvgren pin-up, "Peek a View," 6.25" x 3.5"	15	20
Elsie the Cow Lighted Dial Electric Clock, 1948, 14" dia	300	400
Elsie the Cow Vinyl Bank, 1970s, 9" h	60	80
Endicott Johnson Shoes Whistle	18	25
Equitable Life Insurance Calendar, 1904	100	150
E.R. Durkee and Co. Spices Wooden Box, elephants and India, 1895, 12" x 7"	60	90
Ernie the Keebler Elf Vinyl Squeeze Doll, 1975, 7" h	12	15
Esky Esquire Magazine Cardboard Display, 1960s	100	150
Esso Oildrop Red Plastic Bank, 1960s, 7" h	70	90
Esso Papier-Mâché Dog, polychrome painted	1200	1600
Esso Tiger Pitcher and 6 Glasses, 1950s	50	75
Esso Tiger Plastic Bank, 1960s, 8.5" h	30	40
Eveready Cat Plastic Bank, 1972, 6" h	25	35

Blony Gum Counter Top Display, cardboard truck, wooden wheels, $385. —Photo courtesy of Collectors Auction Services.

	LOW	HIGH
Ever-Ready Safety Razor Clock, diecut wood, man shaving on dial, 22" h	1000	1500
Fairy Soap Tip Tray, "Have you a little 'Fairy' in your home?," litho, 4.25" dia	75	125
Finck's "Detroit Special Overalls" Cardboard Whistle, 2 sided, adv inside, 5" x 3"	95	110
Firestone Tire Ashtray, Texas Central Expo, 1936	20	30
Flavor Kist Saltines Clicker	18	24
Fleet Wing Ethyl Gas Sign, round, tin, yellow and black, 30" dia	90	130
Fletcher Manufacturing Co. Paperweight, glass, oval, factory scene, 2.75" x 4.5"	175	250
Florida Orange Bird Plastic Bank, 1972, 5" h	18	22
Florida Orange Bird Plastic Nodder, 1972, 7" h	20	30
Ford Gramophone Postcard, car, Santa, and R. Clooney, 1956	10	15
Ford Tractor Sign, masonite, 1940s, 11" x 21"	30	50
Foster Hose Supporters Sign, Pulveroid, lady and corset, framed, 16.5" x 8.5"	350	400
Franklin D. Roosevelt Cigar Box Label	25	30
Franklin Shoe Counter Display Sign, cardboard, easel back	50	60
Fred Fossil Resin Statue Store Display	75	125
Freese's Cementing Glue Trade Card, vertical illus, 1885	6	10
Friendship Cut Plug Alarm Clock, depicts man's face chewing tobacco, c1886, 4" h	400	500
Frontenac Brand Peanut Butter Tin, 12 oz	40	50
Funny Face Walkers, 1970, 3" h	60	80
Gabriel's Remedies Easel Back Poster, cardboard, 11" x 14"	35	45
General Electric Refrigerator Clock, 1930s, 9" h	100	150
General Motors Truck Presentation Pen Holder, brass, emb. factory scene	150	200
George Washington Cut Plug Cloth Bag, holds 3 oz tobacco	40	50
Ghirardelli's Cocoa Sign, diecut cardboard, baby in highchair, framed, 13" x 9.5"	400	450
Glendora Coffee Sign, tin, coffee can, 14" x 8.5"	50	75
Glenfiddich Pitcher, black, 1970s	8	12
Globe Gasoline Sign, round, blue, yellow, and white, 30" dia	700	800
GMC Sales and Service Sign, round, orange and blue, 42" dia	250	300
Goodrich Rubber Footwear Blotter, 6.5" x 3.5"	10	12
Goodrich Sport Shoes Blotter, 5.75" x 3.5"	15	20

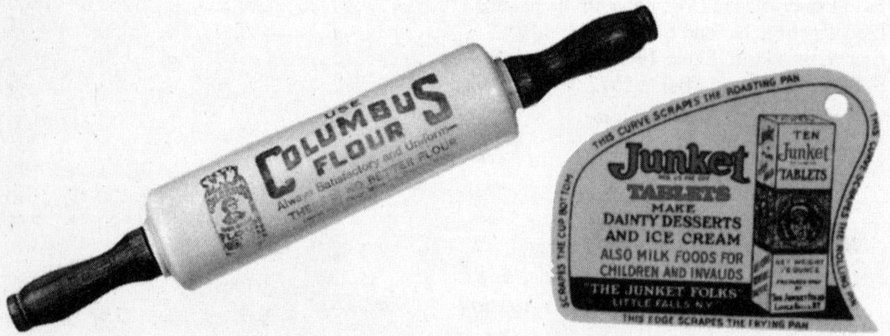

Left to right: Columbus Flour Rolling Pin, white milk glass, wood handles, 17.5" l, 2.5" dia, $880. —Photo courtesy Collectors Auction Services; Junket Powder and Tablets Pot Scraper, litho tin, 2 sided, 2.5" x 3.25", $550. —Photo courtesy Wm. Morford.

	LOW	HIGH
Goodrich Tires Sign, rect., blue, white, green, 18" x 80"	200	300
Grape Nuts Tin Sign, girl and Saint Bernard, 1910, 20" x 30"	1000	1500
Great Lakes Mutual Life Insurance Co. Clicker	15	20
Great Northern Railroad Calendar, Empire Builder, full pad, 1947	125	135
Green River Whiskey Blotter, 9.5" x 4"	20	25
Gulf Pride, magazine adv., 1953	3	5
Hafner's 365 Coffee Clicker	20	25
Hamm's Bear Ceramic Bank, 1980, 11" h	15	20
Hammer's Ice Cream Tray, 1920s	50	70
Happy Foot Composition Store Display, 1950 , 12" h	300	500
Harley-Davidson Motorcycle Oil Can, c1950, 1 qt	150	160
Harold's Club Pin-Up Calendar, by Ren Wicks, 4 pp, 1970, 20" x 26"	30	35
Harry Hood (Milk and Juice) Vinyl Figure, 1970s	60	80
Hartford Tires Sign, metal, painted, early 20th C	1200	1600
Hazard Smokeless Powder Calendar, boy and dog, 1910, 17" x 17"	180	230
Heinz Apple Butter Jar, paper labels, 7.5" h	100	125
Heinz Rice Flakes Trolley Card, 21" x 11"	150	175
Heinz Vinegar Sign, bottle and salad, 1910, 12" x 22"	160	220
Helping Hand Clock, 1985, 6" h	25	35
Henry Hooker & Co. Paperweight, glass, rect., horse-drawn carriage, 2.5" x 4"	150	180
Henry's Drive-In Clicker, "Head for Henry's"	25	35
Hershey's Clicker	38	45
Heywood Shoes Paperweight, glass, rect., vintage shoe, 2.5" x 4"	125	150
Hires Root Beer Clock, light up, "Drink Hires Root Beer with root, barks, herbs," 15" dia	150	175
Hires Root Beer Josh Slinger Baseball Counter, celluloid, 3" x 2.5"	400	450
Hires Root Beer Magic Story Booklet, 1934	10	15
Hires Root Beer Mug, boy w/ mug, "Join Health and Cheer," 1900	150	250
Hires Root Beer Tin Chalkboard, 1940s, 10" x 20"	180	220
Hires Root Beer Tray, 1910	200	500
His Man Figural Cologne Bottle, 1960, 6" h	40	60
Hody's Penaut Butter Tin Pail, kids on peanut seesaw, 1925, 3.5" h	150	200
Honest Weight Chewing and Smoking Tobacco Sign, paper, depicting scale and baby, 15.5" x 11.5"	300	600
Horseford's Self-Rising Bread Preparation Trade Card, 1900	3	5
Hotpoint Wooden Jointed Figure, 1938, 15" h	800	1300
Hoyt's Cologne Trade Card, picturing large frog, 1883	3	5
Humphreys' Remedies Cabinet, tin panel lists remedies, 27.75" x 20" x 10.25"	350	425
Hupmobile Catalog, color, 18 pp, 1929, 9" x 10"	150	160
Hush Puppy Dog Bank, 1970s, 8" h	25	35
Icee Bear Vinyl Bank, 1970s, 8" h	25	45
IGA Oats and Cream Cereal Whistle, wood, 1.5" l	30	40
Illinois Springfield Watches Sign, tin, wood frame, 17.5" x 23.5"	200	250
Imperial Club Cigar Sign, emb. self-framed tin, cigar box, 10" x 13.5"	175	200
Imperial Suspenders Sign, cardboard, "Are good enough for us," framed, 15.5" x 10.5"	75	125
International Trucks Sign, round, red, white, blue, 42" dia	275	475
Iron Fireman Metal Figural Ashtray, 1940s, 5" h	70	90
Jack and Jill Gelatin Dessert Clicker	35	45
Jack Sprat Coffee Clicker	45	50
Jello Hand Puppet, Mr. Wiggle, rubber, 1965, 6" h	70	90
Jersey Cream Blotter, children, 1920s, 4" x 9"	20	30
Jersey Cream Tray, 1915, 12" dia	150	200

	LOW	HIGH
Johnnie Pfeiffer Plaster Store Display, 1955, 8" h	60	80
Johnny Walker Man in Top Hat Store Display, 1950s, 16" h	100	150
Jolly Green Giant Sprout Vinyl Squeeze Doll, 1975, 6.5" h	20	30
Jolly Green Giant Vinyl Squeeze Doll, 1975, 9.5" h	35	45
J.U. Divilbiss Cigar Cutter, emb. cast iron, 1891, 3.25" h	300	350
Juicy Fruit Bus Card, 28" x 11"	475	525
Jumbo Trade Card, P.T. Barnum's circus elephant	6	10
Jumping Jack Shoes Clicker	45	60
Kellogg's Rag Doll, Bo Peep, 14" h	80	100
Kenteria Havana Cigar Cutter, emb. cast iron, shield, 1906, 6" h	500	525
Kern's Bread Flange Sign, metal, 1950s-60s, orig. paper wrapper	150	160
Key Chevrolet Sales Clicker	20	28
King Edward Cigars Window Decal, 8.5" x 7"	20	25
Klene's Buzzer Cigar Box Label	20	25
Kool-Aid Pitcher Man Mechanical Bank, 1970, 7" h	40	60
Libby, McNeill & Libby Calendar, cardboard, girl wearing straw hat, full pad, 1906, 16.5" x 10.75"	40	50
Lifebuoy Soap Poster, "Send for this Baseball Book," 1942, 13" x 17"	150	175
Longine's Watch Clock, brass, 18.5" d	200	300
Lotus Flour Sign, paper, framed, boy doing man's job, 15.25" x 11.5"	100	150
Lovell and Covel Candies Tin Pail, house, 1925, 3" h	120	200
Lucky Strike Cardboard Sign, 1935, 13.5" x 18"	100	150
Lux Soap Poster, Ann Sheridon, "My Beauty Care," 14" x 11"	50	60
Maple Hill Dairy Calendar, "Bare Facts," full pad, 1960, 16" x 32"	40	50
Melorol Ice Cream Whistle, cardboard, metal bird	30	35
Michelin Man (Bibendum) Plastic Ashtray, 1935, 4.5" h	100	150
Miller Locks Display, diecut cardboard, ship passing through Panama Canal, locks on Canal walls, easel back, 1905, 16" x 13"	200	250
Mobil Double-Sided Pegasus Gas Globe, 1920s, 18" dia	300	400
Monarch Paint Sign, 2-sided flange, porcelain, hand holding paint brush, 17" x 15.5"	250	275
Morton's Salt Blotter, "When It Rains It Pours," 6.25" x 3.25"	10	15
Moxie Display Bottle, wood, paper label, tin cap, metal lined to hold ice, 36" h	1000	2000
Moxie Pin, diecut tin, Moxie boy's head shape, 1" h	100	125
Moxie Sign, diecut tin, "I Like It," 6" dia	500	650
Mr. Bubble Plastic Figural Bank, 1970s, 7" h	35	45
Mr. Clean Vinyl Doll, 1960s, 8" h	150	200
Napoleon Cigars Display, cutout cardboard, 27" x 37"	450	600
National Cigar Stand Company Tip Tray, 6" dia	25	50
Nature's Remedy-Vegetine The Blood Purifier Trade Card, girl	4	6
Neco Wafers Sign, paper, 1925, 12" x 20"	200	400
New England Mutual Accident Association Paperweight, glass, rect., vintage railroad and paddle steamboat, 2.5" x 4"	200	250
New & True Coffee Clicker	35	45
New York Grand Central Station Paperweight, glass, rect., "5 Great Limited Trains," 2.5" x 4"	750	900
Newport Culvert Company Calendar, "Lovely Lady," Devores, full pad, 1942, 16" x 33"	125	150
Nobrake Shoe Laces and Corset Laces Poster, paper, 1903, 11" x 9.5"	50	60
Nolde's Bread Clicker	45	50
NuGrape Soda Calendar, 1949	75	100
Occident Flour Sign, tin over cardboard, wheat samples being processed, 9" x 13.75"	150	185

	LOW	HIGH
Odin 5¢ Cigar Sign, emb. tin 19" x 27"	350	375
Old Dutch Cleanser Booklet, 1930s, 3" x 6"	10	12
Old Reliable Coffee Sign, emb. tin, 13.75" x 6.5"	75	85
Old Reliable Coffee Sign, waxboard, 10" x 12"	25	30
Oldsmobile General Motors Sign, marquee shaped, 26" x 60"	550	750
Orange Crush Calendar, 1927	225	300
Oscar Meyer Weiner Mobile, pop-up Oscar, 1955, 4.5" h	175	200
Oscar R. Boehne & Co. Paperweight, glass, rect., gold scale, 2.5" x 4"	100	125
Oshkosh B'Gosh Overalls Sign, porcelain, 10" x 30"	150	200
Oshkosh Clicker	15	18
Oxydol Soap Hanger, diecut cardboard, Mammy, 2-sided, 10" x 9"	400	450
Palmolive Soap Mirror, Dionne quintuplets and doctor	35	50
Patton's Ice Cream Tray, oval logo, glass and dish of ice cream, 1920s, 13.5" sq	90	150
Pepsi-Cola 5¢ Clicker	40	45
Pepsi-Cola Door Push, porcelain, Canadian, 3" x 31"	125	175
Pepsi-Cola Record in Sleeve, "A Recorded Message From Your Man In Service," 1944	25	30
Pepsi-Cola Santa Claus Doll, 36" h	75	80
Peters Diamond Brand Shoes Alarm Clock	45	60
Peters Shoes 6" Ruler	12	12
Peters Shoes Clock, wooden, New Haven	150	175
Peters Weatherbird Pocket Watch, "Shoes For Boys"	175	200
Peters Weatherbird Shoes Clicker	20	25
Peters Weatherbird Shoes Whistle	18	24
Pez Clicker	30	40
Philco Transistor Man Figure, 1960s, 5" h	75	90
Philip Morris Sign, porcelain, cigarette pack, 4" x 25.75"	250	325
Piedmont Cigarettes Folding Chair, wood frame, 2 sided porcelain sign back	100	150
Piper Heidsieck Chewing Tobacco Sign, tin over cardboard, champagne bottle and plug tobacco, 17.5" x 14.5"	50	75
Planters Peanuts, Mr. Peanut, plastic, 2.5" l	15	20
Plymouth Cricket Clicker	15	18
Poll Parrot Bank, metal and cardboard, 2" h	40	50
Poll Parrot Pocket Watch, new dial	40	50
Poll Parrot Shoes Clicker	12	18
Poll Parrot Shoes Coloring Book, Howdy Doody, 8" x 7"	25	30
Poll Parrot Shoes Everyday Cook Book, 1937	15	18
Poll Parrot Shoes Poster, cardboard, easel back, 6" x 9"	20	25

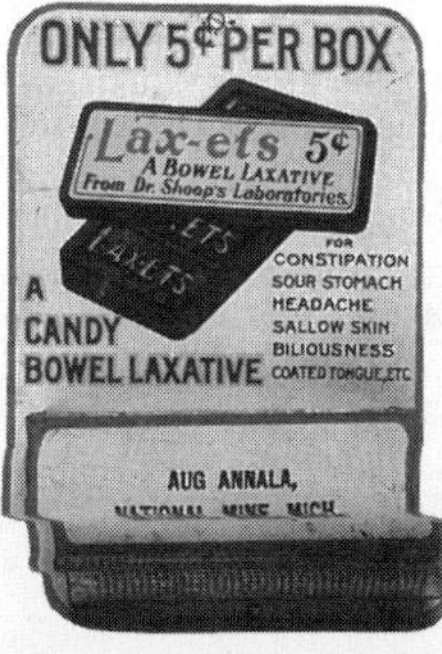

Left to right: DuBelle Grape Juice Pocket Mirror, 2.75" x 1.75", $176. —Photo courtesy Past Tyme Pleasures; Lax–ets Match Safe, litho tin, 4.75" x 3.5", $95. —Photo courtesy Collectors Auction Services.

	LOW	HIGH
Poll Parrot Watch Fob, "Solid Leather Shoes"	145	160
Poll Parrot Wrist Watch, band side mount	125	130
Pratts Veterinary Cabinet, oak display case, tin panel lists remedies, 33" x 16.5" x 7"	300	400
Precision Steel Warehouse Clicker	10	15
Purina Poster, "Fresh Eggs For Sale," 1947, 26" x 19"	40	60
Purity Salt Clicker	25	35
Putnam Fadeless Dyes Fan, General Israel Putnam Escaping British Dragoons, 6.5" x 8.5"	25	35
Quaker City Life Insurance Company Clicker	20	28
Quaker State Motor Oil Clicker	15	20
Raid Bug Remote Control Robot, 1980s, 12" h	150	175
Real Kill Bug Killer Clicker	12	18
Reddy Kilowatt Alarm Clock, Westclox, 5" h	200	250
Red Goose Glider, paper, 9" l	18	20
Red Goose Shoes Blotter, clown, 6" x 3.5"	25	30
Red Goose Shoes Clicker	15	20
Red Goose Shoes Printer's Stamp, 1.5" l	15	20
Red Goose Shoes Pull Toy, wooden elephant, 4" x 3.5"	50	60
Red Goose Shoes Punch Out Book, Chimpanzee Show, St. Louis Zoo, 10.5" x 10"	40	50
Red Goose Shoes String Holder, cast-iron goose, 15" l	400	450
Red Goose Shoes Welcome Mat, rubber	200	225
Red Goose Shoes Whistle, tin, 2.25" l	40	45
Red Man Cigar Leaf Poster, paper, 17.5" x 8"	25	30
Red Race Gingerale Bottle, Tifton, GA, c1910	30	40
Red Spot Coffee Tin Shelf Strip, 20" x 2.75"	25	30
Red Swan Cigar Box Label	10	15
Rinso Lifebuoy Soap Poster, Bob Burns and Amos 'N Andy, 11" x 14"	100	125
Robinson Crusoe Glue Trolley Sign, paper, Crusoe cooking fish glue on beach, framed, 10" x 20"	150	175
Schnapp's Tobacco Cloth Pouch, holds plug chewing tobacco	15	20
Shefford Pimiento Blotter, 6.25" x 3.25"	10	12
Sherwin-Williams Paints and Varnishes Sign, 2-sided flange, porcelain, 16" x 22"	300	350
Shop at Sears Clicker	12	15
Silver Eagle Turkeys Whistle, "Clean as a Whistle"	15	20
Sinclair Opaline Motor Oil Can, 1 qt	30	35
Sparkeeta Up Sign, cardboard, well-dressed lady holding soda bottle, 1946, 29.5" x 23.5"	400	475
Springfield Insurance Ledger Tin, litho, diecut, 12" h	200	275
Squirt Bottle Opener, cast iron, 1930s	20	25
Squirt Ceramic Bank, 1950s, 8" h	150	200
Star Brand Shoes Alarm Clock, "Star Brand Shoes Are Better"	50	60
Star Brand Shoes Calendar, w/ bill clamp	40	50
Sterling Brand Coffee Tin, Corbin Sons Chicago, IL, paper label, 1 lb	125	135
Stollwerck Chocolate & Cocoa Bookmark, celluloid, 5.75" h	20	25
Sunbeam Bread Window Sign, paper, 24" x 10"	25	30
Sundial All Leather Shoes Clicker	15	20
Sundial Shoes Blotter, "Tops Them All," Bonnie Laddie, 6" x 3"	15	18
Sunoco Blue Gas Globe, 1935, 16" dia	200	300
Superior Putting-Out Machine Paperweight, glass, rect., machine, 2.5" x 4"	85	100
Sure Shot Scrap and Chewing Tobacco Clicker	90	110

	LOW	HIGH
Swan Soap Poster, "Get Swan Today," 11" x 14"	20	25
Syracuse Stadium Shoes Bill Clip	45	50
Triple "AAA" Root Beer Decal, 9" x 7"	15	20
Twinkies Shoes Clicker	45	55
Tydol Oil Man License Plate Holder, 1935, 7" h	40	50
Union Trust Cigar Box Label, Tampa, FL	50	55
United Way Clicker	10	15
US Co. Motor Oil Can, 1 qt	25	30
Van Darn Cigars Sign, emb. tin, 28" x 14"	450	525
Walt Whitman Cigar Box Label	15	18
Wampole's Creo Terpin Blotter, 6.25" x 3.5"	10	12
Weather Bird Shoes Clicker	12	18
Weatherbird Pocket Watch	90	120
Weatherbird Shoes Calendar, full pad, 1954, 8" x 13.5"	40	50
Weatherbird Shoes Fan, 1925 June–Sept calendar on reverse	75	80
Weatherbird Shoes Radio Game, framed, 10" x 10"	40	60
Weatherbird Shoes Watch Fob	100	110
Weatherbird Wrist Watch, band side mount	140	150
Wenner Beverage Whistle, bamboo and paper, blue	15	20
Western Assurance Co. Ledger Tin, litho, diecut, 12.5" h	200	275
Weston's Crack-ettes Clicker	18	25
Whistle Soft Drink Whistle, "Thirsty? Just Whistle"	15	20
White's Golden Tonic For Horses Poster, 18" x 23.5"	50	60
White, Warner & Co. Paperweight, glass, rect., 2 men leaning on pot-belly stove, 2.5" x 4"	125	150
Williams Ice Cream Sign, 2-sided flange, tin, 13.5 x 17.5"	75	150
William's Poultry Food Milk Glass Egg w/ Stand, 5" l	150	175
Wrigley's Spearmint Bus Card, "Ride Relaxed Work Relaxed," 28" x 11"	45	60
Wrigley's Spearmint Trolley Card, "Taste the Juice of Real Mint Leaves," 21" x 11"	135	160
Wrigley's Trolley Car Card, "General Store," by John Bliss, 21" x 11"	150	160
Zig Zag Whistle, "The Food Confection"	35	45

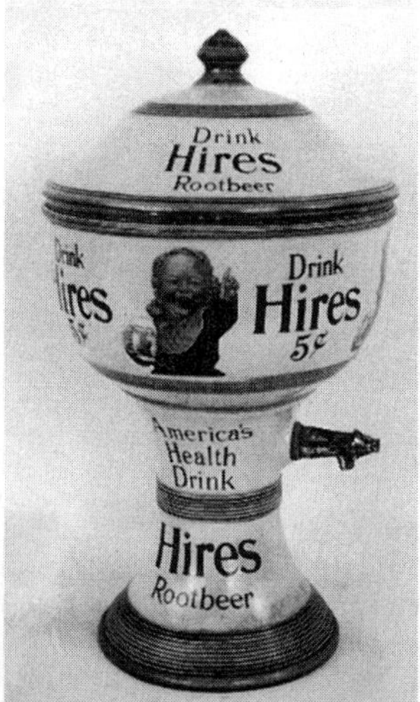

Hires Rootbeer Syrup Dispenser, Mettlach, Villroy & Boch blue version, 19" h, 10.5" dia, $42,000. —Photo courtesy James D. Julia.

Advertising Tins

Collectors judge advertising tins by product, color, design and condition. A tin for expensive candy is more desirable than a tin for acne cream. Similarly, bright reds will generally outperform dull browns. Dents, paint loss and rust severely diminish the value of a tin. The majority of collected tins date from the late 19th and early 20th centuries.

	LOW	HIGH
Bakers Nursery Talcum Powder, multicolor, stork and babies, 6" h	$500	$525
Borden's Challenge Milk, orange, black, and white paper label, 1/2 pt	18	25
Camel 5¢ Cigars, 4.5" w, 5.25" h	150	175
Camel Cigarettes, 100 cigarettes	75	80
Campbell Brand Coffee, camels and desert, bail handle, 4 lb, 8" h	85	100
Chesterfield Cigarettes, 1940s	15	22
Dead Shot Gun Powder, red ground, just-shot flying duck, 1 lb, 5.75" h	160	180
Deep-Rich Coffee, red, black, and white, key wind, 1 lb, 4" h	60	75
Devotion Brand Coffee, black, white, and red on yellow ground, man and woman drinking coffee, 1 lb, 4" h	125	150
Grand Union Baking Powder, multicolor paper label, 2 children, 1 lb	200	235
Herbaline Mountain Rose, multicolor, 3" h	55	65
Honey Moon Tobacco, pocket upright, 1935, 4.5" h	200	250
Lucky Strike Cigarettes, 1930s	25	35
Millar's Magnet Cocoa, multicolor, cocoa harvesting scene, 6" h	100	125
Nabob Brand Baking Powder, multicolor, strawberry cake, 5 lb, 7.5" h	50	65
Old Faithful Lighter Fluid, red, black, and white, geyser, 4" h	50	65
Philip Morris & Co., holds 1 pack	35	40
Pride of Virginia Sliced Plug, flat pocket, 4.5" x 3.75"	30	40
Queen Pine Tar Hair Dressing, trial size	15	18
Santa Fe Pure Ground Mustard, multicolor, paper label, 3.25" h	60	70
Snap Shot Black Sporting Powder, multicolor, duck falling from sky, 1/4 lb, 4.25" h	375	425
Sultana Peanut Butter, A&P Tea Co., NY, 1 lb	50	60
Times Square Tobacco, upright pocket, 1935, 4.5" h	350	425
Uncle Sam Shoe Polish, red ground, Uncle Sam image, 1.5" h	130	145
Wabash Cocoa, man and pile of cocoa beans, red ground, 6" h	200	225

Left to right: Forbes Golden Cup Coffee, black, white, and red, 3 lb, 9.25" h, 6" d, $198; Ramses Condoms, Egyptian bands, 2.75" x 1.75", $85. —Photos courtesy Past Tyme Pleasures.

African-American Memorabilia

For the past century, the depiction of African Americans has been a reflection of this country's fitful growth as a free nation. Although many of the images are derogatory and degrading, both black and white collectors have found them historically interesting. A nation learning from its mistakes will find endless education here.

	LOW	AVG.	HIGH
Advertisement, Georgia Journal, receipt of slaves, 5" x 8"	$30	$40	$50
Aunt Jemima Doorstop, 13.25" x 8"	325	375	425
Bandanna, leaders of Haiti, cotton, 1800, 26" x 28"	1200	1500	1800
Black Cloth Rag Doll, blue overalls, red and white checkered shirt, yarn hair, button eyes, 20" h	275	350	425
Black Cloth Rag Doll, wearing black overalls, gray felt hat, 14" h	100	130	160
Blackface Cast-Iron Pencil Sharpener, insert pencil on side of face and shavings discharge through lips, 1.5" h	125	150	175
Black Gold Movie Press Book, "all colored cast," Norman Studios, Arlington, FL, 4 pp, 22" x 13.5"	50	65	80
Black Panther Magazine, May 19, 1963, Malcolm X issue	140	180	220
Book, *Tell My Horse,* by Zora Neale Hurston, sgd	1500	1750	2000
Book, *The Life and Adventures of Olaudah Equiano,* by Olaudah Equiano, 1829	750	850	950
Book, *Uncle Remus, His Songs and His Sayings,* by Joel Chandler Harris, first edition	700	900	1100
Broadside, address of John Brown, 1859, 13.25" x 11"	3000	3500	4000
Cakewalk Poster, from Danbury Opera House, 1866	630	780	950
Chad Valley Bank, smiling black gentleman on front of round bank, wearing brown checkered jacket, 5" h	250	315	375
Cream of Wheat Chef Cookie Jar, black man in chef's outfit, Japan, 1940s, 10" h	1600	2000	2400

Left to right: Miniature Lawn Jockey Salesman's Sample, painted cast metal, 12.5" h, 4.25" w, $385 at auction. —Photo courtesy James D. Julia; Uncle Tom's Cabin Poster, Robt Kemp artist, 88" x 39.5", framed, $825 at auction. —Photo courtesy Collectors Auction Services.

	LOW	AVG.	HIGH
Face Spoon, sterling silver, handle is black man's face, inscribed "Sunny South," Jacksonville, FL, bears Shiebler emblem, 4" l	90	110	130
Figural Group, 2 children sharing toilet seat, black child on left, white child on right, bisque, c1890, 4" h	100	120	140
Gold Dust Advertising Postcard, black children cleaning globe	40	50	60
Gold Dust Washing Powder Box, orange and black, Gold Dust Twins, 5 oz	30	35	40
Hank Aaron Poster, 23" x 35"	150	175	200
Happy Nig Tobacco Tag, smiling man	100	115	125
Harlem Globetrotters Coca-Cola Sign, 1952	900	1150	1350
"How Ink Is Made" Figurine, black child sitting in tub of black ink, Shelley China, 3.5" h	70	100	110
Joe Louis Movie Handbill, "Roar of the Crowd," pulp paper, late 1930s, 6" x 11.5"	25	35	42
Joe Louis Postcard, real photo, Joe and Marva, "Champion of the World"	20	24	32
Josephine Baker Playbill	30	40	50
Luzianne Coffee & Chicory Tin, Mammy on paper label, 1938, 1 lb	35	40	50
Mammy Doorstop, large, green dress, Hubley, full figure, 12" x 6"	400	450	500
Mammy Doorstop, small, green dress, Hubley, full figure, 8.5" x 4.5"	175	200	225
Mammy Pincushion Tape Measure Doll, orig. box, Japan, 5.5" h	90	110	130
Mammy Still Bank, red dress, white apron and kerchief, 5" h	90	117	140
Martin Luther King Memorial Fan, paperboard on wooden stick, 12" h	30	35	40
Oxydol Mammy Hanger, diecut cardboard, 2-sided, 10" x 9"	380	420	450
Recruiting Poster, "Colored Man Is No Slacker," 19.75" x 16"	500	600	700
Rinso Amos 'N' Andy Poster, paper, "Friday is Amos 'n' Andy Night," 1944, 11" x 14"	95	110	125
Salt and Pepper Shakers, boy w/ watermelon	65	75	85
Sports Illustrated Unsigned Print, "Living Legends," Louis vs Schmeling, 1973, 22" x 18"	20	25	30
Willie Mays Alaga Syrup Poster, 10" x 20"	50	60	70

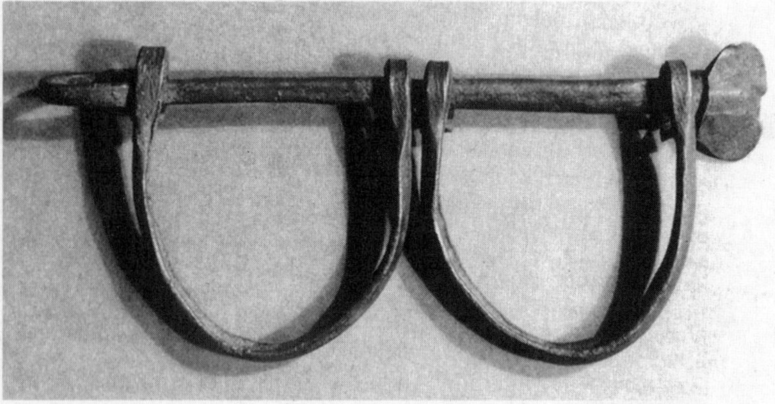

Slave Shackles, for child or young teen, c1800, 4.75" l, 1.5" w wrist bands, $2760. —Photo courtesy Swann Galleries.

Autographs

The personal mark of the famous and revered has always attracted collectors. The following abbreviations are used: *ALS*–Autograph Letter Signed (a letter handwritten by the person who signed it), *LS*–Letter Signed (a letter typed or written out by another person), *DS*–Document Signed (a signed document), *PhS*–Photo Signed, *Cut Sig.*–Cut Signature (a signature cut from a letter, autograph book, or other source).

We have divided this section into Artists, Authors, Civil War Figures, Entertainers, Politicians and Presidents.

Camille Pissaro.

Artists

	ALS		Cut Sig.	
	Low	High	Low	High
Bakst, Leon	$100	$600	$20	40
Beardsley, Aubrey	300	500	50	100
Bierstadt, Albert	380	400	40	75
Braque, Georges	300	1500	60	100
Cassat, Mary	300	1200	50	90
Chagall, Marc	340	400	45	75
Church, Frederick S.	220	280	25	30
Corot, Camille	170	500	35	75
Cruikshank, George	50	300	25	50
Daumier, Honore	400	1000	75	100
DeKooning, Willem	150	300	50	80
Ernst, Max	200	600	50	100
Forain, Jean	24	350	6	8
Forrester, Alfred Henry	56	68	6	8
Fuseli, Henry	300	700	50	100
Gibson, Charles Dana	50	250	15	30
Gifford, R. Swain	16	150	4	8
Gill, Eric	50	100	10	15
Greenaway, Kate	800	1800	150	300
Hassam, Childe	130	300	30	70
Lawrence, Sir Thomas	240	300	12	16
Leslie, C.R.	80	100	8	12
Lipchitz, Jacques	40	100	35	70
Mondrian, Piet	400	1000	60	100
Neiman, LeRoy	100	200	25	30
Picasso, Pablo	800	1600	200	300
Pissarro, Camille	300	2000	50	66
Rackham, Arthur	175	300	20	40
Renoir, Pierre A.	700	5000	120	170
Rossetti, Dante G.	200	2500	60	80
Rouault, George S.	300	1000	50	70
Russell, Charles M.	300	1000	50	100
Segal, George	20	30	10	20
Shahn, Ben	150	200	20	40
Soyer, Raphael	50	100	10	17
Sully, Thomas	220	2000	30	50

Authors

Authors' letters have always been a favorite of collectors. But just like the novels and poems they wrote, content counts! A letter refusing a dinner inviation is worth a fraction of the value of a letter discussing alternative endings of a play.

Examples: France, le Carré, Rice, Updike, Hemingway, and Stowe.

	LS		ALS	
	Low	High	Low	High
Alger, Horatio	$65	$85	$400	$550
Asimov, Isaac	60	140	150	500
Baldwin, James	150	340	150	500
Balzac, Honore	459	1000	400	1500
Baudelaire, Charles Pierre	377	800	700	4000
Baum, Frank	333	1200	373	3000
Beckett, Samuel	199	1500	116	2000
Beerbohm, Max	200	700	73	1000
Bellamy, Edward	100	500	150	1000
Brecht, Bertolt	600	1500	1000	5000
Breton, Andre	100	700	300	1500
Brooke, Rupert	207	1200	500	3000
Browning, Robert	200	1800	305	2500
Bryant, William Cullen	150	190	300	2000
Burnett, Frances H.	50	200	75	500
Burroughs, John	70	100	100	500
Butler, Samuel	90	500	400	1500
Camus, Albert	200	1800	500	5000
Carlyle, Thomas	80	300	300	1300
Cather, Willa	132	500	400	1800
Collins, Jackie	6	13	40	75
Crane, Stephen	400	2500	1300	6000
Curtis, George W.	28	36	32	40
Dana, R.H., Jr.	84	106	200	300
Davis, Richard H.	16	20	28	36
Dos Passos, John	25	200	75	500

	LS		ALS	
	Low	High	Low	High
Durant, Will	10	40	30	200
Durell, Lawrence	20	100	60	150
Fiske, John	20	28	24	30
France, Anatole	100	300	200	400
Frost, Robert	264	564	773	4000
Goldman, William	50	75	100	300
Grass, Gunter	48	114	83	194
Graves, Robert	100	600	200	1800
Grisham, John	25	58	45	99
Hale, Edward E.	28	36	44	56
Harris, Joel C.	200	300	600	5000
Harte, F. Brett	100	400	300	600
Hawthorne, Nathaniel	300	4000	1000	10,000
Hellman, Lillian	50	120	200	800
Hemingway, Ernest	500	5000	1000	10,000
Herbert, Frank	70	170	100	500
Hesse, Hermann	200	600	250	1200
Hubbard, Elbert	36	46	70	80
Irving, Clifford	5	20	25	90
Irving, John	10	30	25	120
Irving, Washington	100	2000	1000	10,000
Kaufman, George S.	45	145	50	500
Kilmer, Joyce	350	450	800	1000
LeCarre, John	20	50	50	150
Longfellow, H.W.	100	500	150	3000
Lowell, James R.	50	150	100	500
Melville, Herman	3000	15,000	5000	20,000
Mencken, H.L.	50	250	100	500
Miller, Henry	300	2500	700	5000
Milne, A.A.	100	600	300	1500
Nash, Ogden	100	500	200	1000
Nin, Anais	80	500	400	2000
O'Neill, Eugene	200	5000	1000	5000
Parker, Dorothy	75	500	300	1500
Pierpont, John	60	80	120	160
Porter, W.S. (O. Henry)	1600	2000	1600	2000
Rice, Ann	30	70	50	150
Roth, Philip	12	30	21	52
Runyon, Damon	147	352	162	376
Salinger, J.D.	1104	2503	722	1802
Solzhenitsyn, Alexander	120	600	400	1800
Stoddard, R.H.	60	80	120	160
Stowe, H.B.	100	500	500	5000
Talese, Gay	50	200	100	700
Tarkington, Booth	350	450	500	700
Taylor, Bayard	80	100	160	200
Thoreau, Henry D.	3000	5000	5000	10,000
Thorpe, Thomas B.	80	100	160	200
Thurber, James	100	600	300	1800
Updike, John	26	63	46	106
Vonnegut, Kurt	30	75	50	150
Wolfe, Thomas	500	1500	1000	5000

Civil War Figures

Not everyone recognizes the officers and heroes of the Civil War. But a sharp eye can still pluck these nuggets from the piles of old letters and documents that still turn up in attics. Condition, content, and date can drive the value above (or below) the ranges noted here.

	ALS		DS		Cut Sig.	
	Low	High	Low	High	Low	High
Anderson, Brigadier General Robert	$60	$75	$25	$33	$7	$11
Andres, John A.	18	23	8	10	3	4
Augur, Christopher C.	14	16	4	7	1	2
Badeau, Adam	14	16	4	7	1	2
Banks, Nathaniel P.	50	65	18	23	8	11
Beuregard, G.T.	275	350	90	110	14	19
Benton, James G.	10	12	8	9	2	3
Berdan, Hiram	43	50	14	18	4	6
Bernard, John G.	18	22	8	10	3	5
Bocock, Thomas S.	20	26	8	10	2	3
Bonham, M.L.	14	18	8	10	2	3
Bragg, Braxton	42	50	18	23	8	11
Buchanan, Thomas M.	125	175	38	50	20	27
Burnside, A.E.	90	120	33	45	12	18
Butterfield, Daniel	20	28	10	15	4	7
Cleburne, Patrick R.	240	300	100	140	35	55
Corse, Brigadier General John M.	14	20	8	11	3	5
Cosby, George B.	20	28	10	15	5	7
Crittenden, Thomas	20	28	10	15	5	7
Custer, George A.	850	875	250	330	60	90
Dahlgren, Rear Admiral J.	33	40	20	28	5	7
Davis, Jefferson	1100	2000	325	475	50	80
Dix, General John A.	45	60	20	28	5	7
Early, Jubal A.	90	130	50	70	8	3
Farragut, Admiral D.G.	275	350	125	200	15	22
Floyd, John B.	20	29	8	13	3	5
Forney, Major General J.H.	20	29	8	13	3	5
Foster, John G.	17	23	8	12	3	5
Fremont, General J.C.	35	43	10	15	6	9
French, Samuel G.	40	56	10	15	6	9
Gardner, Franklin	25	35	8	13	3	5
Garnett, Robert S.	32	43	11	18	3	5
Gilmore, General Quincy A.	25	34	8	11	3	5
Gladden, Adley H.	70	95	21	30	10	15
Gordon, John B.	32	42	10	14	3	5
Gorgas, Josiah	32	42	10	14	3	5
Halleck, H.W.	45	60	22	29	5	8
Hancock, W.S.	35	43	15	20	3	5
Heintzelman, S.P.	22	28	10	14	3	5
Hooker, General Joseph	34	42	12	19	5	8
Humphries, A.K.	34	42	12	19	5	8
Ingraham, Duncan N.	40	58	15	20	5	8
Jackson, "Stonewall"	2800	4500	700	1200	150	200
Jackson, W.H.	36	47	15	20	6	9
Johnston, Joseph E.	45	60	20	32	6	9

Robert E. Lee and G.T. Beauregard.

	ALS		DS		Cut Sig.	
	Low	High	Low	High	Low	High
Jones, David R.	95	130	45	70	15	22
Kearny, Philip	200	275	70	95	20	28
Lee, FitzHugh	32	45	15	20	4	5
Lee, Robert E.	500	900	200	325	80	110
Logan, Major General John A.	26	35	15	10	4	7
Longstreet, James	26	35	10	15	4	7
Luce, Admiral Stephen	33	40	10	15	4	7
Lyon, General Nathaniel	110	150	457	70	20	28
Mahone, William	33	40	10	15	4	7
Mason, James M.	275	350	80	120	20	29
McArthur, John	40	50	15	22	4	7
McClellan, George B.	58	75	22	32	6	9
Meade, George G.	45	58	18	26	6	10
Meagher, Thomas F.	26	36	10	15	4	7
Mosby, John S.	26	36	10	15	4	7
Pickett, George E.	300	415	115	170	18	25
Porter, Admiral David	110	170	50	75	8	12
Porter, FitzJohn	45	65	15	23	5	8
Porter, Horace	33	42	15	23	3	5
Price, Sterling	40	60	20	29	5	8
Pryor, Roger A.	47	75	20	29	5	8
Ransom, Robert, Jr.	80	100	22	30	5	8
Reagan, John H.	33	47	15	22	4	7
Richardson, J.B.	33	47	15	22	4	7
Ripley, R.S.	38	50	15	22	4	7
Rosecrans, W.S.	80	110	22	28	8	12
Scott, Winfield	200	300	80	130	15	20
Seddon, James A.	110	150	35	50	7	12
Seward, William H.	150	210	47	65	10	15
Shrman, William T.	220	300	70	100	15	22
Sigel, Franz	37	50	15	22	4	7
Sneed, John L.T.	40	62	22	28	5	8
Stanton, Edwin M.	130	220	45	85	10	15
Stephens, Alexander H.	80	110	23	32	5	8
Sumner, Charles	80	110	23	32	5	8
Taylor, Richard	100	140	35	50	8	11
Thomas, Major General G.H.	150	200	47	62	11	15
Thompson, M.J.	110	140	35	50	8	11
Toombs, Robert	90	110	22	28	5	9
Twiggs, David E.	40	65	15	22	4	7
Waterhouse, Richard	50	75	15	22	5	8
Welles, Gideon	75	110	22	28	5	8
Wheeler, General Joseph	50	75	22	28	5	8

Entertainers

Who signed that photo? As big stars received more requests for signed photos than they could supply themselves, they (or their studios) hired secretaries to sign photos for them. In the case of Jean Harlow, her mother signed most of the photos picturing this star.

	PhS		PLAIN SIG.	
	Low	High	Low	High
Adams, Don	$10	$13	$7	$9
Aiello, Danny	20	24	6	8
Alda, Alan	14	17	8	10
Allen, Gracie	70	100	10	20
Allen, Woody	30	38	12	15
Alklyson, June	12	18	4	6
Ameche, Don	30	50	10	15
Anderson, Loni	16	19	6	8
Andress, Ursula	23	29	10	13
Andrews, Julie	27	34	7	10
Arness, James	50	70	12	16
Autry, Gene	60	74	16	20
Bach, Barbara	16	22	6	8
Backus, Jim	25	35	12	18
Bacon, Kevin	28	35	6	8
Baker, Carroll	17	21	10	13
Bancroft, Anne	20	24	4	5
Bardot, Grigitte	40	60	15	20
Barkin, Ellen	33	40	9	12
Barr, Roseanne	40	52	12	16
Bartholomew, Freddie	40	70	15	20
Bassinger, Kim	28	35	13	17
Bateman, Justine	20	25	9	13
Beatty, Warren	40	70	15	20
Belafonte, Shari	14	17	3	4

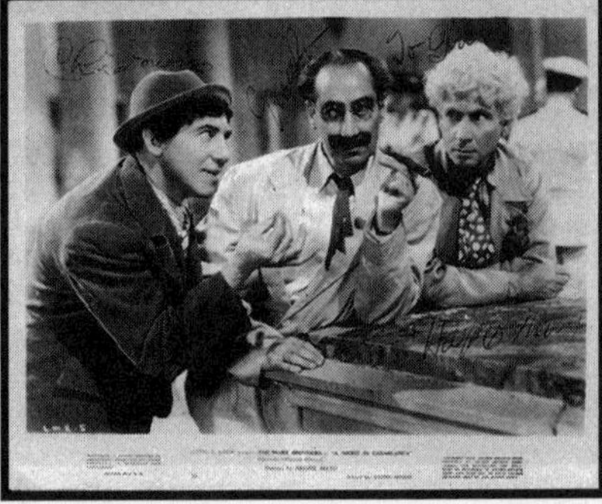

Photo signed by Margaret Hamilton as the Wicked Witch of the West.

Photo signed by Marx Brothers. —Photo courtesy Sotheby's.

	PhS		PLAIN SIG.	
	Low	High	Low	High
Bellamy, Ralph	20	30	7	9
Belushi, John	400	600	80	120
Benatar, Pat	50	60	13	17
Bergan, Candice	23	30	6	8
Bergman, Ingmar	60	80	15	20
Bergman, Ingrid	200	300	70	90
Berle, Milton	23	31	9	12
Bisset, Jaqueline	24	30	16	21
Blair, Linda	14	17	6	8
Blake, Robert	10	13	4	5
Bloom, Claire	15	20	4	6
Bogart, Humphrey	700	1200	300	400
Bowie, David	78	92	23	29
Brinkley, Christie	31	40	6	8
Broderick, Matthew	23	29	6	7
Brolin, James	16	21	10	12
Bronson, Charles	20	30	5	7
Brooks, Mel	15	20	4	6
Brynner, Yul	70	90	18	22
Burnett, Carol	13	16	3	4
Burr, Raymond	35	45	8	12
Burton, Richard	100	150	40	60
Buttons, Red	18	22	4	6
Caan, James	18	22	4	6
Cabot, Sebastian	50	70	10	15
Caesar, Sid	15	20	4	6
Cagney, James	180	220	20	40
Cannon, Diane	14	17	4	5
Cantor, Eddie	70	90	30	40
Cardinale, Claudia	15	25	5	7
Carney, Art	20	30	8	10
Carradine, David	15	20	4	6
Carson, Johnny	20	30	8	10
Carter, Lynda	13	16	4	5
Casidy, David	10	13	3	4
Chaney, Lon	1000	1500	600	800
Chaney, Lon, Jr.	400	600	200	300
Chaplin, Charles	800	1200	200	300
Clapton, Eric	40	60	15	20
Clayberg, Jill	14	17	3	4
Colbert, Claudette	50	61	26	33
Collins, Joan	17	20	9	13
Connry, Sean	50	70	15	20
Conrad, Robert	13	16	4	6
Coogan, Jackie	12	18	30	50
Cooper, Gary	200	400	100	150
Cooper, Jackie	20	30	8	10
Cosby, Bill	21	26	6	8
Crabbe, Buster	40	60	12	18
Crane, Bob	100	200	70	90
Cruise, Tom	56	68	12	17
Crystal, Billy	31	37	13	17

	PhS		PLAIN SIG.	
	Low	High	Low	High
Curtis, Ken	40	60	10	15
Dalton, Timothy	32	40	13	17
Dangerfield, Rodney	14	17	6	9
Danson, Ted	24	29	10	13
Davis, Bette	100	150	40	60
Davis, Sammy, Jr.	132	163	26	32
de Haviland, Olivia	36	45	20	25
De Niro, Robert	30	40	8	10
Denver, Bob	15	22	4	6
Derek, Bo	13	16	6	9
De Vito, Danny	17	21	5	7
Dickinson, Angie	16	21	4	5
Dietrich, Marlene	100	150	30	50
Douglas, Kirk	20	30	8	12
Dreyfus, Richard	26	33	5	6
Duke, Patty	15	20	5	7
Dunne, Irene	30	40	10	15
Durante, Jimmy	30	40	10	15
Durbin, Deanna	25	35	10	15
Easton, Sheena	30	37	7	10
Eastwood, Clint	30	40	8	10
Ebsen, Buddy	20	30	7	8
Eden, Barbara	28	33	7	8
Estevez, Emilio	20	25	6	8
Evans, Linda	31	38	6	8
Fairchild, Morgan	17	21	6	8
Farrow, Mia	19	24	6	8

Poster signed by Marlene Dietrich.
—Photo courtesy Sotheby's.

Bob Hope.

	PhS		PLAIN SIG.	
	Low	High	Low	High
Fawcett, Farrah	17	21	6	8
Feldon, Barbara	24	30	3	4
Field, Sally	18	21	4	6
Fleming, Rhonda	28	34	6	8
Fonda, Henry	70	90	12	18
Fonda, Jane	15	19	4	5
Fontaine, Joan	23	29	7	10
Ford, Glenn	36	43	18	25
Fox, Samantha	30	40	6	8
Foxx, Red	23	30	12	16
Funicello, Annette	16	21	7	8
Gable, Clark	800	1500	300	400
Gabriel, Peter	34	42	10	12
Garbo, Greta	1500	3000	700	1000
Gardner, Ava	77	94	29	40
Gaynor, Janet	40	60	10	15
Gaynor, Mitzi	10	15	4	6
Gere, Richard	52	63	12	17
Gibson, Debbie	21	26	6	8
Gilbert, Melissa	23	29	7	8
Gleason, Jackie	100	150	40	60
Goddard, Paulette	50	70	15	20
Godunov, Alexander	41	50	21	26
Granger, Farley	10	15	3	5
Granger, Stewart	20	30	7	9
Grant, Cary	300	400	100	150
Graves, Peter	15	20	4	6
Greene, Lorne	30	60	15	20
Griffith, Andy	24	30	10	13
Griffith, Melanie	50	60	12	17
Grodin, Charles	10	12	4	5
Hacket, Buddy	17	20	3	4
Hagman, Larry	17	22	45	
Hall, Arsenio	14	17	6	9
Hamilton, Margaret	35	40	16	22
Harlow, Jean	1500	2500	600	900
Harlow, Jean (Mama Jean)	30	50	10	20
Harrison, George	350	450	150	250
Harrison, Rex	64	84	26	33
Hasselhoff, David	28	33	10	13
Hauer, Rutgar	31	38	6	8
Hayworth, Rita	300	400	70	100
Hendrix, Jimi	800	1200	300	400
Hepburn, Audrey	265	323	61	78

	PhS		PLAIN SIG.	
	Low	High	Low	High
Herman, Pee Wee	20	24	8	10
Heston, Charlton	26	32	6	8
Hirsh, Judd	10	12	3	4
Hitchcock, Alfred	400	600	100	150
Hoffman, Dustin	20	30	5	7
Holden, William	70	90	4	6
Holly, Buddy	1500	2500	6	8
Hope, Bob	42	51	6	8
Houston, Whitney	53	65	21	30
Howard, Ron	24	30	6	8
Hudson, Rock	92	120	15	20
Huston, John	30	50	10	15
Huston, Walter	80	120	30	50
Hutton, Betty	21	25	5	6
Hutton, Lauren	17	21	6	8
Hutton, Timothy	24	29	7	10
Idol, Billy	18	21	6	8
Irons, Jeremy	23	30	6	9
Irving, Amy	17	22	5	7
Jaggar, Mick	100	122	32	43
John, Elton	80	120	25	35
Johnson, Don	30	38	9	12
Jolson, Al	300	400	70	90
Jones, Tom	13	17	5	7
Keach, Stacey	13	17	5	6
Keaton, Michael	33	42	6	8
Kerr, Deborah	17	20	10	13
Kirkland, Sally	13	17	3	4

Left to right: Photo signed by Marilyn Monroe; Photo signed by Humphrey Bogart. —Photos courtesy Sotheby's.

Dorothy Lamour, photo ID, $632 at auction. —Photo courtesy Sotheby's.

	PhS		PLAIN SIG.	
	Low	High	Low	High
Knots, Don	15	20	5	7
Ladd, Cheryl	14	17	5	7
Lamour, Dorothy	23	28	6	8
Lancaster, Burt	43	57	16	21
Landon, Michael	70	90	25	35
Lange, Jessica	23	29	5	7
Lansbury, Angela	17	21	3	4
Leigh, Vivian	600	800	200	300
Lemmon, Jack	15	20	4	6
Lennon, John	600	900	300	400
Liberace	70	90	20	30
Loggins, Kenny	17	21	6	8
Lollobrigida, Gina	15	20	4	6
Lombard, Carole	600	800	150	200
Long, Shelly	17	21	6	8
Loren, Sophia	17	22	6	8
Lowe, Rob	31	40	13	16
Loy, Myrna	25	45	8	15
Lucas, George	20	30	7	9
Lunt, Alfred	50	80	20	30
Lupino, Ida	40	60	12	18
Maclaine, Shirley	20	30	8	10
MacMurray, Fred	30	40	10	15
Madonna	157	183	32	43
Majors, Lee	10	12	3	4
Mandrell, Barbara	14	17	4	5
Marx, Chicco	200	300	60	90
Marx, Groucho	300	400	180	220
Marx, Harpo	350	400	200	300
Marx Brothers (3 together)	900	1400	400	700
Marx Brothers (4 together)	1200	1800	600	900
Mason, James	30	40	15	20
Mayo, Virginia	15	20	5	7
McCartney, Paul	340	390	61	86
McDowall, Roddy	15	20	5	7
McGillis, Kelly	23	29	6	8
McGovern, Elizabeth	14	17	3	4

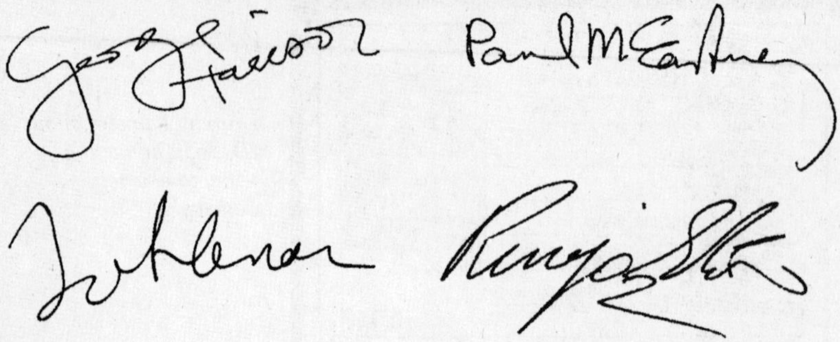

The Beatles: George Harrison, Paul McCartney, John Lennon and Ringo Starr.

	PhS		PLAIN SIG.	
	Low	High	Low	High
McQueen, Steve	150	200	70	90
Mellancamp, John	40	51	22	29
Michael, George	70	81	12	16
Midler, Bette	31	40	9	12
Mitchum, Robert	30	40	6	8
Monroe, Marilyn	1500	4000	800	1500
Montgomery, Elizabeth	15	20	4	6
Moore, Dudley	24	29	6	8
Moore, Mary Tyler	17	21	6	8
Moore, Roger	42	55	6	8
Moranis, Rick	17	20	3	4
Morley, Robert	25	35	8	10
Mostel, Zero	70	90	15	20
Murphy, Eddie	50	65	16	21
Nabors, Jim	12	18	4	6
Newman, Paul	70	100	30	40
Newton-John, Olivia	34	40	9	12
Nicholson, Jack	36	43	31	42
Nielson, Leslie	17	21	6	9
Nimoy, Leonard	70	120	20	30
Niven, David	40	60	15	20
Nolte, Nick	26	34	6	9
Norris, Chuck	26	33	5	7
Novak, Kim	54	66	5	7
O'Brien, Margaret	20	30	5	7
O'Connor, Carroll	14	17	4	5
Oberon, Merle	40	60	15	25
Olivier, Laurence	80	120	25	35
Osmond, Marie	12	18	3	4
Oxenberg, Catherine	26	33	16	21
Pacino, Al	20	30	3	4
Palance, Jack	25	45	5	8
Parker, Fess	20	30	6	8

	PhS Low	PhS High	PLAIN SIG. Low	PLAIN SIG. High
Parton, Dolly	17	21	6	8
Peck, Gregory	25	35	8	12
Penn, Sean	24	30	3	4
Peppard, George	17	21	4	5
Perkins, Tony	30	38	16	20
Perlman, Rhea	10	12	3	4
Peters, Bernadette	17	21	3	4
Pfeiffer, Michelle	57	72	18	25
Pickford, Mary	150	200	30	40
Pidgeon, Walter	30	40	8	12
Plimpton, George	11	15	4	6
Poitier, Sidney	30	36	7	10
Powers, Stephanie	3	5	1	2
Preminger, Otto	25	35	10	15
Presley, Elivs	820	1000	378	535
Prince	140	167	70	93
Pryor, Richard	16	21	5	8
Raft, George	100	150	10	15
Ray, Aldo	8	12	2	4
Raye, Martha	20	30	8	10
Redford, Robert	60	77	25	33
Reynolds, Burt	14	17	5	7
Ringwald, Molly	35	40	12	16
Ritter, John	11	12	3	4
Robards, Jason	20	24	10	13
Roberts, Julia	40	60	15	20
Rogers, Ginger	97	112	25	34
Rogers, Kenny	20	26	6	8
Russell, Jane	17	21	5	7
Russell, Kurt	23	30	10	13
Ryan, Meg	37	44	12	17
Saint, Eva Marie	17	22	6	8
Sales, Soupy	15	20	4	6
Schwarzenegger, Arnold	40	60	15	20
Scott, George C.	57	74	13	17
Scott, Randolph	60	80	15	20
Selleck, Tom	21	25	6	8
Shatner, William	60	80	15	20
Shearer, Norma	150	250	30	50
Shields, Brooke	24	30	6	7
Skelton, Red	52	70	9	13
Spacek, Sissy	26	35	6	8
Spielberg, Steven	80	100	30	50
St. John, Jill	14	17	5	7
Stallone, Sylvester	41	50	9	12
Stanwyck, Barbara	55	70	16	21
Starr, Ringo	200	300	80	120
Stevens, Connie	10	12	4	5
Stewart, James	100	200	30	40
Storch, Larry	10	13	4	5
Streisand, Barbra	200	300	80	120
Struthers, Sally	10	15	3	5

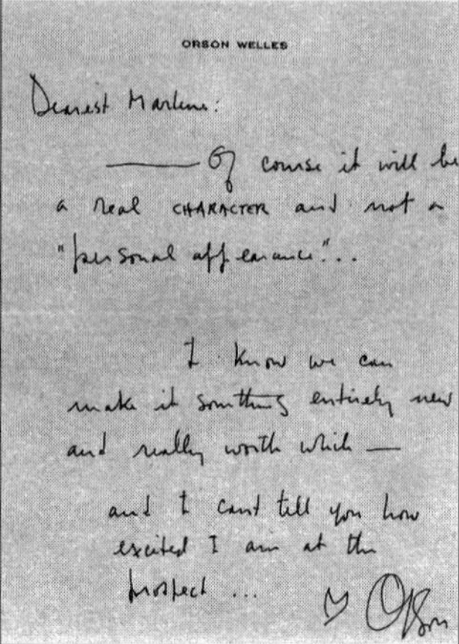
ORSON WELLES

Dearest Marlene:

——Of course it will be a real CHARACTER and not a "personal appearance"..

I know we can make it something entirely new and really worth while —

and I cant tell you how excited I am at the prospect ...

Orson

Orson Welles ALS to Marlene Dietrich, $3,105 at auction. —Photo courtesy Sotheby's.

	PhS		PLAIN SIG.	
	Low	High	Low	High
Summer, Donna	18	21	6	8
Sutherland, Donald	14	17	7	9
Swanson, Gloria	120	180	25	45
Swayze, Patrick	24	28	16	21
Swit, Loretta	20	25	9	13
Tandy, Jessica	30	40	12	15
Tate, Sharon	300	500	100	150
Taylor, Elizabeth	200	300	80	120
Temple, Shirley (as child)	300	500	35	45
Thomas, Heather	25	29	6	9
Thomas, Marlo	10	13	2	3
Tiegs, Cheryl	13	17	5	7
Townsend, Pete	50	80	20	30
Travolta, John	28	34	6	9
Turner, Kathleen	28	34	6	8
Turner, Lana	63	80	13	17
Twiggy	20	24	9	12
Ustinov, Peter	30	40	10	15
Valentino, Rudolph	1200	1800	500	800
Van Dyke, Dick	20	30	4	6
Voight, Jon	18	21	3	4
Wagner, Lindsay	13	17	4	5
Wagner, Robert	21	24	9	13
Wayne, John	400	700	150	250
Weissmuller, Johnny	200	250	40	70
Welch, Raquel	17	21	6	9
Welk, Lawrence	15	20	4	6
Welles, Orson	350	450	40	70
West, Adam	21	21	6	8
West, Mae	200	300	40	60
Wilder, Gene	17	20	6	8
Williams, Esther	14	16	5	7

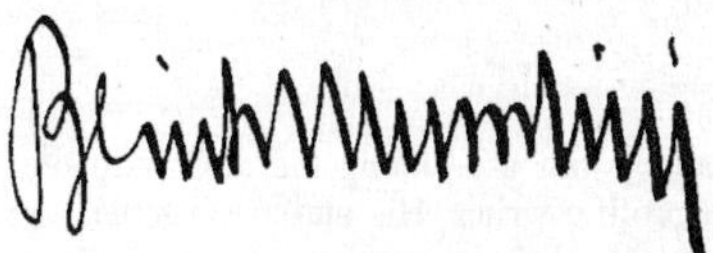

Benito Mussolini

Politicians

	ALS		CUT SIG.	
	Low	High	Low	High
Balfour, Arthur	$44	$100	$15	$40
Bismark, Otto von	300	4000	75	175
Brandt, Willy	70	180	8	18
Bryan, William Jennings	100	300	35	90
Byrd, Robert Co.	35	80	5	11
Castro, Fidel	475	3000	250	600
Chirac, Jacques	67	161	8	20
Churchill, Winston S.	1600	1000	240	500
Delai, Lama (XIV)	70	175	25	50
Ervin, Samuel	25	60	3	7
Fulbright, James	35	80	6	15
Gladstone, William	180	400	20	50
Gorbachev, Mikhail	317	750	150	360
Gromyko, Andrei	110	240	40	90
Heath, Edward	41	120	13	30
Kohl, Helmut	24	55	5	10
McGovern, George	38	85	3	7
McNamara, Robert	42	100	5	710
Mitterand, Francois	100	350	5	10
Mussolini, Benito	1000	5000	120	300
O'Neill, Thomas	33	74	5	10
Rockefeller, Nelson	180	404	10	20
Shriver, Sargent	9	21	1	3
Wagner, Robert F.	70	175	10	20

Admission Ticket, sgd "W.S. Churchill." —Photo courtesy Swann Galleries.

Presidents

Presidential letters and autographs are among the most valuable. George Washington, like many men of his era, was a prolific writer. His autograph letters are often offered at auction. Dwight Eisenhower, however, rarely took a pen to hand for more than a signature. An Eisenhower ALS is often worth more than a Washington ALS! Also beware of auto-pen. This automatic signing device became entrenched in the White House in the early 1960s. It has signed a vast majority of letters coming from the presidents since that time.

ALS and LS

	ALS		LS	
	Low	High	Low	High
Washington, George	$10,000	$150,000	$1000	$100,000
Adams, John	8000	40,000	4000	15,000
Jefferson, Thomas	10,000	50,000	5000	25,000
Madison, James	2000	10,000	1000	5000
Monroe, James	1000	10,000	1000	5000
Adams, John Q.	1000	10,000	500	3000
Jackson, Andrew	1500	10,000	500	5000
Van Buren, Martin	500	2000	300	2000
Harrison, William H.	500	5000	300	3000
Tyler, John	500	4000	300	2000
Polk, James K.	500	5000	300	2000
Taylor, Zachary	500	5000	300	3000
Fillmore, Millard	500	3000	300	3000
Pierce, Franklin	500	2500	200	2000
Buchanan, James	300	2500	250	1000
Lincoln, Abraham	7500	50,000	5000	20,000
Johnson, Andrew	1000	5000	500	2500
Grant, U.S.	500	25,000	300	10,000
Hayes, R.B.	200	1000	100	500
Garfield, James	200	1500	500	2500
Arthur, Chester A.	400	1500	300	2500
Cleveland, Grover	200	5000	200	2500
Harrison, Benjamin	200	2000	150	2500
McKinley, William	200	2000	100	750
Roosevelt, Theodore	500	7500	150	3000
Taft, William H.	200	1000	100	500
Wilson, Woodrow	500	5000	100	500
Harding, Warren G.	500	2000	200	500
Coolidge, Calvin	1000	5000	100	500
Hoover, Herbert	2000	5000	100	400
Roosevelt, Franklin	1000	5000	150	2500
Truman, Harry	1000	3000	150	500
Eisenhower, Dwight	1000	5000	150	500
Kennedy, John F.	1000	10,000	3000	4000
Johnson, Lyndon	1000	5000	150	500
Nixon, Richard M.	1000	10,000	150	1000
Ford, Gerald	1000	3000	150	500
Carter, Jimmy	1000	3000	150	500
Reagan, Ronald	1000	5000	150	1000
Bush, George	500	2500	100	500
Clinton, Bill	1000	2500	100	500

DS, PhS, and Cut Sig.

	DS		PhS		CUT SIG.	
	Low	High	Low	High	Low	High
Washington, George	$8000	$16,000	—	—	$2000	$5000
Adams, John	2000	6000	—	—	1600	2400
Jefferson, Thomas	4000	8000	—	—	200	400
Madison, James	1000	1600	—	—	600	1000
Monroe, James	800	1200	—	—	600	1000
Adams, John Q.	600	1000	—	—	200	400
Jackson, Andrew	800	1400	—	—	600	1000
Van Buren, Martin	600	1000	—	—	300	500
Harrison, William H.	1000	1600	—	—	200	400
Tyler, John	800	1200	—	—	160	240
Polk, James K.	800	1400	—	—	200	400
Taylor, Zachary	1000	1600	—	—	300	500
Fillmore, Millard	300	500	—	—	200	400
Pierce, Frnaklin	800	1200	—	—	200	400
Buchanan, James	400	800	—	—	300	500
Lincoln, Abraham	4000	8000	$15,000	$50,000	1000	3500
Johnson, Andrew	800	1600	3000	5000	400	800
Grant, U.S.	800	1400	1000	1600	500	700
Hayes, R.B.	400	600	600	1000	300	500
Garfield, James	400	800	2000	3000	200	400
Cleveland, Grover	300	500	600	900	200	300
Arthur, Chester A.	600	1000	1200	1800	300	600
Harrison, Benjamin	400	600	2000	3000	300	500
McKinley, William	300	500	1200	1800	200	300
Roosevelt, Theodore	600	1000	800	1200	300	500
Taft, William H.	300	500	800	1200	200	300
Wilson, Woodrow	600	1000	800	1200	300	500
Harding, Warren G.	200	400	400	800	200	300
Coolidge, Calvin	200	400	300	500	100	300
Hoover, Herbert	200	400	200	400	100	300
Roosevelt, Franklin	300	500	600	1000	200	400
Truman, Harry	200	400	400	800	200	400
Eisenhower, Dwight	200	400	400	800	300	500
Kennedy, John F.	300	1500	300	750	200	500
Johnson, Lyndon	200	300	200	600	200	400
Nixon, Richard M.	200	300	200	400	100	200
Ford, Gerald	200	300	200	400	100	200
Carter, Jimmy	200	300	100	300	100	300
Reagan, Ronald	1000	1400	300	500	200	400
Bush, George	200	300	200	300	100	300
Clinton, Bill	200	300	200	300	100	20

Abraham Lincoln.

Zachary Taylor and Richard M. Nixon.

Gerald R. Ford and Jimmy Carter.

Ronald Reagan and George Bush.

Avon Bottles

David Hall McConnell founded The California Perfume Company in New York City at the end of the nineteenth century. The firm changed its name to Avon in 1939. A pioneer in home sales, most people recognize the company's figural decanters produced in the late 1960s to the early 1980s. Prices are based on bottles in mint condition in original boxes of excellent to near mint condition. For further information see Bud Hastin's *Avon & C.P.C. Collector's Encyclopedia, 15th Edition,* published by author, 1998.

Red Cardinal, 1979, $4–$6.

	LOW	HIGH
After Shave on Tap, 1976	$3	$5
Age of the Iron Horse Stein, 1982	20	30
Angler (fishing reel), 1970	5	8
Auburn Boattail Speedster, red and black ceramic, 1983	15	20
Avon Calling Wall Phone, 1973	8	12
Barber Pole, 1974	3	5
Barber Shop Brush, 1976	4	6
Bugatti '27, 1974	8	12
Bunny Salt and Pepper	8	12
Cable Car, 1974	8	10
Camper, 1972	8	12
Casey's Lantern, 1966	45	55
Century of Basketball Stein	40	60
1926 Checker Cab, 1977	7	9
'55 Chevy, 1975	8	12
Chief Pontiac Car Mascot, 1976	8	10
Christmas Carol Stein	40	60
Clock, Léisure Hours, 1970	6	8
Collector's Pipe, 1973	4	6
Colt Revolver 1851, 1975	8	10
'37 Cord, 1974	6	8
Corncob Pipe, 1974	4	6
Corvette Stingray '65, 1975	4	6

	LOW	HIGH
Country and Western Music Stein	30	50
Country Kitchen (rooster), 1973	4	6
Country Store Coffee Mill, 1972	4	6
Country Vendor, 1973	8	12
Covered Wagon, 1970	4	6
Derringer, 1977	6	8
Derringer, Philadelphia, 1980	8	10
Dingo Boot (plastic), 1978	2	3
Dollars and Scents, 1966	8	12
Duck, Mallard, 1967	9	12
Dueling Pistol 1760, 1973	7	9
Dueling Pistol II, 1975	7	9
Dueling Set, Twenty Paces, box, red lining, 1967	30	40
Dueling Set, Twenty Paces, rare raised gun sight, 1967	70	90
Dune Buggy, 1971	7	9
Dutch Pipe, 1973	6	7
Eiffel Tower, 1970	6	8
Eight Ball, 1973	5	7
Express Train, 1876 Centennial, 1978	7	9
1910 Fire Fighter, 1975	6	8
Firm Grip, wrench, 1977	4	6
Flower Maiden, 1973	5	7
Fly-a-Balloon, 1975	6	8
'36 Ford, 1976	6	8
French Telephone, 1971	15	20
Garden Girl, 1975	7	9
Gas Pump, 1979	7	9
Gavel, 1967	8	10
General 4-4-0 Locomotive, 1971	7	9
Gold Cadillac, 1969	8	10
Golden Harvest, ear-of-corn lotion dispenser, 1977	5	8
Golden Rocket Early Locomotive, 1974	7	10
Golf Cart, 1972	7	9
Gone Fishing Boat, 1973	8	12
Greyhound Bus (1931), 1976	7	9
Harvester Tractor, 1973	8	12
Haynes Apperson 1902, 1973	6	8
Highway King, 1977	8	12
Homestead (cabin), 1973	4	5
Indian Head Penny, 1970	5	7
Island Parakeet, 1977	4	6
Jaguar, 1973	6	8
Jeep Renegade, 1981	5	8
Kodiak Bear, 1977	6	8
Library Lamp, 1976	4	6
Longhorn Steer, 1975	6	8
Majestic Elephant, 1977	8	10
Maxwell '23, 1972	6	8
Mini-Bike, 1972	5	7
Mixed Doubles, tennis ball, 1977	4	7
Model A, 1972	5	6
Motocross Helmet, 1976	4	6
Mustang '64, 1976	4	6
One Good Turn, screwdriver, 1976	4	6

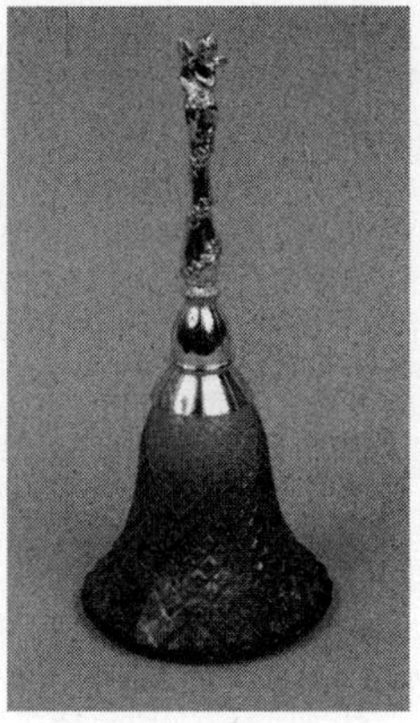

Rosepoint Bell, 1978, $5–$8.

	LOW	HIGH
Packard Roadster, 1970	6	8
Pheasant, 1972	8	10
Pheasant Reissue, 1977	7	9
Pickup Truck, 1973 Ford Ranger, 1978	5	7
Pierce Arrow '33, 1975	6	8
Pipe Dream, 1967	6	8
Pistol, Blunderbuss, 1780, 1976	9	12
Pony Express, 1971	6	8
Pony Post, 1972	3	5
Pony Post Tall, 1966	7	9
Quail, 1973	6	8
Rainbow Trout, 1973	7	9
Red Sentinel Firetruck, 1978	10	12
Remember When (school), 1972	4	6
Revolutionary Cannon, 1975	4	5
Rio Depot Wagon, 1972	6	8
Road Runner, 1973	5	7
Rolls Royce, 1972	7	10
Royal Siamese Cat, 1978	5	7
Scottish Lass, 1975	5	7
Sea Horse, large, 1970	7	9
Sea Horse, miniature, 1973	4	6
Sea Maiden (mermaid), 1971	6	8
Sea Trophy Swordfish, 1972	8	12
Short Pony, 1968	5	6
Side Wheeler, 1971	4	6
Silver Duesenberg, 1970	8	12
Skater's Waltz, 1979	7	9
Skip-a-Rope, 1977	6	8
Smooth Going Oil Can, 1978	4	6
Snoopy Surprise, 1969	8	10
Snow Mobile, 1974	8	10
Spanish Señorita, 1975	7	9
Stage Coach, 1970	5	7
Stanley Steamer, 1971	6	8
Station Wagon, 1971	8	10

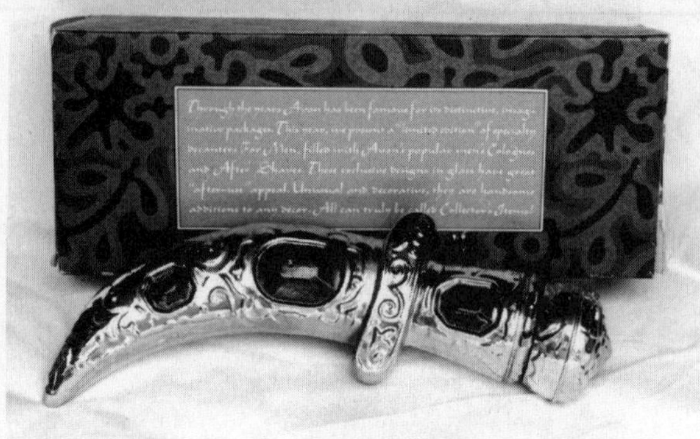

Scimitar, 1968, $10–$15.

	LOW	HIGH
Sterling Six II, 1973	4	6
Sterling Six Silver, 1978	5	8
Stock Car Racer, 1974	5	7
Straight 8, 1969	5	7
Studebaker '51, 1975	5	7
Super Cycle, 1971	6	8
Sure Catch Fishing Lure, 1977	5	6
Sure Winner Race Car, 1972	6	8
Swinger Golf Bag, 1969	8	12
Ten Point Buck, 1973	6	8
Thomas Flyer 1908, 1974	7	9
Thomas Jefferson Hand Gun, 1978	8	10
Thunderbird '55, 1974	5	6
Touring T, 1969	6	8
Touring T Silver, 1978	5	8
Tractor Trailer, Big Rig, 1975	8	12
Triumph TR-3, 1975	8	12
Truck, Big Mack, 1973	7	9
Victorian Pitcher and Bowl, 1971	6	9
Victorian Teddy Collectible Bear, 1995	30	50
Victorian Washstand, 1973	4	6
Volkswagon, black, 1970	7	9
Volkswagon, blue, 1973	7	9
Weather or Not (barometer/thermometer), 1969	8	10
Western Boot, 1973	4	5
Western Choice, 1967	16	22
Winners Circle Stein	40	60

Baskets

There are several types of basket construction. Wickerwork, the most common and widely used technique, is an over-and-under pattern. Twining is similar; two strands are twisted as they are woven over and under, producing a finer weave. Plaiting gives a checkerboard effect in either a tight weave or left with open spaces. Twill work is similar, but with a diagonal effect achieved by changing the number of strands over which the weaver passes. Coiling is the most desirable weave for the collector. This technique has been refined since its conception around 7000 B.C. Fibers are wrapped around and stitched together to form the basket's shape. Most of these pieces were either used for ceremonial purposes or for holding liquids, since these tightly woven containers were leakproof.

Baskets are easy to care for but a few basic rules must be followed: Never wash an Indian basket, especially baskets made of pine needles, straw, grass or leaves. Dust them gently using a soft sable artist's brush. Willow, oak, hickory and rattan baskets may be washed in a mild solution of Murphy's Oil Soap and dried briefly in a sunny location. Baskets continuously exposed to the sun will fade.

Covered Nantucket Basket, $650.
—Photo courtesy Aston Macek.

	AUCTION	RETAIL	
		Low	High
Ash Splint Basket, 8.75" x 6"	$80	$125	$200
Buttoks, 17" 1	250	400	600
Cheese Basket, 6.25" h, 13" dia	245	400	600
Chilcotin Burden Basket, 11"	275	450	750
Chilcotin Burden Basket, 16.5"	275	450	850
Chilcotin Coiled Lidded Basket, 5"	135	250	425
Chilcotin Coiled Pedestal Basket, w/ gallery, 10.5"	300	600	1000
Chicotin Coiled Trinket Basket, 7"	245	425	750
Chilcotin Lidded Basket, w/ tree design, 7"	250	475	825
Chicotin Round Coiled Basket, w/ gallery, 6.5"	240	400	700
Clothes, round w/ 2 handles	175	300	500
Coiled Lilooet Burden Basket, c1900, 15"	1850	3250	6000
Coiled Pomo Basket, w/ arrowhead design	200	375	650

	AUCTION	RETAIL Low	RETAIL High
Covered Oak Splint Basket, 11.5" dia	175	300	500
Drying, New England, shallow rim, c1850, 30" x 48"	300	600	1000
Field Basket, oak splint, c1885	190	350	620
Haida Cedar Bark Basket, 13"	300	550	900
Haida Spruce Root Basket	60	125	200
Hopi Coiled Plaque Caught in Basket Dance, 1991, 9"	60	125	200
Japanese, tightly woven circular, 9" dia	200	375	650
Kilkitatl Salish Basket, 8"	250	475	825
Knitting Basket, fully imbricated, 4.5"	170	320	550
Knob Top Coiled Thompson River Basket, 5.5"	335	620	1200
Knob Top Thompson River Basket, w/ tree design, 8.5"	255	470	830
Laundry, oak splint, 1910	70	130	230
Lidded Salish Basket, w/ butterfly design, c1920, 18"	2250	4300	7500
Lidded Salish Basket, w/ double handles, 28"	475	900	1650
Lilooet Coiled Burden Basket, maker's prov., c1905, 13"	1300	2500	4600
Maine Indian Circular Basket, covered, decorated w/ red and black potato design, 17" dia	8740	12,000	16,000
Maine Indian Rectangular Basket, covered, painted red, blue, and green, 12" l	4000	6500	10,000
Mission Tray, 12" dia	300	600	1000
Nantucket Circular Basket, w/ heart-form side handles, inscribed, 9.5" dia	1800	2500	5000
Nantucket Circular Swing Handle Basket, 7" dia	300	600	1000
Nantucket Lightship, 5" x 10"	600	1150	2000
Nantucket Oval Swing Handle, 13" l	1000	1750	2500
Nantucket Oval Swing Handle, 8"	2000	3500	5500
Nantucket Oval Swing Handle Pocketbook, w/ carved whale motif by Herwin Boyer, 9" l	3000	5000	9000
Nantucket Single Egg Basket, 2.75" dia	500	900	1400
New England Splint Featherbed Storage Basket, covered, painted blue, 30" h	650	100	1750
Nootka Basket, 11"	75	140	240
Nootka Basketry Covered Bottle, 5"	105	200	340
Nootka Basketry Covered Bottle, c1920	100	190	330
Nootka Basketry Covered Cobalt Blue Bottle, w/ thunderbird	120	220	400
Nootka Basketry Covered Jar, w/ animal dec	525	1000	1750
Nootka Lidded Basket, 3.5"	55	100	180
Nootka Lidded Basket, 4"	75	150	250
Nootka Lidded Basket, w/ canoe and bird design, 10"	185	330	600
Nootka Lidded Basket, w/ duck and reindeer design	85	160	280
Nootka Lidded Basket, w/ wolf design, 3"	65	120	200
Nootka Oval Basket, w/ salal berry dye	225	400	700
Nootka Oval Basket, w/ whaling design, 4.5"	475	880	1550
Nootka Round Basket, w/ whale and canoe design, 4.5"	180	330	600
Nootka Round Lidded Basket, 3.5"	60	110	200
Nootka Shell-Covered Basket, w/ animal design	380	700	1250
Nootka Woven Cedar Bark Basket, 12"	130	250	425
Pima Coiled, flaring body, human figures, 10" dia	400	750	1300
Rye Straw, w/ handles, 13" dia	550	100	1600
Rye Straw Charger, 20" dia	900	1750	2500
Salish Basket, 10"	70	130	230
Salish Basket, 11"	25	50	80

	AUCTION	RETAIL Low	RETAIL High
Salish Basket, 15"	90	170	300
Salish Basket, fully imbricated, lidded, 6"	275	510	900
Salish Basket, w/ leather handles, c1920	150	280	500
Salish Basket, zig zag design, 16.5"	275	510	900
Salish Basketry Tray, 18"	80	150	260
Salish Basketry Trunk, 23"	350	650	1140
Salish Boat Shape Basket, w/ gallery, 16.75"	150	280	490
Salish Cradle Basket, 24"'	170	320	550
Salish Female Papoose Cradle Basket, 27.5"	200	370	650
Salish Fishing Creel/Pipe Bag Basket, 12"	450	840	1470
Salish Imbricated Basket, w/ handles, 11.5"	200	370	650
Salish Papoose Cradle Basket, 30"	200	370	650
Salish Rectangular Basket, 13.5"	95	180	310
Salish Rectangular Basket Purse, 7"	75	140	240
Salish Rectangular Lidded Basket, w/ diamond design, 15.5"	225	420	730
Salish Round Lidded Basket, 8.5"	175	330	570
Salish Wool Knitting Basket, 10.5"	250	470	820
Sewing, wicker	40	70	130
Shaker, cheese, round, 12" dia	340	630	1110
Splint, collecting, tightly woven, 8" x 9"	40	70	130
Splint, hickory, open handles	50	90	160
Splint, oval, wooden handles	80	150	260
Splint, oak, buttocks	90	170	300
Thompson River Burden Basket, w/ handles, 22"	200	370	650
Thompson River Coiled Basket, w/ snake design, 8.25"	475	900	1600
Thompson River Pedestal Basket, 10"	60	100	165
Tlingit Knob Top Spruce Root Basket, 19th C, 5.75"	500	1000	1800
Ucluelet Nootka Basket, 4.5"	100	200	350
Winnebago Indian Basket, oval, 21" x 14"	45	100	175

Ohio Mennonite Gathering Basket, wooden bottom sgd "ELI," $675.
—Photo courtesy Aston Macek.

Beer-Related Memorabilia

Advertising and Promotional

	LOW	HIGH
Ballantine Ale Tap Knob Insert, porcelain on metal	$4	$8
Beefeater Gin Figural Composition Display, 1960s	80	100
Bert and Harry Piel Metal Statue, 1955, 9" h	50	80
Bert and Harry Piel Vinyl Store Display, 1965, 11.5" h	40	60
Blatz Beer Display, 3 baseball players, 1968, 11" h	100	150
Budweiser Ashtray, glass, round, 1950s, 5" dia	8	10
Budweiser Beer Booklet, 20 pp, 1965, 5" x 7"	7	9
Budweiser Playing Cards, label	8	12
Budweiser Sign, plastic w/ light-up bottle, 1960s, 5" x 12"	45	75
Bud Man Ceramic Beer Stein, 1989, 8.5" h	20	30
Busch Beer Box of Matchbooks, unused, 1970s	2	5
Corbys Stir Container, plastic, 1950s, 6" h	20	25
Coronet Waiter VSQ Brandy Store Display, 1955, 19" h	125	175
Falstaff Beer Pocket Protector, 1960s	4	6
Gunther's Beer Clicker	20	25
Heinekin Dutch Boy w/ Bottle Figural Display, 1960s, 15" h	80	120
Hines Cognac Bottle Store Display, 1940s, 20" h	25	35
Hyde Park Beer Coaster, blue and orange, 4" dia	4	6
Iroquois Beer Shaving Razor, straight blade, plastic handle	25	35
Labatt's Figural Vinyl Display, 1960s	50	75
Marathon Lager Beer Foam Scraper, 1950s	20	30
Miller High Life Tip Tray, 1940s, 4" l	30	40
Pilsener Brewing Wall Mounted Bottle Opener, cast metal, orig box	25	40
Schlitz Beer Rotating Globe Light, glass and plastic, electric, 1950s, orig box	30	50
Straub's Beer Fly Swatter, plastic, 1950s	2	3

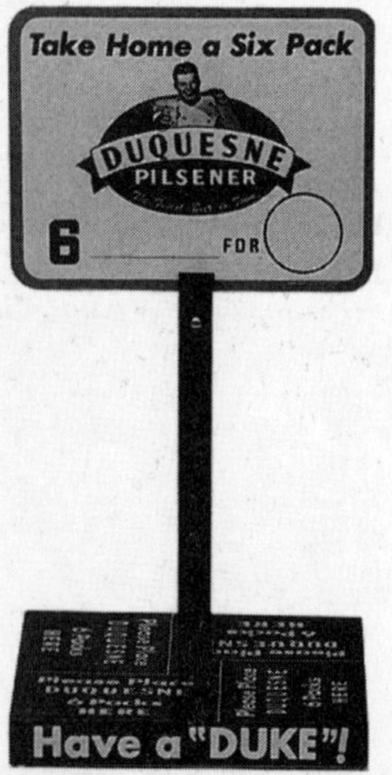

Duquesne Pilsener Display Rack, wood base and pole, fiberboard sign, w/ orig box, new old stock, 58" h, $39 at auction. —Photo courtesy Collectors Auction Services.

Beer Bottles

	LOW	HIGH
"Abner-Drury Brewing Co., Washington, D.C., Registered Not To Be Sold," amber, 9.5", rd.	$5	$7
"The Akron Brewing Co. Akron, O.," lt green, 9.25", rd	4	6
"Andrew Liptak Beer Bottler, 313 7 319 Goodwin St., Perth Amboy N.J.," aqua, 9.25", rd, 1890s	20	30
"The August Wagner & Sons Products Co., Contents 12 Flu. Ozs. Columbus, O.," amber, 9.5", rd	4	6
"B-B-Co Perfectly Brewed, Baltimore, Md," clear, 9.5", rd	5	7
"Blatz," lt aqua, 9.4", rd	5	7
"Chr. Heurich Brewing Co. Washington D.C.," amber, 9.1", rd	7	10
"The Christian Moerlein Brewing Co. Cincinnati, O.," amber, 9.5", rd	5	7
"The E.B. Co. Elkins, W.Va." emb on bottom, "E.B.CO" emb obverse, amber, 9.5", red, 1890s	9	13
"Fred Bauernschmist American Brewery, Balto, Md.," aqua, 9", rd	13	18
"The Geo. Gunther Jr. Brg. Co. Blto, Md., Registered Contents 12 Fl. Oz.," amber, 9.5", rd	5	7
"H.L. Morrison & Co., 16 Mulberry St., Lynn, Mass.," clear, 9.25", rd, 1890s	20	30
"The Herangourt Brewing Co., Cincinnati, O. Union Made," amber, 9.25", rd, 1890s	11	15
"Hoster, Col. O.," amber, 9.4", c1900	11	15
"Hoster, Col, O.," amber, 9.6", rd, 1890s	9	13
"Hoster Columbus A.B. Co.," lt green, 9.4", rd	4	6
"The Huebner Toledo Breweries Co. Toledo, Ohio, Registered 'Pure And Without Drugs Or Poison'," amber, 9.25", rd	9	13
"Hyde Park St. Louis," amber, 9.25", rd	5	7
"J.B. Hankinson U.N.X.L.D. Bottler Freehold, N.J., This Bottle Not To Be Sold," aqua, 9.1", rd, 1890s	23	31
"John Brockhagen, 608 West 47th St., New York," aqua, 9.25", rd, 1890s	22	30
"The John Wagner Brewing Co. Sidney, Ohio," amber, 9.25", rd	4	6
"The Joseph Herb Brewing Co. Milan, Ohio," amber, 9.25", rd, 1900s	16	23
"Lang's Buffalo, N.Y.," lt green, 9.5", rd	5	7
"Lemp, St. Louis" emb in shield, aqua, 9.5", 1890s	20	30
"M. Conway, 16th & Ridge Ave., Philada. Registered" emb obverse, "This Bottle Not To Be Sold" emb verso, clear, 9", rd, 1890s	20	30
"Mcavoy's Alma Water. This Bottle Is The Property Of The Mcavoy Brew Co., Chicago," lt green, 9.25", rd	5	8
"The Ohio Brewing Co. Columbus, O.," amber, 9.5", rd	3	5
"The Pilsener Brewing Co. Cleveland, O.," lt green, 9.5", rd	4	6
"Pilsener's Product Clevelant," lt green, 9.5", rd	4	6
"Renner & Weber Brg. Co., Mansfield, O. Red Band, Contents 13 Fl. Oz.," lt green, 9.4", rd	5	7
"Renner & Weber Brg. Co. Mansfield, O.," lt green, 8.25", rd	4	6
"Robert H. Graupner, Harrisburg, Pa." emb on bottom, lt green, 9.5", rd, 1900s	6	9
"S.B. Co. Galeton, Pa.," amber, 9.4", rd, 1890s	9	13
"Schlitz," label missing dated on bottom "5 50," royal ruby red, 9.6", rd	40	60
"Schmidt's Bottling Works, Hanover, Pa., Registered," aqua, 9.25", 1890s	20	28
"The Standard Brewing Co. Cleveland, O.," lt green, 9.1", rd	8	12
"The Standard Brewing Company Cleveland O.," lt green, 9.1", rd, 1900s	13	18

Beer Cans

A great many peoples' favorite beverage container, the beer can, was introduced by the G. Krueger Brewing Company of Newark, New Jersey in Richmond, Virginia in the spring of 1935. Called flatops, the breweries included opening instructions on the can and gave away millions of "punch type" openers with the purchase of the product.

A different can design, the cone top, was introduced by Jos. Schlitz Brewing Company in August 1935. This and the crowntainer, a third can design, were met with great favor by the smaller brewers as they could be filled on the bottle line and there was not a need to invest in expensive canning equipment. The big problem with cone tops and crowntainers was that they were hard to stack. These cans disappeared in the late sixties when most of the smaller brewers had gone out of business.

The next major innovation was the tab top, which eliminated the punch opener altogether, followed by the aluminum can which greatly reduced shipping weight and was easier to cool.

The following prices are for mint examples opened or unopened. Rust, dents and scratches decrease the value of a beer can. Each entry below begins with the name brand and a description, followed by the type of top, the number of ounces and the brewery name. Abbreviations include *CT* (cone top), *FT* (flat top) and *TT* (tab top).

Many firms produced the same product in other states or licensed others to produce it. This leads to confusion. For detailed information see *The Official Price Guide to Beer Cans, Fifth Edition* by Bill Mugrage, House of Collectibles, Random House, NY, 1993. He is listed in the back of this book. The guide suggests to check older, full cans periodically to make sure they are not leaking and, if you want to drain a full can, open it from the bottom where it can't be seen. Mr. Mugrage also dispels the myth about the value of Billy Beer. He states that any of the five different versions of Billy Beer are worth $2 to $3 each, not hundreds of dollars as rumored. The collector's club is the Beer Can Collectors of America, 747 Mercus Court, Fenton, MO 63026.

	LOW	HIGH
Alpine Brand, premium beer, white and red, round label, FT, 12 oz, Peter Fox	$85	$120
Arrow 77, TT, 12 oz, Cumberland	5	15
Aspen Gold, white and blue, depicting mountain, FT, 12 oz, Tivoli	15	25
Atlas, Prager Bock Beer, gold and red with goat's head, FT, 12 oz, Atlas	90	125
Badger Beer, red and black depicting badger, FT, 12 oz, Whitewater	250	300
Balboa Export Premium Pale Beer, yellow and red, FT, 12 oz, Southern	300	350
Banner Extra Dry, white and red, "Prem. Beer" in blue, FT, 12 oz, Cumberland	35	50
Bantam Ale, squat, white and lt green, FT, 8 oz, Gobel	40	60
Bartels Pure, white and red, man w/ beard, FT, 12 oz, Lion	65	85
Bavarian Jay Vee, blue and white, FT, 12 oz, Grace	115	140
Bavarian's Old Style, white, gold, and red, name/ gold lettering, CT, 12 oz, Bav	15	20
Becker's Best, silver w/ black lettering, FT, 12 oz, Becker	125	175
Ben Brew, yellow and gold, "100% Grain Beer," CT, 12 oz, Franklin	150	175
Beverwyck Ale, Shamrock, CT, 12 oz, Beverwyck	40	60
Big Cat Malt Liquor, white depicting running cat, TT, 16 oz, Pabst	2	5
Black Dallas Malt Liquor, blue and black, evening skyline, TT, 12 oz, Walter	15	30
Blackhawk, Native American profile, CT, 12 oz, Blackhawk	150	200
Blatz, white and brown, TT, 12 oz, G. Heileman	1	3
Bond Hill Beer, blue, gold, and red, FT, 12 oz, Gretz	700	750
Boston Light Ale, black, white, and red, lighthouse, CT, 12 oz, Boston	750	850
Brown Derby Beer, brown and green w/ derby and cane, FT, 12 oz, Humboldt	60	90
Buccaneer Beer, gold and white, pirate, FT, 12 oz, Gulf	650	700
Budweiser Malt Liquor, TT, 16 oz, Anheuser-Busch	2	5
Budweiser, "Tab Top," TT, 16 oz, Anheuser-Busch	1	3

	LOW	HIGH
Burger, white and dark red, no outline name, FT, 12 oz, Burger	12	18
Burgermeister Premium, cream, red, and gold, gold bands, FT, 12 oz, Warsaw	5	9
Cab Cream Ale, copper color w/ horse and buggy, FT, 12 oz, Wehle	850	950
Cascade, "King Size" near top, TT, 16 oz, Blitz Weinhard	12	15
Cee Bee, red and white, TT, 12 oz, Colonial	12	18
Champagne Velvet Beer, gold can, eagle logo, CT, 12 oz, Terre Haute Brewing Co.	350	450
Coal Cracker Beer, multicolor, TT, 12 oz, Yuengling	3	5
Conon's Beer, red and white, script w/ leaf surround, CT, 12 oz, Condon	650	750
Country Club, white, red, and gold, FT, 12 oz, Goetz	20	30
Croft Cream Ale, green can, yellow lettering, 3 heads, Ct, 32 oz, Broston	400	450
Drewry's Malt Liquor, red, green, and white, "A Man's Drink," FT, 12 oz, Drewry	700	900
Frisco Beer, brown, black, and white cartouche of San Francisco skyline, FT, 12 oz, General	600	650
Gerst 77 Beer, metallic gold, red, and white, CT, 12 oz, Gerst	500	600
Gretz Ale, yellow oval, red lettering, CT, 12 oz, Gretz	1000	1200
Highlander Premium, red and white, revised version, FT, 12 oz, Missoula	12	18
Hillman's Superb, blue and gold, FT, 12 oz, Empire	60	80
Hof-Brau, red and white, gray name, blue lettering, TT, 12 oz, Maier	8	12
Hofbrau, cream, white, and red, German inn, FT, 12 oz, Hofbrau	18	22
Hoffman House, white, brown, and red, FT, 12 oz, Walter	4	7
Holiday Special, white and brown w/ blue bands top and bottom, FT, 12 oz, Potosi	12	18
Horton Beer, orange can, block lettering, CT, 12 oz, Horton	400	450
Kingsbury Real Draft, white, brown, and red, wood grain, TT, 12 oz, Kingsbury	8	10
Koehler, dark blue and white, orange trim name, TT, 12 oz, Erie	3	5
Koenig Brau, gold and white, TT, 12 oz, Koenig Brau	8	10
Krueger, yellow, red, and white, "Lt. Lager" in black, FT, 12 oz, Krueger	40	60
Little Dutch Beer, oval w/ Dutch boy and windmills, CT, 32 oz, Wacker	1000	1200
London Bobby Beer, red, black, and white parchment design w/ yellow highlights, CT, 12 oz, Miami Valley	750	850
Lucky Lager, pale blue and gold, name curved, TT, 12 oz, Lucky Lager	5	7
Lucky Malt Liquor, TT, 16 oz, Lucky Lager	30	40
M.C. Beer, yellow can, blue circle, CT, 12 oz, Mt. Carbon	600	650
Maier Select, red, white, and blue, blue leaf near top, TT, 12 oz, Maier	40	60
Malt Duck, purple and white, TT, 12 oz, National	40	60
Manheim, red and white, TT, 12 oz, Reading	9	12
Meister Brau, white, gold, and red, red band at top, FT, 12 oz, Peter Hand	8	12
Mile Hi, red, white, and blue, Colorado mountains, FT, 12 oz, Tivoli	40	60
Miller Select, red, white, and blue, 1/4 moon in blue medallion, FT, 12 oz, Miller	50	60
Milwaukee Premium, white, red, and gold, FT, 12 oz, Waukee	15	20
Milwaukee's Best, blue and white, stein, FT, 12 oz, Gettelman	18	22
Mitchell's Premium, red, white, and blue, FT, 12 oz, Mitchell	100	150
National Ale, green U.S. map, CT, 12 oz, National	500	550
National Beer, red U.S. map, CT, 12 oz, National	1000	1200
North Star XXX Beer, blue and white, silver star, FT, 12 oz, Schmidt	25	35
Old Dutch Beer, brown and orange label w/ windmill, CT, 12 oz, Old Dutch	650	750
P.O.C. Pilsner Beer, maroon, gold label, CT, 12 oz, Pilsner	90	110
Pabst Blue Ribbon, gold, white, and blue, slogan above gold band, FT, 12 oz, Pabst	8	12
Pabst Blue Ribbon, red, white, and blue, FT, 12 oz, Pabst	8	10
Pacific Beer, blue can, white lettering, CT, 12 oz, Rainier	300	500
Pearl Beer, white and blue, TT, 12 oz, Pearl	8	12

Left to right: Mühlheim Draft Beer, TT, 12 oz, $8–$10; Stoney's Pilsener Beer, CT, Jones Brewing, $60–$80.

	LOW	HIGH
Penguin Extra Dry, white and blue, FT, 12 oz, Horlacher	15	25
Pfeiffer's, gold, white, and red, horizon, striping, FT, 12 oz, Pfeiffer	10	15
Pickwick Ale, gold, black, and white, FT, 12 oz, Haffenreffer	125	175
Piel's, gold, silver, and black, white name, FT, 12 oz, Piel's	12	15
Primo Hawaiian, metallic gold, white map, TT, 12 oz, Jos. Schlitz	5	10
Prinz Brau Beer, "Anniversary Offer," TT, 12 oz, Prinz Brau	2	5
Rainier Ale, green, gold label, TT, 12 oz, Rainier	15	20
Red Fox Beer, red can w/ dressed fox, CT, 12 oz, Largay	900	1200
Schlitz Sunshine Vitamin D, brown and white, CT, 12 oz, Schlitz	85	115
Senate Beer, red, brown trim, FT, 12 oz, C. Heurich	150	200
Sick's Select Beer, metallic maroon, yellow, 6 globe, FT, 12 oz, Sick's	150	200
Silver State Beer, blue and white can w/ script lettering, Schneider	1500	1800
Stag, "Half Quart" large white letters near top, TT, 16 oz, Carling	1	3
Stallion XII, gold, white, and red, horse, TT, 12 oz, Gold Medal	85	115
Standard Cream Ale, green, white, and gold, TT, 12 oz, Standard Rochester	35	50
Standard Dry Ale, blue, white, and gold, TT, 12 oz, Eastern	5	7
Stegmaier Bock, brown and white, "Truly Brewed," TT, 12 oz, Stegmaier	2	5
Stegmaier Gold Medal, gold and white, TT, 12 oz, Stegmaier	2	5
Topaz (crowntainer), silver, red stripes near bottom, CT, 12 oz, Koller	135	185
Topper Draught (gal.), CT, 64 oz, Standard	60	80
Tropical Premium, brown and white, "Taste Tells," CT, 12 oz, Florida	300	400
Tru-Blue Ale, blue, green, yellow, and white, 10-star dec, CT, 12 oz, North Hampton	400	600
Valley Forge Beer, yellow lettering in red shield w/ cannons and crest, FT, 32 oz, Adam Scheidt	250	300
Viking Draft Beer, brown and black, FT, 12 oz, Spearman	450	500

Beer Trays

Are they a work of art? Or are they just a bit of nostalgia? Beer trays should have no rust and a minimum of scratches. Valuable trays, like some of the early Anheuser-Busch trays, are now reproduced in large quantities.

Left to right: Cream City Pilsener Beer, Cream City Brewing, Milwaukee, WI, 1930s, 14" dia, $230 at auction; Miller High Lite Beer, Miller Brewing, Milwaukee, WI, 1910s, 15" d, $200 at auction. —Photo courtesy Fink's Off The Wall Auctions.

	LOW	HIGH
Ambassador Beer, Krueger Brewing, Newark, NJ, "Ambassador Export Brewed Beer," 2 sided, 12" dia	$15	$30
Breidt's Beer - Ale, Breidt's Brewing, Elizabethtown, NJ, 12" dia	30	50
Brockert's 3 XXX Ale, Brockert Brewing, Worchester, MA, 1940s, 12" dia	75	90
Budweiser, Anheuser-Busch, St. Louis, MO, 1972 Duquoin State Fair 50th Anniversary, 12" dia	15	25
Budweiser Beer, Anheuser-Busch, St. Louis, MO, glass, bottle, and can, "Ask Your Customers To Make The Budweiser Test," 13.25" dia	75	100
Burkhardt's Beer, Burkardt Brewing, Akron, OH, pretty girl holding glass, pie plate, 1930s, 12" dia	150	175
Christian Feigenspan, Feigenspan Brewing, Newark, NJ, pretty woman, curved rim, 13.25" dia	175	225
Clysmic King of Table, Clysmic Company, Wauekesha, WI, stag and pretty girl, 1930s	65	110
Dickens Ale, Syracuse Brewing, Syracuse, NY, 2 drinking men in goblet, 1930s, 12" dia	70	95
Effinger Fine Beer, Effinger Brewing, Baraboo, WI, saluting Art Deco-style waiter holding tray w/ bottle and glass, 1940s, 12" dia	175	200
Franklin Beer, Franklin Brewing, Wilkes-Barre, PA, "We Serve," 1950s, 13.25" dia	40	60
Franks Old Fashioned Beer, M. Frank & Son Brewing, Mansfield, OH, tavern scene, rectangular, 1930s, 13.5" x 10.5"	110	135

	LOW	HIGH
Free State Supreme, Free State Brewing, Baltimore, MD, tavern keeper and oversized bottle, 1940s, 13.25" dia	25	40
Geidiger & Gesundheit Beer, Geidiger Brewing, Merrill, WI, pretty girl, 1910s, 13.25" sq	245	265
Genesee 12 Horse Ale, Genesee Brewing, Rochester, NY, horse-drawn beer wagon, pie plate, 1930s, 13" dia	25	40
Genesee 12 Horse Ale, Genesee Brewing, Rochester, NY, horse-drawn beer wagon, pie plate, 1930s, 13" dia	35	55
Gettelman Beer, Gettelman Brewing, Milwaukee, WI, logo, 12" dia	40	60
Glennons Beer, Pittston Brewing, Pittston, PA, keystone behind barrel and bottle, 1930s, 12" dia	70	90
Grossvater Beer, Renner Brewing, Akron, OH, hand holding glass of beer, 1930s, 14" dia	165	190
Grossvater Beer, Renner Brewing, Youngstown, OH, men drinking beer, "Grandfather's Drinking...," rectangular, 1910s	85	110
Hampden Mild Ale, Hampden Brewing, Willimansett, MA, man on barrel, 1940s, 13.25" dia	35	60
Hanley's Peerless Ale, James Hanley's Brewing, Providence, RI, bulldog, 1940s, 12" dia	40	60
Hartmann Lager, Ale & Porter, Hartmann Brewing, Bridgeport, CT, porcelain, oval, pre-prohibition, 13" x 16"	165	200
Henslers Popular Beer - Ale, Joseph Hensler Brewing, Newark, NJ, woodgrain, 1930s, 13.5" dia	50	75
Henslers Popular Beer, Hensler Brewing, Newark, NJ, portrait center, "Brewed Today Grandfather's Way, Light, Mild, Satisfying," 1940s, 13.25" dia	15	25
Holihan's Ale, Diamond Springs Brewery, Lawrence, MA, logo, "Pride of the Valley," 12" dia	25	40
Holihan's Extra Fine Ale, Diamond Spring Brewing, Lawrence, MA, logo, 1930s, 12" dia	80	105
Hornung's Beer, Hornung's Brewing, Philadelphia, PA, cartoon man drinking beer, 1930s, 12" dia	75	100
Hull's Ale - Lager, Hull's Brewing, New Haven, CT, HB logo, pie plate, 1930s, 13" dia	40	60
Jax, Jakson Brewing, New Orleans, LA, running waiter carrying tray, 1950s, 13.25" dia	25	35
King's Bohemian Food & Beer, Massachusetts Brewery, Boston MA, trefoil, pre-prohibition, 12" dia	165	185
Koch's Beer, Koch Brewing, Dunkirk, NY, "Drink Koch's Beer," 1950s, 13.25" dia	40	60
Koehler's Beer, Ale - Porter, Erie Brewing, Erie, PA, cartouche with eagle on barrel, 1930s, 14" dia	100	115
Krueger Beer Ale, Brueger Brewing, Newark, NJ, wheat, 2 sided, 12" dia	18	32
Lebanon Valley Export Beer - Ale - Porter, Lebanon Valley Brewing, Lebanon, PA, LV logo, 1950s, 13.25" dia	85	105
Lebanon Valley, Lebanon Valley Brewing, Lebanon, PA, girl's head and hand holding glass of beer, "Pride of the Valley," 1940s, 13.5" dia	125	150
Lucky Lager, Lucky Lager Brewing, San Francisco, CA, compass star, 2 sided, 12" dia	25	40
Mellet & Nichter Beer, Ale & Porter, Mellet & Nicher Brewing, Pottsville, PA, stock tray, woman holding glass of beer and wearing large rose corsage, rectangular, 1910s, 10.5" x 13.25"	1200	1500
Mennel's Extra Beer, Mennel Brewing, Patterson, NJ, "A Product of the Brewers of the Famous Grahams XXX Ale," pie plate, 13.25" dia	70	95
Metz Beer, Metz Brewing, Omaha, NB, M logo, 12" dia	50	75
Miller High Life, Miller Brewing, Milwaukee, WI, girl on the moon, 12" dia	40	65

	LOW	HIGH
Miller High Life Beer, Miller Brewing, Milwaukee, WI, girl on moon, 1940s, 13.25" dia	30	50
Narragansett Ale, Narragansett Brewing, Cranston, RI, logo, pie plate, 1930s, 13" dia	25	40
Old Milwaukee Beer, Schlitz Brewing, Milwaukee, WI, 2 sided, 12" dia	18	30
Old Topper Ale - Beer, Rochester Brewing, Rochester, NY, silhouette man in top hat, 1940s, 12" dia	35	60
Peter Barmann Lager Beer, Ale & Porter, Peter Barmann Brewing, Kingstown, NY, eagle wings logo, 1930s, 12" dia	170	200
Phoenix Beer, Phoenix Brewing, Buffalo, NY, "Buffalo's Famous Brew," 1930s, 12" dia	75	90
R&H Beer, R&H Brewing, Staten Island, NY, 12" dia	20	30
Rheingold Beer, Iron City Brewing, Lebanon, PA, barmaid holding tray w/ 2 glasses of beer, curved rim, 1900s, 13" dia	200	250
Schmidt's Beer – Ale, Schmidt's Brewing, Philadelphia, PA, logo, 1950s, 13.25" dia	12	20
Schmidt's Beer, Schmidt's Brewing, Philadelphia, PA, pretty girl pouring beer from bottle into glass, 1930s, 12" dia	125	135
Standard Ale, Standard Brewing, Rochester, NY, "Properly Aged," pie plate, 1930s, 13" dia	50	75
Standard Dry Ale, Standard Brewing, Rochester, NY, "Ox Cart Dry Beer," 12" dia	30	50
Stanton Beer, Stanton Brewing, Troy, NY, 12" dia	35	55
Sunshine Beer, Barbeys Inc, Reading, PA, 1930s, 12" dia	80	100
Utica Club Pilsener Beer - Cream Ale, West End Brewery, Utica, NY, woman's hand holding pilsener glass, 12" dia	25	40

Left to right: Seitz Beer, Seitz Brewery, Easton, PA, pie plate, 1930s, $150 at auction; Texas Pride, San Antonio Brewing, San Antonio, TX, 1930s, 13.375" x 10.5", $252 at auction. —Photo courtesy Fink's Off The Wall Auctions.

Boxes

During the 18th and 19th centuries, Americans used boxes as utiltarian items. They made specialized boxes for a wide variety of purposes, from containers for food to storage of wedding dresses. Small boxes, for trinkets, matches or cigarettes, are some of the most collectible.

Left: Paint Decorated, early 19th C, 9" w, $2185 at auction. —Photo courtesy Skinner, Inc., Boston, MA.

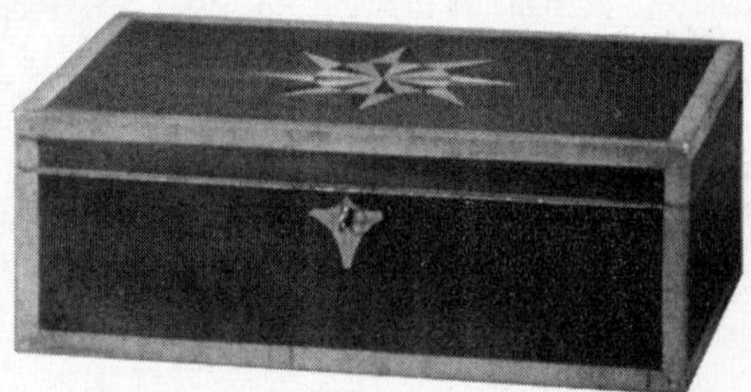

Right: Inlaid Mahogany, 19th C, 12" w, $690 at auction. —Photo courtesy Skinner, Inc., Boston, MA

	AUCTION	RETAIL Low	RETAIL High
Battersea Box, enamel cat form, late 18th C, 3" l	$800	$1500	$2200
Battersea Enamel Necessaire, late 18th C, 3" l	450	800	1250
Bible Box, chip carved oak, 19th C, 29" l	350	700	1100
Bible Box, Chester County, PA walnut w/ inlaid monogram "MG," interior fitted w/ till and 2 secret drawers, raised on ball feet, 10" h, 20.5" w, 14" d	3000	5250	8250
Casket-Form Box, English Regency, rosewood grained, 15" l	200	350	550
Cutlery Box, on mahogany stand, late 19th C, 3" l, 17" l stand	400	700	1100
Decanter Case, French, brass inlaid burl walnut, fitted w/ crystal bottles and wines, 13" l	1600	2800	4400
Humidor, English, inlaid burl walnut dome top w/ oval inlay, fitted on stand w/ drawer on sq legs, 41" h, 25" l	3600	6300	9900
Knife Boxes, pr, Heppelwhite, mahogany urn form, 20" h	1500	3000	4500
Knife Boxes, pr, inlaid mahogany, serpentine form, 15" h	550	960	1510
Lap Desk, brass-bound mahogany, late 19th C	200	350	550
Mechanical Jewelry Box, Continental, faux tortoise finish, brass inlay, 13" l	1000	1750	2750
Pantry Box, New England, painted, double star motif on lid, side w/ pr of shields, 6.5" dia	2300	4000	6000
Pipe Box, American Chippendale, carved mahogany, late 18th C, 16" h	1100	1800	3000

	AUCTION	RETAIL Low	High
Pipe Box, heart cutout in green paint, 20" h	225	400	650
Riding Box, American, red-painted and decorated, front lid dec w/ running horse, ends and back w/ horse motifs, top w/ carrying handle, 22" l	1600	3000	4500
Sewing Box, English, penwork, early 19th C, 6" l	500	900	1400
Sewing Box, late 19th C, leather w/ brass hardware	350	650	1000
Snuff Box, papier-mâché, mid 19th C	150	300	450
Snuff Box, w/ ivory miniature of George Washington, 3.5" dia	1300	2280	3580
Spice Box, English, oak, molded panel door, late 18th C, 13" h	800	1400	2200
Spice Cabinet, English William & Mary, fruitwood w/ drawer, 27" h	1000	1750	2750
Storage Box, New England, painted and decorated pine, dovetailed, swirling blue-green putty dec, side handles, 24" l	800	1400	2200
Tea Caddy, Chippendale, inlaid mahogany, bombé form, 11" l	700	1300	2000
Tea Caddy, English, bowfront mahogany w/ paterae inlay, early 19th C, 8" l	425	740	1170
Tea Caddy, English, brass, mid 19th C, 9" l	300	500	900
Tea Caddy, English, inlaid mahogany w/ paterae and quarter-fan spandrels, early 19th C	400	700	1100
Tea Caddy, English, mahogany, coffin form, 7" l	200	350	550
Tea Caddy, English, penwork, early 19th C, 7" l	400	700	1200
Tea Caddy, hexagonal, quill-work, late 18th C, 13" l	1300	2300	3580
Tea Caddy, Regency style faux tortoiseshell, 12" l	1150	2000	3200
Tunbridge Ware, circular, lidded, c1790, 5.5" h	300	400	500
Work Box, New England, painted and decorated, 15" l	200	350	550

Left to right: Miniature Pantry Boxes, 19th C, $250–$300 each; Polychrome Decorated, attributed to John Colvin, Scituate, RI, early 19th C, 10.5" h, $17,250 at auction. —Photo courtesy Skinner, Inc., Boston, MA.

Cameras

Louis Daguerre invented the first commercial camera in 1839. For the next 30 years nearly all cameras were for professional studios. During the 1870s amateur photography bloomed. The cameras of the late nineteenth century were generally large and bulky box cameras and bellows cameras. But strange and sometimes bizarre novelty cameras also appeared, including cameras designed in the forms of pocket watches, canes, and even neckties. In 1888 the Eastman Dry Plate and Film Company introduced the first commercially available roll film camera, the Kodak. They followed it with the No. 1 Kodak the next year. Soon the Eastman Kodak Company came to dominate the American market. The hundreds of various cameras produced under the Kodak name outstrip any other maker's production record.

Collectors want cameras that are complete and in working order. Some allowance is made for the fragility of leather bellows and rubber parts. For further information see *The Price Guide to Antique and Classic Cameras, 1997–1998, 10th Edition,* edited by Jim and Joan McKeown, Centennial Photo Service, Grantsbury, WI, 1997.

Assorted

	LOW	HIGH
Adox 35	$80	$100
Adox Sport	30	50
Agfa Antar	20	30
Agfa Box	10	20
Agfa Clack	10	20
Agfa Iso	10	15
Agfa Isoflash	10	15
Agfa Isolar	90	120
Agfa Isolette	80	100
Agfa Isolette III	80	100
Agfa Isolette Super	30	50
Agfa Karat 12	80	100
Agfa Karomat	80	100
Agfa Readyset 1	40	50
Agfa Readyset Traveler	40	50
Agfa Selecta-M	190	260
Agfa Shur-Shot	20	25
Agfa Standard (Plate)	50	70
Agfa Super Solinette	70	90
Agfa Synchro-Box	20	25
Agfa View	140	200
Aires 35 IIIC	100	130
Aires 35 IIIL	80	100
Aires 35 V	110	160
Aires Penta 35	110	160
Aires Viscount	70	90
Airesflex	100	130
Altura	110	160
Amerex	60	80
American Camera Mfg. Co., Buckeye No. 2	110	160

	LOW	HIGH
American Camera Mfg. Co., Buckeye Tourist No. 1	290	390
Ansco (Box)	10	20
Ansco Automatic Reflex	240	330
Ansco Buster Brown No. 2	20	25
Ansco Buster Brown No. 2C	20	25
Ansco Buster Brown Junior	20	30
Ansco Cadet Flash	10	15
Ansco Clipper	20	25
Ansco Clipper Special	20	25
Ansco Craftsman	100	130
Ansco Dollar	30	50
Ansco Flash Clipper	20	25
Ansco Folding No. 1	30	40
Ansco Folding No. 1A	30	40
Ansco Folding No. 3	30	50
Ansco Folding No. 4 Model C	50	70
Ansco Folding No. 6	60	80
Ansco Folding No. 9 Model B	60	80
Ansco Lancer	30	40
Ansco Panda	10	20
Ansco Plenax PD-16	30	40
Ansco Readyflash	10	20
Ansco Fediflex	10	20
Ansco Regent	70	90
Ansco Regent Super	90	120
Ansco Shur-Flash	10	15
Ansco Shur-Shot	10	15
Ansco Vest Pocket No. 1	50	70
Ansco Vest Pocket No. 2	60	80
Ansco Vest Pocket Junior	40	50

	LOW	HIGH
Ansco Viking	30	40
Ansco Viking Readyset	30	40
Anscoset	60	80
Anthony Normandie	330	460
Anthony Patent Novelette	520	720
Anthony PDQ	1200	1800
Apparate & Kamerabau Akarette II	120	170
Argus 21 Markfinder	50	70
Argus A	40	50
Argus A2	40	50
Argus A2F	50	70
Argus AA (Argoflash)	60	80
Argus AF	50	70
Argus Argoflex Model 40	30	40
Argus Argoflex Model 75	30	40
Argus Argoflex Model EF	30	40
Argus Argoflex Model EM	30	40
Argus Autronic C3	60	80
Argus C	50	70
Argus C4	70	90
Argus C20	50	70
Argus C44	90	120
Argus FA	50	70
Argus K	380	520
Argus Markfinder (21)	50	70
Arnold Karmaflex	600	900
Arrow	20	30
ASR Foto-Disc	950	1300
Astraflex	330	460
Autoflex (Kiyabashi)	70	100
Automatic Radio Tom Thumb Camera Radio	240	330
Baby Brownie	10	20
Baby Hawkeye	330	460
Balda Baldalette	80	100
Balda Baldarette	70	90
Balda Baldaxette I	90	120
Balda Baldessa Ib	80	100
Balda Baldinette Super	100	130
Balda Juwella	30	50
Balda Poka	20	30
Balda Pontura Super	110	160
Balda Super Baldinette	100	130
Balda Wara	50	70
Baldarette	70	90
Bladaxette	90	120
Baldi	100	130
Bauer	50	70
Beier Beira	330	460
Beier Beirax	50	70
Beier Beirette	330	460
Beier Precisa	80	100
Beil & Freund (Folding Plate)	230	310
Beira	330	460
Beirax	50	70
Beirette	330	460
Belca Belplasca	700	1000
Bell & Howell Foton	1050	1430
Bellieni Jumelle	380	520
Bencini Animatic 600	10	15
Benson Street	330	460
Bentzin Primarflex	330	460
Bentzin Stereo Reflex	800	1100
Bell & Howell TDC Stereo Vivid	190	260
Berning Robot II	170	230
Berning Robot Junior	170	230
Berning Robot Royal 36	570	780

Left to right: Agfa Billy, $30–$40; Goltz & Breutmann Mentor Reflex, $330–$460. —Photo courtesy Auction Team Breker.

	LOW	HIGH
Berning Robot Star	210	290
Berning Robot Star II	290	390
Bettax	60	80
Billy (Agfa)	30	40
Blair Hawkeye Baby	330	460
Blair Hawkeye Folding No. 4 Model 4	130	180
Blair Hawkeye Junior	120	170
Blair Hawkeye Tool-Box Style	400	600
Blair Hawkeye Weno No. 2	50	70
Blair Hawkeye Weno No. 4	50	70
Blair Hawkeye Weno No. 7	50	70
Blair Lucidograph No. 1	1500	2000
Blair Lucidograph No. 3	1500	2000
Blair Stereo Hawkeye	520	720
Blair Stereo Weno	520	720
Blair View	380	520
Bolsey 8	330	460
Bolsey B	50	70
Bolsey B2	50	70
Bosley Bolseyflex	40	50
Bolsey C22 Set-O-Matic	100	130
Bolsey Explorer	80	100
Borsum Reflex New Model	600	900
Boy Scout Kodak	180	250
Boy Scout Memo (Ansco)	310	430
Boyer Altessa	240	330
Brack Field	400	600
Braun Colorette Super	50	70
Braun Paxette 1	50	70
Braun Paxette Super	70	90
Braun Paxina II	40	50
Brooklyn	480	650
Buckeye (Anthony)	100	130
Bullard (Magazine)	570	780
Bullet (Brownie)	10	15
Bulls-Eye (Boston)	110	160
Burke & James Grover	170	230
Burke & James Ideal	190	260
Burke & James Press	200	270
Burke & James Rexo (Box)	20	25
Burke & James Rexo Junior 3	30	50
Burke & James Rexo Vest Pocket	40	50
Burke & James Watson-Holmes Fingerprint	240	330
Busch Verascope F40	750	1000
Butcher Carbine No. 2	20	30
Butcher Carbine Reflex	230	310
Butcher Carbine Watch Pocket	100	130
Butcher Klimax	60	80
Butcher Midg No. 0	70	90
Butcher Midg No. 1	70	90
Butcher Midg No. 2	70	90
Butcher Midg No. 3	70	90
Butcher Midg No. 4	70	90
Butcher Midg No. 4a	70	90
Butcher Midg No. 4b	70	90
Cadet (Ansco)	10	15
Cameo (Butcher)	60	80
Camera Radio (Tom Thumb)	240	330
Candid Perfex Fifty-Five	70	90
Candid Perfex One-O-Two	70	90
Candid Perfex Speed Candid	110	160
Canon Canonet	100	130
Canon III	240	330
Canon IV-F	270	360
Canon IV-S	270	360
Canon IV-S2	270	360
Canon L-1	290	390
Canon P	330	460
Canonet	100	130
Cartridge Hawkeye	20	25
Caspa (Demaria)	400	600
Certo Certonet	60	80
Certo Dollina Super	130	180
Certo Doppel Box	70	90
Certo Folding Plate	100	130
Certosport	90	120
Chase Magazine	240	330
Chevron	330	460
Chicago Ferrotype Co. Mandel Post Card Machine No. 2	240	330
Chiyodo Chiyoko	100	130
Chiyodo Konan Automat 16	240	330
Chiyoko	100	130
Ciro 35 (Graflex)	50	70
Ciro Ciro-flex Model A	50	70
Ciro Ciro-flex Model B	50	70
Ciro Ciro-flex Model C	50	70
Ciro Ciro-flex Model D	50	70
Ciro Ciro-flex Model E	50	70
Ciro Ciro-flex Model F	50	70
Ciro-flex	50	70
Citoskop (Contessa)	620	850
Close & Cone Quad	240	330
CMC	20	30
Columbia Pecto No. 1A	140	200
Compact Graflex	380	520
Compass	1520	2580
Condor (Galileo)	240	330
Conley Folding Plate Camera	100	130
Conley Magazine	110	160
Conley Stereo Box	700	1000
Conley View	240	330
Contessa Altura	110	160
Contessa Cocarette	80	100
Contessa Deckrullo-Nettel	370	510

	LOW	HIGH
Contessa Duchessa	290	390
Contessa Ergo	2200	3000
Contessa Miroflex	520	720
Contessa Onito	80	100
Contessa Piccolette 201	170	230
Contessa Sonnar	80	100
Cornu Reyna Cross III	60	80
Coronet 3-D Stereo	70	90
Coronet Vogue	150	210
Daiichi Kogaku Zenobia	70	90
Dallmeyer Speed	620	850
Darling 16	380	520
Daydark Photo Postcard	290	390
Debrie Sept	330	460
Decora (Dangelmaier)	40	50
Dehel	40	50
Delta Stereo	110	160
Demaria Stereo	480	650
Derby (Foth)	90	120
Derlux	240	330
Detrola 400	570	780
Detrola Model D	40	50
Detrola Model E	40	50
Detrola Model KW	40	50
Devry QRS Kamra	100	130
Dail 35 (Canon)	100	130
Diplomat	20	30
Dollina (Certo)	130	180
Dossert Detective	1810	2470
Dover 620A	30	40
Duchess	380	520
Duchessa (Contessa)	290	390
Duex	30	40
Duo-620	110	160
Durst 66	110	160
Durst Automatica	240	330
Easy-Load	140	200
Ektra	1140	1560
Elega	600	900
Elop Elca	140	200
Enolde	80	100
Ernemann (Box)	50	70
Ernemann Bob I	70	90
Ernemann Bob IV	80	100
Ernemann Ermanox (Folding)	1900	2600
Ernemann Globus	1050	1430
Ernemann Heag II-Series II	70	90
Ernemann Heag XIV	240	330
Ernemann Liliput	140	200
Ernemann Reporter	370	510
Ernemann Rolf	80	100
Ernemann Simplex Stereo	290	390
Ernemann Two-Shuttered	400	600
Eulitz Grisette	100	230

	LOW	HIGH
Esco	240	330
Expo Easy-Load	140	200
Expo Watch	190	260
Fed No. 2	140	200
Fed No. 3	140	200
Fed No. 4	140	200
Feinoptische Astraflex II	380	520
Felica	20	30
Finetta 99	290	390
Fingerprint (Graflex)	210	290
Flat Folding Kodak	2200	3000
Flektar	70	90
Flush Back Kodak	110	160
Foitzik Trier Unca	60	80
Folding Bulls-Eye	240	330
Folding Film Pack Hawkeye	30	50
Folding Montauk	140	200
Foth Derby Model I	90	120
Foth Derby Model II	90	120
Foto-Flex	30	40
Franke & Heidecke Rollei 35	170	230
Franke & Heidecke Rolleicord III	110	160
Franke & Heidecke Rolleicord IV	120	170
Franke & Heidecke Rolleiflex Sport	290	390
Fuji Lyra Semi	90	120
Fuji Mini	180	250
Futura S	120	170
Gaumont Spido Stereo	420	570
Genie	1050	1430
Gennert Montauk (Rollfilm)	60	80
Gevabox	30	40
Gilles-Fallr Studio Camera	600	900
Giobal	40	50
Goerz Ango Stereo	520	720
Goerz Anschutz	240	330
Goerz Anschutz Stereo	530	730
Goerz Minicord	620	850
Goerz Minicord IV	290	390
Goerz Tenax Vest Pocket (Rollfilm)	140	200
Goerz Tengor	70	90
Goldeck-16	290	390
Goltz & Breutmann Mentor Klein	240	330
Graflex 1A	190	260
Graflex 3A	240	330
Graflex Auto	240	330
Graflex Auto R.B.	290	390
Graflex Ciro 35	50	70
Graflex Compact	380	520
Graflex Fingerprint	210	290

	LOW	HIGH
Graflex National Series I	280	380
Graflex National Series II	280	380
Graflex Press	520	720
Graflex R.B. Home Portrait	480	650
Graflex R.B. Super D	400	600
Gray	380	520
Guthe & Thorsch Kawee	110	160
Guthe & Thorsch Prakti	80	100
Guthe & Thorsch Praktica FX	100	130
Guthe & Thorsch Praktiflex	100	130
Hare Stereo	3000	4000
Hare Tourist	1140	1560
Harmony	30	40
Hawkette	50	70
Hermagis Velocigraphe	5600	7800
Hexacon	170	230
Hofert Eho Altiflex	70	90
Hofert Eho Box	110	160
Hofert Eho Stereo Box	180	250
Hollywood	50	70
Homer 16	50	70
Horsman Eclipse No. 3	400	600
Houghton Ensign Reflex	240	330
Houghton Ensignette No. 1	100	130
Houghton Ensignette No. 2	100	130
Hüttig Lloyd	110	160
Hüttig Stereolette	480	650
Hüttig Tropical Plate	1100	1500
Ica Atom Horizontal Format	600	900
Ica Cupido	70	90
Ica Favorit 425	380	520
Ica Halloh 505	80	100
Ica Icar	70	90
Ica Icarette C	80	100
Ica Icarette D	80	100
Ica Maximar	110	160
Ica Minimum Palmos	570	780
Ica Nelson 225	90	120
Ica Niklas	80	100
Ica Nixe	130	180
Ica Teddy	60	80
Ica Trilby 18	190	260
Ica Trona	100	140
Ica Victrix 48	330	460
Ihagee Exa I	80	100
Ihagee Exa Ia	80	100
Ihagee Exakta C	380	520
Ihagee Exakta II	140	200
Ihagee Exakta VX	130	180
Ihagee Exakta Junior	290	390
Ihagee Exakta Night	620	850
Ihagee Ultrix Auto	100	130
Ihagee Ultrix Weeny	140	200
Ikko-Sha Start-35	50	70
Irwin Reflex	20	30
Iso Duplex	290	390
Japy Pascal	1500	2000
Jos-Pe Tri-Color	4750	6500
Joux Alethoscope	380	520
Jumelle (Carpentier)	400	600
Jumelle (Demaria)	400	600
Kalart Press	270	360
Kalimar A	50	70
Kameret Jr. No. 2	30	40

Left to right: Voigtländer Virtus, $330–$460; Revere Stereo-33, $190–$260. —Photo courtesy Auction Team Breker.

	LOW	HIGH
Kenflex	50	70
Kent	30	40
Keystone Street Camera	330	460
Kiev	110	160
Kilfitt Mecaflex	1050	1430
Kinder Kin Dar Stereo	180	250
Kirlg Regula I	50	70
Kiyabashi Autoflex	80	100
Kleffel Field	380	520
Kochmann Korelle K	400	600
Kodak-35	40	50
Kodak Reflex	80	100
Kola	750	1000
Konan (Chiyodo)	240	330
Konishiroku Konica II	100	130
Krauss Eka	2200	3000
Krauss Peggy II	1500	2000
Krauss Rollette	140	200
Kunick Tuxi	110	160
Kunick Tuximat	230	310
Kurbi & Higgeloh Bilora Bella	20	30
Lancaster Merveilleux	290	390
Leidolf Leidox II	100	130
Leidolf Lordomat	60	80
Leidolf Lordomatic	60	80
Leidolf Lordox	80	100
Leitz Leica I g	1200	1800
Leitz Leica II (D)	330	460
Leitz Leica III a (G)	240	330
Leitz Leica III c	240	330
Leitz Leica III c K-Model	1200	1600
Leitz Leica III C. Luftwaffe	1200	1600
Leitz Leica III c Wehrmacht	1200	1600
Leitz Leica III f Black Dial	270	360
Leitz Leica M2	620	850
Leitz Ur-Leica (Replica)	1500	2000
Life-O-Rama III	40	50
Lilliput Detective	5700	7800
Linhof Silar	240	330
Linhof Stereo Panorama	570	780
Linhof Technika I	1000	1370
Lipwa Rollop	170	230
Little Wonder	170	230
Lizars Challenge Dayspool	330	460
Loisir	50	70
Lubitel	60	80
Lumiere Box No. 49	30	40
Lumiere Eljy	140	200
Lumiere Sinox	50	70
Lumiere Sterelux	380	520
Lure	10	15
Lüttke & Arndt Folding Plate	140	200
Macris-Boucher Nil Melior	380	520
Mamiya 6	100	140
Mamiya 16	80	100
Manhattan Bo-Peep	170	230
Manhattan Bo-Peep B	140	200
Manufok Tenax	100	130
Marion Soho Reflex	600	900
Mazo Field Camera	400	600
McBean Stereo Tourist	800	1100
Meopta Mikrcma	190	260
Meridian	380	520
Merit	50	70
Metropolitan Supply Co. King	190	260
Midget (Coronet)	130	180
Minolta 16-EE	60	80
Minolta 16-II	50	70
Minolta 16-MG	50	70
Minolta 16-P	40	50
Minolta A	60	80
Minolta A2	60	80
Minolta Auto Semi-Minolta	100	140
Minolta Semi-Minolta Auto	100	140
Minolta Six	140	200
Minox (Made in USSR)	1500	2000
Minox A	140	200
Minox B	140	200
Minox II	160	220
Minox III	140	200
Minox III-S	130	180
Moller Cambinox	1500	2000
Monroe Model 7	240	330
Montanus Montiflex	190	260
Monti Monte-35	40	50
Moscow-4	240	330
Moscow-5	240	330
Motormatic (Eastman)	80	100
Murer Express	240	330
Murer Reflex	240	330
Megel 18 (Recomar)	140	200
Nagel Junior	40	50
Nagel Recomar 33	110	160
Nagel Vollenda	80	100
National Graflex	280	380
Naturalist's Graflex	5320	7280
Nescon35	50	70
Nettel Argus	2250	3250
Nettel Sonnet Tropical	1200	1800
Newman & Guardia Folding Reflex	400	600
Newman & Guardia Sibyl Baby	600	900
Newman & Guardia Sibyl Deluxe	480	650
Newman & Guardia Special (Magazine Box)	380	520
Nic (Contessa)	60	80

	LOW	HIGH
Nicca IIIS	290	390
Nikkorex	150	210
Nikon S	270	360
Nikon SP	950	1300
Norris	70	90
Olympus Pen	120	170
Ontobloc (Cornu)	100	130
Ontoflex (Cornu)	1100	1400
Opema	480	650
Orion Tio Tropical	1200	1600
Papigny Jumelle Stereo	400	600
Pentacon FB	170	230
Perka	330	460
Perken (Studio)	50	70
Petri	70	90
Phoba Diva	70	90
Photo Master	10	20
Photo Postcard (Daydark)	290	390
Photo See	50	70
Photo-Jumelle (Carpentier)	400	600
Photo-Porst Hapo 36	50	70
Photoscopic	950	1300
Pignons Alpa 9d	570	780
Pignons Bolsey	570	780
Pinetta	50	70
Plaubel (Folding Plate)	80	100
Plaubel Makina	480	650
Plaubel Makina III	320	440
Plaubel Makina Stereo	2250	3250
Plaubel Roll-Op	400	600
Pocket Kodak	190	260
Polaroid J66	20	25
Polaroid Model 80 A (Highlander)	20	30
Polaroid Model 95 (Speedliner)	40	50
Polaroid Model 95 A (Speedliner)	40	50
Polaroid Model 95 B (Speedliner)	40	50
Polaroid Model 100	50	70
Polaroid Model 110 (Pathfinder)	110	160
Polaroid Model 110 B (Pathfinder)	130	180
Polaroid Model 800	20	30
Pontiac Lynx	110	160
Popular Pressman (SLR)	220	300
Post Card Machine (Chicago Ferrotype Co.)	240	330
Pouva Start	40	50
Premium (Plate Box)	380	520
Press Graflex	520	720
Putnam Marvel	330	460
Quad (Close & Cone)	240	330

	LOW	HIGH
Rajar No. 6	50	70
Ray Ray Jr.	110	160
Rectaflex Standard	300	420
Reflex Camera Co. Junior Reflex	300	400
Reflex Camera Co. Reflex	310	430
Revere Eye-Matic EE 127	50	70
Rex Kayson	90	120
Richard Glyphoscope	210	290
Richard Homeos	3800	5200
Ricoh-35	50	70
Ricoh Golden-16	230	310
Rietzschel Heli-Clack	150	210
Rietzschel Cosmo-Clack	330	460
Riken Steky	100	130
Riken Steky II	90	120
Riken Steky III	90	120
Rochester Cyclone Senior	60	80
Rochester Handy	300	420
Rochester Premo B	110	160
Rochester Premo C	110	160
Rochester Premo D	110	160
Rochester Premo No. 4	110	160
Rochester Premo No. 6	150	210
Rolifix (Franka)	50	70
Royer Savoyflex	140	200
Royet Reyna Cross III	60	80
Rubix 16	240	330
Ruthine	50	70
Sabre	20	25]
Saint Louis	330	460
Schleissner Bower	50	70
Schleissner Bower Jr.	30	40
Scovill Detective	950	1300
Scovill Knack	950	1300
Scovill Mascot	800	1100
Scovill Triad Detective	600	900
Screen Focus Kodak	620	850
Secam Stylophot Luxe	330	460
Seroco Delmar	70	90
Shalco	30	40
Shew Xit-Day	330	460
Sida Extra	110	160
Signal Corps Signet-35	240	330
Simda Stereo	950	1300
Simplex Pockette	80	100
Simplex Stereo (Ernemann)	290	390
Sinclair Una	480	650
Soligor I	70	90
Soligor II	70	90
Spartaflex	20	30
Spartas 35F	20	30
Spartus Spartaflex	20	30
Speed Candid Perfex	110	160

	LOW	HIGH
Spiegel Elf	20	30
Starmatic (Brownie)	20	30
Steineck ABC	800	1100
Steinheil Tropical	1100	1500
Stereax (Contessa)	750	1000
Stöckig Union	190	260
Sunart Junior	90	120
Super Dollina (Certo)	130	180
Supersport Dolly (Certo)	100	130
Suter Muro Stereo	750	1000
Taisei Koki Welmy Six	70	90
Taiyodo Koki Beauty Super L	70	90
Taiyodo Koki Beautycord	50	70
Takahashi Gelto D III	140	200
Tanaka Tanack IV-S	240	330
Target (Brownie)	10	15
Taxo	70	90
Tennar	30	50
Tessco (Contessa)	100	130
Thornton-Pickard Puck Stereo	190	260
Thornton-Pickard Ruby Deluxe	330	460
Thornward Dandy	110	160
Thowe Field	290	390
3-D Stereo (Coronet)	70	90
Tower Type 3	240	330
Tri-Color (Devin)	1000	1400
Tropical Deckrullo-Nettel	750	1000
Turret Panoramic	1800	2400
Universal Corsair II	40	50
Universal Mercury II Model CX	70	90
Universal Meteor	30	40
Universal Radio Cameradio	240	330
Universal Uniflex I	40	50
Universal Uniflex II	40	50
Universal Univex Model A	30	40
Utility Falcon	10	20
Utility Falcon Girl Scout	10	20
Utility Falcon Miniature	10	20
Utility Press Flash	10	20
Vanity Kodak	150	210
Vauxhall	80	100
Vega	1200	1800
Venaret	40	50
Vest Pocket Hawkeye	50	70
Vest Pocket Jiffy	30	40
Vest Pocket Kodak	50	70
Vive No. 2	160	220
Vive Stereo	950	1300
Vive Tourist	160	220
Vogue (Coronet)	150	210
Voigtländer Avus	80	100
Voigtländer Bessa RF	220	300
Voigtländer Bessa II	480	650
Voigtländer Bessa Baby	100	130
Voigtländer Bessamatic	140	200
Voigtländer Daguerreotype Cannon	3000	4000
Voigtländer Perkeo	190	260
Voigtländer Perkeo I	80	100
Voigtländer Perkeo II	120	170
Voigtländer Vag	70	90
Voigtländer Vitessa	140	200
Voigtländer Vito B	70	90
Voigtländer Vito C	60	80
Voigtländer Vito II	70	90
Walker Takiv	2200	3000
Walz-Wide	80	100
Walzflex	60	80
Wardflex	60	80
Welta Perle	90	120
Welta Reflekta	60	80
Welta Superflekta	800	1100
Welta Trio	40	50
Welta Weltini	80	100
Welta Weltix	70	90
Welta Weltur	240	330
Wenka	400	600
Western Cyclone Jr.	70	90
Western Cyclone Sr.	80	100
White Realist 35	60	80
Whittaker Micro-16	70	90
Wilca Automatic	950	1300
Windrow	30	40
Wing New Gem	1900	2600
Wirgin Edixa Reflex	100	130
Wirgin Stereo	170	230
Witt Iloca I	60	80
Witt Iloca IIa	60	80
Wollensak Stereo	400	600
Zeiss Adoro	70	90
Zeiss Contax S	400	600
Zeiss Contax I	1140	1560
Zeiss Ikoflex Ic	140	200
Zeiss Kilibri Night	1800	2400
Zeiss Nettel Tropical	1100	1500
Zeiss Nixe	130	180
Zeiss Orix	190	260
Zeiss Palmos Stereo	650	880
Zeiss Piccolette	290	390
Zeiss Sirene	100	140
Zeiss Tenax I	160	220
Zeiss Tenax II	490	680
Zeiss Trix	90	120
Zeiss Werra	110	160
Zenith Edelweiss	30	50
Zenith Kodak	290	390
Zenobia (Daiichi)	70	90
Zion Pocket Z	240	330

Eastman Kodak

	LOW	HIGH
Automatic 35	$40	$55
Baby Brownie	9	14
Bantam Flash	50	75
Bantam RF f3.9	40	50
Beau Brownie	75	100
Brownie Baby	10	14
Brownie (box) No. 0	22	45
Brownie (box) No. I Improved	55	80
Brownie (box) No. 2 (orig)	750	1200
Brownie (box) No. 2	12	18
Brownie (box) No. 2A	10	14
Brownie (box) No. 2C	10	18
Brownie (box) No. 3	12	18
Brownie Folding No. 2	28	40
Brownie Holiday	6	9
Bullet No. 2	60	90
Bullet No. 4	100	150
Bulls-Eye No. 2	40	60
Cirkut No. 10	3000	4000
Cirkut No. 5	850	1250
Cirkut Outfit No. 6	850	1550
Daylight Kodak A	1300	1900
Daylight Kodak B	600	1000
Ektra	650	1100
Eureka No. 2	80	140
Falcon No. 2	75	120
Flexo No. 2	40	60
Flush Back Kodak No. 3	65	115
Folding Kodak No. 4A	70	110
Gift Kodak	85	140
Girl Scout Kodak	120	200
Hawkette No. 2	20	50
Hawkeye Cartridge No. 2	10	16
Hawkeye Film Pack No. 2	15	25
Hawkeye Vest Pocket	25	50
Jiffy Kodak Six-16	19	30
Jiffy Kodak Vest Pocket	16	20
Kodak 35	20	36
Kodak 35 Rangefinder	25	40
Kodak Automatic 35	36	50
Kodak Junior No. 1	20	35
Kodak No. 1	1150	1650
Kodak No. 2	500	700
Kodak No. 3	500	800
Kodak (orig model)	3750	5500
Kodak Reflex Model I	50	75
Kodak Senior Six-16	40	60
Kodak Six-16 Special	50	80
Kodak Six-20	40	70
Kodak Super Six-20	1400	2000
Kodet Folding No. 4	550	850
Kodet No. 4	300	500
Medalist I	150	250
Monitor Six-16	30	50
Motormatic 35	50	75
Nagel Junior	30	45
Petite	150	200
Pony II	10	30
Pony IV	15	25
Premo Cartridge No. 00	50	75
Premo Cartridge No. 2	15	25
Premo No. 12	40	60
Premo Senior	100	150
Premoette No. 1	43	60
Recomar No. 18	80	120
Regent	300	500
Retina Automatic I	150	200
Retina I	74	135
Retina III C	160	270
Retina Reflex	100	150
Retina Reflex IV	160	260
Retinette IA	50	85
Signet 30	35	55
Special Kodak No. 1A	50	75
Speed Kodak No. 1A	220	300
Star Premo	60	100
Super Kodak Six-20	1400	2000
Tourist	14	20
Tourist II	14	20
Vanity Kodak	100	150
Vanity Kodak Ensemble	1150	1650
Zenith Kodak No. 3	210	310

Retina Reflex III, $160–$175.
—Photo courtesy Auction Team Breker.

Canes

Canes are either simple walking sticks or "gadget" canes that conceal a sword, pistol, musical instrument, or other device. The stylish canes of Europe came into vogue in the seventeenth and eighteenth centuries, while the nineteenth century saw gadget canes reaching their peak of popularity. When buying a cane or walking stick, examine it closely for indications of hidden compartments. Many devices go undiscovered for years.

Carved folk art canes are judged by their style and the skill of the carver. Many of the most desirable ones date from the mid nineteenth century. We've seen many of varying quality in the auctions of New England.

"Good" examples are undamaged with simple carving or simple forming. "Best" examples have superior carving or forming and (if wood or metal) a fine patina.

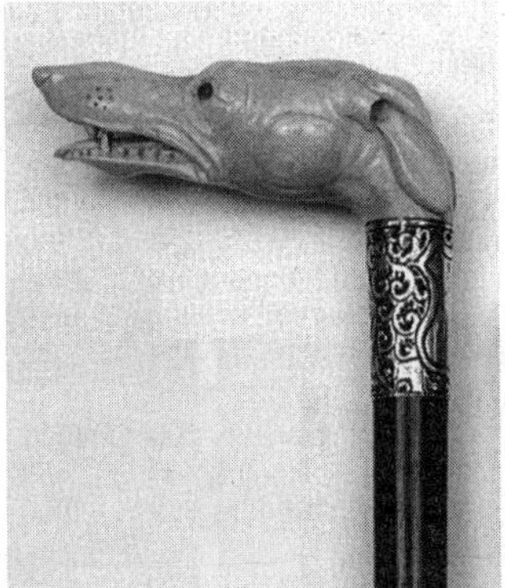

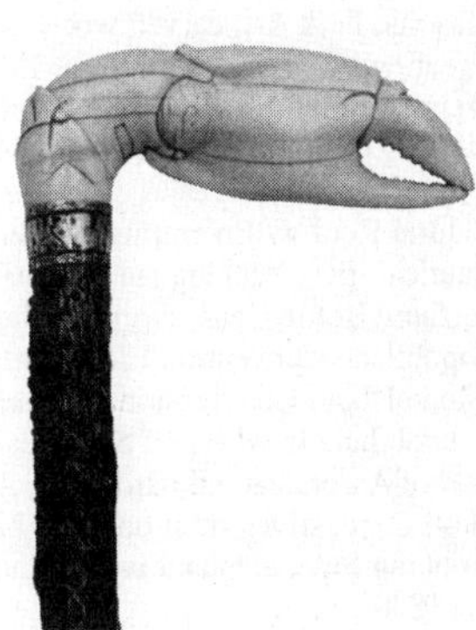

Left to right: English carved elephant ivory Greyhound head cane, glass eyes, c1880, $3300; English carved wood and painted cricket player, c1870, $1485; American carved elephant ivory crab claw cane, c1870, $1650. —Photos courtesy Tradewinds Auction.

	GOOD	BETTER	BEST
American Flag Parade Cane, wood ball handle, c1915	$150	$225	$275
American Folk Art Civil War Cane, Confederate soldier and flag, 1860s	1800	2100	2300
American Indian Basketry, woven sweet grass over wood, c1900	150	225	275
Bakelite Lady's Mirror-Comb Vanity Cane, American, c1920s	650	750	825
Darning Egg, wood egg-shaped darner handle, Continental, c1890	100	175	250
Day's Patent Percussion Gun, English, c1840	825	1200	1800
Dog's Head, carved wood, English, c1890	500	650	715
Dragon Handle, carved ivory, Japanese, c1890	1000	1100	1200
Duck Head, carved ivory, American, c1880	1200	2000	2750
European Folk Art, carved walnut, claw and ball handle, 1903	300	475	525
Folk Art, erotic anti-cleric, carved wood, Continental, c1860	1750	2500	3000
Harmonica Gadget Cane, mahogany, English, early 20th C	1500	2500	3500
Japanese Lady's Cane, elephant ivory tau handle w/ monkeys carved in relief, American, c1890	85	125	165
Lumberman's Measure, brass cap, 8-sided shaft, American	100	150	175

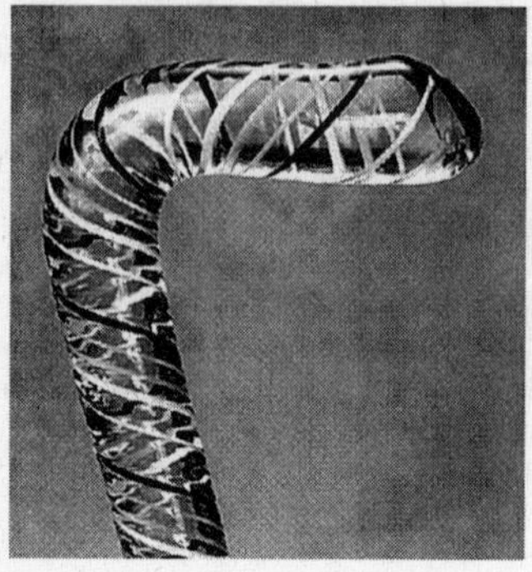

Glass Whimsey, L handle, external striping, American, c1890, $195. —Photo courtesy Tradewinds Auction.

	GOOD	BETTER	BEST
Masonic Folk Art, carved wood and polychrome painted, alligator eating black boy, American, 1926	750	950	1100
Meissen Porcelain Floral Knob, c1900	800	1000	1150
Military Cane, silver plated handle w/ brass overlaid royal coat of arms, WWI	300	425	500
Natural Root w/ Encircling Bronze Snake, Vienna, c1880	175	250	300
Nautical, fist clutching snake, whale ivory, American, c1850	1500	2000	2500
Perfume Bottle Cane, ivory handle, London hallmark, c1900	750	900	1050
Republican Convention Elephant Head, pewter, American, c1890	250	325	375
Rhode Island Congressional Representative's Cane, elephant ivory knob handle w/ inlaid brass seal of Rhode Island	800	1200	1325
Rod of Aaron, carved hardwood, American, mid 20th C	300	400	450
Skull Cane, silver skull on ivory ball, English, c1890	700	825	900
Smoking Pipe, elephant ivory handle, L-shaped pipe, Continental, c1890	600	750	900
Stanhope Souvenir, composition knob handle, stanhope peephole in shaft, photo labeled "Made at Victoria Falls," c1910	175	250	350
Sword Cane, elephant ivory knob, American, c1830	300	450	600
Tau Handle, carved elephant ivory and silver, American, c1890	450	550	600
Tiffany & Co., solid gold and ebony, w/ orig flannel drawstring bag and cardboard box, c1915	1200	1800	2400
Victorian Pistol Handled, cobalt blue porcelain, English, c1870	300	400	500

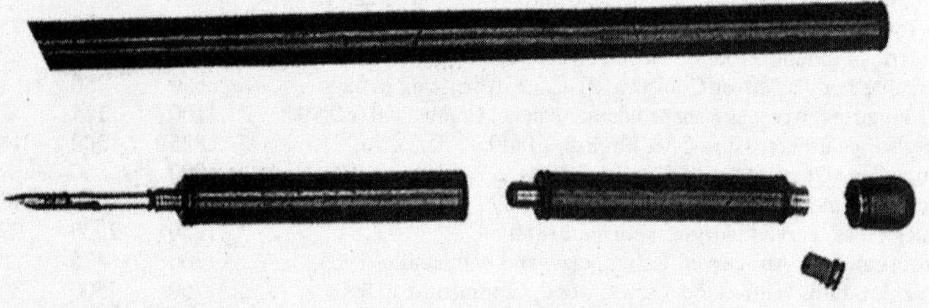

Pen, Pencil and Inkpot Cane, copper knob, glass inkpot, Austrian, c1910, $250. —Photo courtesy Tradewinds Auction.

Cereal Boxes

The breakfast choice for youngsters in post-war America was a break from their parents' waffles, pancakes or eggs. Kids wanted cereal touted on radio, then television. The cereal box became the younger crowd's *New York Times* and *Wall Street Journal* rolled into one. After all, what else was there to do while consuming breakfast before the bus came? Boxes often contained contests, special offers and cutouts ("You have to finish it before you can have the box!"). Boomers are drawn to boxes that remind them of their childhood morning ritual and premium collectors are attracted to the information the boxes provide. Amazingly, boxes have survived and the prices below are for excellent, clean examples.

For further information, see *Cereal Box Bonanza: The 1950's* by Scott Bruce, Collector Books, Paducah, KY, 1995.

	LOW	HIGH
Cheerios, General Mills, Frontier Town, 1948, one of a series of 9, each	$120	$420
Cheerios, w/ Lone Ranger comic book ad on back, 1954	150	350
Coco Flavored Krispies, Kellogg's, Jose the Monkey, 1958	130	180
Coco Puffs, General Mills, conductor's cap cutout, 1959	40	60
Cornflakes, Kellogg's, Dwight Eisenhower and Adlai Stevenson on front, 1952	75	100
Cornflakes, Kellogg's, Norman Rockwell illus, showing signature, 1955	90	125
Count Chocula, General Mills, box w/ disguise stickers ("Star of David" design), 1987	80	120
40% Bran Flakes, Post, "Magic Oven Flavor" w/ cartoon chef, 1955	25	30
Frostie O's, General Mills, cereal bowl on front, 1959	125	150
Grapenuts, Post, thin cartoon mom w/ green apron, 1955	90	125
OKs, Kellogg's, Big Otis Catapult game ad, 1960	90	125
Raisin Bran, Post, Hopalong Cassidy western badge ad, 1950	360	500
Raisin Bran, Post, Looney Tunes Notch-Em toys ad, 1956	130	180
Sugar Coated Cornflakes, Post, Cornelius C. Sugarcoat cartoon ear of corn, 1959	130	180
Sugar Crisp, Post, 3 bears on unicycle, 1955	90	125
Sugar Crisp, Post, 3 bears on unicycle, Blackstone magic trick ad	115	150
Sugar Crisp, Post, Roy Rogers paint set ad, 1954	180	250
Sugar Jets, General Mills, Mickey Mouse ring ad, 1956	270	375
Sugar Pops, Kellogg's, exploding battleship ad, 1958	200	275
Sugar Smacks, Kellogg's, deputy badge ad, 1956	160	220
Sugar Smiles, General Mills, 1953	90	125
Wheaties, General Mills, Hike-o-Meter ad, 1957	270	375

Kellogg's Special K, Kristi Yamaguchi, 1992 Olympic Gold Medalist Women's Figure Skating, $10–$15.

Chalkware

Plaster of Paris figurines painted in bright colors are called chalkware. Originally produced as a cheap imitation of Staffordshire and Bennington wares during the middle and the late 1800s, American companies later manufactured examples as carnival prizes during the first half of the twentieth century. Animals with nodding heads are especially rare. Few were produced and even fewer have survived through the years. They are sometimes found in the Midwest.

Check closely for condition. Because of their fragility, many pieces are restored. Measurements refer to largest dimension. Prices are for perfect (P), minor paint loss (M), and restored (R).

Left to right: Pinocchio, carnival prize, damaged hand, c1940, 15", $77; Betty Boop, carnival prize, repaired, c1930–40, 15", $248. —Photos courtesy Jackson's Auctioneers & Appraisers.

	P	M	R
Basket, c1800s, 8"	$425	$275	$200
Bookends, dogs, c1900s, pr	60	35	25
Boy, seated, c1900s, 10.5"	130	80	55
Buffalo Bank, carnival prize, c1950, 10.5"	28	22	15
Cat, seated, c1800s, 10.5"	300	175	125
Corn in Hand, Iowa Centennial, carnival prize, c1938, 12"	32	28	22
Couple, dancing, c1900s, 14"	40	18	13
Deer, c1800s, 11"	650	500	300
Dove, standing, c1800s, 7"	375	240	175
Eagle, spread winged, c1800s, 9.5"	400	260	180
George Washington, carnival prize, c1940, 11"	40	35	25
Horn of Plenty, c1900s, 14"	38	15	13
Horse and Rider, carnival prize, c1940	95	80	60
Hound, seated, c1900s, 8.5"	180	120	85
Indian w/ Drum, carnival prize, c1940–50, 12.5"	75	65	40
Lamb, c1800s, 8.5"	365	230	165
Lion, standing, c1800s, 6"	500	275	200
Native American, Cigar Store, 23"	350	200	135
Pigeon, c1900, 10"	180	120	85
Rabbit, c1900, 8"	125	90	60
Rooster, c1800s, 6"	450	300	200
Spaniels, c1800, 7.75"	280	175	125
Squirrel, c1800s, 10"	250	165	110
Stag, c1800s, 9.5"	600	450	275
Uncle Sam, carnival prize, c1935, 15"	95	80	50

Clocks, Factory-Made

The types of clocks listed in the selection below include swing clocks in which the clock mechanism itself is imbedded in the pendulum held by a statue. Banjo clocks have a round face, a tapering neck and a square pendulum base. Calendar clocks show the date as well as the time. Carriage clocks are small, intricate clocks generally about four to five inches high, usually with glass sides. Regulator clocks are precise clocks generally with long pendulums but no bells. Statue clocks combine a clock with a bronze or gilt figure. Kitchen clocks are designed for a shelf and are generally upright with ornate decoration on their edges. Ogee clocks are tall, rectangular clocks framed by a convex and concave molding. Novelty clocks are usually small, inexpensive and in whimsical shapes.

The clocks in this section represent the collectible clocks of the late 19th and early 20th centuries. These represent the first factory-produced clocks of the United States which are still frequently seen at auctions and flea markets.

When buying a clock at auction, always factor in the cost of repair. Even if the clock was working during exhibition, by the time it has been moved from display to storage to you, it is often not. Be sure to check for all parts (pendulum, weights, etc.) both before you bid and when you pick it up. Buying from a dealer may cost more money, but can often save on headaches.

Left to right: Parlor Calendar, Ithaca No. 8, $2000–$3000; Teardrop, E.N. Welch, $200–$350.

	LOW	AVG.	HIGH
Ansonia Lever, c1900, Ansonia	$250	$280	$310
Arab Cabinet, New Haven, c1900	310	375	440
Arab Connecticut Shelf, Ansonia, c1890	170	210	250
Arcadian Connecticut Shelf, Ansonia, c1890	190	235	280
Archer Statue, W.L. Gilbert, c1910	440	500	560
Art Nouveau, Seth Thomas, c1910	110	140	170
Art Nouveau Novelty, Ansonia, c1910	140	175	210
Austria Kitchen, Ansonia, c1890	240	280	320
Austrian Calendar, New Haven, c1900	800	1000	1250
Automobile, New Haven, c1920	70	85	100
Avon Kitchen, New Haven, c1900	230	300	360
Aztec Mission, Seth Thomas, c1910	500	600	700
Baghdad Regulator, Ansonia, c1900	1100	1300	1600
Banjo, E. Howard, c1880	3000	3500	4000
Banjo, E. Ingraham, c1920	240	285	330
Banjo, Waltham, c1890	2000	2400	2800
Bank Regulator, Ithaca Calendar, c1880	5300	6750	8500
Barbara Wall Regulator, New Haven, c1890	800	960	1100
Baronet Crystal Regulator, Ansonia, c1910	540	635	730
Baseball, F. Kroeber, c1890	410	630	750
Baseball Pendulum, Lux & Keebler, c1940	260	310	360
Bee Drum Alarm, Ansonia, c1890	70	80	90
Beehive Shelf, E.N. Welsh, c1880	180	215	250
Beehive Shelf, Jerome, c1880	220	280	340
Beehive Shelf, New Haven, c1900	100	120	140
Bisque Novelty, Ansonia, c1890	140	160	180
Black Cat Pendulum, Lux & Keebler, c1940	280	350	400
Black Mantel, E.N. Welsh, c1890	140	160	180
Black Wood Mantel, New Haven, c1900	150	165	180
Blackbird Kitchen, Ansonia, c1890	300	355	410
Boar Hunter Statue, Ansonia, c1890	540	665	790
Bouquet Novelty, New Haven, c1900	190	250	310
Brass Mantel, F. Kroeber, c1890	510	620	730
Brass Novelty, Ansonia, c1890	140	160	180
Brass Novelty, F. Kroeber, c1890	340	415	500

Character, Ingersoll, 1934, $935 at auction. —Photo courtesy James D. Julia.

	LOW	AVG.	HIGH
Brass Plaque, F. Kroeber, c1890	260	330	400
Brest Crystal Regulator, Waterbury, c1910	220	250	280
Bronze and Iron, Mueller & Son, c1900	190	245	300
Bronze Mantel, Ansonia, c1900	540	640	740
Brooklyn Figure Eight Regulator, Ansonia, c1910	2300	3000	3700
Bullfight Alarm, New Haven, c1900	300	340	400
Cabinet, E. Ingraham, c1900	180	195	210
Cabinet, E.N. Welsh, c1890	130	155	180
Cabinet, F. Kroeber, w/ mirrored sides, c1880	380	465	550
Cabinet, Seth Thomas, c1890	260	335	410
Cabinet, Waterbury, c1890	230	275	320
Cabinet, W.L. Gilbert, c1900	240	285	330
Calais Crystal Regulator, Waterbury, c1910	600	750	900
Calendar, F. Kroeber, c1880	350	400	450
Calendar, Jerome, c1900	2200	2500	2800
Calendar, Waterbury, double dial, c1890	1000	1250	1500
Calendar Alarm, Waterbury, c1900	130	155	180
Calendar Eclipse Regulator, E.N. Welsh, c1900	700	790	880
Canada Kitchen, Ansonia, c1890	220	255	300
Capital Kitchen, Seth Thomas, c1910	300	345	400
Carlos Calendar, Ansonia, c1890	400	500	600
Carpenter Iron Novelty, Ansonia, c1890	220	265	310
Carriage, E.N. Welsh, c1900	100	120	140
Carriage, New Haven, c1900	240	285	330
Carriage, Seth Thomas, c1890	140	165	190
Carriage, Waterbury, c1890	190	225	260
Cast Iron Character, Mueller & Son, c1900	300	330	360
Cavalier Statue, Waterbury, c1900	270	330	400
Character, Mueller & Son, c1900	260	315	370
Checkmate Carriage, F. Kroeber, c1890	360	400	440
Chicago Kitchen, Ansonia, c1890	280	335	400
China, New Haven, c1900, 6"	100	115	130
China, New Haven, c1900, 13"	300	355	410
China Novelty, Ansonia, c1890	100	120	140
China Novelty, Seth Thomas, c1900	100	120	140
Christine Kitchen, New Haven, c1900	250	295	340
Cinderella Kitchen, New Haven, c1900	260	300	320
Clifton Regulator, Ansonia, c1910	350	435	520
Colby Crystal Regulator, Ansonia, c1910	340	400	460
College Kitchen, Seth Thomas, c1910	260	305	350
Colorado Kitchen, Ansonia, c1890	300	330	370
Comet Carriage, Ansonia, c1910	270	315	360
Connecticut Shelf, F. Kroeber, c1890	220	245	260
Connecticut Shelf, New Haven, c1900	260	310	360
Connecticut Shelf, Seth Thomas, c1890	190	225	260
Connecticut Shelf Round Top, E. Ingraham, c1880	220	250	280
Connecticut Shelf Split Top, Ansonia, c1890	240	275	310
Connecticut Shelf Split Top, E. Ingraham, c1880	170	215	260
Conroy Kitchen, New Haven, c1900	300	340	380
Cottage Connecticut Shelf, Ansonia, c1890	130	160	190
Cottage Shelf, E. Ingraham, c1900	180	220	260
Cottage Shelf, F. Kroeber, c1890	190	230	270
Cottage Shelf, Jerome, c1880	200	240	280
Cottage Shelf, New Haven, c1900	100	125	150

Left to right: Hanging Office Calendar, Ithaca No. 4, $1000–$2250; Hanging Cottage Calendar, Ithaca No. 7, $1250–$2500; Hanging Office Calendar, Seth Thomas, $1500–$3000.

	LOW	AVG.	HIGH
Cottage Shelf, W.L. Gilbert, c1875	210	255	300
Crystal Palace, Ansonia, c1890	800	900	1000
Crystal Regulator, New Haven, c1900	700	795	900
Crystal Regulator, New Haven, c1920	440	510	580
Crystal Regulator, W.L. Gilbert, c1900	600	670	750
Crystal Regulator, Seth Thomas, c1920	500	630	760
Crystal Regulator, Waterbury, c1910	420	520	620
Cuckoo, Lux & Keebler, c1945	220	265	310
Cuckoo Mantel, F. Kroeber, c1890	540	680	820
Cuckoo Wall, F. Kroeber, c1890	400	480	560
Dauntless Alarm, Ansonia, c1880	260	315	370
Diplomat Crystal Regulator, Ansonia, c1910	740	890	1040
Dog House Pendulum, Lux & Keebler, c1940	220	245	270
Domestic Alarm, Ansonia, c1880	200	240	280
Don Juan Statue, Ansonia, c1890	410	495	580
Don Juan Statue, New Haven, c1900	420	485	550
Dora Carriage, Ansonia, c1880	180	215	250
Double Dial Calendar, New Haven, c1890	1500	1750	2000
Drum Alarm, E. Ingraham, c1920	60	80	100
Drum Alarm, E.N. Welsh, c1890	70	85	100
Drum Alarm, F. Kroeber, c1890	110	125	140
Drum Alarm, Seth Thomas, c1890	100	110	120
Drum Alarm, W.L. Gilbert, c1900	100	125	150
Drum Alarm, Waterbury, c1900	100	125	150
Duchess Crystal Regulator, Ansonia, c1910	500	585	670
Ebony Kitchen Hanging, Ansonia, c1910	610	730	850
Echo Alarm, Ansonia, c1880	300	335	370
Electric, Lux & Keebler, c1960	10	20	30
Elfrida Calendar, New Haven, c1890	1400	1600	1800
Empire Crystal Regulator, Seth Thomas, c1920	500	635	770
Empire Shelf, E.N. Welsh, c1880	420	505	600
Empire Shelf, Seth Thomas, c1875	730	810	890
Enamel Mantel, Ansonia, c1890	580	695	810
English Long Drop Regulator, Ansonia, c1910	570	695	820
Etruscan, Mueller & Son, c1900	220	285	350
Exposition Kitchen, Seth Thomas, c1900	270	340	410
Fancy Alarm, F. Kroeber, c1890	130	155	180

	LOW	AVG.	HIGH
Fancy Alarm, W.L. Gilbert, c1900	140	175	210
Figure Eight, E. Howard, c1880	6500	7500	8500
Figure Eight Calendar, F. Kroeber, c1890	1400	1575	1760
Figure Eight Calendar, New Haven, c1880	1450	1600	1750
Figure Eight Regulator, Ansonia, c1900	420	500	580
Figure Eight Regulator, E. Ingraham, c1900	570	635	700
Figure Eight Regulator, New Haven, c1900	520	580	640
Figure Eight Regulator, Waterbury, c1890	380	470	560
Fleet Kitchen, Seth Thomas, c1910	300	340	400
Floral, Jueller & Son, c1900	220	260	300
Floral China, Ansonia, c1900	60	75	90
Floral Painted, Mueller & Son, c1900	200	235	270
Flute Player Statue, New Haven, c1900	200	240	280
Fulton, Ansonia, c1890	260	330	400
Gallery Brass Lever, W.L. Gilbert, c1875	140	170	200
Gallery, E. Ingraham, c1880	280	330	380
Gallery, E.N. Welsh, c1880	150	175	200
Gallery, F. Kroeber, c1890	760	805	940
Gallery, Jerome, c1890	360	420	480
Gallery, New Haven, c1900	170	200	230
Gallery, Seth Thomas, c1880	240	280	320
Gallery, Waterbury, c1890	170	215	260
Gem Ink Calendar, Ansonia, c1890	380	465	550
Gilt Metal Novelty, Ansonia, c1900	110	125	140
Gilt Metal Novelty, W.L. Gilbert, c1910	130	155	180
Good Luck Alarm, Ansonia, c1880	100	120	140
Gothic Connecticut Shelf, Ansonia, c1890	260	295	330
Gothic Iron, Mueller & Son, c1890	260	315	370
Gothic Shelf, New Haven, c1900	200	240	280
Gothic Shelf, W.L. Gilbert, c1875	260	305	350
Grandfather, Ansonia, c1910	7000	8500	10,000
Grandfather, E. Howard, c1880	15,000	16,500	18,000
Grandfather, New Haven, c1900	4000	4500	5000
Grandfather, Seth Thomas, c1890	3000	3300	3600
Grandfather, Waterbury, c1910	3000	4000	5000
Grandfather No. 83, E. Howard, c1900	4000	5125	6250
Grecian Mantel, E. Ingraham, c1880	320	420	520
Greek Kitchen, Ansonia, c1900	270	345	420
Gypsy Kettle, F. Kroeber, c1890	300	330	370
Hampshire, Ansonia, c1890	300	350	410
Hanging Cottage, Ithaca Calendar, c1890	1250	1500	1750
Hanging Regulator No. 14, E. Howard, c1900	4000	5000	6000
Harlequin Cabinet, New Haven, c1900	300	350	400
Hawk Oak Kitchen, W.L. Gilbert, c1900	300	325	350
Heartbeat, Lux & Keebler, c1930	140	170	200
Helena China, Ansonia, c1900	70	80	90
Herald Kitchen, Ansonia, c1890	240	295	350
Hunter and Dog Statue, New Haven, c1900	600	800	1000
Huron Mantel, E. Ingraham, c1905	330	400	470
Imitation Walnut Kitchen, New Haven, c1900	130	165	200
Inca Cabinet, Ansonia, c1910	180	210	240
Inkstand Brass, Ansonia, c1900	170	205	240
Inkwell Calendar, F. Kroeber, c1880	410	515	620
Ipswich Cabinet, Ansonia, c1910	180	200	220

	LOW	AVG.	HIGH
Iron Case, Ithaca Calendar, c1890	4000	5500	7000
Iron Figural Mantel, F. Kroeber, c1880	260	325	400
Iron Mantel, Ansonia, c1890	210	250	300
Iron Mantel, E.N. Welsh, c1890	200	245	300
Iron Mantel, F. Kroeber, c1890	220	240	260
Iron Mantel, New Haven, c1900	170	205	240
Iron Novelty, Ansonia, c1890	100	120	140
Iron Novelty, E.N. Welsh, c1880	140	170	200
Iron Novelty, Seth Thomas, c1900	100	125	150
Ivanhoe Statue, New Haven, c1900	190	230	270
Japan Kitchen, Ansonia, c1890	270	330	400
Kitchen, E. Ingraham, c1900	300	325	350
Kitchen, E.N. Welsh, c1890	260	295	330
Kitchen, F. Kroeber, c1890	430	485	640
Kitchen, New Haven, c1900	240	280	320
Kitchen, Seth Thomas, c1890	240	295	350
Kitchen, Waterbury, c1890	190	245	300
Kitchen, W.L. Gilbert, c1900	210	245	280
Kitchen, w/ mirrored sides, F. Kroeber, c1890	560	675	790
Kitchen Hanging, New Haven, c1900	360	420	480
Kitchen Wall, Waterbury, c1890	400	470	550
La Cette China, Ansonia, c1890	400	510	620
La Cruz China, Ansonia, c1910	370	420	470
La Nord China, Ansonia, c1910	430	485	540
La Sedan China, Ansonia, c1910	350	435	520
La Tosca China, Ansonia, c1910	430	495	560
Leeds Cabinet, Ansonia, c1880	220	255	300
Library, Waltham, c1920	210	240	270
Lighthouse, New Haven, c1900	420	475	530
Lima, Ansonia, c1890	260	335	410
Little Dorrit Alarm, Ansonia, c1880	230	300	350
Locomotive Iron Novelty, Ansonia, c1890	240	300	340
Lodi Kitchen, Waterbury, c1890	170	205	240
Lusitania Novelty, Seth Thomas, c1900	270	330	400
Lux Art, Lux & Keebler, c1930	140	160	180
Mahogany Mantel, Ansonia, c1920	110	130	150
Mahogany Mantel, E. Ingraham, c1920	100	115	130
Mahogany Mantel, New Haven, c1910	70	80	90
Mahogany Mantel, Seth Thomas, c1910	130	170	210
Major Kitchen, New Haven, c1890	260	295	330
Mandolin Alarm, New Haven, c1900	270	325	380
Mantel, w/ mirrored sides, E. Ingraham, c1900	400	480	570
Mantel, w/ mirrored sides, New Haven, c1890	460	520	580
Mantel Lever, Jerome, c1900	300	340	380
Marble Dial Wall, E. Howard, c1900	2600	3200	3800
Marble Gallery, New Haven, c1910	400	495	600
Marble Mantel, Ansonia, c1900	220	285	350
Marquis Crystal Regulator, Ansonia, c1910	1000	1200	1400
Maryland, Ansonia, c1890	230	285	340
Mayflower Kitchen, New Haven, c1900	240	300	340
Mechanical Bird, F. Kroeber, c1880	3700	4150	4600
Mechanical Ship, F. Kroeber, c1880	3600	4000	4400
Metropolis Kitchen, Ansonia, c1890	280	320	360
Mission, Waterbury, c1910	370	425	480

	LOW	AVG.	HIGH
Mission Cabinet, New Haven, c1910	270	340	410
Mission Kitchen, New Haven, c1910	220	250	280
Mission Kitchen Hanging, New Haven, c1910	510	615	720
Mission Novelty, New Haven, c1910	210	255	300
Mission Octagon Short Drop, New Haven, c1910	350	410	470
Mosel Kitchen, Ansonia, c1890	240	300	360
Musical Mantel, F. Kroeber, c1890	750	1000	1250
Nautical Chronometer, Waltham, c1910	600	700	800
Nectar Kitchen, New Haven, c1900	250	275	300
Nightingale Alarm, Ansonia, c1880	140	160	180
Novelty, Waterbury, c1900	170	210	250
Nymph Statue, Seth Thomas, c1910	140	160	180
Octagon Gallery, F. Kroeber, c1900	220	250	280
Octagon Gallery, Jerome, c1890	250	280	310
Octagon Long Drop Regulator, W.L. Gilbert, c1900	410	500	570
Octagon Peep-o-Day, Ansonia, c1890	50	60	70
Octagon Princess Alarm, Ansonia, c1890	50	65	80
Octagon Regulator Short Drop Calendar, Seth Thomas, c1900	560	645	730
Octagon Short Drop Regulator, F. Kroeber, c1890	470	585	700
Octagon Top Calendar, Ansonia, c1880	410	480	550
Octagon Top Calendar, W.L. Gilbert, c1890	400	485	570
Octagon Top Long Drop, E. Ingraham, c1900	340	395	450
Octagon Top Long Drop Calendar, E. Ingraham, c1910	500	610	720
Octagon Top Long Drop Regulator, E. Ingraham, c1900	500	610	720
Octagon Top Long Drop Regulator, E.N. Welsh, c1900	480	580	680
Octagon Top Long Drop Regulator, New Haven, c1900	340	415	500
Octagon Top Long Drop Regulator, Seth Thomas, c1890	530	640	750
Octagon Top Long Drop Regulator, Waterbury, c1910	520	675	830
Octagon Top Regulator, Ansonia, c1890	430	525	620
Octagon Top Shelf, E. Ingraham, c1880	180	220	260
Octagon Top Shelf, W.L. Gilbert, c1875	170	215	260
Octagon Top Short Drop, E. Ingraham, c1900	270	320	370
Octagon Top Short Drop Calendar, E. Ingraham, c1910	380	500	600
Octagon Top Short Drop Calendar, New Haven, c1900	410	475	540

Shelf, Eli Terry & Sons, $400–$600.

	LOW	AVG.	HIGH
Octagon Top Short Drop Regulator, E. Ingraham, c1900	320	370	420
Octagon Top Short Drop Regulator, E.N. Welsh, c1900	350	425	500
Octagon Top Short Drop Regulator, Seth Thomas, c1890	500	585	680
Octagon Top Short Drop Regulator, Waterbury, c1910	400	445	500
Office Calendar, Seth Thomas, c1900	1500	2000	3000
Office Ink, New Haven, c1900	280	330	380
Ogee Connecticut Shelf, Ansonia, c1890	260	320	380
Ogee Connecticut Shelf, W.L. Gilbert, c1875	240	300	340
Ogee Shelf, E.N. Welsh, c1880	300	345	400
Ogee Shelf, Jerome, c1870	280	325	370
Ogee Shelf, Seth Thomas, c1890	300	320	350
Ogee Shelf, Waterbury, c1890	270	320	370
Olympia Statue, Ansonia, c1890	700	850	1000
Onyx Mantel, Ansonia, c1900	360	440	520
Onyx Mantel, New Haven, c1900	250	315	380
Onyx Mantel, W.L. Gilbert, c1910	320	400	480
Open Swinging Regulator, Waterbury, c1910	1070	1245	1420
Oriole Carriage, Ansonia, c1890	170	195	220
Orpheus Statue, New Haven, c1900	220	250	280
Papier-Mâché Shelf, Jerome, c1890	270	315	360
Parlor Calendar, Seth Thomas, c1900	1280	1600	2100
Parlor Iron, Mueller & Son, c1890	160	205	250
Parlor Shelf Regulator, Seth Thomas, c1900	540	620	700
Parlor Wall Regulator, Ansonia, c1900	640	840	1040
Parlor Wall Regulator, E. Ingraham, c1900	880	1120	1360
Parlor Wall Regulator, F. Kroeber, c1890	1000	1200	1400
Parlor Wall Regulator, New Haven, c1900	790	985	1180
Parlor Wall Regulator, Seth Thomas, c1890	1370	1620	1870
Parlor Wall Regulator, Seth Thomas, c1910	1100	1300	1500
Parlor Wall Regulator, Waterbury, c1890	830	1025	1220
Parlor Wall Regulator, W.L. Gilbert, c1900	1000	1200	1400
Pearl Carriage, Ansonia, c1900	120	145	170
Pearl Inlaid Papier-Mâché, Jerome, c1890	280	360	440
Pendulum, Lux & Keebler, c1930	110	125	140
Pet Alarm, New Haven, c1900	280	335	400
Philosopher Statue, Asnonia, c1890	270	335	400
Pillar and Scroll Shelf, E.N. Welsh, c1880	210	245	80
Pillar and Scroll Shelf, Jerome, c1870	560	645	730
Pillar and Scroll Shelf, Seth Thomas, c1880	270	315	360
Pillar and Scroll Shelf, Seth Thomas, c1900	220	260	300
Planet Calendar Alarm, Ansonia, c1900	160	190	220
Planet Drum Alarm, Ansonia, c1880	180	205	230
Plush Novelty, F. Kroeber, c1890	250	305	360
Plymouth Cabinet, Ansonia, c1880	200	250	300
Porcelain, F. Kroeber, c1900	360	405	450
Porcelain Regulator, Ansonia, c1910	1900	2315	2730
Porcelain Statue, W.L. Gilbert, c1910	350	400	450
Precision Regulator, Seth Thomas, c1890	14,000	16,000	18,000
Prince Crystal Regulator, Ansonia, c1910	900	1100	1300
Princess Drum Alarm, Ansonia, c1880	70	80	90
Racket Drum Alarm, Ansonia, c1900	80	90	100
Rebecca at the Well Statue, Seth Thomas, c1910	250	325	400
Reflector, Ansonia, c1910	830	980	1130
Regulator, New Haven, small second hand, c1900	1100	1400	1700

Left to right: Gothic Four-Poster Shelf, Brewster & Ingraham, $770 at auction; Grecian Shelf, Ingraham, $375 at auction; Zebra Ionic Wall, Waterbury, $468 at auction; Angel Swing Shelf, Kroebler, $1045 at auction. —Photo courtesy York Town Auction, Inc.

	LOW	AVG.	HIGH
Regulator, Seth Thomas, small second hand, c1890	1250	1500	1750
Regulator, Waterbury, small second hand, c1890	1400	1650	2000
Regulator No. 11, Seth Thomas, c1900	2000	2500	3000
Regulator No. 19, Seth Thomas, c1910	1800	2400	3000
Renaissance Crystal Regulator, Ansonia, c1910	1120	1280	1440
Rio Parlor Wall Regulator, Ansonia, c1880	1050	1155	1260
Riverdale Cabinet, Ansonia, c1910	210	260	310
Rockwood Cabinet, Ansonia, c1910	200	245	300
Roman Statue, New Haven, c1900	260	335	410
Rome Parlor Shelf, Seth Thomas, c1920	260	305	350
Rotary, F. Kroeber, c1890	2700	3450	4200
Round Head Regulator, E.N. Welsh, c1900	2400	2995	3600
Round Top Connecticut Shelf, W.L. Gilbert, c1880	170	200	230
Round Top Long Drop Regulator, F. Kroeber, c1890	700	850	1000
Round Top Long Drop Regulator, W.L. Gilbert, c1880	1200	1500	1800
Round Top Long Drop Regulator, Waterbury, c1890	1250	1500	1750
Round Top Mantel, E. Ingraham, c1900	200	235	270
Round Top Shelf, New Haven, c1900	100	115	130
Round Top Shelf, Seth Thomas, c1880	160	205	250
Round Top Short Drop Regulator, E. Ingraham, c1900	320	385	450
Russia Cabinet, New Haven, c1900	260	305	350
Saratoga Wall Regulator, W.L. Gilbert, c1900	650	780	910
Satellite Carriage, Ansonia, c1910	340	415	500
Saxon Statue, New Haven, c1900	300	340	400
Senator Kitchen, New Haven, c1900	210	245	280
Shannon Kitchen, New Haven, c1900	150	185	220
Shaver Alarm, New Haven, c1900	300	330	370
Shelf Regulator, Ithaca Calendar, c1880	3000	4000	5000
Spring Chronometer, Ithaca Calendar, c1890	2000	2400	2800
Sprint Statue, Ansonia, c1890	800	900	1000

	LOW	AVG.	HIGH
Square Top Regulator, Seth Thomas, c1910	1000	1200	1400
Square Top Regulator No. 39, E. Howard, c1900	5500	6750	8000
Square Top Short Drop Regulator, E. Ingraham, c1905	250	305	360
Square Top Short Drop Regulator, New Haven, c1900	400	500	600
Standard Connecticut Round Top, Ansonia, c1890	210	245	280
Steeple Connecticut Shelf, Ansonia, c1890	200	235	270
Steeple Shelf, E.N. Welsh, c1880	170	205	240
Steeple Shelf, F. Kroeber, c1870	220	270	320
Steeple Shelf, Jerome, c1875	280	335	400
Steeple Shelf, New Haven, c1900	160	185	210
Steeple Shelf, Seth Thomas, c1890	140	165	190
Steeple Shelf, W.L. Gilbert, c1870	220	260	300
Stirrup Novelty, New Haven, c1900	280	320	360
Store Regulator, E. Ingraham, c1900	500	565	630
Store Regulator, Seth Thomas, c1910	460	560	660
Summit Cabinet, Ansonia, c1880	230	270	310
Sunlight Alarm, W.L. Gilbert, c1900	220	260	300
Sweep Second Regulator, E.N. Welsh, c1890	2000	2500	3000
Sweep Second Regulator, New Haven, c1900	3800	4600	5400
Sweep Second Regulator, Seth Thomas, c1890	3000	4500	6000
Sweep Second Regulator, W.L. Gilbert, c1890	5000	5500	6000
Sweep Second Regulator, Waterbury, c1890	5500	6500	7500
Swing Arm, Ansonia, c1890	3500	4000	4500
Symbol Crystal Regulator, Ansonia, c1910	750	1000	1250
Teardrop, F. Kroeber, c1890	440	555	670
Teardrop Kitchen, Ansonia, c1890	430	505	580
Teardrop Kitchen, Seth Thomas, c1890	240	280	320
Telephone Pendulum, Lux & Keebler, c1940	100	125	150
Tivoli Cabinet, Ansonia, c1880	250	300	330
Tomahawk Kitchen, New Haven, c1900	250	305	360
Tourist Carriage, Ansonia, c1910	210	250	300
Verdi Crystal Regulator, W.L. Gilbert, c1910	1100	1250	1400
Victorian Kitchen Barometer/Thermometer, Ansonia, c1890	230	285	340
Victory Statue, Seth Thomas, c1900	220	245	270
Watch Form, New Haven, c1900	200	255	310
Watchman's Wall Regulator, E. Howard, c1890	5000	6000	7000
Westminster Chime, New Haven, c1900	330	395	460
Westminster Chimes, Seth Thomas, c1910	320	410	500

Left to right: Mascot Kitchen Clock, Ingraham, $429 at auction; Steeple Clock, New Haven, $1100 at auction. —Photo courtesy York Town Auction, Inc.

Clothing and Accessories

Buttons

Buttons are something we use every day but rarely think about. To the collector, however, buttons are tiny treasures full of history, made of wonderful materials and endless variety. Beautiful, small, and for the most part reasonably priced, buttons make an ideal collectible.

Though buttons date back many centuries, button collecting began in this country in the 1930s. In 1938 the National Button Society was formed. Its members wrote many excellent books in the 1940s and '50s.

Collectors look for a wide range of buttons, from eighteenth century porcelains, hand-painted enamels and carved ivory, to mother-of-pearl, black glass and intricate metals. Most buttons available today are nineteenth or twentieth century. They range in price from as little as 25¢ each to several hundred dollars for some of the rarest varieties. Among the more recent buttons attracting attention are Bakelite, Art Deco and plastic "realistics." Materials include horn, tin, brass, glass, plastic, ivory, porcelain, bone, shell and sterling. They may be plain or highly decorated. There are many good examples of military buttons from the Civil War and earlier. Picture buttons may depict historical or biblical scenes, heads of famous people and animals. As with all collectibles, condition is a major factor in the price. Chips, rust or other damage generally make a button uncollectible.

Our consultant for this area is Adam G. Perl, owner of Pastimes Antiques in Ithaca, NY. He is listed at the back of this book.

	LOW	AVG.	HIGH
Bakelite, fruit, carved orange	$20	$25	$30
Bakelite, round, orange, 1.5"	10	12	15
Black Glass, bird	6	8	12
Black Onyx, ball-shaped, w/ 14k gold, 19th C	65	75	85
Brass, stamped coat of arms	15	25	35
Brass, rooster	12	15	18
Calico, green on white	3	4	5
Celluloid, angel head, gold ground, gilt rims	35	40	45
Ceramic, cat	35	40	45
Cloisonné, fish	80	90	100
Enamel, children playing	65	75	85
Enamel, floral design, 18th C	200	225	250
Enamel, portrait, 18th C	75	100	150
Gay Nineties, brass w/ purple "jewel," 1.75"	25	35	45
Glass, molded opaque, brown bird design	25	33	41
Gold, 14k, button set w/ chain, 19th C	50	75	100
Gold, 18k, ball shape, 19th C	75	100	125
Gold-filled, ball shape w/ ribbing, 19th C	20	25	30
Gold-plated, knot design	15	20	25
Ivory, cutout girl and bird, blue ground	150	175	200
Ivory, painted Cupid	75	100	125
Jasperware, classical figures, white relief on light blue	50	65	75
Pewter, dog	15	20	25
Porcelain, flowers and butterfly, 18th C	15	25	35
Silver, Bacchus, god of wine, etched design	45	65	85
Steel, floral design	5	7	10
Turquoise, w/ 14k gold, button set w/ chain, 19th C	100	125	150
Wedgwood, classical figure, white on royal blue, gilt rim, 18th C	225	250	275

Clothing

Vintage clothing is collected by those who wish to add it to their wardrobes as well as by collectors who wish only to display it. Currently, most market activity is in clothes from the 1920s, 1930s and 1940s. Alterations and construction details are factors in determining price, while skilled workmanship or handmade trims often increase value. Clothing with beadwork is also a good investment.

Vintage clothing requires careful handling. Textiles are perishable: light, humidity, dust and body oil are potentially harmful. The acids in wood, cardboard and tissue paper can also hurt clothing. When storing pieces, it is best to wrap items in white sheets and use mothballs. Hang lightweight clothing on padded hangers, and store heavy clothing laid flat.

For further information, contact The Costume Society of America, PO Box 73, Earleville, MD 21919.

Apparel, Vintage

	LOW	HIGH
Cocktail Dress, black chiffon and wool crepe, c1959	$90	$150
Cocktail Dress, Oleg Cassini, black silk sheath dress w/ fitted corset bodice, white satin underskirt overlaid w/ black lace, 1950s	150	250
Day Dress, Adrian, black crepe, appliquéd yoke, 1940s	2500	3500

Left to right: Campbell's Soup Paper Dress, 1960s, $2185 at auction; Ball Gown, Pierre Balmain, 1961, $4312 at auction. —Photos courtesy William Doyle Galleries.

Evening Dresses, Jean Dessés, c1960, left to right: Lemon Silk Chiffon, $9200 at auction; tomato red silk chiffon w/ satin trim, $6037 at auction; chartreuse silk chiffon, $3450 at auction. —Photo courtesy William Doyle Galleries.

	LOW	HIGH
Day Dress, black and white check heavy cotton w/ white piping and wide sailor collar, c1915	125	200
Day Dress, green and black silk chiffon w/ floral motif, c1925	75	100
Day Dress, white cotton w/ floral print of white and yellow daisies and blue and pink floral sprays, c1930	100	160
Dress, black wool crepe, angel sleeves, net insets, c1930	90	140
Dress, blue and white stripe cotton w/ blue cotton collar and cuffs, c1915	125	190
Dress, Christian Dior, 2-pc, black wool, long sleeves, turned back cuffs, c1950	3000	4000
Dress, ecru lace w/ short cape sleeves and tiered skirt, c1920	125	180
Dress, gray 2-pc hand-loomed knit, trimmed w/ white glass beads, c1920s	95	150
Dress, peach organdy w/ rows of scalloped ruffles edged in lace, c1920s	100	160
Dress, silk taffeta w/ red polka dots and crinoline, c1950	130	200
Dress, white cotton w/ handkerchief hem line trimmed w/ lace, c1920s	50	80
Dress, wool mohair in red and blue plaid, c1965	30	50
Evening Coat, velvet, wide shawl collar, c1910	200	300
Evening Dress, 2-tiered black chiffon w/ rhinestones set in floral motifs, c1920	175	275
Evening Dress, bias cut maroon velvet floor length w/ cream silk ruffle trim, c1930s	100	160
Evening Dress, black velvet bias cut w/ rhinestone buckle, c1930	50	80
Evening Dress, Charles James, black silk satin woven w/ pinstripes, halter neckline, draped at hip, c1945	40,000	50,000
Evening Dress, Herman Patrick Tappé, black silk satin, slip torso, tiered cutaway black tulle skirt, c1930	600	800
Evening Dress, navy blue chiffon w/ navy bugle beads, c1920s	150	250
Evening Dress, Schiaperelli, long slip dress, rayon crepe printed w/ flowers in red, blue, yellow, green, and black on ivory ground, early 1930s	1750	2500
Evening Dress, sheer navy crepe overdress w/ blue and gold geometric underdress, c1920s	120	190

	LOW	HIGH
Evening Dress, silk chiffon w/ red floral patterns and net hem, c1925	125	200
Evening Dress, strapless, short, white silk twill printed w/ island dancers and swriling ribbons, purple, turquoise, rose, gray, green, and black, 1950s	450	600
Evening Gown, black satin, hemmed w/ braid and tassels, c1915	375	575
Evening Grown, cream silk printed w/ blue, green, and pink floral sprays, boned bodice, skirt w/ metallic lace and silk bows, c1920s	225	350
Evening Suit, black crepe w/ diamante buttons, c1930	75	110
Jacket, black wool w/ pink wool bow at neck, c1950	60	90
Jacket, ecru net, cord embroidery, side slits, early 20th C	200	300
Jacket, Fortuny, apricot velvet, gilt stenciled Islamic pattern, kimono style, 1920s	4000	5500
Jacket, purple wool crepe w/ large plastic flower-form buttons, c1940	125	190
Kimono, peach w/ silk floral hand embroidery and sash, c1910	200	350
Nightgown, peach silk w/ lace ruffles at hem, c1923	40	60
Pajamas, silk satin w/ Chinese motif, c1920	150	250
Skirt, black "piano shawl" skirt w/ embroidery and fringe, c1955	75	120
Skirt, black wool w/ fringe at waist, c1950	40	60
Suit, pink wool crepe w/ brass buttons, c1940	130	225
Walking Suit, black wool gabardine 2 pc, early 20th C	2250	400
Walking Suit, purple wool 2 pc w/ black velvet collars and cuffs, early 20th C	400	650
Walking Suit, white linen 2 pc, early 20th C	350	550

Handbags

Afternoon Bag, Christian Dior, briefcase style, 1960s	$90	$115
Afternoon Bag, black alligator w/ black enameled frame, rhinestone catch, 1950s	250	315
Box Bag, Judith Leiber, mottled tan padded plastic outlined w/ brass studs, 1960s	100	175
Box Bag, Koret, brown alligator, gilt metal trim, top mirror, 1960s	290	350

Hatbox Evening Bag, Judith Leiber, black satin w/ rhinestone strap closure and handle, $1265 at auction. —Photo courtesy William Doyle Galleries.

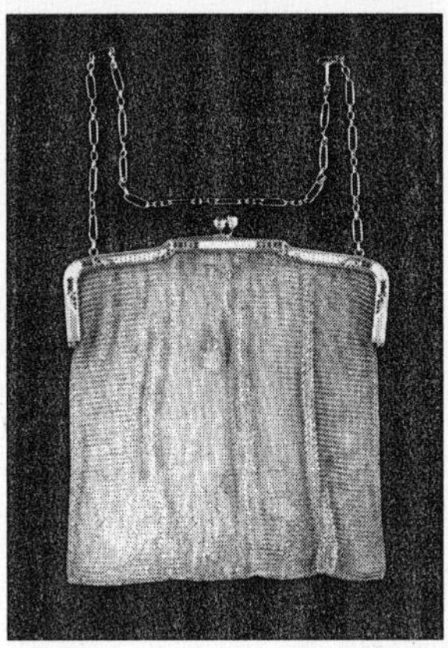

Left to right: Evening Bag, gold mesh with emeralds and diamonds, $2000– $3000; Handbag, lucite, faux tortoiseshell, $50–$85.

	LOW	HIGH
Clutch, Judith Leiber, blue kid, petit point inset, c1978	300	375
Clutch, Judith Leiber, purple snakeskin, oval, gilt metal frame, 1980s	285	350
Drawstring Bag, aluminum w/ brass beads, late 19th C	175	300
Drawstring Bag, green w/ embroidered needlework panel, late 19th C	95	150
Envelope Bag, Germaine Guérin, black lizard, gilt metal handle, 1960s	50	70
Evening Bag, Austrian, black suede w/ mint green enamel, 1930s	350	450
Evening Bag, French, gold lamé woven w/ Indo-Persian floral pattern, gilt metal frame in slate blue Art Deco pattern, 1930s	75	125
Evening Bag, Nettie Rosenstein, blush pink velvet embroidered w/ gold bouillon and rhinestones, 1950s	100	175
Evening Bag, Rosenfeld, gilt metal box w/ molded silver medallion depicting 18th-C outdoor scene, red satin tufted lining, 1950s	80	115
Evening Bag, Tiffany & Co, petit point carpet design in red and green on black ground, 14k gold frame and twisted fringe, orig box	1750	2500
Handbag, Chanel, quilted white linen, black velvet trim and strap, 1980s	175	250
Handbag, Loewe, black crocodile, envelope flap, gilt metal fittings, 1950s	800	1250
Pocketbook, Gucci, white grained leather, bamboo handle and catch, 1960s	300	350
Pouch Bag, Cartier, dark brown suede, silk cord drawstring, 1970s	95	145
Princess Pocketbook, Hermès, brown crocodile, gilt metal push-button clasp, coin purse, early 1950s	1000	1500
Purse, Lucille de Paris, brown alligator, trapezoidal form, fold-over flap w/ gold metal clasp, 1950s	65	100
Reticule, German, drawstring glass beadwork, lined w/ kid, 1820s	230	375
Reticule, glass bead, floral center, white ground, pink, red, green, and blue, 19th C	100	175
Reticule, tulip shaped, linen w/ green silk top and ribbon drawstring, c1800	300	450
Shoulder Bag, Gucci, black suede, green and red fabric strap, 1970s	300	375
Timepiece Bag, French, crocodile, watch clasp sgd "Wyler Incaflex," 1950s	550	700

Hats

	LOW	HIGH
Beret, Christian Dior, oversized, black satin, 1950s	$150	$225
Black Straw, Flo-Raye, fine weave w/ flowers	60	95
Black Straw, Schiaparelli, turned up brim, openwork weave, grosgrain bow, 1950s	75	125
Black Wool, D.E. Bishop, Bloomingdale's	40	55
Chesterfield	5	15
Cloche, straw, silk lined, 1920s	60	75
Derby, black felt, Dobbs Fifth Avenue	80	125
Fedora, felt	5	15
Leopard Hat, Saks Fifth Ave, triangular, folded up brim, pointed crown, 1950s	350	450
Madeline-Style Straw Hat, w/ ribbon	110	180
Masquerade Hat, Schiaparelli, head-hugging form, shocking pink pleated chiffon w/ bird shaped spangles, black velvet mask at back, orig box, 1950s	200	300
Pillbox, mink, brown netting, brown brocade at crown, 1960s	25	50
Pillbox, Norman Durand, edged in black velvet trim w/ rhinestone flowers and butterflies	60	90
Pink Straw, Frank Olive	60	95
Plumed, Grace Emmy	60	95
Poke Bonnet, gray and black cotton, late 1800s	50	75
Straw Hat, Alabert, w/ daisies	40	65
Straw Hat, Frank Olive, navy underbrim, white flower	40	65
Tam, Galanos, black wool w/ white flowers and pumpkin stem, and flower appliqué, 1960s	75	100
Tennis, brown and cream hound's tooth, 1940s	15	25
Toque, Mr. John, magenta velvet, 1950s	70	80
Turban, Lilly Daché, black wool w/ iridescent sequins and black soutache, 1940s	150	225
Turban-Style, turquoise velvet, 1960s	10	20

Left to right: Feather Evening Hat, Jack McConnell, NY, iridescent black feathers on velvet pillbox crown, 1950s, $97 at auction; Cocktail Hat, Hattie Carnegie, black smooth plush w/ black osprey feather spray, 1950s, $23 at auction; Gold Kid Cocktail Hat, Laddie Northridge, NY, toque style, ball fringed veil, 1950s, $172 at auction. —Photo courtesy William Doyle Galleries.

Bakelite Accessories

Bakelite is the trade name of the plastic marketed by the Bakelite Corporation. Leo Hendrik Baekeland invented this form of phenol formaldehyde in 1909. Since then, it has been used for everything from telephones to jewelry to the heat shield on NASA's Jupiter space probe.

Bright colors matter! The selection listed below is based on bright reds, yellows, blues, greens, etc. Dark brown and black will command considerable lesser prices.

	GOOD	BETTER	BEST
Bangle, half inch	$50	$100	$225
Bangle, 1 inch	75	150	350
Bangle, 2 inches	100	200	450
Bangle, figural motif	200	300	475
Bangle, floral motif	100	150	350
Bangle, geometric motif	125	200	400
Bangle, polychrome	90	130	450
Bangle, solid color	30	60	100
Bracelet, figural motif, hinged	225	325	500
Bracelet, figural motif, cuff	225	325	500
Bracelet, floral motif, hinged	125	175	375
Bracelet, floral motif, link	125	175	375
Bracelet, floral motif, stretch	75	125	200
Bracelet, geometric motif, hinged	150	200	350
Bracelet, geometric motif, link	75	125	250
Bracelet, geometric motif, stretch	100	150	400
Bracelet, metal dec	100	200	500
Bracelet, polychrome, hinged	125	250	1000
Bracelet, polychrome, link	75	125	250
Bracelet, polychrome, stretch	100	150	400
Bracelet, rhinestone dec	50	150	350
Bracelet, solid color, hinged	40	70	110
Bracelet, solid color, link	40	70	110
Bracelet, solid color, stretch	30	75	125
Bracelet, wooden dec	50	150	250
Buckle	50	100	150
Button	10	20	30
Charm Bracelet	100	200	450
Dress Clip, pr	40	60	80
Earrings, pr	100	150	200
Necklace, geometric beads	125	250	500
Necklace, polychrome beads	200	300	500
Necklace, solid color beads	50	100	250
Pin, figural	100	200	500
Pin, geometric	100	150	375
Pin, polychrome	80	120	300
Pin, solid color	35	75	100
Ring	50	75	150

Coca-Cola Collectibles

The first batch of Coca-Cola was created by John Pemberton, an Atlanta pharmacist, in 1886. Mr. Pemberton was trying to create a tonic rather than a soft drink. The syrup was soon marketed to Willis Venable, an Atlanta soda fountain manager. As legend has it, a clerk mixed the syrup with soda and an empire was born. In 1894 Joseph Biedenhorn started bottling and distributing Coca-Cola in Vicksburg, MS. Coke became the world's favorite soft drink. With over 100 years of advertisements and promotional material, Coke collectors have an incredible breadth of material from which to draw. The firm has done a great job in promoting its product. One reason collectors love this material is that by viewing it you can draw a time line of our last 100 years. It begins with the Victorian elegance of the 1890s and travels through two World Wars, the Great Depression, Rock 'n' Roll, the country's struggle with the Vietnam War ("I'd Like to Teach the World to Sing"), to today's sports stars' endorsements. Coke ads are usually very appealing and reflective of their time. Since Coca-Cola is now a global entity, the material grows daily, and there are even Coke boutiques specializing in marketing new Coke clothing and products.

The only cautionary note is that there are also many reproductions and items that are done in the style of an earlier era. Such material is often offered as old with prices far beyond their value. Do your homework and deal with knowledgeable people that stand behind their products. The prices below are based on items in excellent or mint condition.

For further information, see *Petretti's Coca-Cola Collectibles Price Guide, 10th Edition,* Allan Petretti, Antique Trader Books, Dubuque, IA 1997. You may also wish to contact the Coca-Cola Collectors Club International, P.O. Box 49166, Atlanta, GA 30359.

Festoon, cardboard, 8' long extended size, $4950 at auction. —Photo courtesy Muddy River Trading Co.

	LOW	AVG.	HIGH
Back Bar Sign, reverse painted glass, "Please Pay When Served, Drink Coca-Cola, Thank You," 1920s, 11.25"	$650	$750	$900
Bank, 5¢, dispenses mini bottles	85	110	125
Bingo Card, c1940	15	18	20
Blotter, "58 Million a Day," 1957	5	8	12
Book Cover, "Always Be Careful," c1951	5	6	7
Book Cover, baseball player, c1939	10	13	15
Bookmark, Hilda Clark, c1900	300	350	400
Bottle, "Best by a Dam Site," c1910	70	80	90

Lillian Nordica Sign, vintage bottle and flared glass, $21,275 at auction. —Photo courtesy James D. Julia.

	LOW	AVG.	HIGH
Bottle, Donald Duck, painted, c1948, 7 oz	15	20	25
Bottle Holder Protector, 6-bottle type, c1933	30	35	40
Bottle Radio, 1933, 24" h	900	1000	1250
Button Sign, tin, "Drink Coca-Cola," 16" dia	450	485	500
Button Sign, tin, "Sign of Good Taste," 1958, 16" dia	275	300	240
Button Sign, w/ attached 20" metal arrow and mounting hardware, 1951, 20" dia	1100	1200	1350
Calendar, nurse holding bottle, 1943	375	410	450
Calendar, pretty girl wearing pink dress, 1914	750	800	875
Calendar, woman wearing hair in scarf, 1953	200	245	270
Calendar Holder, tin, w/ unused 1979 Coke calendar pad, 1953, 8" x 19"	400	440	475
Celluloid Disk, classic "Coca-Cola" and bottle, c1950, 9" dia	230	250	275
Cigarette Lighter, Coke bottle logo, c1965	18	20	22
Cigarette Lighter, Coke bottle shape, c1940	20	25	30
Clock, electric, round, "Drink Coca-Cola" and silhouette girl on button face, c1939	550	600	650
Clock, electric, square wood case, "Drink Coca-Cola In Bottles" button on face, late 1930s, 16" sq	160	175	190
Clock, leather bottle, c1910, 3" x 8"	2100	2350	2750
Coin Purse, emb, c1906	60	75	90
Cooler, painted metal, white lettering on red ground, 1950s, 13" x 19" x 16"	200	230	265
Cooler, stainless steel, orig tray inside, red lettering, 1950s, 20" h	225	250	280
Cooler Radio, red plastic, 1950s	475	510	540
Counter Top Dispenser, 1950s	350	400	500
Cutouts, Toonerville Trolley, uncut, c1932	250	300	350
Cutouts, Uncle Remus, uncut, c1930	300	325	350
Display Bottle, Christmas 1930s, 20" h	180	210	250

	LOW	AVG.	HIGH
Door Plates, pair "Push" and "Pull," 3" x 6" each	950	1100	1250
Door Push Bar, silhouette girl, c1939, 3.5" x 33"	680	715	800
Festoon Centerpiece, diecut cardboard, string and easel back, girl holding glass, "...add Zest to the hour," 1951, 21" x 22"	120	135	150
Flashlight, plastic bottle, c1968	20	25	30
Glass, 5¢ w/ arrow, c1905	300	375	450
Glass, flair type, c1925	60	75	90
Glass, home type, red/white diamond	5	6	7
Ice Pick and Opener, c1940	12	14	16
Key Chain, amber replica bottle w/ brass chain, c1964	15	18	20
Menu Board, tin, profile of woman, c1940	200	240	280
Mirror, pocket, "Bathing Beauty," c1917	900	1100	1300
Mirror, pocket, "Drink Coca-Cola 5¢," c1914	300	400	500
Mirror, pocket, "Elaine" girl w/ bottle turned right, c1917	300	325	350
Mirror, pocket, "Enjoy Thirst," c1930	150	175	200
Mirror, pocket, "Garden Girl," c1920	300	400	500
Mirror, pocket, Juanita w/ pendant and glass, c1909	400	450	500
Mirror, pocket, "Relieves Fatigue," c1906	400	450	500
Mirror, pocket, "St. Louis Exposition," c1904	300	350	400
Mobile, 2 sided, 3 arm, featuring king size bottle w/ rocking sides, 1960s	160	185	210
Neon Sign, "Coke Fountain Service," 3 color, c1960, 22" x 20"	425	440	465
Notebook, brown leather, emb, c1903	160	175	190
Notepad, celluloid cover, 2.5" x 5", c1902	300	350	400
Opener, bone handle knife, c1908	150	175	200
Opener, Nashville Anniversary, c1952	30	35	40

Trays sold at auction, clockwise from top: 1903, 6" d, $1540; 1909, $231; 1906, 4" d, $550; 1910, $66. —Photo courtesy Gene Harris Antique Auction Center.

	LOW	AVG.	HIGH
Opener, skate key style, c1935	12	14	15
Opener, "Starr X," c1930	8	9	10
Paperweight, Coca-Cola gum, c1916	100	125	150
Paperweight, "Coke is Coca-Cola," c1948	30	35	40
Pen, ballpoint w/ telephone dialer	8	9	10
Pen, baseball bat, c1940	20	25	30
Pencil Box, 10-pc set, c1930	25	32	40
Pencil Holder, celluloid, c1910	80	90	100
Pencil Sharpener, plastic, c1960	6	7	8
Pencil Sharpener, red metal, c1933	18	20	24
Plate, glass and Coke bottle motif, c1930, 7.25" dia	200	250	300
Playing Cards, red w/ blue and gold wheat, 1939	35	45	60
Pocket Knife, celluloid key, c1940	70	80	90
Pocket Knife, Chicago World's Fair, 1933, 3.5" l	30	35	40
Pocket Knife, "Enjoy Coca-Cola," c1970	7	8	10
Postcard, "All Over the World," c1913	300	350	400
Postcard, "Duster Girl" driving car, c1906	300	400	500
Postcard, girl w/ clown hat, c1909	300	350	400
Postcard, horse and delivery wagon photo, c1900	100	125	150
Postcard, bottling plant photo, c1905	100	125	150
Poster, cardboard, couple drinking Coke on beach, 1960s	225	250	280
Radio, Model 2001	75	100	125
Record, 45 rpm, "I'd Like to Teach the World to Sing," Canadian, picture sleeve, c1970	18	20	22
Serving Tray, "Duster Girl" replica, c1972	10	13	15
Serving Tray, "Olympic Games," 15" x 11", c1976	20	25	30
Serving Tray, "Sailor Girl," c1940	150	190	230
Serving Tray, "Saint Louis Fair," oval, c1909, 10.75"	1800	2000	2200
Serving Tray, "Santa Claus," c1973, 15" x 11"	12	14	15
Serving Tray, "Soda Fountain Clerk," c1927	300	425	550
Serving Tray, "Springboard Girl," c1939	150	185	220
Serving Tray, "Summer Girl," c1921	500	650	800
Sign, cardboard, Sprite boy w/ 6 pack, 1958, 18" sq	75	90	105
Sign, diecut tin, 6-pack shape, wire handle, 1950, 11" x 13.5"	700	750	825
Sign, emb tin, oval, "Drink Coca-Cola Iced," 1950s, 2' x 3'	200	235	260
Sign, emb tin, "Sign of Good Taste" and bottle, 1958, 18" x 54"	265	285	200
Sign, emb tin, "things go better with Coke" above bottle, 1960s, 18" x 54"	375	400	425
Sign, tin, fishtail flange, "Sign of Good Taste," 1960s	200	235	265
Spinner, diecut tin, 4 wings	1400	1500	1650
Syrup Can, "Drink Coca-Cola, Delicious and Refreshing," white lettering, red ground, 1930s, 1 gal	450	500	575
Thermometer, emb tin, double bottle, 1942, 16" h	450	500	550
Thermometer, diecut tin bottle, gold, 7"	40	50	60
Thermometer, round, fishtail Coca-Cola, "Be Really Refreshed!," c1960, 12" dia	1250	1500	1750
Thermometer, round, white lettering on red ground, "Drink Coca-Cola, Sign of Good Taste," 12" dia	400	425	460
Thermometer, tin, gold bottle, red ground, 1930s, 16"	65	80	100
Tip Tray, "Relieves Fatigue," oval, 6" x 4.25"	275	325	400
Tire Rack, collapsible, wire, tin signs on front and back read "Enjoy Coca-Cola while we check Your Tires," 1952	1450	1550	1700
TV Tray, candle design, c1972	20	25	30
Wallet, script "Coca-Cola," c1922	30	35	40

Coins

The *Maine Antique Digest* reported that the coin world saw a world record set with the highest priced coin of any type or origin selling at Bowers & Merena in Wolfeboro, New Hampshire for $1,815,000 on April 8, 1997. The coin, considered by collectors to be the "King of American Coins," was an 1804 silver dollar, one of only eight known examples.

Beware of altered coins. Some skilled fakers are able to change the date on an otherwise common coin to imitate a rare and valuable example. We have also seen totally fake coins coming from Asia.

The following ratings are from the American Numismatic Association grading system. For more detailed descriptions, write to the American Numismatic Association, 814 N. Cascade Ave., Colorado Springs, CO 80903.

Proof—Refers to method of manufacture, distinguished by sharpness of detail and usually with brilliant mirror surface. Proof coins are in perfect mint state.

Uncirculated (MS–60)—No trace of wear but may show some contact marks; surface may be spotted or lack some luster.

About Uncirculated (AU–50)—Traces of light wear on many of the high points. At least half of mint luster is still present.

Extremely Fine (EF–40)—Design is lightly worn throughout, but all features are sharp and well defined. Traces of luster may show.

Very Fine (VF–20)—Shows wear on high points of design. All major details are clear.

Fine (F–12)—Moderate even wear; entire design is bold with pleasing appearance.

Very Good (VG–8)—Well worn; main feature clear and bold but rather flat.

Good (G–4)—Heavily worn; design visible but faint in areas. many details flat.

About Good (AG–3)—Very heavily worn with parts of lettering and date worn smooth.

For further information see *The Official 1999 Blackbook Price Guide to United States Coins, Thirty-Seventh Edition,* Marc and Tom Hudgeons, House of Collectibles, 1998.

Half Cents

Liberty Cap Type

	AG–3	G–4	VG–8	F–12	VF–20	EF–40
1794–97	$80.00	$200.00	$325.00	$550.00	$1000.00	$2000.00

Draped Bust Type 1800–08

	AG–3	G–4	VG–8	F–12	VF–20	EF–40
1800	$25.00	$45.00	$60.00	$90.00	$250.00	—
1803–08	20.00	30.00	40.00	80.00	200.00	—

Classic Head Type 1809–36

	G–4	VG–8	F–12	VF–20	EF–40
1825–35	$25.00	$35.00	$60.00	$80.00	$300.00

Coronet Type 1840–57

	G–4	VG–8	F–12	VF–20	EF–40
1849–57	$35.00	$45.00	$55.00	$75.00	$200.00

Large Cents

Draped Bust Type 1796–1807

	G–4	VG–8	F–12	VF–20	EF–40	MS–60
1796–1807	$24.00	$35.00	$60.00	$100.00	$300.00	$650.00

Classic Head Type 1808–14

	G–4	VG–8	F–12	VF–20	EF–40	MS–60
1808–14	$30.00	$60.00	$110.00	$350.00	$400.00	$800.00

Coronet Type 1816–57

	G–4	VG–8	F–12	VF–20	EF–40	MS–60
1816–57	$10.00	$12.00	$15.00	$20.00	$55.00	$250.00

Small Cents

Flying Eagle Type 1856–58

	G–4	VG–8	F–12	VF–20	EF–40	MS–60
1856	$2100.00	$2500.00	$3000.00	$3200.00	$3400.00	$5000.00
1857–58	13.00	15.00	18.00	32.00	67.00	250.00

Indian Head Type 1859–1909

	G–4	VG–8	F–12	VF–20	EF–40	MS–60
1860–54	$5.00	$7.00	$15.00	$25.00	$30.00	$100.00
1865	4.00	5.00	7.00	16.00	24.00	60.00
1866–72	20.00	25.00	30.00	60.00	80.00	200.00
1873–76	12.00	15.00	21.00	34.00	55.00	125.00

	G–4	VG–8	F–12	VF–20	EF–40	MS–60
1877	190.00	250.00	360.00	550.00	800.00	2000.00
1878	16.00	24.00	30.00	40.00	50.00	140.00
1879	3.00	4.00	6.00	12.00	21.00	52.00
1880–84	2.00	2.50	3.50	6.00	14.00	40.00
1885	3.00	4.50	9.00	15.00	26.00	60.00
1886–1908	1.00	1.25	1.50	3.50	8.00	28.00

Lincoln Type (Wheat Sheaves) 1909–58

	G–4	VG–8	F–12	VF–20	EF–40	MS–60
1909 v.d.b.	$1.00	$1.50	$2.00	$2.50	$3.00	$30.00
1909S v.d.b.	280.00	300.00	320.00	350.00	400.00	500.00
1909	.50	.60	.75	1.00	2.00	15.00
1916–39	.15	.25	.35	.50	1.00	4.00
1940–42	.10	.15	.25	.40	.60	1.50
1943 (steel)	.20	.25	.40	.75	2.00	4.00
1944–58	.10	.15	.20	.30	.40	2.00
Exceptions						
1913S	7.00	7.50	9.00	11.00	26.00	95.00
1914D	70.00	80.00	100.00	165.00	390.00	750.00
1914S	8.00	10.00	11.00	19.00	36.00	165.00
1915S	7.00	8.00	9.00	12.00	24.00	100.00
1922D	5.00	6.00	7.00	10.00	19.00	80.00
1922 (plain)	165.00	270.00	300.00	500.00	2200.00	4500.00
1924D	9.00	11.00	13.00	20.00	50.00	225.00
1926S	2.00	3.00	4.00	5.00	11.0	100.00
1931D	2.00	2.50	3.50	4.50	7.50	50.00
1931S	32.00	34.00	37.00	40.00	45.00	65.00
1932	1.50	1.75	2.00	2.50	3.00	—
1932D	.70	.90	1.20	1.75	2.50	15.00
1933	.75	.90	1.25	1.50	2.75	16.00
1933D	1.75	2.00	2.25	3.00	4.00	20.00
1944D (stamped over S)	—	—	140.00	170.00	750.00	—
1955 (double die)	—	—	400.00	500.00	1500.00	—

Two-Cent Pieces

1864–73

	G–4	VG–8	F–12	VF–20	EF–40	MS–60
1864 (sm. motto)	$50.00	$65.00	$85.00	$150.00	$225.00	$550.00
1864–71	5.00	7.00	9.0	18.00	30.00	110.00
1872	75.00	100.00	120.00	220.00	325.00	750.00

Silver Three-Cent Pieces

1851–73

	G–4	VG–8	F–12	VF–20	EF–40	MS–60
1851–62	$10.00	$14.00	$18.00	$27.00	$50.00	$160.00

Nickel Three-Cent Pieces

1865–89

	G–4	VG–8	F–12	VF–20	EF–40	MS–60
1865–74	$6.00	$6.50	$7.50	$10.00	$17.00	$80.00
1985–76	7.00	9.00	11.00	17.00	28.00	130.00
1879–80	50.00	75.00	77.00	80.00	100.00	240.00
1881	5.00	6.00	7.00	12.00	18.00	90.00
1882	55.00	65.00	75.00	85.00	110.00	210.00
1883–87	100.00	150.00	185.00	250.00	350.00	600.00
1888–89	40.00	50.00	60.00	80.00	100.00	230.00

Nickel Five-Cent Pieces

Shield Type 1866–83

	G–4	VG–8	F–12	VF–20	EF–40	MS–60
1866	$12.00	$16.00	$20.00	$45.00	$80.00	$200.00
1867–76	8.00	9.00	11.00	18.00	30.00	100.00
1879–80	220.00	260.00	340.00	400.00	500.00	600.00
1881	150.00	175.00	200.00	260.00	350.00	500.00
1882–83	8.00	9.00	11.00	16.00	26.00	100.00

Liberty Head Type 1883–1913

	G–4	VG–8	F–12	VF–20	EF–40	MS–60
1883–84	$6.00	$8.00	$13.00	$22.00	$35.00	$115.00
1885	160.00	220.00	310.0	400.00	600.00	950.00

	G–4	VG–8	F–12	VF–20	EF–40	MS–60
1886	40.00	60.00	100.00	155.00	215.00	450.00
1887–96	4.00	5.00	13.00	17.00	32.00	100.00
1897–1912	.55	1.50	4.00	6.00	20.00	75.00
1912D	1.10	2.00	5.00	10.00	45.00	200.00
1912S	35.00	45.00	60.00	225.00	360.00	500.00
1913 (five known)	—	—	—	—	—	365,000.00

Buffalo Type 1913–38

	G–4	VG–8	F–12	VF–20	EF–40	MS–60
1914D	$25.00	$35.00	$50.00	$70.00	$100.00	$300.00
1914	5.00	6.00	7.00	9.00	16.00	50.00
1915	2.50	3.00	5.00	7.00	13.00	50.00
1915D	6.00	8.00	17.00	35.00	50.00	200.00
1915S	12.00	16.00	30.00	65.00	125.00	500.00
1916	1.00	1.25	1.75	3.00	7.00	50.00
1916 (double die)	11.00	25.00	4000.00	6000.00	8000.00	14,000.00
1921S	12.00	20.00	40.00	250.00	600.00	1000.00
1923–30	.75	1.00	1.50	2.00	6.00	40.00
1923S–26S	.75	.85	1.00	2.00	5.00	40.00
1931S	3.00	4.00	6.00	7.00	10.00	50.00
1934–38	.35	.45	.65	1.20	3.75	15.00
1937D (3 legs)	100.00	155.00	200.00	245.00	310.00	1100.00

Jefferson Type 1938–date

	G–4	VG–8	F–12	VF–20	EF–40	MS–60
1938–42	$.15	$.18	$.20	$.25	$.45	$2.50
1939D	1.50	2.00	4.00	5.00	7.00	40.00
1939S	.50	.60	.75	1.25	2.50	20.00
1942–45 (silver)	.25	.30	.45	.50	1.10	5.00
1946–52	.05	.10	.15	.20	.30	.75

Half Dimes

Flowing Hair Type 1794–95

	AG–3	G–4	VG–8	F–12	VF–20	EF–40
1794–95	$300.00	$700.00	$900.00	$1000.00	$1200.00	$2000.00

Draped Bust Type, Small Eagle

	AG–3	G–4	VG–8	F–12	VF–20	EF–40
1796–97	$350.00	$750.00	$850.00	$1100.00	$1600.00	$2000.00

Draped Bust Type, Heraldic Eagle 1800–05

	AG–3	G–4	VG–8	F–12	VF–20	EF–40
1800–05	$200.00	$500.00	$600.00	$900.00	$1400.00	$2000.00
1802	4000.00	9000.00	15,000.00	21,000.00	30,000.00	50,000.00

Capped Bust Type

	G–4	VG–8	F–12	VF–20	EF–40	MS–60
1829–37	$12.00	$16.00	$25.00	$50.00	$110.00	$400.00
1837 (small 5c)	20.00	30.00	40.00	90.00	150.00	1800.00

Seated Liberty Type 1837–73

	G–4	VG–8	F–12	VF–20	EF–40	MS–60
1837	$25.00	$35.00	$50.00	$100.00	$210.00	$700.00
1838O (no stars)	95.00	100.00	200.00	350.00	700.00	3100.00
1838–73	6.00	7.00	9.00	20.00	43.00	210.00
1844O	60.00	100.00	200.00	350.00	900.00	—
1846	160.00	225.00	350.00	600.00	1200.00	—
1849O	25.00	40.00	75.00	250.00	500.00	—
1852O	20.00	35.00	60.00	150.00	300.00	—
1863	120.00	175.00	225.00	300.00	400.00	750.00
1864	190.00	300.00	350.00	450.00	600.00	1200.00
1864S	25.00	35.00	60.00	100.00	300.00	750.00
1865	200.00	250.00	300.00	350.00	500.00	900.00
1866	125.00	200.00	275.00	350.00	450.00	800.00
1867	250.00	350.00	450.00	550.00	750.00	1250.00
1868	30.00	45.00	70.00	100.00	200.00	400.00

Dimes

Draped Bust Type, Small Eagle

	AG–3	G–4	VG–8	F–12	VF–20	EF–40
1796–97	$400.00	$900.00	$1200.00	$1700.00	$2500.00	$4000.00

Draped Bust Type, Heraldic Eagle

	AG–3	G–4	VG–8	F–12	VF–20	EF–40
1798–1807	$250.00	$450.00	$650.00	$750.00	$1200.00	$1800.00
1804	450.00	1000.00	1500.00	2500.00	3500.00	7000.00

Capped Bust Type 1809–37

	G–4	VG–8	F–12	VF–20	EF–40	MS–60
1809	$85.00	$140.00	$275.00	$450.00	$800.00	$4000.00
1814	25.00	30.00	50.00	150.00	350.00	1500.00
1820–27	15.00	20.00	35.00	90.00	300.00	900.00
1822	250.00	450.00	750.00	1200.00	2000.00	7000.00
1839–37	12.00	15.00	20.00	50.00	175.00	600.00

Seated Liberty Type 1837–91

	G–4	VG–8	F–12	VF–20	EF–40	MS–60
1837	$25.00	$40.00	$65.00	$220.00	$450.00	$1000.00
1838O	30.00	50.00	90.00	275.00	500.00	2400.00
1838–40	6.00	8.00	12.00	25.00	60.00	350.00
1841–52	5.00	8.00	11.00	20.00	45.00	300.00
1841O	7.00	10.00	15.00	35.00	65.00	1000.00
1843O	35.00	70.00	100.00	200.00	550.00	—
1844	30.00	65.00	90.00	200.00	500.00	2000.00
1845O	15.00	25.00	50.00	200.00	500.00	—
1846	75.00	100.00	140.00	300.00	750.00	—
1849O	10.00	20.00	30.00	100.00	300.00	—
1851O	10.00	15.00	25.00	70.00	170.00	1500.00
1853–73	6.00	7.00	8.00	16.00	40.00	300.00
1875–91	5.00	6.00	7.00	12.00	25.00	175.00
1856S	65.00	100.00	150.00	300.00	600.00	—
1858S	60.00	90.00	125.00	250.00	450.00	—
1859S	65.00	100.00	150.00	300.00	650.00	2500.00
1860O	300.00	500.00	700.00	1200.00	2500.00	—
1861S	25.00	40.00	55.00	125.00	250.00	1200.00
1863	175.00	250.00	350.00	450.00	550.00	1100.00
1863S	20.00	30.00	45.00	75.00	200.00	900.00
1864	160.00	225.00	325.00	450.00	500.00	1000.00
1866	175.00	250.00	350.00	500.00	650.00	1200.00
1867	250.00	400.00	500.00	650.00	850.00	1500.00
1868S	12.00	17.00	25.00	60.00	150.00	350.00
1870S	150.00	200.00	250.00	350.00	500.00	1500.00
1871CC	500.00	700.00	900.00	1500.00	2500.00	—
1872CC	250.00	400.00	650.00	1200.00	2500.00	—
1873CC	500.00	800.00	1200.00	2000.00	3500.00	—
1873S	15.00	22.00	30.00	60.00	140.00	900.00
1874CC	1200.00	2000.00	3000.00	3500.00	7000.00	—
1878CC	35.00	50.00	80.00	125.00	250.00	700.00
1879	125.00	180.00	225.00	275.00	400.00	700.00
1880	80.00	120.00	160.00	200.00	350.00	500.00
1881	100.00	175.00	190.00	250.00	350.00	550.00
1884S	12.00	18.00	24.00	45.00	65.00	450.00
1885S	250.00	400.00	500.00	750.00	1000.00	3500.00

	G–4	VG–8	F–12	VF–20	EF–40	MS–60
1886S	20.00	30.00	40.00	60.00	100.00	600.00
1889S	10.00	15.00	20.00	40.00	75.00	400.00

Barber or Liberty Head Type 1892–1916

	G–4	VG–8	F–12	VF–20	EF–40	MS–60
1892	$2.20	$5.00	$9.00	$12.00	$25.00	$115.00
1892O	6.00	9.00	16.00	20.00	30.00	175.00
1892S	25.00	35.00	75.00	125.00	150.00	325.00
1893O	15.00	20.00	50.00	75.00	100.00	250.00
1893S	7.00	12.00	20.00	30.00	50.00	225.00
1894	8.00	14.00	50.00	80.00	100.00	250.00
1894O	30.00	50.00	125.00	175.00	300.00	1000.00
1894S	—	—	—	—	—	275,000.00
1895	60.00	80.00	200.00	300.00	350.00	600.00
1895O	200.00	300.00	450.00	800.00	1200.00	2100.00
1895S	20.00	35.00	75.00	100.00	120.00	350.00
1896O	42.00	65.00	175.00	200.00	300.00	600.00
1896S	40.00	60.00	150.00	200.00	300.00	600.00
1897–1916	1.50	2.00	4.00	7.00	20.00	100.00
1897O	30.00	50.00	150.00	200.00	300.00	650.00
1897S	8.00	15.00	50.00	75.00	100.00	300.00
1900O	5.00	15.00	50.00	75.00	150.00	500.00
1901S	30.00	50.00	175.00	275.00	350.00	700.00
1902S	3.00	7.00	25.00	40.00	100.00	300.00
1903S	15.00	20.00	50.00	90.00	200.00	375.00
1904S	10.00	14.00	20.00	36.00	65.00	300.00
1909D	3.00	10.00	35.00	60.00	90.00	350.00
1909S	4.00	10.00	40.00	60.00	125.00	400.00
1913S	8.00	15.00	50.00	90.00	175.00	425.00

Mercury Type 1916–45

	G–4	VG–8	F–12	VF–20	EF–40	MS–60
1916–31	$1.10	$1.70	$2.50	$4.50	$7.00	$65.00
1916D	350.00	550.00	1000.00	1400.00	2200.00	4000.00
1921	20.00	40.00	70.00	150.00	350.00	1000.00
1921D	30.00	50.00	90.00	175.00	400.00	1200.00

	G–4	VG–8	F–12	VF–20	EF–40	MS–60
1925D	3.00	4.00	10.00	30.00	100.00	450.00
1926S	5.00	7.00	15.00	35.00	200.00	1200.00
1927D	3.00	4.00	5.00	15.00	40.00	350.00
1928D	3.00	5.00	7.00	15.00	40.00	300.00
1930S	2.50	3.00	5.00	6.00	15.00	75.00
1931D	4.50	6.25	10.00	20.00	30.00	75.00
1931S	3.00	4.00	5.00	7.00	15.00	60.00
1934–45	.55	.65	.80	1.10	1.90	9.00

Roosevelt Type 1946–date

	G–4	VG–8	F–12	VF–20	EF–40	MS–60
1946–64	$.20	$.25	$.30	$.35	$.55	$1.00

Twenty-Cent Pieces

1875–78

	G–4	VG–8	F–12	VF–20	EF–40	MS–60
1875–76	$50.00	$60.00	$80.00	$110.00	$200.00	$700.00
1877–78	—	—	—	—	—	(very rare)

Quarter Dollars

Draped Bust, Small Eagle

	AG–3	G–4	VG–8	F–12	VF–20	EF–40
1796	$1500.00	$3000.00	$5000.00	$7500.00	$10,000.00	$15,000.00

Draped Bust, Heraldic Eagle 1804–07

	AG–3	G–4	VG–8	F–12	VF–20	EF–40
1804	$500.00	$800.00	$1100.00	$2200.00	$4000.00	$7000.00
1805–07	100.00	200.00	300.00	450.00	850.00	2000.00

Capped Bust Type 1815–38

	AG–3	G–4	VG–8	F–12	VF–20	EF–40
1815–28	$25.00	$45.00	$65.00	$95.00	$250.00	$600.00
1831–38 (sm.)	15.00	35.00	40.00	50.00	100.00	200.00

Seated Liberty Type 1838–91

	G–4	VG–8	F–12	VF–20	EF–40	MS–60
1838–42	$10.00	$15.00	$25.00	$60.00	$200.00	$1000.00
1843–47	12.00	16.00	20.00	35.00	75.00	600.00
1843O	15.00	25.00	40.00	70.00	200.00	1000.00
1848–53	20.00	35.00	55.00	75.00	150.00	1000.00
1851O	150.00	250.00	400.00	650.00	1000.00	2000.00
1852O	175.00	250.00	400.00	600.00	1200.00	3500.00
1854–55	8.00	11.00	20.00	30.00	90.00	500.00
1855O	35.00	50.00	100.00	200.00	350.00	2000.00
1856–65	8.00	10.00	20.00	27.00	55.00	300.00
1856S	30.00	45.00	75.00	150.00	350.00	1400.00
1857S	50.00	80.00	150.00	300.00	500.00	2000.00
1858S	40.00	60.00	100.00	200.00	400.00	—
1859S	75.00	115.00	175.00	275.00	700.00	—
1859O	15.00	25.00	40.00	75.00	100.00	1000.00
1860S	100.00	150.00	300.00	550.00	1500.00	5000.00
1861S	50.00	75.00	150.00	250.00	450.00	2500.00
1862S	40.00	60.00	100.00	250.00	400.00	2000.00
1864S	150.00	250.00	400.00	750.00	1500.00	—
1864	45.00	65.00	90.00	125.00	250.00	900.00
1865S	65.00	90.00	130.00	275.00	500.00	2500.00
1866	200.00	250.00	350.00	45000	650.00	2000.00
1867–69	100.00	150.00	200.00	300.00	500.00	2000.00
1870–73	20.00	30.00	50.00	80.00	150.00	850.00
1870CC	1200.00	2000.00	4000.00	6000.00	8000.00	—
1872CC	300.00	450.00	800.00	1500.00	3000.00	7500.00
1872S	250.00	400.00	650.00	1000.00	2000.00	5000.00
1873–74	12.00	16.00	30.00	60.00	200.00	850.00
1873CC	800.00	1200.00	2000.00	3500.00	6500.00	15,000.00
1875–91	8.00	10.00	20.00	25.00	50.00	300.00
1875CC	50.00	75.00	120.00	200.00	400.00	1500.00
1878S	60.00	120.00	175.00	250.00	400.00	1500.00
1879–88	100.00	115.00	150.00	180.00	250.00	650.00

Barber or Liberty Head Type 1892–1916

	G–4	VG–8	F–12	VF–20	EF–40	MS–60
1892	$3.50	$5.00	$15.00	$25.00	$50.00	$200.00
1892O	4.00	8.00	18.00	32.00	65.00	250.00
1892S	15.00	25.00	40.00	60.00	120.00	400.00
1893–96	4.00	6.00	18.00	35.00	70.00	300.00
1896O	5.00	10.00	45.00	150.00	300.00	750.00
1896S	150.00	250.00	500.00	850.00	1200.00	3000.00
1897–1916	3.00	4.00	15.00	25.00	60.00	200.00
1899S	8.00	15.00	20.00	35.00	75.00	300.00
1901O	15.00	30.00	60.00	140.00	300.00	700.00
1901S	1000.00	2000.00	3000.00	4500.00	6000.00	10,000.00
1909O	8.00	15.00	40.00	100.00	200.00	600.00
1913	10.00	20.00	50.00	150.00	400.00	1000.00
1913S	300.00	500.00	1000.00	2000.00	3000.00	4500.00

Standing Liberty Type 1916–30

	G–4	VG–8	F–12	VF–20	EF–40	MS–60
1917–24	$11.00	$15.00	$18.00	$30.00	$40.00	$200.00
1916	800.00	1200.00	1600.00	2000.00	2500.00	4000.00
1918D	20.00	25.00	35.00	50.00	80.00	450.00
1919D	40.00	70.00	100.00	150.00	250.00	800.00
1919S	40.00	60.00	100.00	150.00	300.00	1000.00
1921	50.00	80.00	120.00	175.00	250.00	700.00
1923S	100.00	140.00	180.00	250.00	350.00	750.00
1925–30	3.00	4.00	7.00	15.00	30.00	150.00
1927S	9.00	12.00	50.00	150.00	900.00	3300.00

Washington Type 1932–date

	G–4	VG–8	F–12	VF–20	EF–40	MS–60
1932	$3.00	$3.50	$4.00	$6.00	$8.00	$30.00
1932D	31.00	35.00	45.00	60.00	125.00	400.00

	G–4	VG–8	F–12	VF–20	EF–40	MS–60
1932S	20.00	30.00	35.00	45.00	65.00	250.00
1934–38	1.00	1.50	2.00	5.00	10.00	50.00
1936D	2.00	5.00	7.00	14.00	35.00	300.00
1937S	1.00	2.50	5.00	10.00	18.00	90.00
1939S	1.00	2.00	4.00	6.00	10.00	50.00
1940D	1.00	2.00	4.00	6.00	12.00	55.00
1941–46	.50	.75	1.00	1.50	1.75	5.00
1947–55	.50	.75	1.00	1.50	1.75	2.00
1949	.50	.75	1.00	1.50	1.75	18.00
1956–64	.50	.75	1.00	1.50	1.75	2.00

Half Dollars

Flowing Hair Type 1794–95

	AG–3	G–4	VG–8	F–12	VF–20	EF–40
1794	$500.00	$900.00	$1500.00	$2800.00	$4000.00	$8000.00
1795	250.00	400.00	500.00	800.00	1550.00	3500.00

Draped Bust, Small Eagle

	AG–3	G–4	VG–8	F–12	VF–20	EF–40
1796–97	$7000.00	$9000.00	$12,000.00	$15,000.00	$25,000.00	$45,000.00

Draped Bust, Heraldic Eagle 1801–07

	AG–3	G–4	VG–8	F–12	VF–20	EF–40
1801–02	$100.00	$200.00	$300.00	$500.00	$900.00	$1800.00
1803–07	45.00	100.00	125.00	200.00	350.00	600.00

Capped Bust Type 1807–36

	G–4	VG–8	F–12	VF–20	EF–40	MS–60
1807–08	$40.00	$85.00	$150.00	$300.00	$750.00	$1500.00
1809–36	30.00	45.00	85.00	175.00	400.00	100.00
1836 "50 CENTS"	600.00	750.00	1000.00	1200.00	2000.00	7000.00
1837–38	30.00	40.00	50.00	75.00	200.00	900.00
1838O	—	—	—	—	—	50,000.00
1839O	120.00	160.00	250.00	400.00	650.00	3000.00

Seated Liberty Type 1839–91

	G–4	VG–8	F–12	VF–20	EF–40	MS–60
1839–65	$15.00	$20.00	$35.00	$45.00	$75.00	$450.00
1866–78	13.00	18.00	30.00	40.00	60.00	450.00
1842O (small date)	500.00	750.00	1000.00	2000.00	4000.00	—
1848	30.00	40.00	60.00	90.00	150.00	850.00
1850	75.00	100.00	150.00	250.00	450.00	1200.00
1851	75.00	120.00	175.00	300.00	500.00	1500.00
1852	100.00	150.00	250.00	400.00	700.00	1600.00
1852O	40.00	60.00	100.00	150.00	300.00	1000.00
1855S	300.00	400.00	700.00	1200.00	3000.00	—
1857S	25.00	35.00	45.00	100.00	300.00	1300.00
1858S	20.00	25.00	35.00	65.00	140.00	850.00
1862	22.00	30.00	40.00	70.00	100.00	650.00
1870CC	450.00	750.00	1500.00	2500.00	4000.00	—
1871CC	100.00	150.00	250.00	400.00	900.00	4000.00
1872CC	50.00	80.00	150.00	275.00	500.00	2500.00
1873CC	75.00	125.00	200.00	350.00	800.00	4000.00
1874CC	150.00	250.00	400.00	700.00	1200.00	5000.00
1874S	30.00	40.00	60.00	150.00	300.00	1300.00
1878CC	200.00	300.00	450.00	750.00	1500.00	4500.00
1878S	5000.00	6500.00	9000.00	13,000.00	18,000.00	30,000.00
1879–90	110.00	140.00	180.00	240.00	350.00	750.00
1891	20.00	30.00	40.00	60.00	100.00	500.00

Barber or Liberty Head Type 1892–1915

	G–4	VG–8	F–12	VF–20	EF–40	MS–60
1892	$13.00	$25.00	$40.00	$75.00	$200.00	$400.00
1892O	75.00	120.00	170.00	250.00	400.00	800.00

	G–4	VG–8	F–12	VF–20	EF–40	MS–60
1893S	50.00	75.00	120.00	250.00	350.00	900.00
1893–96	6.00	12.00	40.00	70.00	180.00	450.00
1897–1915	5.00	8.00	25.00	50.00	150.00	400.00
1896S	50.00	75.00	100.00	200.00	350.00	1000.00
1897O	50.00	80.00	200.00	400.00	700.00	1400.00
1897S	70.00	100.00	200.00	350.00	550.00	1000.00
1898O	15.00	25.00	70.00	150.00	300.00	650.00
1901S	12.00	20.00	75.00	175.00	450.00	1300.00
1901O	7.00	15.00	40.00	100.00	300.00	1100.00
1904S	10.00	20.00	80.00	200.00	400.00	1200.00
1904O	10.00	15.00	50.00	100.00	300.00	1000.00
1913	15.00	25.00	60.00	175.00	300.00	800.00
1914	18.00	35.00	150.00	275.00	450.00	700.00
1915	16.00	25.00	75.00	200.00	350.00	900.00

Liberty Walking Type 1916–47

	G–4	VG–8	F–12	VF–20	EF–40	MS–60
1916	$20.00	$30.00	$50.00	$100.00	$150.00	$250.00
1916D	12.00	17.00	30.00	65.00	120.00	250.00
1916S	40.00	50.00	100.00	250.00	450.00	800.00
1917–18	5.00	8.00	12.00	25.00	35.00	120.00
1919	12.00	17.00	35.00	120.00	375.00	850.00
1919D	10.00	13.00	30.00	120.00	450.00	2000.00
1919S	10.00	12.00	25.00	100.00	500.00	1700.00
1920–33	6.00	7.00	11.00	20.00	70.00	500.00
1921	50.00	75.00	160.00	450.00	1200.00	2500.00
1921S	15.00	20.00	50.00	400.00	3000.00	7500.00
1934S	3.00	3.50	4.50	6.00	25.00	200.00
1938D	15.00	20.00	25.00	50.00	100.00	320.00
1941S	2.50	3.50	3.75	4.00	7.00	78.00

Franklin Type 1948–63

	VG–8	F–12	VF–20	EF–40	MS–60
1948	$1.75	$3.00	$3.50	$6.00	$16.00
1948D	1.50	1.75	2.50	4.50	11.00
1949	1.50	1.75	2.50	4.50	35.00
1950	1.75	5.00	8.00	12.00	70.00
1951	1.50	1.75	2.50	3.50	11.00
1951D	1.50	1.75	2.50	3.50	30.00
1951S	1.50	1.75	2.50	3.50	30.00
1952–63	1.50	1.60	2.25	3.00	5.00

	VG–8	F–12	VF–20	EF–40	MS–60
1952S	1.50	1.75	2.50	3.50	30.00
1953	1.50	1.75	3.00	6.00	24.00
1953S	1.50	1.60	2.50	4.00	12.00

Silver Dollars

Flowing Hair Type 1794–95

	AG–3	G–4	VG–8	F–12	VF–20	EF–40
1794	$3500.00	$8000.00	$11,000.00	$17,000.00	$25,000.00	$42,000.00
1795	400.00	700.00	900.00	1200.00	2000.00	4000.00

Draped Bust, Small Eagle

	AG–3	G–4	VG–8	F–12	VF–20	EF–40
1794–98	$300.00	$600.00	$800.00	$1000.00	$2000.00	$3500.00

Draped Bust, Heraldic Eagle

	AG–3	G–4	VG–8	F–12	VF–20	EF–40
1798–1804	$300.00	$350.00	$450.00	$700.00	$1300.00	$8000.00

Seated Liberty Type 1840–73

	VG–8	F–12	VF–20	EF–40	MS–60
1840–73	$200.00	$300.00	$350.00	$500.00	$2000.00
1846O	200.00	250.00	325.00	650.00	4000.00
1850	400.00	550.00	800.00	1200.00	4500.00
1851	3000.00	7000.00	8000.00	10,000.00	14,000.00
1852	1500.00	7000.00	8000.00	10,000.00	17,000.00
1858	2500.00	3500.00	5000.00	5500.00	—
1870CC	325.00	450.00	650.00	1000.00	4500.00
1870S	—	50,000.00	70,000.00	90,000.00	—
1871CC	2200.00	3500.00	4500.00	7500.00	20,000.00
1872CC	1000.00	1500.00	2500.00	3500.00	15,000.00

	VG–8	F–12	VF–20	EF–40	MS–60
1872S	300.00	400.00	600.00	900.00	7000.00
1873CC	3000.00	4500.00	7500.00	2,000.00	27,000.00

Liberty Head or Morgan Type 1878–1921

	F–12	VF–20	EF–40	AU–50
1878–1921	$10.00	$12.00	$17.00	$20.00
1879CC	36.00	100.00	170.00	1000.00
1880CC	45.00	70.00	100.00	130.00
1880O	9.00	12.00	22.00	45.00
1881CC	100.00	120.00	130.00	160.00
1882CC	30.00	45.00	50.00	65.00
1883CC	30.00	45.00	55.00	65.00
1883S	13.00	20.00	90.00	350.00
1884S	15.00	35.00	250.00	4000.00
1886O	13.00	18.00	45.00	220.00
1889CC	300.00	650.00	2500.00	6500.00
1889S	20.00	30.00	45.00	90.00
1890CC	30.00	45.00	75.00	200.00
1892CC	50.00	80.00	170.00	300.00
1892S	40.00	100.00	750.00	8000.00
1893	50.00	70.00	140.00	300.00
1893CC	115.00	400.00	700.00	1000.00
1893O	85.00	170.00	350.00	1000.00
1893S	1200.00	2700.00	10,000.00	23,000.00
1894	225.00	350.00	500.00	800.00
1894O	20.00	35.00	125.00	550.00
1895O	100.00	200.00	800.00	8000.00
1895S	175.00	350.00	600.00	1000.00
1896O	12.00	16.00	100.00	650.00
1897O	13.00	17.00	75.00	500.00
1901	25.00	40.00	200.00	1200.00
1903S	55.00	200.00	700.00	2000.00
1904S	35.00	125.00	450.00	850.00

Peace Type 1921–35

	VF–20	EF–40	AU–50	MS–60
1921	$30.00	$40.00	$70.00	$140.00
1922–35	8.00	10.00	12.00	25.00
1924S	14.00	20.00	45.00	130.00
1925S	11.00	15.00	25.00	50.00
1926D	10.00	13.00	27.00	45.00
1927	16.00	22.00	35.00	60.00
1927D	14.00	20.00	155.00	120.00
1927S	13.00	18.00	50.00	85.00
1928	100.00	120.00	140.00	175.00
1928S	15.00	18.00	40.00	65.00
1934D	15.00	18.00	40.00	80.00
1934S	40.00	150.00	400.00	1000.00
1935S	12.00	16.00	60.00	100.00

Gold Half Eagles

Classic Head Type

	VG–8	F–12	VF–20	EF–40	AU–50
1834–38	$225.00	$300.00	$500.00	$850.00	$3000.00

Coronet Type

	F–12	VF–20	EF–40	AU–50
1839–66	$400.00	$1000.00	$2000.00	$6000.00
1873	170.00	225.00	500.00	1800.00
1867–77	500.00	1300.00	4000.00	7000.00
1878–1908	130.00	150.00	175.00	200.00

Indian Head Type

	F–12	VF–20	EF–40	AU–50
1908–29 (most)	$200.00	$225.00	$250.00	$325.00

Decoys

A decoy's value is detemined by the importance of the maker, how it looks and a detailed analysis of its condition. Most decoys are worth no more than a few hundred dollars, many less than $100. However, without actually seeing them, a listing of prices is of little value. Therefore, our list defines the top limit of what decoys by the most important makers have brought at auction and the hypothetical retail range that may be expected. The auction prices that follow are some of those reported by the *Maine Antiques Digest.*

Decoys produced after the mid nineteenth century are most popular among collectors. Famous decoy carvers include Ira Hudson, Charles Wheeler, Albert Laing and Mark Whipple. Enthusiasts usually collect decoys by carver, species or fly-way (path of migration). Decoys made for actual use are more favored by collectors than those intended only for show. Original paint is extremely important to many collectors.

Canada Goose, 28" l, $633 at auction. —Photo courtesy Skinner, Inc., Boston, MA.

	AUCTION	RETAIL	
		Low	High
Black Brant, by "Fresh Air Dick" Janson	$9350	$14,000	$20,000
Black Brant, by Ira Hudson	6600	10,000	14,000
Black Duck, by James T. Holly	1595	2500	3400
Black Duck, by Joe Lincoln	4950	7700	10,000
Black Duck, by N.R. Horner	6050	9400	13,000
Black Duck, by Ward Bros.	12,100	18,000	26,000
Black-Bellied Plover, by N.C. Cobb, Jr.	28,700	44,000	61,000
Black-Bellied Plover, by Tom Wilson	6600	10,000	14,000
Black-Bellied Plover, by "Umbrella" Watson	7150	11,000	15,000
Bluebill, attributed to John Dawson	6,600	10,000	14,000
Bluebill, by A.E. Crowell	2915	4500	6300
Bluebill Hen, by A.E. Crowell	2200	3400	4700
Bluebills, pr, by Obediah Verity	28,600	44,000	61,000

	AUCTION	RETAIL Low	RETAIL High
Brant, by Dave "Umbrella" Watson	31,900	49,000	68,000
Brant, by Harry V. Shourds	8800	13,000	18,000
Brant, by Joe Lincoln	6050	9400	13,000
Brook Trout Head, by Shang Wheeler	11,825	18,000	25,000
Calling Black Duck, by Gus Wilson	7700	11,000	16,000
Canada Goose, by George Warin	5225	8100	11,000
Canada Goose, by Lem Ward	1540	2400	3300
Canada Goose, by Phineas Reeves	10,120	15,000	21,000
Canada Goose, by Thomas Chamber	4950	7700	10,000
Canvasback, by Robert McGaw	2255	3500	4800
Canvasback, by Thomas Chambers	2915	4500	6300
Canvasback, by Ward Bros.	4125	6400	8900
Canvasback Hen, by John Schweikart	2200	3400	4700
Canvasback Hen, by Ward Bros.	5445	8400	11,000
Canvasbacks, pr, by Ward Bros.	10,725	16,000	23,000
Challenge Mergansers, pr, by Mason factory	11,550	17,000	24,000
Curlew, by Daniel Lake Leeds	7150	11,000	15,000
Detroit-Grade Ringbill, by Mason factory	4400	6800	9500
Dowitcher, by Dodge factory	1650	2600	3500
Dowitcher, spring plumage, by William Bowman	14,575	22,000	31,000
Early Blue Goose, by Ben Schmidt	11,550	17,000	25,000
Eider Hen, w/ mussel, by Gus Wilson	5500	8500	11,000
Feeding Willet, by Thomas Gelston	9900	15,000	21,000
Flying Green-Winged Teal, by Ira Hudson	7150	11,000	15,000
Flying Mallard, by Ira Hudson	6600	10,000	14,000
Golden Plover, by A.E. Crowell	7260	11,000	15,000
Goldeneye, by Maurice Eaton	2530	4000	5400
Gondeneye, by Noah Sterling	3190	5000	7000
Gondeneye Hen, by Maurice Eaton	2090	3200	4500
Green-Winged Teal, by Ira Hudson	17,050	26,000	36,000
Green-Winged Teal, by Leonard Pryor	1650	2500	3500
Green-Winged Teal, pr, by Ward Bros	38,500	60,000	82,000
Green-Winged Teal Hen, by Joseph Paquette	1650	2500	3500
High-Neck Pintails, pr, by Ward Bros	52,250	81,000	112,000

Left to right: Common Pintail Drake, Ward Bros, 1930, $1840; Wood Duck Decoy, A. Elmer Crowell, $7188. —Photos courtesy Skinner, Inc., Boston, MA.

	AUCTION	RETAIL	
		Low	High
Kingfisher, by A. Elmer Crowell	8250	12,000	17,000
Long-Billed Curlew, by Thomas Gelston	11,550	17,000	24,000
Lowhead Black Duck, by James Baker	2475	3800	5300
Mallard, by Charles Perdes	2310	3600	5000
Mallard, rectangular brand, by A.E. Crowell	6600	10,000	14,000
Merganser Hen, by Joe Lincoln	27,500	42,000	60,000
Mergansers, pr, by Keyes Chadwick	8250	12,000	17,000
Mini Crook-Necked Canada Goose, by A.E. Crowell	2750	4000	6000
Pheasant, decorative, by A.E. Crowell	15,950	24,000	34,000
Pintail, attributed to John Dawson	13,200	20,000	28,000
Pintail, by Ira Hudson	2200	3400	4700
Pintail, by John Blair	9340	14,000	20,000
Pintail Hen, by Ivar Fernlund	6600	10,000	14,000
Plover, by Morton Rig	7700	11,000	16,000
Premier Merganser Hen, by Mason factory	7150	11,000	15,000
Premier Wigeon, by Mason factory	5500	8500	11,000
Reaching-Head Brant, by N.C. Cobb, Jr.	145,750	200,000	300,000
Red Knot, by John Dilley	10,450	16,000	22,000
Red-Breasted Merganser, attributed to Roger Williams	4400	6800	9500
Red-Breasted Merganser, by A.E. Crowell	7700	11,000	15,000
Red-Breasted Merganser, by Fred Nickerson	7700	11,000	15,000
Red-Breasted Merganser, by George Boyd	7150	11,000	15,000
Red-Breasted Merganser, by George Huey	3630	5000	8000
Red-Breasted Merganser, by Henry Grant	7700	11,000	16,000
Red-Breasted Merganser, Preston Wright	6050	9400	13,000
Red-Breasted Merganser Hen, by Joe King	15,675	24,000	33,000
Red-Breasted Merganser Hen, by N.R. Horner	30,800	47,000	66,000
Red-Breasted Mergansers, pr, by Frank Kellum	1870	2900	4000
Ruddy Duck, by Ned Burgess	13,750	20,000	30,000
Ruddy Turnstone, by Lothrop Holmes	22,550	35,000	50,000
Running Knot, by Arthur Cobb	6875	10,000	14,000
Sleeping Black Duck, by A.E. Crowell	13,200	20,000	30,000
Sleeping Black Duck, by William Quinn	8250	12,000	17,000
Sleeping Goldeneye Hen, by Ed Parsons	3300	5100	7100
Standing Wood Duck, by A.E. Crowell	4675	7200	10,000
Tern, by A.E. Crowell	5500	8500	11,000
White-Winged Scooter, by Samuel Fabens	4070	6300	8000
Wigeon, by George Sibley	5235	8100	11,000
Wigeon, by Joe Lincoln	12,650	19,000	27,000
Willey, attributed to Charles Thomas	5235	8100	11,000
Willet, by John Dilley	10,450	16,000	22,000
Wood Duck, by A.E. Crowell	11,000	17,000	23,000
Wood Duck, by Orel LeBouef	6875	10,000	14,000
Wood Duck, oval brand, by A.E. Crowell	7150	11,000	15,000
Wood Duck Drake, by Shang Wheeler	52,250	80,000	100,000
Wood Duck Hen, by Shang Wheeler	40,700	63,000	85,000
Woodcock, by A.E. Crowell	13,200	20,000	28,000
Yellowlegs, by A.E. Crowell	7700	11,00	16,000
Yellowlegs, by Fred Nichols	8800	13,000	18,000
Yellowlegs, by Ira Hudson	7700	11,000	16,600

Firefighting Memorabilia

Firefighting collectibles run from the leather buckets kept in homes for fire emergencies to full hook and ladder trucks. Much equipment used by firemen received heavy use, so today many early items are scarce. This accounts for price variations and the high price often placed on small items.

Fire Grenade, "Hayward's Hand Fire Grenade," c1871–85, deep yellow olive, $275 at auction. —Photo courtesy Glass-Works Auction.

	LOW	AVG.	HIGH
Alarm Box, oval, Gamewell Grand Central Station, cast iron	$225	$400	$625
Alarm Gong, Gamewell indicator w/ swan-neck pediment, glazed door, and 15" brass bell, 50" h	5225	9000	15,000
Alarm Gong, Moses Crane style, gingerbread pediment, 22" h	1320	2300	3600
Alarm Gong, weight driven, panelled wood case by Charles Chester, New York, w/ 15" bell	2750	5000	8250
Axe, c1870, 43" l	400	600	800
Bell, engine, 10" dia	400	700	1000
Bucket, leather, decorated w/ helmet and hatchet	525	675	825
Bucket, leather, painted	475	650	775
Bucket, leather w/ red design	850	1000	1150
Bucket, owner's name inscribed, c1875	2250	5500	8750
Bucket, tin, painted	475	650	775
Bucket, wooden, iron banding, leather strap handle, 13" h	50	75	100
Buckle, "1811," brass, w/ fire engine, engraved, c1870	200	245	290
Cap, formal, w/ badge, c1900	200	250	300
Drawing, pumpers, fire, c1865	850	1250	1650
Engine, American LaFrance, 6 cyl., pumper, c1948	6500	8500	12,000
Engine, Chevrolet, 4 cyl, 1 ton, fully restored, c1927	12,000	14,500	18,000
Engine, Ford, 8 cyl, restored, c1941	7000	9000	12,000
Engine, Ford F-6, V-S, equipped, c1948	5000	6500	8000
Engine, Ford, unrestored, c1947	3500	4000	4500
Engine, Seagrave, Model "A," 4 cyl, restored, c1928	45,000	55,000	65,000
Extinguisher, brass, c1915	85	120	155
Extinguisher, bulb shape	30	45	60
Extinguisher, glass	140	175	210
Extinguisher, tin	40	55	70
Fire Bell, nickel plated bronze, outside mechanism, mounted on board	400	600	800
Fire Mark, cast iron, c1860	650	760	870
Fire Mark, hands clasped, Germantown National Fire, c1843	400	465	530
Fire Mark, hydrant, F.A., brass plaque, c1817	570	660	750

	LOW	AVG.	HIGH
Fire Mark, hydrant, F.A., brass plaque, c1843	270	310	350
Fire Mark, Insurance Co. of Florida, c1841	700	800	900
Fire Mark, Mutual Assurance Co., iron plaque	350	425	500
Fire Mark, North St. Louis Mutual, late 19th C, 7.5" h	600	650	750
Fire Mark, Portugese, late 19th C	150	175	200
Helmet, 3 cornered, c1870	3600	4200	4800
Helmet, Active Hose Derby, c1875	400	500	600
Helmet, Boston, cataract 10, c1890	350	400	450
Helmet, East Islip, NY, c1890	300	350	400
Helmet, German w/ rolling crest top, c1900	250	275	300
Helmet, hand-painted shield, c1880	1200	1500	1800
Helmet, leather, 6-seam, front shield	170	220	270
Helmet, leather, black w/ emb brass eagle, c1889	260	315	370
Helmet, leather, white w/ eagle, c1890	280	355	430
Helmet, leather w/ trumpet finial	340	405	470
Helmet, Needham, MA, c1945	125	150	175
Helmet, Reading, PA, junior 2, c1880	350	400	450
Hose Nozzle, brass, #12	180	215	250
Hose Nozzle, brass, #15	210	260	310
Hose Nozzle, copper, #25	240	290	340
Lamp, engine, by DeVoursney Bros., New York, silver plated w/ 4 etched colored glass windows	990	1750	2750
Lantern, nickel plated	170	240	310
Lantern, wagon style w/ brass font	430	510	590
Parade Banner, c1890, 39" l	350	375	400
Parade Belt, leather	200	260	320
Parade Belt, leather w/ black, white, and red trim, shield on buckle	120	160	200
Parade Helmet, French brass w/ plume, c1900	200	250	300
Parade Helmet, leather, 18th C	1700	2000	2300
Parade Helmet, spike top	360	440	520
Spotlight, nickel-plated brass	200	300	400
Tickets, fireman's benefit, c1860	20	25	30
Trumpet, brass, engraved	800	1000	12000
Trumpet, nickel plated	425	500	575
Trumpet, silver plated w/ red tassel	800	900	1000
Trumpet, silver presentation, 1867	2000	3200	5000

Helmet, leather, Cairns & Brother, NY, gold painted eagle, $500–$700.

Fishing Tackle

Rods, reels, flies and lures comprise the majoity of collectible fishing tackle. The manufacture of fishing tackle did not begin in the United States until around 1810.

Reels mde by J.F. and B.F. Meeks, B. Milam and Pfleuge are favored, as are rods made by Hiram Leonard. Flies—fake bait made by tying feathers, fur or other materials around the shaft of a hood—are also popular. There are over 5000 patterns and sizes of flies, each with its own name. The manufacturer, or tier, of individual flies is very difficult to discern, unless the fly is in its original marked container.

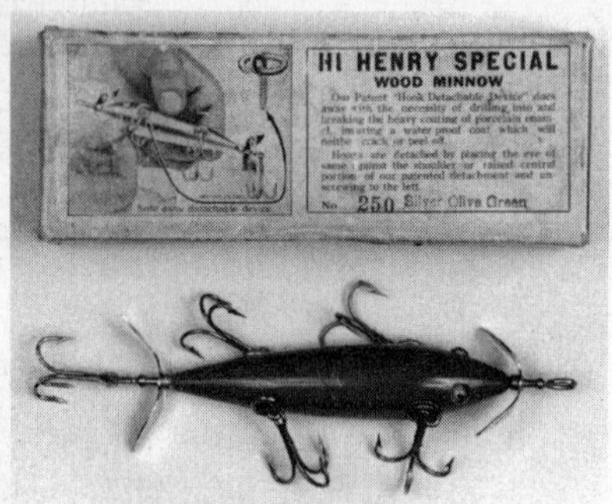

Pfleuger Hi Henry Special Wood Minnow, silver and olive green, orig box, patented Oct. 24, 1911, 3.75" l, $4840. —Photo courtesy Lang's Sporting Collectables.

Lures

	LOW	AVG.	HIGH
Abbey & Imbrie Glowbody Minnow, glass, orig flattened box, c1920	$83	$125	$180
Chippewa Bait, Immell Bait Co., 4" pike size	375	450	550
Harkauf Minnow, H.C. Kaufman Co., Philadelphia, wood, 2.5" l	85	110	135
Hastings Weedless Rubber Frog, hand painted	450	525	650
Heddon Baby Vamp #7400	275	380	450
Heddon Closed Leg Luny Frog	145	200	300
Heddon Deep Diving Wiggler #1600	138	180	250
Heddon No. 150 Minnow, perch finish	650	750	900
Heddon Shrimpy Spook, green and red dots	225	350	500
Heddon Spoony Fish, nickel finish, 1930–31, 4.5" l	225	350	500
Heddon Woodpecker, 4.625" l	775	950	1200
K&K Animated Minnow, jointed, 3.5" l	325	450	600
Kent Floater, bulging eyes, frog finish, orig box, c1911	2500	3250	4500
Klipon Minnow, Green-Wyle Co., Brooklyn, NY, 3.75" l	110	160	225
Lockart Water Witch, white and red, 2.5" l	80	110	160
Rhodes Mechanical Swimming Frog, Kalamazoo Fishing Tackle Co., Kalamazoo, MI, orig box	4125	5000	7500
Rush Deluxe Tango, rainbow victory finish, 4" l	775	900	1100
Rush Tango Minnow, red and white, orig $50 Gold Prize box	525	600	750
Shakespeare Minnow, wooden, orig box, 3.625" l	1825	1950	1200
Thoren Minnow Chaser, minnow and fish	195	250	325
Woods Expert Minnow, 4" l	225	300	425

Reels

	LOW	AVG.	HIGH
Alcedon Micron Spinning Reel	$100	$200	$300
Ambassador Trawling Reel #30, size 4/ 0	150	250	350
Cozzone Squidder	100	150	300
Edward vom Hofe, model 511	200	400	600
Edward vom Hofe, model 621, size 1/ 0	800	1200	1600
Edward vom Hofe, size 00/ 0	400	500	600
Fin-Nor, 9/ 0 size big game casting reel	125	225	325
Hardy LRH, lightweight reel	140	220	340
Hardy Zane Gray, big game reel, 14/ 0 size	3000	5000	7000
Heddon Dominator Reel, model 420	200	400	600
Holiday Spinning Reel, #40	100	200	300
Horton-Meek, #3, Kentucky-style reel	275	375	475
Intrinsic Reel by George Gayle, William Mills & Son, #4	1200	1600	2000
J.A. Coxe, 12/ 0 size, big game reel	800	1400	2000
Julius vom Hofe, #1 casting reel	200	350	500
Julius vom Hofe, bait casting reel, size 1/ 0	350	700	1050
Julius vom Hofe, Leonard trout reel	1000	1700	2400
Kalamazoo Tackle, Alford Meter reel	80	130	200
L.S. Kiefer, German silver	1100	1760	2700
Mitchell Spinning Reel, #300	50	80	110
Ocean City Ike Walton Club Reel	125	225	325
Orvis Madison, #3, fly reel	40	70	100
Otto Schwarg Maximo Reel, size 6/ 0	600	800	1000
Pflueger Alpine Model Reel	40	70	100
Pflueger Altipac #1660, 6/ 0 size	385	620	940
Pflueger Buckeye Reel	100	200	300
Pflueger Portage Cascade Reel	150	250	350
Shakespeare Tournament Reel, #1740	100	200	300
Stan Bogdan, size 50 single-action salmon reel	1400	2500	3600
Stan Bogdan, standard reel	2000	3500	5000

Rods

	LOW	AVG.	HIGH
Abercrombie and Fitch, 6'6" trout rod	$1000	$1600	$2400
Abercrombie and Fitch, 7'6" trout rod	3000	5000	7000
Art Weiler, #193, 6'9" "heritage rod"	450	800	1150
Carlson, Housatonic trout rod, 7.5'	4000	6000	8000
H.L. Leonard, 4 pc, 9'	363	580	890
Heddon #125 "expert," 9'	300	480	740
Kaufman and Benson, 4'6" steel rod w/ reel	100	160	220
Orvis, 2 pc, 6'6"	400	700	1000
Orvis, 2 pc, 9'	137	220	340
Orvis, HLS Graphite, 8'h" fly rod w/ case	176	280	430
Otto Zwarg, model 300, 4/ 0 size	1100	1760	2700
Paul Young Perfectionist Trout Rod, 7.5'	3000	5000	7000
Payne, model 208, 9'	800	1100	2000
Phillipson Deluxe Spinning Rod, model #P64S	168	270	410
Pinky Gillum, 7' light trout rod	8000	10,000	12,000
Swedish Bamboo Rod, 46"	42	70	100

Folk Art

American folk art of the 19th and early 20th centuries has become a sophisticated field. Carvers such as Wilhelm Schimmel and John Bellamy have seen extremely high prices. But beware! Only pieces of the highest quality command the prices listed below. We have included listings for damaged pieces to show how steeply the values can fall. Many pieces are restored. Check closely for condition.

Measurements refer to largest dimension. Prices are for auction (A), damaged (D), and retail (R).

Watercolor on Paper, Bowl of Strawberries, unsgd., 5.5" x 7.25", period gilt gesso frame, $3335 at auction. —Photo courtesy Skinner, Inc., Boston, MA.

	A	D	R
Barber Pole, turned and ptd in red, white, and blue, 38" h	$700	$1250	$2000
Bellamy Eagle, carved wood, 18" l	5000	8000	13,000
Bust, by S.L. Jones, carved wood, polychrome dec, 18" h	10,000	15,000	25,000
Carved Figure, by Edgar Tolson, standing woman in short dress, 14.5" h	1400	2170	4000
Carved Figure, by William Dawson, man in yellow shirt, 14" h	1400	2150	3750
Chocolate Mold, kneeling camel, copper	300	500	900
Fraktur, PA German watercolor and ink, depicting horse and rider, 8" x 9"	2400	3750	7000
Fraktur, PA German watercolor and ink, stylized flowers and hearts, 6" x 7"	1000	1750	2500
French Trade Sign, for hunting lodge, w/ zinc hunting horn in wrought-iron wreath, 19th C	1000	1550	2600
Grotesque Jug, by Lanier Meaders	700	1110	1800
Lobster Claw, ptd depicting Abraham Lincoln w/ Liberty cap, 11" h	2100	3650	5750
Mermaid, by Popeye Reed, carved wood, contemporary	880	1500	2500
Owl, carved stone by Popeye Reed	450	750	1250
Pottery Figure, by Jim Bozeman, bottle form w/ double arm handles	150	250	450
Puppet, carved wood, African American, c1900	1300	2000	3500
Puppet, w/ scull head and moveable jaw, c1900	1000	1500	2000
Skeleton in Coffin, Son Thomas, clay and ptd wood, contemporary, 17" l	385	750	1100
Tin Sign, "Live Bait for Sale"	225	400	650
Trade Sign, "The Ancient Mariner"	350	600	1000
Twig Snake, green and yellow paint	275	500	750
Ventriloquist Head, carved and ptd. w/ glass eyes, early 20th C	1000	1550	2600
Watercolor Theorem on Velvet, depicting openwork basket of fruit on grassy mound, 15.5" x 19"	600	1250	1750
Wooden Figural Pair, by S.L. Jones, carved wood, polychrome dec, depicting rabbit hunters	165	250	400

Furniture

Antique

Antique furniture is a tricky field. The collector needs to be a connoisseur of proportions and alterations. Before the middle of the nineteenth century, cabinetmakers (not carpenters) made furniture by hand. Each piece was unique. The skill of the craftsman and the success of his design are important factors in evaluating furniture. To learn about the proportions and the aesthetics of American antique furniture, see *The New Fine Points of Furniture: Early American* by Albert Sack, Crown, New York, NY, 1993.

Alterations can reduce the value of a piece by over 75%. No collector will sweat over a piece of chipped veneer, but a replaced leg, no matter how skillfully executed, will kill the value of a piece. Also remember that American furniture of the eighteenth century is more valuable than an otherwise identical English piece.

Abbreviations used in this section: *Amer.*–American; *Eng.*–English; *N.E.*–New England; *W. & M.*–William and Mary, c1690–1740; *Q.A.*–Queen Anne, c1720–60; *Chip.*–Chippendale, c1750–90; *Fed.*–Federal, c1780–1820; *Hpwt.*– Hepplewhite; *Prov.*–Provincial; *int*–interior; *dec*–decorated; *min.*–miniature; *mah.*–mahogany; *wal.*–walnut; *uph*–upholstery (upholstered); *circ*–circular; *oct*–octagonal, *rect*–rectangular; *sq*–square. Note that "style" implies a reproduction made at a later date.

	AUCTION	RETAIL	
		Low	High
Armchair, N.E., W. & M., banister back, sausage turnings, splint seat	$500	$880	$1375
Armchair, Edwardian-style, paint dec maple, back inset w/ oval caned panel, medallion adorned w/ putto, caned seat, tapering faux bamboo legs, early 20th C, 35.5" h	1610	2100	3200
Armchair, Flemish Baroque, walnut, rect back, carved scrolled arms, turned legs, molded stretchers, needlework uph, 18th C, 46" h	690	1350	1900
Armchair, Italian Baroque, walnut, rect back w/ foliate carved finials, scrolled arms, needlework uph, 18th C, 54" h	402	800	1200
Armchair, N.E., Pilgrim Century, ladderback, old brown paint	600	1200	2100
Armchair, PA, ladderback, arched slats, bulbous front stretcher, old brown paint	1000	1750	2750
Armchair, Regency, ebonized and parcel-gilt, carved tablet over downswept arms, uph seat, circ tapering legs, first quarter 19th C, 33.5" h	632	1200	1700
Bachelor's Chest, Eng., Chip., mah., dressing slide above 4 drawers, bracket feet, 30" w	2800	5000	7700
Banquette, Gerogian-style, mah., uph top, rope molded frieze, cabriole legs w/ foliate carved knees, pad feet, late 19th/ early 20th C, 86.25" l, 16" dp, 20.5" h	575	1000	1500
Bed, Amer., Classical Revival, mah., tester, front posts w/ barley twist turning and acanthus leaf carving, 60" w, 87" h	1500	3000	5500
Bed, Federal-style, mah., tester, acanthus carved posts, double size	650	1300	2500
Bed, French, Directoire-style, fruitwood	250	440	650
Bed, hired man's, old green paint, 77" l, 49" w	650	1300	2000
Bed, hired man's, rope, red finish, chamfered headposts w/ vase-turned finials, peaked headboard, orig side rails, 54" w	900	1500	2500
Bed, N.E., cannonball, painted red, 55" l, 46" h	200	400	700
Bed, N.E., Sheraton, canopy, birch, arched top, 78" l, 57" w, 86" h	4000	8000	14,000

	AUCTION	RETAIL Low	RETAIL High
Bed, N.E., Sheraton, tall post, cherry, turned and reeded posts, shaped headboard, 76" l, 58" w, 74" h	4750	8000	13,000
Bedroom Suite, Victorian Moorish, walnut, burl walnut, and parcel-gilt, armoire, bedside table w/ marble top, and single bed frame, fourth quarter 19th C, armoire 51" w, 23" dp, 76.5" h, 3-pc set	4025	7500	12,000
Blackamoor Console Table, Milan, Italian Baroque Revival, ebony, ebonized and ivory inlaid, c1880, 43" w, 18.25" dp, 36" h	4887	8500	13,500
Blanket Chest, N.E., grain painted, 2 drawers molded to simulate 4 drawers, 37" w	2000	4000	7000
Blanket Chest, N.E., painted and dec, 43" w	4250	8500	14,000
Blanket Chest, N.E., Pilgrim Century, pine, 48" w	425	850	1400
Blanket Chest, N.E., Pilgrim Century, bootjack ends, orig finish, 57" w	1500	3000	5000
Blanket Chest, PA, Chip., wal., dovetailed, high bracket feet, 47" l	1500	2630	4000
Blanket Chest, PA, grain painted, 42" w	1200	2400	4200
Bookcase, Eng., Chip.-style, mah., 2 sections: upper section w/ geometric glazed doors; lower w/ long drawer over twin doors, 52" l, 88" h	2750	4500	7500
Breakfast Table, cherry, drop-leaf, shaped apron, cabriole legs, pad feet, 36" w	7500	15,000	26,000
Breakfast Table, Eng., Q.A., mah., notched corners, 1 leaf, cabriole legs, pad feet, 34" w	500	1000	1750
Breakfast Table, N.E., tiger maple, drop-leaf, shaped apron, cabriole legs, pad feet, 34" w	3100	6000	10,000
Breakfast Table, NY, Classical Revival, 40" w	1000	2000	3500
Breakfast Table, NY, cherry, drop-leaf, 40" l	300	530	825
Buffet, Louis XV, walnut, rect top, 2 drawers above 2 doors, cabriole legs, 49.5" w, 20.5" dp, 37.5" h	2990	5000	8000
Bull's-Eye Mirror, Fed., gilt w/ applied acorns, 18" dia	1000	2000	3500
Bureau, attributed to Eliphalet Briggs, Keene, NH, Fed., cherry and bird's-eye maple, bowfront, 4 cockbeaded drawers outlined in crossbanded mah. veneer, cyma curved veneer skirt, high French feet, c1810, 39.75" w, 20.5" dp, 38.5" h	9775	18,000	25,000
Butler's Tray, Eng., mah., folding, on new stand, 28" w	500	1000	1700
Butterfly Table, W. & M., splay leg, vase and ring turnings, 39" w	2300	4600	8000
Cabinet, Dutch Baroque, walnut and floral marquetry, bombé base, mid 18th C, 40.5" w, 26" dp, 76.5" h	6325	12,000	18,000
Cabinet on Chest, NH, Fed., inlaid mah., bowfront, 42" w	2500	5000	8750
Cabinet on Stand, German Baroque-style, cabinet w/ panels depicting classical scenes, base w/ griffin and scroll supports, branded "G. Bauer," 45" w, 63" h	3000	5250	8250
Candlestand, Amer., black painted dish top, modified urn standard w/ tripod cabriole legs, pad feet, 21.75" dia, 28.5" h	500	880	1375
Candlestand, Amer., black painted w/ cabriole legs	450	790	1250
Candlestand, Chip.-style, mah., dish top, 20" dia, 29" h	600	1200	2100
Candlestand, CT, cherry, sq molded top, notch carved urn standard, tripod cabriole legs and snake feet, 15" w	2300	4600	8000
Candlestand, CT, inlaid cherry, sq top w/ applied beaded edge and paterae inlay, baluster-turned standard, cabriole legs, 15" l, 26" h	750	1310	2063

	AUCTION	RETAIL Low	RETAIL High
Candlestand, CT, Norwich area, Fed., cherry, molded dish top w/ scalloped lower edge, turned standard, tripod cabriole legs, platform pad feet, 14" dia, 28" h	5000	8750	13,750
Candlestand, CT, Q.A., red painted, circ top, suppressed ball-turned standard, tripod cabriole legs, slipper feet, 16" dia, 27.5" h	2800	4900	7700
Candlestand, CT, River Valley, cherry, sq top, urn-turned standard, cabriole legs, pad feet, 16" d	550	1100	1925
Candlestand, MA, Hpwt., mah., tilt-top, cut corner rect top, spade feet, 22" w	950	1900	3325
Candlestand, mah., dished tilt-top, 20" dia	350	700	1225
Candlestand, N.E., cherry, porringer top, cabriole legs, 15" w	600	1200	2100
Candlestand, N.E., cherry, serpentine top, 14" w	500	1000	1750
Candlestand, N.E., Chip., cherry, oval top, 22" w	400	800	1400
Candlestand, N.E., Fed., birch, oct tilt-top, urn-turned standard, spider legs, spade feet, 21" w, 28" h	800	1400	2200
Candlestand, NH, Fed., birch, tilt-top w/ inlaid diamond, spider legs, 20" w	800	1600	2800
Candlestand, NH, Fed., cherry inlaid, oct cockbeaded tilt-top w/ central oval inlaid mah. veneer panel framed by stringing and set in bird's-eye maple w/ crossbanded mah. border, vase and ring-turned post, tripod cabriole leg base, pad feet, refinished, c1810–20, 18.25" 2, 13" dp, 28" h	1955	2500	5000
Candlestand, NH, Q.A., stained birch, elongated cabriole legs, 17" w, 26.5" h	4500	9000	15,750
Candlestand, turned X-form base, black paint, 25" h	300	600	1000
Canterbury, Eng., Victorian, burl wal., pierced fret sides, 24" l	1600	2800	4400
Card Table, Amer., inlaid mah., demilune, line inlaid apron, 5 sq tapered legs, 36" l	400	700	1100
Card Table, Asia Trade, Sheraton-style, hardwood, long drawer, 35" l	600	1050	1650
Card Table, attributed to Joseph Short, Newburyport, MA, Fed., mah. inlaid, rect folding top, sq tapering legs w/ inlaid paterae, banding, and stringing, 1771-1819, 35.5" w, 16.75" dp, 28.75" h	3335	6000	8500
Card Table, Eng. Hpwt., inlaid mah., demilune, 36" w	540	1000	2000
Card Table, MA, Sheraton, inlaid mah., serpentine front, apron w/ flame birch panels, turned and reeded legs, 35" l	4000	7000	11,000
Card Table, N.E., Fed., mah. carved and inlaid, demilune hinged top, frieze w/ 3 rect inlaid reserves, fluted sq tapered legs, early 19th C, 34.5" w, 17.5" dp, 29" h	1380	2500	4000
Card Table, NE, Hpwt., cherry, oblong top w/ ovolu corners, inlaid shell, sq tapered legs w/ icicle inlay, 35" l	3000	5250	8250
Card Table, Portsmouth, hinged top w/ inlaid edge, apron w/ center inlaid oval panel, ring-turned legs, 36" l	2250	4000	6000
Card Table, RI, Fed., demilune, inlaid mah., sq fluted legs, 36" w	4250	8500	14,000
Carver Armchair, N.E., old surface	4200	8400	14,700
Carver Chair, MA, Pilgrim Century, maple and oak	6750	13,500	23,000
Cassapanca (bench), Italian Renaissance, walnut and marquetry, rect back over hinged seat, scrolled arms, shaped molded base, branded "S.R." in quatrefoil, 70.5" l, 27.5" dp, 37.5" h	1380	2500	4000
Center Table, Amer., Classical Revival, mah., small w/ specimen marble top, base w/ 3 scrolled and reeded legs continuing to triangular plinth raised on ball feet, 21" dia, 28" h	4750	8310	13,000

	AUCTION	RETAIL Low	RETAIL High
Center Table, Boston, Classical Revival, mah., faceted standard, lotus-leaf plinth, 36" dia	800	1600	2800
Center Table, Philadelphia, Empire, marble-top mah., circ top, 3 turned alabaster and mah. legs, shaped plinth base, 30 dia, 31" h	5000	8750	13,750
Center Table, Renaissance Revival, walnut marquetry, ebonized, and parcel-gilt, shaped top, sq tapering stop-fluted legs, stretcher w/ central urn, c1865-75, 54" w, 28.5" dp, 28.5" h	3737	7500	10,000
Chair Table, Early Amer., circ tilt-top above shelf w/ drawer below, sq legs, 48" dia	1000	1750	2750
Chairs, Asia Trade, carved hardwood, shaped back w/ central carved monogram, cane seat, turned and reeded legs, set of 4	1200	2200	3300
Chairs, Biedermeier, walnut, shaped back, uph demilune seat, first quarter 19th C, 37" h, pair	1380	2500	4000
Chest, Amer., Chip., cherry, 4 drawers, ogee bracket feet, 42" w	2000	4000	7000
Chest, Amer., maple and cherry, split-spindle columns, 40" w	300	600	1050

Far Left: New England Banister-Back Side Chair.

Left: New England Child's Rocker, 1860–80.

—Photos courtesy Skinner, Inc., Boston, MA.

Right: Italian Rococo Armchair, third quarter 18th C. —Photo courtesy William Doyle Galleries.

Far Right: Rococo Side Chair.

	AUCTION	RETAIL Low	RETAIL High
Chest, Eng., W. & M., wal., ball feet, 38" w	1500	3000	5250
Chest, Italian Rococo, walnut and olivewood, rect crossbanded top over tapering case w/ 4 drawers, molded base w/ short cabriole legs, 18th C, 19" w, 16.25" dp, 31.25" h	2300	4000	6000
Chest, MA, Sheraton, mah., bowfront, top w/ outset corners, turned posts and legs, 44" w	1300	2300	3500
Chest, N.E. Chip., bracket feet, 36" w	1900	3800	6650
Chest, N.E., Country Q.A., maple, 6 drawers, 33.5" w	2750	5500	9750
Chest, N.E., late Sheraton, mah., bowfront, outset corners, 4 drawers flanked by reeded columns, turned legs, 46" w	1100	1900	3000
Chest, NY, Empire, mah., case w/ carved pineapple, acanthus leaf columns, paw feet, 47" w, 52" h	700	1400	2450
Chest, Spanish Baroque, iron mounted walnut, domed lid, intricately carved front, side handles, 42.5" w, 19.5" dp, 18.5" h	1380	2500	3500
Chest of Drawers, Amer., Hpwt., inlaid mah., 2 short and 3 long drawers, shaped apron, French feet, 37" l	2900	5000	8000
Chest of Drawers, CT, carved cherry, block and shell, rect top w/ molded edge projecting above case w/ 4 long drawers, upper one w/ applied convex shells centering concave carved shell, others w/ conforming blocking on base molding w/ gadrooning, ogee bracket feet, 35.5" w, 17.75" d, 37" h	8000	14,000	22,000
Chest of Drawers, CT, Chip., cherry, reverse serpentine front, top w/ molded edge above 4 drawers, molded base, ogee bracket feet, 36" w, 32" h	9000	15,750	24,750
Chest of Drawers, Dutch Neoclassical-style, mah. and floral marquetry, 4 drawers, plinth base, late 19th C, 40.75" w, 20" dp, 38.5" h	1955	4000	6000

Left: New England Queen Anne High Chest, mid 18th C.

Below: Massachusetts Federal bureau, c1820.

	AUCTION	RETAIL Low	RETAIL High
Chest of Drawers, George III, mah., 4 drawers, bracket base, late 19th C, 32.75" w, 16.5" dp, 34" h	805	1500	2200
Chest of Drawers, George III, mah., rect top, 5 drawers, French feet, late 18th/early 19th C, 42.5" w, 19" dp, 39.75" h	1380	2000	3500
Chest of Drawers, late George III, mah., bowfront, 4 drawers, French feet, early 19th C, 42.5" w, 22" dp, 36" h	1495	3000	5000
Chest of Drawers, MA, Chip., mah., rect top w/ molded edge, 4 drawers, bracket feet, 40.5" w, 32.5" h	3250	5690	9000
Chest of Drawers, N.E., Chip., 4 cockbeaded drawers, bracket feet, late 18th C, 30.5" w, 17.75" dp, 38.25" h	6325	10,000	15,000
Chest of Drawers, NH, Sheraton, mah. and birch, bowfront w/ drop panel, 40" w	900	1580	2475
Chest of Drawers, Spanish Baroque, 2 carved drawers, flattened bun feet, 50" w, 22.5" dp, 37.25" h	1150	2200	3500
Chest on Chest, Eng., Hpwt., mah., French feet, 45" w, 75" h	2000	4000	7000
Chest on Chest, George III, mah., 6 drawers above 4 drawers, fluted sides, bracket feet, 19th C, 42" w, 19.5" dp, 75.75" h	2300	4000	6000
Chest on Frame, N.E., maple, cabriole legs, pad feet, 36" w, 62" h	4500	9000	15,750
Chest on Stand, Eng., W. & M., burl wal., upper section w/ 2 short over 3 long graduated drawers, lower w/ single drawer over spiral-turned legs, 42" w, 51" h	5250	9000	14,500
Chest Over Drawers, MA, Q.A., pine, molded hinged top above deep well, 3 thumbmolded false drawers above 3 working drawers, bracket feet, mid 18th C, 36.5" w, 17.25" dp, 46.5" h	3737	7000	12,500
Child's Armchair, N.E., banister back, black painted, yoked crest, rush seat, 23" h	400	800	1400
Child's Chest of Drawers, N.E., Chip., painted pine, molded rect top, 4 thumbmolded drawers, bracket feet, later Victorian dec including painted floral motifs and scrolls on yellow ground, late 18th C, 24" w, 12" dp, 28" h	3450	6000	10,000
Child's Tall Post Bed, N.E., red painted pine, flat tester w/ chamfered edges, turned tapering posts, ring turned swelled legs, disc feet, c1800, 36" w, 74" dp, 48" h	3737	6500	10,000

Italian Neoclassical Commodes, c1790–1810. —Photo courtesy Skinner, Inc., Boston, MA.

American Chippendale Corner Cupboard, early 19th C. —Photo courtesy Skinner, Inc., Boston, MA.

	AUCTION	RETAIL Low	RETAIL High
Commode, Continental Neoclassical, walnut, burl walnut, and inlay, rect top, 2 drawers, sq tapering legs, 41" w, 20.25" dp, 30.75" h	1610	2500	3250
Commode, French, Louis XIV, ormolu mounted, diminutive, 3 drawers, 25.5" w	3500	6000	9000
Commode, Swedish Rococo-style, walnut and parcel gilt, shaped block fronted top, 3 drawers, carved and gilt skirt, cabriole legs, 19th C, 36" w, 18.25" dp, 30" h	1840	3500	5000
Console Table, Louis XVI-style, demilune, gilt bronze mounted kingwood, tulipwood, and marquetry, marble top, 3 frieze drawers, 3 cabinet doors, tapering legs, late 19th/early 20th C, 43.5" w, 17.5" dp, 36.25" h	1495	3000	4500
Convex Mirror, Fed., gilt, carved eagle and candle arms, 48" h	1200	2400	4200
Corner Chair, Eng., Chip., mah., pierced splats, sq legs	900	1800	3000
Corner Cupboard, pine, raised panel door, white enamel finish, 60" h	110	220	385
Cradle, Amer., Pilgrim Century, pine, orig red paint	450	900	1575
Credenza, Italian, carved wal., 1 drawer over cupboard door, 31" w, 35" h	1100	2200	3850
Cupboard, Scandinavian, green painted, raised panel doors, dated 1844, 58" w, 76' H	2000	4000	7000
Deacon's Bench, Amer., arrow-back, gilt and black painted, 75" w	600	1200	2100
Desk, George I-style, oak and inlay, slant lid, 3 drawers, bracket feet, 19th C, 33.25" w, 19.25" dp, 39.25" h	1092	2000	3000
Desk, George III-style, paint dec satinwood, rect top w/ leather inset writing surface, 2 banks of drawers, circ tapering stop-fluted legs, c1900, 53" w, 21.75" dp, 30.75" h	7475	13,000	20,000

	AUCTION	RETAIL Low	RETAIL High
Desk, MA, Chip., carved mah., oxbow, slant lid, claw feet, 42" w	4000	8000	14,000
Desk, N.E., Chip., cherry, slant lid, stepped int, bracket base, 36" w	900	1800	3250
Desk, NJ, Country Hpwt., lift-top, underside of lid w/ compass star motif and mkd "John S. Schen…desk, New Jersey, Country of Monmouth," high tapered legs, 28" w	800	1400	2200
Dining Chairs, Chip.-style, carved mah., pierced ladderback, needlepoint slip seat, 2 armchairs and 6 side chairs	5200	9000	14,300
Dining Chairs, Chip.-style, mah., armchair and 4 side chairs	1100	1700	3000
Dining Chairs., Eng., Chip., mah., serpentine crest above pierced splat, slip seat, cabriole legs, claw and ball feet, set of 8	10,000	17,500	27,500
Dining Chairs, George III, mah. and inlay, shield-shaped back w/ sheaf of wheat carving, late 18th C, 36.25" h, set of 8	8000	15,000	20,000
Dining Chairs, Philadelphia, Chip., serpentine crest w/ central leaf-carved motif aboved pierced latticework splat, slip seat, sq legs, H-form stretcher, set of 4	4250	7440	11,000
Dining Chairs, NY, Classical Revival, carved mah., Prince of Wales carving on splat, set of 8	7000	14,000	24,500
Dining Chairs, Q.A.-style, walnut and burl walnut, 2 armchairs and 10 side chairs, vasiform splat, slip seat, shell-carved cabriole legs, trifid feet, 20th C, 39.5" h, set of 12	16,100	30,000	45,000
Dining Table, Eng., Q.A., mah., 6-leg drop-leaf, 40" w	600	1299	2199
Dining Table, Eng., Q.A., mah., 8-leg drop-leaf, 56" w, 29" h	1000	2000	3500
Dining Table, Fed.-style, mah., double pedestal, top w/ cross-banded edge, vase-turned pedestals, sabre legs, 44" x 72", w/ pair of 24" leaves	3500	6000	9500

Left to right: William and Mary Fall Front Desk, early 18th C; New England Chippendale Slant Front Desk, c1760–80.

Massachusetts Federal Tambour Desk, c1820.

	AUCTION	RETAIL Low	RETAIL High
Dining Table, George III, mah., 2 pedestal, reeded edge top, molded tripartite base, brass paw feet, early 19th C, 48" w, 25.5" dp, 28.25" h, 48" x 25.5" leaf	3450	6000	9000
Dining Table, George III, mah. D-shaped ends, sq tapering legs, molded feet on brass caps w/ casters, late 18th C, 24.5" w, 48.25" dp, 29.25" h, 48.25" x 26.25" additional leaf	1380	2500	3200
Dining Table, George III-style, mah., 2 pedestal, molded top, turned supports, tripartite splayed legs ending in brass caps on casters, 44" w, 67.5" dp, 29.25" h	1495	3000	4500
Dining Table, N.E., Country Q.A., maple, drop-leaf, pad feet, 47" w	1600	3200	5600
Dining Table, N.E., Hpwt., mah., drop-leaf, 46" w	500	1000	1750
Dining Table, N.E., Country Sheraton, cherry, drop-leaf, rect top, plain skirt, ring-turned legs, 41" x 58" open size	500	880	1375
Dining Table, N.E., Q.A., maple, drop-leaf, oblong top w/ rounded leaves, shaped apron, cabriole legs, pad feet, 41" l	1600	2800	4400
Dining Table, PA., Chip., wal., drop-leaf, arcade apron w/ beaded detail, rect leaves w/ rounded corners, claw and ball feet, 48" open size, 28" w	2200	3850	6000
Dining Table, Philadelphia, Sheraton, mah., 2 part, demilune, reeded legs, 42" w, 80" extended	5750	11,500	20,000
Dining Table, Q.A.-style, walnut, rounded rect top, shell-carved cabriole legs, pad feet, 20th C, 74" w, 42" dp, 30.25" h	16,100	30,000	45,000
Display Cabinet, Aesthetic Movement, arched top w/ gallery above inset panel above galleried shelf, central beveled cabinet door enclosing shelves, flanked by shelves, base drawer, stylized feet, fourth quarter 19th C, 44" w, 79" h	977	1800	2500

	AUCTION	RETAIL Low	RETAIL High
Dressing Mirror, Eng., George III, mah., bowfront, ivory urn finials, 24" h	550	960	1500
Dressing Table, Italian Neoclassical, walnut and inlay, rect molded top, baize lined writing slide flanked by drawers, sq tapering legs, late 18th/early 19th C, 35.25" w, 18" dp, 31" h	1035	2000	2750
Dressing Table, Lancaster County, PA, Q.A., carved walnut, thumbmolded edg top w/ shaped corners, 3 thumbmolded drawers flanked by lambrequin corners, cyma curved skirt, cabriole legs, stockinged pad feet, 1730-60, 29.75" w, 18.5" dp, 30" h	26,450	50,000	68,000
Drop-Leaf Table, PA, Q.A., cherry, cabriole legs, stockinged pad feet, 45" w	550	1100	2000
Drop-Leaf Table, RI, Q.A., tiger maple legs, 48" w	3000	6000	10,000
Dumbwaiter, George III-style, mah., typical form, pad feet on casters, 19th C, 15.5" dia top, 42.5" h	747	1500	2250
Extension Dining Table, Louis XVI-style, brass mounted mah., circ top, drop leaves, 6 tapered legs, 4 additional leaves, late 19th/early 20th C, 43.25" w, 41.25" dp, 30.25" h	9200	15,000	25,000
Extension Dining Table, NY, Classical, carved and veneered mah., circ top w/ molded edge over clustered column-form split pedestal support, foliate and paw feet, 7 additional leaves, c1840, 48" dia, 29.5" h	7475	12,000	20,000
Fancy Chairs, Regency, painted and dec, arched floral painted crests, bamboo turnings, pair	300	530	825
Fancy Chairs, rosewood grained, sabre legs, set of 6	550	960	1500
Fancy Side Chair, Sheraton, tiger maple	200	400	700
Farm Table, French, shaped apron, 3 drawers, 77" w, 29" h	1200	2400	4200
Fire Screen, Aesthetic Movement, ebonized, needlepoint, and beaded, crest figured as cattails and bird heads, trestle base, fourth quarter 19th C, 51" h	1265	2300	4500
Footstool, George II-style, needlepoint uph, cabriole legs, 21" w	400	800	1400
Footstools, Hpwt., mah., sq tapered legs, 13" w, pair	200	400	700
Fret Mirror, Chip., 15" h	225	450	800
Game Table, Regency, mah. and inlay, rect top w/ round corners, ring turned pedestal, 4 splayed legs ending in brass caps on casters, first quarter 19th C, 35" w, 16.5" dp, 29.75" h	1092	2000	3000
Gate-Leg Drop-Leaf Table, CT, maple, vase-turned legs, 44" w	1700	3400	5950
Gate-Leg Drop-Leaf Table, Eng. Prov., oak, deep leaves, ball-turned legs, 19th C, 34" w, 14.75" dp, 29" h	920	1700	2500
Gate-Leg Drop-Leaf Table, late W. & M., shaped top, deep rounded drop leaves, frieze drawer, turned legs, box stretcher, 52" w, 21.5" dp, 29" h	1092	2000	2900
Gate-Leg Table, N.E., maple, vase-turned legs, 41" w	1800	3600	6300
Great Chair, MA Bay Colony, Pilgrim Century, ladderback w/ elongated finials, flat armrests	1600	3200	5600
Gueridon (table), Italian Neoclassical, mah., parcel-gilt, and marble, circ Carrara marble top, plain frieze, bird-form legs, circ marble-top stretcher, early 19th C, 24.5" dia, 28.5" h	747	1500	2300
Hall Tree, Victorian, bamboo, rattan, and tile-inset, arched form w/ double beveled mirrors, umbrella holder base, late 19th C, 32" w, 9.5" dp, 84" h	977	2000	3000

	AUCTION	RETAIL Low	RETAIL High
Hanging Corner Cabinets, green chinoiserie dec, bowed form w/ pr of drawers, late 19th/early 20th C, 23.25" w, 15.5" dp, 37" h, pair	1150	2250	3500
Hanging Corner Cupboard, PA, wal., secret compartment below paneled cupboard door, 28" h	2200	3850	6000
Hanging Cupboard, Continental, wal., 3 raised panels, center long door, 29" h	650	1300	2200
Hanging Cupboard, Early Amer., grain painted, 27" h	1200	2400	4200
Hanging Cupboard, glazed door, H hinges, old red finish, 22" w, 19" h	700	1400	2450
Hanging Shelf, mah., shaped sides, 37.5" w, 29" h	450	800	1200
High Chest of Drawers, Q.A., maple, fan carved drawer fronts, cabriole legs, pad feet, c1760, 39.5" w, 20.25" dp, 74.5" h	27,600	50,000	75,000
Highboy, Amer., maple, bonnet top, cabriole legs, pad feet, 82" h	5250	10,000	18,000
Highboy, N.E., maple, fan-carved, cabriole legs, 40" w, 78" h	4300	8600	15,000
Highboy, N.E., Q.A., maple and pine, case w/ molding and torus drawer above 2 short and 3 long drawers, lower section w/ 5 short drawers above apron w/ drop pendants joining cabriole legs on pad feet, 38" w, 72" h	6750	11,000	18,500
Highboy, N.E., tiger maple, fluted quarter columns, 36" w, 72" h	3500	7000	12,000
Highboy, N.E., wal., fan-carved, bonnet top, 84" h	6000	12,000	21,000
Hutch Table, Early Amer., pine, oval top, shoe foot, 33" w, 40" dp	800	1400	2200
Joint Stool, Eng., Jacobean, carved oak, splayed legs, 19" w	1400	2800	4900
Joint Stool, oak, molded top, splayed legs, 18" w	1000	2000	3500
Kitchen Table, Eng. Prov., oak and elmwood, breadboard top, sq tapering legs, 19th C, 52.5" w, 26.5" dp, 29.25" h	977	1750	2500
Lap Desk, late George III, crossbanded mah., fitted int above long drawer, c1800, 12" l	230	400	600
Lap Desk, mother-of-pearl inlaid rosewood	125	250	400
Library Table, Regency, satinwood, calamander, part ebonized, and parcel-gilt, circ top, fluted column, paw feet, c1810, 42" dia, 28.5" h	7475	15,000	21,000
Linen Press, Amer., Sher., mah., upper section w/ twin panel doors opening to slide-out shelves, lower case projecting and fitted w/ 4 long graduated drawers, turned feet, 58" w, 84" h	1600	2800	4400
Liquor Chest, Dutch, inlaid mah., fitted gilt bottles, 10" w	1100	2200	3850
Lolling Chair, Amer., inlaid wal.	1100	2200	3850
Lowboy, Delaware River Valley, Chip., carved wal., elaborate shell-carved dec	16,250	32,500	56,000
Lowboy, N.E., Q.A., wal., concave carving above shaped apron, cabriole legs, pad feet, 30" w	5250	10,000	18,000
Mantel, attributed to Samuel McIntire, Salem, MA, Federal, center-carved eagle, 72" w, 52" h	5250	9000	14,000
Mantel, VT, Classical, painted and carved pine, 65" w, 47" h	850	1700	3000
Miniature Chest, Eng., Hpwt., inlaid mah., 3 drawers, 11" h	450	900	1575
Miniature Pole Screen, needlework panel, 17" h	125	250	430
Miniature Side Chair, Amer., Victorian, wal., 16" h	550	1100	1900
Mirror, Amer., Chip., walnut veneer and parcel-gilt, scrolled frame, 18th C, 14.5" w, 36.5" h	575	1000	1500
Mirror, Amer., Classical, carved giltwood, twin fruit-filled cornucopia crest, applied pierced shell above oval mirror plate, foliate pendant drop, 30" w, 38" h	5000	8750	13,750

19th-C Miniature Furniture, left to right: Chippendale-style blanket chest, Federal chest of drawers and Federal-style chest of drawers. —Photo courtesy William Doyle Galleries.

	AUCTION	RETAIL Low	RETAIL High
Mirror, Amer., Federal, giltwood, eglomisé harbor scene panel, 31" h	250	440	650
Mirror, Amer., Federal, giltwood, eglomisé tablet w/ colonial building, 33" h	550	960	1500
Mirror, Amer., polychrome dec carved pine, figural jester form, late 19th C, 12" w, 21" h	3737	6000	9000
Mirror, Chip., carved mah., deep crest w/ flanking ears above rect plate, matching pendant drop, 35" h	650	1140	1750
Mirror, Chip., mah., scroll frame w/ giltwood phoenix, 43" h	2200	3850	6000
Mirror, Chip., scrolled crest w/ painted eagle on branch, 42" h	500	880	1375
Mirror, Chip., wal., scroll-form w/ pierced and gilded shell, 39" h	800	1400	2200
Mirror, Continental, giltwood and painted, rect, foliate carved cresting, 19th C, 37" h	287	500	750
Mirror, Continental Baroque-style, black painted and parcel-gilt, raised foliate carved borders, seraphims in corners, 18th C, 50" x 39"	1265	2400	3500
Mirror, Continental Neoclassical, giltwood, oval, borders w/ high relief beasts, foliage, and twist fluting, c1840, 35.5" l	3450	6500	10,000
Mirror, Neoclassical-style, gilt and gilt composition, oval, foliate cresting and pendant, early 20th C, 50.5" h	575	1000	1500
Mirror, Q.A., wal., gilt shell, 29" h	500	1000	1750
Mirror, Q.A., wal., painted shell, 2-part plate, 40" H	2100	4200	7350
Mirror, Q.A.-style, green japanned and verre eglomise, shaped cresting, upper panel painted w/ figures, 19th C, 54" h	862	1600	2400
Mirror, Regency, green and parcel-gilt, carved, drapery, 47" h	300	600	1050
Overmantel Mirror, Victorian Rococo Revival, giltwood, graduated stacked 3-part mirror plate, foliage carved borders, late 19th C, 50" w, 37" h	1380	2500	3750
Patent Folding Armchair, George Hunzinger, NY, Renaissance Revival, walnut and parcel-gilt, collapsible form, green velvet uph, c1866-70	230	425	650
Pedestal, Italian, green marble, circ top, twist fluted standard, late 19th C, 32" h	1265	2400	3500

	AUCTION	RETAIL Low	RETAIL High
Pedestal, Kimbel and Cabus, NY, Aesthetic Movement, ebonized, polychrome incised, and parcel-gilt, oct top, shaped support, stepped plinth base, 37.5" h	977	1000	2000
Pedestal Cabinets, George III, mah., rect molded top over deep drawer over paneled door, plinth base, 19th C, 18.25" w, 16.5" dp, 28" h, pair	977	1000	2000
Pedestal Font, Gothic-style, oak, molded oct form, late 19th/early 20th C, 15.5" w top, 31" h	345	700	1000
Pembroke Table, Amer., Hpwt., inlaid wal., oblong top, shaped leaves, frieze drawer, sq tapering legs w/ diamond inlay and stringing, 36" l	650	1140	1750
Pembroke Table, CT River Valley, Chip., carved cherry, fluted legs, pierced scrolled brackets and cross stretchers, late 18th C, 34.5" w open, 34" dp, 27" h	4887	9000	14,000
Pembroke Table, Hpwt., cherry, X-form stretchers, 35" w	500	1000	1750
Pembroke Table, N.E., Hpwt., mah., frieze drawer, sq tapered legs, X-form stretcher	600	1050	1650
Pier Mirror, Amer., Classical, giltwood, gilt shell, 62" h	1000	1750	2750
Pier Mirror, Continental, Neo-Classical, fruitwood, 46" h	300	600	1100
Pier Mirror, Empire, gilt, carved acanthus leaf spandrels, 60" h	700	1400	2450
Pier Mirror, Federal, giltwood, elaborate crest w/ trophies, 66" h	3800	7600	13,000
Pier Table, Amer., ormolu mounted carved mah., parcel-gilt, 43" w	2500	5000	8750

Left to right: New England Chippendale Desk Bookcase, c1780. —Photo courtesy Skinner, Inc., Boston, MA; American Federal Secretary Bookcase, early 19th C; English George III Secretary. —Photos courtesy William Doyle Galleries.

	AUCTION	RETAIL Low	RETAIL High
Plant Stand, French, white painted wire, 4 tiers, on casters, early 20th C, 75" w, 28" dp, 46.5" h	632	1200	1750
Pole Screen, Fed., inlaid mah., chandle shelf, 60" h	2000	4000	7000
Refectory Table, Spanish Baroque, walnut and iron mounted, rect top, 2 drawers, carved scrolled base w/ iron supports, 18th C, 55" w, 33.5" dp, 32.25" h	4025	7500	12,000
Sawbuck Table, circ top, red paint, 22" dia	400	800	1400
Screen, Late Victorian, oak and crewelwork, 3 panel, 18" w panels, 69" h	230	400	600
Scroll Mirror, Amer., Chip., 25" h	300	530	825
Secretary, MA, Aesthetic Movement, fall-front, dentil molded cornice, mirrored fall-front, carved and fluted sides, base w/ putto heads and paneled door, bracket feet, last quarter 19th C, 39.75" w, 19.5" dp, 68.25" h	2300	4000	6000
Secretary, Hpwt.-style, inlaid mah., glazed doors above tambour slides and writing flap over 2 drawers, sq tapered legs, 40" w, 81" h	2200	3850	6000
Secretary, George III, mah., mullioned doors, 3 drawers, French feet, 49.25" w, 22" dp, 86.5" h	2587	5000	7500
Secretary, N.E., Fed., cherry and inlaid bird's-eye maple, shaped pediment, geometric glazed doors and 2 short drawers above butler's drawer w/ column inlaid prospect door, French feet, 39" w, 84" h	4000	7000	11,000
Server, George III, mah. and boxwood inlaid, tapering molded legs, c1800, 49" w, 20.5" dp, 33" h	1380	2500	4000
Server, Q.A.-style, walnut, rect molded top, 3 drawers, 6 shell-carved cabriole legs, pad feet, 20th C, 77.5" w, 21" dp, 33" h	1380	2500	4000
Settee, Continental, Biedermeier, fruitwood, 60" w	600	1200	2100
Settee, PA, painted and dec triple chair back w/ floral dec, 71" l	500	880	1375
Settle, Eng. Prov., oak, rect paneled back, rope seat w/ loose cushion, 18th/19th C, 74.5" l, 38.5" h	517	1000	1500
Shaving Mirror, George III-style, mah., shield-shaped, serpentine front, bracket feet, 19th C, 18" w, 22" h	230	450	650
Shaving Mirror, NY, Federal, inlaid mah., bowsront, 18" w, 22" h	600	1200	2100
Side Cabinet, Eng. Aesthetic Movement, ebonized, maple, and gilt-incised, mirrored shelf back over shaped top w/ 3 doors, plinth base, fourth quarter 19th C, 71.75" w, 15.5" dp, 84.5" h	1265	2400	3500
Side Chair, Bermudan Q.A., cedarwood, shaped back w/ central splat, uph seat, cabriole legs, Spanish feet, first half 18th C, 40.75" h	1150	2000	3000
Side Chair, Boston, Chip., carved walnut, leaf carved medallion on serpentine crest w/ raked molded ears, pierced and scroll carved splat, pad feet, mid 18th C, 36.5" h	1840	2500	4000
Side Chair, Boston, W. & M., carved and turned maple, leather seat and back	1700	3400	6000
Side Chair, Classical-style, mah., curule-form w/ reeded details and pierced splat	500	1300	2500
Side Chair, CT, Chip., serpentine crest w/ rake molded terminals above pierced splat, crewel-work slip seat, sq beaded legs, 1770-1800, 37.75" h	690	1400	2000
Side Chair, Deerfield, MA region, cherry, ladderback, projecting ears, double curved crest, rush seat, 1785-1810, 39.25" h	805	1500	2200

	AUCTION	RETAIL Low	RETAIL High
Side Chair, MA, Chip., carved mah., serpentine crest w/ central shell above cross-eyed owl splat, carved volutes, slip seat, cabriole legs, pad feet	3200	5600	9000
Side Chair, MA, Q.A., walnut, serpentine crest, raked molded terminals, vasiform splat, front cabriole legs, rear chamfered legs, pad feet, 18th C, 37.25" h	805	1500	2000
Side Chair, N.E., Country Chip., maple, pair	325	650	1100
Side Chair, N.E., Country Q.A., oxbow crest, Spanish feet	550	960	1500
Side Chair, N.E., Q.A., mah., oxbow crest w/ carved shell, block and ring-turned H-form stretcher	5500	11,000	19,000
Side Chair, N.E., W. & M., banister back	200	400	600
Side Chair, PA., Q.A., wal., oxbow crest, vase splat, slip seat, serpentine-form stretcher	1400	2400	3700
Side Chair, Philadelphia, Hpwt., carved mah., sq back w/ urn splat	500	1000	1750
Side Chair, RI, Q.A., maple, oxbow crest, vase splat, cabriole legs, pad feet, turned H-form stretcher	2000	4000	7000
Side Chair, Salem, MA, Hpwt., carved mah., shield back, inlaid fan	1750	3500	6000
Side Chair, School of Samuel McIntire, Salem, MA, Hpwt., mah., shield back w/ foliate carvings and sunburst, serpentine seat, sq tapered legs	1100	1800	3000
Side Chair, Spanish, wal. and tooled leather	700	1230	2000
Side Chairs, Amer., Classical Revival, tablet crest rail, reeded stiles, slip seat, reeded sabre legs, set of 4	1700	3000	4500
Side Chairs, Biedermeier, fruitwood and inlay, stylized foliate back, slip seat, sabre legs, first quarter 19th C, 33" h, set of 4	345	600	950
Side Chairs, CT, Chip., cherry, heart-pierced splat, pair	2000	4000	7000
Side Chairs, Eng., Q.A., wal., shell and tassel carved knees, pair	1400	2800	4900
Side Chairs, Flemish-style, carved oak and cane, pair	400	700	1100
Side Chairs, Louis XVI-style, neoclassical form, green and cream painted, circ stop-fluted legs, uph, late 19th C, 35.25" h, set of 4	1150	2000	3000
Side Chairs, Philadelphia, Chip., carved mah., serpentine crest rail w/ central leaf-carved motif above pierced Gothic splat, slip seat, sq legs w/ molded edge, H-form stretcher, set of 4	12,500	21,000	34,000
Side Chairs, Rococo Revival, rosewood, oval back w/ floral carved crest, uph seat, cabriole legs, third quarter 19th C, 38" h, pair	1150	200	3000
Side Chairs, Victorian, ebonized, polychrome painted, and parcel-gilt, rattan seats, late 19th C, 32.5" h, pair	460	850	1200
Side Table, Continental, wal., single drawer, stretcher base, 28" w	1300	2600	4550
Side Table, Regency, mah., ebonized, and rosewood banded, 2 drawers, 12.5" closed, 17.75" dp, 29.5" h	3250	5500	9000
Sideboard, Amer., Hpwt., inlaid mah., demilune top w/ line inlaid edge above central drawer and twin cupboard doors flanked by bowed cupboard doors, sq tapered legs w/ satinwood inlay, 72" w, 27" dp, 38" h	8000	14,000	22,000
Sideboard, Amer., Hpwt., inlaid mah., serpentine front, central bowed drawer above pair of cupboard doors flanked by concave cupboard doors, sq tapered legs, 70" w, 27" dp, 39" h	4000	7000	11,000
Sideboard, Amer., Sheraton, mah., bowfront, 61" w	7250	14,500	25,000
Sideboard, Amer., Sheraton-style, kidney shape, oblong top above case of drawers and doors, turned reeded legs, 72" w, 28.5" dp	800	1400	2200
Sideboard, Eng., Hpwt., mah., bowfront, 66" l, 36" h	1800	3600	6300

	AUCTION	RETAIL Low	RETAIL High
Sideboard, George III, mah. and satinwood inlay, bowed top w/ crossbanding, sq tapering legs, spade feet, late 18th C, 60.75" w, 25.25" dp, 35.25" h	6900	13,500	25,000
Sideboard, N.E., Hpwt., inlaid mah., diminutive, serpentine top above conforming case w/ 3 line-inlaid drawers above fan-inlaid cupboard doors, line-inlaid sq tapered legs, 58" w, 25" dp, 39.5" h	21,000	36,000	57,000
Sideboard, NY, Hpwt., mah., oblong top w/ bowed front above arrangement of doors, drawers, and bottle drawers, sq tapered legs, 77" l, 23" dp, 45" h	1200	2100	3300
Sideboard, Providence, RI, Fed., mah. inlaid, ovolo corners and dark inlaid edge, 4 drawers and 4 cupboards, 6 sq tapering legs w/ stringing and cuff inlays, oval satinwood inlaid patera in center drawers, c1790-1800, 66" w, 26.5" dp, 40.25" h	39,100	75,000	100,000
Silver Table, Eng., Chip., mah., rect top w/ pierced gallery above blind fret frieze w/ candle slides, sq tapering legs, Marlborough feet, 20" w, 32" dp, 27" h	18,500	32,000	50,000
Silver Table, George III, mah., rect top w/ molded surround, sq tapering legs, block feet, fretwork brackets to sides, late 19th C, 32.75" w, 22.75" dp, 28" h	747	1500	2050
Sofa, Amer., Classical Revival, mah., scrolled crest, carved paw feet, 84" w	700	1400	2450
Sofa, French, Louis XVI-style, painted, 84" w	300	600	1000
Sofa, MA, Federal., mah., bowback, 78" w	3400	6000	9000
Sofa, MA or RI, Chip., mah., camelback, back, scrolled arms, tight seat w/ serpentine overuph seat rail, 1760-80, 78.5" w, 25.5" dp, 35" h	17,250	30,000	45,000
Sofa, MD, Chip., mah. inlaid, camelback, scrolled arms, 6 sq tapering cuff-inlaid legs outlined in stringing, 1780-1810, 75.5" w, 27" dp, 36.75" h	42,550	65,000	85,000

Left to right: Mid-Atlantic States Classical Sideboards, 1840–45; English George III Demilune Sideboard, late 18th/early 19th C. —Photos courtesy Skinner, Inc., Boston, MA.

	AUCTION	RETAIL Low	RETAIL High
Sofa, NH, Sheraton, mah., bird's-eye maple inlay, 74" w	1400	2800	4900
Sofa, Salem, MA, late Federal, mah., scrolled arms, acanthus supports, 70" w	825	1650	2800
Sofa Table, Regency-style, rosewood, rect molded top w/ flaps, 2 drawers, shaped trestle supports, turened stretcher, late 19th C, 27" w, 23.5" dp, 29" h	1955	4000	6000
Sofa Table, Regency-style, yewwood, rect top w/ hinged flaps, 2 frieze drawers opposed by sham drawers, lyre-form trestle support, brass paw feet, late 19th C, 38.75" w, 27.75" h	1495	3000	4500
Stand, Chinese, carved rosewood, late 19th C, 51" h	450	900	1500
Stand, Early Amer., Hpwt., red painted, 1 drawer, splayed legs, 17" sq top	1500	3000	5250
Stand, N.E., Hpwt., painted dec, 1 drawer, 21" w	300	600	1100
Stand, N.E., Sheraton, old red finish, 1 drawer, 19" w	250	500	900
Stand, William IV, rosewood and lacquer, chinoiserie dec top, turned support, reeded brass feet, second quarter 19th C, 14.25" w, 11.25" dp, 17.75" h	575	1000	1500
Step-Back Cupboard, PA., Chip., wal., 2 parts, upper section w/ cove molding above twin glazed doors, lower w/ 5 short drawers over paneled doors, bracket feet, 65" w, 82" h	7500	13,000	20,000
Stool, Classical, mah., curule form	800	1400	2200
Stool, Eng. Jacobean-style, elmwood, pierced top, turned legs joined by stretchers, 17.5" h	258	400	550
Stool, W. & M., turned wal., 19" w	650	1300	2400
Suite, settee and 2 armchairs, Biedermeier-style, fruitwood and inlay, shaped back w/ vertical splats, striped silk uph, sabre legs, late 19th C, settee 67" l, 32" h	3737	6000	8500
Table, Canterbury, NH, red painted pine and maple, scrubbed pine top, painted base w/ drawer, tapering legs, 1820, 47" w, 27" dp, 25.5" h	2530	5000	7500
Table, Eng. Prov., oak, rect top above frieze drawer, turned legs, box-form stretcher, 18th/19th C, 31" w, 28.75" h	1380	2500	4000
Table, George III, mah., oval tilt-top, tripod base, cabriole legs, scroll feet, third quarter 18th C, 33.5" w, 27" dp, 29.25" h	1275	2400	3500
Tall Chest, Concord, NH area, birch, 7 thumbmolded drawers, bracket base, refinished, 35.75" w, 16.25" dp, 54.75" h	4255	8000	12,000
Tall Chest, MA, Chip., cherry and maple, thumbmolded drawers, bracket feet, c1780, 36" w, 17" dp, 52.5" h	3450	6000	9000
Tall Chest, N.E., Chip., maple, cove molding above case w/ 5 long drawers on molded base, bracket feet, 36" w, 50" h	3100	5400	8500
Tavern Table, N.E., pine and cherry, sq tapered beaded legs, c1790, 32" x 34.5" top, 25.5" h	1265	2200	3300
Tavern Table, N.E., W. & M., scrubbed top, turned legs, 31" w	5000	10,000	17,500
Tavern Table, PA, cherry, frieze drawer, vase-turned legs, 51" w, 29" h	1500	3000	5250
Tavern Table, PA, cherry, frieze drawer, sq legs, box stretchers, 48" w, 34" dp, 28" h	1000	2000	3500
Tea Table, George III, carved mah., oct tilt-top w/ pierced gallery, spiral-turned urn standard, cabriole legs w/ leaf carving, scrolled feet, 23" dia, 29" h	2600	4550	7150
Tea Table, MA, Chip., shaped tilt-top w/ molded edge, serpentine sides, spiral carved vase and ring post, tripod cabriole leg base, pad feet, c1780, 28.75" w, 29" dp, 29.5" h	3795	7000	10,500

	AUCTION	RETAIL Low	RETAIL High
Tea Table, N.E., Chip., carved mah., sq serpentine tilt-top w/ molded edge, spiral-twist urn-turned standard, tripod cabriole legs w/ leaf carved knees, claw and ball feet, 29" l, 29" h	2400	4200	6600
Tea Table, Norwich, CT, cherry, circ dished top, birdcage support, cabriole legs w/ carved knees, claw and ball feet, 48" dia	3000	6000	10,000
Tea Table, PA, Chip., circ tilt-top w/ molded edge, birdcage support, ball and ring turned column, tripod cabriole leg base, pad feet on platforms, c1760-80, 26.5" dia, 27.75" h	9775	18,000	26,000
Trunk, China Trade, camphor wood, 36" w	750	1500	2600
Trunk, Continental, dome top, brass mounted leather, polychrome painted, figural and foliate dec, 19th C, 33.25" l, 18.5" dp, 12" h	517	1000	1800
Trunk, dome top, red leather w/ chinoiserie designs in gilt, w/ brass tacks, iron straps, and carrying handles, on matching Q.A.-style frame, 37.5" l stand	1300	2400	3500
Trunk, Salem, MA, brass-studded red leather, John Bott label	200	350	550
Trunk, Spanish or Italian, slightly domed lid, tooled leather cov, iron straps and handles, 19" l	900	1500	2475
Vitrine Table, Edwardian, mah. and inlay, shaped hinged top w/ inset glass, sq tapering legs, medial shelf over shaped stretcher, c1900, 29.5" w, 18" dp, 32.75" h	862	1500	2200
Vitrine Table, Louis XVI-style, gilt metal mounted mah., late 19th/ early 20th C, 59" h, 25.75" dia	3750	7500	10,000
Wardrobe, KY, red painted poplar, 2 recessed paneled doors, int w/ turned Shaker pegs mounted on beaded board, c1850, 48" w, 19" dp, 79" h	2645	4200	6000
Windsor Armchair, Elisha Swan, Stonington, CT, brace back, painted, continuous arm, 6 spindles, shaped handholds, vase and ring turned arm supports and legs, carved saddle seat, 1755-1807, 39" h	2760	5000	7500

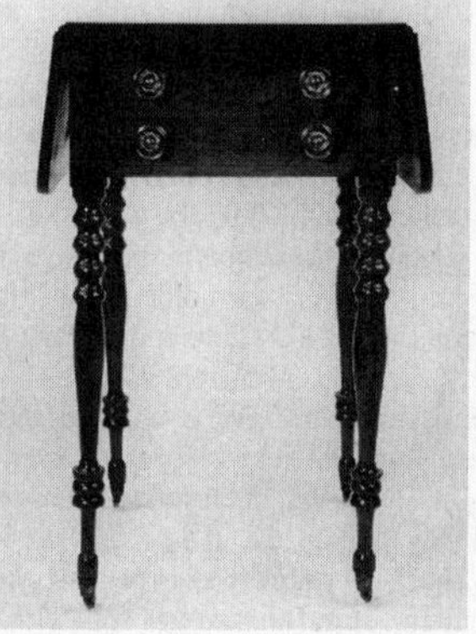

Left to right: New York Classical Drop-Leaf Table, c1815. —Photo courtesy William Doyle Galleries; New York Federal Work Table, c1830. —Photo courtesy Skinner, Inc., Boston, MA.

	AUCTION	RETAIL Low	RETAIL High
Windsor Armchair, Eng. Prov., elmwood and ash, wheel-back, first half 19th C, 45" h	402	700	1000
Windsor Armchair, N.E., painted, fan back, serpentine crest rail, 6 spindles, shaped arms and handholds, vase and ring turned arm supports and legs, c1790, 31" h	6325	12,000	18,000
Windsor Lighting Stand, NH, candle arms, adjustable standard, dished stand, 3 turned splayed legs, late 18th C, 13" dia, 36" h	1840	3500	4700
Windsor Side Chairs, N.E., bow back, 9 bamboo turned spindles, shaped saddle seat, bamboo turned legs, c1810, 36.5" h, set of 4	5175	10,000	15,000
Windsor Stand, northern N.E., bright green paint, early 19th C, 15.5" w, 28.5" h	1265	2100	3200
Wing Chair, Eng., Chip., mah., sq legs, H-form stretcher	2000	4000	7000
Wing Chair, George III, mah. and uph, sq molded legs w/ brass caps, late 18th/early 19th C, 45.5" h	1610	3000	4500
Wing Chair, Hpwt., mah., sq molded legs, H-form stretcher	3400	6800	12,000
Wing Chair, N.E., Chip., maple, sq legs w/ beaded edge, H-form stretcher	1500	3000	5250
Work Table, Amer., Country Hepwt., drop-leaf, 1 drawer, 19" w	550	1100	1925
Work Table, Boston, Classical Revival, carved mah., 2 drawers, 23" w	3400	6800	11,000
Work Table, CT Valley, Sheraton, cherry, 2 drawers, 18" w	1100	2200	3750
Work Table, N.E., Hpwt, mah., 2 drawers, sq tapered legs, 16" w	1000	2000	3500
Work Table, NY, Classical Revival, carved mah., drop-leaf, 2 drawers, paw feet, 18" w	1400	2800	4900
Writing Table, Spanish Baroque, walnut, rect top, 2 carved drawers, 2 secret drawers, scrolled trestle support, 18th C, 41.25" w, 26.25" dp, 29.75" h	2645	5000	7500

New England Decorated Windsor Side Chairs, 1820–30. —Photo courtesy Skinner, Inc., Boston, MA.

Mission

The name of Stickley dominates the field of Mission furniture. Those items produced by Gustav Stickley with the "Als ich kann" (As I can) label are generally the most valuable of the "commercial" makers. Unlike much Early American furniture, makers often labeled Mission pieces. Original (usually dark) finish is an important point in valuing Mission furniture.

Dover Publications and Turn of the Century Editions have reprinted various catalogs of Mission furniture. For further information see also Bruce Johnson's *Arts and Crafts, Second Edition,* published by House of Collectibles, Random House, NY, 1992.

Items are listed under their maker. Prices are given for Refinished and Original Finish. Under each category are values for labeled (L) and unmarked (UM) pieces. Gallery is abbreviated gal.

Gustav Stickley

	REFINISHED		ORIG. FIN	
	L	UM	L	UM
Armchair, high back, sq cutouts, continuous arms, box base w/ cutouts, 32" w, 42.75" h	$5000	$4000	$7000	$6000
Armchair, spindled high back, spindles for each arm, through tenons, 27.5" w, 48.5" h	9000	7000	12,000	10,000
Armchair, V-back rail over 5 splats, corbels for arms, through tenons, 24.5" w, 36" h	400	300	500	400
Bed, double, maple, inverted V head and footboards, arched apron, 54" w, 75" 1	4000	3000	6000	5000
Book Rack, #74, D-form cutouts, "V" shelf	1500	1000	2000	1500
Bookcase, 1 door, 16 glass panes, gal. top, 36" w, 46" h	4000	3000	5000	4000
Bookcase, 2 doors, 8 panes/door, exposed tenons, gal. top, 43" w, 56" h	3000	2000	3500	2500
Bookcase, open, 4 shelves, through tenons, gal. top, 36" w, 56" h	3000	2000	3500	2500
Chair, rabbit ear, keyed through tenons, black leather inset seat w/ brass tacks	800	600	1200	1000
Chair, 3 slats, orig leather seat, 17.5" w, 38" h	400	300	500	400
Chairs, 4 slats, arched lower rail, leather cushion seat, 37" h, set of 4	2500	2000	3500	3000
Chairs, 3 slats, leather seat w/ tacks, 37.5" h, set of 4	2500	2000	3500	3000
Chest, 2 drawers over 4 drawers, paneled sides, brass pulls, 40" w, 48" h	6000	5000	10,000	7000
Chest, 9 drawers, maple, arched apron, wooden pulls, backsplash, 50.5" h	5000	4000	7000	6000
Child's Rocker, 3 slats, arms, 18" w, 25" h	300	200	400	300
China Cabinet, 1 door, 20 panes, paneled back, gal. top, 35.5" w, 66.5" h	9000	7000	15,000	12,000
China Cabinet, 1 door, 9 panes, trapezoidal, butterfly joints, inverted V apron, 37" w, 65" h	10,000	7000	20,000	15,000
China Cabinet, 1 door, glass sides, through tenons, gal. top, 35" w, 57.5" h	5000	4000	7000	6000
China Cabinet, 2 doors, 2 drawers, paneled sides, lower shelf, keyed tenon, 36" h	10,000	7000	20,000	15,000
China Cabinet, 2 doors, 8 panes/door and sides, through tenons, V pulls, gal. top, 42" w, 64" h	5000	4000	7000	6000
Cube Chair, wide splat on each side, caned seat	5000	4000	7000	6000
Day Bed, 5 splats each side, through tenons, 31" w, 29" h	2500	2000	3500	3000

	REFINISHED		ORIG. FIN	
	L	UM	L	UM
Desk, 1 drawer over kneehole shelf, flanked by 4 drawers, copper pulls, exposed tenons, 42" w, 29" h	1000	800	1500	1000
Desk, 2 drawers w/ copper pulls, letter trays, lower shelf, 40" w, 36" h	2000	1500	2500	2000
Desk, 2 drawers over shaped lower shelf, wrought iron V pulls, 40" w, 30" h	800	600	1200	1000
Desk, #730, 42" w, 40" h	2500	2000	3500	3000
Desk, double pedestal, 9 drawers, keyed tenons, 4 corner posts, orig leather top, 47" w, 30.5" h	4000	3000	6000	5000
Desk, drop front, #518, long strap hinges	5000	4000	7000	6000
Desk, fall front, #729, 5 drawers	3000	2000	3500	2500
Desk, slant front, 1 drawer w/ copper pulls, lower shelf, 30" w, 39" h	1000	800	1500	1000
Desk, slant front, fitted int, 1 drawer, platform base, 30" w, 43.5" h	1000	800	1500	1000
Dining Chairs, 3 slats, short corbels, tapered front legs, 17" w, 37.5" h, set of 5	1500	1000	2000	1500
Dining Chairs, 3 slats, double side stretchers, set of 6	2000	1500	2500	2000
Dining Chairs, 3 slats, rush seat, 1 armchair and 8 side chairs	2500	2000	3500	3000
Dining Chairs, 3 splats, arched front and side aprons, set of 6	4000	3000	6000	5000
Dining Chairs, #1297, 4 slats, set of 4	2500	2000	3500	3000

Left to right: Desk, fall front, gallery int., copper V pulls, orig. finish, 32" w, 43" h, $2200 at auction; Dressing Table, #907, swivel mirror, 5 drawers, refinished, 48" w, 29.75" h, $173 at auction. —Photos courtesy David Rago Auctions.

	REFINISHED		ORIG. FIN	
	L	UM	L	UM
Dining Table, pedestal, 54" w	3600	3000	5000	4000
Dresser, 2 short drawers over 2 long drawers, maple, arched apron, tapering standards, mirror, 48" w	2500	2000	3500	3000
Dresser, 2 short drawers over 3 long drawers, mirror, butterfly joints, mortise and tenon, 46" w, 33" h	6000	5000	10,000	7000
Dresser, 4 drawers, mirror, butterfly joints, bowed case, copper V pulls, 48" w, 66" h	4000	3000	6000	5000
Dresser, 6 drawers, reverse V splashboard, paneled sides, wooden pulls, 52.5" h	6000	5000	10,000	7000
Footstool, orig leather top, sq faceted nails, sq flared legs, 12" sq, 4.5" h	500	400	600	450
Footstool, rush top, arched stretchers, 18.5" sq, 18" h	1500	1000	2000	1500
Gout Stool, flared legs, leather top, 4.5" h	500	400	600	450
Letter Rack, rotating, 4 compartments	1500	1000	2000	1500
Library Table, 3 drawers	9000	7000	12,000	10,000
Magazine Stand, #72, 3 shelves, 42" h	3000	2000	3500	2500
Mirror, 3 sections, 4 iron hooks, 48" w	1500	1000	2000	1500
Mirror, cheval, maple, arched stretcher, inverted V top, 34" w, 70" h	1500	1000	2000	1500
Morris Chair, 5 slats for each arm, corbels, side stretcher tenons, shaped top rail, 31" w, 44" h	3500	2500	4500	3500
Morris Chair, #332	2000	7000	14,000	10,000
Morris Chair, bent arm, 18 spindles for each arm, through tenons, 24" w, 36" h	9000	7000	12,000	10,000
Morris Chair, bent arm, 5 splat arms, straight apron, through tenons, 33" w, 40" h	6000	5000	10,000	7000
Morris Chair, spindled, lady's flat arm, 7 spindles each side, 38" h	4000	3000	6000	5000
Office Chair, 11 spindles, flat arms, pedestal base, 25.5" w, 40" h	5000	4000	7000	6000
Office Chair, leather back and seat, flat arms, swivel base, orig leather, 21" w	2000	1500	2500	2000
Office Chair, revolving, leather seat, 18" w, 35" h	800	600	1200	1000
Rocker, 2 slats, concave crest, 26" w, 33.25" h	500	400	600	450
Rocker, 3 slats, curved crest, flat arms, orig leather and tacks, 38.5" h	400	300	500	400
Rocker, 5 slats, corbels for arms, through tenons, 28" w, 38" h	400	300	500	400
Rocker, 11 spindled back, open arms w/ corbels under, uph seat, 26" w, 36" h	2000	1500	2500	2000
Rocker, #373, high spindled back, 7 spindles per side	1000	800	1500	1000
Rocker, V-back, 5 splats, corbels	400	300	500	400
Settle, #171, 6 legs	9000	7000	15,000	12,000
Sewing Rocker, 4 slats, leather seat fits into side stretcher, wide seat rail, 33" h	400	300	500	400
Sewing Table, #630, 26" h	2500	2000	3500	3000
Side Table, #649, 1 drawer	1500	1000	2000	1500
Sideboard, #814, 3 short drawers, 1 long drawer, 2 cupboard doors	6000	5000	10,000	7000
Sideboard, #817, plate rail, 70" w, 50" h	8000	6000	18,000	12,000
Wastebasket, #94, skeletal form	800	400	2500	2000

L. & J.G. Stickley

	REFINISHED		ORIG. FIN	
	L	UM	L	UM
Armchair, 4 splats, long corbels, exposed front tenons, 27" w, 44" h	$300	$200	$400	$300
Armchair, 6 splats in back, 6 splats each arm, corbels, cane seat insert, 28" w, 39.5" h	400	300	500	400
Armchair, #338, Onondaga Shop	2500	2000	3500	3000
Bookcase, 1 door, 16 panes, V-board back, keyed tenons, gal. top, 30" w, 55" h	4000	3000	6000	5000
Bookcase, 2 doors, 12 panes/door, keyed through tenons, gal. top, 49" w, 56.5" h	6000	4000	10,000	7000
Cellaret, 2 doors w/ copper strap work, copper tray, 32" w, 35.5" h	6000	5000	10,000	7000
Chair, 5 splats, arched side rail, leather seat, extended posts, 19.5" w, 36" h	500	400	600	450
Chest, 2 short drawers over 3 long drawers, arched backsplash and apron, paneled sides, 38" w, 40" h	1500	1000	2000	1500
Chiffonier, 2 doors, 4 graduated drawers, arched backsplash, paneled sides, splayed feet, 37" w, 50" h	1500	1000	2000	1500
China Closet, #729, strap hinges	8000	6000	20,000	15,000
China Closet, #719, Onondaga Shop, trapezoidal, 38.5" w, 65" h	10,000	8000	25,000	15,000
Cube Rocker, 4 back and side slats, slightly higher back, 28" w, 30" h	1000	800	1500	1000
Day Bed, canted posts, 4 splats, 30" w, 27.75" h	1500	1000	2000	1500
Desk, 1 drawer, slatted bookshelf sides, 44" w, 29" h	800	600	1200	800
Desk, slant front, fitted int., 2 drawers over 2 drawers, gal. top, 42" w, 42" h	800	600	1200	800
Dining Chairs, 3 slats, extended posts, 2 side stretchers, 1 front and back stretcher, 16.5" w, 35" h, set of 4	3000	2000	3500	2500

Bookcase, keyed through tenons, galleried, orig. finish, 30" w, 57" h, $5225 at auction. —Photo courtesy David Rago Auctions.

	REFINISHED		ORIG. FIN	
	L	UM	L	UM
Dining Chairs, 3 splats, rush seat, arched front and back stretchers, 36" w, set of 4	2500	2000	3500	3000
Dining Chairs, 3 splats, uph seats, double side stretchers, 36" h, set of 6	3000	2000	3500	2500
Dining Table, pedestal, 54" w	4000	3000	9000	6000
Footstool, orig leather top, stretchers, extended posts, 19" w, 18" h	500	400	600	450
Footstool, legs extend above tacked orig leather top, arched apron, 7 spindle sides, 18" w, 17" h	3000	2000	3500	2500
Library Table, #3790, Onondaga Shop, arched apron and medial stretcher, through tenons, 46" w, 29.25" h	4000	3000	6000	5000
Mantel Clock, #85	8000	6000	20,000	15,000
Morris Chair, 5 slats/ arm, long corbels w/ through tenons, spring cushion seat, 34" w, 39" h	1500	1000	2000	1500
Morris Chair, flat arms w/ 16 spindles, leather seat, 36" w, 39" h	2000	1500	2500	2000
Morris Chair, flat arms w/ 6 slats, wide seat rail, 26" w, 41" h	1500	1000	2000	1500
Morris Rocker, open arms, through tenons, leather back and seat, 24" w, 40" h	800	600	1200	800
Rocker, V-back, 5 splats, arched front and side rails	300	200	400	300
Settle, #362, drop arm	4000	3000	9000	6000
Sewing Rocker, 3 slats, leather seat, 16.5" w, 30.5" h	300	200	400	300
Tea Table, #577, circ. top, medial platform stretchers	1000	800	1500	1000

Bookcase, adjustable shelves, orig. finish, 28" w, 55" h, $1540 at auction. —Photo courtesy David Rago Auctions.

Lifetime

	REFINISHED		ORIG. FIN	
	L	UM	L	UM
Bookcase, 3 drawers over 2 doors, through tenons, 48" w, 55" h	$1000	$800	$1500	$1000
Cube Chair, 28" w, 32" h	800	600	1200	800
Desk, 1 drawer, 2 shelves/side, round pulls, 49" w, 29" h	1000	800	1500	1000
Desk, slant front, 1 drawer over 2 doors, extended posts, arched aprons through tenons	400	300	500	400
Dining Chairs, 3 splats, set of 5	800	600	1200	800
Morris Chair, corbels, post tenons, 28" w, 41" h	800	600	1200	1000

Limbert

Armchair, high back, 2 crest rails over 4 splats, exposed faceted leg tenons, 26" w, 40" h	$400	$300	$500	$400
Bed, #470	2000	1500	2500	2000
Bookcase, 1 door, 8 panes, 4 open shelves/side, cutouts on top, 33" w, 47.5" h	6000	5000	10,000	7000
Bureau, #487.5, 5 drawers, mirror	2200	1700	2750	2250
Liquor Cabinet, 2 doors, 1 drawer, full gal., amethyst glass-lined tray, 31" w, 39" h	2000	1500	2500	2000
China Cabinet, 1 door, 2 panes over 1, arched aprons, plate rack, copper hardware, 25" w, 60" h	3000	2000	3500	2500
Desk, 3 drawers w/ wood pulls, arched corbels, shelf w/ through tenons, 60" w, 29.5" h	3000	2000	3500	2500
Dining Chairs, splat cutouts in top rail, arched apron, 18" w, 37" h, set of 6	3000	2000	3500	2500
Footstool, leather top w/ tacks, extended posts, arched aprons, drawer, 18" w, 12.5" h	500	400	600	450
Hall Chair, #81, tall cutout back	4000	3000	5000	4000
Hall Chair, #79, leather and tacks	650	500	100	700
Magazine Stand, #304, inverted V stretchers, 2 slats/side	800	600	1200	800
Occasional Table, #142, circ top, 27" dia	2000	1500	2500	2000
Settle, #649, 14-slat back, drop arm, spade cutouts, 78" w	1500	1000	2000	1500

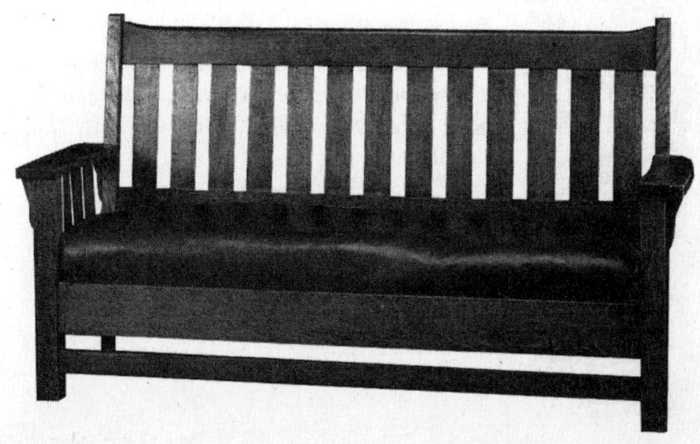

Settle, bowed crest, 13-splat back, replaced brown leather drop-in spring cushion seat, refinished, 74.5" w, $3575 at auction. —Photo courtesy David Rago Auctions.

Roycroft

	REFINISHED		ORIG. FIN	
	L	UM	L	UM
Bookshelf, 4 shelves, vert slats back and sides, 38.5" h	$3000	$2000	$3500	$2500
Bridal Chest, serpentine sides, keyed tenons centering lift top, copper straps, 36.5" w, 26" h	6000	5000	10,000	7000
Chair, #30	1200	900	1500	1200
Footstool, uph, rect., extended posts, 17.75" w, 15" h	500	400	600	450
Mirror, suspended by iron chains from support bar, sq mirror, 29" w, 33" h	1500	1000	2000	1500
Rocker, 4 splats, rounded arms, 31" w, 37" h	2000	1500	2500	2000

Shop of the Crafters

Liquor Cabinet, 2 glazed cupboard doors	$500	$300	$500	$450
Settle, even arm, inlaid	12,000	8000	17,000	14,000

Stickley Brothers

Armchair, high back, 4 splats, tapering feet, 27" w, 44" h	$400	$300	$500	$400
China Cabinet, 1 door, 3 over 2 panes, arched apron, through tenons, copper pulls, 49" w, 56.5" h	2000	1500	2500	2000
China Cabinet, 2 doors, 2 panes over 1 pane/door, arched stretcher, gal. top, 40" w, 54" h	3000	2000	3500	2500
Desk, bookshelf sides, 1 drawer, nickel-washed hardware, 38.5" w, 30" h	500	400	600	450
Dining Chairs, leather back and seat, set of 12	3750	2500	5000	4000
Dining Table, pedestal, 60" w	5775	4500	7000	6000
Footstool, 7 spindles/side, 20.5" w, 15" h	3000	2000	3500	2500
Gout Stool, orig leather drop-in top, through tenons, 12" w	400	300	500	400
Library Table, mortised lower shelf, 60" w	1800	1400	2300	1900

Revolving Bookcase, unknown maker, 4 open sides each fitted with 4 shelves, all within slat-form divisions, 4-legged base on casters, 69.625" h, 24.75" w, $1250.

Wallace Nutting

Wallace Nutting's legacy to collectors includes photographs, ironwares, furniture and an increased public awareness of American antiques. The reproductions of Early American furniture are now seriously collected in their own right, occasionally rising to values over and above some examples of the eighteenth-century originals that they copy.

Nutting's catalog numbers are given in parentheses. When more than one number is given, they refer to two different, but very similar, items with similar values.

	AUCTION	RETAIL	
		Low	High
Armchair, Chip., ribbon back (459-B)	$500	$1100	$1600
Armchair, Federal (438)	940	2000	3000
Armchair, ladderback (490, 492)	900	2000	3250
Armchair, Pilgrim (480, 493)	1000	2100	3700
Armchair, Windsor, bow back (408)	1000	2200	3500
Armchair, Windsor, comb back (415)	1200	2500	3400
Armchair, Windsor, continuous arm (401)	1100	2500	4200
Armchair, Windsor, writing arm (451)	1940	4000	7000
Bed, arched tester, turned feet, 68" h (846-B)	1200	2500	4600
Bed, carved mahogany (826-B)	700	1400	2000
Bed, Federal, tester (832)	2850	6000	10,000
Bed, low urn post (809)	570	1000	2000
Bed, Sheraton, 4-post (846)	2000	4200	7000
Bed, tester, Marlborough feet, 82" h (832-B)	1200	2500	4600
Bookcase Cupboard (927)	2000	4200	6000
Brewster Chair (411)	1440	3000	5000
Candlestand, Federal (644)	1100	2000	3500
Candlestand, turned standard, cross base, 14" dia, 25" h (22)	300	700	1000
Candlestand, Windsor legs, 14" dia, 25" h (17)	300	700	1000
Chair, banister back, carved crest and rush seat, Spanish feet (380)	200	500	700
Chair, Chip., ribbon back (359-B)	300	700	900
Chair, Dutch (361)	690	1400	2800
Chair, Federal (338)	600	1200	2700
Chair, ladderback (374, 290, 392)	330	700	1100
Chair, Pilgrim (393)	200	500	900
Chair, Q.A., shell-carved (399)	700	1500	2200
Chair, Windsor, brace back (301)	400	900	1300
Chair, Windsor, comb/brace back (333)	800	1500	2500
Chest (909, 913, 918, 931)	2500	6000	10,000
Chest, Gottard Townsend-style, 3-shell block front, 39.5" w, 34.75" h (979)	3000	5500	10,000
Corner Chair (430)	650	1400	2000
Day Bed (838)	2160	4500	7600
Desk, Chip., slant front (701)	4500	8000	14,000
Desk, slant front, 3-shell int., 36" w, 49" h (729)	1800	3500	6000
Drop-Leaf Table, butterfly leaves, single drawer (624)	400	1000	1500
Gate-Leg Table (621)	1250	2300	3400
Hat Rack (40)	400	700	1400
Highboy, Chip., broken swan's neck pediment, 39.5" w, 85.5" h (989)	4000	7000	12,000
Library Table (637)	1060	2300	4100

	AUCTION	RETAIL	
		Low	High
Looking Glass, Chip., giltwood, 53" h	1000	1800	3200
Office Chair, Windsor, brace back, swivel (329)	400	900	1300
Refectory Table (601)	980	2300	3300
Secretary, Chip. (729)	9000	15,000	27,000
Settee, low back, Windsor turned legs, 87" l (533)	700	1500	2200
Settle, pine (416)	540	1200	2000
Settle, wainscot, 3-panel, scroll arms, 57" l (589)	500	1200	1600
Slipper Chair, Windsor (349)	660	1450	2500
Sofa, Chip., straight back (525)	1500	3000	5000
Spoon Rack (903)	310	700	100
Stand, Federal (608)	700	1500	2600
Stand, Windsor base, 28" dia, 18" h (605)	1000	2100	3700
Stool (101, 102, 110)	200	500	770
Stool, Gothic (292)	220	550	850
Stool, joined (165)	930	2200	3400
Stool, W. & M. (166, 169)	350	800	1400
Sunflower Chest, lidded, 2 drawers, 48" w, 40.5" h (931)	1500	3500	5500
Table, W. & M. (653)	920	220	3500
Tavern Table, ball-turned, 36" w, 30" h (613)	800	1500	2500
Tavern Table, block-and-ring-turned, 36" w, 27" h (660)	1200	2500	500
Tea Table, Chip., piecrust tilt-top, 33" dia, 27.5" h (693-B)	1800	3500	6000
Trestle Table (610)	1200	2700	5500
Trestle Table, block-and-ring turned, 50" w, 30" h (615)	600	1400	2500
Tuckaway Table (616)	400	900	1300
Welsh Dresser (922)	2700	6000	9000
Wing Chair, Chip. (466)	2500	5500	8000

Banquet Table, Hpwt., mah., 3 part (670), $4125 at auction. —Photo courtesy Michael Ivankovich Antiques.

Wicker

Wicker is the general term for pieces made of woven rattan, cane, dried grasses, willow, reed, or related material. The wicker heyday in the United States was from about 1860 to 1930. Cyrus Wakefield and the Heywood Brothers were the best known wicker manufacturers. They later joined to become the Heywood-Wakefield Company. Other companies include American Rattan Company and Paine's Manufacturing Company.

While nineteenth-century wicker is more valuable, pieces from the 1920s and 1930s are also desirable and easier to find. Natural finish wicker is preferred to painted pieces.

Values quoted are for mid nineteenth century (M–19), painted mid nineteenth century (PM–19), late nineteenth century (L–19), painted late nineteenth century (PL–19), early twentieth century (E–20), painted early twentieth century (PE–20), machine made (M), and painted machine made (PM). Pieces described as ornate have features such as spooling, rolled arms and backs, unusual shapes, weaving between legs, etc. ("Upholstered" is abbreviated as "uph.")

	M–19	PM–19	L–19	PL–19	E–20	PE–20	M	PM
Armchair, ornate	$600	$350	$550	$350	$450	$350	—	—
Armchair, plain	360	210	350	250	270	200	$200	$150
Baby Carriage	770	460	670	440	520	410	460	400
Bassinet, all wicker	—	—	350	230	300	200	—	—
Birdcage	—	—	250	160	200	125	80	50
Boudoir Chair, w/ cushion	300	180	275	180	—	—	—	—
Bread Basket, open top	250	150	200	125	130	100	70	60
Buffet, all wicker, plain	1000	800	800	500	600	400	—	—
Buffet, ornate	1310	750	1100	750	—	—	—	—
Bustle Bench	600	350	580	380	—	—	—	—
Chair, spider caning	830	500	700	450	—	—	—	—
Chaise Lounge, ornate	1100	700	900	600	—	—	—	—
Chaise Lounge, plain	800	500	600	500	500	450	380	320
Chandelier	330	190	400	200	250	150	—	—
Child's Rocker	420	250	370	240	260	200	150	130
Child's Rocker, uph.	420	250	350	230	—	—	—	—
Coffee Table, glass top	—	—	—	—	230	180	150	130
Coffee Table, oak top	—	—	440	300	300	220	190	160
Corner Chair, ornate	1430	850	1300	750	—	—	—	—
Corner Chair, plain	1100	700	1000	600	—	—	—	—
Cornucopia	—	—	—	—	40	40	20	20
Crib	850	550	850	550	570	450	—	—
Crib, swinging frame	—	—	1000	680	850	650	—	—
Desk (2 or more drawers)	1100	850	1000	750	900	700	600	450
Desk, all wicker	950	600	700	500	560	440	460	400
Desk, oak top	860	510	750	500	600	450	—	—
Desk, w/ shelves	1100	760	950	700	780	610	500	400
Desk Accessories Stand	—	—	60	40	60	40	—	—
Desk Chair	150	90	120	80	100	75	—	—
Dining Chair	—	—	150	100	130	100	90	70
Dining Table	—	—	1250	900	730	570	—	—
Doll Carriage	300	180	300	190	210	160	90	70
Dresser	3400	2000	3000	2500	2600	2000	700	500
Dresser, w/ mirror	4000	2400	3700	2400	3000	2300	—	—
Easel, ornate	470	300	280	200	—	—	—	—
Easel, plain	220	150	200	130	—	—	—	—
End Table, ornate	770	460	500	400	300	230	—	—
End Table, plain	550	300	450	250	230	180	—	—

Ornate Rocker.

	M–19	PM–19	L–19	PL–19	E–20	PE–20	M	PM
Etagere, 4 shelves	350	230	280	220	170	130	160	140
Field Basket	150	90	130	90	120	80	90	60
Firewood Holder	270	160	220	135	80	60	—	—
Floor Lamp, no shade	200	160	180	120	—	—	—	—
Floor Lamp, plain shade	340	240	300	200	—	—	—	—
Floor Lamp, ornate shade	720	550	650	500	420	300	400	200
Flower Basket	150	80	120	80	90	70	60	50
Folding Stand	—	—	300	190	260	200	50	30
Footstool, uph.	—	—	200	130	160	120	50	30
Hamper	—	—	—	—	125	75	70	60
Highchair	510	300	530	340	310	240	230	190
Hourglass Chair	—	—	380	250	230	180	150	120
Knitting Basket	100	90	100	75	100	75	50	40
Library Table, all wicker	1000	800	850	600	520	400	270	220
Library Table, oak top	900	750	800	550	400	380	—	—
Lounge Chair	—	—	550	300	340	260	—	—
Loveseat, ornate	950	560	1170	760	800	600	—	—
Loveseat, plain	800	500	900	600	680	500	430	360
Loveseat, uph. seat	1000	700	1000	680	—	—	—	—
Magazine Rack	—	—	440	300	300	250	—	—
Magazine Stand	300	220	270	200	170	100	75	50
Music Cabinet	270	160	—	—	—	—	—	—
Music Stand	190	110	—	—	380	300	—	—
Ottoman	—	—	200	130	180	140	—	—
Photographer's Chair	1400	850	1300	700	—	—	—	—
Picnic Basket, hinged lid	190	110	180	100	140	100	70	40
Picture Frame, 30" h	210	120	190	100	150	80	—	—
Plant Stand	330	190	300	150	220	170	90	55
Plant Table, ornate	550	320	500	300	310	240	—	—
Plant Table, plain	360	210	300	200	160	120	—	—
Platform Rocker, ornate	500	300	550	350	400	300	—	—
Platform Rocker, plain	450	260	380	250	340	260	—	—
Rocker, ornate	740	500	750	500	500	300	180	150

	M–19	PM–19	L–19	PL–19	E–20	PE–20	M	PM
Rocker, plain	310	180	310	200	230	180	—	—
Rocker, uph., w/ pouch	450	260	450	300	360	280	—	—
Settee, ornate	1000	680	1000	680	700	400	—	—
Settee, plain	710	420	820	530	520	400	450	300
Sewing Basket, ornate	270	240	250	200	200	150	—	—
Sewing Basket, plain	190	120	170	100	140	100	—	—
Side Chair, ornate	890	530	800	500	400	200	—	—
Side Chair, plain	600	350	410	270	160	120	110	100
Slipper Chair	510	300	500	320	—	—	—	—
Smoking Stand, ornate	420	250	500	300	300	175	—	—
Smoking Stand, plain	300	180	350	250	200	100	—	—
Sofa, ornate	800	650	800	600	550	430	—	—
Sofa, plain	—	—	640	420	440	340	360	300
Stool, 3-leg	—	—	90	60	60	50	—	—
Stroller	—	—	580	380	500	300	—	—
Swing	—	—	730	480	470	360	—	—
Table, tilt-top	650	400	750	500	—	—	—	—
Table Lamp, no shade	360	200	300	200	170	90	50	40
Table Lamp, ornate shade	450	350	425	325	300	200	180	90
Table Lamp, plain shade	300	220	370	240	300	240	150	130
Teacart	—	—	580	380	550	430	—	—
Tete-a-Tete Chair	1670	990	1640	1000	1000	700	—	—
Tray, all wicker	100	60	90	50	75	60	45	30
Tray, glass bottom	—	—	—	—	60	50	30	20
Umbrella Stand	270	160	250	150	170	130	—	—
Vanity Bench	270	160	220	120	150	100	—	—
Victrola	—	—	—	—	1560	1220	—	—
Wheelchair	—	—	2000	1300	1500	1000	—	—
Wine Rack	—	—	—	—	60	50	50	40

Parlor Suite, armchair, side table, settee, rocker, and lamp, Lloyd Loom, 1928–32, 71.5″ w settee. —Photo courtesy David Rago Auctions.

Glass

Art Glass

Art glass developed to satisfy middle-class Victorians' love for trinkets. In the late nineteenth century more Americans had more money to spend on beautifying the home. The decades surrounding the turn of the century produced much of the finest glass. Many of the firms famous then are still in business today. Some still manufacture designs of sixty years ago.

For all practical purposes, glass cannot be restored. A chip may be ground down, but this alters the shape and thus the value. A crack cannot be painted the way a skilled porcelain restorer can hide a small defect in pottery or porcelain. Glass can be damaged by water if it is allowed to sit in a vase or bowl for weeks on end.

For futher information see *The Official Price Guide to Glassware, Second Edition* by Mark Pickvet, House of Collectibles, NY, 1998.

Amberina

	LOW	HIGH
Bowl, Inverted Thumbprint, bell shape, deep amber to cranberry red, 8" w	$175	$250
Bowl, Inverted Thumbprint, ruffled, 2.5" h, 4.5" w	600	775
Celery Vase, Inverted Thumbprint, sq. top, deep fuchsia red to honey amber, New England, 6" h, 3.25" w	150	300
Cruet, bulbous, applied amber handle, no stopper, 5.5" h	100	250
Cruet, Inverted Thumbprint, amber to rose w/ fuchsia highlights, matching underplate, 6.25" h, 7" dia plate	450	650
Cruet, Inverted Thumbprint, deep ruby to amber, applied amber handle, orig. cut amber stopper, 6.25" h, 4" w	150	300
Jack-in-the-Pulpit Vase, Swirl, deep ruby to amber, applied amber edge, 11" h	350	500
Jug, Swirl, applied reverse amber rope handle, 9" h, 5" w	350	500
Lily Vase, slight ribbing, New England, 10" h	225	400
Miniature Lamp Base, acorn shape, int. ribs, orig. burner, 6" h, 4.5" w	250	400
Pitcher, bulbous, honeycomb design, applied ribbed amber handle, 9" h, 6" w	125	300

Left: Amberina, toothpick holder.

Center: Argy-Rousseau, pate-de-verre lamp. — Photo courtesy Skinner, Inc., Boston, MA.

Right: Bohemian, water goblet.

	LOW	HIGH
Pitcher, Inverted Thumbprint, applied amber loop handle, pale cranberry to deep amber, 7" h, 6" w	100	200
Pitcher, Inverted Thumbprint, bulbous, applied amber reeded handle, 8" h, 6" w	100	250
Pitcher, Inverted Thumbprint, bulbous, applied amber reeded handle, 9" h, 7" w	175	275
Pitcher, Swirl, tankard form, squared handle, applied band of amber around body, ftd, 11.5" h, 5" w	350	500
Pitcher, tankard form, applied amber reeded handle, white enameled flowers, ranches, and butterfly dec., 10" h, 6" w	300	450
Syrup Pitcher, Inverted Thumbprint, deep ruby to honey amber, silver plated handle and lid, New England, 5.75" h, 3.5" w	1300	1500
Tumbler, Swirl, 3.75" h	25	75
Vase, Venetian Diamond, ruffled, deep brown amber on base, applied glass rigaree, 5" h, 5" w	400	500

Argy-Rousseau

	LOW	HIGH
Bowl, pate-de-verre, "Les Oiseaux," amber, circ. ft., dec. w/ band of cranes above flower petals radiating from center, molded signature, c1925, 10.5" dia	$4000	$6000
Butterfly Pendant, pate-de-verre, pierced glass square w/ blue, green, red-orange wings against colorless and gray ground, inscribed "GAR" in design, 2.125" h, 2.25" w	2500	5000
Vase, pate-de-verre, tapering cylindrical body w/ short neck, dec. w/ molded white forsythia, white ground w/ amethyst, amber, and green, imp. mold mark, 5.25" h	4000	6000
Vailleuse, pate-de-verre, ovoid form, tan dec., w/ blossoms separated by amethyst "V" designs, wrought iron base, topped by hand-wrought metal cap and knob finial, 8.5" h	5000	7000

Bohemian

	LOW	HIGH
Bowl, cobalt overlay, cut hobstars and fans, tapered sides, round, 3.5" h, 12" dia	$150	$220
Cake Plate, amethyst overlay, cut wave design, hobstars, and diamonds, notched and scalloped rim, 11.5" dia	100	150
Cologne Bottle, ruby red, frosting at center, medallion w/ etched scene of deer, w/ stopper, 7.5" h, 2.5" dia	350	520
Compote, green overlay, triangles w/ caning, thumbprints and sunburst design, notched and paneled shafts, 6" h, 7.5" dia	75	110
Decanter, cobalt w/ bull's-eye and fan cuts, paneled neck, clear stopper, 12.5" h	125	190
Dish, green overlay w/ 3 cut fans, ftd, round, 3.5" h, 8" dia	100	150
Vase, amethyst overlay, graduated cut panels, 10" h	65	100
Vase, cobalt overlay, trumpet form, graduated cut panels, 7" h	80	120

Bristol

	LOW	HIGH
Cologne Bottle, green satin finish, gilt reeded handles, 9.5" h, 3.5" dia	$130	$200
Jar, pink overlay, silver plated lid, handle, and base rim, white int., blue and white floral dec., enameled duck in flight, 5" h	120	180
Lustres, gilt blue glossy and satin finish, each w/ 8 crystal prisms, 10.5" h, 5" dia, pair	320	480
Vase, flattened oval, enamel bird and flowers, bug dec., 2.5" h, 4.5" dia	200	300
Vase, pink overlay, scalloped cut top w/ gold trim, blue, white, and orange enameled flowers, white heron in blue dot pattern, 15" h	200	300

Burmese

	LOW	HIGH
Bottle Vase, acid finish, salmon pink to yellow, white enameled mums and green foliage, Mt. Washington, 6.5" h, 3.5" dia	$350	$525
Bowl, Diamond Quilted w/ folded edge, pinched basket shape, glossy finish, paper label, Mt. Washington, 2.75" h, 6.5" l	450	680
Chalice, acid finish w/ deep color, ruffled rim, tall standard, c1920s, Pairpoint, 10.25" h, 6" w	350	500
Creamer, applied handle and pedestal base, satin finish, 4" h	350	520
Creamer, Diamond Quilted, glossy finish, Mt. Washington, 4.25" h	450	680
Cruet, acid finish, melon ribbed, Mt. Washington, 6.5" h	1200	1800
Cup and Saucer, matte finish, applied handle, 3" dia cup, 5" dia saucer	500	750
Juice Tumbler, matte finish, handled, Mt. Washington, 3.75" h	175	225
Lemonade Glass, matte finish, applied handle, 5" h	400	600
Lily Vase, matte finish, deep color, orig. paper label, Mt. Washington, 12.5" h	350	500
Lily Vase, matte finish, salmon pink shading to yellow, Mt. Washington, 7" h	165	250
Lily Vase, Queen's pattern, matte finish, Mt. Washington, 8" h	1700	2500
Muffineer, acid finish, white and colored dots form blossoms, attributed to Timothy Canty, Mt. Washington, 4.5" h	1000	1500
Mug, glossy finish, applied loop handle, Mt. Washington, 2.75" h, 3" w	275	400
Mustard Pot, shaded pale yellow ground to white w/ pink wild roses, handled, Mt. Washington, 2.75" h, 2.5" w	400	550
Perfume Bottle, matte finish, branches and pinecones dec., silver cap w/ monogram, 5" h	1200	1800
Punch Cup, matte finish, deep color, handled, Mt. Washington, 3" h, 3" w	200	300
Rose Bowl, satin finish, scalloped edge, 3 applied feet, 3.5"	325	500
Salt and Pepper Shakers, egg shaped, apple blossom dec, Mt. Washington, 2.75" h, pair	200	350
Stick Vase, acid finish, leaves and blueberries dec., gold accent stripe, 10" h	1400	2100
Sugar and Creamer, acid finish, no dec., Mt. Washington, 3.5" creamer	750	1120
Sugar Shaker, shaded ground in beige cream w/ pink flowers and green leaves, orig. top, Mt. Washington, 4.5" h	450	600
Toothpick Holder, acid finish, bulbous w/ sq. top, dec. w/ brown leaves and white and blue enameled flowers, 3" h, 2.5" dia	300	450

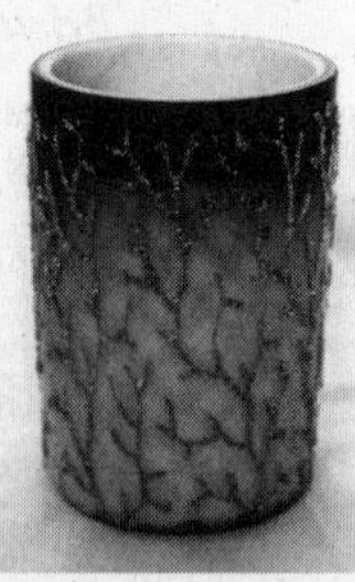

Left: Burmese, Mt. Washington lamp.

Center: Cameo, Muller vase.

Right: Coraline, seaweed pattern tumbler.

—Photos courtesy Skinner, Inc., Boston, MA.

	LOW	HIGH
Toothpick Holder, acid finish, sq. top, 2.5" h, 2.5" dia	200	300
Toothpick Holder, Diamond Quilted, matte finish, all-over enameled floral dec w/ sprays of blue flowers, Mt. Washington, 3" h, 3" w	500	650
Trumpet Vase, acid finish, Mt. Washington, 8" h	450	680
Tumbler, acid finish, 3.75" h	130	200
Tumbler, glossy finish, Mt. Washington, 3.75" h	275	350
Tumbler, satin finish, dec., w/ ivy leaves, gold rim, 3.75" h	400	600
Tumbler, matte finish, deep color, Mt. Washington, 3.75" h	115	185
Vase, fish-in-net, matte finish, blue and purple fish w/ gold, Mt. Washington, 8" h, 6" w	7000	8000
Vase, glossy finish, ruffled top, 3.5" h, 3" dia	220	340
Vase, satin finish, cylindrical, ftd, 9" h	700	1050
Vase, satin finish, pinched top, 3 applied feet and berry pontil, 7.25" h	1000	1500
Whiskey Tumbler, Diamond Quilted, acid finish, yellow edge, Mt. Washington, 2.5" h	250	380

Cameo

Gourd Vase, white over deep cranberry w/ Oriental poppy design, butterfly in flight on reverse, double band on top and base, English, 10" h, 4" w	$2750	$3500
Monumental Vase, frosted, pink, and green ground w/ overlay in shades of green, leaves, berries, and seed pods design, sgd Legras, French, 24" h, 7.5" w	2000	2750
Perfume, citron yellow and white w/ palm leaves, branches, and butterfly in flight, sgd Gorham silver cap, English, 10.5" l	1750	2500
Perfume, sapphire blue and white w/ carved flowers and buds, sgd Gorham silver cap, English, 8.5" l	1500	2000
Vase, 4 layer, opaque yellow over white over transparent yellow w/ deep red exterior layer, stylized rose design w/ morning glories, leaves, branches, poppies, and cut swags and bands, attributed to Thomas Webb & Sons, English, 9" h, 6" dia	6750	8000
Vase, apricot, blue, and frosted ground w/ deep amethyst over medium amethyst design of evergreen trees, mountains, and lake, sgd Muller, French, 12" h, 7" w	3,500	4500
Vase, blue, apricot, pink, and purple ground on frosted, deep amethyst exterior w/ landscape design, sgd "Muller Fres Luneville," French, 12.75" h, 4.5" w	2750	3500
Vase, citron yellow with white, 4 large ostrich plumes w/ carved details, triple border on neck, imp "Theodore B. Starr New York," 13.25" h, 8" w	6500	8200
Vase, deep amethyst on clear frosted and textured ground, poppies design, gold trim, sgd Burgun & Schverer, 7.5" h, 6" w	2000	2500

Cased

Bowl, amethyst, w/ painted butterfly, 7.5" dia	$200	$300
Lustres, white, cranberry banding, circ. medallions, painted flowers, pedestal bases, prisms, 12" h, pair	200	300
Perfume Bottle, dec. yellow, gilt clear ball stopper, applied jewels, 5.5" h, 2.5" dia	200	300
Rose Bowl, amethyst, applied flower and leaves, 3.5" h, 4" dia	300	450

Coraline

Bowl, amberina, box pleated top w/ coraline dec. of fish and pond lilies in white, green, yellow, and orange, one fish yellow, white, and red, other purple and white, gold line dec., sgd "Patent," 7.5" h, 8.5" w	$750	$1000
Jam Jar, MOP satin, blue ground w/ pink coral dec., silver plated cover, 5.75" h, 3" dia	100	200

	LOW	HIGH
Pitcher, orange, coraline beading w/ white and green water lilies and leaves, applied amber handle, 8.5" h, 4" dia	250	350
Vase, Diamond Quilted, pale blue MOP w/ seaweed dec. and coraline blossoms, applied jewel center, 7" h	500	700
Vase, ovoid cased tan body and white lining w/ diamond and fleur-de-lis pattern, coraline beaded dec, 4" h	300	350

Cranberry

Epergne, 4 horns w/ box pleated rims, 3 clear glass canes, ruffled large bowl, English, 21" h	$500	$800
Finger Lamp, applied crystal handle, #1 burner and chimney, 4.5" h	75	100
Lamp, Victorian portrait of young woman w/ blue bonnet, modern fittings, 12.25" h	200	300
Lamp Shade, hanging lamp, Hobnail, brass fixtures, electrified, 8.5" l, 8"	350	500
Pickle Castor, Inverted Thumbprint w/ enameled floral dec., New Haven Silver Plate Company holder, 10.75" h, 4.5" dia jar	450	500
Salt Shakers, figural beets w/ floral dec. and orig. covers, 3" h, pair	575	650
Sugar Shaker, diamond cut, 5.75" h	90	130
Vase, Herringbone, satin finish, 6" h	150	200
Water Set, Victorian, ruffled pitcher w/ applied handles, white, blue, and gold enamel dec., 6 matching tumblers, 11.75" h pitcher, 4" h tumblers	300	375

Crown Milano

Biscuit Jar, starfish and seaweed dec., white, red, and green jewels, Mt. Washington, 9" h, 7" dia	$900	$1000
Bride's Bowl, rect. and bulbous form, pink tracery ground of roses and pink, rose, blue, and white floral dec., sgd Pairpoint silver plated stand, Mt. Washington, 8" h, 9" dia bowl	1650	2000

Left to right: Cranberry, pickle castor. —Photo courtesy James. D. Julia; Crown Milano, vase; D'argental, cameo vase. —Photos courtesy Skinner, Inc., Boston, MA; Daum, vase w/ cameo and enamel design. —Photo courtesy James. D. Julia.

	LOW	HIGH
Cupid Vase, heavy gold dec., deep gold ground, loop handes, sgd, Mt. Washington, 9" h, 7" w	2500	3000
Jardiniere, beige to light brown shaded ground, multicolor oak leveas dec. w/ gold berries, sgd w/ monogram and #598, Mt. Washington, 6" h, 8.25" w	825	1000
Lamp, "Garden of Allah," round globe, Mt. Washington, 10" dia shade, 31" h	10,000	12,500
Pillow Ewer, lavender, cartouche w/ reclining woman and 2 sheep in landscape and floral dec. surrounded by gold leaf and berry wreath, sgd, #504, 10.5" h	3250	4000
Pitcher, beige ground, raised gold azalea blossoms dec., pale pink and gold scrolls around border, gold and pink traceries, Mt. Washington, 8.5" h, 7" w	1500	2500
Rose Jar, charcoal gray w/ multicolor floral bouquets, gold dec., diamond shaped signature, Mt. Washington, 11.5" h, 6.5" w	3500	5000
Vase, bulbous, floral dec and heavy gold scrolls, sgd, #589, Mt. Washington, 13.25" h, 4.5" w	1500	1800
Vase, ducks in flight dec., gold scrolls and floral design top and bottom, double handled, sgd, #518, Frank Guba, 11.25" h, 5.5" w	4500	5500
Vase, melon ribbed, gold daisies w/ jeweled centers, beige and green ground, sgd, #590, 13" h, 7.5" w	1100	1750
Vase, Venetian scene, white shaded to beige ground, scroll and floral cartouche w/ Venetian sailing ship in harbor, Mt. Washington, Frank Guba, 10.5" h, 8" w	5000	5500

D'argental

Bowl, swollen spherical, scalloped undulated rim, yellow ground, overlaid in maroon, cut w/ roses, sgd, c1900, 6" dia	$600	$900
Box, cov, shallow circ. shape, dark yellow ground, overlaid in brown and amber, cut w/ wildflowers, sgd, c1915, 3.5" dia	400	600
Vase, baluster shape, light yellow ground splashed w/ red, overlaid in red, cut landscape of lake, arched bridge, and trees, sgd, c1910, 13.5" h	2000	3000
Vale, baluster shape, turquoise ground, overlaid in dark blue, cut w/ flowers and leaves, sgd, c1900, 7" h	400	600
Vase, cameo, dark brown floral pattern, sgd, 14" h, 6" dia	650	1000
Vase, cameo, lime green ground, Oriental poppy design, 6.25" h, 3.5" w	9000	1000
Vase, cameo, pastoral scene w/ house, trees, and chateau in background, sgd, 6.5" h, 4.5" dia	480	720
Vase, cylindrical, orange-yellow ground, overlaid in red, floral cut, sgd, c1900, 11.5" h	700	1100

Daum

Bowl, mottled green, brown, and purple ground, rose, yellow, and green rose hips and leaves, sgd, 3" h, 6.25" w	$1800	$2200
Bowl, quatrefoil top, yellow and apricot shaded ground, red Oriental poppies, stems, and leaves, cameo cut leaf design, sgd, 2.5" h, 6" w	2000	2750
Box, cov., floral motifs, c1930, 6" dia	1200	1800
Lamp, yellow and apricot ground w/ black and brown boats in harbor design, ball shaped shade, sgd, 20" h, 6.5" dia shade	10,500	12,000
Open Salt, purple and white ground, violets dec., 1.5" h, 2" w	1500	1600
Pillow Vase, pale blue and white mottled ground w/ green harvest scene, sgd, 4.5" h, 7" w	6000	7000
Salt, bucket shaped, cameo and black enamel landscape design, gold trim, 1.75" h, 2" dia	1000	1200
Tumbler, yellow ground, fushia leaf and berry design, sgd, 4.75" h, 2.75" w	1650	1800
Vase, miniature, winter scene, sgd, 2" h	1100	1250
Vase, pale yellow, gold and green peacock feathering, 4" h	1400	2000

De Vez

	LOW	HIGH
Vase, acid finish, blue ground w/ mountain landscape scenes on 3 detailed acid cuttings, sgd, 11.5" h, 3.5" dia	$700	$1100
Vase, acid finish, shell pink ground w/ navy blue shaded to yellow shaded to pink in 3 acid cuttings, mountain scene, sgd, 6.5" h, 2.5" dia	630	940
Vase, bulbous body, long cylindrical neck, light pink ground, overlaid in yellow and blue, cut scene w/ squirrels and mountains, sgd, c1900, 13" h	100	1650
Vase, cylinder shape tapering toward neck, overlaid in lavender shading to pink, cut cartouches enclosing river landscape, sgd, c1900. 9.5" h	800	1200
Vase, cylinder w/ flaring rim and foot, yellow ground splashed w/ orange and green, cut river scene, sgd, c1910, 5.5" h	700	1050
Vase, elongated pear shape, short cylinder neck, yellow ground overlaid in dark blue, cut w/ river scene, sgd, c1910, 5.5" h	700	1050
Vase, pear shape, cylinder neck, flared rim, yellow ground, overlaid in orange and blue, cut river scene, sgd, c1910, 6" h	700	1000

Durand

	LOW	HIGH
Plate, flashed ruby w/ engraving by Charles Link, 8" dia	$325	$500
Vase, baluster, blue iridescent, amber iridescent foot, sgd, 14.5" h	450	680
Vase, brilliant blue w/ heart and vine dec., sgd "Emil Larson," 18.5" h, 8.5" w	6500	7500
Vase, compressed sphere base, cylinder neck expanding to trumpet shape, green ground, undulating bands in amber iridescence, sgd, 1905-30, 12" h	1800	2700
Vase, conical, iridescent gold leaf and vine design, flared rim, 7" h	350	520
Vase, cylindrical, scalloped rim, opalescent glass, dec., w/ hearts and vines, 11" h	1000	1500
Vase, orange-gold ground w/ green and white pulled feather design, random threading, sgd "Durand 17/10," 10.5" h, 9" w	1500	2000
Vase, ovoid, flaring neck, blue iridescent, sgd, 1905-25, 10.5" h	600	900

Gallé

	LOW	HIGH
Cup, miniature, handled, clear w/ rope handle, enameled black and brown dec w/ foliage and bug, sgd, 1.5" h, 2" w	$175	$200
Lamp, miniature, some shade, frosted, deep orange/apricot w/ 3 dragonflies, black rodiron base, sgd, 4.5" h, 2.25" dia shade	1000	1200
Shot Glass, amber w/ blue ribbons and gold banner with "parfait," sgd, 1.75" h	325	400
Vase, elongated cylindrical neck, pale gray ground, deep brown berries and leaves design, sgd with star, 10.5" h, 3" w	1000	1200
Vase, gourd shaped, flaring neck, orange ground, amethyst overlay w/ flowers and leaves, sgd, 5.25" h, 2.25" w	600	700
Vase, orange ground, deep burgundy leaf and berry design, 6" h, 3" w	700	850

Le Verre Francais

	LOW	HIGH
Vase, cameo, orange, red, and white ground colors w/ purple exterior cut layer, Art Deco grapes and vines design, 8" h, 6" w	$750	$900
Vase, cameo, trumpet form, mottled orange and yellow ground, cut bouquets in bright orange to deep purple, sgd, c1920, 18.5" h	400	600
Vase, compressed spherical tapering to trumpet-form neck, green ground overlaid in mottled orange, brown, and green, carved w/ flowers and w/ honeycomb pattern around base, c1920, 16.5" h	800	1200
Vase, spherical w/ cylinder neck, yellow ground, cut flowers and tendrils in blue and orange, sgd, c1925, 12" h	500	750

Left: Durand, vase w/ pulled feather and threading decoration. —Photo courtesy James. D. Julia.

Center: Gallé, vase. —Photo courtesy James. D. Julia.

Right: Le Verre Francais, cameo vase.

Loetz

	LOW	HIGH
Coupe, iridescent green ground w/ all over threaded web-like pattern, bronze base w/ drangonfly handles and pond lilies base, 9.5" h, 4.5" w	$650	$750
Shell, oyster white and clear shell w/ applied rigaree, pale pink base, all over webbing, 5.5" h, 8" l	300	450
Vase, clear ground w/ all over textured design and 3 applied iridescent gold kisses, 5.5" h, 2.75" w	200	300
Vase, cobalt blue iridescent, 4.5" h, 6.5" w	500	600
Vase, cylindrical, pale gold iridescent w/ purple highlights, 7.5" h, 3" w	150	200
Vase, deep brown w/ all over gold octopus dec and gold scroll border, sgd "Pat 9159," 10.5" h, 5" w	1200	1400
Vase, emerald green w/ blue iridescent and bark-like finish, ruffled top, 9" h, 4" w	350	750
Vase, gold w/ all over blue raindrop pattern, sgd w/ cross arrow marks and "Austria," 9" h, 6" w	400	600
Vase, green, purple, and gold iridescent w/ bark-like design, 8-point top, 5.5" h, 3" w	300	375
Vase, jack-in-the-pulpit, iridescent textured ground w/ blue and purple highlights, 5.75" h, 5.5" w	200	300
Vase, purple and rose iridescent, 6.75" h, 4" w	500	750
Vase, red ground w/ purple and gold iridescence, 2 applied double loop handles, 8" h, 3.5" w	275	350
Vase, yellow w/ cranberry and white dec., all over oil spot pattern, 9.5" h, 4.5" w	350	450

Mary Gregory

	LOW	HIGH
Bowl, cranberry, 5" dia	$75	$100
Box, emerald green, puffy shape, lift-off lid, white enamel girl, 3" h, 3.75" dia	1250	1800
Box, lime green, hinged lid, white enamel boy, 1.5" h, 2.5" dia	150	220
Box, sapphire blue, round, hinged lid, white enamel girl, 2.75" h, 3.5" dia	160	240
Cup, cranberry, handled, 3.25" h	75	100
Decanter, cranberry, white enamel girl w/ bouquet, clear bubble stopper, 9" h, 3.5" dia	175	260
Patch Box, green, round, hinged lid, white enamel girl, 1.5" h, 2.5" dia	150	220
Plate, cobalt blue, white enamel girl w/ butterfly net, ormolu compote stand, 3 rings hand from holder, 6.5" dia	150	220

	LOW	HIGH
Tumbler, cranberry, white enamel girl, 4.5" h, 2.5" dia	.75	110
Vase, blue, fluted top, 8" h	.60	90
Vase, cranberry, 5.5" h	.75	100
Vase, cranberry, white enamel boy w/ hat, 7.5" h	.125	200
Vase, sapphire blue, scalloped top, white enamel boy w/ goblet, plated brass base w/ woman's head handles, 14.5" h, 3.5" dia	.250	380
Water Glass, cranberry, 4.5" h	.100	150
Water Set, cranberry, white enameled girl w/ spray of leaves, applied clear reeded handle on pitcher, 4 matching tumblers, 2 w/ boys, 2 w/ girls, 9.75" h pitcher, 4" h tumblers	.400	500

Moser

Bride's Bowl, Swirl over Zipper pattern, deep brown shading to tan, pink int., sq. cut top, silver plated holder, 13.5" h, 12.5" w, 7.5" dia bowl	.$1650	$2000
Decanter, clear to green, orig. stopper, sgd, 8" h	.200	275
Juice Glass, cranberry, polychrome and gilt enamel leaves and acorns, 4" h	.150	225
Perfume Bottle, dec. w/ Egyptian man w/ headdress and staff, hieroglyphics on back, sgd, 11" h, 1.75" w	.750	1000
Pitcher, cylindrical, cranberry, enameled interlocking diamonds w/ pineapple and floral designs, wide gold enameled border, clear applied handles, 11" h, 5" w	.2500	3000
Service Plate, deep ruby w/ white center and border of heavily cut ducks in flight in cameo, gold monogram, 11" dia	.125	200
Vase, opalescent pink to clear, crimped handles burnished w/ gold, gilt polychrome enameled parrot and foliage in relief, sgd, 7.5" h	.900	1300
Vase, sapphire blue ground, brown, maroon, and black dec of 2 raised fish, sea plants and flowers, and insect, 8.5" h, 5" w	.250	400

Left to right: Loetz, green iridescent bowl; Mary Gregory, butter dish. —Photo courtesy Gene Harris Antique Auction Center, Inc.; Opalescent, epergne, blue.

Mother-of-Pearl Satin

	LOW	HIGH
Beverage Set, Diamond Quilted, pitcher and 6 tumblers, ruffled top, deep rose shading to white, white lining, applied camphor handle, 8" h pitcher, 4" h tumblers	$550	$800
Castor Set, Diamond Quilted, 2 apricot to pink shaded cruets w/ thorn handles and orig. thorn stoppers, Mt. Washington, sgd silver plated Webster holder, 9.75" h	700	1200
Cruet, Diamond Quilted, trefoil top, deep raspberry shading to pink, applied loop handle, replaced frosted stopper, 6.25" h, 4" w	225	300
Cruet, shaded yellow to white, applied frosted handle, replaced stopper, 7.5" h, 4" w	275	350
Ewer, Herringbone, ruffled top, applied frosted handle, pink, yellow, and blue, 8.5" h, 4" w	200	300
Fairy Lamp, Swirl, solid deep rose, 5" h, 4.25" dia	1100	1250
Lamp Sahde, Diamond Quilted, ruffled, medium pink shaded, white lining, 4.25" h, 2.25" fitter	200	250
Mug, Zipper, medium yellow, white lining, applied frosted handle, 3.75" h	150	200
Mustard Pot, Coin Spot, deep rose shading to pink to white, orig. silver plated hardware, 4.5" h, 2.5" w	300	400
Sweetmeat Holder, Flower and Acorn, blue w/ pink coraline seaweed dec., orig. silver plated hardware, English, 6" h, 5" w	550	800
Toothpick Holder, Herringbone, pink shaded, silver plated holder sgd "Aurora," 4.75" h, 2" w	750	900
Vase, Diamond Quilted, ruffled rim, applied camphor frosted edge, deep rose shading to pink to white, Mt. Washington, 9.5" h, 6" w	220	350
Vase, Dotted Swiss, melon ribbed, blue shading to pale bluish-white, Mt. Washington, 7.5" h, 5" w	275	350
Vase, Drapery, yellow w/ applied frosted edge, white lining, 8" h, 5" w	220	300
Vase, Flower and Acorn, pouch shape w/ pinched-in sides, purple and lavender, white lining, 8" h, 6.5" w	1200	1500
Vase, Herringbone variation, gourd shape, deep gold over red, white lining, 11.75" h, 4.5" w	250	400
Water Pitcher, Coin Spot, deep rose shading to pink, applied frosted loop handle, white lining, 9" h, 6" w	450	500

Opalescent

	LOW	HIGH
Bowl, Diamond Quilted, light green shaded to pink, ruffled, pewter frame, 17.5" h, 11.5" dia	$350	$550
Bowl, flashed rainbow, fluted edge, enameled floral dec., 5" h	500	750
Fairy Lamp, amber swirl, pyramid shade, sgd Clarke base, 3.5" h, 3.5" dia	200	300
Fairy Lamp, pink and white frosted swirl dec., dome shape, ruffled, sgd Clarke candle cup, 5.5" h, 6" dia	750	1150
Tumbler, cranberry, 10-row hobnailed, 3.5" h, 2.5" dia	250	350
Tumbler, lavender, 8-row hobnailed, 3.5" h, 2.5" dia	225	350
Tumber, peach, dec. w/ white flowers w/ gold leaves and centers, 4" h, 2.5" dia	150	225
Vase, jack-in-the-pulpit, fluted w/ purple edge, 7" h, 4" dia	150	225
Water Set, pitcher and 6 tumblers, deep cranberry w/ white opal polka dots, ruffled rim, applied clear handle, 9" h pitcher, 3.75" h tumblers	385	450

Orrefors, centerbowl w/ frosted leopards and dark blue base. —Photo courtesy Skinner, Inc., Boston, MA.

Orrefors

	LOW	HIGH
Bottle Vase, oval colorless body, internal dec. of alternating vertical aubergine and clear bubble stripes, sgd, Ariel, 7.325" h	$325	$500
Bowl, thick walled, colorless, internal dec. of evenly spaced cobalt blue alternating w/ amber bubble stripes, sgd, Ariel, 7.25" dia	750	1000
Center Bowl, cut and faceted paneled sides w/ frosted leopards, applied dark blue disk base, sgd, Gunnar Cyren, 6" h, 8" dia	1375	1500
Decanter, sq. crystal bottle w/ engraved Romeo and Juliet, sgd, 12.5" h	350	500
Portrait Vase, cylindrical, heavy walled colorless body, internal cobalt blue and amber air trap dec. of boat and gondolier w/ guitar serenading woman, sgd, Ariel, 1974, 6.125" h	5200	5500
Tumbler, pink w/ white and yellow enameled dec., 3.75" h	30	50
Vase, crystal, sq. form, engraved portrait of partially nude woman w/ arms raised, sgd, 1949, 9.5" h	500	700
Vase, heavy walled flattened oval form, colorless w/ internal aubergine-amber bubbles symmetrically arraigned in progression, sgd, Ariel, 5.5" h	1850	2500
Vase, heavy walled oval teardrop form, colorless w/ brown and green fish and plants, sgd, Graal, 1973, 6.75" h	800	950
Vase, swelled baluster body, flared rim, colorless cased to burgundy pink shading to blue, sgd "Orrefors Expo 2641 Nils Landberg," 11.5" h	300	400

Overlay

	LOW	HIGH
Finger Lamp, blue, shaded, emb design, clear reeded applied handle, 6" h, 4.5" dia	$235	$350
Finger Lamp, satin, lemon yellow, emb shell and leaf, frosted reeded applied handle, matching chimney, 5" h	250	380
Goblet, white on crystal, dainty multicolor floral dec, white cut to clear w/ some gold outline, Continental	240	360
Jar, covered, deep pink over white over clear, Sandwich cut ivy leaves and vines on top, and scroll-like cutting around base, morning glory cover, 6" h, 5.5" dia	550	750
Lamp, white cut to cranberry font, mounted on brass stem and double step marble base, 13.5" h	900	1100
Lamp, white cut to medium blue font, mounted on white milk glass base, gold dec. surrounding cut windows, 9.75" h	600	800

	LOW	HIGH
Rose Bowl, Diamond Quilted, rose satin cut velvet, 8-crimp top, white int., 3.5" h, 3.5" dia	280	420
Rose Bowl, fan shape w/ amber applied edging, hobnailed at top, 5.5" h, 9" dia	300	450
Tumbler, pink shade overlay w/ satin blue flowers and green leaves, gold trim, white int., 4.5" h, 3" dia	220	330
Vase, jack-in-the-pulpit, shaded green, clear applied ft, scalloped edges, 6.5" h	175	260
Vase, jack-in-the-pulpit, shaded maroon, white ground, ruffled edge, 7" h, 6.5" dia	200	300
Vases, white w/ enameled blue flowers, clear applied edge, ruffled top, pink int., ormolu-handled holder, 12.5" h, 7" dia	360	540

Peachblow

	LOW	HIGH
Gone With the Wind Lamp, electrified, Wheeling, 15.75" h	$5000	$7500
Lily Vase, matte finish, deep color, New England, 8.75" h, 3" w	400	600
Pilgrim Decanter, glossy finish, applied amber rope handle, orig. cut amber stopper, deep color, Wheeling, 9.5" h, 5.5" w	1650	2000
Pitcher, glossy finish, sq. mouth, applied amber handle, Wheeling, 5" h	650	800
Punch Cup, glossy finish, applied amber loop handle, Wheeling, 2.5" h, 3" w	125	200
Stick Vase, matte finish, bulbous base, deep color, Wheeling, 8.5" h, 3.5" w	1000	1200
Toothpick Holder, cylindrical w/ ruffled rim, 2.5" h	120	150
Tumbler, applied floral dec., Gunderson, 3.75" h	75	100
Vase, ovoid, matte finish, cherry red shading to peach, white lining, Stevens & Williams, 5" h, 3" w	120	200
Whimsy, glossy finish, pear, 5" h	60	100

Pomona

	LOW	HIGH
Beverage Set, first grind, tankard pitcher w/ double cornflower dec., 4 handled lemonades w/ single cornflower dec., 12" h pitcher, 5.5" h lemonades	$1500	$2000
Bowl, fluted, cornflower dec, 2" h, 5.25" dia	70	100
Cruet, first grind, amber staining, applied base, orig. stopper, 7.75" h, 3.75" w	225	350
Fingerbowl and Plate Set, second grind, ruffled fingerbowl w/ matching plate, cornflower pattern, 3" h, 7" dia	120	200
Juice Glass, first grind, delicate hobnailed int., tapered, 3.5" h	120	180
Lemonade Pitcher, first grind, cylindrical, blue-tinted cornflowers, 12" h	1200	1800
Pickle Castor, first grind, cornflower dec., Meriden silver plated holder w/ tongs, 11.5" h, 3.5" w	650	800

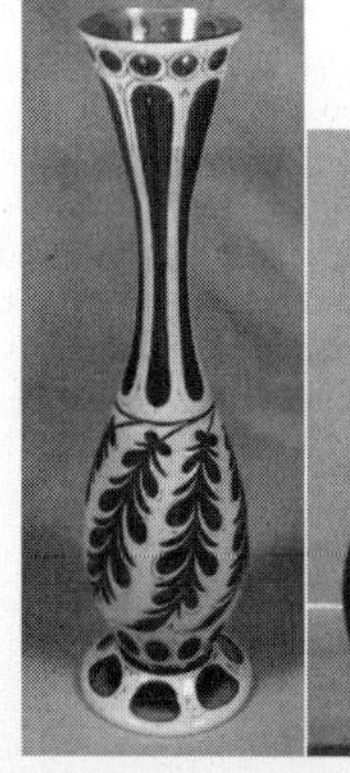

Left: Overlay, vase.

Center: Peachblow, pilgrim decanter, Wheeling. —Photo courtesy James D. Julia.

Right: Pomona, cornflower pitcher.

	LOW	HIGH
Pitcher, first grind, miniature, sq. top	150	220
Ramekin and Underplate, Blueberry pattern, 2.25" h, 4.5" w	100	175
Spooner, second grind, Inverted Thumbprint w/ red stemmed blueberry dec., crimped base, 5" h	150	220
Sugar and Creamer, first grind, ruffled applied wishbone feet, 4" h, 5" dia sugar, 6.5" dia creamer	225	300
Tumbler, first grind, spray of pansies and butterfly, 3.75" h	175	260
Tumbler, second grind, blue cornflower pattern, 3.5" h	250	380
Water Carafe, second grind, cornflower staining	225	340
Water Set, pitcher and 6 tumblers, first grind, 6.5" h pitcher	900	1350

Quezal

Dish, circ., iridescent, 2 ribbed handles, 1901-25, 5.5" dia	$250	$400
Lamp Shade, flower form, flared and scalloped rim, iridescent yellow, sgd, c1900, 5.5" h	300	450
Lamps, iridescent shades w/ white feathering on green w/ gold iridescence, baluster bases, 15.5" h, pair	1000	1200
Sweet Pea Vase, fluted, gold on oyster white w/ green and gold feathering, sgd, 7.75" h, 5" w	2200	2500
Table Lamp, vasiform, pink ground against oyster white w/ gold pulled and hooked feather dec., orig. metal base and fittings, 12.75" h, 6.5" w	1500	1700
Vase, elongated baluster form, domed foot, yellow w/ green feathering, amber iridescence, c1901-25, 19.5" h	2000	3000
Vase, gold iridescent top, green zigzag dec. and gold hooked feather on oyster white ground, 7" h, 3.25" w	2300	2500
Vase, jack-in-the-pulpit, oyster white top shading to green iridescent bottom, 9" h, 8" w	1700	2000
Vase, ovoid, vertical lobing, cylinder neck w/ flaring lip, opalescent ground w/ green and amber iridescent draping, 1901-25, 6.5" h	2500	3750

Satin

Bride's Bowl, Swirl, melon ribbed, gold ext., deep pink int., Meriden silver plated holder, 9.25" h, 11" w	$300	$500
Bride's Bowl, rainbow swirl in pink, yellow, and blue, deep ink int., applied frosted edge, star-shaped bowl, resilvered Victorian silver plated ftd figural holder w/ hummingbird in flight, 5" h, 12" w	1500	2000
Bride's Bowl, swirled melon design, deep rose shading to pink w/ enameled white and orange flowers, ornate sgd Meriden silver plated holder, 16" h, 17" w, 14.5" dia bowl	2400	3000
Cracker Jar, Florette, pink, silver plated cover and handle, 11" h, 6" dia	150	250
Garniture Set, bride's bowl and 2 vases, ftd melon ribbed vases w/ applied frosted thorn handles and camphor edge, deep ink shading to pale pink, sq. shaped bowl w/ petticoat edge and Webster silver plated holder, 11.75" h vases, 11" h bride's bowl	550	750
Miniature Lamp, Diamond Quilted, pink, applied frosted shell feet, 1920s, nutmeg burner, 9.5" h	700	800
Pitcher, Diamond Quilted, sq. form, deep raspberry pink over white, applied frosted loop handle, Mt. Washington, 5" h, 3" w	275	350
Vase, basket weave design, deep gold shading to yellow, turquoise lining, English, 5" h, 3.5" w	275	350
Vase, green shading to olive green, gold butterfly and floral dec., white lining, Webb, 10.5" h, 4" w	750	900

Spatter

	LOW	HIGH
Finger Lamp, peach w/ white and brown spatter, applied handle, matching chimney, 6.5" h, 4.5" dia	$130	$200
Jar, yellow, blue forget-me-nots, applied finial, 6.5" h, 3.5" dia	75	110
Tumbler, green and white emb swirl, 3.5" h, 2.5" dia	60	90
Vase, jack-in-the-pulpit, Diamond Quilted, ruffled, green, white, and peach, 9.5" h, 5.5" dia	80	120
Vase, jack-in-the-pulpit, Diamond Quilted, red and white, 8" h, 5" dia	75	100

Stevens & Williams

	LOW	HIGH
Fairy Lamp, satin finish, striped green and white, sgd Clarke, 5.5" h, 4" dia	$200	$300
Lamp, cranberry over yellow cut in daisy pattern w/ band of diamond point on top and bottom, allover hammered effect, orig. collar and socket, 3" h, 6" dia	900	1200
Plate, Pastil, blue, fleu-de-lis, sgd, 7.5" dia	40	60
Vase, Arbor, frosted cranberry w/ opaque white, frosted, reeded applied handles and pedestal foot, ruffled top, 6.5" h, 3.5" dia	140	200
Vase, clear crystal, double threaded, gourd form w/ cut flowers and leaves, 12.25" h, 5" w	400	500
Vase, Diamond Quilted, sapphire blue cased in purple w/ applied green leaves, stems, and yellow lemons, 4 applied green feet, 12.25" h, 8" w	1200	1500
Vase, green rib design, pinched floral form, 6" dia	35	50
Vase, pale cream w/ applied blue handles, rim, and 4 leaf-like feet, dec. w/ 3 strawberries w/ green leaves, amethyst stems, and applied white blossoms, 12.5" h, 11.5" w	1000	1500
Vase, pink shading to white ground cased in white w/ applied amber edge, dec. w/ branches w/ cherries and leaves and spray of dogwood in pink and white, applied amber handles and 3 thorn feet, 13.75" h, 7.5" w	550	800
Vase, Pompeian Swirl, satin finish, amberina w/ pink lining, 8.25" h, 4" w	225	400
Vase, Swirl, MOP satin, purple on black w/ gold fern and flower dec., 7.25" h, 6" w	875	1000
Vase, Swirl pattern, MOP satin, purple on black w/ gold fern and flower dec., 11" h, 6" w	3250	5000

Left: Quezal, trumpet vase.

Center: Satin, vase, Swirl pattern, English. —Photos courtesy Skinner, Inc., Boston, MA.

Right: Spatter, syrup, cranberry.

Left: Stevens & Williams, vase.

Center: Tiffany Studios, vase w/ pulled feather design.

Right: Webb, cameo glass scent bottle.

—Photos courtesy Skinner, Inc., Boston, MA.

Tiffany Studios

	LOW	HIGH
Cypriote Vase, golds, green, and blue, 4.5" h	$3000	$5000
Lamp, acorn, greens on Greek urn base, 16" dia shade	8000	12,000
Perfume Jar, cylindrical, wave design w/ glass handle, silver plated lid, 3" h	2000	3500
Trumpet Vase, favrille, oyster white w/ green pulled feather and gold iridescent leaves, glass sgd "L.C.T.," bronze holder sgd "Tiffany Studios New York," #1043, 14.75" h, 5.5" w	1500	2000

Webb

Curio Vase, matte finish, bulbous form, fold-over petal top, ivy dec., in green and teal, 3.75" h, 3" w	$250	$400
Curio Vase, matte finish, fuchsia dec., pale pink, patented petal top, sgd, 3.5" h, 3" w	250	450
Curio Vase, matte finish, prunus blossom dec., 3.5" h, 3" w	275	350
Curio Vase, petal top w/ enameled dec. of red flowers and green leaves, 3.75" h, 3" w	225	300
Curio Vase, ruffled, deep color, prunus blossom dec., 4.5" h, 2" w	250	350
Desert Set, Alexandrite, tree bark pattern, ruffled toothpick-like bowl and matching plate, 2.75" h, 5" dia	1000	1500
Ewer, cased, deep cranberry shading to creamy white w/ allover enameled design, applied cranberry handle, 11.25" h, 4" w	165	250
Fairy Lamp, Burmese, matte finish, 3 diamond point sgd Clarke's Cricklite bases on bronze holder w/ full figure frosted and clear dolphin standard, 17" h	1800	2500
Miniature Sugar and Creamer, deep color, currants and leaves dec., 2.75" h, 2.5" dia, pair	450	550
Nut Dish, petal top, matte finish, deep salmon pink shading to deep yellow, 2.25" h, 3.5" w	150	250
Rose Bowl, matte finish, prunus dec., ftd., 3.75" h, 2.5" w	375	500
Sugar and Creamer, matte finish, deep color, pinecone dec., 2.5" h, 3.5" dia bowl, pair	600	700
Tumbler, matte finish, grape and vine dec. w/ leaves, deep color, 3.75" h, 2.5" w	200	300
Vase, crystal, dec., w/ gold bird on branch w/ leaves and berries, Oriental style base w/ allover clear textured glass body in fish scale design, attributed to Jules Barbe, 9.75" h, 6.5" w	325	500
Wine Glass, Alexandrite, Honeycomb, citron to rose to blue, 4.75" h	1100	1500

Bottles

Bitters

	LOW	AVG.	HIGH
Bitters Pharmacy on label, clear, 4.5" h	$5	$10	$15
Celery & Chamomile on label, sq., amber, 10"	24	34	43
Compound Calisaya Bitters, tapered top, sq., amber, 9.5"	33	38	42
Dr. Boyce's Tonic, label, sample size, 12 panels, aqua, 4.5"	20	26	31
Dr. E. Chyder Stomach Bitters, N.C., amber, 10"	35	42	50
Fer-Kina Galeno on shoulder, beer-type bottle brown, 10.5"	21	27	33

Food

	LOW	AVG.	HIGH
Peppermint, marble in neck, aqua, 7.5"	$23	$25	$27
Planters Peanuts, same on back, sq., glass lid w/ peanut finial, clear	65	75	85
Red Snapper Sauce Co., Memphis, 6 sides, clear, 9.5"	19	25	30
Warsaw Pickle Co., aqua, 8.5"	14	18	22

Ginger Beer

	LOW	AVG.	HIGH
A. Goldstein, Rochester, NY, celebrated Ginger Beer	$34	$44	$55
Akron Ginger Beer Co., Akron, OH, English brewed Ginger Beer	15	20	25
Atlantic Bottling Works, Buffalo, New York, Ginger Beer, green glass	5	7	10
Barnum's, Niagara Falls, NY, brewed Ginger Beer	28	36	45
C. Baumgartner, McKeesport, PA, Ginger Beer	24	32	40
C.H. Boll, Albany, NY, incised	60	75	90
Cleverly's, Syracuse, NY, English brewed Ginger Beer	22	28	35
Dr. Browns, New York, NY, Ginger Pop, incised	35	38	40
Flanigan and Murphy, Syracuse, NY, brewed Ginger Beer	23	28	35
Friar's, Niagara Falls, NY, Ginger Beer bottled by A.C. Freir	28	36	45
Gardner's, Elmira, NY, Gardner's Old English style Ginger Beer	24	32	40
Henry Brown Co., Glendale, CA, Sierra Club Ginger Beer	20	30	40
J. Oliver, Savannah, GA, Ginger Pop, incised	35	45	60
J.C. Duffum, Pittsburgh, PA, Ginger Beer	45	58	70
Latter and Co., Seattle, WA, home brewed Ginger Beer	24	32	40

Bitters Bottles. —Photo courtesy Glass-Works Auctions.

	LOW	AVG.	HIGH
Louis Brass, Lancaster, NY, brewed Ginger Beer	24	32	40
Lucas Bros. Auburn, NY, English brewed Ginger Beer	15	20	25
McCoy and Dushnell, Watertown, NY	18	24	29
Niagara Bottling Co., Buffalo, NY, brewed F&M Ginger Beer	24	32	40
Painesville Mineral Springs Co., Painesville, OH	15	18	23
The Double Eagle Bottling Co., Cleveland, OH, painted label, brown glass	6	8	10
William Daft, Tonawanda, NY, brewed Ginger Beer	28	36	45

Ink

	LOW	AVG.	HIGH
135 emb. on bottom, aqua, round, c1800, 2.25" h	$8	$11	$13
210 emb. on bottom, light aqua, cone form, c1880, 3.25" h	10	13	16
Angus 7 Co., cone form, aqua, 3.5" h	10	13	16
Aqua, cone form, c1880, 2.5" h	14	19	23
Arnold's, round, clear or amethyst	15	19	23
Billing & Co., Banker's Writing Ink, aqua, 2" h	35	45	55
BIXBY emb. on bottom, aqua, cone form, c1880, 2.25" h	17	22	27
CARTER'S NO. 724 and *G-128* emb. on bottom, milk glass, round, 3" h	5	7	9
CARTERS 76 emb. on bottom, aqua, cone form, c1880, 2.5" h	17	22	26
CARTERS emb. on bottom, round shoulders, aqua, round, c1880, 2.5" h	16	22	28
Clear, cone form, c1900, 2.25" h	2	3	4
HIGGINS INKS BROOKLYN, N.Y. emb. on bottom, *3/4 OZ.* on shoulder, clear, round, 2" h	2	3	4
S & B, pottery bottle, tan, 7.5" h	16	18	22
STAFFORD'S INK emb. vertically on side of bottle, aqua, round, c1880, 3" h	21	28	34
T emb. on bottom, aqua, cone form, c1880, 2.5" h	10	14	17
WATERMAN'S INK 2 OZ. emb. around shoulder, *THIS CONTAINER MADE IN U.S.A.* emb. on bottom, clear, round, 2.5" h	3	4	4
X emb. on bottom, aqua, cone form, c1880, 2.5" h	10	14	17

Medicine

	LOW	AVG.	HIGH
ABSORBINE JR 4 FL OUNCES emb. on shoulder, *W.F. YOUNG INC. SPRINGFIELD, MASS.* emb. on bottom	$5	$6	$7
Anasarcin Diurectic Elixir, paper label	30	40	50
ANNA ELIZABETH WADE emb. on one side, *A.E.W.* emb. on bottom, *EAST ORANGE, N.J. U.S.A.* emb. on other side	5	7	9
BOYKIN & CARMER CO. DRUGGISTS BALTIMORE, MD. obverse	14	18	22
BROMO. SELTZER EMERSON DRUG CO. emb. upside down at base	9	12	15
CALDWELL'S SYRUP PEPSIN MFG BY PEPSIN SYRUP COMPANY MONTICELLO, ILLINOIS emb. obverse	9	12	15
CAPUDINE FOR HEADACHE emb. on front panel	6	8	10
CHAS. H. FLETCHER'S and *CASTORIA* on sides	5	6	7
CHESEBROUGH MANFG. CO. CD. NEW YORK emb. obverse	4	5	6
CREOMULSION FOR COUGHS DUE TO COLDS emb. obverse	7	9	11
DeWitts Eclectic Cure emb.	18	22	26
DOROTHY PERKINS emb. on both sides	6	8	10
Dr. Ballentine Cure for Whooping Cough NO. 40	25	30	35
Dr. Drakes Glessco Children's Coughs, paper label	25	30	35
DR. KING'S NEW DISCOVERY FOR COUGHS AND COLDS obverse	7	9	11
Dr. Koenig's Hamberg Drops, clear, paper label	25	30	35
DR. MILES MEDICAL CO. emb. obverse	7	9	11

	LOW	AVG.	HIGH
DR. PIERCE PROPR emb. obverse, *DR. SAGE'S* on left, *CATARRH REMEDY* verso, *BUFFALO* on right, aqua, rect., c1870s, 2.5"	267	30	36
DR. TURE'S ELIXIR EXTABLISHED 1851 DR. J.F. TRUE & CO. INC AUBURN, ME. emb. obverse panel	5	7	9
Dr. Vallentine Neurolgia Cure, No. 16, vial	25	30	35
DR. W.B. CALDWELL'S MONTICELLO, ILLINOIS emb. obverse	5	6	7
DR. W.B. CALDWELL'S SYRUP PEPSIN obverse, *PEPSIN SYRUP COMPANY* and *MONTICELLO ILLINOIS*	6	8	10
E. Merck & Co. Apiol Fluid Green, 1 oz., paper label	30	40	50
Fairchild Bros & Foster Enzymol, paper label	9	11	13
FORHAN'S emb. at base on 3 sides	5	6	7
Gardner-Barada Urinary Urisepetin, paper label	9	11	13
GILBERT BROS & CO and *BALTIMORE, MD* on sides	16	20	24
Golden State Liniment, B.F. Hewlett, paper label, clear, 5"	14	17	20
GREEVER, LOTSPEICH MFG CO KNOXVILLE, TENN U.S.A. obverse	10	14	18
HAMLIN'S emb. on right, *WIZARD OIL* emb. obverse, *CHICAGO* emb. on left, aqua, rect., 5.75"	12	15	18
HENRY K. WAMPOLE & COMPANY emb. on both sides	5	7	9
HOOD'S SARSAPARILLA emb. obverse, *LOWELL, MASS* on right, *APOTHECARIES* emb. verso, aqua, rect. c1880s, 9"	20	24	28
Husbans Calcined Magnesum emb.	9	12	15
James Baily & Son, wholesale druggists, Baltimore, MD, paper label	5	6	7
JUDSON B. TODD PHARMACIST ITHACA, N.Y. emb. obverse	25	30	35
KONJOLA MASBY MEDICINE CO. CINCINNATI U.S.A. obverse and *KONJOLA* on sides, male bust on obverse	6	8	10
L.M. GREEN and *WOODBURY, N.J.* on sides	5	7	9
LAVORIS emb. on shoulder and *LAVORIS CHEMICAL CO. MINNEAPOLIS, MINN* emb. on bottom	7	10	13
LEEF BROS DRUGGISTS BALTIMORE emb. obverse	14	20	24
LISTERINE emb. on shoulder and *LAMBERT PHARMACAL COMPANY* at base	5	6	7
LYSOL and measurement marks emb. on side	5	7	9
MARY J. GOLDMAN ST. PAUL MINN emb. obverse	14	18	22
MCELREE'S CARDUI and *THE CHATTANOOGA MEDICINE CO*	3	4	5
MILLER'S / HAYNES GENUINE / ARABIAN BALSAM / E. MARGAN & SONS / PROVIDENCE, R.I. emb. on 5 panels, aqua, 12 sides, c1880s, 4.25"	18	21	24
Mosso's Oil-O-Sol, paper label	8	10	12
Munyons Cough Remedy, vial, paper label	18	22	26
NATIONAL REMEDY COMPANY NEW YORK emb. obverse panel	6	9	12
Norwich Z-L Mouthwash Gargle, paper label	4	5	6
O.W. BRIDGES emb. on right, *LUNG TONIC* emb. obverse, aqua, rect., c1880s, 5"	18	21	24
OTIS CLAPP 7 SONS MALT AND COD LIVER OIL COMPOUND emb. obverse, light amber, rect., 7.5"	12	14	16
PEPTO, MANGAN (GUDE) CONTENTS IN FLUID OUNCES on panel	6	9	12
PHENIQUE CHEMICAL CO. ST. LOUIS MO. emb. on shoulder	2	3	4
PHILLIPS MILK OF MAGNESIA TRADE MARK REG'D IN U.S. PAT. OFFICE AUG. 21, 1906 emb. obverse	6	9	12
PINEX TRADE MARK emb. obverse panel	5	7	9
PISO'S TRADE MARK emb. on one side and *PISO CO. WARREN, PA., U.S.A.* emb. on sides	4	5	6
POLAR STAR COUGH CURE and star emb. obverse, aqua, rect., c1880s, 7"	10	12	14

	LOW	AVG.	HIGH
PURTUSSIN emb. on both sides	5	6	7
R.R.R. RADWAY & CO. NEW YORK obverse, *ENTD ACCORD TO* on left, *ACT OF CONGRESS* on right, aqua, rect., c1880s, 6.5"	13	15	17
R.W. POWERS & CO DRUGGISTS RICHMOND VA. obverse	18	21	24
RED SEA BALSAM / NEW BEDFORD, MASS. all emb. on 2 panels, aqua, 12 sides, c1880s, 4.5"	15	18	21
REV. N.H. DOWNS / VEGETABLE / BALSAMS / ELIXIR all emb. on 4 panels, aqua, 12 sides, 1860s, 4.5"	40	45	50
S.C. WELLS & CO. emb. on right, *SHILOH'S CONSUMPTION CURE* emb. obverse, *LEROY, N.Y.* emb. on left, clear, rect., c1880s, 5.75"	15	18	21
SCOTT'S EMULSION emb. obverse, *COD LIVER OIL* and *WITH LIME & SODA* on sides, aqua, rect., c1880s, 9.25"	18	20	22
SCOTT'S EMULSION TRADE MARK COD LIVER OIL WITH LIME & SODA and man carrying fish emb. obverse	5	6	7
SIMMONS LIVER REGULATOR emb. obverse, *J.H. ZEILIN & CO* emb. verso, *MACON GA* on left, *PHILADELPHIA* on right, aqua, rect., c1870s, 9"	30	40	50
SMITH & ATKINSON obverse panel, *DRUGGIST* and *BALTIMORE* on sides, aqua, rect., w/ panels, c1870s, 6.5"	30	40	50
Southern Pacific Lines Hospital Dept., paper label, clear	14	17	20
St. Joseph's Lax-Ana Tonic, paper label	20	30	40
Sterns Day Cream Liquid Astringent, milk glass, paper label	30	40	50
SYRUP OF BLACK DRAUGHT emb. obverse panel	9	12	15
TANLAC emb. on bottom	7	10	13
THE NAME ST. JOSEPH'S ASSURES PURITY emb. obverse	3	4	5
THE SAYMAN PRODUCTS ARE SUPREME obverse panel and *DR. T.M. SAYMAN* and *ST. LOUIS, MO.* on sides	5	7	9
THREE IN ONE emb. obverse and *3 IN ONE OIL CO* on sides	5	7	9
VASELINE CHESEBROUGH NEW-YORK TRADE MARK obverse	2	3	4
Vick's Va-tro-nol Nose Drops, w/ dropper	14	18	22
VICTOR INFANT'S RELIEF VICTOR REMEDIES CO FREDERICK, MD. emb. obverse, aqua, rect., 1800s, 5.5"	30	35	40
WATKINS TRIAL MARK emb. obverse panel	10	15	20
WHITEHURST emb. vertically obverse	4	5	6
WIZARD OIL obverse, *J.A. HAMLIN & BRO CHICAGO* verso, aqua, rect., w/ indented panels, c1870s, 7.25"	20	25	30

Left: Dr. Townsend's, Sarsaparilla, Albany, N.Y., $143 at auction.

Center: L.Q.C. Wishart's Pine Tree Tar Cordial, $165 at auction.

Right: Bowman's Drug Stores Poison, $253 at auction.

—Photos courtesy Glass-Works Auctions.

Mineral

	LOW	AVG.	HIGH
Mineral, UTE Chief of Mineral Water, U.T. on base, purple, 8"	$10	$16	$20
San Francisco Glass Works, tapered neck, blob top, green, 7"	25	35	45
Saratoga Spring, honey amber, 9.5"	50	70	90
Shasta Water Co., Mineral Water Co., 10.5"	12	18	25
Veronica Mineral Water on shoulder, sq., amber or clear, 10.25"	17	20	28
Weller Bottling Works, Saratoga, N.Y., blob top, aqua	17	23	30

Poison

	LOW	AVG.	HIGH
Baltimore, MD printed on bottom, amber, 3"	$7	$8	$9
DPS, skull and cross, cross on 4 sides, ring top, cobalt	18	22	26
Eli Lilly & Co., Poison printed on panels, amber, 2"	12	18	24
F.S. 7 Co. on base, *Poison* vertically, ring top, amber, 2.5"	15	25	35
R.C. Millings Bed Bug Poison, Charleston, clear, 6.5"	25	35	45
Rat Poison printed on bottle, round, clear or amethyst, 2.5"	35	45	55
Tincture Iodine printed under skull and crossbones, sq., amber	13	18	23
Triloids Poison, paper label, emb. cobalt	80	100	120
Triloids printed on 1 panel, *Poison* on another, cobalt, 3.5"	14	20	25
Wyeth Poison, round ring base and top, cobalt, 2.5"	15	25	30

Pontil

	LOW	AVG.	HIGH
Bake's Dr., printed, tapered top, pale aqua, 5"	$40	$60	$80
Balsam of Honey, printed, round bottle, ring top, aqua, 3"	40	50	60
Brown's, F., Ess. of Jamaica Ginger, Phila., oval, aqua, 5.5"	20	30	40
Cannington Shaw & Co., St. Helens, beading on shoulder	20	35	50
Cooke's Carmine Ink, printed, bell shape, ring top, aqua, 1.5"	30	35	40
Dolby's Criminate, printed, round, light ring top, 3.5"	40	50	60
Harrison's Columbia Ink, printed, round, ring top, cobalt, 4.5"	70	85	100
Hoover Phila., 12 panels, ring top, light green	40	50	60
Snuff, label, flare top, beveled corners, olive amber, 4.5"	25	35	45

Soda

	LOW	AVG.	HIGH
Chero, Cola emb. obverse and *Princeton W.Va.* verso, clear, swirl design, 7.5"	$7	$8	$9
Emmerling Products Co Johnstown, Pa. Registered Contents 7 Fluid Ounces emb. obverse, aqua, round, 8"	10	12	14
Hide's-Franklin Mineral Spring Ballston Spa, N.Y. Registered emb. obverse, clear, round, 8"	8	10	12
Keller Bottling Works Uniontown, Pa. Contents 8 Fluid Oz Registered emb. obverse, *This Bottle Not To Be Sold KBC* emb. verso, clear, round, c1890s, 7.75"	10	12	14
Phillips Bros Champion Bottling Works Trade Mark obverse, 2 men emb. obverse, aqua, round, c1890s, 7.75"	10	12	14
Savannah Consolidated Bottling Co Savannah Ga. and monogram emb. obverse, aqua, round, c1890s, 7.75"	15	20	25
Sun Crest Waynesboro Va., clear, round, 8.5"	5	6	7
Union Bottling Works Uniontown, PA. emb. in circle obverse, light green, round, 7.75"	8	10	12
Wm. O'Gryan Mechanicville, N.Y. Registered emb. obverse, *This Bottle Not To Be Sold* emb. verso, light green, round, 7.5"	8	10	12

Carnival Glass

The turn-of-the-century craze for iridescent art glass spawned the birth of Taffeta (or Carnival) glass in 1905. Using mass production and new chemical techniques, Carnival glass was widely produced toward the end of the Art Nouveau period. Tastes changed, however, ushering in the streamlined Art Deco period. Though produced until 1930, by 1925 Carnival glass was sold by the trainload to fairs and carnivals and given out as prizes (hence, the name Carnival glass). Since the 1970s, Carnival glass has become a desired collectible. For further information see *The Official Price Guide to Glassware* by Mark Pickvet, House of Collectibles, NY.

	GREEN	MARIGOLD	BLUE	AMETHYST
Bowl, Acorn, Fenton, 7"–8.5" dia	$30	$25	$30	$30
Bowl, Apple Blossom, Dugan, 7"–9" dia	42	37	42	42
Bowl, Chrysanthemum, Fenton, flat, 10" dia	50	35	50	—
Bowl, Chrysanthemum, Fenton, ftd, 10" dia	50	35	50	—
Bowl, Elks, Fenton, Detroit	330	—	330	—
Bowl, Elks, Fenton, Parkersburg	360	—	260	—
Candy Dish, Beaded Cable, Northwood	35	25	35	35
Plate, Acorn, Fenton, 9" dia	300	125	300	300
Plate, Apple Blossom, Dugan, 8.5" dia	70	48	70	70
Rose Bowl, Beaded Cable, Northwood	52	35	52	52
Tumbler, Banded Drape, Fenton	—	18	30	30
Water Pitcher, Banded Drape, Fenton	—	72	190	190

Carnival Glass Assortment.

Cut Glass

Cut glass features deep prismatic cutting in elaborate, often geometric designs. Developed during the sixteenth century in Bohemia, it remained popular until the invention of molded pressed glass in America about 1825. It enjoyed a revival during the Brilliant Period of cut glass in America from 1866–1916. The edges are sharp, refracting light clearly. It is thicker and heavier than most blown glass. Round shapes have a distinct bell tone when struck.

Making cut glass required patience and talent. Master craftsmen blew the finest 35%–45% lead crystal or poured it into molds producing a shaped piece called a blank. These blanks measured from .25" to .5" thick, necessary for the deep cutting which distinguished this glass from later periods. The resulting product was exceedingly heavy. Cutting and polishing required four steps. First, the desired pattern was drawn on the blank with crayons or paint. Next, the deepest cuts were made by rough cutting, pressing the blank on an abrasive cutting wheel lubricated by a stream of water and sand. In the third step, the rough cuts were smoothed with a finer stone wheel and water. Finally, the craftsman polished or "colored" the piece on a wooden wheel with putty powder or pumice to produce the gleaming finish.

The prices here are for American cut glass made between 1880 and 1920. They represent an average range for the forms listed. Prices for some highly collected makers (e.g. Libbey and Hawkes) may go for much higher, depending on the piece. For further information see *The Official Price Guide to Glassware, Second Edition* by Mark Pickvet, House of Collectibles, NY, 1998.

	LOW	AVG.	HIGH
Basket, handled, 10"	$430	$455	$480
Bell	120	180	240
Bonbon, diamond shape, 6"	120	160	200
Bonbon, covered, 4.5"–5.5"	160	200	240
Bowl, 9"	110	185	260
Carafe, 10"	120	170	220
Celery, upright	60	80	100
Celery Tray	80	145	210
Champagne Glass	40	60	80
Cheese Dish, covered	320	400	480
Claret Glass	50	75	100
Cologne Bottle, w/ stopper, 6"	60	150	240
Comport, 7"	80	120	160
Comport, 10"	140	200	260
Cordial Glass	50	55	60
Creamer and Sugar	120	165	210
Cruet, 6"	60	95	130
Decanter, 1 pt.	160	200	240
Decanter, handled, 1 pt	200	240	280
Decanter, 1 qt.	400	600	800
Decanter, handled, 1 qt.	600	800	1000
Dish, 4 section, 9"	160	200	240
Dish, 7"–8"	60	110	160
Dish, shell form, 6"	160	200	240
Dish, sq., 8"	120	160	200
Finger Bowl	30	40	50
Fruit Bowl, 8"	80	120	160
Goblet	50	70	90
Ice Cream Dish, 6"	220	270	320
Ice Cream Platter, oval, 13.5"	170	260	350
Inkwell, crystal	40	60	80

	LOW	AVG.	HIGH
Knife Rest, ball ends	40	50	60
Lamp, mushroom shade, 18"	600	800	1000
Lamp Base, 17"	480	600	720
Lemonade Mug	50	55	60
Nappy, 5"	50	65	80
Nappy, 8"	120	155	190
Nappy, handled, 5"	60	80	100
Pitcher, 1 pt.	120	155	190
Pitcher, 1 qt. or 3 pt.	140	190	240
Pitcher, 2 qt.	160	240	320
Powder Jar, covered, 4.5"–5.5"	120	160	200
Powder Puff Box, covered, 4.5"–5.5"	80	100	120
Punch Bowl, 1 piece, 12"	290	505	720
Punch Bowl, 2 part, pedestal base, 14"–15"	1200	1500	2000
Relish Dish, 7"	80	120	160
Salt, open, 2.5"	30	40	50
Shaker	80	120	160
Tobacco Jar, sterling top, 7"	160	200	240
Water Glass	40	50	60
Whiskey Jug, w/ stopper	280	340	400
Vase, 14"	125	175	250
Vase, 18"	150	225	300

Cut Glass Assortment.

Depression Glass

Colored glassware was machine-made during the late 1920s and early 1930s. The glass was available in 10¢ stores, given away at filling stations and theaters and used for promotional purposes. There are over eighty Depression glass clubs that sponsor shows, with attendance in the thousands.

For more information on Depression glass see Mark Pickvet's *The Official Price Guide to Glassware, Second Edition,* House of Collectibles, NY, 1998 and Gene Florence's *Collector's Encyclopedia of Depression Glass, Thirteenth Edition,* Collector Books, Paducah, KY, 1998.

American Sweetheart

	PINK	WHITE	RED	BLUE	CREMAX
Bowl, 6"	$16	$15	$250	$320	$15
Bowl, 9"	28	55	300	355	58
Bowl, 18"	—	400	1100	1270	—
Chop Plate, 11"	18	15	—	—	—
Creamer/Sugar	25	10	195	242	226
Cup/Saucer	17	15	135	173	—
Pitcher, 2 qt.	700	—	—	—	—
Pitcher, 6"–7"	3	5	—	25	—
Pitcher, 8"	12	11	70	115	—
Pitcher, 9"–10"	20	10	110	155	—
Platter, round, 12"	15	15	200	220	—
Platter, oval, 13"	30	50	—	—	—
Salt/Pepper, ftd., pair	400	340	—	—	—
Server, 15.5"	—	250	370	520	—
Server, 3 tier	—	260	740	840	—
Sherbet, ftd., 4"	15	23	—	—	—
Soup Bowl, 4.5"	43	50	—	—	—
Soup Plate, 7.5"	65	—	—	—	—
Soup Plate, 9.5"	50	60	—	—	—
Tumbler, 5–9 oz., 3"–4"	61	—	—	—	—
Tumbler, 10 oz., 4.5"	90	—	—	—	—
Vegetable, oval, 11"	45	50	—	—	—

Block Optic

	GREEN	YELLOW	PINK
Bowl, 4"–5"	$10	$20	$10
Bowl, 7"–9"	22	30	17
Butter Dish, cov	66	75	—
Butter Tub, open	40	60	—
Candlesticks, low, pair	60	70	—
Candy Jar, cov	50	68	56
Comport, 4" w	20	40	—
Creamer/Sugar	31	32	27
Cup/Saucer	21	23	16
Goblet, 9 oz.	27	38	21
Grill Plate, 9"	10	23	17
Ice Bucket	40	50	—
Mug	45	—	—

	GREEN	YELLOW	PINK
Pitcher, 2 qt., 7"–8"	.70	80	—
Pitcher, 3 qt., 8.5"	.45	47	—
Plate, 6"	.2	3	2
Plate, 8"	.5	7	5
Plate, 9"–10"	.21	46	27
Salt/Pepper, pair	.43	95	85
Server, center handle	.61	65	—
Sherbet, 3"–5"	.11	15	10
Tumbler, 5–10 oz.	.21	25	25
Wine Glass, 4.5"	.27	21	—

Bubble, Bull's Eye, Provincial

	CRYSTAL	DK. GREEN	LT. BLUE	DK. RED
Bowl, 4"–5"	.$5	$5	$12	$7
Bowl, 8"–9"	.8	8	15	—
Creamer/Sugar	.6	6	50	—
Cup/Saucer	.3	3	6	10
Grill Plate, 9.5"	.—	—	6	10
Pitcher, cov, 2 qt.	.65	—	—	—
Plate, 6.75"	.2	2	5	—
Plate, 9.5"	.5	5	7	10
Platter, oval, 12"	.8	8	16	—
Server, 2 tier	.10	10	—	—
Soup Plate, 7.75"	.6	6	13	—
Tumbler, 6–12 oz.	.10	10	—	12
Tumbler, 16 oz.	.12	12	—	25

Cameo, Dancing Girl, Ballerina

	GREEN	YELLOW	PINK	CRYSTAL
Bowl, 7"–8"	.$45	—	$180	—
Bowl, 3 ftd., 11"	.65	$100	35	—
Butter, open, 3" h	.175	—	680	$280
Butter Dish, cov	.225	1000	—	—
Cake Plate, 3 ftd., 10"	.22	—	—	—
Cake Plate, flat, 10.5"	.125	—	—	—
Candlesticks, pair, 4"	.100	—	—	—
Candy Jar, cov	.100	82	600	—
Cereal Bowl, 5.5"	.38	36	—	10
Comport, 5" w	.20	—	252	—
Cookie Jar, cov	.63	—	—	—
Cream Soup Bowl, 4.75"	.70	—	—	—
Creamer/Sugar, 3"–4"	.46	31	167	—
Cup/Saucer	.21	15	122	15
Decanter, w/ stopper, 10"	.140	—	—	240
Goblet, 3,5"	.300	—	—	—
Goblet, 4"–6"	.50	—	222	—
Grill Plate, 10"–11"	.12	11	—	57
Jam Jar, cov, 2"	.150	—	—	160
Pitcher, 1.5 pt., 5.75"	.223	293	—	—
Pitcher, 1 qt., 6"	.65	—	—	—
Pitcher, 56 oz., 8.5"	.56	—	1700	520

	GREEN	YELLOW	PINK	CRYSTAL
Plate, 6"	5	3	77	3
Plate, 7"–8"	13	5	30	6
Plate, 8.5" sq	38	140	—	—
Plate, 9"–10"	18	11	53	50
Platter, closed handles, 12"	25	22	—	—
Relish Tray, 3 part, ftd., 7.5"	36	93	—	—
Salt/Pepper, pair	80	—	860	—
Sauce Bowl, 4.25"	—	—	—	7
Server, center handle	3200	—	—	—
Sherbet, 3"	17	25	42	—
Sherbet, 5"	38	37	85	—
Soup Plate, 9"	45	—	—	—
Tumbler, flat, 9–11 oz.	41	45	125	13
Tumbler, flat, 15 oz. 5.25"	68	—	150	
Tumbler, ftd., 3 oz.	70	—	130	—
Tumbler, ftd., 15 oz., 6.38"	400	—	—	—
Vase, 5.75"	200	—	—	—
Vase, 8"	25	—	—	—
Vegetable, oval, 10"	23	35	—	—

Charm, Square

	JADEITE		AZURITE	
	Low	High	Low	High
Bowl, 4.75"	$6	$9	$4	$6
Creamer/Sugar	15	20	10	15
Cup/Saucer	6	9	4	7
Plate, 6.25"	4	6	3	5
Plate, 10"	15	20	12	16
Plate, 8.25"	10	12	8	10
Platter, rect., 12"	15	20	12	15
Salad Bowl, 8"	10	15	8	12
Soup Bowl, 6"	10	15	8	12

Cherry Blossom

	PINK	GREEN	DELPHITE
Bowl, 4.75"	$12	$16	$15
Bowl, 5.75"	36	35	—
Bowl, 8.5"	22	25	55
Bowl, 2 handled, 9"	10	25	20
Bowl, 3 ftd., 10.5"	56	65	—
Butter Dish, cov	88	115	—
Cake Plate, 3 ftd., 10.25"	23	20	—
Coaster	15	16	—
Creamer/Sugar	45	50	75
Cup/Saucer	22	25	25
Grill Plate, 9"	30	30	—
Grill Plate, 10"	—	66	—
Mug, 7 oz.	265	230	—
Pitcher, 1 qt., 7"–8"	52	75	100
Pitcher, 42 oz., 8"	52	67	—

	PINK	GREEN	DELPHITE
Plate, 6"	7	7	15
Plate, 7"	20	25	—
Plate, 9"	18	10	17
Platter, oval, 9"	1000	—	—
Platter, oval, 11"	20	33	48
Platter, 13"	51	55	—
Salt/Pepper, scalloped, pair	1700	1000	—
Server, 10.5"	18	22	23
Sherbet	16	20	20
Soup Plate, 7.75"	63	65	—
Tumbler, 4 oz., 3.75"	18	20	25
Tumbler, 8–9 oz., 4"–5"	26	35	—
Tumbler, 12 oz., 5"	58	70	—
Vegetable, oval, 9"	28	30	65

English Hobnail

	PINK	GREEN	CRYSTAL	AMBER
Ashtray	$30	$30	$5	$5
Bowl, 4"–5"	17	17	10	10
Bowl, 6"	17	17	10	10
Bowl, 8"	27	27	20	20
Bowl, 2 handled, 8"	62	62	35	35
Candlesticks, pair, 3.5"	42	42	16	16
Candlesticks, pair, 8.5"	73	73	50	50
Candy Dish, cov, 3 ftd.	90	90	30	30
Celery Dish, 9"–12"	30	30	18	18
Cigarette Box	40	40	20	20
Cologne Bottle	45	45	20	20
Cordial Glass, 1 oz.	26	26	15	15
Creamer/Sugar	48	48	18	18
Cup/Saucer	20	20	15	15
Cup/Saucer, demitasse	47	47	25	25
Decanter, w/ stopper, 20 oz.	92	92	55	55
Egg Cup	43	43	12	12
Goblet, 8 oz., 6.25"	30	30	10	10
Grapefruit, flange, 6.5"	22	22	12	12
Lamp, 9.25"	185	185	45	45
Marmalade, cov	58	58	20	20
Nappies, 11"–12"	57	57	30	30
Pitcher, 1.5 pt.	213	213	60	60
Pitcher, 1 qt.	215	215	50	50
Pitcher, straight, 2 qt.	300	300	80	80
Plate, 5"–7"	6	6	8	8
Plate, 8"	13	13	8	8
Plate, 10"	35	35	14	14
Relish Tray, 8"–12"	28	28	22	22
Salt/Pepper, pair	125	125	25	25
Sherbet	20	20	15	15
Shot Glass	25	25	10	10
Soup Bowl	25	25	15	15
Tumbler, 5–13 oz.	25	25	12	12
Wine Glass, 2–5 oz.	22	22	10	10

Fire-King Blue

	TURQUOISE BLUE		OVEN GLASS	
	Low	High	Low	High
Ashtray, 3.5"	$3	$5	—	—
Ashtray, 4.5"	5	8	—	—
Ashtray, 5.75"	8	12	—	—
Baker, 1 pt.	—	—	$6	$8
Baker, 1 qt.	—	—	8	12
Baker, 1.5 qt.	—	—	15	20
Baker, 2 qt.	—	—	18	25
Batter Bowl	150	200	—	—
Berry Bowl, 4"–5.5"	4	7	15	25
Casserole, knob lid, 1–4 pt.	—	—	18	25
Casserole, pie plate lid, 1 qt.	—	—	22	28
Casserole, pie plate lid, 1.5 qt.	—	—	25	30
Casserole, pie plate lid, 2 qt.	—	—	30	35
Casserole, tab handle lid, 10 oz.	—	—	20	25
Creamer/Sugar	8	12	—	—
Custard Cup, 5–6 oz.	—	—	5	7
Egg Plate	10	15	—	—
Hot Plate, tab handles	—	—	18	22
Leftover, cov, 5"–9"	—	—	13	25
Loaf Pan, 9"	—	—	20	25
Measuring Cup, 16 oz.	—	—	20	25
Mixing Bowl, round, 1 qt.	8	12	—	—
Mixing Bowl, round, 2 qt.	8	12	—	—
Mixing Bowl, round, 3 qt.	10	15	—	—
Mixing Bowl, round, 4 qt.	20	25	—	—
Mixing Bowl, teardrop, 1 pt.	10	15	—	—
Mising Bowl, teardrop, 1 qt.	12	17	—	—
Mixing Bowl, teardrop, 2 qt.	15	20	—	—
Mixing Bowl, teardrop, 3 qt.	18	22	—	—
Mug	7	10	30	35
Nurser, 4–8 oz.	—	—	18	25
Pie Plate, 8"–9.5"	—	—	15	20
Pie Plate, juice saver, 10.5"	—	—	60	75
Plate, 6"	5	8	—	—
Plate, 7"	7	10	—	—
Plate, 9"	5	7	—	—
Plate, 10"	20	25	—	—
Relish Tray, 3 part	8	12	—	—
Roaster, 8.75"	—	—	40	50
Roaster, 10.5"	—	—	60	75
Soup Bowl, 6.5"	10	15	—	—
Table Server, tab handles	—	—	18	22
Utility Bowl, 7"–10"	—	—	17	22
Utility Pan, 2" x 12.5"	—	—	10	15
Vegetable Bowl, 8"	10	15	—	—

Fire-King Jade-ite

	RESTAURANT WARE		JANE RAY	
	Low	High	Low	High
Bowl, 4"–4.25"	$3	$5	$3	$5
Bowl, 5"	8	10	5	8
Creamer/Sugar, cov	—	—	15	20
Cup/Saucer	6	10	3	5
Cup/Saucer, demitasse	—	—	30	45
Egg Cup	5	10	—	—
Mug, 8 oz.	8	10	—	—
Plate, bread and butter	3	5	—	—
Plate, salad	4	6	3	5
Plate, dinner	8	12	5	7
Plate, divided, 5 part	15	25	—	—
Platter, 10"	15	25	—	—
Platter, 12"	20	30	10	15
Soup Bowl	25	45	10	15
Vegetable Bowl, round, 8"	—	—	10	15

Florentine (#1)

	GREEN	YELLOW	PINK	BLUE
Ashtray, 5.5"	$28	$45	$42	—
Bowl, 5"	12	12	15	$25
Bowl, 6"	15	20	22	—
Bowl, 8.5"	25	37	36	—
Butter Dish, cov	180	225	170	—
Coaster/Ashtray, 3.75"	23	26	35	—
Creamer/Sugar, cov	47	55	53	—
Creamer/Sugar, ruffled	65	—	77	130
Cup/Saucer	13	10	17	100
Grill Plate, 10"	12	16	10	—
Pitcher, flat, 1.5 qt. 7.5"	60	233	140	—
Pitcher, ftd., 1 qt. 6.5"	50	65	65	900
Plate, 6"	5	6	6	—
Plate, 8.5"	10	15	15	—
Plate, 10"	17	25	26	—
Platter, oval, 11.5"	16	21	25	—
Salt/Pepper, pair, ftd.	55	60	76	—
Sherbet, ftd., 3 oz.	10	15	16	—
Tumbler, ftd., 5 oz., 3"–4"	10	25	23	—
Tumbler, ftd., 10–12 oz.	33	30	30	—
Tumbler, 9 oz., 5.25"	—	—	82	—
Vegetable, cov, oval, 9.5"	57	60	65	—

Florentine (#2)

	GREEN	YELLOW	PINK	BLUE
Bowl, 4.5"	$15	$16	$20	—
Bowl, 5.5"	33	25	43	—
Bowl, 6"	20	23	38	—
Bowl, 8"	26	31	31	—

	GREEN	YELLOW	PINK	BLUE
Bowl, 9"	31	—	—	—
Butter Dish, cov	150	—	210	—
Candy Dish, cov	125	165	215	—
Coaster, 3.25"	15	22	27	—
Coaster, 3.75"	23	—	25	—
Coaster, 5.5"	25	—	47	—
Comport, ruffled, 3.5"	20	10	28	75
Creamer/Sugar, cov	55	—	60	—
Cream Soup, 5"	15	15	23	55
Cup/Saucer	13	—	16	—
Custard Cup	73	—	115	—
Gravy Boat, w/ stand	—	115	—	—
Grill Plate, 10.25'	11	—	15	—
Parfait, 6"	35	—	70	—
Pitcher, cone ft., 1.5 pt., 6.25"	—	—	150	—
Pitcher, cone ft., 1.75 pt., 7.5"	32	—	32	—
Pitcher, 4.75 pt., 8"	125	320	280	—
Pitcher, 1.5 qt., 7.5"	75	160	245	—
Sherbet Plate, 6"	5	—	7	—
Plate, indented, 6.25"	22	—	30	—
Plate, 8.5"	10	—	30	—
Plate, 10"	18	22	18	—
Platter, oval, 11"	17	18	10	—
Relish Tray, 10"	22	26	28	—
Salt/Pepper, pair	56	—	65	—
Sherbet, ftd.	10	—	13	—
Soup Plate, 7.5"	—	—	86	—
Tumbler, 5–9 oz., 3"–4"	16	11	26	87
Tumbler, 12 oz., 5"	35	—	48	—
Vegetable, cov, oval, 9"	56	—	75	—

Flower Garden w/ Butterflies

	GREEN	YELLOW	PINK	BLUE
Candlesticks, pair, 4"	$83	$98	$150	$100
Candlesticks, pair, 8"	150	160	235	150
Candy Dish, cov, 6"–7.75"	167	180	265	175
Candy Dish, cov, heart shape	—	540	800	1300
Cologne Bottle, 7.5"	—	300	330	250
Comport, 3" h	28	35	45	30
Comport, 5"–7" h	90	116	135	95
Creamer/Sugar	—	210	—	135
Cup/Saucer	—	163	—	90
Plate, 7"–8"	26	30	43	30
Plate, 10"	55	52	73	50
Platter, 10"–12"	70	100	135	—
Powder Jar, ftd., 6"–7.5"	111	137	200	185
Server, center handle	80	100	135	100
Tumbler, 7.5 oz.	155	—	—	—
Vase, 6.25"	126	150	180	130
Vase, 10.5"	—	172	246	200

Forest Green

	GREEN	CRYSTAL
Ashtray	$4	$5
Bowl, 5"–7.5"	7	10
Creamer/Sugar	10	15
Cup/Saucer	5	8
Mixing Bowl	8	12
Pitcher, 1.5 pt.	18	22
Pitcher, 3 qt.	25	35
Plate, 6.5"	2	3
Plate, 8.5"	5	7
Plate, 10"	25	40
Platter, rect.	15	20
Punch Bowl, w/ stand	30	45
Punch Cup	2	3
Tumbler, 5–10 oz.	4	6
Vase, 4"–9"	5	7

Georgian, Lovebirds

	GREEN	CRYSTAL
Bowl, 4.5"	$5	$7
Bowl, 5.75"	20	25
Bowl, 6.5"	50	70
Bowl, 7.5"	50	65
Butter Dish, cov	75	100
Creamer/Sugar, cov, 3"	40	50
Creamer/Sugar, cov, 4"	100	115
Cup/Saucer	12	17
Plate, 6"	4	5
Plate, 8"	7	10
Plate, 9"	20	25
Platter, 11.5"	60	75
Sherbet	10	12
Tumbler, 9 oz., 4"	45	55
Tumbler, 12 oz., 5.25"	80	120
Vegetable, oval, 9"	60	75

Hobnail

	PINK	CRYSTAL
Bowl, 5"–7"	$7	$5
Creamer/Sugar	12	10
Cup/Saucer	6	6
Decanter, w/ stopper, 1 qt.	25	—
Goblet, 10–13 oz.	10	—
Pitcher, 1 pt.	22	—
Pitcher, 1.5 qt.	40	33
Plate, 6"	2	2
Plate, 8.5"	5	3
Sherbet	5	5
Shot Glass	6	—
Tumbler, 3–15 oz.	8	—

Above, left to right: Bubble Sugar and Creamer; Cherry Blossom Butter Dish.

Above, left to right: Fire-King Blue Oven Glass Roaster; Madrid Luncheon Plate.

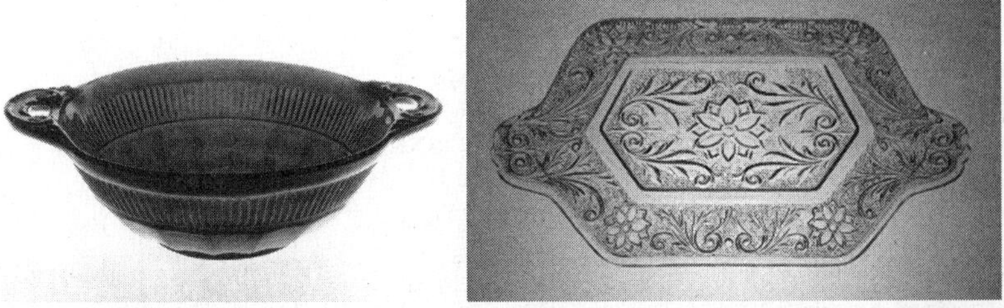

Above, left to right: Royal Ruby Berry Bowl; Sandwich (Indiana Glass Co.) Tray.

Holiday

	PINK	CRYSTAL
Bowl, 5"	$10	$12
Bowl, 8.5"	25	30
Bowl, 11"	80	110
Butter Dish, cov	50	60
Cake Plate, 3 ftd., 10.5"	75	100
Candlesticks, pair, 3"	75	100
Chop Plate, 13.75"	100	120
Creamer/Sugar, cov, ftd.	30	40
Cup/Saucer	12	18
Pitcher, 1 pt., 4.75"	70	90
Pitcher, 3 pt., 6.75"	40	50
Plate, 6"	5	7
Plate, 9"	15	20
Platter, 10.5"–11.5"	17	22
Sherbet	8	12
Soup Plate, 8"	35	45
Tumbler, 10 oz., 4"	35	40
Tumbler, ftd., 6"	100	120
Vegetable, oval, 9.5"	20	25

Lorain, Basket

	CRYSTAL	GREEN	YELLOW
Bowl, 6"	$37	$40	$75
Bowl, 7.25"	55	60	75
Bowl, 8"	100	115	185
Creamer/Sugar	37	40	48
Cup/Saucer	22	25	28
Plate, 5.5"	7	9	11
Plate, 8"	13	15	18
Plate, 10"	46	50	58
Platter, 11.5"	28	30	52
Relish Tray, 4 part, 8"	25	27	30
Sherbet, ftd.	25	28	36
Tumbler, ftd., 9 oz., 4.75"	28	30	30
Vegetable, oval, 10"	57	55	70

Madrid

	AMBER	PINK	GREEN	BLUE
Ashtray, 6" sq	$220	—	$130	—
Bowl, 8"–9.5"	22	$33	25	$40
Butter Dish, cov	87	—	115	—
Cake Plate, 11.25"	16	16	27	
Candlesticks, pair, 2.25"	28	23	—	—
Console, low, 11"	10	13	—	—
Cookie Jar, cov	52	45	—	—
Cream Soup, 4.75"	16	—	—	—
Creamer/Sugar, cov	50	—	65	130
Cup/Saucer	13	15	17	27
Gravy Boat, w/ stand	1600	—	—	—

	AMBER	PINK	GREEN	BLUE
Grill Plate, 10.5"	15	—	25	—
Jam Dish, 7"	20	—	23	35
Lazy Susan, w/ 7 dishes	800	—	—	—
Mold	15	—	—	—
Pitcher, 1 qt., 5.5"	40	—	—	—
Pitcher, 2 qt., 8"	55	60	175	175
Plate, 6"	5	6	5	11
Plate, 7.5"	15	15	13	23
Plate, 9"	10	11	12	23
Plate, 10.5"	45	—	47	80
Platter, oval, 11.5"	10	15	21	20
Relish Dish, 5"	10	10	10	13
Relish Tray, 10.25"	15	15	18	—
Salt/Pepper, pair	65	—	90	168
Sherbet	11	—	13	16
Soup Plate, 7"	15	—	18	16
Trivet, hot dish	45	—	50	—
Tumbler, flat, 5–12 oz., 4"–5.5"	27	10	42	33
Tumbler, ftd., 5 oz., 4"	36	—	50	—
Tumbler, ftd., 10 oz., 5.25"	33	—	40	—
Vegetable, oval, 10"	20	10	25	36

Miss America

	CRYSTAL	PINK	GREEN	RED
Bowl, 4"–6"	$11	$18	$13	—
Bowl, curved-in rim, 8"	57	83	—	$500
Bowl, straight, deep, 8.75"	37	62	—	—
Butter Dish, cov	240	600	—	—
Cake Plate, 12"	26	40	—	—
Candy Jar, cov, 11.5"	70	143	—	—
Celery Dish, 10.5"	13	25	—	—
Coaster, 5.75"	17	27	—	—
Compote, 5"	18	30	—	—
Creamer/Sugar	25	46	—	450
Cup/Saucer	18	32	28	—
Goblet, 3–10 oz., 4"–6"	20	65	265	—
Grill Plate, 10.25"	12	22	—	—
Pitcher, 2 qt., 8"	60	130	—	—
Plate, 5.75"	5	10	8	—
Plate, 8.5"	10	21	13	100
Plate, 10.25"	15	28	—	—
Platter, oval, 12.25"	18	27	—	—
Relish Tray, 4 part, 8.75"	15	21	—	—
Relish Tray, round, divided, 11.75"	20	200	—	—
Salt/Pepper, pair	42	71	430	—
Sherbet	11	17	—	—
Tumbler, 5 oz., 4"	21	57	—	—
Tumbler, 10 oz., 4.5"	21	30	22	—
Tumbler, 14 oz., 5.75"	37	72	—	—
Vegetable, oval, 10"	18	25	—	—

Moderntone

	COBALT	AMETHYST	FIRED-ON
Ashtray, 7.75"	$140	—	—
Bowl, 5"	21	$11	$2
Bowl, 6.5"	62	43	5
Butter Dish, cov	100	—	—
Cheese Dish, cov	250	—	—
Cream Soup, 5"	10	17	—
Creamer/Sugar	25	20	10
Cup/Saucer	17	15	5
Custard Cup	18	15	—
Plate, 6"	6	5	1
Plate, 7"–8"	8	8	3
Plate, 9"	15	11	6
Plate, 10.5"	27	21	6
Platter, oval, 11"–12"	47	25	12
Salt/Pepper, pair	48	46	23
Sherbet	13	12	6
Shot Glass	23	—	—
Soup Plate	60	57	7
Tumbler, 5–9 oz.	25	26	8
Tumbler, 12 oz.	85	60	—

Patrician

	AMBER	PINK	GREEN
Bowl, 5"	$12	$17	$13
Bowl, 8.5"	47	28	20
Butter Dish, cov	110	356	162
Cookie Jar, cov	96	—	475
Cream Soup, 4.75"	16	25	28
Creamer/Sugar, cov	65	95	92
Cup/Saucer	16	22	233
Grill Plate, 10.5"	15	15	16
Jam Dish	25	36	45
Pitcher, 2.25 qt., 8"	110	135	125
Plate, 6"	11	7	8
Plate, 7.5"	18	21	17
Plate, 9"	13	12	12
Plate, 10.5"	10	25	45
Platter, oval, 11.5"	10	18	21
Salt/Pepper, pair	72	100	82
Sherbet	12	15	13
Tumbler, 5–14 oz., 5.25"	35	37	35
Vegetable, oval, 10"	20	25	27

Patrick

	PINK	YELLOW
Bowl, handle, 9"	$35	$30
Bowl, 11"	35	32
Candlesticks, pair	45	40
Candy Dish, 3 ftd.	50	45

	PINK	YELLOW
Cheese Set	55	50
Creamer/Sugar	35	30
Cup/Saucer	18	15
Goblet, 4"–5"	25	20
Goblet, 10 oz., 6"	35	32
Plate, 7"8"	10	8
Sherbet, 4.75"	22	20
Tray, 11"	37	35

Princess

	GREEN	PINK	YELLOW
Ashtray, 4.5"	$92	$95	$115
Bowl, 4.5"–5"	30	25	36
Bowl, octagonal, 9"	35	26	110
Butter Dish, cov	92	120	700
Cake Stand, 10"	23	21	—
Candy Dish, cov	62	70	—
Coaster	37	83	125
Cookie Jar, cov	65	75	—
Creamer/Sugar, cov	50	46	40
Cup/Saucer	18	17	16
Grill Plate, 9"	16	11	10
Pitcher, ftd., 1.5 pt., 7.5"	700	685	—
Pitcher, 1 qt., 6"	61	46	825
Pitcher, 2 qt., 8"	56	58	90
Plate, 6"	10	6	7
Plate, 8"	13	11	12
Plate, 9"	31	20	10
Plate, 11.5"	18	13	15
Platter, 12"	22	18	48
Relish Tray, divided, 7.5"	31	21	81
Religh Tray, plain, 7.5"	100	—	185
Salt/Pepper, pair	70	53	73
Sherbet, ftd.	22	21	42
Tumbler, 5–9 oz., 3"–4"	35	28	32
Tumbler, 10–13 oz., 5.25"	40	26	30
Tumbler, sq., ftd., 9 oz., 4.75"	83	70	—
Tumbler, ftd., 12.5 oz., 6.5"	92	65	126
Vase, 8"	36	28	—
Vegetable, oval, 10"	28	25	60

Royal Ruby

	LOW	HIGH
Ashtray, 4.5" sq	$3	$5
Bowl, deep, 10"	30	40
Berry Bowl, 4.25"	3	5
Berry Bowl, 8.5"	12	17
Bowl, 5.25"	8	12
Card Holder	45	55
Creamer/Sugar, cov	15	20
Creamer/Sugar, flat	10	15

	LOW	HIGH
Creamer/Sugar, ftd.	15	20
Cup/Saucer, round or sq.	6	9
Goblet, ball stem	5	10
Pitcher, tilted or upright, 42 oz.	30	45
Pitcher, tilted, 3 qt.	30	45
Pitcher, upright, 3 qt.	40	60
Plate, 13.75"	20	30
Plate, 7"	3	5
Plate, 7.75"	4	7
Plate, 9"–9.25"	8	12
Punch Bowl, w/ stand	65	85
Punch Cup	2	4
Salad Bowl, 11.5"	25	30
Sherbet, ftd.	5	8
Sherbet Plate, 6.5"	2	4
Soup Bowl, 7.5"	9	12
Tumbler, 5 oz.	5	8
Tumbler, 9 oz.	5	8
Vase, ball-shaped, 4"	3	5
Vase, 6.5"	4	8
Vase, 9"	12	15

Sandwich (Anchor Hocking)

	CRYSTAL	AMBER	RED	DK. GREEN
Bowl, 5"	$5	$5	$16	$30
Bowl, 6.5"	11	10	35	45
Bowl, 7"–8"	12	12	45	60
Bowl, 9"	26	25	—	—
Butter Dish, cov	50	—	—	—
Cookie Jar, cov	40	30	—	—
Cookie Jar, open	—	—	—	20
Creamer/Sugar	28	20	—	45
Cup/Saucer	5	5	—	20
Custard Cup, w/ liner	16	—	—	350
Pitcher, 2 qt.	75	—	—	350
Plate, 7"	12	—	—	—
Plate, 9"	17	10	—	90
Plate, 12"	13	15	—	—
Punch Bowl, w/ stand	40	—	—	—
Punch Cup	2	—	—	—
Tumbler, 3–5 oz.	10	—	—	5
Tumbler, 9 oz.	10	—	—	6
Tumbler, ftd., 9 oz.	27	125	—	—

Sandwich (Indiana Glass Co.)

	PINK	GREEN	BLUE	RED
Bowl, 4"–6"	$6	$6	—	$2
Bowl, hexagonal, 6"	—	—	$12	—
Bowl, 8"–10"	26	26	—	70
Butter Dish, cov	280	280	267	—
Candlesticks, pair, 3.5"	25	25	—	—

	PINK	GREEN	BLUE	RED
Candlesticks, pair, 7"	66	66	—	
Creamer/Sugar	26	26	—	130
Creamer/Sugar/Tray	—	—	40	—
Cruet, w/ stopper, 6.5 oz.	—	212	—	—
Cup/Saucer	12	12	15	47
Decanter, w/ stopper	140	140	—	
Goblet, 9 oz.	25	25	—	60
Pitcher, 2 qt.	145	145	—	—
Plate, 6"–7"	5	5	7	9
Plate, 8"	8	8	12	11
Plate, 10"–13"	21	21	—	—
Server, center handle	45	45	—	—
Sherbet, 3.25"	10	10	11	—
Tumbler, ftd., 3–8 oz.	22	22	—	—
Tumbler, ftd., 12 oz.	42	42	—	—
Wine Glass, 4 oz., 3"	28	28	—	—

Sharon

	AMBER	PINK	GREEN
Bowl, 5"	$10	$10	$13
Bowl, 6"	18	23	20
Bowl, 8.5"	7	28	35
Bowl, 10.5"	25	35	38
Butter Dish, cov	75	60	115
Cake Plate, 11.5"	26	30	70
Candy Dish, cov	61	50	186
Cheese Dish, cov	275	900	—
Cream Soup	28	48	53
Creamer/Sugar	28	31	43
Cup/Saucer	20	21	25
Jam Dish, 7.5"	45	150	55
Pitcher, 2.5 qt.	160	160	533
Plate, 6"	6	6	8
Plate, 8"–10"	18	23	21
Platter, oval, 12.5"	10	23	25
Salt/Pepper, pair	53	55	93
Sherbet	15	16	35
Soup Plate, 7.5"	38	42	40
Tumbler, 9–15 oz., 4"–7"	40	40	80
Vegetable, oval, 9.5"	16	26	25

Ships

	BLUE
Cup/Saucer	$33
Cocktail, w/ stir	30
Cocktail Shaker	33
Ice Tub	40
Pitcher, 2.5 qt.	55
Plate, 6"	17
Plate, 9"	26
Shot Glass	48

Drinking Glasses

	LOW	HIGH
Arby's Looney Tunes, head in star, various designs	$8	$16
Arby's, Zodiac, various designs	4	5
Batman, 1989 Canada, various designs	7	8
Care Bears, 1983 Pizza Hut, various designs	15	20
Circus, Circus Series (Canada), various designs	3	4
Coca-Cola, 1975 Kollect-A-Set, various designs	6	10
Coca-Cola, 1976 King Kong, New York subway train	12	15
Coca-Cola, 1976 King Kong, various designs	4	8
Coca-Cola, 1977 Burger King/Star Wars, various designs	5	11
Coca-Cola, 1980 Burger King/Empire Strikes Back, various designs	4	6
Coca-Cola, 1983 Burger King/Return of Jedi, various designs	4	6
Coca-Cola, 1983 Burger King/Return of Jedi, Ewok Village	9	11
Coca-Cola, Collegiate Crest, various designs	5	10
Coca-Cola, '84 Olympics, Sam the Olympic Eagle, various designs	5	7
Coca-Cola, Historical Mission Series, various designs	9	11
Coca-Cola, World Cup '94, various designs	15	20
Disney, Aristocats, made in France, 3.25"	10	13
Disney, Donald Duck's Collection, made in France, 4.5"	6	7
Disney, Lady and the Tramp, made in France, 3.25"	15	20
Disney, 101 Dalmatians, made in France, 3.25"	10	15
Disney, Peter Pan, 1969 Canada, various designs	25	45
Disney, Rescuers, made in France, 3.25"	11	12
Disney, Sleeping Beauty, 1959 Canada, various designs	15	20
Disney, Snow White and the 7 Dwarfs, 4.25", various designs	18	21
Dr. Pepper, Be a Pepper, rainbow and clouds, flare	5	6
Dr. Pepper, 1978 Star Trek, various designs	25	30
Frostie, Root Beer, figural clear glass mug, 5.75"	4	5
Ghostbusters, 1989 Canada/Sunoco, various designs	5	6
Horse Racing, Kentucky Derby, 1962	40	60
Horse Racing, Kentucky Derby, 1963–1973, various designs	25	35
Horse Racing, Kentucky Derby, 1974–1990, various designs	4	6
Horse Racing, Pepsi/West Virginia Breeders Classics 1989–92, 5.5", various designs	10	13
Horse Racing, Pimlico, Preakness, 1976, various designs	10	20
Horse Racing, Pimlico, Preakness, 1990, various designs	8	14
Iced Teas, Arizona Cactus, various designs	3	4
Iced Teas, Boats of the Ohio River, Great Republic	6	7
Iced Teas, Boats of the Ohio River, New Orleans, tall frosted	8	12
Iced Teas, Boats of the Ohio River, Queen City, tall frosted	8	12
Iced Teas, Florida	8	10
Iced Teas, Kansas, Chisholm Trail, tall frosted	6	7
Iced Teas, Ohio Indians, frosted, various designs	3	4
Iced Teas, Oklahoma Indians, clear, 5.25", various designs	8	10
Iced Teas, Oklahoma Indians, frosted, various designs	5	6
Iced Teas, River Champions/On the Mississippi, white on clear, 5.75"	3	4
Iced Teas, Rush for Gold, tall frosted	3	4
Ivanhoe, Ivanhoe, various designs (Canada)	14	18
McDonald's, 1980 Adventure Series, various McDonald's designs	10	12

	LOW	HIGH
McDonald's, 1989 International Coffee Mug, French Roast	3	4
McDonald's, 1993 Topps Baseball, various desings	5	15
McDonald's, 1995 Three Kings/Coke/Puerto Rico, various designs	6	9
McDonald's, Garfield checkerboard mug, various designs	4	6
McDonald's, Garfield tumbler, Home, James	7	10
McDonald's, Garfield Morning Canada coffee mug	3	4
McDonald's, Grimace, smoke glass mug	3	5
National Flag Foundation, various designs	4	6
National Flag Foundation, Confederate Battle Flag, Pgh Press, pedestal	10	12
Nutella, 1996 Italy, Warner Bros. figures, various designs	8	12
Peanuts, Collage of all Peanuts characters, made in Germany, 5.5"	13	19
Peanuts, Dolly Madison, Back the Beagle, round bottom, 6"	3	4
Pepsi, 1973 Warner Bros. 15 oz. Federal logo, various designs	8	12
Pepsi, 1973 Warner Bros. 16 oz. Federal side logo, various designs	5	15
Pepsi, 1975 Serie de Collectioneur (Canada), various designs	18	23
Pepsi, 1975 MGM characters, various designs	5	10
Pepsi, 1975 MGM 12 oz. action, Tom	3	4
Pepsi, 1976 Jr. Rosebowl Champions, Bakersfield College	4	5
Pepsi, 1977 Warner Bros. Serie de Collectioneur (Canada), various designs	8	16
Pepsi, 1977 Rescuers, various designs	4	6
Pepsi, 1977 Rescuers, Vianca	7	9
Pepsi, 1977 Rescuers, Rufus	20	30
Pepsi, 1977 Hanna-Barbera, various designs	18	22
Pepsi, 1978 Superhero, various designs	8	15
Pepsi, 1978 Superman the Movie, various designs	8	9
Pepsi, 1978 Happy Birthday Mickey, various designs	3	4
Pepsi, 1979 Patterson Thought Factory, various designs	5	6
Pepsi, 1979 Looney Tunes, various designs	7	8
Pepsi, Armchair Quarterback, football-shaped glass	7	9
Pepsi, DC Comics double superheroes, various designs	15	20
Pepsi, Detroit Grand Prix IV	3	4
Pepsi, Go Tigers! Stomp out the Gamecocks! Clemson/SC won-lost record	3	4
Pepsi, Harvey Cartoons, Bib Baby Huey, 16 oz.	14	18
Pepsi, Harvey Cartoons, Casper, blue letters, 16 oz.	10	12
Pepsi, Harvey Cartoons, Hot Stuf	3	4
Pepsi, Harvey Cartoons, Richie Rich	13	16
Pepsi, Leonardo TTV, Simon Bar Sinister, 12 oz.	3	4
Pepsi, Leonardo TTV, Underdog, various designs	4	8
Pepsi, Merry Christmas in different languages in white over holly and berry design	5	6
Pepsi, Pepsi, PAT Ward, various Bullwinkle and Rocky designs	3	4
Pepsi, Pepsi screened on cobalt blue	15	19
Pepsi, Taco Time, orange cactus	4	5
Pepsi, 20 different Pepsi logos, white on clear glass, 5.25"	5	7
Popeye's Fried Chicken, 1978, various designs	14	18
Seven-Eleven, 1977 Marvel Superheroes, various designs	11	14
Sports, Baseball, Detroit Tigers/Burger King/Aren't you hungry?, various designs	4	7
Sports, Baseball, Detroit Tigers/Little Caesar's 1984, various designs	3	4
Sports, Baseball, 1994 Coke/Eat'n Park Clemente Classics, various designs	4	5
Sports, Baseball, World Champions 1960, team logo and signatures	10	12

Flasks

Glass flasks have a broad body and narrow neck, are usually for alcoholic beverages and are often fitted with a closure. Flask collectors search for examples from the early 1800s through the early 1900s. Before 1810, few glass containers were manufactured. Flasks with portraits of presidents or other politicians are highly sought. Many have been reproduced. Color is also an important consideration.

Some of the best flasks pass through Norman C. Heckler's Auction in Auburn, MA.

In this listing, we have used the following abbreviations: *Hist.*–Historical; *GW*–Glass Works; *aqua*–aquamarine; *PS*–pontil scar; *SB*–smooth base; *SM*–sheared mouth; and *CM*–collared mouth. We have also included the McKearin identification number. For the system of identification and an extensive listing, see *American Bottles and Flasks* by Helen McKearin and Kenneth Wilson and *The Official Price Guide to Bottles, Twelfth Edition,* by Jim Megura, House of Collectibles, Random House, NY, 1998.

	LOW	HIGH
Adams – Jefferson Port. Flask, American, light olive yellow, SM, PS, half pt., c1840, GI-114	$400	$600
"Balti./GW" Anchor – Sheaf of Wheat Pictorial Flask, Balti. GW, MD, blue green, double CM, SB, 1 qt., c1865, GXIII-48	3000	4500
Balti. Monument – Sloop Hist. Flask, Balti. GW, MD, smokey, SM, PS, half pt., c1850, GVI-2	3500	5300
Clasped Hands – Clasped Hands Hist. Flask, Midwest, yellow-olive, applied mouth w/ ring, SB, 1 qt., c1870, GXII-37	1000	1500
"Cleve & Steve" Barrel-Shaped Portrait Flask, American, aqua., tooled mouth, SB, 1 pt., c1895, GI-123a	700	1100
Clock Face – Reverse Plain Pictorial Flask, American, yellow amber w/ olive tone, double CM, PS, 1 pt., c1850, GXIII-87	700	1100
Columbia – Eagle Portrait Flask, Kensington Union Co. GW, Phila., PA, aqua., SM, PS, 1 pt., c1826, GI-117	1000	1500
Cornucopia – Large Medallion Pictorial Flask, Midwest, light blue green, SM, PS, half pt., c1830, GIII-1	3500	5300
Cornucopia – Urn Pictorial Flask, Lancaster GW, Lancaster, NY, blue green, SM, iron pontil mark, 1 pt., c1855, GIII-16	1000	1500
Cornucopia – Urn Pictorial Flask, Lancaster GW, Lancaster, NY, light blue green, SM, PS, 1 pt., c1855, GIII-18	2600	3900
Double Eagle Hist. Flask, Coventry GW, CT, yellow olive, SM, PS, half pt., c1840, GII-71	300	500
Double Eagle Hist. Flask, Granite GW, Stoddard, NH, light yellow olive, SM, PS, 1 qt., c1850, GII-80	1000	1500
Double Eagle Hist. Flask, Ky GW, Louisville, KY, sapphire blue, SM, PS, 1 pt., c1850, GII-24	5000	7500
Double Eagle Hist. Flask, Ky GW, Louisville, KY, olive yellow, SM, PS, 1 qt., c1850, GII-26	3300	5000
Double Eagle Hist. Flask, Midwest American, bluish aqua, SM, PS, 1 pt., c1845, GII-20	6500	9800
Double Eagle Hist. Flask, Pittsburgh, PA, aqua., SM, PS, 1 pt., c1830, GII-3	500	800
Double Eagle Hist. Flask, Pittsburgh, PA, pale green, SM, PS, 1 pt., c1830, GII-4a	800	1200
Double Eagle Hist. Flask, Pittsburgh, PA, light yellow green, SM, PS, 1 pt., c1830, GII-5	2000	3000
Double Eagle Hist. Flask, vertically ribbed body, Louisville GW, KY, aqua., SM, PS, 1 pt., c1855, GII-29	500	800

	LOW	HIGH
"E.G. Booz's/Old Cabin/Whiskey" Bottle, Whitney GW, Glassboro, NJ, amber, sloping CM, SB, 1 qt., c1855, GVII-3	2000	3000
Eagle – Cornucopia Hist. Flask, Pittsburgh, PA, pale green, SM, PS, 1 pt., c1830, GII-6	700	1100
Eagle – Cornucopia Hist. Flask, Pittsburgh, PA, sapphire blue, SM, PS, half pt., c1830, GII-16	6500	9800
Eagle – Cornucopia Hist. Flask, Pittsburgh, PA, light blue green, SM, PS, half pt., c1830, GII-69	1700	2600
Eagle – Flag Hist. Flask, Coffin & Hay Manufactory, Hammonton, NJ, dark bluish green, SM, PS, 1 qt., c1840, GII-48	4500	6800
Eagle – Floral Medallion Hist. Flask, Ky GW, Louisville, KY, green aqua., SM, PS, 1 pt., c1850, GII-23	1300	2000
Eagle – Scrolled Medallion Hist. Flask, Pittsburgh, PA, colorless, SM, PS, 1 pt., c1830, GII-8	8300	12,500
Eagle – "Willington/Glass/Co." Hist. Flask, Willington GW, CT, dark forest green, CM, SB, 1 qt., c1865, GII-61	300	500
Eagle – "Willington/Glass/Co." Hist. Flask, Willington GW, CT, yellow olive, double CM, SB, half pt., c1865, GII-63	300	500
"F.L." Eagle – Cornucopia Hist. Flask, Pittsburgh, PA, dark blue aqua., SM, PS, half pt., c1830, GII-15	1000	1500
"General Jackson" – Floral Medallion Portrait Flask, Pittsburgh, PA, dark green aqua, SM, PS, 1 pt., c1830, GI-68	3400	5100
"Genl. Taylor" – Monument Portrait Flask, Balti. GW, MD, amethyst, SM, PS, 1 pt., c1840, GI-73	9000	13,500
"Hard Cider" Barrel – Cabin Hist. Flask, Pittsburgh, PA, dark bluish aqua., SM, PS, 1 pt., c1835, GX-22	7000	10,500
Horseman – Hound Pictorial Falsk, American, yellow amber w/ olive tone, double CM, SB, 1 pt., c1870, GXIII-17	800	1200
Hourglass Masonic Hist. Flask, Coventry GW, CT, light olive yellow, SM, PS, half pt., c1820, GIV-29	8000	12,000
"J.R. & S." Scroll Flask, John Robinson & Son Mfr., Pittsburgh, PA, green aqua., SM, PS, half pt., c1830, GIX-42	800	1200
"Lafayette" – "De Witt Clinton" Portrait Flask, Coventry GW, CT, olive yellow, SM, PS, half pt., c1824, GI-81	1600	2400

Historical Flasks. —Photo courtesy Glass-Works Auctions.

	LOW	HIGH
"Lafayette" – Liberty Cap Portrait Flask, Coventry GW, CT, dark yellow olive, SM, PS, 1 pt., c1824, GI-85	1000	1500
"Lafayette" – Liberty Cap Portrait Flask, Coventry GW, CT, dark yellow olive, SM, PS, half pt., c1824, GI-86	1000	1500
"Lafayette" – Masonic Portrait Flask, Coventry GW, CT, yellow olive, SM, PS, 1 pt., c1824, GI-83	5000	7500
"Lafayette" – Masonic Portrait Flask, Coventry GW, CT, yellow forest green, SM, PS, half pt., c1824, GI-84	5000	7500
Masonic – Eagle Hist. Flask, Keene Marlboro St. GW, NH, colorless, SM, PS, 1 pt., c1820, GIV-1	1300	2000
Masonic – Eagl Hist. Flask, Keene Marlboro St. GW, NH, yellow green, tooled mouth, PS, 1 pt., c1820, GIV-5	900	1400
Masonic – Eagle Hist. Flask, Keene Marlboro St. GW, NH, olive amber, SM, PS, 1 pt., c1825, GIV-19	300	500
Masonic – Eagle Hist. Flask, Keene Marlboro St. GW, NH, dark yellow olive, SM, PS, half pt., c1825, GIV-24	300	500
Masonic – Eagle Hist. Flask, New England, dark yellow olive, sloping CM, PS, 1 pt., c1820, GIV-16	4000	6000
Masonic – Eagle Hist. Flask, White GW, Zanesville, OH, amber, SM, PS, 1 pt., c1825, GIV-32	900	1400
Masonic – Eagle Hist. Flask, White GW, Zanesville, OH, light blue green, SM, PS, 1 pt., c1825, GIV-32	700	1100
Masonic – Eagle Hist. Flask, Pittsburgh, PA, light yellow green, SM, PS, 1 pt., c1825, GIV-36	1700	2600
Masonic Hist. Flask, New England, green, SM, PS, half pt., c1820, GIV-28	1700	2600
"Not For Joe" Girl on a Bicycle – Reverse Plain Pictorial Flask, American, amber, applied mouth w/ ring, SB, 1 pt., c1870, GXIII-1	1700	2600
"Rough & Ready Taylor" – eagle Portrait Flask, Pittsburgh, PA, dark bluish aqua., SM, PS, 1 pt., c1830, GI-76	7500	11,000
"S. McKee" Scroll Flask, Samuel McKee & Co., Pittsburgh, PA, green aqua., SM, PS, 1 pt., c1850, GIX-26	1600	2400
Scroll Flask, American, amber, SM, PS, 1 pt., c1850, GIX-10	700	1100
Scroll Flask, American, sapphire blue, SM, PS, 1 pt., c1850, GIX-19	4000	6000
Scroll Flask, American, aqua., SM, PS, 2 qts., c1850, GIX-29	900	1400
Scroll Flask, Lancaster GW, Lancaster, NY, olive yellow, SM, PS, c1855, GIX-20	3500	5300
Sheaf of Wheat – Star Pictorial Flask, Bulltown GW, Bulltown, NJ, yellow green, double CM, PS, 1 pt., c1860, GXIII-39	1700	2600
Sheaf of Wheat – Tree Pictorial Calabash Flask, American, emerald green, double CM, PS, 1 qt., c1850, GXIII-47	900	1400
Stoddard Flag Hist. Flask, New Granite GW, Stoddard, NH, olive amber, SM, PS, 1 pt., c1865, GX-27	6000	9000
"Success to the Railroad" Hist. Flask, Mt. Vernon GW, Vernon, NY, yellow olive, SM, PS, 1 pt., c1835, GV-5	600	900
Summer Tree – Winter Tree Pictorial Flask, American, medium green, double CM, PS, c1850, GX-19	1700	2600
Sunburst Flask, American, dark wine, SM, PS, half pt., c1825, GVIII-25	4900	7400
Sunburst Flask, American, light blue green, c1825, GVIII-26	1000	1500
Sunburst Flask, Coventry GW, CT, yellow olive, SM, PS, 1 pt., c1820, GVIII-3	1000	1500
Sunburst Flask, Coventry GW, CT, yellow olive, SM, PS, half pt., c1820, GVIII-16	700	1100
Sunburst Flask, Coventry GW, CT, olive amber, SM, PS, half pt., c1820, GVIII-18	600	900

	LOW	HIGH
Sunburst Flask, Keene Marlboro St. GW, NH, light blue green, SM, PS, 1 pt., c1820, GVIII-1	1000	1500
Sunburst Flask, Keene Marlboro St. GW, NH, light green, SM, PS, 1 pt., c1820, GVIII-2	900	1400
Sunburst Flask, Keene Marlboro St. GW, NH, dark olive green, SM, PS, 1 pt., c1820, GVIII-12	7000	10,500
Sunburst Flask, Keene Marlboro St. GW, NH, blue green, SM, PS, half pt., c1820, GVIII-14	1700	2600
Sunburst Flask, Pitkin GW, Manchester, CT, light yellow olive, SM, PS, 1 pt., c1820, GVIII-5a	2700	4100
Sunburst Flask, Pitkin GW, Manchester, CT, olive amber, SM, PS, 1 pt., c1820, GVIII-7	1700	2600
Taylor – "Masterson" Eagle Portrait Flask, Midwest American, dark bluish aqua., SM, PS, 1 qt., c1835, GI-77	3500	5300
Taylor – Ringgold Portrait Flask, Balti. GW, MD, light lavender, SM, PS, 1 pt., c1840, GI-71	2000	3000
"Traveler's/Companion" – "Railroad/Guide" Flask, American, light blue green, SM, PS, half pt., c1850, GXIV-9	700	1100
"Traveler's/Companion" – "Ravenna/Glass Co." Flask, Ravenna GW, OH, yellow w/ olive tone, SM, SB, 1 pt., c1860, GXIV-3	2600	3900
"Traveler's/(Stylized Duck)/Companion" Flask, Lockport GW, NY, blue green, round CM, PS, 1 pt., c1850, GXIV-6	2500	3800
"WC" Eagle – Cornucopia Hist. Flask, Pittsburgh, PA, dark green aqua., SM, PS, half pt., c1830, GII-12	1700	2600
Washington – Taylor Portrait Flask, Dyottville GW, Phila., PA, light yellow green, double CM, SB, 1 qt., c1870, GI-45	500	800
Washington – Taylor Portrait Flask, Dyottville GW, Phila., PA, sapphire blue, CM, PS, 1 qt., c1850, GI-51	2800	4200
Washington – Tree Portrait Calabash Flask, American, aqua, double CM, PS, 1 qt., c1850, GI-36	300	500
Washington – Washington Portrait Flask, Lockport GW, Lockport, NY, pale blue, double CM, iron pontil mark, 1 qt., c1850, GI-60	1700	2600
"Wheeling / Va" – "Old Rye" Lettered Flask, Union GW, Wheeling VA, dark yellow olive, applied mouth w/ ring, SB, 1 pt., c1860, GXV-25	200	300
William Jennings Bryan – Eagle Coin-Shaped Portrait Flask, American, yellow amber, tooled CM, SB, half pt., c1895, GI-126	1400	2100

Scroll Flasks. —Photo courtesy Glass-Works Auctions.

Fostoria

Founded in Fostoria, Ohio, in 1887, Fostoria continues to produce at their Moundsville, West Virginia, factory. Many of their glassware lines are considered as "elegant" Depression-era glass and are avidly sought by collectors.

Fairfax

	GREEN	CRYSTAL	BLUE	YELLOW	PINK
Bowl, ftd., 11.5"	$37	—	$43	$26	$37
Bowl, oval, 19.5"	45	—	60	33	48
Bread and Butter Plate, 6"	7	—	8	5	7
Cereal Bowl, 6"	23	—	29	19	23
Cigarette Box	48	—	66	40	47
Claret Goblet, 4 oz.	43	—	50	37	40
Coaster, 3.5"	7	—	10	5	7
Cocktail Goblet, 3 oz.	38	—	40	33	38
Comport, 7"	35	—	40	30	38
Cream Soup	24	—	27	20	23
Creamer, ftd.	15	—	19	10	15
Cruet, handle, ftd.	200	—	240	170	210
Cup, ftd.	11	—	16	9	10
Dinner Plate, 10.5"	50	—	50	40	47
Fruit Bowl, 5"	12	—	18	10	12
Grill Plate, 10.5"	25	—	33	19	24
Ice Bucket, metal handle	64	—	77	55	63
Luncheon Plate, 9.5"	15	—	18	14	14
Mayonnaise Dish	22	—	28	17	20
Mayonnaise Ladle	27	—	38	27	29
Parfait, ftd., 6.5 oz.	26	—	36	25	28
Pitcher, ftd., 48 oz.	320	—	360	250	325
Platter, oval, 15"	83	—	90	66	83
Relish Tray, 2 section, 8.5"	25	—	27	17	23
Relish Tray, 3 section, 11.5"	34	—	44	25	33
Sauce Boat	55	—	66	48	57
Sherbet, low, 6 oz.	27	—	23	23	26
Sherbet, tall, 6 oz.	25	—	30	26	27
Soup Bowl	29	—	30	24	26
Sugar, ftd.	12	—	22	9	13
Tray, handled, 11"	40	—	55	34	44
Tumbler, ftd., 2.5 oz.	20	—	29	20	20
Tumbler, ftd., 5 oz.	20	—	26	30	20
Tumbler, ftd., 9 oz.	25	—	33	24	25
Tumbler, ftd., 12 oz.	30	—	40	30	33
Water Goblet, 10 oz.	33	—	40	30	34

June

Baking Dish, egg shape, 9" 1	—	$60	$100	$150	$80
Bonbon, stemmed	—	23	19	43	36
Bouillon Bowl, pedestal foot, w/ liner	—	20	67	46	50
Bowl, 10" dia		46	76	64	63
Bread and Butter Plate	—	10	14	13	12
Cake Plate, handled, 10" dia	—	46	93	68	78

	GREEN	CRYSTAL	BLUE	YELLOW	PINK
Canapé Plate	—	18	30	25	26
Candlesticks, pair, 2" h	—	55	87	67	70
Candlesticks, pair, 3" h	—	67	87	78	76
Candlesticks, pair, 5" h	—	—	100	83	90
Candy Jar, cov, 2 cup capacity	—	120	290	200	225
Candy Jar, cov, 6 cup capacity	—	90	300	154	280
Celery Dish, 11" l	—	40	76	65	70
Centerpiece Bowl, oval, 11" l	—	40	85	63	90
Cereal Bowl, 6" dia	—	30	50	56	45
Cheese and Cracker Set	—	45	80	60	85
Chop Plate, 12" dia	—	40	83	70	70
Condiment Bottle, ftd., w/ stopper	—	280	600	450	600
Comport, 5" dia	—	60	60	45	60
Comport, 6" dia	—	75	135	110	115
Comport, 7" dia	—	94	165	115	139
Comport, 8" dia	—	114	180	125	150
Cordial Cup	—	40	100	63	83
Cordial Cup Saucer	—	14	24	17	19
Cordial Glass, stemmed	—	74	130	119	116
Creamer, collar base	—	44	66	45	60
Creamer, pedestal foot	—	34	43	35	30
Cup, pedestal foot	—	29	54	40	43
Decanter, w/ glasss topper	—	550	1000	840	845
Dessert Bowl, handled, 8" dia	—	76	120	85	116
Dinner Plate, 9" dia	—	20	36	44	28
Dinner Plate, 10.5" dia	—	46	80	67	73
Fan Vase, pedestal foot	—	150	260	180	190
Finger Bowl	—	35	66	48	47
Fruit Bowl, 5" dia	—	22	43	35	33
Mayonnaise Comport	—	58	97	60	70
Mint Dish	—	28	57	43	50
Nappy, flat, 7" dia	—	20	40	33	30
Nappy, pedestal foot, 6.5" dia	—	22	40	30	34
Oil Cruet, pedestal foot	—	317	900	550	730
Oyster Plate	—	40	58	40	43
Parfait Glass	—	37	66	84	50
Pitcher	—	—	900	657	650
Platter, 11" dia	—	70	100	85	90
Platter, 15" dia	—	110	245	165	200
Relish Dish, 2 section, 8.5" l	—	30	53	44	50
Sugar Bowl, cov, small	—	45	64	43	58
Tray, loop handle, 11" dia	—	50	100	65	74
Tumbler, 3.5" h	—	43	74	63	67
Tumbler, 5" h	—	30	50	40	40
Vase, 7.5" h	—	70	400	185	190
Water Glass, stemmed	—	38	55	43	60
Whipped Cream Bowl, large	—	140	280	210	250
Whipped Cream Bowl, small	—	35	50	40	43
Whiskey Tumbler, 2.5 oz.	—	40	88	67	60
Wine Glass, stemmed	—	40	100	80	77

Trojan

	GREEN	CRYSTAL	BLUE	YELLOW	PINK
Bonbon Bowl	—	—	—	$25	$25
Bouillon Bowl, ftd.	—	—	—	30	30
Cereal Bowl, 6" dia	—	—	—	33	37
Comport, 6" h	—	—	—	40	45
Creamer, ftd.	—	—	—	30	35
Dinner Plate, 10.5" dia	—	—	—	55	54
Finger Bowl, w/ liner	—	—	—	46	43
Grill Plate, 10" dia	—	—	—	50	50
Luncheon Plate, 8.5" dia	—	—	—	25	23
Mayonnaise Bowl, w/ liner	—	—	—	50	56
Parfait	—	—	—	50	50
Pitcher	—	—	—	475	450
Platter, 12" dia	—	—	—	57	60
Platter, 15" dia	—	—	—	83	90
Relish Dish, 6.5" dia	—	—	—	25	23
Relish Dish, 3 section	—	—	—	47	45
Saucer	—	—	—	16	16
Sherbet, 4.5" h	—	—	—	38	36
Sugar Bowl, ftd.	—	—	—	33	33
Tray, center handle, 11" dia	—	—	—	53	55
Tumbler, 4.5" h	—	—	—	40	38
Tumbler, 5.5" h	—	—	—	29	30
Tumbler, 6" h	—	—	—	40	38
Vase, 8" h	—	—	—	115	110
Whipped Cream Tub	—	—	—	150	130

Versailles

	GREEN	CRYSTAL	BLUE	YELLOW	PINK
Ashtray	$44	—	$57	$53	$45
Bonbon Bowl	25	—	30	23	24
Bread and Butter Plate, 6" dia	8	—	10	8	8
Cereal Bowl, 6" dia	40	—	50	43	38
Chop Plate, 13" dia	60	—	70	67	58
Comport, 6" h	44	—	60	55	46
Comport, 7" h	45	—	67	60	48
Creamer, ftd.	30	—	40	30	30
Decanter	270	—	380	290	280
Demitasse Cup and Saucer	40	—	93	64	44
Finger Bowl, w/ liner	38	—	46	48	23
Fruit Bowl, 5" dia	28	—	34	26	29
Ice Bucket	166	—	158	150	123
Lemon Bowl	20	—	27	24	10
Luncheon Plate, 8.5" dia	15	—	20	20	15
Mayonnaise Bowl, w/ liner	66	—	90	85	75
Parfait	50	—	60	53	47
Pitcher	500	—	700	600	475
Platter, 12" dia	63	—	80	65	60
Platter, 15" dia	85	—	125	100	85
Relish, 8.5" dia	67	—	80	70	60
Sauce Boat, w/ liner	93	—	120	75	84
Soup Bowl, 7" dia	50	—	56	50	50

Fruit Jars

The Mason jar was produced by John Landis Mason in the early 1800s. One of Mason's innovations was a zinc lid which provided greater air tightness.

Nineteenth-century fruit jars for home canning are collected, especially those with the manufacturer's name or a decorative motif embossed on the jar. Before 1810, few glass containers were manufactured.

	LOW	AVG.	HIGH
Agnew, handmade, aqua, qt., wax seal	$45	$50	$55
Alma, handmade, aqua, qt., threaded glass lid	70	75	80
American Soda, machine made, clear, glass lid, wire bail	6	7	8
Anderson Preserving Co., machine made, clear, qt. metal lid	10	12	14
Atlas Good Luck, machine made, clear, glass lid, wire bail, emb shamrock	3	4	5
Atlas Good Luck, machine made, clear, half pt.	4	5	6
Atlas Mason, handmade, aqua, qt., zinc lid	20	25	30
Atlas Special Mason, machine made, clear, metal lid	3	4	5
Atlas Strong Shoulder Mason, machine made, aqua, zinc lid	10	12	14
Atlas Strong Shoulder Mason, machine made, clear, zinc lid	1	2	3
Atlas Whole Fruit Jar, machine made, clear, zinc lid	3	4	5
B&B, machine made, amber, qt., glass lid, metal band	20	25	30
Ball Deluxe Jar, machine made, clear, glass lid, wire bail	3	4	5
Ball Mason's Patent Nov 30th 1858, handmade, aqua, qt., zinc lid, ground lip	3	4	5
Ball Square Mason, machine made, clear, qt., rounded sq., zinc lid	1	2	3
Bamberger's Mason Jar, machine made, aqua, glass lid, wire bail	8	10	12
Beehive, machine made, light blue, glass lid, metal band	50	75	100
Best, machine made, light green, qt., glass lid, metal band	50	55	60
The Best, handmade, light green, qt., glass stopper, lid reads "Aug. 18th, 1868"	70	75	80
Boldt Mason, machine made, aqua/blue, zinc lid	25	30	35
Brighton, handmade, clear, qt., glass lid, toggle top	40	45	50
Buckeye, handmade, aqua, qt., glass lid, iron yoke	140	160	180
Cadiz jar, handmade, aqua, qt., threaded glass lid	80	100	120
The Champion, pat Aug 31, 1869, handmade, aqua, qt., glass lid, iron screw yoke	80	90	100
Crown Mason, machine made, clear, zinc lid	1	2	3
Crystal jar, handmade, clear/amethyst, qt., glass lid	25	38	50
Crystal Mason, handmade, clear, pt./qt., zinc lid	15	20	25
The Dandy, handmade, amber, glass lid, wrie bail	50	55	60
The Dandy, handmade, clear/aqua, glass lid, wire bail	20	25	30
Diamond Fruit Jar, machine made, clear, glass lid, screw band	3	4	5
The Dictator, handmade, green, qt., wax seal	80	90	100
Double Safety, machine made, clear, glass lid, wire bail	4	6	8
Drey Mason, machine made, clear/green, zinc lid	1	2	3
Drey Square Mason, machine made, clear, zinc lid	2	3	4
Dunkley, machine made, clear, qt., hinged glass lid	25	30	35
Electric Fruit Jar, handmade, aqua, qt., glass lid	60	70	80
The Empire, handmade, aqua, qt., glass lid, cam lever	75	80	85
Empress, handmade, clear, qt., glass lid, zinc band	75	80	85
Everlasting Jar, machine made, clear/green, glass lid, toggle	15	20	25
Famous, machine made, aqua, glass lid, wire bail	12	15	18
Faxon, handmade, aqua, glass lid, zinc band	10	12	14
Flickinger, handmade, aqua, qt., glass lid, wire bail	18	20	22
Frank, handmade, aqua, qt., wax seal	40	45	50

	LOW	AVG.	HIGH
The Gem, handmade, aqua, glass lid, screw band, emb ititials	15	18	21
Gem Improved, handmade, green, qt., glass lid, screw band	3	4	5
Glenshaw, machine made, clear, glass lid	3	4	5
Halle, handmade, green, qt., wax seal	50	55	60
Hartells, handmade, aqua, qt., glass lid, metal clamp	60	70	80
Hawley, handmade, green, qt., zinc lid	18	20	22
Hazel Preserve Jar, machine made, clear, glass lid, wire bail	6	8	10
Hero, handmade, green/clear, pt./qt., glass lid, screw band	25	30	35
Hero Improved, handmade, green, pt./qt., glass lid, screw band	15	20	25
Keystone, machine made, clear, pt./qt., zinc lid	8	10	12
Kline, handmade, blue, qt., glass stopper	35	40	45
Knox Mason, machine made, clear, metal lid	1	2	3
Lamb, machine made, aqua/clear, zinc lid	2	3	4
The Leader, handmade, amber, glass lid, wire bail	40	45	50
The Leader, handmade, clear, glass lid, wire bail	20	25	30
Lightning, machine made, clear, glass lid, wire bail, emb anchor	1	2	3
The Marion Jar, handmade, green, zinc lid	8	10	12
Mason, handmade, aqua, zinc lid, emb star and crescent moon	30	35	40
Mason, machine made, clear, zinc lid, emb anchor	1	2	3
Mason Jar, machine made, clear, metal lid, emb star	1	2	3
Mason Jar Improved, handmade, clear, glass lid, screw band	4	5	6
Mason's Union, handmade, aqua, zinc lid, emb shield	10	12	14
Metro Easy-Pack, machine made, clear, zinc lid	1	2	3
Monarch, machine made, clear, glass lid, wire bail, emb shield	4	5	6
Mountain Mason, machine made, clear, zinc lid	12	15	18
Newman's patent, Dec. 20th 1959, handmade, aqua, qt.	100	125	150
The Nifty, handmade, clear, qt., glass lid, clip	25	30	35
The Penn, handmade, green, qt., wax seal	60	70	80
Pine Deluxe Jar, machine made, clear, glass lid, wire bail	4	5	6
Pine Mason, machine made, clear, zinc lid	3	4	5
The Puritan, handmade, aqua, qt., glass lid, clamp	100	125	150
The Queen, handmade, aqua, pt./qt., glass lid, screw band	15	20	25
Rhodes, machine made, aqua, zinc lid	20	25	30
Root, handmade, aqua/green/yellow, pt./qt., zinc lid	5	6	7
The Rose, machine made, clear, qt., zinc lid	12	15	18
Samco, machine made, clear, zinc lid	2	3	4
Sealfast, machine made, clear/aqua, glass lid, wire bail	4	5	6
Security, handmade, clear, qt., glass lid, wire bail	8	10	12
Star, handmade, clear, glass lid, zinc band	50	55	60
Temple, handmade, clear, pt./qt., zinc lid	40	45	50
Veteran, machine made, clear, glass lid, wire bail	20	25	30

Fruit Jars. —Photo courtesy Glass-Works Auctions.

Goofus Glass

When the iridescent glass of Tiffany, Loetz and other makers became popular in the homes of the rich, Goofus Glass answered back with bold, inexpensive lustre painted wares. These pieces date to the first quarter of this century.

	LOW	AVG.	HIGH
Cake Plate, acorn and leaf, 12" dia	$25	$40	$60
Cake Plate, carnation, 12" dia	30	50	80
Cake Plate, morning glory, 12" dia	35	50	90
Decanter, basket-weave, 10" h	50	80	130
Decanter, grape, 7.5" h	50	80	130
Dresser Tray, heart form, 6" l	55	80	140
Nut Dish, cherry, handled, 6.5" l	40	60	100
Perfume Bottle, tulip, 3.5" h	20	30	50
Pitcher, cabbage rose, 5.5" h	45	70	110
Pitcher, strawberries, 6.5" h	45	70	110
Plate, Cupid, 7" dia	40	60	100
Plate, drinking monk, 7" dia	40	60	100
Plate, Gibson Girl, 8.5" dia	40	60	100
Plate, green poppy, 7" dia	30	50	80
Plate, holly, 10.5" dia	50	80	130
Plate, pine cones and leaves, 10" dia	50	80	130
Powder Box, basket-weave, 3.5" l	55	80	140
Powder Box, puffy rose, 3" l	45	70	110
Salt/Pepper, pair, cabbage rose, 3.5" h	40	60	100
Salt/Pepper, pair, dogwood, 4" h	40	60	100
Salt/Pepper, pair, poppies, 3" h	40	60	100
Tumbler, grape, 4" h	30	50	80
Vase, 2 poppies, 12" h	25	40	60
Vase, 3 chrysanthemum, 15" h	60	90	150
Vase, 3 irises, 12" h	50	80	130
Vase, 4 daisies, 12" h	40	60	100
Vase, 4 dogwood blossoms, 15" h	55	80	140
Vase, 4 poppies, 12" h	35	50	90
Vase, 6 clusters of grapes, 10" h	30	50	80
Vase, 6 poppies, 8.5" h	35	50	90
Vase, 6 purple irises, 10" h	30	50	80
Vase, bird and grapevine, 9" h	15	20	40
Vase, birds in dogwood tree, 10" h	40	60	100
Vase, cabbage rose, 12" h	40	60	100
Vase, cluster of dogwood blossoms, 15" h	50	80	130
Vase, dogwood blossoms over hearts, 15" h	40	60	100
Vase, flower on crackle glass, 14" h	60	90	150
Vase, grapes on basket-weave, 10" h	25	40	60
Vase, love birds, 10" h	50	80	130
Vase, mixed fruit, 10" h	40	60	100
Vase, peacock, 10.5" h	100	150	250
Vase, peacock in tree, 15" h	100	150	250
Vase, regal iris, 10" h	75	110	190
Vase, rose in snow, 10" h	20	30	50
Vase, rose tree, 12" h	50	80	130

Heisey Glass

A partnership including George Duncan and Daniel C. Ripley established the A.H. Heisey Glass Co. in the 1860s in Newark, Ohio. Cut and pressed glasswares were manufactured. Heisey glass is high quality. Many patterns are called "elegant Depression glass."

The Heisey Collectors of America, Inc. (169 W. Church St., Newark, OH 43055) publishes *Heisey News,* a newsletter with information on patterns, history of Heisey, and advertisements.

Ipswich

	GREEN	CRYSTAL	BLUE	YELLOW	PINK
Creamer	$32	$14	—	$28	$22
Cruet, ftd., w/ stopper, 2 oz.	85	48	—	75	65
Finger Bowl, w/ liner	40	14	—	34	25
Goblet, 4 oz.	10	—	—	—	—
Goblet, 10 oz.	—	14	—	—	—
Pitcher, 2 qt.	400	95	$300	190	140
Plate, 8" sq	25	15	—	26	22
Sherbet, 4 oz.	20	8	—	20	17
Tumbler, curved rim, 10 oz.	28	8	—	27	24

Lariat

	GREEN	CRYSTAL	BLUE	YELLOW	PINK
Basket, ftd., 10"	—	$125	—	—	—
Bowl, 4"	—	14	—	—	—
Bowl, 12"	—	15	—	—	—
Bowl, 13"	—	18	—	—	—
Bowl, flat, 8"	—	13	—	—	—
Buffet Plate, 21"	—	33	—	—	—
Cake Plate, rolled edge, 12"	—	18	—	—	—
Candlestick, 2 arm	—	11	—	—	—
Goblet, 9 oz.	—	10	—	—	—
Goblet, blown, 10 oz.	—	12	—	—	—
Salad Plate, 7"	—	7	—	—	—
Salad Plate, 8"	—	8	—	—	—
Salt/Pepper, pair	—	140	—	—	—
Sauce	—	3	—	—	—
Server, 2 handles, 14.5"	—	28	—	—	—
Sherbet, low, 6 oz.	—	4	—	—	—

Octagon

	GREEN	CRYSTAL	BLUE	YELLOW	PINK
Bonbon Dish, #1229, 8"	$11	$4	—	$9	$7
Bowl, 6.5"	14	10	—	15	13
Cheese Dish, 2 handles, #1229, 6"	11	4	—	9	7
Hors d'Oeuvre Plate, #1229, 13"	29	14	—	24	19
Plate, 6"	9	3	—	7	5

Old Sandwich

	GREEN	CRYSTAL	BLUE	YELLOW	PINK
Bowl, oval, ftd., 12"	$68	$25	—	$58	$56
Bowl, round, ftd., 11"	58	24	—	46	39
Comport, 6"	78	26	—	74	68

	GREEN	CRYSTAL	BLUE	YELLOW	PINK
Cup	16	7	—	13	11
Decanter, w/ stopper	175	60	320	165	155
Finger Bowl	18	6	—	15	12
Goblet, 4 oz.	20	9	88	18	15
Goblet, 3 oz.	19	8	—	16	14
Mug, 12 oz.	240	24	270	195	185
Mug, 18 oz.	290	28	320	245	220
Pilsener Glass, 8 oz.	33	10	—	28	23
Pilsener Glass, 10 oz.	36	13	—	30	26
Pitcher, 2 qt.	125	55	—	120	115
Pitcher, ice lip, 2 qt.	130	63	—	125	120
Plate, 6" sq	13	4	—	10	8
Plate, 7" sq	15	4	—	14	10
Plate, 8" sq	17	6	—	15	12
Salt/Pepper, pair	58	28	—	48	38
Saucer	14	6	—	12	10
Tumbler, 5 oz.	19	3	—	14	11
Tumbler, 12 oz.	26	9	—	21	16

Pleat and Panel

	GREEN	CRYSTAL	BLUE	YELLOW	PINK
Bouillon Bowl, 2 handles, 5"	$11	$5	—	—	$9
Bouillon Bowl Liner, 6.5"	7	2	—	—	5
Bowl, 4"	9	4	—	—	7
Bowl, 6.5"	11	4	—	—	9
Champagne Goblet, 5 oz.	11	4	—	—	9
Cheese and Cracker Set	34	19	—	—	29
Comport, cov, ftd., 5"	54	24	—	—	44
Creamer, institutional	14	4	—	—	9
Cruet, w/ stopper, 3 oz.	34	16	—	—	29
Cup/Saucer	20	6	—	—	14
Jelly Bowl, 2 handles, 5"	11	5	—	—	9
Marmalade Jar, 4.5"	16	6	—	—	11
Nappy, 4.5"	8	4	—	—	7
Nappy, 8"	16	9	—	—	14
Pitcher	65	30	—	—	50
Pitcher, ice lip	75	40	—	—	60
Plate, 8"	11	4	—	—	9
Plate, 14"	29	14	—	—	24
Platter, oval, 12"	34	18	—	—	29

Provincial

	GREEN	CRYSTAL	BLUE	YELLOW	PINK
Ashtray, 3" sq	—	$11	—	—	—
Bonbon Dish, 2 handles, 7"	$29	9	—	—	—
Buffet Plate, 18"	—	24	—	—	—
Butter Dish, cov	—	55	—	—	—
Candelabra, 3 candles	—	34	—	—	—
Candleholder	—	14	—	—	—
Candy Box, cov, tooled, 5.5"	220	60	—	—	—
Ice Tea Tumbler, ftd., 12 oz.	39	14	—	—	—
Plate, 7"	—	9	—	—	—

Lalique

René Lalique (1860–1945) began his career as a jeweler in Paris and by 1900 had become one of the world's most celebrated Art Nouveau designers. He began to manufacture glass in 1910. Many regard him as the best glass designer of the twentieth century. The company is still in business under the direction of René Lalique's granddaughter Marie Claude Lalique. Most items produced before René Lalique's death in 1945 are marked *R. LALIQUE,* while later pieces are marked *LALIQUE.* Collectors focus on the earlier period, especially pieces in color and rare models. Many fakes and forgeries exist. They are often crude and easily recognizable. When examining Lalique never let a signature authenticate the object, let the object authenticate the signature.

Prices are for items in pristine condition, meaning no cracks, chips, stains, or restorations. For clarification we have included the MA numbers from Felix Marcilhac's *René Lalique,* Edition de L'Amateur, Paris, 1989.

The Lalique Collector's Society can be reached at 400 Veterans Blvd., Carlstadt, NJ 07072, 1–800–CRISTAL.

	LOW	HIGH
Ashtray, Chien, opalescent green, dog, c1926, MA p. 272 #290	$700	$900
Ashtray, Dindon, amber, turkey, c1925, MA p. 272 #287	600	700
Ashtray, Louise, pale gray w/ black enamel detail, c1929, MA p. 275 #301	200	300
Ashtray, Medicis, clear and frosted, female nudes, c1924, MA p. 270 #280	350	450
Ashtray, Vezelay, amber, Art Deco, c1924, MA p. 270 #281	450	600
Automobile Mascot, Tete d'Aigle, clear and frosted w/ chromium plated brass collar and turned wood stand, c1928, 10.7" h wo/ mount, MA p. 499 #1138	2200	3000
Bookends, pair, Chrysis, clear and frosted, kneeling Art Deco female nudes raised on plinths, design #1185400 by René Lalique, c1928, 6.25" h	700	900
Bookends, pair, Reverie, clear and frosted, kneeling female nudes, design #1185000 by Marc Lalique, c1950, 8.75" h	2000	2500
Bowl, Lys, feet modeled as 4 lily pads, c1924, 23.5cm dia, MA p. 292 #382	800	1000
Bowl, Champs Elysees, clear and frosted, foliage pattern, design #1121600 by Marc Lalique, 1956, 18" l	1000	1200
Bowl, Coquilles, opalescent, shells, c1924, 20.7cm dia, MA p. 748 #3201	500	600
Bowl, Ondines Ouverte, opalescent, sirens, c1921, 21cm dia, MA p. 292 #380	1200	1500
Bowl, Perruches, opalescent, parakeets, c1931, 24.5cm dia, MA p. 302 #419	3500	4500
Bowl, Poissons, opalescent, fish, c1921, 20.6cm dia, MA p. 749 #3212	500	600
Bowl, Yeso, clear opalescent green glass applied w/ model of fish, design #1107300 by Marie Claude Lalique, 1976, 9cm dia	750	1200
Box, cov., Coquilles, clear and frosted w/ shells pattern, c1920, MA p. 236 #71	750	850
Box, cov., Copelia, gilt-metal mounted frosted glass, design #1057800 by René Lalique in 1914, 7" l	600	700
Box, Dinard, clear and frosted, Art Deco, c1927, 13cm l, MA p. 237 #78	2300	2500
Box, cov., Quatre Scarabees, black, 4 scarab beetles centering a rosette, c1911, MA p. 225 #15	2000	2500
Brooch, Cabochon Lilas, opalescent, modern metal back, c1920, MA p. 539 M	250	450
Candlesticks, pair, Mesanges, clear and frosted, birds, separate orig. bobeches, design #1090100 by Marc Lalique, c1943, 6.75cm h	900	1200
Carafe, Tokyo, clear, c1930, 17.5cm h, MA p. 848 #5274	250	350
Center Bowl, Aries, clear and frosted, support modeled as ram's head, design #1105800 by Marie Claude Lalique, 1968, 7.5" h	500	700
Center Bowl, Bamako, clear and green glass applied w/ models of salamanders at rim, design #1106900 by MarieClaude Lalique, 1973, 8.75" dia	800	1200
Center Bowl, Deux Moineaux Monquers, clear and frosted applied w/ 2 sparrows, design #1100000 by René Lalique, 1930, 16" dia	1000	1400

	LOW	HIGH
Center Bowl, Stresa, clear and frosted, abstract pattern, design #1122000 by Marc Lalique, 1967, 12" dia	400	600
Center Bowl, Virginia, clear and frosted, design #1105900 by Marie Claude Lalique, 1968, 8.5" dia	600	800
Clock, Deux Colombes, opalescent, lovebirds, c1926, 22.2cm h	4500	6000
Clock, Quatre Perruches, clear and frosted, 4 parakeets, c1920, MA p. 376 #760	1800	2000
Cocktail Shaker, Thomery, clear and frosted, c1928, MA p. 813 #2878	1800	2000
Deep Bowl, Florabella, opalescent w/ sepia patina, c1930, 39cm dia, MA p. 299 #407	4000	6000
Dressing Mirror, Bouton de Roses, clear and frosted, oval, rosebuds on chromium plated easel mount, design # 1065500 by René Lalique in 1939, 9.5" h	800	1000
Figure, Chat Assis, clear and frosted, seated cat, design #1160300 by René Lalique, c1932, 7.5" h	500	700
Figure, Chat Couche, clear and frosted, crouching cat, design #1160200 by René Lalique, 1932, 9" l	500	700
Figure, Colombe Clita, clear and frosted, dove w/ outstretched wings, design #1163400 by Marie Claude Lalique, 1966, 9" h	600	800
Figure, Cygne Haute, clear and frosted, swan swimming w/ head up, w/ orig. flower holder, design #1161600 by Marc Lalique, c1944, 12.5" l	2000	2500
Figure, Cygne Tete Baisee, clear and frosted, swan swimming w/ head down, w/ orig. flower holder, design #1161500 by Marc Lalique, c1944, 14" l	2300	2800
Figure, Danseuse, clear and frosted, female dancer w/ arms up, design #1190800 by Marc Lalique, c1942, 9.5" h	400	600
Figure, Deux Danseuses, clear and frosted, 2 female dancers, design #1190900 by Marc Lalique, c1942, 9.5" h	800	1000
Figure, Gros Poisson Vagues, clear on illuminating bronze base, fish, c1922, 40cm h, MA p. 478 #1100	5000	6000

Top row, left to right: Reverie Bookends, Deux Danseuses Statuette, Danseuse Statuette, Chrysis Bookends. Bottom row: Ganymede Ice Bucket, Masque de Femme Plaque, Bacchantes Vase, Ondines Vase. —Photo courtesy William Doyle Galleries.

	LOW	HIGH
Figure, Motif Ara, clear and frosted, cockatoo, design #1162200 by Marc Lalique, c1953, 11" h	900	1200
Figure, Pigeon Gand, clear, pigeon, design #1160700 by René Lalique, 1932, 12" l	400	600
Figure, Thais, clear and frosted, c1925, 23cm h, MA p. 400 #834	7000	9000
Figure, Zeila, clear and frosted, panther, design #1165200 by Marie Claude Lalique, 1981, 14.5" l	800	1000
Fruit Bowl, Olonne, clear and frosted, foliage pattern, design #11057, discontinued 1990, 10" dia	500	700
Hors d'Oeuvres Server, Nippon, clear, 6 parts, c1931, 34cm dia, MA p. 815 #3888	900	1100
Ice Bucket, cov., Antilles, clear and frosted w/ silvered metal rim, design #11959 by Marc Lalique, c1965, 10.25" h	800	1000
Ice Bucket, Ganymede, clear and frosted, female nudes, design #1195100 by Marc Lalique, c1950, 9" h	1200	1500
Inkwell, Nenuphar, clear and frosted w/ sepia patina, fitted box, c1910, MA p. 315 #425	1500	2000
Inkwell, Sully, black, rect., fitted w/ 2 covered wells, Aztec geometric motif, c1927, 15cm l, MA p. 219 #439	2500	4000
Letter Seal, Tete d'Aigle, black glass w/ white patina, engraved intaglio monogram, c1911, 7.8cm h, MA p. 248 #175	1000	1200
Letter Seal, Tete d'Aigle, clear, 7.8cm h, MA p. 248 #175	600	800
Medallions, pair, Albertville Winter Olympics commemorative, clear and frosted, w/ stands, 1992	500	600
Menu Plaque, Raisin Muscat, clear and frosted, grapes, c1924, 15cm h, MA p. 780 #3475	400	600
Pendant, Cicognes, clear and frosted, exotic birds pattern, silk cord w/ tassels, c1920, MA p. 574 #1635	500	700
Perfume Atomizer, Danseuses Egyptiennes, clear w/ orange enamel detail and gilt-metal top, made for Marcas et Bardel, c1926, MA p. 961	600	800
Perfume Bottle, Ambre, black, for D'Orsay, c1911, 13cm h, MA p.933	1800	2200
Perfume Bottle, Amphitrite, green, c1920, 9.5cm h, MA p. 335 #514	2800	3500
Perfume Bottle, Anges, clear w/ sepia patina, made for Alexander Oviatt store, Los Angeles, c1928, MA p. 339 #531	2500	3500
Perfume Bottle, L'Effleurt, clear and frosted w/ gray patina, for Coty, c1912, MA p. 928/18	6000	8000
Perfume Bottle, Panier de Roses, clear and frosted w/ blue patina, c1912, 10cm h, MA p. 327 #487	1000	1200
Perfume Bottle, Petites Feuilles, clear and frosted w/ gray patina, c1910, 10.2cm h, MA p. 325 #478	900	1000
Perfume Bottle, Sans Adieu, green, Art Deco on ebonized wood and silvered metal stand, for Worth, c1929, 11cm h, MA p. 952 #11	600	750
Plaque, Masque de Femme, clear and frosted, designed as fountain head, w/ orig. chromed metal stand and back plate, design #1164500 by René Lalique in 1928, 12.5" h	4500	6500
Plaque, St. Therese, clear and frosted on ebonized wood base, c1950, 37cm h, MA p. 519 #1221	700	850
Plate, Martigues, opalescent, fish, c1920, 36cm dia, MA p. 290 #377	3500	4500
Plate, Ondines, sirens, c1921, MA p. 292 #3003	1500	1700
Plate, Rosace, opalescent, Art Deco, c1930, 31.5cm dia, MA p. 300 #409	750	900
Powder Box, cov., Degas, ballerina, c1921, Ma p. 235 #66	700	1000
Powder Box, cov., Le Lys, clear and frosted, for D'Orsay, w/ orig. unopened powder and orig. box, c1922, CA p. 964	250	350
Rocker Blotter, Faune et Nymphe, clear and frosted w/ metal mount, c1920, 16cm l, MA p. 245 #153	1600	1800

Perfume Bottles, left to right: Anges, Petites Feuilles, Danseuses Egyptiennes, Ambre, Panier de Roses, Amphitrite. —Photo courtesy William Doyle Galleries.

	LOW	HIGH
Salad Plates, Antibes, teal green, c1960, set of 6	175	300
Spinning Tops, Toupies, clear and frosted, set of 3 in orig. bakelite case, c1929, MA p. 812/D	1200	1600
Table Jardiniere, Chene, clear and frosted, rect., border molded w/ oak leaf and acorn in relief, c1943, 46.6cm l, MA p. 774 #3467	1000	1200
Table Jardiniere, St. Hubert, clear and frosted, handles patterned w/ Art Deco gazelles and foliage, c1927, 48.5cm l, MA p. 773 #3461	450	650
Table Ornament, Groupe Luxembourg, clear and frosted, modeled as 3 cherubs, short-haired version, design #1162000 by René Lalique, c1936, 8cm h	750	900
Tray, Nigeria, clear and frosted, peacocks and foliage, design #11711 by Marc Lalique, c1955, 15.25" dia	700	900
Vase, Antinea, clear applied opalescent green, nymphs, design #1229500 by Marie Claude Lalique, c1969, 8" h	1200	1500
Vase, Archers, deep topaz, male archers, c1921, 26cm h, MA p. 415 #893	3500	4500
Vase, Archers, opalescent w/ blue patina, c1921, 26cm h, MA p. 415 #893	10,000	12,000
Vase, Avalon, opalescent w/ gray patina, c1927, 14.7cm h, MA p. 436 #986	2000	2500
Vase, Bacchantes, clear and frosted, frieze of female nudes in relief, design #11220000 by René Lalique in 1927, c1975, 9.5" h	1700	2000
Vase, Bagatelle, clear and frosted, birds, design #1221900 by René Lalique, 1939, 6.75" h	400	500
Vase, Beliers, opalescent, 2 handles modeled as rams, c1925, 18.8cm h, MA p. 418 #904	3000	4000
Vase, Biskra, light green, Art Deco palm fronds, c1932, MA p. 455 #1078	3500	4500
Vase, Ceylan, opalescent w/ blue-green patina, parakeets, c1924, 25cm h, MA p. 418 #905	5700	7000
Vase, Chevaux, charcoal gray w/ band of horses, Art Deco, c1930, 18.8cm h, MA p. 448 #1047	3000	4000
Vase, Domremy, opalescent, thistle plants, c1926, 22cm h, MA p. 443 #1019	800	1200
Vase, Domremy, opalescent w/ green patina, thistles, c1926, MA p. 443 #1019	1500	2000
Vase, Feuilles, clear and frosted, stylized leaves, design #1220900 by René Lalique, 1933, 7" h	400	600
Vase, Ingrid, clear and frosted, stylized leafage, design #1228900 by Marc Lalique, 1970, 10" h	1000	1500
Vase, Luxembourg, clear and frosted, cherubs in relief, design #1222700 by René Lalique, 1945, 8" h	2300	2800
Vase, Marrakesh, clear and amber, abstract pattern, design #1231100 by Marie Claude Lalique, c1985, 12.25" h	1000	1500
Vase, Mesanges, clear and frosted, birds, design #1226200 by René Lalique, c1931, 12.5" h	1000	1500

	LOW	HIGH
Vase, Ondines, clear and frosted, female nudes, design #1223800 by Marc Lalique, c1950, 9.5" h	1000	1200
Vase, Rose, clear and applied amber, blossoming rose, design #1229400, 8" h	800	1000
Vase, Saghir, clear and applied green, design #1229200, c1971, 8.5" h	800	1000
Vase, Saint Marc, opalescent, fantail pigeons, c1939, 17cm h, MA p. 471 #10-934	1750	2000
Vase, Sauge, deep teal green, sage leaves, c1923, 26cm h, MA p. 425 #935	3500	4500
Vase, Sauterelles, clear and frosted w/ blue and green patina, grasshoppers and grass stalks, c1912, 28cm h, MA p. 414 #888	4500	5500
Vase, Sauterelles, electric blue w/ white patina, grasshoppers and grass stalks, c1920, 28cm h, MA p. 414 #888	8000	10,000
Vase, Serpent, deep amber, modeled as coiled serpent, c1924, 26cm h, MA p. 416 #896	14,000	16,000
Vase, Sirenes et Cabochons, clear and frosted w/ gray patina, c1914, 21cm h, MA p. 417 #899	3500	4000
Vase, Vagues, clear and frosted, waves pattern, design #1229800 by Marc Lalique in 1976, 8.5" h	1800	2300
Vase, Verone, clear and frosted, birds on stylized branches, design #1121800 by Marc Lalique, 1956, 9.75" h	1800	2000
Wall Sconces, pair, Lierre, clear and frosted, Art Deco ivy leaves, 32.5cm l, MA p. 595 #2018	2000	3000
Wall Shelf Supports, pair, Cerf, clear and frosted, modeled as deer, design #1005100 by Marc Lalique, c1955	2500	3500
Wine Goblet, Chien, clear and frosted w/ sepia patina, hunting dogs on foot, c1921, MA p. 806 #3755	200	300
Wine Goblet, Quatre Grenouilles, clear w/ gray patina, frogs, c1912, MA p. 806 #3751	3000	3500
Wine Goblet, Selestat, clear and black, c1925, MA p. 834 #5074	175	250

Vases, top row, left to right: Ingrid, Mesanges, Marrakesh, Vagues. Bottom row: Antinea, Luxembourg, Rose, Saghir. —Photo courtesy William Doyle Galleries.

Paperweights

Glass paperweights were not seen before the 1700s; they are a recent item. The most important examples were made in the nineteenth century. Millefiori weights contain arrays of small ornamental glass beads or stems arranged in a striking pattern. They are quite colorful. Sulfides are ceramic relief plaques encased in glass. Souvenir paperweights featuring some company or place are also common, though not as desirable.

The weight of the specimen is not an indication of quality. Rather, the name of the maker and the level of artistry evident determine the value of a paperweight. Clichy, Baccarat and St. Louis are important producers of artistic glass paperweights. Prices for famous makers are high, although less known craftsmen can also produce exquisite items. Although they sometimes put their initials on one of the canes in a millefiori weight, fakes are not uncommon.

	LOW	AVG.	HIGH
Baccarat, millefiori canes, 1847, 2.75" dia	$1500	$1750	$2000
Baccarat, primrose, pink, red, and green, 3" dia	450	500	550
Baccarat, sulfide, Eleanor Roosevelt	100	175	250
Baccarat, sulfide, John Kennedy	450	500	550
Baccarat, sulfide, Will Rogers	300	400	500
Banford, Ray, stylized roses, c1974	600	700	800
Crider, most designs, large	75	100	125
Crider, most designs, small	48	66	83
Davis, Jim, bell shape, swirl design	29	36	43
Davis, Jim, bird shape, large	19	27	34
Davis, Jim, 5 flowers in vase	38	52	66
Gentile, 3 lilies	25	30	35
Gentile, bubble, clear, small	10	15	19
Gentile, butterfly, small	28	32	35
Gentile, cabbage leaf	36	39	42
Gentile, Elks Lodge	29	34	40
Gentile, millefiori butterfly and flower	75	100	125
Gentile, millefiori pinwheel	61	79	97
Gentile, Remember Pearl Harbor	43	57	71
Gentile, sign of the zodiac	27	34	42
Gentile, white goose	34	40	45
Kazium, Charles, miniature, floral motif, pedestal, 2" h	800	900	1000
New England Glass Co., posy bouquet, millefiori canes, 2.75" dia	850	1000	1150
Oriental, 2 frogs, 4" h	43	52	60
Oriental, flower, elongated pedestal, 5.5" h	52	62	71
Oriental, open rose, 3.5" h	53	63	73
Perthshire, sunflower, 1979, 3.5" dia	278	332	386
St. Clair, bell w/ 5 flowers	22	28	34
St. Clair, floral design	31	39	47
St. Louis, dahlia, star-cut base, 2.5" dia	1500	2000	2500
St. Louis, fruit in a basket, 2.25" dia	4000	4500	5000
St. Louis, King Tut mask, 1979	550	625	700
Tiffany, Favrile, red sides, internal yellow blossoms, 1906	5000	6500	8000
Tiffany, Favrile scarab, c1900, 4" l	1000	1300	1600
Ysart, Paul, clematis in latticinio basket, 2.25" dia	1000	1500	2000
Ysart, Paul, fish w/ multicolored sea bed, 3" dia	900	1100	1300

Pressed Glass

Small, crude objects and feet for footed bowls were first hand-pressed in England in the early 1800s, but pressing glass with machinery appears to have originated in America. Glass companies began producing pressed glass in matching tableware sets during the 1840s.

Although identification of pieces is mainly by pattern name, there is some confusion in this area. Most of the original names have been discarded by advanced collectors who have renamed the pattern in descriptive terms. Manufacturers' marks are exceedingly rare and there are few catalogs available from the period before 1850. By studying the old catalogs that do exist, along with shards found at old factory sites, some sketchy information has been provided. But because the competition quickly copied patterns, absolute verification of the manufacturer is impossible.

Earlier pieces contain many imperfections: bubbles, lumps, impurities and sometimes cloudiness. Reproductions pose a problem to the beginning collector. Two popular patterns, Bellflower and Daisy and Button, have been reproduced extensively. With careful, informed scrutiny, collectors can detect the dullness and lack of sparkle characteristic of remakes. If the reproduction was made from a new mold (formed from an original object), the details will not possess the clarity and precision of the original article. For further information see *The Official Price Guide to Glassware, Second Edition* by Mark Pickvet, House of Collectibles, NY, 1998.

Actress (clear)

	LOW	AVG.	HIGH
Bowl, ftd., 7" dia.	$32	$40	$50
Bread Plate, HMS Pinafore, 7" x 12"	65	80	95
Butter, cov.	65	80	95
Cake Stand, 10"	110	135	160
Candlesticks, pair	175	225	270
Celery Vase, actress head	95	118	140
Comport, cov., 12" dia	220	275	325
Creamer	55	68	80
Goblet	60	75	90
Marmalade, cov.	95	115	135
Milk Pitcher, 6.5" h	200	250	300
Relish, 5" x 8"	24	30	38
Salt, master	50	65	80
Salt Shaker, orig. pewter top	32	40	50
Sauce, ftd.	15	18	24
Spooner	45	55	65
Sugar, cov.	72	90	105
Water Pitcher, 9" h	180	225	270

Baby Face, Cupid (clear w/ frosted stem)

	LOW	AVG.	HIGH
Butter, cov.	$200	$250	$300
Celery Vase	60	75	90
Champagne	80	100	125
Comport, cov., 7"	180	225	265
Comport, open, 7"	80	95	110
Creamer	85	110	140
Goblet	80	100	120
Spooner	82	95	108
Sugar, cov.	150	195	240
Water Pitcher	240	300	365

Cameo (clear)

	LOW	AVG.	HIGH
Butter, cov.	$35	$40	$55
Celery Vase	25	30	35
Comport, cov., high standard	42	50	60
Creamer	28	35	45
Sauce, ftd.	12	15	20
Spooner	20	25	30
Sugar, cov.	32	40	50
Water Pitcher	65	80	95

Cupid and Venus, Guardian Angel

	LOW	AVG.	HIGH
Bowl, cov., ftd., clear, 8"	$30	$35	$40
Bowl, oval, clear, 9"	25	32	40
Bread Plate, amber	60	75	90
Bread Plate, clear	32	40	50
Butter, cov., clear	45	55	65
Cake Plate, clear	38	45	50
Cake Stand, clear	45	60	75
Celery Vase, clear	30	40	50
Comport, cov., high standard, clear, 8"	80	100	120
Comport, cov., low standard, clear, 7"	78	90	105
Creamer, clear	30	35	40
Goblet, clear	60	75	90
Marmalade, cov., clear	70	85	100
Milk Pitcher, amber	140	175	210
Milk Pitcher, clear	60	75	95
Plate, amber, 10" dia.	60	75	90
Plate, clear, 10" dia.	30	40	50
Spooner, clear	30	35	40
Sugar, cov., clear	50	65	80
Water Pitcher, amber	150	195	235
Water Pitcher, clear	50	65	80

Actress *Baby Face* *Cameo* *Cupid and Venus*

—Photos courtesy Gene Harris Antique Auction Center

Jumbo (clear)

	LOW	AVG.	HIGH
Butter, cov., round, Barnum's head	$260	$325	$390
Comport, cov., 7"	320	400	475
Comport, cov., 12"	650	800	950
Creamer, plain Jumbo	180	225	270
Sauce	40	50	60
Spooner, Barnum's head	80	100	125
Sugar, cov., Barnum's head	330	400	475
Water Pitcher	450	550	650

Log Cabin (clear)

	LOW	AVG.	HIGH
Bowl, cov., 8"	$320	$400	$475
Butter, cov.	240	300	360
Comport, high standard, 10.5"	225	275	325
Creamer	80	100	120
Marmalade, cov.	225	275	325
Sauce, flat	60	75	90
Spooner	95	120	150
Sugar, cov.	220	275	325
Water Pitcher	250	300	350

Minerva, Roman Medallion (clear)

	LOW	AVG.	HIGH
Bowl, ftd.	$35	$40	$45
Butter, cov.	65	75	85
Cake Stand, 13"	120	145	170
Comport, cov., high standard, 8"	120	150	180
Creamer	38	45	55
Goblet	75	90	105
Plate, 8"	45	55	65
Sauce, flat	15	18	24
Spooner	32	40	50
Sugar, cov.	55	65	75
Water Pitcher	150	185	220

Jumbo

Log Cabin

Minerva

Powder and Shot

—Photos courtesy Gene Harris Antique Auction Center

Powder and Shot, Horn of Plenty, Powder Horn and Shot (clear)

	LOW	AVG.	HIGH
Butter, cov.	$80	$95	$110
Celery Vase	75	95	105
Comport, cov., high standard	85	100	115
Creamer, applied handle	60	75	90
Goblet	55	65	75
Sauce	18	20	22
Spooner	45	55	65
Sugar, cov.	72	80	90
Water Pitcher	125	150	175

Swan, Plain Swan, Swan with Mesh (clear)

	LOW	AVG.	HIGH
Butter, cov.	$100	$125	$150
Comport, cov., high standard	100	125	150
Creamer	60	75	90
Goblet	70	80	90
Sauce, flat, 4" dia	18	20	24
Spooner, double handles	75	95	115
Sugar, cov., double handles	150	175	200
Water Pitcher	275	350	425

Thistle, Early Thistle, Scotch Thistle (clear)

	LOW	AVG.	HIGH
Bowl, 8" dia.	$25	$30	$35
Butter, cov.	45	55	65
Cake Stand	60	75	90
Comport, cov., low standard	60	75	90
Creamer, applied handle	50	65	80
Goblet	38	45	55
Relish	20	25	30
Sauce, flat, 4"	10	12	15
Spooner	30	35	40
Sugar, cov.	52	65	80
Water Pitcher, applied handle, half gallon	85	100	115

Swan *Thistle* *U.S. Coin* *Westward Ho!*

—Photos courtesy Gene Harris Antique Auction Center

U.S. Coin

	LOW	AVG.	HIGH
Bowl, clear, 6" dia	$150	$175	$200
Bowl, frosted, 6" dia	185	225	275
Bowl, clear, 9" dia	175	215	260
Bowl, frosted, 9" dia	260	325	390
Bread Plate, clear	140	175	210
Bread Plate, frosted	260	325	390
Butter, cov, clear	200	250	300
Butter, cov., frosted	350	435	525
Cake Stand, clear, 10"	185	225	260
Cake Stand, frosted, 10"	220	400	575
CeleryTray, clear	160	200	250
Celery Vase, clear	110	135	160
Celery Vase, frosted	280	350	425
Comport, cov., high standard, clear, 7"	240	300	365
Comport, cov., high standard, frosted, 7"	400	500	600
Comport, open, high standard, clear, 7"	175	215	260
Comport, open, high standard, frosted, 7"	265	325	375
Creamer, clear	285	350	420
Creamer, frosted	490	600	715
Cruet, orig. stopper, clear	300	375	425
Cruet, orig. stopper, frosted	400	500	600
Goblet, clear	250	300	350
Goblet, frosted	370	450	525
Milk Pitcher, clear	510	600	700
Pickle, clear	165	200	240
Sauce, ftd., clear, 4"	85	100	115
Sauce, ftd., frosted, 4"	150	185	220
Spooner, clear	180	225	270
Spooner, frosted	265	325	385
Sugar, cov., clear	190	225	260
Sugar, cov., frosted	260	325	390
Tumbler, clear	110	135	160
Tumbler, frosted	190	235	280
Water Pitcher, clear	325	400	475
Water Pitcher, frosted	675	800	925

Westward Ho!, Pioneer, Tippecanoe (clear/frosted)

	LOW	AVG.	HIGH
Bowl, ftd., 5"	$100	$125	$150
Bread Plate	140	175	210
Butter, cov.	145	185	225
Celery Vase	100	125	150
Comport, cov., high standard, 5"	175	225	275
Comport, cov., low standard, 5"	120	150	180
Creamer	75	95	115
Goblet	70	90	110
Marmalade, cov.	160	200	240
Sauce, ftd., 4.5"	28	35	42
Spooner	68	85	100
Sugar, cov.	150	185	220
Water Pitcher	200	250	300

Sandwich Glass

In 1820, Deming Jarves founded The Boston and Sandwich Glass Company in Sandwich, Massachusetts. The company manufactured lamps, cruets and half pint jugs and was a pioneer in the glass pressing method. Up until 1840, the company specialized in "lacy glass," but moved on to incorporate colored, cut and opalescent glass into its repertoire. Striking colors are highly prized, inlcuding amethyst purple and emerald green. Be forewarned that the tiniest chips greatly affect the value. Also beware of the many high quality reproductions available. Probably the best place to learn more about this glass is the Sandwich Glass Museum at the site of the original company on Cape Cod.

The following prices are for the rarest and finest examples. "B&K" and "McKearin" refer to the Barlow and Kaiser and McKearin reference numbers.

	AUCTION	RETAIL	
		Low	High
Candlestick, clambroth and starch blue acanthus leaf form, B&K #4041, c1850, 10.75" h	$700	$1100	$1500
Candlestick, cobalt blue, lacy candlestick w/ socket #1 and crossbar base, rare, B&K #4006, c1830, 6.75" h	23,000	35,000	50,000
Candlesticks, pair, canary yellow, dolphin form, single step base, B&K #4057, c1855, 10.25" h	2600	4000	5600
Candlesticks, pair, electric blue petal and loop, B&K #4032, c1850, 7" h	3250	5000	7000
Candlesticks, pair, emerald green w/ loop base and hex socket, c1850, 7" h	3750	5800	8000
Candlesticks, pair, pale jade green hex, B&K #4027, c1850, 7.25" h	2000	3000	4500
Candlesticks, pair, plum amethyst w/ petal sockets and hex base, McKearin plate 202 #47, c1850, 7.5" h	5000	7500	10,000
Candlesticks, pair, starch blue and clambroth acanthus leaf form, B&K #4041, c1845, 7.5" h	3000	4500	6500
Candlesticks, pair, starch blue and clambroth, dolphin form, double stepped base, B&K #4058, c1860, 10.25" h	4000	6000	8500
Candlesticks, pair, teal blue Mt. Washington dolphin w/ single step base, B&K p. 69, fig. 3, c1850, 10.25" h	8250	12,500	17,500

Candlesticks, left to right: Canary Petal & Loop; light green canary hexagonal; green canary Petal & Loop; canary hexagonal socket w/ square base; canary hexagonal. —Photo courtesy James D. Julia.

	AUCTION	RETAIL Low	RETAIL High
Decanter, clear glass blown, 3 mold, double pattern, qt., McKearin GIII-5, c1830, 10.5" h	2000	3000	4300
Oil Lamps, pair, canary eye-and-scale w/ hex base, McKearin plate 202 #5, c1855, 9" h	2800	4000	6000
Salt, Lafayette boat form, fiery opalescent medium blue, Neal BT-5, c1830, 3.75" l	1200	2000	2600
Salt, Lafayette boat form, silvery opaque blue, c1830, 3.75" l	550	900	1200
Vases, pair, emerald green, circle and elipse vase w/ gauffered and octagonal base, McKearin plate 202 #51, c1860, 7.25" h	2500	4000	5500
Vases, pair, medium blue, 3 printie block vase w/ gauffered rim and octagonal standard and base, McKearin plate 102 #42, 9.25" h	1200	2000	2600
Vases, pair, twisted loop, amethyst w/ gauffered rim, hex standard, and circ. base, B&K #3027, c1850, 9.25" h	3400	5000	7500
Whale Oil Lamp, electric blue loop pattern, 9.5" h	1400	2200	3000

Blown Molded Decanters, left to right: Arch (Flute & Flute) w/ ribbed ball stopper; Diamond Diaper w/ stopper; Cornucopia (Peacock Tail) w/ stopper; Bull's-Eye Sunburst w/ Diamond Diaper ball stopper; Waffle Sunburst wo/ stopper; Bull's-Eye Sunburst w/ stopper; Heart & Chain w/ stopper; Diamond Diaper w/ stopper; Bull's-Eye Sunburst w/ stopper. —Photo courtesy James D. Julia.

Steuben Glass

The Steuben Glass Company has concentrated on producing fine art glass since its founding in 1903. The Corning Glass Works purchased the company in 1918. Steuben pieces are marked with either the letter "S" or the entire name "Steuben" scratched neatly and in tiny letters on the underside of the base. The model number is usually scratched there as well.

Contemporary Steuben

Many famous designs are still in production. The prices listed include the current retail price when new (NEW), the price of a "second-hand" but perfect condition piece (PERF), and the value if the piece has a small scratch (SM SCR). Also, the size and model number are given after each entry.

	SM SCR	PERF	NEW
Arcus, geometric sculpture, 0217, 5"	$800	$1500	$3850
Archaic Vase, tall, 8584, 13"	490	950	2375
Arctic Fisherman, 1023, 6.5"	800	1500	3850
Athena Candlestick, 8687, 6"	50	90	225
Bear Hand Cooler, 5521, 2.5"	30	60	150
Bull Hand cooler, 5524, 2.5"	30	60	150
Butterfly, 0085, 8"	2600	5750	14,300
Calypso Vase, 8758, 12.5"	170	320	795
Calyx Bowl, 8115, 9.5"	80	140	360
Cat Hand Cooler, 5520, 2.5"	30	60	150
Cat Nap, 8704, 3"	50	90	225
Celestial Bowl, 8563, 8.25"	90	170	425
Christmas Tree, 8498, 6.25"	120	220	560
Chronos Bowl, 8706, 7.5"	70	140	350
Close to the Wind, 1068, 8"	850	1600	4200
Cut Vase, 0098, 6.5"	820	1500	4000
Deep Flower Bowl, 8091, 10"	170	320	800
Deep Pillar Bowl, 8356, 9"	200	380	950
Eagle, 8130, 12"	150	300	740
Eagle, 8304, 5.5"	150	280	710
Eagle Hand Cooler, 5519, 2.75"	30	60	150
Elephant, 8128, 7.5"	170	330	825
Elusive Buck, 0503, 7.25"	1500	3000	7500
Equinox Bowl, 8517, 9.5"	180	350	875
Excalibur, 1000, 8"	650	1240	3100
Fawn, Woodland, 8640, 4.75"	60	120	300
Flower Vase, 7913, 8.5"	110	210	525
Folded Bowl, 8707, 7.25"	40	80	200
Folded Bowl, med., 8708, 9"	60	120	300
Fox, 8582, 3.25"	40	70	185
Framed Vase, 8632, 8.5"	2100	4400	11,000
Frog Hand Cooler, 5510, 2.5"	30	60	150
Galaxy, 8395, 3.5"	160	300	780
Gander, 8358, 5.25"	70	140	350
Gazelle Bowl, 0053, 6.75"	4750	9000	23,000
Glass House, 8633, 3.5"	90	180	450
Goose, 8344, 4"	70	140	350
Handkerchief Vase, 8618, 9.5"	130	250	625
Handkerchief Vase, sm., 8703, 7"	50	90	225

	SM SCR	PERF	NEW
Heart, point down, 8376, 3.5"	90	170	420
Heart, point up, 8377, 4"	90	170	420
Heart Pendant, 1105, 1.75"	580	1100	2800
Heart Throb, 8566, 3.25"	80	160	405
Heart to Heart, 8626, 2.5"	40	70	185
Hellenic Urn, 8592, 9.5"	190	375	925
Heritage Flared Vase, 7706, 12"	150	300	725
Highball, 7923, 6.5"	60	110	275
Horse Head, 7779, 5"	60	120	310
I Love Hope Cube, 8713, 2"	60	120	300
Ice Bear, 1022, 6"	790	1500	3800
Ice Hunter, 1033, 6.25"	860	1600	4150
Juliet Vase, 8629, 5.25"	40	80	195
Lighthouse, 1159, 8.5"	450	860	2150
Lion, 1126, 9.5"	500	960	2400
Low Teardrop Candlestick, 7995, 4.5"	100	200	500
Lyre Vase, 8113, 7.75"	90	160	410
Menorah, 8682, 9.5"	750	1500	3650
Mobius Prism, 0507, 11.5"	1250	3000	8900
Monkey Hand Cooler, 5526, 2.75"	30	60	150
Monument Valley, 0358, 8.75"	900	1750	4300
Moravian Star, 8625, 2.5"	90	180	450
Nut Bowl, 8345, 6"	50	100	245
Old Fashioned Glass, 7933, 3.5"	50	100	240
Olive Dish, 7857, 5.5"	50	120	340
Owl Hand Cooler, 5516, 2.5"	30	60	150
Peach, 8600, 3"	60	110	275
Penguin, 8295, 3.5"	40	80	195
Peony Bowl, 8101, 12.75"	230	450	1100
Pillar of Friendship, 8581, 6.5"	160	300	760
Pisces, 8620, 2.75"	40	70	185
Porpoise, 8126, 9.25"	120	230	580
Prelude and Fugue, 1160, 6"	610	1100	2950
Puppy Love, 8524, 2.75"	40	70	185
Pyramid Block, 8413, 3.5"	80	160	400
Quail, 8533, 5.5"	90	170	435
Rabbit Hand Cooler, 5523, 2.75"	30	60	150
Ram's Head Candy Dish, 7936, 5"	130	260	640
Rising Star, 8621, 4.25"	180	340	850
Rooster Hand Cooler, 5527, 3.25"	30	60	150
Rose Vase, 8090, 11.5"	150	300	740
Rosebud Necklace, 1116, 2"	330	640	1600
Sailboat, 8570, 6.5"	120	230	575
Saturn Paperweight, 8609, 5.5"	100	190	475
Scallop, 8572, 3.5"	40	80	195
Scroll Candlestick, 8735 4.75"	50	100	250
Seashell, 8552, 3.5"	60	120	310
Seawave Vase, 8550, 8"	110	220	540
Ship's Decanter, 7912, 10"	270	520	1300
Shore Bird, 8303, 8.25"	90	180	440
Snail, 7982, 3.25"	40	80	210
Snow Pine, 8611, 4.25"	110	210	525
Spiral Bowl, 8060, 7"	80	150	375
Spiral Vase, 8058, 6.5"	80	150	365

	SM SCR	PERF	NEW
Star of David, 8686, 2.5"	.80	140	360
Star Stream, 8567, 5.25"	.120	220	560
Star-Spangled Banner, 8623, 6"	.330	640	1600
Stardust Decanter, 8580, 9.5"	.260	500	1250
Starfish, 8622, 4.75"	.40	80	195
Strawberry Pendant, 1104, 2"	.230	440	1100
Sunflower Bowl, large, 8531, 15.5"	.200	380	950
Swan, curved neck, 8484, 7.5"	.110	210	515
Swan, straight neck, 8483, 6.5"	.110	210	515
Teardrop Candlestick, 7792, 8.75"	.140	270	675
Trout and Fly, 1002, 8"	.450	860	2150
Turtle Hand Cooler, 5514, 2.5"	.30	60	150
Twist Bowl, 8501, 8.75"	.180	340	840
Twist Bud Vase, 8499, 8"	.60	120	295
Twist Candlestick, 8502, 6"	.130	240	600

Old Steuben

	LOW	HIGH
Candlesticks, pomona green, ribbed double gourd stem, step base, 10" h	$400	$600
Comport, blue Aurene, twisted center, crown top, 7.5" h, 8" w	1400	2200
Crystal Vase, Verre de Soie, yellow reeded dec., Diamond Quilted, 10.25" h, 6" w	.600	900
Cyprian Tri-Footed Centerpiece Bowl, Celeste blue ring, 2.5" h, 10.5" dia	.700	1200
Flower-Form Vase, blue Aurene, sgd. by F. Carder, ribbed and slightly ruffled, 5" h, 5" w	1200	1900
Rosaline Bowl, sgd. by F. Czrder, rolled rim, 2.5" h, 5" dia	.500	800
Scent Bottle, Aurene, gold, blue, and red iridescence	1000	1600
Sherbet Set, Aurene, factory paper label, 4" h, 6" dia liner	.400	600
Urn-Form Vase, Verre-de-Soie, applied foot, 5" h	.300	500
Vase, clear crystal w/ bubbles and green reeded dec., 10" h, 7.5" w	.300	400

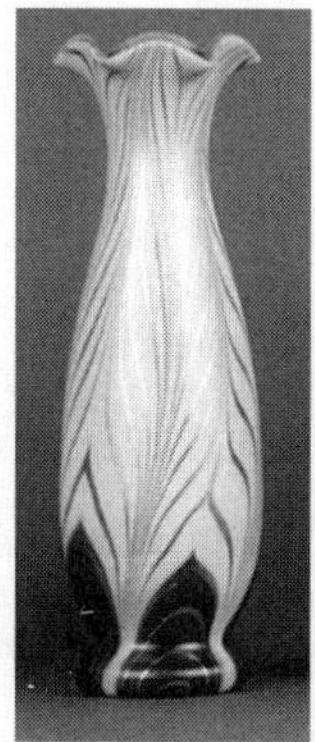
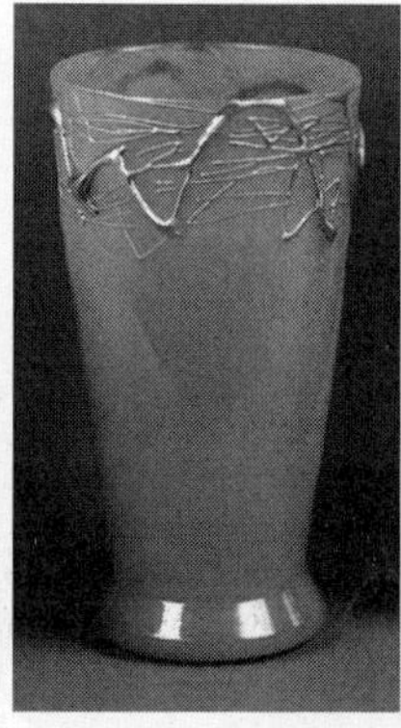

Vases, left to right: Aurene, oyster white and red ground w/ gold pulled feather design, sgd. "Aurene #522," 10.5" h; Green jade w/ blue Aurene random applied threading, 10.5" h; Black Cluthra w/ applied crystal rim. 9.5" h. —Photos courtesy James D. Julia.

Hatboxes

The wallpaper decorated hatboxes of the early nineteenth century are rare finds. Those in good condition with a minimum of slight tears and no loss of original paper command high prices. The values given below are based on pristine examples appearing in New England auctions.

	AUCTION	RETAIL	
		Low	High
"A Peep at Moon," blue wallpaper, 19" l	$850	$1500	$2400
Beaver, w/ inscription "P.C. WillmaRth's Fashionable Hat And Cap Warehouse," 6.25" h, 12" l	1200	1900	2600
Blue Paper, top hat box, inscribed "Peter Higgins, 46 North Market St., Boston," 10" h, 10" l	400	600	900
Canal Scene, 11.5" h, 17.5" l	1400	2200	3000
Castle Garden Lid, rustic bridge base	800	1200	1700
Chapel and Buildings, D.S. Gladding label, 11.5" h, 20.5" l	1500	2300	3200
Chariots, yellow ground, 17" l	150	260	400
Chinese Floral Design on Diamond Grid, red and blue, hat form box, 9.5" h	1100	1700	2400
Classical Views, yellow ground, 17" l	350	610	960
Clayton's Ascent and Boa Constrictor Pattern, 12.5" h, 17.5" l	1500	2300	3200
Coconut Trees and Man in Turban Pulling Horse, 11.25" h, 18.25" l	950	1500	2000
Erie Canal, yellow ground, 16" l	300	530	830
Foliate and White Feather Design, blue ground, 4.5" h, 9.25" l	1800	2500	4000
Floral Design, blue ground, Hannah Davis, labeled	850	1490	2340
Giraffe Design, yellow ground, 19" l	400	700	1100
House and Bridge, 4.5" h, 9.25" l	300	500	600
Hunters, yellow ground, 20" l	200	350	550
Lady's Bonnet, depicted w/ S.A. Brower and Co. label	800	1200	1700
Lute Player, yellow ground, 16" l	350	610	960
Parrot and Lighthouse Design	800	1400	2200
Pink Drapery Swag and Floral Sprays, yellow ground, 10.25" h, 15" l	1000	1600	2200
Rural Life Scene, 11" h, 17" l	1100	1700	2400
Rural Life Scene, yellow ground, 11.25" h, 18.5" l	2500	3900	5400
Yellow Floral Paper, hat form box, "Beebe and Costar, 156 Broadway N.Y.," 9.75" h	550	900	1200

Castle Garden, blue ground, sgd "Joel Post," 23" l, $3300 at auction. —Photo courtesy Garth's Auctions.

Holiday Decorations

Holidays are special events, times when we can get together with friends and family, exchange gifts, observe religious rites or dress in outrageous costumes. Collectors of holiday items can choose from a wealth of material. Many collectors focus on one holiday, such as Christmas or Halloween. Others prefer to specialize in a type of item, such as postcards. Whatever the method, displaying your finds is great fun and collecting can be enjoyed year round. For further information we recommend *Holiday Collectables: A Price Guide* by Pauline and Dan Campanelli, L-W Books, Gas City, IN, 1997, *Christmas Revisited* by Robert Brenner, Schiffer Publishing, West Chester, PA, 1986, and *Collectible Halloween* by Pamela E. Apkarian-Russell, Schiffer Publishing, Atglen, PA, 1997.

Christmas

Figural Light Bulbs

	LOW	AVG	HIGH
Andy Gump, milk glass	$70	$80	$90
Bear, w/ guitar, milk glass	26	30	34
Blue Bird, milk glass	26	30	34
Clock	26	30	34
Clown, milk glass	40	50	60
Elephant, milk glass	50	60	70
Fish, milk glass	20	25	30
Gingerbread Man	30	35	40
Grapes, milk glass	20	25	30
House, milk glass	20	25	30
Humpty Dumpty, milk glass	35	40	45
Lantern	12	15	18
Parrot, milk glass	32	42	52
Pinocchio	32	37	42
Puss N' Boots, milk glass	40	45	50
Santa, painted	60	70	80
Snowman, milk glass	25	30	35
Zeppelin, w/ flag	130	150	170

Greeting Cards

	LOW	AVG	HIGH
A Merry Christmas and Happy New Year, children and Christmas tree, c1870s	$3	$5	$7
A Merry Christmas to You All, family in snowy woodland, c1880	3	4	5
Child, in 19th-C bonnet	3	4	5
Hail, Day of Joy, Prang, angel kneeling w/ dove on finger, c1870	16	19	22
Here, Open the Door, Kate Greenaway, messenger knocking on door, c1880	42	52	62
Here Comes the New Year w/ Lots of Good Cheer, child, tree, and toys, c1870	4	6	8
Ice Pond, boy putting skates on girl, fringed and embroidered, German	3	4	5
Merry Christmas and Happy New Year, children in snow, church, c1880	4	6	8
Merry Christmas to You All, L. Prang, brown-suited Santa, sq.	24	28	32
My Lips May Give a Message, Kate Greenaway, girl holding letter, c1880	42	52	62

	LOW	AVG	HIGH
Prang's American Third Prize Christmas Card, by C. Coleman, Oriental scene	20	24	28
Season's Greetings, card shaped like fan	2	3	4
Season's Greetings, mechanical, boy w/flowers, 19th C	16	20	24
Season's Greetings, river and small boat, 19th C	3	4	5
Victorian Card, paper lace border surrounds "Season's Greeting," c1800s	10	13	16
Wishing You a Happy New Year, Prang, folded, girl on front, old man on back, fringed, w/ tasseled cord, c1884	15	18	21
Wishing You a Merry Christmas, Prang, fireplace, cat, and kittens, sq., c1800s	15	18	21
With Best Christmas Wishes, Tuck, girl w/ spray of flowers, c1885	12	15	18

Ornaments

	LOW	AVG	HIGH
Angel, Dresden	$210	$260	$310
Angel, paper, diecut, trimmed w/ tinsel	50	60	70
Angel, w/ spun glass wings	45	55	65
Angel's Face, blown glass, 2.5" h	40	50	55
Baby in Basket, cardboard, Dresden	200	250	300
Baby in Bunting, blown glass, emb. lettering, 4" l	70	80	90
Ball, amber	22	27	32
Basket, fruit-filled, blown glass	30	35	40
Bear w/ Muff, blown glass	60	70	80
Camel, cardboard, Dresden, flat	50	65	80
Camel, Dresden	55	65	75
Canary, blown glass	28	33	43
Carrot, blown glass, emb. detail, c1901, 4" l	40	50	60
Child, milk glass	22	27	32
Church, blown glass	40	50	60

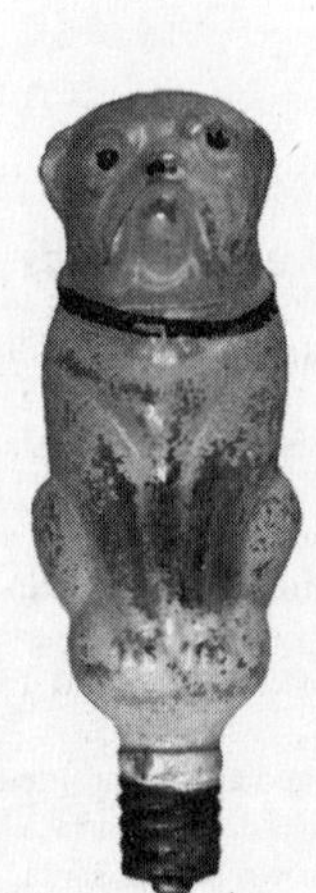

Left to right: Feather Tree; Light Bulb; Scrap Ornament, Father Christmas.

Ornament, dirigible, blown glass, $150–$250.

	LOW	AVG	HIGH
Clown Head, blown glass	40	50	60
Cuckoo Clock, blown glass, emb. and ptd.	50	60	70
Doll's Head, blown glass, silver and flesh color, glass eyes	85	105	125
Elephant, mercury glass w/ milk glass tusks, 4" h	70	80	90
Fish, blown glass	50	55	60
Football Player, milk glass	70	90	110
Foxy Grandpa, blown glass w/ applied legs, 4.5" h	150	175	200
Girl, blown glass	40	60	80
Girl's Head, blown glass w/ blown glass eyes, 2.5" h	50	70	90
Happy Hooligan, blown glass w/ applied legs, 4.5" h	180	205	230
Heart, blown glass, large	40	50	60
Icicle, glass	20	30	40
Kugel, dark blue, grapes w/ metal cap	220	250	280
Lamp	50	70	90
Man in the Moon blown glass, green, 3" h	70	80	90
Monkey Holding Stick, blown glass, 2.5" h	100	130	160
Moon, happy/sad full moon faces, composition squeeze toy, c1890	120	140	160
Peacock, blown glass, brush tail	40	60	80
Pear, pressed cotton	20	25	30
Penguin, blown glass, blue, silver, red, emb. feet	40	50	60
Pinecone, blown glass	15	18	21
Pipe, blown glass	20	25	30
Pocket Watch, blown glass w/ paper face	60	80	100
Purse, blown glass, wire wrapped	60	70	80
Santa, carrying bag of toys, blown glass, 2.5" h	60	80	100
Santa, celluloid, white and red, c1930s, 4.5" h	50	60	70
Santa, plaster face	40	50	60
Scottie Dog, blown glass, yellow and blue	80	90	100
Smiling Snowman, w/ broom, blown glass, c1910, 3.5" h	50	60	70
Snowman, plastic, wearing black stovepipe hat, pipe, red scarf, c1950s, 5" h	10	12	14
Snowman, plastic, wearing blue cap, red mittens, and silver skates, c1950s, 5" h	12	15	18
Stag, blown glass, blue w/ gold antlers, 3" h	40	50	60
Star, Dresden, 2 sided	40	50	60
Swan, blown glass w/ spun glass wings and tail, c1900	90	110	130
Teapot, blown glass	30	35	40
Turkey, blown glass w/ spun glass wings and tail, c1900	90	110	130

Miscellaneous

Bank, Santa, battery operated, w/ orig. box, 10.5" h	$80	$110	$140
Bank, Santa at chimney, plaster, c1950s, 11" h	60	80	100
Bank, Santa in armchair, plaster, c1950s, 10" h	70	90	110
Candy Container, Santa Claus, handpainted, rabbit fur beard, composition hands and face, 7" h	400	500	600

	LOW	AVG	HIGH
Crèche, 17 papier-mâché figures, wooden stable, c1930	110	140	170
Lamp, figural Santa, hard plastic, c1955, 16" h	25	35	45
Light, Santa glass globe on tin battery-box base, c1950	30	40	50
Lights, bells on a string	18	22	26
Pinback Button, "Merry Christmas," Santa w/ pack in household, litho. tin	20	25	30
Pinback Button, "Santa Claus Gave This To Me," c1940s, 5" dia	10	12	14
Pinback Button, Santa reading a book entitled *Good Boys–Good Girls,* 1" dia	10	12	14
Plate, child's ABC, features children and snowman	80	100	120
Postcard, hold-to-light, Santa Claus	125	138	150
Postcard, Santa wearing green, full figure	25	28	30
Postcard, Santa painting sled	10	13	15
Snowdome, figural Santa and reindeer w/ dome center, plastic, c1950s, 5" h	18	21	24
Snowdome, figural Santa w/ dome center, plastic, c1950s, 5" h	16	18	20
Tree, bottle brush, Japan, c1950	4	5	6
Tree, feather, German, c1910, 18" h	220	270	320
Victorian Christmas Stocking	80	100	120

Easter

	LOW	AVG	HIGH
Bunny Mobile, plastic, early style auto, c1950s	$22	$27	$35
Candy Container, Easter egg, red, gold, and white litho. cardboard, c1940	20	25	30
Candy Container, rabbit, pressed cardboard, removable head	90	110	120
Candy Container, rabbit, pressed cardboard, whie, c1950s	35	45	55
Egg Cup, figural bunny and egg, plastic, c1950s, 3" h	4	6	8
Greeting Card, angels on front, by Whitney, NY, 19th C	4	5	6
Greeting Card, Bible verses, birds, late 19th C	2	3	4
Greeting Card, booklet, poem, cross w/ flowers, German	4	6	8
Greeting Card, child coming out of egg, gold-fringed	2	3	4
Greeting Card, cross on reef in sea, by Carter & Karrick, 19th C	3	4	5
Greeting Card, Cupid w/ ribbon holding flowers, 19th C	3	4	5
Greeting Card, floral cross on front, German, 19th C	2	3	4
Greeting Card, girl climbing out of egg shell, fringed, German, 19th C	5	7	9
Greeting Card, heads of children in flower pot, 19th C	2	3	4
Greeting Card, Shakespeare's Heaven Give You Many Merry Days, 19th C	2	3	4
Toy, rabbit pulling cart, tinplate, Chein	75	85	95

Halloween

	LOW	AVG	HIGH
Candlesticks, pair, black cat and jack-o-lantern, plastic, c1950, 2.5" h	$19	$22	$25
Costume, gorilla, gauze mask, orig. Collegetown Costumes box, c1940s	40	45	50
Decoration, black cat, cardboard and honeycomb, 1950s, 20" h	32	37	42
Decoration, jack-o-lantern, cardboard, accordion fold-out, 1950s, 11" h	30	35	40
Decoration, jack-o-lantern scarecrow on wheeled base, orange and black plastic, c1950s, 5" h	22	24	26
Decoration, snowman, orange and black plastic, 5" h	30	35	40
Decoration, witch, bats, and black cat, orange, black, and green pressed cardboard, c1940s, 18" h	50	55	60
Decoration, witch and black cat dancers, accordion-fold crepe paper, 1960s, 28" l	17	19	21
Eyeglasses, figural hissing black cats, plastic	25	30	35

	LOW	AVG	HIGH
Game, Whirl-O-Hallowen Fortune and Stunt Game, card w/ spinner, 7" x 9"	30	40	50
Hat, orange and black crepe paper	8	10	12
Jack-O-Lantern, pressed cardboard w/ insert, 8" h	100	120	140
Jack-O-Lantern, pressed cardboard wo/ insert, 8" h	70	77	85
Lantern, cardboard diecut w/ various Halloween scenes over orange tissue paper, c1935, 12" h	45	55	65
Light, jack-o-lantern glass globe on tinplate battery-box base, c1950	30	40	50
Light, pumpkin, orange plastic, battery operated, c1950s, 2.5" dia	37	42	47
Mask, black cat, paper, round eyes, 11" x 8"	12	15	18
Mask, clown, paper, red, black, and yellow, 8" x 9"	12	15	18
Mask, devil, gauze	15	18	21
Mask, owl, cardboard w/ cat and pumpkin band, 12" x 12"	30	35	40
Noisemaker, cylindrical shake type, litho. tin, jack-o-lanterns and witches, c1950, 4" dia	12	14	16
Noisemaker, paddle type, litho. tin, w/ jack-o-lantern, c1940s, 10" l	26	30	34
Noisemaker, spin type, litho. tin, w/ black cat motif, c1948, 4" dia	10	12	14
Noisemaker, tambourine type, litho. tin, w/ jack-o-lantern, c1940s	30	35	40
Party Favor, basket, black and orange plastic, c1950s, 3.5" dia	12	12	14
Party Favor, black cat, holds lollipop, orange plastic w/ black-striped jersey, c1950s, 5" h	16	19	22
Party Favor, pumpkin, orange plastic, w/ metal bail, c1950s, 3.5" dia	6	8	10
Postcard, Clapsaddle	15	20	25
Postcard, Tuck	12	14	16
Postcard, Winsch	50	58	65

Thanksgiving

	LOW	AVG	HIGH
Candlesticks, pair, cornucopia shape, ceramic, 3" h	$12	$15	$18
Candlesticks, pair, pilgrims, ceramic, 2" h	10	12	14
Candy Container, cornucopia, papier-mâché, c1910	50	60	70
Candy Container, turkey, composition, c1930s	20	30	35
Centerpiece, turkey, Hallmark, c1940	10	12	14
Cornucopia, wicker	12	15	20
Platter, tom turkey design, Japan, c1935	15	18	21
Postcard, Brundage	15	23	28
Postcard, Clapsaddle	8	10	12

Valentine's Day

	LOW	AVG	HIGH
Valentine, children, mechanical pull-down, German, c1915	$6	$8	$10
Valentine, children picking heart-shaped apples from tree, "Hearts Are Ripe"	3	5	7
Valentine, cottage, mechanical, pull-out and stand-up, German, c1910	12	15	18
Valentine, "Cupid's Temple of Love," honeycomb, c1928	6	8	10
Valentine, free-standing folding easel-back, c1900	15	18	21
Valentine, Gibson Girl photo surrounded by lace, cherub heads, Meek and Son, c1890	25	35	45
Valentine, glum-looking woman sewing hat, w/ verse, Elton and Co., NY, c1880	22	26	30
Valentine, heart shaped, little girl on front, folding, Tuck	12	14	16
Valentine, lacy, heart shaped, c1905	9	12	15

	LOW	AVG	HIGH
Valentine, large ship, mechanical pull-down, German	70	80	90
Valentine, little girl holding doll, paper doll mechanical stand-up, Gibson Art, German	20	25	30
Valentine, little girl holding opening parasol, mechanical stand-up, German, c1920	15	20	25
Valentine, Maggie and Jiggs, c1940	18	21	24
Valentine, Popeye, c1940	18	21	24
Valentine, silver, white, and lace, 3 layer, McLoughlin, c1880	20	25	30
Valentine, steam boiler, pull-out and stand-up, German, c1910	12	15	18
Valentine, Temple of Love, young girl and butterfly, Tuck's Betsy Beauties series	12	14	16
Valentine, "To My Valentine," 2 children and verse, Tuck's Innocence Abroad series	12	14	16
Valentine, various animals, mechanical, c1930	10	12	14
Valentine, Victorian, paper lace, fold-out	20	22	24
Valentine, white, gold, and lace, 3 layer, Mcloughlin, c1880	10	12	14

Various Other Holidays

Fourth of July, postcard	$5	$8	$10
Happy Birthday, greeting card, children, 19th C	2	3	4
Happy Birthday, greeting card, floral design, blue fringe, c1880	3	4	5
Happy Birthday, greeting card, maroon floral, fringed, 19th C	3	4	5
Lincoln's Birthday, postcard	8	12	15
Memorial Day, postcard	5	8	10
Washington's Birthday, postcard	5	8	10

Holiday Postcards.

Jewelry

Jewelry divides into two basic groups: precious and non-precious (a.k.a., costume jewelry made after 1920). U.S. custom laws define antique jewelry as jewelry over one hundred years old. Estate or Heirloom jewelry is generally assumed to be over twenty-five years old.

Craftsmanship, aesthetic design, scarcity and current market worth of gemstones and the precous metal are the principal value keys. Antique and period jewelry should be set with the cut of stone prevalent at the time the piece was made. Names (manufacturer, designer, or both) also play a major role in value. Be extremely cautious when buying jewelry. Reproductions and fakes abound. Also be alert for married and divorced pieces.

For further information we recommend *The Official Identification and Price Guide to Antique Jewelry, Sixth Edition* by Arthur Guy Kaplan, House of Collectibles, NY, 1990 and *Warman's Jewelry, 2nd Edition* by Christie Romero, Krause Publications, Iola, WI, 1998.

Abbreviations: Karat *(k)*, carats *(cts)*, yellow gold *(yg)*, white gold *(wg)* and platinum *(plat)*.

	LOW	HIGH
Bracelet, flexible design, set w/ graduated clusters of single and brilliant-cut diamonds, foliate gold spacers, fancy textured link bracelet, 14k yg mount	$3000	$4000
Bracelet, peridot and pearl, silver-topped 18k yg mount	600	800
Bracelet, rect. textured plaques, 14k yg	150	200
Bracelet, scroll motif set w/ clusters of pearls and marquis-, baguette-, and round-cut diamonds, 14k wg mount	2500	3500
Brooch, domed design w/ woven 18k gold wire surmounted by swirl of prong-set round diamonds	1000	1500
Brooch, flower, faceted aquamarine petals w/ diamond-set stems, plat mount	1500	2000
Brooch, pearl, emerald, and ruby serpent, 18k yg mount, c19th C	800	1200
Cocktail Ring, center marquise-cut diamond within abstract butterfly mount, set w/ baguette and round diamonds, plat mount	1500	2000
Ear Pendants, diamond, drop design set w/ round brilliant-cut tapering baguette w/ pear-shaped diamond, plat mount	4000	6000
Earrings, South Sea pearl and diamond, 14k wg findings	6000	8000
Eternity Band, ruby, plat mount	300	400
Line Bracelet, alternating pattern of 6 round diamonds and five channel-set sapphires, plat, sgd. "Tiffany & Co."	5000	7000
Necklace, center bezel-set pear-shaped diamond, 14k yg snake chain, 15" l	3000	4000
Necklace, cultured pearls, 4 strands of graduating pearls, 4.80 to 9.60 mm, baroque pearl and rose-cut diamond 14k gold clasp	1000	1500
Necklace, pink topaz and chrysoberyl festoon mounted to foxtail and curb link chains, c1860	2000	3000
Pendant, round brilliant-cut diamond, 14k wg mount	1000	2000
Pin, Airflow Chrysler, set w/ single-cut diamonds, plat mount	5000	6000
Pin, rhodalite garnet and diamond circle, 18k yg mount	500	700
Ring, diamond cluster, approx. total wt. 2.75 cts., 18k yg mount	600	800
Ring, Edwardian, center antique rect.-cut emerald, plat and diamond-set mount	4000	5000
Ring, geometric design set w/ round diamonds, plat mount, c1940s	2500	3500
Ring, "Peacock Ring," sapphire and diamonds, 14k yg mount, sgd. "Erte"	300	400
Solitaire, center prong-set old European-cut diamond, wide textured 18k yg band	5000	6000
Solitaire, round brilliant-cut diamond flanked by 2 small diamonds, 14k yg and wg mount	1500	2000
Suite, bracelet centered by collet-set diamond surrounded by row of synthetic sapphires and single-cut diamonds on diamond-set box link bracelet, plat mount, millegrain accents, matching ring	1200	1800

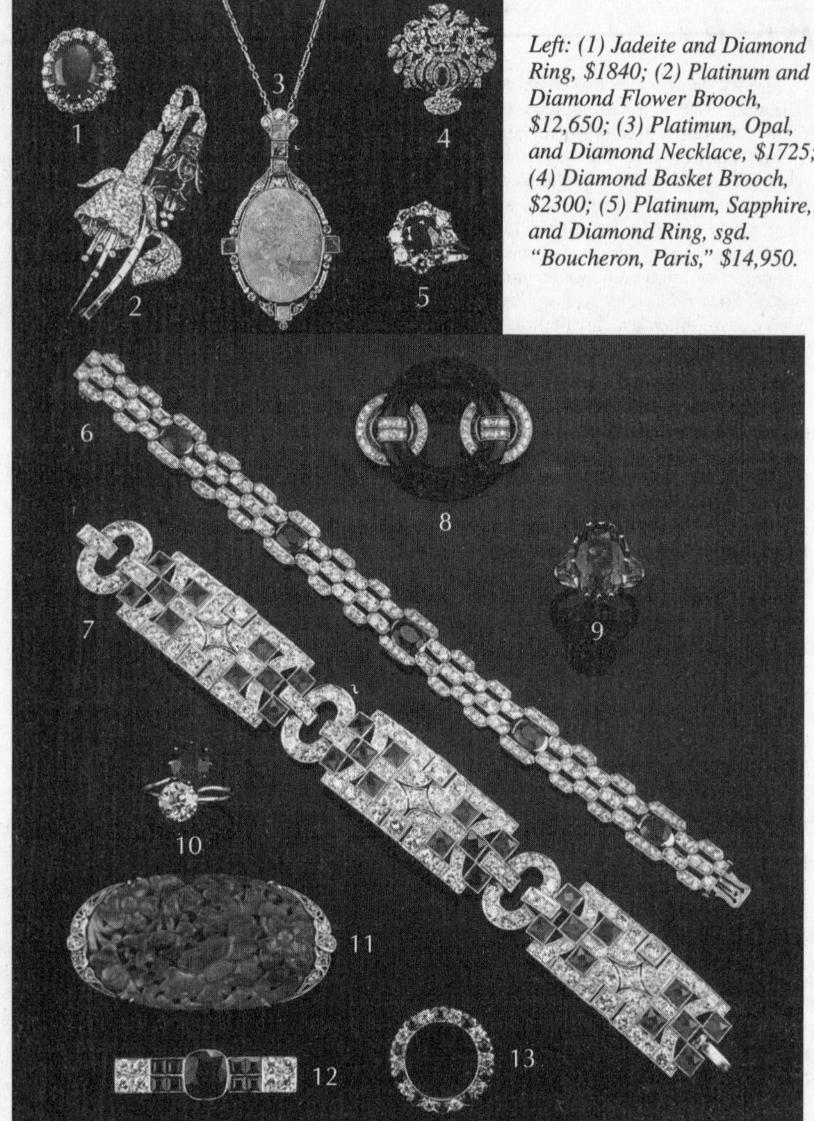

Left: (1) Jadeite and Diamond Ring, $1840; (2) Platinum and Diamond Flower Brooch, $12,650; (3) Platimun, Opal, and Diamond Necklace, $1725; (4) Diamond Basket Brooch, $2300; (5) Platinum, Sapphire, and Diamond Ring, sgd. "Boucheron, Paris," $14,950.

Above: (6) Art Deco Ruby and Diamond Bracelet, $18,400; (7) Diamond and Synthetic Ruby Bracelet, $10,925; (8) Art Deco Onyx, Diamond, and Ruby Circle Pin, J.E. Caldwell & Co., $9775; (9) Art Deco Sapphire Ring, $5750; (10) Diamond and Sapphire Bypass Ring, $5405; (11) Jade and Diamond Brooch, $1380; (12) Sapphire and Diamond Bar Pin, $7475; (13) Sapphire and Diamond Circle Pin, $1380. —Photos courtesy Skinner, Inc., Boston, MA.

Knives

In the 1960s, the United States government began enforcing the law requiring that knife companies mark their knives with the country of origin. This sparked a collectors craze, as dealers sought early unmarked knives. The most desirable pocketknives are those made before World War II. Collectors prefer knives in pristine condition, those neither sharpened nor cleaned.

For further information consult *The Official Price Guide to Collector Knives, Twelfth Edition* by C. Houston Price, House of Collectibles, NY, 1996.

	LOW	HIGH
A. Strauss Co., 1907–1918	$10	$40
A. Ulmer, 1869–1928	20	60
A.W. Wadsworth & Sons, 1905–1936	25	150
Baker & Hamilton, 1853–1981	15	150
Baldwell Cutlery Co., 1879–1929	25	100
Baldwin Cutlery Co., 1912–1981	15	150
Barnsley Bros., 1898–1906	20	150
Barrett-Hicks Co., 1920s	25	125
Beck & Gregg Hdwe. Co., 1890–1894	25	150
Belmont Knife Co., 1920–1930	15	35
Bering-Cortes Hardware Co., 1905–1947	15	55
Berkshire Cutlery Co., 1890	20	45
Best English Cutlery, 1800–1860	35	130
Besteel Warranted, 1930s	10	25
Bighorn, 1971–contemp.	4	10
Billings & Spencer, 1890–1914	25	150
Blue Ribbon, 1910–1950	15	65
Bonsa, 1867–1983	10	50
Booth Bros./Newark, N.J., 1864–1879	25	300
Bowen Knife Co., 1973–contemp	20	150
Bradford & Anthony, 1856–1883	25	200
Bridgeport Knife Co., 1904	40	150
Broch & Thiebes Cutlery Co., 1882–1892	20	150
Brown & Bigelow, 1931–1950s	25	75
Brown Bros. Knife Co., 1902	50	150
Brown Camp Hardware Co., 1907–1959	25	150
Browning, 1969–contemp.	10	75
Brunswick Cutlery Co., 1897–1907	20	75
Buck, 1963–contemp.	20	175
Buck Creek, 1970–contemp.	10	95
Bud Brand Cutlery Co., 1922	25	100
Buffalo Cutlery Co., 1915	25	100
Buhl & Sons Co.	15	65
Bull Brand, 1985–contemp.	15	45
Burgon & Ball, 1873–1917	15	75
Burkinshaw Knife Co., 1881–1920	35	350
Buster Brown Shoe Co., 1930s	15	125
Butler Bros., 1865–1952	25	120
Butler & Co., 1865–1952	25	120
Butterick Pattern Co., 1910	10	25
Cambridge Cutlery Co., 1865	25	350
Camco, 1948–contemp.	5	50
Cameron Knife Co., 1920s	15	65
Camillus, 1902–contemp.	5	110

	LOW	HIGH
Camillus Cutlery Co., 1902–contemp.	10	175
Canton Cutlery Co., 1979-1930	20	175
Canton Hardware Co., 1910	15	150
Capitol Knife Co., 1920s	15	125
Carl Bertram, 1864–1983	20	250
Carl Kammerling & Co., 1904–contemp.	10	90
Carl Klauberg & Bros., 1883–1940	10	90
Carl Linder, 1980–contemp.	25	175
Carrier Cutlery Co., 1900–1921	45	225
Carters, 1969–1983	40	200
Car-Van Cutlery, 1911–1930	10	175
Case XX Metal Stamping Ltd., 1940s	15	75
Catskill Knife Co., 1930s	15	150
Cattaraugus, 1984–contemp.	15	50
Centaur Cutlery, 1893–1913	5	25
Central City Knife Co., 1880–1892	20	200
Central Cutlery Co., 1926	40	130
Challenge Cutlery Co., 1877–1891	25	225
Challenge Cutlery Corp., 1891–1928	20	150
Champion, 1925–1932	15	75
Chapman Cutlery Co., 1915–1931	35	60
Charles Land	60	80
Charles Langbein, 1880–1890	65	125
Charles R. Randall	15	35
Chicago Knife Works, 1911	25	125
Chicago Pocket Knife Co.	25	125
Christy, 1890–contemp.	5	30
Clark Brothers, 1895–1929	25	125
Clark & Carriers Mfg. Co.	35	75
Clauberg Cutlery Co., 1857–contemp.	10	55
Clauss, 1887–contemp.	10	75
Clean Cut, 1880–1912	20	95
Clearcut, 1835–1949	12	30
Clipper Cutlery Co., 1901	10	50
Clover Brand, 1941–1942	15	35
Clyde Cutlrey Co., 1929–1949	12	80
Coles, 1960s	8	50
Collins Bros., 1970–1973	20	75
Colonial, 1926–contemp.	10	55
Colt, 1969–1973	30	350
Col. Coon, 1978–1986	25	150
Commander, 1891–1928	65	100
Concord Cutlery Co., 1880	25	150
Continental Cutlery Co., 1915–1920	25	125
Corning Knife Co., 1930s	10	50
Craftsman, 1940s–contemp.	5	65
Crescent Cutlery Co., 1917–1950	15	50
Cripple Creek, 1986–contemp.	40	150
Cronk & Carrier Mfg. Co., 1900–1921	45	225
Crosman Blades, 1982–contemp.	5	75
Crown Cutlery Co., 1910s–1920s	15	65
Crucible Knife Co., 1925–1932	20	80
Curley Bros., 1885–1905	10	75
Curtin & Clark Cutlery Co., 1898–1910	25	110

	LOW	HIGH
Cussins & Fearn, 1930s	25	75
Cut Sure, 1889–1962	20	150
Cutino Cutlery Co., 1914–1935	20	50
Cutwell Cutlery Co., 1886–1945	20	200
Dame Stoddard & Co., 1901–1930	10	150
Dames & Ball, 1925–1962	65	125
Delmar Cutlery Co., 1910	25	95
Delta, 1878–1953	5	20
Deluxe, 1918–1925	5	20
Depend-On-Me Cutlery Co., 1945	10	75
Diamond Edge Val-Test, 1960–1967	5	50
Diamond Edge, 1967–contemp.	5	15
Dictator, 1930s	10	25
Disston Steel, 1940	10	50
Dixie Knife, 1890–1894	30	60
Dodson Mfg. Co., 1937	25	125
Dollar Knife Co., 1920s	15	150
Dolphin Cutlery Co., 1918–1920s	20	95
Domar Cutlery Co., 1916–1920	15	85
Double Sharp G., 1932–1942	10	40
Drake Hardware Co., 1890	10	50
Duane Cutlery Co., 1910	5	20
Duke Peterson Hdw. Co., 1920s	25	125
Dunlap, 1877–1930	25	150
Dunn Bros., 1927–contemp.	6	25
Duro-Edge, 1928–1930	5	10
Dwight Divine & Sons, 1876–1941	35	175
Eagle Cutlery Co., 1883–1945	10	150
Eagle Knife Co., 1916–1919	20	100
Eagle Pencil Co., 1883–1945	5	25
Eagleton Knife Co., 1890	20	125
Eagle/Phila, 1883–1945	20	70
Eclipse Cutlery Co., 1897–1918	25	125
Edge Mark, 1950–contemp.	3	15
Edgemaster, 1940s	10	45
Edward Parker & Sons, 1900	25	95
Edward Weck, 1893–1943	15	75
Edward Weck & Sons, 1893–1943	25	85
Edward Zin, 1920	5	15
El Gallo, 1968–1970	5	12
Enterprise Cutlery Co., 1920s	25	85
Erber, 1890	5	15
Erma, 1950s	5	50
Ern, 1916–1926	5	15
Ernest Brueckmann, 1891–1956	25	125
Ernest G. Ahrens, 1930s	15	65
Esemco, 1921–1949	5	8
Essem Co., 1921–1949	10	20
Eureka Cutlery Co., 1911–1915	25	175
Excelsior Knife Co., 1880–1884	55	150
Eyre Ward & Co., 1840–1869	25	150
Fabyan Knife Co., 1890	25	110
Fairmont Cutlery Co., 1930s	20	65
Fall River Knife Co., 1900	15	75

	LOW	HIGH
Farwell Ozmun Kirk & Co., 1881–1959	35	110
Fayetteville Knife Co., 1911	30	90
Federal Knife Co., 1920s	20	75
Fife Cutlery Co., 1968–1974	40	150
Finedge Cutlery Co., 1921–1923	15	125
Fletcher Knife Co., 1863–1913	25	175
Fones Brothers, 1881–1914	25	150
Ford & Medley, 1872–1930	20	95
Forest Master, 1934–contemp.	10	25
Fox Cutlery, 1884–1955	35	85
Frank Mills & Co., 1860	8	85
Fred Biffar, 1917–1922	20	75
Frederick Fenney, 1824–1852	25	100
Frederick Westpfal, 1884–1940	25	125
Frost Cutlery Co., 1978–contemp.	5	60
Gamble Stores, 1930s–1950s	10	45
Garland Cutlery Co., 1913	10	25
Gebruder Christians, 1824–contemp.	20	150
Gebruder Krusius, 1856–1983	10	150
Gellman Bros., 1920	15	60
Geneva Cutlery Co., 1902–1934	30	60
Geneva Forge, Inc., 1934–c1948	25	75
George Savage & Sons, 1855	25	150
George Tritch Hdw. Co., 1910	25	85
Gilbert, 1900	60	150
Glenfall Cutlery Co., 1898	15	60
Globe Cutlery Co., 1922	20	55
Gold Top, 1924–1948	10	30
Golden Gate Cutlery Co., 1890s	20	75
Goodell Co., 1913–1948	60	90
Griffon, 1918–1966	30	125
Guttman Cutlery Co., 1947–contemp.	15	75
Hale Brothers, 1871–1907	25	150
Hammer Brand, 1936–contemp.	3	40
Hargreaves Smith & Co., 1866–1920	25	300
Hart Cutlery Co., 1920s	20	200
Hassam Brothers, 1853–1872	25	350
Heller Bros. Co., 1900–1930	25	75
Henckels International, 1970s	10	45
Henry Barge, 1850	25	200
Henry Sears & Son, 1878–1959	40	225
Henry Taylor, 1858–1927	25	300
Herbert Robinson, 1873	15	275
Herder & Co., 1872–contemp.	10	125
Hermitage Cutlery, 1895–1927	8	25
Hike Cutlery Co., 1923	10	45
Hoffritz, 1930–contemp.	5	95
Hollinger	15	150
Hollingsworth Knife Co., 1916–1930	25	200
Hornis Cutlery Co.	20	60
Howard Bros.	15	75
Howard Cutlery Co., 1890	45	200
Howes Cutlery Co., 1900	25	135
Hubertus, 1932–contemp.	20	100

	LOW	HIGH
Hudson Knife Co., 1927	20	65
Hugo Koller, 1861–1980s	15	65
Humason & Beckley, 1852–1914	20	275
Humason & Beckley Mfg. Co., 1852–1916	20	275
Indiana Cutlery Co., 1932	45	95
Industry Novelty Co., 1908–1917	10	75
Jack Knife Ben, 1887–1940s	45	250
Jackmaster, 1938–contemp.	10	60
Jackson Knife & Shear Co., 1900–1914	25	85
James Barlow & Son, 1828–1856	25	200
James Boden, 1860	15	200
James Burnand & Sons, 1865–1970s	25	200
James Cranshaw, 1826	25	200
Jeffrey, 1971	25	95
Jetter & Scheerer, 1880–1932	10	150
John Barber & Son, 1818–1853	25	200
John Chatillion & Sons, 1894–1937	50	300
John Engstrom, 1874–1893	20	45
John Kenyon & Co., 1870–1920	15	150
John Salm, 1918–1935	10	50
John Walters & Co., 1846–1862	25	300
John Wilton	45	125
Jones & Son, 1970	5	15
Joseph Feist, 1898–1924	25	65
Joseph Rodgers & Sons, 1901–1948	25	250
Joseph Thorpe, 1853–1873	25	250
Judson Cutlery Co., 1900–1940	20	65
Kamp Cutlery Co., 1910	8	20
Kamp King, 1935–contemp.	5	25
Ka-Bar, 1951–1966	25	75
Keen Edge, 1901–1927	25	150
Keen Kutter, 1940–1960	25	200
Keener Edge, 1932	10	75
Kendall Mfg. Co., 1948	5	40
Kershaw, contemp.	5	125
Keyes Cutlery Co., 1893	25	150
Keystone Cutlery Co., 1925–1938	45	200
Khyber, 1980s	3	15
Kingston USA, 1915–1958	15	75
Kipsi Kut, 1900	25	150
Klicker, 1958	20	40
Knapp & Spencer, 1895–1905	15	175
Koeller Bros., 1905–1927	10	100
Koeller & Schmidt, 1884–1916	30	90
Korn's Patent, 1883–1907	15	75
Krusius B Brothers K B., 1888–1927	10	150
Kutwell, 1930s	50	300
Kwik Cut, 1921–1926	15	60
Labelle Cutlery Works, 1884–1888	45	120
Lafayette Cutlery Co., 1910–1920s	5	55
Lakota Corp., contemp.	20	100
Landers Frary & Clark, 1863–1954	25	125
Lawton Cutlery Co., 1895	25	75
Layman Carey Co., 1920	25	175

	LOW	HIGH
Lenox Cutlery Co., 1910	10	25
Liberty Knife Co., 1920s	25	60
Lipschultz, 1975	30	90
Long, 1880	25	175
Lord Bros., 1880s	25	175
Luna, 1903–1948	15	75
Lux, 1920	5	55
Lyon Cutlery Co., 1880s	25	95
Magnetic Cutlery Co., 1900–1932	25	95
Majestic Cutlery Co., 1910	5	225
Manhattan Cutlery Co., 1868–1916	25	300
Marshall Field & Co., 1909–1923	15	60
Martin Bros. & Naylor, 1860	60	100
McIntosh Hdw. Co., 1875–1911	20	150
Meridan Cutlery Co., 1855–1925	25	150
Meridan Knife Co., 1917–1932	25	150
Merrimac Cutlery Co.	40	70
Metropolitan Cutlery Co., 1918–1951	10	35
Mill Mfg. Co.	35	90
Miller Bros. Cutlery Co., 1872–1926	25	350
Mitchell & Co. Ltd., 1910	10	150
Mizzoo Cutlery Co., 1906–1918	25	250
Morris Cutlery Co., 1882–1930	35	200
Moslery Cutlery Co.	15	65
Mount Vernon Cutlery Co., 1890	10	50
Mumbley Peg, 1937–1948	50	95
Nash Hdw. Co., 1873–1975	25	150
Nathan Joseph, 1873–1894	25	250
National Silver Co.	10	30
Naugatuck Cutlery Co., 1872–1888	45	175
Naylob & Sanderson, 1810–1830	25	350
Needham Bros., 1860–1900	70	300
Neft Safety Knife, 1920–1930s	65	125
Nelson Knife Co.	15	35
Never Dull Cutlery Co., 1896–1940	20	65
New Britain Knife Co.	10	75
New Century Cutlery Co., 1900	20	55
New England Cutlery Co., 1852–1860	10	150
New England Knife Co., 1910	45	125
New Haven Cutlery Co., 1890s	15	90
New York Cutlery Co., 1890s	10	150
Newton Premier	10	25
Nifty, 1913–1914	4	10
Nippes & Plumacher	15	45
Norberis Cutlery	15	30
North American Knife Co., 1920s	15	65
North West Cutlery Co., 1890	10	90
Northfield Knife Co., 1858–1919	45	300
Norvell's Best, 1902–1917	25	300
Norvell-Shapleigh Hdw. Co., 1902–1917	15	300
Norwich Cutlery Co.	15	60
Noxall Cutlery Co., 1907	5	100
Oak Leaf, 1888–1920	20	200
Oakland Cutlery Co.	5	15

	LOW	HIGH
Occident Cutlery Co., 1910	25	200
Odell Hdw. Co.	25	150
Oehm & Co., 1860–1936	15	275
Ohio Cutlery Co., 1919–1923	40	200
Oklahoma City Hdw., 1911–1951	25	65
Olcut, 1911–1914	45	300
Old American Knife	10	35
Old Cutlery, 1978–contemp.	5	20
Olean Cutlery Co., 1911–1914	50	300
Olsen Knife Co., 1960–1983	10	75
Omega, 1898–1924	5	15
O'Neill & Thompson	6	16
Ontario Knife Co., 1889–contemp.	20	150
Opinel, 1890–contemp.	5	15
Orange Cutlery Co., 1923	25	200
Osgood Bray & Co., 19th C	15	200
Othello, 1923–contemp.	10	150
Oval Cutlery Co.	15	75
Overland, 1951–1953	5	100
Pacific Hdw. & Steel Co., 1901–1918	40	175
Pal, 1924–1939	15	90
Pal Blade Co., 1929–1953	15	90
Pal Cutlery Co., 1929–1953	15	90
Papes Thiebes Cutlery Co., 1903–1929	40	200
Paris Bead, 1920s	25	45
Parisian Novelty Co., 1915	5	20
Parker Bros., 1978–contemp.	5	20
Pastlan Bros. Co.	5	18
Patton & Gallagher, 1864–1959	25	75
Peerless	5	15
Pepsi Cola	15	40
Peters Bros. Celebrated Cutlery, 1870–1886	60	165
Peters Cutlery Mfg. Co., 1876–1886	10	125
Phoenix Knife Co., 1892–1916	45	175
Platts, 1920s	25	175
Pop Cutlery Co.	5	20
Pottery Hoy Hdw. Co.	35	65
Powell Bros.	15	60
Pratt & Co.	70	110
Precise, contemp.	10	125
Press Button Knife Co., 1892–1923	50	190
Presto George, 1925–1945	30	175
Pribyl Bros., 1880–1905	25	45
Progress, 1886–1942	10	150
Pronto, 1926–1952	5	75
Providence Cutlery Co., 1890s–1980s	15	150
Q & Crown, 1932–1955	7	200
Queen City, 1922–1945	20	250
Quick Point, 1930s	25	75
Quick-Kut, Inc.	10	45
Rainbow, 1933–1954	5	15
Randal Hall & Co.	5	15
Raola Cutlery	4	10
Rec-nob Co.	15	30

	LOW	HIGH
Regent	10	30
Rev-O-Nov, 1905–1960	35	40
Richards, 1862–1908	35	40
Richards Bros. & Sons Ltd., 1980s	5	30
Richards & Conover Hdw. Co., 1894–1956	30	55
Richmond Cutlery Co., 19th C	25	100
Rigid Knives, 1970–contemp.	25	150
Riverside Cutlery Co. N.Y., 1918	15	50
Rivington Works, 1900–1946	15	45
Robbins Clark & Biddle, 19th C	25	200
Robert Hartkopf & Co., 1855–1957	15	125
Robert Kerder, 1872–contemp.	15	175
Robert Klaas, 1834–contemp.	15	250
Robert Wade, 1810–1819	25	275
Robinson Bros. & Co., 1880–1925	45	300
Rodgers Wostenholm Ltd., 1971–1984	10	50
Romo, contemp.	3	15
Royal Cutlery Co., 1814–1954	10	25
Royal Oak	15	45
Royce Cutlery Co.	15	35
Runkel Bros., 1920s	15	35
Sabatier	15	35
Salem Co., 1918–1935	15	60
Sam L. Bukley & Son	10	35
Samco	15	30
Samuel Bradford, 1850	15	150
Samuel Bradlee, 1799–1845	25	250
Samuel E. Bernstein, 1890–1950s	15	125
Samuel Hague, 1830s–1950s	25	200
Samuel Hancock & Sons, 1836–1924	25	200
Samuel Wragg & Sons, 1930s–1960s	25	175
Savory Cutlery Co.	5	25
Saxons Cutlery Co.	15	35
Saynor Cooke & Ridal, 1840–1868	45	90
Schmachtenberg Bros. 1887–1939	20	65
Schmidt & Ziegler, 1930s	20	95
Scholfield	8	20
Schrade, 1973–contemp.	10	45
Seaborad Steel Co.	5	65
Seneca Cutlery Co., 1932–1942	15	65
Severing Droeschers, 1891–1924	10	18
Shapleigh, 1920–1960	15	150
Sheldon	15	45
Shur-Snap, 1949	20	45
Simmons Boss, 1940–1960	25	50
Simmons Hdw. Co., 1865–1960	20	300
Simmons, Warden, 1937–1946	20	75
Singleton & Priessman, 1861	50	150
Slash, 1868–1896	25	75
Small Bros. Inc.	10	25
Smith Brothers Hdw. Co., 1903–1959	40	85
Smith & Clark, 1850	25	250
Smith & Hemenway, 1890–1920	25	175
Solidus	10	20

	LOW	HIGH
Southerrn & Richardson, 1846–contemp.	10	40
Southington Cutlery Co., 1867–1914	45	200
Spring Cutlery Co., 1890	45	150
Spyderco	10	45
Sta Sharp	15	30
Sta-Sharp, 1927–1940	20	150
Steelton Cutlery Works	15	25
Stellar	2	5
Stercy	3	15
Stocker & Co., 1897–1970s	15	45
Strauss Bros. & Co.	12	25
Streamline, 1935	15	35
Stringer	35	85
St. Lawrence Cutlery Co., 1886–1916	25	75
Summit Knife Co., 1906	10	35
Superior Cutlery	15	65
Supplee Hdw. Co., 1905–1906	10	35
Swan Works	5	35
Swank	7	15
Syracuse Knife Co., 1930s	15	75
Tammen	5	12
Tampa Hdw. Co., 1910	15	150
Tarry	15	45
Tellin & Co.	8	40
Terrier Cutlery Co., 1910–1916	45	110
Thelco	15	60
Theo M. Green Co., 1916–1920	5	60
Thomas Fenton	14	20
Thomas Wilton	15	75
Thompson	5	15
Thornton, 1950s	5	15
Tina, 1890–contemp.	20	95
Tink Hdw. Co.	35	75
Toledo Cutlery Co.	15	35
Tombay Cutlery Co., 1910	45	200
Twig Brand, 1911	15	75
Two Eagles	10	45
Ulbich	4	15
Universal, 1898–1950	15	35
Universal Knife Co., 1897–1909	10	150
Valley Falls Cutlery Co., 1915	15	75
Valor, 1970–contemp.	3	15
Van Camp Hdw. & Iron Co., 1876–1960	35	275
Veritable Pradel	12	20
Victor Knife, 1907–1913	5	20
Victorinox, 1891–contemp.	10	150
Vignos Cutlery Co., 1879–1948	15	125
Viking, 1931–1934	5	15
Voos Cutlery Co., 1920s–1981	25	150
Voyles Cutlery, 1970s	10	40
Vulcan Knife Co.	5	40
Vulcan & Tellin & Co.	10	35
Wahl Wagner	5	15
Wait Co.	5	30

Walker Cutlery Works	5	35
Wall Bros.	35	150
Wallace Bros., 1895–1955	35	60
Walsh & Lovett	25	150
Waltham Cutlery	5	15
Ward Bros.	5	35
Wardion Cutlery Co.	25	85
Wards, 1935–1950s	10	100
Warren Bros.	35	150
Warwick Knife Co., 1907–1928	35	200
Washington Cutlery Co., 1885–1927	25	175
Water Bros. Cutlery	10	30
Watkins Cottrell Co., 1867	25	150
Weed & Co.	35	75
Wenger, 1908–contemp.	5	100
Weske Cutlery Co., 1946–1952	5	75
Western Cutlery Co., 1874–1914	20	125
Weyhand	10	15
Wherwolf Cutlery Works	10	120

Top, left to right: Colonial, Schrade, Pal Blade Co., and Miller Bros. Cutlery Co.

Bottom: Camillus Cutlery Co., Camco (Dick Tracy and Junior), Victorinox "Swiss Champ" (large), and Victorinox "Classic" (small).

Lamps

The first two decades following World War II were a time of great change in America. It seems that everyone left the inner city for a slice of the American pie: Suburbia. All these new homes had to be furnished and everyone needed lamps. The lamps below were made from the late 1940s to the mid 1960s. There were, of course, more traditional lamps produced but collectors focus on the kitsch, strange and sometimes downright ugly examples that '50s homemakers proudly plugged in. Some have classic themes such as ballet dancers and Harlequin, others, such as sleek panthers, are a carry-over from the Art Deco era of pre-World War II America. The futuristic designs of the third group reflect the era's obsession with technology and UFOs. Shades decorated with abstract splatters reminiscent of an angry Jackson Pollock often top them off. Other examples defy all attempts of categorization.

The lamps listed are in good condition with their original or period shades. Shades are often parchment; red is a common color. Blind shades are metal or plastic and fold down like their window blind namesakes. Base materials range from plaster and porcelain to wood and metal or combinations. Original shades can increase the value of a lamp by more than 50%. Determining if a shade is original is sometimes difficult.

Retailers sold most lamps separately, but those found as matched pairs have a bonus value of 20%–40%. The names represent descriptions, not necessarily manufacturers' listings.

	LOW	AVG.	HIGH
Asian Man and Woman, w/ panther, painted plaster, mkd. Continental Art, 1950, cloth pagoda-style shade, 33" h, matched pair	$200	$250	$300
Ballet Dancers, painted plaster, sgd. E. Bertolozzi, Chicago, w/ oversized cloth shade, 32.5" h, matched pair	100	150	200
Bent Metal Figure 8, centering chrome sphere, red parchment shade, 24" h	20	25	30
Black Horse, porcelain, w/ gold accents, venetian blind shade, 14.5" h	30	45	60
Blackamoor in Turban, black, red, and gold plaster, red parchment shade, 27" h	25	35	45
Brass and Wood Swirl, wooden base w/ swirl design brass support, green parchment shade w/ black and white looping pattern, 23" h	25	35	45
C-Shaped Desk Lamp, black metal base, tubular C support, brass trim, cream parchment shade	20	30	40
Candelabra, black and brass finished metal w/ gold and black mottled parchment shade, 27" h	45	60	75
Dancing X, formed by black-painted wood and tubular brass, black wood base, green parchment shade w/ gold and black highlights, 28.5" h	100	140	180
Deer and Foliage, green porcelain, probably Haeger, pale green parchment shade w/ gold and white brush stroke dec., 26" h, matched pair	120	160	180
Flex Neck Floor Lamp, black w/ brass accents, pierced star pattern parchment shade, 52" h	25	35	45
Futuristic Flowers, large wooden base and stylized leaves, spun plastic shade, matched pair	40	60	80
Genie Lamp (Aladdin style), blue porcelain w/ gold accents, parchment shade, 18" h	25	35	45
Harlequin, painted plaster mkd. Van Cleef Mfg., Mario Montleone ©1950, cloth shade, mask-form finial	40	50	60
Harlequins, painted plaster, mkd. Puccinni Art Co., black and gold swirl parchment shade, 24" h, matched pair	175	225	275
Hula Dancer, copper flash white metal w/ grass skirt and matching shade, dancer's body is articulated so that she dances, 28" h	150	200	250
Leaping Fish w/ Wave, green porcelain, probably Royal Haeger, light green parchment shade, 28" h, matched pair	200	250	300

	LOW	AVG.	HIGH
Oriental Couple, stylized rocky base, tri-form venetian blind shade, 24" h	90	110	130
Oriental Shadow Box, figures on glass panel which conceals lighting unit, metal shadow box frame, 14" x 12", matched pair	50	60	80
Pink Abstract, plaster, bi-level parchment shade, 23" h	80	100	120
Polka Dot, gold-colored metal base w/ 2 porcelain tumblers divided by 2 gold spheres and string and ball dec., gold and turquoise polka-dotted parchment shade, 28" h, matched pair	120	140	160
Prom Queen, porcelain figure w/ layered dress, matching layered shade, 20" h	40	60	80
Robin Hood, painted plaster, mkd. Colonial Art Creations, sgd. S. Nardi, cloth shade, 31" h, matched pair	120	180	240
Sea Shells and Christ, plaster, nightlight concealed in shell, 7" h	8	14	20
Southern Belle, metal shadow box frame featuring light behind painted glass scene of women in layered skirts w/ plantation in background, 14" x 12"	20	25	35
Stalking Panther, black porcelain, 3 hole planter, venetian blind shade, 13" h	30	40	50
Stylized Tree Trunks, white plaster, tan and red mottled parchment shades, 27" h, matched pair	60	80	100
Swirling Cone, pink porcelain w/ gold trim, parchment shade, 24" h	20	30	40
Telephone Lamp, blue plaster w/ clock dial and cigarette lighter in headset, venetian blind shade, 22" h	60	80	100
3-D Last Supper, wall lamp, gold-tone pierced metal frame	20	25	30
3-D Poodle, wall lamp, pierced metal frame, 17" x 21"	45	65	85
Turquoise and Gold Twist, porcelain w/ matching abstract splattered shade, 29" h	90	125	160
Twin Flex Neck Desk Lamp, stylized student's lamp, black w/ turquoise accents and 2 flex necks, fiberglass conical shades, 26" h	24	55	65
Twin Rearing Steeds, black porcelain, venetian blind shade, 13" x 10", matched pair	90	125	160
Vinyl Landscape, wooden frame housing mountain scene screen, backlit, 19" x 27"	25	30	35

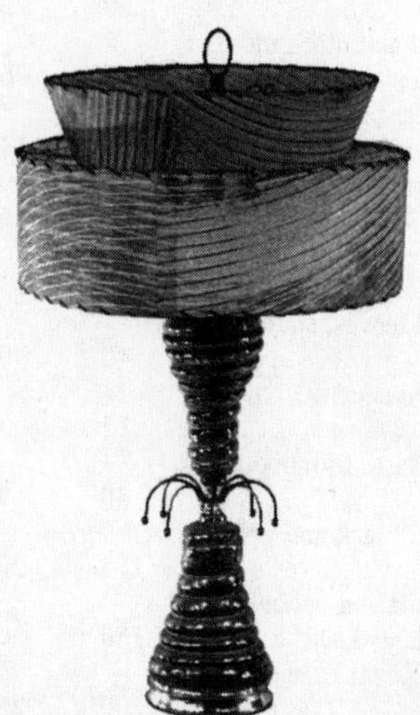

Abstract, ceramic, turquoise w/ gold highlights, 2-tier parchment shade, 30.5" h, pair, $50—$100.

Metallic Collectibles

Aluminum

Although aluminum is a basic element on the periodic table, it was extremely difficult to purfiy. During the nineteenth century it was a luxury metal. Not until after Charles Hill patented an inexpensive smelting method in 1886 did it become a "practical" metal. Nearly all aluminum wares on the market are twentieth century.

Aluminum can be clearned with soap and water or even paste silver polish. Be gentle in cleaning: aluminum dents and scratches easily. Salt will corrode aluminum.

"Good" pieces are not dented or heavily scratched. They are simple in form. "Best" pieces have a fine texture, such as a hammered finish, and have a striking visual appearance. This can be very subjective. One collector's treasure is another collector's junk.

	GOOD	BETTER	BEST
Ashtray	$10	$20	$50
Bowl	10	15	45
Box, cov.	20	40	90
Bread Tray	15	30	50
Butter Dish	8	15	20
Cake Stand	12	20	25
Candelabra, pair	70	100	160
Candlesticks, pair	20	30	50
Candy Dish	10	15	25
Casserole	10	15	20
Cigarette Box	15	30	75
Coaster	2	5	8
Coaster Set	20	30	50
Coffee Urn	40	75	100
Compote	10	20	40
Cream and Sugar	10	18	35
Cup, collapsible	1	3	8
Folding Server	30	50	80
Fondue Pot	15	20	30
Gravy Boat	10	15	20
Hurricane Lamps, pair	20	30	40
Ice Bucket	10	20	40
Matchbox Cover	10	25	50
Meat Platter, well and tree	15	25	40
Napkin Holder	10	15	30
Nut Bowl	15	20	30
Pitcher	20	30	50
Plate, fancy	15	30	50
Powder Box	10	15	20
Sandwich Tray	15	30	50
ServingTray	20	50	80
Silent Butler	20	30	50
Teapot	15	20	40
Tidbit	15	30	45
Tray, whimsical shape	30	50	80
Tumblers	4	8	15
Vase, hammered	20	40	60

Brass

Brass is an alloy of copper and zinc. Early English and Continental pieces are the most valuable. Lighter-weight decorative brassware imported from Asia since the turn of the century often has intricate engraving and tooling, but is less valuable. Objects should be in excellent condition: no dents, no corrosion, even color. Brass may be polished without destroying its value (unlike bronze).

Richard A. Myers in Winston-Salem, North Carolina, sells superb reproductions of seventeenth-century brass candlesticks. They are sand cast with no silver solder used. For those interested in such fine reproductions, contact Richard Myers at 2115 Bethabara Road, Winston-Salem, North Carolina 27106.

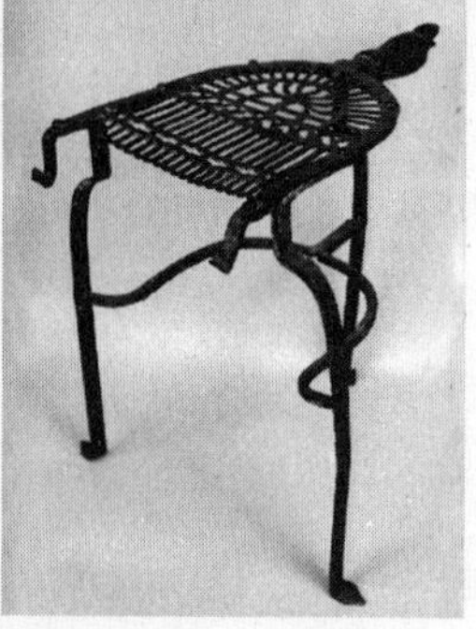

Left: Kettle Stand, reticulated brass trivet, wrought-iron base, turned wood handle, 12" h, $165–$210.

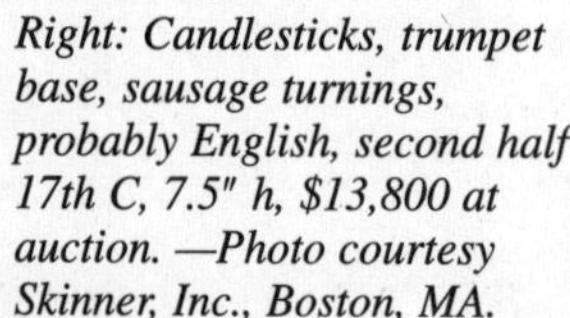

Right: Candlesticks, trumpet base, sausage turnings, probably English, second half 17th C, 7.5" h, $13,800 at auction. —Photo courtesy Skinner, Inc., Boston, MA.

	AUCTION	RETAIL Low	RETAIL High
Andirons, American, banded lemon top w/ spurred carbiole legs, 23" h, pair	$800	$1500	$2500
Andirons, American, spire top w/ spurred cabriole legs, 21" h, pair	900	1500	2500
Andirons, column-form w/ spurred cabriole legs, 22" h, pair	300	600	900
Argan Lamp, column-form w/ plain chimney, 21" h	300	600	900
Argan Lamps, simple column-form w/ plain chimneys, J. & I. Cox, NY label, 19" h, pair	800	1400	2200
Candlesticks, English, stepped hexagonal base, 7.5" h, pair	350	600	1000
Candlesticks, English, tapering fluted column w/ square bobeche, capital, and base w/ gadrooned edge, 11.5" h, pair	900	1600	2500
Candlesticks, English, petal base w/ bobeche and detail on stem, base w/ swirled line on alternating lobes, mid 18th C, 8.5" h, pair	2600	5000	7500
Candlesticks, English, candle cup w/ flaring notched rim, turned stem on circ. base, sq. foot w/ notched corners, mid 18th C, 8.25" h, pair	1300	2400	3500
Candlesticks, English, flaring mid-band candle cup on turned stem and sq. base w/ notched corners, mid 18th C, 7.25" h, pair	950	1750	2750

	AUCTION	RETAIL Low	RETAIL High
Candlesticks, English, shaped petal-form bobeche and base, mid 18th C, 9.5" h, pair	1800	3000	5000
Candlesticks, English, turned stem w/ crimped detail on slightly stepped base w/ notched corners, mid 18th C, 7" h, pair	850	1500	2500
Candlesticks, English, hexagonal base, shaped candle cup, trumpet-turned stem, mid 18th C, 6.25", pair	500	900	1400
Candlesticks, English, petal base, candle cup w/ flaring rim, swelled petal-form detail on stem, mid 18th C, 9" h, pair	1850	3000	5000
Candlesticks, French, 9.5" h, pair	350	600	1000
Candlesticks, baluster-turned stem, square base, fitted for electricity, mid 18th C, 9.5" h, pair	750	1300	2000
Chandelier, Continental, turned 6-scroll arm, 24" dia	3000	5250	8250
Chandelier, Dutch Queen Anne style, 6-arm, 16" h	1600	2800	4500
Chandlelier, painted and decorated metal 3-arm shaft w/ flat disks, curved candlearms w/ candle holders each w/ bobeche, 17" h, 13" dia	600	1150	1750
Door Knocker, cast, eagle form, 10" l	125	220	350
Fire Fender, American, steel wire front, 27" l	120	225	350
Fire Fender, American, pierced, 35" l	170	300	500
Fire Fender, Federal, serpentine front w/ pierced anthemion motif, 41" l	600	1000	1800
Fire Fender, New England, wire and brass, ball finials	400	750	1150
Fire Tools, American, Empire, pair	250	450	700
Fluid Lamp, marble base, Cornelius label, electrified	250	450	700
Girandole Set, hung w/ crystal prisms, tallest piece 13" h, 3-piece set	150	260	425
Measure, English, copper and brass, engraved w/ crest	200	350	550
Planter, Continental, eliptical, 18" l	1200	2100	3300
Planter, Russian, oval, simple repossé on paw feet, 14" l	350	600	1000
Spice Casters, 18th C, 5" h, set of 4	675	1180	2000
Spoon-Maker's Metal Tablespoon Template, 9" l	50	90	135
Warming Pan, Early American, engraved	150	260	425
Warming Pan, engraved peacock, early 19th C, 42" l	225	400	650

Andirons, ball finial, belted, mkd. "Hunneman" (John Hunneman, Boston), c1800, 17" h, $1380 at auction. —Photo courtesy Skinner, Inc., Boston, MA.

Bronze

Though bronze sculpture is of ancient origin, most specimens on the market are Victorian and twentieth century. The name of the artist is the biggest factor in determining value. The name of the foundry is also important.

Don't clean a bronze sculpture with any highly abrasive cleaner. The color and condition of the "patina" is important. Vienna cold painted bronzes should have their original paint in good condition.

Harriet Whitney Frishmuth (1880–1980), Laughing Waters, greenish-brown patina, sgd. "Harriet W. Frishmuth," inscribed "19©29," stamped "Gorham Founders OGOA," 16" h, $11,500 at auction. —Photo courtesy William Doyle Galleries.

	AUCTION	RETAIL Low	RETAIL High
After Antoine-Louis Bayre, seated lion, dark greenish-brown patina, 6.75" h, 5.5" l	$402	$650	$900
After Augustin Pajou (French 1730–1809), maiden and goat, sgd. on base, 33.5" h	4600	7500	10,000
After Model by A. Gory, partially clad Middle Eastern maiden drawing scarf over her head, sgd., 13.5" h	460	750	1000
After Model by Albert Carrier-Belleuse, portrait of a woman w/ hair drawn up and set w/ flowers and ruffled bodice set w/ ribbons, silvered, raised on spreading sq. socle and lion's paw feet, sgd. "Carrier-Belleuse" and "Jules Graux fondeur," 36" h	8575	14,000	20,000
After Model by Antoine Mercie, Gloria Victus, group depicting winged angel w/ parcel gilt armor, supporting fallen soldier, sgd., titled and sgd. "F. Barbedienne Fondeur," 37" h	10,350	17,000	24,000
After Model by Bruno Zach, Art Deco standing figure of a woman w/ cap, 22" h	2875	4000	5500
After Model by Colinet, semi-nude dancer w/ exotic costume, 17" h	1495	2200	3000
After Model by E. Villanis, Tanagra, bust of a woman w/ wide ribbon headband and drawn-up hair, sgd., titled, and w/ foundry mark, c1900, 24.5" h	2645	4000	5500

Pierre Jules Mene (French 1810–1879), "Djinn Etalon Barbe," brown patina, sgd. and dated "1866," horse's name inscribed on base, 11.5" h, $3450 at auction. —Photo courtesy William Doyle Galleries.

	AUCTION	RETAIL	
		Low	High
After Model by Eugene Mariton, "Domitor," depicting standing figure taming a wild cat, sgd., 36" h	2875	4500	6200
After Model by Giovanni Da Bologna, figure of Mercury, black marble base set w/ relief Cupids, 35.5" h	1150	2500	3800
After Model by Giovanni da Bologna, Rape of the Sabine Women, raised on marble base, sgd.	2530	3750	5000
After Model by Hippolyte Moreau, Un Secret, young boy and girl caressing, sgd. and titled, late 19th C, 21" h	3163	5000	6800
After Model by Jean Leon Gerome, equestrian group of Caesar crossing the Rubicon, sgd., 20" l	3737	5500	7000
Alice Carr de Creeft (American, b. 1899), Harold C. Ramser Off to the Hunt w/ His Hounds, group w/ mounted hunter and hounds, dark brown patina, sgd. and inscribed w/ names of the hounds, 17.25" h	4600	7200	10,000
Charles Georges Ferville-Suan (French late 19th C), Musician and Dancer, silvered, 14" h, pair	1265	2500	3200
Continental School, St. Michael slaying demon, medium brown patina, sgd. illegibly, late 19th C, 11" h, 7.5" w	345	550	750
Dan Bates (20th C), coyote, black patina, wood base, sgd "Dan Bates," 5.25" h	460	700	1000
Earl E. Heikka (1910–1941), The Road Agent, brown patina, sgd. "E.E. Heikka," dated "1940," inscribed "© K. Heikka 76 5/36" and "The Road Agent/by Earle E. Heikka," 12.75" h	690	1100	1400
Edouard Drouot (French 1859–1945), Qui Vivi, sgd. on base, 24" h	1035	1700	2400
Emile Antoine Bourdelle (French 1861–1929) Mask of Beethoven, greenish-brown patina, wood base, inscribed w/ artist's monogram, "© By Bourdelle," and "Suisse Fondeur Paris No.3," 8.75" h	1725	2800	3600
Ferdinand Pautrot (French 19th C), pheasant and chicks, medium brown patina, c1870, 21.5" h, 17" l	2070	3200	4100
French, seated Neoclassical female figure, late 19th C, 12.5" l	977	1500	2000
Harriet Whitney Frishmuth (1880–1980), Crest of the Wave, greenish-brown patina, sgd. "Harriet W. Frishmuth," inscribed "©1925," stamped "Gorham Founders QFHL," 21" h	8625	13,500	18,000

	AUCTION	RETAIL Low	RETAIL High
Harry Jackson (b. 1924), The Marshall III, brown patina, marble base, sgd. "Harry Jackson," dated "79," inscribed "©MAIII 306/1000," stamped w/ artist's thumbprint and foundry seal, 10.5" h	6900	10,000	15,000
Isadore Jules Bonheur (French, 1827–1901), The Polo Player, dark brown patina, sgd., 12.5" h	12,650	20,000	27,500
Italian, shepherd holding goat, 19th C, 20" h	690	1100	1500
Jules Moignies (1835–1894), partridge w/ rat, dark brown patina, 7.5" l	402	650	900
Mathurin Moreau (French, 1822–1912), Pandora, light brown patina, etched black marble base, c1870, 24" h	2530	4000	6000
P. Loiseau-Rousseau, ewer, French Art Nouveau, high looped handle molded w/ foliage, light gilt patina, sgd.	143	200	275
P. Tourgueneff (Continental late 19th C), recumbent Alsatian, dark brown patina, Susse Freres foundry marks, 15.5" l, 8" h	546	850	1200
Russian Orientalist, 2 Cossacks on horseback, sgd. on base, 19th C, 20" h	287	450	580
Tiffany Studios, crouching lion, dark brown patina, 4" l	431	725	1000
Unsigned, seated Mercury figure affixing wings to his foot, 25" h	1265	2000	2800
Unsigned, pair of Cupids, each holding a cornucopia, raised on modern marble pedestals, late 19th C, 65" h	20,700	32,000	45,000
Unsigned, standing partially clad warrior w/ pensive expression, holding sword, 21" h	805	1200	1600
Vienna Cold Painted, after model by Namgreb, mummy case opening to reveal gilt nude maiden, sgd., 8" h	1955	3000	4200
Vienna Cold Painted, elaborately caparisoned elephant and rider, 9.5" h	3737	5400	8000
Vienna Cold Painted, equestrian group depicting cowboy shooting revolver on rearing horse, stamped Bergman Foundry mark, 10.5" h	2300	3500	4700
Vienna Cold Painted, jester w/ umbrella under his arm and double base on his back, raised on octagonal onyx base, sgd. "F. Milaui," 14" h	2760	4200	5700
Vienna Cold Painted, kingfisher, 5.5" h	632	1000	1350

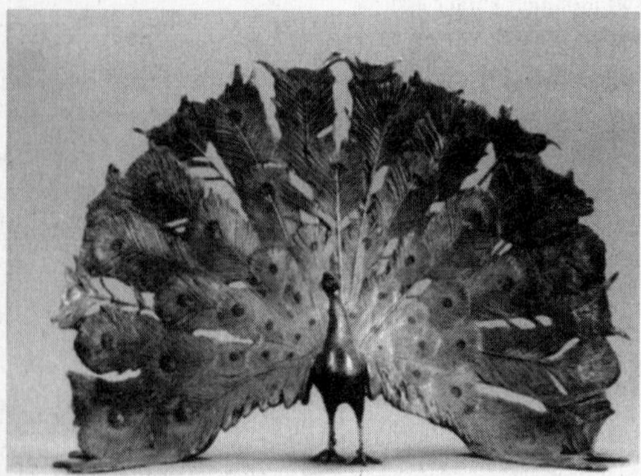

Vienna Cold Painted, peacock, 8" h, $1840 at auction. —Photo courtesy William Doyle Galleries.

Copper

As the price of the metal itself has risen, so has the price for the well-crafted antiques and collectibles. "Good" examples must be in good condition, with only tiny dents. "Best" examples are undented and well proportioned, and show fine workmanship.

Architectural Finial, molded copper, American, 19th C, 61.5" h, $3220 at auction. —Photo courtesy Skinner, Inc., Boston, MA.

	GOOD	BETTER	BEST
Apple Butter Kettle, c1890	$125	$200	$475
Bed Warmer, turned wood handle, pierced lid, early 19th C, 47" l	150	190	300
Bowl, silver gilt int., early 20th C, 10" dia	100	250	400
Bucket, bail handle, early 20th C, 13" h	75	120	200
Candlestick, gilt bronze highlights, late 19th C, 14" h	200	400	600
Chafing Dish, arched supports, w/ burner, c1930	75	110	200
Chamberstick, detachable snuffer, 19th C, 6" dia	125	190	300
Chocolate Pot, wooden side handle, c1800, 7" h	450	700	1500
Coal Scuttle, bail handle, late 19th C, 15" h	125	200	300
Coffeepot, baluster form, 19th C, 12" h	50	80	100
Dipper, 19th C, 14" l	90	125	275
Double Boiler, early 20th C, 1 qt.	60	70	160
Egg Poacher, 2 brass handles, holds 9 eggs, early 20th C	40	60	100
Funnel, late 19th C, 23" h	100	200	300
Hot Water Bottle, bail handle, brass lid, late 19th C	80	100	200
Jelly Kettle, iron bail handle, late 19th C	100	150	300
Kettle, early 19th C	185	250	475
Lamp Filler, dovetail construction, c1800, 4" h	235	375	600
Measure Set, 1 pt. to 2.5 qts., 19th C	275	375	725
Measure Set, harvest measures, 19th C	500	1250	3000
Milk Bucket, iron bail handle, late 19th C	165	225	475
Mixing Bowl, circ. base, handled, 19th C, 14" dia	75	125	250
Mold, animal, 1 pt.	40	75	175
Pudding Mold, early 20th C, 1 pt.	40	70	150
Pudding Mold, early 20th C, 1 qt.	40	75	170
Pitcher, late 19th C, 2 qt.	65	90	200
Pot, hand-crafted, handled, early 19th C, 15" dia	165	210	425
Salt Box, 19th C, 7" w	85	115	250
Saucepan, cov., brass handle, tin-lined, 4 qt.	100	140	350
Serving Spoon, early 19th C, 9" l	75	120	200
Tea Urn, 3 cabriole legs, early 19th C, 19" h	500	800	2000

Graniteware and Enamelware

Graniteware is metalware with an enamel coating. It often has a mottled or marbleized appearance. Most graniteware is made for kitchen use. First featured in 1876 at the Centennial Exposition in Philadelphia, graniteware quickly gained popularity. It has been manufactured from the 1870s to the present.

"Good" pieces should have only traces of rust and no more than a few "dings" in the enamel. "Best" pieces should have no rust and no chipping of the enamel

	GOOD	BETTER	BEST
Baby Food Cup, gray	$15	$30	$50
Baking Dish, blue and white mottled	20	30	38
Baking Dish, brown and white mottled	20	32	40
Baking Dish, dark green, shaded	24	36	46
Baking Dish, red, turquoise, or yellow	12	18	23
Basting Spoon, blue and white mottled	12	18	23
Basting Spoon, brown and white mottled	14	21	27
Basting Spoon, dark purple, shaded	20	30	38
Basting Spoon, gray	10	15	20
Basting Spoon, white	2	4	10
Bedpan, gray, odorless tabbed lid	10	20	40
Berry Bucket, blue and white marbleized swirls, small	10	25	45
Berry Bucket, child's, gray w/ lid and bail handle	55	110	180
Berry Bucket, cobalt and white swirl	53	100	170
Berry Bucket, cobalt diffused	55	110	185
Bowl, blue swirl, 9" dia	30	60	100
Bowl, gray, shallow, 2 qt.	10	25	45
Bread Box, white w/ blue swirls, circ., hinged lid	45	95	150
Bread Pan, gray	10	25	40
Bread Raiser, gray mottled, tin lid w/ wood knob, 15" dia	50	100	175
Bread Tray, blue and white mottled	14	21	27
Bread Tray, brown and white mottled	15	23	29
Bread Tray, dark green, shaded	16	24	30
Bread Tray, gray	12	18	23
Bread Tray, red, turquoise, or yellow and white mottled (late)	10	15	19
Bread Tray, white	5	8	10
Candle Holder, brown and white mottled	39	59	74
Candle Holder, dark purple, shaded	42	63	80
Candle Holder, solid colors, (late)	34	51	65
Cereal Bowl, pink w/ cobalt trim, rabbit dec.	10	20	45
Chamber Pot, cov., brown and white mottled	20	30	38
Chamber Pot, cov., dark purple, shaded	24	36	46
Chamber Pot, cov., white	2	14	7
Cheese Grater, steel handles	35	60	115
Coffee Boiler, blue and white mottled	64	96	122
Coffee Boiler, brown and white marbleized, dome lid, 6 qt.	50	120	190
Coffee Boiler, brown and white mottled	70	105	133
Coffee Boiler, gray	75	100	125
Coffee Boiler, gray mottled, half-moon shape, 5.5" handle, 9" x 5" x 4.5"	25	50	95
Coffee Boiler, gray, bail handle	35	70	125
Coffee Boiler, navy speckled w/ white, U.S. Navy, wire bail w/ wooden handle, large	20	40	80
Coffee Boiler, white	34	51	65
Coffeepot, dark green, shaded	60	90	115

	GOOD	BETTER	BEST
Coffeepot, dark purple, shaded	60	90	115
Coffeepot, gray	46	70	85
Colander, blue and white mottled, large	60	85	90
Colander, brown and white mottled	30	45	60
Colander, dark green, shaded	30	40	50
Colander, dark purple, shaded	38	57	72
Cream Pitcher, white	8	12	15
Cup/Saucer, blue and white mottled	30	45	57
Cup/Saucer, dark green, shaded	38	57	72
Cup/Saucer, dark purple, shaded	38	57	72
Cup/Saucer, red, turquoise, or yellow and white mottled (late)	16	24	30
Cup/Saucer, solid colors (late)	18	27	34
Cup/Saucer, white	10	15	19
Dinner Pail, gray, tin lid, round, striped mottling, bail w/ wood handle, large	30	60	100
Dinner Plate, brown and white mottled	17	26	33
Dinner Plate, gray	12	18	23
Dinner Plate, solid colors (late)	12	18	23
Dinner Plate, white	5	8	10
Dipper, dark purple, shaded	16	24	30
Dipper, red, turquoise, or yellow and white mottled (late)	9	14	17
Dipper, solid colors (late)	10	15	19
Double Boiler, red, turquoise, or yellow and white mottled (late)	28	42	53
Double Boiler, white	18	27	34

Graniteware Auction Prices, clockwise from top left: Pail, cov., blue and white swirl, 7.5" h, $143; Five-Stack Dinner Carrier, white w/ cobalt rims, $93; Milk Can, cov., emerald and white swirl, black rim, 9.25" h, $1375; Berry Pail, red and white swirl, 4.75" h, $2420; Pan, end-of-day, multicolor swirl, cobalt rim, 12" x 7.5", $440. —Photo courtesy York Town Auction, Inc.

	GOOD	BETTER	BEST
Funnel, brown and white mottled	12	18	23
Funnel, gray	10	15	19
Funnel, solid colors	8	12	15
Funnel, white	4	6	8
Invalid Feeder, gray, gooseneck spout	10	20	45
Kerosene Stove, table top, gray, fancy, ornate nickel-coated trim, includes 1 qt. nickel-plated brass tea kettle w/ ornate gooseneck spout and lid, bell-shaped bottom, and wood and bail handle and tray w/ raised rim, by George Haller, 11" dia.	350	725	1150
Ladle, black and white mottled, 12" l	10	20	30
Ladle, cobalt, 12" l	10	20	35
Mixing Bowl, brown and white mottled	18	27	34
Mixing Bowl, dark purple, shaded	21	32	40
Mixing Bowl, solid colors (late)	12	18	23
Mixing Bowl, white	8	12	15
Mustard Pot, blue and white mottled	20	30	38
Mustard Pot, dark purple, shaded	34	51	65
Mustard Pot, solid colors (late)	14	21	27
Pan, blue, 9"	30	48	63
Pan, blue, round, 8"	25	50	80
Pan, blue, round, 11"	20	40	80
Pan, blue and white swirl, round, 8"	25	50	90
Pan, blue swirl, round, 8"	20	40	75
Pan, blue swirl, round, 9"	20	55	95
Pie Plate, blue and white mottled	14	21	27
Pie Plate, brown and white mottled	17	26	33
Pie Plate, dark green, shaded	22	33	42
Pie Plate, dark purple, shaded	22	33	42
Pie Plate, solid colors (late)	12	18	23
Pitcher and Bowl, dark green, shaded	121	181	230
Pitcher and Bowl, white	60	90	114
Skillet, gray	20	30	38
Soap Dish, brown and white mottled	30	45	57
Soap Dish, gray	16	24	30
Soap Dish, white	8	12	15
Soup Plate, blue and white mottled	14	21	27
Soup Plate, brown and white mottled	17	26	33
Soup Plate, dark green, shaded	22	33	42
Soup Plate, red, turquoise, or yellow and white mottled (late)	14	21	27
Soup Plate, solid colors (late)	12	18	23
Soup Plate, white	5	8	10
Spittoon, blue and white mottled	50	75	95
Spittoon, brown and white mottled	56	84	105
Spittoon, gray	40	60	76
Sugar Bowl, dark green, shaded	38	57	72
Tea Kettle, gray	76	114	144
Teapot, blue and white mottled, 1 qt.	80	120	150
Teapot, dark purple, shaded, 1 qt.	95	145	180
Teapot, gray, 1 qt.	80	115	150
Teapot, red, turquoise, or yellow and white mottled (late), 1 qt.	80	115	150
Teapot, white, 1 qt.	40	60	75
Teapot, white, 2 qt.	30	45	58
Tumbler, dark green, shaded	38	57	72
Tumbler, gray	15	20	28

Ironware

Marked ironware pieces have greater value. Dates do not always indicate the year made; some dates stand for the year the patent was issued. Oiling or polishing old ironware decreases its value. Many reproductions are made in Indonesia. Careless welding is a sign of modern work or fakery.

Left: Parrot Bottle Opener, $35–$50.

Top right: "W" windmill weight, $402 at auction. —Photo courtesy Butterfield, Butterfield & Dunning's.

Bottom right: Bootjack, $60–$80.

	AUCTION	RETAIL Low	RETAIL High
Andirons, Easter Island statue form, early 19th C, pair	$1500	$2500	$4500
Andirons, figural cast iron, 15" h, pair	500	1150	1800
Andirons, gooseneck, wrought iron, pair	75	100	200
Axe, hewing, sgd. "William Beatly & Son," Chester NH, 12.25" blade	140	175	220
Barber's Sign, "Haircut and Shave, 25¢," 13.5" l	175	300	500
Barn Hinges, early 19th C, 26.5" l, pair	270	325	375
Beam Spike w/ Hook, 18th C, 6" h	340	410	480
Broiler, rotary, c1800, 23.5" l	450	550	650
Bullet Mold, late 18th C	70	85	110
Candle Snuffer, curved handle, 18th C, 4.75" h	430	520	600
Candlestick, hog scraper, 5.25" h	250	300	350
Candlestick, hog scraper, 9.25" h	330	400	470
Coal Tongs, 10" l	50	60	80
Daybed, swan and lyre-form, painted, 94" l	1400	2500	4000
Eagle Ornament on Sphere, cast, mounted on stand, 23" h	550	960	1500
Ember Shovel, turned wood handle, 18th C, 14" l	325	400	500
Eyeglasses, late 18th C	200	250	325
Fireback, cast, cherubs above swag and date "1687," 30" h	600	1050	1650
Fireplace Crane, c1800, 31" l	240	290	340
Fireplace Crane, wrought, 4 feet, 14" h, 23" w	590	710	830
Fireplace Fork, w/ handle twist, 42.5" l	90	115	140
Fisherman's Ice House Stove, cast, late 19th C, 11" h	340	410	480
Floor Lamp, wrought	100	175	275
Food Chopper, wood handle, early 19th C, 5" w	100	120	140
Griddle, 7-dish form, 19th C, 16.75" l	250	300	350
Hearth Shovel, 24" l	100	130	160
Ice Tongs, hand forged, 12.5" h	80	100	110
Ice Tongs, wood handles, 11.25" L	60	70	80
Lantern Trammel, 18th C, extends to 32"	200	250	320

	AUCTION	RETAIL Low	RETAIL High
Log Lifter, 29.25"	70	90	110
Meat Hook Trammel w/ Hanger, hand forged, 18th C, extends to 35.5"	310	380	440
Pie Lifter, wood handle, c1840, 14" l	450	550	640
Pot Lifter and Trivet Combination Tool, 14" l	70	85	110
Quoits, 19th C, pair	80	100	110
Scissors, blacksmith-made, 18th C	50	65	80
Shooting Gallery Pipe Target, old blue paint	40	45	60
Spatula, blacksmith-made, 20" l	60	75	90
Spatula, heart-formed hanger, 18th C, 16" l	1100	1340	1560
Sugar Block Cutter, spike and hatchet ends, 18th C, 13.5" l	340	410	480
Sugar Devil, wood handle, 19th C, 16.5" l	390	470	550
Sugar Nippers, 18th C, 8" l	240	300	380
Tongs, scissor form, 18th C, 10.5" l	200	240	280
Top Hat, 7" h	550	670	780
Waffle Iron, mid 19th C, 28.5" l	270	330	380
Waffle Iron, United States seal	7000	11,000	13,000
Wall Rack, wrought iron	150	260	415
Warmer, adjustable, hangs from fender, c1800, 13.75" l	280	340	400
Warming Shelf, hanging, 19th C, 12.5" dia	310	280	440
Weaver's Shears, steel, early 19th C	170	210	240

Doorstop Auction Prices, top row left to right: Hubley Jonquils, $330; Roses in Vase, mkd. "Made in USA 445," $880; Hubley French Basket #69, $352; Hubley Flower Vase #465, $660; and Hubley Primrose #488, $385. Bottom row left to right: Hubley Rose Vase #441, $440; Hubley Iris #469, $550; Hubley Tulip Vase, $352; Hubley Tiger Lilies #472, $330; and Hubley Gladiolus #489, $275. —Photo courtesy Bill Bertoia Auctions.

Pewter

Pewter is a tin alloy, often containing copper. It is usually dark gray and soft, but can be light and shiny, almost resembling silver. Early pewter should not be used for eating, drinking or storing food, as it often contains lead, which can poison the food.

"Good" examples must be in reasonable condition, without any large dents. "Best" examples are undented and well proportioned, show exceptional workmanship and usually contain a "touch" or hammered mark of the maker. These marks can be identified by various guides.

Left: Coffeepot, $300–$500.

Right: Teapot, $250–$400.

	GOOD	BETTER	BEST
Candlestick, 19th C, 12" h	$40	$90	$180
Card Tray, peacock form, late 19th C, 5" dia	50	100	150
Chalice, Continental, 19th C, 8" h	85	100	125
Chalice, English, 19th C, 7" h	100	120	140
Chamber Pot, 19th C, 14" dia	80	120	200
Charger, English, 18th C, 18" dia	500	900	1200
Charger, German, 18th C, 15" dia	150	250	500
Coffee Urn, Continental, 19th C, 14" h	75	100	125
Deep Plate, 18th C, 10" dia	225	300	500
Flagon, Continental, spouted, 19th C	250	500	800
Flagon, cov., French, late 18th C, 14" h	600	800	1000
Flagon, octagonal, ram's head thumbpiece, 19th C, 14" h	75	150	225
Flagon, Swiss, Stegkanne form, spouted, 19th C, 12" h	450	600	750

	GOOD	BETTER	BEST
Flask, octagonal, Continental, 18th C, 13" h	750	100	1250
Fluid Lamp, English, 19th C	300	500	700
Funnel, 19th C, 9" l	35	60	90
Lamps, American, acorn form, 11" h, pair	525	700	875
Lavabo, Continental, 2 part, late 18th C	800	1200	1500
Measure, French, 19th C	25	30	50
Measures, English, bulbous form, set of 7	375	500	625
Measures, French, 19th C, set of 7	300	400	500
Mess Bowl, 19th C, 8" dia	20	30	40
Pitcher, French Brocauvin	150	250	500
Plate, American, 18th C, 8" dia	125	180	300
Plate, English, 18th C, 8" dia	100	140	200
Plate, European, 6" dia	25	50	150
Plate, European, 10" dia	50	150	250
Plate, French, wavy edge, 9" dia	25	35	60
Platter, French, wavy edge, 12" l	60	80	100
Porringer, plain tab handle, late 18th C, 5.5" dia	200	800	1200
Porringer, Continental, late 19th C, 5" dia	50	100	300
Porringer, Continental, 2-handled, late 19th C, 6" dia	75	150	400
Pot, cov., French, late 19th C	35	50	90
Serving Spoon, 18th C	50	125	200
Soup Plate, 19th C, 8" dia	20	30	50
Spoon, 18th C	40	100	150
Spoon, 19th C	9	12	15
Tankard, American, 18th C, 8" h	500	800	1500

English Charger and Plates, American Bull's-Eye Magnifying Lamp and Porringer, Fluid Lamp, Candlestick, and Goblet. —Photo courtesy Skinner, Inc., Boston, MA.

Silver

Silver is alloyed with other metals for durability, as pure silver is too soft for most uses. The grade of silver is determined by the amount or percentage of alloy material contained. Sterling silver is 925 parts per 1000 pure (usually stated as .925).

The values listed are primarily for easily found items. However, some rare and valuable examples are included for comparison. "Good" examples are considered to be in excellent condition, but without any superlative features. "Best" examples are perfectly proportioned and show exceptional workmanship. Thicker, and therefore heavier, pieces are generally of better quality than lighter pieces. Although dents can be repaired by a skilled silversmith, the work is not cheap. Also beware that a faker can add new marks, new decoration (such as chasing) or even new parts (such as a new base).

Right: Vase, silver overlay, Loetz, iridescent green glass, 5.75" h, $1870 at auction. —Photo courtesy Jackson's Auctioneers & Appraisers.

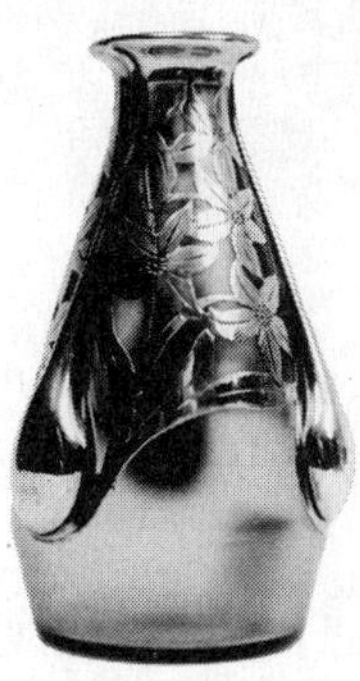

Left: Porringer, Tiffany & Co., enameled rose sprays, matching small plate, $1000 at auction.

	GOOD	BETTER	BEST
Baby Mug, American, repoussé, early 19th C	$200	$270	$400
Baby Mug, English, engraved, late 19th C	100	180	300
Baby Rattle, foliate design, mid 19th C, 3" l	200	270	400
Baby Spoon, American, late 19th C	30	40	60
Beaker, American, C.A. Burnett, incised rings, 4 oz., 3" h	1800	2380	3500
Bodkin, English, early 20th C	50	70	100
Book Cover, late 19th C	150	180	250
Bookmark, American, late 19th C	150	180	250
Bookmark, English, early 20th C	50	90	150
Boson's Whistle, late 19th C	300	360	500
Bottle Opener, early 20th C	30	50	80
Bottle Stopper, simple form, late 19th C	50	70	100
Bottle Stopper, whimsical form, late 19th C	200	220	300
Buckle, Art Deco, engine turned	100	110	150
Buckle, Art Nouveau, late 19th C	150	220	350
Button Hook, Art Nouveau, late 19th C	75	90	125

Silver Hollow Ware, 19th C, coin silver sugars, creamers, beaker, and butter dish and a sterling silver sugar (top right). —Photo courtesy Skinner, Inc., Boston, MA.

	GOOD	BETTER	BEST
Button Hook, repoussé handle, late 19th C	50	70	100
Cake Basket, repoussé	500	760	1200
Calling Card Case, English, late 19th C	200	320	500
Candle Snuffer, mid 20th C	40	50	80
Candlesticks, plain, low, weighted, 20th C, pair	100	160	250
Cane Handle, cast and chased, late 19th C	300	360	500
Christmas Ornament, late 20th C	40	50	80
Cigar Cutter, English, whimsical shape, late 19th C	100	160	250
Cigarette Case, enameled, mid 20th C	200	320	500
Cigarette Case, engraved, early 20th C	100	180	300
Cologne Bottle, silver overlay, clear glass, early 20th C	75	100	150
Cologne Bottle, silver overlay, colored glass, early 20th C	150	220	350
Comport, Ball, Black & Co., .950 silver, 30 oz.	1200	1350	1800
Comport, Ball, Black & Co., medallion pattern, 22 oz., 10" h	1200	1800	2800
Creamer, American, E. Moulton, oval engraved, 5 oz., 5" h	900	1080	1500
Creamer and Sugar, American, E. Moulton, 13 oz.	1800	2840	4500
Darning Egg, silver mounts, early 20th C	40	50	80
Decanter, silver overlay, clear glass, early 20th C	200	270	400
Flask, Art Nouveau, repoussé, late 19th C	500	580	800
Flask, engine turned, late 19th C	300	360	500
Flask, engraved, early 20th C	100	180	300
Flask, Tiffany, Japanese style, late 19th C	2000	2250	3000
Food Pusher, American, mid 19th C	40	50	70
Funnel, early 19th C	500	680	1000
Funnel, early 20th C	100	180	300
Glove Stretcher, American, late 19th C	50	90	150
Inkstand, Georgian style, late 19th C	400	540	800
Inkwell, English, engraved, late 19th C	150	220	350
Judaic Spice Tower, late 19th C, 10"	400	450	600
Letter Opener, engraved handle, mid 20th C	50	70	100

	GOOD	BETTER	BEST
Letter Opener, repoussé handle, late 19th C	100	140	200
Luggage Tag, engraved, late 19th C	50	70	100
Luggage Tag, engraved, mid 20th C	25	40	75
Magnifying Glass, Art Nouveau, late 19th C	300	360	500
Magnifying Glass, engraved, mid 20th C	100	140	200
Match Safe, enameled, 20th C	200	270	400
Match Safe, repoussé, late 19th C	150	220	350
Match Safe, whimsical shape, late 19th C	400	540	350
Miniature Coffeepot, Dutch, late 19th C, 2"	100	180	300
Miniature Sofa, English, early 20th C, 3"	100	140	200
Miniature Table, Continental, early 20th C, 2"	100	140	200
Miniature Tray, English, mid 19th C, 2.5"	300	360	500
Mustache Comb, early 20th C	50	70	100
Napkin Ring, engraved, late 19th C	50	60	75
Napkin Ring, engraved, mid 20th C	10	30	50
Napkin Ring, hand hammered, early 20th C	20	30	50
Napkin Ring, repoussé, mid 19th C	50	70	100
Necessaire, French, early 20th C, 6 implements	200	270	400
Nutmeg Grater, cylindrical, engine turned, early 19th C	300	360	500
Paper Knife, late 19th C	200	270	400
Picture Frame, repoussé, floral dec., late 19th C, 9" h	600	720	1000
Picture Frame, plain, mid 20th C, 6" h	100	180	300
Picture Frame, plain, mid 20th C, 9" h	200	270	400
Pillbox, English, late 19th C	200	270	400
Pincushion, animal shape, late 19th C	200	270	400

Coin Silver, 19th C, wine ewer, pitcher, coffeepot, sugar bowl, bowl, and creamer, and mid 18th C cann (bottom row, second from right). —Photo courtesy Skinner, Inc., Boston, MA.

	GOOD	BETTER	BEST
Pincushion, chatelaine type, late 19th C	100	140	200
Pitcher, silver overlay, clear glass, late 19th C	400	450	600
Place Card Holders, animal shape, early 20th C, set of 4	300	360	500
Place Card Holders, engraved, late 19th C, set of 4	200	270	400
Playing Card Box, English, early 20th C	150	220	350
Porringer, K. Leverett, coin silver, keyhole, 6 oz., 5.25" dia	2500	3380	5000
Posey Holder, Continental, filigree, late 19th C	300	400	500
Posey Holder, English, emb., late 19th C	300	360	500
Posey Holder, paneled, early 20th C	200	270	400
Powder Box, French, engraved, early 20th C	150	220	350
Riding Crop Handle, early 19th C	500	680	1000
Ring Box, English, early 20th C	50	90	150
Scent Bottle, late 19th C	150	220	350
Seal, for sealing wax, late 19th C	200	270	400
Seal, for sealing wax, mid 20th C	50	90	150
Shoe Horn, engraved, early 20th C	75	100	150
Snuff Box, English, late 19th C	300	360	500
Snuff Box, German, early 19th C	600	720	1000
Soap Case, emb., late 19th C	100	110	150
Souvenir Spoon, early 20th C	30	40	70
Souvenir Spoon, late 19th C	50	70	100
Spurs, engraved, early 19th C, pair	400	540	800
Spurs, engraved, early 20th C, pair	200	270	400
Stamp Box, late 19th C	150	180	250
Stamp Box, whimsical form, late 19th C	300	360	500
String Holder, late 19th C	300	360	500
Table Bell, English, late 19th C	150	270	450
Talc Shaker, late 19th C	100	140	200
Tankard, American, R. Humphreys, 21 oz., 7" h	2500	3380	5000
Tatting Shuttle, late 19th C	50	90	150
Tea Infuser, ball form, late 19th C	75	90	125
Tea Infuser, whimsical form, late 19th C	300	360	500
Tea Infuser, whimsical form, mid 20th C	100	110	150
Tea Strainer, late 19th C	100	110	150
Tea Strainer, mid 20th C	50	70	100
Thimble, chased and engraved, early 19th C	300	360	500
Thimble, engraved, late 19th C	100	140	200
Thread Hodler, reticulated, late 19th C	100	140	200
Toast Rack, English, late 18th C	500	630	900
Tobacco Box, English, late 18th C	500	630	900
Toothbrush Holder, early 20th C	50	70	100
Toothpick, early 20th C	20	30	50
Toothpick Holder, engraved, early 20th C	100	180	300
Torah Finials, early 20th C, pair	500	580	800
Trophy Cup, engraved, mid 20th C, 6" h	300	400	600
Vinaigrette, plain, mid 19th C	150	200	300
Vinaigrette, whimsical form, mid 19th C	500	680	1000
Walking Stick Handle, early 20th C	100	180	300
Whistle, penny whistle form, early 20th C	100	140	200
Wine Coaster, mid 19th C	300	360	500
Wine Label, crescent shape, late 19th C	50	90	150
Wine Label, engraved, late 18th C	150	200	300
Wine Taster, Continental, early 19th C	300	360	500
Wine Taster, mid 20th C	100	140	200

Silver Flatware

Silverware includes factory merchandise and products of individual craftsmen. Chief American manufacturers include Gorham, Reed and Barton, Towle, Wallace, Rogers, Oneida, Kirk and International.

Values are given in two sections. In the first we list a large variety of tableware and serving pieces for two patterns (one sterling silver and one silver plated). Values are for excellent condition monogrammed pieces (*M*) and excellent condition pieces with no monogram (*NM*).

In the second section, we list five key pieces for a variety of patterns listed under the name of their manufacturer: Values are for excellent condition pieces with no monogram. Dinner Fork (*DnF*), Salad Fork (*SF*), Tablespoon (*Tb*), Soup Spoon (*SpSp*) and Teaspoon (*Tsp*).

For further information see *Silverware of the 20th Century: The Top 250 Patterns,* by Harry L. Rinker, House of Collectibles, NY, 1997.

Gorham – Buttercup Pattern

(sterling – introduced 1899)

	M	NM
Baby Fork, 4.375" l	$54	$45
Baby Spoon, straight handle, 4.5" l	54	45
Bouillon Spoon, round bowl, 5.25" l	54	45
Butter Serving Knife, flat handle, 6.875" l	32	40
Butter Spreader, hollow handle, stainless blade, 6.25" l	28	35
Cheese Server, stainless blade, 7" l	40	50
Cold Meat Serving Fork, 8.125" l	105	130
Cream Soup Spoon, round bowl, 6.25" l	40	50
Demitasse Spoon, 4.125" l	20	25
Dinner Fork, 7.5" l	48	60
Fish Serving Fork, 8.625" l	110	145
Fruit Spoon, 5.625" l	54	45
Gravy Ladle, 6.125" l	96	120
Ice Cream Fork, 6.375" l	44	55
Ice Cream Slicer, 10" l	112	140
Ice Cream Spoon, 5.625" l	44	55
Iced Tea Spoon, 7.5" l	40	50
Jelly Spoon, 6.25" l	32	40
Knife, hollow handle, blunt blade, 9.625" l	44	55
Knife, hollow handle, modern blade, 8.5" l	32	40
Knife, hollow handle, new French blade, 8.75" l	32	40
Knife, hollow handle, new French blade, 9.625" l	40	55
Punch Ladle, 13.5" l	160	200
Punch Ladle, stainless bowl, 13.5" l	56	70
Salad Fork, 6.375" l	40	50
Salad Serving Spoon, 7.875" l	96	120
Salad Serving Spoon, stainless bowl, 11.25" l	36	45
Salad Set, 8.875" l, 2 pcs	200	250
Soup Spoon, oval bowl, 6.5" l	40	50
Sugar Spoon, 6" l	36	45
Sugar Tongs, 4.625" l	52	65
Tablespoon, 8.375" l	68	85
Teaspoon, 5.875" l	20	25
Vegetable Serving Spoon, 10" l	120	150
Youth Knife, 7.625" l	36	45

Left: Gorham Buttercup. —Photo courtesy Lenox, Inc.

Right: Oneida Silver Artistry. —Photo courtesy Oneida, Ltd.

Oneida Community Plate – Silver Artistry Pattern

(plated – patented 1965)

	M	NM
Baby Fork, 4.75" l	$12	$15
Baby Spoon, straight handle, 4.75" l	12	15
Butter Serving Knife, flat handle, 6.625" l	12	15
Casserole Spoon, shell-shaped bowl, 9" l	26	32
Cold Meat Serving Fork, 8.75" l	24	30
Demitasse Spoon, 4.5" l	8	10
Fork, 7.5" l	12	15
Gravy Ladle, 7.75" l	20	25
Iced Tea Spoon, 7.5" l	12	15
Infant Feeding Spoon, 5.625" l	14	17
Knife, hollow handle, modern blade, 9.25" l	12	15
Pie Server, 9.75" l	36	45
Pie Server, stainless blade, 10.75" l	36	45
Salad Fork, 6.875" l	10	12
Soup Spoon, oval bowl, 7" l	10	12
Steak Knife, 9.125" l	14	17
Sugar Spoon, shell-shaped bowl, 5.75" l	12	15
Tablespoon, 8.5" l	16	20
Tablespoon, pierced bowl, 8.5" l	18	22
Teaspoon, 6.125" l	8	10
Teaspoon, 5 o'clock, 5.5" l	6	7

Other Patterns

	YEAR	DnF	SF	Tb	SpSp	Tsp
ALVIN CO.						
Antique, sterling	1907	$30	$25	$70	$30	$25
Bridal Rose, sterling	1903	75	55	155	60	45
Cellini, sterling	1929	45	35	95	45	30
Della Robbia, sterling	1922	50	40	110	45	35

	YEAR	DnF	SF	Tb	SpSp	Tsp
Flanders, new, sterling	1925	40	30	90	35	25
Florence Nightingale, sterling	1919	40	32	85	38	23
Gainsborough, sterling	1925	35	30	75	30	25
Hamilton, sterling	1913	40	30	55	30	20
Kenmore, sterling	1920	30	25	70	30	25
Lorna Doone, sterling	1925	35	25	70	30	22
Maryland, sterling	1910	50	35	105	40	30
Maytime, sterling	1936	40	30	80	30	20
Miss Alvin, sterling	1931	35	28	70	30	24
Miss America, sterling	1932	30	28	75	35	20
Molly Stark, sterling	1915	40	35	100	38	20
Prince Eugene, sterling	1950	60	50	135	55	30
Raphael, sterling	1903	140	110	250	125	40
Roanoke, sterling	1915	35	30	68	35	22
Rosecrest, sterling	1955	35	25	70	30	20
Southern Charm, sterling	1947	40	30	80	40	20
Spring Bud, sterling	1956	35	28	65	30	17
Star Blossom, sterling	1959	30	25	77	30	18
Winchester, sterling	1915	45	35	90	45	30
Wm. Penn, sterling	1907	35	25	65	30	20
BAKER–MANCHESTER MFG. CO.						
Bridal Wreath, sterling	1919	$37	$28	$75	$33	$30
Roger Williams, sterling	1916	35	30	80	30	24
Spartan, sterling	1914	30	26	85	35	25
DOMINICK & HAFF						
Chippendale, sterling	1880	$34	$28	$81	$33	$32
Gothic, sterling	1900	66	50	150	60	45
Lexington, sterling	1915	45	25	60	28	18
Marie Antoinette, sterling	1917	40	30	90	40	30
Marzarin, sterling	1892	75	50	120	50	30
Priscilla, sterling	1916	30	25	75	35	25
Tradition, sterling	1939	35	30	95	40	30
Virginia, sterling	1912	35	25	70	35	20
DURGIN DIVISION OF GORHAM						
Arts & Crafts, sterling	1906	$45	$30	$80	$35	$24
Bead, sterling	1893	40	30	85	40	25
Chatham, sterling	1915	35	30	85	35	30
Colfax, sterling	1922	45	35	100	40	35
Dartmouth, sterling	1917	40	35	110	50	35
DuBarry, sterling	1901	85	75	195	90	45
English Tip, sterling	1880	45	30	85	35	24
Essex, sterling	1911	45	30	90	40	30
Fairfax, sterling	1910	60	32	65	35	22
Fleur de Lis, sterling	1886	60	50	140	60	30
Hampshire, sterling	1906	65	50	150	60	45
Hunt Club, sterling	1931	50	35	80	35	25
Lenox, sterling	1912	40	30	85	40	20
Louis XV, sterling	1891	95	75	175	90	50
Madame Royale, sterling	1897	80	60	150	60	40
Medallion, sterling	1870	150	135	350	175	75

	YEAR	DnF	SF	Tb	SpSp	Tsp
New Queens, sterling	1900	75	65	170	80	40
No. 19-E, sterling	1912	35	30	75	35	20
No. 19-G, sterling	1912	40	30	75	35	20
Old Standish, sterling	1901	40	25	70	35	18
Princess Patricia, sterling	1927	38	25	65	30	15
Regent, sterling	1901	95	75	175	80	35
Watteau, sterling	1891	50	40	115	50	30
FESSENDEN & CO.						
Antique, sterling	1880	$35	$27	$80	$33	$33
Greenwich, sterling	1890	50	40	110	45	30
Newport, sterling	1905	65	45	150	60	35
Old Boston, hammered, sterling	1880	45	30	100	40	25
FRANK M. WHITING & CO.						
Crystal, sterling	1896	$40	$30	$75	$35	$20
Damascus, sterling	1894	60	50	130	55	35
Esther, sterling	1890	65	50	140	60	40
Genoa, sterling	1893	70	50	135	50	30
George III, sterling	1891	50	40	110	40	25
Georgian Shell, sterling	1948	55	45	105	40	20
Palm, sterling	1887	70	55	145	60	28
Pearl, sterling	1888	50	35	105	40	30
Plain Tip, sterling	1883	55	40	100	45	35
Princess Ingrid, sterling	1945	55	40	110	50	35
Rose of Sharon, sterling	1954	60	45	115	55	30
FRANK SMITH SILVER CO.						
Baronial, sterling	1920	$55	$45	$100	$45	$20
Bostonia, sterling	1914	45	35	90	35	25
Countess, sterling	1920	50	40	100	50	30
Crystal, sterling	1921	55	40	105	50	30
Fiddle, sterling	1886	45	35	85	40	28
Ivanhoe, sterling	1915	50	40	100	45	32
Lion, sterling	1905	95	80	210	95	40
M.W. Lily, sterling	1915	40	30	70	30	20
M.W. Star, sterling	1916	35	25	75	30	25
No. 2, sterling	1918	45	40	115	45	30
No. 10, sterling	1918	50	42	115	45	30
Oak, sterling	1912	75	65	165	70	45
Pilgrim, sterling	1909	35	30	80	35	20
Shell, sterling	1890	45	35	95	40	25
Tokay, sterling	1952	40	30	90	35	20
Tulipan, sterling	1933	50	40	105	45	30
Windsor, sterling	1895	45	30	85	35	24
GORHAM						
Andante, sterling	1963	$55	$35	$60	$45	$30
Camellia, sterling	1942	40	30	60	30	20
Celeste, sterling	1956	50	30	65	35	22
Chantilly, sterling	1895	65	50	85	50	25
Chapel Rose, sterling	1963	55	40	80	45	25
Chateau Rose, sterling	1963	55	35	70	30	22
Decor, sterling	1953	80	80	140	75	45

King Edward – Gorham. *Newport Scroll – Gorham.*

Photos courtesy Lenox, Inc.

	YEAR	DnF	SF	Tb	SpSp	Tsp
English Gadroon, sterling	1939	65	50	80	35	27
Etruscan, sterling	1913	60	45	75	35	20
Greenbrier, sterling	1938	60	35	70	30	25
King Edward, sterling	1936	50	45	90	45	22
Lancaster, sterling	1897	60	45	70	35	25
La Scala, sterling	1964	70	50	100	50	30
Lily of the Valley, sterling	1950	70	50	85	45	25
Lyric, sterling	1940	55	32	80	35	25
Melrose, sterling	1948	65	55	90	55	30
Newport Scroll	1983	65	37	95	40	30
Old English Tipt, sterling	1870	75	50	95	65	32
Old French, sterling	1905	60	50	90	60	30
Rondo, sterling	1951	75	60	100	65	30
Rose Tiara, sterling	1962	65	50	85	50	30
Sea Rose, sterling	1958	60	50	80	45	25
Strasbourg, sterling	1897	60	50	85	45	25
Versailles, sterling	1888	80	90	130	80	50
INTERNATIONAL SILVER CO.						
1810, sterling	1930	$55	$45	$90	$50	$30
Adoration, plated	1930	17	15	27	17	12
Ambassador, plated	1919	15	15	25	18	10
Angelique, sterling	1959	40	40	50	45	25
Blossom Time, sterling	1950	60	35	70	37	22
Brocade, sterling	1950	70	50	80	60	27
Courtship, sterling	1936	60	45	80	45	25
Daffodil, plated	1950	17	15	27	15	10
Danish Princess, plated	1938	18	15	25	15	10

	YEAR	DnF	SF	Tb	SpSp	Tsp
Du Barry, sterling	1968	60	50	75	55	40
Enchantress, sterling	1937	60	45	75	40	25
Eternally Yours, plated	1941	17	15	25	15	10
Exquisite, plated	1940	12	10	17	12	7
First Love, plated	1937	17	17	25	15	7
Flair, plated	1956	17	15	27	17	12
Frontenac, sterling	1903	55	70	95	60	30
Heritage, plated	1953	17	17	25	15	10
Joan of Arc, sterling	1940	55	40	80	45	22
Lovely Lady, plated	1937	15	12	20	12	7
Minuet, sterling	1925	50	32	60	32	20
Old Colony, plated	1911	15	15	22	15	10
Orleans, plated	1964	15	15	20	15	10
Pine Spray, sterling	1957	50	37	80	40	25
Prelude, sterling	1939	50	40	85	45	20
Processional, sterling	1947	45	45	80	45	25
Queen's Lace, sterling	1949	40	40	90	45	27
Reflection, plated	1959	15	15	20	15	10
Remembrance, plated	1948	15	15	20	15	10
Rhapsody, sterling	1957	40	40	85	40	25
Richelieu, sterling	1935	75	50	100	50	30
Royal Danish, sterling	1939	45	37	90	50	25
Serenity, sterling	1940	60	35	65	40	25
Silver Rhythm, sterling	1953	40	40	65	35	20
Southern Colonial, sterling	1945	45	45	80	40	25
Spring Glory, sterling	1942	60	32	70	35	22
Springtime, plated	1957	15	15	20	15	10
Vintage, plated	1904	30	60	40	35	20

Joan of Arc – International Silver Co.

Prelude – International Silver Co.

Photos courtesy International Silver Co./Syratech Corp.

Lady Claire – Kirk Stieff Co.
—Photo courtesy Lenox, Inc.

	YEAR	DnF	SF	Tb	SpSp	Tsp
KIRK STIEFF CO.						
Corsage, sterling	1935	$45	$45	$80	$55	$27
Golden Winslow, sterling, gold accent	1850	75	65	120	70	35
Lady Claire, sterling	1925	70	50	100	60	27
Old Maryland, sterling	1850	50	40	80	35	25
Repoussé, sterling	1828	60	50	85	55	30
Rose, sterling	1937	60	60	100	60	35
Stieff Rose, sterling	1892	45	35	70	40	25
Williamsburg Queen Anne, sterling	1940	60	60	120	50	40
Williamsburg Shell, sterling	1970	75	55	100	35	25
LUNT SILVERSMITHS						
American Victorian, sterling	1941	$65	$35	$70	$35	$22
Bel Chateau, sterling	1983	45	50	80	50	25
Madrigal, sterling	1962	55	30	75	30	25
Mignonette, sterling	1960	70	60	95	65	35
Modern Victorian, sterling	1941	60	40	70	45	25
William & Mary, sterling	1921	55	35	65	40	25
MANCHESTER SILVER CO.						
Abraham Lincoln	1909	$40	$35	$90	$35	$25
American Beauty	1935	55	45	125	50	30
Beacon	1936	35	30	75	30	20
Beaux Art	1920	40	30	90	35	25
Duke of Windsor	1937	50	40	115	45	30
Fleetwood	1934	45	30	90	35	25
Lenore	1939	40	30	80	35	20
Priscilla	1928	40	30	75	35	18
Southern Rose	1933	45	35	100	40	28
Vogue	1932	40	30	70	30	16

Damask Rose – Oneida, Ltd.
—Photo courtesy Oneida, Ltd.

	YEAR	DnF	SF	Tb	SpSp	Tsp
MOUNT VERNON CO.						
Adolphus	1901	$60	$50	$125	$50	$35
Chelsea	1920	40	30	100	35	30
Corinthian	1902	60	45	120	55	30
Florence	1905	60	45	130	50	35
Fontenay	1910	55	45	115	45	32
George II	1912	45	30	90	35	25
Hope	1899	50	40	110	45	25
Kenwood	1916	45	30	90	35	27
Laurel	1905	45	35	90	35	25
Lexington	1900	40	35	95	40	27
Louise	1904	50	45	125	60	30
Medford	1905	45	35	90	35	25
Plymouth	1907	40	30	80	40	22
Pointed Antique	1900	45	30	75	30	20
Princeton	1915	45	32	75	30	18
Queen Anne	1915	40	30	70	35	16
Salem	1912	40	30	80	35	20
Sedgwick	1908	35	25	65	30	15
Tropea	1910	50	40	100	45	30
Warren	1911	35	25	75	30	15
Warwick	1905	45	35	90	40	25
Wentworth	1905	35	25	75	30	18
Westchester	1910	40	30	75	30	18
ONEIDA, LTD.						
Bordeaux, plated	1945	$15	$12	$20	$12	$10
Caprice, plated	1937	15	12	20	12	7
Coronation, plated	1936	15	12	20	12	7
Damask Rose, sterling	1946	50	30	65	35	25
Evening Star, plated	1950	15	12	20	12	8

English Chippendale – Reed & Barton. —Photo courtesy Reed & Barton.

	YEAR	DnF	SF	Tb	SpSp	Tsp
Grenoble, plated	1938	17	15	20	15	10
Grosvenor, plated	1921	15	12	20	12	7
Heiress, sterling	1942	40	30	60	30	20
Lasting Spring, sterling	1949	50	32	60	30	20
Lady Hamilton, plated	1932	15	15	22	17	10
Milady, plated	1940	12	10	20	12	7
Modern Baroque, plated	1969	12	17	22	15	12
Morning Star, plated	1948	15	15	20	15	10
Queen Bess II, plated	1946	12	12	17	12	7
Royal Rose, plated	1939	15	12	20	12	10
Virginian, sterling	1942	45	35	80	38	25
White Orchid, plated	1953	20	17	25	15	12
REED & BARTON						
18th Century, sterling	1971	$60	$45	$100	$50	$30
Autumn Leaves, sterling	1957	60	45	85	40	25
Burgundy, sterling	1949	80	45	90	45	25
Classic Rose, sterling	1954	60	50	90	45	25
English Chippendale, sterling	1984	60	45	90	45	30
Florentine Lace, sterling	1951	60	60	110	65	35
Francis I, sterling	1907	75	50	100	60	40
French Chippendale, plated	1981	17	15	20	15	12
Georgian Rose, sterling	1941	40	30	65	40	20
Grande Renaissance, sterling	1967	60	37	80	40	25
Hampton Court, sterling	1964	55	35	80	40	25
Lark, sterling	1960	60	50	80	50	25
Love Disarmed, sterling	1899	160	100	200	100	80
Marlborough, sterling	1906	60	45	90	50	25
Rose Cascade, sterling	1957	60	60	105	60	50
Savannah, sterling	1962	75	70	120	75	45
Silver Sculpture, sterling	1954	50	50	85	45	27
Silver Wheat, sterling	1952	60	40	70	40	25

	YEAR	DnF	SF	Tb	SpSp	Tsp
Spanish Baroque, sterling	1965	50	45	80	45	25
Tara, sterling	1955	60	50	110	50	30
Woodwind, sterling	1986	60	50	75	60	30
SAMUEL KIRK & SON, INC.						
Calvert, sterling	1927	$45	$39	$105	$48	$30
Ellipse, sterling	1968	45	30	75	35	20
Golden Winslow, sterling	1850	65	50	135	60	25
King, sterling	1827	70	50	125	55	30
Quadrille, sterling	1950	75	55	140	60	35
Rose, sterling	1937	60	50	130	60	35
Severn, sterling	1940	50	35	90	40	25
Wadefield, sterling	1850	50	40	75	40	25
SCHOFIELD CO.						
Clouet, sterling	1910	$38	$30	$75	$35	$20
Frabee, sterling	1936	45	35	95	40	25
Lorraine, sterling	1900	45	40	100	45	28
Raleigh, sterling	1905	35	25	65	25	16
Talbot, sterling	1912	45	35	90	40	22
TIFFANY & CO.						
Audubon, sterling	1871	$95	$95	$150	$100	70
Century	1937	75	65	90	70	45
Chrysanthemum, sterling	1880	130	135	200	150	85
English King, sterling	1885	180	130	210	150	85
Queen Anne	1870	90	85	140	95	65
Rat Tail	1958	65	55	75	60	40
Richelieu	1892	160	120	200	135	80
Shell and Thread	1905	120	100	150	115	75

Chrysanthemum – Tiffany & Co. —Photo courtesy Tiffany & Co.

Queen Anne – Tiffany & Co. —Photo courtesy William Doyle Galleries.

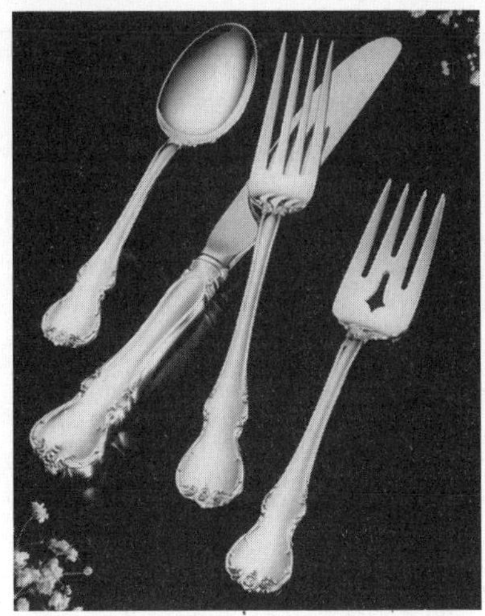

Left: French Provincial – Towle.
—Photo courtesy Towle Silversmiths/ Syratech Corp.

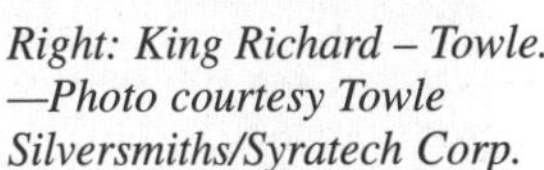

Right: King Richard – Towle.
—Photo courtesy Towle Silversmiths/Syratech Corp.

Left: Old Master – Towle.
—Photo courtesy Towle Silversmiths/Syratech Corp.

	YEAR	DnF	SF	Tb	SpSp	Tsp
TOWLE						
Candlelight, sterling	1934	$50	$35	$80	$40	$22
Chippendale, sterling	1937	65	45	85	50	22
Craftsman, sterling	1932	50	37	80	45	25
Debussy, sterling	1959	60	65	100	60	32

	YEAR	DnF	SF	Tb	SpSp	Tsp
El Grandee, sterling	1964	45	50	95	55	30
Fontana, sterling	1957	50	40	90	50	25
French Provincial, sterling	1948	40	40	80	45	25
King Richard, sterling	1932	60	45	90	50	25
Louis XIV, sterling	1924	65	40	70	45	22
Madeira, sterling	1948	50	32	65	40	20
Mary Chilton, sterling	1912	50	35	60	40	22
Old Master, sterling	1942	40	35	85	45	25
Old Mirror, sterling	1940	75	55	95	50	30
Rambler Rose, sterling	1937	45	37	80	45	22
Rose Solitaire, sterling	1954	40	40	80	45	22
Spanish Provincial, sterling	1967	45	40	85	45	20
TUTTLE SILVER CO.						
Basket-of-Flowers	1928	$35	$25	$70	$30	$15
Classic Antique	1926	40	28	75	35	20
Georgian	1929	40	35	95	40	22
Hannah Hull	1928	45	35	100	40	27
Queen Anne	1928	40	30	75	30	25
WALLACE SILVERSMITHS						
Antique, sterling	1926	$70	$60	$85	$65	$25
Carnation, sterling	1909	75	60	110	70	35
Figured Shell, sterling	1890	85	70	120	75	45
French Regency, sterling	1986	50	40	75	45	27
Golden Aegean Weave, sterling	1971	70	50	115	60	40

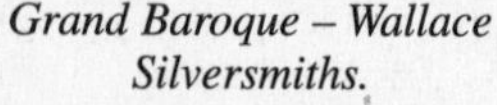

Grand Baroque – Wallace Silversmiths.

Romance of the Sea – Wallace Silversmiths.

Photos courtesy Wallace Silversmiths/Syratech Corp.

Rose Point – Wallace Silversmiths.

Sir Christopher – Wallace Silversmiths.

Photos courtesy Wallace Silversmiths/Syratech Corp.

	YEAR	DnF	SF	Tb	SpSp	Tsp
Grand Colonial, sterling	1942	50	35	80	45	25
Grande Baroque, sterling	1941	45	45	100	55	35
Hamilton, sterling	1911	70	60	90	65	28
Irving, sterling	1900	75	65	115	70	35
La Reine, sterling	1921	75	60	110	50	35
Marie, sterling	1895	70	80	100	75	30
Meadow Rose, sterling	1907	40	37	90	40	27
Nile, sterling	1908	55	45	80	50	25
Old Atlanta, sterling	1975	50	37	95	45	27
Romance of the Sea, sterling	1950	55	50	120	50	40
Rose Point, sterling	1934	40	50	85	45	25
Shenandoah, sterling	1966	40	37	90	45	27
Silver Swirl, sterling	1955	55	45	75	50	18
Sir Christopher, sterling	1936	60	50	95	55	35
Soliloquy	1963	45	40	60	45	17
Spanish Lace, sterling	1964	50	40	90	45	30
St. George, sterling	1890	80	70	100	75	35
Stradivari, sterling	1937	50	40	90	50	25
Versailles, sterling	1914	65	50	85	60	30
Violet, sterling	1904	60	50	80	55	25
Waltz of Spring, sterling	1952	75	60	120	65	35
WATSON CO. (WALLACE)						
Colonial, sterling	1917	$45	$35	$95	$40	$208
Commonwealth, engraved, sterling	1908	65	50	100	60	35
Dorian Rose, sterling	1937	50	45	125	55	25
Etiquette, sterling	1923	35	30	75	30	28
Foxhall, sterling	1942	55	40	70	50	25

	YEAR	DnF	SF	Tb	SpSp	Tsp
Governor Dummer, sterling	1925	45	35	100	40	24
King George, sterling	1920	70	55	150	60	36
King Philip, sterling	1904	45	35	90	40	25
Lady Wellesley, sterling	1921	55	50	115	55	35
Laurel, sterling	1917	35	30	80	30	20
Magnolia, sterling	1908	60	50	80	50	25
Marlborough, sterling	1918	50	45	75	45	25
Martha Washington, sterling	1912	55	35	100	40	24
Mount Vernon, sterling	1907	50	40	65	45	20
Navarre, sterling	1908	45	35	95	35	22
Orleans, sterling	1915	65	45	105	50	25
Plymouth, sterling	1920	45	35	85	40	22
Priscilla Alden, sterling	1923	40	30	80	35	20
Putnam, sterling	1920	95	70	175	75	35
Rochambeau, sterling	1919	80	65	150	70	35
Tuscany, sterling	1930	40	35	90	35	20
Virginia, sterling	1911	70	60	100	65	30
Watteau, sterling	1904	80	75	150	75	38
Wedding Rose, sterling	1900	70	55	145	65	30
Wentworth, sterling	1913	50	40	100	40	25
Windsor, sterling	1920	45	35	85	40	20

WHITING DIVISION OF GORHAM

	YEAR	DnF	SF	Tb	SpSp	Tsp
Adam, sterling	1907	$40	$35	$95	$40	$30
Alhambra, sterling	1870	60	50	140	60	40
Arabesque, sterling	1880	60	45	125	55	30
Athenian, sterling	1890	45	35	90	35	28
Burlington, sterling	1914	50	45	120	45	35
Colonial, sterling	1907	45	35	85	35	25
Diamond, sterling	1875	75	50	140	55	40
Duchess, sterling	1906	45	35	100	40	27
Duke of York, sterling	1900	60	45	140	55	28
Eastlake, sterling	1885	40	35	80	35	20
Egyptian, sterling	1870	60	45	130	55	35
Fruit, sterling	1876	60	55	130	60	38
Honeysuckle, sterling	1870	60	50	135	55	30
Indian, sterling	1875	45	35	90	35	28
Ivy, sterling	1874	55	45	130	50	30
Keystone, sterling	1875	60	50	145	60	35
King Albert, sterling	1919	60	32	65	30	25
Laureate, sterling	1880	50	40	100	45	35
Le Cordon, sterling	1850	45	35	85	40	24
Lily, sterling	1902	95	95	155	70	60
Louis XV, sterling	1891	60	45	120	60	35
Mandarin, sterling	1917	50	35	100	40	30
Old Bead, sterling	1880	45	35	90	35	25
Old English, sterling	1880	40	30	80	35	20
Old King, sterling	1885	55	45	110	55	18
Oriana, sterling	1916	40	30	75	35	22
Oval Twist, sterling	1900	50	35	100	45	24
Pompeian, sterling	1913	45	35	95	35	25
Prince Albert, sterling	1855	60	40	115	45	30
Stratford, sterling	1911	45	35	100	40	25
Tuscan, sterling	1865	45	35	90	35	25

Tinware

Often overlooked, tin collectibles can still be found at many garage sales. "Good" examples must be in good condition, with only small unobtrusive bits of corrosion and only minor dents. "Best" examples are undented and well proportioned, and show fine workmanship. All items are twentieth century unless otherwise noted.

	GOOD	BETTER	BEST
Candle Mold, 12 tubes, strap handle, 19th C	$75	$100	$150
Chamberstick, late 19th C, 8.5" dia	100	150	300
Cheese Mold, floral pattern, 6" w	40	75	190
Cheese Mold, pierced tin, heart form, c1880	36	52	100
Coffee Roaster, mid 19th C, 9" dia	100	200	500
Cookie Cutter, horse, galvanized, air holes, 5" l	20	30	40
Food Mold, cylindrical, c1890	20	30	70
Food Mold, fluted edge, handle, 3" w	20	45	100
Food Mold, lion, 6" w	52	85	200
Foot Warmer, pierced tin panels in wood frame, heart design, c1875	300	400	500
Frying Pan, c1890, 13" dia	40	75	150
Grater, wood handle, c1880, 12" h	25	45	100
Kettle Chain, mesh circles for pot cleaning	8	15	38
Kettle Chain, mesh circles for pot cleaning, w/ steel scraper	10	18	45
Kettle Chain, single ring type	5	12	35
Lunch Pail, dome style, w/ dishes and cup	100	150	200
Lunch Pail, round, handle, 6" dia	36	55	135
Meatloaf Press, tin w/ wood frame, top handle	65	95	200
Milk Pail, oval, c1880	65	95	200
Milk Pail, round, c1880	55	85	190
Milk Skimmer, perforated and stamped, c1890s	15	20	45
Mixing Spoon, adv., pierced bowl, c1880	16	25	55
Mixing Spoon, pierced bowl, wood handle, c1900	10	20	40
Muffin Pan, 8 cups, push-out type, c1910	16	30	50
Muffin Pan, 12 cups, c1870	28	30	80
Muffin Ring, c1875	5	10	25
Nurser, cov., tin can w/ handle and spout, c1880	70	120	250
Nutmeg Grater, handmade, drum type	35	50	125
Pastry Board, w/ hanging loop and trough, 18" l	75	120	250
Pastry Board, w/ rolling pin cradle, 22" x 18.5"	75	120	250
Pie Lifter, shovel type, wood handle, round, c1900	16	28	76
Pie Lifter, wire tines, heavy tin, c1920	8	15	25
Pie Pan, adv., "Balto. Pie Bakery"	25	38	95
Pie Plate, c1880	8	15	42
Plate Warmer, cylindrical, w/ handle, lid, and plate	30	55	100
Plate Warmer, bowl form, w/ legs and handle	145	210	400
Popcorn Popper, factory-made, plain, c1890	20	45	75
Popcorn Popper, rect., wood handle, c1880	82	115	245
Pot, egg form, hinged lid	40	63	150
Pudding Mold, cov., cylindrical, scalloped edge, 2 qt.	26	38	85
Pudding Mold, cov., pan form, c1890	16	25	60
Pudding Mold, oval, serrated rim, 1.5 qt.	23	35	75
Pudding Mold, oval w/ tulip, 2 qt.	28	30	75
Roaster, black, c1890	36	50	100
Roasting Oven, swing top, reflector type, 11" w	163	225	450
Rolling Pin, wood handles	65	95	200

Left to right: Candle Sconces, 13.5" h, pair, $632 at auction. —Photo courtesy Skinner, Inc. Boston, MA; Lantern, pierced, 20" h, $1437 at auction. —Photo courtesy Sotheby's.

	GOOD	BETTER	BEST
Roofer's Stove	35	50	150
Salt Box, hanging	20	45	100
Salt Box, raised letters, "SALT"	33	40	115
Sander, cylindrical, dark finish, 2.5"	25	35	76
Sausage Gun, tapering tube w/ wood plunger	40	75	165
Sausage Stuffer, wood press	42	55	115
Sconces, mirrored backs, circular, c1840, 10" dia, pair	800	1800	5000
Scoop, curved handle, 5" l	16	25	65
Sieve, perforated, c1900	18	28	75
Skimmer, shallow bowl, wood handle	15	25	75
Skimmer, stamped, 19th C	13	10	45
Spice Box Tray, japanned, strap handle	40	70	160
Spice Boxes, enameled, cov. tray, set of 7	75	100	150
Spice Boxes, round boxes w/ wood-handled tray, set of 6	90	125	250
Spice Boxes, sq. boxes w/ wood-handled tray and nutmeg grater, set of 6	100	135	285
Spice Shaker, Norton Brothers, 1890	20	30	65
Steam Cooker, cov., tall cylinder, handle, 12" dia	55	85	190
Stove Board, c1890	25	42	115
Strainer, cone form, loop handle	16	25	65
Strainer, hinged to fit various bowls, c1870	20	30	75
Strainer, perforated bowl w/ wood handle	40	65	150
Sugar Scoop, shovel head, strap handle	25	35	70
Teapot, labeled "HL Piper Co."	60	100	200
Water Pitcher, sloping sides, flared lip, 1 qt.	40	60	150
Water Pitcher, sloping sides, hinged lid, 1 qt.	40	75	170
Wax Skimmer, perforated cov., wood handle	20	30	65
Wine Press, perforated tin w/ wood frame, round	75	100	225

Toleware

Toleware is painted tinware. It ranges from the sophisticated forms produced in eighteenth-century France to the simple pieces from the backwoods of nineteenth-century America.

When buying toleware, pay attention to condition. Many pieces have flaked off much of their original paint and have been heavily restored or entirely repainted. Dents and rust also lower the value. Early American pieces are often reproduced and sometimes faked. Construction technique is often your best clue to authenticity. Modern electrical welding is often smoothed out by grinding the surfaces near the weld. Look for modern grinding marks.

	AUCTION	RETAIL	
		Low	High
Apple Tray, PA, rect. w/ flaring sides and rounded ends, early 19th C, 19.75" l, 7.34" w	$2070	$4000	$6000
Box, domed lid, 9" l	350	650	1000
Bread Basket, 12" l	150	300	700
Clock, French, hanging, early 20th C, 17" dia	75	130	250
Document Box, 8" l	200	400	900
Coffeepot, cov., PA, gooseneck, tapered cylindrical form, domed lid, strap handle, early 19th C, 10.5" h	5175	10,000	15,000
Coffeepot, cov., PA, ovoid diamond form, conical lid, strap handle, flared perforated base, wriggle-work dec., w/ American Eagle and shield, tulips, and serpent, PA, 19th C, 13.75" h	1495	2800	4200
Inkstand, w/ ink castor and undertray, 8" l	100	150	350
Lantern, green-painted, late 19th C, 13" l	50	90	150
Sconces, V-form w/ circ. smokeplate, late 19th C, 17" h, pair	850	1500	2500
Sconces, mirrored backs, twin arms, 15" dia, pair	900	1600	2500
Syrup Jug, 5" h	100	200	400

Toleware Coffeepots, $4312 for lot at auction. —Photo courtesy Sotheby's.

Toleware Box and Trays. —Photo courtesy Sotheby's.

	AUCTION	RETAIL	
		Low	High
Syrup Jug, PA, tapered cylindrical form, hinged lid, strap handle, sparrow's beak spout, early 19th C, 4.25" h	2070	4000	6000
Tea Canister Lamp, 18" h	250	450	700
Tea Canisters, English, gilt chinoiserie dec., fitted as lamps, 32" h, pair	1700	3000	4750
Teapot, 7" h	600	950	1500
Tray, circ., pierced edge, 24" dia	350	650	1000
Tray, rect., floral dec., 20" l	250	400	800
Tray, oval, red, 23" l	400	600	1000

Early Nineteenth-Century Neoclassical French Toleware

(mustard yellow with gilt highlights)

Biscuit Box, cov., oval	$750	$1400	$2500
Box, rect., 10" l	125	230	400
Candlesticks, sq. base, pair	1000	1800	3250
Chestnut Urns, cov., oval, pair	2800	5200	9000
Condiment Set, glass bottles	475	880	1550
Dinner Bell, 7" h	100	200	330
Fruit Basket, oval, reticulated border	800	1500	2600
Peat Bucket	200	370	650
Sauce Boat, reticulated, on secured stand	275	500	900
Tea Kettle, oval, reticulated stand	1300	2400	4000
Tea Urn, burner stand	950	1700	3000
Tray, oval, 18" l	1550	2750	5000
Tray, oval, 26" l	800	1500	2500
Trays, oval, 15" l, pair	500	900	1600

Military Memorabilia

Military memorabilia encompasses items pertaining to all branches of the military. Some hobbyists collect military memorabilia by type of item—for example, badges or swords—while others collect by military branch (Navy, Army or Air Force) or war (Civil War). For more information consult *The Official Price Guide to Military Collectibles, Sixth Edition,* by Richard J. Austin, published by House of Collectibles, NY, 1998.

Warning! Federal law prohibits the sale of American military medals. Recently there has been a crackdown at military memorabilia shows.

Partial grouping of Mexican Border Patrol items of Sergeant Orie Donley. Lot sold for $2750 at auction. —Photo courtesy Jackson's Auctioneers & Appraisers.

Bayonets

	LOW	AVG.	HIGH
#4 Mark II Spike, British	$25	$35	$45
Arisak, Japanese	80	100	140
Baker Bayonet, British	550	650	750
Bayonet Model 1871, Prussian	270	335	400
Brown Bess Socket, British, 19th C	150	225	300
Dahlgren Bowie Knife	1500	1650	1800
Dahlgren Saber Pattern	270	335	400
Enfield Bayonet 1907, British	70	75	80
Fusil Socket, French, early 18th C	800	1100	1400
Imperial German	80	140	200
Imperial Russian, late 19th C	150	225	300
Indian Bayonet, British	80	110	140
Martini Henry, British	175	250	325
Ross Model 1905	190	208	225
Spanish Model 1941	60	72	85

	LOW	AVG.	HIGH
Swiss Model 1931	85	110	135
U.S., late 19th C	100	200	300
U.S. Bannerman Cadet	160	200	250
U.S. Model 1860	270	335	400
U.S. Model 1942	160	192	225

Civil War

The most desirable collectible in this category is that of firearms. This period in time marked a technological transition from a single-shot gun to one that would shoot several times, including the first machine gun. Other collectible areas include uniforms, buttons, belt buckles, canteens, knapsacks, insignia and personal effects, such as diaries, letters and photographs. For more information consult *The Official Price Guide to Civil War Collectibles,* Richard Friz, House of Collectibles, NY, 1995.

	LOW	AVG.	HIGH
Bayonet and Leather Scabbard, 10" l	$400	$450	$500
Belt, Union, infantry, standard issue leather belt w/ U.S. oval buckle	75	80	85
Belt Plate, rect. w/ eagle motif, M1851, used from 1850s	100	125	150
Blanket, Union, Regular Army issue, medium brown	300	400	500
Bond, Confederate States of America, $1000 coupon bond, 1861, pictures C.G. Memminger, printed by B. Duncan, Columbia, SC	160	200	240
Bond, State of Louisiana $500 coupon bond, 1862, typeset, sgd. by governor	185	230	275
Buckle, Confederate, forked tongue, 3.5" x 2.25"	180	200	220
Bugle, cavalry, solid brass, 8.5"	360	385	415
Bullet, .44 cal. Colt Army	1	2	3
Bullet, .52 cal. Sharps carbine	1	2	3
Bullet, .58 cal. U.S. standard "minié ball"	1	2	3
Bullet Mold	50	65	80
Candle Holder, camp, spike on bottom and side, cast iron, 4.5"	45	60	75
Canteen, barrel form, Confederate, iron bands, oval, 10" h	450	500	600
Canteen, circ. form, tin, 7" dia	175	225	250
Cap Pouch, black leather, stamped "Ohio"	70	100	130
Carbine, Burnside, 4th model	1400	1600	1800
Carbine, Joslyn, model 1864	1300	1500	1700
Carbine, Smith, Massachusetts Arms	700	1000	1300
Cartridge and Bullet, .56 cal. Spencer carbine	2	4	6
Cartridge Box, black leather, brass U.S. box plate, tin inserts	75	85	95
Cavalry Boots, leather, tall above-knee type, high heels, no spurs, 31" h, pair	400	500	600
Cavalry Bugle, brass, cord rings, 8.5" l	300	400	500
Dispatch Case, tin, 11.5" x 8"	100	120	140
Drummer's Plate, solid brass, worn on drum sling, iron wire hooks, stamped "C.L. Carrington AP 4th," 3.25" w, 3.5" h	200	250	300
Drumsticks, rosewood, pair	90	100	110
Flag, Confederate, infantry regimental battle flag of the Confederate Army of Northern Virginia, 48" x 48"	8000	10,000	12,000
Grape Shot, solid iron, approx. 4.5" dia	40	60	80
Holster, Confederate, full flap for dragoon-sized revolver, brass stud closure, Richmond leather	475	500	525
Infantry Bugle, brass, engraved, chain guard for mouthpiece, 17.75" l, 6" dia bell	225	300	325

1864 Civil War Diary of Lt. George W. Hill, 7th Michigan Cavalry, $2475 at auction. Sold as part of lot containing over fifty items relating to the military service and family history of Lieutenant Hill. —Photo courtesy Jackson's Auctioneers & Appraisers.

	LOW	AVG.	HIGH
Jacket, Union, artillery shell, regulation issue, dark blue w/ red piping, 20 eagle buttons, fully lined	400	500	600
Knapsack, Confederate, box style, black oil cloth over wood frame w/ leather corners, white straps, from England	150	175	200
Knapsack, Union, "softpack" wo/ wooden frame, tar-covered fabric, leather straps, inspection stamp	35	45	55
Lantern, camp and signal, tin, japanned finish, cylindrical w/ scalloped peaked roof, oil burner, 6.5" h	65	85	105
Letter, by Union Lieutenant writing to wife of a Colonel, reporting on his condition, August 16, 1863	30	50	70
Map, Confederate, pocket map of VA, by West & Johnston, Richmond, 1862	325	350	375
Map Case, black painted tin, 13" x 6.75"	100	140	180
Medicine Kit, Confederate, wood case w/ 42 vials, 5.25" h, 9.75"	500	750	1000
Mess Kit, comprising 2 cups and cover, tin, 4" dia	100	140	180
Musket, Confederate, 3 band rifled, Potts & Hunt, London	700	850	1000
Naval Cutlass, model 1880, brass hilt, halfbasket guard, leather grip, dated 1862, hallmarked U.S.N.	200	300	400
Officer's Frock Coat, Union, field grade officer's model regulation army, double breasted, 18 buttons, RI state seal	800	1000	1200
Sword, foot officer's, double-sided engraved blade, Union inscription, leather grip and scabbard	250	275	300
Sword, officer's, staff and field, rayskin grips, Horstmann blade, etched eagle, brass and steel scabbard	500	600	700
Sword Belt, Confederate, 2-pc sword belt plate, orig. belt, plate mkd. "CS"	900	1000	1100

Epaulets

British, Coldstream Guards, early 1800s	$550	$850	$1150
French Officer's, early 1900s	800	900	1000
German, 19th C	350	525	700
U.S., Civil War officer's	275	600	850
U.S., late 19th C	150	225	300

Guns

	LOW	AVG.	HIGH
Ansley H. Fox A-Grade Double Barrel Shotgun, cal. 12 ga.	$650	$1200	$2000
Armscor AK47/22 Semi-Auto Rifle, cal. 22 LR	250	470	800
Beretta Model 1934 Semi-Auto Military Pistol, cal. 32 ACP	250	470	820
Beretta Model 1934 Semi-Auto Military Pistol, cal. 9 mm Corto	400	740	1300
Browning A-5 F-Grade Semi-Auto Shotgun, cal. 12 ga.	1400	2600	4500
Browning Citori Superlight Over/Under Shotgun, cal. 12 ga.	850	1500	2750
Browning Model 12 Grade-1 Pump Action Shotgun, cal. 20 ga.	300	560	1000
Colt 2nd Generation 1862 Police, cal. 36 percussion	325	600	1000
Colt Frontier Scout Golden Spike Commemorative, cal. 22	325	600	1000
Colt Frontier Scout Lawman Series–Wyatt Earp, cal. 22 LR	350	650	1200
Colt Lightning Small Frame Pump Action Rifle, cal. 22 S	300	560	1000
Colt Model 1903 Large Frame Pocket Pistol, cal. 38 ACP	800	1500	2600
Colt Officers' Model Match Target Revolver, cal. 38 Special	175	330	570
Colt Officers' Model Target Revolver, cal. 22 LR	350	650	1100
Colt Single Action Army Arizona Territorial Centennial Commemorative, cal. 45 Colt	700	1300	2200
Colt-Type AR 15 Vietnam Commemorative, cal. 223	750	1400	2500
Colt Woodsman 3rd Model Sport Semi-Auto Pistol, cal. 22	275	510	900
Deluxe Flobert Action Fluted Barrel Single Shot Rifle, cal. 22	800	1490	2600
English Flintlock Pistol, made by Ketland & Co.	425	790	1400
European Single Barrel Half Stocked Percussion Fowler, mid 19th C	55	100	180
Exel Arms Double Barrel Smooth Bore Slug Gun, cal. 12 ga.	300	560	980
Frank Wesson 2-Trigger Rifle, cal. 38 Tf/Cf	250	470	820
French Model 1886/93 Bolt Action Military Rifle, cal. 8 mm	220	400	700
German Luger Semi-Auto Military Pistol, cal. 9 mm	625	1100	2000
German Over/Under Combination Gun, cal. 9 mm	200	370	650
Harrington & Richardson Defender Revolver, cal. 38 S&W	275	550	900
Ithaca 4-E Single Barrel Trap Gun, cal. 12 ga.	450	840	1500
Ithaca Model 37 Centennial Model Pump Shotgun, cal. 12 ga.	375	700	1220
Ithaca Model 37 Featherlight Bicentennial Pump Shotgun, cal. 12 ga.	400	800	1300
J.P. Sauer & Son Best Quality Double Barrel Shotgun, cal. 12 ga.	800	1500	2600

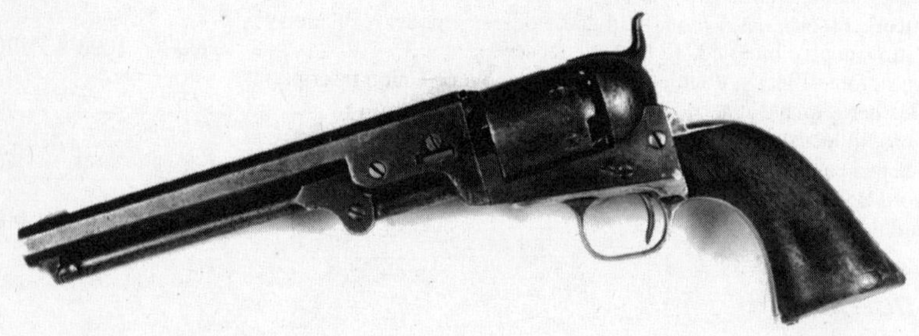

Colt Model 1851 Navy, cal. 36. —Photo courtesy Jackson's Auctioneers & Appraisers.

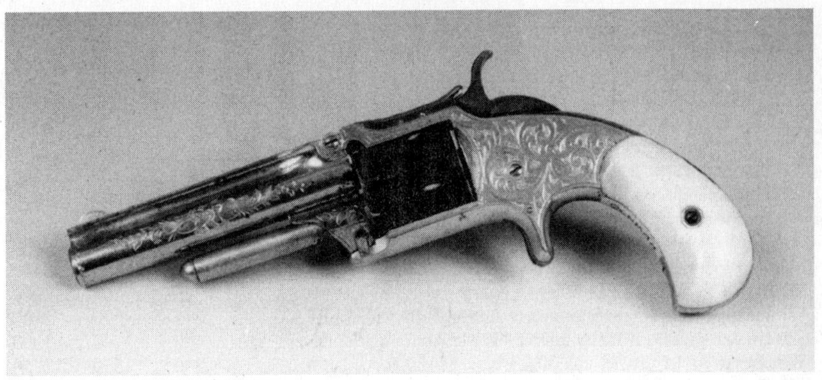

Smith & Wesson Model No. 1½ Ivory-Handled Revolver, 8xx second issue, cal. 32., $1320 at auction. —Photo courtesy Jackson's Auctioneers & Appraisers.

	LOW	AVG.	HIGH
Luger Semi-Auto Military Pistol, cal. 9 mm, 1917 Erfurt	300	600	1000
Luger Semi-Auto Military Pistol, cal. 9 mm, 1939/42	475	880	1500
Luicius W. Pond Single Action Pocket Revolver, cal. 32 rimfire	225	420	730
Marlin Model 1881 Lightweight Lever Action Rifle, cal. 32-40	400	740	1300
Mauser Commercial Obendorf Bolt Action Rifle, cal. 8 x 57	400	740	1300
New England Firearms (H&R) Model R92 D.A. Revolver, cal. 22 LR	60	110	180
Otto Bock Commercial Mauser Bolt Action Rifle, cal. 8 x 57	200	370	650
Parker Double Barrel Hammer Shotgun, cal. 10 ga.	250	470	820
Parker Gh Double Barrel Shotgun, cal. 12 ga.	350	650	1200
Parker N-Grade Damascus Double Barrel Shotgun, cal. 10 ga.	700	1300	2400
Peter Longo Over/Under Deluxe Shotgun, cal. 12 ga.	3000	6000	9000
Remington Model 12a Pump Action Rifle, cal. 22 S, L, LR	225	400	700
Remington Model 8 Takedown Semi-Auto Rifle, cal. 32 Rem	275	500	900
Remington Model 81 Semi-Auto Sporting Rifle, cal. 300 Sav	325	600	1000
Rizzini Model S780c Over/Under Shotgun, cal. 12 ga.	600	1100	1950
Ruger Gp100 D.A. Stainless Steel Revolver, cal. 357 Mag	250	470	820
Ruger Model 77vbz Mkii Stainless Steel Varmint Rifle, cal. 220 Swift	400	740	1300
Ruger Security Six Stainless Steel Revolver, cal. 357 Mag	200	370	650
Ruger T-512 Mk-1 Bumble Bee Special, cal. 22 LR	400	600	1000
Savage Model 1899 Lever Action Takedown Rifle w/ 4 Barrels, cal. 250	800	1500	2600
Savage Model 1905 Semi-Auto Pocket Pistol, cal. 32	200	370	650
Skb Model 505 Crown Field Over/Under Shotgun, cal. 20 ga.	550	1000	1750
Smith Corona Model 03-A3 Bolt Action Rifle, cal. 30-06	325	600	1000
Smith Corona 1903a3 National Match Rifle, cal. 30-06	800	1500	2600
Smith & Wesson Hand Ejector 4th Change, cal. 32-20	150	280	500
Smith & Wesson Model 17-6 Target Revolver, cal. 22 LR	250	475	825
Smith & Wesson Model 31 D.A. Revolver, cal. 32 S&W long	200	370	650
Smith & Wesson Model 67-1 Stainless Steel Revolver, cal. 38 Special	200	370	650
Springfield 1903 National Match-Type Rifle, cal. 30-06	650	1210	2000
Stevens Ideal Rifle No. 44.5, cal. 25 Rf	325	600	1000
Stevens Model 620 Pump Action Shotgun, cal. 16 ga.	120	220	400

	LOW	AVG.	HIGH
Steyr Model 1916 Military Pistol, cal. 9 mm Steyr	175	330	570
Thompson Center High Plains Sporter, cal. 50 percussion	175	330	570
U.S. Model 1816 Musket, percussion Alteration, Type III	1200	2230	4000
U.S. Model 1847 Sappers Musketoon (Composite), cal. 69	700	1300	2250
U.S. Springfield 1903 Bolt Action Military Rifle, cal. 30-06	700	1300	2250
U.S. Springfield Model 1922 M-2 Bolt Action Training Rifle, cal. 22 LR	600	1120	1960
U.S. Springfield Model 1922 Mii Bolt Action Training Rifle, cal. 22 LR	550	1000	1750
Valmet Model 412 Over/Under Combination Gun 2 Bbl Set, cal. 12 x 12 and 12 x 308	750	1400	2450
Valmet Model 412 Over/Under Double Rifle, cal. 9.3 x 74r	750	1400	2450
Webley Mark-V British Military Revolver, cal. 455	325	600	1000
Whitney Howard Single Shot Patent Action Rifle, cal. 44 Rf	275	510	900
Winchester Buffalo Bill Commercial Lever Action Rifle, cal. 30-30	400	740	1300
Winchester M-1 Carbine, cal. 30 Carb	850	1500	2750
Winchester Model '03 Semi-Auto Rifle, cal. 22 Win. Auto	225	400	730
Winchester Model '07 Semi-Auto Rifle, cal. 351 Sl	200	350	650
Winchester Model '12 Custom Engraved Pump Action Shotgun, cal. 12 ga.	400	750	1300
Winchester Model '12 Pump Action Trap Gun, cal. 12 ga.	450	800	1450
Winchester Model 1886 Lever Action Rifle, cal. 40-82	1100	2000	3500
Winchester Model 1886 Standard Grade Lever Action Rifle, cal. 45-70	850	1500	2750
Winchester Model 1892 Lever Action Rifle, cal. 32 Wcf	275	500	900
Winchester Model 1892 Special Order Saddle Ring Carbine, cal. 25-20	450	900	1500
Winchester Model 1894 Saddle Ring Carbine, cal. 30 Wcf	300	560	1000
Winchester Model 1894 Special Order Eastern Carbine, cal. 30 Wcf	425	800	1400
Winchester Model 1894 Special Order Rifle, cal. 38-55	470	870	1600
Winchester Model 1894 Special Order Saddle Ring Carbine, cal. 30 Wcf	375	700	1220
Winchester Model 1895 Takedown Rifle, cal. 30-06	600	1200	1800
Winchester Model 1897 Solid Frame Adams' Express Riot Gun, cal. 12 ga.	750	1400	2500
Winchester Model 61 Pump Action Rifle, cal. 22 S, L, LR	525	1000	1800
Winchester Model 62 Pump Action Rifle, cal. 22 S, L, LR	500	800	1400
Winchester Model 62a Pump Action Gallery Rifle, cal. 22	250	470	820
Winchester Model 62a Pump Action Rifle, cal. 22 S, L, LR	300	560	1000
Winchester Model 71 Custom Engraved Deluxe Rifle, cal. 348	1200	2230	3800
Winchester Model 94 Illinois Sesquicentennial, cal. 20-30	300	560	1000

Headdress

Austrian Dragoon Cap, late 19th C	$270	$335	$400
Austrian Field Artillery Officer's Cap, early 20th C	270	400	550
Austrian Hussar Officer's Shako, early 20th C	2150	2775	3400
Austrian Infantry Shako, 19th C	1500	2000	2500
Austrian Officer's Lancer's Cap (Czapka), late 19th C	2200	2850	3500
Bavarian Officer's Cap, 19th C	540	900	1200
Bavarian Officer's Lancer's Cap, 19th C	1500	2000	2500
Bavarian Shako, 19th C	1500	2000	2500
British Infantry Officer's Shako, 19th C	2200	2850	3500
British Mounted Police Officer's Pillbox Cap, late 19th C	375	425	475
British Officer's Fur Busby, late 19th C	800	1100	1500
British Officer's Lancer's Cap, late 19th C	4000	4750	5500
British Officer's Patrol Cap, late 19th C	400	550	700
British Other Ranks Fur Busby, late 19th C	400	550	700
British Other Ranks Lancer's Cap, late 19th C	2200	2850	3500

Japanese WWII Admiral's Cap, $275 at auction. —Photo courtesy Jackson's Auctioneers & Appraisers.

	LOW	AVG.	HIGH
British Royal Scots Bearskin Cap, early 20th C	800	1100	1400
British Staff Officer's Cocked Hat, early 19th C	1000	1350	1700
Canadian Militia Officer's Forage Cap, late 19th C	350	400	450
French Foreign Legion Cap	55	65	75
French Officer's Lancer's Cap, 19th C	2500	4000	5500
French Officer's Shako, 19th C	1500	2000	2500
French Other Ranks Lancer's Cap, 19th C	1500	2000	2500
German Hussar's Officer's Cap	540	850	1250
German Imperial Infantry Shako, late 19th C	1000	1500	2000
German Imperial Lancer's Cap, late 19th C	1000	1350	1750
German Imperial Officer's Busby, late 19th C	5000	6500	8000
German Imperial Other Ranks Busby, late 19th C	2500	3250	4000
Nazi Admiral's Visor Cap	4000	5500	7000
Nazi Airforce Officer's Visor Cap	270	400	525
Nazi Diplomatic Corps Visor Cap	5000	6000	7000
Nazi General Staff Officer's Cap	1500	1750	2000
Nazi Infantry Cap	270	400	525
Nazi Police Officer's Shako	550	700	850
Nazi SS Coffee Can Cap	2500	4000	5500
Prussian Officer's Black Beaver Hat, early 19th C	800	1100	1400
Prussian Other Ranks Black Felt Hat, late 18th/early 19th C	540	800	1200
Prussian Shako, 19th C	1000	1500	2000
Royal Fusiliers Officer's Racoon Skin Cap, late 19th C	1500	1750	2000
Royal Italian Cavalry Busby, early 20th C	1300	1650	2000
Russian Hussar's Shako, 19th C	2200	2850	3500
U.S. Enlisted Man's Artillery Hat, 19th C	800	1100	1400
U.S. Enlisted Man's Fatigue Cap, early 29th C	270	335	400
U.S. Enlisted Man's Forage Cap, early 19th C	400	450	500
U.S. Enlisted Man's Shako, 19th C	800	1250	1700
U.S. First Guard Other Ranks Grenadier Cap, 19th C	4000	5500	7000
U.S. Officer's Cocked Hat, early 19th C	1500	1750	2000
U.S. Officer's Tricorn Hat, late 18th/early 19th C	1500	1750	2000

Molds

Before ice cream producers could send the various shapes of ice cream now offered in the freezer of the corner maket, local merchants made their own ice cream and sold it in shapes they pressed into molds themselves. Homemade ice cream also found its way into these molds. Because some pewter contains lead, it is not advisable to continue the practice.

All of the ice cream molds are pewter unless otherwise indicated. Chocolate molds are tin.

Stork, E. & Co. N.Y. #7032, $90–$125.

Chocolate

	LOW	HIGH
Air Ship, Anton Reiche #25647, 2.75" h	$110	$130
Basket	45	70
Cat, 8"	100	125
Christmas Stocking	115	175
Dog Head, 4"	17	25
Eagle, #10, 4.625" h	45	75
Girl and Rabbit, Anton Reiche #21889S, 4.25" h	80	100
Jack-O-Lantern	35	50
Kewpies, #1980, 3 part, Germany, 6" h	85	120
Naked Child, Anton Reiche, #17499, 10.875" h	155	200
Owl, #18, 4" h	20	35
Rabbit Playing Drum, Anton Reiche #26024, 6" h	85	115
Rabbit Riding Rooster, 6"	46	70
Rabbits and Egg on Gondola, Anton Reiche, 1.75" h	15	25
Santa	23	35
Sitting Cat, #14, 3" h	20	32
Sitting Rabbit, 3.5"	23	35
Snowman, 4"	46	70
Teddy Bear, #2644, 11"	175	260
Turkey, 3-part	52	80

Strawberry Medallion, #414, $60–$80.

Ice Cream

	LOW	HIGH
Asparagus Bunch	$50	$80
Bell, Krauss #285	50	80
Chicken, E. & Co. N.Y. #652	50	80
Christmas Stocking, #596	100	150
Christmas Tree w/ Ornaments, #641K	50	80
Christmas Wreath, E. & Co. N.Y. #1146	100	160
Chrysanthemum, Krauss #313	65	100
Conch Shell, S. & Co. #270	85	130
Corn on the Cob, S. & Co. #270	60	90
Cornucopia, #287	30	45
Cornucopia, E. & Co. #1004	85	130
Cupid, Krauss #492	63	100
Daisy, E. & Co. N.Y. #317	50	80
Dove in Flight, E. & Co. N.Y. #677	100	150
Drum, 3 part, Krauss #511A	85	130
Duck, Krauss #187	50	80
Flaming Hearts, Krauss #300	60	90
George Washington, Krauss #460	75	115
Grapes, Krauss #159	50	80
Native American, Krauss #458	85	130
Pumpkin, S. & Co.	40	60
Rabbit, Krauss # 190	50	80
Roasting Turkey, Krauss #364	45	70
Rocking Horse, E. & Co.	85	130
Rose, Krauss #582	60	90
Rose w/ Bud and Leaves, S. & Co.	65	100
Santa at Chimney, E. & Co. N.Y. #1171	85	130
Santa, S. & Co. #427	50	80
Standing Rabbit, Krauss #189	60	90
Strawberry, Krauss #503	75	115
Train Engine, #477	85	130
Triple Rose, Krauss #391	50	80
Triple Strawberry, S. & Co.	65	100
Turkey, E. & Co. N.Y. #650	50	80
Witch's Cat, E. & Co. N.Y. #1175	85	130

Motion Lamps

Animated motion lamps draw the eye by presenting an illusion of a waterfall, a ship at sea or a variety of action-packed images. The heat of the light bulb causes the cylinder to revolve inside a painted shade creating the illusion of a moving image. The light of the bulb shining through the shade casts a beautiful glow. The most prominent manufacturers were Scene in Action and National in the 1920s, and Econolite and L.A. Goodman in the 1950s through the 1960s. Prices are guided by condition, availability and collector demand. Care must be taken to ensure that the original cylinder is inside the lamp because cylinders are not interchangeable. Values are given for lamps in mint condition.

Our consultants for this section are Jim and Kaye Whitaker, owners of Eclectic Antiques. They are listed in the back of this book.

Antique Autos, Econolite, 1957, 11" h, $110–$130.

	LOW	HIGH
Bicycles, plastic, Econolite, 1959, 11" h	$130	$160
Birch Trees w/ Ducks, plastic, L.A. Goodman, 1956, 11" h	95	105
Blacksmith, Gritt Co., 1920s, 11" h	75	100
Boy Scout and Girl Scout, plastic, Rotovue Jr., Econolite, 1950, 10" h	175	250
Butterflies, plastic, Econolite, 1954, 11" h	110	150
Christmas Tree, paper, 1951, 10.5" h	40	75
Church Snow Scene, plastic, Econolite, 1957, 11" h	130	140
Colonial Fountain, Scene in Action Co., 1930s, 10" h	140	170
Fireplace, plastic, Econolite, 11" h	70	80
Forest Fire, glass, Scene in Action Co., 9" h	130	150
Forest Fire, Ignition Co., 1940s, 8" h	35	55
Forest Fire, plastic, Econolite, 1955, 11" h	85	100
Forest Fire, plastic, L.A. Goodman, 1956, 11" h	65	80
Fountain of Youth, plastic, Rotovue Jr., Econolite, 1950, 10" h	90	110
Hawaiian Scene, palm trees, plastic, Econolite, 1959, 11" h	90	120
Indian Chief, plaster, Gritt Inc., 1920s, 11" h	45	60
Indian Maiden, plaster, Gritt Inc., 1920s, 11" h	45	60
Japanese Twilight, Scene in Action Co., 1931, 13" h	140	170
Ko-Pak-Ta Nut Machine, chrome, Roy Stringer Co., 1930s, 15" h	250	350

	LOW	HIGH
Lighthouse/Ship, glass and paper, Scene in Action Co., 1930s, 10" h	110	140
Lighthouse/Ship, plastic, L.A. Goodman, 1950s, 11" h	85	95
Marine Scene, glass and white metal, Scene in Action Co., 1930s, 9" h	90	110
Merry Go Round, yellow, Rotovue Jr., Econolite, 1950s, 10" h	85	95
Mill Stream, plastic, Econolite, 1956, 11" h	65	80
Miss Liberty, plastic, Econolite, 1957, 11" h	135	155
Mother Goose, plastic, Econolite, 1948, 11" h	90	110
Mountain Waterfall (campers), plastic, L.A. Goodman, 1956, 11" h	55	70
Niagara Falls, glass, Scene in Action Co., 1931, 10" h	100	125
Niagara Falls, plastic, Econolite, 1955, 11" h	50	65
Niagara Falls, plastic, L.A. Goodman, 1957, 11" h	35	50
Niagara Falls, plastic, Rotovue Jr., Econolite, 1950, 10" h	55	70
Niagara Falls, rainbow, plastic, Econolite, oval, 1960, 11" h	60	75
Op Art Lamp, black plastic, Visual Effect Inc., 1970s, 13" h	35	55
Oriental Fantasy, volcano, plastic, L.A. Goodman, 1957, 11" h	70	90
Pot Belly Stove, plastic, black or silver, Econolite, 1950s, 12" h	120	150
Santa and Reindeer, plastic, L.A. Goodman, 1950s, 12" h	100	140
Seattle World's Fair, plastic, Econolite, 1962, 11" h	130	160
Ships, Rev-O-Lite, 1930s, 10" h	75	95
Snow Scene w/ Cabin, plastic, Econolite, 1950s, 11" h	100	120
Spirit of '76, plastic, Creative Light Products, 1973, 11" h	45	60
Steamboats, plastic, Econolite, 1957, 11" h	100	120
Story Book, "Hey Diddle Diddle," plastic, L.A. Goodman, 1956, 11" h	80	95
The Bar Is Open, black plastic, Visual Effects, 1970s, 13" h	25	40
Trains, plastic, Econolite, 1956, 11" h	100	125
Trains Racing, plastic, L.A. Goodman, 1957, 11" h	85	100
Truck and Bus, plastic, Econolite, 1962, 11" h	130	160
Venice Grand Canal, plastic, Econolite, 1963, 11" h	125	140
Water Skiers, plastic, Econolite, 1950s, 11" h	100	145
White Christmas, flat front, plastic, Econolite, 1953, 11" h	120	150
Yellowstone, framed wall mounting, wood and glass, Econolite, 1953, 10" h	40	65

Hopalong Cassidy, $400–$600.

Music

CDs

Although they first appeared on the market only 15 years ago, compact discs are already collector items. Music fans collect CDs for the sound they contain, often unique recordings that can't (or no longer can) be picked up by a quick visit to the local music emporium. Most of the more valuable CDs are promotional discs. Often companies only produced relatively few such promos, but not always. Although most promos have a somewhat higher value, there are enough exceptions to trip up the unwary.

When we have listed only the recording artist, the price reflects the average range for this performer. Some noteworthy exceptions for individual albums are listed as such. All prices are for near mint examples. For further information refer to *The Official Price Guide to Compact Discs* by Jerry Osborne and Paul Bergquist, House of Collectibles, NY, 1994.

	LOW	HIGH
Aerosmith	$8	$12
B-52's	6	7
Bad Company	5	7
Beastie Boys	7	15
Benatar, Pat	6	8
Black Crowes	6	10
Black Sabbath	7	8
Blue Nile	5	7
Bolton, Michael	6	8
Bonjovi	6	12
Bowie, David	6	25
Brooks, Garth	8	10
Brown, James	8	10
Campbell, Kevin	5	7
Carey, Mariah	6	10
Cash, Johnny	6	7
Chapman, Tracy	5	10
Cher	6	8
Chicago	5	6
Chicago: Chicago II, promo	25	30
Clapton, Eric	6	8
Cocker, Joe	5	6
Cole, Natalie	5	8
Cole, Natalie: Pink Cadillac, promo	10	12
Costello, Elvis	4	8
Crowded House	5	12
Cure	5	8
Cure: Hot, Hot, Hot, promo	20	25
Dead Milkman	5	7
Denver, John	5	6
Depeche Mode: Strange Love, promo	15	17
Duran Duran	6	10
Earth, Wind, and Fire	4	8
Estefan, Gloria	5	10
Eurythmics	6	8
Fine Young Cannibals	4	15
Flack, Roberta	4	6

	LOW	HIGH
Fleetwood Mac	4	8
Fleetwood Mac: Behind the Bask (oversized box)	25	30
Franklin, Aretha	5	8
Gabriel, Peter	5	8
Gabriel, Peter: Shaking the Tree, Geffen 4217, promo	4	10
Genesis	5	6
Great White	4	8
Great White: Live at the Ritz, promo	15	18
Guns n' Roses	8	12
Hammer	4	6
Happy Mondays	4	7
Harrison, George: Cheer Down	6	8
Harrison, George: Cloud Nine, promo	50	60
Harrison, George: Got My Mind Set on You, Dark Horse 2846, promo, special envelope	100	120
Heart	8	12
Hitchcock, Robyn	4	12
Houston, Whitney	5	10
Hurricane	4	8
Ice-T	4	6
Indigo Girls	6	10
INXS	5	8
INXS: Master of Rock, promo, 2 CDs	45	50
Jackson, Janet	8	12
Jackson, Michael	6	10
Jethro Tull	6	7
Jett, Joan	6	7
John, Elton	5	8
Khan, Chakha	4	6
Kiss	8	15
Kravitz, Lenny	5	8
LaBelle, Patti	6	7
lang, k.d.	6	7
Lauper, Cyndi	5	7
Little Feat	4	5
Little Feat: Waiting for Columbus (radio show), promo	25	30
Lovett, Lyle	4	7
Madonna	5	8
Manilow, Barry	6	8
Marx, Richard	4	6
McCartney, Paul	6	8
Mellencamp, John	5	7
Metallica	10	20
Midler, Bette	5	6
Mills, Stephanie	5	6
Morrison, Van	5	8
Motley Crue	6	8
Motley Crue: Angela, promo	6	7
Neville Brothers	4	5
Newton-John, Olivia	7	10
Nirvana	6	9
Orbison, Roy	6	8
Overkill	4	5
Palmer, Robert	4	8

Boston, $5–$7.

	LOW	HIGH
Petshop Boys	6	10
Pixies	4	6
Pop, Iggy	4	6
Presley, Elvis: Elvis (RCA PCD11382)	500	600
Presley, Elvis: Elvis Gold Records Volume 2 (RCA PCD1-5197), only 50 copies made	3500	4000
Presley, Elvis: My Happiness (RCA 2645, promo)	40	45
Prince	6	10
Queen	7	12
Raitt, Bonnie	5	6
Red Hot Chili Peppers	6	8
REM	5	19
Rolling Stones	12	20
Rolling Stones: The Interview, promo	30	35
Ronstadt, Linda	5	6
Roth, David Lee	5	8
Shocked, Michelle	5	8
Simply Red	5	8
Smashing Pumpkins	5	6
Soul Asylum	5	8
Sprinsteen, Bruce	8	15
Stewart, Rod	4	7
Sting	5	8
Streisand, Barbra	6	8
Sweat, Keith	4	6
Tears for Fears	5	7
10,000 Maniacs	4	8
Thorogood, George	6	8
TLC	5	7
Turner, Tina	5	8
U2	8	12
Van Halen	5	8
Vandross, Luther	4	6
White, Karyn	4	8
Williams, Hank, Jr.	4	5
Winwood, Steve	5	6
Young, Neil	6	8

Records, Albums

Many people who discarded their record collections in the 1980s are buying them back in the 1990s. Collectors feel that the sound quality on albums is richer and more subtle than on CDs. People also love the photos and artwork of the covers. The nostalgic appeal of records is very strong; music is often a reminder of happy moments. Many collectors remember records as their first independent purchase as a teenager.

The following is a cross-section of LPs; 45s are not covered. Each entry consists of the performer's name, the title of the LP, the company that produced it, the stock number and the date. Condition is all important for records; collectors usually grade both the record and the album cover. Scratches on the record that interfere with sound quality can destroy the price of a record. Worn, torn, or stained covers also decrease their prices. The prices below are for records in excellent condition with excellent condition covers. That means that the record may have small scratches that can be seen but not heard. The covers should be crisp and clean with only slight wear. Near mint or mint examples will command higher prices than those listed below.

The world of records is filled with rare variations. Often these are subtle differences such as misspellings. Some people put more value on stereo or mono versions of the same record. In general, the prices below reflect the prices of the more common variations. For further reading, see *The Official Price Guide to Records, Twelfth Edition,* Jerry Osborne, House of Collectibles, NY, 1997, and *Goldmine's Price Guide to Collectible Record Albums, Fifth Edition,* Neal Umphred, Krause Publications, Iola, WI, 1996.

	LOW	HIGH
Abba, Waterloo, Atlantic, SD-18101k 1974	$3	$5
AC/DC, Highway to Hell, Atlantic, SD-19244, 1979	2	4
Aerosmith, Get Your Wings, Columbia, KC-32847, 1974	3	5
Allman Brothers Band, Eat a Peach (2 records), Capricorn 2CP-0102, 1972	6	10
America, Holiday, Warner Bros., BS-2808, 1974	2	4
Animals, Eric Is Here, MGM, E-4433, 1967	6	15
Animals, The Animals, MGM, E-4264, 1964	20	32
Anka, Paul, Strictly Nashville, RCA Victor, LSP-3580, 1966	6	15
Archies, The Archies, Calandar, KES-101, 1968	12	18
Association, Stop Your Motor, Warner Bros., WS-1927, 1971	5	7
Avalon, Frankie, You're Mine, Chancellor, CHLS-5027, 1962	25	45
Average White Band, Cut the Cake, Atlantic, SD-18140, 1975	4	5
Bailey, Pearl, Cultured Pearl, Coral, CRL-57162, 1957	20	30
Barry, Chuck, Chuck Barry in London, Chess, LPS-1495, 1965	15	30
Baxter, Les, Thinking of You, Capitol, T-474, 1954	20	32
Beach Boys, Little Deuce Coupe, Capitol, ST-1998, 1963	20	32
Beach Boys, Surfin' USA, Capitol, ST-1890, 1963	25	45
Bee Gees, Horizontal, Atco, SD-33-233, 1968	8	20
Bennett, Tony, Blue Velvet, Columbia, CL-1292k 1959	15	20
Benton, Brook, Singing the Blues, Mercury, SR-60740, 1962	18	30
Berry, Chuck, Berry Is on Top, Chess, LP-1435, 1959	90	165
Berry, Chuck, Golden Hits, Mercury, MG-21103, 1967	12	15
Big Brother and the Holding Company, Be a Brother, Columbia, C-30222, 1970	15	25
Black Sabbath, Paranoid, Warner Bros., WS-1887, 1971	6	15
Blondie, Autoamerican, Chrysalis, CHE-1290, 1980	3	5
Blood, Sweat and Tears, New Blood, Columbia, KC-31780, 1972	3	5
Boone, Pat, Star Dust, Dot, DLP-3118, 1958	15	20
Bostick, Earl, Dance Time, King, KSD-525, 1966	6	15
Bowie, David, Aladdin Insane, RCA Victor, AYL1-3890, 1980	3	5
Boxtops, Non-Stop, Bell, S-6023, 1968	6	15
Brewer, Teresa, Music, Music, Music, Coral, CRL-57027, 1956	15	22

Left to right: Big Brother and the Holding Company, Cheap Thrills, *$10–$12; Doors,* The Best of Doors, *$5–$8.*

	LOW	HIGH
Broonzy, Big Bill, Country Blues, Folkways, FA-2326, 1957	25	45
Brown, James, Handfull of Soul, Smash, SRS-67084, 1966	20	40
Browne, Jackson, For Every Man Asylum, SD-5067, 1974	3	5
Browne, Jackson, For Everman, Asylum, SD-5067, 1973	8	14
Bruce, Lenny, I Am Not a Nut, red vinyl, Fantasy, 7007, 1960	50	100
Buffett, Jimmy, Volcano, MCA, 5102, 1979	3	5
Butler, Jerry, Sweet Sixteen, Mercury, SRM-006, 1974	4	10
Byrds, Farther Along, Columbia, KC-31050, 1971	5	7
Byrds, Turn! Turn! Turn!, Columbia, CL-2454, 1965	15	22
Cannon, Ace, Aces Hi, Hi, SHL-32016, 1964	10	20
Carpenters, Close to You, A & M, SP4271, 1970	6	10
Carpenters, Close to You, A & M, QU-54271, 1973	8	10
Charles, Ray, The Genius of Ray Charles, Atlantic, 1312, 1960	15	20
Charles, Ray, The Great Ray Charles, Atlantic, SD-1259, 1960	6	15
Checker, Chubby, Let's Twist Again, Parkway, P-7004, 1961	25	45
Checker, Chubby, Limbo, Parkway, SP-7020, 1962	18	30
Cher, Backstage, Imperial, LP-12373, 1968	6	12
Chiffons, Sweet Talkin' Guy, Laurie, LLP-2036, 1966	40	75
Christy, June, Big Band Specials, Capitol, T-1845, 1962	10	18
Clapton, Eric, No Reason to Cry, RSO, 3004, 1976	3	5
Clark, Dave, Five By Five, Epic, BN-26236, 1967	15	35
Coasters, Greatest Hits, Atco, 33-111, 1960	25	45
Cooke, Sam, My Kind of Blues, RCA Victor, LPM-2392, 1961	20	30
Cooper, Alice, Billion Dollar Babies, Warner Bros., BS-2685, 1974	3	5
Cream, Fresh Cream, Atco, SD-33-206, 1967	15	25
Creedence Clearwater Revival, Cosmo's Factory, Mobile Fidelity, MFSL-037	30	50
Crosby, Bing, In a Little Spanish Town, Decca, DL-8846, 1959	12	18
Darin, Bobby, Earthy, Capitol, ST-1826, 1963	10	18
Darin, Bobby, Twist With Bobby Darrin, Atco, 33-138, 1961	20	30
Davis, Skeeter, The End of the World, RCA Victor, LSP-2699, 1962	20	30
Day, Doris, Day in Hollywood, Columbia, CL-749, 1955	10	16
Denny, Martin, Exotica, Liberty, LRP-3034, 1957	18	25
Diamond, Neil, Velvet Gloves and Spit, Uni, ST-93030, 1971	4	6
Dire Straits, Making Movies, Warner Bros., 3480, 1980	3	5
Domino, Fats, A Lot of Dominos, Imperial, LP-12066, 1964	20	35
Drifters, Under the Boardwalk, white cover, Atlantic, 8099, 1964	35	65
Elliott, Ramblin's Jack, Country Style, Prestige, PRLP-13045, 1962	18	22

Left to right: Genesis, Foxtrot, *$8–$12; Iron Butterfly,* In A Godda Da Vida, *$15–$18.*

	LOW	HIGH
Everly Brothers, Gone, Gone, Gone, Warner Bros., WS-1585, 1965	30	45
Everly Brothers, The Everly Brothers Best, Cadence, CLP-3025, 1969	40	80
Fabian, The Fabulous Fabian, Chancellor, CHLX-5005, 1959	40	60
Fifth Dimension, Portrait, Bell, 6045, 1970	5	7
Fireballs, Sugar Shack, Dot, DLP-25545, 1963	30	50
Fisher, Eddie, I'm In the Mood for Love, RCA Victor, LPM-1180, 1955	18	22
Flatt & Scruggs, Foggy Mountain Jamboree, Columbia, CL-1019, 1957	20	35
Fleetwoods, Goodnight, My Love, Dolton, BST-8025, 1963	15	35
Fleetwoods, Mr. Blue, Dolton, BST-8001, 1959	50	86
Ford, Tennessee Ernie, Spirituals, Capitol, T-818, 1957	15	20
Four Seasons, Rag Doll, Philips, PHM-200-146, 1964	18	22
Four Tops, Four Tops, Motown, MS-622, 1964	20	30
Francis, Connie, Who's Sorry Now?, MGM, E-3686, 1959	20	30
Franklin, Aretha, The Electrifying…, Columbia, CL-1761, 1962	25	35
Franklin, Aretha, Unforgettable, Columbia, CS-8963, 1964	18	25
Fugs, The Fugs First Album, ESP-Disk, 1018, 1966	20	35
Funicello, Annette, Annette's Pajama Party, Buena Vista, STER-3325, 1964	50	90
Garland, Judy, The Wizard of Oz, Decca, DL-8387, 1957	30	40
Gaye, Marvin, Marvin Gay's Greatest Hits, Tamla, TS-252, 1964	18	26
Gibson, Don, No One Stands Alone, RCA Victor, LSP-1918, 1959	25	35
Gore, Lesley, Boys, Boys, Boys, Mercury, MG-20901, 1964	12	20
Gorme, Eydie, Love Is a Season, ABC-Paramount, ABCS-273, 1958	12	18
Grand Funk Railroad, Survival, Capitol, S@-764, 1972	3	5
Grateful Dead, The Grateful Dead, Warner Bros., WS-1689, 1967	30	45
Guy, Buddy, A Man and the Blues, Vanguard, VSD-79272, 1968	10	15
Hendrix, Jimi, Pie, Live 'n' Dirty, Nutmeg, NUT-1001, 1978	18	22
Herman's Hermits, Introducing…, MGM, E-4282, 1965	12	19
Hooker, John Lee, Travelin', Vee Jay, LP-1023, 1960	45	65
Hopkins, Lightin', Double Blues, Fantasy, F-24702, 1972	6	15
Horne, Lena, At the Waldorf Astoria, RCA Victor, LSO-1028, 1957	30	40
Ian, Janis, Society's Child, Verve, V05027, 1967	10	18
Impressions, Keep on Pushing, ABC-Paramount, ABCS-493, 1964	18	24
Ives, Burl, Down to the Sea in Ships, Decca, DL-8245, 1956	14	18
James, Tommy, I Think We're Alone Now, Roulette, R-25353, 1967	14	20
Jerry & The Pacemakers, Greatest Hits, Laurie, SLLP-2031, 1965	18	26
Joel, Billy, Glass House, Columbia, FC-36384, 1980	2	4
King, B.B., My Kind of Blues, Crown, CLP-5188, 1961	15	22

	LOW	HIGH
King, B.B., Singin' the Blues, Crown, CLP-5020, 1957	40	80
King, Ben E., Greatest Hits, Atco, SD-33-165, 1964	20	32
Kingston Trio, String Along, Capitol, ST-1407, 1960	18	22
Kinks, Schoolboys in Disgrace, RCA Victor, AYL1-3749, 1980	3	5
Knight, Gladys, Everbody Needs Love, Soul, SS-706, 1967	12	18
Leadbelly, Huddie Ledbetter's Best, Capitol, T-1821, 1962	35	60
Lee, Brenda, This Is Brenda, Decca, DL-74082, 1960	15	20
Lennon, John and Yoko Ono, Sometime in NYC, Apple, SVBB-3392, 1972	20	30
Lewis, Jerry Lee, The Return of Rock, Smash, SRS-67063, 1965	30	40
Liberace, Sincerely Yours, Columbia, CL-800, 1955	12	18
London, Julie, About the Blues, Liberty, LST-7012, 1958	20	30
Lovin' Spoonful, Do You Believe in Magic, Kama Sutra, KLPS-8050, 1965	18	24
Lynn, Loretta, Hymns, Decca, DL-74695, 1965	15	20
Mancini, Henry, The Mancini Touch, RCA Victor, LSP-2101, 1960	12	15
Martin, Mary, South Pacific, Columbia, OL-4180, 1949	18	25
Mathis, Johnny, Warm, Columbia, CL-1078, 1957	20	30
McCartney, Paul, Band on the Run, w/ poster, Capitol, SO-3415, 1973	18	22
McGuire Sisters, While the Lights Are Low, Coral, CRL-57145, 1957	18	25
Mommas and the Poppas, California Dreaming, Pickwick, SPC-3352, 1972	3	5
Monkees, Monkey Flips, Rhino, RNLP-1113, 1984	3	5
Monroe, Marilyn, Some Like It Hot, United Artists, UAL-4030, 1959	40	75
Muddy Waters, Muddy, Brass and Blues, Chess, LPS-1507, 1966	25	38
Nelson, Rick, Ricky, Imperial, LP-9048, 1964	15	24
Nelson, Rick, Ricky Sings Again, Imperial, LP-12090, 1962	75	135
Nelson, Tracy, Deep Are the Roots, Prestige, PRLP-7393, 1965	15	20
Nelson, Willie, And Then I Wrote, Liberty, LRP-3238, 1962	20	30
Orbison, Roy, There Is Only One Roy Orbison, MGM, SE4308, 1965	15	22
Owens, Buck, I've Got a Tiger By the Tail, Capitol, ST-2283, 1965	15	20
Page, Patti, This Is My Song, Mercury, MG-20102, 1955	15	20
Partridge Family, Partridge Family, w/ photo, Bell, 6050, 1970	15	20
Paul, Les and Mary Ford, Bye Bye Blues, Capitol, T-356, 1955	25	40
Peter, Paul and Mary, In the Wind, Warner Bros., W-1507, 1963	12	18
Platters, Moonlight Memories, Mercury, MG-20759, 1963	15	20
Preston, Johnny, Running Bare, Mercury, MG-20592, 1960	60	90
Price, Ray, Talk to Your Heart, Columbia, CL-1148, 1958	15	20
Queen, Live Killers, Elektra, BB-702, 1979	4	5
Ramones, Ramones, Sire, SASD-7520, 1976	15	20
Rascals, Once Upon a Dream, Atlantic, SD-8148, 1968	12	18
Redding, Otis, Soul Ballads, Volt, 411, 1965	40	60
Reed, Jimmy, Just Jimmy Reed, Vee Jay, LP-1050, 1962	18	28
Reese, Della, Della, RCA Victor, LSP-2157, 1960	15	20
Reeves, Jim, Jim Reeves Sings, Abbott, LP-5001, 1956	10	15
Reeves, Jim, The Intimate Jim Reeves, RCA Victor, LSP-2216, 1960	20	30
Reynolds, Debbie, Am I That Easy to Forget?, Dot, DLP-25295, 1960	18	22
Rich, Charlie, The Best Years, Smash, SRS-67078, 1966	18	24
Righteous Bros., You've Lost That Loving Feelin', Philles, PHLP-4007, 1965	15	20
Rodgers, Jimmie, Twilight on the Trail, Roulette, R-25081, 1959	15	20
Rogers, Roy, Song Wagon, Golden, GRC-6, 1958	60	80
Rolling Stones, Satanic Maj. Request, 3D, stereo, London, NPS-2, 1967	25	35
Rolling Stones, Some Girls, Mobil Fidelity, MFSL-087	18	25
Ruby and The Romantics, Our Day Will Come, Kapp, KL-1323, 1963	15	22
Rydell, Bobby, Bobby Sings, Cameo, C-1007, 1960	20	35
Sam the Sham and The Pharoahs, Wooly Bully, MGM, SE-4297, 1965	18	28
Searchers, Meet the Searchers, Kapp, KL-1363, 1964	15	22

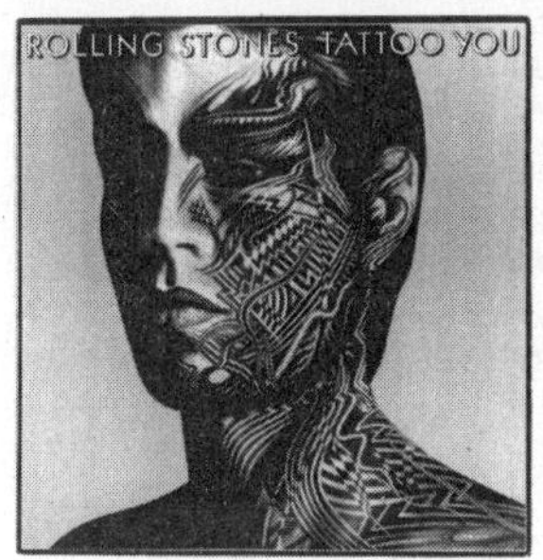

Left to right: Rolling Stones, Tattoo You, *$3–$5; Santana,* Santana, *$8–$10.*

	LOW	HIGH
Seeger, Pete, Pete Seeger at Carnegie Hall, Folkways, FA2351, 1958	15	20
Shannon, Del, The Best of Del Shannon, Dot, DLP-25824, 1967	20	30
Sharp, Dee Dee, It's Mash Potato Time, Cameo, D-1018, 1962	25	40
Shirelles, Golden Oldies, Scepter, SPS-516, 1964	25	40
Shore, Dinah, Dinah Down Home, Capitol, ST-1655, 1962	12	18
Sinatra, Frank, Come Dance With Me, Cpitol, SW-1069, 1959	10	15
Sinatra, Frank, Days of Wine and Roses, Reprise, FS-1011, 1964	10	15
Sinatra, Frank, High Society, Capitol, SW-750, 1958	12	18
Snow, Hank, Railroad Man, RCA Victor, LPM-2705, 1963	18	22
Sonny and Cher, Look at Us, Atco, 33-177, 1965	12	15
Sons of the Pioneers, Favorite Cowboy Songs, RCA Victor, LPM-1130, 1955	30	45
Starr, Kay, The Hits of Kay Starr, Capitol, T-415, 1950s	14	18
Statler Brothers, Flowers on the Wall, Columbia, CL-2449, 1966	10	15
Stevens, Cat, Catch Bull at Four, A & M, QU-54365, 1974	10	16
Stone Poneys, The Stone Poneys, Capitol, ST-2666, 1967	20	30
Supremes, Supremes A'Go-Go, Motown, M-649, 1966	18	24
Taylor, James, James Taylor, Apple, SKAO-3352, 1969	18	25
Temptations, Meet the Temptations, Gordy, GS-911, 1964	20	30
The Band, Music From Big Pink, Capitol, SKAO-2995, 1968	10	15
The Band, Stagefright, Capitol, SW-425, 1972	3	5
Tubb, Ernest, Ernest Tubb Favorites, Decca, DL-8291, 1956	35	65
Turtles, Happy Together, White Whale, WWS-7114, 1967	10	25
Twitty, Conway, Lonely Blue Boy, MGM, SE-3818, 1960	50	90
Valens, Ritchie, The Original Ritchie Valens, Guest Star, GS-1469, 1963	20	30
Vanilla Fudge, Vanilla Fudge, Atco, 33-224, 1967	8	12
Vee, Bobby, Bobby Vee, Liberty, LST-7181, 1961	25	38
Ventures, Walk—Don't Run, Dolton, BST-8003, 1963	18	24
Wagoner, Porter, The Bluegrass Story, RCA Victor, LPM-2960, 1964	12	18
Washington, Dinah, In the Land of Hi Fi, EmArcy, MG-36073, 1956	20	34
Watson, Doc, Doc Watson, Vanguard, VSD-79152, 1964	10	15
Weavers, The Best of the Weavers, Decca, DL-8893, 1959	20	35
Wells, Kitty, Kitty's Choice, Decca, DL-78979, 1960s	18	24
Williams, Andy, Under Paris Skies, Cadence, CLP-3047, 1961	8	12
Wonder, Stevie, Down to Earth, Tamla, TS-272, 1966	15	25
Wonder, Stevie, Stevie at the Beach, Tamla, T-255, 1964	35	45
Young, Neil, On the Beach, Reprise, MS-2180, 1974	2	4

Records, 45s

	LOW	HIGH
Abba, Atlantic, 3372, Dancing Queen, 1976	$2	$3
AC-DC, Atlantic, 3761, You Shook Me All Night Long, 1980	2	3
Archies, Calendar 1008, Sugar Sugar, 1969	8	12
Association, Warner Bros. 7195, Time For Livin', 1968	4	6
Baez, Joan, Vanguard 35138, The Night They Drove Old Dixie Down, 1971	3	5
Band, Capitol 2635, Up On Cripple Creek, 1969	5	7
Beach Boys, Capitol 6094, Surfin' U.S.A., 1966	15	23
Bee Gees, Atco 6639, I Started a Joke, 1968	5	7
Blondie, Chrysalis 2295, Heart of Glass, 1979	2	3
Blood, Sweat and Tears, Columbia 44776, You've Made Me So Very Happy, 1969	4	6
Booker T and MG's, Stax 0037, Mrs. Robinson, 1969	6	9
Bowie, David, RCA Victor PB-10320, Fame, 1975	4	6
Box Tops, Mala 593, Crys Like a Baby, 1968	6	9
Campbell, Glen, Capitol 4095, Rhinestone Cowboy, 1975	2	3
Cash, Johnny, Columbia 44944, A Boy Named Sue, 1969	6	9
Cher, Kapp 2146, Gypsies, Tramps and Thieves, 1971	2	3
Clapton, Eric, RSO 1039, Tulsa Time, 1980	2	3
Clark, Petula, Warner Bros. 7216, Don't Give Up, 1968	6	9
Cocker, Joe, A & M 1174 PS, The Letter, 1970	2	3
Collins, Judy, Elektra 45680, Turn! Turn! Turn!, 1969	5	7
Cooper, Alice, Warner Bros. 8349, You and Me, 1977	2	3
Cream, Atco 6455, Sunshine of Your Love, 1967	5	7
Creedence Clearwater Revival, Fantasy 622, Bad Moon Rising, 1969	4	6
Crosby, Stills, Nash and Young, Atlantic 2740, Ohio, 1970	2	3
Deep Purple, Tetragrammation 1514, River Deep-Mountain High, 1969	6	9
Diamond, Neil, Uni 55264, He Ain't Heavy, He's My Brother, 1970	4	6
Donovan, Hickory 1309, Catch the Wind, 1965	8	12
Doors, Elektra 45635, Hello, I Love You, 1968	8	12
Dovells, Parkway 845 PS, Hully Gully Baby, 1962	19	29
Dramatics, Volt 4058, Whatcha See Is Whatcha Get, 1971	5	7
Dylan, Bob, Columbia 45913, Knockin' on Heaven's Door, 1973	4	6
Earth, Wind and Fire, Columbia 10090, Shining Star, 1975	2	3
Facenda, Atlantic 2057, Little Baby, 1959	19	29
Fifth Dimension, Soul City 772, Aquarius—Let the Sunshine In, 1969	5	7
Franklin, Aretha, Atlantic 2751, Don't Play That Song, 1970	4	6
Gaye, Marvin, Tamia 54176, I Heard It Through the Grapevine, 1968	6	9
Genesis, Atlantic 3751, Turn It On Again, 1980	8	12
Golden Earring, Track 40202, Radar Love, 1974	4	6
Goldsboro, Bobby, United Artists 50525, I'm a Drifter, 1969	5	7
Grand Funk Railroad, Capitol 4002 PS, Some Kind of Wonderful, 1974	4	6
Grass Roots, Dunhill 4237, Baby Hold On, 1970	6	9
Greenbaum, Norman, Reprise 0885, Spirit in the Sky, 1970	5	7
Guess Who, RCA Victor 74-0325, American Woman, 1970	4	6
Harrison, George, Apple 1862, Give Me Love, 1973	6	9
Heart, Portrait 70004, Barracuda, 1977	2	3
Herman's Hermits, MGM 13885, I Can Take or Leave Your Loving, 1968	5	7
Hollies, Epic 10871, Long Cool Woman (in a Black Dress), 1972	3	5
Holly, Buddy, MCA 60004, Peggy Sue, 1973	8	12
Jackson 5, Motown 1186, Maybe Tomorrow, 1971	5	7
Jackson, Michael, Motown 1207, Ben, 1972	4	6
James, Tommy and The Shondells, Roulette 7008, Mony Mony, 1968	8	12
Jay and The Americans, United Artists 50475, This Magic Moment, 1968	8	12

Left to right: David Cassidy, Bell 45–150, Cherish, *1971, $4–$6; Tom Jones, Parrot 9765,* What's New Pussycat?, *1965, $6–$8.*

	LOW	HIGH
John, Elton, MCA 40364 PS, Philadelphia Freedom, 1975	4	6
Jones, Tom, Parrot 40018, I'll Never Fall in Love Again, 1967	5	7
King, B.B., Blues Way 61032, The Thrill Is Gone, 1969	6	9
Kinks, Reprise 0930, Lola, 1970	6	9
Kiss, Casablanca NB 873, Hard Luck Woman, 1976	46	
Knight, Gladys, and The Pips, Buddah 393, I've Got to Use My Imagination, 1973	2	3
LaBelle, Patti, Epic 50048, Lady Marmalade, 1975	2	3
Lennon, John and Yoko Ono, Apple 1830, Power to the People, 1971	8	12
Lennon, John, Apple 1868 PS, Mind Games, 1973	8	12
Lennon Pipers, Buddah 23, Green Tambourine, 1967	8	12
Lightfoot, Gordon, Reprise 0974, If You Could Read My Mind, 1970	2	3
Lindsay, Mark, Columbia 45180, Silver Bird, 1970	4	6
Lopez, Trini, Reprise 0700, If I Had a Hammer, 1968	5	7
Lovin' Spoonful, Kama Sutra 211 PS, Summer in the City, 1966	15	23
Mamas and The Papas, Dunhill 4107, Glad to Be Unhappy, 1967	5	7
McCartney, Paul, Apple 1875, Junior's Farm, 1974	5	7
Monkees, Colgems 1019, Valleri, 1968	8	12
Moody Blues, Threshold 67004, Question, 1970	3	5
Morrison, Van, Warner Bros. 7462, Blue Money, 1971	3	5
Mountain, Windfall 532, Mississippi Queen, 1970	3	5
Nash, Johnny, Epic 10902, I Can See Clearly Now, 1972	3	5
Nashville Teens, London 9689, Tobacco Road, 1964	11	17
Nelson, Rick, Decca 32980, Garden Party, 1972	2	3
Nitty Gritty Dirt Band, United Artists XW 544-X, Battle of New Orleans, 1974	3	5
O'Kaysions, North State 1001, Girl Watcher, 1968	45	55
Osmond, Marie, MGM K-14609, Paper Roses, 1973	5	7
Ozark Mountain Daredevil, A & M 1888, You Know Like I Know, 1976	4	6
Page, Patti, Mercury 72013, The Boys' Night Out, 1962	8	10
Palmer, Robert, Island 7-99570, Addicted to Love, 1986	3	5
Pink Floyd, Columbia 1-11187, Another Brick in the Wall (Part II), 1979	6	8
Platters, Mercury 71847, I'll Never Smile Again, 1961	12	15
Rydell, Bobby, Capitol 5305, I Just Can't Say Goodbye, 1964	10	12
Simon, Paul, Warner Bros. 28667-7, You Can Call Me Al, 1986	2	4
Taylor, Livingston, Critique 7-99255, City Lights, 1988	4	6
Village People, Casablanca NB 973, In the Navy, 1979	8	10
Vinton, Bobby, Epic 5-9382, Roses Are Red, 1962	10	12
Who, The, MCA 40475, Squeeze Box, 1975	24	30

Sheet Music

Sheet music is a musical composition. It was the first way of mass merchandising popular music. Tin Pan Alley originated off-Broadway on 28th Street in New York City. It was the center of American popular music in the late nineteenth and early twentieth centuries. Publishers sought recognition for their songs. They backed shows and employed song pluggers to popularize their music. Waiters often supplemented their wages by belting out tunes.

Condition, rarity and image establish the value of sheet music. Some collectors want the music, but many others are more interested in the graphics. Sheet music represents a great area for cross-over collecting. It includes themes such as movies, WWI and WWII, Disney, character and illustration art. Winslow Homer and Norman Rockwell ("Over There") are a couple of artists that drew covers. Since sheet music was mass produced, most often in huge quantities, it is still relatively inexpensive. It can, however, be fragile, and mint examples are harder to find. Specimens are not always in top condition due to music store stamps, tape marks, staples, binder holes, and ownership signatures. Worn, incomplete copies sell for considerably less than those in mint condition described below. Garage sales are a good source for sheet music, but be prepared to sort through stacks of material. Dealers that frame sheet music realize that they have a decorative item and reflect that in the price. Sheet music is best stored in unsealed plastic containers designed for paper conservation. If framing, use acid-free backing and make sure the process is reversible, i.e., don't use methods which can damage the sheet music.

Names following the titles listed below are descriptions of the cover; a celebrity's name denotes a photo of that person.

	LOW	HIGH
A Man Doesn't Know, Damn Yankees, 1955	$3	$6
Alright Okay You Win, 1959	2	3
And There You Are, 1945, Ginger Rogers, Lana Turner, Pidgeon, Johnson, Cugat	5	8
Are You Sorry, 1925, Cliff Edwards	3	5
As We Follow the Sun, 1976, York, Agutter, Fawcett-Majors	5	8
Be Still My Heart, 1934	2	4
Brother Can You Spare a Dime, 1932	4	6
Busy Doin' Nothing, 1948, Bing Crosby, Rhonda Fleming	8	12

Left to right: All the Way, *1957, Frank Sinatra, Mitzi Gaynor, Jeanne Crain, $5–$8;* From Here To Eternity, *1953, Lancaster, Clift, Kerr, Reed, Sinatra, $10–$12.*

	LOW	HIGH
California Moon, 1951, Mitzi Gaynor, Dale Robertson, Dennis Day	5	8
Call of Love, 1934, Ramon Nevarro, Lupe Velez	7	12
Call of the Range, 1943, Johnny Mack Brown, Nell O'Day, Fuzzy Knight	10	15
Can't You Do a Friend a Favor, A Connecticut Yankee, 1944	8	12
Captain Swagger, 1928	8	12
Celeste's Theme, 1991, Kevin Kline, Whoopi Goldberg, Sally Field, Morton Downey, Jr.	3	6
Champagne Charlie, 1960	2	5
Chantilly Lace, 1958	4	8
Chim Chimenea, 1963, Dick VanDyke	5	10
Cinnamon Cinder, 1963	5	8
Cocoanut Grove, 1965	2	4
College Rhythm, 1934, Joe Penner, Lanny Ross, Helen Mack, Jack Oakie	8	12
Come On Over Here, The Doll Girl, 1913	6	10
Come Saturday Morning, 1969, Liza Minelli	2	4
Come Summer, Come On Strong, 1962	4	8
Come Where My Love Lies Dreaming	2	5
Continental Polka, 1945, Van Johnson, Esther Williams, Lucille Ball	9	12
Count Your Blessings, 1933	7	10
Cow Bell Song, 1947	4	6
Dames At Sea, 1969	3	6
Dance of the Nightingales, 1908	6	10
Dancing the Blues Away, Dancing Around, 1914, Jolson	6	10
Diga Diga Doo, 1928, Leena Horne, Bill Robinson, Cab Calloway	8	12
Do You Know What It Means to Miss New Orleans, 1946	2	4
Don't Sleep in the Subway, 1967	1	3
Down By the Station, 1948	2	5
Dreamsville, Peter Gunn, 1960	3	6
Ebb Tide, 1953	1	3
El Capitan March, 1896	6	10
Emerald Song, Magdalena, 1948	4	8
For the Good Times, 1968	1	3

Left to right: If It Wasn't For Mother's Love, *$6–$10;* Never Can Say Goodbye, *The Jackson 5, $2–$4.*

	LOW	HIGH
Forty Hour Week For a Livin', 1985	1	3
Frankie and Johnny, 1923, Mae West	50	85
Gentle On My Mind, 1967, Glen Campbell	1	3
Good Man Is Hard to Find, A, 1917	1	3
Hittin' the Ceiling, 1929	9	12
Have You Changed, 1941	2	5
Heart and Soul, 1938	1	3
Hi Lili Hi Lo, 1932, Claudia	2	5
Historia De Amor, 1970, Ryan O'Neal, Ali McGraw	2	5
Hold On Partner, 1991	3	5
House of the Rising Sun, 1975	4	6
How Far Away Is Far Away, Come Summer, 1969	8	12
How Long Has This Been Going On, 1927	3	5
I Can't Cry Anymore, 1952, Don Corness	2	4
I Could Make You Care, 1940, Wayne Morris, Rosemary Lane	12	18
I Found a Dream, 1935, John Boles, Dixie Lee	8	12
I Love You, Michael Todd's Mexican Hayride, 1943	1	3
I See the Moon, 1953, The Mariners	2	4
I Won't Take Less Than Your Love, 1988	2	4
I'll Be Seein' You In Dallas Alice, 1939	3	6
I'll Walk Alone, 1944, Dinah Shore	2	4
I'm Coming Back, 1947	3	5
I'm Head and Heels In Love With You, 1907	1	3
If I Had a Hammer, 1962	1	3
If You Can Dream, 1955, Cyd Charisse	8	12
Imperial March Darth Vader's Theme, 1980	4	6
Indiscretion, 1954, Jennifer Jones, Montgomery Clift	5	8
Is My Baby Blue Tonight, 1953, Dick Haymes	2	4
It Makes No Difference, 1967, Vic Damone	2	4
Jean, 1969, Oliver	2	4
Just For Fun, 1949, John Lund, Diana Lynn, Martin and Lewis	7	10
Keep That Twinkle In Your Eye, 1936, Jane Withers	15	20

Left to right: On the Atchison, Topeka and the Santa Fe, *1934, Judy Garland, $12–$18;* Picnic, *William Holden, Kim Novak, $8–$10.*

	LOW	HIGH
Lady In Red, 1935, Dolores Del Rio	5	8
Let the Worry Bird Worry For You, 1951	4	7
Let's Have Another, 1936, Mae Clark, John Payne	8	12
Little Bird, Little Bird, Man of La Mancha, 1968	4	8
Lonely Acres In the West, 1926	3	7
Love On a Greyhound Bus, 1945, Van Jonnson, Pat Kirkwood, Cugat, Lombardo	5	8
Love Theme, Flashdance, 1983, Jennifer Beals	4	7
Loveliest Night of the Year, 1951	2	4
Lovely to Look At, 1935, Astaire, Rogers, Dunne	3	6
Lover Come Back to Me, 1928, Jose Ferrer, Helen Traubel	5	8
Lucky In Love, 1927, June Allyson, Peter Lawford	3	5
Macho Man, 1978, The Village People	4	7
Magic Moon in Rio, 1943, Enric Madriguera	3	6
Mame, Mame, 1966, Gaylea Byrne	5	8
Marriage Type Love, Me and Juliet, 1953	5	8
Meet Me Tonight In Dreamland, 1936, Judy Garland, Van Johnson	15	20
Miranda, Bravo Giovanni, 1962	8	12
Motorcycle Mama, 1972, Sailcat	2	4
Mr. Clown, Maggie Flynn, 1969	7	10
My Melody of Love, 1974, Bobby Vinton	2	4
My Own True Love, 1948, Phyllis Calvert, Melvin Douglas	6	10
Never Again, The Amazing Adele, 1955	18	25
On My Way, 1964	7	10
One Boy, Bye Bye Birdie, 1960	2	5
Only a Back Street Girl, 1932, Irene Dunne	8	12
Our Love Affair, 1940, Judy Garland, Mickey Rooney	10	15
Page Miss Glory, 1935, Marion Davies	6	10
Paradise, 1931	1	3
Piano Selection, Carousel, 1945	4	7
Poor Jud, 1943, Shirley Jones, Gordon MacRae	3	6
Poor Little Hollywood Star, Little Me, 1962	10	15
Poppy of Sacrifice, 1951	8	12

Left to right: Ring Out, Wild Bells, *1912, $20–$25;* Sh-Boom (Life Could Be a Dream), *The Crew-Cuts, $4–$8.*

	LOW	HIGH
Pretty Girl Is Like a Melody, A, 1919	5	8
Proud Mary, 1968, Credence Clearwater Revival	2	4
Rhythm of Life, 1969	5	8
Rhythm On the River, 1940, Bing Crosby, Mary Martin	16	20
Rififi, 1955	6	10
Right Under My Nose, 1949, Ginger Prince	6	10
Rose of Washington Square, 1946	3	5
Ruby Don't Take Your Love to Town, 1977	2	5
Samba De Orfeu, 1959	6	10
She's My Love, Carnival, 1961	3	5
Shenanigans, 1937	12	15
So o o o o In Love, 1945, Danny Kaye, Virginia Mayo	8	12
Song of Surrender, 1949, Macdonald Carey, Wanda Hendrix	1	3
Song of the Islands, 1944, Betty Grable	7	10
Spinning Wheel, 1968, Blood, Sweat and Tears	2	5
Survive Theme, 1976	4	8
Swedish Rhapsody Love Theme, 1948, Lana Turner, Kier Dullea, Burgess Meredith	10	15
Thanks To You, 1952, Betty Hutton, Ralph Meeker	6	10
They Were You, The Fantasticks, 1960	8	12
Third Man Theme, 1950	4	8
Thorn Birds Theme, 1983, Chamberlain	3	5
Time Is Tight, 1969, Raymond St. Jacques	5	8
To Know You Is to Love You, 1928, Willie Lightner, Joe E. Brown	6	10
Touch a Hand Make a Friend, 1974, Staple Singers	2	4
Twelfth Regiment, 1908	8	12
View to a Kill, 1985, Roger Moore, Grace Jones	4	8
What's the Use, Candide, 1957	4	8
Where Have You Been All My Life, 1934, Mae Clark, John Payne	10	15
Where There's a Will There's a Way, 1921	3	5
While There's a Song to Sing, Music In My Heart, 1947	7	12
Wyoming In the Spring, 1939	6	10
You Are So Beautiful, 1974	2	4

Left to right: Turn Me Loose, *Fabian, $5–$8;* Written On the Wind, *1956, Rock Hudson and Lauren Bacall, Four Aces inset, $4–$8.*

Native American Collectibles

American Indian artifacts range from jewelry and woven products to weapons.

Collected items date from prehistoric to contemporary times. Quality of workmanship is key to value.

Artifacts may originate throughout the United States, but most items come from the Plains and the Southwest. Likewise, the majority of dealers will be found in the Southwest, particularly in the area of Santa Fe, New Mexico.

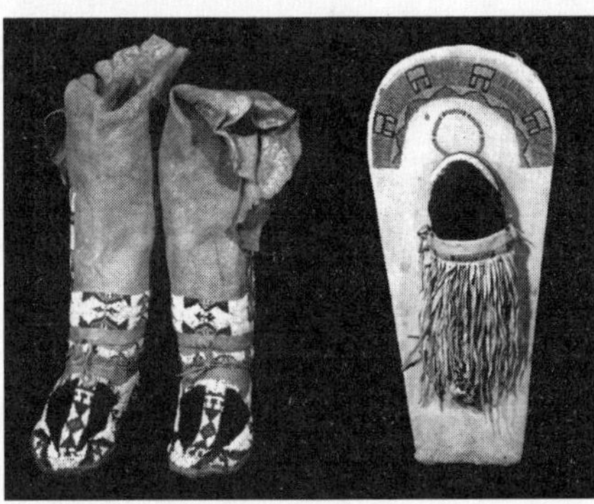

Left: Arapaho Beaded Hightop Moccasins, c1890, pair, $2310 at auction.

Right: Ute Beaded Toy Cradleboard, c1875, 19" l, $1320 at auction.

—Photos courtesy W.E. Channing & Co.

	AUCTION	RETAIL Low	RETAIL High
Alder Feast Ladle, c1920	$25	$50	$80
Athabaskan Bead and Sinew Game Bag, c1890, 13.5"	550	1000	1800
Athabaskan Sheep Horn Ladle	550	1000	1800
Beaded Blue and Yellow Pouch, c1910, 5.5"	350	650	1100
Beaded Jacket, w/ lupins	130	240	420
Beaded Moccasins, c1925	60	110	200
Beaded Snake Necklace, 16"	55	100	180
Beadwork Jacket, w/ animal design	100	190	330
Bella Bella Wood Figure, 12"	120	220	400
Bella Coola Hand-Hammered Copper Frontlet	210	390	680
Black Chevron Trade Bead Necklace	150	280	500
Blue Chevron Trade Bead Necklace	65	120	210
Button Blanket, bear design, 65"	300	560	980
Button Blanket, by Lisa Hanuse, 74" x 48"	650	1200	2200
Casa Grande Pottery, by Lidia Quezada, 13"	20	40	70
Casa Grande Pottery, from the Quick Collection	100	190	330
Casa Grande Pueblo Bird Effigy Bowl, polychrome, 9"	95	180	300
Cedar Box, w/ rounded lid, painted West Coast design, c1950	55	100	180
Cedar Indian Face, carved by Howard Williams	25	50	80
Cedar Rattle, w/ cedar bark, c1900, 12"	200	370	650
Cherokee Horsehair Hat Band	55	100	180
Chilcotin Coiled Tray, w/ swastika design, 9.25"	300	560	1000
Chilcotin Coiled Tray, 18.75"	310	580	1000
Cowichan Indian Sweater	10	20	30
Cree Beaded Gauntlets, c1915	140	260	460
Cree Embroidered Doeskin Pouch, c1920	145	270	470
Cree Embroidered Vest	75	140	240

Left: Tlinget Rattle-Top Basket, $2750 at auction.

Center: Northwest Indian Figural Carved Knife, $6435 at auction.

Right: Northwest Indian Open-Top Basket, $1100 at auction.

—Photo courtesy James D. Julia.

	AUCTION	RETAIL	
		Low	High
Crow Parfleche Container, 23.5"	600	1120	2000
Crow Quirt, c1890	1700	3000	5500
Dance Apron, w/ coppers, 28"	475	880	1550
Deerskin Fringed Cushion, w/ beads and embroidered silk	32	60	110
Dentalium Shell and Trade Bead Necklace	140	260	460
Dovetail Blade, Ohio, 3.25"	70	130	230
Drum, by Randy Bell, 20"	425	790	1500
Eagle and Bear Totem Pole, carved, 13"	55	100	180
Eastern Athabaskan Moccasins, 19th C	60	110	200
Eastern Canada Beaded Purse, on green velvet, c1880	100	190	330
Frontlet Headress, copper, 10"	250	470	820
Haida Carved Horn Ladle, 19th C	875	1600	2750
Haida Model Canoe, c1900, 9.5"	110	200	360
Hopi Child's Flat Kachina Doll, w/ dance wand	85	160	280
Hopi Kachina Doll, 9.5"	275	510	900
Hopi Longhair Kachina Doll, by Sam Leslie	25	50	80
Hopi Maiden Kachina Doll, c1970, 2nd Mesa	75	140	240
Hopi Wicker Plaque, Turtle Clan design, 3rd Mesa, 12"	80	150	260
Hudson Bay Coat, white w/ stripe, c1930	55	100	180
Hudson Bay Coat, red, c1930	75	140	240
Inuit Carved Wooden Dog Sledding Scene, 24"	80	150	260
Inuit Dance Figure, w/ drums, 5"	200	370	650
Inuit Soapstone Seal	35	70	110
Kispiox Totem Pole, 21.5"	95	180	310
Kwakiutl Killer Whale Rattle, carved and painted, c1940, 11"	370	700	1250
Kwakiutl Seal Bowl, carved and painted, 35"	500	930	1600
Kwakiutl Totem Pole, carved bone, c1930	130	240	420
Kwakiutl Yellow Cedar Ladle, c1880, 9.5"	75	140	240
Lapland Boot Cushion, 19th C	15	30	50
Lillooet Tray, diamond design, 14.5"	165	300	540
Moon Mask, carved and painted by Jay Brabant, 19"	675	1260	2200
Mountain Goat Horn Ladle	60	110	200
Native Feather Headdress	85	160	280
Navajo Blanket, c1960s, 86" x 46"	650	1200	2250
Navajo Rug, Gray Hills, 45" x 27"	320	600	1000
Nootka Carved and Painted Bird Rattle, 13.5"	225	420	730
Nootka Double Woven Cedar Painted Hat, 19th C, 16"	3000	5500	9000
Nootka Model Canoe, c1900, 12"	110	200	360
Nootka Sea Serpent Design Model Canoe, w/ 2 paddles, 14.75"	300	560	1000
Northeast Adze, L.M. Crosbie Collection	210	390	680
Norval Morresseau Drawing of Loon Family, 8.5" x 13"	120	220	400

	AUCTION	RETAIL Low	RETAIL High
Owl Mask, carved and painted by Jay Brabant, 12"	550	100	1790
Pipe Tomahawk, 20"	80	150	260
Plains Beaded Dance Necklace, c1910, 54"	300	560	1000
Plains Beaded Jacket	200	370	650
"Poochie" Beaded Ceremonial Moosehide Dog Coat, c1940	95	180	300
Salish Carved Cedar Figure, 12"	45	80	150
Salish Coiled Tray, w/ handles, 15.5"	230	430	750
Salish Chest, cov., 17"	300	560	1000
Salish Picture Frame, 14"	130	240	420
Salish Round Tray, dated May 1, 1920	120	220	400
Salish Suitcase, 14"	200	370	650
Seal Skin Moccasins, pair	45	80	150
Silver and Turquoise Navajo Bear Paw Buckle	150	280	490
Silver Bracelet, w/ killer whale design	185	340	600
Sioux Club, c1930, 25"	130	240	420
Sioux Moccasins, c1920, pair	450	840	1470
Spindle Whorl, carved by Charles Elliott, 9"	130	240	420
Thunderbird Rattle, rawhide	65	120	200
Thunderbird Totem Pole, carved, 17"	50	90	160
Totem Pole, 3 figure, c1950, 59"	950	1750	3000
Totem Pole, carved and painted, 19.5"	40	70	130
Totem Pole, carved by Ida Jack of Port Renfrew, 25"	150	280	500
Totem Pole, sgd. "R.G.," 13"	25	50	80
Trade Bead Necklace	75	140	240
Trade Bracelet, copper, Kingcome Inlet	75	140	240
Turquoise Necklace	75	140	240
Turtle Back Adze, Jersey Co., IL	50	90	160
Turtle Rattle, rawhide	80	150	260
Uvalde Blade	50	90	160
West Coast Mountain Goat Horn Ladle, w/ abalone inlay, 6.5"	55	100	180
Wooden Inuit Spoon, c1850, 12.5"	260	480	850
Woodlands Beaded Bag	100	190	330

Southwestern Hopi Kachina Dolls. —Photo courtesy Skinner, Inc., Boston, MA.

Nautical Memorabilia

Items from the eighteenth and nineteenth centuries, the Age of Sail, are highly prized. Fine specimens command high prices. Finds can still be made in small New England auctions and estate sales.

Mast Head Lantern, "Shubert & Cottingham Philadelphia" label, Coin Dot pattern cranberry glass shade, $4600 at auction. —Photo courtesy James D. Julia.

	AUCTION	RETAIL Low	RETAIL High
Brass Bell, from steamship *Massachusetts,* 1907, 17" h	$2000	$3750	$6500
Campaign Chest, English, mahogany, brass-bound, top drawer fitted as desk, 38" w case	1700	3000	5500
Colonial Yacht Club Davidson Trophy For Runabouts, sterling w/ enamel pennant, Old Newbury Crafters, 84 oz., 13" h	1500	3000	5000
Dry Compass by Robert Merrill, NY, 11" dia	350	650	1150
Eskimo Engraved Pipe, stem bowed and depicting various ships and wagon, 10" l	1300	2500	4500
Folk Art Carving of American Clipper Ship Game Cock, 22.5" l	750	1400	2500
Marine Compass by Thaxter, Boston, mustard painted drum, 7" dia	450	850	1450
Nantucket Pocketbook by Jose Formoso Reyes, oval w/ ivory clasp and twin gull ivory ornaments carved by Aletha L. Tacy on lid, 11" l	3500	6500	11,000
Navigational Octant, by Ripley and Son, London, wooden case w/ painted inscription "Samuel Woodburry, 1826," 17" h case	1200	2230	4000
Pocket Compass by Le Maire Fils, Paris, French silver, octagonal form, obverse engraved w/ dial rings, 3" l	1400	2600	4500
Sea Chest, blue and red painted, w/ rope handles and ship portrait on lid interior, 39" l	2250	4000	7500
Shadowbox of American Bark by Wm. F. Gill, w/ cloth sails, 23" x 38" frame	1500	3000	5000
Shadowbox Diorama of American Ship, 17.25" x 26.25"	400	740	1300
Shadowbox Diorama of Gloucester Fishing Vessel, 19.25" x 20.25"	550	1000	1800
Shadowbox Diorama of Ship *Avon,* 18.25" x 34.25"	800	1500	2500
Ship Captain's Wheel, mahogany and brass, 8 spokes, 36" dia	450	850	1450
Swift, whalebone, finely carved, mounted on inlaid ivory and exotic wood table grip, 19" h	3400	6500	11,000
Telescope, engraved w/ manufacturer's name "Dolland, London," 52" l	1000	2000	3500
Tiller, mahogany, w/ dolphin and rope carving, 46" l	1300	2500	4500
Walking Stick, oriental hardwood w/ octagonal carved whale's tooth knopped handle, 34" l	150	300	500

Orientalia

Chinese Export Porcelain

The word "china," as in "fine china," derives from the time when all porcelain came from China. Before Europeans learned the secrets of kaolin clay and the firing process, kings and princes spent fortunes (literally) on their porcelain collections. Even after Western entrepreneurs cracked these secrets, merchants imported shiploads of Chinese porcelain for an ever-growing number of dinner services. The Chinese fed this demand with pieces designed for the West. Chinese Export Porcelain (CEP) developed more or less standard designs that crossed the oceans throughout the nineteenth century. Canton, Nanking and Fitzhugh are the well-known blue and white designs, while polychrome favorites are Rose Mandarin and Rose Medallion.

Pieces marked "Made in China" date after 1894. Some unscrupulous dealers have ground out this mark. Look for suspicious grinding marks or related flaws on the undersides of pieces. For further information see *Chinese Export Porcelain: Standard Patterns and Forms, 1780–1880* by Herbert, Peter and Nancy Schiffer, Schiffer Publishing, Exton, PA, 1975.

Armorial Pieces

	AUCTION	RETAIL	
		Low	High
Deep Plate, reticulated, crested, 11" dia	$900	$1700	$3000
Deep Plates, 9.25" dia, pair	2000	3200	5000
Hot Water Plate, Arms of Snodgrass, 11" l	425	800	1400
Mug, coat-of-arms and spearhead border, 7" h	3250	6000	10,000
Plate, Burrell impaling Raymond, 9" dia	320	600	1000
Plate, coat-of-arms, 10" dia	850	1500	2500
Plate, elaborate arms, 9" dia	2750	4400	6900
Plate, octagonal, elaborate arms, 8.75" w	1600	2600	4000
Plates, Arms of Parker, 8.5" dia, pair	700	1300	2300
Platter, green and gilt floral and bird dec., 17.5" l	1750	2800	4400
Platters, green and gilt floral and bird dec., 14.5" l, pair	4600	7400	11,500
Soup Plate, elaborate arms, 9" dia	1000	1600	2500

Chinese Export Armorial Plates amd Soup Plate. —Photo courtesy Sotheby's.

	AUCTION	RETAIL Low	RETAIL High
Soup Tureen w/ Underplate, strap handle, green and gilt floral and bird dec., 13.5" l	10,000	16,000	25,000
Teapot, crested, 9" h	1400	2600	4600
Vegetable Dishes, green and gilt floral and bird dec., 9.5" l, pair	2000	3200	5000
Vegetable Dishes, cov., strap handles, crested, pair w/ liners and undertray	12,000	22,000	40,000

Canton

	AUCTION	RETAIL Low	RETAIL High
Bowl, 8.5" sq	$850	$1400	$2300
Bowl, scalloped edge, 10" dia.	350	600	900
Bowl and Tray, oval, reticulated, 11" l	700	1160	1860
Candlesticks, 11" h, pair	5250	8400	13,000
Cider Pitcher, 9" h	850	1300	2000
Creamer, baluster form, 5.5" h	900	1350	2500
Creamer, helmet form, 4.5" h	500	830	1330
Deep Dish, circ., scalloped edge, 9.5" dia	450	740	1190
Deep Dish, oblong, 11" l	250	410	660
Dinner Plate, 9" dia	100	170	270
Dish, scalloped edge, 10" l	550	910	1460
Egg Cup, ftd.	75	120	200
Fruit Bowl, oval, reticulated, 11" l	500	800	1300
Ginger Jar, cov., 10" h	150	250	400
Hot Water Plate, 9" dia	200	330	530
Leaf Dish, 8" l	150	250	400
Milk Pitcher, 6.5" h	450	700	1100
Mug, strap handle, 4" h	400	660	1060
Platter, 13.5" dia	650	1100	1750
Platter, octagonal, 15" l	150	200	400
Salad Bowl, lobed, 10.5" dia	700	1160	1860
Sauce Boat, strap handle, 7" l	275	450	730
Shrimp Dish, 9" l	500	850	1400
Tureen Stand, 15" l	450	700	1100
Vegetable Dish, cov., 8" sq	250	410	660
Vegetable Dish, cov., rect., pod finial, 8" l	350	600	900
Vegetable Dishes, 8" l, pair	400	600	1000
Vegetable Dishes, oval, pod finials, graduated set of 4	1800	3000	4500

Canton Platter and Covered Urn. —Photo courtesy Sotheby's.

Orange Fitzhugh Platter, Plate, and Cups and Saucers. —Photo courtesy Sotheby's.

Fitzhugh

	AUCTION	RETAIL	
		Low	High
Comport, boat shaped w/ scroll handles and crest, 12.5" l	$3000	$4800	$7500
Dinner Plates, blue, 10" dia, set of 14	550	910	1460
Dinner Plates, orange, 10" dia, set of 6	1400	2310	3710
Luncheon Plates, orange, 8" dia, set of 16	3500	5780	9280
Mug, strap handle, 8" h	700	1100	1800
Plate, green w/ American eagle, 8" dia	500	800	1300
Platter, green w/ American eagle, 11.5" l	3100	5120	8220
Platter, orange, oval, 13.5" l	550	900	1400
Platter, oval, orange, 15" l	1750	2890	4640
Platter, orange, oval, 17" l	950	1500	2400
Platter, w/ mazzarin liner, 18.5" l	1700	2700	4300
Platters, oval, 13" l, pair	2900	4600	7300
Razor Box, 7" l	1000	1600	2500
Sauce Dish, green	80	130	210
Serving Dish, brown, 9.25" sq	6750	10,000	17,000
Soup Plates, blue, set of 19	600	990	1590
Soup Plates, orange, 10" dia, set of 6	1000	1600	2500
Soup Plates, orange, 10" dia, set of 11	2000	3300	5300
Soup Plates, orange, 10" dia, set of 13	3600	5940	9540
Soup Tureen, cov., blue, strap handles, pod finial	2100	3470	5570

Nanking

	AUCTION	Low	High
Bowl, fluted and ftd., 5" h, 10" dia	$2500	$4000	$6300
Cider Jug, 6.5" h	500	800	1300
Cider Jug, 8.5" h	1000	1900	3300
Coffeepot	2200	4100	7200
Creamer	150	300	500
Hot Water Plate	200	400	700
Platter, 18.5" l	800	1300	2000
Platter, oval, 18" l	500	800	1300
Platter, oval, 19" l	500	900	1600
Platter and Strainer, 15.5" l	1100	2400	4500
Platters, oval, 13" l, pair	800	1300	2000

	AUCTION	RETAIL	
		Low	High
Sauce Boats, strap handles, 7" l, pair	700	1200	2100
Serving Dishes, oval, pair	2000	3700	6500
Soup Tureen, cov., 14" l	1000	1800	3000
Tureen and Undertray, cov., strap handles, pod finial, 14" l	1100	1800	2800
Vases, baluster form, "chicken skin" finish, pair	900	1700	2900
Vases, ovoid, "chicken skin" finish, pair	900	1700	2900
Vegetable Dish, cov., oval, 11" l	350	700	1100
Water Bottle	550	1000	1800

Rose Mandarin

Charger, 14" dia	$650	$1000	$1750
Cider Jug, cov., 11" h	3000	4800	7500
Hot Water Plates, 10.5" l, pair	1900	3000	4800
Mug, underglazed blue dec., 5.5" h	650	1000	1750
Platter, bird dec., 19" l	2000	3300	5300
Punch Bowl, 12" dia	900	1500	2700
Punch Bowl, 15" dia	4750	7500	12,000
Soup Plates, 10" dia, pair	500	850	1400
Vase, court scene dec., 20" h	2400	4000	6500
Vase, cylindrical, 6" h	300	500	800
Vegetable Tureens, 10" l, pair	2800	4500	7000

Rose Medallion

Candlesticks, 6.5" h, pair	$500	$900	$1600
Candlesticks, 8" h, pair	1000	1600	2500
Charger, 15" dia	500	900	1500
Charger, 18.5" dia	2250	3600	5600
Chop Dish, oval, ftd., 16" l	800	1500	2600
Coffeepot, butterfly dec., 8" h	500	900	1800
Dish, 9" sq	350	700	1100
Garden Barrel, pierced, vignettes of figures, gilt, 19" h	2200	4000	7200
Garden Barrels, 18" h, pair	5200	9000	17,000
Garden Seat, hexagonal, 18" h	1750	2800	4400
Garden Seat, hexagonal, scenic vignettes and panels, gilt, 18" h	2300	4300	7500
Hot Water Plate, knobbed lid, 11" l	675	1300	2200
Milk Jug, octagonal, 6.5" h	475	900	1500
Punch Bowl, 14" dia	2200	3750	5000
Punch Bowl, 14.5" dia, 6.5" h	1200	2200	4000
Punch Bowl, 15.25" dia	1500	2400	3800
Punch Bowl, gold ground, 14" dia	1300	2100	3300
Razor Box, 8" l	550	1000	1800
Sauce Tureen, oval, ftd. base, 7.5" l	900	1400	2300
Sauce Tureen and Undertray, cov., 9" l	750	1300	2000
Soup Tureen, cov., strap handles, pod finial, 14" l	1400	2450	3850
Teapot, 7" h	500	900	1700
Temple Jar, cov., 18" h	1800	3300	5900
Tray, trefoil-shaped, 11" l	350	600	900
Vase, double gourd form, 10" h	250	500	900
Vase, animal-form handles, applied serpent dec., 17.5" h	700	1100	1800
Wash Basin, 16" dia	750	1200	1900

Left to right: Plate w/ Grisaille Border; Tobacco Leaf Platter. —Photos courtesy Sotheby's.

Miscellaneous

	AUCTION	RETAIL	
		Low	High
Deep Plate, Continental ship, 8" dia	$450	$800	$1500
Deep Plate, Grisaille scene of European children, 8" dia	175	300	600
Deep Saucer, Docai dec. w/ deer on terrace, reign mark, 6" dia	850	1600	3000
Dish, Tobacco Leaf variant, 9" dia	850	1600	2800
Garden Seats, octagonal, celadon ground, 19" h, pair	2000	3700	6500
Garniture Vase, cov., blue urn dec., 12" h	425	800	1400
Ice Pail and Undertray, sepia landscapes, 7.5" h	3100	5800	10,000
Mug, masonic dec., strap handle, 6" h	1600	2800	4400
Platter, octagonal, blue and white pagoda dec., 16" l	500	900	1600
Punch Bowl, Famille Rose, floral and picket fence dec., 10" dia	1800	2900	4500
Razor Box, orange, sacred bird and butterfly, 7" l	900	1700	2900
Rice Bowl, Famille Rose, 11" dia	550	900	1400
Sauce Tureen and Undertray, scenic medallion, 9" l	600	1100	2000
Shrimp Dish, Famille Rose, orange peel finish, 11" l	450	800	1500
Strainer, Imari-style dec., fitted bamboo-turned stand, 14" dia	650	1200	2100
Teapot, floral, domed lid, 7" h	1200	2100	3300
Trays, oval, reticulated, monogrammed, 8" l, pair	2100	3900	6800
Tureen and Undertray, cov., strap handles, pod finial	6750	12,500	22,000

Famille Rose Plates. —Photo courtesy Sotheby's.

Cinnabar

Cinnabar is Chinese carved lacquer. Layers are built up over wood, porcelain, or metal thick enough to carve ornate designs. The color is usually deep red. Although cinnabar has been made continuously for over three hundred years, the majority of the collected pieces currently available date from the turn of the century, as do all pieces listed below.

"Good" pieces may show some wear with some minor flecks of lacquer chipped away. "Best" pieces must be in perfect condition with no chipping or cracks.

Snuff Bottle, 2.75" h, $200–$400.

	GOOD	BETTER	BEST
Ashtray, 5" dia	$80	$170	$400
Bowl, landscape, black on red, 9" dia	170	250	500
Bowl, cov., pedestal foot, 6" dia	200	300	650
Bowl, cov., red flower design, black ground, 6" dia	170	300	700
Bowl, scalloped rim, red, 6.5" dia	170	270	600
Box, cov., floral design, black on red, 6" dia	230	400	800
Box, cov., floral design, red on green, 6.5" dia	460	700	1300
Box, cov., oblong, carved view, 6.5" w	230	350	750
Box, cov., sports scene, black on red, 15" dia	630	900	2300
Box, melon shape, 6.5" dia	170	350	800
Box, scenic views, 6.5" sq	200	350	750
Cigarette Box, 11.5" dia	250	400	860
Cup, dragon handles, 4.5" dia	250	400	900
Cup, floral design, flared rim, 4.5" dia	300	480	1100
Cup, footed, 5.5" dia.	200	300	700
Dish, floral design, 9.5" dia	300	500	1000
Ginger Jar, landscape scene, red on cream, 8.5" h	400	600	1300
Mirror, rust-colored landscape, 19.5" w	230	350	700
Plate, double dragon design, 12.75" dia	600	1000	2200
Plate, floral design, ftd. base, 8" dia	250	450	900
Plate, floral design, red on green, 13" dia	650	1100	2500
Plate, flower and butterfly design, 10.5" dia	380	550	1300
Plate, geometric design, red on black, 8" dia	170	300	580
Pot, Taoist markings, ftd., 7" dia	450	700	1400
Stool, Greek key border, floral medallion, 18" h	1840	2900	6600
Tray, flower and bird design, red, yellow, and green, 15" w	900	1400	3200
Tray, flower and bird design, reddish-brown, 15" w	980	1500	3500
Tray, flowering tree, 12.5" w	350	500	1200
Tray, gilded rim, 17" w	300	500	1000
Urn, red flower, black ground, 6.5" h	100	200	450
Vase, dragon design, green, yellow, and red, 15" h	1600	2760	6500
Vase, dragon design, red, 12" h	400	800	1750
Vase, fish design, 15" h	750	1800	4000
Vase, fish shape, red, 7.5" h	290	460	1100

Nippon Porcelain

Nippon porcelain resulted from the 1893 American tariff act requiring imports to be marked (in English) with the country of origin. "Nippon" was an accepted name for Japan at that time. Nippon ware also represents Satsuma, Noritake, Imari and other Japanese wares of that period.

The marks most frequently depict an "M" within a green wreath, and the word "Nippon" printed in curved letters underneath. There are many, many variations, however. By the late 1920s, "Japan" replaced "Nippon." Nippon ware has been faked and reproduced.

Ashtray, continuous scene w/ reclining dog, 5.75" dia, $75–$125.

	LOW	AVG.	HIGH
Bowl, blue, pink, and red floral medallions, white ground, handles, green M mark, 7" dia	$15	$20	$25
Bowl, enameled, raised chestnut motif, handles, green M mark, 8" dia	25	30	35
Bowl, bisque, walnut motif, green M mark, 9" dia	75	100	125
Bowl, mustard color, gold jewels, rose motif, blue M mark, 9" dia	60	70	80
Bowl, red and black scenic motif, unmkd., 9" dia	60	70	80
Bowl, square, green M mark, hand-painted Nippon mark, 6.5" w	40	50	60
Bowl, strawberries, leaves, and flowers, leaf-shaped handle	350	375	400
Box, blue, gold raised motif, green M mark, 2" h	100	120	140
Candy Bowl, floral design, beaded gold rim, blown-out sides, 2 gold handles, 6" sq	80	100	120
Candy Bowl, palm trees and sailboat, pastel colors, beaded gold rim, pierced handles	65	70	75
Candy Dish, oval, scenic motif, open-work handles, hand-painted M wreath, green mark, 7" x 5"	50	55	60
Celery Dish, floral dec. and small houseboat w/ sail, satin finish, 9" x 4"	35	40	45
Cocoa Set, consisting of cov. pot and 6 cups and saucers, rose sprays on turquoise ground	400	425	450
Comport, Chicago Post Office medallion, flowers, and insects, Oriental China Nippon mark	90	100	110
Cookie Server, floral motif, yellow ground, gold handle, M mark, 10" dia	25	35	45
Creamer, gold foliage motif, hand-painted Nippon mark	14	16	18
Creamer and Sugar, flowers and leaves, gold trim	55	65	75
Cruets, oriental garden motif, M mark, 6" h, pair	80	100	120
Cup, grapevine motif, gold, green M mark, 3" h	18	22	26
Cup and Saucer, multicolored Art Nouveau floral motif, green M mark	10	14	18
Demitasse Coffee Set, consisting of cov. pot and 5 cups and saucers, Art Deco black outline, Nippon mark	175	200	225
Demitasse Coffee Set, consisting of cov. pot and 5 cups and saucers, M mark, 9" h pot	175	200	225
Desk Set, scenic cameos, 5-pc set	325	375	425
Dish, yellow ground, tan floral motif, green stems, black ribbons, lined in gold, green M mark, 12" x 6"	14	18	20
Dish, cream ground, multicolor design, raised gold trim, M mark, 6" dia	18	22	26

	LOW	AVG.	HIGH
Dish, fish shape, mythological bird motif, bordered, unmkd., 7" l	80	90	100
Dish, gold ground, floral and foliage motif, M mark, 7" x 6"	35	40	45
Dish, cov., brown and tan panel, floral motif, gold handle, rising sun mark, 8" x 6"	65	70	75
Dish, handled, green M in wreath, hand-painted Nippon mark, 7.5" l	45	50	55
Dish, handled, red and green RC, hand-painted Nippon mark, 5.5" dia.	55	65	75
Dresser Set, consisting of 7" l tray, 3" h stoppered bottle, and 2 cov. patch boxes, white ground, gold trim	70	80	90
Egg Cup, white ground, blue and amber butterflies	30	35	40
Egg Warmer, green M in wreath, 5" dia	140	160	180
Ewer, bulbous body, band of violets, greens and purples, unmkd., 10" h	200	250	300
Ewer, bulbous body, floral design, red and violet, 1900s, 12" h	300	350	400
Fruit Bowl, geometric designs and flowers, scalloped gold rim, handles, blue leaf mark	100	120	140
Hat Pin Holder, floral design, dark blue ground, gold trim	55	65	75
Jar, multicolored floral design, gold-green M mark, 4" h	25	30	35
Napkin Ring, windmill scene, satin finish	80	100	120
Nappy, green M in wreath, hand-painted Nippon mark, 6" dia	40	45	50
Nut Bowl, green M in wreath, hand-painted Nippon mark, 6" dia	70	80	90
Nut Cup, blue maple leaf, Nippon mark, 3.5" w	25	30	35
Nut Set, consisting of 4 ftd. dishes, floral design, gold outline	45	50	55
Plate, multicolored floral design, green M mark, 10" dia	20	25	30
Plate, red floral design, raised gold, pierced handles, mkd.	75	90	100
Plate, Art Nouveau floral design, green M mark, 5" dia	10	15	20
Plate, oval floral medallions, gold outline, blue mark, 6" dia	50	60	70
Plate, child holding bouquet, blue M mark, 7" dia	15	20	225
Plate, children playing and elephant, hand-painted Nippon, 7" dia	25	30	35
Plate, enameled leaves, vines, and oval medallions w/ gold outline, green M mark, 8" dia	30	35	40
Platter, autumn scene of lake and path into forest, applied handles, 11" dia	80	100	120
Relish Dish, blue Komaru symbol, hand-painted Nippon mark, 8.25" l	45	50	55
Salt Dip, polychrome floral motif, gold outline, green M mark	15	20	25
Shakers, pink floral motif, gold handles, rising sun mark, 2" h, pair	25	30	35
Spoon Holder, floral motif, 2 handles, M mark	55	65	75
Vase, green M in wreath, hand-painted Nippon mark, 10.5" h	400	425	450
Vase, green M in wreath, hand-painted Nippon mark, 5" h	60	67	85
Vase, green M in wreath, hand-painted Nippon mark, 6" h	75	90	100

Left: Vase, lake scene, gold handles, green M in wreath mark, hand-painted Nippon mark, 8.75" h, $150–$250.

Right: Vase, tan ground, beaded llama and trim, green M in wreath mark, hand-painted Nippon mark, 4.5" h, $60–$85.

Rugs, Oriental

Oriental rugs older than 50 years have long been collected and used in fine homes throughout the United States. They originated in Persia (modern Iran), Turkey and the surrounding areas. The following representative examples show prices realized at auction (wholesale) and the corresponding retail range. "Karastan" rugs are machine made and not collected by anyone we know. All the rugs listed here are hand-woven. European examples from the nineteenth century are particularly valuable.

	AUCTION	RETAIL	
		Low	High
Afghanistan War Rug, dark blue field depicting helicopters, rifles, and planes, 2'8" x 6'4"	$400	$600	$900
Baktiari Carpet, dark blue field w/ repeating rows of multicolored lobed medallions surrounded by light blue floral border, 6'10" x 10'7"	3250	5000	7000
Baktiari Long Scatter Rug, midnight blue field filled w/ ascending design of cedar trees, birds, and palmettes, 3'5" x 9'	2750	3400	6300
Bidjar Runner, blue field w/ overall Herati design within pale rust floral-filled main border, 3'11" x 15'4"	3000	3800	7000
Bordjalou Scatter Rug, tomato red field w/ overall floral motif, 3'4" x 4'	550	900	1200
Caucasian Long Rug, field w/ alternating red and white medallions within ivory border w/ ascending bird motif, 3'9" x 8'6"	750	1200	1800

Left to right: Bidjar Carpet, midnight blue field w/ overall Afshan design, red turtle border, 9'2" x 12'4", $3220 at auction; Chinese Rug, gold field w/ circular medallions set w/ a dragon, cloudbands, and Buddhist motifs, mountains, clouds, and waves end borders, 4'2" x 7'4", $862 at auction. —Photos courtesy Skinner, Inc., Boston, MA.

	AUCTION	RETAIL Low	RETAIL High
Caucasian Runner, brown field filled w/ geometric medallions within ivory border, 3'6" x 10'10"	1400	2200	3000
Caucasian Scatter Rug, modern, 3' x 4'5"	600	800	1600
Chinese Carpet, modern, ivory field, blue border, 6' x 8'	430	500	1000
Chinese Scatter Rug, tan field filled w/ coin motifs and companion border, 3'2" x 4'6"	860	1100	2100
Daghestan Prayer Rug, ivory field w/ blue lattice filled w/ floral devices surrounded by red main border, 3'6" x 4'6"	1500	2000	3800
Daghestan Scatter Rug, 3'6" x 4'11"	2200	2400	5000
Ersari Turkoman Camel Bag, 15" x 53"	640	800	1500
Ersari Turkoman Main Carpet, 4 rows of 12 Ersari guls interspersed w/ diamonds, 11'2" x 19'5"	2400	3500	5000
Fereghan Sarouk Rug, floral design, 3'10" x 6'3"	2200	2800	5000
Fereghan Sarouk Scatter Rug, midnight blue field w/ soft brick red medallion and complementary border, 3'4" x 5'3"	1300	2000	2800
Hamadan Corridor Carpet, dark blue field w/ overall red and blue Herati design w/ floral-filled main borders, 6'1" x 13'9"	900	1400	2000
Hamadan Rug, 6'4" x 4'10"	2200	2800	5500
Hamadan Runner, light camel field w/ trellis design w/ ivory medallions within an ivory floral border and wide camel margin, 3'1" x 12'7"	1800	2300	4500
Hamadan Runner, midnight blue field w/ overall floral design within an ivory floral border, 2'8" x 6'4"	860	1100	2000

Left to right: Daghestan Prayer Rug, ivory field w/ serrated hexagonal lattice w/ flowering plants, red interrupted vine border, 3'9" x 4'6", $3450 at auction; Ersari Main Carpet, rust-red field w/ 2 columns of 6 guls, ashik gul-in-diamond border, 7'8" x 10'4", $4600 at auction. —Photos courtesy Skinner, Inc., Boston, MA.

	AUCTION	RETAIL Low	RETAIL High
Hamadan Runner, midnight blue field w/ overall Herati design within a red floral and vine border, 3'3" x 16'2"	6880	8000	16,000
Hamadan Runner, predominantly red, 2'6" x 13'	500	600	1300
Hamadan Runner, small medallions and elliptical stylized floral motifs within a camel hair border, 3'4" x 17'3"	4000	5200	10,000
Hamadan Scatter Rug, 6'11" x 5'5"	170	200	400
Hamadan Scatter Rug, tomato red field w/ red and blue boteh within multiple borders, 4'4" x 7'1"	1000	1400	2700
Heriz Carpet, madder ground w/ medallion, 9'6" x 6'	3000	3800	7000
Heriz Carpet, russet field w/ central dark blue medallion w/ attached pale green pendants and elongated pale blue spandrels, 8' x 12'	18,000	22,000	40,000
Heriz Carpet, rust field w/ oversized blue and ivory medallion, ivory spandrels, and rust main border, 9'7" x 11'5"	5000	7800	10,000
Heriz Carpet, tomato red field w/ central blue medallion and ivory spandrels within blue border, 9' x 12'	5000	7800	10,000
Heriz Carpet, tomato red field w/ red and blue central medallion and ivory and green spandrels within a dark blue border, 9' x 12'	9000	14,000	20,000
Heriz Rug, stylized tree design, 4'1" x 4'11"	2200	2800	5500
Heriz Runner, tomato red ground w/ 4 pulled medallions within a camel hair border w/ geometric motifs, 2'7" x 8'5"	15,000	20,000	37,500
Indian Mugal Fragment, soft raspberry field w/ overall floral design within a pale brown border, 6" x 3'	860	1100	2100

Left to right: Fereghan Rug, terra–cotta field w/ stepped diamond medallion and spandrels inset w/ rosette lattice, reciprocal border, 4'8" x 6'5", $2645 at auction; Heriz Carpet, terra-cotta field w/ curved serrated leaves and blossoming vines, midnight blue turtle border, 8'2" x 11'3", $8625 at auction. —Photo courtesy Skinner, Inc., Boston, MA.

	AUCTION	RETAIL Low	RETAIL High
Indo-Kashan Carpet, light blue field w/ overall latticework w/ small yellow medallions, 10' x 12'4"	3000	4700	6500
Ispahan Carpet, gold flower-filled field w/ central blue medallion w/ rust spandrels within a blue main border, 7'5" x 10'6"	2500	3900	5400
Joshagan Rug, dark blue field w/ diamond floral forms within a central red medallion with a red border 5' x 7'11"	800	1200	1700
Karabagh Corridor Carpet, cochineal field w/ overall green and light blue Herati design surrounded by dark blue main border, 8'2" x 21'7"	4000	6200	8600
Karabagh Long Rug, alternating blue and white diagonal stripes filled w/ pinwheels, ivory border w/ multicolored 8-point stars, 8'8" x 4'4"	3200	4000	7500
Karabagh Long Rug, dark blue field w/ diagonal rows of flowering shrubs within a wide tomato red border w/ stylized endless knot border, 3'9" x 11'9"	1000	1600	2200
Karabagh Runner, Shikli Kazak design, 4' x 8'10"	200	300	400
Karabagh Runner, tomato red field w/ 9 serrated-edge geometric motifs within green, white, and tomato red borders w/ stylized flowers, 3'1" x 12'8"	8200	10,000	20,000
Karachov Kazak Long Rug, medium blue field w/ alternating ivory and red medallions within an ivory border w/ latchwork designs, 4'7" x 9'2"	7500	8800	18,000
Karachov Kazak Scatter Rug, 3'10" x 5'9"	600	900	1300

Left to right: Karabagh Eagle Rug, red field w/ 2 sunburst medallions, ivory crab border, 4'x 6'9", $3105 at auction; Karachov Kazak Rug, red field w/ octagonal medallion and 4 star-filled squares, wine glass border, 5'9" x 6'6", $3565 at auction. —Photos courtesy Skinner, Inc., Boston, MA.

	AUCTION	RETAIL Low	RETAIL High
Karagashli Kuba Scatter Rug, light blue field w/ geometric and stylized motifs in ivory, tomato red, yellow, and soft blue within 3 borders, 4'2" x 5'	7500	8800	18,000
Karaja Carpet, rust field w/ medium blue central medallion, ivory and blue spandrels, and complementary border, 10'2" x 12'2"	5000	7800	10,000
Karaja Scatter Rug, red field w/ 3 medallions within light blue main border, 2'11" x 4'4"	1000	1300	2100
Karaja Scatter Rug, rust field w/ 3 Karaja medallions within dark blue main border, 4'10" x 6'1"	850	1300	1800
Kashan Carpet, modern, ivory field, 8'6" x 11'7"	3000	3800	7000
Kazak Cloud Band Rug, rust field, w/ 2 large blue medallions w/ light blue flowering border, 4'3" x 7'3"	1500	2300	3200
Kazak Double-Eagle, abrashed red field w/ 2 large eagle medallions, 5' x 8'3"	9000	11,000	21,000
Kazak Long Rug, 2 parallel rows of memling guls surrounded by an ivory border, 3'8" x 8'	2200	2800	5500
Kazak Long Rug, pale rust field w/ 3 Sewan Kazak medallions within a dark brown main border filled w/ geometric devices, 4'3" x 12'	3200	4000	7500
Kazak Prayer Rug, blue-green field w/ stylized flowerheads and animals within an ivory border, 4' x 6'	900	1400	2000
Kazak Prayer Rug, light blue field w/ 2 diamond medallions within an ivory border, 3'8" x 4'10"	700	1100	1500

Left to right: Kazak Rug, red field w/ 3 quatrefoil medallions, ivory crab border, 4'4" x 7'6", $4600 at auction; Kirman Rug, tan field w/ rosette medallion and matching spandrels, ivory floral meander border, 4'7" x 6'7", $2070 at auction. —Photos courtesy Skinner, Inc., Boston, MA.

	AUCTION	RETAIL Low	RETAIL High
Kazak Rug, red field w/ 3 large medallions within an ivory border, 5'1" x 7'1"	2200	3400	4700
Kazak Rug, red field w/ 3 latch hook medallions within a midnight blue border, 5' x 7'	2200	3400	4700
Kazak Rug, rust field w/ 4 starburst medallions within ivory geometric border, 4'2" x 8'4"	2200	3400	4700
Kazak Scatter Rug, red open field w/ large blue medallion enclosing smaller red medallion, 3'11" x 6'4"	1100	1700	2500
Kazak Scatter Rug, tomato red field w/ 5 geometric medallions within an ivory border, 4'4" x 8'2"	2300	3600	5000
Khorassan Rug, military figures, 10' x 11'7"	11,000	13,000	27,000
Kirman Carpet, cream field w/ large scale foliate medallion and urn and floral spandrels surrounded by ivory floral main border, 6'10" x 10'2"	5250	8000	11,000
Kirman Carpet, ivory field w/ cedar trees, flowering bushes, and floral sprays, ivory main border w/ similar motifs, 8'9" x 11'9"	3440	4300	8400
Kirman Carpet, pale magenta field w/ overall latticework, flowerheads, and buds within a dark blue main border filled w/ flowerheads and leaves, 8' x 16'4"	9000	11,000	21,000
Kirman Carpet, rose flower-filled field w/ central blue medallion and gold spandrels w/ complementary border, 8'2" x 12'3"	2500	3900	5400
Kirman Mat, ivory floral field w/ dark blue medallion within an ivory floral border, 2'3" x 3'1"	500	600	1300
Kirman Millefiore Prayer Rug, dark blue field w/ flowering vase flanked by cedar trees w/ gold spandrels, 4'2" x 8'	4500	7000	10,000
Kirman Scatter Rug, midnight blue field filled w/ large raspberry medallions within 3 complementary borders, 3'2" x 5'2"	600	800	1500
Konya Prayer Rug, 3'6" x 5'	13,000	16,000	33,000
Kuba Blossom Carpet, medium blue field w/ overall large-scale shields and flowerheads within a narrow red and blue reciprocal trefoil main border, 7'6" x 18'3"	7500	8800	18,000
Kuba Dragon Carpet Fragment, large octagonal medallion w/ geometric devices flanked by stylized dragons, 5'3" x 7'4"	8200	10,000	20,000
Kuba Prayer Rug, ivory field w/ diamond motifs and mirab w/ 2 stylized trees, 2'8" x 5'5"	1500	2000	3800
Kuba Prayer Rug, soft gold field filled w/ floral sprays within multiple borders w/ small flowerheads, 4'4" x 6'8"	1500	1900	3800
Kuba Runner, black field w/ trellis design, 6'8" l	860	1100	2100
Kuba Scatter Rug, corroded black field w/ yellow latticework filled w/ floral devices surrounded by an ivory stepped medallion main border, 3'1" x 4'7"	1300	1700	3400
Kuba Scatter Rug, dark blue field w/ geometric devices within a pale gold kufic border, 3'10" x 5'8"	1200	1500	2900
Kuba Scatter Rug, midnight blue field w/ latticework framing stylized floral motifs within 5 borders, 4'4" x 7'4"	2200	3400	4700
Kuba Soumak Rug, 4' x 4'10"	3000	3800	7000
Kurdish Bidjar Rug, midnight blue field w/ green and peach oversized medallion, 4' x 6'10"	1100	1700	2400
Kurdish Scatter Rug, dark blue field w/ latticework containing flowers and trees, 3'1" x 6'2"	550	900	1200
Lavar Kirman Rug, ivory floral field w/ central blue medallion and raspberry spandrels within multiple floral borders, 6' x 9'	2700	3400	6700

	AUCTION	RETAIL Low	RETAIL High
Lori Runner, 4'11" x 9'6"	3440	4400	8400
Mahal Carpet, dark blue field w/ large-scale floral motifs within a pale gold main border w/ palmettes and geometric leaves, 8'7" x 11'10"	7200	8800	17,500
Mahal Carpet, light blue field w/ overall Herati design surrounded by soft red main border, 7'7" x 9'6"	5750	8900	12,500
Malayer Scatter Rug, blue field w/ red medallion and ivory spandrels within a gold border, 4'4" x 5'9"	700	1100	1500
Marasali Scatter Rug, blue field w/ overall small geometric motifs, ivory predominant, within 2 ivory borders and 1 blue border, 3'4" x 6'9"	4400	5600	10,000
Marasali Shirvan Prayer Rug, 3'5" x 3'11"	5100	6500	12,500
Moteham Kashan Carpet, palmette medallion, 4'7" x 6'7"	5100	6500	12,500
Mustafi Palace Carpet, midnight blue field filled w/ interlacing foliate scrolls within a tomato red border w/ Persian inscriptions, 11'10" x 20'	13,000	20,200	28,000
Northwest Persian Runner, diagonal rows of stylized flowers within an ivory main border w/ large stylized flowers, 2'11" x 12'5"	3440	4400	8400
Northwest Persian Scatter Rug, medium blue field w/ oversized Bidjov design within a pale rust border w/ flowerheads and leaves, 3'2" x 6'6"	1800	2300	4600
Oushak Carpet, red medallion, 12'6" x 15'11"	7740	9600	18,000

Left to right: Marasali Prayer Rug, midnight blue field w/ staggered rows of serrated and zig-zag striped boteh, ivory boteh variant border, 3'6" x 5'2", $4600 at auction; Northwestern Persian, rust field w/ indented diamond medallion and spandrels, midnight blue border, 4'5" x 7', $1610 at auction. —Photos courtesy Skinner, Inc., Boston, MA.

	AUCTION	RETAIL Low	RETAIL High
Persian Heriz Carpet, red field w/ ivory and midnight blue medallion and ivory spandrels within a blue border, 8'6" x 11'5"	3750	5800	8100
Persian Ispahan Rug, ivory field w/ overall dense floral motif surrounded by abrashed floral main border, 4'7" x 6'10"	1050	1600	2300
Persian Kashan Scatter Rug, dark blue field w/ red medallion, floral sprays, and botch spandrels within a red main border, 4'5" x 6'10"	1600	2500	3400
Persian Rug, gold field w/ blue lobed medallion and rose spandrels, 3'9" x 6'4"	1400	1800	3600
Persian Rug, ivory and blue repeating medallion field filled w/ vines and flowers, 4'7" x 7'8"	4400	5600	11,000
Sarouk Carpet, gold field filled w/ birds, trees, and flowering shrubs w/ central blue, red, and ivory concentric medallions and spandrels within a dark blue floral main border, 12'3" x 18'4"	9000	14,000	20,000
Sarouk Carpet, ivory floral field w/ alternating taupe and pink medallions within a taupe main border w/ russet and blue flowerheads, 8' x 11'	8600	10,000	21,000
Sarouk Prayer Rug, rose field w/ vase of flowers, floral sprays, and ivory spandrels within a blue border, 3'4" x 4'9"	750	1200	1600
Sarouk Rug, soft rose field w/ dark blue medallion, cloud bands, cypress trees, and light blue spandrels surrounded by dark blue main border w/ scrolling vine, 4'5" x 6'8"	1750	2700	3800

Left to right: Sarouk Rug, red field w/ serrated diamond medallion and floral sprays, midnight blue floral border, 3'6" x 5', $1150 at auction; Shirvan Rug, midnight blue field w/ keyhole medallion inset w/ 3 star-in-octagon motifs, diagonal stripe border, 3'7" x 5'8", $2530 at auction. —Photos courtesy Skinner, Inc., Boston, MA.

	AUCTION	RETAIL Low	RETAIL High
Sarouk Scatter Rug, ivory floral field w/ dark blue medallion and pale rose floral spandrels, 3'3" x 4'11"	1200	1900	2600
Schikli Kazak Rug, dark blue field w/ central medallion and pinecone motif, 3'8" x 6'3"	1100	1700	2400
Seichor Scatter Rug, black field filled w/ boteh, 3'7" x 5'6"	860	1100	2100
Senna Carpet, midnight blue field w/ small-scale overall Herati design within a wide rust border w/ bird and palmette motifs, 11'8" x 19'3"	13,000	16,000	33,000
Shirak Carpet, 3 bird-filled ivory medallions, 5'6" x 9'5"	1100	1700	2400
Shiraz Scatter Rug, midnight blue field w/ 3 medallions, figures, and horse within an S-design border, 4'6" x 9'2"	2580	3300	6300
Shirvan Long Rug, midnight blue field w/ alternating rows of pale green and red boteh within a main border of red and white diagonal stripes, 3'1" x 11'	3000	3800	7000
Shirvan Runner, ivory field w/ repeating rows of flowering plants surrounded by red reciprocal border, 3'7" x 10'7"	1500	2200	3300
Shirvan Scatter Rug, midnight blue field w/ 3 blue and red medallions within 3 geometric borders, 3'11" x 5'1"	2100	3300	4500
Suzani Silk Carpet, soft palette w/ multiple circular medallions, 6'7" x 14'	10,000	14,000	25,000
Suzani Silk Rug, soft palette w/ stylized lotus motif, 4'1" x 7'2"	860	1000	2100
Tabriz Carpet, rust field w/ latticework of flowerheads and small vases within a dark blue border, 10'10" x 16'5"	9500	15,000	20,000

Left to right: Shirvan Rug, navy blue field w/ hexagonal medallion and 6 large rosettes, gold spandrels, red interrupted vine border, 3'6 x 5', $805 at auction; Shrivan Rug, midnight blue field w/ 3 star-in-octagon motifs, red and ivory striped border, 3'7" x 5'8", $2530 at auction. —Photos courtesy Skinner, Inc., Boston, MA.

Satsuma

Satsuma is a cream-colored Japanese pottery, usually with a delicate crackled glaze, elaborately painted, and gilt. Although it dates to the seventeenth century, most pieces seen today are from the nineteenth and twentieth centuries. The following are nineteenth-century examples.

Satsuma Tea Bowl and Vase. —Photos courtesy Skinner, Inc., Boston, MA.

	AUCTION	RETAIL Low	RETAIL High
Box, cov., circ., fan dec., interior dec., w/ butterflies, 3.5" dia	$2250	$4000	$7500
Bowl, flaring rim, 7" dia	650	1000	1800
Bowl, lobed, Thousand Face interior, 16" dia	2250	3850	6000
Bowl, ribbed, 6" dia	500	850	1300
Box, circ., old men dec., 5"	400	500	750
Cabinet Cup, parading children and chrysanthemum border w/ matching interior base dec., 2.5" dia	900	1400	1800
Charger, Thousand Butterflies dec., 13"	950	1500	2000
Jar, cov., old man and children in landscape, winged Foo dog finial, 20.5" h	1900	3500	5500
Koro, rect., 8.5" l	850	1530	2300
Plate, 9" dia	250	400	750
Snuff Box, 2.5" dia	600	1000	1800
Teapot, 7" h	750	1300	2000
Vase, baluster form, 11" h	400	650	950
Vase, elephant handles, figural patterns and high relief, 24.5" h	2900	5000	8000
Vase, figural dec., 7" h	250	375	600
Water Bottle, gilt flowers and tendrils on shoulders, body w/ foliate motifs, 20" h	8000	12,000	18,000

Snuff Bottles

Snuff bottles appeared with the growing popularity of snuff in China during the latter part of the seventeenth century. Originally a practical item, like a cigarette case, craftsmen of all sorts decorated these pieces with greater and greater sophistication. Eventually snuff bottles gained a life of their own. Collected and produced long after the fad of using snuff died out, they are still made today.

Judging snuff bottles is highly subjective. Craftsmanship and beauty are the dominant factors, but rarity of materials also plays a part. Some jade examples are valued almost solely on the quality of the piece of jade, rather than age, craftsmanship, or design.

Cloisonné

	LOW	AVG	HIGH
Blue, yellow dragon, white cloud motifs, c1800s	$400	$500	$600
Green, dragon motif, double bottle shape, c1900s	600	700	800
Yellow, blue clouds, dragon motif, c1900s	600	700	800

Enamel

	LOW	AVG	HIGH
Blue, gourd shape, fruit and foliage motif, c1800s	$687	$838	$990
White, plants and dragonfly motif, c1800s	750	1000	1250

Jade

	LOW	AVG	HIGH
Streaked, green and gray, toad and landscape, c1800s	$646	$788	$920
White, scenic motif, inscribed, c1900s	1000	1300	1600
Yellow, streaked beige, double-bottle shape, c1800s	1300	1600	1900

Lacquer

	LOW	AVG	HIGH
Black, irovy rim, purse shaped, c1900s	$700	$850	$1000
Brown, green, mother-of-pearl, shore line, water motif, c1900s	750	950	1150
Gold and Black, c1900s	225	300	375
Real Gourd, lacquered black, c1800s	584	727	870

Porcelain

	LOW	AVG	HIGH
Blue and White, 2 figures under tree, c1800s	$500	$600	$700
Blue and White, dragon motif, c1800s	240	300	360
Blue and White, scenic motif, c1800s	300	400	500
Blue, Red, and White, courtyard motif, c1800s	440	545	650
Fish Lotus Motif, paneled, c1800s	500	625	750
Green, red figural motif, red seal on bottom, c1800s	400	500	600
Green and White, dragon and cloud motif, c1800s	600	750	900
Red, dragon motif, seal on base, c1800s	280	340	400
Red, warrior motif, c1800s	500	640	780
Red Foo Dog and Pup, c1900s	400	500	600

Rock Crystal

	LOW	AVG	HIGH
Clear, basket-work motif, square shape, c1800s	$1500	$1900	$2300
Clear, thin black lines, fish motif, c1800s	600	750	800
Thin Brown Hairlines, c1900s	1000	1200	1400
Thin Lines, reclining horse motif, c1800s	261	315	370

Paper Collectibles

Cranberry Labels

	LOW	HIGH
Battleship, depicts battleship, 7" x 10.25"	$15	$25
Battlehsip, depicts battleship, 15.5" dia	50	75
Beacon, depicts man w/ lantern in window, 7" x 10.25"	50	75
Bluebird, depicts bluebird on branch, 13.5" x 8"	30	40
Bunker Hill, depicts Bunker Hill Monument, 7" x 10.25"	25	35
Capitol, depicts Capitol dome, 13.5" x 8'	9	12
Chanticleer, depicts rooster, blue ground, 7" x 10.25"	6	8
Chipmunk, depicts chipmunk on branch, 13.5" x 8"	30	40
Dragon, depicts gargoyle, 15.5" dia	120	180
Eagle, depicts eagle on branch, 7" x 10.25"	40	55
Harvard, depicts college campus, 13.5" x 8"	15	25
Holiday, depicts young boy, tree, Noah's Ark, toys, 13.5" x 8"	18	26
Honker, geese in flight, 12" dia	100	140
Inspected, depicts sprigs of cranberries, 7" x 10.25"	3	5
Iris, depicts iris, 7" x 10.25"	25	35
John Alden, depicted at desk, 7" x 10.25"	25	35
John S. Burgess, Plymouth, Mass., red star, depicts star in triangle, red, white, and black	20	30
Lion, depicts lion, 7" x 10.25"	9	12
Lone Pine, depicts pine tree, cranberry bog in background, 7" x 10.25"	17	25
Louis Taylor & Sons, Lotas Brand, depicts sprig of cranberries, light blue, green, and red	15	25
Magnolia, depicts flowering branch, 13.5" x 8"	35	45
Mayflower, depicts sailing ship, 15.5" dia	30	40
Minots Light, depicts lighthouse, 13.5" x 8"	45	60
Mistletoe, depicts sprig of mistletoe, 7" x 10.25"	3	4
Myles Standish, depicts colonial man w/ gun, beach in background, 7" x 10.25"	30	40
Ocean Spray, depicts cranberries at top and bottom, wave in center, black, red, white, and blue	3	4
Paul Revere, depicts man on horseback, 7" x 10.25"	37	51
Peacock, depicts peacock w/ spread tail, 13.5" x 8"	7	10
Pheasant, depicts pheasant, 7" x 10.25"	10	15
Pilgrim, depicts Pilgrims, 13.5" x 8"	17	23
Pilgrim, depicts Pilgrims coming ashore, 7" x 10.25"	4	6
plymouth Rock, depicts rock and Pilgrims coming ashore, 13.5" x 8"	29	40
Pocohontas, depicts kneeling Indian maiden, 7" x 10.25"	15	21
Priscilla, depicts woman at spinning wheel, 7" x 10.25"	21	29
Puritan, depicts men in forest, 7" x 10.25"	25	34
Red Cedar, depicts tree leaning over water, 7" x 10.25"	3	5
Red Honker, depicts geese in flight, red background, 13.5" x 8"	20	27
Samoset, depicts Indian brave w/ arms outstretched, 7" x 10.25"	17	23
Samoset, depicts Indian hand extended palm up, 13.5" x 8"	21	30
Santa Claus, depicts Santa at chimney, 13.5" x 8"	15	20
Santa Claus, depicts Santa at chimney, 7" x 10.25"	10	15
Skipper, depicts captain at helm, 13.5" x 8"	7	10
Skipper, depicts captain at helm, 15.5" dia	30	40
White House, depicts the White House, 7" x 10.25"	18	26
White Springs Co., depicts Indian maiden and sprig of cranberries, red and green	40	55

Fruit Crate Labels

The decorative labels that adorned the sides of wooden fruit crates are popular collectibles. The oldest and rarest date to the 1880s. Rarity and design are the important variables with fruit crate labels. California labels are usually worth more than Florida labels, and orange labels usually have more ornate designs. Label designs changed over the years, and some collectors focus on labels that have undergone design changes.

Emblem, CA, grapes, red and white lettering, black ground, $3–$8.

	LOW	AVG.	HIGH
Briant, WA, apple, Washington State map, white and blue lettering, blue ground	$3	$5	$8
Broadway, CA, pear, red and black graphic-type lettering, gold leaf, blue ground, blue-green border	5	8	11
Brownie's, CA, citrus, Brownies preparing orange juice, yellow sun and blue ground, 10" x 11"	3	5	8
Buddy, MI, broker label, smiling baby, blue ground, green border, 1920	8	12	16
Bunting, WA, apple, red apple, ribbon sash through center, red lettering, blue ground	7	10	13
Butler's Pride, WA, apple, branch w/ large red apple, white lettering, graphic, blue ground	3	5	8
Cal-Flavor, CA, citrus, oranges, blossoms and leaves against wood-grained and black ground, 10" x 11"	3	5	8
Cho Paks, WA, apple, trees, mountains, and distant orchard scene, blue ground	20	23	27
Circle A&F, WA, apple, yellow and black lettering, circle in center w/ A&F in white letters, black ground	7	11	14
Clasen, WA, apple, old litho of orchard homes and Mt. Adams in background, 2 red apples on limb, red lettering, 40 lbs.	6	10	13
Clipper, FL, citrus, 3-mast schooner, 7" x 7"	2	4	6
Coed, CA, ctirus, smiling girl in graduate cap and gown, purple ground, 10" x 11"	3	5	8
Color Guard, WA, apple, blue bottom, yellow lettering, graphic, black ground	5	8	11
Congdon Refrigerated, WA, apple, first edition label, red apple frozen in block of ice, Art Deco lettering, black ground	32	40	48
Congdon Refrigerated, WA, pear, pear frozen in block of ice	9	13	17
Corona Uly, CA, citrus, white and gold speckled lily, black ground, 10" x 11"	3	6	9
Desert Bloom, CA, citrus, white, blooming yucca w/ desert greenery and mountains, blue sky ground, 10" x 11"	3	6	9

Camel, CA, pears, multicolor, orange sky background, 7.5" x 10.25", $12–$19.

	LOW	AVG.	HIGH
Dewy Fresh, WA, apple, modern green leaf, fairy in leafy skirt holding wand, believed to be one of the last labels printed, white and red ground, 1958	3	7	10
Diamond, OR, pear, Mt. Hood scene, red diamond shipper is apple growers service	4	8	12
Diamond S, CA, pear, 2 horse heads, blue diamond	14	17	20
Diving Girl, CA, apple, 1920s girl in swimming suit diving into lake	13	19	24
Dixie Boy, FL, ctirus, black boy, 9" x 9"	4	7	10
Don Juan, CA, pear, orchard scene upper left corner, blue, black, and red ground	3	6	9
Don't Worry, WA, apple, blond boy holding apple w/ bite taken out, white script letters, shiny black ground	10	14	17
Double A, CA, citrus, train supported by 2 capital letter "A"s on trestle, 10" x 11"	2	4	5
Duckwall, OR, apple, stone wall w/ colorful duck in front, red ground	32	40	40
Dunbar, OR, pear, cartoon pear skiing down snowy hill, yellow lettering, blue sky	6	10	14
Eagle, CA, pear, eagle and 2 pears, red lettering, blue ground, yellow border	8	12	16
Eatum, WA, apple, 1 red and 1 golden apple, yellow lettering, graphic-type label, blue and black ground	2	5	8
El Mejor, CA, citrus, Sunkist orange, 10" x 11"	2	4	5
Emerald Green, WA, apple, suit of armor head w/ shield w/ large emerald on it, green ground	7	10	13
Empire, WA, apple, evaporated apples, old litho of mountains, orchards, and trees	7	11	15
Empire Builder, WA, apple, mountains, large warehouse, trucks, train, orchards, large apple-covered wagon, and 4 oxen	3	6	9
Endurance, CA, citrus, night scene w/ camels against purple and black background, 10" x 11"	12	16	19
Esporanza, CA, citrus, señorita w/ carnation in her hair, wearing lace mantilla and holding lace fan, blue ground 10" x 11"	2	4	5
Fillmore Crest, CA, citrus, blue border frames 3 oranges and green leaves against turquoise ground, 10" x 11"	2	4	6
First Blue, WA, apple, photo of 3 apples, light blue and orange lettering on yellow sash, blue ground	3	6	9
Flavor Crest, treasure chest full of red and golden apples (apple label from New York), blue ground	12	16	20
Florida Cowboy, FL, citrus, cowboy astride bucking bronco w/ Diamond K brand palm trees in background, 9" x 9"	6	12	18

Repetition Pears, WA, yellow lettering, black ground, 7.5" x 11", $23–$36.

	LOW	AVG.	HIGH
Florita, CA, citrus, dancing señorita and 2 guitarists against black ground, 10" x 11"	7	11	14
Flying V, WA, apple, photo of red apple, yellow script lettering and winged "V," blue ground	7	15	22
Foothills, OR, pear, old stone litho of orchard, mountain, river, and 2 pears	10	14	17
Full O'Juice, CA, citrus, half-peeled orange and glass of juice, lavender ground, 10" x 11"	2	5	8
Galleon, CA, citrus, galleon sailing on open sea, sky background, 12.5" x 8.5"	3	6	9
Gladiola, CA, citrus, 2 gladiola sprays on gold and tan ground, 10" x 11"	3	6	9
Globes O' Gold, CA, citrus, 3 oranges, blossoms, and leaves, 10" x 11"	3	6	9
Gold Circle, CA, pear, gold circle, yellow circle, and 2 pears, graphic, blue ground	4	8	11
Kings Park, CA, citrus, waterfall and mountain stream, 10" x 11"	3	6	9
Lake View, WA, apple, 1 red apple flanked by 2 golden apples and Pajaro Valley scene, blue ground, green border	12	16	19
Lakecove, CA, pear, barefoot boy w/ straw hat leaning against tree, lake and mountain in background	12	16	19
Laurel, CA, citrus, oranges, berries, and laurel leaves, blue ground, 10" x 11"	2	3	4
Laurie, CA, apple, little girl wearing pink dress holding apple in each hand, blue ground, 1930s, rare	22	27	31
Leavenworth, WA, pear, 2 green pears, white lettering, blue ground	3	7	10
Legal Tender, CA, citrus, U.S. currency in $250 bundle, blue and black ground, 10" x 11"	2	5	8
Loch Lomond, CA, citrus, Scottish scene on blue and green plaid ground, 10" x 11"	2	3	4
Luxor, WA, apple, big red Maltese cross w/ name "Luxor" in white lettering, blue ground	23	27	31
Nimble, CA, citrus, orange and blossoms against orchard landscape, aqua ground, 10" x 11"	2	3	4
Nob Hill, CA, pear, metropolitan skyscrapers, autos, and street cars	11	15	19
Orland, CA, citrus, old dam scene, 10" x 11"	9	14	18
Our Pride, WA, apple, parrot sitting on twig, 1 red apple, black ground, blue border, ©1923, 40 lbs.	11	15	19
Prinoeso, CA, citrus, princess in royal robes and crown jewels, grapefruits, and leaves on blue ground, dated 1911	3	5	7
Pyramid, Canada, apple, 3 pyramids w/ river, palm trees, and camel and rider, blue ground	23	28	32

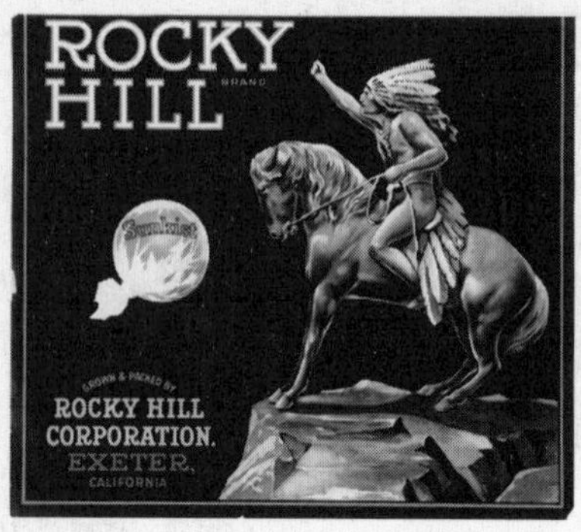

Rocky Hill, CA, oranges, dark blue ground, 9.5" x 10.75", $12–$18.

	LOW	AVG.	HIGH
Queen Esther, CA, citrus, elegant queen dressed in turquoise gown and wearing golden crown, 10" x 11"	5	8	11
Quercus Ranch, CA, pear, orchard, sky, lake, mountains, and 2 pears	7	10	13
Rancheria, CA, pear, Indian Chief on horse, maiden, and teepees, black ground	5	9	13
Red Bird, CA, citrus, large red eagle, black ground, 10" x 11"	2	3	4
Red Peak, CA, citrus, landscape scene, 10" x 11"	2	3	4
Red Star, CA, apple, big red star in center, red and white lettering, black ground, red border	9	13	16
Red Wagon, WA, apple, cartoon boy pulling red wagon full of red and golden apples, black ground, yellow border	18	24	28
Redlands Best, CA, citrus, 4 blue arrows pointing to big orange in center, 10" x 11"	4	8	12
Reindeer, CA, citrus, reindeer and grove, yellow ground, 10" x 11"	4	8	12
Repetition, WA, apple, 3 identical boys in front of 3 identical labeled boxes of apples, black ground	23	30	36
Rose, WA, apple, 2 large red roses w/ thorns and leaves, white lettering, blue ground	7	12	17
Round Robin, OR, pear, big red robin standing on hill, blue ground	18	24	30
Royal Feast, CA, citrus, orange, blossoms, dark blue leaves, and 2 lions in black framed by black checkered border, 10" x 11"	2	3	4
Sails, WA, apple, large sailing ship on choppy seas, yellow and red lettering, blue ground, red pen line border, 40 lbs.	12	16	20
Sam Birch, OR, apple, red apple, yellow strip through label w/ blue lettering, blue ground	19	23	26

Exposition, CA, cherries, wood-grained lettering, red ground, $5–$8.

Maps

Maps have a long collecting history. Those listed here are some of the earliest still available on the market. You won't find these in the glove compartment of your car, but we've seen these treasures at estate sales and small auctions throughout the country.

Maps are more valuable with original hand coloring, but beware of old maps with new hand coloring. Tears, stains, poor printing and trimmed margins all reduce value. Maps of the New World are more valuable than those of Europe, especially those of obscure Central European areas. A map is almost always more valuable when sold in the area it depicts. The more important the mapmaker, the more valuable the map.

For further information see *Mercator's World* magazine, 845 Williamette St., Eugene, OR 97401.

In the following entries, the region is listed first, followed by the map's maker, the title of the map, the date and the size.

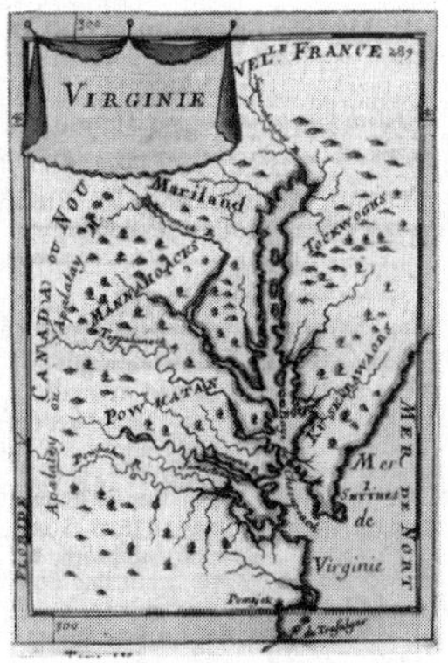

Above: When detail is lacking because the map maker was trying to save time and space, the value is decreased. Below: When detail is lacking because the area was unexplored, the value is increased. —Photos courtesy Swann Galleries.

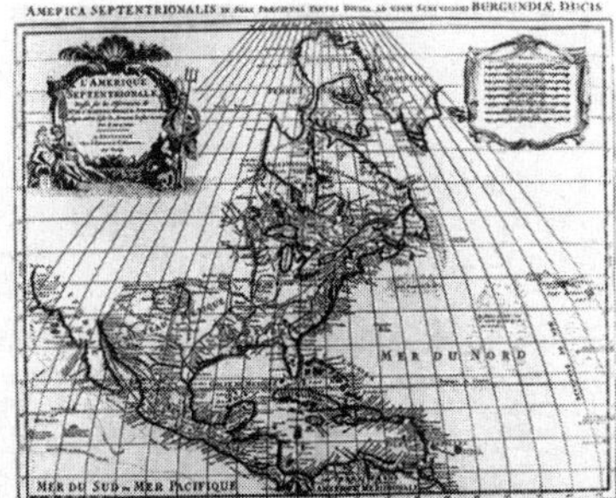

	LOW	AVG.	HIGH
Africa, N. De Fer, 1717, 13" x 9"	$150	$170	$190
Alabama, Rand, McNally, 1890s, 12" x 19"	20	30	40
Arctic Regions, Edward Weller, 1858, 16.75" x 12"	20	30	40
Arizona, G. Cram, 1885, 20" x 12"	20	30	40
Arizona, Rand, McNally, 1890s, 12" x 19"	30	40	50
Arizona/New Mexico, Mitchell, 1882, 14" x 22"	60	70	80
Arkansas, G.W. Colton, 1857, 14.5" x 11.75"	40	50	60
Arkansas, Rand, McNally, 1890s, 19" x 26"	30	40	50
Arkansas/Mississippi/Louisiana, Johnson, 1864, 17.5" x 24"	40	50	60
Baltimore, G.W. Colton, 1864, town plan, 14" x 11"	40	50	60
Bohemia, A. Zatta, 1781, 16" x 13"	70	80	90
Boston, G.W. Colton, 1857, town plan, 11.75" x 14.5"	40	50	60
Boston, Rand, McNally, 1912, 26" x 19"	30	40	50
Brazil Guayana, G.W. Colton, 1859, 13" x 15.5"	40	50	60
Brooklyn, Rand, McNally, 1912, 19" x 26"	30	40	50
Bucarelli, Alaska, J. La Perouse, 1979, 20" x 27"	310	360	400
California, Rand, McNally, 1890s, 12" x 19"	30	40	50
California/Nevada/Utah/Colorado/New Mexico/Arizona, Johnson, 1864, 16.5" x 24"	160	190	220
Canada, G. De l'Isle, 1703, 20" x 23"	1250	1440	1630
Canada East, Colton, 1859, 12.5" x 15.75"	50	60	70
Canada West, Colton, 1859, 12.5" x 15.75"	50	60	70
Carolina, John Speed, 1676, A New Description of Carolina…, 20" x 15"	1200	1600	2000
Carolina/Florida, G. Robert de Vaugondy, c1765, la Floride Divisee En Floride Et Caroline, 6.75" x 6.5"	90	110	120
China, H. Moll, 1701, 9" x 9"	100	120	130
Cincinnati, Rand, McNally, 1896, 12" x 19"	30	40	50
Cleveland, Rand, McNally, 1896, 12" x 19"	30	40	50
Colorado, Rand, McNally, 1890s, 19" x 26"	30	40	50
Colorado, Rand, McNally, 1912, 19" x 26"	30	40	50
Connecticut, Rand, McNally, 1890s, 12" x 19"	20	30	40
Cuba, R. Bonne, 1780, 8" x 12"	120	150	170
Cuba/Jamaica/Puerto Rico, Colton, 1859, 12.5" x 15"	40	50	60
Delaware/Maryland, G.W. Colton, 1857, 15.5" x 12.5"	30	40	50
Delaware/Maryland, G.W. Colton, 1864, 15.5" x 12.5"	40	50	60
Delaware/Maryland, Greenleaf, 1840, 10" x 12"	90	110	130
Delaware/Maryland, Johnson & Ward, 13" x 16"	70	90	100
East Indies (Singapore, Java, etc.), A. Zatta, 1784, 13" x 16"	220	250	280
Eastern Hemisphere, J. Colton, 1857, 13" x 16"	50	60	70
England/Wales, Mitchell, 1860, 10.75" x 13.25"	40	50	60
Essex, J. Pigot, 1842, 14" x 9"	60	70	80
Europe, Colton, 1855, 12.5" x 15.5"	60	70	80
Florida, Baldwin & Craddock, 1834, 16" x 14"	150	170	190
Florida, Johnson, 1863, 12.5" x 15.5"	80	100	110
Florida, Rand, McNally, 1890s, 12" x 19"	30	40	50
France, J. Tallis, 1851, 13" x 10"	50	60	70
France/Spain/Portugal, Mitchell, 1860, 11.25" x 13.25"	30	40	50
Georgia, Rand, McNally, 1890s, 12" x 19"	30	40	50
Germany, Colton, 1895, 13" x 16"	40	50	60
Idaho, Rand, McNally, 1890s, 12" x 19"	30	40	50
Idaho, Rand, McNally, 1912, 19" x 26"	30	40	50
Illinois, Rand, McNally, 1896, 26" x 19"	30	40	50
Indiana, Rand, McNally, 1890s, 26" x 19"	20	30	40

	LOW	AVG.	HIGH
Iowa, G.W. Colton, 1857, 12" x 15.5"	40	50	60
Iowa, G.W. Colton, 1864, 15.75" x 12.75"	30	40	50
Iowa, Rand, McNally, 1912, 19" x 26"	30	40	50
Iowa/Nebraska, Johnson & Ward, 1864, 23" x 17"	40	50	60
Italy (Northern), Colton, 1859, 15" x 13"	30	40	50
Kansas, Rand, McNally, 1890s, 19" x 26"	30	40	50
Kansas, Rand, McNally, 1912, 19" x 26"	30	40	50
Kansas City, Rand, McNally, 1912, 19" x 26"	30	40	50
Kansas/Nebraska, Mitchell, 14" x 21.5"	60	70	80
Kansas/Nebraska, Mitchell, 1882, 14" x 22"	50	60	80
Kentucky/Tennessee, G.W. Colton, 1864, 15.75" x 12.75"	30	40	50
Kentucky/Tennessee, Rand, McNally, 1890s, 19" x 26"	30	40	50
Lake Champlain, J.N. Bellin, 1744, 12" x 6"	90	110	120
Lake Superior/Michigan, G.W. Colton, 1857, 14.5" x 11.75"	30	40	50
Libya/Egypt, G. Ruscelli, 1561, 8" x 10"	80	90	100
Louisiana, G. Robert de Vaugondy, c1768, Cours Du Mississipi et La Louisiane…, 6.5" x 8.5"	90	110	120
Louisiana, G.W. Colton, 1864, 14" x 11"	40	50	60
Louisiana, Joseph Hutchins Colton, 1858, 14.5" x 11"	30	40	50
Louisiana, Rand, McNally, 1890s, 12" x 19"	30	40	50
Maine, G.W. Colton, 1857, 11.75" x 14.5"	40	50	60
Maine, Rand, McNally, 1890s, 12" x 19"	20	30	50
Martinique/Dominica, J. Thomson, 1817, 20" x 24"	90	110	120
Maryland/D.C./Delaware, Rand, McNally, 1890s, 19" x 26"	20	30	40
Massachusetts/Connecticut/Rhode Island, Mitchell, 1860, 11.5" x 13.75"	40	50	60
Massachusetts/Rhode Island, G.W. Colton, 1857, 14.5" x 11.75"	40	50	60
Mexico, Conrad Malte-Brun, 1837, Carte Des Etats-Unis Du Mexique, 12" x 8.5"	50	60	70

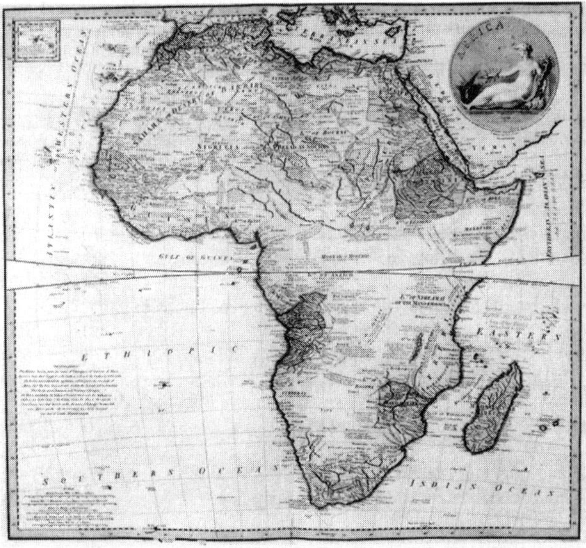

Africa, James Wyld, London, 1823, $488 at auction. —Photo courtesy Swann Galleries.

	LOW	AVG.	HIGH
Mexico, Jan Janson, 1647, Nova Hispania Et Nova Galicia, 19" x 13"	290	340	390
Michigan, Colton, 1855, 12.75" x 15.5"	80	90	100
Michigan-Northern Peninsula, Rand, McNally, 1896, 26" x 19"	30	40	50
Michigan-Southern Part, Rand, McNally, 1890s, 19" x 26"	30	40	50
Minnesota, Mitchell, 11.5" x 14"	40	50	60
Minnesota, Rand, McNally, 1912, 26" x 19"	30	40	50
Missouri, Tand, McNally, 1912, 19" x 26"	30	40	50
Montana/Idaho,Wyoming, Smith, 14" x 20"	50	60	70
Montana, Rand, McNally, 1912, 19" x 26"	30	40	50
Natal, J. Tallis, 1851, 13" x 10"	70	80	90
Nebraska, Rand, McNally, 1896, 19" x 26"	30	40	50
Nebraska/Dakota/Colorado/Idaho/Kansas, Johnson & Ward, 12" x 15"	60	70	80
Nevada, Rand, McNally, 1896, 19" x 12"	40	50	60
New England, G. Robert de Vaugondy, c1765, Nouvelle Angleterre Nlle. York Nlle. Jersey Pensilvanie Mariland Et Virginie…, 6.25" x 7.5"	90	110	120
New Hampshire, G.W. Colton, 1857, 11.75" x 14.5"	30	40	50
New Hampshire, J. Colton, 1857, 15" x 13"	50	60	70
New Hampshire, Johnson & Ward, 12" x 15"	50	60	70
New Hampshire, Rand, McNally, 1896, 19" x 26"	20	30	40
New Jersey, G.W. Colton, 1857, 11.75" x 14.5"	50	60	70
New Jersey, Johnson & Ward, 12" x 15"	50	60	70
New Jersey, Rand, McNally, 1890s, 12" x 19"	20	30	40
New Jersey/Pennsylvania, Asher & Adams, 1872, 15.75" x 22.25"	50	60	70
New Mexico, Rand, McNally, 1890s, 19" x 12"	30	40	50
New Mexico, Rand, McNally, 1912, 26" x 19"	30	40	50
New York, Colton, 1855, 16.5" x 25"	70	80	90
New York, G.W. Colton, 1864, 25" x 17"	60	70	80
New York, G.W. Colton, 1864, town plan, 26" x 16"	60	70	80
New York, Henry S. Tanner, 1825, 26" x 21"	380	440	490
New York, Mitchell, 1877, 14" x 21.25"	50	60	70
New York, Rand, McNally, 1896, 19" x 26"	20	30	40
New York-Brooklyn/Jersey City, Rand, McNally, 1912, 19" x 26"	30	40	50
New York City, Colton, 1859, 16" x 26"	60	70	80
New York/Massachusetts/Connnecticut/Pennsylvania, Asher & Adams, 1872, 16.5" x 22.5"	40	50	60
New York State, G.W. Colton, 1857, 14.75" x 11.75"	40	50	60
North America, Charles Smith, 1824, 14" x 10.5"	40	50	60
North America, Colton, 1859, 12.75" x 15.5"	70	80	90
North America, Conrad Malte-Brun, 1837, Amerique Sepentrionale, 12" x 8.5"	40	50	60
North America, G. Robert de Vaugondy, c1768, Amerique Sepentrionale…, 7.5" x 6'2"	80	100	110
North America, M. Seutter, c1730, 8" x 10"	470	550	630
North America, Mitchell, 1882, 14" x 11"	50	60	70
North America, Thomas Brown, 1801, A New and Accurate Map of North America From the Best Authorities, 13" x 11"	70	90	100
North Carolina, Colton, 13" x 16"	90	110	120
North Carolina, Rand, McNally, 1890s, 12" x 19"	30	40	50
North Dakota, Rand, McNally, 1890s, 13" x 23"	30	40	50
North Pole, C. Weigel, c1730, 13" x 14"	250	300	340
Ohio, Rand, McNally, 1890s, 19" x 26"	20	30	40
Oregon, Rand, McNally, 1890s, 19" x 26"	30	40	50
Oregon/Washington, Johnson, 1866, 11" x 16"	70	90	110

	LOW	AVG.	HIGH
Oregon/Washington/Idaho/Montana, Mitchell, 11.5" x 14"	50	60	70
Panama, John Tallis, 1851, Isthmus of Panama, 13" x 9.75"	30	40	50
Pennsylvania, Mitchell, 1877, 17" x 23"	50	60	70
Pennsylvania/New Jersey, Henry S. Tanner, 1825, 28" x 20"	320	380	430
Persia/Arabia, Colton, 1855, 12.5" x 15.5"	40	50	60
Peru/Boliva, Colton, 1859, 12.5" x 15.5"	40	50	60
Philadelphia, G.W. Colton, 1857, town plan, 11.75" x 14.5"	40	50	60
Philadelphia, S.D.U.K., c1844, town plan, 15" x 12"	40	50	60
Port des Francais, Alaska, J. La Perouse, 1797, 20" x 27"	310	360	400
Prussia/Saxony, Colton, 1859, 15" x 13"	40	50	60
Prussia/The German States, Mitchell, 1882, 10" x 13"	30	40	50
Rutland, W. Blaeu, 1635, 15" x 20"	190	220	240
Saxon Britain, W. Rogers, 1600, 8" x 6"	160	180	200
Scotland, Colton, 1859, 12.5" x 15.5"	70	80	90
Scotland, Tunison, 1887, 12" x 10"	30	40	50
South America, Colton, 1859, 12.5" x 15.5"	70	80	90
South Carolina, Mitchell, 11.5" x 14"	90	110	120
South Dakota, Rand, McNally, 1890s, 14" x 22"	30	40	50
St. Louis/Chicago, G.W. Colton, 1857, town plan, 14.5" x 11.75"	30	40	50
St. Paul/Minneapolis, Rand, McNally, 1912, 26" x 19"	30	40	50
Switzerland, Colton, 1859, 15" x 13"	40	50	60
Texas, J. Colton, 1857, 16" x 23"	180	220	250
Texas, Rand, McNally, 1890s, 19" X 26"	40	50	60
Texas, W. Bradley, 1886, 17" x 22"	70	90	100
The World, Conrad Malte-Brun, 1837, Mappe Monde En Deux Hemispheres, 18" x 9.75"	60	70	80
Tokyo (Jedo), J.N. Bellin, 1752, 10" x 10"	150	170	190
United States, Charles Smith, 1822, 14" x 10.25"	40	50	60
United States/Antilles, Conrad Malte-Brun, 1829, Etats Unis et Grandes Antilles, 8.75" x 11.75"	60	80	90
United States of America, Conrad Malte-Brun, 1837, Carte Des Etats-Unis D'amerique, 11.75" x 8.75"	70	80	90
Utah/Nevada, Mitchell, 1867, 11.5" x 14"	70	80	90
Utah/Nevada, Mitchell, 1882, 14" x 23"	60	70	80
Utah/Nevada, Smith, 13" x 20"	40	50	60
Vermont, G.W. Colton, 1857, 11.75" x 14.5"	30	40	50
Virginia, Rand, McNally, 1896, 19" x 12"	20	30	40
Virginia/West Virginia, Mitchell, 1882, 11" x 13"	50	60	70
Washington, Rand, McNally, 1890s, 19" x 26"	30	40	50
Washington D.C., Mitchell, 1882, 11" x 13"	50	60	70
West Indies/Mexico/Central America, Mitchell, 1860, 13" x 21"	60	70	80
West Virginia, Rand, McNally, 1890s, 12" x 19"	30	40	50
Western Hemisphere, Colton, 1859, 14" x 16"	70	80	90
Western Hemisphere, John Thomson, 1817, circular, 20" dia	50	60	70
Western Hemisphere, Mitchell, 1877, 9.75" x 14"	40	50	60
Western Hemisphere, Sidney Hall, 1830, circular, 16" dia	40	50	60
Western Hemisphere, Sidney Hall, 1857, circular, 16" dia	30	40	50
Wisconsin, G.W. Colton, 1864, 11" x 14"	40	50	60
Wisconsin, Rand, McNally, 1890s, 26" x 19"	20	30	40
World, Conrad Malte-Brun, 1829, Mappe-Mondes Sur Diverses Projections, 18" x 12.5"	170	210	240
World, Conrad Malte-Brun, 1837, Mappe-Monde Suivant La Projection De Mercator, 17" x 12"	50	60	70

Movie Memorabilia

In 1909, the Motion Picture Patents Company standardized the size and purpose of posters. Currently, there are seven poster sizes. "Half sheets" (or display cards) are posters 28" x 22"; "one sheets" are 41" x 27"; "three sheets" are 81" x 41". Lobby cards are a set of eight photos, each 11" x 14", depicting eight different scenes from the movie. Sets that have four one-quarter-inch triangular cuts on the photos from mounting are worth 30% to 50% less. Window cards measure 22" x 14" and inserts are 36" x 14". Probably the most extensive listing of movie posters is the *Movie Poster Price Almanac,* edited by John Kisch and published by Separate Cinema Publications in Hyde Park, NY. See also *Warren's Movie Poster Price Guide, Fourth Edition* by John R. Warren, American Collectors Exchange, Chattanooga, TN, 1997.

IMPORTANT: Movie titles and dates followed by "R" refer to a re-release of the film, not the first release.

Lobby Cards

	LOW	HIGH
Andy Hardy Comes Home, 1959, M. Rooney	$21	$26
Anna Lucasta, 1949, P. Goddard	41	61
Anything Can Happen, 1952, J. Ferrer	20	25
Arena, 1953, G. Young	19	25
Around the World in 80 Days, 1958, D. Niven	22	25
Ask Any Girl, 1959, D. Niven	18	27
Atomic Submarine, 1959, A. Franz	20	27
Auntie Mame, 1958, R. Russell	20	27
Bachelor Party, 1957, D. Murray	21	27
Bamboo Prison, 1954, R. Francis	22	26
Beyond the Time Barrier, 1959, R. Clarke	20	27
Bhowani Junction, 1955, A. Gardner	20	26
Bigamist, 1953, E. O'Brien	21	27
Bitter Creek, 1954, B. Eliott	20	26
Black Orchid, 1959, S. Loren	22	27
Blue Denim, 1959, M. Carey	20	25
Brigand, 1952, A. Dexter	21	27
Brothers Rico, 1975, R. Conte	21	26
Caddy, 1953, J. Lewis	20	26
Calypso Heat Wave, 1957, J. Desmond	21	26
Calypso Joe, 1957, H. Jeffries	20	25
Chain of Evidence, 1957, B. Elliot	21	27
City of Fear, 1959, V. Edwards	21	27
Crash Landing, 1958, G. Merill	21	25
Crime and Punishment USA, 1959, G. Hamilton	20	25
Crimson Kimono, 1959, V. Shaw	21	26
Crooked Web, 1955, F. Lovejoy	21	25
Cry Terror, 1958, J. Mason	21	27
Dangerous Crossings, 1953, J. Crain	20	27
Detective, 1954, A. Guinness	21	27
Devil's Disciple, 1959, B. Lancaster	20	27
Disc Jockey, 1951, G. Simms	21	26
Domino Kid, 1957, R. Calhoun	18	24
Don't Give Up the Ship, 1959, J. Lewis	21	25
Duel on the Mississippi , 1955, L. Barker	22	27
El Alamein, 1953, S. Brady	21	27
Encore, 1952, G. Johns	21	26

	LOW	HIGH
Everybody's Dancing, 1950, R. McDowall	21	26
Faust and the Devil, 1950, I. Tajo	21	27
Fiend Without a Face, 1958, M. Thompson	250	350
Fighting Lawmen, 1954, W. Morris	21	26
Finders Keepers, 1951, T. Ewell	21	26
Finger of Guilt, 1956, R. Basehart	21	27
Fire Over Africa, 1954, M. O'Hara	20	25
Francis, 1949, D. O'Conner	50	70
Frontier Marshall, 1939, R. Scott	155	227
Goddess, 1958, K. Stanley	20	25
Golden Hawk, 1952, R. Fleming	20	27
Golden Mask, 1954, V. Heflin	21	26
Goliath, 1958	21	26
Great Diamond Robbery, 1954, R. Skelton	20	27
Great Man, 1956, J. Ferar	20	25
Gun Belt, 1953, G. Montgomery	21	27
Gun for a Coward, 1956, F. MacMurray	21	27
Gun That Won the West, 1955, D. Morgan	21	27
Gunfight at OK Coral, 1957, K. Douglas	200	300
Gunmen From Loredo, 1958, Knapp	21	26
Handle With Care, 1958, D. Jones	21	25
Haunted Strangler, 1958, B. Karloff	20	27
He's a Cockeyed Wonder, 1950, M. Rooney	20	26
Hiawatha, 1952, V. Edwards	21	27
High Flight, 1957, R. Milland	21	27
House of Numbers, 1957, J. Palance	21	25
House of Seven Hawks, 1959, R. Taylor	22	27
Indian Fighter, 1955, K. Douglas	21	27
Innocent Sinners, 1958, F. Robson	20	26
Inside Detroit, 1955, P. O'Brien	21	27
It Should Happen To You, 1954, J. Holiday	21	26
It Started With a Kiss, 1959, G. Ford	21	27
It's Always Fair Weather, 1955, S. Donen	21	26
Jacqueline, 1956, J. Gregson	21	27
Jayhawkers, 1959, J. Chandler	21	26

Left to right: Ambush Trail, 1946, Bob Steele, $20–$25; Arizona Whirlwind, Ken Maynard, Hoot Gibson, and Bob Steele, 1944, $22–$27.

	LOW	HIGH
Jesse James vs. the Daltons, 1954, B. King	20	25
John and Julie, 1957, C. Gibson	20	27
Juggler, 1953, K. Douglas	21	27
Jupiter's Darling, 1955, E. Williams	20	26
Kidnappers, 1954, D. Macrae	21	27
Lady Says No, 1951, D. Niven	20	25
Lafayette Escadrille, 1958, T. Hunter	21	25
Last Angry Man, 1959, P. Muni	21	27
Last of the Comanches, 1952, B. Crawford	21	27
Last Posse, 1954, B. Crawford	21	25
Last Stagecoach West, 1957, J. Davis	20	26
Lawless Street, 1955, R. Scott	21	27
Let's Do It Again, 1954, J. Wyman	21	26
Life In the Balance, 1955, R. Montalban	21	27
Living Idol, 1956, S. Forrest	20	26
Living It Up, 1954, J. lewis	21	27
Long Gray Line, 1954, T. Power	22	27
Looking For Danger, 1957, Bowery Boys	20	26
Louisiana Hussy, 1959, N. Peterson	20	26
Mad At the World, 1955, F. Lovejoy	21	27
Man From Bitter Ridge, 1955	20	26
Man In the Dark, 1954, E. O'Brien	21	27
Man On Fire, 1957, B. Crosby	21	27
Man Who Turned to Stone, 1957, V. Jory	21	26
Mask of the Avenger, 1951, J. Derek	20	26
Massacre Canyon, 1954, P. Carey	21	26
Masterson of Kansas, 1954, G. Montgomery	21	27
Miss Robin Crusoe, 1954, A. Blake	21	26
Mission Over Korea, 1954, J. Hodiak	21	25
Mr. Drake's Duck, 1951, D. Fairbanks, Jr.	20	25
My Sister Eileen, 1955, J. Lemmon	21	26
Navy Air Patrol, 1955, J. Derek	21	27
Never Let Me Go, 1953, C. Gable	20	25
New Orleans Uncensored, 1955, A. Franz	21	25
Night Holds Terror, 1955, J. Kelly	21	27
Night of the Quarter Moon, 1959, J. London	20	26
Nowhere to Go, 1959, G. Nadler	21	26
Odds Against Tomorrow, 1959, H. Belafonte	21	25
Passage Home, 1954, A. Steel	21	26
Pharoah's Curse, 1957, M. Dana	20	26
Phffft, 1954, J. Holiday	21	27
Pickup, 1951, H. Haas	21	26
Port Afrique, 1956, C. Lee	21	26
Port Sinister, 1953, J. Warren	21	27
Prisoner of War, 1954, R. Reagan	20	27
Private's Affair, 1959, Weisbart	21	27
Problem Girls, 1953, H. Walker	21	26
Rack, 1956, P. Newman	21	27
Rebel Set, 1959, G. Palmer	21	27
Redhead and the Cowboy, 1952, G. Ford	21	26
Rich, Young and Pretty, 1951, J. Powell	21	26
Ride the High Iron, 1956, R. Burr	21	26
Riot In Juvenile Prison, 1959, J. Thor	20	26
Rogue Cop, 1954, R. Taylor	20	26

	LOW	HIGH
Royal Tour of Queen Elizabeth, 1954	21	26
Scapegoat, 1959, A. Guinness	21	25
Shadow of the Eagle, 1955, R. Greene	21	27
Silk Stockings, 1957, F. Astaire	150	250
Silken Affair, 1957, D. Niven	21	25
Sitting Bull, 1954, D. Robertson	20	25
Slight Case of Larceny, 1953, M. Rooney	22	27
Slightly Scarlet, 1956, J. Payne	21	26
Sniper, 1952, A. Menjou	21	27
Snowfire, 1958	21	26
Solid Gold Value, 1957, R. Hudson	21	25
Spin a Dark Web, 1956, F. Domergue	20	26
Storm Over the Nile, 1956, T. Young	22	27
Stowaway Girl, 1957, T. Howard	20	26
Strange One, 1957, G. Peppard	21	27
Svengali, 1955, H. Neff	21	27
Sweethearts on Parade, 1953, R. Middleton	21	26
Tamango, 1959, C. Jurgens	22	25
Teahouse of the August Moon, 1956, M. Brando	21	26
Teenage Crime Wave, 1955, T. Cook	20	26
Tempest, 1959, V. Heflin	20	26
Teresa, 1951, J. Ericson	21	26
These Thousand Hills, 1959, D. Murray	21	26
This Could Be the Night, 1957, A. Franciosa	20	26
Trail Blazers, 1953, A. Hale, Jr.	21	26
Trap, 1959, R. Widmark	21	26
True Story of Lynn Stuart, 1958, B. Palmer	21	26
Uranium Boom, 1956, D. Morgan	20	25
Vice Squad, 1953, E.G. Robinson	20	27
Vintage, 1957, P. Angeli	20	27
Violent Men, 1955, B. Stanwyk	21	26
Volcano, 1953, A. Magnani	20	27
When You're Smiling, 1950, F. Lane	21	27
Where's Charlie?, 1952, R. Bolger	21	25
Whistle at Eaton Falls, 1951, L. Bridges	20	27

Left to right: The Little Red Schoolhouse, 1930s, $20–$26; A Very Special Favor, 1965, Rock Hudson, Leslie Caron, Charles Boyer, $22–$27.

All Hands On Deck, 1961, Pat Boone, Buddy Hackett, Barbara Eden, $20–$30.

Movie Posters, One Sheets

	LOW	HIGH
Air Force One, Harrison Ford	$14	$18
Alice's Restaurant, 1969, Arlo Guthrie, Pat Quinn	40	60
Anaconda, Jon Voight	14	18
Arizona Raiders, 1965, Audie Murphy	35	60
Avalanche Express, 1979, Robert Shaw, Lee Marvin	5	10
Baby the Rain Must Fall, 1965, Lee Remick	20	30
Batman Forever, Val Kilmer, Jim Carrey	14	18
Batman Returns, Keaton, Pheiffer, DeVito	14	18
Batman and Robin, George Clooney	14	18
Brass Bottle, The, 1964, Tony Randall	10	20
Breakdown, Kurt Russell	14	18
Broken Arrow, John Travolta, Christian Slater	14	18
Busy Body, The, 1967, Sid Ceasar, Robert Ryan	30	50
Camille, 1936, Greta Garbo	3500	5000
Casanova's Big Night, 1954, Bob Hope	30	50
Charlie Chan at the Olympics, W. Oland	1500	2000
Charlie the Lonesome Cougar, 1967, Ron Brown	20	30
Chocolate Soldier, R-1962, N. Eddy	10	15
City Lights, R-1972, Charlie Chaplin	10	15
Con Air, Nicholas Cage	14	18
Contact, Jodie Foster	14	18
Cop Land, Sylvester Stallone, Robert DeNiro	14	18
Darby O'Gill and the Little People, R, Sean Connery	10	15
Donnie Brasco, Al Pacino, Johnny Depp	10	14
Dr. Cadman's Secret/Silent Death, R, Boris Karloff	10	15
English Patient	14	18
Every Which Way But Loose, 1978, Clint Eastwood	30	50
Excess Baggage, Alicia Silverstone	14	18
Face Off, John Travolta, Nicholas Cage	14	18
Father's Day, Billy Crystal, Robin Williams	14	18
Featurettes, 1949	10	15

Invitation to a Gunfight, 1964, Yul Brynner, Louis Rule, $20–$30.

	LOW	HIGH
Firefly, 1937, J. MacDonald	230	320
Firestarter, 1984, Drew Barrymore, Martin Sheen	25	35
Five Miles to Midnight, 1963, Sophia Loren	40	60
For the First Time, 1959, Mario Lanza	10	15
Four Sons, 1940, Don Ameche	80	114
Four Wives, 1939, P. Lane	110	154
Four's a Crowd, 1938, Errol Flynn	250	350
Free Willy 2	14	18
G.I. Jane, Demi Moore	14	18
Gauntlet, 1977, Clint Eastwood, Sondra Locke	40	60
Get Shorty, John Travolta, Gene Hackman	14	18
Grand Hotel, R-1970, Greta Garbo	10	15
Great Dan Patch, R-1960, D. O'Keefe	10	15
Great Dictator, R-1972, Charlie Chaplin	10	15
Great Guns, 1941, Laurel & Hardy	1000	1500
Great Lie, 1941, Bette Davis	600	900
Greek Tycoon, 1978, Anthony Quinn, Jacqueline Bisset	20	30
Green Light, R, duotone	10	15
Greyfriars Bobby, 1961, Donald Crisp, Laurence Naismith	25	35
Gross Pointe Blank, John Cusack	14	18
Hail Mafia, 1964, Jack Klugman, Henry Silva	10	20
Harrigan's Kid, 1943, B. Readick	50	65
He Married His Wife, 1939, Joel McCrae	80	115
Hero at Large, 1980, John Ritter, Anne Archer	10	20
House of Wax, R-1981, Vincent Price	10	15
In Old Kentucky, 1935, Will Rogers	400	600
In the Meantime Darling, 1944, J. Crain	70	100
Invasion of the Body Snatchers, 1978, Donald Sutherland	20	30
Irish Eyes Are Smiling, 1944, J. Haver	80	115
Janie, 1944, J. Leslie	70	96
Janie Gets Married, 1946, J. Leslie	50	65
Julius Caesar, 1953, Marlon Brando	80	150
Keeper of the Flame, 1953, Spencer Tracy, Katherine Hepburn	300	600
King of the Lumberjacks, 1940, J. Payne	70	100

The Great Victor Herbert, 1939, Allan Jones, Mary Martin, Walter Connolly, $150–$200. —Photo courtesy Poster Mail Auction.

	LOW	HIGH
Lady Let's Dance, 1944, Belita	40	56
Leaving Las Vegas, Nicholas Cage, Elisabeth Shue	14	18
Lili, 1952, L. Caron	80	140
Little Men, 1935, R. Morgan	20	32
Little Women, R-1962, Elizabeth Taylor	10	15
Lost World Jurassic Park	14	18
Love Finds Andy Hardy, 1938, Judy Garland	300	500
Mad Max, 1979, Mel Gibson	40	60
Magnificent Obsession, R-1947, Irene Dunne	40	60
Major Bowes Amateur Theatre, 1935	90	160
Make Your Own Bed, 1944, Jane Wyman	60	86
Man Who Knew Too Much, R-1983, Jimmy Stewart	10	15
Marvin's Room	14	18
Mask, Jim Carrey	14	18
Michael, John Travolta	14	18
Miss Susie Slagels, 1946, V. Lake	150	200
Monkeys, Go Home!, 1967, Maurice Chevalier	45	65
Monsieur Verdoux, R-1972, Charlie Chaplin	10	15
Monsignor, 1983, Christopher Reeve	10	20
Moon Is Blue, R-1960, William Holden	10	15
Mother Carey's Chickens, 1938, R. Keeler	250	350
Mr. Skeffington, 1943, Bette Davis	250	350
Muscle Beach Party, 1964, Frankie Avalon	40	60
Mutiny on the Bounty, R-1971, C. Gable	10	15
Never Say Never Again, 1983, Sean Connery	30	50
Nightmare on Elm Street, 1984, Robert Englund	50	70
Nightmares, 1983, Christina Raines, Timothy James	10	20
Nightwatch	14	18
Old Maid, 1939, Bette Davis	1500	2000
Old Yeller, R-1965, T. Kirk	900	1200
Out of This World, 1945, V. Lake	80	115
Pardners, R-1965, Martin & Lewis	10	15
Park Avenue Logger, 1937, G. O'Brien	80	115
People vs. Larry Flint	14	18

Woman in White, 1948, Sydney Greenstreet, Eleanor Parker, Alexis Smith, $75–$100. —Photo courtesy Poster Mail Auction.

	LOW	HIGH
Perilous Holiday, 1946, Pat O'Brien	60	86
Philadelphia Story, R, Cary Grant	10	15
Pope of Greenwich Village, The, 1984, Eric Roberts	20	30
Prairie Thunder, R, D. Foran	40	60
Pride and Prejudice, R-1962, L. Olivier	10	15
Rainbow on River, 1937, B. Breen	90	125
Ransom, Mel Gibson	14	18
Ring-A-Ding Rhythm, 1962, Helen Shapiro, Craig Douglas	20	30
Romance and Rhythm, R-1953, Phil Silvers	10	15
Rose Marie, R-1962, H. Keele	10	15
Royal Scandal, 1945, T. Bankhead	160	230
Rumble Fish, 1983, Matt Dillon, Mickey Rourke	10	20
Samson and Delilah, R-1968, V. Mature	10	15
San Francisco, R-1971, C. Gable	10	15
Say It in French, 1938, Ray Milland	70	95
Sayonara, 1957, Marlon Brando	10	15
Selena, Jennifer Lopez	14	18
Sense and Sensibility, Kate Winslett	14	18
Seven Years in Tibet, Brad Pitt	14	18
Shaggy Dog, R-1967, T. Kirk	10	15
Skipper Surprised His Wife, 1950, R. Walker	10	15
Stablemates, R-1975, Mickey Rooney	10	15
Starman, 1984, Jeff Bridges, Karen Allen	30	50
Station West, R-1954, Dick Powell	10	15
Stranger At My Door, 1956, M. Carey	10	15
Strawberry Blonde, 1941, James Cagney	550	750
Striptease, Demi Moore	14	18
Support Your Local Sheriff, 1969, James Garner	30	50
Sure Thing, The, 1985, John Cusack	10	20
Sweet Rosie O'Grady, 1943, Betty Grable	250	350
Sweethearts, R-1962, J. MacDonald	10	15
Tale of Two Cities, R-1962, R. Colman	10	15
Tammy and the Millionaire, 1967, Debbie Watson	25	35
They Only Kill Their Masters, 1972, James Garner	20	30

	LOW	HIGH
This Is Cinerama, R-1973	10	15
This Is the Life, Jane Withers	90	125
Those Calloways, 1964, Brian Keith, Vera Miles	20	30
Three Secrets, 1950, E. Parker	15	25
Three Sons of Guns, 1941, S. Morris	20	30
Thunderhoof, 1948, P. Foster	20	30
Twinkle in God's Eye, 1955, Mickey Rooney	20	30
Ulysses, R-1960, Kirk Douglas	10	15
Vanquished, 1953, J. Payne	20	30
Virginia, 1941, M. Carrol	200	300
Viva Cisco Kid, 1940, C. Romero	160	230
Wallflower, 1948, J. Reynolds	10	15
Westward Ho the Wagons, 1956, Fess Parker	35	45
When's Your Birthday, J. E. Brown	150	200
Wild and Wolfy, R, T. Avery	40	53
Wild Life, The, 1984, Eric Stolz	5	10
Wild Rebels, 1967, Steve Alaimo	40	60
Windjammer, 1937, G. O'Brien	90	125
Women of Paris, R-1953, G. Sanders	10	15
Yes My Darling Daughter, 1939, P. Lane	90	125
You Can't Ration Love, 1944, B. Rhodes	70	100
You Can't Run Away From It, 1956, Jane Allyson	20	30
Young As You Feel, 1940, Jones Family	80	115

Pressbooks

Animal Crackers, R-1974, Marx Brothers	$12	$16
Buccaneer, 1958, Yul Brynner	8	10
Dancing Pirate, 1936, C. Collins	12	16
Gold Rush, R-1973, Charlie Chaplin	8	10
Imitation of Life, R-1965, Lana Turner	8	10
Jamboree, 1957, Fats Domino	6	8
Limelight, R-1972, Charlie Chaplin	8	10
Man Who Knew Too Much, R-1963, Jimmy Stewart	12	16
Pack Train, 1953, Gene Autry	12	16
Streetcar Named Desire, R-1970, Marlon Brando	10	12
Ten Seconds to Hell, 1959, J. Chandler	9	11
Thunder Over Arizona, 1956, S. Momeier	8	10
White Christmas, R-1961, Bing Crosby	8	10
Words and Music, R-1962, Judy Garland	8	10

Other

Chatterbox, 1943, J. Canova, insert, 36" x 14"	$33	$43
Evening With Batman and Robin, R-1966, insert, 36" x 14"	27	35
Gone With the Wind, R-1954, 3-sheet, 81" x 41"	350	600
Henry and Dizzy, 1942, J. Lyden, insert, 36" x 14"	18	30
I Was a Teenage Caveman, 1958, R. Vaughn, insert, 36" x 14"	90	120
Jailhouse Rock, R, Elvis Presley, 40" x 30"	30	40
Masquerade in Mexico, 1945, Dorothy Lamour, insert, 36" x 14"	33	45
She Devil, 1957, M. Blanchard, 60" x 40"	36	45
Vertigo/To Catch a Thief, R-1963, window card, 22" x 14"	30	40
What Price Glory, 1952, James Cagney, insert, 36" x 14"	35	45
Wild One, R, Marlon Brando, 40" x 30"	30	40

Postcards

Picture postcards in the United States were introduced in 1893 at the Columbian Exposition. By 1910 they were a national craze with nearly a billion cards being sent through the mail. In 1914, the introduction of the folding greeting card began the rapid decline of this "Golden Age" of postcards. While collectors are mainly looking for postcards from this early period, there are many wonderful cards from the 1920s through the present day that are also prized by collectors.

Postcards are roughly divided into three categories: greeting cards, view cards and real photo cards. A greeting card is any card designed by an artist. This includes all the holidays (including the popular Halloween and Santa cards), children, animals, advertising, romance, Art Nouveau, etc. Many of the better greeting cards are embossed, highly colorful and beautifully designed. Some of the best-known publishers include Tuck, Winsch and PFB. Many of these cards are "artist signed," meaning that the artist's name is on the front of the card. Some of the rarer types of greetings include hold-to-the-lights and mechanicals.

View cards are pictures of specific places, typically prints made from a photograph. They may be black and white or colored and were usually mass produced. Views are the most widely collected postcards since nearly every city, town or hamlet in the United States can be found on a postcard. Many collectors are interested in how their hometown looked at the beginning of the century. Expositions, transportation (trains, planes, autos, ships), commercial enterprises and Main Streets are among the views prized by collectors. Things that have changed little, such as monuments and waterfalls, as well as frequently visited tourist areas (Niagara Falls, Washington, D.C., national parks, etc.) are common and not very desirable.

The real photo card, our third category, has skyrocketed in value over the past decade. A real photo card is simply a photograph printed directly onto a postcard. Usually black and white, they are occasionally colored. The reason for the interest in these cards is their subject matter and scarcity. While the bigger cities had millions of published views, many small towns and villages are represented only on photo postcards. Unidentified views and family occupational photos, political and social themes (e.g. suffragettes, presidential campaign stops, criminals), postal and photographic history and any other unique subject matter is of great interest to collectors.

Condition is a major factor in determining value. Prices listed are for mint condition. A slight flaw will reduce the value considerably while a serious flaw may render the card uncollectible. For more information see *Postcard Collector* magazine, PO Box 1050, Dubuque, IA 52004.

Our consultant for this section is Adam G. Perl, owner of Pastimes Antiques in Ithaca, New York (he is listed in the back of this book).

Advertising Postcards, left to right: Bear Brand Hosiery, 1910, $15–$20; Chevrolet Impala Custom Coupe, 1970, $4–$6.

	LOW	AVG.	HIGH
Advertising, "Broadway's Favorite, Dolly Dimples," 1906	$20	$25	$30
Advertising, Campbell Kids, vertical	75	88	100
Advertising, linen, "Chicken in the Rough"	5	10	15

	LOW	AVG.	HIGH
Advertising, linen, "Pastel Swann Hats," 3 men and 5 hats	15	18	20
Advertising, Red Star Line, poster style	25	35	45
Antelope Hunting, 2-tone, undivided back, Wild West Series, Ridley, artwork by Charles M. Russell	20	25	30
April Fool, sgd. Hutaf	15	20	25
Austrian Cavalry Patrol Crossing River, Underwood & Underwood, color	8	10	12
Beef Herd on Water, black and white, undivided back, Morris & Kirby	4	6	8
Branding Calves, 2-tone, undivided back, Holmes & Warren	6	8	10
Children, sgd. Clapsaddle	10	15	20
Christmas, children w/ toys	4	6	8
Christmas, Santa in green, full figure	25	30	35
Christmas, Santa painting sled	10	13	15
Columbian Exposition, 1893, pub. Goldsmith	20	25	30
Fur Canoe, color, undivided back, Wild West Series, MacFarlane	10	12	14
Halloween, 2 jack-o-lanterns in orange blimp, sgd. Clapsaddle	20	25	30
Halloween, scared boy, jack-o-lantern in window, sgd. Clapsaddle	20	25	30
Halloween, Tuck	20	25	30
Halloween, Winsch	50	75	125
Hold-to-Light, 1904 St. Louis Expo	25	30	35
Hold-to-Light, Santa Claus	125	150	175
Home Sweet Home, color, undivided back, Tammen	12	14	15
Horse-Drawn Double Decker Buses in London's Ludgate Circus, color, Louis Levy, divided back	5	7	10
Hudson-Fulton Expo, Redfield Floats	3	5	8
Indian Encampment on River Bank, color, undivided back, Illinois Postcard Co.	5	7	10
Indians, Chief Spotted Tail, color, undivided back, Leighton	5	7	10
Iron Ore Docks of Toledo, color, undivided back, Clinton & Close	5	7	10
Kewpies, sgd. Rose O'Neill	25	32	40
Levee Scene, color, undivided back, Erker #221	5	6	7
Lewis and Clark Exposition, pub. B.B. Rich	10	13	15
Missouri State Building, color, undivided back, *Sun Post Dispatch* (St. Louis), 1900	7	9	11
Oklahoma Building, color, undivided back, Samuel Cupples	7	9	11

Artist Signed Postcards, left to right: Arth. Thiele, $15–$25; Ellen Clapsaddle, $25–$30; F. Earl Christy, $15–$25.

Left to right: Elephant Landmark at South Atlantic City, color, $5–$10; Real Photo, early aviation, black and white, c1908, $40–$50.

	LOW	AVG.	HIGH
Pan-American Expo, 1901, pub. Niagara Env.	15	20	25
Patriotic, Fourth of July	5	8	10
Patriotic, Lincoln	8	12	15
Patriotic, Memorial Day	5	8	10
Patriotic, Washington	5	8	10
Political, Bryan campaign	15	25	35
Political, Prohibition	15	25	45
Political, Taft campaign	10	13	15
Political, Teddy Roosevelt campaign	10	20	25
Political, Teddy Roosevelt family	5	7	8
Railroad Station, Honesdale, PA, w/ train	6	8	12
Real Photo, 2 men on railway handcar	40	50	60
Real Photo, blacksmith w/ tongs at forge	25	35	45
Real Photo, dry goods store interior	25	30	35
Real Photo, exaggeration, "Salted," giant rabbits, sgd. W. Martin	15	20	25
Real Photo, girl w/ doll	15	20	25
Real Photo, horse-drawn milk wagon w/ adv.	65	75	85
Real Photo, musicians on steps (6 male and 2 female)	15	20	25
Real Photo, railroad station, Wellsburg, NY, w/ stationmaster	40	50	65
Real Photo, Spencer, NY, parade on Main St.	20	25	30
Real Photo, train in station, good detail	45	50	55
Red River Carts, color, divided back, Wild West Series, MacFarlane	10	12	14
Red Roof Tower at Left of Mountains, German Tyrolean Alps Series, Samuel Cupples	15	18	20
Residence House at Roof Square, German Tyrolean Alps Series, Samuel Cupples	15	18	20
Roper, 2-tone, undivided back, Wild West Series, Ridley, artwork by Charles M. Russell	20	25	30
Soulard Market, color, undivided back, Erker #246	5	6	7
Suffragette Comic, sgd. Donald McGill, rooster and duck, "Since my wife…she wants me to lay half the eggs"	20	25	30
Thanksgiving, sgd. Brundage	15	20	25
Two Crow Papooses, black and white, undivided back, Miller	5	8	10
Valentine, The Westmount Club of Montreal, color, divided back	6	7	8
Valentine, Tuck, "New Outcault Series," No. 7, "Will you be my Valentine? Read the answer in the stars"	10	12	15
Village Square, German Tyrolean Alps Series, Samuel Cupples	16	18	20

Road Maps

At one time, the local gas station gave these maps away free of charge to any customer. They are now collected as memorabilia of the post-war car culture. Folds should not be taped or worn through. Colors should be fresh and stain-free. There should be no added pen marking of routes or circled towns.

Mid-Atlantic States Road Maps, $2–$3 each.

	LOW	HIGH
Boston and Cape Cod, Esso, 1962	$1.50	$2.50
Boston, Cape Cod, Esso, depicts Faneuil Hall, 1958	2.00	3.00
Cape Cod and Boston, Gulf, c1964, depicts Minuteman, Paul Revere	1.75	2.75
Cape Cod, Sunoco, 1962-63, depicts Sunoco station	2.50	4.50
Connecticut/Massachusetts/Rhode Island/Long Island, Texaco, 1949	9.00	14.00
Illinois, A.A.A., 1963	2.75	4.20
Lost River Reservation, N. Woodstock, NH, 1949	2.50	4.50
Maine, Maine State Highway Commission, 1971	1.75	2.75
Massachusetts/Connecticut, Rhode Island, Atlantic, c1945, depicts Atlantic sign, highway	15.00	25.00
Massachusetts/Connecticut/Rhode Island/Cape Cod, Flying A Service, 1963	1.75	2.75
Massachusetts, MA Dept. Public Works, 1971	2.50	4.50
Michigan, Michigan State Transportation, 1983	1.80	2.80
New England, Esso, 1963, depicts lobsterman, Rockport, Mass.	1.75	2.75
New England, Esso, depicts Roger Williams Park, R.I., 1957	1.75	2.75
New England, Ford, 1950s, depicts beach scene	3.50	5.00
New England, Ford Dealers, scenic views, 1956	3.50	5.00
New England, Gulf, 1934, service station, attendants	18.00	28.00
New Hampshire/Vermont/Maine, Richfield, 1960, Richfield sign, scenic view	3.50	5.00
New Jersey, Esso, Hudson River Palisades, 1957	1.80	2.80
New York City Subway Map, Transit Authority, 1980	2.50	4.50
New York/New Jersey/Pennsylvania/Maryland/Delaware/South Atlantic States, Scarboro's Map Service, 1936	15.00	20.00
Ontario and North Central States, Imperial Oil Ltd., 1929	18.00	28.00
Philadelphia, Flying A Service, 1960	1.50	2.50
Socony, Long Island, 1932, depicts Long Island	20.00	30.00
Texas, Gulf, 1940s, depicts Gulf sign and auto	10.00	15.00
United States, Esso, 1964	2.50	4.50
War Map II, Esso, Featuring the World Island-Fortress Europe	9.00	14.00
Waterbury, Connecticut, Red Arrow Guide, 1925	10.00	15.00
World Atlas, Shell, soft cover, 32 pages, c1960	5.00	8.00
Yellow Octagon Guide, 4" x 9" folds out to 8" x 9", 20 full pages, 1930, A Handbook for the Motorist	7.00	11.00

Pens and Pencils

Pens can be either dip pens (the earliest type), fountain pens or ballpoint pens, Dip pens are the style of modern calligraphy pens: a pointed nib is dipped in ink and used quickly. Fountain pens (FP) contain their own ink supply, as do ballpoints (BP) and roller balls (RB). Pencils are either traditional or mechanical.

The fountain pen, invented in the 1880s by Lewis Waterman, is the most collectible type. It experienced its heyday in the 1920s and 1930s. The important makers from that time are Waterman, Parker, Conklin, Sheaffer and Wahl. Rarity and condition are very important. Historical importance may also play a part, though only in isolated instances, such as a presidential pen used to sign important legislation into law.

We have seen some pens listed on the Internet. For further information see *Collecting Pen World Magazine,* PO Box 6007, Kingswood, TX 77325.

	LOW	AVG.	HIGH
Aikin Lambert, swirl jade green plastic, FP, 1927	$225	$250	$275
Bayard 2000, dark purple, FP, 1950	65	72	80
Cartier, sterling silver w/ gold mount, pencil, 1982	30	37	45
Chilton, cream and gold, marbled, gold plated trim, golf pencil, 1930	60	75	90
Conklin, desk pen, black and orange taper, FP, 1933	50	70	90
Conklin, Endura, black, gold trim, FP, 1925	45	55	65
Conklin, Endura, orange, lever filler, gold plated trim, 1920s	80	100	120
Conklin, Nozak, gray and red pearl, gold plated trim, 1931	70	100	130
Conklin, orange and gold, FP, 1925	85	95	105
Conklin, 2P, black chased hard rubber, crescent filler, 1918	70	100	130
Crocker, black zigzag dec. hard rubber, FP, 1916	65	75	85
Cross, Townsend, black lacquer, FP and pencil set	80	100	120
Cross, Townsend, Medalist gold filled, FP and RB set	80	100	120
Doric, pearly lined nickel plated trim, pencil, 1935	50	85	120
Eagle, Epenco Merlin, red w/ gold stars and moons, FP, 1937	35	50	65
Eclipse, Gothic, gold filled, FP, 1932	85	100	115
Eveready, yellow, FP, 1930	45	55	65
Eversharp, green, chrome, gold banded cap, 1951	60	80	100
Eversharp, Skyline, black, 1945	40	50	60
Gold Bond, lapis blue color, yellow ends, FP, 1928	175	200	225
Lincoln, red marbled, 1926	60	85	110
Majestic, black and cream, 1930s	70	85	100
Mont Blanc, Monte Rosa, black, gold trim, FP, 1950	120	140	160
Mont Blanc, 146 FP and pencil set, black	150	175	200
Moore, Fingertip, cream and gold, FP, 1946	200	225	250
Parker, burgundy and black streamline pencil	25	30	35
Parker, Deluxe Challenger, gold plated trim, 1930s	80	100	120
Parker, Duofold International, burgundy, flat band	90	125	160
Parker, Duofold, red w/ gold trim, pencil, 1922	40	50	60
Parker, Duofold, gold pearl and black, gold plated trim, 1939	150	175	200
Parker, Duofold Jr., black, gold plated trim, 1927	100	110	120
Parker, Duofold Sr., Big Red, gold plated trim, 1924	250	350	450
Parker, Duofold Sr., red w/ gold trim, FP, 1926	175	225	275
Parker, gold filled metal, button filler, 1926	130	170	210
Parker, Lady Duofold, pearl finish, FP, 1930	100	150	200
Parker, Lady Duofold, red, gold plated trim	90	130	170
Parker, Premier, gold filled w/ black stripes	90	125	160
Parker, Premier, gold barley corn pattern	90	125	160
Parker, Premier, lacquer, FP and pencil set	90	125	160

Shaeffer, black, gray, and white striped, $50–$80.

	LOW	AVG.	HIGH
Parker, Premier, sterling grid pattern	90	125	160
Parker, Pastel, blue, gold plated trim, 1926	90	120	150
Parker, silver plated, pencil, 1921	150	180	210
Parker, Sonnet, 23 GP Laque, FP and pencil set	150	200	250
Parker, Sonnet Sterling Fougere	80	100	120
Parker, T-1 set, FP and BP	500	600	700
Parker, Vacumatic, black, 1947	60	85	110
Parker, 51, demi size black barrel, gold filled cap	30	40	50
Parker, 51s, Lustraloy cap	30	35	40
Parker, 75, burgundy set, FP and BP	60	75	90
Parker, 75, tortoise lacquer, FP, pencil, and RB set	80	100	120
Parker, 75, GF stripe pattern, FP and BP set	100	150	200
Peerless, black and cream, gold plated trim, lever filler, 1930	50	70	90
Peerless, gold plated trim, black veined cream, lever filler, 1920s	50	70	90
Recife, brown, flat top model	60	75	90
Royal, Parker Duofold imitation, yellow, gold plated trim, 1928	100	115	130
Saltz, black hard rubber, cream ends, nickel trim	25	30	35
Sanford and Bennett, black, eye dropper filler, 1904	90	125	160
Sheaffer, 30, black, gold plated trim, lady's, lever filler, 1930s	40	55	70
Sheaffer, Balance, pearl and black marbled, pencil, 1931	120	155	190
Sheaffer, black, gold plated trim, pencil, 1925	80	115	150
Sheaffer, Crest, colored	60	75	90
Sheaffer, Crest, silver plated, FP and RB set	100	150	200
Sheaffer, Lifetime, black and pearl, gold plated trim, lever filler, 1932	230	270	310
Sheaffer, sterling silver, lady's, early feed, lever filler, 1916	110	130	150
Sheaffer, Targas, colored	75	100	125
Swann, 14K gold, fine point, 1920s	160	210	260
Wahl, #4, gold filled metal, 1924	210	250	290
Wahl, gold filled, lever filler, 1926	100	125	150
Wahl-Eversharp, gold filled metal, pen and pencil set, 1924	270	335	400
Waterman, black, chased hard rubber, pencil, 1920	40	55	70
Waterman, Commando, black, gold trim, FP, 1943	55	65	75
Waterman, Gentleman, sterling, FP and pencil set	150	200	250
Waterman, LeMan 100, black	100	150	200
Waterman, LeMan 200s (smaller size)	80	100	120
Waterman, Olive Wood LeMan 100 (large size)	150	200	250
Waterman, Opera	70	90	110
Waterman, Patrician (modern version), blue	150	175	200
Waterman, Rhapsody (first of the modern version editions), gray	80	100	120
Waterman, Rhapsody, blue	80	100	120
Waterman, Rhapsody, red	80	100	120
Waterman, Taperite, gold filled cap, 1946	60	75	90
Waterman, #52, black chased hard rubber, nickel plated trim, 1923	60	80	100
Waterman, #452, Gothic, sterling silver, 1925	320	350	380
Waterman, #513, pearl finish, FP, 1939	150	175	200
Waterman, #516, ink view, gray pearl, gold plated trim, 1939	110	140	170

Phone Cards

Phone cards are one of the newest collectibles. They provide an easy entrance for novice collectors since many cards sell for under $10 and you can store thousands in a very small space. They appeal to a cross section of collectors because the themes are nearly endless, including sports, personalities and cartoon characters. They seem to be a great Internet collectible since there are so many auctions of them on the Web. This is a young market and therefore volatile. It will be interesting to see how the area develops. Are phone cards today's postal stamps? Time will tell.

	LOW	HIGH
Ameritech, $1, Frank Thomas	$1	$2
Amerivox, $1, American Telecard Expo Texas '95, cut in shape of American Map, active	15	25
Amerivox, 1 unit, Elvis ID Card	6	10
Amerivox, 10 units, Promotional Harley Davidson	30	45
Amerivox, $5, AIDS Memorial Quilt	20	30
Assets Racing '96, $2, Dale Earnhardt, active	4	7
AT&T, 10 units, Apples/Oranges Competitive AT&T Price, expired	3	5
AT&T, 10 units, General Foods Coffee, expired	4	7
AT&T, 30 minutes, Healthy Choice, expired	5	8
AT&T, 5 units, rec.collecting.phonecards, active	12	22
AT&T, Chicago Bulls Championship Rings, 10 minutes, active	50	75
AT&T, Die Cut "1996" Olympics, expired	5	8
AT&T, Healthy Choice—3 Cards, 10, 20, and 30 minutes, expired	6	10
AT&T, NYNEX Pioneers, $4.95, The First Telephone 1875, expired	5	9
AT&T, rec.collecting.phonecards, JUMBO 5 units, #7/25, active	35	50
AT&T, Rock & Roll Hall of Fame, 10 minutes, expired	6	10
B&J, Telecard Times Expo '95, 3 minutes, expired	3	5
Blockbuster Video, Power Rangers	8	13
C&W, 10 units, Canadian Mist, expired	3	5
C&W, 10 units, Tropicana Orange Juice, active	10	17
C&W, 5 minutes, Telecard World NY '96, active	8	13
C&W, Dallas Convention '96, 5 units, desert scene, active	5	8
C&W, Dunkin Donuts, 10 units, expired	6	10
C&W, Fetzer Vineyards Chardonnay, active	6	10
C&W, Telecard Times Expo '95 NY, $2, expired	6	10
C&W, Telecard World 1996, New York Skyline animated, 5 minutes, active	6	10
Canadian, Hello Canada, $10, Snowman	4	7
Captain Munchies, Australia, Coke Souvenir Pack, $5	12	19
Card Caller Canada, $100, Niagara Falls, expired	13	21
Card Caller Canada, $20, Canadian Rockies, expired	7	11
Card Caller Canada, $50, Niagara Falls, expired	11	19
CDG, 5 minutes, Earth Day '95, expired	3	5
Clear Assets, $1, Dale Earnhardt, active	3	5
Clear Assets, $2, Dale Earnhardt, active	4	7
Clear Assets, $5, Dale Earnhardt, active	12	21
Clear Assets, $5, Keyshawn Johnson, active	4	16
Collector's Advantage, $10, Motorcycle Series 1940 Indian Inline, expired	4	7
Collector's Advantage, $20, Motorcycle Series 1941 Military Scout, expired	1	2
Collector's Advantage, $5, Motorcycle Series 1949 Indian Arrow, expired	1	2
Colorado Democrats, Clinton and Gore '96	10	17
Comic Images, "War Machine," 10 units, Heavy Metal	4	7
Czech Republic, Wooly Mammoth Chip Card, expired	6	10
Destiny, 10 units, 150th Anniversary Mormon Trail, active	3	5

Card Caller Canada, $10, Mounties, $10–$18.

	LOW	HIGH
Destiny, 10 units, Hale Bopp Charity Card, active	12	20
Diet Coke – NBC Friends Card, 15 minutes, expired	10	18
Disney, Chile "Pocohontas," various designs, original packaging	7	11
Doral & Co., 10 minutes	4	7
East West Telecom, The Card Mall, 10 minutes, expired	18	28
Flying Buffalo, $7.50, Software Gaming Co., expired	3	5
Fone America, $10, "Glendale Galleria"	2	3
France, Lipton Tea, Jimmy Connors, expired	7	12
Frontier, $10, Beverly Hills 90210, expired	7	12
Frontier, $10, Melrose Place, expired	4	7
Frontier, $10, Simpsons, Bart in Phonebooth, expired	4	7
Frontier, $10, Simpsons, Homer wrapped in phone cord, expired	4	7
Frontier, $10, X-Files, expired	11	18
Frontier, 5 minutes, "Kleenex" On the Go, expired	6	10
Frontier, Betty Boop Southern California Expo, 3 units, active	5	8
Frontier, Bozo the Clown, 3 units, Southern California Expo, active	8	14
Frontier, Kit Kat, 10 minutes, expired	8	13
Frontier, Maxwell House, 10 minutes, expired	12	19
Frontier, Pepperidge Farms, expired	5	9
Gem International $3, Marilyn Monroe Southern California Expo, active	12	20
Glen Ellen Winery, 10 units, expired	3	5
Globalcomm, 20000, $20, Marilyn Monroe, photo in heart, expired	20	35
Grapevine AT&T, 10 units, LPGA McDonald's Card 1, active	8	14
GTI, $10, Casper, Bill Pullman and Ghost	3	5
GTI, $10, Flintstones, bowling, expired	3	5
GTI, $10, Flintstones, in car, expired	6	10
GTI, 10 unit, World Cup '94 South Korea Soccer	5	8
GTI, Budweiser Blimp	11	18
GTI, Star Wars, Darth Vader, $10, active	25	45
GTI/Fuji Film, K-Mart, American Flag, 4 units	5	8
GTI/Suncoast Video, 5 units, Pulp Fiction, active	5	8
GTS, $10, NHL Chicago Blackhawks, expired	6	10
GTS, $10, NHL New Jersey Devils, expired	7	11
GTS, $10, NHL NY Islanders, expired	6	10
GTS, $10, NHL NY Rangers, expired	6	10
GTS, $10, NHL Philadelphia Flyers, expired	4	7
GTS, Klaas Foundation	6	10
Hard Rock Café, 25th Anniversary, $10, active	10	17
Hawaiian Tropics, 10 minutes	3	5
HT, 10 units, 9th Avocado Festival 1995	3	5

	LOW	HIGH
HT, 10 units, NIKE 1995, Portland Marathon	3	5
HT, "Happy Holidays," Victorian House, 10 units, expired	5	8
HT, "Partners For the Planet" Youth Summit, 5 units	2	3
IGN, $3, Space View of Earth and Moon, expired	5	8
Innovative Nickelodeon, 10 minutes, expired	6	10
Innovative Telecom, 5 minutes, Doan's Back Specialist, active	1	2
Interactive "Consecutive Games 2131," Cal Ripken, expired	4	7
Japan, Hideo Nomo, Toyota Challenge, expired	5	8
K-Mart, James Dean, various designs, original packaging	6	10
Karis Commission Liberty Series '96, $5, Statue of Liberty, active	6	10
L'Eggs Silken Mist, 10 minutes	5	8
LCI, $10, Fed/EX St. Jude Classic, expired	3	5
LCI, 10 units, "Sunflower," expired	3	5
LCI, 5 units, Campus Talk 800, expired	3	5
LCI, Campus Talk 800	1	2
LDDS, Fiberweb, $5, "Sailing," active	5	8
LDDS, Kickoff Classic '95, 10 units, NY Jets, expired	2	3
LDDS, License Plates – Pennsylvania, expired	5	8
LDDS, Pepsi, 15 minutes, Pepsi points 1996, blue card, expired	6	10
LDDS, Pepsi, 15 minutes, Pepsi Points 1996, white card, expired	6	10
Levi's Bealls, jeans, 15 minutes	6	10
License Plates, Texas, 10 minutes	12	20
Lipton Recipe Secrets, 5 minutes, expired	9	15
Looney Tunes, 10 minutes, Bugs Bunny	20	30
Looney Tunes, 10 minutes, Daffy Duck	20	30
Marc's "Fun For Your Money," 60 minutes, expired	5	8
MCI, $10, American Flag, Mt. Rushmore, expired	3	5
MCI, $50, American Airlines Advantage, expired	3	5
MCI, Fox Sliders	2	3
MCI, Sliders, 5 minutes	3	5
Mothers Schnapps, 10 minutes, expired	6	10
National, Betty Boop, 10 units, "Merry Christmas," in folder	3	5
New Media, $20, Season's Greetings from NYC, expired	3	5
Omnitel, 5 minutes, Dunkin Donuts, 1995 Beanpot, Boston Gardens	5	8
Omnitel, 5 minutes, Xerox/Mail Boxes Etc., expired	9	15
Omnitel, 5 units, "The Beatles" Abbey Road, expired	15	25
Omnitel, NBC Media Week, 10 minutes, expired	8	13
PacificNet, Australia, $3, Janet Jackson, Sony Sig, Rolling Stone cover	5	9
PacificNet, Australia, X-Files $10, Card #1 "Screaming Face"	6	10
PacificNet, Australia, X-Files $10, Card #3 "Mulder & Scully"	8	13
Palmolive, 10 minutes, expired	6	10
PATCO, 25 units, "Hot Tuna" Band, expired	3	5
PATCO, Pamela Anderson, Triumph Motorcycles, 10 minutes, active	14	24
Phase Four, "The Campbell Card"	6	10
Planet Telecom, $1, National Convention St. Louis, expired	1	2
Planet Telecom, $6, Charlotte Speedway, Coca-Cola 600 '95, expired	4	7
Planet Telecom, $6, Lug Nut, Coca-Cola 600 '95, expired	4	7
Platinum Telecom, $5, Platinum Phone Card, expired	3	5
Proline Intense, $3, John Elway, active	7	12
Proline Intense, $5, Keyshawn Johnson, active	2	3
Provident, $10, Picasso, "The Woman With a Yellow Hat 1962," expired	2	3
Quest, Sears Phone Card Dept., 10 units, expired	10	17
Schneider Commission, 10 minutes, Rayovac Batteries, expired	6	10
Smartel Dexter USA, 10 minutes, expired	4	7

Telecom, Ireland, 5 units, Kellogg's, $12–$20.

	LOW	HIGH
Snapple Calling Card, expired	5	9
SNET 5 unit, Caller ID, expired	2	3
Speed Call, $6, NAPA 500 Nov '95, expired	12	20
Sprint, 15 minutes, Casual Corner	3	5
Sprint, $3, Monsters of the Gridiron, expired	3	5
Sprint Hallmark Telephone, "Merry Christmas"	3	5
Sprint/Classic, $5, Coke National Gold, "Coke Logo 5 Cents"	1	2
Sprint/Classic, $5, Coke National Silver, "Get in Line"	1	2
STS, 10 unit, Baby Wildlife Series in Card, deer	18	28
STS, 10 unit, Baby Wildlife Series in Card, porcupine	16	26
STS, 10 units, clouds, expired	6	10
STS, 150 units, clouds, expired	10	17
STS, 5 units, 1st Anniversary Phone Chip	15	25
STS, Family Movie Review Card, 20 units	6	10
STS, Good as Gold, 10 units, active	8	13
STS, Greeting Card, 10 units, "Udderly Ridiculous," active	6	10
STS, Greeting Card, 10 units, "Wish We Had Time," active	5	8
STS, Roaming Call Back, active	4	6
STS, Ski Spree Dallas Convention 1996, active	6	10
STS/MCI, Connecting Your Tommorrows, 5 units, expired	7	11
Talk N Toss, Children's Miracle Network, 10 minutes	1	2
TCI, "Sound Garden" Band Card, expired	2	3
TCM, $1, Milk and Cookies Santa	1	2
TCM, $10, Air Force F-117 Stealth Fighter, expired	11	19
TCM, $15, American Classics Bicycle Museum 1950 Schwinn, expired	4	7
TCM, $20, Air Force B-2 Bomber, expired	11	18
TCM, $5, Annie w/ Daddy Warbucks, expired	5	8
TCM, $5, Dick Tracy w/ Flattop and Pruneface, expired	6	10
TCM, $5, Heroes of Extinction Saurosuchus, dinosaur, expired	4	7
Telefiesta, $5, parrot and palm trees	5	8
Teletrading, 3 units, Babe Ruth and Lou Gehrig, expired	2	3
Tell One, 5 minutes, TCW East '96, PCM Report Magazine, active	3	5
Tell One, Microsoft Windows '95, expired	15	25
US West, $1, Chip Card, Telecard Times 3rd Anniversary	4	7
US West, $5, Chip Card, Valentines, Cupid, active	25	45
USA Card, $5, Marilyn Monroe/Long Beach Show, June 1997, active	12	20
USA Card, $5, Paper Money Expo '96, active	6	10
USA Card, New Cracker Jack, butter toffee, active	10	17
USA Card, Pink Panther Olympics 1996, 10 units, active	17	29
Weberg, Hot Country KICKS '96, active	7	11

Photographs

Assorted Subjects

In the following entries, photographs are listed by subject matter. The values quoted are the average retail price for various types of prints. Daguerreotypes (D) generally average 4" x 3" on silver plates; Tintypes (T) generally average 3" x 2" (these values are not for the thumbnail-size variety); Carte-de-Visites (CdV) average 4" x 2.5" on cardboard; Studio Photos (SP) are about 6" x 4" on cardboard; and Stereopticon Cards (Str) have a double image for observing in one of a variety of viewers.

The value of photographs is determined by age and subject matter. Prints made in the studios of important photographers such as Edward Cuttis, Matthew Brady, Alfred Stieglitz and Carleton Watkins command high prices.

Tintypes were invented in 1858 and declined in popularity by the 1870s. Stereographs with a revenue stamp on the back date between 1864 and 1866. In 1868, many publishers listed the views in a particular stereographic series by underlining or outlining a card number or title. After 1880, curved stereographs appeared, believed to have a more three-dimensional quality.

Due to the fragility of paper, *An Ounce of Preservation: A Guide to the Care of Papers and Photographs,* by Craig Tuttle, Rainbow Books, Highland City, FL, 1995, is worth consulting.

Left: Typical cabinet card.

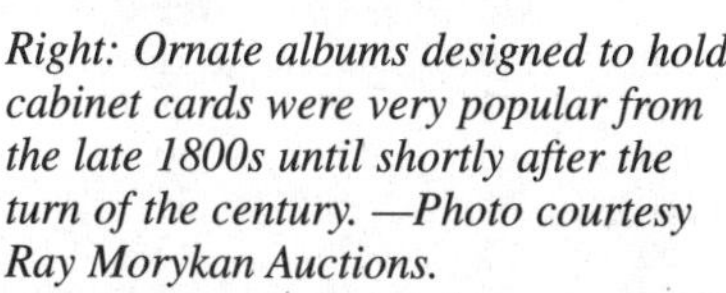

Right: Ornate albums designed to hold cabinet cards were very popular from the late 1800s until shortly after the turn of the century. —Photo courtesy Ray Morykan Auctions.

Historical Events

	D	T	CdV	SP	Str
Chicago Fire of 1871	$900	$250	$40	$65	$15
Mill Creek Flood of 1874	500	150	—	45	10
San Francisco Earthquake, 1906	—	300	150	250	30
Spanish American War	—	75	25	35	20
World War I	—	—	—	10	6

Left to right: Daguerreotypes are cased to protect the image. Although they can be cleaned, many amateur attempts have destroyed such photos; Gutta percha cases are valued for their elaborate decoration, but not if they are chipped.

Landscapes

	D	T	CdV	SP	Str
Death Valley	$550	$200	—	$45	$7
France	75	25	$10	15	5
House	35	15	5	10	10
Landscape	100	50	—	30	7
Mining Scene	400	200	—	50	10
New York City, landmark	250	75	40	50	10
Niagara Falls	750	175	—	50	10
Street Scene	100	45	—	15	12
Western USA landscape, w/ mountains	200	100	—	50	8
Yosemite Falls	400	200	50	75	30

People and Portraits

	D	T	CdV	SP	Str
Actor/Actress	$45	$15	$7	$12	$12
African American	200	120	40	55	25
Booth, Edwin	300	75	35	45	20
Booth, John Wilkes	750	500	300	350	200
Bryan, William Jennings	300	80	40	55	20
Circus Performer	150	55	25	45	30
Civil War Officer	200	125	35	50	15
Civil War Soldier	175	75	30	50	40
Cowboy	75	25	10	15	19
Edison, Thomas Alva	—	225	75	100	60
Ford, Henry	—	150	50	75	50
Lindbergh, Charles	—	—	75	120	35
Native American	260	150	50	85	25
Nude, woman	260	75	35	50	25
Opera Star	65	25	15	20	15
Portrait of a Beautiful Woman	50	7	7	12	—
Portrait of a Cat (or other pet)	100	25	10	15	7
Portrait of a Child	50	1	1	1	—

	D	T	CdV	SP	Str
Portrait of a Man	.15	1	1	1	—
Portrait of a Woman	.15	1	1	1	—
Professional (subject holding tools, etc.)	.100	50	20	30	15
Rockefeller, John D.	.—	—	50	75	25
Sporting Figure	.350	200	35	50	35
Thumb, Tom	.300	200	75	100	40

Presidents

	D	T	CdV	SP	Str
Arthur, Chester A.	.—	$75	$20	$35	$35
Buchanan, James	.$300	100	50	50	20
Cleveland, Grover	.—	125	25	50	40
Garfield, James	.—	75	20	35	35
Grant, U.S.	.750	175	45	90	45
Harrison, Benjamin	.—	65	20	40	35
Hayes, R.B.	.—	75	20	35	35
Johnson, Andrew	.400	100	50	65	12
Lincoln, Abraham	.rare	rare	2000	4000	50
McKinley, William	.—	100	25	50	40

Left: Steroscope Viewer and Cards.

Below: Comic scenes are a common subject matter for stereopticon photos.

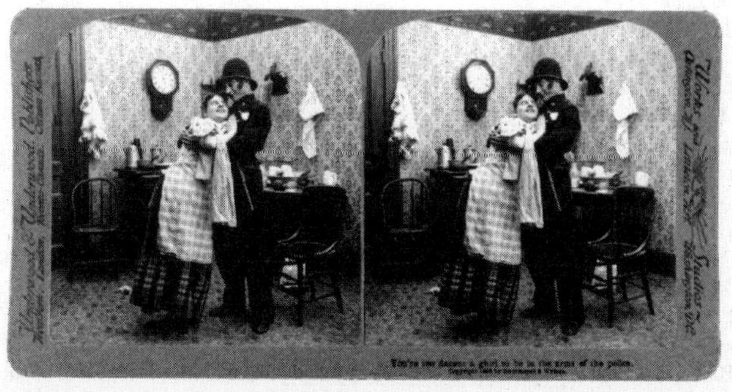

Wallace Nutting

At the same time he was reproducing American antique furniture, Wallace Nutting funded his many projects with money earned from selling photographs of quaint scenes. Often signed, these photographs have been collected since their first appearance.

	AUCTION	RETAIL Low	RETAIL High
Affectionately Yours, 10" x 12"	$127	$160	$200
Almost Ready, 9" x 12"	66	85	100
Among October Birches, 9" x 11"	105	130	160
Awaiting an Opening, 10" x 15"	176	220	260
At the Fender, 11" x 14"	193	250	300
At the Fender, 16" x 20"	330	410	500
At the Well, Sorrento, 9" x 15"	330	400	480
Auspicious Entrance, 13" x 16"	77	100	120
Autumn Grotto, 13" x 16"	160	200	240
Autumn Nook, 14" x 17"	138	175	215
Awaiting a Guest, 11" x 14"	165	200	240
Barre Brook, 10" x 20"	28	35	42
Barre Brook, 11" x 17"	39	50	60
Barre Brook, 12" x 20"	160	200	240
Barre Brook, 16" x 20"	105	130	160
Below the Arches, 10" x 12"	105	125	150
Benedict Door, 9" x 11"	204	250	300
Berkshire Crossroad, 14" x 17"	237	300	360
Between Hill and Tree, 13" x 15"	94	120	150
Birch Brook, 13" x 16"	94	125	150
Birch Grove, 11" x 14"	44	55	65
Birch Strand, 13" x 16"	61	85	110
Bit of Paradise, 10" x 12"	165	205	250
Blooms at the Bend, 11" x 17"	149	185	220
Blossom Valley, 8" x 14"	99	125	150
Blossoms at the Bend, 13" x 15"	39	50	60
Bonnie Dale, 10" x 12"	50	62	75
Bonnie May, 16" x 20"	39	50	60
Braiding a Rug, 10" x 12"	132	165	200
Caherlough, 20" x 28"	743	900	1050
Call for More, 11" x 14"	193	250	300
Call of the Road, 11" x 14"	66	80	95
Canal Road, 12" x 16"	198	250	300
Canterbury Close, 13" x 16"	193	250	300
Champlain Shores, 13" x 15"	440	550	660
Cliff Corner, 11" x 14"	825	1000	1250
Cluster of Zinnias, 13" x 16"	330	415	500
Colonial Home Room, 13" x 16"	88	110	130
Coming Out of Rosa, 11" x 14"	132	160	200
Coming Out of Rosa, 14" x 17"	138	175	215
Como Crest, 13" x 16"	935	1250	1500
Concord Banks, 14" x 17"	72	90	110
Connecticut Blossoms, 10" x 16"	44	50	60
Cup that Cheers, 10" x 12"	99	125	150
Decked as a Bride, 16" x 20"	83	100	125

	AUCTION	RETAIL Low	RETAIL High
Dixie Creek, 14" x 17"	160	200	240
Durham, 14" x 17"	55	70	85
Early Foliage, 10" x 16"	83	120	140
Early June Brides, 14" x 20"	116	150	180
Elaborate Dinner, 9" x 15"	143	175	210
Enticing Waters, 13" x 16"	88	100	120
Enticing Waters, 15" x 18"	61	75	90
Evangeline Bough, 13" x 15"	182	225	260
Eventful Journey, 13" x 16"	468	600	750
Farm Cart Track, 9" x 11"	121	150	175
Fine Effect, 12" x 20"	369	450	500
Fleur-de-lis and Spirea, 13" x 16"	682	850	1000
Foral Miniature, 4" x 5"	253	300	350
Foot Bridge and Ford, 13" x 16"	264	325	400
From the Mountain, 11" x 17"	143	175	210
Fruit Luncheon, 9" x 12"	187	230	270
Glance in Passing, 13" x 16"	165	200	245
Going Back to Nature, 10" x 16"	88	100	120
Grafton Windings, 10" x 16"	44	55	65
Greeting Card, 4" x 5"	83	100	120
Harmony, 14" x 17"	160	200	240
Hawthorne Cottage, 12" x 20"	28	35	42
High Rollers, 10" x 16"	165	200	250
High Rollers, 13" x 16"	83	100	120
Hint of September, 15" x 22"	72	90	110
His First Letter, 10" x 16"	176	220	260
His Rose, 11" x 17"	132	170	200
Hollyhock Cottage, 18" x 22"	209	250	300
Home Charm, 13" x 16"	83	100	120
Home Charm, 15" x 22"	154	200	240
Home Hearth, 10" x 16"	105	125	150
Home Room, 14" x 17"	182	225	260
Homestead in Blossom Time, 10" x 20"	55	70	85
Honeymoon Drive, 10" x 12"	44	55	65
Honeymoon Stroll, 10" x 12"	83	100	120
Hope of the Year, 9" x 11"	72	90	110
In Tenderleaf, 12" x 20"	66	80	95
In Tenderleaf, 16" x 20"	165	200	240
Informal Call, 11" x 14"	116	140	165
Inside the Gate, 13" x 16"	209	250	300
Into the West, 10" x 16"	44	50	65
LaJolla, 9" x 15"	138	175	220
LaJolla, 13" x 16"	77	90	125
Lake Brandt Birches, 13" x 16"	149	180	220
Lambs at Rest, 11" x 14"	187	240	270
Lane to Uncle Jonathan's, 10" x 17"	88	100	120
Langdon Door, 9" x 11"	149	175	225
Larkspur, 10" x 12"	61	75	90
Larkspur, 14" x 17"	110	140	165
Larkspur, 18" x 22"	165	200	240
Last Furrow, 13" x 16"	330	410	500
Leaf Stream Brook, 10" x 12"	105	130	160

	AUCTION	RETAIL Low	RETAIL High
Leaf Strewn Brook, 16" x 20"	116	145	180
Lined with Petals, 14" x 17"	160	200	240
Lingering Water, 10" x 12"	72	90	110
Litchfield Minster, 13" x 16"	187	235	280
Little Killarney Lake, 13" x 16"	193	250	300
Little River, 12" x 20"	99	125	150
Little River and Mt. Washington, 12" x 16"	116	145	175
Lost in Admiration, 12" x 15"	88	100	120
Maiden Reveries, 13" x 15"	127	150	180
Maine Coast Sky, 11" x 14"	198	250	300
Maine Coast Sky, 13" x 16"	385	475	580
Maple Sugar Cupboard, 12" x 16"	66	80	100
Maple Sugar Cupbaord, 16" x 20"	165	200	250
Mary Ball Washington's Parlor, Fredericksburg, 13" x 16"	303	375	450
Mary's Little Lamb, 13" x 16"	231	280	350
Meandering Battenkill, 13" x 22"	50	72	85
Meeting of the Ways, 10" x 16"	138	170	200
Memories of Childhood, 12" x 16"	154	200	240
Middlesex Glen and Camel's Hump, 13" x 15"	220	275	330
Mills at the Turn, 13" x 17"	220	275	325

Bucolic landscapes were a popular Wallace Nutting theme. —Photo courtesy Michael Ivankovich Antiques, Inc.

	AUCTION	RETAIL Low	RETAIL High
Mirror with "A Call at the Squire's" Scene, 8" x 28"	248	300	360
Morning Duties, 10" x 12"	132	165	200
Mossy Stair, 16" x 20"	143	175	210
Mountain Ledges, 12" x 16"	116	150	180
Natural Bridge (miniature), 4" x 5"	39	50	60
Nest, The, 11" x 14"	127	150	180
Nest, The, 13" x 16"	154	200	240
Nethercote, 8" x 10"	83	100	120
Newton October, 12" x 14"	39	50	60
Notch Mountain, 13" x 16"	105	125	150
Nuttingham Blossoms, 14" x 16"	94	120	140
Oak Palm Drive, 12" x 16"	385	270	360
October Array, 9" x 11"	61	75	90
October Splendors, 12" x 16"	66	80	95
October Waters, 13" x 22"	94	120	150
Old Drawing Room, 12" x 16"	50	72	85
Old Home, 12" x 20"	282	350	425
Old Village Street, 14" x 17"	303	375	450
Orchard Brook, 13" x 16"	77	100	120
Out of a Garden Fair, 11" x14"	127	150	180
Over the Wall, 13" x 15"	149	200	235
Palmetto Grace, 14" x 17"	440	550	650
Paradise Portal, 15" x 19"	413	420	525
Paradise Valley, 10" x 16"	127	150	185
Parlor Corner, 13" x 16"	330	400	480
Parting of the Ways, 13" x 17"	171	220	260
Path Among Blossoms, 12" x 15"	187	230	275
Path of Roses, 10" x 12"	292	370	420
Patty's Favorite Walk, 10" x 12"	194	250	300
Peaceful Stretch, 10" x 16"	160	200	250
Pennsylvania Arches, 14" x 17"	292	375	425
Petals Above and Below, 10" x 12"	61	75	90
Pilgrim Daughter, 14" x 16"	110	140	160
Pine Landing, 13" x 16"	220	275	325
Plymouth Curves, 14" x 17"	88	100	125
Porta Della Carta, 11" x 14"	303	375	450
Presidential Range, 7" x 9"	77	95	120
Purity and Grace, 13" x 16"	94	90	115
Quilting Party, 11" x 14"	154	200	240
Quilting Party, 13" x 16"	94	125	150
Red Eagle Lake, 9" x 11"	105	130	160
Reeling the Yarn, 14" x 17"	143	180	220
River Meadow, 16" x 20"	132	170	210
River Meadow, 18" x 22"	237	300	360
Roadside Brook, 10" x 16"	160	200	240
Romance of the Revolution, 10" x 12"	165	205	250
Roses and a Bud, 13" x 15"	413	500	600
Sallying of Sally, 14" x 17"	165	200	250
Season of Rejoicing, 14" x 17"	94	125	150
Sewing by the Fire, 10" x 12"	127	160	200
Shadowy Orchard Curves, 11" x 14"	83	100	120
Shore Battle, 11" x 14"	149	185	225

	AUCTION	RETAIL	
		Low	High
Sip of Tea, 13" x 15"	149	180	220
Slack Water, 9" x 14"	44	55	65
Spanning the Glen, 10" x 12"	132	170	200
Spring Colors, 10" x 16"	72	90	110
Spring in the Dell, 10" x 12"	94	120	140
Spring Pageant, 10" x 16"	83	100	125
Stamford Roadside, 10" x 12"	66	85	100
Stepping Stones at Bolten Abbey, 13" x 16"	633	800	1000
Still Depths, 10" x 12"	138	175	210
Stitch in Time, 12" x 15"	193	240	300
Street Border, 12" x 16"	231	290	370
Summer On the Avon, 11" x 15"	88	105	130
Swimming Pool, 8" x 10"	83	100	120
Swimming Pool, 16" x 20"	88	105	125
Swimming Pool, 18" x 22"	44	55	65
Swimming Pool, 18" x 26"	105	125	150
Tea for Two, 14" x 17"	143	180	220
Tea Maid, 13" x 15"	110	140	200
There's Rosemary!, 12" x 15"	330	400	500
Three Chums, 10" x 12"	165	200	250
To the End Porch, 12" x 16"	309	375	425
Treasure Bag, 8" x 10"	72	90	110
Treasure Bag, 18" x 22"	198	250	300
Tunnel of Bloom, 14" x 17"	127	150	180
Twix't Apple and Birch, 18" x 22"	149	185	225
Under the Blossoms, 14" x 17"	259	325	400
Untitled Cow Scene, 7" x 11"	121	150	180
Untitled English Cottage, 7" x 9"	50	65	80
Untitled House, 14" x 17"	121	150	180
Untitled Interior, 7" x 9"	83	100	125
Untitled Sheep Scene, 7" x 9"	94	120	150
Valley in the Pyrenees, 13" x 15"	94	120	145
Vermont Road, 13" x 22"	99	125	150
Very Satisfactory, 18" x 22"	121	150	180
Village Vale, 11" x 17"	88	100	120
Vines and Thatch, 11" x 14"	132	165	200
Waiting Bucket, 9" x 11"	127	150	190
Walk Under the Buttonwood, 14" x 17"	66	80	95
Walpole Road, 9" x 17"	105	125	150
Warm Spring Day, 12" x 16"	165	200	250
Warm Spring Day, 13" x 20"	220	275	320
Warwick Castle, 11" x 17"	413	500	600
Waterford Streamside, 13" x 16"	127	150	175
Way It Begins, 11" x 14"	198	250	300
Way Through the Orchard, 13" x 16"	121	150	180
Wayside Inn Garden, 14" x 17"	105	130	160
Weaver, The, 14" x 17"	154	190	240
Westfield Water, 13" x 16"	88	100	125
Westfield Water, 16" x 20"	72	85	110
What a Beauty!, 14" x 16"	308	375	450
Where Grandma Was Wed, 16" x 20"	220	275	325
Witch Water, 11" x 17"	83	100	125

Plates, Collector

Collector plates were introduced in 1895 with the issue of Bing and Grøndahl's Christmas plate. Despite much publicity about increasing values, selling a collection of plates may realize only pennies on the dollar. First and last issues within a series are generally valued higher than the other plates in the same series. As with all collectibles, buy what you love because you love it, not because it might increase in value. For more information consult *The Official Price Guide to Collector Plates, Seventh Edition,* Rinker Enterprises, House of Collectibles, NY, 1999.

The following entries are listed by company name, with series' titles indented. Original issue prices (Issue) are listed first, followed by current secondary market values for plates within that series. Issue prices have been rounded up to the nearest dollar.

	ISSUE	LOW	HIGH
American Artists			
Family Treasures	$40	$20	$30
Famous Fillies	65	50	80
Fred Stone Classic	75	80	85
Horses of Fred Stone	55	40	125
Mare and Foal Miniature	25	15	25
Racing Legends	75	50	75
Sport of Kings	65	75	100
Zoe's Cats	30	20	30
American Express Company			
Birds of North America	38	25	35
Four Freedoms	38	30	40
Songbirds of Roger Tory Peterson	48	30	40
American Heritage			
Africa's Beauties	65	40	50
American Sail	40	30	40
Celebrity Clowns	50	35	50
Craftsman Heritage	40	30	40
Sawdust Antics	50	35	45
Vanishing West	60	40	50
American Legacy			
Children to Love	60	50	125
Penni Anne Cross	55	40	50
Special Heart	35	20	30
Anheuser-Busch, Inc.			
Archive Plates	28	15	20
Civil War	45	30	40
Holiday Plates	28–30	20	45
Man's Best Friend	28–30	20	40
Anna-Perenna			
American Silhouettes	75	85	400
Arctic Spring	75	50	70
Bashful Bunnies	63	50	60
Capricious Clowns	95	50	70
Celebration	100	80	150
Children of Mother Earth	250	200	250
Christmas Magic	68–85	60	300
Flowers of Count Lennart Bernadotte	75	60	95
Happy Village	55	40	50
Heartland	90	75	80
Mother's Love	80–85	60	75

	ISSUE	LOW	HIGH
Rhythm and Dance	30	15	30
Uncle Tad's Cat	75–80	65	150
Uncle Tad's Golden Oldies	40	30	60
Anri			
Christmas	38–300	50	300
Disney Four Star Collection	40–50	40	95
Father's Day	35–60	90	100
Ferràndiz Christmas	35–150	85	225
Ferràndiz Mother's Day	35–150	100	200
Ferràndiz Wooden Birthday	15–22	100	200
Ferràndiz Wooden Wedding	40–60	90	150
Mother's Day	35–60	50	60
Sarah Kay Annual	120	80	100
Antique Trader			
Bible Series	11	5	10
C.M. Russel	12	5	10
Currier & Ives	9	5	10
Armstrong's/Crown Parian			
American Folk Heroes	35	20	30
Beautiful Cats of the World	60	50	80
Buck Hill Bears	30	20	30
Constitution	40	30	40
Eyes of the Child	65	40	55
Faces of the Wild	25	10	20
Lovable Kittens	30	15	25
Moments of Nature	40	30	40
Portraits of Childhood	65	50	60
Reflection of Innocence	38	30	35
Sporting Dogs	55	45	100
Statue of Liberty	40	30	40
Three Graces	50	40	50
Wells Fargo	65	55	65
Artaffects			
America's Indian Heritage	25	35	45
American Blues Special Occasions	35	25	35
Angler's Dream	55	45	55
Baby's Firsts	22	15	20
Bessie's Best	30	50	65
Bring Unto Me the Children	30	20	30
Carnival	40	30	40
Children of the Prairie	30	20	30
Classic American Trains	35	30	65
Colts	40	30	55
Council of Nations	30	30	40
Gift Edition	38	25	35
Heavenly Angels	27	20	25
How Do I Love Thee?	40	30	40
Magical Moments	30	45	80
North American Wildlife	30	20	30
Nursery Pair	25	35	40
Old Fashioned Christmas	30	25	30
On the Road	35	45	55
Playful Pets	45	55	60
Portraits	25	30	35

	ISSUE	LOW	HIGH
Reflections of Youth	30	25	50
Rockwell Americana	75	100	125
Rose Wreaths	27	20	25
Sailing Through History	30	40	45
Simpler Times	35	50	55
Studies of Early Childhood	35	20	55
Tender Moments, set of 2	150	200	250
Timeless Love	35	25	30
Unicorn Magic	50	40	50
War Ponies of the Plains	27	20	25
Young Chieftains	50	70	75
Artists of the World			
Celebration	40	35	40
Children at Play	65	100	150
Children of Don Ruffin	50–60	40	50
Children of the Sun	35–38	50	75
Fiesta of the Children	35	20	30
Western Series	65	90	100
Woodland Friends	60	45	55
World of Game Birds	45–50	40	80
Art World of Bourgeault			
English Countryside	70–95	200	250
Royal Literary Series	60–65	75	80
Where Is England?	525	500	600
Bareuther			
Christmas	12–60	15	60
Father's Day	11–43	8	50
Mother's Day	11–43	8	75
Thanksgiving	14–43	10	35
Berlin Design			
Christmas	15–80	25	125
Father's Day	15–25	20	40
Historical	30–48	20	40

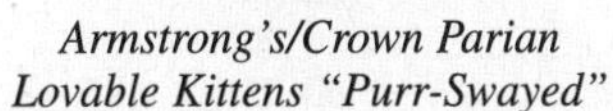

Armstrong's/Crown Parian
Lovable Kittens "Purr-Swayed"

Artaffects
On the Road "City Pride"

	ISSUE	LOW	HIGH
Holiday Week of the Family Kappelmann	33–35	20	25
Bing & Grøndahl			
Carl Larsson Miniature	15	5	10
Cat Portraits	40	25	35
Centennial Collection	60	45	55
Composers of Classical Music	38	25	30
Gentle Love	45	30	40
Hans Christian Andersen	43	28	35
Moments of Truth	30	5	15
Seasons Remembered	35	20	30
Windjammers	95	75	85
Blue Delft			
Christmas	12	5	25
Father's Day	12	25	30
Mother's Day	12	5	8
Boehm Studios			
Award-Winning Roses	45	60	100
Banquet of Blossoms and Berries	63	45	55
Butterflies of the World	62	45	55
Favorite Florals	58	40	50
Gamebirds of North America	63	45	55
Hummingbird Collection	63	50	80
Life's Best Wishes	75	60	70
Roses of Excellence	62	55	85
Tribute to Award-Winning Roses	63	50	60
Bradford Exchange			
Alice in Wornderland	33	20	25
Battles of American Civil War	30	20	25
Bygone Days	30	20	25
Charles Wysocki's Hometown Memories	30	20	25
Charles Wysocki's Peppercricket Grove	25	15	18
Christmas in the Village	30	20	25
Classic Cars	55	40	50
Classic Roses	35	25	30
Currier & Ives Christmas	35	20	25
Deer Friends at Christmas	30	20	25
Divine Light	35	15	20
Enchanted Charms of Oz	33	20	25
Family Affair	30	20	25
Family Circles	30	15	25
Field Pup Follies	30	20	25
Forever Glamorous Barbie	50	35	45
Fracé's Kingdom of the Great Cats: Signature Collection	40	30	40
Freshwater Game Fish of North America	30	20	25
Great Superbowl Quarterbacks	30	20	25
Heart to Heart	30	15	20
Heaven's Little Sweethearts	30	20	25
Heirloom Memories	30	20	25
Hidden Garden	30	20	25
It's a Wonderful Life	35	20	30
Lena Liu's Beautiful Gardens	35–47	25	35
Life of Christ	30–35	20	25
Mysterious Case of Fowl Play	30	15	20
Mystic Spirits	30–33	15	20

	ISSUE	LOW	HIGH
Native Visions	.30	20	25
Our Heavenly Mother	.35	20	25
Pathways of the Heart	.30	20	25
Pinegrove Winter Cardinals	.30	20	25
Santa's Little Helpers	.25	15	20
Silent Journey	.30	20	25
That's What Friends Are For	.30	20	25
Thomas Kinkade's Illuminated Cottages	.35–38	30	40
Timberland Secrets	.30	20	25
Trains of the Great West	.30	25	30
Triumph of the Air	.35	25	30
Two's Company	.30	20	25
Warm Country Moments	.30	20	25
When All Hearts Come Home	.30	20	25
Where Eagles Soar	.30	20	25
Winter Shadows	.30	20	25
Byliny Porcelain			
Flights of Fancy: Ornamental Art of Old Russia	.30–33	15	55
Jewels of the Golden Ring	.30–35	15	25
Legend of the Scarlet Flower	.30–33	20	65
Legend of Tsar Saltan	.40	25	75
Russian Seasons	.30–35	20	80
Tale of Father Frost	.30–33	20	90
Village Life of Russia	.36–41	20	30
Castleton China			
Bicentennial	.60	40	50
Natural History	.40	25	30
Christian Bell Porcelain			
Age of Steam	.65	40	200
Preserving a Way of Life	.60–65	50	55
Christian Fantasy Collectibles			
Christian Fantasy	.50	30	40
Fantasy Cookbook	.50	30	40

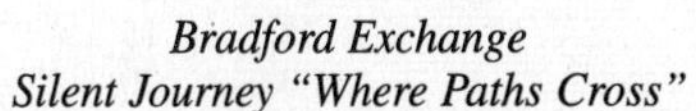

Bradford Exchange
Silent Journey "Where Paths Cross"

Byliny Porcelain
Village Life of Russia "Merry Musicians"

	ISSUE	LOW	HIGH
Realms of Wonder	50	30	40
Christian Seltmann			
Luekel's Idyllic Village Life	25–30	15	20
Velvet Paws	30–36	25	100
Crestley Collection			
Backyard Buddies	20	10	15
Heavenly Hearts	20	10	15
Picture Purrfect Cats	20	10	15
Teddy Bear Fair	20	10	15
Trolls	20	10	15
Vision Quest	20	10	15
Crown Delft			
Christmas	10	5	30
Father's Day	10	4	8
Mother's Day	10	4	8
CUI-Arolina Collection-Dram Tree			
Great American Sporting Dogs	40	20	30
Native American	40	20	30
Danbury Mint			
Bicentennial Silver	125	80	120
Christmas	25–30	15	20
Currier & Ives Silver	125	80	120
Michelangelo Crystal	75	50	60
Michelangelo Silver	125	80	120
Pigs in Bloom	30	15	25
Pride of the Wilderness	30	15	25
D'Arceau Limoges			
Cambier Four Seasons	105	90	125
Christmas	25–31	20	45
Lafayette Legacy	15–20	10	15
Les Douze Sites Parisiens	23–27	15	30
Les Femmes du Siècle	15–23	15	45
Les Tres Riches Heures	76	50	60
Dave Grossman Creations			
Boy Scout Annual	30	30	45
Children of the Week	30	20	25
Emmett Kelly Christmas	20–30	35	300
Margaret Keane	25	20	40
Miniature Bas Relief	25–27	30	40
Native American	45	30	40
Norman Rockwell–Tom Sawyer	26	35	40
Saturday Evening Post	25	15	20
Davenport Pottery			
Attwell's Silver Linings	25	20	50
Cottages of Olde England	75	65	125
Gardens of Victoria	60–65	50	100
Toby Plate Collection	35–40	25	30
Treasury of Classic Children's Verse	29–34	20	50
World of Beatrix Potter	59–69	60	140
Delphi			
Adventures of Indiana Jones: The Last Crusade	25	20	60
Beatles	25–30	20	65
Beatles '67-'70	28	15	25
Commemorating the King	30	20	25

	ISSUE	LOW	HIGH
Dream Machines	.25–28	15	20
Elvis on the Big Screen	.30–35	25	95
Elvis Presley Hit Parade	.30–37	20	30
Elvis Presley: In Performance	.25–32	25	85
Elvis Presley: Looking at a Legend	.25–35	20	70
Fabulous Cars of the Fifties	.25–28	15	20
Legends of Baseball	.25–32	15	25
Magic of Marilyn	.25–28	25	30
Marilyn Monroe Collection	.25–32	60	75
Portraits of the King	.28–33	25	75
Take Me Out to the Ballgame	.30–35	20	25
Diana Art			
Backyard Birds	.30	20	25
Ducks for All Seasons	.30	20	25
Endangered Species	.30	20	25
Exotic Animals	.30	20	25
Farm Animals	.30	20	25
Dominion China, Ltd.			
Be My Baby	.30	15	20
Birds of the North	.35–40	15	50
Heartfelt Traditions	.35	25	70
Joys of Childhood	.30–35	25	75
Lords of the Wilderness	.35–38	30	70
Moments of Serenity	.30–33	20	25
Portraits of the Wild	.30–35	25	60
Proud Passage	.30–33	25	50
Reflections of Canadian Childhood	.25–30	15	25
"The Loon" Voice of the North	.30–40	25	55
Treasures of the Arctic	.30–33	15	45
Victorian Christmas	.40–47	25	40
Wild and Free: Canada's Big Game	.30–35	20	25
Wings Upon the Wind	.22–25	15	60
Edna Hibel Studios			
David Series	.250–275	300	1200
Edna Hibel Holiday	.50	70	85
Famous Women and Children	.350	400	1200
Flower Girl Annual	.79	200	225
Mother and Child	.40–85	90	500
Mother's Day Annual	.30–37	250	300
Oriental Gold	.275–325	375	650
Tribute to All Children	.55	70	100
World I Love	.85	175	300
Edwin M. Knowles			
Americana Holidays	.26	10	15
American Innocents	.20	10	25
Carousel	.25	10	20
Casablanca	.35–38	30	45
Christmas in the City	.35	25	50
Classic Mother Goose	.30	20	45
Eve Licea Christmas	.45–50	40	65
Gone with the Wind	.22–30	30	100
Heirlooms and Lace	.35–38	30	80
Jessie Wilcox Smith Childhood Holidays	.20–23	10	15
Mary Poppins	.30–33	25	40

	ISSUE	LOW	HIGH
Old-Fashioned Favorites	30	60	140
Purrfect Point of View	30	25	50
Pussyfooting Around	25	10	15
Season for Song	35	40	65
Singin' in the Rain	33	25	45
Snow White and the Seven Dwarfs	30–37	30	45
Upland Birds of North America	25–28	15	20
Wizard of Oz: A National Treasure	30–35	20	50
Enesco			
Barbie–Glamour	30	20	25
Calico Kittens	35	20	25
Cherished Teddies–Christmas	35	20	30
Cherished Teddies–'Tis the Season	13	8	10
Precious Moments Four Seasons	40	30	50
Precious Moments Holly-Day Greetings	10	5	8
Star Trek	8	4	5
Star Trek: The Next Generation	30	15	25
Fairmont China			
Famous Clowns	55	35	275
Gnome Four Seasons	30	20	25
Long Road West	40	20	30
Memory Annual	77–80	70	85
When I Grow Up	30	20	25
Fenton Art Glass			
Alliance	15–18	25	30
American Craftsman Carnival	10–18	50	200
Christmas in America	13–25	10	50
Christmas Star	65–85	60	90
Mother's Day I	11–35	10	35
Mother's Day II	45–50	35	45
Valentine's Day	15	20	25
Fleetwood Collection			
Birds and Flowers of the Meadow and Garden	40	20	30

Enesco
Calico Kittens "Friendship Is Heavenly"

Fenton Art Glass
Christmas Star "Silent Night"

	ISSUE	LOW	HIGH
Blossoms of China	50	30	40
Christmas	45–50	40	55
Golden Age of Sail	39	20	30
Mother's Day	45–50	40	60
Pandas of Wu Zuoren	40	20	30
Franklin Mint			
American Portrait	30	15	25
American Revolution	75	50	65
Arabian Nights	28	15	20
Audubon Society	125	50	75
Bernard Buffet	150	250	275
Birds and Flowers of Beautiful Cathay	35	20	25
Birds and Flowers of the Orient	55	35	40
Clipper Ships	55	30	40
Country Year	55	30	45
Currier & Ives	40	40	40
Days of the Week	39	20	30
Fairy Tales Miniatures	15	8	10
Flowers of the American Wilderness	40	20	30
Garden Birds of the World	55	35	45
Grimm's Fairy Tales	42	20	30
International Gallery of Flowers	55	35	45
Mark Twain	38	30	55
Poor Richard	13	5	10
Roberts' Zodiac	150	150	165
Rockwell American Sweethearts	120	140	160
Songbirds of the World	55	35	45
Songbirds of the World Miniatures	15	5	10
Woodland Birds of the World	65	40	50
World's Great Porcelain Houses	20	10	15
Frankoma Pottery			
Bicentennial	5	30	40
Christmas	4–12	15	300
Madonna Plates	13–15	10	25
Teenagers of the Bible	5–12	30	45
Furstenberg			
Christmas	15–25	20	35
Easter	15–25	20	150
Mother's Day	15–25	20	45
Muninger's Romantic Winter Impressions	35–40	20	30
Wild Beauties	35–43	30	70
Ghent Collection			
Christmas Wildlife	20–32	20	55
Country Diary of an Edwardian Lady	80	60	70
Mother's Day	22–32	20	40
Goebel/M.I. Hummel			
Christmas in Kinderland	50	40	60
M.I. Hummel Club Celebration	90–120	120	150
M.I. Hummel Little Music Maker	30–40	60	75
Mothers	45–75	30	60
Gorham			
American Landscapes	45–60	30	50
Boy Scout	20	30	75
Charles Russell	38–45	65	100

	ISSUE	LOW	HIGH
Christmas	13–38	25	65
Clowns	45	30	60
Four Seasons–A Boy and His Dog, set of 4	50	150	175
Four Seasons–Dad's Boy, set of 4	135	90	120
Grande Copenhagen	25–45	20	70
Irene Spencer	38–40	50	100
Lewis and Clark Expedition	55	45	75
Moppets Christmas	10–12	8	35
Remington Western	25–38	20	60
Time Machine Teddies	33–38	30	45
Ugly Duckling	29–32	15	25
Greentree Potteries			
American Landmarks	10	5	8
Grant Wood	10	5	7
Mississippi River	20	10	15
Motorcar	20	10	15
Hackett American			
Classical American Beauties	60	40	50
Endangered Species	35–40	30	75
Everyone's Friends	43	30	35
Favorite Dreams	40	25	30
Friends of the Forest	50	30	40
Horses in Action	50	30	40
Mother and Child	43	25	35
Ocean Moods	50	30	40
Owl and the Pussycat	40	25	30
Snow Babies	40–43	35	65
Waterbird Families	43	30	40
Hadley House			
American Memories	85	75	150
Annual Christmas	65	50	225
Birds of Prey	75	50	60
Country Doctor	30	20	25
Glow Series	55	85	325
Mountain Majesty	50	40	50
Navajo Woman	50	30	40
North American Legacy	60	40	50
Retreat Series	65	85	120
That Special Time	65	60	95
Windows to the Wild	65	50	60
Hallmark Galleries			
Days to Remember–Norman Rockwell	35–45	30	40
Enchanted Garden	25–45	20	40
L. Votruba Collection	8–9	5	10
Marjolein Bastin's Seasons of Nature	38	20	30
Hamilton Collection			
American Civil War	38	45	75
American Rose Garden	30	20	25
America's Greatest Sailing Ships	30	40	50
Andy Griffith	30	30	75
Bundles of Joy	25	30	100
Butterfly Garden	30	20	40
Childhood Reflections	30	20	65
Classic TV Westerns	30	45	95

	ISSUE	LOW	HIGH
Coral Paradise	30	30	40
Country Garden Calendar Collection	55	35	45
Country Garden Cottages	30	20	35
Curious Kittens	30	25	35
Delights of Childhood	30	20	25
Elvis Remembered	38	65	100
English Country Cottages	30	20	75
Eternal Wishes of Good Fortune	35	35	70
Farmyard Friends	30	20	25
Favorite American Songbirds	30	20	35
Good Sports	30	20	50
Great Fighter Planes of World War II	30	20	35
Japanese Floral Calendar	33	25	40
Jeweled Hummingbirds	38	40	45
Majesty of Flight	38	30	50
Mystic Warriors	30	20	25
Nature's Quiet Moments	38	40	75
North American Gamebirds	38	30	45
Official Honeymooners	25	115	140
Proud Indian Families	30	20	50
Proud Nation	25	20	50
Rockwell's Mother's Day	24–33	25	85
Saturday Evening Post	35	30	60
Seasons of the Bald Eagle	38	50	75
Star Trek 25th Anniversary Commemorative	35–38	35	150
Star Wars	30	150	200
Vanishing Rural America	30	25	45
West of Frank McCarthy	38	40	60
Wizard of Oz–Portraits from Oz	30	200	300
Haviland			
Bicentennial	40	30	50
French Collection Mother's Day	30–55	15	45
Historical	100	50	75

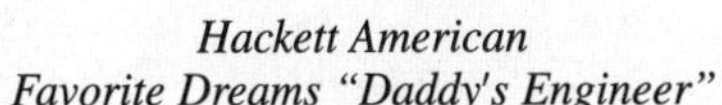

Hackett American
Favorite Dreams "Daddy's Engineer"

Hadley House
Glow Series "Evening Glow"

	ISSUE	LOW	HIGH
Theatre des Saisons	120	130	140
Heinrich Porzellan			
Fairies of the Fields and Flowers	35	75	125
Flower Fairy	35	30	50
Russian Fairy Tales	70	40	50
Historic Providence Mint			
Alice in Wonderland	30	20	25
America the Beautiful	38	20	30
Li'l Peddlers	30	20	25
Vanishing American Barn	40	25	30
Hoyle Products			
Norman Rockwell Clowns	45	35	75
Norman Rockwell Salesman	35–45	20	30
Nostalgia	25–30	25	65
Remember When	30	20	25
Wings of the Wild	30	20	25
Hutschenreuther			
Bouquets of the Season	25–30	15	20
Country Birds of the Year	30	20	25
Flowers That Never Fade	28	15	20
Glory of Christmas	80	100	125
Gunther Granget	30–125	50	200
Legend of St. George	100	70	80
Zodiac	125	120	135
Imperial Ching-Te Chen			
Beauties of the Red Mansion	28–35	10	20
China's Imperial Palace: The Forbidden City	40–46	15	25
Legends of West Lake	30–35	15	20
Maidens of the Folding Sky	30–33	30	50
Incolay Studios			
Christmas Cameos	60–65	40	50
Four Elements	25	15	20
Majestic Sailing Ships	65	40	50
Romantic Poets	60–70	50	80
Voyages of Ulysses	50–55	40	60
Kaiser			
Anniversary	17–40	20	30
Christmas	13–40	20	40
Classic Fairy Tales	40	30	50
Faithful Companion	50	30	45
Glen Loates' Feathered Friends	70–80	75	100
Mother's Day	13–40	10	85
On the Farm	50	60	75
Racing for Pride and Profit	50	25	40
Romantic Portraits	175–200	150	225
Treasures of Tutankhamen	90	100	120
Water Fowl	50–55	40	75
Wildflowers	40–50	50	55
Wildlife, set of 6	100	100	125
Kern Collectibles			
Adventures of the Old West	65–75	50	60
Child's World	45	25	35
Companions	40–55	40	90
Favorite Pets	40	30	85

	ISSUE	LOW	HIGH
Sugar and Spice	40–50	60	130
Konigszelt Bayern			
Deutches Fachwerk	25–27	15	20
Grimm's Fairy Tales	23–29	10	15
Hedi Keller Christmas	30–35	15	20
Sulamith's Love Song	30	15	20
Lenox			
American Wildlife	65	40	50
Boehm Birds	35–93	25	90
Boehm Woodland Wildlife	50–100	75	100
Colonial Christmas Wreath	65–75	60	150
Garden Birds	48	30	35
Lenox Christmas Trees	50–80	40	70
Royal Cats of Guy Coheleach	40	20	25
Lihs Linder			
America the Beautiful	42	30	35
Christmas	25–40	20	35
Easter	22–28	30	45
Mother's Day	20–28	15	90
Playmates	45	40	55
Lladró			
Christmas	28–90	20	75
Lladró Plate Collection	32–50	20	40
Mother's Day	28–90	30	125
Lowell Davis Farm Club			
Davis Cat Tales	38	75	85
Davis Christmas Annual	45–48	50	125
Davis Country Pride	35	100	200
Davis Red Oak Sampler	45–53	110	125
Lynell			
American Adventures	50	40	60
Betsy Bates Annual	25–39	20	45
Famous Clowns of the Circus	39	20	30
How the West Was Won	39	20	25
Little Traveler	45	15	20
Norman Rockwell Mother's Day	30	25	40
Marmot			
Christmas	13–40	30	60
Father's Day	12	40	100
Mother's Day	16–40	45	140
Presidents	25	15	20
Metal Arts Company			
Children of Norman Rockwell	21	10	15
Norman Rockwell Christmas	48	30	35
Norman Rockwell Man's Best Friend	40	40	60
Modern Concepts Limited			
Nursery Rhyme Favorites	39	25	30
Signs of Love	40	30	40
Special Moments	35–39	35	50
Modern Masters			
Babes in the Woods	45–50	35	45
Litter Baskets	35	20	25
Wings of Nobility	43–50	30	40

	ISSUE	LOW	HIGH
Morgantown Crystal			
Heavens Above	65	40	50
Star of Bethlehem	35–38	20	25
Yate's Country Ladies	75	70	90
Osiris Porcelain			
Cleopatra: Queen of Ancient Egypt	40	60	95
Egypt: Splendors of an Ancient World	79–84	60	75
Legend of Tutankhamen	40–45	30	75
Pemberton & Oakes			
Adventures of Childhood	20–25	40	60
Best of Zolan in Miniature	13	40	110
Childhood Discoveries–Miniature	15–17	15	40
Childhood Friendship	20	35	60
Children and Pets	19	35	70
Children at Christmas	48	60	100
Moments to Remember–Miniature	17	15	55
Nutcracker II	25	35	70
Special Moments of Childhood	19–25	30	95
Swan Lake	35	45	65
Wonder of Childhood	19–22	20	35
Zolan's Children	19–25	35	90
Pickard			
Christmas	60–90	60	90
Children of Renoir	50–60	65	125
Gems of Nature	29–34	20	60
Lockhart Wildlife	150–200	110	650
Romantic Castles of Europe	55	40	50
Symphony of Roses	85–100	95	135
Porsgrund			
Christmas	12–42	35	120
Father's Day	8–22	10	20
Mother's Day	8–25	5	20
Princeton Gallery			
Circus Friends	30	20	25
Cubs of the Big Cats	30	20	25
Enchanted World of the Unicorn	30	20	25
R.J. Ernst Enterprises			
Beautiful World	28	15	20
Elvis Presley	40	20	30
Hollywood Greats	30	40	85
Hollywood Walk of Fame	40	25	35
Liebchen	20	10	15
Republic Pictures Library	38	20	30
Seems Like Yesterday	25	20	35
Star Trek	30–40	65	150
Star Trek Commemorative	30	75	150
Yesterday	25	15	20
Reco International			
Barefoot Children	30	20	60
Becky's Day	25–28	20	35
Bohemian Annual	130–150	155	160
Childhood Almanac	30–35	30	35
Grafburg Christmas	20–22	20	60
Hearts and Flowers	30–35	30	55

	ISSUE	LOW	HIGH
King's Christmas	100–200	225	265
King's Flowers	85–130	130	175
Little Professionals	40	45	95
McClelland Children's Circus	30	30	50
Mother Goose	23–28	20	65
Vanishing Animal Kingdoms	35	20	30
World of Children	50	35	45
Reed and Barton			
Audubon	60–65	50	150
Christmas Carols	55–60	65	200
Kentucky Derby	75	80	85
River Shore			
Baby Animals	50	65	90
Children of the American Frontier	25	25	40
Little House on the Prairie	30	40	45
Puppy Playtime	25	20	30
Remington Bronze	55–60	60	70
Rockwell Four Freedoms	65	100	425
Signs of Love	19–27	10	15
We the Children	25	15	20
Rockwell Museum			
American Family I	29	35	60
American Family II	35	30	55
Christmas Collectibles	55–75	50	75
Shirley Temple Collectibles	75	80	100
Rockwell Society			
Christmas	25–35	20	90
Coming of Age	30–35	25	65
Mother's Day	25–33	15	60
Rockwell Heritage	15–30	15	60
Rockwell's American Dream	20–25	10	30
Rockwell's Golden Moments	20–25	15	30
Rockwell's Rediscovered Women	20–23	10	30

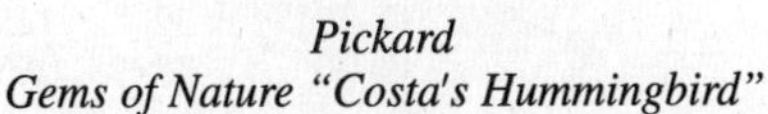

Pickard
Gems of Nature "Costa's Hummingbird"

R.J. Ernst
Hollywood Greats "John Wayne"

	ISSUE	LOW	HIGH
Roman, Inc.			
Child's Play	30	35	40
Frances Hook Legacy	20–23	30	35
Love's Prayer	30	20	25
Masterpiece Collection	65–95	60	80
Sweetest Songs	40	40	45
Rorstrand			
Christmas	12–93	10	475
Father's Day	15–43	10	30
Mother's Day	15–43	20	30
Rosenthal			
Classic Rose Christmas	84–195	50	160
Wiinblad Christmas	100–375	200	750
Wiinblad Crystal	150–295	270	400
Royal Bayreuth			
Antique American Art	50–65	60	70
L. Henry Series	50–55	50	60
Mother's Day	17–65	50	130
Royal Copenhagen			
America's Mother's Day	35–45	25	35
Christmas in Denmark	7–75	60	70
Historical	30–95	30	90
Motherhood	30–32	35	50
Mother's Day	13–38	25	130
Royal Cornwall			
Alice in Wonderland	45	25	35
Beauty of Bouguereau	35	30	65
Bethlehem Christmas	30–35	40	85
Classic Christmas	55	65	85
Crystal Maiden	58	75	80
Five Perceptions of Weo Cho	55	75	125
Legendary Ships of the Sea	50	30	40
Puppy's World	50	30	40
Windows on the World	45	30	40
Royal Doulton			
Behind the Painted Masque	95	150	175
Beswick Christmas	35–55	30	45
Celebration of Faith	250	250	300
Children of the Pueblo	60	80	100
Commedia Dell' Arte	50–70	75	175
Flower Garden	60–85	75	90
Grandest Gift	75	80	100
I Remember America	70–95	70	90
Portraits of Innocence	65–95	115	125
Reflection on China	70–85	75	90
Victorian Childhood	29–34	30	85
Victorian Era Christmas	25–42	30	55
Royal Worcester			
Birth of a Nation	45–65	120	275
Doughty Birds	150–330	140	300
Kitten Encounters	30	25	50
Royale			
Christmas	12–30	30	125
Father's Day	13–30	35	80

	ISSUE	LOW	HIGH
Game Plates	180–265	200	250
Mother's Day	12–30	35	80
Royale Germania			
Christmas Annual	200–450	310	650
Mother's Day Crystal	135–350	225	650
Royal Grafton	28–33	15	20
Braithwaite Game Birds	25–30	15	30
Schmid–Germany			
Beatrix Potter	50	35	40
Berta Hummel Christmas	15–65	5	55
Berta Hummel Mother's Day	15–55	10	70
Friends of Mine	53–55	40	50
My Name Is Star	30	20	25
Prairie Women	35	20	25
Schmid–Japan			
Disney Characters	23–37	20	60
Disney Christmas	10–19	10	150
Disney Mother's Day	10–19	15	50
Kitty Cucumber Annual	25	25	45
Paddington Bear Annual	13	10	30
Peanuts Christmas	10–19	10	100
Peanuts Valentine's Day	13–18	10	35
Raggedy Ann Annual	18–19	15	70
Raggedy Ann Christmas	13–18	10	45
Seven Seas			
Christmas Carols	15–25	15	25
Historical Events	14–15	20	150
Mother's Day	15	20	30
New World	15–18	10	30
Sports Impressions			
Best of Baseball	30	15	20
Golden Years	60	40	50

Royal Copenhagen
Motherhood
"Mother Robin with Babies"

Schmid-Germany
Berta Hummel Mother's Day
"Mother's Little Athlete"

	ISSUE	LOW	HIGH
NFL Platinum Edition	50	30	40
Regular Edition	50	30	40
Sterling America			
Mother's Day	18–24	15	25
Twelve Days of Christmas	18	20	25
Studio Dante de Volteradici			
Christmas Crèche	55–60	40	100
Gates of Paradise	75–80	50	115
Grand Opera	35–40	20	25
Renaissance Madonnas: Gifts of Maternal Love	65–70	50	80
Vague Shadows			
Chieftains I	65	80	300
Masterpieces of the West	35	30	75
Motherhood	50	60	75
Pride of America's Indians	25	20	75
Princesses	50	100	175
Storybook Collection	30	40	45
Tribal Ponies	65	100	150
Waterford–Wedgwood USA			
Avon Christmas	15–25	10	30
Avon Mother's Day	15–17	20	30
Bicentennial	40–45	30	100
Christmas	25–80	20	90
My Memories	27–29	20	50
Winston Roland			
Best of Loates	39	20	25
Brush with Life	43	30	40
Faithful Companions	50	35	40
Olde Country Cottages	46	35	40
W.S. George			
Alaska: The Last Frontier	35–38	25	55
America's Pride	30–35	25	45
America the Beautiful	35–40	15	30
Art Deco	40	30	60
Baby Cats of the Wild	30–33	30	45
Bear Tracks	30	20	25
Black Tie Affair: The Penguin	30	25	50
Country Nostalgia	30–35	20	45
Critic's Choice: Gone with the Wind	28–35	20	50
Delicate Balance: Vanishing Wildlife	30–33	20	40
Dr. Zhivago	40	20	50
Eyes of the Wild	30	15	20
Flowers of Your Garden	25–30	15	50
Garden of the Lord	30–35	25	40
Gentle Beginnings	35–38	30	80
Lena Liu's Basket Bouquets	30–33	20	50
Loving Look: Duck Families	35–38	20	30
Majestic Horse	35	30	75
Memories of a Victorian Childhood	30–33	20	60
Nature's Playmates	30–37	20	45
On Gossamer Wings	25–30	15	35
Spirits of the Sky	30–35	25	75
Vanishing Gentle Giants	33–36	20	50
Victorian Cat Capers	25–30	20	50

Political Memorabilia

Every political campaign from dog catcher to president produces memorabilia. In addition to the familiar campaign buttons, there is literature of all types, including posters, pictures, brochures and newpaper ads. Such variety and the number of candidates over the years create a rich and broad collecting field. Political memorabilia offers a history lesson, a chance to discover the movers and shakers of other eras. Most collectors concentrate on national elections and well-known politicians. There are others that focus on third party and more obscure candidates.

Buttons are a favorite area of specialization for many collectors. There are several types of buttons. Celluloid buttons are produced by placing a thin piece of paper over a metal disc and then sealing it with a coating of celluloid. Tin lithograph buttons are produced by printing directly onto the tin. A curious term to novices is "jugates," which are buttons picturing both the presidential and vice-presidential candidates.

Although some items are worth thousands of dollars, this collecting field offers items for every budget.

Franklin Roosevelt, litho cardboard fan, adv for Boyd School, Washington, D.C. on back, 7.5" x 10.5", $35–$40.

Assorted Memorabilia

	LOW	HIGH
Blaine, ribbon, black and white, 1884, 9" l	$50	$75
Blaine, James and John Logan, campaign bandanna, 18" sq	180	220
Bryan, postcard, "Back to the Farm–Three Strikes and Out," anti-Bryan cartoon	14	20
Bryan, postcard, "Bottom Is Out of the Full Dinner Pail," 1908	10	20
Bryan, postcard, "Next Occupant of the White House"	8	14
Bryan, ribbon, black and white, 1908, 5"	35	55
Bryan, watch fob, brass and enamel, 1908	40	60
Carter, pencil, "Carter-Mondale '76," green lettering, 7" l	5	8
Carter, "The Interview, Carter Talks in *Playboy,*" *Playboy* magazine folder with 2.5" dia button	8	12
Cleveland, stickpin, brass portrait, 1888, 2.5"	30	50
Cleveland, Grover and Thomas Hendricks, bandanna, 18" sq	200	300
Eisenhower, sticker, "I Like Ike," 1952 or 1956, 3" x 3.5"	6	9

	LOW	HIGH
Garfield, cologne bottle, clear glass, bust of Garfield, 9" h	800	1200
Garfield, ribbon, black and blue, 1880, 7" l	120	180
Grant, ribbon, black and white, 1868, 7.5" l	250	450
Harrison, Benjamin, bandanna	300	500
Johnson, pennant, red, white, and blue, "Win with Johnson," triangular, felt, 1964, 30" l	10	15
Kennedy, pennant, red, white, and blue, "Kennedy–Johnson," 1960, felt, 30" l	15	20
Kennedy, doll, sitting in rocking chair, musical	200	300
Lincoln, cigar box label, "Lincoln Bouquet," colored and emb., c1910, 6" x 10"	10	25
McCarthy, scarf	6	8
McGovern, litho, "McGovern for McGovernment," by Alexander Calder	375	400
McKinley, tile, glazed pottery, 3" sq	40	50
Nixon, ribbon, red, white, and blue, 1960, 6" l	15	20
Nixon, sticker, "Let's Back Nixon," Nixon pointing finger at Krushchev, 1960 campaign, 4" x 6"	15	20
Roosevelt, Franklin, poster	15	25
Roosevelt, Franklin, mug, "Happy Days Are Here Again"	30	50
Roosevelt, Teddy, postcard, "Dee Lighted," 1905	12	20
Roosevelt, Theodore, *Puck* magazine, issue contains 2 large political cartoons, one of Teddy Roosevelt, 1906	15	25
Roosevelt, Theodore, serving tray, Roosevelt as Rough Rider on horseback, polychrome tin	500	750
Taft, postcard, "Nation's Choice," emb., Taft and Sherman image	10	15
Taft, postcard, "Our Next President William H. Taft: Glory and Prosperity For Our Country," color Taft image	8	12
Taft, postcard, "Our Next President and Vice President," Taft and Sherman	8	12
Wilson, sheet music, "I Think We've Got Another Washington and Wilson Is His Name," 1915	15	20
Wilson, sheet music, "Never Swap Horses When You're Crossing a Stream," Wilson portrait, 1916	15	20

Pinback Buttons

Carter, "The Grin Will Win Jimmy in '76, Carter for President"	$6	$10
Chafin, "Eugene Chafin for President," 1908 Prohibition Party candidate, black and white, .875"	36	40
Coolidge, litho tin, blue and white	14	18
Coolidge/Davis, jugate, celluloid, black and white, .875"	35	45
Cox, black and white, portrait in ring, 1920, 1.25"	200	300
Eisenhower, "I Like Ike," litho tin, red lettering on white ground, 1952	2	3
Hoover, black and white, 1.25"	45	50
Hoover, litho tin, red, white, and blue, .875"	4	8
Johnson/Humphrey, jugate, photos in outline of U.S., "Vote Democratic," red, white, and blue, 3.5"	10	15
Johnson, Lyndon, "Sterilize LBJ: No More Ugly Children," 1.25"	15	25
Kennedy, profile portrait, "Youth for Kennedy," red, white, and blue, 1960, 4"	250	450
Kennedy, "For President John F. Kennedy," red, white, blue, and black	10	15
Landon, brown, white, and yellow picture in sunflower, 1936, 1.75"	12	18
McKinley/Hobart, jugate, mechanical gold button, 1896	200	250
McKinley/Theodore Roosevelt, jugate, "Employment for Labor, A Full Dinner Bucket," sepia, 1.25"	100	145
Nixon/Lodge, jugate, litho tin, 1960	3	5
Quayle, Daniel, "We are the Most Powerful Planet on Earth," 1.25"	2	4

	LOW	HIGH
Reagan, "Ronald Reagan for Governor," litho tin, white border	2	3
Roosevelt, red rose w/ "VELT" on leaves, red, white, and blue, 1940, 1.25"	40	60
Roosevelt, "Carry On," litho tin, 1"	4	8
Roosevelt, "Rally Round Roosevelt, The People's Choice for President, RRR," red, white, and blue	25	35
Roosevelt, Franklin/Wallace, jugate, sepia w/ red, white, and blue border	42	52
Roosevelt, Teddy, portrait	20	30
Smith/Robinson, jugate, litho tin, 1926	20	30
Stevenson, "Our Next President Adlai Stevenson," red, white, and blue, 1.75"	10	14
Taft, name only, red and white, 1908, .75"	10	15
Taft, polychrome portrait, 1908, 4"	225	300
Taft, celluloid, multicolor	35	40
Taft/Sherman, jugate, gray and white	100	140
Truman, Inauguration, January 20, 1949, red, white, and blue w/ gray photo, 1.75"	18	22
Willkie, "If I Were 21 I'd Vote for Wilkie," green and white, 1.25"	6	9
Willkie, portrait surrounded by Stars and Stripes, red, white, and blue, 1940, 1.75"	30	50
Willkie, white and black w/ shoulder length portrait, "For President" at top	18	22
Wilson, polychrome portrait, "Win with Wilson," 1916, 1.25"	30	50
Wilson/Marshall, jugate, celluloid, black and white, "Win With Wilson and Marshall," .875"	32	40

Campaign Buttons. Above left to right: Harding, brown, .75" d, $10–$15; Willkie, red, white, and blue, 1" w, $5–$10; Keep Coolidge, blue, white, and black, .75" d, $10–$15. Below: Lydon Johnson plastic flasher button, $12–$18.

Pottery & Porcelain: Manufacturers

For more information on pottery and porcelain, consult *The Official Price Guide to Pottery and Porcelain, Eighth Edition* by Harvey Duke, House of Collectibles, NY, 1995 and *Dinnerware of the 20th Century: The Top 500 Patterns* by Harry L. Rinker, House of Collectibles, NY, 1997.

J.A. Bauer Pottery

The J.A. Bauer Company began producing clay flowerpots in 1909. After the introduction of stoneware and art pottery, the company added colored dinnerware in 1930, which it produced until 1962.

Marks: an impressed mark with *Bauer* or a combination of the words *Bauer, Los Angeles, Pottery* and *USA.* Many items are unmarked or simply stamped *Made in USA.*

Monterey (1936–1945)

Orange, red, and burgundy are the most desirable of the ten colors.

	LOW	AVG.	HIGH
Butter Dish	$60	$73	$86
Cake Plate, pedestal	80	90	100
Candle Holder	25	30	35
Chop Plate, 13"	30	40	50
Coffee Server	32	37	42
Dish, 6"	11	14	17
Fruit, ftd., 8" to 9"	27	36	44
Fruit, ftd., 12"	45	54	63
Gravy Boat	33	38	43
Pitcher, 2 qt.	33	38	42
Plate, 6" to 7.5"	8	10	12
Plate, 9"	13	15	17
Plate, 10.5"	26	29	31
Platter, oval, 12" to 17"	30	37	45
Relish Tray, 3-pc., 11.5"	42	50	58
Salad, 11.5"	31	36	42
Salt/Pepper	12	16	19
Sauce Boat	38	42	46
Soup Plate, 7"	16	19	21
Tumbler, 8 oz.	15	18	21
Vegetable, oval, 10.5"	30	38	45

Ring (c. 1931)

Ring is Bauer's most popular pattern. It is reputedly the line that influenced Homer Laughling to create Fiesta. The pattern appears in many colors. Black pieces are worth more than the values quoted below.

	LOW	AVG.	HIGH
Baking Dish, cov., 4"	$20	$23	$26
Batter Bowl, 1 to 2 qt.	60	80	100
Butter Dish	110	130	150
Candlestick, spool	30	35	40
Canister, 4" to 6"	60	80	100
Casserole, individual, 5.5"	65	70	75

Ring, nesting bowls, green, yellow, cobalt blue, and orange-red, set of 4, $175. —Photo courtesy Ray Morykan Auctions.

	LOW	AVG.	HIGH
Casserole, metal holder, 6.5" to 7.5"	45	60	75
Chop Plate, 12" to 14"	42	55	68
Chop Plate, 17"	75	90	106
Coffeepot, 8 cup	120	160	180
Cream Pitcher, 1 pt.	35	45	55
Custard	8	10	12
Egg Cup	65	74	82
Fruit Dish, 5"	13	15	17
Gravy Bowl	38	44	50
Mixing Bowl, 1 pt.	13	16	19
Mixing Bowl, 1.5 pt.	16	19	22
Mixing Bowl, 1 qt.	20	23	25
Mixing Bowl, 1.5 qt.	22	25	27
Mixing Bowl, 1 gal.	42	48	56
Mustard	100	125	150
Pickle Dish	16	19	22
Pitcher, 1.5 pt.	21	25	28
Pitcher, 1 qt.	26	30	33
Pitcher, 2 qt.	33	38	43
Pitcher, 3 qt.	42	52	62
Pitcher, ball form	65	75	85
Pitcher, ice lip, metal handle, 2 qt.	68	80	93
Plate, 5" to 9"	12	16	20
Plate, 10.5"	31	36	40
Platter, oval, 9"	22	24	26
Platter, oval, 12"	27	30	33
Punch Bowl, 9"	100	130	160
Punch Bowl, pedestal base, 14"	160	180	200
Punch Cup	16	19	22
Relish Tray, 5-pc.	36	43	50
Salad, low, 9"	31	36	41
Salad, low, 12" to 14"	60	75	90
Saucer	5	7	9
Shaker, barrel shape	5	7	9
Shaker, low	5	7	9
Sherbet	32	38	44
Soufflé Dish	138	150	163
Soup Plate	27	30	32
Storage Jar, open	15	18	21
Sugar Bowl	50	60	70
Teapot, 2 to 6 cup	50	60	70
Tumbler, barrel shape, metal handle	32	37	42
Vegetable, oval, 8" to 10"	26	28	30
Vegetable, oval, divided	45	55	65

Jim Beam Bottles

Jim Beam bottle figural liquor containers were first issued in the 1950s. The company produces a variety of themes including the Executive Series, Regal China Series and Political Figures Series. Early Beam bottles made before the figural series are also collectible. In 1953, the company produced its first figural decanter. When the decanters sold well, Beam began producing decorative bottles on a large scale.

Arizona, 1968, $5–$10.

	LOW	AVG.	HIGH
Beam Pot, 1980, 7.25" h	$25	$30	$35
Bob Hope Golf, 1973, 11" h	15	20	25
Buffalo Bill, 1971, 10.5" h	6	10	12
Cedars of Lebanon, 1971, 9.75" h	5	10	12
Chicago Art Museum, 1972, 8.75" h	15	20	25
Circus Wagon, 1979, 13.25" l	30	35	40
Coho Salmon, 1976, 10.5" h	8	10	12
Delco Freedom Battery, 1978, 5" h	12	10	20
Dial Telephone, 1980, 13.5" h	18	20	22
Emmett Kelly Clown, 1973, 14" h	50	60	70
French Cradle Telephone, 1979, 7.25" h	20	22	30
Great Dane, 1976, 11.5" h	8	10	12
Hongie Hika Maori Warrior, 1980, 13" h	150	160	200
Hoola Bowl, football, 1975, 11.25" h	10	12	20
Jackelope, 1971, 14" h	8	10	12
Maine, 1970, 13" h	5	8	10
Mister Goodwrench, 1978, 13.5" h	9	10	12
Model T Ford, 1974, 9.5" h	45	50	60
Northern Pike, 1978, 8.75" h	10	12	20
Pearl Harbor, 1972, 11.75" h	24	30	35
Ramada Inn, 1976, 11" h	8	10	12
Screech Owl, 1979, 9.75" h	20	22	30
Short Timer, army boots and helmet, 1975, 8" h	30	35	40
Shriner's Pyramid, 1975, 5" h	16	20	24
Sidney Opera House, 1977, 8.5" h	26	30	40
Stone Mountain, 1974, 10.5" h	7	10	12
Sturgeon, 1980, 6.25" h	15	18	20
Texas Rabbit, 1971, 12.25" h	8	10	12
Thomas Flyer 1907, 1976, 16" l	65	70	90
Trout Unlimited, 1977, 12" h	10	12	20
Uncle Sam Fox, 1971, 12.5" h	10	12	20
Viking, 1973, 14" h	8	10	10
Yellowstone, 1972, 11.25" h	7	8	10

Bennington Pottery

The period of true Bennington was brief, from 1842 to 1858, but this is deceiving since the output during those sixteen years was heavy. In 1842 Julius Norton (a grandson of the founder) went into partnership with Christopher Fenton. Norton and Fenton set out to duplicate the surface of Rockingham wares. From the original name of "Norton and Fenton," it became "Fenton's Works," then "Lyman, Fenton and Co." Finally, the company used the name "United States Pottery" from 1850 until its collapse in 1858.

The earliest mark of Norton and Fenton, in 1842, was a circular wording of *NORTON & FENTON, BENNINGTON, Vt.* Block lettering was used without any symbol. When the company name changed, after Norton left in 1847, the mark became *FENTON'S WORKS, BENNINGTON, VERMONT* enclosed in a rectangular decorative border. This distinctive mark was set in two styles of lettering with *FENTON'S WORKS* in slanting characters resembling italics. The address was set in standard vertical lettering. The next mark, that of Lyman, Fenton and Co., sat within a plain oval frame and read *LYMAN FENTON & CO., FENTON'S ENAMEL, PATENTED 1849, BENNINGTON, Vt.* This ushered in the era of colored glazes. Within this mark, the year (1849) is prominently displayed. The United States Pottery Co. era introduced two different marks, both reading *UNITED STATES POTTERY Co., BENNINGTON, VT.* One carries the wording in an oval frame with two small ornamental flourishes; the other is a modified diamond shape composed of decorative printer's type, but without further ornamentation.

Flint Enamel "Rockingham" Glazed Pieces

	AUCTION	RETAIL	
		Low	High
Baking Dish, 1849 mark, 7" dia	$175	$400	$660
Book Flask, 4 qt. largest size	1600	3500	6000
Book Flask, "Bennington Battle," 7.5" h	700	1650	2650
Book Flask, "Departed Spirits," 5" h	425	1000	1600
Book Flask, "Departed Spirits," 8" h	700	1650	2650
Book Flask, extended spout, rare small 1849 mark, 6" h	900	2120	3400
Book Flask, "Hoo Doo King," 5.5" h	1300	3000	5000
Book Flask, "Lexington Battle," 7" h	600	1420	2250
Candlesticks, 8" h, pair	500	1180	1900
Candlesticks, 9.25" h, pair	725	1700	2750
Chamber Pitcher, scalloped rib pattern, 1849 mark, 12.75" h	750	1750	2700
Chamber Pot, cov., diamond pattern, 10" dia	350	830	1330
Coffeepot, 1849 mark	250	600	950
Coffeepot, scalloped rib pattern, 12" h	650	1500	2500
Cow Creamer, cov., 7" l	350	830	1330
Creamer, tulip and heart pattern, 1849 mark, 6" h	300	700	1140
Curtain Tieback, 3.5" l, 4.5" dia	30	70	100
Cuspidor, scalloped rib pattern, 1849 mark, 8.25" dia	100	240	380
Doorknob	25	60	90
Foot Warmer, 9" h	100	240	380
Goblet, 4.75" h	200	470	760
Goblet, ftd., handle, 4.5" h	250	590	950
Mold, Turk's head, 6.5" dia	150	350	570
Mug, 3.25" h	60	140	230
Nameplate, 8" l	125	300	470
Picture Frame, oval, 8" x 7"	400	850	1400
Picture Frame, Rococo, 10" x 9"	1600	3500	6000
Picture Frame, scalloped or serpentine, 5.75" x 6.75"	150	350	570

	AUCTION	RETAIL Low	RETAIL High
Pipkin, cov., 7.5" h	450	1000	1700
Pitcher, 8-panel, molded tulips and hearts, 7" h	450	1000	1700
Pitcher, alternate rib pattern, 6.75" h	150	350	570
Pitcher, alternate rib pattern, 1849 mark, 10" h	900	2000	3400
Pitcher, diamond pattern, 9" h	350	800	1350
Pitcher, early, "Norton & Fenton East Bennington VT," 8" h	800	2000	3000
Pitcher, mask under spout, 8.75" h	200	450	750
Relish Dish, 10" l	350	800	1350
Slop Jar Base, 1849 mark	450	1000	1700
Tile, 1849 impressed mark, 7" sq	400	940	1500
Tobacco Jar, cov., alternate rib pattern, 6.75" h	300	700	1100
Toby Creamer, 1849 mark	550	1300	2000
Toby Pitcher, honey-colored coachman, 1849 mark, 10.5" h	475	1200	1800
Toby Pitcher, vintage handle, 6" h	350	830	1300
Toby Snuff Jar, cov., dark greenish-brown glaze	600	1400	2200
Toothbrush Holder, cov., alternate rib pattern	500	1200	1900
Tulip Vase, fine and colorful glaze, 10" h	600	1400	2250
Wash Bowl, paneled, 1849 mark, 13.5" dia	475	1100	1800
Wash Bowl and Pitcher, 1849 mark	375	900	1420

Parian Pieces

	AUCTION	RETAIL Low	RETAIL High
Bust, girl w/ bird, 5" h	$50	$120	$190
Creamer, Bennington-type handle, 4.25" h	55	120	190
Doorknob, rosette pattern	25	50	80
Pitcher, pond lily pattern, U.S. Pottery ribbon mark, 10" h	175	410	660
Pitcher, wild rose pattern, 10" h	200	470	760
Trinket Box, blue and white, 5" l	30	70	110
Trinket Box, cov., molded flower lid, 5.5" l	15	25	40
Vase, hand holding flower, miniature, 3" h	15	20	40
Vase, molded grapevine pattern, scalloped rim, 4.5" h	50	120	200
Vase, songbird pattern, blue and white, 4" h	25	60	90

Left: Rockingham Glazed Pitcher, seated hunter and hound, 9" h, $200–$300.

Right: Parian Pitcher, Paul and Virginia pattern, dark blue ground, ribbon mark, 10.75" h, $300–$400.

Ezra Brooks Bottles

Ezra Brooks produces figural bottles with themes ranging from sports and transportation to antiques. The antique series includes an Edison phonograph and a Spanish cannon. Ezra Brooks rivals Jim Beam as one of the chief whiskey companies manufacturing figural bottles.

Ram, 1972, $12–$16.

	LOW	AVG.	HIGH
American Legion, Miami Beach, 1973	$12	$14	$16
Amvet, Polish Legion, 1973	22	27	32
Antique Cannon, 1969	8	9	10
Antique Phonograph, "morning glory" horn, gold trim	12	14	15
Arizona, 1969, man w/ burro in search of "Lost Dutchman Mine"	7	9	10
Auburn 1932 Classic Car, 1978	45	50	55
Badger No. 3, Hockey, 1974	24	28	30
Baltimore Oriole Wild Life, 1979	53	60	70
Baseball Hall of Fame, Heritage China, 1973	22	26	30
Bengal Tiger Wild Life, 1979	50	55	60
Big Daddy Lounge, white, green, and red, 1969	7	8	9
Bighorn Ram, 1973	11	13	15
Bordertown, Borderline Club, club building w/ vulture on roof stopper	7	8	9
Brahma Bull, 1972	17	20	23
Clown, Imperial Shrine, 1978	28	32	38
Club Bottle, 3rd commemorative, shape of America, gold stars represent locations of Ezra Brooks Collectors Clubs, 1973	30	35	40
Colt Peacemaker, gun-shaped flask, 1969	6	7	8
Conquistador's Drum and Bugle, 1972	15	18	20
Corvette Indy Pace Car, 1978	62	68	73
Giant Panda, 1972 Maine Lobster, lobster-shaped, 1970	28	32	36
Minnesota Hockey Player, 1975	27	30	33
Missouri Mule, 1972, brown	17	20	22
Mr. Foremost, bottle-shaped symbol of Foremost Liquor stores, 1969	13	15	17
Mr. Maine Potato, 1973	9	10	11
Mr. Merchant, shopkeeper leaping w/ arms outstretched, 1970	12	14	16
Nebraska "Go Big Red," Heritage China, game ball and fan, 1972	15	17	19
New Hampshire State House, eagle stopper, 1970	15	17	19
North Carolina Bicentennial, 1975	15	18	21
Oil Gusher, oil drilling rig, all silver, black stopper as gushing oil	7	9	11
Old Ez, No. 1, barn owl, 1977	67	76	86
Penguin, Heritage China, 1972	12	14	16
Sailfish, blue-green fish, green "waves" base, 1971	11	14	17
Sea Captain, holding pipe, "wooden" stanchion base, 1971	15	17	19
Senators of the U.S., "Old Time" senator, Heritage China, 1972	17	20	22

Buffalo Pottery

Buffalo Pottery Company was established in 1901 by the Larkin Soap Company for the purpose of producing mail order premiums. Early production consisted mainly of semi-vitreous dinnerware. The company's most famous line, Deldare Ware, was produced from 1908 to 1909 and from 1921 to 1923. Emerald Deldare, which used scenes from Goldsmith's *The Three Tours of Dr. Syntax,* was made in 1911.

	AUCTION	RETAIL	
		Low	High
Chamberstick Holder, village scene border, 1.75" h, 5" dia	$550	$675	$800
Chop Plate, The Fallowfield Hunt–The Start, 1908, 13.5" dia	550	675	800
Cup/Saucer, The Fallowfield Hunt, 1909, 2" h cup, 5.75" d saucer	303	380	450
Hair Receiver, Ye Village Street, 1908, 2.75" h, 4.75" dia	605	750	900
Mug, At the Three Pigeons, 1908, 4.5" h, 5.25" d	495	625	750
Pitcher, The Fallowfield Hunt–The Return, 1909, 7.25" h	825	950	1100
Plate, Dr. Syntax Pursued By a Bull, 1911, 9.325" dia	935	1050	1300
Plate, The Fallowfield Hunt-The Death, 1909, 8.25" dia	193	240	300
Shaving Mug, Ye Razor, 1910, 3.75" h, 4.5" d	1210	1500	1800
Soup Bowl, The Fallowfield Hunt-Breaking Cover, 1909, 2" h, 9" dia	495	625	750
Sugar, open, Breaking Cover, 6-sided, 1908, 2.75" h, 3.75" dia	385	480	575
Tankard, The Great Controversy, 1908, 12.25" h	1040	1300	1500
Vase, baluster form, 3 ladies in formal gowns 1 side, gentleman and lady other side, 1908, 8" h, 7.5" dia	1320	1650	2000
Wall Plaque, The Fallowfield Hunt-Breakfast at the Three Pigeons, 1908, 12" dia	523	650	775
Wall Plaque, An Evenin at Ye Lion Inn, 1908, 13.5" dia	385	480	575

Left to right: Deldare Charger "The Fallowfield Hunt–The Start"; Emerald Plate "Dr. Syntax Presenting A Floral Offering"; Deldare pitcher "The Fallowfield Hunt–Breaking Cover"; Emerald Powder Jar w/ birds, flowers, and butterflies; Deldare Pitcher "To Spare An Old Broken Soldier–To Advise Me In A Whisper"; Deldare Egg Cup "Village Scene"; Deldare Pitcher "Their Manner of Telling Stories–Which He Returned With A Curtsey". —Photo courtesy Smith & Jones.

Camark Pottery

The Camark Pottery Company operated from 1926 (as Camden Art and Tile Company) until 1982, but it produced few pieces for the last decade and a half. Early "Le-Camark" pieces are wheel-thrown and of the hand-decorated line. Most pieces, however, are molded. The most desired are Le-Camark pieces, animal figurals, and pitchers with figural handles. Reproductions, notably the cat with fish bowl (Wistful Kitten) are on the market.

Marks: most often impressed *CAMARK*.

Planter, swans, white, gold trim, $20–$35.

	LOW	AVG.	HIGH
Ashtray, green	$7	$9	$12
Ashtray, shell	12	16	29
Bowl, cabbage leaf	10	15	20
Bowl, hand-thrown, ruffled edge	40	45	50
Bowl, onion, large	35	40	45
Bowl, pumpkin, large	12	16	20
Bowl, pumpkin, small	7	9	11
Bowl, swans	12	16	20
Bud Vase, star	14	18	22
Console Bowl, floral and cones decoration	30	35	40
Cream/Sugar, on stand	15	20	25
Creamer	10	12	14
Dog, miniature	8	10	12
Flower Frog, dancer	20	25	30
Flower Frog, round	10	15	20
Flower Frog, swans	15	19	22
Humpty Dumpty	20	25	30
Mug	20	25	30
Pitcher, corn-form body	25	30	50
Pitcher, cornucopia	40	45	50
Pitcher, parrot handle	45	60	75
Planter, elephant	55	60	65
Planter, wood barrel	20	25	30
Vase, cornucopia	24	28	32
Vase, double handled	24	28	32
Vase, fan, black, early	60	65	70
Vase, flower handles	22	26	30
Vase, hand-thrown, rings and fluted top	45	50	55
Vase, leaf, large	30	35	40
Vase, leaf, small	24	28	32
Vase, mirror black, early	60	65	70
Vase, ribbon	28	32	36
Vase, twist, large	40	45	50

Canonsburg Pottery

The Canonsburg Pottery manufactured dinnerware for the first three quarters of this century. It is often marked by a backstamp with a cannon.

Keystone (1934)

	LOW	AVG.	HIGH
Casserole	$15	$20	$25
Cream/Sugar	9	16	23
Cup/Saucer	5	7	9
Plate, 6" to 7"	6	7	8
Plate, 9"	8	9	10
Platter, oval, 11"	10	12	14

Priscilla (1932)

	LOW	AVG.	HIGH
Casserole	$25	$30	$35
Cream/Sugar	12	16	18
Cup/Saucer	4	6	8
Plate, 6" to 7"	2	3	4
Plate, 9"	4	5	6
Teapot	15	20	25

Ceramic Arts Studio, Snuggles

Ceramic Arts Studio is famous for its novelties manufactured between 1941 and 1955. They are usually stamped with the words "Ceramic Arts Studio" underlined or with a half circular "Madison, Wisconsin." Sometimes the piece is named.

Snuggles or Lap-Sitters are pairs of figures that fit together.

	LOW	AVG.	HIGH
Bear, mother and baby	$18	$25	$32
Boy w/ Chair	16	22	28
Clown and Clown Dog	16	22	28
Cow and Calf	16	22	28
Dog w/ Doghouse	18	25	32
Elephant and Native Boy	30	35	40
Girl w/ Chair	16	22	28
Kangaroo Mother and Baby	18	25	30
Kitten and Pitcher	20	25	30
Monkey Mother and Baby	18	25	30
Mouse and Cheese	18	25	30
Native Boy on Alligator	35	40	45
Oak Sprite, sitting on leaf	16	22	28
Oak Sprite, straddling leaf	16	22	28
Oriental Girl and Boy	28	32	38
Seahorse and Coral	15	20	25
Skunk Mother and Baby	20	25	30
Suzette on Pillow	15	20	25

Crooksville China

The Crooksville China Company manufactured semiporcelain dinnerware and kitchenware from 1902 until 1959. Several backstamps exist.

Petit Point House

	LOW	AVG.	HIGH
Casserole, 8"	$20	$25	$30
Coaster, 4"	8	12	16
Coffeepot	35	40	45
Cream/Sugar	12	16	18
Cup/Saucer	4	6	8
Custard Cup	2	3	4
Plate, 6"	1	2	3
Plate, 9" to 10"	5	6	7
Platter, rectangular, 11" to 15"	5	10	15
Pudding Dish	4	5	6
Syrup Pitcher	15	20	25
Tea Tile	16	18	20
Vegetable, rectangular, 9.25"	8	10	12

Silhouette Pitcher, $20–$25.

Silhouette

	LOW	AVG.	HIGH
Cream/Sugar	$14	$18	$20
Cup/Saucer	5	7	9
Custard Cup	3	4	5
Plate, 6"	2	3	4
Plate, 9" to 10"	6	8	10
Platter, 11" to 13"	8	14	20
Pudding Dish	4	5	6
Tea Tile	18	20	24

Southern Belle

	LOW	AVG.	HIGH
Coaster, 4"	$8	$12	$16
Cream/Sugar	12	16	18
Cup/Saucer	4	6	8
Custard Cup	2	3	4
Plate, 6"	1	2	3
Plate, 9" to 10"	4	5	6
Platter, rectangular, 11" to 13"	6	12	18
Pudding Dish	4	5	6
Tea Tile	17	20	23

Dedham Pottery

Dedham Pottery was originally founded as the Chelsea Keramicworks, but changed its name in 1895 after the company relocated to the town of Dedham, Massachusetts. The company was renowned for its gray stoneware pottery with crackle glazing and blue border designs of animals, flowers and birds.

Plate Patterns

See low end for 6" plates and high end for 10" plates.

	AUCTION	RETAIL Low	RETAIL High
Azalea	$75	$250	$300
Birds in Orange Tree	200	600	800
Butterfly	100	300	600
Crab	250	600	900
Duck	125	300	500
Elephant	300	700	900
Grape	125	250	350
Horse Chestnut	100	300	350
Iris	100	300	350
Lobster	250	700	900
Magnolia	125	250	300
Mushroom	300	400	500
Polar Bear	400	800	1200
Pond Lily	125	300	400
Rabbit	75	175	250
Turkey	175	400	800

Dedham patterns, top row left to right: Magnolia, Horsechestnut, Polar Bear, Poppy, and Strawberry. Bottom row left to right: Swan, Horsechestnut, Polar Bear, and Rabbit. —Photo courtesy Smith & Jones.

Dedham patterns, top row left to right: Rabbit cookie jar, embossed Night & Morning pitcher w/ embossed Owl & Prey decoration w/ moon on reverse, Poppy plate. Bottom row left to right: Pond Lily plate, Duck cup and saucer, Rabbit child's plate; Rabbit open nappy #2. —Photo courtesy Smith & Jones.

Other Forms

	AUCTION	RETAIL	
		Low	High
Bacon Rasher, swan pattern	$825	$1320	$2100
Bowl, cov., swan border, 7.25"	400	650	1100
Bowl, square, rabbit pattern	550	890	1400
Candlestick, elephant w/ baby pattern	715	1150	1900
Cereal Bowl, rabbit border	175	360	500
Creamer, rabbit pattern	360	580	1000
Cruet, rabbit pattern w/ standing rabbit stopper	2750	4400	7000
Cupboard Bowl, rabbit pattern	550	850	1400
Demitasse Cup and Saucer, rabbit patter	350	540	900
Egg Cup, rabbit pattern	300	460	800
Mug, elephant pattern, 3"	4000	6000	8000
Fruit Bowl, floral border	175	280	500
Milk Pitcher, global, rabbit pattern	825	1310	2100
Mug, baluster form, rabbit pattern	825	1340	2100
Pickle Dish, rabbit pattern	600	930	1600
Sugar Bowl, rabbit border, 4.25" dia	175	260	400
Sugar Bowl, rabbit pattern	1760	2680	4700
Water Pitcher, rabbit pattern	1430	2250	3700

Frankoma Pottery

In 1933, while working at the University of Oklahoma Ceramics Department, John Frank started Frank Potteries. By 1938, he had left the university, moved to Sapulpa, Oklahoma, and renamed his company Frankoma Pottery. Joh Frank designed all of Frankoma's dinnerware lines such as Mayan-Aztec (1945), Lazybones, Plainsman, Wagon Wheel and Westwind. Most are still in production.

Marks: impressed *Frankoma*; some early pieces have *Frankoma* stamped in black. A mark featuring an impressed panther in front of a vase appeared from 1936 to 1938.

Frankoma impressed mark.

	LOW	AVG.	HIGH
Ashtray, Dutch shoe, #914, 6"	$18	$22	25
Batter Pitcher, #87	25	30	35
Bowl, #45, 12"	24	30	35
Bowl, carved, #202, 11"	26	30	35
Bowl, swirled, #209, 12"	16	20	25
Bud Vase, #32	8	12	15
Bud Vase, #43, crocus	12	15	18
Cornucopia, #57, 7"	8	10	12
Cornucopia, #222, 12"	15	20	25
Eagle Pitcher, miniature, #555	20	24	30
Flower Bowl	20	24	30
Honey Jug, #8	12	15	20
Lazy Susan, #838	35	40	45
Leaf Dish, #227	25	30	35
Planter, mallard, #208A	10	12	15
Match Holder, #89A	35	40	45
Mug, #C2	4	5	6
Pitcher, #835, 24 oz.	12	15	20
Plate, Texas State	8	10	12
Rice Bowl, #F34	4	6	8
Vase, free form, #6	25	30	32
Vase, fan, #19	28	30	35
Vase, pedestal, #23A	6	8	12
Vase, fan shell, #54	35	40	45
Vase, swan, #228	12	15	20
Vase, ringed, #272	5	7	10
Vase, orbit, #F36	8	10	15

Lazybones (1953)

	LOW	AVG.	HIGH
Cereal Bowl, #4X	$4	$5	$7
Mug, #4M, 16 oz.	4	5	7
Soup Cup, #4SC	5	7	10

Plainsman (1948)

Item			
Baker and Warmer, #5W, 3 qt.	$20	$25	$30
Creamer, #5A	4	5	6
Mug, #5M	8	10	12
Plate, #5F, 10.5"	10	12	15
Plate, #5G, 8"	4	5	6
Platter, #5Q, 13"	12	15	18
Salad Bowl, #5X	4	5	6
Salt/Pepper, #5H	4	6	8
Sauce Boat, #5S	20	25	30
Teacup, #5CC, 5 oz.	5	8	10
Tumbler, #51C	4	6	8

Wagon Wheel (1941)

Item			
Baker, #94W, 3 qt.	$30	$40	$50
Bean Pot, individual, #94U	30	40	50
Candle Holder, #454	20	25	30
Casserole, #94V	30	35	40
Chili Bowl, #94XL	8	10	12
Cream/Sugar, #94A&B	20	25	30
Cream/Sugar, miniature, #510	15	20	24
Cup, #94C	7	10	12
Dessert Bowl, #94XO	6	8	10
Fruit Bowl, #94XS	8	10	12
Mug, #94M	9	12	15
Pitcher, #94D	20	25	30
Plate, #94F, 9"	8	10	13
Plate, #94FL, 10"	10	12	15
Plate, #94G, 7"	8	10	13
Platter, #94Q, 13"	16	20	25
Salt/Pepper, #94H	10	14	20
Saucer, #94E	5	6	7
Server, divided, #94QD	20	25	30
Serving Dish, #94N	10	15	18
Sugar, miniature, #510	5	10	12
Teapot, cov., #94T	30	35	42

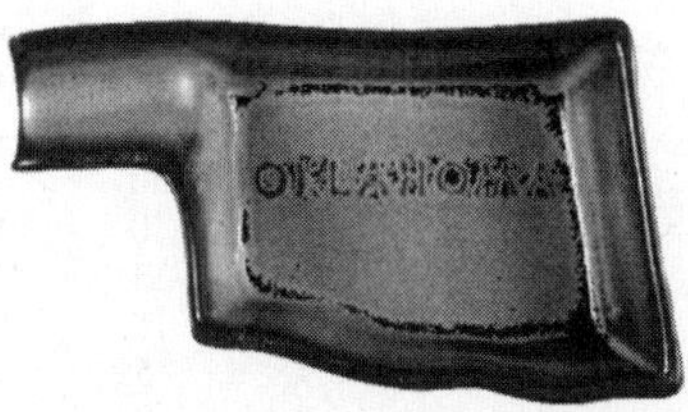

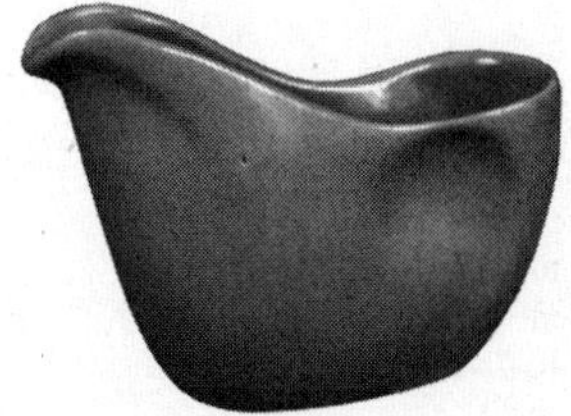

Left to right: Lazybones Creamer, $5–$8; Ashtray, Oklahoma State, $12–$15.

French-Saxon China

The Sebring family of Sebring, Ohio, owned both the French China Company and the Saxon China Company. The bankruptcy of the American Chinaware Company pulled both under in 1932. W.V. Oliver bought the Saxon plant and named his company French-Saxon. It made semiporcelain kitchenware and dinnerware. Royal China bought the company in 1964.

Marks: backstamps included a knight and shield graphic backstamp and a circular Union mark. Romany and Rancho have only their names stamped.

French-Saxon backstamp.

Rosalyn (1937)

	LOW	AVG.	HIGH
Casserole	$9	$12	$15
Cream/Sugar	22	26	30
Cup/Saucer	7	9	11
Dish, 5" to 6"	2	3	4
Gravy Boat	15	18	20
Plate, 6" to 7"	4	5	6
Plate, 9" to 11"	7	8	9
Salt/Pepper	11	15	18
Soup Plate, 7.75"	7	8	9
Vegetable, 8.5"	16	17	18

Zephyr (1938)

Solid colors decorated with decals. The two solid-color lines are called Romany (red, yellow, dark blue, and green) and Rancho (maroon, gray, chartreuse, and dark green).

	LOW	AVG.	HIGH
Bowl, 36s	$7	$8	$9
Chop Plate, 13"	9	12	15
Coffeepot	36	40	45
Cream/Sugar	25	30	35
Cup/Saucer	8	10	12
Dish, 5" to 6"	2	3	4
Gravy Boat	15	18	21
Plate, 6" to 7"	4	5	6
Plate, 9" to 11"	8	10	12
Salt/Pepper	12	16	18
Soup Plate, 7.75"	8	10	12
Vegetable, 8.5"	16	18	20

Fulper Potter

The Fulper Pottery produced an Arts and Crafts-style ware from c1913 through the 1920s.

	AUCTION	RETAIL	
		Low	High
Bowls, leopard skin crystalline glaze, 5" d, set of 6	$425	$525	$650
Cabinet Vase, dark brown and gray matte crystalline glaze, 4" h, 3" w	375	450	525
Effigy Bowl, cat's-eye flambé glaze interior, mustard matte and brown exterior	750	900	1050
Vase, baluster, mirrored black to copperdust crystalline flambé glaze, 7" h	600	750	900
Vase, bottle shape, mauve, mustard, and leopard skin crystalline flambé glaze, 11.25" h	2700	3200	4000
Vase, bulbous, ribbed, 2 handles, ivory, mahogany, and mirrored black flambé glaze, 12" h	1000	1250	1500
Vase, corseted, 2 handles, copperdust crystalline to Flemington green flambé glaze, 10" h	550	675	800
Vase, gourd shape, mirrored black to Flemington green flambé glaze, 5.5" h	400	500	600
Vase, ovoid, 2 handles, green to cobalt crystalline flambé glaze, 7.75" h	300	375	450
Vase, tall and tapering form, 2 handles, cucumber crystalline to cucumber matte glaze, 13" h	1000	1250	1500
Vessel, bell pepper shaped, cat's eye to Chinese blue flambé glaze, 4.25" h	350	400	475
Vessel, 2 buttressed handles, leopard skin crystalline glaze, 6.5" h	550	675	800

Assortment of Fulper Pottery. —Photo courtesy Smith & Jones.

Garnier Bottles

The Garnier Company began producing figural bottles in 1899. Those produced prior to World War II are scarce. Some of the better known include the Cat, 1930; Clown, 1910; Country Jug, 1937; and Greyhound, 1930.

	LOW	AVG.	HIGH
Bellows, Figural Specialties, #232, 1969	$12	$18	$24
Broc, #88, 1936	15	23	30
Broc Decor Cerises, #42, 1935	24	36	48
Broc Lijay, #60, 1936	24	36	48
Broc Six Sides, #65, 1935	24	36	48
Bull, Wildlife Figurals, #202, 1963	15	23	30
Candlestick, Figural Specialties, #134, 1955	24	36	48
Clown, Figurines, #137, 1955	18	27	36
Coffeepot, Figural Specialties, #192, 1962	21	32	42
Country Jug, #103, 1937	21	32	42
Diamond Bottle, Glass Specialties, #234, 1969	9	14	18
Drunkard, Figurines, #145, 1956	15	23	30
Duckling, Wildlife Figurals, #148, 1956	24	36	48
Duo, Multi-Compartment Glass, #168, 1959	9	14	18
Falcon Trocadero, Glass Specialties, #113, 1949	15	23	30
Five-Handle Jug, #170, 1959	13	20	36
Glass Decanter, Glass Specialties, #94, 1935	15	23	30
Goddess, Figurines, #196, 1963	27	41	54
Goose, Wildlife Figurals, #141, 1955	15	23	30
Grendadier, Figurines, #109, 1949	45	68	90
Hoola Hoop, Glass Specialties, #173, 1959	18	27	36
Horse Pistol, Figural Specialties, #205, 1964	12	18	24
Inca, Figurines, #236, 1969	15	23	30
Lafayette, Figurines, #107, 1949	48	72	96
Liquer D'Or, Glass Specialties, #101, 1938	12	18	24
Locomotive, Transportation Series, #101, 1938	12	18	24
Marquise, Figurines, #55, 1931	48	72	96
Musical Lamp, Glass Specialties, #209, 1964	27	41	54
Partridge, Wildlife Figurals, #177, 1961	27	41	54
Penguin, Wildlife Figurals, #50, 1932	45	68	90
Petanque, Figural Specialties, #217, 1966	21	32	42
Rainbow, Multi-Compartment Glass, #143, 1955	12	18	24
Rocket, Figural Specialties, #217, 1966	21	32	42
Rooster, Wildlife Figurals, #132 (black), 1952	15	23	30
Round Log, Figural Specialties, #156, 1958	27	41	54
Sheriff, Figurines, #164, 1953	15	23	30
Sommelier, Glass Specialties, #159, 1958	24	36	48
St. Tropez Jug, #182, 1961	15	23	30
State Bird Series, 1969	9	14	18
Three-Decanter Oak Tantalus, Glass Specialties, #93, 1938	24	36	48
Three-Decanter Tantalus, Glass Specialties, #140, 1955	24	36	48
Trio, Multi-Compartment Glass, #144, 1955	11	17	22
Trout, Wildlife Figurals, #224, 1967	11	17	22
Two-Legged Lamp, Glass Specialties, #157, 1958	17	26	34
Violin, Figural Specialties, #219, 1966	13	20	26
Woman w/ Jug, Figurines, #49, 1930	36	54	72
Young Deer, #207, 1964	18	27	36

W.S. George Pottery

In 1903 William S. George bought the East Palestine Pottery Company from the Sebring brothers from whom he had leased the plant. The plant produced his semiporcelain dinnerware for the next half century. The company used many different backstamps; some were unique to their shape.

W. S. GEORGE
MADE IN U.S.A.

W.S. George
Georgette

W.S. George backstamps.

Lido (1932)

	LOW	AVG.	HIGH
Bowl, 36s	$5	$6	$7
Butter Dish	19	22	24
Candlestick	18	20	22
Casserole	18	22	25
Cream/Sugar	15	18	21
Cup/Saucer	5	7	9
Dish, 5" to 6"	1	2	3
Egg Cup	6	8	10
Gravy Boat	10	12	14
Pickle Dish, 7.5"	4	5	6
Plate, 6" to 8"	2	3	4
Plate, 9" to 10"	5	6	7
Platter, 11" to 13"	6	8	10
Salt/Pepper	12	15	17
Soup Plate, 7.75"	5	6	7
Teapot	33	35	37
Vegetable, 9"	10	12	15

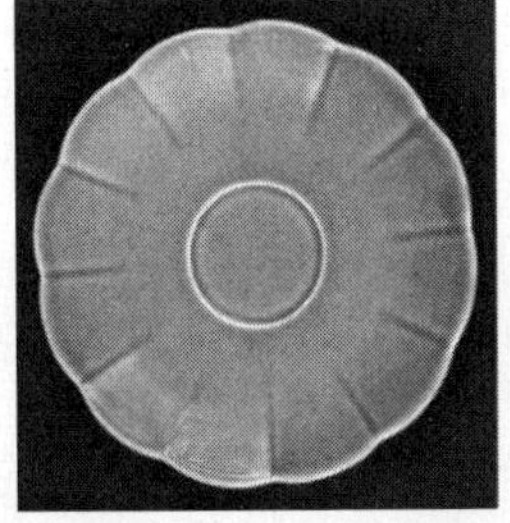

Petalware Saucer.

Petalware

	LOW	AVG.	HIGH
Bowl, 36s	$4	$5	$6
Casserole	15	20	25
Cream/Sugar	12	16	18
Cup/Saucer	4	6	8
Dish, 5" to 6"	1	2	3

	LOW	AVG.	HIGH
Gravy Boat	8	12	16
Pickle Dish	3	4	5
Plate, 6" to 8"	4	5	6
Plate, 9" to 10"	4	5	6
Platter, 11" to 16"	5	10	15
Soup Bowl	4	5	6
Teapot	15	20	25
Vegetable, cov.	15	20	25
Vegetable, open	8	10	12

Rainbow

Casserole	$18	$20	$22
Cream/Sugar	17	19	21
Cup/Saucer	5	6	7
Custard Cup	3	4	5
Dish, lug handle, 6.5"	2	3	4
Gravy Boat	12	13	14
Pickle Dish	3	5	6
Plate, 6" to 8"	2	3	4
Plate, 9" to 10"	4	5	6
Platter, 11" to 12"	7	8	9
Relish, shell-form	7	8	9
Salt/Pepper	12	16	19
Soup Plate	5	6	7
Teapot	29	31	33
Vegetable	10	12	14

Ranchero

Butter Dish	$15	$20	$25
Casserole	23	27	30
Coffeepot	30	35	40
Cream/Sugar	19	22	25
Cup/Saucer	6	8	10
Dish, 5" to 6"	2	3	4
Egg Cup	8	9	10
Gravy Boat	15	17	18
Plate, 6" to 7"	2	3	4
Plate, 9"	6	7	8
Platter	15	17	19
Salt/Pepper	15	17	19
Teapot	20	25	30
Vegetable	12	15	18

Sailing Pattern — Georgette Shape

Bowl, 36s	$5	$6	$7
Cream/Sugar	16	19	22
Cup/Saucer	5	7	9
Dish, 5" to 7"	1	2	3
Gravy Boat	11	12	13
Plate, 6" to 8"	4	5	6
Plate, 9" to 10"	6	7	8
Vegetable, oval, 9"	11	12	13

Gladding, McBean

The Gladding, McBean & Company began operating as a sewer pipe manufacturer in 1875. It introduced its famous earthenware Franciscan line of dinnerware in 1934. In 1963 the company changed its name to the Interpace Corporation. Wedgwood (England) purchased it in 1979 and continued production until 1986. Franciscanware is now produced in England.

Franciscan Classics was Gladding, McBean's name for its three most popular patterns of embossed, hand-painted underglaze dinnerware. These were Apple, Desert Rose and Ivy. Both Apple and Desert Rose have seen continuous production since the early 1940s.

Marks: various backstamps and decals, including *GMB* in an oval and *F* in a box for Franciscan. Contemporary pieces are backstamped *England.*

Apple (1940)

	LOW	AVG.	HIGH
Butter Dish, cov., 1/4 lb.	$30	$36	$45
Cake Plate, 12.5"	28	35	40
Casserole, individual	75	84	90
Cereal Bowl, 6"	6	10	15
Cookie Jar, cov.	200	250	300
Cream Soup	8	10	12
Cup/Saucer, jumbo	50	58	65
Fruit Dish	3	4	5
Gravy Boat, w/ liner	30	38	45
Milk Pitcher, 6.25" h	70	75	85
Plate, 6.5"	3	4	5
Plate, 8.5"	7	8	9
Plate, 9.5"	9	10	11
Plate, 10.5"	13	16	20
Platter, oval, 14"	40	55	70
Salad, crescent	25	32	40
Salad Bowl, 10"	115	145	165
Salt/Pepper, large	50	65	75
Salt/Pepper, small, apple shape	15	18	20
Soup Bowl, 8.5"	12	20	25
Tea Cup/Saucer	6	9	11
Teapot	75	95	125
Vegetable, oval, divided, 10.75" l	38	42	48
Water Pitcher	105	125	160

Desert Rose (1941)

	LOW	AVG.	HIGH
Butter Pat	$17	$18	$20
Cereal Bowl, 6"	13	14	16
Chop Plate, 14"	55	75	90
Coffeepot	85	95	110
Cup/Saucer	8	10	12
Demitasse Cup/Saucer	40	45	50
Egg Cup, single	20	28	35
Gravy, w/ liner	35	42	50
Milk Pitcher, 1 qt.	75	84	90
Plate, 6.5"	6	7	8
Plate, 8.5"	12	13	15

Left: Desert Rose Plate.
Right: Ivy Plate.

	LOW	AVG.	HIGH
Plate, 9.5"	13	15	20
Plate, 10.5"	15	17	19
Platter, 14.5"	35	40	45
Salt/Pepper, large	28	35	40
Salt/Pepper, small, rosebud	20	22	25
Soup, ftd., 5.5"	18	24	30
Vegetable, divided, 10"	38	45	50
Water Pitcher	100	115	125

Ivy

Butter Dish	$20	$25	$30
Casserole, 1.5 qt.	45	50	60
Cheese Server	42	50	55
Chop Plate, 12" to 14"	28	38	48
Cigarette Box	46	50	55
Coffeepot	40	48	55
Comport	25	40	55
Cookie Jar	80	90	100
Cream/Sugar	28	34	40
Crescent Dish	10	12	16
Cup/Saucer	8	10	14
Cup/Saucer, 12 oz.	16	18	20
Dish, 5" to 6"	7	12	14
Gravy Boat	20	24	28
Ladle	40	45	48
Mixing Bowl	35	50	65
Mug, 7 oz. to 12 oz.	14	20	26
Party Plate, round	16	18	20
Pitcher, 1 pt. to 2.5 qt.	15	35	55
Plate, 6" to 8"	7	10	13
Plate, 9" to 10"	10	15	20
Platter, 12" to 14"	25	38	50
Platter, 17"	90	115	140
Relish Tray	12	20	28
Salad	45	50	60
Salt/Pepper	22	28	34
Tidbit, 2-tier	34	40	45
Sherbet	12	15	18
Soup Plate	12	16	20
Teapot	42	48	55

Grueby Potteries

Grueby Potteries operated from 1891 to 1907. After 1907 all Grueby pottery was manufactured and sold under the name of Tiffany. Grueby produced expensive, high quality vases, ornamental wares including statuettes, and decorative tiles. These usually have a factory stamp and an artist's mark, either straight-line or circular.

	AUCTION	RETAIL Low	RETAIL High
Paperweight, scarab, curdled green matte glaze, 4" l	$770	$850	$950
Paperweight, scarab, leathery mustard matte glaze, 3" l	770	850	950
Paperweight, scarab, leathery teal matte glaze, 3.5" l	523	600	675
Tile, cuenca w/ 3-masted ship, brown, ivory, and French blue matte glaze, 6" sq	660	750	820
Vase, bottle-shaped, matte green glaze, 6" h	1045	1200	1350
Vase, corseted, tooled and applied leaves, matte green glaze, 8" h	2860	3200	3600
Vase, cylindrical, thick honey matte glaze, 7" h	1870	2000	2200
Vase, cylindrical, matte leathery blue-gray glaze, 9" h	825	940	1050
Vase, ovoid, incised ridges, matte green glaze, 5.5" h	1540	1750	2000
Vase, spherical, semimatte leather green glaze, 5" h	880	1000	1200
Vessel, squat, green matte glaze, 3.5" h	1045	1200	1350
Vase, squat, modeled leaves, thick white dead matte glaze, 4.75" h	1650	1900	2150
Vase, squat w/ flared rim, stylized leaf design, dark blue matte glaze, 3.75" h	1980	2200	2500
Vase, tapering, ridged, cucumber matte green glaze, 9" h	1540	1750	2000
Vessel, coupe-shaped, modeled leaves, pumpkin matte glaze, 3.5" h	2200	2900	3500

Grueby Pottery. —Photo courtesy David Rago Auctions.

Hall China

Robert Hall named his 1903 acquisition the Hall China Company and continued making the semiporcelain dinnerware and toiletware the old company had produced. After his death, his son experimented with firing the body and the glaze at the same time. He introduced the process in 1911. Hall still makes this vitrified hotel and restaurant ware. In 1920, the famed gold-decorated teapots appeared. In 1931, decal-decorated kitchenware and dinnerware were introduced. Hall reissues many classic designs. All are decorated in solid colors (no decal or gold decorated pieces). Many pieces are in new colors or color combinations.

Early marks read *HALL'S CHINA* in a circular frame containing a mold or pattern number. *MADE IN U.S.A.* sometimes appears beneath the stamp. Later, a rectangular frame surrounded *HALL'S SUPERIOR QUALITY KITCHENWARE* or *HALL*, with a trakemark *R*.

Autumn Leaf Teapot. —Photo courtesy Ray Morykan Auctions.

Autumn Leaf (1933)

Produced for the Jewel Tea Company.

	LOW	AVG.	HIGH
Baker, open, 6.5"	$32	$35	40
Ball Jug, #3	20	22	25
Bean Pot, cov., 1 handle	400	465	525
Bean Pot, cov., 2 handles	170	190	230
Bowl, Radiance, 6" to 7.5"	7	8	9
Bowl, Radiance, 9"	22	25	28
Butter Dish, 1/4 lb.	22	25	28
Coaster	3	4	5
Coffeepot, rayed, w/ drip, 8 cup	50	55	62
Condiment Bowl, w/ liner	20	22	25
Cookie Jar, cov., Zeisel	100	110	125
Custard Cup, Radiance	3	4	5
Drip Jar, cov., 5"	10	11	12
French Baker, 4.25"	10	11	12
Fruit Dish	6	7	8
Gravy Boat	18	20	24
Jug, rayed, 2.5 pt.	20	22	25
Mug, conic	35	38	42
Plate, 6"	2	3	4
Plate, 7"	3	4	5
Plate, 8"	4	5	6
Platter, oval, 11.5"	25	28	32

	LOW	AVG.	HIGH
Platter, oval, 14"	18	18	20
Salad Bowl, 2 qt.	10	12	15
Soup Bowl	12	15	18
Sugar, cov., ruffled	10	12	15
Teapot, Aladdin shape	100	120	138
Teapot, Newport shape	100	115	130
Tidbit, 2-tier	62	70	80

Blue Bouquet Ball Jug.

Blue Bouquet (early 1950s)

	LOW	AVG.	HIGH
Baker	$28	$36	$45
Ball Jug, #3	125	175	200
Bean Pot, cov., #4	100	110	125
Bowl, 6"	10	13	15
Bowl, 9"	18	24	30
Cake Stand	18	24	30
Casserole, cov.	24	30	35
Cereal Bowl, 6"	12	15	18
Coffeepot	100	125	150
Cream/Sugar	35	45	52
Cup/Saucer	18	22	26
Custard Cup	12	15	18
Fruit Dish, 5.5"	8	9	10
Gravy Boat	34	42	50
Jug, Radiance	60	65	75
Leftover, rectangular	50	55	62
Mixing Bowl, 6" to 8.5"	28	35	42
Pitcher	28	36	45
Plate, 6"	5	6	7
Plate, 6.5"	9	12	15
Plate, 9"	10	12	15
Platter, 10" to 13"	24	30	38
Salt/Pepper	32	38	46
Soup Plate, 8.5"	20	25	30
Soup Tureen	115	148	180
Tea Tile	92	115	135
Teapot, Aladdin shape	95	115	135
Vegetable, 9.5"	42	54	65

Cameo Rose (1950s)

Produced for the Jewel Tea Company.

	LOW	AVG.	HIGH
Casserole, cov., tab handles	$50	$60	$70
Cereal Bowl, 6"	7	9	12
Cream/Sugar	15	18	22
Cup/Saucer	14	18	22
Fruit Dish, 5.5"	5	6	7
Gravy Boat	24	30	36
Plate, 6.5" to 8"	5	6	7
Plate, 9.5"	7	9	11
Plate, 10"	9	12	15
Platter, 11"	20	25	30
Platter, 13"	24	30	35
Relish Dish, 9"	18	22	26
Soup Plate	12	15	18
Teapot	60	80	100
Vegetable, oval	20	25	30
Vegetable, round, 9"	15	20	25

Crocus Tidbit. —Photo courtesy Ray Morykan Auctions.

Crocus

	LOW	AVG.	HIGH
Ball Jug	$175	$195	$225
Cake Plate	28	30	35
Casserole, cov.	55	60	70
Cup/Saucer	16	18	20
Drip-O-Lator, Medallion shape	75	82	100
Gravy Boat	32	35	40
Mixing Bowl	45	50	58
Plate, 8.25"	8	10	12
Plate, 9"	10	12	15
Plate, 10"	32	35	40
Platter, oval, 13.25"	32	35	40
Soup Tureen	375	425	490
Teapot, Banded shape	160	175	200
Tidbit, 3-tier	45	50	58

Heather Rose Pie Baker.

Heather Rose

	LOW	AVG.	HIGH
Cake Plate	$12	$15	$18
Jug, Rayed	15	18	20
Pie Baker	15	18	20
Platter, oval, 13.25"	12	15	18
Soup, flat, 8"	10	12	15
Sugar, cov.	10	14	16

Orange Poppy

	LOW	AVG.	HIGH
Ball Jug, #3	$60	$66	$75
Bowl, Radiance, 6"	10	12	15
Cake Plate	22	25	30
Canister, Radiance	250	275	310
Casserole, cov., oval, 8"	58	65	74
Casserole, cov., oval, 9"	50	55	62
Drip Jar, cov., Radiance	18	20	24
Drip-O-Lator, Bricks and Ivy shape	18	20	26
Leftover	68	75	85
Plate, 6"	5	6	8
Plate, 9"	12	15	18
Salt/Pepper	58	65	75
Sugar, cov.	22	25	28
Teapot, Donut shape	360	425	500
Teapot, Melody shape	180	200	240

Pastel Morning Glory (1930s)

	LOW	AVG.	HIGH
Ball Jug, #3	$45	$58	$70
Bean Pot, cov., 1 handle	100	120	140
Bowl, 5.5"	10	12	14
Bowl, 6"	12	15	18
Bowl, 9"	24	30	36
Casserole, cov., tab handles	58	72	85
Cream/Sugar	12	15	18
Drip Jar	35	40	48
Gravy Boat	42	54	65
Plate, 6"	5	6	7

	LOW	AVG.	HIGH
Plate, 8.5"	7	9	10
Plate, 9"	20	25	30
Platter, 11" to 13"	36	45	55
Salt/Pepper	36	45	55
Soup Plate, 8.5"	20	28	34
Vegetable, oval	30	38	45

Poppy and Wheat

Ball Jug, #3	$70	$80	$90
Bean Pot, cov., #4 and #5	100	120	140
Bowl, Sunshine, #1	15	20	25
Bowl, Sunshine, #3	30	40	50
Butter Dish, Bingo	300	350	400
Cake Plate	40	50	60
Casserole, Sunshine	50	60	70
Cream/Sugar	40	50	60
Cup/Saucer	15	20	25
Dish, 5" to 6"	5	10	15
Gravy Boat	30	40	50
Leftover, MaryLou	60	70	80
Mug	60	70	75
Pie Baker	30	40	50
Pitcher, Sunshine	50	60	70
Plate, 6" to 8"	5	10	15
Plate, 9" to 10"	20	30	40
Platter, 11" to 13"	30	35	40
Pretzel Jar	120	140	150
Server	20	30	40
Shaker, handled	20	30	40
Soup Plate, 8.5"	20	30	40
Soup Tureen, cov.	260	300	330
Vegetable, 9" to 10"	30	40	50

Range Poppy (1933)

Produced for the Great American Tea Company.

Baker	$24	$30	$36
Ball Jug, #3	35	45	55
Bean Pot, cov., 1 handle	90	105	125
Bowl, 6" to 7.5"	20	25	30
Bowl, 9" to 10"	36	45	54
Cake Plate	25	30	36
Casserole, cov., oval, 8"	45	55	65
Casserole, cov., oval, 11"	130	165	200
Casserole, cov., round, 2 handles	35	46	58
Coffeepot	75	90	110
Cream/Sugar	42	54	68
Cup/Saucer	12	16	20
Custard Cup	30	38	48
Drip Jar	32	40	48
Plate, 7"	8	10	12
Plate, 7.5"	9	12	14
Plate, 9"	14	18	22

	LOW	AVG.	HIGH
Platter, 11.5" to 13.5"	34	45	56
Pretzel Jar, 11.5" to 13.5"	85	119	135
Salt/Pepper	14	16	20
Soup Plate, 6.5"	20	24	30
Spoon	70	85	105
Vegetable, 9.5"	45	55	65

Red Poppy Salt and Pepper Shakers.

Red Poppy (early 1950s)

Produced for the Grand Union Tea Company.

Ball Jug, #3	$50	$65	$75
Bowl, 6"	20	25	30
Bowl, 9"	40	48	55
Cake Plate	25	30	35
Cereal Bowl, 6"	12	15	20
Cup/Saucer	10	12	15
Custard Cup	18	20	24
Drip Jar	27	30	36
Fruit Dish, 5.5"	8	10	12
Gravy Boat	45	55	65
Mixing Bowl, Radiance, #5	8	10	12
Pie Baker	22	25	28
Plate, 6"	4	5	6
Plate, 7"	8	10	12
Plate, 9" to 10"	12	16	20
Platter, 11"	30	35	45
Platter, 13"	35	45	55
Salt/Pepper	20	22	25
Soup Plate	20	28	35

Rose Parade (1940s)

Baker	$25	$30	$38
Bean Pot, cov., tab handles	75	90	110
Bowl, 6"	20	25	30
Bowl, 7.5"	25	30	36
Bowl, 9"	28	36	45
Casserole, cov., tab handles	38	45	55

	LOW	AVG.	HIGH
Cream/Sugar	30	38	45
Custard Cup	10	12	14
Drip Jar	35	42	50
Pitcher, 5" to 7.5"	50	65	75
Salt/Pepper	25	30	35
Teapot, 4 cup	40	50	60

Rose White (1940s)

Bean Pot, cov., tab handles	$60	$75	$95
Casserole, cov., tab handles	45	55	65
Cream/Sugar	28	35	40
Custard Cup	10	12	15
Drip Jar, cov., tab handles	25	30	35
Pie Baker	20	24	30
Pitcher, 5" to 7.5"	35	45	55
Salad Bowl, 9"	20	25	30
Salt/Pepper	25	30	36
Teapot, 6 cup	40	52	65

Serenade (1930s)

Produced for the Eureka Tea Company.

Ball Jug, #3	$50	$55	$60
Bowl, 7.5"	20	25	30
Bowl, 9"	26	35	40
Casserole, cov.	48	60	75
Cereal Bowl, 6"	10	12	14
Coffeepot	40	45	56
Cup/Saucer	10	13	15
Fruit Dish, 5.5"	8	9	10
Gravy Boat	25	30	35
Plate, 6"	2	3	4
Plate, 8.5"	7	9	11
Plate, 9"	8	10	12
Platter, 11" to 13"	32	38	45
Pretzel Jar, cov., tab handles	95	120	150
Salt/Pepper	36	45	55
Soup Plate, 8.5"	18	24	30

Springtime

Ball Jug, #3	$48	$58	$70
Bowl, 6"	16	20	26
Cake Plate	12	15	18
Casserole, cov., tab handles	48	60	75
Cream/Sugar	24	30	38
Cup/Saucer	14	18	20
Custard Cup	8	10	12
Drip Jar	24	30	36
Fruit Dish, 5.5"	7	9	12
Gravy Boat	38	44	52
Pie Baker	24	30	38
Plate, 6"	2	3	4

	LOW	AVG.	HIGH
Plate, 8.5"	8	10	12
Plate, 9.5"	20	28	35
Platter, 11"	28	34	40
Platter, 13"	30	40	48
Salad Bowl, 9"	20	28	35
Salt/Pepper	35	45	55
Soup Plate, 8.5"	18	22	26

Taverne

Ball Jug, #3	$60	$75	$90
Bean Pot, #4	200	250	300
Bowl, 6"	15	20	25
Bowl, Colonial, #3 to #5	30	35	40
Bowl, Sunshine, #3 to #5	40	45	50
Casserole, cov.	50	60	75
Coffeepot, Banded	90	110	130
Cream/Sugar, Colonial	60	70	80
Cream/Sugar, MaryLou	50	60	70
Cup/Saucer	12	15	18
Drip Jar, cov.	25	30	36
Fruit Dish, 5.5"	7	9	10
Leftover, cov., rectangular	38	46	54
Leftover, cov., square	50	60	70
Pie Baker	30	40	50
Pitcher	35	45	55
Plate, 6" to 8"	10	15	20
Plate, 9.5"	12	15	18
Platter, 11" to 13"	30	35	40
Pretzel Jar, cov., tab handles	95	125	150
Salad Bowl, 9"	20	25	30
Salt/Pepper	20	24	30
Shaker, handled	50	60	70
Soup Plate, 8.5"	20	28	35
Vegetable, oval, 10.5"	30	35	45

Tulip

Produced for the Cook Coffee Company.

Cream/Sugar	$30	$38	$45
Cup/Saucer	12	15	20
Deca Coffee	45	50	60
Drip-O-Lator, Banded Ball shape	37	42	50
Fruit Dish, 5.5"	9	10	12
Gravy Boat	22	25	28
Mixing Bowl, 6"	25	28	35
Mixing Bowl, 7.5"	32	36	40
Nested Bowls, thick rims, set of 3	68	75	85
Plate, 6"	3	4	5
Platter, oval, 13.25"	38	42	48
Saucer, St. Denis	6	8	10
Sugar, cov.	22	25	30
Vegetable, oval, 10.25"	30	35	42

Wildfire Gravy Boat.

Wildfire (1950s)

Produced for the Great American Company.

	LOW	AVG.	HIGH
Bowl, 9"	$20	$24	$28
Cereal Bowl, 6"	9	12	14
Cream/Sugar	24	32	38
Cup/Saucer	15	18	21
Custard Cup	10	12	14
Fruit Dish, 5.5"	7	9	11
Gravy Boat	24	30	38
Jug, Radiance, #5	32	35	40
Mixing Bowl, large	42	54	65
Mixing Bowl, small	14	18	22
Pie Baker	19	24	30
Plate, 9"	12	15	18
Platter, oval, 13.25"	28	30	34
Soup Plate, 8.5"	12	15	18
Tidbit, 3-tier	85	90	95
Vegetable, oval, 9"	28	30	34

Drip-O-Lators

	LOW	AVG.	HIGH
Ball, Bird of Paradise	$30	$35	$45
Banded Ball, floral decal	45	50	60
Bricks and Ivy	18	20	28
Cathedral, orange, floral decal, large	15	17	25
Cathedral, plain, large	18	22	30
Crest, Minuet decal	28	33	42
Drape, floral decal, aluminum insert	22	25	30
Lattice, floral decal	30	33	40
Meltdown, ivory and red, platinum trim	20	25	32
Monarch, floral lattice design	40	45	55
Perk, Shaggy Tulip pattern	50	55	65
Rounded Terrace, floral decal, small	18	20	25
Rounded Terrace, plain, small	10	12	18
Sash, white ground, blue sash w/ white stars	60	65	75
Scoop, floral decal	32	35	40
Sweep, blue and orange tulips, aluminum insert	25	28	35
Target, Dutch decal	25	28	35

	LOW	AVG.	HIGH
Terrace, light blue, gold flowers	18	20	28
Trellis, floral decal	48	52	60
Trellis, plain	20	22	30
Viking, Cactus	42	45	54
Viking, flamingo decal	35	38	45
Waverly, floral decal, aluminum insert, large	20	22	28
Waverly, plain, small	18	20	25

Teapots

Airflow, gold w/ gold, 8 cup	$60	$70	$82
Boston, cadet blue w/ gold, 2 cup	90	105	125
Boston, Dresden w/ gold, 6 cup	70	78	90
Boston, gray w/ gold, 6 cup	55	62	70
Boston, light green w/ gold, 2 cup	75	85	98
Connie, green	55	62	70
French, avocado green w/ gold floral dec., 12 cup	35	42	48
French, brown w/ gold, 6 cup	60	70	80
French, maroon, 4 to 6 cup	35	42	48
Los Angeles, cobalt blue w/ gold, 6 cup	45	54	60
Los Angeles, ivory w/ gold, 6 cup	35	42	48
Moderne, ivory, 6 cup	30	35	42
Moderne, yellow, 6 cup	20	24	28
Moderne, yellow w/ gold, 6 cup	50	58	70
New York, green w/ gold, 6 cup	40	46	52
New York, yellow rose decal	85	98	112
Parade, canary, 6 cup	45	50	58
Parade, canary w/ gold, 6 cup	50	58	65
Philadelphia, brown w/ gold, 6 cup	30	35	40
Philadelphia, turquoise w/ gold, 6 cup	45	54	62
Windshield, cadet blue w/ rose decals	50	58	66
Windshield, Dot pattern, ivory w/ gold, 6 cup	30	35	40

Assortment of Hall Teapots and one Drip-O-Lator (bottom left).
—Photo courtesy Gene Harris Antique Auction Center.

Harker Pottery

The Harker Pottery Company began in 1890. In 1931, it bought the E.M. Knowles plant in Chester, West Virginia, and closed its own East Liverpool, West Virginia operations. The Chester plant operated until 1972. The Cameoware line and the Hotoven Kitchenware are popular favorites. An arrow backstamp is common

Harker backstamps.

Amy

	LOW	AVG.	HIGH
Box, cov.	$35	$40	$45
Casserole, 7" to 9"	25	30	35
Casserole Tray, 8" to 10"	7	8	10
Cookie Jar	25	30	35
Custard Cup	4	5	6
Leftover, round, 4" to 6"	6	10	14
Mixing Bowl, 10"	26	38	30
Salt/Pepper	15	18	20
Serving Bowl, 6" to 9"	10	18	24
Stack Set, 3-piece	35	40	45
Teapot, 5 cup	30	35	40
Tray, round, 10"	10	12	14

Gadroon Creamer.

Gadroon

	LOW	AVG.	HIGH
Chop Plate	$12	$14	$16
Cream/Sugar	24	28	34
Cup/Saucer	10	15	20
Dish, 5" to 6"	4	5	6
Dish, cov.	12	14	16
Gravy Boat	16	18	20
Pickle Dish	8	10	12

	LOW	AVG.	HIGH
Plate, 6" to 8"	4	6	8
Plate, 8" to 9" sq	6	9	12
Plate, 9" to 10"	8	9	10
Platter, 11" to 15"	10	15	20
Salad Bowl	16	18	20
Salt/Pepper	10	14	16
Soup Bowl	8	9	10
Soup Plate, 8.5"	8	9	10
Teapot	30	36	42
Tidbit, 3-tier	18	20	24
Vegetable, 9"	18	20	22

Hotoven Kitchenware (1926)

Bean Pot, individual	$4	$5	$6
Cake Server	14	16	18
Casserole, 7" to 9"	18	20	24
Cup/Saucer, 10 oz.	9	10	12
Custard Cup	2	4	6
Drip Jar, Skyscraper	14	16	18
Leftover, paneled	14	16	18
Mixing Bowl, 9" to 10"	12	14	18
Pie Baker, 9" to 10"	6	8	10
Pitcher	18	20	22
Rolling Pin	40	45	50
Salad Set (fork and spoon)	30	50	70
Scoop	24	26	28
Stack Set, 4-piece	30	38	48
Tea Tile, octagonal	20	22	24
Teapot	30	32	35

Virginia

Bowl, 36s	$8	$9	$11
Casserole	22	26	30
Cream/Sugar	25	30	34
Cup/Saucer	10	14	18
Dish, 5" to 6"	2	3	4
Plate, 6" to 8"	4	6	8
Plate, 9" to 10"	8	9	10
Platter, 11" to 14"	10	14	16
Soup Plate, 7.75"	8	9	10
Vegetable, 8.25"	14	15	16

Zephyr

Casserole, 7" to 9"	$26	$32	$38
Casserole Tray, 8" to 10"	7	8	9
Cookie Jar	25	30	35
Custard Cup	4	5	6
Leftover, round, 4" to 6"	8	12	16
Mixing Bowl, 10"	28	30	32
Salt/Pepper	18	19	20

A.E. Hull Pottery

Begun as a stoneware company, the A.E. Hull Pottery Company moved on to semiporcelain dinnerware in 1907 with the purchase of the Acme Pottery Company. It slowly added various lines until the late 1930s, when Hull introduced its famous matte-finished pastel art pottery. Production continued through the 1950s when manufacturing operations ceased.

Prices for gilt pieces are higher, glossy pieces somewhat less. The listings include pattern numbers. Early marks include an impressed *H* in a circle or diamond. Later marks include *Hull, Hull Art,* or *Hull Ware* written in block or script lettering.

For further information contact the Hull Pottery Association at 4 Hilltop Road, Council Bluffs, IA 51503.

Bow-Knot (1949)

Bow-Knot is decorated with high-relief multicolored flowers and bows in matte finish on a background of pink with blue or blue with blue or turquoise.

	LOW	AVG.	HIGH
Basket, B25, 6.5"	$160	$175	$190
Candle Holders, B17, pair	120	140	160
Console Bowl, B16, 13.5"	200	220	245
Cornucopia, B5, 7.5"	70	85	100
Cornucopia, double, B13, 13"	165	170	175
Creamer, B21	80	90	100
Ewer, B1, 5.5"	80	100	120
Ewer, B15, 13.5"	1100	1300	1500
Jardiniere, B19, 9.75"	1500	1900	2300
Sugar Bowl, B22	80	90	100
Teapot, B20	300	350	400
Vase, B14, 12.5"	1650	2150	2650

Butterfly

Butterfly has pink and blue flowers and butterflies with black decorating either cream-colored matte with turquoise interior or glossy all-white pieces.

	LOW	AVG.	HIGH
Basket, B13, 8"	$100	$110	$120
Basket, B17, 10.5"	170	200	230
Bonbon Dish, B4, 6.5"	130	170	210
Bud Vase, pitcher shape, B1	56	64	70
Candle Holders, B22, pair	70	82	94
Candy Dish, urn shape, open, B6	40	45	50
Console Bowl, 3 ftd., B21	110	135	160
Cornucopia, B2, 6.5"	27	35	43
Cornucopia, B12	60	70	80
Cream/Sugar, B19/20	80	100	125
Ewer, B15, 13.5"	125	145	160
Fruit Bowl, B16	90	100	110
Lavabo Set, B24/B25, 16"	160	190	220
Pitcher, handled, B11	81	94	110
Serving Tray, B23, 11.5"	150	200	250
Teapot, B18	150	175	200
Window Box, B8	56	68	80

Calla Lily

Calla Lily is also called Jack-in-the-Pulpit. It has embossed flowers in matte-color combination with green leaves.

	LOW	AVG.	HIGH
Bowl, 500-32, 10"	$140	$170	$200
Candle Holders, 508-39, pair	135	150	165
Console Bowl, 500-32, 10"	330	430	530
Cornucopia, 570-33, 8"	85	95	105
Ewer, pink and blue, 506, 10"	450	590	730
Vase, 520-33, 10"	350	455	460
Vase, brown and tan, 530-33, 9"	510	665	820
Vase, cream and blue, 560-33, 13"	310	405	500

Dogwood

This line has embossed dogwood flowers.

	LOW	AVG.	HIGH
Basket, 501, 7.5"	$200	$250	$300
Bowl, low, 521, 7"	90	110	130
Candle Holders, 512, 4", pair	140	170	200
Console Bowl, 511, 11.5"	180	220	260
Cornucopia, 522, 4"	50	62	75
Ewer, 505, 5.5"	370	485	600
Ewer, 505, 8.5"	135	168	200
Ewer, 519, 13.5"	500	620	740
Teapot, 507, 6.5"	200	250	300
Window Box, 508, 10.5"	100	125	150

Ebbtide

Ebbtide has glossy fish and seashell designs on various backgrounds.

	LOW	AVG.	HIGH
Candle Holder, E13, 2.5", pair	$38	$45	$50
Console Bowl, E12, 15.75"	130	145	160
Cornucopia, E3/E9, 7" to 12"	90	105	120
Cream/Sugar, E15/E16	100	125	145
Ewer, E10, 13"	210	270	330
Pitcher Vase, E1, 8.25"	90	100	110
Pitcher Vase, E10, 14"	200	250	300
Teapot, E14	180	200	220

Iris (1940)

Iris has embossed irises on matte-finished bodies.

	LOW	AVG.	HIGH
Basket, 408, 7"	$200	$240	$280
Candle Holders, 411, 5", pair	125	135	145
Console Bowl, 409, 12"	200	220	240
Ewer, 401, 5"	70	80	90
Ewer, 401, 8"	145	160	175
Rose Bowl, 413, 7"	100	115	130
Console Bowl, 409, 12"	320	420	520
Vase, 403, 10.5"	370	485	600
Vase, 404, 10.5"	450	590	730
Vase, pink and blue, 414, 16"	700	900	1100

Hull Little Red Riding Hood. —Photo courtesy Gene Harris Antique Auction Center.

Little Red Riding Hood

This was a popular figural line with Little Red Riding Hood and the Wolf.

	LOW	AVG.	HIGH
Batter Pitcher, 5.5"	$200	$260	$320
Butter Dish	500	550	600
Canister	800	900	1000
Cream/Sugar, ruffled skirt	510	580	650
Cream/Sugar, side open	250	285	315
Creamer, spout on top of head	180	200	220
Grease Jar, Wolf	800	950	1100
Jar, cov., basket in front, 8.5"	400	450	500
Jar, cov., basket on side, 9"	350	400	450
Mustard Jar, 4.5"	500	550	600
Mustard Jar, w/ spoon, 5.5"	400	440	480
Milk Pitcher, 8"	325	335	345
Salt/Pepper, 3.5"	60	65	72
Salt/Pepper, 5.5"	120	135	150
Spice Jar	600	750	900
Sugar Shaker, 4 holes on top	180	200	220
Sugar Bowl, "creeping," hands on table	180	200	220
Teapot	300	350	400

Magnolia, Glossy

Glossy Magnolia has embossed magnolia flowers on colored backgrounds.

	LOW	AVG.	HIGH
Basket, H14, 10.5"	$200	$230	$260
Cornucopia, H10, 8.5"	80	90	100
Cream/Sugar, H21/H22	83	98	112
Ewer, H11, 8.5"	85	90	96
Ewer, H19, 13.5"	325	375	425
Teapot, H20	125	135	145

Magnolia, Matte (1946)

Matte Magnolia has embossed magnolia flowers on colored backgrounds.

	LOW	AVG.	HIGH
Candle Holders, 27, 4.5", pair	$80	$90	$100
Console Bowl, 26, 12.5"	125	130	135
Cornucopia, 19, 8.5"	60	65	70
Cream/Sugar, 24/25	80	90	100
Ewer, 14, 4.75"	45	50	55
Ewer, 18, 13.5"	200	230	260
Teapot, 23	125	135	150

Open Rose

Also called Camellia, this pattern has polychrome roses on pastel matte backgrounds.

	LOW	AVG.	HIGH
Basket, 107, 8"	$200	$275	$350
Basket, 140, 10.5"	550	700	850
Candle Holders, dove shape, 117, 6.5", pair	160	200	260
Console Bowl, 116, 12"	200	250	300
Cornucopia, 101, 8.5"	98	120	145
Cornucopia, 141, 8.5"	115	135	160
Cream/Sugar, 111/112, 5"	110	140	170
Ewer, 115, 8.5"	145	185	225
Hanging Basket, 132, 7"	180	230	280
Teapot, 110, 8.5"	230	290	350

Parchment and Pine

Parchment and Pine has pinecones on glossy backgrounds.

	LOW	AVG.	HIGH
Basket, S3, 6"	$60	$75	$90
Basket, S8, 16"	100	125	150
Candle Holders, S10, 2.75", pair	40	50	60
Console Bowl, S9, 16"	60	75	85
Cornucopia, S2, 8"	40	55	65
Cornucopia, S6, 12"	70	90	110
Cream/Sugar, S12/S13	50	60	75
Ewer, S7, 13.5"	120	150	180
Teapot, S11	70	90	110
Teapot, tall, S15, 8"	115	150	185

Serenade

Serenade is decorated with birds on branches.

	LOW	AVG.	HIGH
Basket, S14, 12"	$250	$320	$380
Fruit Bowl, ftd., S15, 11.5"	75	100	125
Candle Holders, S16, 6.5", pair	60	70	80
Cornucopia, S10, 11"	50	60	70
Cream/Sugar, S18/S19	60	70	80
Ewer, S8, 8.5"	75	85	95
Ewer, S13, 13.25"	250	330	410
Pitcher, S21	100	110	120
Pitcher Vase, S2, 6.5"	55	60	65
Window Box, S9, 12.5"	50	60	65

Sunglow

Sunglow has different combinations of flowers, butterflies, and bows.

	LOW	AVG.	HIGH
Basket, 84, 6.5"	$54	$60	$65
Bowl, 50, 5" to 10"	22	34	48
Casserole, 51, 7.5"	42	48	54
Cornucopia, 96, 8.5"	65	675	80
Drip Jar, 53	32	38	44
Ewer, 90, 5.5"	35	38	42
Pitcher, 52, 24 oz.	45	48	52
Pitcher, 55, 7.5"	90	100	110
Salt/Pepper, 54	18	21	24

Tokay (1958)

Also called Tuscany, Tokay has embossed grapes and leaves on high-gloss backgrounds.

	LOW	AVG.	HIGH
Basket, 11, 10.5"	$70	$78	$85
Basket, 15, 12"	85	110	135
Candy Dish, cov., 9C, 8.5"	60	70	80
Consolette, 14, 15.75"	110	125	145
Cornucopia, 6" to 11"	30	45	60
Cream/Sugar, 17/18	80	90	100
Ewer, 13, 12"	200	250	300
Fruit Bowl, 7, 9.5"	110	130	150

Woodland

Woodland has twig handles and embossed twigs and flowers on a glossy finish.

	LOW	AVG.	HIGH
Basket, W9	$225	$250	$265
Candle Holders, W30, pair	45	50	60
Console Bowl, W10, 11"	40	45	50
Cornucopia, W10	115	130	150
Hanging Basket, W17, 7.5"	130	150	170
Vase, W18	50	55	60
Wall Pocket, conch shell shape, W13	60	68	75

Hull Pottery. —Photo courtesy Gene Harris Antique Auction Center.

Hummel Figurines

Hummels are ceramic figurines, usually of children. Berta Hummel, an artist and nun, created the concept and the original designs in 1935.

Each design has a title and a number. In the first section, we have listed the designs by number, followed by the title. Through 1991, all marks fall into six basic categories (although variations exist): Crown Mark (CM), 1935–49; Full Bee Mark (FB), 1950–59; Stylized Bee Mark (SB), 1957–72; Three Line Mark (3–L), 1964–72; Last Bee Mark (LB), 1972–79; and Missing Bee Mark (MB), 1979–91. Items produced after 1991 are marked with a New Crown Mark.

In the second section, we have listed auction prices achieved at recent auctions which featured substantial selections of Hummel figurines.

Above, left to right: Crown Mark, Full Bee Mark, Stylized Bee Mark.
Below, left to right: Three Line Mark, Last Bee Mark, Missing Bee Mark.

	CM	FB	SB	3–L	LB	MB
1, Puppy Love	$340	$250	$170	$120	$100	$80
2/I, Little Fiddler (brown hat)	670	580	300	300	180	190
2/II, Little Fiddler (brown hat)	1700	1480	980	850	800	660
2/III, Little Fiddler (brown hat)	2630	1960	1460	880	820	590
2/4/0, Little Fiddler (brown hat)	—	—	—	—	—	40
3/II, Bookworm	1450	1230	1180	940	790	640
3/III, Bookworm	2720	2200	1000	950	780	750
6/I, Sensitive Hunter	980	590	220	160	100	90
6/II, Sensitive Hunter	1460	770	420	340	300	190
7/I, Merry Wanderer	990	760	740	260	190	170
7/II, Merry Wanderer	1830	1500	1300	850	670	630
7/III, Merry Wanderer	2620	2100	1150	900	750	680
7/X, Merry Wanderer	—	—	—	—	12,000	12,000
9, Begging His Share, w/ candle holder	—	360	270	120	—	—
10/I, Flower Madonna, brown	770	780	270	180	—	—
10/I, Flower Madonna, blue	370	240	160	130	110	100
10/III, Flower Madonna, white	460	210	200	150	160	160
10/III, Flower Madonna, brown	2860	1910	420	310	—	—

	CM	FB	SB	3–L	LB	MB
10/III, Flower Madonna, blue	630	400	260	280	250	270
11/0, Merry Wanderer	490	250	200	190	90	70
11/0, Merry Wanderer, large	570	240	140	100	80	70
11/2/0, Merry Wanderer, large	350	200	160	100	90	80
12/I, Chimney Sweep	370	270	130	110	70	70
13/0, Meditation	290	240	190	120	80	100
13/II, Meditation	3110	2620	2140	—	250	190
13/2, Meditation	1990	2000	1780	—	160	160
13/V, Meditation	—	2560	1730	1220	770	680
13/5, Meditation	—	3480	4000	3900	430	420
14A & B-III, Bookworm Bookends	2000	2250	2180	2340	—	—
15/I, Hear Ye, Hear Ye	520	300	200	150	120	90
15/II, Hear Ye, Hear Ye	1000	650	440	310	230	170
16/I, Little Hiker	380	260	150	120	100	80
17/2, Congratulations	6620	—	—	—	—	—
18, Christ Child, white	420	380	290	250	—	—
21/0 1/2, Heavenly Angel	350	250	160	100	90	70
21/I, Heavenly Angel	420	300	280	150	100	90
21/II, Heavenly Angel	1140	840	410	320	190	200
22/I, Angel w/ Birds	500	290	230	—	—	—
23/II, Adoration	—	2100	—	—	—	—
23/III, Adoration	1000	920	750	300	240	160
24/III, Lullaby	1630	1290	560	—	360	250
26/I, Child Jesus	540	330	260	—	—	—
27/III, Joyous News	2210	1830	1000	—	270	100
28/2, Wayside Devotion	470	430	360	250	200	—
28/III, Wayside Devotion	840	660	470	400	260	210
29/0, Guardian Angel	1640	1280	1000	—	—	—
29/I, Guardian Angel	2000	1790	1180	—	—	—
32, Little Gabriel	—	—	—	—	70	60
32/I, Little Gabriel	1610	1270	1100	920	—	—
35/I, Good Shepherd	630	280	140	—	—	—
36/I, Angel w/ Flowers	360	300	180	90	—	—
III/38/0, Joyous News w/ Lute	160	100	70	50	40	30
III/38/I, Joyous News w/ Lute	340	260	160	120	—	—
III/39/0, Joyous News w/ Accordion	120	110	50	40	40	20
III/39/I, Joyous News w/ Accordion	240	210	150	100	—	—
III/40/0, Joyous News w/ Trumpet	120	100	60	50	30	30
III/40/I, Joyous News w/ Trumpet	280	190	160	60	—	—
42, Good Shepherd	—	—	—	—	90	70
42/I, Good Shepherd	4800	3400	3000	—	—	—
45/0/W, Madonna w/ Halo	60	100	70	60	40	30
45/I, Madonna w/ Halo	140	110	90	60	40	30
45/I/W, Madonna w/ Halo	260	180	110	80	80	30
45/III, Madonna w/ Halo	520	390	150	140	130	90
45/III/W, Madonna w/ Halo	260	150	120	80	80	80
46/0/W, Madonna wo/ Halo	60	130	100	90	50	50
46/I, Madonna wo/ Halo	270	190	120	100	60	60
46/III, Madonna wo/ Halo	430	360	260	210	150	100
46/III/W, Madonna wo/ Halo	300	180	110	100	90	70
47/0, Goose Girl	470	390	170	120	100	90
47/II, Goose Girl	1000	640	400	300	240	220
48/0/W, Madonna Plaque	170	80	—	—	—	—
48/II, Madonna Plaque	680	340	190	130	100	100

Hummel Nativity Set. —Photo courtesy Gene Harris Antique Auction Center.

	CM	FB	SB	3–L	LB	MB
48/II/W, Madonna Plaque	1620	1340	—	—	—	—
48/V, Madonna Plaque	1640	1400	960	—	—	—
48/V/W, Madonna Plaque	2000	1200	—	—	—	—
49/0, To Market	480	280	190	150	130	110
49/I, To Market	—	—	—	—	290	250
50, Volunteers	1300	900	—	—	—	—
50/0, Volunteers	780	500	310	190	200	140
50/I, Volunteers	1100	830	500	360	240	230
51/0, Village Boy	400	300	190	150	100	100
51/I, Village Boy	760	410	290	—	140	120
51/2/0, Village Boy	150	160	100	70	60	60
52, Going to Grandma's	1400	—	—	—	—	—
52/I, Going to Grandma's	1200	850	680	—	510	230
57/I, Chick Girl	470	290	180	140	110	110
58/I, Playmates	500	290	200	150	110	80
65, Farewell	360	220	130	100	80	90
65/I, Farewell	370	280	150	120	110	—
68, Lost Sheep	540	350	240	250	—	—
68/0, Lost Sheep	220	170	160	110	90	80
68/2/0, Lost Sheep	190	130	110	80	60	60
70, The Holy Child (over 7")	330	260	—	—	—	—
78/I, Infant of Krumbad	210	160	40	30	30	20
78/II, Infant of Krumbad	250	220	40	40	30	30
78/III, Infant of Krumbad	320	190	60	40	40	30
78/V, Infant of Krumbad	490	440	160	120	100	60
78/VI, Infant of Krumbad	750	460	260	190	190	130
78/VIII, Infant of Krumbad	970	750	390	350	280	230
81, School Girl	350	280	—	—	—	—
81/0, School Girl	350	180	150	90	80	70
82/0, School Boy	350	250	160	110	90	90
82/II, School Boy	900	830	400	—	260	190
84/V, Worship	2800	1750	880	870	710	590
85/II, Serenade	910	650	260	220	230	180
88/II, Heavenly Protection	830	750	470	260	240	230
89/II, Little Cellist	940	550	310	290	220	200
94, Surprise	470	270	190	—	—	—
94/I, Surprise	460	300	190	120	120	90
98, Sister	340	230	180	—	—	—
98/0, Sister	180	130	140	90	80	80
109, Happy Traveler	980	710	—	—	—	—

	CM	FB	SB	3–L	LB	MB
109/II, Happy Traveler	520	600	340	290	240	210
110, Let's Sing	380	250	—	—	—	—
110/I, Let's Sing	210	230	110	100	80	70
111, Wayside Harmony	440	280	200	140	—	—
111/I, Wayside Harmony	290	190	130	80	80	60
112, Just Resting	520	350	270	140	—	—
112/I, Just Resting	420	250	190	130	100	80
124/I, Hello	1000	560	350	—	100	70
136, Friends	2300	—	—	—	—	—
136/V, Friends	2000	1720	860	630	570	290
137/B, Child in Bed	530	350	130	60	—	—
141/I, Apple Tree Girl	440	270	190	130	120	90
141/V, Apple Tree Girl	610	560	420	—	—	—
141/X, Apple Tree Girl	—	—	—	—	13,500	12,000
142/I, Apple Tree Boy	80	440	400	300	70	100
142/V, Apple Tree Boy	—	—	—	610	580	530
142/X, Apple Tree Boy	—	—	—	—	12,000	13,300
143, Boots	750	490	300	200	—	—
143/I, Boots	540	360	230	170	150	120
145, Little Guardian, blue flowers	300	170	80	—	—	—
150, Happy Days	260	1170	—	—	—	—
150/0, Happy Days	430	360	190	—	150	130
150/I, Happy Days	120	1000	790	—	530	250
151/W, Madonna Holding Child	2340	1910	1990	—	190	190
152A/II, Umbrella Boy	—	1560	990	860	840	820
152B/II, Umbrella Girl	—	1540	1040	890	840	770
153, Auf Wiedersehen	1060	590	490	—	—	—
153/0, Auf Wiedersehen	—	290	200	140	100	100
153/I, Auf Wiedersehen	1030	560	470	350	160	130
154, Waiter	950	—	—	—	—	—
154/0, Waiter	410	260	180	130	110	90
154/I, Waiter	760	380	230	140	130	120
164, Worship	250	170	60	50	40	30
165, Swaying Lullaby	1080	880	510	—	90	80
166, Boy w/ Bird	410	250	140	140	90	90
167, Angel Bird	220	150	60	50	30	30
168, Standing Boy	1080	860	600	—	90	90
169, Bird Duet	260	190	130	90	90	60
170/I, School Boys	—	—	710	580	560	550
170/III, School Boys	2560	2130	1490	1360	1360	1440
171, Little Sweeper	240	140	120	90	70	70
172, Festival Harmony w/ Mandolin	2570	2990	—	—	—	—
172/0, Festival Harmony w/ Mandolin	—	—	—	150	150	110
172/II, Festival Harmony w/ Mandolin	—	1050	370	300	230	210
173, Festival Harmony w/ Flute	2650	2750	—	—	—	—
173/0, Festival Harmony w/ Flute	—	—	—	150	130	120
173/II, Festival Harmony w/ Flute	700	1130	360	280	210	190
174, She Loves Me, She Loves Me Not	370	270	150	120	80	70
175, Mother's Darling	400	220	150	130	100	80
176, Happy Birthday	810	510	—	—	—	—
176/0, Happy Birthday	300	290	180	130	110	100
176/1, Happy Birthday	690	530	340	280	170	150
177, School Girls	2350	2090	1640	—	—	—
177/I, School Girls	—	—	790	610	570	510

	CM	FB	SB	3–L	LB	MB
177/III, School Girls	2660	2150	1540	1370	1460	1360
178, The Photographer	480	280	180	130	110	120
179, Coquettes	440	270	170	110	120	100
180, Tuneful Goodnight	420	250	140	120	98	80
183, Forest Shrine	1680	1070	620	280	280	—
184, Latest News (square base)	390	300	220	170	150	110
185, Accordion Boy	690	230	160	90	90	80
186, Sweet Music	730	250	150	120	100	90
187, Store Plaque in English	1490	870	540	370	—	—
188, Celestial Musician	740	340	190	150	140	90
192, Candlelight	670	690	300	130	90	80
193, Angel Duet	460	230	140	110	100	90
194, Watchful Angel	670	370	260	180	150	140
195/I, Barnyard Hero	370	280	230	160	140	120
195/2/0, Barnyard Hero	220	210	140	100	100	70
195, Barnyard Hero	600	550	—	—	—	—
196/0, Telling Her Secret	430	320	220	150	160	140
196/I, Telling Her Secret	840	780	480	270	240	230
197, Be Patient	560	500	—	—	—	—
197/I, Be Patient	300	240	170	130	110	100
197/2/0, Be Patient	—	220	130	120	90	80
198, Home From Market	490	370	—	—	—	—
198/I, Home From Market	310	230	170	120	100	90
198/2/0, Home From Market	150	150	100	70	70	60
199, Feeding Time	470	420	—	—	—	—
199/0, Feeding Time	310	250	170	130	100	90
199/1, Feeding Time	360	290	240	160	110	100
200, Little Goat Herder	450	420	360	—	—	—
200/0, Little Goat Herder	250	200	180	90	90	90
200/1, Little Goat Herder	270	220	180	220	110	90
201, Retreat to Safety	530	340	—	—	—	—
201/1, Retreat to Safety	350	380	190	170	100	100
201/2/0, Retreat to Safety	180	190	140	100	80	80
203, Signs of Spring	460	300	—	—	—	—
203/I, Signs of Spring	260	230	200	120	110	90
203/II/0, Signs of Spring	400	180	130	100	90	70
204, Weary Wanderer	460	320	220	150	100	100
206, Angel Cloud	560	440	290	90	40	30
207, Heavenly Angel	260	110	40	40	30	30
217, Boy w/ Toothache	—	170	140	100	80	80
218, Birthday Serenade	—	770	590	—	—	—
218/0, Birthday Serenade	—	720	690	580	130	120
218/2/0, Birthday Serenade	—	460	470	400	100	80
220, We Congratulate	—	200	170	100	90	80
223, To Market	—	580	320	290	230	250
224, Wayside Harmony	—	540	470	—	—	—
224/I, Wayside Harmony	—	320	240	220	200	180
224/II, Wayside Harmony	—	540	380	300	240	230
225/I, Just Resting	—	340	250	230	190	190
225/II, Just Resting	—	500	430	290	280	220
226, Mail Is Here	—	810	510	430	300	250
227, She Loves Me, She Loves Me Not	—	580	310	190	200	180
228, Good Friends	—	540	310	200	180	180
229, Apple Tree Girl	—	710	280	210	180	170

Auction Results

	AUCTION	RETAIL Low	RETAIL High
16/I, Littler Hiker, SB	$121	$135	$165
95, Brother, SB	99	125	155
96, Little Shopper, LB	66	125	155
98/0, Sister, SB	99	125	155
109/II, Happy Traveler, LB	176	215	265
142/V, Apple Tree Boy, LB	495	530	610
177/I, School Girls, 3-L	468	550	670
184, Latest News, SB	121	200	240
196/0, Telling Her Secret, 3-L	132	135	165
198, Home From Market, FB	193	340	400
201/2/0, Retreat to Safety, SB	99	125	155
255, Stitch In Time, 3-L	143	150	180
256, Knitting Lesson, LB	154	165	200
304, The Artist, LB	132	140	170
305, The Builder, 3-L	110	130	158
306, Little Bookkeeper, LB	99	125	155
307, Good Hunting, SB	275	300	360
308, Little Tailor, LB	121	140	170
328, Carnival, LB	99	125	155
331, Crossroads, LB	176	200	240
334, Homeward Bound, LB	143	165	200
337, Cinderella, LB	90	100	120
340, Letter to Santa, LB	132	145	175
342, Mischief Maker, LB	110	125	150
317, Not For You, LB	143	160	185
345, A Fair Measure, LB	138	150	180
367, Busy Student, 3-L	99	125	155
369, Follow the Leader, LB	440	500	600
371, Favorite Pet, LB	143	160	190
381, Flower Vendor, LB	132	150	180
385, Chicken Licken, LB	121	140	170
386, On Secret Path, LB	154	165	200
396, Ride Into Christmas, LB	176	190	230

471, Harmony in Four Parts, missing bee mark, $1155 at auction. —Photo courtesy Jackson's Auctioneers & Appraisers.

Iroquois China

The Iroquois China Company produced hotel ware from 1905 until 1969. The company is best known to collectors today for its dinnerware lines designed by Russell Wright (Casual China) and Ben Seibel (Impromptu and Informal).

Casual China (1946)

	LOW	AVG.	HIGH
Bowl	$30	$33	$36
Carafe	80	100	120
Casserole, 2 qt. to 4 qt.	40	55	70
Casserole, 6 qt.	70	85	100
Chop Plate, 14"	32	36	40
Coffeepot	55	60	65
Cream/Sugar	28	34	40
Cup/Saucer	9	12	16
Cup/Saucer, After Dinner	60	64	68
Dish, 5" to 7"	8	9	10
Dutch Oven	85	100	115
Frying Pan, cov.	60	70	80
Gravy, cov.	30	37	45
Mug	60	70	80
Party Plate	30	35	40
Pitcher	65	75	80
Plate, 6" to 8"	6	8	10
Plate, 9" to 10"	9	12	14
Platter, 12" to 14"	18	24	30
Salad Bowl, 10"	25	30	35
Sauce Pan, cov.	60	65	75
Shaker, stacking	12	15	18
Soup Plate, 8.5"	20	24	28
Teapot	45	60	75
Vegetable, 8" to 10"	22	30	36
Vegetable, cov., divided	50	55	60

Impromptu

	LOW	AVG.	HIGH
Butter Dish	$17	$20	$24
Casserole, cov.	22	25	28
Coffeepot	30	35	40
Comport	18	20	22
Cream/Sugar	14	16	18
Cup/Saucer	6	9	12
Gravy Boat	14	16	18
Plate, 6" to 8"	2	4	6
Plate, 9" to 10"	4	5	6
Platter, 12" to 15"	6	9	11
Relish Tray	6	7	8
Salt/Pepper	14	16	18
Soup Plate	7	8	9
Vegetable	9	12	15

Informal

	LOW	AVG.	HIGH
Butter Dish	$18	$21	$24
Casserole, 2 qt.	24	26	30
Coffeepot, 9 cup	48	54	60
Cream/Sugar	13	16	20
Cup/Saucer	5	6	7
Dish, 5" to 6"	1	2	3
Dutch Oven, cov.	24	26	30
Frying Pan, cov.	24	26	30
Gravy Boat	14	16	18
Plate, 6" to 8"	2	4	6
Plate, 9" to 10"	4	5	6
Platter, 12" to 15"	7	9	11
Salt/Pepper	14	16	18
Samovar, w/ stand	36	42	48
Sauce Pan, cov.	22	26	30
Soup Plate	7	8	9
Soup, cov.	13	15	17
Vegetable	9	12	15

James River Pottery

Originally the Hopewell China Compnay, the James River Pottery's best known designer was Simon Slobodkin. He designed the pieces, which are part of the Cascade pattern (1935). Pieces are usually unmarked. Some have an impressed or stamped *JR*.

James River backstamp.

	LOW	AVG.	HIGH
Cream/Sugar	$20	$23	$26
Cup/Saucer	7	9	11
Dish, 6"	3	4	5
Pickle Dish, 11"	7	9	11
Plate, 6" to 7"	3	4	5
Plate, 9" to 10"	6	8	10
Platter, 12" to 14"	8	10	12
Relish Tray	10	12	14

Josef Originals

Muriel Joseph George of Arcadia, California, designed Josef Originals figurines from 1946 until 1982. (The "Josef" spelling resulted from a printing error on the labels which could not be corrected due to a lack of time.) In 1982 she sold the company to her long-time partner and representative George Good, but she continued designing figures through 1985. These pieces were produced in California through 1960, when production was moved to Japan. Examples below are from the 1940s through the 1980s. In this time period the girls were all made with black eyes and a glossy finish, the animals with a semigloss finish. Figures are now produced by Applause, which purchased the firm in 1985.

Prices are for figurines in perfect condition. All original figurines are marked on the bottom, either incised or ink-stamped "Josef Originals ©" and have a Josef oval sticker with either the California or Japan designation. Beware of copies, which have only a Josef label. Our consultants for this area are Jim and Kaye Whitaker, co-authors of *Josef Originals,* Schiffer Publishing, Atglen, PA, 1997, and owners of Eclectic Antiques. They are listed in the back of this book.

Animals

	LOW	HIGH
Buggy Bugs Series, various poses, w/ wire antenna, Japan, 3.25" h, price each	$10	$13
Dalmatian, Kennel Club series, Japan, 3.5" h	12	14
Elephant, flower on head, 4.5" h	35	45
Frogs, various poses, price each	10	14
German Shepherd, 3"	18	22
Kangaroo Mama w/ Baby in Pouch, Japan, 6" h	65	75
Mama Camel, standing, Japan, 6.75" h	65	75
Mice, various poses and costumes, price each	14	18
Monkeys, various poses and costumes, price each	14	18
Ostrich Babies, 5" h, price each	20	25
Ostrich Mama, 5" h	40	55
Poodle, Kennel Club series, Japan, 3.5" h	12	14
Rabbits, various poses, price each	10	14
Reindeer, Christmas trim, Japan, 6" h	20	24
Skunk, w/ perfume atomizer, Japan, 2.5" h	10	12
Tawny, Character Cat, Siamese, Japan, 4" h	12	14
Wee Three, 3 kittens in basket, California, 3" h	15	17

Teddy, 1945–62, 4.5" h, $45–$55.

Josef Originals of California (1945–62)

Doll of the Month Series, 12 different, trimmed w/ stones, 3.5" h, price each	$35	$40
Hedy, girl in pink dress w/ hat holding gift, 4.25" h	40	55
Kandy, blue or pink, gold trim, w/ colored stones, 4.5" h	40	45
Little TV Cowboy, large hat, rope in hands, 5.25" h	60	70
Mama, blue dress, sitting w/ book, 7.25" h	75	85

	LOW	HIGH
Missy, blue or pink, gold trim, w/ colored stones, 4.5" h	35	40
Monday, Days of the Week series, pink, washing clothes, 4" h	33	37
Penny, little girl sitting, blue, green, pink, or white, 4" h	40	45
Pitty Sing (first Chinese boy), large hat	42	48
Prince, boy sitting w/ thumb in mouth, 3.75" h	45	55
Sakura, Chinese lady w/ fan, white, green, blue, or pink, 10.75" h	90	110
Saturday, Days of the Week series, yellow w/ pie, 4" h	30	40
Sylvia, lime green, holding rose bouquet, 5.75" h	55	60
Taffy, pink or green, gold trim w/ colored stones, 4.5" h	30	34
Teddy, boy in gray suit holding flowers, 4.5" h	40	50
Victoria, holding muff, green or mauve, 6" h	55	58
Wee Ching, Chinese boy w/ dog	35	45
Wee Ling, Chinese girl w/ kitten	35	45
Wu Fu and Wu Cha, Chinese couple, ecru w/ gold trim, 10" h, pair	85	95
Yvette, Morning-Noon-Night series, aqua gown w/ scissors, 5.5" h	60	65

Josef Originals of Japan (1960–85)

Baby w/ Kitten, blue, pink, or yellow, 3" h	$28	$32
Birthday Girls, #1 to #16, black eyes, 2.75" h to 6.5" h, price each	25	35
Birthstone Dolls, colored stone in flower, 12 different, 4" h, price each	15	26
Blue Bird, girl in yellow dress w/ bird on hand, 9" h	80	100
Bridal March Music Box, couple in tuxedo and bridal gown	65	75
Christmas Girl, red dress w/ green front, cape, 6" h	25	35
Debby, First Formal series, yellow gown, holding mirror, 5.25" h	30	32
Debby, First Love series, pink dress w/ hat, 5" h	22	28
Doll of the Month, 12 different poses and colors, 4" h, price each	25	35
Engagement, Romance series, blue dress w/ ring, 8" h	90	120
Flutist, Classical Touch series, green, w/ flute, 6" h	35	40
Gigi Series, pink dress, w/ hat and puppy, 6" h, price each	80	100
Happiness Is, boy in bed, puppy	30	40
High Heels, Sweet 16 series, green dress, 7.5" h	90	120
Holiday in Hawaii, Holiday Girls series, girl w/ lei, 5.5" h	45	50
Housekeepers Series, green dress w/ teapot, 3" h	25	30
Jeanne, Colonial Days series, lavender dress, 9.5" h	90	120
Jill, Nusery Rhymes series, green dress, w/ bucket, 4" h	25	30
Lara's Theme Music Box, couple wearing green suit and rose dress	65	75
Lilacs, Flower Girl series, pink gown, holding lilac bouquet, 5.5" h	35	38
Lipstick Holder, lavender, aqua, or pink, 4" h, price each	22	25
Little International Series, 3.5" h to 4" h, price each	25	35
Louise, Colonial Days series, white gown, 9.5" h	95	120
Love Letter, Sweet Memories series, lavender gown, 6" h	75	80
Love Rendezvous, girl w/ light blue dress and hat, 9" h	90	120
Marie, XVII Century French series, white w/ veil, 7" h	75	87
Mary Holding Jesus, white gown, 5" h	25	35
Mighty Like a Rose, Favorite Sayings series, rose hat, 4" h	23	29
New Baby, Special Occassion series, girl holding teddy bear, 4.5" h	20	23
New Hat, A Mother's World series, blue and yellow dress and hat, 7.5" h	90	120
Pianist Music Box, Classical Touch series, plays *Fur Elise,* 5" h	60	65
Pixies, varous poses, green, w/ red and gold trim, 2" to 3.25" h, price each	12	14
Portraits, Ladies of Song series, pink w/ parasol, 6" h	45	50
Robin, Musicale series, blue dress w/ harp, 6" h	55	65
Santa, w/ boy on his lap, 6.25" h	45	47
School Belle, yellow dress w/ apple, 3" h	22	28

Edwin M. Knowles China

Edwin M. Knowles, son of the founder of Knowles, Taylor, Knowles, manufactured his own semiporcelain from 1901 until 1963. There are many different backstamps

Edwin M. Knowles backstamp.

Bench

	LOW	AVG.	HIGH
Bowl, 36s	$8	$9	$10
Bowl, coupe, 6"	4	5	6
Butter, open	21	23	25
Casserole	30	36	41
Chop Plate	12	15	17
Cream/Sugar	24	28	32
Cup/Saucer	10	15	20
Custard Cup	4	5	6
Dish, 6"	2	3	4
Gravy Boat	14	16	18
Pickle Dish	6	7	8
Plate, 6" to 8"	4	6	8
Plate, 9" to 10"	8	9	10
Platter, 8" to 12"	11	18	25
Salt/Pepper	24	28	32
Soup Plate	8	9	10

Beverly (1941)

	LOW	AVG.	HIGH
Bowl, 36s	$8	$9	$10
Bowl, coupe, 8"	10	12	14
Butter, open	21	23	25
Candle Holders, pair	24	27	29
Casserole	20	25	30
Chop Plate	12	14	16
Cream/Sugar	18	22	26
Cup/Saucer	10	15	20
Dish, 6"	2	3	4
Gravy Boat	12	14	16
Plate, 6" to 8"	4	6	8
Plate, 9" to 10"	8	9	10
Platter, 8" to 12"	12	16	20
Salt/Pepper	24	28	32
Soup Plate	8	9	10
Teapot	25	30	35

Deanna (1938)

	LOW	AVG.	HIGH
Bowl, 36s	$7	$8	$10
Casserole	27	31	34
Chop Plate	14	16	18
Coaster	14	16	18
Cream/Sugar	21	24	27
Cup/Saucer	9	13	16
Dish, 4" to 5"	2	3	4
Gravy Boat	14	16	18
Pickle Dish	5	7	9
Plate, 6" to 8"	4	6	7
Plate, 9" to 10"	7	8	9
Platter, 8" to 12"	8	13	18
Salt/Pepper	21	24	27
Soup, coupe	7	8	9
Teapot	27	31	34
Vegetable, 7" to 10"	13	15	17

Esquire (1956)

	LOW	AVG.	HIGH
Comport	$58	$61	$64
Cream/Sugar	42	44	46
Cup/Saucer	15	19	22
Dish, 5" to 7"	12	14	16
Gravy Boat	36	40	42
Pitcher, 2 qt.	85	95	105
Plate, 6" to 7"	9	12	14
Plate, 9" to 10"	15	16	18
Platter, 9" to 14"	26	30	36
Salt/Pepper	25	32	40
Server, 22"	45	50	55
Teapot	100	110	120
Vegetable	45	58	70

Yorktown (1936)

	LOW	AVG.	HIGH
Bowl, coupe, 6"	$4	$5	$6
Candle Holders, pair	24	28	32
Casserole	30	36	40
Chop Pltae	12	15	17
Coaster	10	13	16
Cream/Sugar	24	28	32
Cup/Saucer	24	28	32
Custard Cup	4	5	6
Dish, 6"	2	33	4
Gravy Boat	14	16	18
Pickle Dish	6	7	8
Plate, 6" to 8"	4	6	8
Plate, 9" to 10"	8	9	10
Platter, 8" to 12"	12	18	25
Salt/Pepper	24	28	32
Soup Plate	8	9	10

Homer Laughlin China

Founded in 1874 as the Laughlin Brothers Pottery, it became the Homer Laughlin China Company in 1896. Homer's brother, Shakespeare, withdrew in 1877. Homer Laughlin mainly produced semiporcelain. In 1959, vitreous dinnerware and institutional ware lines were introduced. The company is one of the largest still manufacturing today.

Homer Laughlin is most famous for its Fiesta dinnerware. The company is also well known because of its dinnerware designed by Frederick Rhead, head designer from 1928 to 1942, and Don Schreckengost, head designer from 1945 to 1960. Laughlin used a variety of backstamps.

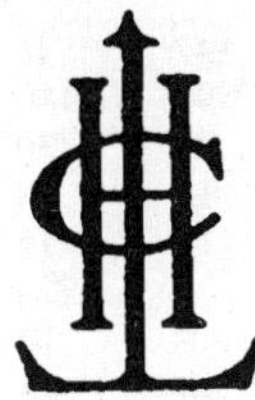

Early Homer Laughlin backstamps.

Brittany

	LOW	AVG.	HIGH
Bowl, 6"	$6	$8	$10
Cream/Sugar	25	30	35
Cup/Saucer	10	15	20
Dish, 5"	5	6	7
Egg Cup	15	20	25
Gravy Boat	18	22	26
Pickle Dish	10	12	14
Plate, 6" to 7"	4	7	10
Plate, 9" to 10"	7	10	13
Plate, 8" sq.	9	14	20
Platter, 11" to 13"	25	30	35
Platter, 15"	25	28	31
Soup Plate, 9"	20	22	24
Teapot	35	45	55
Vegetable, 8" to 9"	20	30	40

Century (1931)

Century is an early square shape in dinnerware.

Batter Pitcher	$80	$100	$120
Butter Dish	75	85	95
Casserole	34	40	46
Cream/Sugar	18	22	26
Cup/Saucer	12	14	16
Dish, 5"	6	7	8
Dish, 6"	12	14	16
Gravy Boat	15	20	25
Pickle Dish	16	17	18
Plate, 6" to 7"	6	8	10
Plate, 9" to 10"	15	20	25

	LOW	AVG.	HIGH
Platter, 11" to 15"	16	24	30
Soup Bowl/Saucer	50	60	70
Soup Plate, 8"	12	14	16
Syrup Pitcher	80	85	95
Teapot	75	85	95
Vegetable, 9"	20	22	24

Epicure

Epicure was designed by Don Schreckengost and glazed in solid colors.

	LOW	AVG.	HIGH
Casserole	$42	$46	$50
Coffeepot	95	110	125
Cream/Sugar	25	30	34
Cup/Saucer	15	18	20
Dish	12	15	18
Gravy Boat	21	23	25
Plate, 6" to 8"	8	10	12
Plate, 9" to 10"	12	15	18
Salt/Pepper	20	24	26
Soup Plate	11	14	16

Fiesta Ware

The Homer Laughlin China Company introduced this brightly colored pottery tableware in 1935. Frederick H. Rhead's graduated ring design was one of the most widely manufactured tablewares of the twentieth century.

Colors include red, rose, dark green, medium green, light green, chartreuse, yellow, old ivory, gray, turquoise, and cobalt blue. Pieces are trademarked in the mold or with an ink hand-stamped mark. Reissued and restyled from the originals in 1986, Fiesta is still being produced. Prices are for old, not reissued pieces. Medium green in the most valued, followed by rose, gray and forest green.

	AUCTION	RETAIL	
		Low	High
Bread and Butter Plate, 6" dia., chartreuse	$9	$11	$12
Bread and Butter Plate, 6" dia., dark green	10	12	14
Bread and Butter Plate, 6" dia., ivory	7	9	11
Bread and Butter Plate, 6" dia., medium green	18	21	25
Bread and Butter Plate, 6" dia., rose	9	11	12
Bread and Butter Plate, 6" dia., turquoise	5	6	7
Bread and Butter Plate, 6" dia., yellow	5	6	7
Carafe, red	200	250	300
Casserole, cov., chartreuse	300	350	400
Casserole, cov., cobalt	150	175	200
Casserole, cov., dark green	300	350	400
Casserole, cov., light green	125	150	175
Casserole, cov., rose	200	230	260
Chop Plate, 13" dia., ivory	40	45	50
Chop Plate, 13" dia., rose	50	60	70
Chop Plate, 13" dia., turquoise	50	60	70
Chop Plate, 15" dia., cobalt	40	45	50
Coffeepot, light green	190	220	250

	AUCTION	RETAIL Low	RETAIL High
Cream Soup, light green	42	50	55
Creamer, cobalt	25	30	35
Creamer, gray	35	40	45
Creamer, rose	35	40	45
Creamer, turquoise	20	22	24
Creamer, yellow	20	22	24
Creamer, individual, red	200	240	280
Creamer, stick handle, ivory	50	55	60
Creamer, stick handle, yellow	45	52	60
Creamer, stick handle, red	60	70	80
Cup/Saucer, chartreuse	35	40	45
Cup/Saucer, cobalt	30	40	45
Cup/Saucer, dark green	40	45	50
Cup/Saucer, ivory	34	40	47
Cup/Saucer, medium green	65	75	85
Cup/Saucer, red	35	40	45
Cup/Saucer, rose	35	45	55
Cup/Saucer, turquoise	25	30	35
Cup/Saucer, yellow	25	30	35
Deep Plate, chartreuse	60	70	80
Deep Plate, gray	60	70	80
Deep Plate, ivory	45	55	65
Deep Plate, light green	40	45	50
Deep Plate, red	50	60	70
Deep Plate, turquoise	40	45	50
Deep Plate, yellow	35	40	45
Demitasse Cup/Saucer, turquoise	70	80	90
Dessert Bowl, turquoise	40	46	57
Dinner Plate, 10" dia., chartreuse	45	53	61
Dinner Plate, 10" dia., ivory	40	45	50
Dinner Plate, 10" dia., light green	30	35	40
Dinner Plate, 10" dia., medium green	100	125	150
Dinner Plate, 10" dia., red	40	45	50
Dinner Plate, 10" dia., rose	50	55	60
Dinner Plate, 10" dia., turquoise	30	35	45
Dinner Plate, 10" dia., yellow	28	34	38
Dinner Plate, 9" dia., chartreuse	20	25	28
Dinner Plate, 9" dia., cobalt	17	21	23
Dinner Plate, 9" dia., dark green	25	32	35
Dinner Plate, 9" dia., gray	20	25	28
Dinner Plate, 9" dia., ivory	17	20	23
Dinner Plate, 9" dia., light green	12	15	17
Dinner Plate, 9" dia., medium green	40	50	60
Dinner Plate, 9" dia., red	17	20	24
Dinner Plate, 9" dia., rose	20	25	28
Dinner Plate, 9" dia., turquoise	12	15	18
Dinner Plate, 9" dia., yellow	11	13	15
Disk Juice Pitcher, yellow	40	47	53
Disk Pitcher, chartreuse	300	350	400
Disk Pitcher, ivory	155	180	210
Disk Pitcher, red	150	175	200
Disk Pitcher, rose	100	120	140

Fiesta Lazy Susan, multicolor, $250–$350.

	AUCTION	RETAIL Low	RETAIL High
Disk Pitcher, turquoise	90	100	110
Disk Water Pitcher, cobalt	90	110	130
Disk Water Pitcher, dark green	220	260	300
Disk Water Pitcher, ivory	150	175	200
Disk Water Pitcher, yellow	100	120	140
Fork, light green	85	100	115
Fruit Bowl, 4.75" dia., chartreuse	35	45	50
Fruit Bowl, 4.75" dia., gray	30	35	40
Fruit Bowl, 4.75" dia., ivory	33	40	46
Fruit Bowl, 4.75" dia., rose	35	42	49
Fruit Bowl, 4.75" dia., turquoise	28	35	37
Fruit Bowl, 4.75" dia., yellow	22	27	29
Fruit Bowl, 5.5" dia., cobalt	30	35	40
Fruit Bowl, 5.5" dia., ivory	30	35	40
Fruit Bowl, 5.5" dia., medium green	70	80	90
Fruit Bowl, 5.5" dia., turquoise	20	25	30
French Casserole, yellow	200	230	260
Gravy, chartreuse	75	87	100
Gravy, red	60	70	80
Gravy, rose	75	87	100
Juice Tumbler, cobalt	35	40	45
Juice Tumbler, red	35	40	45
Juice Tumbler, turquoise	35	40	45
Luncheon Plate, 7" dia., chartreuse	12	14	18
Luncheon Plate, 7" dia., cobalt	9	11	13
Luncheon Plate, 7" dia., dark green	15	18	20
Luncheon Plate, 7" dia., gray	12	14	16
Luncheon Plate, 7" dia., light green	7	9	11
Luncheon Plate, 7" dia., medium green	30	35	40
Luncheon Plate, 7" dia., red	9	11	13
Luncheon Plate, 7" dia., rose	12	15	16
Luncheon Plate, 7" dia., yellow	7	9	11
Marmalade, coablt	300	370	400
Marmalade, red	280	340	400
Mixing Bowl, #2, light green	85	100	120
Mixing Bowl, #4, yellow	120	140	160
Mixing Bowl, #5, cobalt	110	120	130
Mixing Bowl, #6, cobalt	125	140	165
Mixing Bowl, #6, yellow	160	180	200

	AUCTION	RETAIL	
		Low	High
Mug, medium green	60	75	90
Mug, turquoise	23	27	30
Mustard, light green	190	235	250
Mustard, yellow	160	190	220
Nappy, 8.5" dia., chartreuse	30	38	40
Nappy, 8.5" dia., light green	30	35	40
Nappy, 8.5" dia., rose	55	65	75
Nappy, 8.5" dia., turquoise	19	23	25
Nappy, 8.5" dia., yellow	28	33	37
Nappy, 9.5" dia., ivory	40	50	54
Nappy, 9.5" dia., yellow	30	35	40
Onion Soup, cov., yellow	400	450	500
Plate, divided, 10" dia., cobalt	40	50	56
Plate, divided, 10" dia., gray	75	85	95
Plate, divided, 10" dia., yellow	35	42	47
Plate, divided, 12" dia., ivory	50	60	70
Platter, oval, chartreuse	80	100	120
Platter, oval, cobalt	42	49	56
Platter, oval, gray	80	100	120
Platter, oval, red	42	52	57
Platter, oval, yellow	30	35	42
Relish Tray	250	300	350
Salad Bowl, individual, medium green	100	120	140
Salad Bowl, individual, red	80	97	100
Salad Bowl, individual, turquoise	70	80	90
Salad Bowl, individual, yellow	80	90	100
Salt/Pepper, chartreuse	40	45	50
Salt/Pepper, cobalt	26	32	35
Salt/Pepper, ivory	26	32	34
Salt/Pepper, light green	20	25	27
Salt/Pepper, rose	40	45	50
Salt/Pepper, yellow	20	25	28
Syrup Pitcher, red	385	465	520
Teapot, medium, turquoise	130	150	170
Teapot, medium, yellow	135	160	180
Teapot, rose	150	180	210
Utility Tray, cobalt	25	30	35
Utility Tray, red	55	65	75
Vase, 8", cobalt	600	700	800
Water Tumbler, cobalt	60	70	80

Fiesta Teapot.

Harlequin (1938)

Similar to Fiesta, it has bright colors, simple shapes and a series of rings, but not on the rim. Pieces were unmarked.

	LOW	AVG.	HIGH
Ashtray, basketweave, rose	$40	$50	$60
Bowl, 36s, gray	50	60	70
Bowl, 36s, rose	25	35	45
Butter, 1/2 lb.	60	85	110
Candlesticks, pair	100	130	160
Casserole	50	75	100
Cream/Sugar	25	50	75
Creamer, maroon	20	24	28
Creamer, individual, yellow	18	22	26
Cup/Saucer, dark green	18	20	22
Cup/Saucer, gray	14	16	18
Cup/Saucer, yellow	12	15	18
Deep Plate, chartreuse	25	30	35
Deep Plate, turquoise	18	22	26
Demitasse Cup/Saucer, turquoise	55	65	75
Dish, 5.5"	6	9	12
Dish, 6.5"	16	20	24
Egg Cup	9	12	14
Egg Cup, double, yellow	15	18	21
Fruit Bowl, 5.5", gray	10	12	14
Gravy Boat, rose	20	25	30
Gravy Boat, yellow	18	22	26
Jug, 22 oz., gray	70	80	90
Jug, 22 oz., red	50	60	70
Jumbo Cup/Saucer	55	65	75
Marmalade	100	125	150
Nut Dish, maroon	14	16	18
Oatmeal Bowl, rose	20	25	30
Oatmeal Bowl, yellow	15	20	25
Plate, 7", dark green	12	15	18
Plate, 7", yellow	8	10	12
Plate, 9", gray	12	14	16
Plate, 9", rose	12	14	16
Plate, 9", turquoise	8	10	12
Plate, 9", yellow	10	12	14
Plate, 10", rose	20	25	30
Plate, 10", turquoise	15	20	25
Platter, 11", light green	16	18	20
Platter, 11", rose	14	16	18
Platter, 11", turquoise	14	16	18
Platter, 11", yellow	14	16	18
Relish Tray, 4-part	175	200	225
Salad, individual, dark green	30	35	40
Salad, individual, rose	30	35	40
Salad, individual, turquoise	20	25	30
Salad, individual, yellow	20	25	30

	LOW	AVG.	HIGH
Sauce Boat, rose	24	28	32
Shaker	8	10	12
Soup Plate, chartreuse	30	35	40
Soup Plate, red	25	30	35
Soup Plate, rose	25	30	35
Sugar, cov., rose	20	24	28
Sugar, cov., turquoise	18	22	26
Teapot	52	64	75
Tumbler	24	28	32
Vegetable, 9"	13	18	23
Water Pitcher, turquoise	50	75	100

Rhythm

Rhythm was designed by Don Schreckengost.

	LOW	AVG.	HIGH
Cream/Sugar	$25	$29	$33
Cup/Saucer	10	14	18
Dish, 5" to 6"	4	5	6
Gravy Boat	16	18	20
Pickle Dish, 9"	8	9	10
Pitcher, 2 qt.	50	60	70
Plate, 6" to 8"	4	6	8
Plate, 9" to 10"	8	9	10
Platter, oval, 11" to 15"	15	20	24
Salt/Pepper	12	15	18
Soup Plate, 8"	8	9	10
Spoon Rest	130	165	200
Teapot	43	48	53
Vegetable, cov.	30	34	38
Vegetable, open, 9"	17	19	20

Riviera

Riviera was based on the Century design.

	LOW	AVG.	HIGH
Batter Pitcher	$145	$182	$220
Butter Dish	150	165	180
Casserole	135	145	155
Creamer/Sugar	34	42	50
Cup/Saucer	25	28	31
Dish, 5"	12	14	16
Dish, 6"	37	44	52
Gravy Boat	31	40	48
Pickle Dish	30	34	38
Plate, 6" to 7"	12	16	20
Plate, 9" to 10"	30	40	50
Platter, 11" to 15"	31	46	62
Soup Plate, 8"	24	28	31
Syrup Pitcher	130	155	180
Teapot	150	175	200
Vegetable, 9"	40	45	50

Serenade (1939)

Serenade used an embossed wheat sheaf decoration.

	LOW	AVG.	HIGH
Casserole	$15	$20	$25
Chop Plate, 13"	8	10	12
Cream/Sugar	12	16	20
Cup/Saucer	5	9	13
Dish, 6"	2	3	4
Gravy Boat	8	10	12
Pickle Dish, 9"	4	5	6
Plate, 6" to 7"	3	4	5
Plate, 9" to 10"	4	5	6
Platter, oval, 12.5"	6	7	8
Salt/Pepper	12	15	18
Soup Plate, 8"	5	6	7
Teapot	15	20	25
Vegetable, 9"	8	10	12

Swing (1938)

Swing has delicate round handles and finials.

	LOW	AVG.	HIGH
Butter Dish	$19	$22	$25
Casserole	31	34	38
Coffeepot	30	34	38
Cream/Sugar	28	32	36
Cup/Saucer	8	10	12
Egg Cup	10	13	15
Muffin Cover	29	36	42
Plate, 6" to 8"	4	5	6
Plate, 9" to 10"	8	9	10
Platter, 11" to 13"	10	11	12
Salt/Pepper	14	16	18
Soup Bowl/Saucer	25	30	35
Soup Plate, 8"	8	9	10
Teapot	31	36	40
Vegetable, oval, 9"	12	14	16

Tango

Tango is rare and widely sought.

	LOW	AVG.	HIGH
Casserole	$30	$45	$55
Cream/Sugar	35	45	55
Cup/Saucer	10	13	15
Dish, 6"	6	8	10
Egg Cup	35	45	55
Plate, 6" to 7"	6	8	10
Plate, 9" to 10"	10	13	15
Platter, 11.5"	16	18	20
Salt/Pepper	17	22	27
Soup Plate	17	19	21
Vegetable, 8" to 9"	19	21	23

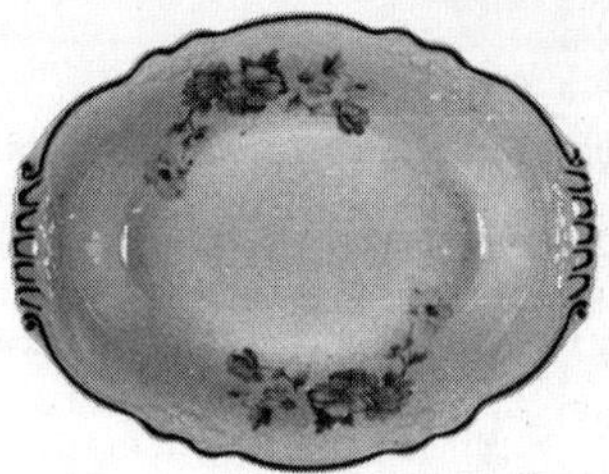

This pink floral decal is commonly found on Virginia Rose pieces. —Photo courtesy Ray Morykan Auctions.

Virginia Rose

Virginia Rose is the name of a shape, rather than a pattern. Pieces were decorated with a variety of floral decals and trimmed in either silver or gold.

	LOW	AVG.	HIGH
Butter, cov.	$40	$45	$50
Cake Plate	14	18	22
Cream/Sugar	22	25	28
Cup/Saucer	3	5	7
Fruit Bowl, 5.25"	3	5	7
Gravy	5	7	10
Mixing Bowl, 10"	48	55	62
Oatmeal Bowl, 6"	6	8	10
Plate, 6" to 7"	4	6	8
Plate, 9" to 10"	10	12	15
Platter, 11" to 13"	16	20	25
Salt/Pepper	8	10	12
Saucer Boat/Liner	24	30	36
Soup Plate, 8"	8	10	12
Vegetable, cov.	42	48	54
Vegetable, open, oval	16	20	25

Wells (1930)

Wells was designed by Frederick Rhead. It has a thin rim and open handles.

	LOW	AVG.	HIGH
Bowl, 36s	$11	$13	$15
Casserole	44	52	60
Coffeepot	45	53	61
Cream/Sugar	35	40	46
Cup/Saucer	12	15	18
Dish, 5"	3	5	6
Egg Cup	14	18	22
Gravy Boat	22	25	28
Pickle Dish	9	12	14
Plate, 6" to 8"	6	9	11
Plate, 9" to 10"	12	14	15
Plate, square	11	13	14
Platter, 11" to 15"	14	22	30
Soup Plate	22	26	30
Teapot	52	57	62
Vegetable, round, 8" to 9"	14	16	18

Limoges China

The Sterling China Company changed its name to Limoges early in this century. After WWII, legal action brought by Limoges of France forced the name change to American Limoges. Production halted in 1955. Viktor Schreckengost designed some American Limoges lines. The quality of American Limoges dinnerware is not as high as dinnerware produced by the French company of the same name. Don't pay French Limoges prices for American Limoges pieces.

Limoges backstamp.

Casino (c. 1954)

Casino has the shape of playing card suits, with matching decal decorations.

	LOW	AVG.	HIGH
Cream/Sugar, diamond	$20	$30	$40
Cup, club	10	14	18
Dish, diamond	6	7	8
Plate, spade	9	13	16
Platter, diamond	18	22	24
Saucer, heart	4	5	6

Thin Swirl

	LOW	AVG.	HIGH
Butter Dish	$20	$22	$24
Casserole	20	23	26
Cream/Sugar	12	14	16
Cup/Saucer	4	5	6
Gravy Boat	12	14	16
Plate, 6" to 7"	2	3	4
Plate, 9"	7	8	9
Teapot	30	35	40

Triumph (1937)

	LOW	AVG.	HIGH
Casserole	$20	$23	$26
Chop Plate, 11" to 13"	12	16	20
Coffeepot	40	45	50
Cream/Sugar	13	15	17
Cup/Saucer	4	5	6
Dish, 5" to 6"	1	2	3
Gravy Boat	8	9	10
Plate, 6" to 7"	1	2	3
Plate, 10" to 11"	4	5	6
Platter, oval, 11" to 15"	10	14	18
Salt/Pepper	8	10	12
Soup Plate, 8.25"	10	11	12
Vegetable, round, 8.75"	15	17	20

Lladró Figurines

The famous porcelain figurines made by Lladró in Labernes Blanques, Spain, are popular, limited edition collectibles.

	LOW	HIGH
Adolescence, #4878	$360	$480
Angel Tree Topper, blue, #5719	90	120
Angel Tree Topper, rose, #5831	90	120
Attentive Polar Bear, #1207	60	80
Bear Seated, #1206	110	150
Best Friend, #7620	220	290
Boy Awakening, #4870	70	90
Can I Play, #7610	320	420
Christmas Morning, #5940	90	120
Clean Up Time, #4838	160	220
Destination Big Top, #6245	320	430
Duck Jumping, #1265	60	80
Female Tennis Player (matte finish), #1427	630	830
Flower Song, #7607	450	590
Garden Classic, #7617	450	590
Garden Song, #7618	360	470
Holy Family, #5657	90	120
Holy Shepherds, #5809	90	120
King Balthasar, #5481	230	300
King Melchior, #5479	230	300
Koala Bear, #5461	260	340
Leopard Butterfly, #1584	180	230
My Buddy, #7609	360	480
Naptime, #5448	190	250
Pekinese Sitting, #4641	320	420
Picture Perfect, #7612	410	540
Pierrot w/ Concertina, #5279	120	160
Polar Bear, #1208	60	80
Practice Makes Perfect, #5462	380	500
Precocious Courtship, #5072	630	830
Pretty Butterfly No. 10, #1682	200	260
Queen Butterfly No. 14, #1686	140	190
Saint Nicholas, #5427	630	830
School Days, #7604	360	480
Sea Saw, #1255	540	710
Snuggle Up, #6226	140	190
Spotted Butterfly No. 11, #1683	190	260
Still Life, #5363	310	410
Summer Stroll, #7611	300	400
Teaching to Pray, #4779	150	200
The Architect, #5214	430	570
Three Kings, #5729	90	120
Valencian Girl, #4841	190	260
Valencian Harvest, #5668	410	540

Metlox Pottery

Metlox makes art ware, novelties, and Poppytrail dinnerware. Although solid color wares may date to 1927, decorated wares date from the 1940s through the present.

California Ivy

	LOW	AVG.	HIGH
Butter Dish, cov.	$50	$55	$60
Chop Plate, 13"	30	35	40
Coaster	12	15	18
Coffeepot	100	120	140
Cream/Sugar	30	35	40
Cup/Saucer	14	18	22
Dish, 5" to 7"	11	17	22
Gravy Boat	35	38	41
Mug	22	25	28
Pitcher, 2.5 qt.	50	60	70
Plate, 6" to 8"	14	18	20
Plate, 10"	21	25	28
Platter, oval, 9" to 13"	34	46	58
Salad Bowl, 11"	343	38	42
Salad Plate	8	12	16
Salt/Pepper	14	21	28
Soup Bowl, 5"	8	10	12
Soup Plate, 7"	17	19	21
Teapot	100	125	150
Tumbler, 13 oz.	40	45	50
Vegetable, 9" to 11"	40	45	50

Homestead Provincial

	LOW	AVG.	HIGH
Butter Server, rectangular, 9.5"	$50	$60	$70
Butter Dish, rectangular	50	55	60
Canister Set, 4-pc.	225	250	275
Casserole, hen lid, 1 qt.	57	64	71
Chop Plate, 12.25"	30	35	40
Coaster, 3.75"	11	14	17
Coffeepot, 7 cup	100	112	125
Cookie Jar	70	85	100
Cream/Sugar	30	35	40
Cruet	50	55	60
Cup/Saucer	16	22	28
Dish, 5" to 6"	8	12	12
Egg Cup	23	25	27
Gravy Boat	32	38	43
Lazy Susan, 7-pc.	90	115	140
Mug, 8 oz.	16	19	21
Pitcher, 1 qt. to 2 qt.	50	60	70
Plate, 6" to 8"	12	16	20
Plate, 10"	23	26	28
Platter, oval, 11" to 16"	40	55	70
Salad Bowl, 11"	34	38	42
Salt/Pepper	14	22	30

Left: Homestead Provincial.
Right: Red Rooster.

	LOW	AVG.	HIGH
Shakers, hen/rooster	45	48	52
Soup Plate, 8"	16	20	23
Tankard, 1 pt.	45	50	55
Teapot	110	125	140
Tumbler, ftd., 11 oz.	110	125	140
Vegetable, 7" to 12"	30	40	50
Vegetable, cov., 1 qt.	58	62	68

Red Rooster

Butter, rectangular	$70	$80	$90
Butter, rectangular	60	65	70
Canister Set, 4-pc.	200	250	300
Casserole, hen lid, 1.25 qt.	65	75	85
Casserole, individual, hen lid	110	120	130
Chop Plate, 12"	30	32	36
Coaster, 3.75"	14	18	20
Coffeepot	110	130	150
Cookie Jar	150	170	180
Cream/Sugar	36	44	50
Cup/Saucer	22	28	32
Dish, 6"	18	22	25
Egg Cup	30	32	36
Gravy Boat	42	48	52
Lazy Susan, 7-pc.	450	500	550
Marmalade	130	150	170
Mug, 8 oz.	28	32	36
Pitcher, 1.5 pt. to 2.25 qt.	50	70	90
Plate, 6" to 8"	11	18	25
Platter, oval, 9" to 16"	40	60	80
Salad, 11.5"	40	48	54
Salt Box	170	185	200
Salt/Pepper	18	26	35
Salt/Pepper, hen/rooster	50	60	70
Salt/Pepper Mill	150	160	170
Soup, individual, 5"	11	13	15
Soup Plate, 8"	22	26	30
Tankard, 1 pt.	50	60	70
Teapot	135	155	175
Tumbler, ftd., 11 oz.	140	160	180
Tureen	500	750	1000
Vegetable	40	60	80

Newcomb Pottery

The Newcomb College Art Department in New Orleans began producing pottery for sale in 1896. Newcomb wares carry underglaze designs picturing subjects from nature.

There are usually five marks on each piece: the mark of Newcomb (a white-on-black vase with the initials *N.C.*, with the *N* within the *C*, or *NEWCOMB COLLEGE* spelled out), a potter's mark, an artist's or decorator's mark, a recipe mark and a registration mark.

	AUCTION	RETAIL	
		Low	High
Bud Vase, M. DeHoa LeBlanc, tall corseted shape, carved w/ white flowers on dark blue-green glossy ground, impressed "NC/MHLB/CV11/Q/JM," 1909, 9.5" h, 3.5" dia	$6600	$8000	$9500
Cabinet Vase, Sadie Irvine, live oak and Spanish moss in denim blue against pale blue ground, mkd. "NC/2/SL80/S," 1930, 2.25" h, 2.75" dia	1430	1750	2000
Cabinet Vase, Henrietta Bailey, pink blossoms and green leaves on purple ground, mkd. "NC/JS26/236/JM/HB," 1918, 4.25" h, 3" dia	1980	2500	3000
Low Bowl, green and brown hare's fur glaze, impressed "NC/JMF/F/D," 2.5" h, 4.75" dia	495	650	800
Pitcher, Harriet Joor, high glaze w/ incised yellow daffodils and green stems on ivory and pale blue ground, mkd. "NC/JM/Q/AR13/JH," 1905, 8" h	9350	12,000	15,000
Vase, Anna F. Simpson, bulbous w/ white irises and green stems on mottled blue-green ground, mkd. "NC/JM/K/DV38/AFS," 1910, 8.5" h, 6" dia	7700	9500	11,000
Vase, Anna F. Simpson, spherical w/ 4 handles, carved w/ white lilies on green stems against blue ground, impressed "NC/JM/IJ25/AFS/274," 1916, 4.5" h, 5.75" dia	3020	3800	4600
Vase, Sadie Irvine, carved w/ moonlit landscape, Spanish moss, and oak trees, mkd. "NC/211/N178/SI," 1923, 11" h, 6.5" dia	5500	6800	8200
Vessel, R.B. Kennon, squat, incised w/ grapevines in cobalt and blue-green on glossy blue ground, mkd. in ink "NC/R.B.K./W37," 1902, 6" h, 7.5" dia	8250	10,000	12,000
Vase, Sadie Irvine, purple flowers and green stems on blue-green semigloss ground, impressed "NC/SI/133/HO13," 1915, 11.25" h, 4" dia	5750	7000	9200

Newcomb College Pottery. —Photo courtesy David Rago Auctions.

Niloak Pottery

Niloak Pottery is old classic redware, influenced by Greek, Roman and Native American design, but with a striking marbleized texture. Potters threw Niloak ware on a wheel. Many pieces have only an inside glaze. The word "niloak" is kaolin (the chief ingredient in porcelain) spelled backwards. Niloak pottery is completely unlike porcelain. Most successful during the 1920s, the firm survived until 1946.

The pottery had an impressed mark or a circular paper label, reading simply *NILOAK POTTERY.* Paper labels became standard in later years.

	AUCTION	RETAIL	
		Low	High
Candlestick, slender form, broad steel blue and cerulean blue swirls and narrow terra cotta, ivory, chocolate, and beige swirls, first impressed mark w/ early art letters, 6.5" h	$138	$175	$200
Vase, baluster shape w/ trumpet neck, broad swirls w/ cerulean blue, terra cotta, chocolate, ivory, and beige, first impressed mark w/ early art letters, 6.75" h, 3.75" dia	293	400	500
Vase, flared rim, deep gray bands contrasted against narrow cerulean blue, chocolate, ivory, and terra cotta swirls, paper label, 5.25" h, 3.75" dia	165	210	270
Vase, flat rim, broad beige and ivory swirls w/ narrow terra cotta, cerulean blue, and chocolate accents, first impressed mark w/ early art letters, 4.5" h, 3" dia	77	100	130
Vase, miniature w/ flared lip, narrow swirls in shades of brown, terra cotta, ivory, and steel blue, impressed die stamp w/ early art letters, 5.25" h, 3.25" dia	293	400	500
Vase, miniature w/ rolled rim, narrow swirls of terra cotta and beige w/ accents of cerulean blue, ivory, and beige, early paper label, 4.5" h, 2.75" dia	110	140	170
Vase, ovoid w/ protruding lip, broad swirls in shades of brown w/ terra cotta, ivory, and sky blue, impressed die stamp w/ early art letters, 8.5" h, 4" dia	275	360	450
Vase, short neck, broad swirls of cerulean blue, beige, and terra cotta w/ ivory and gray accents, first impressed mark w/ early art letters, 6.75" h, 4" dia	165	220	280

Niloak Mission Ware. —Photo courtesy Smith & Jones.

George Ohr Pottery

George Ohr of Biloxi, Mississippi, designed and manufactured all pieces himself. Ohr pottery was produced between the early 1880s and 1906. Most pieces are marked *G.E. OHR, BILOXI.*

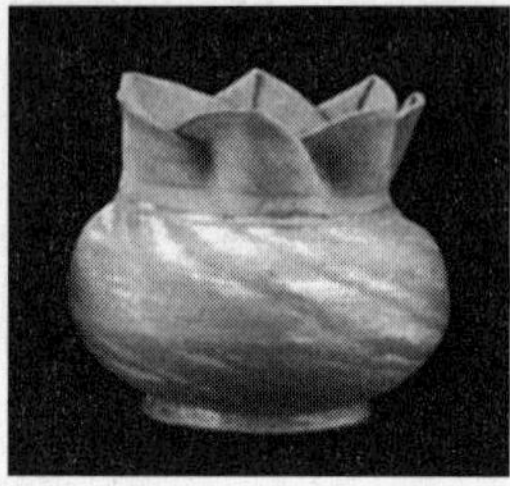

Vessel, bisque scroddled clay w/ folded rim, script signature, 4" h, 4.75" dia., $1210 at auction. —Photo courtesy David Rago Auctions.

	AUCTION	RETAIL Low	RETAIL High
Bud Vase, conical base, in-body twist, cupped top, dead matte black crystalline glaze, die stamped "G.E. Ohr/Biloxi," 5.25" h	$1540	$2000	$2500
Candle Holder, organic, pinched ribbon handle, in-body twist, ribbed base, yellow, green, and raspberry matte mottled glaze, script mark, 6.5" h	3630	4800	6000
Chamberstick, flattened bulbous base, deep red, green, and yellow matte mottled glaze, hand incised "GE Ohr," 4" h, 3.75" dia	1650	2200	2800
Demitasse Cup, green, cobalt, and raspberry marbleized glazed exterior, sponged cobalt and raspberry volcanic glazed interior, die stamped "G.E. Ohr/Biloxi, Miss," 2.5" h	1650	2200	2800
Jar, cov., spherical, gunmetal and green glazed dripping over mottled raspberry ground, die stamped "G.E. Ohr/Biloxi, Miss," 4.25" h, 5" dia	1650	2200	2800
Mustache Cup, occupational, hand built as shirt cuff w/ ribbon handle, sponged blue glazes, die stamped "Geo. E. Ohr/Biloxi, Miss," 2.75" h, 4" dia	2200	3000	3700
Pitcher, pinched handle, pink and green volcanic glaze, die stamped "G.E. Ohr/Biloxi, Miss," 4" h, 4.25" dia	2420	3200	4000
Vase, bottle shaped, brown, green, and amber speckled lustered glaze, die stamped "G.E. Ohr/Biloxi, Miss," 8.5" h	1320	1750	2250
Vase, corseted w/ flaring folded rim, top covered in blue-green glaze, bottom w/ added mottled raspberry glaze, die stamped "Biloxi, Miss/Geo. E. Ohr," 4" h, 3.75" w	4675	6000	7200
Vase, cupped top, deep in-body twist, pinched ribbon handles, green and purple mottled glaze, die stamped "G.E. Ohr/Biloxi, Miss," 4.75" h	4675	6000	7200
Vessel, bulbous, severely folded and pinched top, leathery gunmetal glaze over amber base, die stamped "G.E. Ohr/Biloxi, Miss," 5.5" h, 4.25" w	2640	3300	4000
Vessel, heavily dimpled front and back, folded rim, green speckled glossy glaze, die stamped "G.E. Ohr/Biloxi, Miss," 5.5" h, 4.75" dia	3300	4400	5500
Vessel, tapered neck, squat base, gunmetal over mottled raspberry glaze, script signature, 4.25" h, 3.75" dia	1650	2200	2800
Vessel, unglazed scroddled clay, assymetrically pinched into wave-like folds, script mark, 4.5" h, 6.5" dia	9625	11,000	12,500

Paden City Pottery

The Paden City Company manufactured semiporcelain dinnerware from 1914 through 1963. It exhibited at the 1938–39 World's Fair. The Caliente line is the favorite of collectors.

Shenandoah Ware, Poppy pattern.

Caliente (1936)

	LOW	AVG.	HIGH
Casserole	$22	$27	$31
Cream/Sugar	19	21	23
Cup/Saucer	6	8	10
Dish, 5" to 6"	2	3	4
Plate, 6" to 7"	3	4	5
Plate, 9" to 11"	6	7	8
Platter, oval, 12" to 16"	9	12	15
Salt/Pepper	18	21	23
Teapot	44	48	52
Vegetable, 9" to 10"	12	14	16

Shellcrest (1937)

	LOW	AVG.	HIGH
Casserole	$15	$20	$25
Cream/Sugar	12	16	20
Cup/Saucer	4	6	8
Dish, 5" to 6"	2	3	4
Plate, 6" to 7"	2	3	4
Plate, 9" to 11"	4	5	6
Platter, oval, 12" to 16"	6	10	14
Salt/Pepper	12	15	18
Teapot	30	35	40
Vegetable, 9" to 10"	8	10	12

Shenandoah Ware — Jonquil or Poppy Pattern

	LOW	AVG.	HIGH
Casserole	$15	$20	$28
Cream/Sugar	12	16	21
Cup/Saucer	5	10	15
Pickle Dish, 9"	3	4	5
Plate, 6" to 7"	2	3	4
Plate, 9" to 10"	5	7	9
Platter, oval, 13" to 16"	5	10	16
Salt/Pepper	12	18	25

Purinton Pottery

Bernard Purinton moved the company from its 1936 home of Wellsville, Ohio, to Shippenville, Pennsylvania, in 1941. It remained there until its close in 1959. Purinton is best known for its dinnerware, kitchenware and novelties with under-the-glaze hand-painted slip decoration. Many pieces are unmarked.

Apple

	LOW	AVG.	HIGH
Bean Pot	$30	$40	$45
Bowl, rectangular, 14.5"	70	85	100
Butter Dish	60	90	120
Casserole, 9"	50	70	90
Chop Plate, 12"	45	60	75
Coffeepot, 8 cup	55	70	85
Cream/Sugar	30	40	50
Cup/Saucer	12	16	202
Dish, 5" to 7"	10	12	14
Fruit Bowl, 12"	30	40	50
Party Plate, 8.5"	20	25	30
Pickle Dish, 6"	9	12	15
Plate, 6" to 8"	9	12	15
Plate, 9" to 10"	15	20	25
Platter, 11" to 12"	20	30	40
Relish Tray, 3-pc.	30	40	50
Salad Bowl, 11"	41	50	60
Teapot, 2 cup	19	24	28
Teapot, 6 cup	40	50	58
Tray, 11"	35	45	55
Vegetable, 8"	25	30	35
Vegetable, divided	40	50	60

Brown Intaglio

	LOW	AVG.	HIGH
Butter Dish	$72	$84	$96
Casserole, 9"	48	56	64
Chop Plate, 12"	24	28	32
Coffeepot, 8 cup	60	70	80
Cookie Jar	60	70	80
Cookie Jar, w/ wooden lid	96	112	128
Cream/Sugar	36	42	48
Cup/Saucer	14	17	19
Dish, 5" to 7"	11	13	14
Fruit Bowl, 12"	38	43	50
Marmalade	48	56	64
Pickle Dish, 6"	11	13	14
Plate, 6" to 8"	11	13	14
Plate, 9" to 10"	20	24	27
Platter, 11" to 12"	30	35	40
Relish Tray, 3-pc.	42	50	56
Salad Bowl, 11"	48	56	64
Teapot, 2 cup	24	28	32
Vegetable, 8.5"	24	28	30

Fruit

	LOW	AVG.	HIGH
Cream/Sugar	$35	$40	$45
Cup/Saucer	10	12	14
Plate, 9" to 10"	18	22	26
Relish Tray, 3-pc.	50	60	70
Salt/Pepper, jug style	16	20	25
Sugar Canister, 9"	60	70	82

Pennsylvania Dutch

	LOW	AVG.	HIGH
Bean Pot	$45	$55	$65
Butter Dish	90	108	126
Casserole, 9"	60	72	84
Chop Plate, 12"	30	36	42
Coffeepot, 8 cup	80	95	110
Cookie Jar	75	90	105
Cookie Jar, w/ wooden lid	120	144	168
Cream/Sugar	45	54	64
Cup/Saucer	18	22	25
Dish, 5" to 7"	14	16	20
Fruit Bowl, 12"	48	56	65
Marmalade	60	72	84
Pickle Dish, 6"	14	16	20
Plate, 6" to 8"	14	16	20
Plate, 9" to 10"	26	30	36
Platter, 11" to 12"	38	45	54
Relish Tray, 3-pc.	54	64	74
Salad Bowl, 11"	60	72	84
Teapot, 2 cup	30	36	42
Tray, 11"	38	45	54
Vegetable, 8.5"	30	35	40

Tea Rose

	LOW	AVG.	HIGH
Butter Dish	$80	$95	$110
Casserole, 9"	60	72	84
Chop Plate, 12"	30	36	42
Coffeepot, 8 cup	75	90	100
Cookie Jar	75	90	100
Cream/Sugar	45	54	64
Cup/Saucer	18	22	25
Dish, 5" to 7"	14	16	18
Fruit Bowl, 12"	48	56	65
Pickle Dish, 6"	12	16	18
Plate, 6" to 8"	14	16	18
Plate, 9" to 10"	26	30	36
Platter, 11" to 12"	38	45	54
Relish Tray, 3-pc.	54	64	74
Salad Bowl, 11"	60	72	84
Teapot, 2 cup	30	36	42
Tray, 11"	38	45	54
Vegetable, 8.5"	28	34	56

Red Wing Pottery

The Red Wing Potteries, Inc., traces its roots to 1878, although it operated under that name only from 1936 until its close in 1967. The early Red Wing stoneware and dinnerware produced from the 1930s onward are collected.

Backstamps often use a wing motif.

Bob White (1955)

	LOW	AVG.	HIGH
Beverage Server, w/ lid	$80	$90	$100
Bread Tray, 24"	60	75	90
Butter Dish	70	80	90
Butter Warmer, cov.	45	60	75
Casserole, 1 qt. to 4 qt.	50	75	100
Cocktail Tray	30	45	60
Coffee Cup	20	28	36
Cookie Jar	40	60	80
Cream/Sugar	60	75	90
Cruet, w/ stopper	140	160	180
Dish, 5" to 6"	20	30	40
Gravy Boat, cov.	45	58	70
Lazy Susan	90	95	100
Mug	58	64	70
Pepper Mill, tall	450	475	500
Pitcher, 1.5 qt.	60	72	85
Pitcher, 3.5 qt.	140	170	200
Plate, 6" to 8"	11	17	22
Plate, 10"	23	26	29
Platter, 13"	11	17	22
Platter, 20"	30	38	44
Relish Tray, 3-pc.	40	50	60
Salad Bowl, 12"	58	66	74
Shaker, tall	28	36	43
Soup Plate	28	36	44
Teapot	60	80	100
Trivet	100	105	110
Tumbler	175	200	225
Vegetable	30	44	60
Water Jar, w/ base, 2 gal.	450	530	610

Fondoso (1939)

Belle Kogan designed Fondoso as one of four shapes for Gypsy Trail Hostessware (also Chevron, Reed and Plain). It appeared in many pastel colors.

	LOW	AVG.	HIGH
Batter Pitcher	$60	$65	$70
Batter Set Tray	45	50	55
Butter Dish, large	35	38	40
Casserole, 8.5"	60	75	90
Chop Plate, 14"	28	34	40
Coffeepot	40	50	60
Coffee Server	36	44	52
Console Bowl	30	38	46
Cookie Jar	30	50	70

Fondoso Teapot.

	LOW	AVG.	HIGH
Cream/Sugar, large	60	64	68
Cream/Sugar, small	36	40	46
Cup/Saucer	25	32	40
Custard Cup	24	28	30
Dessert Cup, ftd., 4"	11	15	20
Dish, 5" to 6"	18	24	30
Mixing Bowl, 5" to 7"	14	21	28
Mixing Bowl, 8" to 9"	34	44	55
Pitcher, straight, 1 pt. to 5 pt.	40	60	80
Pitcher, tilt, 2 qt.	58	66	74
Plate, 6" to 8"	12	16	20
Plate, 9" to 12"	20	27	34
Platter, oval, 12"	30	32	36
Relish Tray	24	32	40
Salad Bowl, 12"	35	40	45
Salt/Pepper	30	38	44
Soup Plate, 7.5"	18	20	24
Syrup Pitcher	42	50	58
Teapot	40	50	60
Tumbler, 7 oz. to 10 oz.	25	35	45
Vegetable, round, 8"	25	30	35

Pepe

Beverage Server, w/ lid	$80	$90	$100
Bread Tray, 24"	60	75	90
Butter Dish	70	80	90
Casserole, 1 qt. to 4 qt.	50	75	100
Cream/Sugar	60	75	90
Cruet, w/ stopper	140	160	180
Cup/Saucer	20	28	36
Dish, 5" to 6"	20	30	40
Gravy Boat, cov.	45	58	70
Lazy Susan	90	95	100
Mug	58	64	70
Pitcher, 1.5 qt.	60	72	85
Plate, 6" to 8"	11	17	22
Plate, 10"	24	26	30
Platter, 13"	30	38	44
Platter, 15"	60	80	100
Relish Tray	40	50	60
Salad Bowl, 12"	58	66	74

	LOW	AVG.	HIGH
Shaker, tall	28	36	44
Soup Plate	28	36	44
Vegetable	30	44	60
Water Jar, w/ base, 2 gal.	450	530	610

Tampico

Beverage Server, w/ lid	$80	$90	$100
Butter Dish, cov.	70	80	90
Casserole, cov.	50	75	100
Coffee Cup	20	28	36
Coffee Mug	20	28	36
Cream/Sugar	60	75	90
Dish, 5" to 6"	20	30	40
Gravy Boat, w/ lid	45	57	70
Nappy	30	35	40
Pitcher, 1.5 qt.	60	72	85
Pitcher, 3.5 qt.	140	170	200
Plate, 8.5"	23	26	29
Plate, 10.5"	11	17	22
Platter, 13"	30	38	44
Platter, 15"	60	80	100
Relish Dish	40	50	60
Salad Bowl, 12"	58	66	74
Salt/Pepper	28	36	44
Soup Plate	28	36	44
Teapot	60	80	100
Vegetable	30	44	60
Water Jar, w/ base, 2 gal.	450	530	610

Town and Country (1947)

Bean Pot	$140	$160	$180
Casserole	50	65	80
Casserole, individual	28	33	38
Cream/Sugar	30	36	42
Cruet, cov.	38	40	42
Cup/Saucer	22	26	30
Dish, 5" to 6"	12	14	18
Mixing Bowl, 9"	70	90	110
Mug	40	50	60
Mustard Jar	40	52	64
Milk Pitcher	50	65	90
Syrup Pitcher	50	60	70
Plate, 6" to 8"	6	9	12
Plate, 10" to 11"	10	14	18
Platter, 9" to 15"	26	38	50
Relish Tray, 7"	20	25	30
Salad Bowl, 13"	35	55	75
Salt/Pepper, large	30	45	60
Salt/Pepper, small	20	25	30
Teapot	100	112	125
Vegetable, oval, 8"	30	35	40

Rookwood

Rookwood manufactured pottery from 1879 to 1967. Its heyday was from 1890 to 1930. Standard glaze pieces feature a large, bold underglaze painting.

	AUCTION	RETAIL Low	RETAIL High
Basket, K. Shirayamadani, gondola shape, standard glaze, yellow slip-painted daisies on shaded green ground, impressed flame, "374/S," and artist cipher, 1888, 8" h, 15.5" w	$660	$850	$1100
Bowl, Z-Line, low, impressed geometric pattern, matte green glaze, flame mark and "IV/16DZ," 1940, 2.25" h, 6" dia.	413	550	700
Ewer, Anna M. Valentien, standard glaze, clover blossoms on luminous shaded yellow, green, and brown ground, flame mark and "537D/WAMV," 1894, 10" h, 7" w	715	950	1200
Ewer, Sallie Toohey, standard glaze, oak leaves on shaded brown and umber ground, flame mark and "611A/ST," 1899, 11" h, 8" w	413	550	700
Ewer, William McDonald, standard glaze, berries on shaded brown ground, flame mark and "WPMD/387W," 1892, 12.5" h, 6.25" w	715	925	1200
Humidor, Constance A. Baker, standard glaze, pipes, matches, and cigars on shaded ocher, orange, and green ground, flame mark and "66S/CAB," 1896, 5.5" h, 6" dia	660	850	1000
Jardiniere, faience, emb. steer skulls and garlands, matte green glaze, impressed flame mark, some chips, 11.5" h, 14" dia	715	950	1100
Pitcher, A.M. Valentien, Limoges-style cameo design w/ white narcissus on salmon pink ground, flame mark and "343/W/A.M.V.," 1890, 8.75" h, 6.25" w	440	600	800
Potpourri Jar, Charles McLaughlin, vellum glaze, band of pink cherry blossoms on ivory ground, flame mark and "XVII/321CB/CJM," 1917, 6" h, 5.5" dia	550	700	870
Tile, Faience, dec. in cuenca w/ Glasgow rose in pink w/ green leaves, mounted in new Arts & Crafts frame, impressed "Rookwood Faience/1281Y," 6" sq.	1430	1800	2200
Urn, cov., mustard microcrystalline glaze, flame mark and "X/339B," 1910, 12.75" h, 9.5" w	1430	1800	2200

Rookwood Pottery. —Photo courtesy David Rago Auctions.

	AUCTION	RETAIL Low	RETAIL High
Vase, A.M. Valentien, standard glaze, green palm fronds on shaded brown and green ground, flame mark and "A.M.V. 814A/X," 1900, 10" h, 6.25" dia.	935	1250	1500
Vase, bottle shaped, standard glaze, blue and yellow pansies on shaded ground, flame mark and "352/VI," 1894, 6" h, 3.5" dia.	385	500	630
Vase, Elizabeth Lincoln, wax matte, purple bell-shaped flowers and green leaves on blue, red, and yellow butterfat ground, flame mark and "XXVI/1841/LNL," 1926, 10.25" h, 3.25" dia.	1320	1750	2100
Vase, Jeanette Swing, standard glaze, brown poppies w/ green stems on amber ground, flame mark and "III/JS/901D," 1903, 7.25" h, 3.25" dia.	605	800	1000
Vase, Kataro Shirayamadani, tiger eye w/ amber heron on brown ground, impressed flame mark, artist signature illegible, 7.5" h, 3.5" dia.	1210	1600	2000
Vase, Rose Reschheimer, carved indigo irises and green leaves on red and green ground, flame mark and "VI/932D/P.F.," 1906, 8.5" h, 3.5" dia.	6050	8000	10,000
Vase, Sallie Toohey, standard glaze, ovoid bocy w/ red and yellow tulips on shaded green and orange ground, flame mark and "III/932/CC/ST," 1903, 10" h, 4" dia.	715	850	1000
Vase, Sara Sax, jewel porcelain, Art Deco flowers in pink, green, and blue, flame mark and "XXX/6180/SX," 1930, 6" h, 5.5" w	2310	4000	4800
Vessel, spherical, hand modeled w/ large leaves under matte mottled green and brown glaze, flame mark and "XIII/2037," 1913, 5.25" h, 7" dia.	880	1100	1400
Wall Pocket, cicada, matte green glaze, impressed flame mark and "VIII/1636/V," short glazed-over firing line, 1908, 9" h, 4.5" w	1320	1800	2200
Wall Sconce, deeply emb. w/ pair of owls, green and brown matte glaze, flame mark and "X/1688," minor repair to candle holder and sides, 1910, 11.25" h, 6" w	990	1200	1500

Rookwood vases with scenic vellum decoration. Left to right: Carl Schmidt, 1920, 10.25" h, $4125 at auction; Elizabeth McDermott, 1917, 7" h, $1540 at auction; E.T. Hurley, 1943, 7.75" h, $2640 at auction; Ed Diers, 1917, 9.25" h (chipped), $1320 at auction. —Photo courtesy David Rago Auctions.

Roseville Pottery

The Roseville factory opened in 1885 in Roseville, Ohio. In 1902, the factory bought a stoneware plant in Zanesville and made art pottery there until 1954. In 1910, the Roseville arm of the company closed. Roseville called it art ware "Rozane" (the sum of *RO*seville and *ZANE*sville).

Beware of recent reproductions. They are generally easy to spot by their color and lack of quality. For further information see *The Collectors Encyclopedia of Roseville Pottery, First Series* (1976, 1997 value update), and *Second Series* (1980, 1997 value update) by Sharon and Bob Huxford, Collector Books, Paducah, KY.

The following listings are arranged by pattern name, with individual forms indented under each pattern.

	AUCTION	RETAIL	
		Low	High
Apple Blossom			
Basket, 309-8", green	$220	$240	$260
Basket, 310-10", blue	165	180	200
Ewer, 318-15", blue	715	775	850
Vase, 389-10", blue	138	150	165
Vase, 392-15", pink	275	300	325
Wall Pocket, 366-8", pink	248	270	300
Bleeding Heart			
Console Bowl, 382-10", green	138	150	165
Ewer, 972-10", pink	248	275	300
Fan Vase, 970-9", blue	220	240	260
Pitcher, 1123, green	385	425	460
Wall Pocket, 1287-8", pink	385	425	460

Roseville Baskets. —Photo courtesy Gene Harris Antique Auction Center.

	AUCTION	RETAIL Low	RETAIL High
Bushberry			
Bookends, 9, orange, pair	138	150	165
Console Set, centerbowl (415-10"), flower frog (45), and 2 candlesticks (1147-C.S.), orange	193	220	240
Pitcher, 1325, blue	248	265	300
Umbrella Stand, 779-21", orange	550	600	660
Vase, 38-12", orange	165	180	200
Clematis			
Console Set, centerbowl (1159-10") and 2 candlesticks (1159-4"), blue	138	150	165
Cornucopia Fan Vases, 193-6", green, pair	99	110	125
Urn, 111-10", brown	66	75	80
Vase, 107-8", blue	77	85	95
Vase, 111-10", blue	77	85	95
Freesia			
Basket, 391-8", blue	193	210	230
Candlesticks, 1161-4½", blue, pair	165	180	200
Ewer, 19-6", brown	99	110	125
Jardiniere, 669-8", blue	275	300	325
Pitcher, 21-15", brown	220	240	260
Vase, 125-10", brown	99	110	125
Vase, 598-8", brown	220	240	260
Vase, 895-7", blue	275	300	325
Wall Pockets, 1296-8", brown, pair	248	300	350
Magnolia			
Basket, 384-8", brown	138	150	165
Conch Shell, 453-6", green	99	110	125
Conch Shell, 454-8", blue	110	120	135
Creamer and Sugar, 4S and 4C, brown	44	50	60
Floor Vase, 98-15", blue or brown	303	340	370
Vase, 91-8", green	77	85	95
Ming Tree			
Basket, 509-12", blue	330	360	390
Vase, 585-14", white	413	450	500
Wall Pocket, 566-8", white or pink	248	275	300
Pinecone			
Bud Vase, 112-7", brown	193	220	250
Cornucopia, 128-8", blue	220	240	265
Cornucopia, 422-8", green	88	100	120
Double Wall Pockets, 1273-8", brown, pair	413	450	500
Fan Vase, 472-6", blue	468	500	550
Flower Pot, 633-5", green	88	100	115
Flower Pot and Saucer, 636-5", green	138	150	165
Pillow Vase, 845-8", green	220	250	270
Pitcher, 415-9", blue	715	775	825
Planter, 379-9", brown	303	330	360
Vase, 704-7", blue	275	300	325
Vase, 705-9", brown	165	180	200
Vase, 712-12", brown	660	320	400
Vase, 747-10", brown	358	390	420
Vase, 847-9", blue	413	450	490
Vessel, 278-4", brown	165	180	200

	AUCTION	RETAIL Low	RETAIL High
Snowberry			
Basket, IBK-8", green	138	150	170
Basket, 1BK-10, green	165	175	200
Jardiniere, KJ-8", pink	275	300	330
Urn, IV-15", pink	440	480	520
Water Lily			
Conch Shell, 438-8", blue	138	150	170
Floor Vase, 85-18", blue	550	600	650
Urn, 175-8", blue	110	120	135
White Rose			
Basket, 363-10", blue	220	245	270
Basket, 363-10", pink	193	210	230
Cornucopia, 144-3", green	88	100	115
Pillow Vase, 987-9", brown	165	175	200
Vase, 982-7", pink	165	175	200
Vase, 991-12", blue	220	245	270
Vase, 992-15", pink	248	275	300
Wincraft			
Boat Dish, 227-10"	33	40	45
Fan Vase, 272-6"	66	70	80
Vase, 234-10"	165	180	200
Vase, 283-8"	55	60	70
Vase, 285-10"	220	240	260
Vase, 286-12"	110	120	130
Window Box, 268-12"	88	100	110
Zephyr Lily			
Basket, 393-7", blue	165	175	200
Cornucopias, 204-8", green, pair	165	175	200
Ewer, 24-15", brown	193	210	230
Floor Vase, 142-18", green	660	710	780
Hanging Basket, blue	275	300	325
Vase, 131-7", green	110	120	130
Vase, 137-10", brown	220	240	260
Vase, 139-12", brown	275	300	325

Left to right: Pinecone vase, Snowberry basket, Zephyr Lily flower pot, Carnelian I vase (back), Foxglove jardiniere, and Dahlrose vase. —Photo courtesy Gene Harris Antique Auction Center.

Royal Doulton

Royal Doulton figures are ceramic works of art. Although the English company produces other items, its HN series is the best known. The company was begun in the early 1800s by John Doulton. The HN series was introduced in 1913 and named after Harry Hixon, head colorist at the time.

Besides their figurines, there are many different Royal Doulton collectibles, including Toby jugs, plates, limited editions, and bird and animal figures. Royal Doulton figures are identified by the HN prefix followed by numbers in a chronological sequence. Subjects in this series are highly diverse representing the works of many different artists at different time periods.

The earliest Royal Doulton figures (with the lower HN numbers) are usually the most desirable to collectors. For more information consult *The Charlton Standard Catalogue of Royal Doulton Beswick Figurines, Fifth Edition* by Jean Dale, Charlton Press, Toronto, Canada, 1996.

	LOW	AVG.	HIGH
HN3, Milking Time	$3500	$3900	$4300
HN9A, Crinoline	1600	1900	2200
HN10, Madonna of the Square	1600	1800	2000
HN13, Picardy Peasant	2300	2700	3000
HN21, Crinoline	1600	1900	2200
HN21A, Crinoline	1600	1900	2200
HN24, Sleep	2900	3300	3600
HN24A, Sleep	2900	3300	3600
HN34, Moorish Minstrel	2900	3100	3300
HN38, Carpet Vendor	4100	4800	5500
HN38A, Carpet Vendor	4100	4800	5500
HN45, Jester	1900	2100	2300
HN48, Lady of the Fan	1900	2100	2300
HN59, Upon Her Cheeks She Wept	2300	2600	2900
HN64, Shy Anne	2300	2700	3000
HN67, Little Land	2400	2700	3000
HN69, Pretty Lady	900	1100	1200
HN72, An Orange Vendor	1200	1500	1800
HN79, Shylock	2900	3100	3300
HN82, Afternoon Call	3500	3900	4300
HN87, Lady Anne	3500	3900	4300
HN91, Jack Point	2300	2700	3000
HN98, Guy Fawkes	1400	1600	1800
HN305, Scribe	1100	1300	1600
HN310, Dunce	3200	3450	3600
HN313, Summer Seasons	1900	2000	2200
HN317, Shylock	2900	3100	3300
HN319, Gnome	1300	1600	1800
HN327, Curtsey	1700	1900	2100
HN334, Curtsey	1600	1800	2000
HN336, Lady with Rose	1900	2100	2300
HN337, Parson's Daughter	800	1000	1100
HN356, Sir Thomas Lovell	2900	3300	3600
HN359, Fisherwomen	4700	5100	5500
HN359, Double Jester	4700	5400	6100
HN375, Lady and Blackamoor, 2nd version	2900	3300	3600
HN390, Little Mother	2900	3100	3300
HN404, King Charles	2300	2500	2700
HN405, Japanese Fan	2300	2700	3000

	LOW	AVG.	HIGH
HN440, Goosegirl	3200	3450	3600
HN456, Welsh Girl	2900	3100	3300
HN458, Lady with Shawl	4900	5300	5700
HN459, Omar Khayyam and the Beloved	5300	5700	6100
HN461, Mandarin, 3rd version	3500	3900	4300
HN464, Captain MacHeath	700	900	1000
HN466, Tulips	1900	2100	2300
HN474, Autumn Seasons	1800	2100	2300
HN476, Fruit Gathering	3000	3200	3400
HN486, Balloon Seller	2000	2300	2600
HN490, One of the Forty	1250	1300	1500
HN503, Fruit Gathering	2900	3300	3600
HN504, Marie	2900	3100	3400
HN505, Marie	2900	3100	3400
HN506, Marie	2900	3100	3400
HN507, Pussy	8800	10,000	11,500
HN512, Spook	1500	1700	2000
HN517, Lady with Rose	1900	2100	2300
HN528, One of the Forty	1600	1800	2000
HN535, Pecksniff, 1st version	20	90	160
HN536, Stiggins	20	90	160
HN540, Little Nell	10	80	160
HN543, Cobbler	1300	1500	1600
HN550, Polly Peachum	420	540	670
HN554, Uriah Heep, 2nd version	300	420	540
HN561, Fruit Gathering	2900	3300	3600
HN570, Womand Holding Child	2300	2500	2700
HN573, Madonna of the Square	1900	2000	2200
HN576, Madonna of the Square	1900	2000	2200
HN580, Chelsea Pair	900	1100	1200
HN588, Girl with Yellow Frock	2900	3300	3600
HN593, Nude on Rock	1500	1700	2000
HN598, Omar Khayyam and the Beloved	5300	5700	6100
HN601, Mandarin, 3rd version	3500	3900	4300
HN608, Falstaff, 1st version	1300	1600	2000
HN626, Lady with Shawl	4900	5300	5700
HN628, Crinoline	1500	1700	1800
HN631, Fisherwomen	4700	5100	5500
HN635, Harlequinade	1300	1400	1600
HN641, Mandarin	3500	3900	4300
HN648, One of the Forty	1400	1600	1800
HN657, Mask	1800	2000	2000
HN661, Boy with Turban	900	1100	1200
HN678, Lady with Shawl	4900	5300	5700
HN701, Welsh Girl	2900	3100	3300
HN704, One of the Forty, 2nd version	1400	1600	1800
HN705, Gainsborough Hat	1300	1500	1600
HN713, One of the Forty, 12th version	1400	1600	1800
HN728, Victorian Lady	330	450	570
HN735, Shepherdess, 2nd version	1700	1900	2100
HN741, Geisha	2900	3300	3800
HN742, Victorian Lady	540	720	910
HN751, Shepherd, 3rd version	2600	2800	3000
HN769, Hearlequinade Masked	2600	3000	3300

Above, top row left to right: HN1926, Roseanna; HN2792, Christine (2nd version); HN1962, Genevieve; HN1948, Lady Charmain. Bottom row: HN2148, The Bridesmaid; HN2059, The Bedtime Story; HN1417, Marie; HN1908, Lydia; HN2107, Valerie.

Below, top row left to right: HN1977, Her Ladyship; HN2839, Nicola; HN1901, Penelope; HN2193, Fair Lady. Bottom row: HN1941, Peggy; HN2865, Tess; HN2864, Tom; HN2048, Mary Had a Little Lamb; HN2799, Ruth; HN1889, Goody Two Shoes.

—Photos courtesy Gene Harris Antique Auction Center.

	LOW	AVG.	HIGH
HN784, Pierette	1600	1800	2000
HN788, Proposal	1600	1800	2100
HN792, Welsh Girl	2900	3100	3300
HN794, Bouquet	2900	3300	3600
HN797, Moorish Misntrel	3700	4000	4300
HN1201, Hunts Lady	2300	2700	3000
HN1203, Butterfly	1700	2000	2300
HN1208, Victorian Lady	650	840	1000
HN1211, Quality Street	1100	1300	1500
HN1223, Geisha, 2nd version	1100	1300	1600
HN1225, Boy with Turban	1000	1200	1300
HN1233, Susanna	1200	1300	1500
HN1236, Tete-a-Tete, 2nd version	1000	1300	1600
HN1246, Baba	800	1000	1200
HN1250, Circe	2300	2500	2700
HN1255, Circe	2300	2500	2700
HN1259, Alchemist	1700	1900	2200
HN1267, Carmen	1400	1500	1600
HN1272, Negligee	2200	2400	2700
HN1279, Kathleen	700	800	1000
HN1292, Geisha, 2nd version	1100	1300	1600
HN1298, Sweet and Twenty	200	360	450
HN1304, Harlequinade Masked	2600	3000	3300
HN1305, Siesta	2900	3300	3600
HN1306, Midinette	2800	3100	3300
HN1310, Geisha, 2nd version	1100	1300	1600
HN1316, Toys	4700	5100	5500
HN1333, Jester, 2nd version	2200	2300	2400
HN1340, Priscilla	350	400	450
HN1357, Kathleen	890	1000	1100
HN1369, Boy on Pig	4700	5100	5500
HN1372, Darling	800	1100	1300
HN1374, Fairy	1100	1300	1600
HN1375, Fairy	1000	1200	1400
HN1376, Fairy	700	900	1100
HN1378, Fairy	700	900	1100
HN1380, Fairy	1250	1500	1750
HN1390, Doreen	900	1000	1200
HN1392, Paisley Shawl	420	540	670
HN1408, John Peel	3500	3900	4300
HN1409, Hunting Squire	2900	3300	3600
HN1413, Margery	450	550	650
HN1414, Patricia	650	810	970
HN1417, Marie	300	400	500
HN1428, Calumet	1100	1200	1300
HN1432, Barbara	800	1000	1200
HN1434, Little Bridesmaid	270	380	480
HN1437, Sweet and Twenty	620	800	970
HN1440, Midd Semure	650	810	970
HN1453, Sweet Anne	330	420	510
HN1455, Molly Malone	2300	2600	2900
HN1458, Monica	480	600	730
HN1459, Monica	480	600	730
HN1496, Sweet Anne	180	280	390

	LOW	AVG.	HIGH
HN1502, Lucy Ann	240	340	450
HN1504, Sweet Maid	1300	1600	1800
HN1506, Rose	300	390	480
HN1512, Kathleen	800	1000	1100
HN1514, Dolly Vardon	1300	1500	1700
HN1521, Eugene	900	1100	1200
HN1523, Lisette	1100	1200	1300
HN1531, Marie, 2nd version	300	420	540
HN1552, Pinkie	800	1000	1200
HN1558, Dorcas	360	480	600
HN1562, Gretchen	1000	1200	1500
HN1574, Rhoda	650	840	1000
HN1575, Daisy	480	660	850
HN1578, Hinged Parasol	600	760	910
HN1581, Rosebud	800	1000	1200
HN1588, Bride	800	1000	1200
HN1616, Bookend, Tony Weller	2300	2700	3000
HN1618, Maisie	600	700	800
HN1620, Rosabell	1400	1700	1900
HN1623, Bookend, Pickwick	2300	2700	3000
HN1625, Bookend, Sairey Gamp	2300	2700	3000
HN1638, Margot	900	1100	1200
HN1633, Clemency	900	1100	1200
HN1637, Evelyn	1100	1300	1500
HN1642, Granny's Shawl	480	600	730
HN1646, Herminia	1300	1600	1800
HN1653, Margot	950	1100	1250
HN1654, Rose	300	400	450
HN1656, Dainty May	480	600	730
HN1668, Sibell	1130	1350	1570
HN1670, Gillian	770	900	1030
HN1679, Babie	70	130	190
HN1680, Tootles	30	120	210
HN1681, Delicia	1400	1500	1700
HN1685, Cynthia	800	900	1100
HN1688, Rhoda	700	900	1000
HN1689, Calumet	800	900	1000
HN1694, Virginia	800	1000	1200
HN1699, Marietta	770	900	1030
HN1709, Pantalettes	100	1200	1400
HN1714, Millicent	1600	1800	2000
HN1717, Diana	400	500	600
HN1721, Frangcon	1000	1200	1500
HN1723, Coming of Spring	2900	3300	3600
HN1727, Celia	1100	1300	1600
HN1734, Kate Hardcastle	1300	1500	1700
HN1741, Sonia	1300	1600	1800
HN1744, Mirabel	1200	1400	1500
HN1756, Lizana	700	900	1100
HN1771, Maureen	700	800	900
HN1773, Delight	480	600	730
HN1807, Spring Flowers	425	500	650
HN1812, Forget-Me-Not	650	780	900
HN1815, Huntsman, 2nd version	3500	3900	4300

	LOW	AVG.	HIGH
HN1828, Salome	5300	5700	6100
HN1830, Lady of the Snows	4700	5100	5500
HN1837, Mariquita	2500	2800	3000
HN1848, Reflections	1200	1400	1500
HN1849, Top o' the Hill	100	200	300
HN1853, Mirror	2900	3300	3600
HN1858, Dawn with Headdress	2500	2800	3000
HN1859, Tildy	1000	1200	1300
HN1864, Sweet and Fair	1000	1200	1500
HN1867, Wedding Morn	2600	2800	3000
HN1871, Annabella	600	780	970
HN1885, Nadine	1100	1300	1500
HN1886, Nadine	1100	1300	1500
HN1889, Goody Two Shoes	480	600	730
HN1899, Midsummer Noon	700	800	900
HN1900, Midsummer Noon	1700	1900	2200
HN1901, Penelope	270	390	500
HN1903, Rhythm	2300	2700	3000
HN1905, Goody Two Shoes	480	600	730
HN1908, Lydia	100	200	300
HN1916, Janet, 2nd version	270	360	450
HN1917, Meryll	4100	4500	4900
HN1926, Roseanna	480	600	720
HN1928, Marguerite	330	440	540
HN1930, Marguerite	800	1000	1150
HN1935, Sweeting	90	180	270
HN1938, Sweeting	650	760	880
HN1940, Toinette	1600	1900	2100
HN1941, Peggy	270	360	450
HN1944, Daydreams	900	1100	1200
HN1948, Lady Charmain	180	280	380
HN1949, Lady Charmain	210	300	390
HN1955, Lavinia	60	140	210
HN1956, Chloe	650	810	970
HN1961, Daisy	540	700	850
HN1962, Genevieve	325	430	530
HN1967, Lady Betty	300	390	480
HN1972, Regency Beau	1250	1440	1630
HN1973, Corinthian	1250	1400	1600
HN1977, Her Ladyship	275	350	500
HN1982, Sabbath Morn	240	340	450
HN1984, Patchwork Quilt	270	380	480
HN1991, Market Day, Country Lass	270	380	480
HN1992, Christmas Morn	80	100	140
HN1993, Griselda	450	560	670
HN2043, Poacher	210	300	390
HN2047, Once Upon a Time	400	500	600
HN2048, Mary Had a Little Lamb	110	170	230
HN2049, Curly Locks	400	500	600
HN2050, Wee Willie Winkie	390	500	600
HN2056, Susan	400	500	600
HN2057, The Jersey Milkmaid	300	450	520
HN2059, The Bedtime Story	493	600	750
HN2103, Mask Seller	240	300	360

	LOW	AVG.	HIGH
HN2104, Abdulah	540	660	790
HN2106, Linda	60	150	240
HN2107, Valerie	100	170	240
HN2111, Betsy	400	500	600
HN2148, The Bridesmaid	175	250	350
HN2193, Fair Lady	150	220	300
HN2214, Sleepyhead	1100	1300	1500
HN2141, Choir Boy	50	130	210
HN2149, Love Letter	240	360	480
HN2151, Mother's Help	180	270	360
HN2157, Gypsy Dance	500	600	700
HN2158, Alice	90	160	240
HN2165, Janice	500	600	700
HN2173, Organ Grinder	700	800	900
HN2179, Noelle	400	500	600
HN2184, Sunday Morning	260	360	450
HN2203, Teenager	210	300	390
HN2205, Master Sweep	600	700	800
HN2209, Hostess of Williamsburg	120	220	330
HN2218, Cookie	90	180	270
HN2229, Southern Belle	270	300	390
HN2233, Royal Governor's Cook	390	480	570
HN2240, Blacksmith of Williamsburg	130	230	330
HN2242, First Steps	480	600	730
HN2246, Cradle Song	420	540	670
HN2250, Toymaker	390	500	600
HN2262, Lights Out	180	270	360
HN2270, Pillow Fight	180	270	360
HN2304, Adrienne	170	240	300
HN2312, Soiree	100	180	270
HN2319, Bachelor	300	400	510
HN2338, Penny	50	120	180
HN2352, Stitch in Time	90	180	270
HN2361, Laird	240	300	360
HN2373, Joanne	100	160	230
HN2380, Sweet Dreams	170	240	300
HN2382, Secret Thoughts	290	360	420
HN2393, Rosalind	120	210	300
HN2417, Boatman	150	260	360
HN2435, Queen of the Ice	90	180	270
HN2437, Queen of the Dawn	90	160	230
HN2438, Sonata	90	160	230
HN2440, Cynthia	140	220	300
HN2442, Sailor's Holiday	180	270	360
HN2443, Judge, matte finish	120	210	300
HN2466, Eve	890	990	1090
HN2477, Denise	100	160	230
HN2677, Taking Things Easy	210	300	390
HN2712, Mantilla	300	390	480
HN2713, Tenderness, white	70	140	210
HN2715, Patricia	50	120	200
HN2724, Clarinda	120	210	300
HN2731, Thanks Doc	290	360	430

	LOW	AVG.	HIGH
HN2732, Thank You	120	200	270
HN2733, Officer of the Line	120	210	300
HN2736, Tracy	100	170	240
HN2738, Columbine	1000	1100	1200
HN2743, Meg	170	240	300
HN2744, Modesty	100	170	240
HN2745, Florence	170	240	300
HN2756, Musicale	90	160	220
HN2759, Private, Rhode Island Reg., 1781	830	990	1150
HN2770, New Companions	150	240	330
HN2780, Corporal, 1st New Hampshire Reg., 1778	1000	1200	1300
HN2788, Marjorie	120	210	300
HN2789, Kate	130	230	350
HN2792, Christine, 2nd version	300	400	500
HN2799, Ruth	210	320	430
HN2803, First Dance	210	280	340
HN2808, Balinese Dancer	710	840	970
HN2810, Solitude	120	210	300
HN2811, Stephanie	210	280	360
HN2814, Eventide	210	280	360
HN2824, Harmony	120	210	300
HN2839, Nicola	360	430	500
HN2842, Innocence	80	160	250
HN2862, First Waltz	150	250	350
HN2864, Tom	350	425	510
HN2865, Texx	200	275	350
HN2898, Ko-Ko, 2nd version	650	810	970
HN2902, Elsie Maynard	830	920	1020
HN2906, Paula	120	210	300
HN2907, Piper	360	450	640
HN2918, Boromir, J.R.R. Tolkien	50	130	210
HN2923, Barliman Butterbur	40	120	210
HN2937, Gail	210	300	380
HN2938, Isadora	170	240	300
HN2939, Donna	100	170	240
HN2954, Samantha	50	120	200
HN2955, Nancy	100	160	230
HN2956, Heather	100	160	230
HN2958, Amy	60	140	210
HN2961, Carol	100	160	220
HN2967, Please Keep Still	30	100	180
HN2981, Stick 'Em Up	30	100	180
HN3002, Marilyn	140	220	300
HN3016, Graduate, girl	140	220	300
HN3032, Tom, Tom, the Piper's Son	50	120	180
HN3038, Yvonne	160	230	300
HN3041, Lawyer	130	220	300
HN3042, Gillian	160	230	300
HN3045, Demure	110	180	240
HN3051, Country Girl	70	140	210
HN3077, Windflower	110	180	240
HN3091, Summer Darling	160	230	300
HN3096, Merry Christmas	200	280	360
HN3127, Playmates	150	220	300

Salem China

The Salem China Company reached its 100th year in 1968 solely as a distributor. Its semi-porcelain dinnerware, famous in the 1930s and 1940s, ceased production in 1967.

Briar Rose (c1930)

	LOW	AVG.	HIGH
Butter Dish, open	$14	$16	$18
Cake Plate, 10"	5	6	7
Casserole	20	23	26
Cream/Sugar	13	16	18
Cup/Saucer	7	9	11
Dish, 5" to 6"	3	4	5
Gravy Boat	11	13	15
Pickle Dish	4	5	6
Plate, 6" to 7"	4	6	8
Plate, 9" to 10"	9	11	13
Platter, 11" to 13"	7	9	10
Platter, 22"	40	50	60
Soup, coupe, 7"	5	6	7
Vegetable, 8" to 9"	11	13	15

Tricorne (1934)

	LOW	AVG.	HIGH
Casserole	$31	$34	$37
Comport	18	20	22
Cream/Sugar	25	30	35
Cup/Saucer	13	16	19
Dish, 5" to 6"	3	4	5
Nut Dish, 4"	6	7	8
Plate, 5" to 6"	3	4	5
Plate, 9" to 12"	8	12	14

Victory (1938)

	LOW	AVG.	HIGH
Bowl, 6" to 7"	$6	$8	$10
Cake Plate, 10"	5	6	7
Candle Holder	15	17	19
Casserole	22	28	34
Coffeepot	30	40	50
Cream/Sugar	12	15	17
Cup/Saucer	6	9	12
Dish, 5" to 7"	2	3	4
Gravy Boat	10	12	13
Plate, 6" to 7"	1	3	5
Plate, 10"	8	11	13
Platter, oval, 11" to 13"	7	8	9
Salt/Pepper	13	16	19
Soup Bowl/Saucer	8	10	12
Soup Plate, 8.25"	5	6	7
Vegetable, round, 8"	10	12	14

Sebring Pottery

The Sebring family established the town of Sebring, Ohio, in 1899. There they consolidated their various business ventures and built the Sebring Pottery to produce semiporcelain dinnerware. Some art ware and kitchenware were made in the 1930s. The name Sebring vanished in the 1943 takeover by National Unit Distributors, although some patterns continued being manufactured.

Aristrocrat (1932)

	LOW	AVG.	HIGH
Casserole	$18	$22	$25
Coffeepot	24	30	34
Cream/Sugar	13	15	17
Cup/Saucer	6	7	8
Plate, 6" to 7"	3	4	5
Plate, 9"	5	6	7
Platter, 13"	8	10	12
Salt/Pepper	10	12	14
Soup Plate, 7.5"	5	6	7
Teapot	25	30	35

Doric (1930)

	LOW	AVG.	HIGH
Batter Pitcher	$20	$22	$25
Cream/Sugar	13	16	20
Cup/Saucer	4	5	6
Dish, 5" to 6"	1	2	3
Gravy Boat	8	10	12
Plate, 6" to 7"	2	3	4
Plate, 9"	4	5	6
Platter, rectangular, 11" to 13"	5	6	7
Soup, coupe, 7.5	4	5	6
Vegetable, 8"	7	9	11

Trojan

	LOW	AVG.	HIGH
Casserole	$21	$25	$28
Coffeepot	22	26	30
Cream/Sugar	15	18	21
Cup/Saucer	8	10	12
Dish, 5" to 6"	2	3	4
Egg Cup	7	9	11
Gravy Boat	12	14	16
Plate, 6" to 7"	2	3	4
Plate, 9" to 11"	6	8	10
Vegetable, oval, 9"	12	14	16

Shawnee Pottery

The Shawnee Pottery Company produced earthenware art pottery and brightly colored dinnerware and kitchenware from 1937 through 1961.

Marks include an embossed *USA*, and/or *Shawnee*, and/or a shape number. Some pieces are unmarked. Items trimmed in gold command a premium.

Corn King

	LOW	AVG.	HIGH
Cereal Bowl, #94	$50	$55	$60
Casserole, cov., #74	75	85	95
Cookie Jar	140	160	190
Creamer, #70	25	30	35
Dish, 6"	10	12	14
Mixing Bowl, #5	35	40	45
Mixing Bowl, #6	36	40	44
Mug, #69, 8 oz.	40	45	50
Pitcher, 1 qt.	80	90	100
Plate, 7.25"	32	36	40
Plate, 10"	35	50	65
Platter, 12"	50	60	70
Relish Tray, #79	35	40	45
Salt/Pepper, #76	26	30	34
Salt/Pepper, #77	32	38	44
Teapot, 30 oz.	60	80	100
Tumbler	30	35	40
Utility Jar	40	50	60

Shawnee Corn King and Corn Queen patterns. The first six pieces on the top row are Corn Queen. Note the difference in leaf style. Also, Corn Queen featured almost white corn with dark green leaves, while Corn King had yellow corn with avocado green leaves. —Photo courtesy Gene Harris Antique Auction Center.

Corn Queen

	LOW	AVG.	HIGH
Butter Dish, cov., #72	$25	$30	$35
Cookie Jar, #66	120	145	175
Fruit Bowl, #92, 6"	10	12	14
Mixing Bowl, #5, 5"	12	15	18
Mixing Bowl, #6, 6.5"	15	20	25
Mixing Bowl, #8, 8"	20	24	28
Mug, #69, 8 oz.	18	22	26
Pitcher, #7, 1 qt.	40	48	54
Plate, 7.25"	2	3	4
Plate, 10.5"	7	9	12
Platter, #96, 12"	20	24	28
Shaker, #76, 3.25" h	3	4	5
Shaker, #77, 5.25" h	4	5	6
Teapot, #75	100	125	150
Vegetable, #95, 9"	24	28	32

Miscellaneous

	LOW	AVG.	HIGH
Cookie Jar, Jack, gold trim	$285	$325	$380
Cookie Jar, Jack, yellow pants	65	75	85
Cookie Jar, Muggsy	375	425	475
Cookie Jar, Muggsy, gold trim	750	850	950
Cookie Jar, Puss 'N Boots	180	225	260
Cookie Jar, Puss 'N Boots, gold trim	500	595	700
Cookie Jar, Smiley, all white	65	75	85
Cookie Jar, Smiley, blue bib, cold paint	65	75	85
Cookie Jar, Smiley, shamrock	210	250	300
Cookie Jar, Smiley, yellow bib, gold trim	275	300	325
Cookie Jar, Winnie, blue collar	220	250	275
Planter, bird and cup, #502	10	12	14
Planter, boy and wheelbarrow, #750	12	15	18
Planter, butterfly, #524	12	14	16
Planter, clown, #607	30	35	40
Planter, cockatiel, #522	6	8	12
Planter, elf shoe, white, gold trim, #765	10	14	18
Planter, man w/ pushcart, #621	12	15	18
Planter, rocking horse, pink, #526	18	22	26
Planter, rooster, #503	15	18	22
Planter, windmill, blue, #715	16	20	24
Salt/Pepper, chanticleer, large	50	55	60
Salt/Pepper, flower pots, small	18	22	26
Salt/Pepper, fruit, small	20	24	28
Salt/Pepper, Jack/Jill, large	80	100	125
Salt/Pepper, Jack/Jill, small	38	42	48
Salt/Pepper, milk cans, small	16	20	25
Salt/Pepper, Muggsy, large	120	150	180
Salt/Pepper, Muggsy, small	60	70	80
Salt/Pepper, owls, blue eyes, small	10	14	18
Salt/Pepper, owls, gold trim, small	30	35	40
Salt/Pepper, Puss 'N Boots, small	32	38	45
Salt/Pepper, Smiley, large	100	125	150
Salt/Pepper, Smiley/Winnie, small	40	50	60

Southern Potteries

Southern Potteries, Inc., operated from 1920 to 1957. The company is best known for its hand-painted under-the-glaze Blue Ridge line of dinnerware, usually featuring floral designs. The pottery also produced decal-decorated hotel ware and dinnerware.

Candlewick

	LOW	AVG.	HIGH
Butter Dish	$23	$34	$48
Cake Plate, round, 10.5"	23	31	40
Cake Plate, square, 12"	33	43	54
Cake Server	23	31	40
Celery	15	24	30
Chop Plate, 11" to 12"	24	30	40
Coffeepot, Art Deco	68	92	120
Cream/Sugar	24	28	32
Cup/Saucer	8	14	20
Dish, 5" to 6"	6	8	12
Egg Cup	24	32	40
Fork/Spoon	68	80	94
French Casserole, 5" to 7"	24	34	48
Gravy Boat	12	20	28
Grill Plate	28	38	48
Party Plate, 8.5"	18	24	32
Pickle Dish	15	20	24
Plate, 6" to 8"	6	9	12
Plate, 9" to 10"	10	15	25
Plate, square	10	15	25
Platter, oval, 9" to 15"	38	54	70
Salad Bowl, large	24	30	40
Salt/Pepper	12	20	30
Sherbet	15	24	30
Soup Plate, 8"	12	15	20
Teapot	60	95	130
Tidbit, 3-tier	24	32	40
Vegetable, cov.	54	72	94
Vegetable, open	15	20	28

Colonial (1939)

	LOW	AVG.	HIGH
Butter Dish	$18	$28	$38
Butter Pat, 4"	18	20	25
Cake Plate, round, 10.5"	18	25	30
Cake Plate, square, 12"	26	35	44
Cake Server	18	25	30
Celery Tray	12	18	25
Chop Plate, 11" to 12"	18	25	30
Coffeepot	78	92	106
Coffeepot, Art Deco	54	74	94
Covered Toast	84	98	114
Cream/Sugar	19	22	25
Cup/Saucer	6	10	15
Dish, 5" to 6"	5	7	9

	LOW	AVG.	HIGH
Egg Cup	18	25	32
Fork/Spoon	54	64	75
French Casserole, 5" to 7"	18	28	38
Gravy Boat	10	16	24
Grill Plate	22	30	38
Party Plate, 8.5"	14	20	25
Pickle Dish	12	15	20
Plate, 6" to 8"	5	7	10
Plate, 9" to 10"	7	14	20
Plate, square	6	12	20
Platter, oval, 9" to 15"	12	20	30
Salt/Pepper	10	18	25
Sherbet	12	18	25
Soup Plate, 8"	10	12	15
Teapot	50	75	105
Tidbit, 3-tier	18	25	32
Vegetable, cov.	42	58	75
Vegetable, open	12	18	24

Trellis

	LOW	AVG.	HIGH
Butter Dish	$34	$50	$58
Butter Pat, 4"	34	40	45
Cake Plate, round, 10.5"	34	45	56
Cake Plate, square, 12"	50	64	78
Caker Server	34	45	56
Celery Tray	24	34	45
Chop Plate, 11" to 12"	34	45	56
Coffeepot	145	170	190
Coffeepot, Art Deco	100	135	170
Covered Toast	158	180	200
Cream/Sugar	36	40	45
Cup/Saucer	12	20	28
Dish, 5" to 6"	9	12	16
Egg Cup	34	45	56
Fork/Spoon	100	120	135
French Casserole, 5" to 7"	34	50	68
Gravy Boat	18	30	40
Grill Plate	42	54	58
Party Plate, 8.5"	28	36	45
Pickle Dish	24	28	34
Plate, 6" to 8"	9	14	18
Plate, 9" to 10"	14	24	34
Plate, square	12	24	34
Platter, oval, 9" to 15"	24	40	56
Salad Bowl, large	56	80	100
Salt/Pepper	18	32	45
Sherbet	24	34	45
Soup Plate, 8"	18	24	28
Teapot	90	140	190
Tidbit, 3-tier	34	45	56
Vegetable, cov.	80	105	135
Vegetable, open	24	32	41

Stangl Pottery

In 1926, John M. Stangl, acting as president of Fulper, bought the Anchor Pottery Company of Trenton and began manufacturing there as the Stangl Pottery Company. The company manufactured dinnerware and decorative accessories, including their famous bird figures, produced from 1940 until 1972. Several birds were reissued between 1972 and 1977. These versions are dated on the bottom and worth approximately one half the value of the original birds.

After Stangl's death in 1972, the Wheaton Glass Company purchased and ran the company until 1978.

Birds

	AUCTION	RETAIL	
		Low	High
3250A, Standing Duck, 3.25"	$125	$150	$180
3250C, Feeding Duck, 1.375"	75	90	110
3250F, Quacking Duck, 3.625"	125	150	175
3275, Turkey, 3.375"	375	450	525
3276, Bluebird, 5.125"	70	85	100
3276D, Bluebirds, reissued, 8.25"	200	220	240
3405D, Cockatoos, reissued, 9.5"	120	130	140
3443, Flying Duck, 9"	225	275	325
3446, Hen, 7.5"	185	220	250
3450, Passenger Pigeon, 9.25" x 19.25"	1100	1320	1550
3451, Willow Ptarmigan, 11"	2500	3000	3500
3453, Mountain Bluebird, 6.375"	1100	1300	1500
3454, Key West Quail Dove, wings raised, 9"	800	950	1100
3490D, Redstarts, 9.5"	210	250	290
3491/3492, Hen/Cock Pheasant, 6.625" and 6.125"	275	325	375
3518D, White-Crowned Pigeons, 7.875" x 12.5"	600	720	840
3480, Cockatoo, 8.75"	110	130	150
3581, Chickadees, 5.75" x 8.25"	350	420	490
3582D, Parakeets, 7.5"	250	300	350
3599D, Hummingbirds, reissued, 8.75"	275	300	325
3627, Rivoli Hummingbird, 6.125"	175	210	250
3628, Rieffers Hummingbird, reissued, 4.825"	80	90	100
3717D, Bluejays, 13"	3700	4500	5200
3749S, Western Tanager, 5"	325	380	420
3750D, Western Tanagers, 8"	425	500	580
3752D, Red-Headed Woodpeckers, 7.75"	325	390	450
3755, Audubon Warbler, 4.5"	425	500	580
3852, Cliff Swallow, 3.5"	185	210	250
3853, Golden Crowned Kinglets, 5.5"	600	720	780
3868, Summer Tanager, 3.625"	425	500	575
3924, Yellow-Throated Warbler, 5.75"	350	420	500

Blueberry Dinnerware

	LOW	AVG.	HIGH
Butter Dish	$7	$9	$11
Casserole, 5" to 8"	30	40	50
Coaster	10	12	16
Coffeepot	46	60	75

Cream/Sugar	26	32	38
Cup/Saucer	16	20	24
Dish, 6"	12	15	18
Egg Cup	11	14	17
Gravy Boat	22	28	34
Mixing Bowl, 5" to 14"	30	38	45
Mug	12	15	18
Pitcher, 2 qt.	46	58	70
Plate, 6" to 8"	6	7	8
Plate, 9" to 10"	12	16	20
Platter, oval, 15"	17	21	24
Salad Bowl, lug, 12"	24	32	40
Soup Bowl, cov.	21	28	34
Syrup Pitcher	28	34	42
Teapot	50	60	70

Colonial Dinnerware

Ball Pitcher	$46	$58	$70
Bean Pot	45	55	65
Casserole, 5" to 8"	30	40	50
Chop Plate, 12" to 14"	30	38	46
Coffeepot	46	60	75
Cream/Sugar	26	32	38
Cup/Saucer	16	20	24
Dish, 6"	12	15	18
Egg Cup	12	14	18
Gravy Boat	22	28	34
Hors d'Oeuvre, 9" to 12"	28	36	45
Mixing Bowl, 5" to 14"	30	38	45
Pie Baker	25	35	45
Plate, 6" to 8"	6	7	8
Plate, 9" to 10"	13	17	20
Platter, oval, 12" to 14"	18	20	24
Salt/Pepper	18	24	28
Syrup Pitcher	28	34	40
Teapot, 6 cup	50	60	70
Vegetable, oval, 10"	18	24	28

Tulip Dinnerware

Casserole, 5" to 8"	$30	$40	$50
Coffeepot	46	60	75
Cream/Sugar	26	32	38
Cup/Saucer	16	20	24
Dish, 6"	12	15	18
Egg Cup	12	14	18
Gravy Boat	22	28	34
Grill Plate, 10"	18	22	26
Mixing Bowl, 5" to 14"	30	38	45
Pitcher, 2 qt.	46	58	70
Plate, 6" to 8"	6	7	8
Plate, 9" to 10"	14	18	22
Salad Bowl, lug, 8" to 10"	24	32	40
Syrup Pitcher	28	34	42
Teapot	50	60	70

Taylor, Smith and Taylor China

In 1901 the Taylor, Smith and Lee Company changed its name to Taylor, Smith and Taylor. It produced semiporcelain toilet ware, dinnerware, kitchenware and specialties. Its most famous dinnerware line is Lu-Ray, produced in solid-colored pastels. Anchor Hocking bought the company in 1972.

Lu-Ray (1938)

	LOW	AVG.	HIGH
Butter Dish	$30	$35	$40
Cake Plate, lug, 11"	25	30	35
Casserole, 8"	70	75	80
Chop Plate, 14" to 15"	20	25	30
Coaster	25	30	35
Dish, 5"	2	3	4
Egg Cup	12	15	18
Epergne	60	70	80
Gravy Boat	15	20	25
Grill Plate, 10"	15	18	22
Mixing Bowl, 5" to 7"	45	52	60
Mixing Bowl, 8" to 10"	50	62	75
Muffin Cover	60	65	75
Nut Dish, 4.5"	20	25	30
Pitcher, 1 qt.	60	68	75
Pitcher, 2 qt.	35	42	50
Plate, 6" to 8"	3	5	7
Plate, 9" to 10"	7	9	11
Platter, 11" to 14"	10	12	14
Relish Tray, 4-pc.	75	80	85
Salad Bowl, 10"	30	35	40
Salt/Pepper	8	12	14
Soup Plate, 8"	8	10	12
Teapot	45	55	65
Tumbler, 5 oz.	20	25	30
Tumbler, 9 oz.	40	45	50
Vegetable, 9" to 11"	8	10	12

Vistosa

	LOW	AVG.	HIGH
Ball Pitcher	$40	$50	$60
Chop Plate, 11" to 14"	15	20	25
Cream/Sugar	25	30	35
Cup/Saucer	15	20	25
Dish, 5"	8	10	12
Egg Cup	25	30	35
Gravy Boat	125	150	175
Plate, 6" to 7"	4	7	10
Plate, 9" to 10"	8	12	16
Salad Bowl, ftd.	125	150	175
Salt/Pepper	15	20	25
Soup Bowl, 6.5"	25	30	35
Soup Plate, 7.5"	15	18	20

Van Briggle Pottery

Artus and Anne Van Briggle founded this arts and crafts pottery in 1901. It dominated the western market with pots and vases of stylized tree limbs, cactus and other plants. Glaze colors included Mountain Craig (green to brown), Midnight (black), Moonglo (off-white), Persian Rose, Turquoise Ming and Russet.

The first and most famous mark consisted of the letters *AA*, the initials of Van Briggle and his wife, Anne. Prior to 1920, the mark often included the date of production. These are the most desirable pieces. A stock number often appeared, especially on later pieces. The words *HAND CARVED* are often found on pieces with raised decoration.

	AUCTION	RETAIL Low	RETAIL High
Mug, matte green glaze, incised "AA/COLO SPRINGS/1907/ 28B," 1907, 4½" x 5"	$358	$425	$500
Vase, cylindrical, blossoms and leaves, burgundy glaze, incised "AA/VAN BRIGGLE/1903/III," 1903, 10" x 4"	2750	3200	3700
Vase, tall, daffodils, matte turquoise and blue glaze, incised "AA/ VAN BRIGGLE/COLO SPGS.," 1920s, 13" x 5"	770	900	1000
Vase, tall tapering, daffodils, curdled brown matte glaze with brown clay showing through, incised "AA VAN BRIGGLE/Colo. Sprgs. 1906," 1906, 9½" x 3½"	2970	3500	4100
Vase, ovoid, dogwood blossoms, sheer dark green glaze, incised "AA/VAN BRIGGLE/COLO.SPRINGS/1906," minor kiln kiss to side, 1906, 8¼" x 5"	2420	3000	3500
Vase, bulbous, leaves, amber clay under gunmetal-brown glaze, incised "AA," stamped "1913/849," 1915, 4¾" x 3½"	1210	1400	1600
Vase, bulbous, leaves, green on burgundy ground, incised "AA/19--," 1910s, 8" x 5"	715	850	1000

Van Briggle Pottery. —Photo courtesy Gene Harris Antique Auction Center.

	AUCTION	RETAIL Low	RETAIL High
Vase, bulbous, leaves, matte white and pink glaze, illegible marks, pre-1905, 5" x 4"	880	1050	1120
Vase, bulbous, leaves, mauve glaze with clay showing through, incised "AA/VAN BRIGGLE/Colo.Spgs./742," 1908–11, 8" x 5½"	1320	1580	1850
Vase, tall tapering, lilies, matte dark purple glaze, incised "AA/ VAN BRIGGLE/1903/ III/3," minor grind at base from in-fire stilt pull, 1903, 14" x 5¾"	5225	6200	7200
Vase, tall, morning glories, matte yellow glaze, incised "AA VAN BRIGGLE/1903/228," small base chip repair, 1903, 10¾" x 5"	4400	5200	6000
Vase, tall tapering, peacock feathers, green glaze on blue ground, incised "AA VAN BRIGGLE, 1904/174," 1904, 11" x 4"	3850	4500	5200
Vase, bulbous, poppies, speckled matte green glaze with brown clay showing through, incised "AA/VAN BRIGGLE/1903/ 204/ III," 1903, 4" x 4¼"	2200	2600	3000
Vase, ovoid, poppies, turquoise matte glaze, incised "AA/1916," 1916, 7½" x 4"	935	1100	1250
Vase, broad-shouldered, poppy pods and stems, mottled red, blue, and mauve matte glaze with brown clay body showing through, incised "AA VAN BRIGGLE/1902/III," 1902, 9" x 6"	14,300	17,000	19,500
Vase, ovoid, poppy pods and stems, dark brown clay, ivory matte glaze, incised "AA VAN BRIGGLE/Colo.Sprg./1907," 1907, 6½" x 5¼"	3850	4500	5200
Vase, spherical, stylized design, matte green glaze, incised "AA/ VAN BRIGGLE/ 1904/V/148," restored lines to body, 1904, 4½" x 5"	413	500	580
Vase, bulbous, stylized feathers, leathery dark green matte glaze, incised "AA," 1907–12, 7" x 6"	1210	1400	1600
Vase, bulbous, stylized floral design, matte green and speckled mustard ground, incised "AA/VAN BRIGGLE/20," 1915–20, 4" x 4"	523	620	720
Vase, spherical, stylized poppies, dark blue matte glaze, incised "AA/190" under glaze, pre-1910, 5½" x 6½"	990	1200	1400
Vase, tall tapering form, stylized yucca leaves, purple glaze, green ground, incised "AA," impressed "1915/157," 1915, 15½" x 7"	5225	6200	7200
Vase, bulbous, trefoils, black-green matte feathered glaze, incised "AA/Colorado Springs," 1907, 7¼" x 5½"	2970	3500	4200
Vase, ovoid, trefoils, matte green glaze, incised "AA/VAN BRIG-GLE/1904/176/V," three hairlines from rim, 1904, 7¼" x4¾"	1210	1500	2000
Vase, tapering w/ closed-in rim, vertical ribs, pale blue micro-crystalline glaze with dark brown clay body showing through, incised "AA," early, 5½" x 4"	1045	1250	1500
Vessel, squat, gooseberry leaves and fruit, two-handled, green glaze, raspberry ground, incised "AA VAN BRIGGLE/1905/82," 1905, 7½" x 9½"	2750	3000	3500
Vessel, squat, holly, speckled matte green glaze with brown clay showing through, incised "AA VAN BRIGGLE/Colo.Spgs./ 1906," 1906, 2" x 5½"	880	1050	1175
Vessel, squat, matte green glaze, incised "AA/VAN BRIGGLE/ Colo. Spgs./1910," 1910, 4" x 5½"	440	520	600
Vessel, squat, triangular leaves, matte light green glaze, incised "AA/VAN BRIGGLE/1906/428/3," 1906, 4" x 7"	2200	2600	3000

Watt Pottery

The Watt Pottery Company operated in Crooksville, Ohio. After producing stoneware crocks during the 1920s, the company introduced several kitchenware lines featuring simple, hand-painted decoration. Many pieces were stamped with advertising and issued as premiums. The following designs were manufactured between 1936 and 1965.

Apple

	LOW	AVG.	HIGH
Baker, cov., #66, 7.25"	$110	$125	$140
Baker, cov., #96, 8.5"	80	100	120
Bowl, #5, 5.25"	50	60	70
Bowl, #8	60	70	80
Bowl, #39, 13"	110	135	160
Bowl, #60, 6.25"	80	90	100
Bowl, #66, 7.25"	40	50	60
Bowl, #73, 9.5"	60	75	90
Casserole, cov., #5, 5"	130	150	170
Creamer, #62	100	110	120
Ice Bucket, cov., #59, 7"	200	250	300
Pie Plate, #33, 9.25"	110	125	140
Pitcher, #16, 6.5"	90	100	110
Pitcher, #17, 8"	230	280	330
Platter, #49, 12"	300	350	400

Double Apple

	LOW	AVG.	HIGH
Bowl, #5, 5.25"	$80	$90	$100
Bowl, #6, 6.25"	60	70	80
Pitcher, #15, 5.25"	275	325	375

Dutch Tulip

	LOW	AVG.	HIGH
Bowl, #7	$100	$130	$160
Casserole, cov., #18, 5"	250	300	350
Pitcher, #16, 6.5"	175	200	225

Rio Rose

	LOW	AVG.	HIGH
Bowl, #39, 13"	$80	$90	$100
Bowl, #44, 8"	20	25	30
Pie Plate, #33, 9.25"	125	150	175
Pitcher, #15, 5.25"	200	250	300
Plate, 8.5"	20	25	30
Platter, #31, 15"	90	105	120

Rooster

	LOW	AVG.	HIGH
Bowl, #60, 6.25"	$90	$105	$120
Bowl, #66, 7.25"	80	90	100
Casserole, #5, 5"	150	175	200
Creamer, #62, 4.25"	200	250	300
Pitcher, #15, 5.25"	110	125	140
Pitcher, #16, 6.5'	110	135	160

Watt Pottery. —Photo courtesy Gene Harris Antique Auction Center.

Starflower

	LOW	AVG.	HIGH
Bean Cup, #75, 3.5"	$30	$40	$50
Bowl, #52, 6.25"	25	30	35
Bowl, #53, 7.25"	30	35	40
Canister, #81, 6.5"	250	300	350
Cookie Jar, #21, 7.5"	170	200	230
Creamer, #62, 4.25"	200	250	300
Grease Jar, cov., #47, 5"	200	250	300
Ice Bucket, cov., #59, 7"	150	175	200
Mug, #501, 4.5"	80	90	100
Pitcher, #15, 5.25"	60	65	70
Salt/Pepper, hourglass, 4"	200	250	300

Tear Drop

	LOW	AVG.	HIGH
Bean Pot, #76, 6.5"	$90	$110	$130
Bowl, #6, 6.25"	30	40	50
Bowl, #7, 7.25"	30	44	55
Bowl, #39, 13"	300	350	400
Pitcher, #15, 5.25"	50	60	70
Pitcher, #16, 6.5"	110	125	140
Salt/Pepper, hourglass, 4"	175	200	225

Tulip

	LOW	AVG.	HIGH
Bowl, #39, 13"	$300	$350	$400
Bowl, #602, 4"	200	250	300
Bowl, #603, 5"	200	250	300
Pitcher, #16, 6.5"	130	150	170
Pitcher, #17, 8"	250	300	350

Weller Pottery

The Weller Pottery Company was founded in 1882 in Zanesville, Ohio, and became famous for its whimsical artware and novelty glazes. The Second Line Dickens was one of its signature collections. It was based on characters from Charles Dickens novels, decorated with animal and human figures and most frequently shaded in turquoise and light brown.

In 1903 Weller Pottery began its Jap Birdimal line based on themes incorporating Japanese landscapes. The Hudson artware line, developed in the early 1920s, is among the most desired by collectors and features pastoral scenes and floral backgrounds. The company closed in 1948.

Umbrella Stand, Ardsley, 1920–28, 19" h, $500–$650. —Photo courtesy Gene Harris Antique Auction Center.

	AUCTION	RETAIL Low	RETAIL High
Bud Vase, La Sa, trapezoidal, pines, 6.25" h	$275	$325	$375
Bud Vase, Woodcraft, trunk-shaped, 8.25" h	100	120	140
Charger, Sicard, peacock feathers, 10.5" dia	800	950	1100
Figure, frog, Coppertone, 6.25" x 6.25"	850	1000	1150
Figure, pop-eyed dog, 9.5" x 8.5"	3250	3900	4600
Flower Frog, Moskota, fish, 2.5" x 4.5"	275	330	385
Flower Frog, Woodcraft, frog and water lily, 5"	375	450	525
Hanging Basket, Woodcraft, fox heads and apples, 4.25" x 8.5"	650	780	910
Jardiniere, satyrs in Bacchanalian scene, A. Lorber	225	270	320
Low Bowl, Sicard, stylized flowers and leaves, 5" dia	300	360	420
Mug, ribbed corsetted body, matte green glaze w/ frosted black throughout, 5.125" h, 5.25" dia	99	120	140
Pillow Vase, Louwelsa, Persian cat portrait, Hester Pillsbury, 7.5" h	3190	3700	4300
Pitcher, Dickensware, melon form w/ over-the-body handle, monk and floral design, 6" h	495	600	700
Syrup Pitcher, Mammy, 6.25" h	770	920	1070
Vase, applied frog and snake, mottled blue-gray matte glaze, 8" h	1870	2500	2800
Vase, Baldin, bulbous, 2-handled, 10.25" h	500	600	700
Vase, Bronzeware, 11.5" h	300	350	410
Vase, Bronzeware, ovoid, hammered body, blue mottled mouth, 11" h	770	920	1100
Vase, Chase, fan shape, 8.5" h	250	300	350
Vase, Dickensware II, corseted, woman golfer, 12" h	1300	1500	1750
Vase, Dickensware II, monk, Gibson, 13" h	935	1100	1300
Vase, Eocean, bulbous, mauve and gray leaves, 6.5" h	375	450	525
Vase, Eocean, cactus blossoms, Claude Leffler, 9.5" h	900	1075	1250

	AUCTION	RETAIL Low	RETAIL High
Vase, Eocean, flowers, berries, and green leaves, 10.25" h	600	720	840
Vase, Eocean, tapering, irises, 10.25" h	475	570	660
Vase, Eocean, jonquils, 2-handled, 11.5" h	800	950	1100
Vase, Etna, bulbous, stylized cherry design, lavender glaze, 3.125" h, 4.75" dia.	110	130	150
Vase, Etna, corseted, grapes and leaves, 15.5" h	700	840	980
Vase, Etna, corseted, poppy, 10" h	150	180	210
Vase, Etna, embossed chrysanthemums, 14.5" h	750	900	1050
Vase, Hudson, broad-shouldered, flowers on royal blue ground, 9.75" h	358	425	500
Vase, Hudson, bulbous, 2-handled, white roses, Mae Timberlake, 7" h	800	960	1120
Vase, Hudson, bulbous, lotus flower, 10" h	150	180	210
Vase, Hudson, classic shape, nasturtium, McLaughlin, 11.75" h	950	1150	1300
Vase, Hudson, corseted, daisies, M. Ansel, 8.75" h	450	540	630
Vase, Hudson, cylindrical, pink roses, 13.5" h	475	575	675
Vase, Hudson, ovoid, blue irises, Hester Pillsbury, 7" h	750	900	1050
Vase, Hudson, ovoid, pink flowers and leaves, 7" h	450	540	640
Vase, Hudson, closed mouth, floral design, royal blue ground, 8.75" h	385	460	550
Vase, Hudson, tapering, swans and lake, 6.25" h	2900	3500	4000
Vase, La Sa, ovoid, landscape, 8.5" h	225	270	310
Vase, La Sa, ovoid, palm trees at sunset, 6.25" h	475	575	675
Vase, Louwelsa, bulbous, roses, 8.5" h	150	180	310
Vase, Louwelsa, flower and leaf, 6.5" h	425	510	600
Vase, Louwelsa, ovoid, nasturtium and stylized stems, 12" h	385	460	530
Vase, Sicard, 2-sided, daisies, scalloped rim, 5.5" h	1500	1800	2100
Vase, Sicard, 3-sided, scalloped, maple leaves, 7.25" h	600	720	840
Vase, Sicard, 4-sided, spider chrysanthemums and foliage, 11" h	1500	1800	2100
Vase, Sicard, cylindrical, grape clusters, 15.5" h	2600	3000	3500
Vase, Sicard, fig-shaped, 4" h	400	480	550
Vase, Sicard, tapered w/ flaring rim, stars and butterflies, 14.5" h	2200	2600	3000
Vase, tapering, embossed beetles and leaves, glossy dark purple glaze, 4.75" h	440	520	600
Vase, Woodcraft, cylindrical, squirrel and nut, 17.75" h	1500	1800	2100
Wall Pocket, Glendale, 12"	600	720	810

Weller Eocean Vases. —Photo courtesy David Rago Auctions.

Zsolnay Pottery

With the opening of Eastern Europe, we have seen more of the quality pottery and porcelain from that part of the world. The Zsolnay factory in Hungary originally produced cement in the middle of the nineteenth century. By the 1870s, the company produced fine art pottery. Many of the best pieces date near the turn of the century.

	LOW	HIGH
Bottle, #6918, wine flask form, raised relief dec., c1902, 6.5" h	$400	$600
Cachepot, #5686, green and gold eosin glaze, Secession stylized floral dec., factory mark, c1899, 9.75" h, 10.75" w	3600	5000
Cachepot, #5897, Secession design, metallic eosin glaze, factory mark, c1900, 4.5" h, 5" w	900	1200
Charger, #3968, historical style, factory mark, c1880, 13.5" dia	2500	3500
Goblet, #5668, Secession style, 4 flower stem handles, green and blue eosin glaze, factory mark, c1899, 6" h	1800	2500
Pitcher, #1009, yellow glaze, c1885, 10.5" h	500	600
Pitcher, #1152, rooster form, green metallic eosin glaze, factory mark, c1900, 5.5" h	1100	1600
Pitcher, #4115, oak leaves, eosin glaze, red beetle in relief, c1893, 15.5" h	5900	8000
Pitcher, #5064, maroon metallic eosin ground w/ cream and pale brown floral dec., factory mark, c1898, 7.5" h	700	900
Pitcher, #7766, women farm workers, earth tones, c1906, 6.5" h	1100	1600
Vase, #262, yellow glaze w/ gilt highlights on relief dec., c1873, 13" h	400	500
Vase, #359, leaf and red berry dec. on purple ground, c1900, 3" h	1800	2500
Vase, #2289, Persian style dec., factory mark, c1882, 4.25" h	1500	2000
Vase, #3939, red and putty dec. on white glaze, Turkish design, c1893, 10.5" h	2500	3400
Vase, #5288, landscape, rainbow metallic eosin colors, c1898, 7.75" h	5400	7500
Vase, #5330, gold Secession style dec. on maroon ground, factory mark, c1898, 4.5" h	1500	2000
Vase, #5551, organic form, blue, green and gold glaze, c1900, 9.75" h	7500	10,000
Vase, #5743, green eosin glaze on dark blue ground, factory mark, c1898, 8" h	3000	4100
Vase, #6171, Hungarian folk design, blue and yellow stylized flowers on red ground, c1900, 9" h	2700	3800
Vase, #6173, tulip form, metallic red, green, and blue eosin glaze, c1900, 8.5" h	7000	9000

Pottery & Porcelain: Miscellaneous

Banks

Collecting piggy banks is not limited to pigs. Many of the highly collected pottery companies found it worth their while to include banks in their lines.

Smiley Pig, cookie jar bank, Shawnee Pottery, $200–$300. —Photo courtesy Ray Morykan Auctions.

	LOW	AVG.	HIGH
Barber Head, Ceramic Arts Studio	$70	$90	$110
Bulldog, Shawnee Pottery	65	75	85
Bulldog, brown, Morton Pottery, 3.75" x 3"	30	40	50
Cat, reclining, yellow, Morton Pottery, 4" x 6"	22	28	32
Corky Pig, Hull Pottery, c1957	30	36	42
Dime Bank, Hull Pottery	44	50	58
Eagle, McCoy	30	34	38
Elephant, Frankoma	20	25	30
Hen, white, Morton Pottery, 4" x 3"	25	30	35
Little Audrey, American Bisque	475	500	525
Little Red Riding Hood, wall bank, Hull Pottery	700	800	900
Mr. Blankety Blank, Ceramic Arts Studio	75	90	115
Mrs. Blankety Blank, Ceramic Arts Studio	70	90	110
Pig, black, Morton Pottery, 5.5" x 7"	38	45	52
Pig, Franciscan	275	325	375
Pig, Hull Pottery, 14" l	60	70	80
Pig, small, Purinton Pottery	35	50	65
Piggy Bank, Gladding, McBean	30	35	40
Popeye, American Bisque	325	360	400
Sailor, Seaman's Bank for Savings adv., McCoy	45	50	55
Sinclair Oil Dinosaur, Hull Pottery	85	100	115
Treasure Chest, Bowery Savings Bank adv., McCoy	35	42	50
Uncle Sam, Purinton Pottery	45	50	55
Uncle Sam, Morton Pottery, 4" x 2"	15	20	25
Winnie Pig, cookie jar bank, Shawnee Pottery	200	250	300

Bookends

Dating back to before either television or the Internet, bookends were considered far more a necessity than today. But for those of us who can find no end to our books, these pottery shelf stoppers are well worth their collectors' dollars. Look for bold forms and, as always, beware of cracks and chips. Prices below are for pairs of bookends.

Pinecone, Roseville, 4.75" x 4.25", $220 at auction. —Photo courtesy David Rago Auctions.

	LOW	AVG.	HIGH
Calla Lily, Royal Haeger, 5.5"	$25	$30	$35
Clydesdale, Frankoma, 5"	320	420	520
Dolphin, Abingdon, 5.5"	22	28	32
Dreamer Girl, Frankoma, 6"	130	155	180
Duck Head, Frankoma, 5.5"	155	180	205
Eagles, Morton, 6"	42	52	62
Fern Leaf, Abingdon, 5.5"	52	62	72
Flying Geese, Shawnee, 6"	32	42	52
Foxglove, Roseville, #10, pink and blue	85	100	115
Horse, Royal Haeger, 8.5"	36	44	50
Horse Head, Abingdon, 7"	45	60	75
Horse Head, Royal Haeger, 7.5"	28	35	44
Irish Setter, Frankoma, 6"	115	145	175
Leopard, Frankoma, 7"	100	125	150
Leopard, Royal Haeger, 15"	58	74	88
Lion Head, Royal Haeger, 7.5"	28	35	42
Monk, Catalina, 7"	400	500	600
Mountain Girl, Frankoma, 7"	75	100	125
Owl, Van Briggle, 6"	275	345	415
Owls, Rookwood, blue/green matte	410	460	510
Owls, Rookwood, wine madder	240	280	320
Panthers, Rookwood, wine madder	300	350	400
Parrots, Morton, 6"	34	44	52
Quill, Abingdon, 8.25"	80	95	110
Ram's Head, Royal Haeger, 5.5"	26	32	38
Ramses, Fulper	650	700	750
Rook, Rookwood, black matte	400	450	500
Scotty, Abingdon, 6"	50	60	70
Sea Gull, Abingdon, 7.5"	70	90	110
Seahorse, Frankoma, 6"	300	400	500
Temple Gate, Fulper	4000	4500	5000
Water Lily, Royal Haeger, 5"	20	28	35
Woodpeckers, Cliftwood, 6.5"	130	160	185

Cookie Jars

These beloved containers of the kitchen hold the comforting treat we have pursued for years. Cookie jar collecting gained momentum in the early 1980s. Sotheby's 1988 auction of the estate of pop artist Andy Warhol catapulted figural cookie jars to national prominence. Hearing a cookie jar brought over $20,000 (it was actually for a lot of several jars), people scrambled to their kitchens and attics in hopes of striking gold. Following the sale, cookie jar collecting flourished and today many jars command hundreds, and even thousands, of dollars.

Collectors can specialize in manufacturers, themes or characters. Many times jars by one firm are referred to by the same name as similar jars by another producer. Make sure you know which jar you are purchasing. Recently, crossover interest from character memorabilia collectors fueled a rapid rise in prices of jars such as the Flintstones series (which has been reproduced), Casper the Ghost, Popeye and others. Collectors of black memorabilia seek the Mammy cookie jars.

The prices below are for jars in excellent condition, with a minimal amount of paint loss, and no chips or cracks. The amount these faults affect value depends on severity, how it alters the jar's visible appeal and personal tolerance. Cookie jar collectors are generally more tolerant of paint loss than other collectors, but top condition still brings a premium price. For more information consult *The Complete Cookie Jar Book,* Mike Schneider, Schiffer, West Chester, PA, 1991.

	LOW	HIGH
Albert Apple, Pitman-Dreitzer	$100	$150
Alice in Wonderland, Regal	—	2600+
Alpo Dog	45	60
Animal Crackers, McCoy	60	80
Apollo 11, McCoy	875	1150
Apple, Doranne	10	20
Apple, Metlox	35	100
Apple, yellow, McCoy	40	50
Apple in Barrel, Metlox	25	65
Asparagus Bunch, McCoy	35	75
Astronauts, McCoy	600	1000
Baby Pig, Regal	400	500
Ball of Yarn, w/ kittens, American Bisque	90	140
Ballerina Bear, Metlox	90	130
Bananas, McCoy	80	100
Barnum's Animals, McCoy	300	400
Barrel, American Bisque	25	35
Baseball Boy, McCoy	200	300
Basket of Eggs, McCoy	40	60
Basket of Fruit, McCoy	45	65
Basket of Strawberries, McCoy	40	60
Basket w/ Dog Lid, McCoy	50	70
Basket w/ Duck Lid, McCoy	50	70
Basket w/ Kitten Lid, McCoy	45	65
Basket w/ Lamb Lid, McCoy	50	60
Bear, cookies in pocket, cold painted, McCoy	50	70
Bear, w/ open eyes, American Bisque	70	90
Bear and Beehive, McCoy	30	40
Beehive w/ Cat, American Bisque	45	65
Betsy Baker, McCoy	200	350
Big Bird, California Originals	60	80
Bird Feed Sack, McCoy	25	45
Black Cat, McCoy	300	400
Bugs Bunny, McCoy	200	250

	LOW	HIGH
Butter Churn, McCoy	180	240
Casper the Ghost, American Bisque	1000	1500
Chef w/ Spoon, American Bisque	90	140
Chef's Head, McCoy	80	120
Chick, wearing beret, American Bisque	60	80
Chiffonnier, McCoy	50	70
Chipmunk, McCoy	80	120
Christmas Tree, California Originals	200	300
Christmas Tree, McCoy	450	650
Circus Horse, Brush	700	1400
Circus Horse, McCoy	180	220
Clock, #653, Abingdon	70	100
Clown Head, Metlox	100	270
Clown in Barrel, tan and white, McCoy	80	120
Clown on stage, #805, American Bisque	200	425
Coalby Cat, McCoy	380	450
Coffee Grinder, McCoy	25	40
Coffee Mug, McCoy	30	40
Coffeepot, metal handle, American Bisque	30	40
Conestoga Wagon, Brush	500	700
Collegiate Owl, American Bisque	65	85
Conestoga Wagon, McCoy	55	85
Cookie, girl's face w/ glasses and pigtails, Abingdon	80	100
Cookie Box, McCoy	100	150
Cookie Boy, McCoy	200	300
Cookie Jug, dark brown top, white bottom, McCoy	20	25
Cookie Monster, California Originals	40	60
Cookie Time Clock, #203, American Bisque	60	80
Cookie Train, American Bisque	80	100
Cookie Truck, American Bisque	80	100
Cow, American Bisque	70	90
Cow Jumped Over the Moon, flasher, American Bisque	800	1300
Cowboy, Lane	400	700
Cowboy Boots, American Bisque	180	230

Left to right: Hen, Farmyard Follies, Doranne, #CJ-100, $30–$50. —Photo courtesy Ray Morykan Auctions; Cow, brown, cat finial, Brush, $125–$200.

	LOW	HIGH
Dalmatians on Rocking Chair, McCoy	350	450
Davy Crockett, boy, American Bisque	300	500
Davy Crockett, bust, McCoy	450	650
Davy Crockett, bust, Regal	500	700
Davy Crockett, man, American Bisque	800	1100
Davy Crockett, w/ gold trim, Brush	500	800
Davy Crockett, wo/ gold trim, Brush	250	350
Dino, Flintstones, American Bisque	900	1300
Dog and Basket, Brush	250	300
Dog in Doghouse, McCoy	180	220
Donald Duck on Pumpkin, California Originals	150	200
Donkey and Cart, Brush	250	450
Drum, McCoy	60	80
Drum, Metlox	100	150
Drum Majorette, American Bisque	300	450
Duck, McCoy	200	300
Dutch Boy, cold painted, American Bisque	35	45
Dutch Boy, cold painted, Shawnee	80	120
Dutch Boy, McCoy	45	55
Dutch Girl, cold painted, American Bisque	35	45
Dutch Girl, Regal	600	900
Dutch Girl and Boy, McCoy	100	150
Eagle Basket, McCoy	30	40
Ear of Corn, McCoy	100	150
Elephant, w/ beanie, American Bisque	90	130
Elephant, whole trunk, McCoy	300	400
Elephant, w/ ice cream cone, Brush	400	500
Elsie the Cow, barrel, Pottery Guild	250	350
Farmer Pig, American Bisque	100	150
Fat Boy, #495, Abingdon	300	400
Fish, Brush	400	500
Football Boy, McCoy	200	250
Formal Pig, black coat, Brush	180	220
Fred Flintstone, American Bisque	900	1500
Friar Tuck, blue, Red Wing	90	110
Frog, Holiday	25	35
Frontier Family, McCoy	30	50
Frosty the Snowman, Robinson-Ransbottom	450	650
Goldilocks, Regal	300	400
Grandma, Brayton Laguna	400	500
Granny, American Bisque	140	180
Granny, Brush	300	400
Granny, McCoy	80	120
Hamm's Bear, McCoy	200	250
Happy Hippo, #549, Abingdon	300	400
Hen on Nest, McCoy	70	90
Hippo, monkey handle, Brush	500	700
Hobby Horse, McCoy	100	150
Hocus Rabbit, McCoy	40	50
Honey Bear, yellow, McCoy	80	120
Honeycomb Jar, McCoy	55	75
Howdy Doody, Purinton	700	900
Hubert Lion, Regal	800	1000
Humpty Dumpty, w/ beanie, Brush	200	250

	LOW	HIGH
Humpty Dumpty, in cowboy outfit, Brush	200	300
Indian Head, McCoy	250	350
Jack-in-the-Box, American Bisque	100	150
Jack O' Lantern, #674, Abingdon	300	400
Jack O' Lantern, McCoy	400	600
Kangaroo, blue, McCoy	250	300
Kangaroo, tan, McCoy	360	420
Katrina, Dutch girl, green, Red Wing	150	200
Katrina, Dutch girl, brown, Red Wing	90	120
King of Hearts, Red Wing	650	800
Kitten on Basket, McCoy	90	110
Kitten on Beehive, American Bisque	50	75
Koala Bear, McCoy	75	95
Lady Pig, American Bisque	90	120
Lamb in Hat, American Bisque	100	150
Lamb on Basket, McCoy	100	150
Lemon, McCoy	40	60
Leprechaun, McCoy	1000	1300
Liberty Bell, American Bisque	90	110
Little Boy Blue, w/ gold trim, Brush	600	800
Little Girl, #693, Abingdon	90	100
Little Miss Muffet, #662, Abingdon	200	250
Little Red Riding Hood, pointsettias, Hull	700	1000
Little Red Riding Hood, Pottery Guild	125	175
Little Red Riding Hood, w/ gold stars, Hull	250	400
Little Red Riding Hood, w/ gold trim, Brush	800	1600
Little Red Riding Hood, wo/ gold trim, Brush	400	800
Little Red Riding Hood, wo/ gold trim, Hull	225	350
Log Cabin, McCoy	70	90
Lollipops, McCoy	60	80
Ludwig Von Drake, American Bisque	900	1200
Ma and Pa Owls, McCoy	85	105
Mammy, aqua or yellow, McCoy	600	900
Mammy, Brayton Laguna	900	1200
Mammy, cauliflowers, McCoy	900	1200
Mammy, cold painted, McCoy	180	220
Mammy, red, Metlox	700	800
Mickey and Minni, turnabouts, Leeds	300	400
Milk Can, McCoy	35	45
Monk, McCoy	35	45
Mother Goose, McCoy	100	150
Mouse, McCoy	35	45
Mugsey the Dog, w/ gold trim, Shawnee	800	1100
Mugsey the Dog, wo/ gold trim, Shawnee	325	500
Oaken Bucket, McCoy	30	40
Olive Oyl, American Bisque	2400	2900
Orange, McCoy	45	55
Oscar the Grouch, California Originals	60	80
Owl, glossy brown, McCoy	30	40
Owl, winking, white and brown, Shawnee	100	150
Peek-A-Boo Bear, Regal	900	1300
Penguins, kissing, white, McCoy	60	80
Peter Pan, w/ gold trim, Brush	550	850
Picnic Basket, McCoy	55	65

	LOW	HIGH
Pig, sitting, Brush	400	500
Pineapple, McCoy	70	100
Pineapple, Metlox	90	110
Pirate Chest, McCoy	80	100
Pot Belly Stove, black, McCoy	30	40
Pumpkin Coach, Brush	250	300
Puppy Holding Sign, McCoy	80	100
Puppy in Blue Pot, American Bisque	45	65
Quaker Oats, Regal	90	130
Rabbit in Hat, American Bisque	55	75
Raggedy Ann, McCoy	90	110
Rooster, McCoy	75	85
Saddle, American Bisque	200	300
Sailor Boy, white, Shawnee	90	110
Sandman, flasher, American Bisque	250	350
Santa, winking, American Bisque	350	550
Schoolhouse Bell, American Bisque	35	55
Spaceship, American Bisque	250	350
Spaceship w/ Spaceman, American Bisque	800	1100
Squirrel on Log, Brush	200	250
Strawberry, 1950s, McCoy	50	70
Strawberry, 1970s, McCoy	30	40
Tattle Tale Lady, Helen Hutula	500	1200
Teapot, black, McCoy	45	55
Thinking Puppy, McCoy	25	40
Toby, Regal	850	1100
Train, #651, Abingdon	120	160
Tug Boat, American Bisque	150	250
W.C. Fields, McCoy	150	250
Whale, Robinson-Ransbottom	600	800
Windmill, #678, Abingdon	200	250
Windmill, McCoy	100	150
Wise Bird, Robinson-Ransbottom	60	90
Wishing Well, McCoy	30	50
Woodsy Owl, McCoy	100	150
Wren House, McCoy	120	160

Left to right, Shawnee Pottery: Smiley Pig, chrysanthemum, $193 at auction; Winnie Pig, blue, $253 at auction; Smiley Pig, pink and blue flower, $193 at auction. —Photo courtesy Gene Harris Antique Auction Center, Inc. Far right: Sheriff Pig, Robinson-Ransbottom, $120–$160. —Photo courtesy Ray Morykan Auctions.

Earthenware Pottery

Using less sophisticated kilns and whatever clays were found locally, country potters produced a diverse array of beautiful and imaginative kitchenwares and tablewares. Design and coloration are key in determining values. But a crack or chip puts a major dent in the price.

Mochaware was decorated in various methods that included finger-painting (to create "earthworm" designs) and spitting a tobacco juice concoction (to create "seaweed" designs). Redware gets it name from the red clay used. Spatterware designs were achieved with a paint brush, often requiring several hundred touches per square inch. Spongeware decoration was applied with sponges, most commonly in blue. Yellowware gets its name from the yellow glaze in which it was dipped.

Mochaware

	AUCTION	RETAIL	
		Low	High
Chamber Pot, 2-tone blue bands, black stripes, black and white earthworm design, leaf handle, 8.75" dia	$121	$170	$220
Creamer, brown stripes, white band w/ blue seaweed dec., 4.75" h	440	600	800
Jar, cov., pale blue band, black stripes, white, black, and blue earthworm and cat's eye dec., 5" h	495	700	900
Milk Pitcher, dark glue-gray band, black stripes, embossed band w/ green and black seaweed dec., leaf handle, 4.625" h	440	600	800
Mug, dark brown band and stripes w/ blue, white, and tan earthworm dec., leaf handle, 3.75" h	550	800	950
Mug, white band w/ teal stripes and seaweed dec., ribbed leaf handle, 3.625" h	248	350	450
Mustard Pot, cov., tan band w/ black stripes and white, yellow, and black earthworm dec., ribbed handle, 2.5" h	605	850	1000
Salt, gray band, black stripes, white wavy lines, 3" dia, 2.125" h	330	470	600
Shaker, black, tan, and blue stripes, 4.875" h	330	450	550
Shaker, blue band, black stripe, brown, black, and white earthworm dec., blue top, 4.875" h	330	450	550
Shaker, tan bands, brown stripes, black seaweed dec., 4.125" h	220	300	400
Waste Bowl, amber band w/ black seaweed design separated into 5 segments by squiggly lines, green molded lip band, 4.75" dia	275	330	440
Waste Bowl, orange-tan band, dark brown stripes, embossed green band w/ blue, white, and dark brown earthworm dec., 5.625" dia, 2.875" h	550	800	950

Redware

	AUCTION	RETAIL Low	RETAIL High
Book Flask, 4.5" h	$100	$150	$300
Deep Dish, circular, yellow slip spiraling and scalloped line on dark brown ground, plain rim, 14" dia	450	700	1200
Deep Dish, circular w/ crimped rim, yellow slip triple-serpentine motif, 13" dia	2400	4000	6500
Deep Dish, oblong, 2 yellow slip stylized evergreens on brown ground, plain rim, 14" x 16"	2300	4000	6000
Deep Dish, oblong, brown slip feather combed dec., 12" x 15"	1000	1700	2600
Deep Dish, oblong, alternating serpentine and wavy lines on brown ground, plain rim, 12" x 14"	1800	3000	5000
Deep Dish, rectangular w/ coggled rim, brown slip pinsripe motif on yellow ground, 13" x 11"	1700	3000	4420

Mochaware Mug and Waste Bowl.

Redware Tomato Bank and Turk's Head Food Mold. —Photo courtesy Aston Macek.

Spongeware Teapot.

Yellowware Mixing Bowls. —Photo courtesy Collectors Auction Services.

	AUCTION	RETAIL Low	RETAIL High
Food Mold, oval w/ arched sides, crimped edge, and center ear of corn, applied feet, clear glaze w/ sponged rim, 7.875" l	440	650	850
Jar, ovoid, ribbed strap handle, green tint glaze, 9" h	220	450	700
Jug, slip leaf dec. and owner's name, 12" h	350	600	900
Mariner's Jug, English, slip dec., 11" h	850	1400	2200
Mug, strap handle, 5" h	300	500	800
Plate, floral design in sgraffito, white, green, and orange stripes, German inscription on rim in black	660	900	1200
Shaving Mug, 4" h	375	640	970

Spongeware

	AUCTION	RETAIL Low	RETAIL High
Bank, bottle form, blue polka dots, stenciled initials, 6" h	$743	$850	$1000
Batter Bowl, straight sided, 6.75" dia	330	450	550
Bean Pot, cov., 4.625" h	413	550	650
Bowl, dark blue sponging, 8.5" sq, 2.375" h	358	500	600
Bowl, molded ribs, 11.25" dia, 4.25" h	77	100	125
Butter Crock, cov., blue sponging, molded rim, 5.5" h	110	150	200
Butter Crock, cov., center white band w/ dark blue label "Butter" on front and "Village Farm Dairy" on back, 5.75" h	165	200	250
Butter Crock, cov., molded pinwheels, wire bail handle, 7.5" dia	220	300	400
Cooler, cov., mkd. "8," nickel-plated spigot, 18" h	341	500	650
Creamer, tnakard shape, 3.375" h	303	420	540
Crock, straight sided, brown Albany slip interior, 7.75" dia, 7.25" h	110	150	200
Cuspidor, miniature, corset shaped, blue stripes, 3.25" dia	275	400	500
Dish, cov., miniature, 3.25" dia	935	1200	1500
Pitcher, bulbous base, labeled "UHL Pottery Co.," 6.5" h	770	1000	1300
Pitcher, tankard shaped, 6.75" h	413	500	700
Pitcher, barrel shaped, stripes near rim and base, 8.625" h	303	420	530
Platter, oval, 13" l	303	400	520
Soap Dish, 8-sided, 3.5" x 4.75"	61	80	110
Teapot, cov., ball shaped, 7" h	825	1100	1400
Wash Bowl and Pitcher, blue stripes around middle, 14.5" dia bowl, 12" h pitcher	330	450	550

Yellowware

	AUCTION	RETAIL Low	RETAIL High
Bank, house shape, molded details highlighted in black, "For My Dear Girl" on roof, 3.625" h	$660	$950	$1200
Bottle, mermaid form, 19th C, 8.5" h	150	200	350
Crock, banded	80	120	240
Crock, cov., blue and white bands	200	350	600
Deep Dish, crimped rim, brown slip stripes, 11" x 13"	1300	2210	3380
Deep Dish, notched rim, brown slip combed feather design, 13" x 17.5"	1500	2550	3900
Deep Dish, notched rim, combed brown slip design, 13.5" dia	1000	1700	2600
Deep Platter, brown, feathered and combed design, 16" x 20.5"	2100	3570	5460
Figure, "Staffordshire" dog, Rockingham glaze, 9.875" h	110	150	200
Milk Pitcher	75	100	200
Mixing Bowl, molded shoulder, brown bands, 12.5" dia	70	90	120
Pitcher, light blue and white stripes, ribbed handle w/ leaf, 5.25" h	358	450	600

English and Continental Pottery and China

With few potteries of its own, the early Americans imported from Europe many tablewares. Delftware is the generic name for the tin-glazed earthenwares made in great numbers in Holland and England during the seventeenth and eighteenth centuries. The name comes from the Dutch city where many of these pieces originated. Do not confuse these pieces with those made by the modern corporation "Delft," whose wares pay tribute to the fine early pieces. The pitchers made in Liverpool, England, often called "Liverpool Jugs," sported many patriotic American themes. Lustreware is decorated in a bright metallic finish. Majolica was the tradename used by the Minton Company in England to describe wares that imitated Majolica pieces from the Italian Renaissance. Collectors now use the term to refer to similar pieces made by many English potters of the mid nineteenth century.

Beware of English eighteenth century-style earthenware pieces of various glazes, especially tortoiseshell glaze. The Dewitt Wallace Decorative Arts Gallery at Colonial Williamsburg in Virginia has documented many modern fakes including candlesticks and teapots. Some brilliant examples potted by Guy Timothy Davies have fooled many knowledgeable dealers and collectors.

Delft

	AUCTION	RETAIL	
		Low	High
Charger, Dutch, blue and white floral dec., 14" dia	$550	$950	$1500
Charger, Dutch, polychrome parrot dec., 13" dia	850	1500	2250
Charger, Dutch, polychrome bird and vase dec., 13" dia	1000	1700	2600
Charger, Dutch, polychrome bird and flower pot dec., 13" dia	900	1600	2400
Charger, Dutch, manganese and yellow putti dec., 14" dia	950	1600	2500
Charger, English, blue and white floral dec., 12" dia	400	700	1000
Figure, recumbent horse, blue and white, 6" w	1500	2550	3900
Figures, cow w/ milker, 7" h, pair	200	350	550
Flower Brick, English, blue and white, 5" w	350	600	900
Garniture Vase, Dutch, blue and white, fitted as lamp	310	530	800
Garniture Vases, blue and white biblical scenes, 10" h, set of 5	550	1000	1500
Plaques, Dutch, manganese figures and animals, 11" h, pair	1300	2200	3400
Tankard, Dutch, pewter-mounted, 10" h	500	850	1300
Tazza, English, blue and white, 7" dia	450	760	1170

Gaudy Dutch

	AUCTION	Low	High
Cup/Saucer, handless, Butterfly pattern	$660	$900	$1200
Cup/Saucer, handleless, Sunflower pattern	358	500	650
Cup/Saucer, handleless, Urn pattern	303	450	600
Cup/Saucer, War Bonnet pattern	369	500	650
Plate, Double Rose pattern, 10" dia	935	1200	1600
Plate, Urn pattern, 8.25" dia	908	1200	1600
Plate, War Bonnet pattern, 8.125" dia	880	1150	1500

Gaudy Ironstone

	AUCTION	Low	High
Bud Vase, blue floral transfer w/ red, pink, and green enamel, 7.125" h	$61	$90	$120
Coffeepot, paneled, blue transfer War Bonnet pattern w/ red, orange, and yellow enamel, mkd. "Ironstone China," 10" h	220	320	420
Cup/Saucer, handleless, seaweed in underglaze blue w/ red and green enamel	83	120	160

	AUCTION	RETAIL Low	RETAIL High
Cup/Saucer, handleless, urn in underglaze blue w/ red, pink, and green enamel	275	400	525
Plate, bittersweet in underglaze blue w/ red and green enamel w/ luster, impressed "Walley Paris White Ironstone," 9.625" dia	220	320	420
Plate, black transfer w/ 3 frogs and flowers, red, blue, green, and yellow flowers, 9.375" dia	468	700	950
Plate, black transfer w/ 8 rabbits, red, blue, green, and yellow flowers, 9.5" dia	358	500	650
Plate, black transfer w/ 9 rabbits, 3 cabbages, 3 frogs, and three trees, red, blue, green, and yellow flowers, 9.375" dia	385	530	680
Plate, strawberry in underglaze blue w/ red, pink, and green enamel, impressed "Elsmore Forster and Co.," 8.625" dia	220	320	450
Plate, center flower in underglaze blue w/ red, pink, and green enamel and luster, 9.75" dia	275	400	525
Platter, black transfer w/ 8 rabbits, 4 frogs, and flowers, red, blue, green, and yellow flowers, 14.875" l	1100	1600	2200
Platter, blue War Bonnet pattern transfer w/ red, orange, and yellow enamel, mkd. "Ironstone China," 14.75" l	165	240	320

Gaudy Staffordshire

	AUCTION	RETAIL Low	RETAIL High
Cup/Saucer, handleless, Adam's Rose pattern, red, green, and black, imp. "Adams"	$220	$300	$400
Plate, Adam's Rose pattern, red, green, and black, imp. "Adams," 10.5" dia	138	200	275
Platter, oblong, Adam's Rose pattern, red, green, and black, imp. "Adams," 13.5" l	385	500	620

Gaudy Welsh

	AUCTION	RETAIL Low	RETAIL High
Bowl, blue transfer w/ red enameling, transfer label "Mason's Patent Ironstone China," 12" dia, 3" h	$220	$300	$400
Cup, floral w/ oriental pagoda in underglaze blue w/ red and green enameling, 3.125" h	358	500	650
Pitcher, paneled, dragon handle, underglaze blue w/ red and green enamel and luster, imp. "Mason's Patent Ironstone China," 8" h	688	900	1200
Pitcher, paneled, snake handle, blue transfer w/ red and green enamel, mkd. "Mason's Patent Ironstone China," 9.75" h	275	375	500
Platter, blue "Amherst Japan" transfer w/ red and yellow enameling, imp. "Improved Stone China," 16.5" l	358	500	650
Punch Bowl, molded scrolls and beaded panels, balloon pattern in underglaze blue w/ red and green enamel and gilt, 10.75" dia, 6" h	523	725	1000

Liverpool

	AUCTION	RETAIL Low	RETAIL High
Pitcher, American market w/ American ship in polychrome, American eagle, seal, "SW" in wreath; reverse w/ "The Parting Lovers" and verse "my love is fix'd...", 9.5" h	$5000	$8750	$13,750
Pitcher, American market transfer-printed depiction of Salem shipyards, 8" h	3200	4500	7500
Pitcher, American market transfer printing, "Washington in Glory" Memorial, "Peace, Plenty & Independence," traces of orig. gilt, 11" h	4800	8000	12,000

	AUCTION	RETAIL Low	RETAIL High
Pitcher, "Success to the Caledonia," Captain Francis Mallaby	3000	5000	9000
Red Ale Mug, American market transfer-printed w/ portrait medallion, "James Lawrence, Esq., Late of The United States Navy," 6" h	5250	9000	14,500

Lustres

	AUCTION	RETAIL Low	RETAIL High
Creamer, canary yellow w/ silver luster resist bands w/ floral dec., 3.75" h	$121	$200	$300
Creamer, copper luster, canary band w/ white reserves and black transfer scenes of "Cornwallis" and "Lafayette," 4" h	660	950	1200
Creamer, copper luster, canary band w/ white reserves w/ purple transfer of woman and child in classical attire, polychrome enamel, 4.125" h	182	240	350
Cup/Saucer, canary	100	175	275
Punch Bowl, ships, bridge, mottos, and sailors, Sunderland, 11" dia	2000	3000	5000
Tea Set, w/ tea plates, pink luster, house pattern 30 pcs	400	700	1100

Majolica

	AUCTION	RETAIL Low	RETAIL High
Cake Stand, Wedgwood, round dish w/ reticulated Greek Key border, supported by 3 entwined dolphins on shaped plinth, 1864, 7" dia	$862	$1200	$1500
Centerpiece, Sarreguemines, modeled as putto holding bowl formed from broad leaves and grapevines, standing on square plinth w/ molded masks at corners, c1885, 15.5" h	2070	3000	4000

With the exception of the English sweetmeat dish (top row second from left) and the Victorian sardine box (bottom row right), all the majolica items pictured above are by George Jones. Top row left to right: Oyster Plate; English Sweetmeat Dish; Table Center; Oyster Plate. Bottom row left to right: Sardine Box; Fish Server; and Victorian Sardine Box. —Photo courtesy William Doyle Galleries.

	AUCTION	RETAIL Low	RETAIL High
Cuspidor, Victorian, blossoming branches on brown rustic ground, c1875, 7" h	143	200	280
Fish Server, cov., George Jones, oval twig basket holding modeled salmon on leafage bed, c1871, 19.5" l	2875	4000	5400
Jardiniere, George Jones, lozenge-form bowl supported by pair of winged sphinxes on oval pedestal, c1875, 9" l	3565	5000	6500
Jug, Simon Fielding, modeled as branch of coral encrusted w/ shells and resting on waves, c1880, 7.75" h	230	320	450
Jug, William Brownfield, modeled as 2 intertwined Renaissance-style scaly fish, 1879, 11.75" h	1955	2800	3500
Oyster Plate, Minton, green center, pale blue oyster pockets, 1872, 9" dia	690	1000	1200
Planter, Royal Worcester, modeled by James Handley as circus elephant w/ howdah, 1869, 9" l	1495	2200	3000
Sardine Box, w/ lid and standard, George Jones, radiating stiff leaves, lid molded w/ 3 fish, c1872, 8.5" l base	1150	1500	2200
Sweetmeat Dish, modeled as putto seated on conch shell, raised on dolphin and oval plinth, c1870, 7" h	1725	2500	3300
Teapot, Minton, modeled as monkey wearing Japanese-style tunic and clutching coconut, 1874, 6" h	4830	6500	9000
Teapot, Victorian, modeled as cauliflower head, c1865, 5.25" h	977	1400	2000
Vase, Continental, modeled as ear of corn, c1890, 10.5" h	747	1000	1500
Wall Tile, Copeland, modeled w/ round panel of disguised cupid representing Winter, c1875, 8" x 8"	258	350	500

Quimper

	AUCTION	RETAIL Low	RETAIL High
Bottle, geometric design, early 20th C	$300	$450	$650
Bowl, Shield of Brittany, scalloped edge	700	1000	1500
Figural Group, 7" h	1200	1800	2500
Figure, man, 6" h	325	450	700
Holy Water Font, Benitier, late 19th C, 5" h	160	250	350
Holy Water Font, Benitier, 20th C, 6" h	140	200	300
Platter, oval, 13"	800	1200	1800
Snuff Container, donut form, 19th C	600	1000	1500
Snuff Container, donut form, early 20th C	300	450	650
Snuff Container, baluster form, early 20th C	300	450	650
Snuff Container, frog form, early 20th C	750	1200	1800
Snuff Container, shield form, early 20th C	100	200	300
Snuff Container, butterfly form, early 20th C	850	1400	2000
Snuff Container, hear form, early 20th C, 4" h	450	800	1200
Tray, scalloped edge, w/ handles, late 19th C	1700	2500	3500
Vase, baluster form, 11.5" h	850	1400	2000
Vase, geometric dec., 9" h	560	900	1400

Spatterware

	AUCTION	RETAIL Low	RETAIL High
Creamer, brown and black rainbow spatter, 4.375" h	$440	$650	$900
Creamer, green spatter, black edge stripe, black, yellow ochre, and blue peafowl, leaf handle, 3.75" h	495	750	1000
Cup/Saucer, handless, blue spatter, molded panels, red, green, and black hollyberry	259	350	450
Cup/Saucer, handless, blue spatter, red, green, and yellow star	330	450	570

Spatterware Peafowl creamer and sugar and Rainbow Loop pitcher. —Photo courtesy Jackson's Auctioneers & Appraisers.

	AUCTION	RETAIL Low	RETAIL High
Cup/Saucer, handleless, blue spatter, red, yellow, green, and black peafowl	660	900	1200
Cup/Saucer, handleless, green spatter, black, red, blue, green, and yellow ochre peafowl on bar	1595	2200	3000
Cup/Saucer, handleless, green spatter, blue, yellow, red, and black peafowl	605	850	1000
Cup/Saucer, miniature, green spatter, red, blue, yellow, and black peafowl	330	450	570
Cup/Saucer, handless, purple spatter, red and green thistle	523	800	1000
Cup/Saucer, handleless, red and purple rainbow spatter, blue, yellow ochre, red, and black peafowl	578	850	1100
Cup/Saucer, handleless, red spatter, blue, green, red, and black open body peafowl, green tree	1705	2500	3300
Mug, maroon and green spatter, 2.75" h	248	350	470
Piggy Bank, black spatter, 5" l	69	100	130
Pitcher, blue spatter, leaf handle, 7" h	143	200	270
Plate, blue spatter, blue, orange, red, and black peafowl, 8.25" dia	550	800	1000
Plate, blue spatter, red, blue, green, and black peafowl in unusual shape, 8.75" dia	1100	1600	2000
Plate, blue spatter, red, blue, green, and black pomegranate, 8.5" dia	385	450	600
Plate, blue spatter, red, green, black, and yellow peafowl, 8.25" dia	495	750	1000
Plate, blue spatter, red, green, yellow, and black tulip, 8.875" dia	385	450	575
Plate, red spatter, blue, yellow, green, and black peafowl, 8.125" dia	440	700	900
Platter, octagonal, red spatter, blue, yellow, green, and black peafowl, 13.5" l	908	1300	1700
Soup Plate, blue spatter, blue, yellow ochre, red, and black peafowl, 10.5" dia	2090	3000	4000
Soup Plate, red spatter, green, purple, red, blue, and black columbine, 10.5" dia	330	450	600
Sugar Bowl, red and green rainbow spatter, 4.375" h	248	350	450
Teapot, blue spatter, green and black tree, molded flower finial and handle, 6" h	330	450	600
Toddy, scalloped rim w/ red, green, and blue rainbow spatter, impressed "Adams," 6.375" dia	165	240	320

Figurines

Artisan modeled figurines in pottery and porcelain are a mainstay of the collecting market. Often, the most valuable pieces are not those produced as "limited edition." Quality of design and craft are the most important factors, but condition, rarity and size are also important.

The listings here are by title, followed by maker.

	LOW	AVG.	HIGH
Ann, Florence Ceramics	$50	$55	$60
Arabesque, Ceramic Arts Studio	30	35	40
Attitude, Ceramic Arts Studio	30	35	40
Autumn Andy, Ceramic Arts Studio	20	25	30
Bali Hai, Ceramic Arts Studio	30	35	40
Balinese Dance Boy and Girl, Ceramic Arts Studio	100	110	120
Ballerina Child, Florence Ceramics	80	90	100
Ballet en Pose, Ceramic Arts Studio	80	90	100
Bandanna Duck, Hull, #74	35	40	50
Bandanna Duck, Hull, #76	15	20	18
Bass Viola Boy, Ceramic Arts Studio	40	50	60
Bedtime Boy and Girl, Ceramic Arts Studio	30	35	40
Berty, Ceramic Arts Studio	80	90	100
Beth, Florence Ceramics	60	65	70
Billikin Doll, Cliftwood Potteries, 7.5"	60	65	70
Billikin Doll, Cliftwood Potteries, 11"	100	110	120
Birthday Girl, Florence Ceramics	120	135	150
Black Girl, Brayton Laguna	220	250	280
Black Girls, Brayton Laguna	150	170	190
Black Panther, Royal Haeger, 18"	35	40	50
Black Panther, Royal Haeger, 24"	95	110	125
Blackamoor, Abingdon, 7.5"	40	45	50
Blackamoor, Brayton Laguna	30	35	40
Blynken, Florence Ceramics	60	65	70
Blythe and Pensive, Ceramic Arts Studio	100	110	120
Bo Peep, Ceramic Arts Studio	30	35	40
Boy, in tuxedo, Florence Ceramics	80	90	100
Boy and Girl, standing, Ceramic Arts Studio	40	45	50
Boy and Tiger, Ceramic Arts Studio	40	45	50
Boy Blue, Ceramic Arts Studio	15	20	25
Boy w/ Dog, Ceramic Arts Studio	40	45	50
Boy w/ Fiddle, Florence Ceramics	90	100	110
Bride, Florence Ceramics	340	380	420
Bride and Groom, Ceramic Arts Studio	60	65	70
Bull, miniature, Frankoma	60	70	80
Bust, Florence Ceramics	80	90	100
Calico Cat and Gingham Dog, Ceramic Arts Studio, pair	25	30	35
Camille, Florence Ceramics	80	90	100
Carol, Florence Ceramics	200	220	240
Caroline in Brocade, Florence Ceramics	340	380	420
Cat, angry, Kay Finch, 10.25"	80	90	110
Cat, Cliftwood Potteries, 1.5"	90	100	110
Cat, Cliftwood Potteries, 5.75"	90	100	110
Cat, Cliftwood Potteries, 6"	40	45	50
Cat, Cliftwood Potteries, 8.5"	40	45	50
Cat, climbing, large, Camark, #058	35	40	45

Crane, Midwest Pottery, $20–$30.

	LOW	AVG.	HIGH
Cat, climbing, small, Camark, #N155	18	20	22
Cat, contented, Kay Finch, 6"	40	50	60
Cat, Egyptian, Royal Haeger, 7.5"	17	20	23
Cat, Morton Pottery Co., 6"	10	15	20
Cat, Persian, Kay Finch, 10.75"	80	90	100
Cat, playful, Kay Finch, 8.5"	60	65	70
Cat, sitting, Royal Haeger, 6"	26	30	34
Cat. sleeping, Royal Haeger, 7"	25	30	34
Cat, standing, Royal Haeger, 7"	25	30	35
Cat, tiger, Royal Haeger, 11"	29	30	38
Cat, tigress, Royal Haeger, 8'	28	30	34
Catherine, Florence Ceramics	140	160	180
Cats, Puff and Muff, Ceramic Arts Studio, pair	28	30	38
Centaur, Vernon Kilns	660	735	810
Centaurette, Vernon Kilns	370	410	450
Chanticleer, Kay Finch, 10.5"	100	110	120
Charles, Florence Ceramics	90	100	110
Charmaine, Florence Ceramics	70	80	90
Cherub Head, Kay Finch, 2.75"	5	10	15
Chicken Biddy, Kay Finch, 8.25"	30	35	40
Chinese Boy, Kay Finch, 7.5"	20	25	30
Chinese Boy and Girl, Ceramic Arts Studio	30	35	40
Chinese Couple, Ceramic Arts Studio	15	20	25
Chinese Girl, Florence Ceramics	40	45	50
Chipmunk, Ceramic Arts Studio	20	25	30
Choir Boy, Florence Ceramics	50	55	60
Cinderella and Prince, Ceramic Arts Studio	40	45	50
Cindy, Florence Ceramics	50	55	60
Clarissa, Florence Ceramics	50	55	60
Claudia, Florence Ceramics	90	100	110
Cocker Pup, Royal Haeger, 4"	15	20	25
Cocker Spaniel, Ceramic Arts Studio, pair	29	30	38
Cocker Spaniel, miniature, Frankoma	100	120	140
Colleen, Florence Ceramics	60	65	70
Colonial Boy and Girl, Ceramic Arts Studio	40	45	50
Colonial Lady and Man, Ceramic Arts Studio	40	45	50
Colt, prancing, miniautre, Frankoma	380	430	480
Colts, Balky and Frisky, Ceramic Arts Studio, pair	52	60	68
Comedy and Tragedy, Ceramic Arts Studio	90	100	110

Delia, Florence Ceramics, 7.75" h, $120–$150. —Photo courtesy Ray Morykan Auctions.

	LOW	AVG.	HIGH
Court Lady, Kay Finch Ceramics, 10.5"	30	35	40
Cowboy, Frankoma	200	220	240
Cowboy on Bronco, Midwest Pottery, 7.5"	30	35	40
Cowgirl and Cowboy, Ceramic Arts Studio	50	55	60
Crane, Midwest Pottery, 6"	15	20	25
Cuban Child, Ceramic Arts Studio	20	25	30
Cuban Woman, Ceramic Arts Studio	30	35	40
Cynthia, Florence Ceramics	200	220	240
Dancing Dutch Boy and Girl, Ceramic Arts Studio	80	85	90
Dancing Woman, Midwest Pottery, 8.5"	20	25	30
Dachshund, Hull, 14"	85	100	115
Dachshund, Royal Haeger, 14.5"	44	50	58
Deer, Midwest Pottery, 8"	15	20	25
Deer, Midwest Pottery, 12"	30	35	40
Deer, Morton Pottery, 4.5"	5	10	15
Diane, Florence Ceramics	90	100	110
Dogs, Fifi and Fufu, Ceramic Arts Studio, pair	28	30	40
Donkey, Morton Pottery, 2"	30	35	40
Douglas, Florence Ceramics	70	75	80
Drummer Girl, Ceramic Arts Studio	40	50	60
Dutch Boy and Girl, Ceramic Arts Studio	15	20	25
Dutch Boy and Girl, sitting, Ceramic Arts Studio	20	25	30
Dutch Love Boy and Girl, Ceramic Arts Studio	30	35	40
Edith, Florence Ceramics	60	65	70
Edward, Florence Ceramics	120	135	150
Elaine, Florence Ceramics	40	45	50
Elephant, Cliftwood Potteries, 6"	40	50	60
Elephant, Cliftwood Potteries, 9"	40	45	50
Elephant, "GOP/candidate," Morton Pottery	10	15	20
Elephant, Kay Finch, 5"	20	25	30
Elephant, Kay Finch, 6.75"	40	50	60
Elephant, Kay Finch, 17"	340	380	420
Elephant, miniature, Frankoma	80	100	120
Elephant, Morton Pottery, 2.5"	5	10	15
Elephant, Royal Haeger, 5"	20	30	40
Elephant, Royal Haeger, 9"	65	80	85
Elephant, Vernon Kilns	320	355	390
Elisha, Florence Ceramics	90	100	110
Elizabeth, Florence Ceramics	140	155	170

Doves, Kay Finch, #5101 and #5102, 5.25" h, 8.25" l, pair, $200–$300. —Photo courtesy Ray Morykan Auctions.

	LOW	AVG.	HIGH
Ellen, Florence Ceramics	70	75	80
Emily, Brayton Laguna	30	35	40
English Setter, Frankoma, 3"	50	60	70
Ethel, Florence Ceramics	60	65	70
Eugenia, Florence Ceramics	1780	190	210
Evangeline, Florence Ceramics	50	55	60
Fair Lady, Florence Ceramics	290	325	360
Fall, Florence Ceramics	40	45	50
Fan Dancer, Frankoma	140	160	180
Fawn, standing, Ceramic Arts Studio	20	25	30
Female Bust, Midwest Pottery	70	75	80
Female Nude, Midwest Pottery, 11.5"	110	125	140
Female Torso, abstract, Brayton Laguna, 10.5"	70	75	80
Figaro (Disney), Brayton Laguna	100	110	120
Fighting Cock, Midwest Pottery, 6.5"	20	25	30
Fire Couple, Ceramic Arts Studio	180	205	230
Fishing Boy and Farmer Girl, Ceramic Arts Studio	30	35	40
Flame Couple, Ceramic Arts Studio	180	205	230
Flower Girl, Frankoma	70	80	90
Flute Girl, Ceramic Arts Studio	40	50	60
Fox and Goose, Ceramic Arts Studio, pair	50	60	70
Frances, Brayton Laguna	30	35	40
Frog, Midwest Pottery, 1"	5	10	15
Fruit Girl, Abingdon, 10"	90	100	110
Gardener Boy, Frankoma	90	100	110
Gardner Girl, Frankoma	70	80	90
Gary, Florence Ceramics	70	80	90
Gay 90s Lady and Man, Ceramic Arts Studio	40	45	50
Genevieve, Florence Ceramics	100	110	120
Georgia in Brocade, Florence Ceramics	340	380	420
Geppetto (Disney), Brayton Laguna	220	250	280
Geppetto w/ Pinocchio (Disney), Brayton Laguna	300	335	370
Giraffe and Young, Royal Haeger, 13.5"	105	120	135
Giraffes, Brayton Laguna, 18", pair	300	330	36-
Giraffes, Royal Haeger, 15", pair	120	130	140
Girl and Boy, sitting, Ceramic Arts Studio	40	45	50
Girl w/ Cat, Ceramic Arts Studio	40	45	50
Girl w/ Pail, Florence Ceramics	100	110	120
Godey Lady, Kay Finch, 7.5"	30	35	40
Godey Lady, Kay Finch, 9.5"	30	35	40

	LOW	AVG.	HIGH
Godey Man, Kay Finch, 7.5"	30	35	40
Godey Man, Kay Finch, 9.5"	30	35	40
Goose, Abingdon, 5"	45	50	58
Grace, Florence Ceramics	60	65	70
Grandmother and I, Florence Ceramics	280	310	340
Guitar Boy, Ceramic Arts Studio	40	50	60
Gull, Abingdon, 5"	75	80	92
Gypsy Girl and Boy, Ceramic Arts Studio	130	145	160
Hansel and Gretel, Ceramic Arts Studio	50	55	60
Hare, Florence Ceramics	90	100	110
Harlem Hoofer, Frankoma	470	525	580
Harlequin Boy and Girl, Ceramic Arts Studio	140	160	180
Harlequin Cat, Homer Laughlin	120	140	160
Harlequin Donkey, Homer Laughlin	105	120	135
Harlequin Duck, Homer Laughlin	95	110	125
Harlequin Fish, Homer Laughlin	95	110	125
Harlequin Lamb, Homer Luaghlin	111	130	146
Harlequin Penguin, Homer Laughlin	89	110	130
Harmonica Boy, Ceramic Arts Studio	40	50	60
Hen, Royal Haeger, 4"	25	30	35
Her Majesty, Florence Ceramics	70	75	80
Heron, Abingdon, 5.5"	45	50	55
Hiawatha, Ceramic Arts Studio	20	25	30
Hindu Boys, Ceramic Arts Studio	40	45	50
Hippo, Vernon Kilns	320	355	390
Horse, Royal Haeger, 7"	25	30	35
Horse, Royal Haeger, 13"	70	80	90
Hound Dog, Brayton Laguna	35	45	45
Irene, Florence Ceramics	50	55	60
Jeanette, Florence Ceramics	70	75	80
Jennifer, Florence Ceramics	130	145	160
Jim, Florence Ceramics	50	55	60
John Kennedy, Jr., Morton Pottery	30	35	40
Jon, Brayton Laguna	30	35	40
Josephine, Florence Ceramics	70	75	80
Joy, Florence Ceramics	50	55	60
Joyce, Florence Ceramics	190	215	240
Julie, Florence Ceramics	70	75	80
Kangaroo, Abingdon, 7"	88	100	118
Kangaroo, Morton Pottery, 2.75"	5	10	15
Kay, Florence Ceramics	60	65	70
King's Jester and Musicians, Ceramic Arts Studio	200	225	250
Kissing Girl and Boy, Ceramic Arts Studio	40	45	50
Kitten, sleeping, Kay Finch, 3.25"	5	10	15
Kiu, Florence Ceramics	40	45	50
Kneeling Nude, Abingdon, 7"	170	190	210
Lady Diana, Florence Ceramics	140	160	180
Lady Rowena, Ceramic Arts Studio	70	80	90
Lamb, Kay Finch, 2.75"	5	10	15
Lamb, Morton Pottery, 3.5"	5	10	15
Lantern Boy, Florence Ceramics	40	45	50
Laura, Florence Ceramics	100	110	120
Leading Man, Florence Ceramics	140	160	180
Leopard, pacing, miniature, Frankoma	290	310	330

	LOW	AVG.	HIGH
Lillian, Florence Ceramics	90	100	110
Lillian Russell, Florence Ceramics	340	380	420
Linda Lou, Florence Ceramics	70	75	80
Lion, Cliftwood Potteries, 14"	60	70	80
Lioness, Cliftwood Potteries, 12"	60	65	70
Lisa, Florence Ceramics	90	100	110
Little Jack Horner, Ceramic Arts Studio	15	20	25
Lorry, Florence Ceramics	120	135	150
Louis XV, Florence Ceramics	200	220	240
Louis XVI, Florence Ceramics	140	160	180
Louise, Florence Ceramics	100	110	120
Love Birds, Hull, #93	25	30	35
Macaw, Royal Haeger, 14"	36	40	46
Madame Pompadour, Florence Ceramics	200	220	240
Madonna Plain, Florence Ceramics	50	55	60
Madonna w/ Child, Florence Ceramics	70	75	80
Male, abstract, Brayton Laguna	250	280	310
Man in Knickers, Morton Pottery, 7.5'	10	15	20
Mare and Foal, Royal Haeger, 9"	65	70	84
Margot, Florence Ceramics	190	215	240
Marie Antoinette, Florence Ceramics	140	160	180
Marleen in Brocade, Florence Ceramics	340	380	420
Marsie, Florence Ceramics	70	75	80
Martin, Florence Ceramics	170	190	210
Mary and Little Lamb, Ceramic Arts Studio	30	35	40
Matilda, Florence Ceramics	100	110	120
Melanie, Florence Ceramics	70	75	80
Mexican Boy and Girl, Ceramic Arts Studio	60	65	70
Mikado, Florence Ceramics	140	160	180
Mike, Florence Ceramics	50	55	60
Minnehaha, Ceramic Arts Studio	20	25	30
Miranda, Brayton Laguna, 6.5"	30	35	40
Miss Muffet, Ceramic Arts Studio	15	20	25
Modern Dance Woman, Ceramic Arts Studio	60	65	70
Monk, Frankoma	120	130	140
Musette, Florence Ceramics	100	110	120
Nancy, Florence Ceramics	50	55	60
Nita, Florence Ceramics	70	75	80
Nubian Centaurette, Vernon Kilns	370	410	450
Our Lady of Grace, Florence Ceramics	50	55	60
Owl, Kay Finch, 3.75"	15	20	25
Owl, Kay Finch, 8.75"	30	35	40
Oxen, Morton Pottery, 3.25"	30	35	40
Pamela, Florence Ceramics	70	75	80
Parakeets, Ceramic Arts Studio, pair	30	35	38
Parasol, Florence Ceramics	190	215	240
Parrots, Pete and Polly, Ceramic Arts Studio, pair	74	90	105
Patricia, Florence Ceramics	90	100	110
Peacock, Abingdon, 8"	45	50	55
Peasant Boy, Kay Finch, 6.75"	30	35	40
Peasant Girl, Florence Ceramics	60	65	70
Peasant Girl, Kay Finch, 6.75"	30	35	40
Peasant Woman, Brayton Laguna	30	35	40
Pekingese, miniature, Frankoma	250	275	300

	LOW	AVG.	HIGH
Pelican, Abingdon, 5"	45	50	55
Penguin, Abingdon, 5.5"	45	50	55
Penguins, Ceramic Arts Studio, pair	30	34	38
Peter Pan, Ceramic Arts Studio	50	55	60
Pheasant, Royal Haeger, 6"	27	30	34
Pied Piper, Ceramic Arts Studio	30	35	40
Pied Piper Child, Ceramic Arts Studio	20	25	30
Pierrene and Pierrott, Ceramic Arts Studio	80	90	100
Pinocchio (Disney), Brayton Laguna	220	250	280
Pioneer Sam and Susie, Ceramic Arts Studio	40	45	50
Polar Bear, Royal Haeger, 7"	26	30	34
Polar Bear, Royal Haeger, 16"	66	70	82
Polar Bear Cub, Royal Haeger, 3"	14	16	20
Polish Boy and Girl, Ceramic Arts Studio	30	35	40
Pouter Pigeon, Abingdon, 4.5"	44	50	55
Prima Donna, Florence Ceramics	250	280	310
Princess, Florence Ceramics	170	190	210
Priscilla, Florence Ceramics	60	65	70
Puma, miniature, Frankoma	44	50	56
Puppy, Shawnee	20	25	30
Rabbit, Ceramic Arts Studio	20	25	30
Rabbit, Hull, 5.5"	35	40	56
Rabbit, Midwest Pottery, 2.5"	5	10	15
Rabbit, Morton Pottery, 3"	5	10	15
Rabbit, Shawnee	20	25	30
Rabbits, Midwest Pottery, 2.5"	20	25	30
Race Horse, Midwest Pottery, 7.25"	60	65	70
Racing Horse, Royal Haeger, 9"	30	34	38
Rebecca, Florence Ceramics	100	110	120
Reclining Sprite, Vernon Kilns	150	165	180
Rhett, Florence Ceramics	80	90	100
Rooster, Hull, #951	37	40	48
Rooster, Royal Haeger, 5"	20	30	40
Roosters, Ceramic Arts Studio, pair	30	33	37
Rosalie, Florence Ceramics	90	100	110
Rose Marie, Florence Ceramics	90	105	120
Russian Boy and Girl, Ceramic Arts Studio	60	65	70
Russian Wolfhound, Royal Haeger, 7"	28	30	33
Sailing Ship, Midwest Pottery, 2"	5	10	15
Sally, Brayton Laguna	20	25	30
Sally, Florence Ceramics	60	65	70
Samoan Mother and Child, Gladding, McBean	60	65	70
Santa Claus and Evergreen Tree, Ceramic Arts Studio	20	25	30
Sarah, Florence Ceramics	60	65	70
Satyr, Vernon Kilns	140	160	180
Saxophone Boy, Ceramic Arts Studio	40	50	60
Scandie Boy, Kay Finch, 5.25"	20	25	30
Scandie Girl, Kay Finch, 5.25"	20	25	30
Scarf Dancer, Abingdon, 13"	170	190	210
Scarlett, Florence Ceramics	140	160	180
Scotties, Ceramic Arts Studio, pair	25	30	35
Shen, Florence Ceramics	110	125	140
Shepherdess and Faun, Abingdon, 11.5"	90	100	110
Sherri, Florence Ceramics	140	160	180

	LOW	AVG.	HIGH
Shirley, Florence Ceramics	120	135	150
Smiley Pig, Kay Finch, 6.75"	30	35	40
Southern Belle and Gentleman, Ceramic Arts Studio	40	45	50
Spaniel, Midwest Pottery, 6"	40	45	50
Spanish Dance Couple, Ceramic Arts Studio	90	100	110
Spring Sue, Ceramic Arts Studio	20	25	30
Sprite, Vernon Kilns	150	165	180
Square Dance Couple, Ceramic Arts Studio	40	45	50
St. Francis, Ceramic Arts Studio	80	90	100
St. George, Ceramic Arts Studio	90	100	110
Stag, Royal Haeger, 14.5"	42	50	55
Stallion, Midwest Pottery, 6"	10	15	20
Stallion, Midwest Pottery, 10.75"	30	32	34
Stork, Morton Pottery, 4"	5	10	15
Stork, Morton Pottery, 7.5"	15	20	25
Story Hour, Florence Ceramics	220	250	280
Sue, Florence Ceramics	50	55	60
Sue Ellen, Florence Ceramics	80	85	90
Sultan and Harem, Ceramic Arts Studio	70	75	80
Summer Sally, Ceramic Arts Studio	20	25	30
Susan, Florence Ceramics	200	225	250
Swan, Abingdon, 3.75"	70	80	90
Swan, Hull, #69, 8.5"	25	30	35
Swan, miniature, Frankoma	45	50	55
Swordfish, Abingdon, 4.5"	45	50	55
Taka, Florence Ceramics	120	135	150
Temple Dancer, Ceramic Arts Studio	170	190	210
Tom Tom the Piper's Son, Ceramic Arts Studio	40	50	60
Torch Singer, Frankoma	450	500	550
Toucans, Brayton Laguna, pair	220	250	280
Turkey, wild, Midwest Pottery, 11.5"	40	45	50
Turtle, Midwest Pottery, 1"	5	10	15
Unicorn, Vernon Kilns	320	355	390
Victor, Florence Ceramics	110	125	140
Victoria, Florence Ceramics	200	220	240
Victorian Lady and Man, Ceramic Arts Studio	40	45	50
Virginia in Brocade, Florence Ceramics	340	380	420
Vivian, Florence Ceramics	120	135	150
White Rabbit and Alice, Ceramic Arts Studio	60	65	70
Winged Sprite, Vernon Kilns	150	165	180
Winney, Ceramic Arts Studio	70	80	90
Wee Chinese, Ceramic Arts Studio	20	25	307
Wee Dutch, Ceramic Arts Studio	20	25	30
Wee Eskimos, Ceramic Arts Studio	20	25	30
Wee French, Ceramic Arts Studio	20	25	30
Wee Swedish, Ceramic Arts Studio	20	25	30

Head Vases

Head vases are figural vases most often depicting women and young girls. They were popular in the 1950s and 1960s. Ladies with thick eyelashes, long gloves, dangle earrings and elaborate hats capture an exaggerated 1950s look. Although the United States manufactured some vases, Japan produced the majority. Identification is difficult because many were unmarked or had only paper labels.

When handling a head vase, be careful not to harm the label, the finish or delicate details such as jewelry. Beware of cracks and chips that decrease value. Watch out for reproductions or new head vases. Interest in head vases has intensified in the last five years and prices have risen accordingly. For further reading see *The Encyclopedia of Head Vases* by Kathleen Cole, Schiffer Publishing, Atglen, PA, 1996.

	LOW	HIGH
Bonnie, Ceramic Arts Studio, 7" h	$100	$120
Clown, w/ patched hat and bowtie, Relpo, 5.5" h	45	60
Girl, in bonnet, holding bouquet, w/ plaid side bow, Relpo, 5.5" h	55	75
Girl, in wide-brimmed hat, wall pocket, Royal Copley, 8" h	25	35
Girl, w/ closed eyes, applied eyelashes, hat and cutout bangs, Napco, 6" h	40	50
Girl, applied flowers in hair, w/ umbrella, mkd. "CN," 5" h	30	40
Manchu, Chinese man, Ceramic Arts Studio, 7.5"	100	150
Mei Ling, Chinese woman, Ceramic Arts Studio, 5" h	90	120
Svea, girl w/ pigtail, Ceramic Arts Studio, 6" h	70	90
Woman, in black lace, black eyelashes, dangle pearl earrings, Enesco, 5.5" h	60	80
Woman, closed eyes, painted lashes, honey blond hair, turquoise blouse, 5.5" h	25	35
Woman, in green, w/ gold accents, hat, and lashes, 4" h	15	20
Woman, black glove and lashes, pearl necklace, mkd. "C3282B Napco, 1956," 5" h	60	80
Woman, black hair, applied black lashes, molded hood, Inarco, 6" h	40	60
Woman, brown gloves and eyelashes, mkd. "4228 Lefton," 6" h	80	100
Woman, closed eyes, painted lashes, flower in blond hair, blue blouse, 4" h	20	25
Woman, wall pocket, lashes, black hair, wide-brimmed green hat, 7" h	20	30

Variety of Head Vases. —Photo courtesy Gene Harris Antique Auction Center.

Hotel and Restaurant China

China and silver patterns, with unique and prominently displayed names and logos, have been in frequent use since the late nineteenth century by restaurant, lodging and entertainment businesses to help distinguish their operations by creating favorable customer impressions. China items are often styled in such a way as to nostalgically evoke a particular era or regions, and range from simply designed and effective advertising to multicolored and highly sophisticated decorative pieces. Often, these pieces are among the only surviving artifacts of once legendary places, such as the Astor Hotel, Chicago's Blackstone Hotel (home of the original "smoke-filled room" of political image fame), or of earlier eras of modern operations, like the Pennsylvania Hotel. Some of the most sought-after designs include figures of people, animals, buildings and monuments. Some people collect all china and silver pieces from a particular establishment, city or region. Others collect by form (e.g. teapot or ashtray), manufacturer (Buffalo China Co.) or by pictorial subjects (Indians) from various businesses. Condition is important to the value of an object, especially if it is damaged by chips, cracks, scratches or heavy wear. Our consultants for this area are Christopher Wolfe and Scott Townsend of Townsend, Wolfe & Company. They are listed in the back of this book.

	LOW	AVG.	HIGH
Ashtray, Horn & Hardart Automat, top and back marked, thistle border, c1935	$60	$75	$85
Ashtray, "Luchows Restaurant—Since 1882," 6" beer stein design	35	50	65
Ashtray and Match Holder, Hotel Dennis, Atlantic City	25	35	40
Bouillon Cup, The William Foor Hotels, double handled, 1920s–30s	12	17	20
Bread Plate, Desert Inn, Las Vegas, c1960, 5.5"	10	15	18
Bud Vase, Bellevue Stratford Hotel, Philadelphia, gold crest, 4.5" h	20	25	28
Butter Pat, Broadway Central Hotel, New York City, top mkd. w/ full name, c1910s, 2.875" dia	50	55	65
Celery Tray, Hotel Astor, New York, thistle border, c1925	25	35	40
Celery Tray, Oriental Cafe, Detroit, Chinese room scene, c1920	60	70	85
Child's Dinner Plate, Holiday Inn, back mkd. only, c1962	20	28	35
Coffee Mug, Dunkin Donuts, pink side logo, 1970s	8	12	15
Coffee Mug, Playboy Club, ftd., side mkd. w/ Key Club logo, Hall China, early 1970s, 5.375" h, 3" dia	35	38	42
Compote, Hotel Lennox, New York, ftd., c1925, 4.5" dia	35	40	45
Creamer, Holiday Inn, individual size, older sign logo, c1965	12	18	25
Creamer, New Yorker Hotel, individual size, molded name, yellow glaze, 1.5 oz.	22	24	28
Creamer, Queen Hotel, Halifax, Nova Scotia, individual size, c1930	12	18	25
Cup/Saucer, The Biltmore, Los Angeles, c1940	15	22	27
Cup/Saucer, Toddle House, side and top mkd., 1964	15	20	28
Demitasse Cup/Saucer, Astor Hotel, New York, c1925	30	45	55
Demitasse Cup/Saucer, Fairmont Hotel, Shenango, c1970	15	20	25
Dinner Plate, Battle Creek Sanitarium, green, red and gold border, c1925, 9.75"	45	50	60
Dinner Plate, Columbia Hotel, Kalamazoo, Michigan, c1940, 10"	20	30	40
Dinner Plate, Everglades Hotel, Miami, c1945, 9"	15	25	40
Dinner Plate, Harrison Orange Drink distinctive logo, 1920s–30s, 10"	70	85	110
Dinner Plate, Hotel Traymore, Atlantic City, c1940, 9"	25	30	35
Dinner Plate, Howard Johnson's, divided, orange Pie Man logo, 1960s–70s	17	28	35
Dinner Plate, Liggetts Drug Store, Indian Tree pattern, 1940s–50s, 9"	15	18	22
Dinner Plate, St. Francis Hotel, San Francisco, c1945, 9.5"	25	30	40
Dresser Plate, Statler Hotel, 1935–40	35	40	50

	LOW	AVG.	HIGH
Ice Cream Shell, La Concha Hotel, Key West, wave and palm tree border, 1920s	35	45	60
Luncheon Plate, The Blackstone Hotel, Chicago, Buffalo, 1925	40	45	55
Mustard Pot, cov., Horn & Hardart Automat, back mkd., 1940s, 3.25" h	50	60	70
Mustard Pot, cov., Stevens Hotel, Chicago, 1940s–50s	10	13	18
Mustard Pot, open, "Liberty Hospital" and Statue of Liberty, c1910s–20s	35	40	50
Nut Dish, Hotel Peabody, Memphis, c1950	10	14	20
Pitcher, "Cosmopolitan," side mkd. in light brown w/ green floral top border, c1910s, 8 oz.	45	50	55
Plate, Bungalow Cafe Dearborn, oval, top mkd w/ same and "So Little More for the Best/Established Since 1925," Shenango, 7.5" x 5"	40	43	45
Plate, Chicken in the Rough, top mkd. w/ chicken logo, Syracuse China, 7.25" dia	35	40	48
Plate, The Monson, St. Petersburg, FL, oval, name in logo w/ palm tree and lighthouse in green, w/ green and red pinstripes, Syracuse China, 10.5" x 7.25"	30	35	40
Platter, Howard Johnson's, traveling scenes and compass border, 1950s	20	25	35
Salad Bowl, United Hotels Co., double, c1940	20	25	30
Salad Plate, Mayflower Hotel, Washington D.C., Buffalo, c1925	15	20	25
Sauce Boat, Hilton Hotels, c1945	12	15	20
Service Plate, Howard Johnson's, top mkd. w/ Pie Man logo, Walker, 11.5" dia	40	45	55
Service Plate, "Sarah Siddons," Ambassador East Hotel, Chicago, Syracuse China	80	95	110
Soup Plate, Astor Hotel, New York, c1925, 9" dia	35	50	65
Souvenir Plate, John Wanamaker, 50 Year (Philadelphia) Jubilee, 1911, 4.375"	45	55	70
Sugar Bowl, open, Howard Johnson's, 1960s	20	28	35

Left to right: Plate, Canadian National System, railroad, Royal Doulton, 8.75" dia., $40–$50; Saucer, "The Wanamaker Store, Philadelphia, Largest In the World, 1861 – Jubilee Year – 1911," green and white, Buffalo China, 4.375" dia, $60–$80.

Planters

Are planters the final frontier in figural ceramic collecting? Planter collectors think so, but something new is always being discovered. Collectors boast that planters are the perfect size; they demand less shelf space than cookie jars and display better than the smaller salt and pepper shakers. Shawnee, McCoy and other firms that produced cookie jars and salt and pepper shakers made many planters. So far, planters don't enjoy the widespread collecting base of cookie jars and salt and pepper shakers, but they're gaining momentum.

We listed style numbers of the various pieces and the manufacturer when known, and "Japan" for items so identified.

Shawnee often marked pieces with "USA," sometimes with a style number. This attribution is not foolproof because other firms also used the "USA" mark. Many planters had a paper label or were unmarked, so do your homework.

We recommend *Collector's Encyclopedia of Figural Planters & Vases: Identification & Balues,* by Betty and Bill Newbound, Collector Books, paducah, KY, 1997..

	LOW	HIGH
Angel Fish, Japan, 3.5" h	$8	$10
Baby Carriage and Lady, blue, Royal Haeger, 7.5" h	28	34
Berry and Leaf, McCoy, 8" l	12	18
Bird on Bamboo, 5.25" h	7	9
Bowling Boy, blue, Royal Haeger, 6" h	25	35
Box Car, Shawnee, #552	20	30
Bug, metal feet, 3" h	15	20
Bulldog and Drum, 3" h	18	24
Burro, Abingdon, #673, 4.5" h	30	35
Canopy Bed, Shawnee, #734, 8" l	75	95
Cat, black, painted eyes, 15" l	30	40
Cat, plaid, Japan, 5.25" h	6	8
Cat Playing Saxophone, Shawnee, #729	32	52
Chick w/ Cart, Shawnee, #720	15	20
Chick w/ Egg, Shawnee, #730, 3.5" h	15	20
Chinese Girl, Royal Copley, 7" h	25	35
Circus Wagon, Shawnee	30	35

Left to right: Bird on Stump, 4.5" h, $12–$15; Boat, green, 8" l, $15–$20. —Photos courtesy Ray Morykan Auctions.

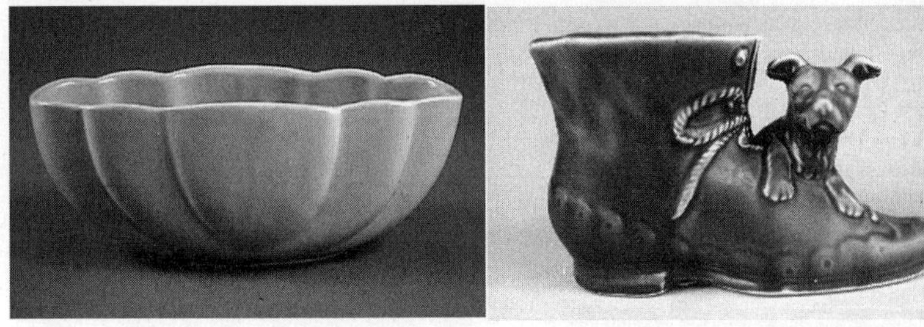

Left to right: Bowl, light blue, Shawnee, 9.5" l, $35–$40; Pup and Shoe, burgundy, Shawnee, $10–$15. —Photos courtesy Ray Morykan Auctions.

	LOW	HIGH
Conestoga Wagon, Shawnee, #617, 3.5" h	20	26
Coolie w/ Basket and Umbrella, Shawnee, #617, 4.5" h	15	20
Cow Skull, McCoy, 8" h	30	40
Cowboy Boot, Shawnee, 6.5"	10	15
Diamond Design, McCoy, 7" l	10	12
Doe and Fawn, McCoy, 7" h	32	38
Dog Cart, McCoy, 5" h	25	30
Dog Profiles, 5" h	15	20
Donkey, Abingdon, #669, 7.5" h	38	48
Donkey w/ Basket, Shawnee, #722, 5.5" h	15	20
Duck and Logs, Occupied Japan, 3" h	15	18
Dutch Boy and Girl, 6.5" h	20	30
Dutch Boy at Wall, 5.5" h	12	14
Dutch Shoe, Abingdon, 5" l	30	50
Elephant, Shawnee, #759	8	10
Elephant and Leaf, Shawnee, #501	50	70
Elf w/ Green Shoe, Shawnee, #765, 5.75" h, 6.5" l	30	50
Fawn, Abingdon, #672, 5" h	20	30
Fawn, Morton Potter, #645, 6.5" h	10	15
Fish, black bass, 4.5" h	20	30
Fish in Swirling Waves, green, 7.5" h	18	24
Flamenco Dancers, 9" h	30	40
Flamingo and Foliage, 9.5" h	30	40
Flower and Bird, raised base, 4" h	15	20
Flying Bird, w/ flowers, 5" h	10	15
Gazelle, Royal Haeger, 17" l	90	130
Girl and Basket, Shawnee, #534	10	15
Gondolier, Royal Haeger, #6578, 19.5" l	30	50
Horse, rearing, 9.5" h	25	35
Igloo and Penguin, yellow, 3.25" h	9	12
Jaguar, rocky base, 9" l	20	25
Jalopy, Relpo, 7" l	7	9
Lady w/ Donkey Cart, Japan, 5.5" h	15	20
Leopard, Royal Haeger, #760	25	35
Lily Pad and Frog, 3.75" h	9	12
Lovebirds on Pinecone, 4" h	20	30

	LOW	HIGH
Madonna, blue, Royal Windsor, 4.5" h	15	20
Madonna, white, Royal Haeger, #650, 9" h	25	35
Masks, Tragedy and Comedy, McCullogh, 3.5" h	10	12
Mexican Child, Royal Copley, 5.5" h	30	40
Oxcart and Dutch Girl, Japan, 3.5" h	12	18
Pelican on Bamboo Log, Japan, 9" l	65	90
Pheasant, black, gold highlights, 17" l	20	30
Piano, Shawnee, #528	20	30
Pirate, Brush, 3.5" h	25	35
Pixie, winged, Shawnee, #536, 4" h	7	10
Poodle, green, 7" h	15	20
Poodle, yellow, whimsical, 5" h	12	16
Pot and Saucer, button-tufted design, McCoy, 3.5" h	9	14
Rabbit, 7" h	10	14
Racing Horses, Royal Haeger, #883, 11" l	30	50
Rickshaw and Driver, Shawnee, 5" l	7	9
Rocking Horse, #526, 5.5" h	30	40
Rooster, Camark, #501	18	22
Santa and Chimney, Morton Pottery, 7" h	20	25
Shell, Shawnee, #2005, 4" x 7.75"	20	30
Sleeping Peasant w/ Burro, 5.75" h	30	40
Sofa, Germany, 4.5" h	8	12
Swan, black, 5.5" h	15	20
Swan, blue w/ gold floral dec., 6" h	15	20
Three-Piece Band, Napco, 7.5" h	70	100
Three Pigs, Shawnee	8	10
Top Hat, star-spangled, Shawnee, 3" h	7	9
Train Caboose, Shawnee, #553	30	40
Train Engine, Shawnee, #550	50	60
Train Set, Shawnee, #550, #551, #552, and #553	130	190
Train Tender, Shawnee, #551	25	35
Tree Stump w/ Boy, Shawnee, #533	9	14
Turkey, Morton Pottery, 5" h	10	15
Turtle, green, McCoy, 7" l	30	40
Violin, Royal Haeger, 17" l	25	35
Wishing Well w/ Dutch Boy and Girl, Shawnee, #710, 5.75" h, 8.25" w	30	50

Left to right: Shell Motif, pink and white, 7.5" l, $18–$24; Twin Swans, yellow, cold painted features, Brush-McCoy, 11.5" l, $35–$45. —Photos courtesy Ray Morykan Auctions.

Staffordshire

Staffordshire pottery refers to pottery produced in and around Staffordshire, England, from the mid eighteenth century through the end of the nineteenth century. Originally conceived as an affordable alternative to Chinese porcelain, Staffordshire wares are now recognized in their own right. Important makers include Enoch Wood, Ridgway and Clews. With the development of the transfer decoration process, manufacturers covered dinnerware with scenes of popular landmarks and historical vignettes. "Historical Blue" had its heyday in the second half of the nineteenth century. Many popular designs are still produced.

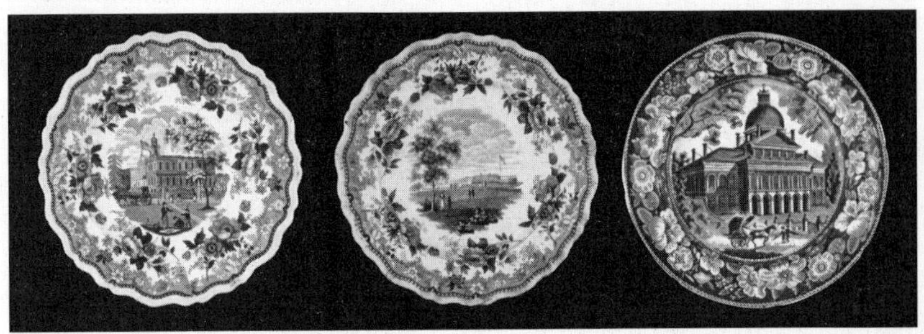

Left to right: At Richmond, Virginia, American Scenery, Job and John Jackson, purple, plate, 6.75" dia., $150; Battery 8c, New York, American Scenery, Job and John Jackson, green, plate, 7.75" dia., $125; Boston State House, floral border, Enoch Wood & Sons, dark blue, plate, 8.5" dia., $275.

Dinnerware

	AUCTION	RETAIL	
		Low	High
Alms House Boston, Stevenson, dark blue, platter, 14.5" l	$1650	$2400	$3200
Anti-Slavery (Lovejoy/Tyrant's Foe), light blue, cup plate, 4" dia	275	400	500
Arms of New York, T. Mayer, dark blue, plate, 10" dia	440	600	850
Arms of Rhode Island, T. Mayer, dark blue, plate, 8.625" dia	385	530	720
Arms of South Carolina, T. Mayer, dark blue, plate, 7.5" dia	550	800	1000
Baltimore & Ohio Railroad, Shell Border, Enoch Wood, dark blue, plate, 10.125" dia	990	1400	1900
Baltimore & Ohio Railroad, Shell Border, Enoch Wood, dark blue, soup plate	1100	1650	2200
Beaver, Quadrupeds series, Hall, dark blue, plate, 8.75" dia	209	300	400
Beehive, Stevenson & Williams, dark blue, plate, 6.125" dia	176	250	320
Boston Mails…Saloon, Edwards, black, platter, 19.875" l	330	480	620
Cambrian, Phillips, light blue, set of 12 plates, 6.625" dia	495	800	1000
Capitol at Washington, Shell Border, Enoch Wood, dark blue, plate, 6.5" dia	358	500	650
Castle Forbes, Aberdeenshire, Grapevine Border series, Wood, dark blue, plate, 6.625" dia	110	160	210
Castle Garden, Battery New York, Wood & Sons, dark blue, platter, 18.625" l	2750	4000	5500

Left to right: City Hall New York, Beauties of America, J. & W. Ridgway, dark blue, plate, 10" dia., $250; Giraffe, Quadruped series, Adams, red, saucer, $120; Harper's Ferry, U.S., William Adams and Son, red, platter, 15.25" x 13", $475.

	AUCTION	RETAIL Low	RETAIL High
Catskill House, Hudson, Shell Border, Enoch Wood, dark blue, plate, 6.5" dia	358	500	700
Catskill Mountains, Hudson River, Shell Border, Enoch Wood, dark blue, gravy boat, 4.75" h	358	500	700
Chief Justice Marshall Troy, Wood, dark blue, plate, 8.5" dia	495	750	900
Chillicothe, Cites series, Davenport, dark blue, gravy boat, 5.25" l	6600	9500	12,500
Christmas Eve, no border, Wilkie series, Clews, dark blue, cup plate, 3.5" dia	303	450	600
City of Albany of State of New York, Shell Border, Enoch Wood, dark blue, plate, 10.25" dia	660	900	1200
Columbia College N.Y., Acorn and Oakleaf Border, Clews, medium blue, plate, 6.375" dia	385	480	650
Commodore MacDonnough's Victory, Wood, dark blue, plate, 10.125" dia	605	900	1200
Death of the Bear, Indian Sporting series, Spode, medium blue, hot water plate, 11.5" dia	770	1000	1300
Eagle on Urn, Clews, dark blue, teapot, 7" h	1870	2500	3200
Esholt House, Yorkshire, Grapevine Border, Enoch Wood, dark blue, plate, 10" dia	248	350	450
Fair Mount Near Philadelphia, Eagle Border, Stubbs, blue, plate, 10.25" dia	275	380	500
Fair Mount Near Philadelphia, Eagle Border, Stubbs, blue, shallow bowl, 9.25" dia	550	750	1000
Fair Mount Near Philadelphia, Eagle Border, Stubbs, light blue, plate, 10.25" dia	193	270	350
Fonthill Abbey, Wiltshire, Bluebell Border series, Clews, dark blue, platter, 17" l	990	1400	1800
Franklin's Morals, Davenport, dark blue, plate, 7.625" dia	303	450	600
Gilpin's Mills on the Brandy, Shell Border, Enoch Wood, dark blue, plate, 9.125" dia	1320	1900	2500
Halifax (from Dartmouth), British America series, Podmore, Walker & Co., brown, platter, 19.25" l	660	950	1200

Left to right: Hartford, Connecticut, American Scenery, Job and John Jackson, red, plate, 10.25" dia., $135; Harvard Hall, Mass., American Scenery, Job and John Jackson, red, plate, 7" dia., $150; Junction of the Sacondaga and Hudson Rivers, Picturesque Views, Clews, brown, plate, 7" dia., $175.

	AUCTION	RETAIL	
		Low	High
Harvard College, Acorn and Oakleaf Border, Clews, medium blue, plate, 10.125" dia	550	750	950
Highlands at West Point Hudson River, Shell Border, Enoch Wood, dark blue, plate, 6.5" dia	990	1300	1600
Hospital Boston, Vine Border, Stevenson, dark blue, plate, 9" dia	330	450	600
Hudson River View, Shell Border, Enoch Wood, dark blue, plate, 5.75" dia	605	800	1000
India Pattern, medium blue, plate, 8.375" dia	72	100	120
Insane Hospital, Boston, Beauties of America, Ridgway, dark blue, gravy tureen lid	198	300	400
Lafayette at Franklin's Tomb, Enoch Wood, dark blue, wash bowl, 4.25" h, 10.75" dia	935	1200	1500
Lake George, State of New York, Shell Border, Enoch Wood, dark blue, platter, 16.5" l	1650	2300	3000
Landing of General Lafayette, Clews, dark blue, basin, 12.125" l, 4.5" h	1210	1700	2200
Landing of General Lafayette, Clews, dark blue, plate, 8.875" dia	330	430	550
Landing of General Lafayette, Clews, dark blue, platter, 15.25" l	1760	2500	3300
Nahant Hotel New Boston, Eagle Border, Stubbs, dark blue, plate, 8.875" dia	413	600	800
New York from Heights Near Brooklyn, Stevenson, dark blue, platter, 16.25" l	6050	8000	11,000
Niagara From the American Side, Wood and Sons, dark blue, platter, 14.875" l	2640	3700	4800
Octagon Church Boston, Beauties of America series, Ridgway, dark blue, soup plate, 9.75" dia	385	500	650
Oxburgh Hall, Acorn and Oakleaf Border, dark blue, openwork undertray, 10.625" l	715	1000	1250
Park Theatre, New York, Acorn and Oakleaf Border, Clews, blue, soup plate, 10" dia	385	500	650
Pass in the Catskill Mountains, Shell Border, Enoch Wood, dark blue, plate, 7.5" dia	550	750	950

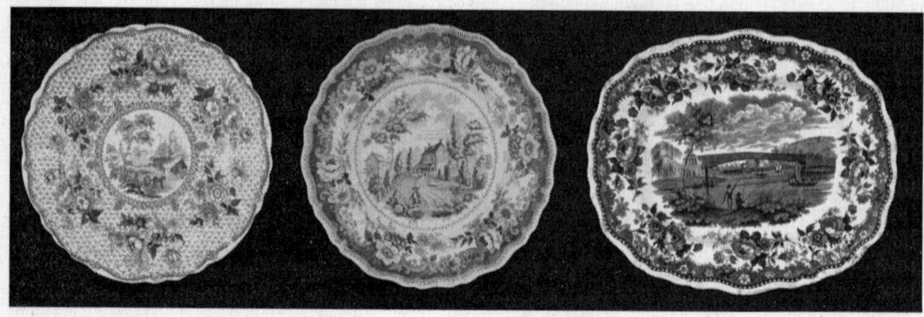

Left to right: New Orleans, Lace Border, Ralph Stevenson, red, plate, 8.25" dia., $120; Residence of the Late Richard Jordan, J.H. & Co., light blue, plate, 9" dia., $185; Upper Ferry Bridge Over the River Schuylkill, American Scenery, Job and John Jackson, black, platter, 10" x 8", $275.

	AUCTION	RETAIL Low	RETAIL High
Pine Orchard House, Catskill Mountains, Shell Border, Enoch Wood, dark blue, plate, 10.25" dia	660	850	1000
Quebec, British America series, Podmore, Walker & Co., brown, strainer, 12.75" l	495	700	800
Quebec, Shell Border, Enoch Wood, dark blue, vegetable dish, 9.5" sq	825	1100	1400
Residence of the Late Richard Jordan, New Jersey, J.H. & Co., blue, plate, 10.375" dia	165	240	320
Residence of the Late Richard Jordan, New Jersey, J.H. & Co., brown, plate, 7.75" dia	99	130	170
Residence of the Late Richard Jordan, New Jersey, J.H. & Co., light blue, cup plate, 3.75" dia	275	350	470
Residence of the Late Richard Jordan, New Jersey, J.H. & Co., light blue, plate, 9" dia	165	240	320
Residence of the Late Richard Jordan, New Jersey, J.H. & Co., light purple/lavender, handled mug, 3.25" h	248	350	450
Residence of the Late Richard Jordan, New Jersey, J.H. & Co., purple, plate, 5.625" dia	77	100	130
Residence of the Late Richard Jordan, New Jersey, J.H. & Co., purple, plate, 8.75" dia	88	110	150
Residence of the Late Richard Jordan, New Jersey, J.H. & Co., purple, plate, 9" dia	143	200	250
Residence of the Late Richard Jordan, New Jersey, J.H. & Co., purple, plate, 10.25" dia	88	110	150
Residence of the Late Richard Jordan, New Jersey, J.H. & Co., purple, platter, 9.75" l	385	500	650
Residence of the Late Richard Jordan, New Jersey, J.H. & Co., purple, soup, 7.75" dia	154	220	300
Residence of the Late Richard Jordan, New Jersey, J.H. & Co., red, plate, 5.625" dia	220	300	400
Residence of the Late Richard Jordan, New Jersey, J.H. & Co., red, plate, 7.5" dia	99	130	160

Left to right: English Scenery, Enoch Wood, brown w/ yellow, green, and blue accents, creamer, 4.5" h, $85; Near Fort Miller, Hudson River, Clews, red, pitcher, 8" h, $400; Tributes to the State of New York w/ DeWitt Clinton "Governor" eulogy and to the city of Utica, New York, dark blue, creamer, 5.75" h, $1200.

	AUCTION	RETAIL	
		Low	High
Residence of the Late Richard Jordan, New Jersey, J.H. & Co., red, plate, 10.5" dia	165	220	300
Rural Homes, Wood, dark blue, plate, 7.5" dia	94	125	150
Sandusky w/ Steamship *Henry Clay,* I.M. Thompson & Co., Wheeling Va., dark blue, platter, 16.5" l	8250	12,000	16,000
State House Boston, Beauties of America series, Ridgway, dark blue, sauce boat, 6.5" l	330	450	600
States, America and Independence, Clews, dark blue, pitcher, 9.75" h	2530	3500	4500
States, America and Independence, Clews, dark blue, plate, 8.75" dia	303	400	500
States, America and Independence, Clews, dark blue, plate, 10.5" dia	358	420	520
States, America and Independence, Clews, dark blue, platter, 11.75" l	1540	2200	3000
The Capitol, Washington, Shell Border, Enoch Wood, dark blue, plate, 7.5" dia	715	1000	1300
Transylvania University, Lexington, Shell Border, Enoch Wood, dark blue, plate, 9.25" dia	385	520	680
Union Line, Wood, dark blue, plate, 10.25" dia	715	1000	1300
View Near Sandy Hill, Hudson, emb. rim, black transfer, pink luster border, plate, 4.75" dia	220	300	400
View of Greenwich, Grapevine Border, Enoch Wood, platter, 14.875" l	605	800	1000
View of Trenton Falls, Shell Border, Enoch Wood, dark blue, plate, 7.5" dia	303	400	500
Villa in the Regent's Park, London, Regent's Park series, Adams, dark blue, plate, 9" dia	182	270	360
Warwick Castle, Grapevine Border, Enoch Wood, plate, 10" dia	165	240	320
Water Works, Philadelphia, Acorn and Oakleaf Border, Clews, blue, plate, 10.125" dia	605	850	1100
West Point Military Academy, Shell Border, Enoch Wood, dark blue, vegetable dish, oval, 10.75" l	1045	1400	1900
Winter View of Pittsfield, Mass, Clews, dark blue, open vegetable, 12.5" l	1870	2500	3400
Winter View of Pittsfield, Mass, Clews, dark blue, plate, 8.875" dia	220	300	400

Left to right: Cipsus, 14" h, $185; Cow, spill vase, 8.5" h, $300.

Figures & Miscellaneous

	AUCTION	RETAIL Low	RETAIL High
Baby in Cradle, 2.25" l	$40	$90	$175
Bear w/ Cub, 3" h	100	215	375
Ben Franklin, holding paper titled "Freedom," black, red, and flesh tones, 15.75" h	2090	4000	5500
Billy Goat, 2.5" h	60	135	200
Boy, wearing blue coat, 3.25" h	100	215	375
Boy, riding rooster, wearing tricorn hat, 3.5" h	125	275	425
Boy w/ Net, unglazed, 4" h	20	45	90
Boy w/ Rooster, 3.75" h	100	215	375
Camel,2.75" h	60	125	200
Cow, 2" h, 3.5" l	70	150	250
Dog, sitting, 2.75" h	90	175	250
Dog, standing, 2.5" h	60	125	200
Dogs, recumbent, on mottled bases, early 19th C, 6.5" l, pair	1100	2000	3000
Dogs, recumbent, w/ red and black markings, 4.5" l, pair	100	175	275
Dogs, w/ russet markings, 7" l, pair	700	1200	1900
Horse, reclining, 3.25" h	100	225	400
King Charles Spaniels, standing, 13" l, pair	1800	3000	5000
Lamb, 2.5" h	60	125	200
Lamb, reclining, 3.5" h	100	225	400
Lion, 3.5" h	100	225	375
Monkey in Tree, 4" h	250	450	650
Ostrich, running, 4.5" h	85	175	300
Poodle, seated, 3.75" h	95	200	350
Poodles, mother w/ 3 pups on scrolled bases, 5" h, pair	450	775	1250
Rooster, 3.75" h	120	250	400
Rooster, 4.5" h	100	225	400
Spaniel, seated, black and white, 3" h	100	225	400
Spaniel, seated, orange and white, 3.5" h	130	275	425
Spaniels, seated, red and white, 7.5" h, pair	400	700	1200
Stag, reclining, 2.5" h	90	175	300
Turkey, 3" h	70	150	250
Zebra, black and green, 6.5" h	248	450	700

Steins

Europeans have produced steins since the thirteenth century. Collections of early steins can be very valuable. However, steins from the nineteenth and twentieth centuries are widely available. Collectors of modern steins prize those made by Villeroy & Boch Company of Mettlach, Germany. They also seek those manufactured by Merkelbach & Wick and Simon Peter Gerz. For more information see *The Mettlach Book* by Gary Kirsner, Glentiques, Ltd., Coral Springs, FL, 1994.

Stein auction prices, left to right: Mettlach, inlaid lid, #3329, 1 liter, $4025; Mettlach, inlaid lid, #1856, 1 liter, $3680; Mettlach, inlaid lid, #2717, .5 liter, $4600; Hauber & Reuther, golfer, pewter top, .5 liter, $2530. —Photo courtesy Gary Kirsner Auctions.

	AUCTION	RETAIL Low	RETAIL High
Capo di Monte type, classical motif, inlaid lid, mkd w/ crown over "N," 4L	$1495	$1650	$2000
Character, artillery shell, lithophane, .5L	403	450	550
Character, double skull, mkd. "E. Bohne Söhne," .4L	1064	1200	1400
Character, football, baseball pitcher dec., Harvard University, .5L	253	300	380
Character, man w/ beard, #46, .5L	661	720	850
Character, monk, #572, .5L	403	470	550
Character, owl, #7682, .5L	299	350	420
Character, student cat, Gerz, #061, .5L	518	600	700
Delft, hand painted, pewter lid, Royal Bonn, 4L	374	420	500
Faience, Nürnberg, pewter lid and footring, mid 18th C, 1L	403	450	550
Faience, Berlin, pewter lid and footring, lid dated 1784, 1L	2300	2500	3000
Faience, pewter lid and footring, lid dated 1779, 1L	1208	1400	1800
Lithophane, 2 women reading letter, pewter lid, .5L	403	450	550
Lithophane, transfer dec., "All Heil!, Deutscher Rad-Fahren Bund," pewter lid, .5L	345	400	500
Mettlach, barmaid, inlaid lid, #2939, .5L	748	830	950
Mettlach, bicycle rider, pewter lid, 3.1L	2530	2750	3200
Mettlach, bicycle riders, cameo type, inlaid lid, #2686, 2.5L	1783	1970	2100
Mettlach, carpenter, inlaid lid, #2723, .5L	1070	1200	1500
Mettlach, cherub drinking, inlaid lid, #1396, .5L	547	620	750
Mettlach, Cornell Universtity, inlaid lid, #2001, .5L	5635	6000	7000
Mettlach, courier, inlaid lid, #2720, .5L	1610	2100	2500
Mettlach, couple dancing, inlaid lid, #1162, .5L	547	600	750

	AUCTION	RETAIL Low	RETAIL High
Mettlach, couple sitting at table, cameo type, inlaid lid, #2773, 2.3L	1380	1500	1750
Mettlach, crest, cameo type, pewter lid, #2951, .5L	661	720	850
Mettlach, crusader, pewter lid and alligator head, 1786, 1L	1265	1400	1700
Mettlach, dancers, inlaid lid, #1655, .5L	431	500	600
Mettlach, Falstaff, PUG, pewter lid, #983, .5L	265	300	350
Mettlach, gnome, inlaid lid, #2133, .5L	2415	2600	3000
Mettlach, Hamburg crest, relief, silver lid, #62	345	400	500
Mettlach, John C. White, White & Crafts Malsters, PUG, pewter lid, #2118, 2L	949	1100	1300
Mettlach, knight, inlaid lid, #2765, .5L	1840	2000	2400
Mettlach, man serenading woman, inlaid lid, #2780, .5L	431	500	600
Mettlach, men drinking, inlaid lid, #2639, .5L	690	750	900
Mettlach, mosaic, inlaid lid, #1989, 1.5L	431	500	600
Mettlach, Seidel-Science, inlaid lid, #2831, .5L	5290	5700	6700
Mettlach, student association crest, "Teutonia sei's Panier!," dated 1899, pewter lid	431	500	600
Mettlach, woman and bicycle, inlaid lid, #2635, .5L	1064	1200	1400
Occupational, fireman, "Hoch! Dreimal Hoch der Feuerwehr!," pewter lid, .5L	374	400	470
Occupational, Müller, pewter lid, .5L	230	250	300
Pottery, artillery scene, "Königl. Preussische Feld Artillerie," relief, pewter lid, #1271, .5L	276	300	400
Pottery, Heidelberg scene, sgd. "KB," inlaid lid, #820, .5L	546	600	720
Pottery, medical books, inlaid lid, mkd. "Coblenz," #1714, .5L	518	580	700
Pottery, tavern scene, inlaid lid, J.W. Remy, #717, 1L	219	250	280
Rauenstein, hand-painted floral dec.	575	720	750
Regimental, "1. Comp. Bay̆r. Inft. Regt. Nr. 12, Neu Ulm (1900–02)," medical scenes, .5L	2875	3200	3800
Regimental, "7. Comp. Eisenbahn Regt. Nr. 1, Berlin - Schöneberg (1909–11)," .5L	1553	1700	2000
Regimental, "2. Comp., Bay̆r. Jäger Batl. Nr. 2, Aschaffenburg (1909–11)," .5L	1438	1600	1900
Regimental, "2. Comp. Bay̆r. Train Batl. Nr. 1, München (1907–08)," .5L	1035	1200	1400
Regimental, "9. Comp., Bay̆r. Inft. Regt. Nr. 2, München (1906–08)," .5L	575	640	750
Regimental, "4. Comp. Inft. Regt. Nr. 88, Mainz (1910–12), .5L	546	600	720
Regimental, "9. Comp. Sächs. Inft. Regt. Nr. 103, Bautzen (1909–11), .5L	776	830	950
Souvenir, transfer dec. of little boy peeing in stream, "Trinkt nur kein Wasser! Sevilla-Biltmore, Havana, Cuba," Marzi & Remy, pewter lid, .5L	311	350	420
Souvenir, transfer dec. of University of Michigan, pewter lid, .5L	184	200	240
Third Reich, "Masch. Gew. Komp. Geb. Jäger-Batl. 19," pewter lid, .5L	834	910	1100
Third Reich, "3 Komp. Inft. Regt. Regensburg," pewter lid, .5L	265	300	360
Third Reich, "2./Pz. Abw. Abt. 27, Augsburg," pewter lid inscribed "Uffz. Kast 12.6.37," .5L	431	480	570
Third Reich, faience, towns incorporated into Munich in 1938, pewter lid, 1L	1150	1250	1500
Third Reich, "18./E.J.G./Inft. Regt. 75 Donaueschingen," pewter lid w/ helmet finial w/ swastika, .5L	1380	1500	1800

Tiles

	AUCTION	RETAIL Low	RETAIL High
Grueby, 1 w/ mermaid, 1 w/ monk playing cello, red clay w/ matte mustard ground, 6" sq, pair	$385	$425	$475
Grueby, 2-tile frieze, stylized Viking ship on high waves, cuenca, blues, greens, and browns, new Arts & Crafts frame, 9" x 18"	2750	3000	3300
Grueby, 6-tile frieze spelling out in cuerda seca "Kelsey Ranch L exington/Supplying Waldorf Lunches" in green and ivory, Arts & Crafts frame, 3" x 30"	990	1100	1250
Grueby, cuenca w/ oak tree against cloud-filled sky in shades of green, blue, and white, Arts & Crafts frame, 6" sq	1980	2200	2500
Grueby, "Pines," cuenca w/ trees in landscape in greens, blues, and brown, new Arts & Crafts frame, 6" sq	2310	2500	2800
Grueby, stylized monk at lectern in bisque red clay against heavily curdled matte ochre ground, Arts & Crafts frame, 6" sq	440	500	550
Grueby, white tulip w/ green leaves on matte mustard ground, 6" sq	1870	2000	2250
Marblehead, cluster of trees in dark green under blue overcast sky, ship mark, paper label, 4.25" sq	880	950	1000
Marblehead, landscape of trees in dark green reflected in lake, small chip to front and back, ship mark, paper label, 4.25" sq	770	820	900
Marblehead, large tree in forest in shades of brown and umber matte against moss green matte ground, Arts & Crafts frame, impressed ship mark, 6" sq	1430	1500	1700
Mosaic, dec. in cuenca w/ ship on water in taupe, orange, and green against dark blue sky, company logo "MTC" on sail, small nicks around edges, Arts & Crafts frame, 6" sq	440	500	550
Owens, mountain landscape in cuenca in shades of green and ochre matte glazes, new Arts & Crafts frame, impressed "Owens," 11.75" sq	2970	3200	3500
Owens/Empire, dec. in cuenca w/ ship on water in shades of ochre and brown, Arts & Crafts frame, 11.75" sq	1540	1700	1900
Rookwood Faience, decorated in cuenca with Glasgow rose in pink w/ green leaves, new Arts & Crafts frame, impressed "Rookwood Faience/1281Y," 6" sq	1430	1600	1800
Rookwood Faience, geometric design, matte ochre glaze, wood box frame, 6" sq	110	125	150
Tiffany, set of 3 w/ molded dec, blue thistle, chartreuse fleur-de-lis, and blue stylized blossoms, largest tile 3.5" sq	330	380	420

Rookwood Faience, 5-tile frieze, cottage scene with rolling hills and trees in polychrome cuenca, impressed marks, 60" x 12", $18,700 at auction. —Photo courtesy David Rago Auctions.

TV Lamps

TV lamps have been described as outrageous forms for subtle lighting. We define TV lamps as those lamps and lamp/planter or lamp/clock combinations that produce an indirect light either shaded by its position within its figural structure or by a screen shade or an insert shade. These lamps serve in many capacities but are now categorized as TV lamps. The need for TV lamps arose from the fear that flickering TV images could harm eyestight if not offset by another source of light. The lamps also allowed 1950s homemakers a means to lessen the intrusiveness of the electronic box. In the early 1950s manufacturers such as Royal Haeger often revamped vases and figural pieces based on pre-war designs. It is not uncommon to see a vase produced in the late 1930s fitted as a lamp in the 1950s (collectors avoid home conversions). As the fifties progressed makers integrated bold and sometimes bizarre themes of fashion and design into TV lamps. They produced lights in the shape of pink poodles, Siamese cats and flying ducks.

Avoid chipped or cracked examples, especially when these defects detract from the lamp's visual appeal. When using a lamp make sure it is wired properly. One common mistake is using a higher wattage bulb than the lamp's sepcification. This causes the singe marks sometimes seen on shade screens and cracks around the lighting fixtures of many lamps. Low-wattage low-heat bulbs are recommended. For futher reading we recommend *Turned On: Decorative Lamps of the 'Fifties* by Leyland and Crystal Payton, Abbeville Press, NY, 1989.

Gazelle, green and white, Royal Haeger, 10.5" x 13.5", $72 at auction. —Photo courtesy Collectors Auction Services.

	LOW	HIGH
Blue Birds, double, plaster tray, Lane, 11" x 13"	$50	$75
Chinese Figures, pierced gold fixtures, 13" h, pair	90	130
Chinoiserie Double Planter, green, brass surround, 7.5" x 11"	18	24
Conch Shell, pink w/ white and gold, Premco, 11" h	35	55
Cougars, double, brown and cream, 8" x 11"	30	40
Cowboy Horse, red fiberglass conical shade, 11" x 11"	25	35
Criss-Cross Sides, green shade insert, 7" x 12.5"	60	90
Dancer, leaping, gold and black plaster, 13" x 15"	40	60
Deer, porcelain w/ plaster tray, 13" x 13.5"	50	70
Deer, running, green w/ leaf and vine, 5" x 10"	15	20
Doves, white and gold, Royal Fleet Company	20	30
Farm Scene, vinyl, cylindrical, pierced gold metal base, 11.5" h	15	20
Fawn, white w/ pink planter, Electrolite, 8" h	25	35
Fish, double, gray and maroon	50	70
Flower in Basket, green, 9" h	25	35
Galleon, multicolor 9.5" x 12"	45	55
Galleon Clock/Lamp, wooden, Gilbrator Precision, 18" x 13"	30	45
Gazelle, leaping, black, swirling base, 11" x 16"	45	65
Gazelles, leaping twins, planter, swirl plume base, 11" x 14"	35	65

Sampan, brown w/ gold highlights, Premco Mfg., 7" x 16", $35–$45.

	LOW	HIGH
Horse, porcelain, on plaster rocky bluff base, Lane, 11" x 13.5"	30	40
Horse, black, 5.5" x 10.5"	20	30
Horse, on rocky plateau, white, 13" h	35	45
Horse Head, brown, 14.5" h	25	35
Horse Head, knight style, gray, coutout eyes, 14" h	45	55
Leaf Form, 5" x 12"	25	35
Leaf, green, triple frond, 5" x 13.5"	25	35
Leopard in Forest, green screen, 9" h	35	45
Mallard in Flight, planter surround, 11.5" x 14.5"	35	50
Mare and Colt, brown, 8.5" x 11"	30	40
Mare and Colt, gray, 9.5" x 10"	35	45
Mermaid, deep sea background, 7.5" x 9.5"	100	150
Owl, cutout eyes, mkd. "Kron, Texans Inc.," 12" h	80	100
Owl, whimsical, Maddux	25	35
Panther, black planter, 22" l	25	45
Panther, black w/ rhinestone eyes, 22" l	25	45
Panther, brown planter, 22" l	25	45
Panther, cutout eyes, lime green, Royal Haeger, 20" l	35	50
Panther, gray leaf and log base, 9" x 15"	30	50
Panther, pink and gray leaf and log base, 9" x 15"	45	55
Panther, plaster w/ green screen background, 8.5" x 17"	45	65
Panther, small, black w/ gold accents, 15" l	25	30
Panther, small, green, 5" x 11"	20	30
Panther, small, pink, 6" x 9"	25	35
Panther, white screen, oval base, Royal Haeger	40	60
Pierced Metal, black, inner shade and wire legs, 13" h	12	18
Plastic Surround Landscape, 10" h	12	18
Poodles, double, pink, 10" x 13"	100	150
Rooster, crowing, maroon, 10" h	25	35
Sailboat Planter, gray waves base, 11" h	30	40
Sampan, w/ Asian couple, green, gold highlights, 6" x 16"	35	45
Ship, green stylized wave base, 10" x 11"	30	40
Siamese Cats, coutout eyes, mkd. "Kron, Texans Inc.," 13" h	50	70
Stag, leaping, green, 11.5" x 10.5"	20	30
Stallion, running, black, yellow, and white highlights, 11" x 15"	40	60
Swan, small, pink w/ plastic rose, 10" h	10	15
Swan, white, blue water base, Maddux, 11" h	20	30
Television Set, stylized, metal, porthole w/ scene, 7" x 11"	30	40
Tree Trunk, stylized, brown, green, and white, 10" h	20	25
Tropical Leaves, Lane, 13.5" x 10.5"	50	70

Wall Pockets

	LOW	AVG.	HIGH
Acanthus Bracket, Abingdon, #589, 7"	$50	$60	$75
Acanthus Bracket, Abingdon, #649, 8.75"	40	55	65
Acanthus Wall Vase, Abingdon, #648, 8.75"	45	55	65
Basketweave, Catalina, 9.5"	215	225	235
Bird and Bamboo, Japan, 6.5"	20	24	28
Birdhouse, Shawnee, #830	15	20	25
Blackamoor, holding planter above head	150	160	175
Book, Abingdon, #676, 6.5"	55	70	80
Bow, gold highlights, Shawnee, #534, 3.5" h	15	20	25
Bucking Bronco, Brush	110	115	125
Butterfly, Abingdon, #601, 8.5"	30	40	48
Calla Lily, Abingdon, #586, 9"	32	38	45
Camellia, Hull, #125, 8.5"	245	270	300
Carriage Lamp, Abingdon, #711, 10"	55	65	70
Cherub, Abingdon, #587, 7.5"	60	70	80
Cookbook, Abingdon, #676	55	60	68
Cup and Saucer, Hull, Bow-Knot, #B24	100	115	125
Cup and Saucer, Hull, Sunglow, #80	38	40	45
Daisy, Abingdon, #379, 7.75"	50	60	70
Dutch Boy Planter, Abingdon, #489, 10"	80	90	100
Dutch Girl Planter, #490, 10"	80	90	100
Dog in Cup, 5" h	12	15	18
Female Mask, Abingdon, #376F, 7.5"	115	120	130
Fish, green and yellow, 8" h	30	40	50
Girl w/ Rag Doll, Shawnee, #810	18	24	30
Grape Vine, Royal Haeger, #745	20	25	28
Ionic, Abingdon, #457, 9"	55	65	70
Iron, Hull, Sunglow	40	48	55
Ivy Basket, Abingdon, #590, 7"	90	95	100
Leaf, Abingdon, #724	50	65	75
Little Jack Horner, Shawnee, #585	20	25	30
Male Mask, Abingdon, #376M, 7.5"	115	120	130
Mantel Clock, Shawnee, #530	20	25	30
Match Box, Abingdon, #675, 5.5"	35	45	55
Morning Glory, Abingdon, #377, 7.5"	20	25	30
Morning Glory, double, Abingdon, #375, 6.5"	30	35	40
Pear and Apple, Lefton, #3850, 7.25"	10	12	15
Pitcher, Hull, Bow-Knot, #B26	90	100	110
Pitcher, Hull, Sunglow, #81	30	35	40
Poppy, Hull, #609, 9"	240	250	265
Rocking Horse, Royal Haeger, #724	18	20	25
Rosecraft Vintage, brown w/ fruit and grapevines, Roseville	90	120	150
Rosella, Hull, #R10	60	65	70
Scoop, embossed flowers, Camark, #N45	18	20	25
Shell, Abingdon, #508, 7"	40	48	55
Telephone, Shawnee, #529	22	25	30
Whisk Broom, Hull, Bow-Knot, #B27	90	100	115
Whisk Broom, Hull, Sunglow, #82	35	38	40
Woodland Glossy, Hull, 7.5"	48	55	60
Woodland Matte, Hull, 7.5"	95	110	120
Woodpecker and Tree Stump, American Art Pottery	12	15	18

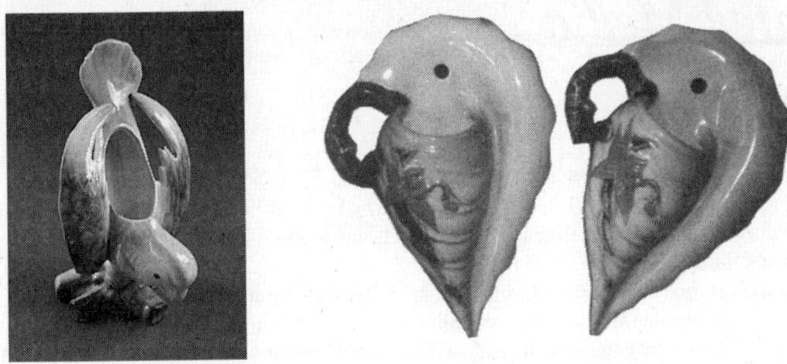

Left to right: Cockatiel, green body, yellow, purple, and burgundy highlights, Morton, 8", $20–$25. —Photo courtesy Ray Morykan Auctions; Conch Shells, Woodland, Hull, #W-13, 7.5", pair, $121 at auction. —Photo courtesy Collectors Auction Services.

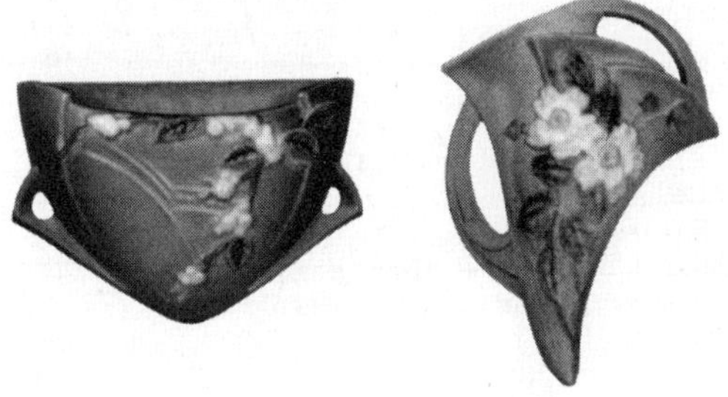

Left to right: Snowberry, Roseville, #1WP-8, 8", $80–$100; White Rose, Roseville, #1289-8, 8.5", $150–$175. —Photo courtesy Gene Harris Antique Auction Center.

Left to right: Embossed Bird and Flower, Italy, 8", pair, $18–$25; Right: Floral, blue luster band, Japan, 5.5", $35–$45. —Photo courtesy Ray Morykan Auctions.

Printed Media

Bibles

Johann Gutenberg printed the first typeset Bible in 1455. Since then, the Bible has been reprinted more than any other book. Some collectors buy only rare Bibles of the fifteenth and sixteenth centuries. Others specialize in miniature Bibles (12mo, 24mo or 32mo), or Bibles translated into exotic languages.

Almost everyone has an old family Bible, but most nineteenth-century examples are worth about $50; most eighteenth-century examples are worth around $100. However, there are many valuable Bibles. For an extensive listing of Bibles sold at auction consult *American Book Prices Current,* edited by Katherine and Daniel Leab, at American Book Prices Current, Box 1236, Washingon, CT 06793.

	AUCTION	RETAIL	
		Low	High
1649: London, Companie of Stationers, (Eng.)	$175	$300	$400
1657: Cambr., John Field, 16mo, (Eng.)	100	170	230
1696: New Test. of Our Lord, Oxford Univ., 12mo, (Eng.)	130	230	300
1715: Oxford, John Baskett, (Eng.)	100	170	250
1716: Edin., James Watson, 12 mo, (Eng.)	100	170	250
1736: Nuremberg, Endters, (German)	170	300	400
1791: Dublin, 2 vols., (Eng.)	600	1000	1400
1791: The Holy Bible, Phila., W. Young, 2 vols., 12mo, (Eng.)	3400	6000	8000
1791: Trenton, Isaac Collins, (Eng.)	150	260	350
1792: NY, T. Allen, (Eng.))	275	500	640
1795: Holy Bible Abridged, Bost., S. Hall, 32mo, (Eng.)	300	500	900
1796: Curious Hieroglyphick Bible for the Amusement of Youth, London, R. Bassam, 12mo, (Eng.)	160	280	375
1800: London, T. Macklin, 6 vols., (Eng.)	500	890	1100
1836: [New Test.] London, S. Bagster, (Eng.)	200	350	475
1837: [New Test.] London, S. Bagster, (Eng.)	750	1335	1770
1846: The Illuminated Bible, NY, (Eng.)	200	355	475
1848: London, W. Pickering, trans. by J. Wycliffe, (Eng.)	400	710	900
1856; Genesi, Park Hill, OK, Mission Press, (Cherokee)	200	350	470
1856; Iu Otoshki, New Test., trns. into Ojibwa, NY, 8vo	120	200	280
1866: Tours, illus. by G. Dore, 2 vols., (French)	130	200	300
1876: Hartford, trans. by J.E. Smith, (Eng.)	50	80	100
[1900]: London, Grolier Soc., 1 of 1000, 14 vols., (Eng.)	80	140	180
1910–11: London, Ballantyne Press, 1 of 750, 3 vols., (Eng.)	225	400	530
[1934–36]: New Test., London, illus. by E. Gill, 4 vols., (Eng.)	350	600	825
[1934]: Bost., R.H. Hinkley, 1 of 488, 14 vols., (Eng.)	200	350	470
1941: [New Test.], NJ, St. Anthony Guild, 1 of 1000, (Eng.)	120	210	280
1949: Cleveland, 1 of 975, designed by B. Rogers, (Eng.)	400	710	950
1959: NY, Abradale Press, (Eng.)	70	125	165
1961: Paterson and NY, Pageant Books, 1 of 1000, 2 vols., facsimile of Gutenberg Bible, (Latin)	1500	2670	3500
1965: Cleveland, World Publishing Co., facsimile of 1st Ed. of King James version, 1611, (Eng.)	340	600	800
1970: Jerusalem Bible, Garden City, illus. by S. Dali, (Eng.)	65	115	150
1974: Leaf from 1st Ed. of Coverdale Bible, 1535, San Francisco, Book Club of Calif., 1 of 425, 4to	200	355	470

Books

Classic Books

Books were first printed around 1450, although handwritten books date back thousands of years. Many book collectors limit themselves to one or two favorite writers or a favorite subject, since the field of book collecting is vast. A collection is judged on quality rather than quantity. Books with water damage, broken bindings, or missing pages are usually worth almost nothing.

For an extensive listing of books sold at auction consult *American Book Prices Current,* edited by Katherine and Daniel Leab, at American Book Prices Current, Box 1236, Washington, CT 06793. For information on books traded at many flea markets, consult *The Official Price Guide to Old Books,* by Marie Tedford and Pat Goudey, House of Collectibles, Random House, NY.

Values quoted are for First Editions (F), Leather-bound copies (L), Limited Edition Club copies (LEC), Heritage Press copies (HP), and Cloth-bound copies (C).

	F	L	LEC	HP	C
Adams, H., *Education of Henry Adams*	$3800	$27	$75	$13	$11
Aeschylus, *Oresteia*	—	18	45	9	8
Aesop, *Fable*	—	45	100	16	14
Allen, Hervey, *Anthony Adverse*	550	25	55	10	8
Aristotle, *Politics and Poetics*	—	29	75	13	11
Bacon, Francis, *Essays or Counsels...*	5500	25	55	10	8
Balzac, Honore de, *Droll Stories*	—	35	90	13	10
Baudelaire, Charles, *Flowers of Evil*	—	27	70	12	10
Bellamy, Edward, *Looking Backward*	330	25	65	10	7
Benet, Stephen V., *John Brown's Body*	340	40	100	14	12
Bierce, Ambrose, *Devil's Dictionary*	—	23	70	11	8
Blake, William, *Poems*	—	29	75	13	10
Boccaccio, Giovanni, *Decameron*	—	25	65	11	8
Boswell, James, *Life of Samuel Johnson*	4000	40	100	14	12
Bradbury, Ray, *Fahrenheit 451*	300	40	100	14	11
Bradbury, Ray, *Martian Chronicles*	750	50	120	17	13
Brecht, Bertolt, *Threepenny Opera*	—	25	65	11	8
Browning, E. *Sonnets From the Portuguese*	—	35	80	15	12
Browning, Robert, *Ring and the Book*	200	25	50	8	6
Bryant, William Cullen, *Poems*	6500	25	65	10	7
Bunyan, John, *Pilgrim's Progress*	—	30	80	15	12
Burns, Robert, Poems	5000	22	50	8	6
Butler, Samuel, *Ereshon*	—	32	80	15	12
Caesar, Julius, *Gallic Wars*	—	35	80	14	11
Camus, Albert, *The Stranger*	—	37	90	13	10
Casanova, Giacomo, *Memoirs*	—	30	70	12	10
Cellini, Benvenuto, *Life of Benvenuto Cellini*	—	36	90	13	10
Cervantes, Miguel de, *Don Quixote*	—	32	80	14	11
Chaucer, Geoffrey, *Canterbury Tales*	—	35	85	15	12
Cicero, Marcus Tullius, *Orations and Essays*	—	16	50	8	6
Clemens, Samuel, *Huckleberry Finn*	1350	45	100	14	12
Clemens, Samuel, *Life on the Mississippi*	480	50	170	18	14
Clemens, Samuel, *Prince and the Pauper*	—	35	90	12	10
Clemens, Samuel, *Puddin-head Wilson*	550	30	70	12	10
Clemens, Samuel, *Roughing It*	450	30	75	13	10
Clemens, Samuel, *Tom Sawyer*	4500	55	170	18	14
Colette, Sidonie, *Break of Day*	—	25	70	11	8

	F	L	LEC	HP	C
Collier, John Payne, *Punch and Judy*	1500	35	90	13	10
Collins, Wilkie, *Woman in White*	3850	20	50	8	6
Confucius, *Sayings*	—	32	75	13	10
Conrad, Joseph, *Nostromo*	350	29	65	11	8
Crane, Hart, *The Bridge*	2600	22	55	9	7
Crane, Stephen, *Red Badge of Courage*	3400	34	80	14	11
Dante Alighieri, *Divine Comedy*	—	25	70	12	10
Darwin, Charles, *Descent of Man*	—	30	80	15	12
Darwin, Charles, ...*Voyage of the* HMS Beagle	9500	35	90	12	10
Darwin, Charles, *On the Origin of Species*	16,000	50	130	17	13
De Quincey, T., *Confession of an... Opium-Eater*	—	25	70	11	8
Defoe, Daniel, *Moll Flanders*	—	18	55	9	7
Defoe, Daniel, *Robinson Crusoe*	9000	35	70	12	10
Diaz, Bernal, ...*Conquest of Mexico*	—	30	80	15	12
Dickens, Charles, *Chimes*	—	50	230	18	15
Dickens, Charles, *A Christmas Carol*	2600	20	50	9	7
Dickens, Charles, *Cricket on the Hearth*	350	37	90	13	10
Dickens, Charles, *Pickwick Papers* (book)	1600	35	85	15	12
Dickinson, Emily, *Poems*	3500	27	60	10	8
Dodgson, Charles, *Alice... in Wonderland*	4000	55	400	22	18
Dodgson, Charles, *Through the Looking Glass*	700	55	450	22	18
Donne, John, *Poems*	13,500	22	45	8	6
Dostoevsky, Fyodor, *Brothers Karamazov*	—	30	75	13	10
Dostoevsky, Fyodor, *Crime and Punishment*	—	25	55	10	7
Dostoevsky, Fyodor, *House of the Dead*	—	22	50	9	7
Dostoevsky, Fyodor, *Idiot*	—	25	60	10	7
Dostoevsky, Fyodor, *Possessed*	—	40	100	16	13
Doyle, A.C., *Adventures of Sherlock Holmes*	2600	35	85	15	12
Doyle, A.C., *Later Adventures of Sherlock Holmes*	—	25	55	10	7
Dreiser, Theodore, *An American Tragedy*	400	25	65	10	7
Dreiser, Theodore, *Sister Carrie*	—	35	90	13	10
Dumas, Alexandre, *Camille*	—	55	450	—	—
Dumas, Alexandre, *Count of Monte Cristo*	—	35	85	15	12
Emerson, Ralph Waldo, *Essays, 1st & 2nd Series*	2600	22	50	8	6
Erasmus, Desiderius, *In Praise of Folly*	—	25	65	11	8
Fielding, Henry, *History of Tom Jones*	3500	22	55	9	7
Fitzgerald, F. Scott, *Great Gatsby*	650	22	50	9	7
Flaubert, Gustave, *Madame Bovary*	—	22	50	9	7
Francis of Assisi, *Little Flowers*	—	25	65	11	8
Franklin, Benjamin, *Autobiography*	550	22	45	8	6
Frazer, James George, *Golden Bough*	300	25	60	10	7
Frost, Robert, *Complete Poems*	—	50	350	20	16
Garcia Marquez, Gabriel, *100 Years of Solitude*	—	25	65	11	8
Gibbon, E., ...*Fall of the Roman Empire,* 7 vols.	2700	100	220	30	30
Gilbert and Sullivan, *1st Night...*		40	100	14	11
Grahame, Kenneth, *Wind in the Willows*	2600	60	600	23	18
Grass, Gunter, *Flounder*	—	45	220	19	16
Graves, Robert, *Poems*	—	22	50	9	7
Grimm Brothers, *Fairy Tales,* (English 1823–26)	4000	38	85	14	11
Hardy, Thomas, *Far from the Madding Crowd*	1500	20	60	10	7
Hardy, Thomas, *Jude the Obscure*	625	26	80	13	10
Hardy, Thomas, *Tess of the D'Urbervilles*	—	30	80	15	12
Hawthorne, N., *House of the Seven Gables*	900	22	50	9	7
Hawthorne, N., *Scarlet Letter*	800	30	80	13	10

	F	L	LEC	HP	C
Hawthorne, N. *Twice-Told Tales*	—	23	70	11	8
Hemingway, E., *For Whom the Bell Tolls*	400	50	250	20	16
Hesse, Herman, *Steppenwolf*	—	25	50	10	7
Homer, *Iliad*	—	45	100	16	13
Homer, *Odyssey*	—	50	200	19	16
Hugo, Victor, *Battle of Waterloo*	—	20	45	8	6
Hugo, Victor, *Notre-Dame de Paris*	—	55	150	18	14
Hugo, Victor, *Toilers of the Sea*	—	25	55	10	7
Irving, Washington, *Alhambra*	200	22	50	9	7
Irving, Washington, *Rip Van Winkle*	300	27	60	10	8
James, Henry, *Portrait of a Lady*	1200	22	50	10	9
Joyce, James, *Dubliners*	2200	50	150	18	14
Joyce, James, *Ulysses*	7800	140	4000	50	40
Kafka, Franz, *Metamorphoses*	—	50	160	18	14
Keats, John, *Poems*	4000	22	50	9	7
Kingsley, Charles, *Westward Ho!*	400	22	45	8	7
Kipling, Rudyard, *Jungle Book*	1200	27	60	10	8
La Fontaine, Jean de, *Fables*	—	25	60	10	7
Le Sage, Alain-Rene, *Adventures of Gil Blas*	—	30	70	12	10
Lewis, Sinclair, *Main Street*	200	45	220	19	16
Lewis and Clark, *Journals*	8500	60	125	17	15
Livius, Titus, *History of Early Rome*	—	30	70	12	10
London, Jack, *Call of the Wild*	800	36	90	12	10
London, Jack, *White Fang*	350	22	45	8	6
Lytton, Edward, *Last Days of Pompeii*	385	25	55	10	7
Machiavelli, Niccolo, *The Prince*	—	25	55	10	8
Malory, Thomas, *Le Morte D'Arthur*	—	40	100	16	13
Mann, Thomas, *Magic Mountain*	—	30	75	13	10
Marlowe, Christopher, *Four Plays*	—	27	65	11	8
Marquez, Gabriel (see Garcia Marquez, Gabriel)					
Maugham, W.S., *Of Human Bondage*	200	55	410	21	17
Melville, Herman, *Moby Dick*	16,000	45	100	15	15
Melville, Herman, *Typee*	1350	32	80	14	11
Merimee, Prosper, *Carmen*	—	26	60	10	7
Miller, Arthur, *Death of a Salesman*	270	50	350	20	16
Milosz, Czeslaw, *Captive Mind*	—	22	50	9	7
Milton, John, *Masque of Comus*	—	28	80	14	11
Mitchell, M., *Gone With the Wind*	2200	30	80	15	12
Moliere, Jean, *Tartuffe*	—	16	50	8	6
More, Sir Thomas, *Utopia*	—	26	65	10	7
Mietzsche, F., *Thus Spake Zarathustra*	—	23	70	11	8
Nordhoff and Hall, *Mutiny on the Bounty*	450	30	80	15	12
Omar Khayyam, *Rubaiyat*	—	30	80	15	12
O'Neill, Eugene, *Ah, Wilderness!*	270	30	70	13	10
Ovid, *Metamorphoses*	—	40	100	14	11
Paine, Thomas, *Rights of Man*	—	27	65	11	8
Parkman, Francis, *Oregon Trail*	200	44	130	17	13
Paz, Octavio, *Three Poems*	—	51	3500	20	16
Pepys, Samuel, *Diary*	—	30	85	15	12
Plato, *Republic*	—	30	70	12	10
Plato, *Trial... of Socrates*	—	33	100	13	10
Poe, Edgar A., *Fall of the House of Usher*	—	50	260	19	16
Poe, Edgar A., *...Arthur Gordon Pym*	660	22	45	8	6
Poe, Edgar A., *Tales of Mystery...*	250	21	60	10	7

	F	L	LEC	HP	C
Polo, Marco, *Travels*	—	25	70	12	10
Porter, William, *Voice of the City...*	—	46	200	18	14
Prescott, William, ...*Conquest of Peru*	350	25	70	12	10
Proust, Marcel, *Swann's Way*	—	50	180	19	16
Pushkin, Aleksandr, *Golden Cockerel*	—	47	110	17	13
Rabelais, F., *Gargantua and Pantagruel*	—	35	85	15	12
Raspe, Rudolph, ...*Baron Munchausen*	—	30	70	13	10
Rimbaud, Arthur, *A Season in Hell*	—	76	1800	30	24
Rostand, Edmond, *Cyrano de Bergerac*	—	22	45	8	7
Scott, Sir Walter, *Ivanhoe*	570	16	50	8	7
Shakespeare, William, *Hamlet*	—	50	180	18	14
Shakespeare, William, *Poems and Sonnets*	—	55	170	18	14
Shelley, Mary, *Frankenstein*	—	30	75	13	10
Sheridan, Richard, *Rivals*	400	27	60	10	7
Sheridan, Richard, *School for Scandal*	—	21	65	10	7
Sienkiewicz, Henryk, *Quo Vadis?*	—	25	65	11	8
Sinclair, Upton, *The Jungle*	—	25	60	10	8
Singer, Isaac, *Gentleman From Cracow*	—	38	90	13	10
Singer, Isaac, *Magician of Lublin*	—	45	210	19	16
Spenser, Edmund, *Faerie Queene*	22,000	35	75	13	10
Steinbeck, John, *Grapes of Wrath*	1350	53	470	21	17
Steinbeck, John, *Of Mice and Men*	1000	25	50	9	8
Stephens, James, *Crock of Gold*	200	25	60	12	10
Sterne, Laurence, *Tristram Shandy*	6750	35	80	14	11
Sterne, Laurence, *A Sentimental Journey*	1100	30	85	15	12
Stevenson, R.L., *Child's Garden of Verses*	750	23	65	11	8
Stevenson, R.L., *Dr. Jekyll and Mr. Hyde*	1100	26	60	10	7
Stoker, Bram, *Dracula*	1850	25	60	10	7
Stowe, Harriet B., *Uncle Tom's Cabin*	2200	55	200	18	14
Swift, Jonathan, *Gulliver's Travels*	11,000	40	90	13	11
Tennyson, Alfred, *Idylls of the King*	—	30	70	12	10
Thackeray, William M., *Henry Esmond, Esq.*	650	22	45	8	6
Thackeray, William M., *The Newcomes*	200	25	55	10	7
Thackeray, William M., *Vanity Fair*	2800	35	50	15	12
Thoreau, Henry David, *Cape Cod*	550	24	65	10	7
Thoreau, Henry David, *Walden*	2600	50	375	18	16
Thucydides, *Peloponnesian War*	—	27	60	10	7
Tolstoy, Leo, *War and Peace*	—	50	110	16	13
Verne, Jules, *From the Earth*	—	24	60	10	8
Verne, Jules, *Mysterious Island*	—	47	110	17	13
Virgil, *Aeneid*	—	30	65	11	8
Virgil, *Georgics*	—	32	80	14	11
Voltaire, Francois, *Candide*	—	22	45	8	6
Wallace, Lew, *Ben-Hur*	—	22	45	8	6
Walton, I. and Cotton, C., *Compleat Angler*	—	55	150	18	16
Warren, Robert P., *All the King's Men*	—	45	110	16	13
Whitman, Walt, *Leaves of Grass*	16,000	60	600	22	18
Wilde, Oscar, *Lady Windemere's Fan*	400	23	50	9	8
Wilde, Oscar, *Picture of Dorian Gray*	—	33	80	14	11
Wilde, Oscar, *Salome*	1600	50	110	16	13
Wilder, Thornton, *Bridge of San Luis Rey*	525	30	75	13	10
Wilder, Thornton, *Our Town*	275	25	70	12	10
Williams, T., *A Streetcar Named Desire*	—	50	140	17	14
Wister, Owen, *The Virginian*	—	22	50	9	7

Little Golden Books

The first twelve Little Golden Books® titles produced in 1942 sold for the bargain price of 25¢ apiece. Early books have a dust jacket and blue spine. Many titles were reprinted for years. Some books give the date and printing up front. More often the book has a code on the lower portion of the last page squeezed next to the back cover. "A" refers to a first printing, "B" to a second, and so on. Prime condition "A" printings command the highest prices. Collectors are a little more willing to accept a later printing on rare or early titles. *A Poky Little Puppy®* from the 1970s will command a fraction of the price of a first printing. Currently titles based on television series are very popular. Books with dolls, puzzles, and games are difficult to find intact; complete examples are worth several times the value of incomplete examples.

Several Little Golden Book series have been included in the listing. In the No. column, book numbers preceded by "A" are from the Little Golden Activity series; "D" is for Disney; "Din" is for Ding Dong School; and, four-digit numbers beginning with "5" indicate books from the Giant Little Golden Book series. The prices quoted are for first printings in excellent condition showing minimal wear on the covers and pages.

Our consultant for this area is Rebecca Greason, owner of Rebecca of SunnyBook Farm, author of *Tomart's Price Guide to Little Golden Books,* Tomart Publications, Dayton, OH, 1991, and editor of *The Gold Mine Review,* PO Box 209, Hershey, PA 17033. She is listed in the back of this book.

	YEAR	NO.	LOW	HIGH
ABC Around the House, w/ spin dial	1957	A18	$15	$35
Aladdin and His Magic Lamp	1959	371	7	12
Albert's Stencil Zoo, punched	1951	112	20	30
Albert's Stencil Zoo, unpunched	1951	112	50	60
Ali Baba	1958	323	10	15
All Aboard	1952	152	18	22
Alphabet from A to Z, 42 pgs., w/ dust jacket	1942	3	45	120
Alphabet from A to Z, 42 pgs., wo/ dust jacket	1942	3	10	20
Animal Stories	1957	5006	8	12
Annie Oakley and the Rustlers	1955	221	15	25
Baby Listens, Eloise Wilkin	1960	383	15	45
Baby Looks, Eloise Wildin	1960	404	20	50
Baby's House, w/ puzzle	1950	80	35	130
Baby's House, wo/ puzzle	1950	80	7	12

Left to right: Captain Kangaroo and the Panda, *1951, #278, $12–$18;* Dennis the Menace and Ruff, *1959, #386, $10–$15.*

Left to right: The Flintstones, *1961, #450, $15–$20;* Goofy, Movie Star, *1956, D52, $18–$25.*

	YEAR	NO.	LOW	HIGH
Benji, Fastest Dog in the West	1978	165	8	12
Birds	1958	5011	18	25
Bobby the Dog	1961	440	18	26
Bow Wow! Meow!	1963	523	15	20
Brave Cowboy Bill, w/ puzzle	1950	93	70	120
Brave Cowboy Bill, wo/ puzzle	1950	93	12	18
Buffalo Bill, Jr.	1956	254	12	20
Bugs Bunny Gets a Job	1952	136	15	20
Bullwinkle	1962	462	18	22
Busy Timmy, Eloise Wilkin	1948	50	18	24
Captain Kangaroo	1956	261	10	18
Cars	1956	251	9	18
Cars and Trucks	1959	366	10	15
Cave Kids	1963	539	15	18
Charmin' Chatty	1964	554	18	24
Chitty Chitty Bang Bang	1968	581	12	18
Christmas ABC, Eloise Wilkin	1962	478	24	30
Christmas in the Country	1950	95	12	15
Christopher and the Columbus	1951	103	12	18
Cinderella	1950	D13	18	24
Cinderella's Friends	1950	D17	18	24
Circus Time, w/ dial	1955	A2	18	35
Color Kittens	1949	86	18	25
Come Play House, Eloise Wilkin	1948	44	12	20
Cowboys and Indians	1958	5019	20	30
Daddies	1953	187	8	16
Dale Evans and the Coyote	1956	253	20	30
Danny Beaver's Secret	1953	160	8	14
Davy Crockett's Keelboat Race	1955	D47	25	35
Day at the Beach	1951	110	30	35
Dick Tracy	1962	497	25	30
Disneyland on the Air	9155	D43	12	28
Doctor Dan at the Circus, w/ Band-Aids	1960	399	90	150
Doctor Dan at the Circus, wo/ Band-Aids	1960	399	16	20
Donald Duck in Disneyland	1955	D44	15	20
Donald Duck Prize Driver	1956	D49	15	20

Left to right: Howdy Doody and Santa Claus, *1955, #237, $18–$25;* Lassie and the Lost Explorer, *1958, #343, $15–$20.*

	YEAR	NO.	LOW	HIGH
Dumbo, w/ dust jacket	1942	D3	90	150
Dumbo, wo/ dust jacket	1942	D3	30	40
Emerald City of Oz	1952	151	12	30
Five Little Firemen	1949	301	14	18
Fix It, Please, Eloise Wilkin	1947	32	18	48
Flintstones	1961	450	15	20
Fly High	1971	597	9	15
Four Puppies	1960	405	9	12
Gaston and Josephine	1958	65	18	30
Gay Purree	1962	488	7	18
Gene Autry	1955	230	20	30
Giant With Three Golden Hairs	1955	219	15	20
Ginger Paper Doll, uncut	1957	A32	65	110
Gingerbread Shop	1952	126	14	18
Golden Egg Book	1962	456	6	12
Grandpa Bunny	1951	D21	20	35
Gunsmoke	1958	320	25	35
Hansel and Gretel	1954	217	8	12
Happy Birthday, uncut	1949	384	24	40
Happy Family, The, Elliott illus.	1947	35	7	16
Happy Family, The, Malvern illus.	1955	216	15	30
Hey There, It's Yogi Bear	1964	542	18	24
Hi Ho! Three In a Row, Eloise Wilkin	1954	188	25	35
Howdy Doody and Mr. Bluster	1954	204	12	32
Howdy Doody's Animal Friends	1956	252	25	30
I Have a Secret	1962	495	6	14
J. Fred Muggs	1955	234	12	18
Jamie Looks, Eloise Wilkin	1963	522	30	40
Jenny's New Brother	1970	596	25	50
Jetsons	1962	500	20	30
Kitten's Surprise, The	1951	107	9	18
Lassie and Her Day in the Sun	1958	307	12	18
Leave It to Beaver	1959	347	20	25
Let's Go Shopping	1948	33	5	14
Life and Legend of Wyatt Earp	1958	315	10	28
Little Black Sambo, 42 pgs.	1948	57	85	135

	YEAR	NO.	LOW	HIGH
Little Boy With a Big Horn	1950	100	10	15
Little Engine That Could	1954	548	4	15
Little Eskimo	1952	155	12	15
Little Fat Policeman	1950	91	14	18
Little Golden Book of Uncle Wiggly	1954	148	15	18
Little Golden Holiday Book, Eloise Wilkin	1951	109	18	26
Little Indian	1954	202	10	15
Little Man of Disneyland	1955	D46	10	14
Lone Ranger and the Talking Pony	1958	310	30	40
Lucky Mrs. Ticklefeather	1951	122	18	24
Lucky Puppy	1960	D89	15	20
Lucky Rabbit	1955	Din7	10	14
Mad Hatter's Tea Party	1951	D23	20	30
Madeline	1954	186	15	25
Magic Compass, The, Mary Poppins	1953	146	8	18
Make Way For the Thruway	1961	439	12	18
Marvelous Merry Go Round	1950	87	8	12
Maverick	1959	354	18	24
Mickey Mouse and His Space Ship	1952	D29	20	30
Mickey Mouse Christmas Shopping	1953	D33	20	25
Mister Ed the Talking Horse	1962	483	20	25
More Mother Goose Rhymes	1958	317	12	18
Mr. Noah and His Family	1948	49	7	16
My Baby Sister	1958	340	12	20
My Christmas Treasury, 72 pgs.	1957	5003	12	20
My First Book of Bible Stories, w/ dust jacket	1943	19	45	135
My Kitten, Eloise Wilkin	1953	528	10	24
My Magic Slate Book, intact w/ pencil	1959	5025	45	90
Name For Kitty, A	1948	55	8	14
New Baby, Eloise Wilkin, w/ pink title	1948	412	20	45
New Brother, New Sister	1966	564	14	18
New Kittens	1957	302	9	14
Noises and Mr. Flibberty Jib, Eloise Wilkin	1947	290	20	25
Nurse Nancy, yellow cover, w/ Band-Aids	1952	154	45	160

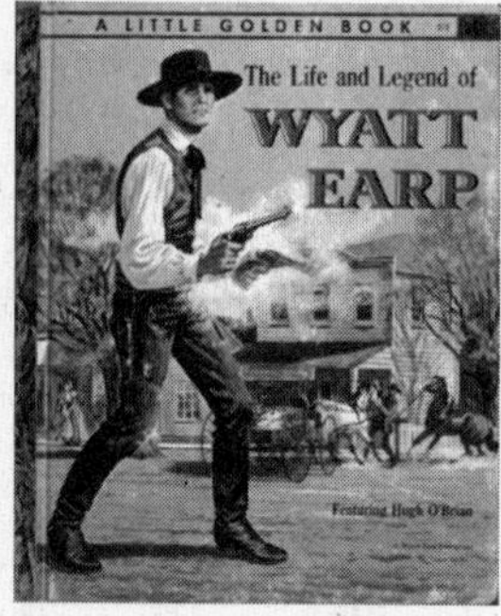

Left to right: The Life and Legend of Wyatt Earp, *1958, #315, $10–$28;* The Little Golden Book of Words, *1948, #45, $12–$15.*

Left to right: Steve Canyon, *1959, #356, $18–$24;* Supercar, *1962, #492, $25–$35.*

	YEAR	NO.	LOW	HIGH
Nurse Nancy, yellow cover, wo/ Band-Aids	1952	154	15	30
Nursery Rhymes	1948	59	14	18
Off to School	1958	5015	18	30
Once Upon a Wintertime	1948	D12	18	22
Ookpik, the Arctic Owl	1968	579	12	15
Open Up My Suitcase	1954	207	9	16
Our Puppy	1948	56	7	14
Our World	1955	242	8	12
Out of My Window	1955	245	15	20
Pantaloon	1951	114	18	24
Pebbles Flintstone	1963	531	9	28
Pepper Plays Nurse	1964	555	7	14
Peter Pan and the Pirates	1952	D25	18	30
Pinocchio	1948	D8	20	30
Play Street	1962	484	18	24
Poky Little Puppy, w/ dust jacket	1942	8	100	180
Poky Little Puppy, wo/ dust jacket	1942	8	50	75
Prayers for Children, Eloise Wilkin	1952	205	8	10
Puss in Boots	1953	137	9	15
Quick Draw McGraw	1960	398	14	18
Raggedy Ann and Andy Help Santa	1979	156	7	10
Rags	1970	586	5	12
Rin Tin Tin and Rusty	1955	246	18	22
Rocky and His Friends, campfire cover	1960	408	8	18
Rocky and His Friends, portrait cover	1960	408	9	20
Ronald McDonald and the Talking Plant	1984	—	18	24
Rootie Kazootie, Detective	1953	150	25	35
Rootie Kazootie Joins the Circus	1955	226	38	36
Roy Rogers and the Mountain Lion	1955	231	24	32
Roy Rogers and the New Cowboy	1953	177	18	25
Saggy Baggy Elephant	1947	385	12	16
Santa's Toy Shop	1950	D16	8	14
Scuffy the Tugboat	1946	30	20	30
Seven Sneezes, The	1948	51	9	18
Sleeping Beauty Paper Doll, uncut	1959	A33	90	140
Smokey and His Animal Friends	1960	387	14	18
Smokey the Bear and the Campers	1961	423	14	18

	YEAR	NO.	LOW	HIGH
Snow White and Rose Red	1955	228	15	18
Steve Canyon	1959	356	18	24
Supercar	1962	492	25	35
Tales of Wells Fargo	1958	328	9	22
Taxi That Hurried	1946	25	20	30
This Little Piggy, w/ dust jacket	1942	12	65	120
This Little Piggy, wo/ dust jacket	1942	12	10	30
Tin Woodman of Oz	1952	159	20	30
Tom and Jerry	1951	117	12	18
Tootle	1945	21	15	20
Touché Turtle	1962	474	20	30
Twelve Days of Christmas	1963	526	8	12
Two Little Gardeners	1951	108	10	15
Ugly Duckling	1952	D22	15	20
Ukelele and Her New Doll, w/ puzzle	1951	102	90	150
Ukelele and Her New Doll, wo/ puzzle	1951	102	18	25
Uncle Remus, Disney	1947	D6	15	30
Up in the Attic	1948	53	15	20
Visit to the Children's Zoo (Central Park, NYC)	1963	511	6	12
Wacky Witch	1973	416	4	10
Wagon Train	1958	326	25	30
Waltons, Birthday Present	1975	134	7	10
We Help Daddy	1962	468	12	20
We Help Mommy	1959	352	12	18
When I Grow Up, w/ puzzle	1950	96	60	140
When I Grow Up, wo/ puzzle	1950	96	12	20
Where Is the Bear?	1967	568	8	10
Whistling Wizard, Bill Baird	1953	132	10	18
Wiggles, Eloise Wilkin	1953	166	12	38
Winky Dink	1956	266	18	22
Wonders of Nature	1957	293	9	16
Words, w/ spin dial	1955	A1	15	30
Yanky Doodle and Chopper	1962	449	9	18
Zorro	1958	D68	20	25

Left to right: This World Of Ours, *1959, #5026, Eloise Wilkin, $20–$28;* Through the Picture Frame, *1944, #D1, $25–$32.*

Comic Books

Comic book collecting enjoys a huge following. Collectors have actively pursued this area for years but it gained prominence in the early 1990s. There is an endless number of characters and new, exciting books appear each day. The selection below covers a tiny area of the comic book world and concentrates on early, well-known characters. Because comic books (especially early ones) are fragile, condition is crucial to determining value. Grading a comic book is both an art and a science. We suggest you consult the *Overstreet* guide cited below. We list two ranges of prices. The first is loosely described as average condition (what collectors generally refer to as very good). This means the book is intact but shows wear, the color of the paper may be brownish and there may be minor inside creases or a small tear or two. Our second range is superior, although not near mint; it is what collectors consider fine condition. Near mint and, where available, mint condition books bring considerably more than the values listed below. There are reissues of many books, and some bear a striking resemblance to the original but command only a fraction of the original's price. As in any collecting area, do your homework.

The following listings are organized by publisher with the subhead being the name and date of the series. Individual entries begin with the issue number. For more information and extensive listings, refer to *The Overstreet Comic Book Price Guide,* Robert M. Overstreet, Confident Collector, New York, 1995.

D–C / National Periodical Publication

ACTION (1938)	VERY GOOD	FINE
1, no number, Superman, origin retold	$10,000–$15,000	$30,000–$50,000
7, Superman (Pep Morgan, Scoop Scanlon), Adventures of Marco Polo, Superman on cover	400–500	800–1200
14, Superman vs. Ultra (Pep Morgna, Chuck Dawson, Clip Carson), Adventures of Marco Polo, Zatara on cover	300–500	800–1000
17, Superman vs. Ultra, last installment of Adventures of Marco Polo, Superman on cover	300–400	500–800
18, Three Aces, begins	200–300	500–800
19, Superman vs. Ultra (Chuck Dawson, Clip Carson, Three Aces), Superman on cover	200–300	500–800
20, Superman vs. Ultra	200–300	500–800
22, Last Chuck Dawson, had appeared continuously from #1	200–300	500–800
23, Superman vs. Luthor, Luthor shown w/ red hair initially, first appearance of The Black Pirate. Created by Sheldon Moldoff, this short-lived series ran for only 19 issues and was never regarded as a major feature, but it was superbly illustrated	300–400	500–600
24, Flag Cover	250–350	500–700
33, Mr. America, origin, created by artist Bernard Bailey	150–250	300–400
37, Superman Charged with Violation of Law, first appearance of Congo Bill, created by Whitney Ellsworth, first appeared as minor feature in D-C's More Fun comics for 11 issues. One month later, Action comics introduced a new series of Congo Bill in which he became a movie star. The movie serial turned out to be one of the better ones of the 1940s	120–180	200–300
42, Origin of The Vigilante, last Black Pirate, Mr. America uses his cape as a flying carpet fo the first time. Vigilante soon became one of D-C's star attractions and he headlined their new entry, Leading Comics, which began as a quarterly publication in January 1942	100–175	200–300
43, The Vigilante vs. The Shade (Billy Gunn)	100–175	200–300

	VERY GOOD	FINE
45, The Vigilante, first appearance of Stuff, the Chinatown Kid	100–175	200–300
46, The Vigilante vs. Rainbow Man	100–175	200–300
51, Superman vs. The Prankster (first appearance)	100–150	200–300
52, Origin of Americommando, cover features montage w/ Superman, Zatara, Congo Bill and The Vigilante	100–150	200–300
56, Americommando vs. Dr. Ito	90–110	150–200
60, Lois Lane, Superwoman	90–110	150–200
64, Superman vs. The Toyman (first appearance)	90–120	150–200
68, Lois Lane, niece Susie is introduced	90–120	220–280

BATMAN (1940)

	VERY GOOD	FINE
1, Origin Retold	$4000–6000	$15,000–25,000
2, The Crime Master (Adam Lamb), The Case of the Missing Link (Hackett and Snead, Professor Drake)	1000–1500	2000–3000
3, The Ugliest Man in the World (Carlson, Ugly Horde, Detective McGonicle), The Crime School for Boys (Big Boy Daniels), Batman vs. the Cat Woman, first appearance of Cat Woman in costume, cover: Batman and Robin running toward reader w/ capes flying	600–800	1000–2000
4, More Whirlwind Adventures of Batman and Robin, Blackbeard's Crew and the Yacht Society (Thatch), cover: Batman climbing rope ladder	500–700	1000–1500
5, The Case of the Honest Crook (Smiley Sikes), The Riddle of the Missing Card (Queenie), Diamond Jack Deegan (Clumbsy), cover: Batman weighs fugitives on "scales of justice." Last issue published quarterly, switches to 6 issues per year 2/ #6	500–700	1000–1500
6, Suicide Beat (Jimmy Kelly, Fancy Dan, Alderman Skigg)	500–600	800–1000
7, The Trouble Trap (Linda Page, Commissioner Gordon), The People vs. the Batman (Horatio Delmar, Weasel Venner, Freddie Hill)	550–650	800–1000

D.C. Comics, Batman No. 1, Spring 1940.

	VERY GOOD	FINE
8, The Strange Case of Professor Radium (Professor Rose), Stone Walls Do Not a Prison Make, The Superstition Murders (Johnny Glim), The Cross-Country Crimes (Namtab/Batman)	500–600	800–1000
9, The Case of the Lucky Law Breaker, The White Whale (Capt. Burly, Bob Cratchit, Timmy Cratchit)	500–600	800–1000
10, Sheriff of Ghost Town (Five Aces Frogel), Report Card Blues (Tommy Trent)	550–600	800–1000
11, Four Birds of a Feather (Buzzard Benny, Joe Crow, Canary, The Penguin), Payment in Full (Joe Dolan)	500–600	900–1200
12, The Wizard of Words (The Joker), They Thrill to Conquer (Joe Kirk)	400–500	600–800
13, The Story of the 17 Stones (Rocky Grimes), Comedy of Tears (The Joker)	400–450	600–800
14, Prescription for Happiness (Pills Mattson), Swastika Over the White House (Count Felix, Fitz Hoffner), The Case Batman Failed to Solve	475–525	700–1000
15, Your Face Is Your Fortune (Elva Barr), The Loneliest Man in the World (Kirk Dagner, Tom Wick), The Boy Who Wanted to be Robin (Knuckles Conger, Bobby Deen)	350–550	700–900
16, Grade-A Crime (Winthrop, character without first name), Here Comes Alfred, Adventures of the Branded Tree (Squidge, character without first name), The Joker Reforms (Joe Kerswag)	200–300	500–600
17, Adventure of the Vitamin Vandals (Archie Gibbons), The Penguin Goes a-Hunting, Rogues Pageant (Alfred the Butler)	150–250	400–600
18, The Secret of the Hunter's Inn (Alfred the Butler, Tweed Cousins), first appearance of Police Stories	150–250	400–600
19, Collector of Millionaires (Ali, Ali's Health Resort), The Case of the Timid Lion (the Joker), Atlantis Goes to War (Emperor Taro, Empress Lanya)	150–250	400–600
20, The Centuries of Crime (Ecla Tate, Swami Meera Kell, The Joker), Bruce Wayne Loses the Guardianship of Dick Grayson (Alfred the Butler, Fatso Foley), The Trial of Titus Keyes (Slick Fingers/George Collins)	150–250	400–600
21, Batman and Robin Whoop It Up in Four Whirlwind Action Stories, The Streamlined Rustlers (Brule, character without first name), His Lordship's Double (Lord Hurley Burleigh, C.L.J. Carruthers), The Three Eccentrics (The Penguin), Blitzkrieg Bandits (Chopper Gant, Hannibal B. Brown)	150–250	350–450
47, Special! The Peril-Packed Inside Story of the Origin of Batman (retold), The Chain Gang Crimes (Warden Beltt, Whiskers Mob), cover: Batman as a boy reading *Gotham Gazette* w/ headline "Socialite Thomas Wayne Slain by Mystery Killer!" Thomas Wayne was Batman's father. The *Gotham Gazette* neglected to mention that Batman's mother was killed at the same time	250–350	700–900
48, The Thousand Secrets of the Batcave (Wolf Brando), Fowls of Fate (the Penguin), Crime from Tomorrow (Morton, character without first name)	120–160	200–300
49, Scoop of the Century (Jervis Tetch, Vicki Vale), Batman's Arabian Nights (The Crier, Professor Carter Nichols, The Joker)	180–220	300–400
50, The Second Boy Wonder (Waxey Wilson), Lights-Camera-Crime (Vicki Vale, Stilts Tyler, Tom Macon)	100–150	200–300

	VERY GOOD	FINE
51, The Stars of Yesterday (Rufus Lane), Pee-Wee the Talking Penguin, The Wonderful Mr. Wimble (Warts)	90–120	150–200
52, Batman and the Vikings (Olaf Erickson, Professor Carter Nichols), The Man with the Automatic Brain (Alfred the Butler), The Happy Victims (The Joker, Mrs. Carlin)	100–150	200–300
57, The Walkiing Mummy (Andrews, character without a first name, he was a museum curator), The Funny Man Crimes (The Joker)	90–120	150–250
58, The Brand of a Hero (Joaquin Murieta), The State Bird Crimes (the Penguin), The Black Diamond (Bulls-Eye Kendall, Barracuda Brothers, Nitro Nelson). Joaquin Murieta was a real-life desperado of the Old West, here worked into a time-travel piece	90–120	150–250
59, Batman in the Future (Erkham, character without first name), The Man who Replaced Batman (Deadshot/Floyd Lawton, Commissioner Gordon), The Forbidden Cellar (Professor Vincent)	90–120	150–250
60, The Auto Circus Mystery (Lucky Hooton)	90–120	150–250
61, The Birth of Batplane II (Boley Brothers), Wheelchair Crime Fighter (Vicki Vale), Mystery of the Winged People (The Penguin)	75–100	175–275

SUPERMAN (1939)

2, Superman vs. Luthor (first appearance)	$1000–1500	$2000–3000
4, Superman vs. Luthor	500–700	1000–2000
10, Superman vs. Luthor	400–450	600–000
12, Superman vs. Luthor	275–325	700–800
19, Superman Movie Cartoons, redone into book format	220–260	600–700
30, Superman vs. Mr. Mxyztplk, 1st appearance of Mr. Mxyztplk; in later issues the name was spelled Mxyzptlk	220–260	600–700
45, Lois Lane, Superwoman (Hocus, Pocus)	90–130	250–300
53, Anniversary Issue, origin retold	375–425	800–1200
54, Superman vs. The Wrecker (first appearance)	90–110	200–250
61, Superman Returns to Krypton, first Kryptonite story	190–210	450–500
76, Guest Appearances by Batman and Robin	200–250	550–650
78, Lois Lane's Meeting with Lana Lang	80–90	180–220
81, Superman's Secret Workshop, discovered by arch-foe Luthor	80–90	180–220
100, Origin Retold, for the second time	200–250	700–800
113, The Superman of the Past, part I	35–45	90–110
114, The Superman of the Past, part II	35–45	70–90
115, The Superman of the Past, part III	25–35	70–90
123, Girl of Steel	25–35	70–90
125, Clark Kent in College	25–35	70–90
127, Return of Titano	25–35	70–90
128, Kryptonite Story	25–35	70–90
130, Krypton Grows Up	25–35	70–90
133, How Parry White Hired Clark Kent	20–25	50–70
135, Lori Lemaris	20–25	50–70
138, Lori Lemaris	20–25	50–70
139, Story of Red Kryptonite	20–25	50–70
140, Superman and the Son of Bizarro	20–25	50–70
141, Superman Returns to Krypton and Meets Lyla Lorry	15–20	40–50
142, Guest Appearances by Batman and Robin	15–20	40–50

	VERY GOOD	FINE
143, Return of Bizarro	15–20	40–50
144, Superboy's First Public Appearance	15–20	40–50
145, Great Boo-Boo	15–20	40–50
146, Superman's Life Story	20–25	50–70
147, Superman vs. The Legion of Super Villains (first appearance)	18–22	45–60
149, Death of Superman (fantasy)	18–22	45–55
156, Last Days of Superman, w/ appearances by Batman and Robin	8–10	20–25
158, Nightwing and Flamebird	8–10	20–25

Fawcett

CAPTAIN MARVEL ADVENTURES (1941)

1, no number, Origin Retold	$1000–2000	$4000–6000
19, Cover: Santa Claus riding on Captain Marvel's back, w/ Mary Marvel, wording (at upper right): "On sale every third Friday"	70–90	180–220
26, Cover: Captain Marvel soaring skyward against huge American flag, wording "War, Stamps for Victory"	60–70	150–175
27, Captain Marvel Joins the Navy, cover: Captain Marvel rearing back to hurl bomb as if it were a football, wording "This is the insignia recently adopted by a naval air squadron" (referring to the lightning bolt on Captain Marvel's shirt front)	60–70	150–175
28, Cover: Captain Marvel standing at attention w/ hands at sides, receiving medal from Uncle Sam while column of soldiers watch	60–70	150–175
31, Captain Marvel in Buffalo, City Saved From Doom; Captain Marvel Fights His Own Conscience, cover: Captain Marvel in close-up w/ angel on one shoulder and devil on other	55–65	140–160
42, Cover: close-up portrait of Captain Marvel in Christmas wreath, "Season's Greetings"	40–50	90–110
47, Cover: Captain Marvel stands facing old man w/ long beard who holds scroll. On wall are names Solomon, Hercules, Atlas, Zeus, Achilles, Mercury, and "Seventh War Loan, buy stamps and bonds"	30–40	90–110
60, Captain Marvel Battles the Dread Atomic War, cover: Captain Marvel in nuclear-devastated city, poised to catch falling atomic bomb	30–40	60–70
70, Captain Marvel and the Horror in the Box, cover: Captain Marvel peering into box that has a question mark on the lid	28–32	50–60
73, Cover: Captain Marvel speeds past the Woolworth Building in New York City	28–32	50–60
97, Captain Marvel Is Wiped Out, cover: Captain Marvel standing full-length, a hand w/ an eraser is "wiping out" the drawing. He exclaims, "Holy moley! What goes on?"	25–30	75–85
104, Mr. Tawny's Masquerade, cover: Mr. Tawny (w/ cape) delivering knockout punch, Captain Marvel exclaims, "Attaboy, Mr. Tawny"	20–25	50–60
112, Captain Marvel and the Strange Worrybird, cover: Worrybird pacing ground w/ dark cloud of gloom overhead, as Captain Marvel stands by mystified	20–25	50–60

Marvel Comics

THE AMAZING SPIDERMAN (1963)	VERY GOOD	FINE
1, Origin Retold, Spiderman vs. Chameleon (John Jameson), Fabulous Four, Ditko artwork, Lee stories, inking unknown	$800–1200	$3000–4000
2, Duel to the Death with the Vulture, Uncanny Threat of the Terrible Tinkerer, Kitko artwork, Lee stories, Duffy lettering	250–350	400–800
4, Nothing Can Stop the Sandman (Betty Brant), Kitko artwork, Lee stories	100–200	300–600
5, Marked for Destruction by Dr. Doom (Fabulous Four), Kitdo artwork, Lee stories, Rosen lettering	100–200	300–600
6, Face to Face with the Lizard, Ditko artwork, Lee stories, Simek lettering	100–200	300–600
7, Return of the Vulture, Ditko artwork, Lee stories, Simek lettering	80–160	300–500
8, Living Brain, Spiderman Tackles the Human Torch (Fabulous Four), Kirby and Ditko artwork, Lee stories, Simek lettering, Ditko inking	100–150	300–400
9, A Man Called Electro, Ditko artwork, Lee stories, Simek lettering	120–160	300–600
10, Enforcers (Fredrick Foswell, The Ox, Montana, Fancy Dan), Ditko artwork, Lee stories, Rosen lettering	100–150	380–420
11, Turning Point (Spiderman, Tracer, Dr. Octopus), Ditko artwork, Lee stories, Rosen lettering	60–80	180–200
12, Unmasked by Dr. Octopus, Ditko artwork, Lee stories, Simek lettering	60–80	180–200
13, Menace of Mysterio, Ditko artwork, Lee stories, Simek lettering	80–100	250–300
14, Green Goblin (Hulk, Enforcers, Ox, Montana, Fancy Dan), Ditko artwork, Lee stories, Simek lettering (premium value because of Hulk appearance)	450–550	800–900
15, Kraven the Hunter (Chameleon), Ditko artwork, Lee stories, Simek lettering	80–100	200–250
50, Classic Cover, Kingpin (first appearance)	50–75	100–150
100, Anniversary Issue Special	20–30	50–100
121, Death of Gwen Stacy	15–25	50–75
122, Death of Green Goblin	15–25	50–75
129, Jackal and The Punisher (first appearance)	20–40	50–100

Magazines

Magazines are history in the first person. Few things capture the mood of the American nation as the magazines we read. Few things are as American as *Life Magazine.* But magazines, unlike books, were meant to be read and discarded. Although publishers printed large numbers, readers saved only a small percentage. These saved copies may turn up anywhere, from a church bazaar to the bottom of an auction box lot.

Collectors of magazines want clean, crisp copies. They should not be marked, torn or frayed. The best copy is an unread copy

	LOW	AVG.	HIGH
Action Packed Western, May 1957	$2.70	$3.00	$3.80
Action Packed Western, July 1957	2.70	3.00	3.80
Advanced Scholars Quarterly, April 1905	4.50	5.00	6.30
Air Force, Jan. 1944	2.70	3.00	3.80
Air Force, April 1944	2.70	3.00	3.80
Air Force, May 1944	2.70	3.00	3.80
Air Force, Dec. 1944	2.70	3.00	3.80
Air Force, May 1945	2.70	3.00	3.80
Alaska Sportsman, July 1955	2.70	3.00	3.80
American Cookery, Feb. 1942	3.60	4.00	5.00
American Home, Sept. 1942	0.90	1.00	1.30
American Home, Aug. 1945	0.90	1.00	1.30
Argosy, 1882–90	4.00	4.75	6.00
Argosy, 1891–1900	3.25	4.00	4.75
Argosy, 1901–10	2.75	3.38	4.00
Argosy, 1911–20	2.25	2.75	3.25
Argosy, July 1914	10.80	13.00	15.00
Argosy, Sept. 1914	10.80	13.00	15.00
Arizona Highways, Feb. 1959	4.50	5.00	6.30
Arizona Highways, Jan. 1962	4.50	5.00	6.30
Arizona Highways, April 1962	4.50	5.00	6.30
Arizona Highways, May 1962	4.50	5.00	6.30
Arizona Highways, Nov. 1962	4.50	5.00	6.30
Art News, 1942, 10/14 (Charles Dana Gibson)	20.00	23.50	27.00
Asia, Jan. 1929	26.00	29.50	32.00
Association Men (YMCA Publication), 1917	5.00	6.00	7.00
Atlantic Monthly, June 1887	14.00	15.00	16.50
Atlantic Monthly, 1950–59	2.75	3.00	3.25
Atlantic Monthly, 1960–69	2.00	2.38	2.75
Audio, Feb. 1966	2.30	3.00	3.10
Audio, Oct. 1967	2.30	3.00	3.10
Audio, April 1975	1.80	2.00	2.50
Audio, Aug. 1975	1.80	2.00	2.50
Audio, Feb. 1976	1.80	2.00	2.50
Audubon Magazine, 1950–55	4.50	5.75	7.00
Audubon Magazine, 1956–60	4.00	5.00	6.00
Backyard Mechanic, 1976	4.50	5.00	6.30
Bandleaders, June 1946	11.50	12.50	13.50
Baseball Magazine, 1923	12.00	14.00	16.00
Baseball Magazine, 1955	3.25	3.88	4.50
Beatles Monthly Book, Mar. 1965	20.00	23.50	27.00
Best of the Wrestler, Fall 1976	1.80	2.00	2.50
Best of the Wrestler, Fall 1977, Andre the Giant	1.80	2.00	2.50

	LOW	AVG.	HIGH
Best of the Wrestler, Spring 1977	1.80	2.00	2.50
Better Homemaking, Oct. 1939	1.80	2.00	2.50
Better Homes and Gardens, 1920–30	6.75	8.00	9.50
Better Homes and Gardens, 1950–60	3.25	4.00	5.00
Better Homes and Gardens, 1961–70	2.25	2.75	3.25
Better Roads, Jan. 1938	9.00	11.00	12.50
Big Book of Wrestling, Mar. 1975	1.80	2.00	2.50
Black Mask, Feb. 1927	70.00	75.00	80.00
Black Mask, Jan. 1935	60.00	65.00	70.00
Black Mask, May 1936	70.00	75.00	80.00
Bluebook, April 1955	4.50	5.00	6.30
Bow and Arrow, Nov.–Dec. 1968	4.50	5.00	6.30
Brigitte Bardot, 1958	40.00	45.00	50.00
Brown Book of Boston, 1903–05	7.00	9.00	11.00
Brown Book of Boston, April 1905	17.50	18.50	19.50
Candid, Sept. 1953, Vol. 1, #1 (Marilyn Monroe)	9.00	11.00	12.50
Captain Future, 1940–42	15.00	22.50	30.00
Car and Driver, Aug. 1981	1.40	1.90	2.40
Car and Driver, Mar. 1984	1.40	1.90	2.40
Carnival, 1953-54	1.75	2.00	2.25
Cars, Nov. 1953	3.60	4,00	5.00
Cartoon Comedy Parade, 1963	1.00	1.25	1.50
Cartoon Parade, 1962–68	1.00	1.50	2.00
Cavalier, Aug. 1960	2.70	3.00	3.80
Cavalier, Feb. 1961	2.70	3.00	3.80
Celebrity Swimwear, April 1985	2.70	3.00	3.80
Century Magazine, Oct. 1887	14.50	15.50	16.50
Century Magazine, Feb. 1892	8.00	9.00	10.00
Clic, 1938–40	4.00	5.50	7.00
Collier's, 1902–10	18.00	25.00	32.00
Collier's, 1910–20	15.00	20.00	25.00
Collier's, 1920–60	8.00	14.00	20.00

Left to right: Collier's, *Nov. 12, 1921;* Collier's, *Dec. 6, 1941.*

	LOW	AVG.	HIGH
Collier's, 1937, 11/6 (Mickey Mouse)	42.00	47.00	52.00
Collier's, 1951, 2/17 (Herbert Hoover's Memoirs)	11.00	12.00	13.00
Comedy, 1956-60	1.00	1.75	2.50
Complete Detective, May 1938, first issue	45.00	50.00	55.00
Complete Photographer, 1941	6.00	7.00	8.00
Complete Sports, Jan. 1966	3.60	4.00	5.00
Complete Wrestling, Feb. 1975	1.80	2.00	2.50
Complete Wrestling, June 1975	1.80	2.00	2.50
Consumer Reports, April 1973	1.80	2.00	2.50
Cosmic Science Fiction, 1941	40.00	42.50	45.00
Cosmopolitan, 1890–99	16.75	20.88	25.00
Cosmopolitan, 1900–10	13.50	16.75	20.00
Cosmopolitan, 1911–20	12.00	14.38	16.75
Cosmopolitan, 1921–30	2.75	6.38	10.00
Cottage Hearth, June 1891	7.20	9.00	10.00
Country Gentleman, 1853–60	7.75	11.00	14.00
Country Gentleman, 1861–70	6.75	9.00	12.00
Country Gentleman, 1871–80	4.00	5.38	6.75
Country Gentleman, July 1950	3.60	4.00	5.00
Current History, Nov. 1925	8.10	10.00	11.30
Current History, Oct. 1927	6.30	8.00	8.80
Current Opinion, July 1923	5.40	6.00	7.50
Current Opinion, Nov. 1924	8.10	10.00	11.30
Custom Rodder, Sept. 1964	2.70	3.00	3.80
Daughters of the American Revolution, May 1932	3.60	4.00	5.00
Daughters of the American Revolution, Oct. 1933	2.70	3.00	3.80
Delineator, 1881–90	4.50	6.00	7.50
Delineator, Jan. 1902	9.00	11.00	12.50
Delineator, Aug. 1907	9.00	11.00	12.50
Dexter Smith's Musical Journal, 1875	3.60	4.00	5.00
Doc Savage, Sept. 1933	200.00	220.00	240.00
Doc Savage, Jan. 1935	65.00	70.00	75.00
Doc Savage, Jan. 1939	50.00	55.00	60.00
Doc Savage, 1939–48	20.00	30.00	40.00
Doc Savage, Dec. 1944	70.00	75.00	80.00
Double Action Western, April 1956	2.70	3.00	3.80
Double Detective, 1937–40	50.00	55.00	60.00
Electric Journal, Jan. 1910	4.50	5.00	6.30
Electronics World, April 1961	0.90	1.00	1.30
Electronics World, Dec. 1962	0.90	1.00	1.30
Electronics World, May 1963	0.90	1.00	1.30
Electronics World, Nov. 1964	0.90	1.00	1.30
Electronics World, Sept. 1965	0.90	1.00	1.30
Esquire, Nov. 1942 (Rita Hayworth)	13.50	16.00	18.80
Esquire, 1944–55	14.00	15.00	16.00
Esquire, Sept. 1951 (Marilyn Monroe)	47.00	52.00	57.00
Esquire, 1956–66	2.00	3.00	4.00
Esquire, 1967–72	2.50	3.50	4.50
Etude, 1900–10	1.35	2.05	2.75
Etude, Feb. 1914	5.00	6.00	6.90
Family Circle, 1950–59	1.00	1.18	1.35
Family Circle, 1960–69	0.75	0.88	1.00
Famous Western, Feb. 1957	2.70	3.00	3.80
Famous Western, April 1957	2.70	3.00	3.80

	LOW	AVG.	HIGH
Farm Journal, Aug. 1903	3.60	4.00	5.00
Farm Journal, Oct. 1903	3.60	4.00	5.00
Farmer's Wife, 1928-31	2.00	3.50	5.00
Farmer's Wife, Feb. 1933	10.80	13.00	15.00
Farmer's Wife, Feb. 1936	10.80	13.00	15.00
Field and Stream, 1896–1900	3.75	4.50	5.25
Field and Stream, 1901–10	3.25	3.75	4.25
Field and Stream, 1911–20	3.00	3.38	3.75
Field and Stream, 1921–30	2.00	2.50	3.00
Film Weekly, 1931–37	25.00	32.50	40.00
Filmland, 1951–57	10.00	15.00	20.00
Flying, Feb. 1971	1.80	2.00	2.50
Flying, Oct. 1971	1.80	2.00	2.50
Focus, April 1938	5.00	6.00	7.00
Focus, 1951–53	1.75	2.00	2.25
Foreign Car, Aug. 1960	2.70	3.00	3.80
Fotorama, 1955–61	1.75	2.00	2.25
Fotorama, July 1959 (Elvis Presley)	3.50	4.00	4.50
Frank Leslie's Popular Monthly, Dec. 1885	12.00	15.00	18.00
Frank Leslie's Weekly, 1890–99	7.00	9.00	11.00
Frank Leslie's Weekly, 1900–10	5.75	7.25	8.75
Frank Leslie's Weekly, 1911–20	4.00	5.00	6.00
Front Page Detective, April 1938	4.50	5.00	6.30
Fun House Comedy, 1964	1.00	1.25	1.50
Fur-Fish-Game, Feb. 1943	4.50	5.00	6.30
Game, Harvard Football News, Nov. 24, 1962 (Harvard vs. Yale)	7.20	9.00	10.00
Gangsters, 1975, #1	5.50	6.00	6.50
General Electric Review, Dec. 1912	5.40	6.00	7.50
General Electric Review, May 1913	5.40	6.00	7.50
General Electric Review, June 1913	5.40	6.00	7.50
General Electric Review, Sept. 1913	5.40	6.00	7.50
Godey's Lady's Book, 1844–53	9.00	12.00	15.00
Godey's Lady's Book, late 1860s	6.75	8.50	10.00
Good Housekeeping, 1902–20	9.00	11.00	13.00
Good Housekeeping, 1921–28	5.00	6.00	7.00
Good Housekeeping, 1929–39	3.25	3.88	4.50
Good Househeeping, 1940–49	2.25	2.75	3.25
Good Housekeeping, 1950–61	1.50	1.75	2.00
Good Housekeeping, Aug. 1961 (Caroline Kennedy)	4.00	5.00	6.00
Good Literature, 1907	2.00	3.00	4.00
Groove, 1947–49	10.00	11.00	12.00
Gun World, April 1974	2.70	3.00	3.80
Guns, Feb. 1977	2.70	3.00	3.80
Guns and Ammo, May 1975	2.70	3.00	3.80
Gunsport, July 1965	2.70	3.00	3.80
Gunsport, June 1973	2.70	3.00	3.80
Hall of Fame Wrestling, Fall 1974	1.80	2.00	2.50
Ham News, Jan–Feb. 1952	1.80	2.00	2.50
Ham News, July–Aug. 1953	1.80	2.00	2.50
Ham News, Nov.–Dec. 1953	1.80	2.00	2.50
Harper's Bazaar, 1893	4.00	4.75	5.50
Harper's Monthly, 1850	7.00	8.00	9.00
Harper's Monthly, 1851–55	11.00	15.50	20.00
Harper's Weekly, 1850–59	5.50	6.63	7.75

	LOW	AVG.	HIGH
Harper's Weekly, 1860–65	10.00	25.00	40.00
Harper's Weekly, 1860, 4/21 (Stephen Douglas)	27.50	30.00	32.50
Harvard Football News, Oct. 24, 1964	7.20	9.00	10.00
Headline Detective, July 1940	4.50	5.00	6.30
High Fidelity, April 1971	0.90	1.00	1.30
High Fidelity, Aug. 1981	0.90	1.00	1.30
High Society, July 1981 (Nastassja Kinski)	14.00	15.00	16.00
Home Arts, May 1933	7.20	9.00	10.00
Home Arts, Nov. 1936	7.20	9.00	10.00
House and Garden, Jan. 1929	7.20	9.00	10.00
House Beautiful, 1919–29	7.00	8.50	10.00
House Beautiful, 1930–45	4.00	5.00	6.00
House Beautiful, 1946–60	2.00	3.00	4.00
Household, Aug. 1899	7.20	9.00	10.00
Household, Dec. 1899	7.20	9.00	10.00
Hunting and Fishing, Mar. 1939	4.50	5.00	6.30
Hunting and Fishing, Mar. 1948	2.70	3.00	3.80
Illustrated Blue Book, 1926–29	25.00	30.00	35.00
Imported Cars, Mar. 1971	1.80	2.00	2.50
Inside Detective, 1936–58	9.00	11.00	13.00
Inside Detective, 1959–70	6.00	7.00	8.00
Inside Detective, Mar. 1970 (Charles Manson)	9.00	10.00	11.00
Inside Wrestling, Aug. 1974	1.80	2.00	2.50
Inside Wrestling, April 1975	1.80	2.00	2.50
Inside Wrestling, Sept. 1975	1.80	2.00	2.50
Ladies' Home Journal, 1890–10	15.00	18.50	22.00
Ladies' Home Journal, 1911–29	10.00	11.50	13.00
Ladies' Home Journal, 1930–40	5.00	7.00	9.00
Life Magazine *(see separate listing)*			
Literary Digest, 1910–29	0.75	1.00	1.25
Literary Digest, 1920s (Norman Rockwell covers)	4.50	5.25	6.00
Literary Digest, 1924	3.00	4.00	5.00
Literary Digest, 1924, 6/25 (Lindberg)	9.00	10.00	11.00
Literary Digest, 1930–38	0.75	0.88	1.00
Look, Aug. 1, 1950	3.60	4.00	5.00
Look, Dec. 18, 1951	4.50	5.00	6.30
Look, Jan. 15, 1952	3.60	4.00	5.00
Look, July 21, 1959	3.60	4.00	5.00
Look, July 23, 1968 (The Beatles, Ronald Reagan by Norman Rockwell)	13.50	16.00	18.00
Look, Oct. 19, 1971	3.60	4.00	5.00
Mad, #164, Nov. 1979, Alien	15.00	20.00	25.00
Mad, #169, July 1980, Star Trek	20.00	25.00	30.00
Mad, #175, Jan. 1981, M*A*S*H	13.00	16.00	19.00
Mad, #176, Mar. 1981, B. Miller	8.00	10.00	12.00
Mad, #177, May 1981, Hulk	8.00	10.00	12.00
Mad, #215, June 1980, Apple/Worm	7.00	10.00	12.00
Mad, #216, July 1980, Elevators	7.00	10.00	12.00
Mad, #218, Oct. 1980, Vote!	14.00	17.00	20.00
Mad, #220, Jan. 1981, Yoda	18.00	22.00	26.00
Mad, #222, April 1981, Coffee Break	7.00	9.00	11.00
Mad, #228, Jan. 1982, Raiders	14.00	17.00	19.00
McCall's, 1873–1910	6.00	8.50	11.00
McCall's, 1911–20	4.00	6.00	8.00

	LOW	AVG.	HIGH
McCall's, 1921–30	3.75	5.18	6.60
McCall's, 1931–45	3.25	4.63	6.00
McCall's, Mar. 1936	6.30	8.00	8.80
McCall's, 1956–75	1.00	2.50	4.00
McClure's Magazine, 1899–1904	8.00	10.00	12.00
Men, Feb. 1947	1.80	2.00	2.50
Mentor, July 1921	10.80	13.00	15.00
Miss America For Teenagers, May 1945	2.70	3.00	3.80
Modern Movies, 1937–38	20.00	23.50	27.00
Modern Priscilla, 1887–99	12.00	15.00	18.00
Modern Priscilla, 1913–25	10.00	12.50	15.00
Modern Priscilla, 1921–30	9.00	11.00	12.50
Modern Romances, 1937–39	7.00	8.50	10.00
Modern Romances, Sept. 1944	3.60	4.00	5.00
Modern Screen, 1931–39	25.00	35.00	45.00
Modern Screen, 1940–45	22.00	26.00	30.00
Modern Screen, Jan. 1943 (Ronald Reagan and Jane Wyman)	70.00	80.00	90.00
Modern Screen, 1946–53	15.00	17.50	20.00
Modern Screen, Aug. 1948 (Shirley Temple)	27.00	29.50	32.00
Modern Screen, Oct. 1953 (Marilyn Monroe)	45.00	50.00	55.00
Modern Screen, 1954–59	8.00	10.00	12.00
Modern Screen, Oct. 1955 (Marilyn Monroe)	38.00	41.00	43.00
Modern Screen, June 1959 (Rock Hudson)	20.00	22.50	25.00
Modern Screen, 1960–64	5.00	6.50	8.00
Modern Screen, Nov. 1962 (Marilyn Monroe)	25.00	27.50	30.00
Modern Screen, Dec. 1964 (JFK and Jackie)	25.00	27.50	30.00
Modern Screen, 1965–68	2.00	3.50	5.00
Modern Screen, 1969–79	1.00	1.50	2.00
Modern Screen, June 1979 (Elvis Presley)	8.00	9.00	10.00
Mothers, Nov. 1935	2.70	3.00	3.80
Motion Picture, pre-1920	14.50	17.50	21.00
Motion Picture, 1921–30	30.00	32.50	35.00
Motion Picture, 1931–40	20.00	22.50	25.00
Motion Picture, 1941–50	10.00	12.50	15.00
Motion Picture, 1951–55	7.00	9.50	12.00
Motion Picture, 1955–64	5.00	7.50	10.00
Motion Picture, 1965–70	2.00	3.00	4.00
Motion Picture, 1971–75	1.00	1.50	2.00
Motion Picture News, pre-1930	5.50	6.50	7.50
Motor Age Magazine, May 1924	15.30	18.00	21.30
Motor Guide, Mar. 1959	2.70	3.00	3.80
Motor Sport, Jan. 1952	3.60	4.00	5.00
Motor Sport, May–June 1955	3.60	4.00	5.00
Motor Sport, Nov. 1963	4.50	5.00	6.30
Motor Trend, Feb. 1954	3.60	4.00	5.00
Motor Trend, June 1955	3.60	4.00	5.00
Motor Trend, June 1962	2.70	3.00	3.80
Motor Trend, June 1963	2.70	3.00	3.80
Motor Trend, Jan. 1973	1.80	2.00	2.50
Movie Classic, 1933–42	27.00	37.00	47.00
Movie Classic, 1940–45	20.00	27.50	35.00
Movie Mystery, Sept. Oct. 1946	4.50	5.00	6.30
Movie People, May 1954 (w/ 3-D glasses)	60.00	65.00	70.00
Movie Show, 1946–48	20.00	22.50	25.00

	LOW	AVG.	HIGH
Movie Stars Parade, 1944–60	15.00	20.00	25.00
Movie Stars Parade, Oct. 1953 (Marilyn Monroe)	45.00	50.00	55.00
Movie Story, 1937–49	20.00	27.50	35.00
Movie Story, 1950–onwards	15.00	17.50	20.00
Movie World, 1952–54	14.00	16.00	18.00
Movieland, 1947–60	20.00	35.00	50.00
Movies, 1935–48	20.00	32.50	45.00
Munsey, 1895–1896	7.00	9.00	11.00
N.E. Plumbing & Heating, Sept. 1929	1.80	2.00	2.50
National Geographic, 1880, Vol. 1, No. 1	550.00	613.00	676.00
National Geographic, 1880, Vol. 1, No. 2	200.00	262.50	325.00
National Geographic, 1888	320.00	420.00	520.00
National Geographic, 1890–94	80.00	115.00	150.00
National Geographic, Mar. 1898	45.00	52.50	60.00
National Geographic, 1899	25.00	37.50	50.00
National Geographic, 1900–04	20.00	30.00	40.00
National Geographic, 1905–13	13.50	16.75	20.00
National Geographic, 1914–19	5.00	6.50	8.00
National Geographic, 1920–29	2.00	3.00	4.00
National Geographic, 1930–49	1.00	2.00	3.00
National Geographic, 1950–95	1.00	1.50	2.00
National Monthly, 1913–16	4.00	5.00	6.00
National Sportsman, Jan. 1922	6.30	8.00	8.80
National Sportsman, May 1927	13.50	16.00	18.80
Nature, pre-1920	1.00	1.50	2.00
Nature, 1920–29	0.75	1.05	1.35
Nature, 1945–46	1.50	1.75	2.00
Needlecraft, Aug. 1928	10.80	13.00	15.00
New Amstel Magazine, May 1919	3.60	4.00	5.00
New England Homestead, Feb. 11, 1899	4.50	5.00	6.30
New England Homestead, Sept. 1969	1.80	2.00	2.50
New Far East, June 1926	4.50	5.00	6.30

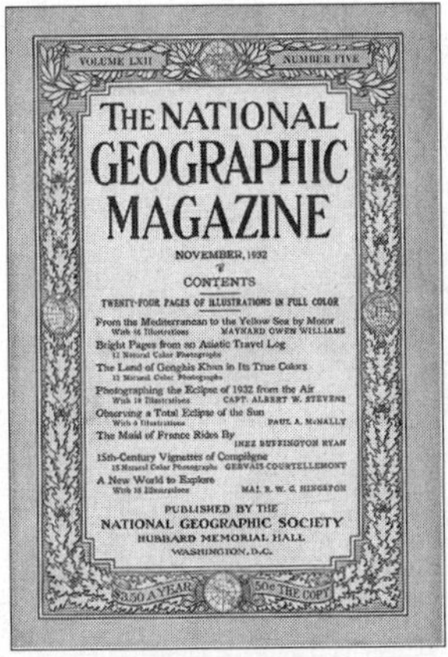

Left to right: National Geographic, *Nov. 1932;* National Geographic, *Dec. 1962.*

	LOW	AVG.	HIGH
New Movie, 1930–33	30.00	35.00	40.00
Newsweek, 1950–55	2.00	2.63	3.25
Newsweek, 1956–60	1.76	2.26	2.75
Newsweek, 1961–65	1.36	1.68	2.00
Newsweek, 1966–70	1.00	1.18	1.35
Official Detective, 1937–56 (13" x 10.5")	6.00	8.00	10.00
Official Wrestling, July 1974	1.80	2.00	2.50
Old West, Summer 1974	2.70	3.00	3.80
Old West, Winter 1969	3.60	4.00	5.00
Oui, Oct. 1972 (first issue)	20.00	22.50	25.00
Oui, 1973–74	2.50	3.00	3.50
Our Young Folks, Nov. 1866	9.00	11.00	12.50
Outdoors, Dec. 1943	5.40	6.00	7.50
Outdoorsman, Dec. 1943	6.30	8.00	8.80
Penthouse, 1972–74	4.00	6.00	8.00
People Today, 1954	1.50	2.00	2.50
People's Home Journal, 1902	3.00	4.00	5.00
People's Popular Monthly, Mar. 1930	4.10	5.00	5.60
Peterson's Magazine, 1844–59	4.50	5.25	6.00
Peterson's Magazine, 1860–65	6.00	7.25	8.50
Photo, 1952–55	2.00	2.25	2.50
Photo Play, 1919–29	50.00	62.50	75.00
Photo Play, 1930–37	27.00	38.50	50.00
Photo Play, 1938–43	22.00	27.50	33.00
Photo Play, 1944–45	18.00	21.50	25.00
Photo Play, 1946–50	15.00	17.50	20.00
Pic, 1940–45	3.00	5.50	8.00
Pictorial Review, World War I era	2.75	4.50	5.75
Picture Digest, 1956–57	1.00	1.25	1.50
Picture Play, 1930–38	20.00	30.00	40.00
Picture Show, 1945–49	15.00	17.50	20.00
Playboy, 1954–55	30.00	45.00	60.00

Playboy, *Sept. 1971.*

	LOW	AVG.	HIGH
Playboy, 1956	18.00	20.00	22.00
Playboy, 1957–66	10.00	12.50	15.00
Playboy, 1967–75	7.00	8.50	10.00
Playboy, 1976–79	3.00	5.00	7.00
Playboy, Dec. 1953	90.00	100.00	110.00
Playboy, Jan. 1954	90.00	100.00	110.00
Popular Imported Cars, Dec. 1965	3.60	4.00	5.00
Popular Mechanics, 1900–10	10.00	15.00	20.00
Popular Mechanics, Dec. 1949	1.80	2.00	2.50
Popular Mechanics, 1951–53	2.00	2.50	3.00
Popular Mechanics, 1960–69	0.75	1.13	1.50
Popular Photography, Dec. 1939	5.40	6.00	7.50
Popular Radio, Dec. 1926	5.40	6.00	7.50
Popular Science, pre-1900	20.00	27.50	35.00
Popular Science, 1901–10	20.00	22.50	25.00
Popular Science, 1911–30	15.00	17.50	20.00
Popular Science, May 1931	4.50	5.00	6.30
Prairie Farmer, 1920–29	1.00	1.50	2.00
Pro Wrestling Illustrated, Jan. 1984	0.90	1.00	1.30
Puck, late 1800s	7.00	11.38	15.75
Puck, early 1900s	4.00	5.38	6.75
Pulse, 1954–55	1.50	2.00	2.50
Radio, Feb. 1942	2.70	3.00	3.80
Radio and T.V. News, Aug. 1957	2.70	3.00	3.80
Radio and T.V. News, Dec. 1958	2.70	3.00	3.80
Radio and Television, Sept. 1941	1.80	2.00	2.50
Radio and Television Maintenance, April 1950	3.60	4.00	5.00
Radio Broadcast, 1929	5.00	6.00	7.00
Radio Craft, Oct. 1929 (first issue)	15.00	18.00	22.00
Radio Craft, 1929–40	9.00	12.50	15.00
Radio Craft, May 1946	2.70	3.00	3.80
Radio Craft, Sept. 1947	2.70	3.00	3.80
Radio-Electronics, Aug. 1949	1.80	2.00	2.50
Radio-Electornics, Feb. 1950	0.90	1.00	1.30
Radio-Electronics, July 1951	0.90	1.00	1.30
Radio-Electronics, Mar. 1952	0.90	1.00	1.30
Radio-Electronics, May 1964	0.90	1.00	1.30
Radio-Electronics, Oct. 1964	0.90	1.00	1.30
Radio News, May 1938	4.50	5.00	6.30
Radio News, Nov. 1939	4.50	5.00	6.30
Radio News, Nov. 1940	4.50	5.00	6.30
Radio News, Oct. 1941	4.50	5.00	6.30
Radio-Television News, Dec. 1948	1.80	2.00	2.50
Radip-Television News, July 1949	1.80	2.00	2.50
Radio-Television News, July 1950	0.90	1.00	1.30
Radio-Television News, June 1951	0.90	1.00	1.30
Radio-Television News, Mar. 1953	0.90	1.00	1.30
Radio-Television News, Mar. 1954	3.60	4.00	5.00
Radio-Television News, Mar. 1956	0.90	1.00	1.30
Radio-Television News, Mar. 1957	1.80	2.00	2.50
Reader's Digest, 1930s	0.75	1.05	1.35
Reader's Digest, 1940–60	0.50	0.75	1.00
Redbook, 1950–60	2.00	3.50	5.00
Richardson's Musical Hours, Feb. 1880	3.60	4.00	5.00

	LOW	AVG.	HIGH
Road and Track, Feb. 1959	2.70	3.00	3.80
Road and Track, Feb. 1975	1.80	2.00	2.50
Rodding and Restyling, Mar. 1966	2.70	3.00	3.80
Saga, April 1954	2.70	3.00	3.80
Saga Annual, 1972	3.60	4.00	5.00
Saturday Evening Post, 1900–07	10.00	13.38	16.75
Saturday Evening Post, 1908–10	8.00	9.00	10.00
Saturday Evening Post, 1911–20	5.00	7.50	10.00
Satruday Evening Post, 1921–30	4.00	5.00	6.00
Saturday Evening Post, 1931–40	2.75	3.38	4.00
Saturday Evening Post, 1933–37 (Norman Rockwell covers)	20.00	25.00	30.00
Saturday Evening Post, Mar. 25, 1950	4.50	5.00	6.30
Saturday Evening Post, Nov. 3, 1951	5.40	6.00	7.50
Saturday Evening Post, April 6, 1963 (Kennedy)	4.50	5.00	6.30
Saturday Evening Post, Dec. 1978 (Bob Hope, Raquel Welch)	3.60	4.00	5.00
Science and Invention, Dec. 1926	5.40	6.00	7.50
Science and Mechanics, 1942–56	3.00	5.00	7.00
Science and Mechanics, June 1952	3.60	4.00	5.00
Science and Mechanics, Feb. 1954	3.60	4.00	5.00
Scientific American, 1950–60	1.25	1.50	1.75
Screen Album (quarterly), 1951–54	15.00	17.50	20.00
Screen Book, 1929–39	25.00	37.50	50.00
Screen Guide, 1939–45	15.00	22.50	30.00
Screen Guide, 1956–51	8.00	11.50	15.00
Screen Hits Annual, 1949–52	10.00	15.00	20.00
Screen Play, 1936–37	30.00	35.00	40.00
Screen Romances, 1934–38	22.00	31.00	40.00
Screen Stars, 1946–49	12.00	14.00	16.00
Screen Stars, 1950–57	5.00	7.50	10.00
Screen Stories, 1948–55	8.00	11.00	14.00
Screen Stories, 1956–60	5.00	6.50	8.00

Left to right: Saturday Evening Post, *Mar. 30, 1918;* Saturday Evening Post, *Aug. 16 1958, Norman Rockwell Cover.*

Sports Illustrated, Feb. 1986, Elle Macpherson swimsuit issue.

	LOW	AVG.	HIGH
Screen Stories, 1961–72	2.00	4.00	6.00
Screenland, 1924–32	22.00	27.00	32.00
Screenland, 1933–39	17.00	20.00	23.00
Screenland, 1940–48	12.00	15.00	18.00
Screenland, 1949–55	7.00	9.50	12.00
Screenland, 1956–65	2.00	4.00	6.00
Scribner's Magazine, 1881–94	8.00	10.00	12.00
Scribner's Monthly, World War I era	1.50	2.00	3.00
Shooting Times, Oct. 1968	2.70	3.00	3.80
Shooting Times, Sept. 1969	2.70	3.00	3.80
Silver Screen, 1939–64	10.00	15.00	20.00
Small Cars Illustrated, Jan. 1959	2.70	3.00	3.80
Small Cars Illustrated, Mar. 1959	2.70	3.00	3.80
Speed Age, June 1953	3.60	4.00	5.00
Speed and Custom, Dec. 1963	2.70	3.00	3.80
Speed and Custom, Dec. 1964	2.70	3.00	3.80
Sport Fishing and Boating Illustrated, Summer 1966	1.80	2.00	2.50
Sports Afield, 1890–1940	3.25	5.00	6.75
Sports Car Illustrated, April 1957	3.60	4.00	5.00
Sports Car Illustrated, Aug. 1958	2.70	3.00	3.80
Sports Illustrated, Feb. 1986 (Elle Macpherson)	2.70	3.00	3.80
Sports Review, Wrestling, July 1975	1.80	2.00	2.50
Sports Review, Wrestling, July 1977	1.80	2.00	2.50
Stage, 1935–34	20.00	25.00	30.00
Star Quest Comix, #1, Oct. 1978	5.40	6.00	7.50
Stereo, Fall 1971	1.80	2.00	2.50
Stereo Review, Aug. 1976	0.90	1.00	1.30
Stereo Review, Nov. 1978	0.90	1.00	1.30
Stereo Review, Sept. 1981	0.90	1.00	1.30
Street Rod Pictorial, 1969	9.00	11.00	12.50
Success, April 1940	4.50	5.00	6.30
Tab, 1952–66	2.00	2.25	2.50
Tab, Aug. 1966 (Sophia Loren)	4.00	5.00	6.00
Technical World, July 1915	3.60	4.00	5.00

	LOW	AVG.	HIGH
Telephone Topics, Oct. 1921	4.50	5.00	6.30
Theatre, 1910–14	25.00	27.50	30.0
Theatre Magazine, 1925–26	20.00	27.50	35.00
Think, Nov 1936	3.60	4.00	5.00
Time, 1932–39	6.00	7.00	8.00
Time, Dec. 25, 1939 (Gone With the Wind)	25.00	27.50	30.00
Time, 1940–59	1.50	2.00	2.50
Time, 1960–66	1.00	1.50	2.00
Tops, Nov. 1955	3.60	4.00	5.00
Tower Radio, Aug. 1935	12.60	15.00	17.50
True Adventures, Nov. 1955	2.70	3.00	3.80
True Detective, 1924–39	11.00	16.00	21.00
True Detective, 1940–61	8.00	10.00	12.00
True Experiences, June 1938	7.20	9.00	10.00
True Love and Romance, Aug. 1939	3.60	4.00	5.00
True Story, Sept. 1935	7.20	9.00	10.00
True Story, Mar. 1939	7.20	9.00	10.00
True West, non-fiction, Feb. 1970	2.70	3.00	3.80
True's Gun Annual, #1, 1962	3.60	4.00	5.00
True's Gun Annual, #2, 1963	2.70	3.00	3.80
TV Guide *(see separate listing)*			
U.S. Camera, Mar. 1944	3.60	4.00	5.00
U.S. Camera, May 1947	3.60	4.00	5.00
Victory Sports Series, Inside Wrestling, Nov. 1977	1.80	2.00	2.50
Wacko, #1, 1980	24.00	29.00	34.00
Wacko, #2, April 1981	23.00	27.00	31.00
Western Action, May 1957	2.70	3.00	3.80
Wild West, Dec. 1969	2.70	3.00	3.80
Woman's Day, Feb. 1940	2.70	3.00	3.80
Woman's Day, Mar. 1941	2.70	3.00	3.80
Woman's Day, Sept. 1941	2.70	3.00	3.80
Woman's Home Companion, 1900–10	4.00	5.38	6.75
Woman's Home Companion, Mar. 1952	2.70	3.00	3.80
Woman's World, Nov. 1914	7.20	9.00	10.00
Wrestler, Feb. 1975	1.80	2.00	2.50
Wrestler, July 1979	1.80	2.00	2.50
Wrestling Monthly, June 1974	1.80	2.00	2.50
Wrestling Revue, Mar. 1973	1.80	2.00	2.50
Wrestling Revue, May 1974	1.80	2.00	2.50
Wrestling Revue, Oct. 1976	1.80	2.00	2.50
Wrestling Superstars, Winter 1976	2.70	3.00	3.80
Wrestling World, Summer, 1974	1.80	2.00	2.50
Yankee Plumber, Nov. 1934	1.80	2.00	2.50
Your Car, April 1954	3.60	4.00	5.00
Youth's Companion, Feb. 18, 1926	1.80	2.00	2.50
Youth's Companion, Oct. 28, 1926	1.80	2.00	2.50
Zane Grey Western, Feb. 1972	3.60	4.00	5.00

Life Magazine

		LOW	AVG.	HIGH
1937, Jan. 4	Franklin Roosevelt	$25	$30	$35
1937, May 3	Jean Harlow	27	29	32
1937, May 17	Quintuplets	40	50	60
1938, Apr. 25	John Thomas Winsett, Brooklyn Dodgers World Series	20	24	28
1938, Oct. 31	Abe Lincoln on Broadway	13	16	18
1939, May 13	World's Fair	25	27	30
1939, Sep. 11	Mussolini	19	20	21
1939, Dec. 25	Merry Christmas	13	16	18
1940, Apr. 29	Winston Churchill	10	13	15
1940, May 20	General Weygand	7	9	11
1941, Sep. 15	Captain Lord Louis Mountbatten	7	9	11
1942, Apr. 27	Nelson Rockefeller	8	9	10
1947, Sep. 1	John Cobb and Racing Car	7	9	11
1948, Feb. 9	Robert Taft, 49th State	7	9	11
1948, Aug. 9	Grandmother Dietrich	10	13	15
1948, Nov. 22,	Truman	9	10	11
1948, Dec. 6	Montgomery Clift	14	17	20
1949, Mar. 14	Dorothy McGuire's Baby	8	10	12
1949, Apr. 18	Mary Martin, South Pacific	10	13	15
1949, Oct. 10	Oppenheimer	12	15	17
1950, Mar. 13	Spring Fashions, Buster Keaton	6	8	10
1950, Apr. 10	Young Horsewoman, Toys	4	5	6
1950, Jun. 12	Hopalong Cassidy	30	35	40
1950, Jun. 19	Children's Sand Styles	5	6	7
1950, Sep. 25	Swedish Red Cross Girls	4	5	6
1950, Oct. 2	Stuart Symington, Alaska	5	6	7
1951, Jan. 29	Betsy Von Furstenburg, Ted Williams	5	6	7
1951, Feb. 5	NY Police Commissioner Tom Murphy	10	13	15
1951, Mar. 12	Paul Douglas	5	6	7
1951, Mar. 26	Young Choir Singer, Fred Astaire	5	6	7
1951, Apr. 16	Esther Williams	7	9	11
1951, Oct. 22	Bronc Rider Casey Tibbs, Howdy Doody	8	10	11
1951, Nov. 12	Anthony Eden, Roy Rogers	5	6	7
1951, Dec. 10	Harry Truman, Audrey Hepburn	8	10	12
1952, Apr. 14	Italian Fashions	4	5	6
1952, May 5	Dianna Lynn	10	13	15
1952, Jun. 16	Eisenhower, Dionne Quints, Ben Hogan	12	15	17
1952, Jul. 21	Dwight D. Eisenhower	5	6	7
1952, Aug. 18	Marlene Dietrich	8	10	12
1952, Sep. 15	Rita Gam, Musual and Mantle	8	10	12
1953, Jun. 29	Cyd Charisse, Marilyn Monroe	9	12	13
1953, Jul. 6	Terry Moore	8	10	12
1953, Jul. 20	Jack and Jackie	22	27	31
1953, Aug. 3	Nicole Maurey	7	9	11
1953, Nov. 2	Churchill, Disney	12	15	17
1953, Dec. 14	Nixon, Ronald Reagan	10	13	15
1954, Mar. 1	Rita Moreno, Marilyn Monroe	8	10	12
1954, Mar. 15	Mrs. Rockefeller	4	5	6
1954, May 31	William Holden	10	13	15
1954, Jul. 12	Pier Angeli	10	13	15
1954, Aug. 2	Summer Show Whale	5	6	7

		LOW	AVG.	HIGH
1954, Sep. 6	Dior, Rock Hudson	7	9	11
1954, Sep. 13	Judy Garland, Willie Mays	19	24	27
1954, Oct. 11	Mountain Climber	5	6	7
1954, Nov. 8	New Jersey Deer, Liz Taylor	5	6	7
1954, Nov. 22	Judy Holliday	10	13	15
1955, Feb. 7	Festival of Lights	5	6	7
1955, Feb. 28	Shelley Winters	8	10	12
1955, Mar. 7	Buddha, Jimmy Dean, Disney	6	8	10
1955, Apr. 11	Grace Kelley	16	19	22
1955, Jun. 6	Henry Fonda	7	9	11
1955, Jul. 11	Susan Strasberg, Girl Scouts	4	5	6
1955, Aug. 22	Sophia Loren	10	13	15
1955, Oct. 3	Rock Hudson, Marciano-Moore	16	19	22
1955, Nov. 14	Eisenhower, Hunting Dogs	8	10	11
1955, Nov. 28	Carol Channing, Tyrone Power	5	6	7
1955, Dec. 26	Christmas Special	5	6	7
1956, Jan. 30	Henry Ford II	4	5	6
1956, Mar. 12	Eisenhower, Panco Gonzales	5	6	7
1956, Jul. 16	Gary Cooper, Marilyn's Wedding	10	13	15
1956, Aug. 6	Andrea Doria	7	9	11
1956, Aug. 20	Audrey Hepburn	8	10	12
1956, Nov. 12	Rosalind Russell	8	10	12
1957, Jan. 28	B-52, Wilt Chamberlain	12	15	17
1957, Mar. 11	John Kennedy	16	19	22
1957, May 6	Sophia Loren, Buster Keaton	8	10	12
1957, Jun. 3	Making of a Satellite	5	6	7
1957, Dec. 9	Nixon, N.C. Wyeth	8	10	11
1958, Jan. 27	Ski Fashions, Jayne Mansfield Wedding	7	9	11
1958, Apr. 7	Sugar Ray Robinson, Elvis Drafted	13	16	18
1958, Apr. 28	Willie Mays	27	32	37

Left to right: March 30, 1942, Shirley Temple; April 13, 1962, Elizabeth Taylor and Richard Burton.

		LOW	AVG.	HIGH
1959, Aug. 3	Kingston Trio	7	9	11
1959, Sep. 14	7 Astronauts, Debbie Reynolds	8	10	12
1960, Jan. 11	Dina Merrill, Bobby Darin	8	10	12
1960, Feb. 22	Henry and Jane Fonda	8	10	12
1960, Mar. 7	Hypnosis, Squaw Valley Olympics	5	6	7
1960, Apr. 4	Marlon Brando, Chuck Dressen	4	5	6
1960, May 9	Yvette Mimieux, Art Carney	5	6	7
1960, Jun. 6	Lee Remick, Kim Novack	5	6	7
1960, Nov. 21	Jack and Jackie Winners, Marilyn Monroe	10	13	15
1960, Nov. 28	Carroll Baker, Clark Gable	4	5	6
1960, Dec. 26	25 Years of Life, Marilyn Monroe	18	22	25
1961, Jan. 27	Kennedy Inauguration, Ann Margret	10	13	15
1961, Feb. 17	Shirley MacLaine, Art Linkletter	5	6	7
1961, May 19	Alan Shepard	3	4	5
1961, Jun. 9	Kennedy, DeGaulle, Golf	3	4	5
1961, Sep. 1	Jackie Kennedy	3	4	5
1961, Oct. 6	Elizabeth Taylor	4	5	6
1961, Nov. 17	Minnesota Vikings	3	4	5
1962, Feb. 2	John Glenn	4	5	6
1962, Apr. 20	Audrey Hepburn, Ben Casey M.D.	4	5	6
1962, May 4	Mono-Rail at Seattle World's Fair	7	9	11
1962, May 11	Bob Hope	4	5	6
1962, Aug. 10	Janet Leigh, 007 Ian Fleming	6	8	10
1962, Sep. 28	Don Drysdale, Joan Crawford	22	27	31
1962, Oct. 12	Pope John XXII	3	4	5
1962, Nov. 2	Cuba, Natalie Wood	8	10	12
1963, Feb. 15	Lincoln's Body, Cassius Clay	7	9	11
1963, Mar. 8	Jean Seberg, Ted Williams	8	10	12
1963, Apr. 26	Young Jackie Kennedy	6	8	10
1963, May 10	Bay of Pigs, Marlon Brando	8	10	12
1963, Aug. 2	Sandy Koufax, Sonny Liston	22	27	31
1963, Nov. 29	JFK Assassination	30	40	50
1963, Dec. 13	Lyndon B. Johnson	8	10	12
1964, Jan. 31	Geraldine Chaplin, The Beatles	14	17	20
1964, Apr. 3	Carol Channing, James Bond	6	8	10
1964, May 1	World's Fair	8	10	12
1964, May 22	Barbra Streisand	10	13	15
1964, Jul. 17	Carroll Baker, General MacArthur	8	10	11
1964, Oct. 23	Leonid Brezhnev, The Beatles	8	10	12
1964, Dec. 18	Elizabeth Taylor	8	10	12
1964, Dec. 25	Moses by Rembrandt	3	4	5
1965, Jan. 15	Ted Kennedy, The XB-70	10	12	14
1965, Feb. 26	North Vietnam Stamp	3	4	5
1965, Mar. 5	Negro Upheaval	7	9	11
1965, Mar. 19	Civil Rights March in Alabama	4	5	6
1965, Apr. 2	Gemini's Journey	3	4	5
1965, Jul. 16	JFK Summer Movies	3	4	5
1965, Jul. 30	Mickey Mantle at 33	45	54	62
1966, Jan. 14	Ho Chi Minh, Wilt Chamberlain	4	5	6
1966, Apr. 15	Louis Armstrong	6	8	10
1966, May 6	Jackie Kennedy	6	8	10
1966, May 27	Disco, Dick Tracy	5	6	7
1966, Sep. 9	LSD Art, Muhammad Ali	7	9	11
1966, Oct. 7	Ian Fleming, James Bond	6	8	10

		LOW	AVG.	HIGH
1966, Nov. 25	A Matter of Reasonable Doubt	6	8	10
1967, Jul. 14	Princess Lee Radziwill, Joe Frazier	7	9	11
1967, Nov. 17	Jackie Kennedy, Soviets 50th	5	6	7
1968, Mar. 29	Jane Fonda	8	10	11
1968, May 10	Paul Newman, Steam Car	5	6	7
1968, Jun. 21	James Earl Ray, Sirhan Sirhan	5	6	7
1968, Sep. 20	Arthur Ashe, The Beatles	15	18	21
1968, Oct. 25	Apollo 7, Mickey Mouse	5	6	7
1968, Nov. 1	Jackie O Wedding, Apollo 7	6	8	10
1969, Jan. 10	The Incredible Year 1968	7	9	11
1969, Feb. 14	Barbra Streisand	7	9	11
1969, Mar. 21	Woody Allen	8	10	12
1969, May 23	Rowan and Martin	5	6	7
1969, Jun. 20	Joe Namath, Apollo 10	8	10	12
1969, Aug. 8	Neil Armstrong on the Moon	7	9	11
1969, Oct. 31	Marijuana, The Muppets	8	10	12
1969, Sep. 5	Peter Max	10	13	15
1969, Nov. 21	Johnny Cash	6	8	10
1969, Dec. 12	Apollo 12 on the Moon	7	9	11
1970, Jan. 23	Johnny Carson	3	4	5
1970, Feb. 6	Robert Redford	4	5	6
1970, Mar. 13	The Great Hemline Hassle	2	3	4
1970, Apr. 3	Lauren Bacall	4	5	6
1970, Apr. 24	Jim Lovell, The Beatles	4	5	6
1970, May 1	Evelyn Trop, Apollo 13	2	3	4
1970, May 15	Tragedy at Kent State	3	4	5
1970, Jun. 19	Dennis Hopper	4	5	6
1970, Jun. 26	Americans in Foreign Jails	2	3	4
1970, Jul. 24	Candice Bergen	5	6	7
1970, Aug. 14	Summer Nomads	2	3	4
1970, Oct. 23	Muhammad Ali	7	9	11
1970, Nov. 27	Khrushchev Remembers	2	3	4
1971, Feb. 19	Movie Queens	6	8	10
1971, Mar. 5	Ali vs. Frazier	8	10	11
1971, Apr. 23	Jane Fonda, Circus	6	8	10
1971, Jul. 23	Clint Eastwood	6	8	10
1971, Jul. 30	Chou En-Lai	2	3	4
1971, May 7	Germaine Greer	2	3	4
1971, Oct. 1	The Brain	2	3	4
1971, Oct. 29	David Cassidy	4	5	6
1971, Dec. 10	Cybil Sheperd	4	5	6
1972, Aug. 18	Mark Spitz	4	5	6
1972, Mar. 10	Marlon Brando	5	6	7
1972, Mar. 31	Jackie Onassis	4	5	6
1972, May 12	Vietnam Retreat	2	3	4

TV Guide

TV Guide is a weekly magazine that includes local television listings and articles about Hollywood stars. The nationally distributed editions began in 1953. Before 1953, there were local forerunners. Season preview issues, and issues featuring popular Hollywood stars and television shows on the cover are usually more valuable than other editions.

Left to right: #163, Richard Green of Robin Hood, May 12–18, 1956, $9–$12; #587, Mr. and Mrs. Johnny Carson, June 27, 1964, $8–$12.

	LOW	HIGH
#1 Lucy's $50,000,000 Baby	$700	$1200
#5 Eve Arden	60	90
#10 Martin and Lewis	90	120
#16 Lucy and Desi	350	420
#17 Groucho	130	180
#27 Red Skelton	40	60
#23 Warren Hull	20	30
#38 Bob Hope	60	90
#41 Joan Caufield	20	30
#42 Martha Raye	20	30
#44 Robert Montgomery	20	30
#56 Lucille Ball	90	120
#72 Martin and Lewis	60	90
#137 Liberace	20	30
#184 Gale Storm	10	20
#235 Burns and Allen	20	30
#305 George Gobel	9	13
#420 Mitch Miller	9	11
#421 Garry Moore	9	13
#424 Lorne Green of Bonanza	30	40
#428 Efrem Zimbalist, Jr.	8	12

	LOW	HIGH
#429 Lawrence Welk	8	12
#506 Dick Van Dyke	30	35
#509 Edie Adams	10	15
#511 Arnold Palmer	6	9
#513 Milner and Maharis of Route 66	50	70
#514 Jack Webb	20	25
#516 Princess Grace	14	20
#517 Carol Burnett	7	10
#520 Richard Chamberlain	7	10
#521 Andy Williams	6	9
#522 Cast of Bonanza	50	80
#524 Richard Egan of Empire	5	8
#525 Red Skelton	10	15
#527 Cast of The Virginian	10	14
#529 Cast of The Defenders	20	30
#530 Lawrence Welk	7	10
#531 Garry Moore and Dorothy Loudon	10	16
#532 Johnny Carson	10	20
#534 Kirby and Funt of Candid Camera	6	9
#535 Donna Reed and Carl Betz	9	13
#539 Game Show Contestants	5	10
#541 Cast of I've Got a Secret	5	8
#542 Fred MacMurray	6	9
#545 Irene Ryan and Donna Douglas	10	15
#546 Special Fall Preview Issue	90	120
#547 Richard Chamberlain	12	16
#549 Phil Silvers	6	9
#551 Judy Garland	50	70
#555 Cast of Mr. Novak	8	12
#557 George C. Scott	10	20
#560 Merry Christmas	9	13
#562 Cast of Dick Van Dyke Show	20	40
#564 Pernell Roberts of Bonanza	60	80
#566 Danny Kaye	10	14
#567 Petticoat Junction Girls	30	40
#568 Andy Williams and Claudine Spachek	10	18
#569 David Janssen as The Fugitive	90	120
#571 Richard Chamberlain	7	10
#575 Vince Edwards as Ben Casey	9	13
#576 Cast of My Favorite martian	10	15
#579 Cast of The Farmer's Daughter	10	15
#580 Cast of Combat!	40	60
#592 Cast of Today	5	8
#595 E.G. Marshall of The Defenders	5	8
#597 Lucille Ball	20	40
#600 Dan Blocker of Bonanza	10	20
#601 Mia Farrow of Peyton Place	8	12
#616 Bob Hope	8	12
#620 Andy Williams	5	8
#624 Cast of Bonanza	20	30
#625 Dorothy Malone of Peyton Place	5	8
#627 Vince Edwards	5	8
#637 Amanda Blake and Milburn Stone	6	9
#640 Jimmy Dean	5	6

	LOW	HIGH
#642 Cast of McHale's Navy	30	50
#646 Lassie and Robert Bray	20	30
#647 Fess Parker as Daniel Boone	6	9
#652 Jackie Gleason	10	15
#655 Red Skelton	10	15
#656 Chuck Conners of Branded	10	14
#659 Joey Heatherton	8	14
#660 Efrem Zimbalist, Jr. of F.B.I.	6	9
#663 Cast of F Troop	20	30
#667 Gabor and Albert of Green Acres	30	40
#669 David Janssen of The Fugitive	10	20
#674 Barbara Stanwyck of Big Valley	10	20
#679 Dean Martin	10	15
#683 Lucille Ball by Searle	10	15
#685 Frank Sinatra	20	30
#687 Sally Field of Gidget	10	16
#688 Andy Griffith	10	20
#692 Walter Cronkite	5	6
#696 Johnny Carson	7	10
#697 Clarence Thompson of Daktari	13	18
#698 Larry Storch of F Troop	18	25
#702 Special Fall Preview Issue	60	90
#703 Joey Heatherton	10	14
#705 Vietnam War	6	9
#706 Jim Nabors	14	15
#708 Lucy Goes Mod in London	20	30
#713 Ron Ely as Tarzan	10	20
#715 James Arness as Matt Dillon	10	15
#719 Ben Gazarra of Run For Your Life	10	15
#720 Art Carney	4	5
#722 The Monkees	80	110
#723 Dale Robertson of Iron Horse	7	10
#725 Dean Martin and Friends	6	9
#726 Phyllis Diller	4	5
#727 Shatner and Nimoy of Star Trek	150	210
#728 Dorothy Malone	6	9
#729 Jackie Gleason	9	13
#730 Culp and Cosby of I Spy	18	25
#731 Cheryl Miller and Judy of Daktari	5	8
#732 Dick Van Dyke	12	16
#733 The Starlet: 1967	6	9
#735 Lawrence Welk	10	14
#736 Harry Morgan and Jack Webb of Dragnet	5	8
#739 Cast of F Troop by Searle	18	25
#740 Duff and Cole of Felony Squad	5	6
#741 Smothers Brothers	4	5
#742 Ed Sullivan	4	5
#744 Chet Huntley and David Brinkley	5	6
#756 Lucille Ball	20	30
#747 Cast of Bonanza	20	30
#750 Mike Douglas	5	8
#752 Gomer Pyle by Searle	10	14
#753 Gabor and Albert of Green Acres	18	25
#754 Special Fall Preview Issue	40	60

	LOW	HIGH
#759 Johnny Carson	5	8
#760 Mia Farrow	10	15
#762 Stuart Whitman of Cimmarron Strip	8	12
#768 Sebastian Cabot	5	8
#769 Merry Christmas	9	13
#772 Bob Hope	5	6
#773 Cast of High Chaparral	18	25
#775 Ben Gazzara of Run For Your Life	4	5
#776 Smothers Brothers	18	25
#778 Joey Bishop	4	5
#780 Jackie Gleason	9	13
#782 Bill Cosby and Robert Culp of I Spy	18	25
#783 Lucille Ball	18	25
#784 Barbara Anderson of Ironside	13	18
#787 Leslie Uggams	6	9
#790 Mike Conners of Mannix	5	6
#799 Cast of The Big Valley	50	70
#802 Cast of Gentle Ben	4	5
#803 Cast of Gunsmoke	6	9
#804 Cast of Star Trek	120	160
#805 Johnny Carson by Searle	5	6
#807 Special Fall Preview Issue	23	30
#809 Dean Martin	14	15
#811 Olympics Preview	7	10
#812 Jim Nabors	7	10
#815 Get Smart Wedding	10	15
#816 Cast of The Good Guys	10	15
#819 Robert Morse of That's Life	10	15
#820 Diahann Carroll	5	6
#821 Merry Christmas	4	5
#826 Cast of Land of the Giants	50	70
#830 Cast of Lancer	10	15
#833 Foster and Barry of Mayberry R.F.D.	5	8
#839 Jack Paar	5	8
#841 TV's Role in Space Shots	5	6
#843 Cast of Today	5	6
#846 Glen Campbell	5	8
#847 Jackie Gleason	4	5
#848 Cast of Julia	4	5
#854 Soaring Costs of TV Sports	4	5
#855 Merv Griffin	4	5
#859 Special Fall Preview Issue	20	30
#862 Bill Cosby	5	8
#864 Cast of Mission: Impossible	8	12
#866 Cast of Room 222	6	9
#868 Cast of Governor and J.J.	6	9
#870 Cast of Bonanza	20	30
#874 Remember 1969?	5	8
#877 Cast of Ironside	7	10
#879 Debbie Reynolds	5	6
#881 Bracken's Girls	5	6
#882 Daly and Everett of Medical Center	5	6
#884 Cast of Hee Haw	5	8
#890 Cast of The Bold Ones	5	6

	LOW	HIGH
#892 Glen Campbell	4	5
#893 David Frost	5	6
#894 Spiro T. Agnew by Norman Rockwell	5	8
#897 Robert Young	5	6
#898 Johnny Cash	4	5
#904 Cast of Mayberry R.F.D.	7	10
#906 Bessell and Thomas of That Girl	5	8
#907 Johnny Carson by Norman Rockwell	7	10
#909 Eddie Albert of Green Acres	5	6
#911 Special Fall Preview Issue	20	30
#913 Cast of Room 222	6	9
#914 Red Skelton	4	5
#917 Don Knotts	5	8
#925 Merry Christmas	4	5
#926 Cast of Julia	4	5
#931 James Arness	7	10
#932 Cast of The Odd Couple	13	18
#933 Goldie Hawn	5	8
#935 Hal Holbrook of The Senator	4	5
#940 Cable TV	4	5
#943 Cast of Marcus Welby, M.D.	5	8

Left to right: #614, Cast of The Munsters, January 2–8, 1965, $30–$60; #1181, Starsky & Hutch, November 15–21, 1975, $9–$12.

Newspapers

Valuable newspapers are those with major events in the headlines. One of the most valuable twentieth-century papers carries the premature "Dewey Defeats Truman" headline.

Prices are for whole issues, not just front pages. Front pages alone are worth less than the prices shown. The major papers of the major American cities are the most valuable, for example *The New York Times, The Chicago Tribune* and *The Washington Post.*

	LOW	HIGH
American and Commercial Advertiser, Baltimore, Apr. 15, 1865, Lincoln assassination	$600	$1000
American and Commercial Advertiser, Baltimore, Feb. 3, 1865, Kentucky legislature debates abolition of slavery, Negro slavery	12	20
American Journal, Providence, 1779	160	260
American Mercury, Hartford, Aug. 19, 1793	35	60
Baltimore Sun, Apr. 13, 1945, Roosevelt dies	20	35
Baltimore Sun, Aug. 7, 1945, atomic bomb	25	45
Boston Chronicle Extradordinary, Dec. 2, 1768	45	75
Boston Daily Advertiser, Oct. 12, 1871, Chicago fire	25	40
Boston Gazette, 1770, w/ Paul Revere masthead	450	700
Boston Gazette, Sept. 1, 1760	300	500
Boston Transcript, Jan. 12, 1864, "Colored Soldiers of Louisiana"	15	25
Boston Transcript, Oct. 13, 1858, Lincoln–Douglas debate	120	200
Boston Transcript, Sept. 17, 1849, California Gold Rush	13	20
British Apollo or Curious Amusements For the Ingenious, London, 1709	15	25
Charleston Daily News, 1870	3	5
Chicago Journal of Commerce, May 2, 1945, Hitler dies	15	25
Chicago Record-Herald, Dec. 19, 1903, Wright brothers' flight	40	650
Chicago Tribune, Aug. 9, 1974, Nixon resigns	15	30
Chicago Tribune, Paris Edition, Nov. 12, 1918, Armistice Day	15	25
Cleveland Daily Herald, Sept. 11, 1876, James Gang bank robbery	75	125
Cleveland Weekly Herald, Apr. 7, 1882, Jesse James dies	300	500
Cleveland Weekly Herald, Ohio, Sept. 23, 1881, Garfield dies	50	80
Columbian Centinel, Boston, Jan. 28, 1795	30	50
Columbian Centinel, Boston, Oct. 3, 1795	20	30
Columbian Centinel, Boston, Mar. 16, 1793, Washington inaugurated	500	900
Connecticut Courant, Hartford, Feb. 26, 1787, Shays' Rebellion	250	350
Connecticut Courant, Hartford, 1781	150	240
Continental Journal, Boston, 1780	175	275
Daily Alta California, San Francisco, Apr. 20, 1865, Lincoln assassination	65	100
Daily Colorado Tribune, Denver, 1868	25	45
Daily Delta, New Orleans, Mar. 11, 1862, *Merrimac* battles	160	250
Daily Globe, Washington, Mar. 11, 1862, *Monitor* vs. *Merrimac*	50	80
Daily National Intelligencer, Washington, Feb. 12, 1829, Andrew Jackson elected	30	50
Daily State Journal, Austin, TX, Sept. 17, 1870	15	25
Daily State Register, Des Moines, IA, Nov. 4, 1868, Grant elected president	60	90
Davenport Daily Gazette, IA, Nov. 24, 1863, Lincoln's Gettysburg address	200	300
Deseret Evening News, July 12, 1876, Custer's Last Stand	75	125
Deseret Semi-Weekly News, Salt Lake City, Apr. 8, 1882, Jesse James dies	225	350
Detroit Daily Tribune, July 22, 1861, First Battle of Bull Run	75	120
Dublin Evening Post, Ireland, 1803	6	9
Dunlap's American Daily Advertiser, Philadelphia, May 3, 1793	20	30
Essex Gazette, Salem, MA, Aug. 27, 1771	250	450
Essex Gazette, Salem, MA, May 8, 1770	200	300

	LOW	HIGH
Essex Gazette, Salem, MA, Nov. 22, 1774, First Continental Congress	3000	5000
Essex Journal and New-Hampshire Packet, Newburyport, MA, Apr. 3, 1793, Louis XVI sentenced	60	90
Evansville Weekly Journal, IN, Aug. 22, 1850, California joining U.S.	30	50
Evening News, Newark, NJ, July 21, 1969, moon landing	13	20
Examiner, London, 1710	14	20
Federal Gazette and Baltimore Daily Advertiser, Aug. 13, 1796	30	50
Fitchburg (MA) Sentinel, Apr. 14, 1841, William H. Harrison dies	60	90
Freeman's Journal, Philadelphia, July 4, 1781	150	240
Gazette of the U.S., Philadelphia, Jan. 12, 1791	35	60
Gazette of the United States, NY, Oct. 28, 1789, president's salary set	160	270
Gazette of the United States, NY, Sept. 23, 1789, Bill of Rights	2000	3500
Gazette of the United States, Philadelphia, Dec. 4, 1790	20	35
General Avertiser, Philadelphia, May 3, 1797	20	35
Gentleman's Magazine, London, July 1815, Battle of Waterloo	60	90
Georgetown Gazette, CA, Feb. 2, 1899	7	12
Golden Era, San Francisco, Dec. 14, 1862, Battle of Fredericksburg	13	20
Guardian, London, 1713	13	22
Harper's Weekly, Apr. 21, 1877, Frederick Douglas	40	65
Harper's Weekly, NY, June 22, 1861	20	30
Herald: A Gazette For the Country, NY, Jan. 7, 1795, $10 reward for runaway slave	25	45
Honolulu Star-Bulletin, May 7, 1945, "EXTRA," V-E Day	35	65
Independent Chronicle, Boston, Apr. 10, 1777	400	600
Independent Chronicle, Boston, Dec. 17, 1798	35	65
Independent Chronicle, Boston, Sept. 1, 1814, Washington DC burns	135	235
Independent Press, Lawrenceburgh, IN, Apr. 7, 1852	7	12
Intelligencer Journal, Lancaster, PA, Aug. 9, 1974, Nixon resigns	15	25
Intelligencer Journal, Lancaster, PA, July 21, 1969, moon landing	20	30
Journal of Commerce, Chicago, Nov. 2 & $, 1908, Taft elected	10	20
Lancaster Intelligencer, May 12, 1869	50	85
Leavenworth Daily Conservative, KS, Nov. 9, 1861, Lincoln elected	140	200
Liberator, Boston, 1846, abolitionist newspaper of William Lloyd Garrison, slavery	25	45
London Chronicle, 1762	6	10
London Gazette, 1694	40	60
Long Beach Press-Telegram, Dec. 8, 1941, Pearl Harbor	10	20
Los Angeles Evening Express, Sept. 5, 1872, speech by Frederick Douglas	25	40
Los Angeles Evening Herald, Apr. 16, 1912, 5th Extra, *Titanic* sinks	200	330
Los Angeles Evening Herald, Apr. 16, 1912, Sunset Edition, *Titanic* sinks	250	400
Los Angeles Evening Herald Express, Apr. 30, 1945, Mussolini dies	15	25
Los Angeles Herald Examiner, July 21, 1969, moon landing	35	50
Marysville (CA) Daily Appeal, Apr. 16, 1865, Lincoln assassination	1000	1750
Massachusetts Spy or Worcester Gazette, Oct. 7, 1790	25	45
Massachusetts Spy or Worcester Gazette, July 12, 1797	20	30
Massachusetts Spy or Worcester Gazette, Paul Revere masthead, 1784	200	340
Memphis Press-Scimitar, Aug. 17, 1977, Elvis Presley dies (beware of reprints)	25	40
Mercurious Reformatus, or The New Observator, London, 1691	25	40
Miami Student, Miami University, Oxford, OH, Apr. 12, 1945, FDR dies	25	40
Minneapolis Journal, Oct. 10, 1892, Lizzie Borden	20	35
N.Y. Daily Tribune, Aug. 1, 8161, Bull Run	25	45
N.Y. Semi-Weekly Tribune, Apr. 18, 1865, Lincoln assassination	360	600
N.Y. Times, July 21, 1969, moon landing	25	45
Napa (CA) Register, Apr. 12, 1945, FDR dies	30	50

	LOW	HIGH
Napa (CA) Register, May 7, 1945, V-E Day	25	40
National Intelligencer, Feb. 21, 1846, includes news of Liberia as a possible colonization site, slavery	20	35
National Intelligencer, Feb. 22, 1828, Washington dies	12	18
National Intelligencer, Nov. 4, 1868, Grant elected	30	50
National Intelligencer, Washington, D.C., Jan 23, 1862, Tyler dies	15	25
National Intelligencer, Washington, D.C. Feb. 10, 1825, John Quincy Adams elected	30	50
Nevada Daily Transcript, Nevada City, CA, Feb. 22, 1873	7	12
New Orleans Daily Crescent, 1859, Negroes For Sale adv.	15	25
New York Herald, Dec. 12, 1862	25	40
New York Herald, Dec. 25, 1862	25	45
New York Herald, July 19, 1861	35	60
New York Journal, July 6, 1775, Bunker Hill	450	750
New York Journal and Patriotic Register, June 23, 1792	25	40
New York Observer, Oct. 24, 1846	10	15
New York Times, Dec. 26, 1863	8	14
New York Times, Feb. 20, 1863	15	20
New York Times, Feb. 24, 1864	12	18
New York Times, July 27, 1861	11	17
New York Times, Mar. 11, 1862, *Monitor* vs. *Merrimac*	75	125
New York Times, Nov. 17, 1862	15	25
New York Times, Nov. 18, 1861	12	18
New York Times, Oct. 31, 1863	20	30
New York Times, Sept. 20, 1864	12	18
New-Hampshire Gazette and General Advertiser, Portsmouth, May 17, 1783, Revolutionary War ends	60	100
New-York Gazette, or The Weekly Post-Boy, Oct. 27, 1755, French and Indian War	500	750
Newes, Published For Satisfaction and Information of the People, London, 1664	125	200
Nile's Weekly Register, Baltimore, July 19, 1817, on illegal kidnapping of free blacks sold on the slave market, slavery	25	40
Oakland (CA) Herald, Apr. 18, 1906, San Francisco earthquake	450	700
Observator, London, 1686	25	35
Pennsylvania Evening Post, Apr. 26, 1777	235	400
Pennsylvania Gazette, July 3, 1766, repeal of Stamp Act	250	450
Pennsylvania Gazette, Philadelphia, July 14, 1773, Slave insurrection	75	120
Pennsylvania Gazette, Philadelphia, July 6, 1749, printed by Ben Franklin	2000	3500
Pennsylvania Gazette, Philadelphia, Aug. 4, 1773	160	240
Pennsylvania Gazette, Philadelphia, Nov. 21, 1765, Stamp Act	1500	2500
Pennsylvania Packet, 1781	135	230
Pennsylvania Packet, Philadelphia, Apr. 13, 1789, Washington elected	2750	4750
Philadelphia Evening Bulletin, Sept. 20, 1881, Garfield dies	15	25
Philadelphia Inquirer, Apr. 10, 1867, Alaska purchase	100	170
Pittston Gazette, PA, Aug. 4, 1914, W.W. I begins	14	20
Porcupine's Gazette, Philadelphia, June 22, 1797	20	30
Post-Standard, Syracuse, NY, July 21, 1969, moon landing	20	30
Prices Current and Shipping List, San Francisco, Oct. 31, 1853, California gold rush	60	100
Providence Gazette, RI, Feb. 5, 1785	30	50
Rambler, London, ed. by Samuel Johnson, 1750	12	20
Redwood City (CA) Tribune, July 21, 1969, moon landing	20	30
Sacramento Weekly Union, July 11, 1863, Gettysburg	300	450

	LOW	HIGH
Salem Gazette, Jan. 23, 1783	45	70
Salinas Weekly Index, CA, Apr. 25, 1889	9	14
San Diego Union, CA, 1873	15	25
San Francisco Bulletin, Sept. 4, 1886, Geronimo surrenders	60	100
San Francisco Call Bulletin, Aug. 14, 1945, V-J Day	15	25
San Francisco Call Bulletin, San Francisco Chronicle, and San Francisco Examiner, issued together as one paper, Apr. 19, 1906, San Francisco earthquake	600	1000
San Francisco Chronicle, Aug. 3, 1923, Harding dies	45	70
San Francisco Chronicle, Aug. 9, 1974, Nixon resigns	17	25
San Francisco Chronicle, July 21, 1969, moon landing	20	30
San Francisco Daily Herald, Nov. 26, 1853, California gold rush	36	60
San Francisco Examiner, Apr. 13, 1945, FDR dies	17	25
San Francisco Examiner, Aug. 3, 1923, Harding dies	25	40
San Francisco Examiner, Extra, Apr. 20, 1906, San Francisco earthquake	300	500
San Francisco Examiner, June 1, 1889, Johnstown flood	60	90
San Francisco Examiner, June 5, 1968, Robert Kennedy shot	12	18
San Francisco Examiner, May 7, 1945, "Extra," V-E Day	13	20
San Francisco Examiner, Oct. 15, 1912, Teddy Roosevelt shot	35	60
San Francisco Examiner, Sept. 11, 1889, Jack the Ripper	200	300
San Francisco News, Apr. 12, 1945, FDR dies	25	45
San Francisco News, Aug. 6, 1945, atom bomb	25	45
San Francisco News, Feb. 10, 1942, *Normandie* sinks	9	13
Santa Ana (CA) Register, Nov. 11, 1918, Armistice Day	35	55
Scientific American, NY, Mar. 2, 1895	12	20
Seattle Daily Times, Aug. 3, 1923, Harding dies	30	50
Seattle Post Intelligencer, Apr. 15, 1912, *Titanic* sinks	200	350
Seattle Post Intelligencer, Dec. 8, 1941, Pearl Harbor	70	100
Sentinel, Richmond, VA, July 27, 1863, Gettysburg, Confederate paper	750	1250
Shipping and Commercial List, NY, 1840	4	7
Spectator, London, 1711-12, Addison and Steele's	15	25
St. Louis Globe-Democrat, Sept. 14, 1876, Northfield bank robbery	150	250
St. Louis Post-Dispatch, Apr. 13, 1945, FDR dies	15	25
Stockton (CA) Daily Independent, Nov. 4, 1868, Grant elected	22	35
Tatler, London, 1709	15	25
Texas State Gazette, Aug. 1, 1863, Gettysburg	120	200
Tombstone Epitaph, Tombstone, Arizona Territory, Aug. 6, 1881, Billy the Kid dies	1250	2000
Torrance (CA) Daily Breeze, Aug. 17, 1977, Elvis dies	20	35

Prints and Lithographs

Audubon

John James Audubon is a name synonymous with bird pictures. His "Birds of America" series is recognized worldwide. Between 1826 and 1842, Audubon travled throughout the United States and Canada gathering material to paint this famous work.

Today, experts believe there are less than 200 sets of "Birds of America" actually bound in volumes. The work was engraved by R. Havell and Son in London. There are 435 plates in a complete set. In 1971 an exact facsimile edition of 250 copies was printed in Amsterdam.

We list the original Havel prints, first with a typical auction range; next, a retail price is given (R), followed by retail prices for the later Bien edition (B) and the Amsterdam printing (A). Entries are listed sequentially by plate number, followed by subject.

All photos used for this category are courtesy of Sotheby's, New York.

		AUCTION RANGE		R	B	A
7	Purple Grackle	$3200	$4500	$8800	$750	$600
9	Selby's Flycatcher	825	1100	2200	200	160
10	Brown Titlark	5500	700	7100	1250	1100
12	Baltimore Oriole	3200	5500	11,000	750	600
13	Snow Bird	825	1100	2200	200	160
15	Blue Yellow-Backed Warbler	1500	2150	4400	380	300
16	Great-Footed Hawk	3200	4500	8800	750	600
18	Bewick's Wren	825	1100	2200	200	160
19	Louisiana Water Thrush	825	1100	2200	200	160
21	Mockingbird	4500	5500	11,200	1100	825
22	Purple Martin	2150	3200	6200	500	400
24	Roscoe's Yellow Thorat	825	1100	2200	200	160
25	Song Sparrow	825	1100	2200	200	160
27	Red-Headed Woodpecker	2150	3200	6200	500	400
29	Towhe Bunting	825	1200	2500	200	160
31	Shite-Headed Eagle	3200	5500	11,000	750	600
32	Black-Billed Cuckoo	4500	5500	12,500	1100	825
33	American Goldfinch	2500	3540	7600	620	500
34	Worm-Eating Warbler	1100	1500	3100	250	200
35	Children's Warbler	600	1100	2150	150	120
36	Stanley Hawk	2150	2500	5600	500	400
38	Kentucky Warbler	825	1200	2500	200	160
40	American Redstart	2150	2500	5600	500	400
41	Ruffed Grouse	4500	6500	12,500	1100	825
42	Orchard's Oriole	825	1200	2500	200	160
43	Cedar Bird	2150	3200	6200	500	400
45	Traill's Flycatcher	600	925	1900	150	120
46	Barred Owl	3200	5500	11,000	750	600
47	Ruby-Throated Hummingbird	11,000	16,000	31,200	2500	2150
48	Azure Warbler	825	1200	2500	200	160
50	Black and Yellow Warbler	600	925	1900	150	120
51	Red-Tailed Hawk	3200	4500	8800	750	600
52	Chuck Will's Widow	2150	4500	8500	500	400
53	Painted Finch	2150	3200	6200	500	400
54	Rice Bird	825	1200	2500	200	160
55	Cuvier's Regulus	825	1200	2500	200	160

		AUCTION RANGE		R	B	A
57	Loggerhead Shrike	1100	1500	3100	250	200
58	Hermit Thrush	825	1200	2500	200	160
60	Carbonated Warbler	1200	1800	3800	300	240
61	Great Horned Owl	6500	10,000	17,500	1500	1200
63	White-Eyed Flycatcher or Vireo	825	1200	2500	200	160
65	Rathbon's Warbler	825	1200	2500	200	160
67	Redwinged Starling	2150	3200	6200	500	400
69	Bay-Breasted Warbler	1100	1800	3500	250	200
70	Henslow's Bunting	1200	1800	3800	300	240
71	Winter Hawk	2150	3200	6200	500	400
73	Wood Thrush	1100	1500	3100	250	200
74	Indigo Bunting	1200	1800	4000	300	240
75	Le Petit Caporal	1100	1500	3100	250	200
76	Virginia Partridge	3200	5500	11,000	750	600
77	Belted Kingfisher	2150	4500	7500	500	400
78	Great Carolina Wren	2150	2500	6200	500	400
79	Tyrant Flycatcher	1100	1500	3100	250	200
80	Prairie Titlark	1100	1500	3100	250	200
81	Fish Hawk or Osprey	15,000	25,000	50,000	3950	3200
82	Whip-Poor-Will	1700	7000	11,000	380	310
83	House Wren	2150	3200	6200	500	400
84	Blue-Gray Flycatcher	825	1200	2500	200	160
85	Yellow-Throated Warbler	825	1200	2500	200	160
86	Black Warrior	2150	3200	6200	500	400
87	Florida Jay	2150	4500	7500	500	400
88	Autumnal Warbler	825	1200	2500	200	160
89	Nashville Warbler	825	1200	2500	200	160
90	Black and White Creeper	700	925	2150	180	140
91	Broad-Winged Bunting	600	925	1900	150	120
95	Blue-Eyed Yellow Warbler	825	1200	2500	200	160
97	Little Screech Owl	2150	4500	7500	500	400
98	White-Bellied Swallow	600	925	1900	150	120
99	Cow Pen Bird	825	1200	2500	200	160
101	Raven	2150	4500	7500	500	400
102	Blue Jay	825	1200	2500	200	160
103	Canada Warbler	850	1250	2700	200	160
104	Chipping Sparrow	700	1100	2100	180	140
105	Red-Breasted Nuthatch	600	925	1900	150	120
107	Canada Jay	1100	1500	3100	250	200
108	Fox-Colored Sparrow	825	1200	2500	200	160
109	Savannah Finch	825	1200	2500	200	160
113	Blue Bird	1200	1800	3800	300	240
114	White-Crowned Sparrow	600	925	1900	150	120
115	Wood Pewee	600	925	1900	150	120
116	Ferruginous Thrush	1500	2500	5500	380	300
117	Mississippi Kite	1500	2500	5500	400	300
118	Warbling Flycatcher	1500	2500	5500	380	300
120	Pewee Flycatcher	500	700	1500	120	100
121	Snowy Owl	27,000	37,000	80,000	6250	5500
122	Blue Grosbeak	825	1200	2500	200	160
124	Green-Black Capped Flycatcher	825	1200	2500	200	160
125	Brown-Headed Nuthatch	600	825	1800	150	120
127	Rose-Breasted Grosbeak	2150	4500	7500	500	400
128	Cat Bird	825	1200	2500	200	160

Left: #1, Great American Cock Male.

Right: #17, Carolina Pigeon or Turtle Dove.

Left: #26, Carolina Parrot.

Right: #27, Red Headed Woodpecker.

Left: #61, Great Horned Owl.

Right: #82, Whip-Poor-Will.

		AUCTION RANGE		R	B	A
130	Yellow-Winged Sparrow	700	1100	2100	180	140
131	American Robin	4500	6500	13,500	1100	825
132	Three-Toed Woodecker	2150	4500	7500	500	400
133	Black Poll Warbler	8225	1200	2500	200	160
134	Hemlock Warbler	825	1200	2500	200	160
135	Blackburnian Warbler	1100	1500	3100	250	200
136	Meadow Lark	10,000	13,000	26,000	2150	1600
137	Yellow-Breasted Chat	3200	5500	11,000	750	600
138	Connecticut Warbler	1200	1800	3800	300	240
139	Red Sparrow	825	1200	2500	200	160
140	Pine-Creeping Warbler	1100	1500	3100	250	200
141	Goshawk	2150	3200	6200	500	400
143	Golden Crowned Thrush	700	1100	2100	180	140
144	Small Green-Crested Flycatcher	1100	1500	3100	250	200
146	Fish Crow	2150	3200	6200	500	400
147	Night Hawk	3200	5500	10,000	750	600
148	Pine Swamp Warbler	600	925	1900	150	120
150	Red-Eyed Vireo	600	925	1900	150	120
152	White-Breasted Nuthatch	2150	4500	7500	500	400
153	Yellow-Rump Warbler	1500	2500	5500	380	300
155	Black-Throated Blue Warbler	1100	1500	3300	250	200
157	Rusty Grackle	600	925	1900	150	120
158	American Swift	500	700	1500	120	100
160	Black-Capped Titmouse	825	1200	2500	200	160
161	Caracara Eagle	4500	6500	12,500	1100	825
162	Zenaida Dove	825	1200	2500	200	160
164	Tawny Thrush	1100	1500	3100	250	200
165	Bachman's Finch	1200	1800	3800	300	240
168	Fork-Tailed Flycatcher	3200	5500	11,000	750	600
169	Mangrove Cuckoo	1500	2500	5500	380	300
170	Gray Tyrant	825	1200	2500	200	160
171	Barn Owl	7750	11,000	23,000	1750	1400
173	Barn Swallow	2150	3200	6200	500	400
174	Olive-Sided Flycatcher	825	1200	2500	200	160
175	Marsh Wren	600	925	1900	150	120
176	Spotted Grouse	3200	5500	11,000	750	600
178	Orange-Crowned Warbler	500	700	1500	120	100
179	Wood Wren	825	1200	2600	200	160
180	Black-Capped Titmouse	825	1200	2600	200	160
182	Ground Dove	2600	3600	7500	620	500
183	Golden-Crested Wren	600	925	2100	150	120
185	Bachman's Warbler	1100	1500	3300	250	200
186	Pinnated Grouse	3200	5500	11,000	750	600
188	Tree Sparrow	700	1100	2100	180	140
189	Snow Bunting	825	1200	2500	200	160
191	Willow Grouse	3200	5500	11,000	750	600
192	Great American Shrike	825	1200	2600	200	160
194	Canadian Titmouse	500	700	1500	120	100
195	Ruby-Crowned Wren	825	1200	2500	200	160
196	Labrador Falcon	2600	3600	8000	620	500
197	American Crossbill	1200	1800	3800	300	240
198	Worm-Eating Warbler	825	1200	2500	200	160
200	Shore Lark	600	925	1900	150	120
201	Canada Goose	4500	6500	12,500	1100	825

#6, Great American Hen & Young.

#31, White-Headed Eagle.

#71, Winter Hawk.

#176, Spotted Grouse.

#234, Tufted Duck.

#266, Common Cormorant.

#296, Barnacle Goose.

#297, Harlequin Duck.

		AUCTION RANGE		R	B	A
203	Fresh Water Marsh Wren	1100	1500	3100	250	200
204	Salt Water Marsh Wren	600	825	1800	150	120
205	Virginia Rail	700	1100	2100	180	140
206	Summer or Wood Duck	10,000	13,000	27,000	2150	1800
208	Esquimaux Curlew	825	1200	2500	200	160
209	Wilson's Plover	500	700	1500	120	100
210	Least Bittern	1500	2600	5500	380	300
213	Puffin	2150	3200	6200	500	400
214	Razor Sill	825	1200	2500	200	160
215	Phalarope	600	925	1900	150	120
217	Louisiana Heron	16,000	27,000	55,000	4000	3400
218	Foolish Guillemar	825	1200	2500	200	160
219	Black Guillemar	1500	2500	5500	380	300
220	Piping Plover	600	925	1900	150	120
221	Mallard Duck	20,000	30,000	62,500	5500	4500
222	White Ibis	3200	5500	10,000	750	600
223	Pied Oyster Catcher	1100	1500	3300	250	200
224	Kittiwake Gull	600	925	1900	150	120
225	Kildeer Plover	500	700	1500	120	100
226	Whooping Crane	11,000	16,000	31,200	2500	2150
227	Pin-Tailed Duck	5500	7750	16,000	1250	1100
228	Green-Wing Teal	3200	5500	11,000	750	600
229	Scaup Duck	2150	4500	7500	500	400
230	Ruddy Plover	600	825	1800	150	120
232	Hooded Merganser	3200	5500	11,000	750	600
233	Sora or Rail	500	700	1500	120	100
235	Night Heron	4500	6500	12,500	1100	825
237	Great Exquimaux Curlew	1100	1500	3100	250	200
238	Great Marbled Codwit	1100	1500	3100	250	200
240	Roseate Tern	2150	3200	6200	500	400
241	Black-Backed Gull	1100	1500	3100	250	200
242	Snowy Heron	16,000	27,000	55,000	3750	3200
243	American Snipe	2150	3200	6200	500	400
245	Thick-Billed Murre	600	825	1800	150	120
246	Eider Duck	11,000	16,000	33,000	2600	2150
248	American Pied-Bill Dobchick	1500	2500	5500	380	300
249	Tufted Auk	1100	1500	3100	250	200
251	Brown Pelican	13,000	19,000	40,000	3600	2400
252	Florida Cormorant	1500	2500	5500	380	300
255	Red Phalarope	825	1200	2500	200	160
256	Purple Heron	4500	6500	12,500	1100	825
257	Double-Crested Cormorant	1500	2500	5500	380	300
259	Horned Grebe	1200	1900	3800	300	240
260	Fork-Tail Petrel	825	1200	2500	200	160
262	Tropic Bind	2150	4500	8000	500	400
263	Curlew Sandpiper	825	1200	2500	200	160
264	Fulmar Petrel	825	1200	2500	200	160
266	Common Cormorant	1100	1500	3400	250	200
267	Arctic Jager	1100	1500	3100	250	200
268	American Woodcock	2150	3200	6900	500	400
269	Greenshank	1200	1800	3800	300	240
271	Frigate Pelican	2150	4500	8000	500	400
272	Richardson's Jager	600	925	2100	150	120
274	Semipalmated Snipe	825	1200	2500	200	160

Left: #97, Little Screech Owl.

Right: #107, Canada Jay.

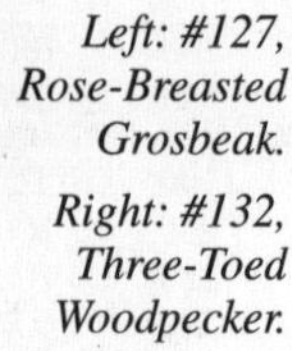

Left: #127, Rose-Breasted Grosbeak.

Right: #132, Three-Toed Woodpecker.

Left: #162, Zenaida Dove.

Right: #171, Barn Owl.

		AUCTION RANGE		R	B	A
275	Noddy Tern	500	700	1500	120	100
277	Hutchins' Barnacle Goose	1500	2600	5500	400	300
278	Schinz's Sandpiper	600	925	1900	150	120
280	Black Tern	600	825	1800	150	120
282	White-Winged Silvery Gull	825	1200	2500	200	160
283	Wandering Shearwater	600	825	1800	150	120
284	Purple Sandpiper	600	925	1900	150	120
285	Fork-Tailed Gull	825	1200	2500	200	160
287	Ivory Gull	1200	1800	4200	300	240
288	Yellow Shank	3200	5500	11,000	750	600
289	Solitary Sandpiper	1200	1800	3800	300	240
291	Herring Gull	3200	5500	11,000	750	600
292	Crested Grebe	2150	3200	6200	500	400
295	Manx Shearwater	500	700	1500	120	100
297	Harlequin Duck	1200	1800	4200	300	240
299	Dusky Petrel	600	925	1900	150	120
300	Golden Plover	400	600	1200	100	80
301	Canvasback Duck	600	925	1900	150	120
302	Black Duck	2150	3200	6200	500	400
303	Upland Sandpiper	1500	2500	5500	380	300
305	Purple Gallinule	2150	3200	6200	500	400
306	Common Loon	1500	2600	5500	380	300
308	Greater Yellow Legs	825	1200	2500	200	160
310	Spotted Sandpiper	825	1200	2500	200	160
312	Long-Tailed Duck	1200	1800	3800	300	240
314	Laughing Gull	825	1200	2500	200	160
315	Sandpiper	600	925	1900	150	120
317	Surf Duck	1100	1500	3100	250	200
318	Avocet	1200	1800	3800	300	240
319	Lesser Tern	1500	2500	5500	380	300
320	Little Sandpiper	825	1200	2500	200	160
322	Red-Head Duck	2150	4500	7500	500	400
323	Black Skimmer	2150	3200	6200	500	400
324	Bonaparte's Gull	825	1200	2500	200	160
325	Bufflehead	2150	3200	6200	500	400
328	Long-Legged Avocet	1500	2500	5500	380	300
329	Yellow Rail	600	925	1900	150	120
330	Plover	500	700	1500	120	100
332	Labrador Duck	1500	2500	5500	380	300
333	Green Heron	3200	5500	11,000	750	600
334	Black-Bellied Plover	400	600	1200	100	80
335	Red-Bellied Sandpiper	825	1200	2500	200	160
337	American Bittern	1500	2500	5500	380	300
338	Bemaculated Duck	3200	5500	11,000	750	600
339	Little Auk	600	925	1900	150	120
340	Stormy Petrel	600	925	1900	150	120
341	Great Auk	2150	3200	6200	500	400
343	Ruddy Duck	1500	2500	5500	380	300
344	Long-Legged Sandpiper	600	925	1900	150	120
345	American Widgeon	1500	2500	5500	380	300
346	Black-Throated Diver	4500	6500	13,500	1100	825
347	American Bittern	1500	2500	5500	380	300
348	Gadwall Duck	2150	3200	6200	500	400
350	Rocky Mountain Plover	500	700	1500	120	100

#305, Purple Gallinule.

#381, Snow Goose.

#391, Brant Goose.

#392, Louisiana Hawk.

#397, Scarlet Ibis.

#401, Red-Breasted Merganser.

#404, Eared Grebe.

#429, Western Duck.

		AUCTION	RANGE	R	B	A
352	Black-Winged Hawk	825	1200	2500	200	160
353	Chestnut-Backed Hawk	825	1200	2500	200	160
354	Louisiana Tanager	2150	4500	7500	500	400
355	MacGillivray's Finch	825	1200	2500	200	160
356	Marsh Hawk	3200	5500	11,000	750	600
357	American Magpie	1200	1900	4200	300	240
360	Winter and Rock Wren	700	1100	2100	180	140
361	Long-Tailed Grouse	1500	2500	5500	380	300
363	Bohemian Chatterer	825	1200	2500	200	160
364	White-Winged Grossbill	1100	1500	3100	250	200
365	Lapland Longspur	500	700	1500	120	100
366	Iceland Falcon	13,000	19,000	40,000	3200	2400
367	Band-Tailed Pigeon	3200	5500	11,000	750	600
368	Rock Grouse	1200	1800	3800	300	240
369	Mountain Mockingbird	1200	1800	3800	300	240
372	Common Buzzard	1100	1500	3100	250	200
374	Sharp-Shinned Hawk	825	1200	2500	200	160
375	Lesser Red Poll	825	1200	2500	200	160
376	Trumpeter Swan	3200	5500	10,000	750	600
379	Ruff-Necked Hummingbird	3200	5500	11,000	750	600
380	Tengmalm's Owl	600	925	1900	150	120
381	Snow Goose	2150	4500	7500	500	400
382	Sharp-Tailed Grouse	1200	1800	3800	300	240
383	Long-Eared Owl	1200	1800	3800	300	240
384	Black-Throated Bunting	700	1100	2100	180	140
385	Bank Swallow	200	1200	1800	50	40
386	Great American Egret	13,000	19,000	37,500	3200	2400
388	Glossy Ibis	3200	5500	11,000	750	600
391	Brant Goose	2150	3200	6200	500	400
392	Louisiana Hawk	1200	1800	3800	300	240
383	Blue-Winged Teal	600	925	1900	150	120
394	Buntings and Finches	1100	1500	3300	250	200
395	Audubon's Warbler	825	1200	2500	200	160
396	Burgomaster Gull	1500	2500	5500	380	300
398	Lazuli Finch	600	925	1900	150	120
399	Black-Throated Warbler	825	1200	2500	200	160
401	Red-Breasted Merganser	2150	4500	8000	500	400
403	Golden-Eyed Duck	1200	1800	3800	300	240
406	Trumpeter Swan	3200	5500	11,000	750	600
408	American Scooter Duck	1200	1800	3800	300	240
409	Havell's Tern	1200	1800	3800	300	240
411	Common American Swan	13,000	19,000	40,000	3200	2500
412	Violet Green Cormorant	1100	1500	3100	250	200
413	California Partridge	1100	1500	3100	250	200
414	Golden-Winged Warbler	600	925	1900	150	120
417	Maria's Woodpecker	2150	3200	6200	500	400
418	American Ptarmigan	825	1200	2500	200	160
421	Brown Pelican, young	10,000	13,000	27,000	2150	1600
423	Plumed partridge	1200	1800	3800	300	240
424	Lazuli Finch	500	700	1500	120	100
425	Columbian Hummingbird	1500	2500	5500	380	300
427	White-Legged Oyster Catcher	1200	1800	3800	300	240
428	Townsend's Sandpiper	500	700	1500	120	100
429	Western Duck	825	1200	2500	200	160

Currier and Ives

In 1835, Nathaniel Currier started a lithography company in New York. James Ives joined in 1852 as a bookkeeper. Currier and Ives was unique in its ability to combine artistic talent, skilled craftsmanship, appropriate technology and merchandising acumen into a successful business enterprise. It employed well-known artists of the day, including Maurer, Palmer, Tait and Worth. The finest materials were used: stones from Bavaria (where lithography was invented), lithographic crayons from France and colors from Austria. The firm invented a lithographic crayon, reputed to be superior to all others, and produced a lithographic ink of beef suet, goose grease, white wax, castile soap, gum mastic, shellac and gas black. Mass distribution and low cost were the keys to success. Uncolored prints were sold for as little as 6¢ each and even large-colored folios sold for no more than $3. Prints were sold door-to-door by peddlars and in the streets by pushcart vendors, and even overseas through agents. The firm of Currier and Ives was dissolved in 1907. Although an estimated ten million prints sold, only a small percentage survive today.

Published in various sizes, the prints are commonly grouped into folio sizes: *Very Small* (up to approximately 7" x 9"), *Small* (approximately 8.8" x 12.8"), *Medium* (approximately 9" x 14" to 14" x 20") and *Large* (anything over 14" x 20"). The sizes pertain to the image only, not the margin. Often, print owners trimmed the margins of the pictures, so an uncut print is more valuable than a pared one.

Most prints were struck in black and white and then hand colored. Because of this method, different colorings of the same print are found. Folio sizes *Very Small, Small* and *Medium* were completed in this manner. However, the *Large* folios were sometimes partially printed in color and then finished by hand, usually by only one artist. Many of these prints have been reprinted often. Beware buying a modern calendar print.

Each print is given with its Conningham number (C#), a reference to the checklist by Frederic A. Conningham, *Currier and Ives Prints: An Illustrated Check List, Revised,* Crown, NY, 1970, out-of-print. Photos illustrating this category are courtesy Sotheby's in New York.

Large Folio

C#	LOW	HIGH
1090, City of Baltimore, 1880	$5000	$8100
2458, Government House	900	1500
2956, House, Kennel and Field	800	1400
3247, Jib and Main Sail Race, 1882	1750	2700
3291, Jolly Smoker, 1880	400	700
3336, King of the Road, 1869	2300	3900
3863, Magadino, Lake Maggiore	600	900
3943, Mama's Darling	250	400
4126, Mill River Scenery	2000	3300
4637, Our Cabinet, 1885	400	600
4775, Pic-Nic Party, 1858	1000	1600
5043, Race to the Wire, 1891	2000	3000
5264, Rush for the Pole, 1877	2000	4000
5455, See My Boots!	500	700
5688, Stag at Bay	500	900
5880, Summer's Afternoon	1500	2500
5914, Surrender of Napoleon III	280	500
6040, Three Little Maids from School	440	700
6273, Two to Go, 1892	1500	2500
6443, View on the Housatonic, 1867	2000	3500
6570, Waterfall-Moonlight	800	1400
6725, Winning the Card	2000	3000

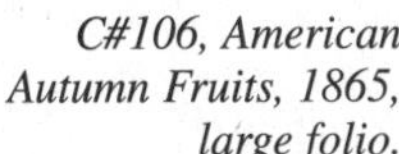
C#106, American Autumn Fruits, 1865, large folio.

C#161, American Fruit Piece, 1859, large folio.

C#1107, The City of New York, 1876, large folio.

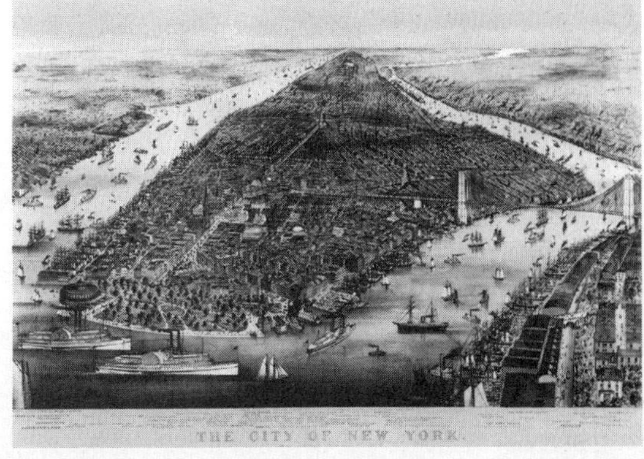

Medium Folio

C#	LOW	HIGH
131, American Farm Life, 1868	$1000	$1600
181, American Patriot's Dream, 1861	320	500
276, Arthur Chamber's "Lightweight Champion"	500	800
478, Begging a Crust	210	300
521, Big Thing on Ice, 1862	1000	1800
689, Brigham Young	180	300
760, By the Seashore, 1868	530	900
841, Castle Howard	190	300
1023, Cherry Time, 1866	700	1200
1182, Coaching Four-in-Hand, 1876	1000	1800
2132, Free Lunch, 1872	370	600
2608, Great Exhibition of 1860	600	900
3436, Landscape and Cattle	600	900
4125, Mill in the Highlands	650	100
4132, Miller's Home	600	1000
4273, Mustang Team	700	1100
4668, Over the Garden Wall	220	400
4689, Paddy and the Pigs	390	600
4832, Pond in the Wood	520	900
5052, Rail Candidate	330	600
5158, River Road	1130	1900
5178, Robert Burns	150	200
5427, School Rewards	550	900
5441, Scottish Boarder	240	400
5815, Still Hunting on the Susquehanna	1040	1600
5843, Stride of a Century, 1876	560	1000
5874, Summer Ramble	530	900
5889, Sunny Morning	440	800
6121, Training Day	350	600
6388, View of Astoria, L.I.	2000	3500
6681, Will He Bite?, 1868	320	500
6757, Won By a Dash, 1892	900	1500

Small Folio

C#	LOW	HIGH
126, American Eclipse, 1879	$450	$800
162, American Fruits, 1861	250	400
213, Among the Hills	400	700
220, Angel Gabriel	30	100
251, Aquarium	180	300
284, Ascension of Christ	30	100
293, Astoria Institute	300	500
319, Autumn Fruits, oval	260	400
340, Bad Dream	270	400
347, Bad Streak, 1879	190	300
367, Barefaced Cheek, 1881	380	6003
381, Battle of Boyne	100	200
388, Battle of Bunker's Hill	400	700
400, Battle of Cole Harbor, VA	330	500
404, Battle of Fort Douglas	310	500
454, Beautiful Dreamer	110	200
474, Bedtime	100	200

C#	LOW	HIGH
484, Bell Ringers	100	200
533, Bird's Nest	60	100
557, Black Rock Castle	120	200
564, Blarney Castle	110	200
576, Blue-Eyed Beauty	110	200
622, Boss Team	410	700
736, Burial of the Bird	130	200
782, Canary Bird	130	200
800, Captive Night	150	200
1009, Charles Sumner	150	200
1124, Clam Boy on His Muscle	280	400
1217, Come Into the Garden, Maude	170	300
1255, Corned Beef	300	500
1332, Curfew Bell	200	300
1455, David and Goliath	150	200
1466, Dead Beat	280	500
1567, Desperate Peace Man	300	500
1579, Dexterous Whip, 1876	440	700
1597, Domestic Bliss	140	200
1731, Emmet's Betrothed	110	200
1761, Etta	110	200
1816, Fairy Isle	150	200
1844, Family Record	80	100
1934, Feast of Fruits, oval	250	400
1961, First Blood	100	200
1999, First Violet	140	200
2044, Flower Piece	200	300
2123, Frankie and Tip	130	200
2196, Fruits of the Garden	240	400
2230, Gems of American Scenery	600	1000
2291, General Robert E. Lee	260	400
2311, General Trochu	100	200
2334, Genuine Havana	170	300
2389, Go As You Please	120	200
2431, Good Friends	120	200
2545, Grandma's Treasures	150	300
2557, Grant in Peace	150	300
2674, Growling Match	180	300
2696, Hambrino, 1879	460	800
2737, Harry Bluff	150	200
2758, Havana	140	200
2826, Highland Mary, 1876	120	200
2853, How Pretty!	150	200
2991, Hungry Little Kittens	220	400
3070, In the Indian Past	500	800
3110, Infant Toilet	170	300
3140, Ivanhoe	100	200
3204, Jersey Litchfield Bull	200	300
3257, John Bull Makes a Discovery	200	300
3331, Kelleney Hill, Dublin	140	200
3360, Kitty and Rover	220	400
3449, Last Shake, 1885	120	200
3537, Lilliputian King	140	200
3617, Little Fannie	130	200

C#1896, Fashionable "Turn-Outs" in Central Park, 1869, large folio.

C#1907, Fast Trotters on Harlem Lane N.Y., 1879, large folio.

C#2597, The Great East River Suspension Bridge, 1886, large folio.

C#	LOW	HIGH
3661, Little Mamie	140	200
3726, Little Thoughtful	130	200
3809, Lover's Leap, 1886	140	200
3845, Luxury of Tobacco	400	600
4062, Mary's Little Lamb	200	300
4170, Momentous Question	420	800
4195, Morning Glories	180	300
4303, My Hearts Treasure	120	200
4408, Nelson	470	800
4424, New Hat Man	300	500
4544, Off the Port	1300	2300
4564, Old Ironsides	400	700
4800, Playing Dominos	250	400
4943, Prize Setter	450	700
4978, Pussie's Return	200	300
5110, Rejected	120	200
5149, Ripe Strawberries	240	400
5252, Ruins of the Abbey	120	200
5262, Rural Scenery	250	400
5307, Saint Anne	30	100
5470, Settling the Question, 1885	400	700
5508, Siege of Charleston	620	1000
5543, Sisters Prayer	80	100
5549, Sleeping Beauty	130	200
5734, Southern Rose	110	200
5323, St. Francis of Assisi	30	100
5719, Steadfast in the Faith	30	100
5834, Story of the Great King	70	100
5852, Summer Afternoon	260	400
5928, Sweet Sixteen	160	300
5950, Taking a Breath	120	200
5970, Tea With Dolly	180	300
5977, Temple of Jupiter	40	100
6003, Thatched Roof	200	300
6020, This Man Was Talked to Death, 1873	220	400
6082, Tobogganing in the Alps	950	1600
6253, Twilight Hour	250	400
6349, Up in a Balloon, 1876	310	500
6393, View of Chicago	1000	1700
6459, Village Beauty	120	200
6486, Wait for Me	160	300
6560, Watch on the Rhine	120	200
6592, We Sell for Cash, 1875	630	1000
6649, Who Said Rats?	210	400
6659, Widow's Son	120	200
6832, You Will! Will You?, 1868	230	400

Trade Cards

366, Bare Chance, 1879	$120	$200
730, Bull Dozed!!, 1877	100	200
1313, Crowing Match	100	200
1456, Dawn of Love	100	200
3487, Liberty Frightening the World	150	300

C#	LOW	HIGH
3841, Luke Blackburn, 1881	130	200
4087, Maxy Cobb, 1882	150	250
4499A, Nobby Tandem, 1879	90	200
4586, Old Suit and the New, 1880	120	200
4705, Parole, 1881	150	250
4747, People's Evening Line, 1881	150	250
5029, Queen's Own, 1880	120	200
5384A, Santa Claus, 1882	130	200
5570, Smoking Run, 1880	120	200
5624, Sorrel Dan, 1881	150	250
5959, Taking It Easy	100	200
6063, Tip-Top, 1880	100	200
6120, Training a Trotter, 1881	125	200

C#3522, The Life of a Hunter, "A Tight Fix," 1861, large folio.

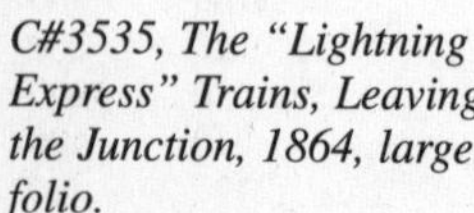

C#3535, The "Lightning Express" Trains, Leaving the Junction, 1864, large folio.

Louis Icart Prints

Louis Icart's works demonstrate a mastery of dry point, line etching, aquatint, and their variations. Icart produced up to 500 prints each of over 1,000 subjects. However, his works are scarce because many have been lost or destroyed.

Most prints bear his hallmark near the edge of the print. His signature is also easily identifiable, although subject to fogery and sometimes found on lithographic reproductions of his prints. Earlier works will have his signature but may not bear the hallmark. Most will, however, bear the stamp of his gallery, an oval shape with the letters EM for "estampe moderne." It is possible to have an original Icart with no hallmark at all, but this is rare. Icart often pulled two editions, one for Europe and one for American distribution. Sometimes the number is preceded by the letter "A" for an American edition, for example "A 75/120." Not all prints were numbered.

Left: Departure, 21.5" x 15.5", $1093 at auction.

Right: Homage to Guynemere, 26" x 21", estimated $1500–$2000 at auction.

Photos courtesy James D. Julia.

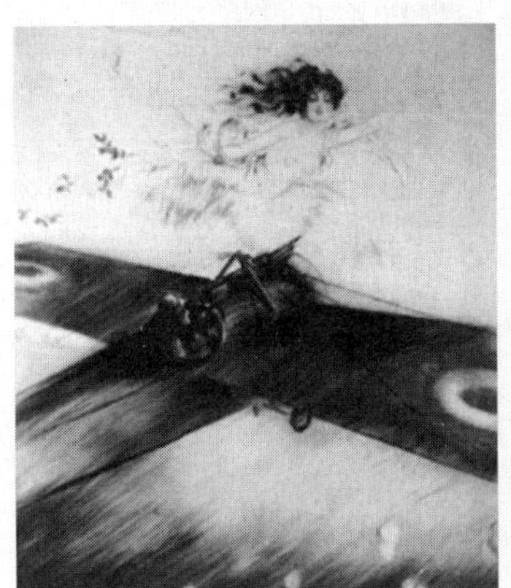

	LOW	AVG.	HIGH
Alighting From the Carriage, 22.25" x 29.5"	$1600	$2500	$3400
Autumn, 9" x 6.75"	715	1100	1500
Ballerina, 19.75" x 23.25"	950	1500	2000
Basket of Apples, 22" x 16"	1100	1700	2400
Bathing Beauties, 24" x 16.5"	2700	4200	5800
Best Friends, 16.75" x 13.25"	1400	2200	3000
Blue Buddha, 16" x 20.25"	1800	2800	3900
Casanova, 21" x 14"	1300	2000	2800
Choice Morsel, 18.5" x 14"	400	600	900
Coach, The, 21" x 14"	1000	1600	2200
Conchita, 21.25" x 14.25"	1300	2000	2800
Coursing, 12" x 16.5"	5500	8500	11,500
Coursing II, 15.25" x 25.25"	2500	3900	5400
Coursing III, 16" x 25.75"	4300	6700	9200
D'Artagnan, 19.5" x 15.5"	1400	2200	3000
Daisy, The, 17" x 12"	1300	2000	2800
December, 15" x 19.5"	1400	2200	3000
Don Juan, 21" x 14"	800	1200	1700
Eve, 13" x 9"	900	1400	1900
Fair Dancer, 19.5" x 23"	2000	3100	4300
Faust, 20.25" x 12.75"	1400	2200	3000
Flower Seller, 19.75" x 15"	600	900	1300
Forbidden Fruit, 16" x 12"	1500	2300	3200

	LOW	AVG.	HIGH
Frolicking, 14.75" x 19"	1000	1600	2200
Gilda, 18.5" x 13"	4700	7300	10,000
Green Robe, 13.75" x 17.5"	800	1200	1700
Greyhounds, 19" x 25"	2500	3900	5400
Gypsy, 18" x 21.5"	1000	1600	2200
Joan D'Arc, 28" x 21.5"	1300	2000	2800
Joy of Life, 24.5" x 16"	3500	5400	7500
Kiss of Motherland, 22" x 13.75"	1100	1700	2400
Lady of the Camellias, 7.25" x 5.5"	250	400	500
Laziness, 15" x 19.25"	1200	1900	2600
Leda, 24.75" x 25.25"	4000	6200	8600
Lillies, 28.5" x 19.25"	4000	6200	8600
Little Bo Peep, 20.25" x 13.5"	1000	1600	2200
Little Prisoner, 15" x 19"	950	1500	2000
Masked, 12" x 8"	900	1400	1900
My Model, 21" x 16.5"	3300	5100	7100
Old Yarn, 17" x 21.25"	700	1100	1500
Orange Cellar, 19" x 14.5"	1800	2800	3900
Passion Cat, 17.75" x 14"	2200	3400	4700
Pink Lady, 8.5" x 11.25"	800	1200	1700
Poem, 18.75" x 22.25"	2300	3600	4900
Roses, 14.5" x 18.25"	3300	6100	7100
Sleeping Beauty, 15.5" x 19.25"	1200	1900	2600
Smoke, 14" x 19"	1400	2200	3000
Snow, 20" x 14.25"	1150	1800	2500
Spanish Dancer, 21.25" x 14"	1100	1700	2400
Speed, 19.75" x 28.25"	2750	4300	5900
Speed II, 15" x 24.75"	1700	2600	3700
Sulking, 13.25" x 18"	1150	1800	2500
Summer, 9.5" x 7"	1800	2800	3900
Tennis, 19" x 13.75"	1700	2600	3700
Tsar, 10.5" x 8.25"	800	1200	1700
Unmasked, 12" x 8"	800	1200	1700
Waltz Echoes, 19" x 19"	1900	2900	4100
Winter, 9" x 6.5"	825	1300	1800
Zest, 19.25" x 14.25"	1000	1600	2200

Left: Les Lis, 27.75" x 18.875", estimated $3250–$3500 at auction.

Right: Orchids, 32.5" x 23.5", $2875 at auction.

—Photos courtesy James D. Julia.

Maxfield Parrish Prints

Maxfield Parrish illustrated magazine and advertisements for various national companies during the early 1900s. He also created many limited edition prints. There are many reproductions on the market.

Sing A Song Of Six-Pence, c1910, 10.375" x 22.5", $3685 at auction. —Photo courtesy Wm. Morford.

	LOW	AVG.	HIGH
Aladdin and the Lamp, 10" x 12"	$200	$240	$280
Aladdin in Cave of Forty Thieves, 12" x 16.5", on quality paper	225	275	300
Argonauts, In Quest of the Golden Fleece	125	160	200
Arizona, landscape of mountain, rich blues, 11" x 13"	125	160	200
Atlas, giant holding up sky	200	240	280
Aucassin Seeks Nicolotte, knight on horse, bookplate SM	60	80	100
Autumn, maiden standing on hilltop	175	225	275
Below the Balcony, knaves and maidens in garden	100	125	150
Brazen, The Boatman, 10" x 12"	160	200	240
Brown and Bigelow Landscape, The Village Church, 24" x 27"	400	500	600
Cadmus Showing the Dragon's Teeth, 10" x 12"	125	160	200
Canyon, maiden in canyon, 12" x 5"	300	375	450
Century, The, Midsummer Holiday Number, August, 1897, color litho., 19.75" x 13.5"	4000	5000	6000
Century, The, Midsummer Holiday, poster, Thomas and Wylie Co., 1897, 20" x 13"	2000	3000	4000
Circles Palace, maiden standing on porch	125	160	200
Cleopatra, rare, large	1000	1300	1600
Community Plate, 1918, 11" x 13"	70	85	100
Contentment, large Edison Mazda calendar	750	950	1150
Dawn, maiden sitting on rock, Edison Mazda Calendar, color litho., 1918, 23" x 14.5"	2000	3000	4000
Dawn, maiden sitting on rock, Mazda print	125	160	200
Daybreak, nude and maiden on porch, large size	475	575	675
Daybreak, nude and maiden on porch, small size	250	350	450
Daybreak, nude and maiden on porch, photo litho., 17.75" x 29"	125	160	200

Above: Old King Cole, cigar box, c1915, $688 at auction.

Left: Sunrise, Forbes calendar, 1933, 38.5" x 19.375" overall, $8140 at auction.

—Photos courtesy Wm. Morford

Above: Get Together, Edison Mazda adv. tape measure, 1.5" dia., $275 at auction.

Left: Get Together, Edison Mazda bulb tester, c1921, 23.25" x 15.625" x 12", $3685 at auction.

—Photos courtesy Wm. Morford.

	LOW	AVG.	HIGH
Dinkey Bird, nude on swing, 1904, 13.5" x 18"	250	350	450
Djer-Kiss Ad, maiden on swing in forest, 10.5" x 14"	120	150	180
Dream Castle in the Sky, 9" x 12"	100	125	150
Dreaming, nude sitting under oak tree, large size	475	575	675
Dreaming, nude sitting under oak tree, medium size	400	500	600
Dreamlight, maid on swing, Edison Mazda calendar, 1925, 9.5" x 20.5"	500	650	800
Duchess at Prayer, L'Allegro illustration, 1901, 10" x 15"	60	75	90
Ecstasy, maiden standing on rock, large Edison Mazda calendar	1200	1500	1800
Ecstasy, maiden standing on rock, small size	225	300	375
Enchantment, maiden standing on stars at night, Edison Mazda calendar, color litho., 1926, 26" x 15.75"	1500	2000	2500
Enchantment, maiden standing on stars at night, large size, 9.5" x 20.5"	850	1100	1350
Errant Pan, Pan sitting by stream, 6" x 8"	70	90	120
Evening, nude sitting on rock in lake, 13" x 17"	180	225	270
Fisherman and the Genie, The, 10" x 12"	150	185	225
Florentine Fete, maidens in garden, 10" x 16"	80	100	120
Garden of Allah, 3 maidens sitting in garden, 15" x 30"	200	300	400
Garden of Allah, 3 maidens sitting in garden, color litho., 18" x 30"	400	600	800
Garden of Allah, 3 maidens sitting in garden, large Edison Mazda calendar	550	750	950
Garden of Opportunity, prince and princess	650	850	1050
Garden of Opportunity Triptych, 10" x 13"	125	160	200
Golden Hours, maidens in forest, large Edison Mazda calendar	850	1100	1350
Harper's Weekly, poster	2800	3400	4000
Hilltop, youths sitting on mountain, House of Art, large size	1000	1250	1500
Hilltop, youths sitting on mountain, House of Art, small size	175	200	225
His Christmas Dinner, tramp eating dinner	125	160	200
Interlude, maidens in garden playing lutes	240	300	360
Isola Bella Scene, 9" x 10"	60	80	100
Jack Sprat and Wife, Swift Ham adv.	100	125	150
Jason and His Teacher Chiron the Centaur, 1910	100	125	150
John Cox–His Book, bookplate	60	75	90
King of the Black Isles, king on throne, quality paper, 9" x 11"	180	230	280
King's Son, Arab in garden by fountain	125	160	200
Knaves and Maidens, conversing in garden	125	160	200
Lamplighters, Mazda calendar, 1924, 9" x 13"	200	250	300
Lampseller of Baghdad, The, maiden on steps, Mazda calendar	650	850	1050
Land of Make-Believe, The, maiden in garden	125	160	200
Little Princess, princess sitting by fountain	60	75	90
Lute Players, House of Art, large size	800	1100	1400
Lute Players, House of Art, small size	150	175	200
Milkmaid, maiden walking on mountain	60	75	90
Morning, maiden sitting on rock, 13" x 16"	260	325	390
Night Call, bare-breasted girl in surf, 6" x 8"	60	80	100
Old Romance, nude sitting in pool, 8" x 8"	130	170	210
Pandora's Box, maiden sitting by large box	160	200	240
Pierrot, clown w/ lute, sky glittering, 1912	240	300	360
Pipe Night, comical men w/ pipes and coffee urns sitting facing each other at table, 9" x 12.5"	75	95	115
Pool of the Villa D'Este, nude lying beside luminous pool, 7.5" x 10.5"	60	80	100
Post Standing, by river in forest	70	85	105
Potpourri, nude in garden picking flowers	125	160	200

	LOW	AVG.	HIGH
Prince, from Knave of Hearts, 10" x 12.5"	275	350	425
Prince Goodad, pirates on boat	160	200	240
Prosperina, maiden in the sea, 10" x 12"	160	200	240
Providing It By the Book, 2 gents at table	60	80	100
Queen Guinare, maiden on porch, 10" x 12"	160	200	240
Reveries, large Edison Mazda calendar	450	550	650
Sandman, w/ full moon, 6" x 7.5"	80	100	120
Sea Nymphs, 1914, 12" x 14"	125	160	200
Search for the Singing Tree	90	120	150
Seven Green Polls at Cintra, 6" x 8"	70	90	110
Shepherd w/ Sheep, 8.5" x 13.5"	60	80	100
Ship in Ocean, 11" x 13.5"	100	125	150
Sinbad and the Cyclops, 10" x 12"	100	125	150
Singing Tree, The, 10" x 12"	100	125	150
Spirit of the Night, Edison Mazda calendar, color litho, 1919	3000	4000	5000
Stars, nude sitting on rock, House of Art, large size	1100	1300	1500
Stars, nude sitting on rock, House of Art, medium size	500	700	900
Story From Phoebus, 1901, 8" x 10"	50	65	80
Sunlit Valley, scenic of river and mountains	270	340	405
Turquoise Cup, man sitting in villa	60	80	100
Twilight Had Fallen, 2 figures on beach	65	90	115
Valley of Diamonds, Arab in valley	100	125	150
Venetian Lamplighter, Edison Mazda calendar, 1924	160	210	260
Villa D'Este, nude sitting by pool	100	125	150
Walls of Jasper, youth and castle, 12" x 14"	150	200	250
Waterfall, large Edison Mazda Calendar	1250	1500	1750

Left, top and bottom: Soldier Ten Pins, Parker Bros. game, c1921, 11.5" x 19.5" x 1.75" game box (above) and soldiers (below), $1870 at auction.

Right: Soldier Puzzle, Parker Bros., cardboard, 24" x 9.5", $908 at auction.

—Photos courtesy Wm. Morford.

Radios

The following section encompasses several areas of radio collecting. Included are early examples from the 1920s, Catalin plastic case radios from the 1930s and 1940s, later Bold War-era radios from the 1950s and 1960s, early transistor radios from the same era and novelty and advertising radios.

Catalin radios are the beautiful marbleized or mottled-look radios. They are often mistakenly called Bakelite. Catalin refers to a clear plastic that can be colored, first developed by the Catalin Corporation. The prices of Catalin radios shot up dramatically in the late 1980s to early 1990s. Interest has cooled but they still draw great interest. In the case of Catalin radios many collectors suggest "don't touch that dial" because heat can crack the cases. Catalins have also been known to shrink, crack and fade.

There are those who prefer the early wooden case models. Many new collectors, however, or those frustrated by Catalin's prices, have turned to what we call the dashboard-type radios, due to their ultrasleek "techno" designs. Others pursue newer advertising radios.

In the following entries, each radio is first listed by make, followed by the type of radio: (N) *novelty, includes character and interestingly shaped radios,* (P) *portable,* (TR) *transistor,* (C) *crystal,* (A) *advertising* and (F) *floor models.* Next follows a brief description, along with the approximate date of manufacture. All prices are for radios in complete and excellent condition. Radios should also be in working order with the possible exception of some of the plastics (since heat can crack the case).

We suggest these books: *Guide to Old Radios, Second Edition,* David and Betty Johnson, Wallace-Homestead, Radnor, PA, 1995; *Collector's Guide to Antique Radios, Fourth Edition,* Marty and Sue Bunis, Collector Books, Paducah, KY, 1997; and *Collector's Guide to Novelty Radios,* Marty Bunis and Robert F. Breed, Collector Books, Paducah, KY, 1995.

Left: Addison, Model 5F "Theater," red Catalin case w/ yellow grill bars and knobs, c1940, $1200–$1500.

Below left to right: Addison Model A2A, dark blue Plaskon case and knobs w/ white trim, c1940, $600–$800; Addison Model A2A, maroon Catalin case and knobs w/ yellow trim, c1940, $600–$800.

—Photos courtesy Gene Harris Antique Auction Center.

Fada Model 1000 "Streamliner," yellow Catalin case and trim, 1946, $600–$800. —Photo courtesy Gene Harris Antique Auction Center.

MAKE	TYPE	DESCRIPTION	DATE	VALUE
Admiral 4L26	T	yellow plastic, overlap dial	1958	$12–$18
Admiral 5X12	T	plastic, round dial, 2 knobs	1948	25–35
Admiral 5Z22	T	brown plastic, metal dial	1952	35–45
Admiral 7C65W	F	4 knobs	1950	50–80
Air Castle 5003	T	plastic, slide rule dial, louvers	1947	35–45
Air King Comet 815	T	wood, cloth grill	1938	50–65
Arvin Velvet Voice 8583	P	rotating handle	1959	35–55
Baseball	N	trophy	1941	800–1200
Bendix 55L3	T	white plastic, slide rule dial	1949	40–50
Bendix 55X4	P	plastic, hinged front	1949	50–80
Bowling Ball	N	trophy	1941	550–750
Bulova 120	T	plastic, logo centered grill	c1955	35–45
Bulova 670 Bantam	TR	jewel dec.	1960	200–300
California Raisin	A	California Raisins	1988	30–40
Channel Master 6506	TR	pocket	1958	30–40
Charlie McCarthy	N	Majestic	1938	900–1200
Charlie the Tuna	A	Star Kist Tuna	1970	60–80
Clarion C100	T	plastic, sq. dial, louvers	1946	40–50
Coca-Cola Cooler	A	Coca-Cola	1950	600–800
Crosley 538	T	wooden slant front	1926	80–100
Crosley X	T	wooden	1922	150–200
Crosley VI VR78	T	wooden	1922	100–150
Dahlberg Pillow Speaker	N	coin operated	1955	250–350
DeForest D10	T	wooden, loop antenna	1923	400–600
DeForest D6	T	wooden, rectangular	1923	900–1100
DeForest DT600	T	wooden, crystal "Everyman"	1923	250–350
Detrola 219 Pee Wee	T	plastic	1940	300–500
Emerson 888 Vanguard	TR	pink or blue	1960	80–20
Emerson Patriot 400	T	Catalin case	1940	1000–1500
Emerson Tombstone	T	Catalin	1940	1000–1500
Fada 252 Temple	T	Catalin	1940	300–500
Fada 115 Bullet	T	Catalin	1941	600–800
Federal 57	T	wooden, 1 dial	1922	400–500
Federal 61	T	metal, 3 dials	1923	700–900
Federal 58DX	T	metal, "Orthosonic"	1922	400–500
Freshman SF2	T	wooden, 3 dials, "Masterpiece"	1924	90–120
G.E. Clock Radio	T	pink plastic	1960	18–22
General Electric 675	TR		1956	80–100
Goulden's Mustard Jar	A	Goulden's Mustard	1982	30–40

MAKE	TYPE	DESCRIPTION	DATE	VALUE
Grand Old Granddad Bottle	A	Whiskey	1965	45–65
Grebe CR5	T	wooden, 3 dials	1921	400–500
Grebe MU1	T	wooden, "Synchrophase"	1925	150–200
Helping Hand	A	Hamburger Helper	1980	30–40
Hitachi 666	TR	pocket, red or gray	1958	80–120
Hopalong Cassidy	N	Arvin	1950	300–400
Kadette Jewel	T	plastic, various models	1935	200–300
Knight's Helmet w/ Crest	N		1970	30–40
Lafayette D140	T	ivory plastic, Deco	1939	90–110
Little Sprout	A	Green Giant	1980	30–40
Lone Ranger	N	Airline	1951	500–800
Magnavox TRF5	T	wooden, doors	1925	80–125
Manola	TR	table, red plastic	1958	20–30
Mercedes Auto Grill	N		1965	30–40
Mickey Mouse	N	brown case	1940	1200–1800
Mork Egg	N		1978	30–50
Motorola	T	aqua plastic clock radio	1958	20–30
New World Glove and Stand	N	Colonial	1933	800–1200
Philco	T	brown plastic, "services" dial	1954	25–40

Top row, left to right: Fada Model 652 "Temple," yellow Catalin case and trim, 1946, $500–$650; Fada Model 659 "Temple," shortwave, insert grill, maroon Catalin case w/ yellow trim, 1946, $850–$100.

Bottom row, left to right: Sentinel Model 284, wavy-grill, yellow Catalin case w/ yellow trim, 1947, $600–$750; Sentinel Model 284, outline-grill, yellow Catalin case w/ red trim, $1000–$1200. —Photo courtesy Gene Harris Antique Auction Center.

Westinghouse, Model H124 "Little Jewel," transistor, 1945, $70–$90.

MAKE	TYPE	DESCRIPTION	DATE	VALUE
Philco 49501	T	boomerang Transitone	1949	200–300
Philco T7	TR	black and white	1956	80–120
Polaroid 600 Plus	A	Polaroid Film	1980	25–35
Punchy	A	Hawaiian Punch	1972	40–60
Raid Bug Clock Radio	A	Raid Insecticide	1980	100–150
RCA Aeriola Jr.	C		1922	120–180
RCA Radiola X	T	wooden	1925	300–400
RCA Radiola 26	P	wooden	1925	300–400
RCA 7QBK	F		1940	80–100
Regency TR1	TR	white or black, pocket	1954	250–350
Snow White	N	Emerson, tan case	1938	1000–1500
Sony TR63	TR	pocket	1957	300–500
Spartan 558	T	blue mirror, Deco	1937	2000–3000
Stromberg Carlson Clock Radio	T	gray and salmon plastic	1957	20–30
Tide Box	A	Tide Detergent	1980	40–50
Tony the Tiger	A	Sugar Frosted Flakes	1980	35–45
Toshiba 5TR	TR	lacy face plate	1958	150–200
Westinghouse	A	aqua plastic, tapering shield	1960	18–25
Westinghouse H685	TR	table top w/ clock	1959	20–30
Zephyr 41X6	T	wooden, grill left, 3 knobs	—	40–60

Salt and Pepper Shakers

Salt and pepper shakers are on most dinner tables (very few of us use salt cellars). Although people obtain shakers to match table settings, we listed shakers that are considered novelty or figural shakers; some even advertise products. Collectors are drawn to the strange forms and bright colors. Many shakers match a more expensive cookie jar by the same manufacturer such as Shawnee or Regal. Shakers draw collectors not only from the cookie jar field but from the fields of black Americana, comic character and advertising memorabilia. With so many shapes and themes, crossover collecting is nearly endless. Collectors talk about sets such as one piece (one container), nodders (which sit in a base and rock back and forth), nesters (which sit one inside the other), or huggers (which fit together).

Sometimes a pair of salt and peppers aren't really a pair, but two different forms that share a theme, such as a cow jumping over the moon or a bowling ball and pin. Many times there are other pieces, such as a condiment jar, a tray or a bench, that are required in order to complete the set. Be alert to reproductions of expensive shakers and missing pieces. Prices listed are for excellent condition examples—no chips, cracks, flaking finish, or missing parts.

The shakers below usually range from 1" to 5" in height, so nearly everyone has room for two or three…hundred. Many common shakers can be purchased for less than $10.

For further reading we recommend *The Complete Salt and Pepper Shaker Book* by Mike Schneider, Schiffer, Atglen, PA 1993 and *Salt and Pepper Shakers, Vols. I–IV* by Helene Guarnaccia, Collector Books, Paducah, KY.

Above: Auction prices for plastic gas station advertising shakers, 2.75" h. Left to right: Texaco, $44; Conoco, $55; and Phillips 66, $44. —Photo courtesy Collectors Auction Services.

Left: Advertising Shakers, RCA, Nipper, "His Master's Voice" impressed on base, Lenox China, 1930s, 3" h, $50. —Photo courtesy Ray Morykan Auctions.

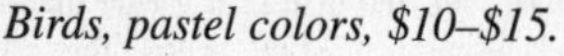

Birds, pastel colors, $10–$15.

Dogs, 1 winking, 1 laughing, Japan, $12–$18.

	LOW	HIGH
Apes, in fancy dress	$10	$17
Birds, lusterware, 1.25"	6	11
Budweiser Budman, red w/ blue cape, ceramic	13	22
Campbell Kids, plastic, 1950s, 4.5" h	32	42
Campbell Soup Kids, new, ceramic	10	17
Cambell Soup Kids, old, plastic	42	73
Cats, black, wooden, leather ears	6	9
Cats, wooden, w/ hats, Japan, c1950s, 4"	11	20
Chanticleers, small, wo/ gold, Shawnee, 3" h	25	35
Chef and Aunt Jemima, Brayton	160	210
Child Couple, boy w/ carrots, girl w/ basket, LEGO, Japan, 4"	14	24
Coca-Cola Cooler, ceramic	9	15
Colonel and Mrs. Sanders, plastic, 1960s, 4" h	65	85
Cow Jumping Over Moon, 5" l	28	36
Dachshund, 1-pc., Japan, 10" l	10	15
Dogs, playing cards, Clay Art	10	18
Ducks, Shawnee, 3" h	20	30
Dutch Couple, lusterware	12	21
Dutch Kids, wo/ gold, Shawnee, 5" h	40	50
Dutch Shoes, Frankoma	20	30
Elephant, Frankoma	60	70
Elephants, painted to resemble cloth	8	14
Elsie and Elmer, ceramic, 1950s, 4" h	65	85
EverReady Batteries, metal	10	17
Fifi and Fido, Ken-L Ration Dogs, plastic, 1960s, 3.5" h	25	35
Fish, in base, 3-pc. nodder	50	70
Flamingos, 1 head up, 1 down	12	18
Flower Pots, wo/ gold, Shawnee, 3.25" h	18	22
Gavels, red plastic, 1950s, 3" l	11	20
German Kissing Couple, Napco	16	28
Gingham Dog and Calico Cat, Brayton	35	55
Giraffe, 1-pc., Japan, 10" l	10	15
Greyhound Bus, metal	40	70
Hamms Beer Bears, ceramic	19	34
Handy Flame, ceramic, 1950s, 4" h	18	25

Elephants, green, Japan, $8–$14.

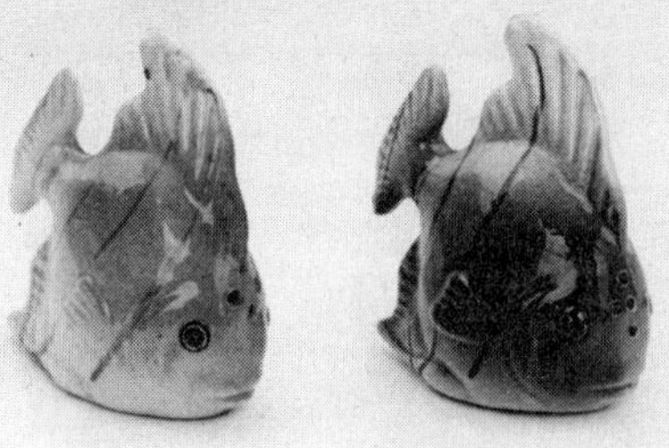

Fish, 1 blue, 1 brown, Japan, $10–$15.

	LOW	HIGH
Harlequin Clown	11	20
Hedgehog Chefs	12	18
Heinz Catsup Bottles, plastic	8	14
Hershey Kisses, ceramic	13	22
Hersheys Unsweetened Chocolate Bar, ceramic	32	56
Huggies, bears, Van Telligen, Regal	20	30
Huggies, boy and dog, Van Telligen, Regal	70	90
Huggies, ducks, Van Telligen, Regal	30	50
Huggies, Dutch boy and girl, Van Telligen, Regal	35	45
Huggies, Mary and lamb, Van Telligen, Regal	40	60
Humpty Dumpty, before the fall, plastic	10	15
Humpty Dumpty, Regal	150	200
Ice Cream Cones, glass and tin, Enesco, 4" h	20	30
Jack and Jill, Shawnee, 5" h	40	60
Jugs, Frankoma	14	18
Magic Chef, ceramic, 1950s, 5" h	55	75
Magic Chef, plastic, 1950s, 5" h	35	45
Max and Ray Camels, ceramic	24	42
Mice, wearing pajamas	4	7
Milk Bottles, Sealtest	25	35
Milk Cans, Shawnee, 3.25" h	18	24
Monkey in Tree, Dee Lee Imports, 4.5" h	6	8
Morton and Leslie Salt Minis, cardboard	11	20
Mount Rushmore	6	9
Mr. and Mrs. Mushroomhead, 6" h	8	12
Mrs. and Mrs. Snowman, formal attire	10	12
Mr. Peanut, beige plastic, 3" h	9	15
Mr. Peanut, red plastic, 3" h	9	15
Mr. Peanut, tan and black, 4" h	13	22
Mr. Peanut, yellow w/ black top hat	30	40
Mugsey, small, wo/ gold, Shawnee, 3" h	35	55
Native Americans, Syrocowood, c1950, 2.5" h	10	17
New Era Potato Chip Cans, metal	26	45
Niagra Falls, *Maid of the Mist* boat, 3-pc nester	100	150
Nipper and Phonograph, ceramic	10	17

Lobsters, Japan, 3" h, $15–$20.

Urns, hand painted, 4" h, $10–$15.

	LOW	HIGH
Nipper and Phonograph, plastic, 1950s, 3" h	25	35
Old Salt and Pepper, his wife, Purinton	100	150
Old Woman Who Lived in a Shoe, 4" h	15	20
Owls, wo/ gold, Shawnee, 3.25" h	20	30
Pepsi Bottles, glass	12	21
Pigs, Brayton	35	45
Pigs, pink and white w/ polychrome painting under glaze, 2" x 2.75"	8	14
Pillsbury Doughboy and Girl, ceramic, 1988	13	22
President Kennedy in Rocking Chair	45	55
Puss 'N Boots, wo/ gold, Shawnee, 3.25" h	15	25
"S" and "P" letters, Camark	10	15
7-Up Bottles, glass, 1950s	10	12
Skunks, w/ hats	9	12
Smiley Pigs, blue or red scarves, Shawnee, 5.5" h	70	90
Smoky Bear, ceramic, 1960s, 4" h	22	30
Spot, tall tan and white dogs	8	12
Squirt Bottles, glass	10	18
Statue of Liberty and Empire State Building, on tray	20	30
Steam Irons, plastic	8	12
Stuffed Puppies, red w/ white painted stitching, Japan, 3" h	12	20
Sunshine Bakers, ceramic	10	18
Sword Fish, Japan, 4.5" h	6	8
Tappan Chefs, ceramic, 1960s, 4" h	22	32
Teddy Bears, w/ bows, Clay Art	8	14
Teepee, Frankoma	25	35
Toaster, removable toast, plastic, 2.5" h	10	15
Tomatoes, 1.5" h, 2" dia	11	20
Trader Vic Tiki's, ceramic	6	11
Willie and Millie Penguins, plastic, 1950s, 3" h	10	15

Scrimshaw

Scrimshaw is artwork done on bone. It can be carved or painted. Carved scrimshaw, which seldom has any painted decoration, is mostly in the nature of little trinkets, boxes, pins, or forks, for example. Painted scrimshaw is done directly on the tooth or bone. It is accomplished by scratching the design into the surface with needles, then working India ink into the scratches. Whalebone is the most commonly found material, followed by walrus tusk. Occasionally a low-grade ivory such as whale tooth is used.

The age, size, artistic quality, subject matter and state of preservation all go into determining the value of scrimshaw. Beware of fakes made from polymers (see *Fakeshaw: A Checklist of Plastic "Scrimshaw"* by Stuart Frank, Kendall Whaling Museum, 1988). Also beware of various endangered species laws. Differences in federal and state regulations make this a tricky topic. Check with local authorities before buying or selling scrimshaw.

Above: Whale Bone Busks. Top to bottom: Whaling vignettes, $518 at auction; Whaling scene, hearts w/ sweetheart portraits, cityscape and country scene, and inscription "on Board Brig Bruce," $2530 at auction; Whaling scenes, $1380 at auction. —Photo courtesy Skinner, Inc., Boston, MA.

Below: Eskimo Cribbage Boards. Top to bottom: Polar bear eating seal, caribou pulling sled, native couple, early 20th C, 7.5" l, $1380 at auction; Myriad of arctic mammals including polar bear, walrus, and arctic fox finial, carved in the round, c1920s, 19" l, $4313 at auction. —Photo courtesy Skinner, Inc., Boston, MA.

	AUCTION	RETAIL Low	RETAIL High
Busk, dec. w/ pinwheels, hearts, and basket of flowers, bearing date "1872," 12" h	$650	$1210	$2120
Busk, engraved w/ lighthouse below public buldings, 13" l	550	1020	1790
Cane, w/ turned ivory and baleen details, 34" l	500	930	1630
Cribbage Board, Eskimo, walrus tusk, hawk and sea animals, sgd. "Herman Toolie, Alaska," 24.25" l	450	850	1500
Cribbage Board, Eskimo, walrus tusk, sea animals and hunters, 18.5" l	500	930	1630
Cribbage Board, Eskimo, walrus tusk, tip in form of open-mouth fish, 13.5" l	550	1020	1790
Cribbage Board, Eskimo, walrus tusk, tip in form of fish, mounted on carved seals, 17" l	500	930	1630
Cribbage Board, Eskimo, walrus tusk, whale, walrus, and foxes, 24.25" l	450	840	1470
Coconut Shell Dipper, w/ vine motifs, scrimshaw end, 15"	600	1120	1960
Double-Block, w/ rope fitting, 2.5"	325	600	1060
Fid, carved, pierced hearts, 6.5"	700	1300	2300
Jagging Wheel, block baluster handle, 5.5" l	920	1750	3000
Jagging Wheel, finely shaped and pierced handle, 6" l	1100	2000	3600
Jagging Wheel, floral engraved handle, 7.5" l	500	850	1500
Jagging Wheel, fluted wheel, 6" l	350	550	1000
Jagging Wheel, inlaid w/ abalone diamond, 6.5" l	700	1300	2280
Jagging Wheel, plain curved handle, 7.5" l	230	500	900
Jagging Wheel, unicorn, 7" l	4600	8000	12,000
Knife Sharpener, bone handle carved in form of gloved hand, 16" l	400	750	1300
Nantucket Pocketbook, w/ scrimshaw shale by Jose Formosc Reyes, oval, 10" l	800	1500	2600
Net Mender, 14" l	100	190	330
Pie Crimper, tapering fluted form, inlaid w/ abalone heart, 7" l	500	930	1630
Pie Crimper, w/ hand-form handle and sawtooth dec. wheel, 6" l	2300	4500	7500
Rope Seamer, sailor-made, 5.5"	400	750	1300
Teeth, by R.E. Spring, depicting whaling scenes, 7.25" l, pair	1500	2750	4000
Teeth, engraved w/ floral panels, 4" l, pair	500	930	1630
Teeth, w/ anchor, sailor, whale, oriental figure, ship, Scotsman, palm tree, and pelican, 5" l, pair	1700	3250	5500
Tooth, 3-masted vessel on obverse and verso, 8.5" l	900	1750	3000
Tooth, allegorical representation of Neptune on shell pulled by sea horses and mermaid, 7.5" l	1600	2980	5220
Tooth, American eagles, whales, ship, sailors, and sailor's sweethearts, 6.5" l	7000	12,000	20,000
Tooth, bark flying American flag, 7" l	650	1250	2250
Tooth, by R.E. Spring, depicting whale attack after Garneray print, 6.5" l	750	1400	2500
Tooth, polychrome dec. w/ whaling scenes, sea captain, and glove, 8.5" l	450	850	1500
Tooth, scene of sailor at cannon holding flag	450	850	1500
Tooth, "The Only Daughter" and "The Queen of Candy," 6.5" l	400	800	1200
Walrus Tusks, vignettes of women, ships, walrus, and penguin, each mkd. "Susan," 13" l, pair	550	1020	1790
Watch Hutch, mahogany stand w/ facing engraved teeth and panbone watch holder, teeth w/ fanciful dolphin motifs, 7.5" h, 12" l	3000	5580	10,000

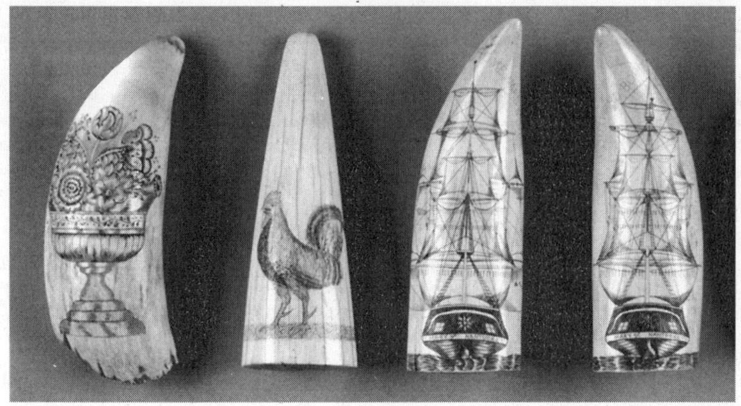

Left to right: Whale's Tooth, urn of flowers, 19th C, $1840 at auction; Walrus Tusk, rooster, 20th C, $345 at auction; Whale's Teeth, Mary of Nantucket *"Homeward Bound" and "Outward Bound," matched pair, $1265 at auction.*

Above: Whale's Tooth (front and back), by Edward Burdett (1805–33), depicts whaleship Elizabeth of London, *$60,250 at auction.*

Above left: Walrus Tusks, Nathaniel Sylvester Finney, 17.5" l, matched pair, center inset shows enlargement of inscription, estimated $15,000–$20,000 at auction.

—Photos courtesy Skinner, Inc., Boston, MA.

Shaker Collectibles

The Shakers formed a socioreligious organization in England in 1747. Their doctirnes advocated simplicity and celibacy. They were nicknamed "Shakers" because of their devotional dancing in religious services. Ann Lee led a group to America in 1776 and attracted many converts. Known for their fine quality, Shakers made products that symbolized beliefs of purity and utility from the early nineteenth century to the twentieth century. Although the Shakers made furniture for their own use, much was made for commercial sale.

Pieces are worth more if the collector can identify the Shaker community of origin. For the sampling of pieces listed below, the following abbreviations are used: Alfred, Maine = *ALF;* Canterbury, New Hampshire = *CANT;* Enfield, Connecticut = *ENF;* Harvard, Massachusetts = *HAR;* Hancock, Massachusetts = *HAN;* Mt. Lebanon, New York = *MtL;* New Lebanon, New York = *NL;* Pleasant Hill, Kentucky = *PLH;* Sabbathday Lake, Maine = *SDL;* and Watervliet, New York = *WVLT.*

Identifying Shaker pieces can be difficult. There are large numbers of fakes and countless reproductions. For further information see *Shaker Woodenware: Vol. 1* by June Sprigg and Jim Johnson, Berkshire House, Great Barrington, MA, 1991.

	LOW	HIGH
Armchair, #3, maple, tape seat, MTL, c1870	$1250	$1850
Armchair, #7, maple, rush seat, MTL, c1870	5500	8500
Basket, ash and hickory, rect. w/ hoop handle, PLH, c1850, 20" w	1800	2700
Basket, maple, 2-handled, double-wrapped rim, ENF, c1850, 7.5" dia	1650	2500
Basket, maple and ash, flared top, ENF, c1850, 29" h, 17" sq	4200	6300
Basket, oak, swing handle, wrapped rim, SDL, c1840, 14" dia	1500	2250
Basket, splint, attached lid, hoop handle, sgd., HAR, c8150, 9" w	1800	2700
Blanket Chest, pine, red paint, cutout base, ENF, c1850, 41" w	2400	3600
Bonnet, #5, linen trimmed, paper label	600	900
Box, oval, 1 finger on lid and base, 3.5" l, 2" w	100	200
Box, oval, 3 fingers, 11 copper brads, c1840, 6.25" l, 4.5" w	435	650
Box, oval, pine and birch, orig. white paint, 5 fingers, c1840, 12.5" l	4500	6750
Box, oval, pine and maple, orig. varnish, 3 fingers, SDL, c1850, 3.25" l	1800	2700
Box, pine, orig. red stain, molded lid, NL, c1830, 14.5" w	1500	2250
Box, poplar, rect., blue stain, SDL, 5.5" w	150	220
Bucket, cov., pine, blue paint, MTL, c1850, 9.75" dia	2400	3600
Bucket, cov., pine, orig. red paint, sgd. "Enfield," 9.75" dia	3000	4500
Bucket, pine, orig. paint, wire bail handle, NL, c1820, 6.25" dia	1000	1500
Candlestand, snake leg, orig. finish, NL, c1840, 23.5" h, 16" dia	8000	12,000
Cape, wool, mother-of-pearl buttons, initialed, 32" l	680	1000
Carrier, oval, orig. yellow varnish, 2 fingers, CANT, c1830, 10" dia	2700	4000
Carrier, round, pine and maple, HAR, c1830, 10.75" dia	2250	3400
Carrier, round, poplar and maple, orig. green paint, swing handle, 9" dia	1500	2250
Cheese Basket, black ash, ALF, c1840, 21" dia	2400	3600
Child's Rocker, #0, maple, tape seat, MTL decal, 23" h	6500	9500
Child's Side Chair, #1, dark varnish, orig. tape seat, MTL decal, 28" h	4500	7000
Child's Tilt Chair, birch, orig. varnish, tape seat, ENF, c1830, 32" h	6000	9000
Cloak, blue wool and satin, labeled "Enfield, N.H.," 56" l	900	1350
Clothes Brush, horsehair, 8.75"	450	680
Clothes Hanger, pine, initialed, NL, c1850, 17" w	200	320
Clothes Hanger, pine and hickory, CANT, c1850	220	340
Clothes Hanger, walnut, ENF, c1840, 12.5" w	600	900
Cream Tub, orig. blue paint, wire handles, ENF, c1840, 10" dia	2550	3820
Desk Box, CANT, c1840, 18" w	3300	5000
Desk Box, chestnut, cherry, and pine, orig. red stain, c1850, 16" w	2100	3150

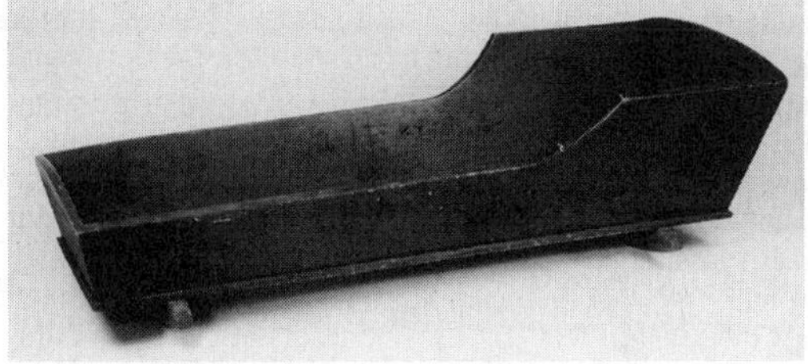

Above: Adult Cradle, maple and pine, orig. red wash, dovetailed and nailed sides possibly HAR, 19th C, 78.75" l, $978 at auction.

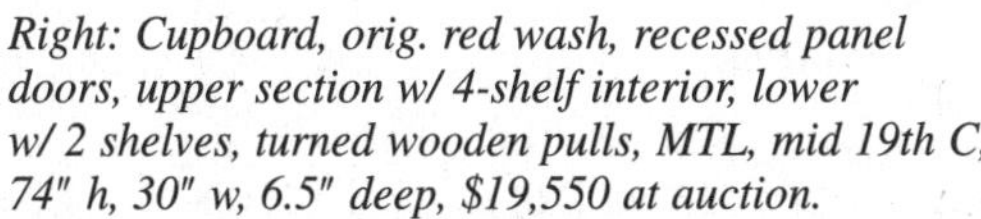

Right: Cupboard, orig. red wash, recessed panel doors, upper section w/ 4-shelf interior, lower w/ 2 shelves, turned wooden pulls, MTL, mid 19th C, 74" h, 30" w, 6.5" deep, $19,550 at auction.

Left to right: Deaconess' Desk, butternut and tiger maple, refinished, hinged lid, desk box rests on pedestal base, ENF, 1830, 29" h, $6900 at auction; Rocker, #6, old finish, replaced gold and pink tape seat, MTL, 1880–1930, 40" h, $403 at auction.

—Photos courtesy Skinner, Inc., Boston, MA.

	LOW	HIGH
Dipper, ash, orig. cream-yellow paint, 6.5" l	1650	2480
Document Box, pine, orig. blue paint, SDL, c1850, 6.5" w	1650	2480
Dry Sink, pine, refinished, NL, c1830, 35" h, 31" w	2700	4000
Drying Rack, arched base, orig. red paint, WVLT, c1850, 55" h	3000	4500
Drying Rack, folding, orig. salmon paint, 4-part, ENF, c1840, 60" h	3300	5000
Footstool, #0, maple, orig. dark varnish, rush seat, MTL decal, 13" w	1500	2250
Knife Basket, ash, carved medial handle, 17" w	3300	5000
Knife Box, canted sides, finger holes, c1850, 5" h, 13.25" l	900	1350
Land Grant, 12" w	1350	2000
Medicine Bottle, green, orig. stopper, mkd. "New Leb., NY," 9.25" h	1720	2500
Neckerchief, hand-woven silk, initialed, 1846, 35" sq	1350	2000
Peg Rail, pine w/ birch pegs, 60" l	600	900
Pie Lifter, wood, w/ spring action and locking ring, 17" l	145	250
Rocker, #3, shawl bar, ebony finish, tape seat, MT>, c1870	1500	2250
Rocker, #4, maple, stained finish, shawl bar, MTL, c1870	1950	2920
Rocker, #5, maple, black walnut finish, old tape seat	3900	5850
Rocker, #7, cherry, shawl bar, tape seat, MTL, c1870	2700	4000
Rocker, #7, maple, shawl bar, tape seat, MTL, c1870	4200	6300
Rocker, #7, maple, tape seat, MTL decal, c1900	2700	4000
Rug, silk, cotton backing, black border, polychrome field, 24" x 40"	450	680
Seed Box, orig. red paint, "Shakers Seeds, Mt. Leb.," 3.5" h, 23.5" w	3900	5800
Seed Box, pine, label "Fresh Garden Seeds Raised," 5.5" h, 14" w	2000	3000
Seed Carrier, pine, orig. red stain, CANT, c1830, 9.5" h, 10.5" sq	3000	4500
Sewing Basket, maple, side handles, 15.5" sq.	1350	2000
Sewing Basket, splint, fitted lid, MTL, 3.5" h, 5.75" sq	2400	3600
Sewing Stand, orig. red stain, 1 drawer, HAN, c1850, 22" w	3000	4500
Shawl, wool, striped border, fringe, SDL, 64" sq	900	1350
Side Chair, #3, cherry, orig. varnish, tilters, split reed seat	1650	2500
Side Chair, bird's-eye maple, fitted w/ tilters	2450	3850
Side Chair, maple, mustard yellow paint, tape seat, ALF, c1830, 41" h	2700	4000
Spice Chest, walnut, 4 drawers, 7.25" h, 13" w	550	750
Spice Chest, walnut, 13 drawers, WVLT, c1850, 17" h, 17" w	2400	3500
Spool Holder, orig. varnish, tomato pincushion, thimble holder, 5.5" dia	1500	2250
Stand-Up Desk, lift lid, dovetailed drawer, shelf, 51" h, 28" w	3900	5850
Storage Box, orig. brown paint, WVLT, c1840, 7.5" h, 15.5" w	2700	4000
Storage Box, yellow paint, CANT, 11" h, 25" w	1400	2200
Stove, iron, canted sides, straight legs, NL, c1840, 19" h, 29" l	1800	2700
Swift, maple, orig. mustard paint, 21" h	1350	2000
Triple Hanger, walnut stain, initialed, PLH, c1850, 6.25" h, 14" w	1350	2000
Wool Basket, carved double handles, 13" h, 27.5" w	1650	2400
Wool Wheel, weathered finish, initialed, SDL, c1830	1000	1580
Work Stand, cherry, 1 drawer, CANT, c1840, 27" h, 17" w	5100	7500
Work Stand, cherry and pine, 1 drawer, MTL, 27.5" h, 20" w	2800	4000
Work Table, pine and birch, red base, scrubbed top, round tapered legs, CANT, c1820, 28" h, 63" w	5500	7700
Work Table, pine and maple, orig. red finish, turned legs, ALF, c1820, 28" h, 34" w	4250	6500
Work Table, pine and oak, red stain, 1 drawer, chamfered legs, SDL, c1860, 27.5" h, 20.5" w	1000	1500
Yarn Winder, maple, clock reel, CANT, c1839, 37" h	1750	2500

Ship Models

There are four main types of ship models. *Wright's models (W)* were made by a shipwright (a ship builder) as a working model for an actual ship. *Sailor's models (S)* were made while the sailor served on a ship. *Collector's models (C)* were made after the ship was constructed, often after it ceased to exist, using photographs or drawings in books. *Kit models (K)* are built from components and directions furnished in a commercially sold kit.

Wright's models are the most desired and expensive. Sailor's models may be crude, but they are often highly regarded. The value of a collector's model is determined by age, size, intricacy of detail and state of preservation. Models of steamships are generally not as valuable as sailing vessels.

Schooner, half hull model, 19th C, 46.5" l (W), $2185 at auction. —Photo courtesy Skinner, Inc., Boston, MA.

	AUCTION	RETAIL	
		Low	High
Bark *Nabob,* half hull model, c1862, 63" l (W)	$3500	$6600	$9500
Brilliant, decorative half hull model, 47" l (C)	1700	3500	4500
Cabin Cruiser, painted wood model, 24.5" l (C)	400	800	1000
Clipper Ship *Flying Cloud,* 28" l (C)	2000	3500	5000
Destroyer, scratch-built model, 50" l (C)	400	800	1000
Frigate, plank on frame model, carved figurehead, 56" l (C)	1000	1800	2600
Frigate *Española* of Boston, carved sternboard and billet head, 42" l (C)	1000	1800	2600
Half Hull, w/ alternating lifts, 48" l (W)	3000	5500	7500
Patent Model for Ship's Windlass, 17.5" l	1600	2900	4200
Sail and Steam Vessel, copper, 36" l (C)	500	1000	1300
Schooner, 3 masts, in shadowbox, 23" l (C)	200	400	500
Shield's Class 1 Design Yacht Model, built by Stephen Pinney, 31" l (C)	1200	2200	3300
Sloop, half hull model, 44" l (C)	1300	2400	3500
Stag Hound of Dennis, MA, w/ eagle sternboard, 30" l (C)	2000	3500	5000
Steam and Sail Tender, scratch-built model, 26" l (C)	200	400	500
Steam Yacht *Piet Hein,* scratch-built model, 30" l (C)	500	900	1300
Swedish Steam and Sail Freighter, Kronan of Gotegorg, scratch-built model, 42" l (C)	300	500	800
Three-Masted Ship, elaborate brass and bone fittings, 41" l (S)	4000	7800	10,000
Two-Masted Merchant Ship, bone model, fitted w/ long boat and oars, 7" h, 11" l (S)	5000	9500	13,000
U.S.S. Constitution, carved and painted, fully rigged, 44" l (C)	1600	3000	4500
Whaler *Charles W. Morgan,* by Piel Craftsmen of Newburyport, MA, 20" l (C)	200	400	500
Whaler *Wanderer,* w/ long boats and oars, 26" l (C)	1300	2500	3500
Yacht, varnished, brass fittings, 24" h (C)	300	500	800

Silhouettes

Silhouettes are profiles cut out of one color paper and mounted to a contrasting-colored background. Sometimes detail is added in chalk, pen or watercolor. Most collected silhouettes date to the first half of the nineteenth century. Value depends on age, quality and size of the specimen. The fame of the subject is also very important. Modern and semimodern silhouettes have little or no value.

Group of Eight, American School, hollow-cut w/ cutwork background, probably Pennsylvania, unsgd., together in a common period frame, 19th C, 7.125" x 9.125", $575 at auction. —Photo courtesy Skinner, Inc., Boston, MA.

	AUCTION	RETAIL Low	RETAIL High
Child, full-length, early 19th C, 5.5" h	$400	$700	$1100
Child Holding Flower, by "M. Gapp," 4.5" h	450	650	1200
Couple, by Augustus Day, hollow-cut, pencil details, sgd., 8" h, pair	800	1400	2200
Couple, by Samuel Metford, chalk and gilt details, sgd., 11.5" h, pair	300	530	830
Couple, hollow-cut, eglomisé frame, 5.5" h, pair	300	530	830
Couple, hollow-cut, man w/ striped vest, young woman, stamped "Williams" (Henry Williams, American, 1787–1830), pair	125	220	340
Family Group, William Henry Brown (1808–83), full-length, chalk details, sgd. and dated "1849"	1000	1750	2750
Family Group, couple and 2 children, hollow-cut, 6.5" x 9", pair	350	750	1100
Gentleman, full-length, wearing top hat, bird's-eye maple frame, 13" h	250	470	820
Gentleman, full-length, interior scene background, gilt frame, 14.5" h	400	740	1300
Gentleman, hollow-cut, pencil details, sgd., 5.75" h	350	650	1000
Gentleman, w/ umbrella, full-length, gilt highlights, w/ stamp of Master Hankes on reverse, 13.5" h	200	350	550
Gentleman, mechanical silhouette, stamped (William) King, hollow-cut, 5" h	275	480	760
Man, profile, 4" h	50	90	150
Man and Child, full-length, gilt highlights, 10" h	250	500	900
Seated Matron, sgd. (Samuel) Metford, full-length, 12.25" h	150	260	410
Triple Silhouettes of Gentlemen of the Leighton Family of Yarmouthport, ME, watercolor and ink dec., depicting 2 generations, rare, 3.75" x 8.25"	900	1580	2480
William Westerfield, full-length, w/ inscription, dated 1852, 10" h	350	700	1100
Woman, in manner of Miers	75	140	240
Woman, hollow-cut, in blue watercolor dress w/ floral sprig and parasol, attributed to William Chamberlain, Dunbarton, NH, c1830, 3.5" h	3250	5690	8940
Youth, by Master Hankes, full-length, stamped on reverse, 11.75" h	200	350	550

Stoves

Collectible stoves are those made in the nineteenth and early twentieth centuries. They are usually sought by kitchen enthusiasts. Before the early nineteenth century most cooking was done over an open hearth fire. In 1850 the first gas cookers arrived on the market. Electric cookers were introduced in 1894 and stoves equipped with thermostats appeared in 1923.

	LOW	AVG.	HIGH
Acme, Sunburst, hard coal base burner, silver nickel swing top, a dome, artistic urn, tea kettle attachment, smoke collar, large double front doors, ash door w/ screw register, nickel-plated foot rails and base	$1400	$1600	$1800
Acme, Triumph, polished blue plate, high warming closet, coal feed pouch and broiler door, wood feed door, duplex grate, fire box, oven thermometer, reservoir tanks, early 20th C	4000	5050	6100
European Make, cast iron, small, hot plate underneath removable cover, 3-ftd., early 20th C, 15" x 38" surface area	700	750	800
European Make, cast iron, fully nickel plated, openwork cover, removable for stoking, early 20th C, 17" x 37"	1100	1550	2000
European Make, enameled in dark red, handle in the shape of a winged creature, early 20th C, 27" x 11"	700	950	1200
European Make, some brass and copper, numerous tiles, 65" h	1600	1950	2300
European Make, stands on hearth that comes out, enameled in green, hot plate, openwork cover, early 20th C, 17" x 45"	700	750	800
Excelsior, small, rounded shape, burns wood or coal	100	150	200
Franklin, stands on 3 legs, brass tip on top, bird, fruit and flower motifs, 35" x 42" surface area	200	250	300
Norwegian, w/ burning box at base, 3 sections above, each holding a hot plate, c1890, 26" x 78"	1200	1600	2000
Norwegian, wood burning, cast iron, black leading, c1915, 16" x 58"	500	600	700
Scandinavian Make, cast iron, a trio of ovens above hearth, wooden base, late 18th C, 88" x 30"	7000	9000	11,000
Scandinavian Make, mid 19th C, 55" x 35"	2000	2300	2600
Sears, step, 2 burners on top and double burner on step, early 20th C, 14" x 22" surface area	1800	2450	3100
Sears, wood burning	100	200	300
Wehrle, combination stove, 4-hole, coal and wood, pig iron, rococo design, 4 slightly splayed legs, early 20th C	1200	1650	2100
Wehrle, see-through door, early 20th C, 66" h	3200	3850	4500
Westminster, green enamel, removable hearth, c1910, 28" x 28"	1000	1100	1200
Wildwood, return flue, Tood Stove, rococo design, silver nickeled ornaments, smoke collar, swing top, early 20th C	600	700	800
Windsor, gas, porcelain lined, blue and white enamel	400	700	1000

Accessories

	LOW	AVG.	HIGH
Stove Handles, iron coated w/ porcelain, c1910	$15	$20	$25
Stove Lid Lifters, factory made, coil handle	6	12	18
Stove Lid Lifters, hand wrought	10	20	30
Stove Poker, wire handled, curved	9	16	21
Stove Poker, wire handled, straight	9	16	21

Textiles

Coverlets

Coverlets are bedspreads woven on a loom. They fall into two categories: geometrics and Jacquards. The geometrics generally date earlier and have small simple designs such as the star, diamond or snowball. The Jacquards, produced using a loom device made by Frenchman Joseph Jacquard, have curving, ornate designs such as flowers, birds and trees.

The early geometric coverlets were woven at home usually by women. The Jacquards were more often made by professional male weavers. The Jacquard device enabled the weaver to put his name on his work; the simple loom didn't. Two threads are used in weaving. The warp threads (vertical) are usually cotton, and the weft threads (horizontal) are usually wool. Red and blue dye was primarily used until the middle of the nineteenth century when synthetic dyes brought a greater color variety. The development of the power loom brought an end to most manual loom weaving.

Most collected coverlets date to the middle of the nineteenth century. Jacquards are more popular with collectors than the geometrics. Expect higher prices for the rare all-cotton or all-wool coverlets. The listings are identified as geometric or Jacquard. Following the identification are color, description and dates, when available.

Geometric coverlets have simple, repetitive designs.

Geometric

	LOW	AVG.	HIGH
Black and White, 44" x 60"	$500	$650	$800
Blue and White, 60" x 60"	300	350	400
Blue and White, c1850, 55" x 62"	400	500	600
Indigo and Cream, double weave	500	600	700
Log Cabin design, 45" x 55"	500	650	800
Red and White, c1830, 45" x 55"	600	650	700
Red, White, and Blue, center seam	425	500	575
Red, White, and Blue, c1850, 50" x 60"	450	550	650

Jacquard coverlets have more elaborate designs and are often labeled and dated at the corner.

Jacquard

	LOW	AVG.	HIGH
Black and White, animals, 45" x 57"	$700	$800	$900
Black and White, floral, 42" x 54"	500	650	800
Blue and White, American shield motif, c1860	1500	2000	2500
Blue and White, floral and geometric motifs, house, horse, and tree border, double weave, center seam, c1835	800	900	1000
Blue and White, floral medallions and American eagles and star border, double weave, c1830	900	1200	1500
Blue and White, garlands and flowers, spread-winged eagle, double weave, center seam, c1855	800	900	1000
Blue and White, rose sprays and stars center, eagle corners, double weave, c8150	1200	1300	1400
Blue and White, rosettes, leaves, and snowflakes, double weave	800	900	1000
Red and White, floral, 46" x 59"	500	650	800
Red and White, spread-winged eagle motif, unsgd.	600	700	800
Red and White, spread-winged eagle motif, sgd.	650	750	850
Red, Green, and White, oak leaf and flower design	600	700	800
Red, Gold, and Blue, stars and leaves w/ grapes on border, center seam, c1850	1000	1200	1400
Red, Tan, and Ivory, eagle motif, "Independence, Virtue, Liberty"	1400	1600	1800
Red, White, and Blue, exotic birds, 44" x 60"	1200	1400	1600
Red, White, and Blue, star and flower motif, 42" x 58"	600	700	800
Red, White, and Gold, bird medallions, double weave	550	650	750
Red, White, and Green, flowers, stars, and spread-winged eagle	650	750	850
Red, White, Gold, and Green, medallion and floral borders, double weave	600	700	800
Tree of Life, sgd., c1848	1200	1400	1600

Reproduction

	LOW	AVG.	HIGH
Bear Paw, 24-panel, 3-color, triple weave, 48" x 68"	$60	$100	$140
Everlasting, 24-panel, 3-color, triple weave, 48" x 68"	60	100	140
Old Colony, white and blue rosettes, double weave, 48" x 68"	40	75	110
Starburst, 6-panel, 3-color, triple weave, 48" x 68"	60	100	140
Victorianna, white and blue, house border, double weave, 48" x 68"	40	75	110

Hooked Rugs

Hooked rugs made from discarded rags or scraps from the cutting room show a wealth of American imagination. The best are nineteenth-century examples with scenes and/or figures, but those are difficult to find in good condition. Collectors can find fine examples from the early twentieth century more easily.

Watch out for rotted and unraveled examples. They may look good from the back of the auction hall, but restoring them can cost more than the value of the rug itself.

	AUCTION	RETAIL Low	RETAIL High
Apple Basket, late 19th C, 35" x 25"	$325	$500	$900
Automobile, sgd., early 20th C, 38" x 50"	1000	2000	3500
Bird, early 20th C, 42" x 27"	150	275	450
Cart, early 20th C, 33" x 46"	175	300	500
Flowers, late 19th C, 60" x 100"	460	700	1500
Fruit Basket, circ., late 19th C, 32" dia	725	1400	2200
Geometric, early 20th C, 45" x 66"	300	500	900
Horse, surrounded by leafy boughs, 15" x 35"	650	1200	2100
House, early 20th C, 24" x 37"	275	425	725
Sleigh Ride in Town, early 20th C, 31" x 41"	350	700	1100
Stars, 6-pointed, brown, black, red, and white, 30" x 36"	315	600	1000
Whaling Ship, late 19th C, 39" x 55"	1500	2700	4500

Grenfell Pictorial Hooked Rug, Newfoundland or Labrador, label on reverse, early 20th C, 27.25" x 39", $2185 at auction. —Photo courtesy Skinner, Inc., Boston, MA.

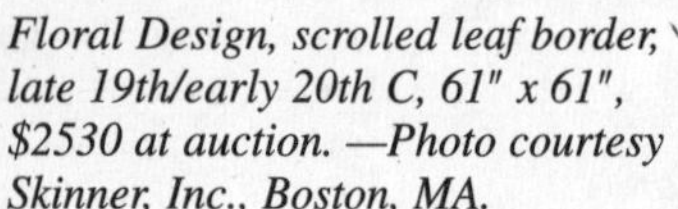

Floral Design, scrolled leaf border, late 19th/early 20th C, 61" x 61", $2530 at auction. —Photo courtesy Skinner, Inc., Boston, MA.

Needlework

Embroidery or decorative needlework uses diverse threads such as silk, gold, wool, or cotton stitched into any type of fabric including cloth or leather. The most valuable and rarest embroidery work is from the 1700s. Embroidery pieces from the 1800s and 1900s are more readily available. The condition, workmanship, materials, design and age of a piece are equally important in determining value. Many hobbyists collect all types of embroidery while others collect by motif, stitch, or country of origin.

Memorial, "By Elizabeth Shute 11 years old," ink highlights, early 19th C, 15.25" x 15", $1150 at auction. —Photo courtesy Skinner, Inc., Boston, MA.

	AUCTION	RETAIL Low	RETAIL High
Bell Pull, Victorian, brass tip, 66" l	$125	$200	$300
Bellows, w/ floral needlework panel	55	100	150
Berlin Woolwork Square, 9 red and blue circles, divided by brown crosses, each circle w/ mouse, mid 19th C, 5" x 5"	40	60	140
Berlin Woolwork Square, diagonal rows of roses in orange, red, purple, and green, mid 19th C, 5" x 5"	30	50	120
Bonnet, Colonial period	650	1000	1500
Book Cover, William and Mary, 12" h	750	1200	2000
Courting Couple and Landscape, w/ animals and brick mansion, English Queen Anne, 25" x 20"	7250	12,000	18,000
Floor Cloth, from ship *Nancy Louise,* Deer Isle, ME, dated 1939, 46" x 22"	600	1000	1500
Memorial, for William Weston, by Caroline Weston, 1837, 16" x 13"	1200	2000	3000
Petit Point, silk on linen, flowers in yellow, brown, and green, mid 19th C, 7" x 2"	25	45	100
Pictorial, by Eliza Greenawalt, depicting shepherd and sheep, 1822, 15" x 17"	900	1500	2500
Pocketbook, "John Clark, 1757," flame-stitched	450	750	1250
Sampler, American, sgd. and dated, vases and baskets of flowers and birds in brown, green, and ivory on linen, early 19th C, 18" x 17"	800	1200	1800
Sampler, English, woolwork, sgd. and dated, alphabet in 2 scripts, dog and cat on cushions w/ yellow tassels, bird on branch, floral border, mid 19th C, 14" x 12.5"	500	900	1500

	AUCTION	RETAIL Low	RETAIL High
Sampler, "Hope Beside an Anchor, and Adam and Eve," 1800, 18" x 14"	1400	2500	3500
Sampler, Portsmouth, "wrought by Mary Elizabeth Coffin," 20" x 17"	650	1000	1500
Sampler, verse on education, 1797, 18" h	1000	1750	2500
Valentine, punch card, German, embroidered meandering vine in wool and gold metallic thread, w/ gold leaf and green painted highlights, mid 19th C, 8" x 11"	70	120	250

Picture, "Edgar & Matilda," sgd. "Sally Aldrich," w/ watercolor and sequin highlights, early 19th C, 16" dia., $978 at auction.

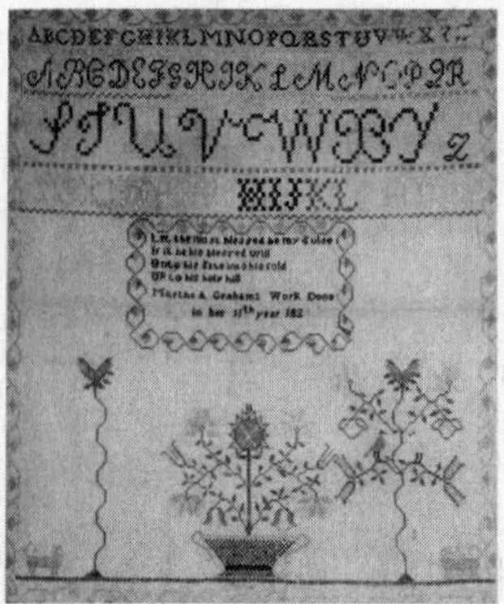

Samplers, above left to right: "Martha A. Grahams Work Done in her 11th year 182...," 18.625" x 16.25", $805 at auction; "Haverhill August 29 Betsey Gage Plummer Born AD 1782 this wrought in the 14 year of her age...," MA, 19.375" x 15.75", $10,925 at auction.

—Photos courtesy Skinner, Inc., Boston, MA.

Quilts

Amish quilts are the leaders in hobbyist appeal, and usually, though not always, the most valuable.

Potted Tulip Appliqué, green and red calicos on white ground, 19th C, 92.5" x 94.5", $978 at auction. —Photo courtesy Skinner, Inc., Boston, MA.

	AUCTION	RETAIL Low	RETAIL High
Barn Raising Log Cabin, Mennonite, Lancaster Co., PA, c1870, 89" x 88"	$1500	$2000	$2750
Barn Raising Log Cabin, PA, red and white, c1910, 78" x 63"	250	500	700
Bedcover, American, quilted sateen, pink and beige striped fabric, 75" x 77"	150	260	400
Bedcover, European, floral chintz quilted, wide goldenrod border, 82" x 106"	300	550	850
Broken Star, polychrome, new, crib size, Amish, Franklin Co., PA, 39" x 39"	150	200	450
Burgoyne Surrounded/Homestead, pink and white, Bowmansville, PA, c1930, 79" x 79"	300	500	700
Checkerboard, red and white, crib size, PA, c1880, 37" x 26"	200	350	550
Checkerboard Windows, red, white, cream, and blue, PA, c1900, 88" x 86"	325	450	650
Cherry Baskets, blue and white, Ohio, c1930, 79" x 76"	350	550	750
Coverlet, quilted whitework, floral motifs, 75" x 89"	175	350	550
Crazy Quilt, polychrome, sgd., MD, c1880, 77" x 76"	800	1100	1600
Double Wedding Ring, red, green, and white, PA, c1930, 84" x 72"	150	250	450
Dresden Plate, white and green, PA, c1930, 90" x 70"	350	550	750
Floral and Vine Appliqué, w/ drapery swag border and elaborate stitching overall, 100" x 100"	150	250	400
Golden Gate, Mennonite, Lancaster Co., PA, c1900, 78" x 76"	1000	1350	1850
Lone Star, reds and greens, minor stains, 73" x 81"	400	650	1000
Oak Leaf Appliqué, New Hampshire, c1880, 83" x 83"	1000	1750	2250
Pineapple Log Cabin, polychrome, PA, c1910, 78" x 77"	500	700	900
Pinwheel, brown and blue, cut corners, 61" x 81"	350	600	900
Puss in Corner, blue and white, PA, c1880, 86" x 68"	500	800	1200
Repeating Triangles, pieced, cut corners, print fabrics, 84" x 84"	375	650	1000
Rose of Sharon, white, yellow, and green, ME, c1930, 77" x 65"	350	600	900

	AUCTION	RETAIL Low	RETAIL High
Stairway to Heaven, crib size, new, Amish, PA, 38" x 39"	125	200	350
Sunshine and Shadow, Amish, Lancaster Co., PA, c1940, 80" x 80"	800	1200	1800
Sunshine and Shadow, yellow, red, green, and blue, crib size, new, Amish, Franklin Co., PA, 39" x 39"	150	200	300
Whig Rose and Vine Appliqué, red and green, PA, c1850, 89" x 86"	700	1200	1800
Wild Goose Chase, red and white, PA, c1860, 80" x 65"	500	800	1200

Pieced Star of Bethlehem w/ Appliquéd Potted Plants, plain and printed cottons on white ground, 19th C, 85" x 88", $748 at auction. —Photo courtesy Skinner, Inc., Boston, MA.

Thermometers

	LOW	HIGH
Calotabs, wood, Atlanta	$100	$140
Calumet Baking Powder, can and child, 1920s, 21" h	300	500
Clemmons, tin, NC	20	30
Cream of Kentucky, heart-shaped, plastic, 1950s, 10.5" h	50	70
Dr. Pepper, 10-2-4, dial, c1965	60	80
Dr. Pepper, bottle and clock, 10-2-4, 1930s, 17" h	220	340
Dr. Pepper, Drink a Bite to Eat at 10-2-4, c1935	500	600
Ex-Lax Prescription Drugs, porcelain, sq. corners, horizontal temperature scale, 8" x 36"	230	320
Gold Coke, orig box, 7" l	25	30
Hires Draft Root Beer, dial, glass, c1965	60	80
Hires Root Beer, bottle shape, 1930s, 7" h	100	160
Kayo Chocolate, 5.75" x 13.5"	150	175
Leak's, tin, Danbury, VA	20	30
Mason's Root Beer, c1940	180	250
Mason's Root Beer, c1955	50	60
Occident Flour, tin	140	190
Orange Crush, bottle form, c1958, 30" h	110	160
Orange Crush, bottle cap, c1955, 16" h	110	160
Pepsi-Cola, dial, glass, c1951, 12" dia.	140	190
Pepsi-Cola, Light Refreshment, bottle cap, c1954, 27" h	90	130
RCA Victor Radio, 30" h	250	450
Seven-Up, We Proudly Serve, circ., bottle image, c1945, 10" dia	270	380

Left to right: Whistle, 1940s, 12" dia.; Alka Seltzer, 1950s, 12" dia.; and Dr. Pepper, 1950s–60s, 11" dia. —Photo courtesy Muddy River Trading Co.

Tools

Hand tools of the eighteenth, nineteenth and twentieth centuries often represent fine craftsmanship and engineering. Values vary with quality, rarity and also usability. Many craftsmen prefer the high quality of some antique tools over those now available. Watch out for missing parts.

"Good" pieces show wear but no damage and are still capable of use. "Best" pieces are in perfect condition with superior quality manufacture. For further information see *The Antique Tool Collector's Guide to Value, Third Edition* by Ronald S. Barlow, Windmill Publishing, El Cajon, CA, 1991.

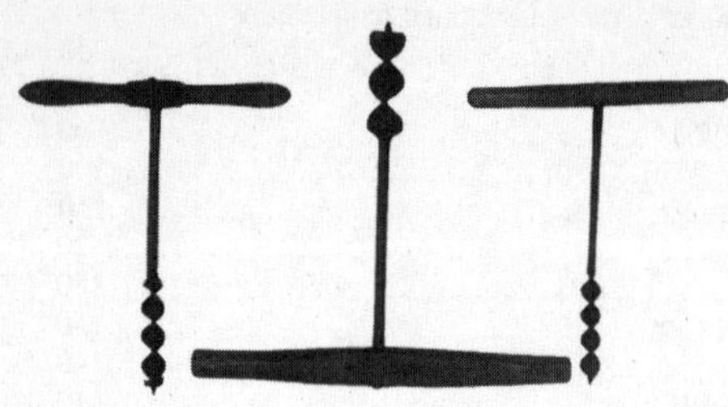

T-Handle Augers, $10 each.

	GOOD	BETTER	BEST
Adz	$16	$42	$105
Anvil, bench	15	45	100
Anvil, jeweler's	12	30	75
Auger, handled	20	50	100
Axe, cooper's	20	35	75
Axe, hewing	30	60	100
Axe, ice	11	22	43
Axe, Kent	15	30	50
Axe, mortising	30	45	75
Boring Machines	70	100	170
Brace	10	30	100
Brace, 18th C	80	60	320
Brace, Sheffield	60	100	310
C-Clamp, 4"	5	8	15
C-Clamp, 8"	8	12	25
Calipers	6	18	50
Chisel, wood carving	9	16	35
Chisels, set of 14	110	220	450
Clamp, violin	10	18	30
Clamp, floor	25	40	80
Clamp, mitre jack	15	25	45
Cobbler's Bench	100	200	500
Compass, drafting	5	10	30
Compass, woodworker's, 8"	5	10	25
Draw Knife	10	15	30
Drill, bow	150	275	650
Drill, breast	20	42	85
Drill, hand	10	20	40
Hacksaw	20	30	50
Hammer, ball peen	10	20	40

Pulley Block, $30.

	GOOD	BETTER	BEST
Hammer, claw	5	15	35
Hand Screw, all wood	10	20	35
Lathe, w/ treadle	150	330	600
Level, 6"	8	15	30
Level, 15"	15	40	75
Marking Gauge	8	20	75
Plane, badger	12	34	80
Plane, block	12	40	120
Plane, compass	18	45	160
Plane, horn	30	85	225
Plane, jack	20	35	80
Plane, joiner	25	45	125
Plane, molding	10	20	40
Plane, plow	12	35	100
Plane, smoothing	30	60	175
Pliers	5	15	30
Plumb, 5"	10	18	40
Plumb Bob	10	30	50
Router, hand	15	40	80
Saw, bow	50	100	200
Saw Set, sharpener	20	40	60
Screwbox	30	50	150
Screwdriver	6	12	25
Sextant	100	250	500
Sextant, boxed	150	300	750
Sharpening Stone, Arkansas	10	20	50
Shears	8	15	25
Spokeshave	10	20	50
Square, steel	10	15	35
Square, rosewood	15	20	50
Surveying Compass	50	100	275
Tool Chest, machinist's	80	130	275
Trammel	30	60	120
Vise, bench	50	90	180
Vise, swivel	40	70	100
Whetstone, turning wheel	30	60	140
Wrench, wooden handle	10	20	45

Toys and Playthings

Baby Rattles

Baby rattles are a universal toy. Almost every culture in the world has its own traditions and superstitions surrounding them. Available examples range from Georgian coral-and-bells to the plastic ones of today. Rattles can be made of gold, silver, ivory, tin, celluloid, paper and plastic. Collectors must compete with silver collectors and toy collectors for the prime examples, but flea markets, antique shows and some auctions are still good resources.

Prices give a typical retail range. Our consultant for this section is Marcia Hersey, author of *Collecting Baby Rattles and Teethers: Identification & Value Guide,* Krause Publications, Iola, WI, 1998.

	LOW	AVG.	HIGH
American, Art Nouveau jester, silver, c1910	$300	$450	$550
American, Bakelite and celluloid Humpty Dumpty, c1940	85	100	150
American, celluloid doll w/ tennis racquet, c1920	140	170	200
American, painted tin boy's head, c1900	85	120	175
American, painted tin pony cart, c1910	200	250	300
American, scrimshaw, ivory or whalebone, c1840	300	375	450
American, silver and mother-of-pearl, Tiffany, c1920	475	575	675
American, silver Art Deco bell, c1930	75	100	135
American, silver child reaching for moon, c1925	60	90	110
American, silver tambourine, c1875	400	525	650
American, stuffed cloth, Disney Minnie Mouse	50	75	100
American, wood ice cream sandwich, hand carved, c1991	20	25	30
Austrian, adapted silver coin w/ bells, c1750	375	475	575
Brazilian, straw man w/ bells, c1900	250	300	425
Chinese, silver lock, c1900	35	60	80
Dutch, silver-gilt, carnelian handle, c1850	450	550	650
English, Birmingham, silver w/ mother-of-pearl, 1869	300	375	450
English, Birmingham, silver gilt and coral, 1807	600	725	850
English, celluloid sheep, c1930	20	30	40
English, George II, silver w/ coral handle, 1735	1750	2000	2250
English, Georgian, gold coral and bells, c1780	2500	5000	9000
English, Georgian, silver coral and bells, c1790	800	1000	1250
English, silver Golliwog, c1917	150	200	225
English, silver jester, mother-of-pearl handle, c1900	250	300	350
English, silver w/ stained ivory handle, 1745	1750	2250	2650
English, silver plate London bobby, c1920	40	65	75
English, silver plate whistle, c1930	40	65	75
French, Art Deco, silver w/ ivory ring, c1930	125	165	200
French, Art Nouveau, silver w/ ivory ring, c1910	85	110	140
French, gold w/ mother-of-pearl handle, c1800	3500	4000	4500
French, Marotte, c1900	200	350	750
French, prisoner's work, ivory, c1840	400	550	700
German, silver butterfly, c1905	200	250	300
German, silver house, ivory handle, c1902	300	400	500
Indian, silver mallet, c1900	50	60	75
Japanese, celluloid Santa Claus, "Made in Occupied Japan"	75	100	125
Japanese, leather and wood, c1900	225	275	325
Portuguese, silver fish w/ ivory handle, c1940	80	100	120
Russian, silver w/ niello, bracelet attached, c1900	1000	1250	1500

Banks

Mechanical Banks

The values indicated for mechanical banks in this section reflect prices realized at private sales and recent public auctions. When evaluating a bank, one must consider market trends, subject matter, personal taste, and, most importantly, the subtleties of condition. Prices are given for each bank in three condition categories. We define fair as working, with 60% original paint, minor repairs and some professional restoration. Average is working with 80% original paint and perhaps a minor repair. Our highest category is not mint but superb, with 98% original paint, no repairs and working. Superb condition banks are rare and collectors pay a premium price for them. Many banks have been reproduced and most of these are poor quality and easy to detect. Beware of banks that are badly rusted and look like they have been buried in someone's backyard, since that may have been done in order to simulate age. Banks that bear the mark "The Book of Knowledge" are 1950s reproductions that are handsome but worth only a fraction of the value of the originals. Repairs and some reproductions are harder to detect but, with practice, these skills can be developed. As in all areas of collecting, do your homework.

Our consultant for this area is Sy Schreckinger, collector, dealer, appraiser and contributing author to *Antique Toy World Magazine.* Mr. Schreckinger is also a member of the Mechanical Bank Collectors of America, the Still Bank Collectors Club of America and the Toy Collectors of America. He is listed in the back of this book. For further reading we recommend *The Bank Book: The Encyclopedia of Mechanical Bank Collecting* by Bill Norman, Accent Studios, San Diego, CA, 1984, and *Penny Lane: A History of Antique Mechanical Toy Banks* by Al Davidson, Longs Americana, Mokelumne Hill, CA, 1987.

Left to right: Trick Dog; Elephant and 3 Clowns. —Photo courtesy Bill Bertoia Auctions.

	FAIR	AVG.	SUPERB
Acrobat	$2000	$5500	$11,000
Artillery	375	1100	4500
Bad Accident	1200	3200	8500
Bank Teller	20,000	45,000	75,000
Bear and Tree Stump	200	550	1700
Bird on Roof	750	1600	6500
Boy Robbing Bird's Nest	1850	6800	22,000
Boy Scout Camp	2000	7500	20,000
Boys Stealing Watermelons	1200	3000	8500

Left to right: Uncle Sam; Jonah and the Whale; Mammy and Child. —Photo courtesy Bill Bertoia Auctions.

	FAIR	AVG.	SUPERB
Boy on Trapeze	1300	2900	9800
Bucking Mule	400	1200	2500
Bull Dog, coin on nose	650	1400	5200
Bull Dog Savings	1800	3500	13,000
Butting Buffalo	1800	5500	17,000
Butting Goat	250	550	1600
Cabin	350	650	2500
Calamity	3000	12,000	35,000
Cat and Mouse, balance	700	3000	8500
Chief Big Moon	550	2500	5500
Chimpanzee	1800	4200	15,000
Circus	5500	16,500	45,000
Clown on Globe	750	2750	11,000
Confectionery	4500	9500	28,000
Creedmore	200	450	2000
Darktown Battery	900	2300	90000
Dentist	3000	9200	25,000
Dinah	350	900	3200
Dog on Turntable	200	400	1800
Dog Tray Bank	1700	4500	9500
Eagle and Eaglets	275	650	2500
Elephant, 3 clowns	750	2000	6000
Elephant Howdah, man pops out	250	550	3000
Elephant Pull Tail	150	450	1200
Frog on Rock	200	500	1500
Frog on Round Base	350	700	2500
Frogs Two	650	2000	8500
Gem	200	400	1200
Girl Skipping Rope	5500	18,000	65,000
Girl in Victorian Chair	2500	6500	17,000
Goat, Frog, Old Man	200	3500	12,000
Halls Excelsior	100	250	2000
Halls Liliput, w/ tray	200	500	2500
Hen and Chick, white hen	2500	5500	24,000
Hen and Chick, brown hen	2000	4500	18,000

Left to right: William Tell; Creedmore; Indian Shooting Bear. —Photo courtesy Bill Bertoia Auctions.

	FAIR	AVG.	SUPERB
Hindu	800	2500	10,000
Hold the Fort	2000	5000	11,000
Home Bank	550	1500	5800
Horse Race, flanged base	3500	10,000	30,000
Humpty Dumpty	3500	10,000	30,000
Indian Shooting Bear	650	2000	8000
Initiating, First Degree	3500	8500	23,000
Jolly N Bank	75	125	550
Jonah and the Whale, Jonah tosses coin into whale's mouth	1200	2500	10,000
Leap Frog	1300	2500	9500
Lion and Two Monkeys	600	2500	8000
Lion Hunter	2500	6500	15,000
Little Joe	100	350	750
Magic Bank	550	1500	3500
Magician	1700	4500	14,000
Mammy and Child	1850	6500	21,000
Mason	1700	6500	15,000
Milking Cow	4000	10,000	35,000
Monkey Bank (Hubley)	200	550	1500
Monkey and Coconut	800	3000	6000
Mosque	500	1550	3500
Mule Entering Barn	400	750	4500
New Creedmoor	200	550	2000
Novelty Bank	450	1400	4100
Organ Bank, boy and girl	500	1450	3500
Organ Bank, cat and dog	200	750	2500
Organ Bank, medium	300	550	1600
Organ Bank, miniature	350	750	2500
Organ Grinder and Performing Bear	2500	3500	14,000
Owl, slot in head	350	750	1500
Owl, turns head	200	500	1600
Paddy and the Pig	1500	3800	9500
Panorama	2000	8000	20,000
Patronize the Blind Man and His Dog	2000	6000	14,000
Peg-Leg Beggar	800	2500	5000
Pelican	1000	2000	4500
Picture Gallery	5500	16,000	32,000

Left to right: Presto Bank; Halls Liliput; Independence Hall; Halls Excelsior; Cabin. —Photo courtesy Bill Bertoia Auctions.

	FAIR	AVG.	SUPERB
Pig in a High Chair	300	700	2700
Presto Bank, trick drawer	100	250	1200
Professor Pug Frogs	3200	9500	28,000
Pump and Bucket	750	1500	3500
Punch and Judy	750	2000	5500
Rabbit in Cabbage	250	400	1600
Reclining Chinaman	2500	6500	18,000
Rooster	200	450	2000
Santa Claus at Chimney	1000	2500	6500
Speaking Dog	550	1800	5000
'Spise a Mule, bench	600	1800	4300
'Spise a Mule, jockey	400	1800	5000
Springing Cat, lead	5000	12,000	24,000
Squirrel on Tree Stump	750	2000	4500
Stump Speaker	1500	3500	9500
Tabby	450	1200	2500
Tammany	200	800	2000
Teddy and the Bear	750	1800	4500
Toad on Stump	350	600	2500
Trick Dog, 6-part base	400	1200	3500
Trick Pony	550	1800	4000
Uncle Remus	2000	5000	12,000
Uncle Sam	1500	3500	8500
Uncle Tom	200	650	2500
U.S. and Spain	2000	3500	12,000
Watchdog Safe	200	400	2500
Weedens Plantation, tin	800	2000	5500
William Tell	250	750	2500
Wireless	200	400	1200
World's Fair, Columbus	350	850	3000
Zoo Bank	600	1200	3500

Still Banks

Still banks are aptly named since there are no mechanical actions required to make the deposit. When collecting still banks, beware of rust, reproductions and repaints.

The M numbers in the following listing refer to *The Penny Bank Book: Collecting Still Banks* by Andy and Susan Moore, Schiffer Publishing, Exton, PA, 1984. The book includes photographs and names of manufacturers of most of the banks listed below. Unless specified, the following banks are made of cast iron. When bronze or copper is noted this refers to the type of finish, just as gold and silver refer to paint colors. Banks featuring several colors are described as "multi."

Prices are for examples in excellent condition (at least 90% paint intact). These pieces should have no major paint loss, no cracks, repairs, or repaints. Such faults decrease the value of a bank. Mint or near mint condition examples will command premium prices, 20% to 50% more than the prices listed below.

Our consultants for this area are Leon and Steven Weiss, owners of Gemini Antiques in Bridgehampton, New York, who specialize in antique toys and still and mechanical banks (they are listed in the back of this book).

Left to right: General Eisenhower Bust; General MacArthur Bust; Tank Bank.

	LOW	HIGH
1884 Bank, small rabbit, oval base, green and white, 2.25" h, M569	$1200	$1500
Air Mail on Stand, red, blue, and white accents, 6.38" h, M848	250	500
Andy Gump, 4.38" h, M217	700	1200
Arabian Safe, 4.5" h, M882	150	250
Bank of Columbia, nickel, 4.88" h, M906	100	200
Baseball Player, gold, red, and flesh tone, 5.75" h, M18	350	550
Basket, woven, bronze finish, 2.88" h, M917	75	125
Basset Hound, gold, 3.13" h, M380	800	1200
Bean Pot Nickel Register, red, nickel finish top, 3.5" dia., M951	150	200
Billiken, gold, 4.13" h, M74	50	100
Billiken, on throne, gold, red and black accents, 6.38" h, M73	100	200
Blackpool Tower, unpainted, 7.38" h, M984	250	350
Bucket Penny Register, nickel, 2.75" h, M912	100	150
Buffalo, small, gold, 4.38" l, M560	100	150
Buffalo Amherst Stoves, black, 4.38" h, M556	150	250
Bungalow, 3.75" h, M999	250	500
Buster Brown and Tige, gold, red, and multi, 5.5" h, M241	150	250
Captain Kidd, multi, 5.75" h, M38	300	500
Castle, bronze, 4" h, M1088	600	950
Cat, w/ ball, gray, 2.5" h, M352	200	250
Cat on Tub, gold, 4.13" h, M358	150	200

Left to right: Three Skyscraper Banks; Domed Bank Building; Presto Bank.

	LOW	HIGH
Church Towers, 6.75" h, M956	1200	1500
Clown, gold, red accents, 6.25" h, M211	75	100
Clown w/ Crooked Hat, 6.75" h, M210	1500	2500
Colonial House, w/ porch, gold, 3" h, M993	150	200
Cupola Bank, red, 5.5" l, M1145	350	800
Dog on Tub, gold, 4" h, M359	150	200
Dog Seated, "Cutie," black, red accents, 3.88" h, M414	100	150
Domed Bank Building, silver, 4.75" h, M1183	150	200
Double-Door Bank Building, dark, gold accents, 5.5" h, M1125	150	250
Eiffel Tower Bank, 10.38" h, M1075	700	1200
Elephant w/ Chariot, gray, red, and yellow, 7.25" l, M467	300	500
Elephant w/ Howdah, gray, silver, and gold, 3.5" h, M477	75	100
Elephant w/ Howdah, large, gold, 4.88" h, M474	125	175
Elephant w/ Howdah, small, 3" h, M459	100	150
Elephant on Tub, gold, 5.5" h, M483	75	100
Elephant on Wheels, 4" h, M446	250	350
Empire State Building, lead, 5.63" h, M1046	100	150
Fidelity Safe, large, black or green, gold trim, 3.5" h, M863	200	350
Fidelity Trust Vault, 6.5" h, M903	350	700
Fido, black and gold, red and white trim, 5" h, M417	50	100
Flat Iron Building, silver, gold trim, small trap, 5.75" h, M1160	300	500
Frowning Face, 5.75" h, M12	1000	1500
General Butler, multi, 6.5" h, M54	2000	3500
General Eisenhower Bust, white metal, 5.5" h, M133	50	75
General MacArthur, white metal, 5.625" h, M132	50	75
Give Billy a Penny, silver or red, black, and flesh tone, 4.75" h, M15	300	500
Globe Savings Fund 1888, multi, 7" h, M1199	1200	2500
Golliwog, multi, 6.25" h, M85	400	600
Hen on Nest, 3" h, M546	700	1100
High Rise, silver, gold accents, 5.5" h, M1217	300	500
Home Bank, bronze w/ green wash, 4" h, M1019	400	500
Horse on Tub, silver, 5.5" h, M510	200	250
House w/ Chimney, 4.5" h, M996	1500	2000
Independence Hall, 9.38" l, M1242	1000	1500
Independence Hall, gold, 15.5" l, M1243	2000	4000
Independence Hall, bronze, 9.38" h, M1244	700	900

Left to right: Elephant w/ Howdah (small); Statue of Liberty; Mulligan Policeman; Santa w/ Tree.

	LOW	HIGH
Independence Hall Tower, 9.5" h, M1202	400	700
Indian w/ Tomahawk, multi, 6" h, M228	200	350
Labrador, black, gold collar, 4.65" h, M412	300	400
Liberty Bell, Harper, bronze, 3.75" h, M780	500	700
Lighthouse, 10" h, M1115	1800	4000
Lion, gold, red accents, 4" h, M755	50	75
Lion, gold, red accents, 5" h, M754	50	75
Lion on Tub, decorated, gold, red, and blue, 5.5" h, M746	100	150
Lion on Tub, small, gold, 4.13" h, M747	100	150
Lion on Wheels, gold, 4.63" h, M760	250	300
Litchfield Cathedral, 6.5" h, M968	200	300
Man on Cotton Bale, 5" h, M37	800	1750
Main Street Trolley, no passengers, gold, 6.75" l, M1469	250	350
Middy Bank, metallic finish, 5.13" h, M36	100	200
Mosque Bank, w/ combination door, gold, 5.13" h, M1176	300	400
Mulligan Policeman, 5.75" h, M177	200	300
Old Doc Yak, multi, 4.5" h, M30	600	800
Old Doc Yak, silver, 4.5" h, M30	500	600
Old South Church, 5.63" h, M990	5000	6500
Old South Church, 13" h, M991	8000	18,000
One-Car Garage, gold, 2.5" h, M1009	200	300
Palace, black, gold accents, 7.5" h, M1116	1500	2200
Pershing, copper, 7.75" h, M150	100	150
Policeman, Arcade, 5.5" h, M182	250	400
Polish Rooster, 5.5" h, M541	1200	2400
Porky Pig, M264	200	300
Prancing Horse, large, gold, 7.25" h, M520	100	150
Prancing Horse, oval base, black, 5.13" h, M513	100	150
Presto Bank, silver, 4.063" h, M1167	150	200
Presto Trick Bank, black and red, 4.5" h, M1171	400	500
Puppo on Pillow, black and white, 5.5" h, M442	150	300
Rabbit, begging, gold, red accents, 5.13" h, M566	150	300
Roof Bank, dark, gold accents, 5.25" h, M1122	150	300
Rooster, 4.75" h, M548	100	150

Left to right: Fidelity Trust Vault; Independence Hall Tower.

	LOW	HIGH
Safe, Arabian, desert scenes, 4.5" h, M882	100	150
Safe, Security, black, gold accents, 6" h, M889	150	200
Safe, Time, nickel, 7.13" h, M895	350	450
Santa w/ Tree, Hubley, 6" h, M61	400	750
Save and Smile Money Bank, black w/ red lips, 4.25" h, M24	350	450
Scottie, white metal, red, white, or black, 4.75" h, M433	50	75
Six-Sided Building, 2.5" h, M1007	150	300
Skyscraper Building, 2.5" h, M1007	75	125
Soldier, gold, 6" h, M44	300	500
Spitz, gold, 4.25" h, M409	300	500
St. Bernard, w/ pack, dark, gold and silver, 5.38" h, M437	100	150
State Bank, brown, gold accents, 5.75" h, M1080	75	150
Statue of Liberty, silver, 6.063" h, M1164	75	150
Statue of Liberty, silver, 6.38" h, M1165	100	150
Stork Safe, 5.5" h, M651	800	1000
Tally-Ho, brown, gold, and silver, 4.5" h, M535	125	175
Tank Bank, 3.625" l, M1435	125	175
Teddy Roosevelt, gold, silver, and red, 5" h, M120	200	250
Three "No Evils" Monkeys, gold, 3.5" l, M743	200	400
Three Wise Monkeys, 3.25" h, M743	200	300
Tower Bank, combination lock, red and black, gilt, 7" h, M1198	1000	1500
Turkey, large, bronze w/ red accents, 4.25" h, M585	300	500
Two-Car Garage, silver and blue, 2.5" h, M1010	200	300
Two-Faced Black Boy, large, black and gold, 4.13" h, M83	150	225
Two-Faced Black Boy, small, black and gold, 3" h, M84	75	125
Two-Faced Devil, red, black, and white, 4.25" h, M31	700	1000
Two Kids, black, green, and silver, 4.38" h, M594	700	1200
U.S. Mail, silver, red trim, combination trap, 4.75" h, M835	100	150
Villa, 4" h, M959	300	500
Westminster Abbey, 6.38" h, M974	200	250
Woolworth Building, gold, no base, 7.88" h, M1041	150	200

Board Games

Board games are a part of practically everyone's lives. Beginning in the 1840s, mass-produced games have offered hours of fun and provided glimpses of their eras. A large number of those listed below are based on television shows, a theme that dominates post-war collecting. There are also examples of card, skill and target games included. The majority are by American companies.

The following prices are for games ranging from the 1880s to the 1980s. There are differences between post-WWII and pre-war collecting but condition and quality are sought by all collectors. Prices for post-war games are for *near mint complete.* These examples must have no tears, stains, broken corners, or missing pieces. Prices of the pre-war games, particularly for those dating before 1920, are a bit more lenient on condition due to age. They reflect examples that are complete with no stains or tears on the box or board image, but may have minor flaws: repaired inner corner or small skirt tears, and some dirt but nothing that affects the illustrations.

For further reading see *Antique Trader's Guide to Games & Puzzles* by Harry L. Rinker, Antique Trader Books, Dubuque, IA, 1997, and *Baby Boomer Games: Identification & Value Guide* by Rick Polizzi, Collector Books, Paducah, KY, 1995.

Across the Yalu, Milton Bradley, c1905, $150–$200.

Adventures of the Nebbs, Milton Bradley, c1925–27, $75–$100.

	LOW	HIGH
A-Team, Parker Brothers, 1984	$10	$15
ABC Monday Night Football, Aurora, 1972	35	45
Acquire, 3M, 1968	12	18
Across the Continent, Parker Brothers, 1952	35	45
Across the Continent, Parker Brothers, 1960	15	25
Across the Yalu, Milton Bradley, c1905	150	200
Addams Family Game, Ideal, 1965	50	70
Addams Family Reunion Game, Pressman, 1991	8	12
Admiral Byrd's South Pole Game, Parker Brothers, c1934	325	375
Adventures of Robin Hood, Bettye-B, 1956	50	70
Adventures of the Nebbs, Milton Bradley, c1925–27	80	90
Aero-Chute Target Game, American Toy Works, c1930s	60	70
Aggravation, Lakeside, 1970	4	6
Air Ship Game, McLoughlin Brothers, 1904	325	375
Airline, Mulgara Products, 1985	8	12
Alee-Oop, Royal Toy, 1937	18	24
Alfred Hitchcock Why Mystery Game, Milton Bradley, 1967	20	28
All-American Football Game, Cadaco, 1960	25	35
All in the Family, Milton Bradley, 1972	12	18
All My Children, TSR, 1985	5	10
All-Star Bowling, Gotham, 1960s	18	24

All–Star Baseball, Cadaco-Ellis, 1957, $40–$60.

Annie Oakley, Milton Bradley, 1958, $30–$40.

	LOW	HIGH
Allan Sherman's Camp Granada Game, Milton Bradley, 1965	30	35
Amateur Golf, Parker Brothers, 1928	60	70
Amazing Dunninger, Hasbro, 1967	18	24
American Boy Game, Milton Bradley, 1924–26	125	175
American Derby, Cadaco-Ellis, 1945	35	45
American Derby, Cadaco, 1951	30	38
American History in Pictures, Interstate School Service, c1920s	22	28
Amusing Game of Innocence Abroad, Parker Brothers, 1888	275	350
Anagrams, Peter G. Thomson, c1885	18	25
Angel Spiel, German, c1910–20	70	80
Animal Game, Saalfield Publishing, c1920s	45	60
Annie, Parker Brothers, 1981	8	12
Ant Farm Game, Uncle Milton's Industries, 1969	18	24
Anti-Monopoly, Ralph Anspach, 1973	35	45
Ants in the Pants, Schaper, 1970	8	12
Apollo A Voyage to the Moon, Tracianne, 1969	20	30
Are You Being Served?, Toltoys, 1977	18	25
Arrest and Trial, Transogram, 1963	30	38
Art Linkletter's House Party Game, Whitman, 1968	20	28
Astro Launch, Ohio Art, 1963	45	55
Authors, E.E. Fairchild, c1945	12	18
Authors Illustrated, Clark & Sowdon, 1893	30	40
Auto Race Game, Milton Bradley, c1925	225	275
Babar and His Friends, See-Saw Game, Milton Bradley, 1961	15	25
Balance the Budget, Elten Game Corp., 1938	18	25
Bamboozle, Milton Bradley, 1962	30	38
Bandit Trail Game, Kenon Hardware Co., 1950s	70	80
Bantu, Parker Brothers, 1955	18	25
Barbie Game, Queen of the Prom, Mattel, 1964	50	60
Bargain Hunter, Milton Bradley, 1981	12	18
Baron Munchausen Game, Parker Brothers, 1933	20	30
Baseball, Parker Brothers, 1959	25	35
Batman Pin Ball Game, Marx, 1966	75	125
Battleship Game, Whitman, 1940	12	18
Beatles Flip Your Wig, Milton Bradley, 1964	100	150
Bermuda Triangle, Milton Bradley, 1976	12	18
Big Business, Transogram, 1937	20	30
Big Foot, Milton Bradley, 1977	10	15

Archie Bunker's Card Game, Milton Bradley, 1972, $12–$18.

'Babe' Ruth's Baseball Game, Milton Bradley, c1926–28, $700–$800.

	LOW	HIGH
Big Sneeze, Ideal, 1968	15	20
Big Town News Reporting & Printing Game, Lowel, 1955	70	80
Billionaire, Parker Brothers, 1973	10	18
Billy Blastoff Space Game, Danlee, 1969	25	35
Billy Whiskers, Saalfield Publishing, c1923–26	45	60
Bionic Crisis, Parker Brothers, 1975	18	25
Black Beauty, Transogram, 1958	30	40
Blockade, Milton Bradley, c1898	28	35
Blondie and Dagwood's Race for the Office Game, Jaymar, 1950	40	50
Blox-O, Lubbers & Bell Mfg. Co., 1923	18	25
Bobbin Noggin, Milton Bradley, 1964	12	18
Bobbsey Twins on the Farm, Milton Bradley, 1957	25	35
Boom or Bust, Parker Brothers, 1951	100	150
Boy Scouts, McLoughlin Brothers, c1910s	225	275
Bozo the Clown Circus Game, Transogram, 1960s	20	30
Breakthru, 3M, 1965	18	25
Bridge Keno, Milton Bradley, 1930	12	18
Bruce Force–Lost in Outer Space, Ideal, 1963	45	55
Buck Rogers Battle for the 25th Century, TSR, 1988	12	18
Bug-A-Boo, Whitman, 1968	12	18
Bullwinkle and Rocky, Ideal, 1963	55	65
Buy and Sell, Whitman, 1953	12	18
Cabby, Selchow & Righter, 1938–40s	55	65
Cake Walk Game, Parker Brothers, c1900s	1000	1400
Camouflage, Milton Bradley, 1961	20	30
Campaign, Waddington, 1971	30	40
Campus Queen, King-Sealey, 1967	20	30
Capture Hill 79, Hasbro, 1968	40	50
Car 54 Where Are You?, Allison, 1962	70	80
Careers, Parker Brothers, 1958	25	35
Casey Jones Game Box, Saalfield, 1959	45	55
Cat, Carl F. Doerr, c1915	25	35
Championship Base Ball Parlor Game, Grebnelle Novelty Co., 1914	1100	1500
Charge It!, Whitman, 1972	18	25
Charlie's Angels, Milton Bradley, 1978	20	30
Cherry Ames' Nursing Game, Parker Brothers, 1959	45	55
Chestnut Burrs, Fireside Game Co., 1896	35	45
Cheyenne, Milton Bradley, 1958	60	70

Cheyenne Game, Milton Bradley, 1958, $60–$70.

Coon Hunt Game, Parker Brothers, 1903, $350–$400.

	LOW	HIGH
Chicklets Gum Village Game, Hasbro, 1959	25	35
Chit Chat, Milton Bradley, 1963	15	20
Chivalry, George S. Parker & Co., 1888	90	110
Christmas Goose, McLoughlin Brothers, 1890	700	800
Chutes and Ladders, Milton Bradley, 1943	20	30
Chutes and Ladders, Milton Bradley, 1950s	18	25
Cinderella or Hunt the Slipper, McLoughlin Brothers, 1887	55	65
Clean Sweep, Schaper, 1967	25	35
Coast to Coast, Ewing, 1955	20	30
Commanders of Our Forces, E.C. Eastman, 1863	80	120
Concentration, Milton Bradley, 1964	12	18
Cootie, Transogram, 1939	20	30
Crazy Car Race, Steven Mfg., 1972	18	25
Crows in the Corn, Parker Brothers, 1930	90	110
Day at the Circus, 1898	900	1100
Decoy, Selchow & Righter, plastic ducks, 1956	35	45
Dewey at Manila, Chaffee & Selchow, 1899	50	60
Dig, Parker Brothers, 1959	8	12
Disneyland, Whitman, 1965	35	45
Doctor Dolittle, Mattel, 1967	40	50
Dodging Donkey, Parker Brothers, c1924	60	70
Donkey Kong, Milton Bradley, 1981	12	18
Don't Bug Me, Hasbro, 1967	8	12
Dungeons & Dragons, Tactical Studies Rules, 1974	18	25
Easy Money, Milton Bradley, 1936	20	30
Eddie Cantor's Automobile Game "Tell It to the Judge," Parker Brothers, 1930s	25	35
Electric Football, Electric Game Co., 1940s	45	55
Emergency Game, Milton Bradley, 1973–74	12	18
Espionage, Transogram, 1963	35	45
Excursion to Coney Island, Milton Bradley, c1885	25	35
F Troop, Ideal, 1965	100	120
Face the Facts, Lowell Mfg., 1961	30	40
Familiar Quotations, McLoughlin Brothers, c1890	20	25
Fantastic Voyage, Milton Bradley, 1968	20	30
Fantasy Island, Ideal, 1978	15	20
Farmer Jones' Pigs, McLoughlin Brothers, c1885	110	130
Fast Eddie, Mattel, 1970	8	12

Fox Hunt, Milton Bradley, 1905, $40–$60.

The Hand of Fate, McLoughlin Brothers, 1901, $900–$1100.

	LOW	HIGH
Feed the Elephant, Cadaco, 1952	25	35
Felix the Cat, Milton Bradley, 1960	35	45
Ferrilude or Game of Beasts, West & Lee Game Co., 1873	30	35
Fireball XL5, Milton Bradley, 1964	80	100
Fish Bait, Ideal, 1965	50	60
Flapper Fortunes, The Embossing Co., 1929	15	20
Flash, Justice League of America, Hasbro, 1967	125	175
Flintstones Game, Milton Bradley, 1971	20	30
Flying the Beam, Parker Brothers, 1941	70	80
Foot Race, Parker Brothers, c1900	15	20
Frontier Fort Rescue Race, Gabriel, 1956	25	35
Fugitive, Ideal, 1964	115	135
Game of Black Sambo, Samuel Gabriel Sons & Co., c1939	225	275
Game of Dragnet, Transogram, 1955	45	55
Game of Jack Straws, Parker Brothers, 1900s	18	24
Game of Jumping Frog, J.H. Singer, c1890	18	25
Geography Up to Date, Parker Brothers, c1890	12	18
Giant Barrel of Monkeys, Lakeside, 1969	12	18
Gilligan's Island, Game Gems/T. Cohn, 1964	70	80
Go to the Head of the Class, Milton Bradley, 1955	8	12
Going to Market, Beech-Nut Packing Co., 1915	100	120
Goodbye Mr. Chips, Parker Brothers, 1969	25	30
Grandma's Game of Useful Knowledge, Milton Bradley, c1910	20	25
Green Hornet Quick Switch Game, Milton Bradley, 1966	200	275
Happy Face, Milton Bradley, 1968	12	18
Hats Off, Kohner, 1967	12	18
Hawaiian Eye, Lowell, 1963	75	85
Hee Haw, Dooley Fant, Inc., 1975	12	18
Hen That Laid the Golden Egg, Parker Brothers, 1900	225	275
Hogan's Heroes Bluff Out Game, Transogram, 1966	60	70
Home Fish Pond, McLoughlin Brothers, c1890	90	110
Hotels, Milton Bradley, 1987	15	20
Howdy Doody's T.V. Game, Milton Bradley, 1953	35	45
Illya Kuryakin Card Game, Milton Bradley, 1965–66	25	35
India Bombay, Cutler & Saleeby Co., c910	20	30
Ironside, Ideal, 1967	80	100

Little Orphan Annie Game, Milton Bradley, 1927, $100–$150.

NBC-TV News Game, Dadan, Inc., 1962, $20–$30.

	LOW	HIGH
Jack & Jill, Milton Bradley, 1909	50	60
Jackie Gleason's "And AW-A-A-Ay We Go!," Transogram, 1956	90	110
Jeopardy, Milton Bradley, 1964	10	15
Jetsons Game, Milton Bradley, 1985	8	12
Johnny Ringo, Transogram, 1960	80	100
Journey to the Unknown, Remco, 1968	90	100
Junk Yard, Ideal, 1975	18	25
Kick Back, Schaper, c1965	10	12
Knight Rider, Parker Brothers, 1983	8	12
Lancer, Remco, 1968	50	65
Lazy Pool, Dashound, 1965	4	6
Leave It to Beaver Rocket to the Moon, Hasbro, 1959	30	40
Letters or Anagrams, Parker Brothers, c1889	18	25
Lindy, Parker Brothers, 1927	20	30
Little Beaver's 3 Game Set, Built-Rite, 1956	50	60
Little Mother Goose, Parker Brothers, c1890	25	35
Lobby, Milton Bradley, 1949	18	25
Lone Ranger Game, Milton Bradley, 1966	18	25
Lost in Space, Milton Bradley, 1965	50	65
Lot the Calf, Brown Games Inc., 1964	18	25
Lucky Star Gum Ball Game, Ideal, 1961	25	35
Madam Morrows Fortune Telling Cards, McLoughlin Brothers, 1886	25	35
Major Matt Mason Space Exploration, Mattel, 1967	55	65
Man From U.N.C.L.E. Shoot Out!, Milton Bradley, 1965	45	55
Masquerade Party, Bettye-B, 1955	70	80
Mel Allen's Baseball Game, Radio Corp. of America, 1959	175	225
Merry Game of Old Bachelor, McLoughlin Brothers, 1892	30	40
Mexican Pete, Parker Brothers, 1940s	25	35
Monopoly, Parker Brothers, 1935	34	45
Monopoly, Parker Brothers, 1957	12	18
Mork & Mindy Card Game, Milton Bradley, 1978	8	12
Mr. Bug Goes to Town, Milton Bradley, 1955	30	40
Mr. T. Game, Milton Bradley, 1983	8	12
Mystic Wanderer, J.H. Singer, c1890–95	70	80
National Velvet Game, Transogram, 1961	30	40
New Fox and Geese, McLoughlin Brothers, c1888	18	25
Newlywed Game, Chuck Barris Productions, 1979	8	12
Notch, Remco, 1960	10	15
Old Maid, Milton Bradley, c1905	12	18

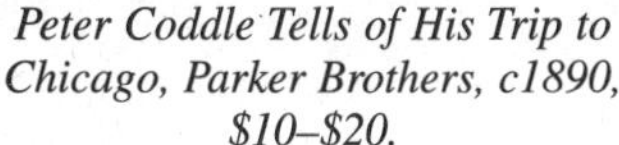
Peter Coddle Tells of His Trip to Chicago, Parker Brothers, c1890, $10–$20.

Round the World with Nellie Bly, McLoughlin Brothers, c1904, $175–$225.

	LOW	HIGH
Old Woman Who Lived in a Shoe, Parker Brothers, c1895	100	120
Our National Ball Game, McGill & Delany, 1886	600	700
Parcheesi, Selchow & Righter, 1940s	25	35
Patty Duke Game, Milton Bradley, 1964	25	35
Peeko, Watkins-Strathmore, 1964	8	12
Peter Coddle's Trip to the World's Fair, Parker Brothers, 1939	10	15
Philip Marlowe Game, Transogram, 1960	35	45
Pigs in the Clover, Milton Bradley, c1930	18	25
Pinhead, Remco, 1959	20	30
Pink Panther Game, Warren, 1977	18	25
Pirate and Traveler, Milton Bradley, 1911	55	65
Pivot Golf, Milton Bradley, 1973	35	45
Point of Law, 3M, 1972	8	12
Poison Ivy Game, Ideal, 1969	18	25
Pollyanna, Parker Brothers, 1915–20s	25	35
Pop Yer Top!, Milton Bradley, 1968	18	25
Post Office, Hasbro, 1968	20	25
Pot of Gold, Parker Brothers, 1897	100	150
Pursuit, Aurora, 1973	15	20
Puzzle-Peg, Lubbers & Bell Mfg. Co., c1920	10	18
Quick Draw McGraw Private Eye Game, Milton Bradley, 1960–61	20	30
Quiz Kids Own Game Box, 1940	18	25
Race Trap, Multiple Toymakers, 1960s	30	40
Rack-O, Milton Bradley, 1961	5	10
Raggedy Ann's Magic Pebble Game, Milton Bradley, 1940–41	55	65
Red Skelton's "I Dood It!," Zondine Game Co., 1947	65	75
Ripcord, Lowell, 1962	50	60
Rip-Van Win-kle, Parker Brothers, c1890	100	150
Robot Sam the Answer Man, Jacmar	30	40
Rodeo the Wild West Game, Whitman, 1957	25	35
Rook, Parker Brothers, 1936	5	10
Ruff and Reddy Circus Game, Transogram, 1962	25	35
Salute, Selchow & Righter, 1940s	25	35
Score Four, Funtastic, 1968–75	8	12

Scooby Doo Where Are You?, Milton Bradley, 1973, $18–$24.

Game of Strategy, McLoughlin Brothers, c1891, $200–$300.

	LOW	HIGH
Scrabble, Selchow & Righter, 1953	8	12
Scru-unch, Mattel, 1967	35	45
Sharp's Shooter, Sharp	70	80
Shotgun Slade Game, Milton Bradley, 1960	20	30
Silly Safari, Topper, 1966	45	55
Skittle Pool, Aurora, 1972	25	35
Smitty Game, Milton Bradley, c1930s	100	120
Snoopy's Doghouse Game, Milton Bradley	10	15
Soli-Peg, Rosebud Art Co., c1930s	18	25
Soupy Sez Go-Go-Go!, Milton Bradley, 1961	60	70
Space Game, Parker Brothers, 1953	40	50
Speedway, Ideal, 1961	35	45
Spider and Fly Game, Milton Bradley, c1925	45	55
Spring Chicken, Mattel, 1968	18	25
Star Wars, Parker Brothers, 1982	20	30
Steeple Chase, J.H. Singer, c1890	90	100
Stop and Go, Shell Oil, c1930s	35	45
Straight Away, Selchow & Righter, 1961	45	55
Stratego, Milton Bradley, 1962	10	18
Sub Attack Game, Milton Bradley, 1965	20	30
Super Market, Selchow & Righter, 1953	18	25
Superman Quoit & Horseshoe Set, Super Swim, Inc., 1950s	90	110
Swap, Ideal, 1965	12	18
Sweepstakes, WM, 1970s	25	35
Take It or Leave It, Zondine, 1942	35	45
Talk to Cecil, Mattel, 1961	35	45
Tee Party, Milton Bradley, 1968	20	30
Ten Commandments Bible Game, Cadaco, 1964	10	20
Terrytoon Hide & Seek Game, Transogram, 1960	40	50
Texas Checkers, Asco, 1960s	8	12
Things and Places, Pressman, 1960	20	30
Think-A-Thon, Hasbro, 1961	70	80
Three Chipmunks Cross Country Game, Hasbro, 1960	30	40
Through the Locks to the Golden Gate, Milton Bradley, c1905	80	90
Ticker, Glow Products Co., 1929	70	80
Tiddledy Winks, Milton Bradley, c1905	10	18
Tip Top Fish Pond, Milton Bradley, c1930s	18	25
To Tell the Truth, Lowell, 1957	25	35
To the North Pole by Airship, McLoughlin Brothers, 1897	800	900

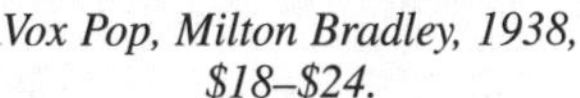
Vox Pop, Milton Bradley, 1938, $18–$24.

Zorro, Whitman, 1959, $30–$50.

	LOW	HIGH
Tobogganing at Christmas, McLoughlin Brothers, 1899	1500	2000
Tom and Jerry Game, Milton Bradley, 1968	18	25
Tootsie Roll Train Game, Hasbro, 1964	20	30
Toss Across, Ideal, 1969	12	18
Touché Turtle, Transogram, 1962	55	65
Touring, Parker Brothers, 1958	5	10
Toy Town Telegraph Office, Parker Brothers, c1910	300	350
Train for Boston, Parker Brothers, 1900	1000	1500
Trap the Rat, Hasbro, 1964	12	18
Trip Around the World, Parker Brothers, c1920	50	60
Triple Play, National Games Inc., c1930s	8	12
Trolley, Snyder Bros. Game Co., 1904	40	50
Truth or Consequences, Gabriel, 1955	25	35
TV Jackpot Game, Milton Bradley, 1975	8	12
Uncle Wiggily Game, Milton Bradley, 1920s	30	40
Universe, Parker Brothers, 1967	12	18
Victory Bomber, Whitman, 1940s	20	30
Voodoo Doll Game, Schaper, 1967	25	35
Voyage of Fear Game, Whitman, 1979	10	18
Voyage to the Bottom of the Sea Card Game, Milton Bradley, 1965	20	30
Wackiest Ship in the Army Game, Standard Toykraft, 1964–65	40	50
Walt Disney's Babes in Toyland, Parker Brothers, 1961	25	35
Walt Disney's Tomorrowland Rocket to the Moon Game, Parker Brothers, 1956	35	45
Wells Fargo Game, Milton Bradley, 1959	35	45
What's My Name!, Jay Mar Specialty, c1940	30	40
Whirly Bird, Schaper, 1958	10	18
Wild Bill Hickok's the Cavalry and the Indians Game, Built-Rite	45	55
Wogglebug Game of Conundrums, Parker Brothers, 1905	90	100
Woody Woodpecker Game, Milton Bradley, 1958	35	45
Wow Pillow Fight Game for Girls, Milton Bradley, 1964	18	25
X-Plor US, Alderman-Fairchild, c1922	80	90
Yacht Race, Clark & Sowdon, c1895	50	60
Yankee Doodle, Parker Brothers, 1895	600	650
Yankee Trader, Corey Games, 1941	25	35
Yogi Bear Game, Milton Bradley, 1971	18	25
You Don't Say Game, Milton Bradley, 1964–69	8	12
Zaxxon, Milton Bradley, 1982	8	12
Zippy Zepps Air Game, Alderman-Fairchild	375	450
Zok, Hasbro, 1967	18	25

Character Toys

Character toys and memorabilia charm children and adults alike. They are based on familiar faces seen in the comics, heard on the radio or seen on a movie screen or TV. The following items range from the Yellow Kit (turn of the century) to Pee Wee Herman (1980s). Since there is such a diversity of materials, collecting criteria varies a bit. Most of the keywind tinplate character toys have a lithographed or printed finish while cast-iron toys are usually painted. Overall the condition reported below is for excellent and better. Prices are given for the item and in many cases a separate range is listed for the item in its original box or package. We do not give a range for toys that are unlikely to be found with their original box nor do we give a price for items that have little value without their packaging, such as records.

For futher information about character and other toys we suggest *Hake's Price Guide to Character Toys, 2nd Edition* by Ted Hake, Avon Books, New York, Gemstone Publishing, Timonium, MD, 1998; *The Official Price Guide to Action Figures* by Stuart Wells III and Jim Main, House of Collectibles, NY, 1997; *Toys & Prices, 5th Edition* edited by Sharon Korbeckl, Krause Publications, Iola, WI, 1997; and *Toys of the Sixties* by Bill Bruegman, Cap'n Penny Productions, Akron, OH, 1992.

There are also character items in the following sections of this book: Advertising, Board Games, Comic Books, Comic Character Watches, Dolls, Little Golden Books, Premiums, Radios, Robots, Space Toys and Viewmaster.

Left to right: Addams Family Jigsaw Puzzle, Milton Bradley, 14" x 24.125" assembled size, $10–$15; Amos 'N' Andy, Fresh Air Taxi Cab, keywind, tinplate, Marx, 8" l, $1000–$1500.

	UNBOXED	BOXED
Addams Family, Gomez Hand Puppet, Ideal, c1965, 11" h	$90–120	$200–300
All in the Family, Mug, 1970s	9–12	—
Amos 'N' Andy, Amos Walker, keywind, tinplate, Marx, c1930, 12" h	700–1000	—
Amos 'N' Andy, Taxicab, cast iron, 6" l	800–1000	1200–1800
Andy Gump, Andy Walker, keywind, tinplate, Marx, c1930, 12" h	700–1000	—
Andy Gump, Car, cast iron, Arcade, c1924, 5.75" l	1200–1800	—
Aquaman, Figure, plastic, Comic Action Heroes, Mego, c1975, 3.75" h	20–25	50–70
Archies, Archie Doll, Marx, c1975, 10" h	12–18	35–65
Archies, Betty Doll, Marx, c1975, 10" h	12–18	35–65

	UNBOXED	BOXED
Archies, Jalopy, Marx, c1975, 10" h	25–30	50–70
Archies, Jughead Doll, Marx, c1975, 10" h	12–18	35–65
Archies, Sabrina Paper Doll	9–12	18–22
Archies, Veronica Doll, Marx, c1975, 10" h	12–18	35–65
Babar, Arthur Figure, Bilikin, c1989	2–3	8–10
Babar, King Babar Figure, plastic, Bilikin, c1989	2–3	8–10
Babar, Queen Celeste Figure, Bilikin, c1989	3–4	10–12
Bambi, Bambi Soakie, c1960s	20–30	—
Bambi, Thumper Soakie, c1960s	20–30	—
Banana Splits, Bingo the Bear Doll, Sutton, c1970	40–60	90–120
Banana Splits, Drooper the Lion Doll, Sutton, c1970	40–60	90–120
Banana Splits, Fleagle Beagle the Dog Doll, Sutton, c1970	40–60	90–120
Banana Splits, Snorky the Elephant Doll, Sutton, c1970	40–60	90–120
Barnacle Bill the Sailor, Bill and Punching Bag, keywind, tinplate, Chein, 7.5" h	500–800	—
Barney Google, Barney Figure, jointed wood, Schoenhut, c1922, 8.5" h	400–650	—
Bat Masterson, Holster Set, w/ cane and vest, Carnell, c1960s	100–150	250–350
Batman, Batbike, Corgi, 4.25" l	40–60	80–100
Batman, Batcave, Toy Biz, c1989	8–12	20–30
Batman, Batcycle, Toy Biz, c1989	4–6	10–15
Batman, Batman and Robin Bookends, 1966, 4" x 7"	70–90	100–150
Batman, Batman and Robin Bank, figural, ceramic, 1966	60–80	90–150
Batman, Batman and Robin Society Member Button, full color, 1960s	30–40	—
Batman, Batman Bank, figural, ceramic, c1966, 7" h	60–70	80–100
Batman, Batman Figure, magnetic w/ fly-away action, Mego, c1979, 12.5" h	60–90	120–180
Batman, Batman Flashlight, 1976	10–12	20–30
Batman, Batman Music Box, figural, ceramic, Price/National, c1970s, 7" h	50–70	100–150
Batman, Batmobile, remote control, Toy Biz, c1989	15–20	30–40
Batman, Batmobile Bubble Bath, plastic, Avon	10–15	20–30
Batman, Batmobile Gold Hubs, Corgi, 1966, 5" l	200–250	350–500
Batman, Batphone, Marx, c1966, 8" l	90–110	140–180
Batman, Batwing, Toy Biz, c1989	9–14	20–30
Batman, Book, *From Alfred to Zowie!,* Golden Press, 1966	15–20	—
Batman, Charm Bracelet, w/ 5 charms, on orig. store card, 1966	30–40	80–100
Batman, Coloring Book, Batman Meets Blockbuster, Whitman, 1966	8–12	40–60
Batman, Coloring Book, Western Publishing Co.	8–10	40–60
Batman, Flying Copter, Remco, c1966	50–70	90–130
Batman, Fork, metal, Imperial, 1966, 6" l	8–10	15–20
Batman, Hair Brush, plastic, figural handle, Avon, 1976, 8.5" l	8–12	20–25
Batman, Halloween Costume, w/ mask, Ben Cooper, 1960s	20–25	40–60
Batman, Joker Music Box, figural, ceramic, Price/National, c1970s, 7" h	50–70	100–150
Batman, Joker Van, Toy Biz, c1989	7–9	18–22
Batman, License Plate, 1966, 4" x 7.5"	10–15	20–30
Batman, Mug, white plastic w/ Batman and Robin illus.	70–90	—
Batman, Paint By Numbers Set, Hasbro, c1966	60–80	100–160
Batman, Penguin Music Box, figural, ceramic, Price/National, c1970s, 7" h	50–70	100–150
Batman, Record, 45 rpm, diecut sleeve in form of Batman's head, c1966	—	50–70
Batman, Record, Soundtrack LP, 20th Century Fox, 1966	—	120–160
Batman, Riddler Music Box, figural, ceramic, price/National, c1970s, 7" h	50–70	100–150

	UNBOXED	BOXED
Batman, Robin Flashlight, 1976	8–10	20–25
Batman, Utility Belt, Ideal, c1966	500–700	800–1200
Batman, Wallet, 1966	20–30	—
Beatles, George Doll, Remco, c1964, 5" h	70–90	150–200
Beatles, John Doll, Remco, c1964, 5" h	70–90	150–200
Beatles, Paul Doll, Remco, c1964, 5" h	70–90	150–200
Beatles, Ringo Doll, Remco, c1964, 5" h	70–90	150–200
Betty Boop, Acrobat, keywind, celluloid and tinplate, 8.5" h	500–750	—
Betty Boop, Doll, composition head, Cameo, 12" h	400–700	—
Betty Boop, Figure, composition, c1940, 14" h	500–800	—
Beverly Hillbillies, Car, plastic, Ideal, 1963, 22" l	200–250	400–600
Bewitched, Broom, Amsco, c1965, 36" l	30–50	80–120
Bewitched, Samantha Doll, Ideal, c1965, 12" h	200–250	400–600
Bionic Woman, Bionic Beauty Salon, Kenner, c1976	15–20	30–40
Bionic Woman, Jamie Sommers Figure, Kenner, c1976	18–22	40–60
Bionic Woman, Sports Car, Kenner, c1976	20–30	50–70
Blondie and Dagwood, Blondie's Jalopy, keywind, tinplate, Marx, 15" l	1500–2000	2200–2800
Blondie and Dagwood, Dagwood the Driver Car, keywind, tinplate, Marx, c1935, 8" l	400–600	900–1400
Blondie and Dagwood, Dagwood's Solo Flight Airplane, keywind, tinplate, Marx, 9" l	500–700	900–1200
Bonanza, 4-in-1 Wagon, plastic, American Character, c1966	90–140	250–350
Bonanza, Album, *Party Time*	—	25–35
Bonanza, Ben and Palomino, plastic, American Character, c1966	65–85	180–220
Bonanza, Hoss and Stallion, plastic, American Character, c1966	75–95	200–250
Bonanza, Jigsaw Puzzle, Ponderosa Ranch	—	25–35
Bonanza, Little Joe and Pinto, plastic, American Character, c1966	75–95	200–250
Bonanza, Movie Viewer, National Broadcasting Co.	10–15	20–30
Bonanza, Holster Set, Halpern Nichols, c1960	90–120	150–220
Bonanza, Paperback Book, *One Man With Courage,* Media Books, 1966	7–9	—
Bonanza, Paperback Book, *The Living Legend of Bonanza*	8–10	—
Bonzo, Scooter, tinplate, Chein, 7" h	500–750	—
Boob McNutt, Figure, wooden, jointed, Schoenhut, 9" h	1000–1500	—
Bozo the Clown, Soakie, c1960s	20–30	—
Brady Bunch, Coloring Book, Whitman, c1970s	8–10	25–35
Buck Rogers, Ardella Figure, plastic, Mego, c1979, 3.75" h	4–6	10–15
Buck Rogers, Atomic Pistol, chrome plated, Daisy, c1930s	100–150	200–300
Buck Rogers, Battlecruiser, Tootsie Toy, c1937	100–150	200–300
Buck Rogers, Buck Figure, plastic, Mego, c1979, 3.75" h	4–6	10–15
Buck Rogers, Buck Figure, plastic, Mego, c1979, 12" h	15–20	40–60
Buck Rogers, Combat Holster Set, Daisy, c1934	180–220	300–400
Buck Rogers, Copper Disintegrator Cap Gun, cast iron, c1930s	100–150	300–400
Buck Rogers, Draco Figure, plastic, Mego, c1979, 3.75" h	10–12	20–30
Buck Rogers, Laserscope Fighter, plastic, Mego, c1979	12–15	25–40
Buck Rogers, Pencil Case, cardboard, c1938	35–55	—
Buck Rogers, Pocket Pistol, Daisy, c1930s	120–180	250–350
Buck Rogers, Police Patrol Spaceship, keywind, tinplate, Marx, c1939, 12" l	800–1200	1800–2200
Buck Rogers, Printing Set	60–80	150–200
Buck Rogers, Rubber Band Gun, large litho cardboard punch-out, Onward, c1930s	30–40	60–80

Left to right: Batman Figure, Bilikin, c1989, $3–$4; Charlie Chaplin Candy Container, glass, Borgfeldt, 3.75" h, $150–$200; Donald Duck on Tricycle, bisque, Japan, 3.25" h, $250–$350.

	UNBOXED	BOXED
Buck Rogers, Sonic Ray Gun, plastic, battery powered, Norton Engineering, 1950s	60–90	120–180
Buck Rogers, Star Fighter Command Center, Mego, c1979, 3.75" h figures	25–35	40–70
Buck Rogers, Strato-Kite, Aero Kite, c1946	45–65	—
Buck Rogers, Tiger Man Figure, plastic, Mego, c1979, 12" h	15–20	30–50
Buck Rogers, Walking Twiki, plastic, Mego, c1979, 12" h	20–30	45–65
Buffalo Bill Jr., Western Outfit, c1950s	70–90	100–150
Bugs Bunny, Doll, talking, pull string, Mattel, c1970s	30–40	80–120
Buster Brown, Dog Cart, cast iron, 7.5" l	400–600	—
Buttercup and Spare Ribs, Pull Toy, tinplate, Nifty, c1925, 7.5" h	900–1600	—
Captain America, Figure, plastic, Comic Action Heroes, Mego, c1975, 3.75" h	15–20	40–50
Casper, Talking Ghost Doll, Mattel, c1960s, 15" h	50–80	150–200
Charlie Chaplin, Doll, jointed, Boucher, 7.5" h	1800–2200	—
Charlie Chaplin, Walker, keywind, Boucher, 8" h	1000–2000	—
Charlie McCarthy, Benzine Buggy, keywind, tinplate, Marx, 8" l	600–900	1000–1500
Charlie McCarthy, Drummer, keywind, tinplate, Marx, 8" h	500–700	800–1200
Charlie McCarthy, Ventriloquist Doll, composition, Effanbee, 20" h	500–800	1000–1500
Charlie McCarthy, Walker, keywind, tinplate, Marx, 8" h	250–350	400–600
Charlie's Angels, Gift Set, Sabrina, Kelly, and Kris Dolls, Hasbro, c1977, 8.5" h	30–40	60–90
Charlie's Angels, Jill (Farah Fawcett) Doll, Hasbro, c1977, 8.5" h	25–35	50–70
Charlie's Angels, Kelly (Jaclyn Smith) Doll, Hasbro, c1977, 8.5" h	20–30	35–45
Charlie's Angels, Kris (Cheryl Ladd) Doll, Hasbro, c1977, 8.5" h	20–30	35–45
Charlie's Angels, Sabrina (Kate Jackson) Doll, Hasbro, c1977, 8.5" h	20–30	35–45
Cinderella, Drinking Glass, #8, fitted for shoe, c1950, 4.63" h	9–12	—
Creature From the Black Lagoon, Soakie, Colgate Palmolive, c1963, 10" h	80–120	—
Daniel Boone, Flintlock Pistol, Marx, 1960s	60–80	150–200
Dick Tracy, Police Squad Car, friction, tinplate, Marx, 6.75" l	120–160	200–300
Dick Tracy, Police Station, w/ car, keywind, tinplate, Marx, 7.5" l	250–350	400–600
Dick Tracy, Siren Squad Car, friction and battery powered, tinplate, Marx, 11" l	250–350	400–600

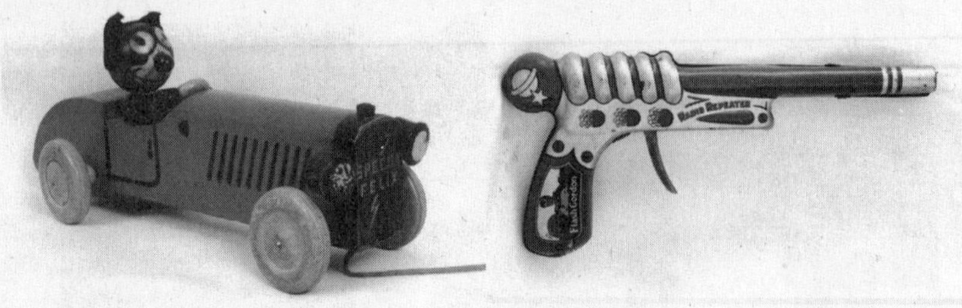

Left to right: Felix the Cat, Speedy Felix Car, wooden, Nifty, c1935, 12" l, $700–$900; Flash Gordon Radio Repeater Gun, litho tin, Marx, 1930s, $200–$250.

	UNBOXED	BOXED
Dick Tracy, Squad Car #1, keywind, tinplate, Marx, c1939, 11" l	300–400	500–700
Donald Duck, Bubble Duck, plastic, Morris Plastics, c1955	90–130	—
Donald Duck, Cowboy Bank, figural, ceramic, c1940, 6.5" h	80–130	—
Donald Duck, Doll, composition and cloth, wearing Russian costume, 9" h	1000–1500	—
Donald Duck, Donald Duck Duet, keywind, Donald and Goofy dancing, c1946, 10.5" h	700–900	1000–1500
Donald Duck, Donald on Tricycle, tinplate, Linemar, 4" h	300–400	600–800
Donald Duck, Milk Pitcher, figural, ceramic, c1940, 6.5" h	80–120	—
Donald Duck, Paint Box, litho tin, c1930s	80–120	—
Donald Duck, Rowboat, wood and paper, Chad Valley	700–900	—
Donald Duck, Sunshine Straws, c1950s	—	20–30
Donald Duck, Toothbrush Holder, figural, bisque, double Donald, c1940, 4.5" h	200–250	—
Donald Duck, Watering Can, tin, Ohio Art, c1930s, 6" h	120–190	—
Dr. Dolittle, Doll, Mattel, c1967, 6" h	30–50	100–150
Dr. Seuss, Cat in the Hat Jack-in-the-Box, c1960s	50–60	90–130
Dumbo, Dumbo Figure, composition, swiveling trunk, googlie eyes, Cameo Doll, c1941, 9" h	300–600	
Dumbo, Timothy Mouse Doll, cloth, 14" h	300–400	—
Family Affair, Buffy and Mrs. Beasley Doll Set, Mattel, c1967	30–40	80–120
Farfel, Hand Puppet, vinyl and flannel, Juro, c1950s	60–80	90–140
Felix the Cat, Doll, cloth, 14.5" h	500–700	—
Felix the Cat, Doll, Schuco, 10.5" h	200–300	—
Felix the Cat, Figure, composition, 13" h	500–700	—
Flash Gordon, Arresting Ray Gun, Marx, 1930s	180–230	300–400
Flash Gordon, Easter Egg Decals, features The Phantom and others, c1940	20–30	80–100
Flash Gordon, Figure, standing at attention, wood, 5" h	250–350	—
Flash Gordon, Flash Dueling Ming Button, 1970s	6–9	—
Flash Gordon, Rocket Fighter, litho tin, Marx, c1930s, 13" l	500–700	800–1200
Flash Gordon, Solar Commando Figures, litho card w/ three 3" plastic figures, premier, 1952	50–70	120–160
Flash Gordon, Space Compass, flexible plastic band, 1950s	30–40	60–80
Flintstones, Bamm-Bamm Doll, Ideal, c1963, 16" h	60–80	150–200
Foghorn Leghorn, Figure, Dakin, c1970, 6" h	20–30	50–75
Foxy Grandpa, Bell Ringer Toy, cast iron, 6.75" h	800–1200	—
Foxy Grandpa, Doll, composition, 17" h	900–1400	—

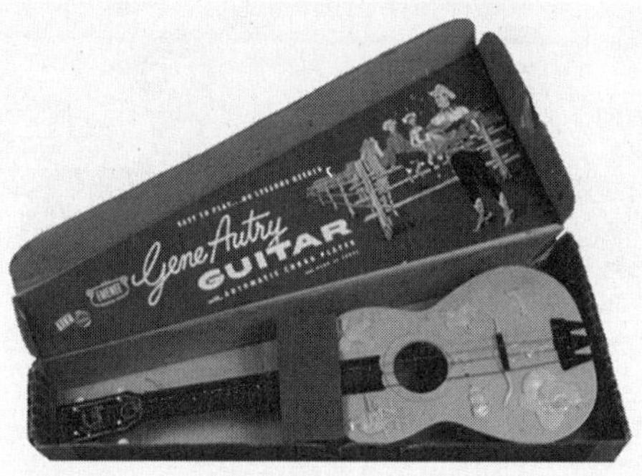

Left to right: Gene Autry Guitar, plastic, Emenee, $200–$275; Get Smart Paperback Book, Get Smart Once Again!, *1966, $10–$14;*

	UNBOXED	BOXED
Frankenstein, Soakie, c1960s	90–120	—
Gabby Hayes, Foldout Book, Bonnie Book, c1954	80–100	—
Gene Autry, Cowboy Spurs, c1950	40–60	70–90
Get Smart, Agent 86 Pen/Radio, c1966	20–30	40–60
Goofy and Wilbur, Drinking Glass, Disney All Star Parade, c1939, 4.88" h	25–35	—
Green Goblin, Figure, plastic, Comic Action Heroes, Mego, c1975, 3.75" h	20–25	45–50
Green Hornet, Billfold, c1966	20–30	40–60
Green Hornet, Black Beauty Car, Corgi, c1966, 5" l	150–240	350–500
Gumby, Electronic Drawing Set, Lakeside, c1966	20–25	50–70
Gunsmoke, Handcuffs, c1950s	15–20	30–40
Happy Hooligan, Donkey Cart, tinplate, Ingap, 7.5" l	1200–1800	—
Happy Hooligan, Goat Cart, cast iron, 7.5" l	1800–2200	—
Happy Hooligan, Nodder Donkey Cart, cast iron, 6.5" l	500–700	—
Happy Hooligan, Nodder Horse Cart, cast iron, Kenton, 10.5" l	1000–1500	—
Happy Hooligan, Walker, keywind, tinplate, Chein, 6" h	300–600	—
Happy Hooligan and Rabbit, Candy Container, 7.5" h	1200–1800	—
Harold Lloyd, Donkey Cart, litho tin, Spain, c1929, 9" l	3000–5000	—
Harold Lloyd, Walker, keywind, tinplate, Marx, 10.75" h	600–900	—
Henry on Elephant, keywind, celluloid, c1934, 8" h	1200–1800	2000–3000
Henry on Trapeze, keywind, celluloid, 7.75" h	300–500	700–900
Hogan's Heroes, Peri-Peeper Periscope, w/ ID card and badge	30–40	60–80
Honey West, Doll, plastic, Gilbert, c1965, 12" h	90–130	200–250
Hopalong Cassidy, Holster Light, Aladdin, c1950s	250–350	—
Hopalong Cassidy, Leather Belt	20–30	40–60
Hopalong Cassidy, Milk Container, c1955, 1 pt.	80–100	—
Hopalong Cassidy, Pocket Knife, black w/ image of Hoppy and Topper	25–35	—
Hopalong Cassidy, Record Album	—	60–80
Hopalong Cassidy, Wallet	20–30	30–40
Horace Horsecollar, Drinking Glass, red figure, c1936, 4.75" h	25–35	—
Howdy Doody, Clarabelle Cow Drinking Glass, red, seated w/ mirror, c1936, 4.75" h	20–30	—

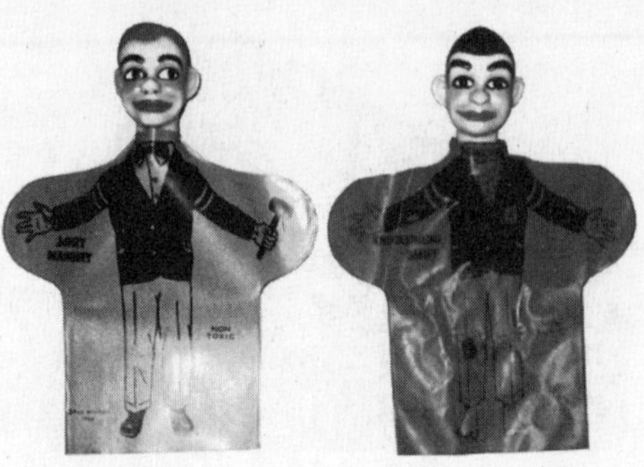

Left to right: Howdy Doody Coloring Book, Whitman, 1950, 8.5" x 11", $30–$40; Jerry Mahoney and Knucklehead Smiff Hand Puppets, vinyl, c1966, $125–$150 each.

	UNBOXED	BOXED
Howdy Doody, Ear Muffs, figural	20–30	70–90
Howdy Doody, Howdy Figure, wooden, jointed, c1950, 12.5" h	400–700	—
Howdy Doody, Howdy Piggy Bank, figural, porcelain, c1950s	180–220	—
Howdy Doody, Piano Band, keywind, tinplate, Unique Art, c1940, 8.5" h	700–900	1200–1500
Huckleberry Hound, Bank, figural, hard plastic, c1960s, 10" h	25–35	—
Huckleberry Hound, Soakie, c1960s	25–35	—
Humphrey, Mobile, keywind, tinplate, Wyandotte, 9" l	300–500	800–1000
I Dream of Jeannie, Jeannie Doll, Ideal, c1966, 18" h	200–300	400–600
Indiana Jones, Cairo Swordsman Figure, Kenner, c1982, 3.75" h	8–12	20–30
Indiana Jones, Desert Convoy Truck, Kenner, c1982	18–22	35–45
Indiana Jones, Indy Figure, German uniform, Kenner, c1982, 3.75" h	12–16	28–32
Indiana Jones, Indy Figure, plastic, Kenner, c1982, 3.75" h	15–20	60–90
Indiana Jones, Marion Ravenwood Figure, on card, Kenner, c1982, 3.75" h	30–40	180–220
It Takes a Thief, Paperback Book, #1	12–18	—
Jackie Coogan, Walker, keywind, tinplate, German, c1920, 7" h	600–900	—
James Bond, Aston Martin Car, battery operated, Gilbert, c1965, 12" l	200–250	400–500
James Bond, Attaché Case, MPC, c1965, 18" x 12"	200–250	400–600
James Bond, Doll, plastic, wearing suit, orig. issue, Gilbert, c1964, 12" h	120–180	300–400
Jetsons, Rosy the Robot, keywind, tinplate, Marx, c1965	180–200	350–450
Katzenjammer Kids, Mama Katzenjammer Figure, ball-jointed, 7" h	400–600	—
Katzenjammer Kids, Mama Katzenjammer Figure, celluloid, 5" h	300–400	—
Katzenjammer Kids, Mama Katzenjammer Tea Cozy, Steiff, c1908, 15" h	2000–3000	—
Katzenjammer Kids, Spanking Toy, cast-iron donkey wagon, Kenton, c1906, 11.75" l	2500–3500	—
Komical Kat, Walker, keywind, tinplate, Gama, c1929, 7" h	400–600	—
Krazy Kat, 3-Wheeled Scooter, keywind, c1925, 7.75" l	500–700	—
Krazy Kat, Ignatz Mouse Car, litho tin, Ingap, c1930, 6" l	2500–3500	—
Krazy Kat, Krazy Kat Chasing Mice, tinplate wheeled platform, Nifty, c1932, 7.5"	600–900	—

Left to right: Jetsons Frame Tray Puzzle, Whitman, $12–$20; Joe Penner and His Duck Goo Goo Walker, keywind, litho tin, Marx, 1930s, 9" h, $1200–$1400; Lone Ranger Coloring Book, Whitman, 1974, 8" x 11", $18–$22.

	UNBOXED	BOXED
Krazy Kat, Krazy Kat Doll, cloth, c1916, 3" l	600–800	—
Land of the Giants, Signal Ray Space Gun, Remco, c1968	50–70	100–150
Land of the Giants, Target Rifle, Remco, c1968, 28" l	90–140	200–300
Lassie, Lassie Doll, stuffed cloth, c1950s	70–120	—
Laurel and Hardy, Oliver Hardy Doll, cloth, Lenci, 10" h	700–1000	—
Laurel and Hardy, Stan Laurel Doll, cloth, Lenci, 10" h	700–1000	—
Li'l Abner, Dog Patch Band, keywind, tinplate, Unique Art, c1950, 9" h	500–700	800–1200
Little Lulu, Cloth Doll, Georgene Novelties, c1944, 13.5" h	400–600	—
Little Nemo, Dr. Pimm Roly Poly, Schoenhut, 11.5" h	3000–4000	—
Lone Ranger, Holster Set, fiberboard, set of 2, c1945, 11" l	20–30	50–70
Lone Ranger, Lone Ranger and Silver, keywind, tinplate base, Marx	200–250	350–600
Lone Ranger, Lone Ranger Doll, composition and cloth, Dollcraft, 20" h	600–900	1200–1700
Lone Ranger, Tonto Doll, composition and cloth, Dollcraft, 20" h	500–700	1000–1500
Lost in Space, Robot, plastic, AHI, c1977, 12" h	50–75	100–150
Lost in Space, Robot, plastic, Remco, c1966, 12" h	250–350	500–700
Lost in Space, Roto Jet Gun, Mattel, c1966	700–900	1500–2000
Maggie and Jiggs, Jazzcar, keywind, tinplate, Nifty, c1924, 6.5" l	2000–3000	—
Maggie and Jiggs, Jiggs Doll, cloth, c1925, 18" h	1200–1800	—
Maggie and Jiggs, Jiggs Doll, composition and cloth, 7.5" h	200–300	—
Maggie and Jiggs, Maggie Doll, cloth, c1925, 18" h	1200–1800	—
Maggie and Jiggs, Squeeze Toy, c1925, 8" l	1000–1500	—
Man From U.N.C.L.E., Car, blue, fires missiles, Corgi, 1966	50–80	120–160
Man From U.N.C.L.E., Illya Kuryakin Doll, plastic, Gilbert, c1965, 12" h	120–180	300–350
Man From U.N.C.L.E., Illya Kuryakin Gun Set, Ideal, c1965, 8" l	200–250	400–600
Man From U.N.C.L.E., Napoleon Solo Doll, plastic, Gilbert, c1965, 12" h	60–80	180–230
Man From U.N.C.L.E., Napoleon Solo Gun Set, Ideal, c1965	250–320	600–800
Man From U.N.C.L.E., Paperback Book, *ABC's of Espionage*	8–12	—
Man From U.N.C.L.E., Passport Set, Ideal, c1965	45–60	90–130
Man From U.N.C.L.E., Promotional Still, MGM	30–40	—
Man From U.N.C.L.E., Record Album, LP, RCA, 1966	—	45–75

Left to right: Maggie and Jiggs Dolls, Schoenhut, $1100 at auction. —Photo courtesy Gene Harris Antique Auction Center; Mickey Mouse the Unicyclist, keywind, tinplate, Linemar, $1800–$2000.

	UNBOXED	BOXED
Man From U.N.C.L.E., Thrush Rifle, Ideal, c1966, 36" l	800–1300	1700–2200
Merrymakers Mouse Band, keywind, tinplate, Marx, 1930s, 9" h	700–900	1200–1500
Mickey and Donald, Fire Truck, hard rubber, Sun Rubber, c1950	90–140	—
Mickey and Donald, Sand Pail, w/ Daisy and Nephews, Chein, 1930s, 4.5" h	100–150	—
Mickey and Minnie, Car, wooden, Gong Bell, c1933, 10.75" l	1200–1900	—
Mickey and Minnie, Drinking Glass, black on pink, c1950, 5.88" h	15–20	—
Mickey and Minnie, Playland, keywind, Japan, 10.5" h	2500–3500	—
Mickey and Minnie, Toothbrush Holder, bisque, c1930, 4.5" h	250–350	—
Mickey, Donald, and Pluto, Cup, tug-of-war, Patriot China, c1930s	20–30	—
Mickey Mouse, Cloth Doll, Knickerbocker, c1930, 15" h	900–1200	—
Mickey Mouse, Cowboy Doll, cloth, Knickerbocker, c1935, 19.5" h	2500–3500	—
Mickey Mouse, Drummer, battery operated, Linemar, c1955, 11" h	600–800	1000–1500
Mickey Mouse, Mickey and Cat Pull Toy, wooden, 13.5" l	500–700	—
Mickey Mouse, Mickey in Rowboat, wooden, Fun-E-Flex, 10.75" l	2000–3000	—
Mickey Mouse, Mickey the Magician, battery operated, tinplate, Linemar, 10" h	900–1400	1800–2400
Mickey Mouse, Piano, litho wood, Marks Brothers, c1935, 10" h	1500–2000	—
Mickey Mouse, Recipe Scrap Book, Peter Pan Bread, premium, c1930	50–80	—
Mickey Mouse, Seed Packets, Colorforms, c1977	—	5–7
Mickey Mouse, Spoon, Mickey on handle, Bransford, c1935, 5.5" l	32–42	—
Mickey Mouse, Tumbling Toy, keywind, Schuco, 4" h	200–250	300–400
Milton Berle, Crazy Car, keywind, tinplate, Marx, c1950s	180–220	300–350
Minnie Mouse, Cloth Doll, Knickerbocker, c1930, 15" h	900–1200	—
Minnie Mouse, Minnie Knitting, keywind, tinplate, Linemar, c1950, 6.5" h	500–700	900–1200
Monkees, Monkees Mobile Car, battery operated, ASC, c1967, 12" l	200–300	500–600
Moon Mullins and Kayo, Handcar, Marx, c1940, 6" h	500–700	800–1000
Mortimer Snerd, Walker, keywind, tinplate, Marx, 8.5" l	200–300	400–600
Mr. Ed, Hand Puppet, talking, pull string, Mattel, c1962, 12" h	20–30	60–90
Mr. Magoo, Automobile, battery operated, tinplate and plastic	90–150	300–400
Mr. Magoo, Soakie, c1960s	28–36	—
Mummy, Soakie, Colgate Palmolive, c1963, 10" h	80–120	—
Munsters, Herman Doll, Remco, c1964, 6" h	160–220	350–550

Left to right: Moon Mullins Police Patrol, cast iron, Tootsie Toys, 1930s, 3", $200–$300; Mortimer Snerd Doll, composition and wire, Ideal, 13" h, $500.

	UNBOXED	BOXED
Munsters, Herman Hand Puppet, talking, pull string, Mattel, c1964, 12" h	150–200	300–400
Munsters, Hypodermic Needle Squirt Gun, Hasbro, c1964, 8" l	60–80	150–200
Munsters, Koach, AMT, c1964, 12" l	200–300	500–700
Mutt and Jeff, Jeff Doll, stuffed felt, c1930, 12" h	100–150	—
Mutt and Jeff, Jeff Figure, jointed metal, Boucher, c1922, 6.5" h	300–500	—
Mutt and Jeff, Mutt Doll, stuffed felt, c1930, 14" h	100–150—	—
Mutt and Jeff, Mutt Figure, jointed metal, Boucher, c1922, 6.5" h	300–500	—
My Favorite Martian, Beanie w/ Antenna, c1960s, 7" dia	50–80	—
Orphan Annie, Sandy the Dog, playing w/ ball, Marx, 8" l	350–450	500–600
Orphan Annie, Sandy w/ Suitcase, keywind, tinplate, Marx, c1937, 4.5" h	250–350	600–800
Osmonds, Pictorial Activity Book, c1970s	7–9	12–18
Peanuts, Snoopy See and Say, Mattel, c1960s	25–35	60–80
Peanuts, Snoopy Soap Dish, figural, soft plastic	10–14	18–22
Pee-Wee's Playhouse, Pee-Wee Herman Doll, talking, c1988, 18" h	20–30	60–80
Pee-Wee's Playhouse, Playset, Matchbox, 1988	18–22	30–50
Pinocchio, Jiminy Cricket Christmas Light Bulb, c1950	25–35	—
Pinocchio, Jiminy Cricket Drinking Glass, w/ poem on reverse, c1940, 4.75" h	10–15	—
Pinocchio, Jiminy Cricket Hand Puppet, vinyl and cloth, Gund, c1960	25–35	50–80
Pinocchio, Pinocchio the Acrobat, keywind, tinplate, Marx, c1939, 14.75" h	300–400	700–900
Planet of the Apes, Cornelius Doll, Mego, c1973, 8" h	35–45	100–150
Planet of the Apes, Zira Doll, Mego, c1973, 8" h	35–45	100–150
Popeye, Bluto Dippy Dumper Truck, tinplate and celluloid, Marx, 8.75" l	400–600	700–900
Popeye, Brutus Soakie, c1960s	25–30	—
Popeye, Bubble Blowing Popeye, battery operated, tinplate, Linemar, c1950s, 8.5" h	900–1100	1800–2200
Popeye, Eugene the Jeep Figure, painted and jointed wood, 7" h	700–1000	—
Popeye, Handcar, tinplate and rubber, Marx, c1935, 6.5" h	700–900	1200–1500
Popeye, Heavy Hitter Hammer and Bell Toy, keywind, Chein, c1932, 11.5" h	1800–2800	3500–5000

Left to right: Orphan Annie Skipping Rope, keywind, tinplate, Marx, 1930s, 5" h, $300–$400; Popeye Express, litho tin, Marx, 8" h, $250–$450; Rocky and Bullwinkle, Rocky Soaky, Colgate-Palmolive, 1962, $30–$40; Tennessee Tuxedo Soaky, Colgate-Palmolive, 1965, $35–$40.

	UNBOXED	BOXED
Popeye, Lamp, cast iron w/ litho paper shade, c1935, 17" h	700–1000	—
Popeye, Olive Oyl Ballet Dancer Top, tinplate, Linemar, c1950	200–250	400–500
Popeye, Popeye and Olive Oyl Ball Toss, keywind, tinplate, Linemar, c1950, 19" l	700–900	1200–1900
Popeye, Popeye and Olive Oyl Handcar, tinplate, Linemar, 9.5" l	700–900	1000–1300
Popeye, Popeye and Olive Oyl Roof Band, Marx, c1935, 9.5" h	700–900	1200–1800
Popeye, Popeye Dippy Dumper Truck, tinplate and celluloid, Marx, 8.75" l	500–700	800–1400
Popeye, Popeye Figure, jointed wood, c1932, 10" h	300–400	—
Popeye, Popeye Figure, jointed wood, c1935, 11" h	450–650	—
Popeye, Popeye Figure, jointed wood, w/ cap and pipe, c1935, 14" h	400–600	—
Popeye, Popeye in Rowboat, keywind, tinplate, Hoge, c1935, 15.5" l	6000–8000	—
Popeye, Popeye on Motorcycle, cast iron, Hubley, c1938, 9" l	2000–3000	—
Popeye, Popeye on Tricycle, keywind, tinplate, Linemar, 4" h	300–500	600–800
Popeye, Popeye the Champ Boxing Toy, keywind, tinplate and celluloid, Marx, c1936, 7" x 7"	2000–2500	3000–5500
Popeye, Punching Bag, overhead, keywind, tinplate, Chein, c1932, 9.75"	2000–3000	3500–5500
Popeye, Punching Bag, upright, keywind, tinplate, Chein, c1935, 8" h	1000–1600	—
Popeye, Rooftop Jigger, keywind, tinplate, Marx, c1936, 9.75" h	700–900	1000–1300
Popeye, Smoking Popeye, tinplate, Linemar, 8.5" h	800–1000	1500–2000
Popeye, Soakie, c1960s	25–35	—
Popeye, Somersaulter, keywind, tinplate, Linemar, 5" h	700–1000	—
Popeye, Sparkler, tinplate, Chein, c1959, 5" h	200–300	400–600
Popeye, Spinach Delivery Motorcycle, cast iron, Hubley	600–900	—
Popeye, Thimble Theatre Mystery Playhouse, w/ 3 walkers, c1939, 9.5" x 12"	1800–2500	—
Porky Pig, Cowpuncher Porky, keywind, tinplate, Marx, 8" h	200–400	500–800

Snow White Kitchen Appliance Set, litho tin, Wolverine, 1970s, $100–$200.

	UNBOXED	BOXED
Porky Pig, Porky w/ umbrella, keywind, tinplate, Marx, c1939, 8.5" h	300–400	500–600
Porky Pig, Soakie, c1960s	20–30	—
Powerful Katrinka Lifting Jimmy, keywind, tinplate, c1925, 6.75" h	3000–4000	—
Rin-Tin-Tin, Cloth Doll, Smile Novelty, c1959	80–120	—
Rocky and Bullwinkle, Bullwinkle Soakie, c1960s	25–35	—
Roy Rogers, Bedspread, c1950s	125–175	—
Roy Rogers, Fix-It Stage Coach, plastic, Ideal, c1956	90–130	220–280
Roy Rogers, Guitar, litho cardboard, c1950s	80–100	120–160
Roy Rogers, Lantern, battery operated, tinplate, c1956	70–90	100–150
Shazam, Figure, plastic, Comic Action Heroes, Mego, c1975, 3.75" h	15–20	40–50
Six Million Dollar Man, Steve Austin Doll, bionic grip, Kenner, c1976	12–18	30–60
Snow White and the Seven Dwarfs, Bashful Doll, Ideal, 7" h	200–300	400–600
Snow White and the Seven Dwarfs, Doc Doll, Ideal, 7" h	200–300	400–600
Snow White and the Seven Dwarfs, Dopey Doll, Ideal, 7" h	200–300	400–600
Snow White and the Seven Dwarfs, Dopey Figurine, plaster, c1930s, 14" h	70–100	—
Snow White and the Seven Dwarfs, Dopey Soakie, c1960s	20–30	—
Snow White and the Seven Dwarfs, Grumpy Christmas Light Bulb, c1940	25–35	—
Snow White and the Seven Dwarfs, Grumpy Doll, Ideal, 7" h	200–300	400–600
Snow White and the Seven Dwarfs, Happy Doll, Ideal, 7" h	200–300	400–600
Snow White and the Seven Dwarfs, Sleepy Doll, Ideal, 7" h	200–300	400–600
Snow White and the Seven Dwarfs, Sneezy Doll, Ideal, 7" h	200–300	400–600
Snow White and the Seven Dwarfs, Snow White Doll, Ideal, 15.5" h	300–400	500–700
Snowflakes and Swipes, Pull Toy, litho tin, c1929, 7.5" l	900–1200	—
Sparkplug, Racing Platform, keywind, litho tin, c1924, 9" h	5000–7000	—
Sparkplug, Figure, jointed wood, 9" h	400–600	—
Superman, Badge, movie promotional, emblem shape (*Superman I*)	18–22	—
Superman, Belt Buckle, tin, blue and red, chains portrait, 1940s	120–160	—
Superman, Button, Kellogg's Pop Cereal premium, multicolor litho tin, 1950s	25–35	—
Superman, Candy Coated Peanuts, box only, illustrated lid, 1966, 5" l	—	30–40
Superman, Dime Register Bank, litho tin, 1940s	260–320	—
Superman, Doll, composition and wood, painted and jointed, w/ cape, Ideal, 13" h	1200–1800	—

Left to right: Sylvester and Tweety Frame Tray Puzzle, Whitman, 1982, $15–$20; Tarzan Cartoon Kit, Colorforms, 1966, $30–$40; Zorro Halloween Costume, Ben Cooper, $70–$100.

	UNBOXED	BOXED
Superman, Doll, stuffed cloth, w/ cape, Toy Works, 1970s, 25" h	10–15	22–28
Superman, Figure, Syrocco, 1940s, 5" h	3000–4000	—
Superman, Music Box, figural, ceramic, Price/National, c1970s, 7" h	50–70	100–150
Superman, Pencil Case, Mattel, 1960s	18–22	—
Superman, Records and Booklet, *The Magic Ring,* 2 records, 78 rpm, Musette, c1947	—	100–150
Superman, Rollover Airplane, keywind, tinplate, Marx, c1940, 6" l	800–1000	—
Superman, Toothbrush, battery operated	20–30	50–70
Superman, Turnover Tank, keywind, tinplate, Marx, c1940, 4" l	400–600	700–1000
Sylvester and Tweety, Sylvester Soakie, c1960s	25–35	—
Sylvester and Tweety, Tweety Bird Figure, Dakin, c1960s, 6" h	8–12	18–22
Tarzan, Thingmaker Mold, Mattel, c1966	20–25	40–50
Three Little Pigs, Big Bad Wolf Doll, stuffed cloth, c1930s, 21" h	700–900	—
Three Little Pigs, Pig Figure, keywind, Schuco, 4.75" h	100–150	200–250
Tom and Jerry, Jerry Doll, stuffed cloth, Merry Thought, c1950s, 6" h	45–60	—
Topo Gigio, Doll, nodding head, c1960	20–30	50–70
Toonerville Trolley, tinplate, c1925, 7" h	400–600	700–900
Uncle Wiggily, Crazy Car, 7" l	300–500	600–800
W.C. Fields, Doll, Effanbee, 19" h	400–600	1000–1500
Wagon Train, Frame Tray Puzzle, Whitman, c1960, 14" x 11"	—	10–15
Wagon Train, Record, 45 rpm, w/ picture sleeve, Mitch Miller Orchestra, 1957	—	20–30
Waltons, Paper Dolls	6–8	15–20
Wild, Wild West, Writing Tablet	12–15	—
Winky Dink and You, Magic TV Kit, Standard Toy, 1960s	50–70	—
Wolfman, Soakie, Colgate Palmolive, c1960s, 10" h	80–120	—
Woody Woodpecker, Frame Tray Puzzle	—	18–22
Woody Woodpecker, Soakie, c1960s	25–35	—
Yellow Kid, Figure, cast iron, burlap dress, 6.5" h	700–1000	—
Yellow Kid, Goat Cart, cast iron, 7.5" l	400–600	—
Yogi Bear, Magic Slate, c1960s	20–30	—

Character Watches

Mention "character watches" and you will invariably hear the reply, "You mean like a Mickey Mouse watch?" It was Mickey who ushered in the first comic character watch in 1933 and the market has been thriving ever since. Prices for watches in their original, colorful boxes have skyrocketed due to scarcity and increasing demand. Promotional watches requiring boxtops or proof of purchase and acquired by mail have gained in popularity.

The prices listed in the MNP column are for mint condition working watches, without their packaging or original boxes; the second price range (MIP) is for working, mint in the package examples. MIP for promo watches means that they come with their original mailing material. We have substituted AC for alarm clock, PW for pocket watch and WW for wristwatch.

The following are our codes for manufacturers: *BR*–Bradley; *BY*–Bayard; *CT*–Columbia Time; *EX*–Exacta Time; *FW*–Fawcett; *GC*–Glen Clock; *GT*–Gilbert; *HD*–Haddon; *HL*–Helbros; *IG*–Ingraham; *IN*–Ingersol; *L*–Lorus; *PWC*–Patent Watch Company; *RT*–Ralston; *SF*–Starkist Foods; *SK*–Seiko; *SM*–Smith; *SW*–Swiss (maker unknown); *UK*–Unknown; *UST*–U.S. Time; *W*–Wilane; and *WB*–Warner Brothers.

Our consultant for this section is Howard S. Brenner, collector and author of *Comic Character Clocks and Watches,* Books Americana, 1987 (he is listed in the back of this book).

	COMPANY	CIRCA	MNP	MIP
Alice in Wonderland WW, plastic teacup pkg.	UST	1950	$75–$100	$275–$325
Babe Ruth WW, plastic baseball pkg.	EX	1949	150–200	750–1000
Bambi AC	BY	1964	150–200	200–300
Batman WW	TX	1978	60–80	140–160
Betty Boop PW	IG	1934	750–900	1500–2000
Buck Rogers PW, light, bolt hands, monster bk.	IG	1935	800–900	1400–1600
Bugs Bunny AC	IG	1951	400–450	700–800
Bugs Bunny WW	WB	1951	350–400	700–800
Captain Marvel WW (deluxe), 1 jewel	FW	1948	250–300	550–600
Captain Marvel WW (larger than deluxe)	FW	1948	350–400	700–750
Charlie McCarthy AC, animated	GT	1938	1500–2000	3000–3500
Charlie the Tuna WW, promo	SF	1971	60–80	90–120
Cinderella WW, porcelain statue pack	TX	1958	75–100	150–200
Cinderella WW, slipper box	UST	1950	75–100	375–425
Dale Evans WW, pop-up display box	IG	1951	150–200	400–600
Dan Dare PW, double animation	IN	1953	700–750	900–1000
Davy Crockett Clock	UK	1955	200–300	400–450
Davy Crockett Clock, electric, animated	HD	1954	400–475	500–600
Davy Crockett WW, 3-D pop-up display box	BR	1956	75–140	425–525
Davy Crockett WW, powder horn box	UST	1954	75–140	400–500
Dick Tracy WW	NH	1948	180–220	450–550
Donald Duck Clock, animated	BY	1964	180–220	280–320
Donald Duck Clock, animated	GC	1950	380–420	600–700
Gene Autry WW	W	1948	250–300	500–600
Gene Autry WW, 6-shooter, animated	NH	1951	500–550	750–850
Goofy WW, runs backwards	H	1972	550–650	750–1000
Hopalong Cassidy AC	UST	1950	350–450	600–700
Hopalong Cassidy PW	UST	1950	500–600	900–1100
Howdy Doody WW, moving eye, window box	PWC	1954	250–300	500–650
Lone Ranger PW, w/ pistol and holster	NH	1939	400–450	750–850
Lone Ranger WW	NH	1939	320–380	650–750
Little Pig (Disney Fiddler Pig) WW	UST	1947	350–400	650–750
Mickey Mouse AC, animated, round case	IN	1934	850–950	1900–2100
Mickey Mouse AC, animated, wind-up	IN	1933	850–950	1900–2100

	COMPANY	CIRCA	MNP	MIP
Mickey Mouse AC, electric, revolving Mickey Mouse	IN	1933	1000–1200	2200–2600
Mickey Mouse AC, moving feet	BR	1983	60–80	100–150
Mickey Mouse AC, PW form	BR	1979	60–80	100–150
Mickey Mouse Clock, Magic Castle, animated	BR	1979	300–350	450–550
Mickey Mouse Clock, square case	IN	1933	850–950	1900–2100
Mickey Mouse PW, Bicentennial	BR	1976	100–125	200–300
Mickey Mouse PW, debossed back, round fob	IN	1933	600–650	1000–1200
Mickey Mouse PW, shield fob	IN	1933	600–650	1000–1200
Mickey Mouse WW, 1973 first issue	BR	1973	160–180	200–230
Mickey Mouse WW, 50th Birthday	BR	1978	250–300	350–400
Mickey Mouse WW, "Ambassador to the World"	SK	1986	350–400	450–500
Mickey Mouse WW, deluxe, Mickey on second hand	IN	1938	500–600	1000–1300
Mickey Mouse WW, digital	BR	1973	180–200	250–300
Mickey Mouse WW, electric	TX	1968	475–525	650–750
Mickey Mouse WW, "Mickey #1," steel band	IN	1933	500–600	750–850
Mickey Mouse WW, Pluto wagging head (200 made)	BR	1978	750–850	900–1100
Mickey Mouse WW, wagging head, animated	BR	1978	200–250	320–380
Mickey and Donald WW (first time together)	L	1986	175–200	220–260
Mickey and Minnie WW, promo	SW	1976	60–80	90–110
Minnie Mouse WW, 1973 first issue	BR	1973	170–200	220–260
Minnie Mouse WW, animated, wagging head	BR	1978	375–425	500–600
Mister Peanut WW, promo	SW	1975	60–80	90–110
Orphan Annie WW	NH	1948	250–300	450–500
Popeye AC, animated	SM	1968	250–300	400–500
Popeye PW	NH	1935	450–500	700–800
Popeye PW, animated, Thimble Theatre char. face	NH	1934	650–700	850–950
Popeye WW	NH	1935	400–450	850–950
Porky Pig WW, round case	IG	1949	300–350	500–550
Raid WW, promo	SW	1975	60–80	90–110
Roy Rogers AC, animated	IG	1951	350–400	550–700
Roy Rogers PW, w/ charm	BR	1959	350–400	700–800
Roy Rogers WW, round case, pop-up box	IG	1951	300–350	500–600
Roy Rogers WW, Roy and Trigger posing on face	IG	1951	350–400	500–600
Snow White WW, large size, pre-war	IN	1939	350–400	550–600
Snow White WW, magic mirror box	UST	1959	75–100	350–400
Star Trek WW, Spock	BR	1979	25–35	40–50
Star Wars WW, Darth Vader	BR	1977	35–45	50–85
Superman PW	BR	1959	400–500	750–1000
Superman WW	NH	1948	350–400	1400–1600
Superman WW, large	TX	1976	110–125	175–200
Superman WW, large, pre-war	NH	1939	500–550	1600–1800
Superman WW, small	TX	1976	90–125	150–175
Three Little Pigs AC, animated Wolf	I	1934	400–450	2200–2600
Three Little Pigs PW, animated, debossed back	IN	1934	800–900	2200–2600
Three Little Pigs WW, figural steel band	IN	1934	1000–1200	2800–3200
Tom Mix WW, promo	RT	1983	300–350	450–550
Woody Woodpecker AC, animated	CT	1950	350–400	750–850
Zorro WW, sombrero package	UST	1957	75–90	250–300

Left: Star Wars WW, R2D2 and C3PO, Bradley Time, 1977, $50–75.

Right: Hopalong Cassidy WW, in saddle stand box, U.S. Time, 1950, $400–$450.

Mickey Mouse Clocks by Ingersoll. —Photo courtesy Bill Bertoia Auctions.

Cracker Jack

F.W. Ruckenheim and his brother developed this famous mixture of popcorn, peanuts and molasses. In 1893 they sold it at the Columbian Exposition in Chicago where it was an overnight sensation. In 1896 it was named Cracker Jack and soon after prizes were introduced. At first coupons were used which the customer could trade for various prizes. The company began putting the actual prize in each box by 1912. Cracker Jack prizes have been made of lead, paper, porcelain, plastic, tin, paper and wood. The little sailor, Jack, is based on the founder's grandson Robert (for trivia fans, the dog's name is Bingo).

The following prices are for items in excellent to mint condition; dates are approximate. For more information see *Cracker Jack Prizes,* Alex Jarmillo, Abbeville Press, NY, 1989.

	LOW	HIGH
Air Corps Wings, emb. metal	$50	$75
Badge, junior detective, emb. metal, 1.25" h	50	60
Booklet #12, Bess and Bill, paper, 2.5" h	70	90
Charm, blue celluloid, comical man's head	20	30
Clicker, metal, black and silver, instructions on front, 2.13" h	20	30
Clicker Whistle, metal, emb. "Cracker Jack," 2" w	20	30
Coconut Corn Crisp, tin, round, full-color, 3.5" h	70	90
Corkscrew, Angelus, metal, 3.75" w	55	75
Flip Book, Charlie Chaplin, pre-1922	90	130
Frog, paper, green, black, and white outside, opens to red and tan inside	45	65
Game #1, red, white, and blue, 2.5" w	40	50
Golf Top, paper, red, white, and blue, rules on back	40	60
Horse and Wagon, diecast metal, 3" l	200	300
Hummer Band, emb. metal, 1" dia	35	45
Iron-Ons, paper, 4/sheet, 1945	8	12
Jumper, frog, tin, green and silver, 1935, 1.88" l	25	35
Magazine Ad, *Saturday Evening Post,* June 1919, red, white, and blue	20	30
Magic Puzzle, donkey, paper and plastic, 1.5" w	12	18
Magic Puzzle, fish	12	18
Magic Puzzle, man w/ cigar, mkd. "Cracker Jack Co." on reverse	15	20
Paper, Jack at blackboard, turn dial, he writes and erases name, 2" sq	145	195
Pin, lady, celluloid, paper insert in back for "Cracker Jack 5 Cents"	30	40
Pocket Watch, tin, gold, black, and white, 1.5" dia	50	70
Postcard, bears #13	30	40
Postcard, bears #15	30	40
Puzzle Book #1, ©1917, 4" h	30	40
Puzzles #1–#15, complete set	200	350
Rainbow Spinner, cardboard, 1920s, 2.5" l	15	25
Sign, cardboard, red, white, and blue box on blue ground, 11" x 15"	400	700
Spinner, tin, red, white, and blue illus. of Cracker Jack pkg., 1.5" w	25	45
Standup, Harold Teen, tin	50	90
Standup, Orphan Annie, tin	70	130
Standup, Perry, tin	25	35
Top, fortune teller, tin	40	60
Truck, plastic, emb. on 4 sides, gold, 1940s, 1.63" l	30	40
Truck, tin, red, white, and black, "Cracker Jack" one side, "Angelus" other side, 1.63" l	75	95
Whistle, metal, emb. "Cracker Jack"	40	60
Whistle, paper, red and white, reverse mkd. "Cracker Jack Whistle," 2" h	25	35
Whistle, tin, silver and blue, 1940s, 2.5" l	15	25

Dollhouses

Dollhouses and dollhouse furniture are difficult areas to evaluate because of their diversity. Quality craftsmanship and attention to detail are important considerations for wooden items. Because most earlier dollhouses are hand crafted, price is often determined by a collector's individual taste. Collectors of paper on wood examples rely on manufacturer, style and condition. Tinplate dollhouses made by Marx and other firms are worth more money if unassembled in the original box with all accessories intact. Dollhouse furniture and accessories have similar criteria; elaborate, well-crafted early items in excellent condition command the highest prices. Many items have been reproduced or created in the style of earlier periods; these items are not worth as much as similar period pieces. Color variations can occasionally affect the prices of plastic dollhouse accessories; prices listed are for more common colors. Our consultants for this area are Joan and Gaston Majeune of Toys in the Attic; they are listed in the back of this book.

Tootsietoy Victorian Cottage, wooden, yellow w/ red trim and green shingled roof, 2 rooms 1st floor, 1 room 2nd floor, early 20th C, 23" h, 26" w, 23.75" deep, $460 at auction. —Photo courtesy Skinner, Inc., Boston, MA.

	LOW	HIGH
Arcade Toy Company, cast-iron living room sofa and chair, painted pink, removable cast-iron pillows, c1927	$1000	$1400
Bliss, Alphabet House, paper litho on wood, full front porch, 2nd floor balcony, 2 side balconies, unusual litho interior w/ alphabet border, border on 1st floor missing letter "Z", 24" h, 19" w, 12" deep	3000	3800
Bliss, Doll Furniture, wood w/ paper litho designs of children at play, soft blues and reds, 1890s, 7 pcs.	600	950
Bliss, Seaside Residence, paper litho on wood, mkd. "Bliss" on front door, 3 rooms, front and side openings, 24" h, 18" w, 10" deep	2500	3600
Bliss, Semi-Detached House, paper litho on wood, mkd. "Bliss" on front door, 4 rooms, opens on both ends, 24" h, 18" w, 10" deep	2200	3200
German, "Blue Roof" by Maurice Gottschalk, paper litho on wood, unmkd., 2 rooms, front opening, 20" h, 14" w, 11.5" deep	1950	2400
German, Grocery Store, dark wood frame, counter, and shelves, green patterned paper walls, porcelain drawer tags, "parquet" paper floor, w/ dolls and many accessories, 1910	2800	3600
German, Kitchen, wooden, blue and white paper on floors and walls, blue and white painted wood furnishings, many accessories, 1900, 14" h, 30" w, 15" deep	2750	3800
German, "Red Roof," painted wood, 2 floors and hinged dormer to attic rooms, 21.5" h, 17" w, 9.5" deep	1700	2700

	LOW	HIGH
German, Stable by Maurice Gottschalk, paper litho and painted wood, 4 horse and carriage stalls, metal feed racks, 2nd floor doors open, w/ horses and wagons, 15" h	1100	1650
House, paper litho on wood, 2 rooms, front opening, unmkd., 14" h, 11" w, 8" deep	1050	1750
Marklin, Bentwood Metal (Solarium) Furniture, painted black, 6 pcs	550	850
Marx, Colonial House, tinplate, red upper story, white below, tinplate awnings, chimney, garage w/ deck above, 5 rooms, unboxed, c1950, 18.75" h, 33.5" w, 12" deep	85	150
McLoughlin 1894 Folding Doll House, litho on hinged cardboard which folds flat to fit in box, 4 rooms	550	850
Playsteel, Buck's County House, tinplate, 5 rooms, unboxed, c1948, 19" h, 22" w, 12" deep	65	125
Rich, Colonial House, gypsum and hardboard, steel reinforced edges, steel interior stairs, 6 rooms, 1930s, 25" h, 35" w, 14" deep	275	450
Schoenhut 1928 Model, wood and fiberboard painted yellow, red "tile" roof, 8 rooms, interior stairs, window boxes, metal Schoenhut tag attached to side base, 24" h, 23" w, 24" deep	1000	1600
T. Cohn, House, tinplate, red and white, red "tile" roof, tin windows do not open, 5 rooms, unboxed, c1941	40	90
Two-Part House, paper litho on wood, smaller room and roof fit into larger room for storage, unusual interior lithography, larger room 17" h, 11" w, 8" deep	2800	4200

Left to right: McLoughlin Bros., Dolly's Play House (photo of box only), litho paper on board, folding, 2 rooms, folding printed paper furniture, late 19th C, 18.5" h house, $375 at auction; Bliss, Half-Timber House, litho paper on wood, late 19th/early 20th C, $460 at auction; Stable, litho paper on wood, late 19th C, 15.625" h, 19" w, 9.5" deep, $115 at auction; Stirn & Lyon, Combination Dollhouse (photo of box only), stenciled wood building sections, litho paper illus. on lid, patented 1881, 15" h, $173 at auction. —Photo courtesy Skinner, Inc., Boston, MA.

Dolls

Doll collecting has grown remarkably in the last twenty-five years to become one of the top hobbies in the United States. It rivals stamps and coins. Individual appeal seems to be the magic ingredient which drives the marketplace. The prices of dolls cover such a wide range that any collector can find a category to fit his budget. Interesting and varied collections can be assembled by specializing in dolls of a certain era, made from a specific material or all the various dolls produced by a single manufacturer.

In doll collecting, condition is all important. Prices given here are for dolls in excellent condition. Dolls with original or true period clothes will carry an incrementally higher value depending on quality. Deductions must be made for any missing or replaced parts, worn-out or faded clothes and wigs, and most importantly, broken, chipped or cracked heads.

For further reading see *13th Blue Book Dolls & Vallues* by Jan Foulke, Hobby House Press, Grantsville, MD, 1997 and *200 Years of Dolls: Identification and Price Guide* by Dawn Herlocher, Antique Trader Books, Dubuque, IA, 1996. Our consultant for the bisque doll portion of this section is Matrix Quality Antique Dolls.

Antique

	LOW	HIGH
Armand Marseille, 326, German bisque socket head baby w/ solid crown, glass sleep eyes, open mouth w/ 2 teeth, 5-pc composition baby body, 10" h	$340	$360
Armand Marseille, 326, 15" h	525	575
Armand Marseille, 326, 20" h	675	750
Armand Marseille, 341, known as Dream Baby, German bisque head w/ flange neck, solid crown, glass sleep eyes, closed mouth, cloth body w/ celluloid hands, 9" h	180	220
Armand Marseille, 341, 13" h	360	380
Armand Marseille, 341, 20" h	625	675

Left to right: Armand Marseille Dream Baby; Armand Marseille 390.

	LOW	HIGH
Armand Marseille, 351, known as Dream Baby, German bisque head w/ flange neck, solid crown, glass sleep eyes, open mouth w/ 2 teeth, cloth body w/ celluloid hands, 9" h	180	220
Armand Marseille, 351, 13" h	350	400
Armand Marseille, 351, 20" h	625	750
Armand Marseille, 390, German bisque socket head child w/ wig, glass sleep eyes, open mouth w/ 4 teeth, ball-jointed composition body, 12" h	180	220
Armand Marseille, 390, 20" h	375	425
Armand Marseille, 390, 24" h	475	525
Armand Marseille, 390, 30" h	750	850
Armand Marseille, 971, German bisque socket head baby w/ wig, glass sleep eyes, open mouth w/ 2 teeth, 5-pc. composition baby body, 10" h	300	350
Armand Marseille, 971, 20" h	475	600
Armand Marseille, 971, 24" h	700	850
Armand Marseille, 990, German bisque socket head baby w/ wig, glass sleep eyes, open mouth w/ 2 teeth, 5-pc. composition baby body, 10" h	275	350
Armand Marseille, 990, 20" h	460	500
Armand Marseille, 990, 24" h	675	750
Armand Marseille, Florodora, German bisque shoulder head child w/ wig, glass sleep eyes, open mouth w/ 4 teeth, kid leather body w/ bisque arms, 12" h	140	180
Armand Marseille, Florodora, 15" h	180	240
Armand Marseille, Florodora, 20" h	360	400
Bebe Jumeau, "Déposé, Tete Jumeau, Bte SGDG" in red ink, French bisque socket head child w/ cork pate and wig, glass paperweight eyes, open mouth w/ 6 teeth, pierced ears, ball-jointed composition body, 16" h	1800	2200
Bebe Jumeau, "Déposé, Tete Jumeau, Bte SGDG," 20" h	2400	2600
Bebe Jumeau, "Déposé, Tete Jumeau, Bte SGDG," 24" h	2800	3200
Bebe Jumeau, "Déposé, Tete Jumeau, Bte SGDG" in red ink, French bisque socket head child w/ cork pate and wig, glass paperweight eyes, closed mouth, pierced ears, ball-jointed composition body, 16" h	3500	3800
Bebe Jumeau, "Déposé, Tete Jumeau, Bte SGDG," 20" h	3800	4200
Bebe Jumeau, "Déposé, Tete Jumeau, Bte SGDG," 24" h	4000	4500

Bebe Jumeau.

	LOW	HIGH
Bye-Lo Baby, Grace S. Putnam, German bisque head w/ flange neck, solid crown, glass sleep eyes, closed mouth, cloth body w/ celluloid hands, 12" h	500	550
Bye-Lo Baby, Grace S. Putnam, 15" h	650	750
Bye-Lo Baby, Grace S. Putnam, 20" h	1200	1500
Bye-Lo Baby, Grace S. Putnam, German bisque socket head, solid crown, glass sleep eyes, closed mouth, 5-pc. composition baby body, 13" h	700	900
Bye-Lo Baby, Grace S. Putnam, 15" h	900	1100
Bye-Lo Baby, Grace S. Putnam, German composition head w/ flange neck, solid crown, painted eyes, closed mouth, cloth body w/ composition hands, 13" h	340	360
Bye-Lo Baby, Grace S. Putnam, German bisque socket head, solid crown w/ wig, glass sleep eyes, closed mouth, all bisque baby body w/ jointed limbs, 4" h	700	750
Bye-Lo Baby, Grace S. Putnam, 8" h	1100	1300
China Head, molded hairdo w/ curly waves, sometimes showing ears, black or blonde hair, painted blue eyes, closed lips, cloth or leather body w/ cloth, leather, china, or bisque arms, 8" h	90	125
China Head, 12" h	200	250
China Head, 16" h	275	325
China Head, 24" h	500	600
EffanBee, Lovums, American composition, swivel head w/ sleep eyes, open mouth w/ teeth, molded or wigged hair, shoulderplate on cloth body w/ 3/4 composition limbs, period clothes, 16" h	300	350
EffanBee, Lovums, 18" h	350	400
EffanBee, Lovums, 24" h	500	600
EffanBee, Lovums, 28" h	650	850
Heinrich Handwerck, 69, German bisque socket head child w/ wig, glass sleep eyes, open mouth w/ 4 teeth, pierced ears, ball-jointed composition body, 16" h	625	675
Heinrich Handwerck, 69, 24" h	750	850
Heinrich Handwerck, 69, 30" h	1200	1400

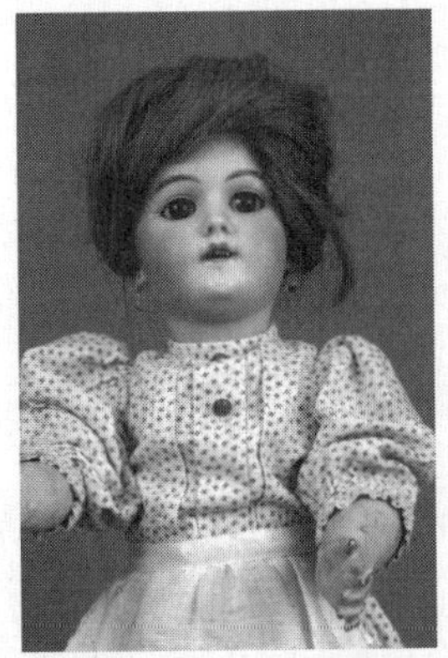

Left to right: Heinrich Handwerck 69; Heinrich Handwerck 109.

	LOW	HIGH
Heinrich Handwerck, 79, German bisque socket head child w/ wig, glass sleep eyes, open mouth w/ 4 teeth, pierced ears, ball-jointed composition body, 16" h	625	675
Heinrich Handwerck, 79, 24" h	750	850
Heinrich Handwerck, 79, 30" h	1200	1400
Heinrich Handwerck, 89, German bisque socket head child w/ wig, glass sleep eyes, open mouth w/ 4 teeth, pierced ears, ball-jointed composition body, 16" h	725	775
Heinrich Handwerck, 89, 24" h	850	950
Heinrich Handwerck, 89, 30" h	1400	1600
Heinrich Handwerck, 99, German bisque socket head child w/ wig, glass sleep eyes, open mouth w/ 4 teeth, pierced ears, ball-jointed composition body, 16" h	600	650
Heinrich Handwerck, 99, 24" h	750	850
Heinrich Handwerck, 99, 30" h	1100	1300
Heinrich Handwerck, 109, German bisque socket head child w/ wig, glass sleep eyes, open mouth w/ 4 teeth, pierced ears, ball-jointed composition body, 16" h	600	650
Heinrich Handwerck, 109, 24" h	750	850
Heinrich Handwerck, 109, 30" h	1100	1300
Heinrich Handwerck, 119, German bisque socket head child w/ wig, glass sleep eyes, open mouth w/ 4 teeth, pierced ears, ball-jointed composition body, 16" h	625	675
Heinrich Handwerck, 119, 24" h	750	850
Heinrich Handwerck, 119, 30" h	1200	1400
Ideal, Baby Shirley, composition head w/ flirty eyes, open mouth, socket head on shoulder plate w/ cloth torso and composition limbs, orig. wig and baby dress w/ label, 12" h	900	1100
Ideal, Baby Shirley, 18" h	1400	1600
Ideal, Shirley Temple, all composition head and body (in good condition) mkd. "Shirley Temple" w/ size number, socket head, sleep eyes, jointed body, orig. wig, orig. dress w/ label, 11" h	650	850
Ideal, Shirley Temple, 13" h	575	625
Ideal, Shirley Temple, 15" h	600	700
Ideal, Shirley Temple, 18" h	700	800
Ideal, Shirley Temple, 20" h	850	950
Ideal, Shirley Temple, 25" h	950	1150
Ideal, Shirley Temple, 27" h	1150	1350
Ideal, Shirley Temple, all composition head and body (in good condition) mkd. "Shirley Temple" w/ size number, socket head, sleep eyes, jointed body, orig. wig, orig. Captain January blue sailor suit w/ label and white cap, 11" h	550	650
Ideal, Shirley Temple, 13" h	850	950
Ideal, Shirley Temple, 15" h	800	900
Ideal, Shirley Temple, 18" h	900	1100
Ideal, Shirley Temple, 20" h	1000	1200
Ideal, Shirley Temple, 25" h	1200	1400
Ideal, Shirley Temple, 27" h	1400	1600
Ideal, Shirley Temple, all composition head and body (in good condition) mkd. "Shirley Temple" w/ size number, socket head, sleep eyes, jointed body, orig. wig, orig. Texas Ranger cowgirl outfit w/ label, gun, holster, and hat, 11" h	900	1100
Ideal, Shirley Temple, 13" h	900	1000
Ideal, Shirley Temple, 15" h	1000	1200
Ideal, Shirley Temple, 18" h	1100	1300

	LOW	HIGH
Ideal, Shirley Temple, 20" h	1200	1400
Ideal, Shirley Temple, 25" h	1400	1600
Ideal, Shirley Temple, 27" h	1600	1800
Ideal, Shirley Temple, all composition head and body (in good condition) mkd. "Shirley Temple" w/ size number, socket head, sleep eyes, jointed boy, orig. wig, orig. Little Colonel southern belle outfit w/ label and large bonnet, 11" h	900	1100
Ideal, Shirley Temple, 13" h	900	1000
Ideal, Shirley Temple, 15" h	1000	1200
Ideal, Shirley Temple, 18" h	1100	1300
Ideal, Shirley Temple, 20" h	1200	1400
Ideal, Shirley Temple, 25" h	1400	1600
Ideal, Shirley Temple, 27" h	1600	1800
Ideal, Shirley Temple, all composition head and body (in good condition) mkd. "Shirley Temple," brown color tone, black wig, orig. Hawaiian grass skirt and lei, 18" h	900	1100
J.D. Kestner, 129, German bisque socket head child w/ plaster pate and wig, glass sleep eyes, open mouth w/ 4 teeth, composition ball-jointed body, 16" h	750	850
J.D. Kestner, 129, 24" h	900	1100
J.D. Kestner, 129, 30" h	1300	1500
J.D. Kestner, 148, German bisque shoulder head child w/ plaster pate and wig, glass sleep eyes, open mouth w/ 4 teeth, kid body w/ bisque arms, 12" h	425	475
J.D. Kestner, 148, 16" h	500	550
J.D. Kestner, 148, 20" h	650	750
J.D. Kestner, 152, German bisque socket head child w/ plaster pate and wig, glass sleep eyes, open mouth w/ 4 teeth, composition ball-jointed body, 16" h	750	850
J.D. Kestner, 152, 24" h	900	1100
J.D. Kestner, 152, 30" h	1300	1400
J.D. Kestner, 154, German bisque shoulder head child w/ plaster pate and wig, glass sleep eyes, open mouth w/ 4 teeth, kid body w/ bisque arms, 12" h	375	425
J.D. Kestner, 154, 16" h	450	500
J.D. Kestner, 154, 20" h	575	625
J.D. Kestner, 161, German bisque socket head child w/ plaster pate and wig, glass sleep eyes, open mouth w/ 4 teeth, composition ball-jointed body, 16" h	750	850
J.D. Kestner, 161, 24" h	900	1100
J.D. Kestner, 161, 30" h	1300	1500
J.D. Kestner, 167, German bisque socket head child w/ plaster pate and wig, glass sleep eyes, open mouth w/ 4 teeth, composition ball-jointed body, 16" h	700	800
J.D. Kestner, 167, 24" h	900	1000
J.D. Kestner, 167, 30" h	1100	1300
J.D. Kestner, 171, German bisque socket head child w/ plaster pate and wig, glass sleep eyes, open mouth w/ 4 teeth, composition ball-jointed body, 16" h	675	725
J.D. Kestner, 171, 24" h	850	900
J.D. Kestner, 171, 30" h	1100	1300
J.D. Kestner, 174, Geman bisque socket head child w/ plaster pate and wig, glass sleep eyes, open mouth w/ 4 teeth, composition ball-jointed body, 16" h	800	900
J.D. Kestner, 174, 24" h	1000	1200
J.D. Kestner, 174, 30" h	1400	1600

	LOW	HIGH
J.D. Kestner, 195, German bisque shoulder head child w/ plaster pate and wig, glass sleep eyes, inset fur eyebrows, open mouth w/ 4 teeth, kid body w/ bisque arms, 15" h	425	475
J.D. Kestner, 195, 20" h	525	575
J.D. Kestner, 211, German bisque socket head baby w/ plaster pate and wig, glass sleep eyes, open mouth w/ 2 teeth, 5-pc. composition baby body, 12" h	650	750
J.D. Kestner, 211, 16" h	800	900
J.D. Kestner, 211, 20" h	1100	1300
J.D. Kestner, 214, German bisque socket head child w/ plaster pate and wig, glass sleep eyes, open mouth w/ 4 teeth, composition ball-jointed body, 16" h	725	775
J.D. Kestner, 214, 24" h	900	1000
J.D. Kestner, 214, 30" h	1100	1300
J.D. Kestner, Hilda, German bisque socket head baby w/ solid crown or plaster pate w/ wig, glass sleep eyes, open mouth w/ 2 teeth, 5-pc. composition baby body, 15" h	3400	3600
J.D. Kestner, Hilda, 20" h	4200	4800
J.D. Kestner, Hilda, 24" h	5500	6500
J.D. Kestner, JDK, German bisque socket head baby w/ solid crown, glass sleep eyes, open mouth w/ 2 teeth, 5-pc. composition baby body, 12" h	550	650
J.D. Kestner, JDK, 16" h	700	800
J.D. Kestner, JDK, 24" h	1300	1500
Kämmer and Reinhardt, 100, known as Kaiser baby, German bisque socket baby head w/ solid crown, painted blue eyes, open/closed mouth, 5-pc. composition baby body, 12" h	550	600
Kämmer and Reinhardt, 100, 15" h	700	750
Kämmer and Reinhardt, 100, 20" h	950	1200
Kämmer and Reinhardt, 121, German bisque socket head baby w/ wig, glass sleep eyes, open mouth w/ 2 teeth, 5-pc. composition baby body, 12" h	600	650
Kämmer and Reinhardt, 121, 15" h	750	800
Kämmer and Reinhardt, 121, 20" h	900	1100

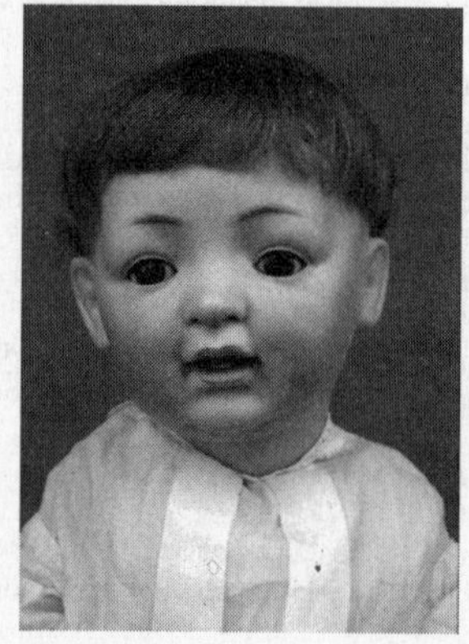

J.D. Kestner 211.

	LOW	HIGH
Kämmer and Reinhardt, 122, German bisque socket head baby w/ wig, glass sleep eyes, open mouth w/ 2 teeth, 5-pc. composition baby body, 12" h	600	700
Kämmer and Reinhardt, 122, 15" h	750	850
Kämmer and Reinhardt, 122, 20" h	900	1200
Kämmer and Reinhardt, 126, German bisque socket head baby w/ wig, glass sleep eyes, open mouth w/ 2 teeth, 5-pc. composition baby body, 12" h	475	525
Kämmer and Reinhardt, 126, 15" h	625	675
Kämmer and Reinhardt, 126, 20" h	800	900
Kämmer and Reinhardt, 403, German bisque socket head child w/ wig, glass sleep eyes, open mouth w/ 4 teeth, pierced ears, ball-jointed composition body, 12" h	725	775
Kämmer and Reinhardt, 403, 16" h	725	775
Kämmer and Reinhardt, 403, 24" h	900	1200
Kämmer and Reinhardt, 403, 30" h	1300	1500
Kewpie, Rose O'Neil, all bisque standing figure, w/ side glancing eyes, stiff neck w/ little blue wings, feet joined in standing position, jointed arms w/ starfish hands, 2" h	60	80
Kewpie, Rose O'Neil, all bisque standing figure, 4" h	100	125
Kewpie, Rose O'Neil, all bisque standing figure, 6" h	150	200
Kewpie, Rose O'Neil, all bisque standing figure, 8" h	400	500
Kewpie, Rose O'Neil, all bisque standing figure, 10" h	900	1000
Kewpie, Rose O'Neil, all bisque standing figure, 12" h	1200	1500
Kewpie, Rose O'Neil, composition standing figure, w/ side glancing eyes, stiff neck w/ little blue wings, feet joined in standing position, jointed arms w/ starfish hands, 12" h	250	350
Lenci, Laura, Italian felt child w/ wig, painted eyes, closed mouth, felt body jointed at shoulders and hips, wearing felt clothes, w/ label, 16" h only	850	1500
Lenci, Lucia, Italian felt child w/ wig, painted eyes, closed mouth, felt body jointed at shoulders and hips, wearing felt clothes, w/ label, 14" h only	400	900
Lenci, Mascott, Italian felt child w/ wig, painted eyes, closed mouth, felt body jointed at shoulders and hips, wearing felt clothes, w/ label, 8"–9" only	250	600

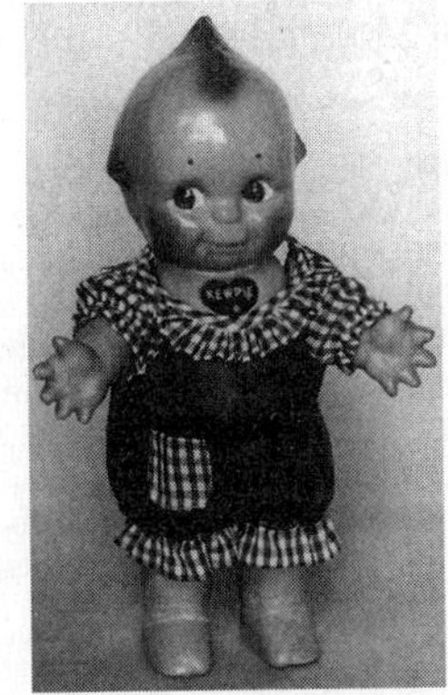

Left to right: Kämmer and Reinhardt 403; Composition Rose O'Neil Kewpie.

	LOW	HIGH
Madam Alexander, Cissy, American hard plastic head w/ sleep eyes, wig, closed mouth, hard plastic body w/ jointed legs and vinyl jointed arms, all slender. Value is very dependent on and varies w/ condition and clothing, 21" h simple example	300	450
Mask Face Googly, composition face w/ wig, big round glass eyes, watermelon smile, cloth body, 10" h	500	650
Mask Face Googly, 14" h	750	950
Mask Face Googly, 16" h	1000	1400
Monica, American composition socket head w/ wig, painted eyes, closed mouth, 5-part composition body w/ period clothes, unmkd., 14" h	500	600
Monica, 18" h	650	700
Monica, 20" h	750	850
Schoenhut Baby, wooden socket head w/ or wo/ wig, painted eyes, open or closed mouth, 5-pc. wooden body, orig. paint, normal wear, 12" h	500	600
Schoenhut Baby, 15" h	650	800
Schoenhut Carved Hair, wooden socket head child w/ hair carved in various hairdos, sometimes w/ carved ribbon, carved eyes, closed mouth, spring-jointed wooden body, orig. paint, normal wear, 14" h	1200	1600
Schoenhut Carved Hair, 17" h	1500	1800
Schoenhut Carved Hair, 21" h	1800	2500
Schoenhut Character, wooden socket head child w/ wig, carved eyes, closed mouth or showing teeth, spring-jointed wooden body, orig. paint, normal wear, 14" h	700	900
Schoenhut Character, 17" h	900	1200
Schoenhut Character, 21" h	1200	1500
Schoenhut Dolly, wooden socket head child w/ wig, decal eyes, open mouth showing teeth, spring-jointed wooden body, orig. paint, normal wear, 14" h	400	550
Schoenhut Dolly, 17" h	550	750
Schoenhut Dolly, 21" h	800	950
Schoenhut Walker, wooden socket baby head w/ or wo/ wig, painted eyes, open or closed mouth, wooden bent arms and straight hinged legs, orig. paint, normal wear, 12" h	700	850
Schoenhut Walker, 16" h	800	950
SFBJ, 301, French bisque socket head child w/ wig, glass sleep eyes, open mouth w/ 4 teeth, pierced ears, ball-jointed composition body, 15" h	750	850
SFBJ, 301, 20" h	900	1000
SFBJ, 301, 24" h	1100	1300
Simon & Halbig, 550, German bisque socket head child w/ wig, glass sleep eyes, open mouth w/ 4 teeth, ball-jointed composition body, 16" h	475	525
Simon & Halbig, 550, 24" h	650	750
Simon & Halbig, 550, 30" h	1400	1600
Simon & Halbig, 1078, German bisque socket head child w/ wig, glass sleep eyes, open mouth w/ 4 teeth, ball-jointed composition body, 16" h	525	575
Simon & Halbig, 1078, 24" h	725	775
Simon & Halbig, 1078, 30" h	1000	1200
Simon & Halbig, 1079, German bisque socket head child w/ wig, glass sleep eyes, open mouth w/ 4 teeth, ball-jointed composition body, 16" h	525	575
Simon & Halbig, 1079, 24" h	725	775
Simon & Halbig, 1079, 30" h	1000	1200

Barbie

Barbie was born in 1959, arriving as a svelte, young woman, Mattel founders Elliot and Ruth Handler had already bought out their partner Harold Matson when they introduced the doll named after their daughter. She was modern and little girls could role play with her, dressing her in countless costumes. Barbie had elegant gowns, mirroring many of the best designers of the day, as well as work togs and casual clothes. Barbie was advertised on "The Mickey Mouse Club." Barbie rapidly became the "must have" doll of the baby-boomer generation. Ken (named after the Handler's son) and a group of friends soon joined Barbie. The doll is still going strong after forty years. Many adults who adored her as a child now collect her today. Her thirtieth birthday in 1989 was a gala event covered by news services around the world.

Collectors look for condition. The most desirable Barbies are pristine examples from the 1950s and 1960s. Collectors shy away from much of the 1970s material because there is a perception of inferior quality.

The prices below are based on items in near mint to mint condition. Since the same item can be bought at a variety of locations and prices, and many dolls are no longer in their original boxes, we have devised a double range system. The low range (MNP) includes items that are near mint to mint without packaging. The higher end range (MIP) reflects the prices of near mint to mint items in near mint to mint original boxes. Therefore, prices below are for the best items available; scratched, chipped, or altered examples are not included. Cut hair, missing clothes and cracked or stained plastic greatly reduces Barbie's value. Each entry lists the approximate year of introduction and the item number.

See *The Collectors Encyclopedia of Barbie Dolls and Collectibles* by Sybil DeWein and Joan Ashabraner, Collector Books, Paducah, KY, 1977, 1996 value update and *The Barbie Doll Years: 1959–1996, Second Edition* by Patrick C. Olds and Myrazona Olds, Collector Books, Paducah, KY, 1997.

Barbie and Friends

	YEAR	NO.	MNP	MIP
Barbie #1, blonde	1959	850	$1900–2600	$3500–5500
Barbie #1, brunette	1959	850	2400–3000	4000–6000
Barbie #2, blonde	1959	850	1600–2000	2600–3500
Barbie #2, brunette	1959	850	1900–2600	3500–4500
Barbie #3, blonde	1960	850	400–500	700–800
Barbie #3, brunette	1960	850	450–550	800–1000
Barbie #4, blonde	1960	850	200–250	400–600
Barbie #4, brunette	1960	850	250–300	500–700
Barbie, bendable legs, American girl hairdo	1965	1070	300–400	700–900
Barbie, bendable legs, American girl hairdo	1966	1070	300–400	900–1200
Barbie, bendable legs, rare side flip hairdo	1965	1070	1800–2400	3200–3600
Benefit Performance Porcelain Barbie	1988	5475	100–140	340–420
Bubble Cut Barbie	1961	850	140–160	250–350
Bubble Cut Barbie	1962	850	140–160	250–300
Color Magic Barbie	1966	1150	650–750	1200–2000
Fashion Queen Barbie	1963	870	100–150	400–500
Francie, bendable legs, black	1967	1100	300–350	700–900
Francie, bendable legs, white	1966	1130	60–90	200–300
Francie Twist 'N' Turn, bendable legs	1967	1170	70–90	260–320
Free Moving Barbie	1975	7270	12–18	50–70
Free Moving Ken	1975	7280	10–15	30–40
Gold Medal Olympic Skater Barbie	1975	7262	12–16	80–100
Happy Holidays Barbie, red velvet gown	1988	170	120–180	380–420
Happy Holidays Barbie, white satin gown	1989	3253	50–80	120–160
Hawaiian Barbie	1977	7470	25–35	70–90

	YEAR	NO.	MNP	MIP
Hawaiian Ken	1978	2960	15–20	30–40
International Barbie, Canadian	1988	4928	8–12	25–32
International Barbie, Eskimo	1982	3898	60–80	120–160
Julia, 1-pc. nurse outfit	1970	1127	40–60	100–150
Julia, 2-pc. nurse outfit	1969	1127	150–80	120–180
Julia, talking	1969	1128	50–80	120–180
Ken, bendable legs	1965	1020	90–130	200–300
Ken, bendable legs	1970	1124	25–35	80–120
Ken, flocked crew cut hair	1961	750	50–70	130–180
Ken, painted crew cut hair	1962	750	40–50	100–150
Live Action Barbie, blonde	1971	1155	30–50	90–130
Malibu Barbie	1971	1067	12–18	40–50
Midge, bendable legs	1965	1080	200–250	400–500
Midge, straight legs	1964	860	40–60	140–180
Miss Barbie (sleep-eye)	1964	1060	250–350	700–900
Mod Hair Ken	1973	4224	40–50	90–120
Pink Jubilee Barbie (1200 made)	1989	—	700–900	1400–1800
Quick Curl Barbie	1973	4220	12–18	60–90
Ricky, straight legs	1965	1090	50–60	90–120
Skipper, bendable legs	1965	1030	40–60	90–110
Skipper, straight legs	1964	950	40–60	100–150
Skipper, straight legs, reissues, pinker skin	1970	950	50–70	120–180
Skooter, bendable legs	1966	1120	60–80	220–280
Standard Barbie	1967	1190	80–100	280–320
Swirl Pony Tail Barbie	1964	850	200–250	400–700
Talking Barbie	1969	1115	60–80	200–250
Talking Ken	1969	1111	40–60	110–130
Talking P.J.	1969	—	50–70	120–160
Talking Truly Scrumptious	1969	1107	120–160	320–360
Truly Scrumptious, straight legs	1969	1108	100–150	350–450
Twiggy	1967	1185	70–90	220–320
Twist and Turn Barbie	1967	1160	80–100	280–340
Walk Lively Barbie	1972	1182	50–70	120–180
Walk Lively Ken	1972	1184	25–35	60–80

Clothing

	YEAR	NO.	MNP	MIP
Aboard Ship	1965	1631	$90–$140	$200–$250
American Airlines Stewardess	1961	984	50–75	150–200
Arabian Knights	1964	874	90–120	200–250
Ballerina	1961	989	40–60	130–160
Barbie in Japan	1964	821	190–220	360–420
Barbie-Q Outfit	1959	962	55–75	140–180
Beautiful Bride	1967	1698	300–500	800–1000
Benefit Performance	1966	1667	300–350	600–800
Campus Sweetheart	1964	1616	200–300	400–600
Career Girl	1963	954	60–80	180–220
Cheerleader	1964	876	60–80	150–200
Commuter Set	1959	916	300–400	600–800
Debutante Ball	1966	1666	200–300	400–700
Doctor Ken	1963	793	50–70	90–120
Easter Parade	1959	971	750–1000	1500–2000
Gay Parisienne	1959	964	400–600	1200–1800
Gold 'N Glamour	1965	1647	300–400	700–800

Above: Suburban Shopper outfit, blue striped dress, 1961, $140.

Left: Hispanic Barbie, 1979, #1292, $50–$60.

	YEAR	NO.	MNP	MIP
Here Comes the Bride	1966	1655	350–400	700–900
Ken Campus Hero	1961	770	20–30	50–70
Ken Country Clubbin'	1964	1400	40–60	90–110
Ken Fraternity Meeting	1964	1408	25–35	60–70
Ken Here Comes the Groom	1966	1426	250–350	600–900
Ken Mr. Astronaut	1965	1415	180–240	400–500
Ken Tuxedo	1961	787	40–60	100–140
Little Red Riding Hood & the Wolf	1964	880	180–220	380–420
Miss Astronaut	1965	1641	300–350	600–700
Modern Art	1965	1625	150–200	280–320
Nighty-Negligee	1959	965	40–50	90–130
Pajama Party	1964	1601	12–18	50–80
Pan American Stewardess	1966	1678	500–800	1500–2000
Poodle Parade	1965	1643	200–250	400–500
Roman Holiday	1959	968	1200–1800	2200–2800
Saturday Matinee	1965	1615	320–380	600–800
Shimmering Magic	1966	1664	450–500	900–1300

Gift Sets and Accessories

	YEAR	NO.	MNP	MIP
Barbie Beautiful Blues Gift Set	1967	303	$300–$350	$700–$900
Barbie and Ken Tennis Gift Set	1962	892	250–350	800–1200
Barbie's Sparkling Pink Gift Set	1964	1011	250–350	600–800
Barbie's Sport Plane (Irwin)	1964	—	300–400	600–900
Barbie's Wedding Party Gift Set	1964	1017	400–600	1000–1800
Casey Goes Casual Gift Set	1967	3304	300–400	700–1000
Fashion Queen Barbie and Ken Trousseau Gift Set	1964	864	250–350	800–1000
Midge's Ensemble Gift Set	1964	1012	300–400	800–1000

G.I. Joe

Joe is thirty-five and still going strong. Hasbro introduced him in 1964. The Irwin Company produced some of Hasbro's early vehicles for Joe. Plastic and 11.5" tall, Joe was marketed as a fighting or action figure and not as a doll. Thus the action figure toy was created. A huge success with boys, girls often substituted him for Ken, to act as Barbie's date. Joe has changed with the times. In 1977 Hasbro reduced his height to 8.5". Following the enormous success of the *Star Wars* action figure line, Joe was reintroduced in the 3.75" size in 1982, and is still being produced. Collectors are beginning to seek these smaller figures. The following list, however, focuses on the earlier 11.5" figures.

The prices below are based on items in excellent or mint condition. Since the same item can be bought at a variety of locations at different prices we devised a range system. The low range (MNP) covers complete, near mint to mint items without the original box or packaging. The higher range (MIP) reflects the prices of complete, near mint to mint items in near mint to mint boxes. Prices below are for complete "like new" items. Completeness is an important factor for G.I. Joes.

The Complete Encyclopedia of G.I. Joe, 2nd Edition by Vincent Santelmo, Krause Publications, Iola, WI, 1997, describes in great detail what each set contained.

The year listed is the year of introduction, unless it's a reissue or update. Following the date is the series: Action Marine–*AM*; Action Girl–*AG*; Action Sailor–*ASL*; Action Soldiers of the World–*ASW*; Action Solder–*ASD*; Action Pilot–*AP*; Adventure Team–*ADT*; and Adventure Pack–*ADP* (a designation, not a series). Words are abbreviated to conserve space. Following the series is the product number. We have put in *Fig.* (figure), *Unf.* (uniform), or *Equip.* (equipment) to avoid confusion between similarly named sets. Each term encompasses everything that originally came with the set.

	YEAR	SERIES	NO.	MNP	MIP
Action Black Soldier Fig.	1965	ASD	7900	$700–$900	$1000–$1600
Action Marine Fig.	1964	AM	7700	120–180	320–380
Action Nurse Fig.	1967	AG	8060	1300–1600	2000–3200
Action Sailor Fig.	1964	ASL	7600	150–200	300–400
Action Soldier Fig.	1964	ASD	7500	120–180	260–320
Air Acad. Cadet Unf. Set	1967	AP	7822	400–500	800–1000
Air Sea Rescue Unf. Set	1967	AP	7825	400–600	1500–2000
Annapolis Cadet Unf. Set	1967	ASL	7624	400–500	800–1200
Astronaut Unf. Set	1967	AP	7824	300–400	1200–1500
Austr. Jungle Ftr. Deluxe Set, fig. and equip	1966	ASW	8105	500–700	2000–2600
Austr. Jungle Ftr. Standard Set, w/ fig.	1966	ASW	8205	400–600	1200–1400
Basic Foot Locker	1965	AS	8000	40–50	90–140
Beachhead Flamethrower Set	1964	AM	7718	50–60	80–100
Bivouac Sleeping Bag	1964	ASD	7515	25–35	60–80
British Com. Deluxe Set, fig. and equip.	1966	ASW	8104	500–600	2000–2500
British Com. Equip.	1966	ASW	8304	160–200	300–350
British Com. Standard Set, w/ fig.	1966	ASW	8204	400–500	1000–1600
Combat Fatigue Pants	1964	ASD	7504	40–50	80–100
Combat Fatigue Shirt	1964	ASD	7503	30–40	90–120
Combat Field Jacket	1964	ASD	7505	60–90	180–240
Command Flag Set	1964	AM	7704	200–250	400–500
Command Post Field Radio Tel. Set	1964	ASD	7520	40–50	80–100
Command Post Poncho	1964	ASD	7519	30–50	90–120
Crash Crew Fire Truck Set	1967	AP	8040	1800–2200	3000–3500
Deep Freeze Unf. Set	1967	ASL	7623	300–400	900–1400
Deep Sea Diver Unf. Set, reissue	1968	ASL	7620	300–500	900–1300
Desert Patrol Jeep Set, w/ fig.	1967	ASD	8030	800–1000	1500–2200
Dress Unf.	1964	AP	7803	300–500	1400–2000

	YEAR	SERIES	NO.	MNP	MIP
Fighter Pilot Unf. Set	1967	AP	7823	500–700	1500–2000
Forward Base Set, w/ fig. (Sears)	1966	ASD	5969	300–400	600–900
Fr. Res. Ftr. Deluxe Set, w/ fig. and equip.	1966	ASW	8103	300–500	1800–2200
Fr. Res. Ftr. Equip.	1966	ASW	8303	120–180	250–300
German Soldier Deluxe Set, w/ fig. and equip.	1966	ASW	8100	400–500	1800–2200
German Soldier Equip.	1966	ASW	8300	160–200	300–350
German Soldier Stnd. Set, w/ fig.	1966	ASW	8200	300–500	1200–1400
Green Beret Equip.	1966	ASD	7533	70–90	200–300
Green Beret Fig.	1966	ASD	7536	400–500	1800–2200
Green Beret Mach. Gun Outpost, w/ 2 figs.	1966	ASD	5978	600–800	1200–1500
Japanese Imp. Soldier Deluxe Set, w/ fig. and equip.	1966	ASW	8101	600–700	2200–2600
Japanese Imp. Soldier Standard Set, w/ fig.	1966	ASW	8201	550–650	1300–1600
Jet Fighter Airplane	1967	ASD	5396	400–500	800–1000
Jungle Fighter Unf. Set	1967	AM	7732	600–900	1800–2200
M.P. Duffel Bag	1964	ASD	7523	25–35	50–70
M.P. "Ike" Jacket	1964	ASD	7524	50–70	90–120
Machine Gun Set, w/ fig. (Sears)	1965	ASD	7531	350–450	700–1100
Marine Demo. Set (reissue)	1968	AM	7730	100–150	350–450
Marine Weapons Rack	1967	AM	7727	120–160	350–500
Military Staff Car	1967	ASD	5652	300–350	500–700
Official Jeep Set, w/ engine sound	1965	ASD	7000	250–350	500–600
Russian Soldier Deluxe Set, w/ fig. and equip.	1966	ASW	8102	500–600	1800–2200
Russian Soldier Standard Set, w/ fig.	1966	ASW	8202	400–500	1200–1400
Sea Sled and Frogman Fig. Set	1966	ASL	8050	180–220	350–500
Ski Patrol Equip. Set	1965	ASD	7531	300–350	600–900
Space Capsule Set (Sears)	1966	AP	5979	300–350	600–800
Special Forces Unf. Set, w/ bazooka	1966	ASD	7532	300–400	700–900
Talking Action Marine Fig.	1967	AM	7790	200–300	600–800
Talking Action Pilot Fig.	1967	AP	7890	450–650	1200–2000
Talking Action Sailor Fig.	1967	ASL	7690	300–400	600–900
Talking Action Soldier Fig.	1967	ASD	7590	190–230	350–450
Talking Adv. Team Black Com. Fig.	1974	ADT	7291	250–350	600–800
Talking Fig., w/ command post items	1968	ADP	90517	500–600	1600–2200
Talking Fig., w/ LSO equip.	1968	ADP	90621	600–800	2000–2500
Talking Fig., w/ Special Forces items	1968	ADp	90532	600–800	2000–2500
Talking Marine Fig., w/ field pack equip.	1968	ADP	90712	400–600	1600–2000
Tank Com. Unf. Set	1967	AM	7731	350–450	900–1400
West Point Cadet Unf.	1967	ASD	7537	400–500	800–1000

Paper Dolls

Paper dolls date to the 1400s and appeared as children's toys in the late 1700s. Collectors usually specialize either in antique examples or in specific types such as celebrity, advertising or works of favorite artists or companies. Dolls based on movie and TV stars attract collectors from other areas.

A paper doll's collectibility depends upon artist, subject, age, construction, condition and size. Prices below are for uncut near mint condition examples. Near mint, cut dolls may command prices only 20% to 50% of the value of the same uncut dolls. Abbreviations have been used throughout the listings; for example: *lg.*–large; *asst.*–assorted; *num.*–numerous; *cstms.*–costumes; *acces.*–accessories; and *clr.*–color.

Darling Dolls with Wavy Hair, Saalfield #6039:100, $8–$12.

	LOW	HIGH
Career Girls, Samuel Lowe, 1950	$20	$35
Carmen, Rita Hayworth, 2 dolls, asst. outfits, thin cover, 1948	60	80
Carmen Miranda, Saalfield #1558, 2 dolls, asst. outfits, 1952	80	110
Carmen Miranda, Whitman #995, 1942	90	125
Carmen Miranda Paper Dolls, by Tom Tierney, 1 doll, asst. cstms.	8	15
Dolls Across the Sea, by Queen Holden, Platt and Munk, Hans, Ingrid, Yvonne, and Juliane, foreign cstms., boxed, 1969	8	12
Dolls for All Nations–Russia, *Boston Sunday Globe*	12	18
Dolls of Other Lands, Watkins, 6 dolls, 42 cstms., 1968	8	12
Dolly Dingle's World Flight, 4 dresses, June 1932	30	40
Dolly Dingle's World Flight in Italy, boy doll, 3 cstms., Dec. 1932	30	40
Dolly Dingle's World Flight in Russia, 1 doll, pets, Mar. 1933	30	40
Dolly Dingle's World Flight in Sweden, 1 boy, cstms., Feb. 1933	30	40
Dolly Dingle's World Flight in Switzerland, Sep. 1931	30	40
Donna Reed, Saalfield #4412, 2 dolls, asst. clothes, folder, 1959	50	75
Doris Day, Whitman book #1179:15, 2 dolls, 8 pages of outfits, 1954	60	80
Doris Day, Whitman book #1952, statuette dolls, asst. clothes, folder, 1955	60	80
Doris Day, Whitman book #1952, asst. outfits, 1956	50	75
Doris Day, Whitman book #210325, statuette dolls, asst. outfits, folder, 1952	50	75
Dorothy Provine, Whitman book #1964, 1 doll, asst. outfits, folder w/ handle, 1962	35	45
Dr. Kildare and Nurse Susan, #2740, punch-outs, 3 dolls, asst. outfits	25	35
Dr. Kildare Play Book, Samuel Lowe	25	35
Dress-Up Doll Book, by Sally de Frehn Ogg, Treasure book #T-167, 5 dolls, asst. outfits to be colored, 1953	20	25

	LOW	HIGH
Hansel and Gretel Push-Out Book, Whitman, 1954	12	18
Happiest Millionaire, Saalfield, 1967	10	14
Happy Bride, Whitman book #1958, 4 dolls, 1960s-style clothes, 1967	18	22
Happy Days Playset Characters, various scenes, characters, includes Arnold's Drive-In and Fonzie's motorcycle	18	22
Happy Family, Samuel Lowe, 1973	6	8
Happy Holiday, reprint of Carmen Miranda, Saalfield book #2722, 2 dolls, asst. outfits	20	35
Hayley Mills in *Summer Magic,* Whitman book #1966, 1 doll, asst. cstms., folder, 1963	50	70
Hayley Mills in *The Moon Spinners,* Whitman book #1960, 1 doll, asst. cstms., 1964	50	70
Hedy Lamarr, Merrill #3482, 2 dolls, 22 outfits, 29 access., 1942	50	60
Hedy Lamarr, Saalfield, 1951	50	60
Hee-Haw, punch-out, by George and Nan Pollard, C.B.S Artcraft book #5139, Gunilla, Lulu, Kathy, and Jeannie, 1971	15	20
In Old New York, Saalfield book #1772, 2 dolls, 2 pages of cstms., thin cover	25	35
In Our Background, Samuel Lowe, 1941	25	35
Jack and Jill, book #1561, 4 dolls, animals, asst. storyland cstms.	15	20
Jack with Magic Eyes, Queen Holden, James and Jonathan #9301-P, lg. doll, disc eyes, 1963	50	70
Jackie and Caroline, #107	60	80
Journey Friends, toy from Germany, by Ann Eshner, Jack and Jill set, Dec. 1952	10	12
Judy, Merrill, 1951	10	15
Judy and Jim, by Hilda Miloche and Wilma Kane, Simon and Shuster, asst. cstms.	40	50
Judy Garland, Queen Holden, Whitman #996, 1940	100	150
Judy Garland, Queen Holden, Whitman #999, 2 dolls, lg. asst. of cstms., 1945	100	150
Judy Holiday, Saalfield book #159110, 3 dolls, 4 pages of cstms., thin cover, 1954	45	55
Julia, Saalfield, 1968	35	50
Julie Andrews, Saalfield, 1958	35	50
June Allyson, Whitman book #970, 2 dolls, asst. outfits, 1950	50	70
June Allyson, Whitman book #1173:15, 2 dolls, 8 pages of dresses and cstms., 1953	50	75
June Allyson, Whitman book #2089, 2 dolls, 6 pages of clothes, 1957	50	75
June Allyson, Whitman book #119015, 8 pages of outfits, 1950-52	50	75
June Allyson, Watkins/Stratemore book #1820, 2 statuette dolls, 1 green, 1 pink and gray, asst. clothes, 1960s	50	75
June and Stu Erwin, w/ Jackie and Joyce (*Trouble With Father*), #159210, 1954	50	70
June Bride, by Art Tanchon, Stephens Company book #136, 1946	25	35
Jungletown Jamboree, Samuel Lowe	6	8
Junior Miss, Saalfield book #250, lg. dolls, 1942	35	45
Junior Prom, Saalfield, 1942	35	45
Karen Goes to College, Merrill, 1955	35	45
Keepsake Folio-Mini Doll, Samuel Lowe, 1964	15	20
Keepsake Folio-Trudy Doll, Samuel Lowe, 1964	20	30
Kewpie Kin, by Joseph Kallus, Saalfield book #4413, punch-out, wrap-around dresses, blue cover, 1967	22	34
Kewpies, lg. Skootles on cover, 2 smaller Kewpies on back, asst. clothes, 1963	25	38
Kewpies in Kewpieville, Saalfield, Rose O'Neill's dolls, 1966	22	34
Kiddie Circus, Saalfield	10	12
Little Ballerina, Whitman book #1963, 4 dolls, asst. outfits, folder, 1969	10	15
Little Brothers and Sisters, Whitman, 4 dolls, asst. outfits, 1953	15	20
Little Cousins, Samuel Lowe, 1940	15	20

	LOW	HIGH
Little Dolls, Samuel Lowe, 1972	6	8
Little Fairy, Merrill book #154715, 4 children w/ asst. cstms., 1951	30	40
Little Folks Dolls Set, Milton Bradley #4727, 3 True-Life dolls, 3 sheets of colored clothing, 25 sheets of clothes to color, 1900s	70	100
Little Girls, Samuel Lowe, 1969	6	8
Little Joy San, *McCalls,* 1 Japanese girl doll, dress, toy lantern, Oct. 1919	12	18
Little Kitten to Dress, Samuel Lowe, 1942	20	30
Party Time, Whitman, 1952	10	15
Pat Boone, Whitman book #1968, 2 statuette dolls in folder, asst. clothes, 1959	50	70
Pat Boone, Whitman book #1985, 1959	50	70
Pat Crowley, Whitman book #2050, 2 dolls, 8 pages of clothes, 1955	50	70
Pat the Stand-Up Doll, Lowe book #1042, front and back dresses, asst. clothes, 1946	35	45
Patches and Petunia, by Betty Bell Rea, Saalfield book #2160, lg. doll, asst. clothes, 1937	35	45
Patchwork, Saalfield, 1971	8	12
Patchy Annie, Saalfield, 1962	7	10
Patience and Prudence, Abbott book #1807, 2 dolls, asst. outfits, thin cover, 1959	35	45
Patti Page, Abbott book #1804, 2 dolls, asst. outfits, thin cover, 1958	40	60
Patty Duke, Whitman book #1991:59, 2 dolls, 6 pages of punch-out clothes, 1965	50	75
Polly Pal, Samuel Lowe, 1976	4	6
Preschool, Saalfield, 1958	10	15
Pretty As a Rose, Saalfield, 1963	15	20
Prince and Princess, Saalfield book 34464, coloring book and paper dolls, punch-outs, horse and rider, medieval cstms.	40	50
Princess Diana Paper Doll Book of Fashion, by Clarissa Harlow and Mary Anna Bedford, num. outfits, 40-page book	6	8
Prom Home Permanent, Samuel Lowe, 1952	20	30
Puppy and Kitty Cut-Outs, Florence Salter, 21 pcs. of clothing, 1938	20	30
Quiz Kids, Saalfield, 1942	35	45
Raggedy Ann, by Ethel Hays Simms, Saalfield book #369, thin cover	40	50
Raggedy Ann, Whitman, 1970	6	9
Raggedy Ann and Andy, by Ethel H. Simms, coloring book and paper dolls, Saalfield book #4409, Marcella and the Raggedies, 1944	40	50
Raggedy Ann and Raggedy Andy, book #1728, 2 dolls, yellow cover, 1961	20	30
Raggedy Ann and Raggedy Andy, by Ethel Hays Simms, Saalfield book #2715, Raggedies on front, Marcella on back, 1961	30	40
Raggedy Ann and Raggedy Andy Sticker Kit Circus, #546, sticker pictures, 1941	25	35
Ranch Family, Merrill, 1957	25	35
Rave Doll Dressing Book, England, possibly based on "The Avengers"	50	60
Ricky Nelson, Whitman book #2081, 2 dolls, 6 pages of clothes, 1959	70	90
Ride a Pony–Judy and Jill, Merrill, 1944	12	18
Rita Hayworth, Merrill book #3478, 2 dolls, asst. outfits, 1942	60	80
Robin Hood, Walt Disney, press-out finger puppets, scenery and castle, 1973	12	17
Robin Hood and Maid Marian, Saalfield book #2784, asst. cstms., diecut covers	50	60
School Friends, Merrill book #1556, Linda, Bobbie, and Diane, dresses and cowgirl suits, 1955	20	30
School Girl, Saalfield book #2400, lg. dolls, asst. clothes, 1942	35	45
Schoolmates, Saalfield, 1947	12	18
Sesame Street Characters, Whitman, Big Bird, Oscar, Cookie Monster, etc., 1976	6	8
Seven and Seventeen, Merrill book #3441, 4 dolls, asst. clothes, 1954	35	45
Seven Children, by Queen Holden, lg. asst. of clothes	50	70
Shari Lewis, Saalfield, 1958	40	60
Shari Lewis and Her Puppets, Saalfield, 1960	35	45

	LOW	HIGH
Sheree North, Saalfield book #1728, front and back dolls, 4 pages of dresses, thin cover, 1957	40	60
Sherlock Bones, Samuel Lowe, 1955	8	12
Sherry and Terry, Lowe book #1847, Kewpie-style dolls	12	18
Shirley Temple, diecut teenage set, 2 dolls, yellow formal, asst. outfits, thin cover, 1942	150	200
Shirley Temple, front and back doll, blue plaid dress, white collar, black tie, 1930s adv.	50	70
Shirley Temple, Gabriel #300, statuette doll, snap-on clothes, real picture faces, num. outfits, 1950s	40	65
Shirley Temple, Saalfield book #1761, 2 toddler dolls, 2 dresses, 1937	50	90
Shirley Temple, Saalfield book #2112, 4 dolls, asst. clothes, num. access., 1934	100	150
Shirley Temple, Saalfield book #5110, statuette doll, asst. dresses, folder, 1958	80	100
Shirley Temple, Whitman book #1986, 1 doll, asst. clothes, pink tote bag, 1976	8	12
Shirley Temple–Her Movie Wardrobe, 1 doll in pink slip, asst. cstms., 1938	80	120
Sparkle Plenty, baby from the Dick Tracy comic strip, 1948	30	50
Sports Time, Whitman book #2090, blonde doll in white slip, 1952	18	24
Square Dance, Saalfield #2717, 5 dolls, 6 pages of cstms., 1950	20	30
Stand-Up Dolls, Artcraft, 6 dolls, 1960s	8	10
Star Babies, Merrill, 1945	20	25

Left to right: Gone With the Wind, Merrill #3404, 18 dolls and costumes, $300–$400; White House Party Dresses, Merrill #1550, ©1961, $30–$40.

Hess Trucks

Every year around Thanksgiving Hess gas stations announce the arrival of the latest Hess toy. Since 1964, these vehicles have been sold for a limited time only during the Christmas season. Collectors pay top prices for earlier toys or rare variations. We have listed price ranges for mint in box (MIB) examples. Boxes and packaging materials are crucial in determining value. The MIB prices listed are for items that are practically in the same condition as they were when purchased. Assessing value is tricky because sometimes the same truck is used two different years with only minor changes to the truck but with different boxes. The box therefore becomes the determing factor in dating an item.

Our consultant for this section is Jim Glaab, owner of Jim Glaab's Collectors Showcase in Greene, NY (he is listed in the back of this book). Mr. Glaab notes that on June 1, 1998, Hess issued its first miniature truck (Matchbox scale). This white tanker truck, similar to the 1990 truck, sold for $3.99 at stations. It sold out in one day. The miniature truck was billed as a "promotional offering being test marketed." Chances are that future promotions of miniatures will be offered.

	LOW	HIGH
1964, Model B Mack Tanker Truck, w/ funnel	$2000	$2500
1965, Model B Mack Tanker Truck, w/ funnel	2000	2500
1966, Voyager Tanker Ship, w/ stand	2000	3000
1967, Split Window Tanker Truck, w/ red velvet base box	2400	2800
1968, Split Window Tanker Truck, wo/ red velvet base, Perth Amboy, NJ	650	750
1969, Split Window Tanker Truck, Woodbridge, NJ on box	700	800
1969, Amerada Hess Split Window Tanker Truck (not issued to the public)	2000	3000
1970, Red Pumper Fire Truck	700	800
1971, Red Pumper Fire Truck in Season's Greetings box	2500	3000
1972, Split Window Tanker Truck	300	400
1974, Split Window Tanker Truck	300	400
1975, Box Truck, w/ 3 unlabeled oil drums, 1-pc. cab, made in Hong Kong	300	400
1976, Box Truck, w/ 3 Hess labeled oil drums, 2-pc. cab, made in Hong Kong	300	400
1977, Tanker Truck, w/ large rear label	180	220
1978, Tanker Truck, w/ slightly smaller label than 1977 version	180	220
1980, GMC Training Van	350	450
1982, '33 Chevy, "The First Hess Truck," red switch	80	120
1983, '33 Chevy, "The First Hess Truck," bank	80	120
1984, Hess Tanker Truck Bank, similar to 1977 truck	80	120
1985, '33 Chevy, "The First Hess Truck," bank, reissue of 1983 truck	90	120
1985, Hess Tanker Truck Bank, reissue of 1984 truck	90	120
1986, Red Aerial Ladder Fire Truck	100	150
1987, White Box Truck, w/ 3 labeled oil drums	60	90
1988, Slant Bed Truck, w/ race car	75	95
1989, White Ladder Fire Truck	45	65
1990, White Tanker Truck	40	50
1991, Slant Bed Truck, w/ race car, similar to 1988 truck	30	40
1992, Race Car Hauler, car inside	30	50
1993, Patrol Car, w/ 2 sirens and flashing lights	25	30
1993, Premium Diesel Tanker Truck (not issued to the public)	900	1200
1994, Rescue Truck	20	25
1995, Truck and Helicopter	25	35
1996, Emergency Truck	18	30
1997, Toy Truck and Racers	18	30
1998, Recreation Van w/ Dune Buggy and Motorcycle	18	35
1998, Hess Miniature Tanker Truck (for children 4 years and older), 1st mini	30	60

Hot Wheels

Hot Wheels burst onto the toy scene in 1968 as Mattel's answer to Matchbox Toys. Their popularity soared because the product lived up to its name:

- The design of the axles and wheels produced a smooth fast ride
- They emulated the souped-up drag racing cars popular at the time
- The metallic paint was attractive

The amazing aspect of collecting Hot Wheels is the number of variations possible for what seems to be the same model. Most differences in value are due to the different paint jobs or details such as wheels, applied logos and decoration. Many times a model is introduced in a more desirable paint color. Early vehicles finished in metallic pink seem to command higher prices, as the color was discontinued after a short production run. Conversely, common colors produced in huge quantitites or for several years often deflate the price of a vehicle. The same model (with slight changes such as color) was introduced over the years but age doesn't necessarily constitute value. The year 1973 was disastrous for Mattel. Trying to cut costs, the company removed the button from the package and changed the paint from the metallic Spectra Flame finish to less costly enamels. Sales plummeted. Although terrible for the company, it was a boon for collectors. The 1973 line is more difficult to find than other years, thus prices are consistently higher. Collectors can be fickle; what is thought rare and sought after one year may be displaced by something else the next.

Since the same item can be bought at a variety of locations and because condition and color variations further complicate pricing, we have devised a range system. The low range includes items that are in excellent to mint condition without packaging (MNP). The higher end price reflects the prices of excellent to mint items in excellent to mint boxes (MIP). Therefore prices below are for the best items available; scratched, chipped or altered examples are not included. We have seen poor condition Hot Wheels ranging from $1 to the prices listed below and beyond. In our opinion, bad condition models are worth little unless extremely rare. On the other hand, some special colors (frequently metallic pink) are rare and worth considerably more than the general prices listed here. Because of the many variations, exact identification can be tricky. We have also used the following abbreviations within the description: *rt.*–redline tires; *bwl.*–blackwall tires; *var.*–various paint finishes, *met.*–metallic paint (other colors may also be abbreviated). For each entry, date of manufacture and model number are also listed.

We suggest *The Complete Book of Hot Wheels* by Bob Parker, Schiffer Publishing, Atglen, PA, 1995. This guide has an excellent wheel dating chart and many photos. You may also want to consult *Hot Wheels Newsletter,* 26 Madera Ave., San Carlos, CA 94070.

	DATE	NO.	MNP	MIP
Alive '55, blue	1974	6968	$70–$90	$300–$400
Alive '55, chrome rl. or bwl.	1977	9210	15–20	30–40
Alive '55, dk. gren., op. hood	1983	6968	50–70	90–110
Alive '55, var.	1973	6968	90–140	300–450
Ambulance, var.	1970	6451	40–60	45–75
Ambulance, white	1970	6451	80–100	100–150
American Tipper, red	1976	9089	16–22	26–36
American Victory, lt. blue	1975	7662	15–20	30–40
AMX/2, met. pink	1971	6460	60–70	80–100
AMX/2, var.	1971	6460	35–45	60–80
Backwoods Bomb, grn. rl. or bwl.	1977	7670	30–40	70–90
Backwoods Bomb, lt. blue	1975	7670	30–40	60–80
Beatnik Bandit, var.	1968	6217	15–25	30–50
Boss Hoss, var.	1971	6406	50–70	100–150
Bragham Repco F1, var.	1969	6264	10–15	25–35
Bugeye, var.	1971	6178	35–45	70–90
Buzz Off, blue	1974	6976	35–45	70–90

	DATE	NO.	MNP	MIP
Buzz Off, var.	1973	6976	90–120	250–350
Bye-Focal, var.	1971	6187	70–90	200–250
Carabo, lt. grn.	1974	7617	30–40	50–60
Carabo, pink	1970	6420	60–70	90–110
Carabo, yellow	1974	7617	250–350	400–600
Carabo, var.	1970	6420	25–35	45–55
Cement Mixer, var.	1970	6452	25–35	35–45
Chapparal 2G, pink	1969	6256	40–70	90–140
Chapparal 2G, var.	1969	6256	15–20	30–40
Chevy Monza 2+2, grn.	1975	7671	180–220	250–300
Chevy Monza 2+2, orange	1975	7671	40–50	70–90
Chief's Special, red	1975	7665	30–40	40–60
Classic '31 Ford Woody, var.	1969	6251	12–18	40–60
Classic '32 Ford Vicky, var.	1969	6250	18–22	45–55
Classic '36 Ford Coupe, lt. blue	1969	6253	35–45	50–70
Classic '36 Ford Coupe, pink	1969	6253	70–90	100–150
Classic '36 Ford Coupe, var.	1969	6253	12–18	30–50
Classic '57 T-Bird, pink	1969	6252	70–90	100–150
Classic '57 T-Bird, var.	1969	6252	20–30	50–70
Classic Cord, var.	1971	6472	125–175	300–400
Classic Nomad, var.	1970	6404	40–60	70–90
Cockney Cab, var.	1971	6466	40–50	70–90
Corvette Stingray, red	1976	9241	30–40	55–70
Custom AMX, var.	1969	6267	40–60	80–100
Custom Barracuda, var.	1968	6211	50–60	200–300
Custom Camaro, var.	1968	6208	40–70	200–300
Custom Charger, var.	1969	6268	50–80	120–160
Custom Convertible Mark III, var.	1969	6266	20–30	40–60
Custom Corvette, var.	1968	6215	50–80	200–250
Custom Cougar, var.	1968	6205	60–80	300–400
Custom Eldorado, var.	1968	6218	30–50	100–150
Custom Firebird, var.	1968	6212	40–60	200–250
Custom Fleetside, var.	1968	6213	40–60	150–200
Custom Mustang, var.	1968	6206	60–80	300–400
Custom Police Cruiser, white	1969	6269	50–60	100–150
Custom T-Bird, var.	1968	6207	60–80	200–300
Custom VW Bug, var.	1968	6220	12–20	40–60
Demon, var.	1970	6401	15–20	30–40
Deora, var.	1968	6210	40–60	300–350
Double Header, var.	1973	5880	80–100	250–350
Double Vision, var.	1973	6975	80–100	200–300
Drag Race Act. Set (add val. 2 cars in set)	1968	6202	20–30	50–70
Dump Truck, var.	1970	6453	18–22	30–40
Dune Daddy, var.	1973	6967	80–100	250–350
El Rey Special, var. grn.	1974	8273	40–60	70–90
Emergency Squad, red	1975	7650	12–16	40–50
Evil Weevil, var.	1971	6471	35–45	60–80
Ferrari 312P, met. red, wht. int.	1970	6417	100–150	180–220
Ferrari 312P, var.	1970	6417	15–20	30–40
Ferrari 312P, var.	1973	6973	200–250	600–800
Ferrari 512S, var.	1972	6021	80–100	180–240
Fire Chief Cruiser, red	1970	6469	10–14	18–22
Fire Engine, var.	1970	6454	30–50	50–70
Ford J-Car, var.	1968	6214	10–15	30–50

	DATE	NO.	MNP	MIP
Ford Mark IV, var.	1969	6257	8–12	25–35
Fuel Tanker, white enamel	1971	6018	50–70	100–150
Full Curve Pak	1968	6225	8–10	18–22
Funny Money, gray	1972	6005	50–60	180–220
Funny Money, magenta	1974	7621	30–40	40–60
Grass Hopper, engine on hood, green	1974	7622	35–45	40–50
Grass Hopper, var.	1971	6461	30–40	50–75
Gremlin Grinder, green	1975	7652	25–35	40–50
Gun Slinger Jeep, olive	1975	7664	25–35	40–50
Hairy Hauler, var.	1971	6458	30–40	35–45
Heavy Chevy, var.	1970	6408	35–45	50–70
Heavy Chevy, var.	1974	7619	45–55	80–90
Heavy Chevy Silver Special, chrome	1970	6189	40–50	90–110
Hiway Robber, var.	1973	6979	80–100	200–250
Hood, met. pink	1971	6175	60–80	60–80
Hood, var.	1971	6175	30–40	40–60
Hot Heap, var.	1968	6219	12–18	30–50
Ice "T," var.	1973	6184	40–50	120–180
Ice "T," var.	1973	6980	90–140	300–500
Indy Eagle, gold chrome	1969	6263	50–70	160–200
Indy Eagle, var.	1969	6263	10–15	30–40
Jack Rabbit Jack-in-the-Box promo	1970	6421	100–150	200–250
Jack Rabbit Special, white	1970	6421	10–15	35–45
Jet Threat, var.	1971	6179	50–70	100–150
King 'Kuda, chrome club kit	1970	6190	50–60	80–120
King 'Kuda, var.	1970	6411	30–40	60–80
Light My Firebird, var.	1970	6412	18–22	50–60
Lola GT 70, var.	1969	6254	8–12	20–30
Lotus Turbine, var.	1969	6226	10–15	25–35
McLaren M6A, var.	1969	6255	8–12	30–40
Mercedes 280SL, var.	1969	6275	18–22	35–45
Mercedes 280SL, var.	1973	6962	90–120	300–400
Mercedes C-111, var.	1972	6169	80–100	200–250
Mercedes C-111, var.	1974	6978	180–220	300–400
Mighty Maverick, var.	1970	6414	35–45	60–80
Mod Quad, var.	1970	6456	18–22	30–40
Mongoose II, met. blue	1971	5954	60–90	200–300
Mongoose Funny Car, red	1970	6410	50–60	120–160
Mongoose Rail Dragster (2 pk.), blue	1971	5952	70–90	500–600
Moving Van, var.	1970	6455	35–45	70–90
Mutt Mobile, var.	1971	5185	50–80	90–120
Nitty Gritty Kitty, var.	1970	6405	35–55	100–150
Noodle Head, var.	1971	6000	50–80	90–140
Olds 442, var.	1971	6467	200–250	500–600
Open Fire, var.	1972	5881	80–100	200–300
Paddy Wagon, dk. blue	1970	6402	9–12	25–35
Peppin Bomb, var.	1970	6419	10–15	25–35
Pit Crew, white	1971	6183	60–80	300–500
Porsche 917, var.	1970	6416	12–18	30–40
Porsche 917, var.	1973	6972	180–220	400–700
Power Pad, var.	1970	6459	30–40	60–90
Python, var.	1968	6216	15–20	35–50
Racer Rig, white or red	1971	6194	70–90	250–350
Rear Engine Mongoose, blue	1972	5699	140–180	300–500

	DATE	NO.	MNP	MIP
Rear Engine Snake, yellow	1972	5856	140–180	300–500
Red Baron, red, black interior	1970	6400	20–30	30–40
Rocket Bye Baby, var.	1971	6186	50–70	120–180
Rolls Royce Silver Shadow, var.	1969	6276	25–45	50–70
S'Cool Bus, yellow	1971	6468	100–150	600–700
Sand Crab, var.	1970	6403	12–18	30–40
Scooper Dump Truck, var.	1971	6193	80–100	200–300
Seasider, var.	1970	6413	50–70	100–150
Shelby Turbine, var.	1969	6265	12–18	30–50
Short Ofder, var.	1971	6176	40–50	80–120
Side Kick, var.	1972	6022	80–100	175–225
Silhouette, var.	1968	6209	12–18	35–50
Six Shooter, var.	1971	6003	60–80	125–175
Sky Show Fleetside, var.	1970	6436	350–500	600–700
Snake II, white	1971	5953	50–60	200–250
Snake Funny Car, yellow	1970	6409	50–80	200–250
Snake Rail Dragster, white	1971	5951	70–90	500–600
Snorkel, var. (2 pak)	1971	6020	60–80	120–160
Special Delivery, blue	1971	6006	40–60	150–200
Splittin' Image, var.	1969	6261	10–15	30–40
Staff Car	1976	9521	500–700	—
Street Eater, yellow	1975	7669	30–50	80–100
Street Snorter, var.	1973	6971	90–110	250–350
Strip Teaser, var.	1971	6188	50–80	150–200
Sugar Caddy, var.	1971	6418	40–60	60–80
Super Van, black	1975	7649	30–40	40–60
Super Van, King Radio	1975	7649	80–100	120–180
Super Van, Toys R Us	1976	7649	125–175	200–250
Superfine Turbine, var.	1973	6004	200–300	500–900
Sweet-16, var.	1973	6007	80–100	200–300
Swingin' Wing, var.	1970	6422	20–30	40–50
T-4-2, var.	1971	6177	40–50	90–140
Talking Serv. Center	1969	5159	40–70	80–120
Team Trailer, white or red	1971	6019	60–80	150–200
TNT Bird, var.	1970	6407	30–40	60–80
Torero, pink	1969	6260	60–70	80–100
Torero, var.	1969	6260	12–15	30–50
Torino Stocker, red	1975	7647	30–40	40–60
Tough Customer, olive	1975	7655	14–20	40–60
Tow Truck, var.	1970	6450	25–35	45–55
Tri Baby, var.	1970	6424	20–30	40–50
Turbofire, var.	1969	6259	10–15	40–60
Twin Mill, var.	1969	6258	12–22	40–50
Twin Mill II, orange	1976	8240	18–22	25–30
Vega Bomb, orange	1975	7658	35–45	70–90
VW Beach Bomb, surf bds./side, var.	1969	6274	40–50	80–100
Volkswagen Bug, orange, bug on roof	1974	7620	30–40	50–60
Volkswagen Bug, orange w/ stripes	1974	7620	140–180	300–400
Waste Wagon, var.	1971	6192	70–90	200–300
What 4, gold	1971	6001	80–100	180–220
What 4, var.	1971	6001	60–80	100–150
Whip Creamer, var.	1970	6457	20–40	40–60
Winnipeg, yellow	1974	7618	60–90	95–135
Xploder, var.	1973	6977	90–120	300–350

Japanese Automotive Tinplate Toys

Two decades before Japan threatened Detroit for the auto market they dominated the post-war tinplate toy industry. Ford, GM and American Motors refined the art of the automobile in the 1950s and Japan replicated their efforts in toys. A score of Japanese toy companies produced these toys. Even four decades later, very little is known about these firms.

Collectors of post-war Japanese automotive toys favor those models in the 10" to 16" category, followed by the 8" category. Many oversized models are less popular because of the amount of shelf space they require. The *créme de la créme* of this area is the 16" 1962 Chrysler Imperial, a car any collector will find space for.

When collecting these vehicles examine them carefully and make sure there are no missing parts, including mirrors and trim. Make sure there is no restoration; battery boxes should be examined closely for corrosion. Never leave a battery in a toy; it can leak and cause damage. The prices below are for mint without box (MNB) and mint in the box (MIB) examples. Rust, scratches and restoration will lower these prices. All dates refer to the year the vehicle most closely resembles; production is usually around the same time. These are toys and not exact replicas, so there are differences between them and their real life counterparts. In the cases where a model looks the same for several years, we used *c.* Abbreviated company names are unidentified firms, as in *UK* (unknown). Regarding power, *BT* stands for battery operated, *BR* for battery operated with remote control, *BL* is battery operated with lights, and *F* is friction powered.

An excellent source of information on this subject is *Collecting the Tin Toy Car 1950–1970,* Dale Kelly, Schiffer Publishing, Extón, PA, 1984. Our consultant for this area is Jack Herbert, collector and contributing author to *Antique Toy World Magazine,* a must-have publication for toy collectors (see our list of publications). Mr. Herbert's address is listed in the back of this book.

Mercedes Benz 300SE (reissued), 1970, Ichiko, friction, 24" l, MIB. —Photo courtesy Collectors Auction Services.

MODEL	YEAR	CO.	SIZE	POWER	MNB	MIB
Aston-Martin (James Bond car)	1965	Gilbert	11"	BT	$350–$400	$600–$800
Austin Healy Sports Car	1954	Bandai	8"	F	300–400	400–600
BMW 600 Isetta, 4 whls.	c.1950	Bandai	9"	F	500–700	600–800
Buick	1949	Nomura	16"	F	800–1000	1000–1200
Buick	1953	Marusan	7"	F	600–800	700–800
Buick	1959	Nomura	11"	F	600–700	900–1200
Buick	1960	Ichiko	17.5"	F	700–800	900–1200
Buick Convertible	1949	UK	8.5"	F	250–350	400–500
Buick Emergency Car	1961	Nomura	14"	F	500–600	800–900

Left: Chevrolet Impala, friction, 11.25" l.

Right: Cadillac, Marusan, friction, some rust spotting, 12" l. —Photos courtesy Collectors Auction Services.

MODEL	YEAR	CO.	SIZE	POWER	MNB	MIB
Buick Future Car Convertible	1951	Yonezawa	7.5"	F	800–900	1000–1200
Buick LeSabre	1966	Asahi	19"	F	700–900	800–1000
Buick Sportswagon	1968	Asakusa	15"	F	700–900	800–1000
Buick Station Wagon	1954	UK	8"	BT	400–600	500–700
Cadillac	1951	Marusan	11"	BT	1200–1500	1500–1600
Cadillac	1960	Yonezawa	18"	F	1600–1900	2000–2500
Cadillac	1962	Yonezawa	22"	F	1000–1200	1400–1600
Cadillac	1967	Ichiko	28"	F	1600–2200	2000–2200
Cadillac, 4-door	1959	Bandai	11"	F	300–400	500–700
Cadillac, 4-door	1965	Ichiko	22"	F	700–900	1200–1400
Cadillac Convertible	1952	Alps	11.5"	F	1800–2200	2200–2500
Cadillac Convertible	1952	Nomura	13"	BL	400–600	500–800
Cadillac Convertible	1959	Bandai	11"	F	300–400	500–700
Cadillac Convertible	1960	Bandai	11"	F	400–600	600–800
Cadillac Eldorado	1967	Kosuge	10.5"	F	800–900	1200–1500
Cadillac Eldorado	1968	Ichiko	29"	F	500–700	800–1000
Cadillac Eldorado Convertible	1967	UK	10.75"	F	300–500	400–600
Cadillac Fleetwood	1961	S.S.S.	17.5"	F	300–400	500–700
Champion's Racer	c.1954	Yonezawa	18"	F	1200–1500	1400–2000
Chevrolet	1955	Marusan	11"	BL	500–700	700–900
Chevrolet	1962	Asahi	11"	F	400–500	600–700
Chevrolet Camaro	1971	Taiyo	9.5"	BT	150–200	250–300
Chevrolet Convertible	1959	S.Y.	11.5"	F	600–800	800–900
Chevrolet Corvette	1962	Bandai	8"	BT	400–500	500–600
Chevrolet Corvette	1963	Bandai	8"	F	300–350	400–500
Chevrolet Corvette	1968	Taiyo	9.5"	BT	150–200	250–300
Chevrolet Impala Convertible	1961	Bandai	11"	F	700–800	900–1200
Chevrolet Impala Sedan	1961	Bandai	11"	F	600–800	700–1000
Chevrolet Pick-Up	1963	UK	8"	F	100–125	150–200
Chevrolet Wagon	1960	UK	12"	F	400–500	500–600
Chrysler Imperial	1962	Asahi	16"	F	10–15,000	15–18,000
Chrysler Sedan	1967	Nomura	12"	F	300–350	400–600
Citroen	1955	Bandai	12"	F	400–600	500–800
Datsun 280Z	1976	Alps	19"	F	300–350	450–550
Dodge	1958	Nomura	11"	F	600–800	700–800

MODEL	YEAR	CO.	SIZE	POWER	MNB	MIB
Dodge Pick-Up	1959	M.	18.5"	F	1000–1200	1200–1600
Edsel	1958	Asahi	10.75"	F	700–800	900–1200
Edsel Convertible	1958	Haji	10.25"	F	1200–1500	1500–2000
Edsel Station Wagon	1958	Haji	10.5"	F	800–900	1000–1200
Ferrari 250G Convertible	1957	Asahi	9.5"	F	500–600	600–800
Fiat Hardtop Sedan	1955	Nomura	15"	F	200–300	300–500
Ford	1957	Ichiko	12"	F	800–1200	1000–1400
Ford	1957	Yonezawa	12"	F	800–1000	1000–1200
Ford, 2-door	1956	Marusan	13"	F	1800–2200	2500–2800
Ford Convertible	1956	Haji	11.5"	F	4000–5000	5000–7500
Ford Convertible, trunk opens	1955	Bandai	12"	F	800–900	900–1200
Ford Country Sedan Station Wagon	1961	Bandai	10.5"	F	400–600	500–700
Ford Country Sedan Station Wagon	1962	Asahi	12"	F	800–900	900–1200
Ford Fairlane Convertible	1957	Ichiko	10"	F	400–600	500–800
Ford Flower Delivery Wagon	1955	Bandai	12"	F	700–800	900–1200
Ford Galaxie	1965	Mod. Toys	11"	F	400–600	500–700
Ford GT	c.1968	Bandai	10"	BT	400–600	500–700
Ford Gyron	1960	Ichida	11"	BT	400–600	500–700
Ford Mustang	1965	Bandai	11"	BT	300–500	400–600
Ford Mustang	1967	Bandai	13"	BT	400–600	500–700
Ford Ranchero	1955	Bandai	12"	F	400–600	500–800
Ford Ranchero	1957	Bandai	12"	F	500–600	600–700
Ford Sedan	1952	H	7.5"	F	200–250	300–400
Ford Station Wagon	1955	Bandai	12"	F	400–600	500–800
Ford Station Wagon	1957	Bandai	12"	F	400–600	500–700
Ford T-Bird Convertible, retractable roof	1962	Yonezawa	11"	BT	400–500	500–800
Ford Thunderbird	1956	Nomura	11"	BL	600–700	700–800
Good Humor Truck	1950	K.T.S.	10.75"	F	700–900	1000–1200
International Cement Truck	c.1955	S.S.S.	19"	F	1200–1500	1500–2000
Isetta 3-Wheeler	c1950	Bandai	6.5"	F	500–700	600–800
Jaguar SKE	c.1965	T.T.	10.5"	F	400–600	500–700
Jaguar XK-120	1965	Alps	6.5"	F	300–500	400–600

Right: Ford Convertible, Irco, friction, 7" l.

Left: Chevrolet, 1954, Linemar, friction, 11.25" l.

—Photos courtesy Bill Bertoia Auctions.

MODEL	YEAR	CO.	SIZE	POWER	MNB	MIB
Jeepster Station Wagon	1966	Daiya	10.5"	F	150–250	300–400
Land Rover	1960	Bandai	7.5"	F	400–600	600–700
Lincoln	1955	Yonezawa	12"	F	900–1200	1000–1400
Lincoln	1960	Yonezawa	11"	BT	600–800	800–1000
Lincoln Futura	1956	Alps	11"	BT	800–1200	1200–1500
Lincoln Mark II	1956	Line Mar	12"	B	2500–3000	3000–3500
Lincoln Mark II	1956	Line Mar	12"	F	2500–3000	3000–3500
Lincoln Mark III	1958	Bandai	11"	F	500–700	600–800
Lincoln Sedan	1963	Nomura	10.5"	BT	300–350	400–500
Lotus Elite	c.1958	Bandai	8.5"	F	150–200	200–250
Mercedes Benz 220S	1962	S.S.S.	12"	BT	600–800	700–1000
Mercedes Benz 250 SE	1965	Ichiko	13"	BT	200–300	300–400
Mercedes Benz 300 SL	c.1958	Cragstan	9"	BT	600–800	700–900
Mercedes Benz Racer	1955	Line Mar	9.5"	F	700–900	800–1000
Mercury	1958	Yonezawa	11.5"	F	900–1000	1000–1200
Mercury Cougar	1967	Taiyo	10"	BT	400–600	500–800
Messerschmitt	1957	Bandai	8.5"	F	500–600	700–1000
MG 1600 Mark II	c.1958	Bandai	8.5"	F	175–225	300–400
MG A	1957	Asahi	10"	F	400–600	500–700
MG TD	1955	S.S.S.	6.5"	F	125–175	150–200
MG TF	1952	UK	8.5"	F	300–500	400–600
MG TF	1955	Bandai	8"	F	300–400	400–600
Olds Toronado	1966	Bandai	11"	BT	400–600	500–700
Oldsmobile	1956	UK	10.5"	F	600–800	700–900
Oldsmobile	1958	Yonezawa	16"	F	1200–1800	1800–2200
Opel	c.1955	Yonezawa	11.5"	BL	500–600	600–700
Packard Convertible	1953	Alps	16"	F	5000–7000	7–10,000
Packard Sedan	1953	Alps	16"	F	4000–6000	5000–8000
Plymouth	1956	Alps	12"	BT	500–700	700–800
Plymouth	1961	Ichiko	12"	F	600–900	800–1000
Plymouth Ambulance	1961	Bandai	12"	F	600–700	700–800
Plymouth Convertible	1959	Asahi	10.5"	F	600–700	700–900
Plymouth Hardtop Convertible	1959	Asahi	10.5"	F	600–900	800–1000
Pontiac Firebird	1967	Bandai	9.5"	BT	500–600	600–700
Porsche Rally 911	c.1965	Alps	9.5"	BT	300–500	400–600
Rambler (Nash) Sedan	1953	K	8"	F	250–300	400–500
Rambler Station Wagon	1959	Bandai	11"	—	400–500	500–700
Renault 750	1958	Masudaya	7"	F	400–600	500–700
Renault 750	1958	Yonezawa	7.5"	F	400–600	500–700
Rolls Royce	c.1958	Bandai	12"	BT	400–600	500–700
Rolls Royce	1960	UK	10.5"	F	1000–1200	1200–1500
Rolls Royce Convertible	c.1955	Bandai	12"	F	400–600	500–700
Studebaker	1953	UK	9"	F	500–600	600–800
Studebaker Avante	c.1955	Bandai	8"	F	500–600	600–700
Toyota 2000 GT	1967	Asahi	15"	F	200–250	250–300
Volkswagen Bug	c1960	Bandai	15"	BT	450–500	550–600
Volkswagen Bus	c.1965	Bandai	9.5"	BT	400–600	500–700
VW Convertible Bug	c.1960	Masudaya	9.5"	F	500–700	700–800
VW Convertible Bug	c.1960	Taiyo	10.5"	BT	400–600	500–700
VW Karman-Ghia Convertible	c.1960	Bandai	7.5"	F	300–350	400–600
VW Pick-Up Truck	c.1965	Bandai	8"	BR	250–350	400–500

Lionel Trains

Joshua Lionel Cohen founded America's best-known toy train producer, Lionel, in 1901. In the following descriptions we give the numbers and titles of various locomotives *(Loco)* and cars. Descriptions of locomotives contain the wheel configuration, such as 4-4-4 (four forward wheels, four wheels in the middle and four in the back). Locomotive descriptions contain engine type, steam or electric (elec.). This describes the style of the locomotive, not the power that runs the toy. Unless otherwise noted, electricity is the power source. The number of some locomotives is followed by *E*, which refers to an E-Unit reverse system. *Sp* following a number stands for Special. Gauge for cars and locomotives is listed, such as *Std.* (Standard), and *O*. Gauge refers to the track width. Although specific years are not listed, *post* and *pre* indicate if an item was produced before WWII (pre) or after WWII (post).

The following prices are given in a double range format. The first range is for items in good condition, having scrapes and many scratches and/or some light corrosion. The second range is for items in excellent or like-new condition.

There are many variations of Lionel trains. Color and stylistic differences can dramatically influence prices. The prices below, unless otherwise specified, are for the most common variations. We strongly recommend you consult the large Greenberg Guides for information on variations.

For further information we recommend *Greenberg's Pocket Price Guide to Lionel Trains,* Kent J. Johnson, editor, Kalmbach Books, Waukesha, WI, 1998 and *Greenberg's Guide to Trains, 1901–42, Volumes I–IV* and *Greenberg's Guide to Trains, 1945–69, Volumes I–VII,* Kalmbach Books, Waukesha, WI. The Train Collector's Association can be reached at TCA, P.O. Box 248, Strasburg, PA 17579, 717-687-8623.

Our consultant for this area is collector Michael Brinkmann.

NO.		GOOD	EXCELLENT
1	Trolley, 4 wheel, Std., pre	$450–$550	$1300–$1500
2	Trolley, 4 wheel, Std., pre	550–650	1300–1550
3	Trolley, 8 wheel, Std., pre	1200–1400	3000–3500
4	Trolley, 8 wheel, Std., pre	2000–2250	6000–6500
5	Loco 0-4-0, steam, Std., pre	400–500	900–1000
6	Loco 4-4-0, steam, Std., pre	400–500	900–1000
7	Loco 4-4-0, steam, Std., pre	1500–1700	2800–3000
8	Loco 0-4-0, elec., St., pre	75–85	150–200
9E	Loco 0-4-0, elec., Std., pre	500–600	1000–1100
10	Loco 0-4-0, elec., Std., pre	85–95	175–200
16	Ballast, Std., pre	60–70	120–140
17	Caboose, Std., pre	35–45	80–85
31	Combine, Std., pre	40–45	80–90
32	Mail, Std., pre	40–45	80–90
33	Loco 0-4-0, elec., Std., pre	60–70	130–140
33	Loco 0-6-0, elec., Std., pre	250–300	700–800
34	Loco 0-6-0, elec., Std., pre	300–350	800–900
38	Loco 0-4-0, elec., Std., pre	70–80	150–175
42	Loco 0-4-4-0, square, elec., Std., pre	180–200	425–450
50	Loco 0-4-0, elec., Std., Pre	80–90	175–200
53	Loco 0-4-4-0, elec., Std., pre	1200–1500	3000–4000
53	Loco 0-4-0, elec., Std., pre	100–125	250–300
54	Loco 0-4-4-0, elec., Std., pre	1700–1900	3800–4000
61	Sp., Loco 0-4-4-0, Schwartz, elec., Std., pre	1300–1500	2800–3000
117	Caboose, Std., pre	30–35	60–70
150	Loco 0-4-0, elec., O, pre	55–60	150–175
152	Loco 0-4-0, elec., O, pre	50–60	150–175
153	Loco 0-4-0, elec., O, pre	50–55	160–170

Above: 385E Locomotive and 385W Tender, gunmetal, standard gauge.

Above: No. 381E Bild-A-Loco w/ Coaches, 4-4-4, green w/ apple green subframe, includes Illinois, Colorado, California, and New York coaches.

Above: No. 402E Passenger Set, includes 402E Locomotive, #429 Combo, #418 Pullman, and #490 Observation Car, mauve, orig. boxes, locomotive overhauled and rewheeled. —Photos courtesy Bill Bertoia Auctions.

NO.		GOOD	EXCELLENT
154	Loco 0-4-0, elec., O, pre	45–50	140–150
156	Loco 4-4-4, elec., O, pre	225–250	725–750
158	Loco 4-4-4, elec., O, pre	60–75	200–225
201	Loco 0-6-0, steam, O, pre	250–275	525–550
202	Trolley, 4 wheel, Std., pre	900–1000	2800–3000
203	Loco 0-6-0, steam, O, pre	175–200	375–400
203	Loco 0-4-0, armored, elec., O, pre	850–900	1700–1850
204	Loco 2-4-2, steam, O, pre	40–50	110–115
214R	Refrigerator, Std., pre	175–200	550–600
224E	Loco 2-6-2, steam, O, pre	70–80	150–175
225E	Loco 2-6-2, steam, O, pre	130–140	275–300
226E	Loco 2-6-4, steam, O, pre	275–300	625–650
227	Loco 0-6-0, steam, O, pre	575–600	1100–1200
228	Loco 0-6-0, steam, O, pre	575–600	1100–1200
229	Loco 2-4-2, steam, O, pre	35–40	90–100
233	Loco 0-6-0, steam, O, pre	575–600	1200–1300
238	Loco 4-4-2, steam, O, pre	130–140	285–295
248	Loco 0-4-0, elec., O, pre	60–75	140–160
249	Loco, steam, O, pre	90–100	200–220
250	Loco 0-4-0, elec., O, pre	45–50	140–150
250E	Loco 0-4-0, Hiawatha, steam, O, pre	650–700	1400–1500
251	Loco 0-4-0, elec., O, pre	90–100	250–275
252	Loco 0-4-0, elec., O, pre	50–60	140–150
253E	Loco 0-4-0, elec., O, pre	80–90	250–275
254	Loco 0-4-0, elec., O, pre	100–120	230–250
255E	Loco 2-4-2, steam, O, pre	250–275	575–600
256	Loco 0-4-4-0, elec., O, pre	225–250	725–750
258	Loco 2-4-2, 2nd version, steam, O, pre 1930	65–75	175–185
259	Loco 2-4-2, steam, O, pre	35–40	85–95
260E	Loco 2-4-2, steam, O, pre	240–250	525–550
261	Loco 2-4-2, steam, O, pre	110–120	235–245
262	Loco 2-4-2, steam, O, pre	85–90	200–215
263E	Loco 2-4-2, gunmetal, steam, O, pre	225–250	525–550
263E	Loco 2-4-2, blue, steam, O, pre	300–325	675–700
264E	Loco 2-4-2, steam, O, pre	150–165	300–325
309	Pullman, Std., pre	70–80	160–175
310	Baggage, Ste., pre	70–80	160–175
318E	Loco 0-4-0, elec., Std., pre	90–100	175–200
322	Observation, Std., pre	70–80	160–175
380E	Loco 0-4-0, elec., Std., pre	160–175	325–350
381E	Loco 4-4-4, elec., Std., pre	1000–1200	3000–3200
384	Loco 2-4-0, steam, Std., pre	225–250	500–525
385E	Loco 2-4-2, steam, Std., pre	325–350	700–725
390	Loco 2-4-2, black, steam, Std., pre	400–425	700–750
390E	Loco 2-4-2, blue, steam, Std., pre	550–600	1200–1300
392E	Loco 4-4-2, steam, Std., pre	450–500	1000–1100
400E	Loco 4-4-4, steam, Std., pre	600–700	1800–2000
400E	Loco 4-4-4, blue, steam, Std., pre	800–1000	2500–2700
402E	Loco 0-4-4-0, elec., Std., pre	250–275	500–550
408E	Loco 0-4-4-0, elec., Std., pre	600–700	1300–1500
431	Diner, Std., pre	300–325	600–625
450	Loco 0-4-0, Macy's Sp., elec., O, pre	225–250	700–750
600	Pullman Car, O, pre	20–28	70–75
601	Pullman Car, O, pre	15–20	55–60

NO.		GOOD	EXCELLENT
652	Gondola, O, pre	10–12	40–45
653	Hopper, O, pre	15–20	55–60
671	Loco 6-8-6, steam, O, post	75–90	175–200
681	Loco 6-8-6, steam, O, post	80–90	175–200
700	Loco 0-4-0, elec., O, pre	200–225	525–550
700E	Loco 4-6-4, Scale Hudson 5344, steam, O, pre	1300–1500	4200–4500
701	Loco 0-4-0, elec., O, pre	175–200	625–650
703	Loco 0-4-0, elec., O, pre	375–400	1100–1200
708	Loco 0-6-0, steam, O, pre	1000–1100	2400–2500
726	Loco 2-8-4, steam, O, post	200–225	400–425
736	Loco 2-8-4, steam, O, post	175–200	350–375
752E	Loco Streamliner, w/ 2 passenger cars, diesel, O, pre	300–375	700–725
763E	Loco 4-6-4, Scale Hudson, steam, O, pre	1000–1200	2200–2400
773	Loco 4-6-4, Hudson, steam, O, post	650–700	1200–1300
804	Tank, Shell, O, pre	12–15	30–35
805	Box Car, O, pre	12–15	30–35
806	Cattle, O, pre	12–15	35–45
807	Caboose, O, pre	10–12	25–30
820	Floodlight, O, pre	55–60	190–200
831	Flat, O, pre	10–12	30–35
1100	Handcar Mickey and Minnie, pre	300–325	800–900
1103	Handcar Bunny and Basket, pre	350–375	1000–1100
1105	Handcar Santa, pre	400–425	1300–1400
1107	Handcar Donald Duck, pre	350–375	1000–1100
1651E	Loco 0-4-0, elec., O, pre	70–75	140–150
1661E	Loco 2-4-0, steam, O, pre	30–35	90–100
1662	Loco 0-4-0, steam, O, pre	125–150	325–350
1663	Loco 0-4-0, steam, O, pre	125–150	375–400
1664	Loco 2-4-2, steam, O, pre	35–40	80–85
1666	Loco 2-6-2, steam, O, post	50–55	125–135
1684	Loco 2-4-2, steam, O, pre	30–35	70–75
1689E	Loco 2-4-2, steam, O, pre	40–45	95–100
1835E	Loco 2-4-2, steam, Std., pre	425–450	725–750
1910	Pullman, Std., pre	500–550	1000–1100
1911	Loco 0-4-0, early, elec., Std., pre	900–1000	2000–2100
1911	Sp., Loco 0-4-4-0, elec., Std., pre	1200–1300	2500–2700
1912	Loco 0-4-4-0, elec., Std., pre	1300–1500	2700–3000
1912	Sp., Loco 0-4-4-0, elec., Std., pre	2000–2200	4750–5000
2037	Loco 2-6-4, steam, O, post	45–50	90–100
2055	Loco 4-6-4, steam, O, post	65–70	130–140
2056	Loco 4-6-4, steam, O, post	70–75	140–150
2810	Derrick, O, pre	140–150	375–395
2816	Hopper, O, pre	60–65	240–250
3357	Hydraulic Maint. Car, O, post	20–25	60–65
3409	Helicopter Car, O, post	40–45	110–120
3413	Mercury Capsule Car, O, post	60–65	145–155
3470	Target Launcher, O, post	30–35	75–80
3472	Automatic Milk Car, O, post	25–30	70–80
3510	Satellite Car, O, post	40–45	150–160
3859	Dump, O, pre	35–40	80–85

Lunch Boxes

Steel lunch boxes produced from the 1950s to the 1980s were one of the last holdouts of the lithographed metal process once prevalent in the production of toys. In order to deter sandlot warriors from injuring each other, steel boxes were discontinued in the 1980s. Soon after, they burst onto the collecting scene. Buying back a box from their youth, collectors relived grade school memories and the late summer ritual of shopping for school supplies. Collectors also love the diversity of topics represented. Many of the boxes are based on classic TV shows, and they frame their topics like small screens. Steel boxes are not the only ones sought by collectors; some of the vinyl examples are among the costliest. After a meteoric rise, the market cooled in the early '90s. However, today's growing interest in TV memorabilia is bringing in a new group of collectors.

We devised a range system for pricing. Since bottles often become separated from the box, we have given estimates for boxes and bottles separately. The prices below reflect items that are in excellent to mint condition. Rust and dents decrease the value of boxes and bottles. The "NB" designation in the bottle column means that a bottle was not produced for that particular box.

For more information consult *The Illustrated Encyclopedia of Metal Lunch Boxes* by Allen Woodall and Sean Brickell, Schiffer Publishing, West Chester, PA, 1992.

We used several abbreviations in this listing. "The" was removed from titles such as "The Munsters." We have listed distinguishing features such as *emb.* for embossed and *dome* to denote a box with a domed lid. All boxes are steel, unless *vinyl* appears in the description. Dates reflect our best approximation.

	BOX	BOTTLE
Adam-12, emb., Aladdin, 1973	$60–$80	$18–$22
Addams Family, King Seeley Thermos, 1974	80–120	30–50
America on Parade, Aladdin, 1976	15–20	5–7
Annie, The Movie, Aladdin, 1982	18–22	5–7
Apple's Way, King Seeley Thermos, 1975	30–40	8–10
Archies, emb., Aladdin, 1970	55–75	18–22
Astronaut, dome, King Seeley Thermos, 1960	120–180	40–50
Atom Ant, King Seeley Thermos, 1966	150–200	45–55
Back in '76, Aladdin, 1975	20–30	8–10
Batman, emb., Aladdin, 1966	140–180	50–60
Beatles, emb., Aladdin, 1966	300–350	90–110
Beatles Air Flite, vinyl, Air Flite, 1965	400–500	NB
Beatles Kaboodle, vinyl, Standard Plastic Products, 1965	500–700	NB
Beverly Hillbillies, emb., Aladdin, 1963	120–160	40–60
Bionic Woman, car/bk., Aladdin, 1977	25–30	8–10
Black Hole, emb., Aladdin, 1980	35–45	8–12
Bonanza, black rim, Aladdin, 1968	110–140	50–70
Bond XX, Ohio Art, 1966	130–170	NB
Bozo the Clown, Aladdin, 1964	200–250	60–80
Brady Bunch, King Seeley Thermos, 1970	200–250	50–75
Brave Eagle, King Seeley Thermos, 1955	220–260	50–80
Buccaneer, dome, Aladdin, 1957	180–220	60–90
Bullwinkle, vinyl, blue steel glass bottle, King Seeley Thermos, 1962	400–500	90–130
Bullwinkle and Rocky, steel, Universal, Landers, Frary & Clark, 1962	500–700	190–230
Captain Kangaroo, vinyl, King Seeley Thermos, 1964	200–250	40–50
Carnival, Universal, Landers, Frary & Clark, 1959	400–500	180–230
Casey Jones, dome, Universal, Landers, Frary & Clark, 1960	500–700	80–120
Charlie's Angels, emb., Aladdin, 1978	40–50	10–15
Chitty Chitty Bang Bang, King Seeley Thermos, 1969	70–90	30–40
Chuck Wagon, dome, Aladdin, 1958	120–180	60–80
Close Encounters, King Seeley Thermos, 1978	60–80	10–12

Left to right: Munsters by King Seeley; Beatles by Aladdin; Gene Autry by Universal, Landers, Frary & Clark. —Photo courtesy Collectors Auction Services.

	BOX	BOTTLE
Daniel Boone, Aladdin, 1965	90–130	40–50
Davy Crockett/Kit Carson, AL, 1955	190–210	80–100
Disney Fire Fighters, dome, Aladdin, 1969	70–90	15–20
Disney School Bus, Aladdin, 1961	30–40	12–16
Doctor Dolittle, emb., Aladdin, 1968	75–95	30–40
Dr. Seuss, emb., Aladdin, 1970	70–95	20–30
Dr. Seuss, vinyl, Aladdin, 1970	250–400	20–30
Dudley Do-Right, steel, Universal, Landers, Frary & Clark, 1962	500–800	180–240
E.T., emb., Aladdin, 1983	25–35	7–9
Eats 'n Treats, vinyl, King Seeley Thermos, 1959	180–220	30–40
Emergency, dome, Aladdin, 1977	70–90	8–12
Empire Strikes Back, King Seeley Thermos, 1980	35–45	8–12
Family Affair, King Seeley Thermos, 1969	60–80	25–30
Fat Albert and The Cosby Kids, King Seeley Thermos, 1973	25–35	5–7
Fess Parker/Daniel Boone, King Seeley Thermos, 1965	120–160	40–60
Fireball XL-5, King Seeley Thermos, 1964	120–180	40–60
Flag-O-Rama, UN flags, Universal, Landers, Frary & Clark, 1954	320–420	70–90
Flintstones, 2nd design, Aladdin, 1964	80–100	30–40
Flintstones and Dino, emb., Aladdin, 1962	80–120	35–45
Flipper, King Seeley Thermos, 1966	90–140	40–50
Flying Nun, emb., Aladdin, 1968	80–130	30–40
Fraggle Rock, King Seeley Thermos, 1984	12–15	4–6
Gene Autry, Universal, Landers, Frary & Clark, 1954	250–300	90–110
Gentle Ben, Aladdin, 1968	60–80	15–20
Get Smart, King Seeley Thermos, 1966	140–180	35–45
Girl and Poodle, vinyl, Ardee, 1960	80–100	8–12
Gomer Pyle, emb., Aladdin, 1966	90–140	30–40
Green Hornet, King Seeley Thermos, 1967	260–320	60–90
Gremlins, emb., Aladdin, 1984	12–15	4–6
Grizzly Adams, dome, Aladdin, 1978	55–75	20–30
Gunsmoke, red rim, emb., Aladdin, 1962	140–180	45–55
Gunsmoke, Splash/bk., Aladdin, 1972	50–70	18–25
Gunsmoke, Stage/bk., Aladdin, 1973	90–110	18–25
H.R. Pufnstuf, emb., Aladdin, 1970	90–110	18–22
Hair Bear Bunch, King Seeley Thermos, 1972	30–40	12–20

	BOX	BOTTLE
Happy Days, King Seeley Thermos, 1977	45–55	15–20
Hogan's Heroes, dome, Aladdin, 1966	200–250	60–80
Hopalong Cassidy, curve decal, Aladdin, 1950	100–150	40–60
Hopalong Cassidy, full picture, Aladdin, 1954	200–250	60–80
Hot Wheels, King Seeley Thermos, 1970	50–70	18–24
Indiana Jones, King Seeley Thermos, 1984	15–20	5–8
It's About Time, dome, Aladdin, 1967	190–210	50–70
James Bond–Agent 007, emb., Aladdin, 1966	180–220	50–70
Jet Patrol, Aladdin, 1957	250–300	55–75
Jetsons, dome, Aladdin, 1963	750–950	180–240
Johnny Lightning, emb., Aladdin, 1971	60–80	20–30
Kiss, King Seeley Thermos, 1979	50–70	12–20
Lance Link, King Seeley Thermos, 1971	80–120	35–45
Land of the Giants, emb., Aladdin, 1969	120–160	35–45
Laugh-In, Aladdin, 1969	90–110	20–30
Little House on the Prairie, King Seeley Thermos, 1979	35–45	7–9
Lone Ranger, Aladdin, 1954	380–420	NB
Lost in Space, emb., King Seeley Thermos, 1967	500–600	50–70
Man From U.N.C.L.E., King Seeley Thermos, 1966	120–180	50–70
Masters of the Universe, emb., Aladdin, 1983	9–14	2–3
Mickey Mouse/Donald Duck, Adco Liberty, 1954	200–250	80–100
Monkees, vinyl, King Seeley Thermos, 1967	250–300	50–70
Mork and Mindy, King Seeley Thermos, 1980	28–34	8–10
Munsters, King Seeley Thermos, 1965	150–200	50–80
Partridge Family, King Seeley Thermos, 1971	40–50	20–30
Pigs in Space, King Seeley Thermos, 1979	18–22	4–6
Planet of the Apes, emb., Aladdin, 1975	80–100	20–30
Porky's Lunch Wagon, dome, King Seeley Thermos, 1959	300–350	50–80
Red Barn, closed doors, King Seeley Thermos, 1957	50–60	18–22
Red Barn, dome, open doors, King Seeley Thermos, 1958	40–50	18–22
Return of the Jedi, King Seeley Thermos, 1983	30–40	7–9
Roy Rogers Chow Wagon, dome, King Seeley Thermos, 1958	180–240	40–60
Roy Rogers and Dale Evans, wood bk., bd., King Seeley Thermos, 1953	100–130	30–40
Roy Rogers and Dale Evans, hide/8 scns, King Seeley Thermos, 1955	80–100	30–40
Scooby Doo, King Seeley Thermos, 1973	30–40	6–8
Sesame Street, emb., Aladdin, 1980	8–12	4–5
Space: 1999, King Seeley Thermos, 1976	30–40	7–9
Space Explorer, Aladdin, 1960	300–350	60–80
Star Trek, dome, Aladdin, 1968	550–650	140–180
Star Wars, King Seeley Thermos, 1978	35–45	7–9
Stewardess, vinyl, Aladdin, 1962	300–500	40–60
Supercar, steel, Universal, Landers, Frary & Clark, 1962	200–250	90–120
Superman, metal handle, Universal, Landers, Frary & Clark, 1954	600–800	150–200
Tom Corbett Space Cadet, curve decal, Aladdin, 1952	190–230	60–70
Tom Corbett Space Cadet, full picture, Aladdin, 1954	450–500	70–90
Under Dog, steel, Okay Industries, 1973	700–900	200–250
Waltons, emb., Aladdin, 1974	25–35	4–6
Welcome Back Kotter, emb., Aladdin, 1977	28–36	4–6
Wild, Wild West, emb., Aladdin, 1969	150–200	45–55
Winnie the Pooh, vinyl, Aladdin, 1967	400–450	40–50
Yellow Submarine, King Seeley Thermos, 1969	350–450	90–130
Zorro, blue sky, Aladdin, 1958	120–160	40–60

Matchbox Toys

Leslie Smith and Rodney Smith (no relation) started Lesney Toys in England in 1947. They produced their first toys in 1948 and had a huge success with a coach produced in 1952 for the Queen's coronation in 1953. In 1953 they started producing small diecast vehicles packed in what appeared to be matchboxes. These toys are known as the 1-75 Series. They range from approximately 1.5" to 3". Lesney has produced other series over the years but the list below refers mainly to the 1-75 Series. Exceptions are the early toys which have no product number, and the Yesteryear Series, denoted by Y as the first letter in the product code. Cars in both these series are larger than those in the 1-75 series. Matchbox toys are still produced, but the Lesney name was removed in 1982.

Since the same item can be bought at a variety of locations at different prices, we devised a range system. The low range *(MNB)* covers complete, near mint to mint items without the original package. The higher range *(MIB)* reflects the prices of complete, near mint to mint items in the original near mint to mint boxes. Prices below are for complete like-new examples. Prices of scratched, chipped or altered examples are not included. Beware of high prices for poor quality. We have seen many poor condition Matchbox vehicles ranging in price from $1 to the prices listed below. In our opinion these poor condition models are worth very little unless they are extremely rare.

In the listings *sf* stands for super fast wheels and axles, a feature Lesney developed to battle Hot Wheels. For the most part, collectors prefer the regular wheels *(rw)*. The numbering system is not foolproof; sometimes a model produced for this country has a different number than the same vehicle originally sold exclusively in England. The letters that precede a number refer to a system designed by collectors to distinguish different models with the same number; the earlier the letter, the earlier the model. Because there are so many variations, exact identification can be tricky. For more information we suggest *The Encyclopedia of Matchbox Toys* by Charlie Mack, Schiffer Publishing, Atglen, PA, 1997.

	YEAR	NO.	MNB	MIB
1862 Am. General Loco.	1959	U-13-A	$35–$45	$50–$70
1909 Thomas Flyabout	1967	Y-12-B	18–22	25–35
1924 Fowler "Big Lion" Showman's Engine	1958	Y-9-A	55–65	75–85
Articulated Trailer	1980	50-F	2–3	6–8
Austin A50 Seday	1957	36-A	20–30	35–40
Austin Mk 2 Radio Truck	1959	68-A	25–35	40–50
Bedford Milk Delivery Van	1956	29-A	25–30	35–40
Bedford Tipper Truck	1957	40-A	25–35	40–50
Bedford Ton Tipper	1961	3-B	18–22	28–32
Berkley Cavalier Travel Trailer	1956	23-A	28–32	35–45
BMW M1, opening hood, LESNEY	1981	52-E	2–3	4–6
Boat and Trailer, rw.	1966	9-C	8–12	18–22
Cadillac Ambulance, rw.	1965	54-B	18–24	28–32
Cadillac Ambulance, sf.	1970	54-C	6–8	10–12
Cadillac Sedan	1960	27-C	30–35	40–50
Caterpillar Crawler	1954	18-D	22–28	32–42
Caterpillar D8, w/ red blade	1956	18-A	28–32	40–50
Caterpillar Tractor	1955	8-A	40–50	60–80
Cement Mixer	1953	3-A	32–38	45–55
Chevrolet Impala	1961	57-B	25–30	32–38
Chop Suey Motor Cycle	1973	49-D	2–3	4–67
Citroen DS19	1959	66-A	30–35	4–48
Claas Combine Harvester	1967	65-C	7–9	12–18
Commer 30 CWT Van "Nestle's"	1959	69-A	30–35	40–50
Commer Milk Truck	1961	21-C	28–32	34–38

Right: Muir Hill Site Dumper #2.

Left: Cement Mixer #3.

Right: Quarry Truck #6.

Left: London Bus #5.

Right: Massey-Harris Tractor w/ Fenders #4.

Left: MG Midget #19.

	YEAR	NO.	MNB	MIB
Conestoga Wagon, w/ barrels	1955	—	140–180	200–250
Curtis-Wright Rear Dumper	1961	K-7-A	18–24	28–34
Daimler Ambulance	1956	14-A	30–35	40–50
Dennis Fire Escape Engine, metal wheels	1955	9-A	30–40	50–60
Dodge Cattle Truck, sf.	1970	37-E	5–7	9–12
Dodge Charger	1970	52-C	5–7	9–12
Dodge Crane Truck, rw.	1968	63-C	10–14	16–22
Dodge Dump Truck, rw.	1966	48-C	12–15	18–22
Dodge Stake Truck, rw.	1967	4-D	8–10	12–16
Dodge Tractor w/ Twin Tippers	1966	K-16-A	28–32	38–44
Dodge Wreck Truck, "BP," rw.	1965	13-D	14–16	20–25
Dumper	1953	2-A	45–50	55–70
ERF 686 Truck	1959	20-B	35–45	50–60
Euclid Quarry Truck	1957	6-B	28–38	44–54
Ferrari F1 Racing Car	1962	7-B	30–36	40–46
Ford Customline Station Wagon	1957	31-A	28–34	40–50
Ford Fairlane Station Wagon	1960	31-B	25–35	35–40
Ford Galaxie Fire Chief Car, rw.	1966	59-C	10–14	18–22
Ford Galaxie Police Car	1966	55-C	15–20	25–30
Ford Mustang Fastback, rw.	1966	8-E	8–10	12–16
Ford Pickup, rw.	1968	6-D	10–14	15–20
Ford Thunderbird	1960	75-A	32–38	45–52
Ford Zodiac Convertible	1957	39-A	40–50	60–80
GMC Tipper Truck, small, sf.	1970	26-D	8–10	12–16
Harley Davidson Motorcycle Sidecar	1962	66-B	40–45	55–65
Hatra Tractor Shovel	1965	69-B	30–40	50–70
Honda Motorcycle and Trailer, rw.	1967	38-C	12–15	20–25
Honda Motorcycle and Trailer, sf.	1970	38-D	6–8	10–15
Horse-Drawn Milk Float, gray metal wheels	1954	7-A	50–65	80–100
Hot Rocker Mercury Capri	1973	67-D	5–7	9–12
Hoveringham Tipper	1963	17-C	12–18	24–32
Jaguar, 3.4 litre	1959	65-A	18–22	28–34
Jaguar, D-type	1957	41-A	35–40	45–55
Jeep Gladiator Pickup Truck	1964	71-B	18–25	28–32
Land Rover, w/ driver	1955	12-A	30–40	45–55
Leyland Royal Tiger Coach	1961	40-B	15–38	22–28
Lincoln Continental, rw.	1964	31-C	15–18	22–28
Lincoln Continental, sf.	1969	31-D	6–8	10–15
London Bus	1954	5-A	38–44	50–60
Mack Dump Truck, rw.	1968	28-D	8–12	18–22
Massey Harris Tractor, w/ fenders	1954	4-A	35–45	60–70
MG Sports Car	1956	19-A	42–48	55–65
Mobile Canteen Refreshment Bar	1959	74-A	40–45	55–65
Peterbilt Conventional	1982	49-H	4–7	6–12
Pontiac Convertible	1962	39-B	40–45	55–65
Quarry Truck	1954	6-A	38–42	50–60
Rolls Royce Silver Cloud	1958	44-A	25–35	45–65
Saracen Personnel Carrier	1959	54-A	28–32	35–55
Scammell Breakdown Truck	1959	64-A	20–25	32–38
School Bus	1985	47-H	1–2	2–3

Pez Dispensers

Pez is so American, a part of growing up from the 1950s to present day. Like most of us, Pez has its roots in a different country. Eduard Haas introduced it in 1927 in Austria. It takes its name from the German word for peppermint, *pfefferminz*. Originally sold as a breath mint/candy, it came with a handy dispenser with grip (called regulars). Pez redesigned its product for the American market in 1952. They added character heads and introduced fruit flavors. Pez became a kids' candy.

In recent years, Pez collecting has been very active. Christie's auction house even included a section of Pez in one of its sales. Collectors tend to concentrate on the head of a Pez dispenser; most do not collect based on stem or container differences. That is because heads can be switched from stem to stem. There is a feet versus no-feet controversy. Most containers have a rounded base. Some people call them shoes but they are more often referred to as no feet *(nf)*. Feet *(f)* are the bases that appeared on figures beginning around 1987. They are thin, flat, and have a stylized "V" indentation. Many collectors prescribe to the "only the head matters" theory, while others place a higher value on no-feet examples. Collectors contend that packaging for the most part does not matter since early Pez containers came in unattractive bags or boxes. The matter is harder to determine when evaluating Pez sold on blisterpacks or blistercards. We feel that original packaging will increase the value of an item, especially the more elaborate and interesting packaging. Most notable is the Stand-By-Me Pez, which must have the original packaging, including the movie poster, or it is just a Pez Pal Boy.

The prices below are for mint nonpackaged examples except where noted differently. Pez dispensers are hard to date, so the decades we suggest are only our best guess. For further reading we recommend *PEZ Collectibles* by Richard Geary, Schiffer, Atglen, PA, 1994.

	LOW	HIGH
Annie, nf, 1980s	$32	$42
Arithmetic, nf, 1960s	200	300
Arlene, f, 1980s	3	5
Astronaut A, sm. helmet, nf, 1955	150	250
Astronaut B, pointed helmet, nf, 1970s	75	100
Baloo, blue head, f, 1980s	15	20
Bambi, f, 1980s	6	12
Barney Bear, f, 1980s	10	16
Baseball Glove, ball, nf, 1960s	130	220
Baseball Glove, ball, bat, plate base, 1960s	225	350
Batgirl, soft head, nf, 1970s	60	80
Batman, w/ cape, nf, 1960s	100	150
Batman, soft head, nf, 1970s	70	100
Betsy Ross, nf, 1970s	40	75
Big Top Elephant, w/ pointed hat, nf, 1960s	50	60
Big Top Elephant, flat hat, nf, 1960s	35	55
Big Top Elephant, hair, nf, 1960s	160	300
Bouncer Beagle, f, 1990s	3	5
Bozo, cutout side, nf, 1960s	80	140
Brutus, nf, 1950s	90	150
Bullwinkle, nf, 1960s	150	200
Candy Shooter Gun, Pez on grip, 1970s	90	140
Captain, nf, 1970s	50	70
Captain America, nf, 1980s	45	65
Captain Hook, nf, 1970s	25	35
Casper, nf, 1960s	60	80
Casper, w/ "Casper" on side, nf, 1960s	80	125

	LOW	HIGH
Clown, collar, nf, 1960s	25	35
Cockatoo, nf, 1970s	0	50
Cocoa Marsh Astronaut, nf, 1950s	90	170
Cowboy, nf, 1960s	220	350
Creature From the Black Lagoon, green head, nf, 1960s	200	250
Crocodile, nf, 1960s	55	85
Daffy Duck, f, 1980s	3	5
Dalmatian Pup, f, 1980s	22	32
Daniel Boone, nf, 1970s	100	150
Dino, f 1990s	2	3
Doctor, nf, 1960s	45	65
Donald Duck, diecut face, nf, 1960s	90	120
Dopey, nf, 1960s	100	150
Droopy Dog, attached ears, f, 1980s	8	10
Eerie Spectres Air Spirit, fish head, nf, 1980s	35	50
Eerie Spectres Diabolic, nf, 1980s	35	50
Eerie Spectres Scarewolf, nf, 1980s	35	50
Eerie Spectres Spook, nf, 1980s	35	50
Eerie Spectres Vamp, nf, 1980s	50	75
Eerie Spectres Zombie, nf, 1980s	50	75
Engineer, nf, 1960s	25	38
Fireman, nf, 1960s	12	18
Fishman, looks like Black Lagoon Creature, nf, 1970s	100	150
Foghorn Leghorn, nf, 1980s	32	45
Fozzie Bear, f, 1980s	3	5
Frankenstein, nf, 1960s	175	250
Garfield, w/ smile, hat, f, 1980s	2	3
Giraffe, nf, 1960s	40	50
Girl, f, 1980s	2	4
Girl, Pez Pal, nf, 1960s	15	20
Green Hornet, nf, 1960s	200	300
Groom, nf, 1960s	150	250
Henry Hawk, f, 1980s	25	38
Hulk, f, 1990s	2	3
Hulk, nf, 1970s	20	30
Indian Brave, nf, 1970s	125	180
Indian Chief, nf, 1970s	50	75
Indian Maiden, nf, 1970s	50	80
Jerry, nf, 1990s	2	4
Jerry, inside of ears pink, nf, 1990s	15	20
Jerry (Tom and Jerry), nf, 1980s	10	18
Jiminy Cricket, nf, 1970s	30	50
Joker, soft head, nf, 1970s	75	90
Mary Poppins, nf, 1960s	325	525
Mickey Mouse, f, 1980s	3	5
Mickey Mouse D, removable nose, nf, 1970s	10	15
Olympic Snowman, 1976	200	350
One-Eye Monster, nf, 1960s	50	75
Orange, nf, 1970s	70	90
Penguin (Batman), soft head, nf, 1970s	60	90
Petunia Pig, nf, 1980s	12	16
Pilgrim, nf, 1970s	70	90
Pineapple, nf, 1970s	700	1100

	LOW	HIGH
Psychedelic Eye, hand holding eye, nf, 1960s	300	400
Regular, w/ advertising, 1950s	275	450
Road Runner, nf, 1980s	1	5
Santa, full body, 1950s	150	200
Santa, w/ small head, painted face, nf, 1950s	100	150
Snoopy, f, 1980s	3	5
Snowman, nf, 1990s	2	4
Space Trooper, full body, 1950s	300	400
Spaceman, nf, 1950s	90	130
Spike (bulldog), nf, 1980s	10	25
Stand-By-Me, must be MIP, 1980s	170	250
Sylvester, nf, 1980s	2	4
Tinkerbell, nf, 1980s	75	125
Tom C (Tom and Jerry), f, 1990s	2	4
Uncle Scrooge McDuck, nf, 1980s	8	12
Wile E. Coyote, nf, 1980s	18	25
Witch, 1-pc. head, emb. stem, nf, 1950s	125	175
Wolfman, nf, 1960s	200	300
Wounded Soldier, nf, 1970s	90	150
Zorro, nf, 1960s	30	50
Zorro, w/ Zorro logo on side, nf, 1960s	75	100

Selection of Pez Dispensers.

Playing Cards

Over the past fifteen years, interest in collecting playing card decks has grown considerably.

Since their introduction in Europe some six centuries ago, many thousands of different designs have adorned playing cards. But because most decks of cards get used and tossed away, complete packs of some issues are exceedingly rare.

The 52-card pack of spades, hearts, diamonds and clubs, introduced by French printers, has become the international standard. Other deck arrangements, still being published today, are the Italian and Spanish traditional suits (swords, batons, cups and coins), and the German-suited packs (leaves, hearts, acorns and bells). Rare and desirable packs of all traditions command quite high prices.

Earliest packs were cut with square corners, and usually lacked any design on their cardbacks. After 1875, cards with rounded corners became the norm, as back designs became elaborate. Corner symbols, known as indexes (or indices), became standard about 110 years ago. Even today, packs are usually undated. However, the spade ace and joker cards may yield useful information.

Besides innovative design variants, card decks have cultural relevancy: Advertising, souvenir, entertainment, commemorative, political and transportation-related packs are a few examples.

Maximum value goes to packs that are complete, including Joker (first introduced about 125 years ago) and still with original box or wrapper. Except for the rarest of packs, value seriously declines when cards are damaged, soiled or missing. Among older packs, "wide" (2.5" x 3.5") is valued over "narrow" or "bridge" size (2.25" x 3.5").

In purchasing playing cards, you'll find prices fluctuate greatly. For the lucky and knowledgeable buyer, valuable decks can still be found at small cost. Reproductions of interesting old packs will have a bit of value, but don't mistake them for the real thing.

Our consultant for this area is David Galt, owner of Games and Names. He is listed in the back of this book.

	LOW	AVG.	HIGH
'53 Vargas Girls, Creative Card Co., St. Louis, by famed pin-up artist, 1955	$70	$100	$150
Allied Armies, Montreal Litho. Co., several different editions, shows Allied leaders of WWI, 1915–17	250	300	350
American Indian Souvenir, Lazarus & Melzer, oval photos on faces, blanket on back, 1900	100	150	250
Anti-Religions, made in USSR, world religions mildly lampooned, 1928	200	500	800
Bezique, Samuel Hart, 32 cards, square corners, 1865	100	200	300
Bicycle, U.S. Playing Card Co., depending on Joker and back design, pre-1915	20	36	500
Black Velvet, double deck, Heublein Liquor advertising, red and white suits on black background, 1974	10	16	22
Bowl Up, Creative Sales Co., St. Louis, 1954	15	22	30
Brown Derby, Brown & Bigelow, Hollywood star caricature on every card, 1950	35	55	75
Bud Light, Spuds MacKenzie	10	15	20
C&O Rail Road, wide size, oval souvenir photos on each card (several versions), 1900	50	100	150
Canadian Pacific, blue, logo, checkered flags	10	25	40
Canary Islands, Fournier, Spain, souvenir photos on each card, 1959	20	30	40
Century of Progress, 1933/34 Chicago World's Fair, depending on style and advertising	20	60	100
Cir-Q-Lar, Waddington's, London, round cards, 1930	10	17	25
Coca-Cola, first Coke advertising pack, 1907	1000	2000	3000

	LOW	AVG.	HIGH
Coca-Cola Spotter, airplane silhouettes on each card, Coke services gal on backs, 1943	50	80	125
Comic Political, A.H. Caffee, Cleveland kayoing Harrison, 1888	1000	1200	1400
Comic Political, A.H. Caffee, Harrison kayoing Cleveland, 1888	700	750	800
Congress 606, U.S. Playing Card Co., wide, "named" backs, depending on subject, 1899–1918	10	65	300
Culbertson's Own, Russell, NY bridge tips in card margins, 1932	15	22	30
DeLand's Automatic, S.S. Adams, NJ, marked cards, depending on age and design, 1913–50	20	50	75
Eagle-Picher White Lead, advertising, double deck, Eagle Joker, 1929	20	65	110
Eagles, Lawrence & Cohen, NY, ornate, "illuminated," lots of gold, 1865	700	1550	2400
Fauntleroy, miniature cards by U.S. Playing Card Co., 1910–30	10	22	35
Goldwater Campaign Pack, AuH20 backs, Goldwater on face cards, 1964	35	45	60
Great Northern Pacific, steamship souvenir photos of ship and snowy Northwest, 1900	200	400	600
Green Spade Tarot, August Petrtyl, 78 cards, Native American theme, 1922	250	775	1200
Hard-A-Port Tobacco Insert Cards, pin-ups acquired card by card, several versions, complete pack, 1890	700	1100	1500
Harlequin, Tiffany & Co., comic transformation pack, 1879	800	1400	2000
Hart's Linen Eagle, Sam'l Hart, Phila. & NY, Faro cards, no indices, 1880-1910	75	150	200
Hercules Buggy, advertising, wide, horses and buggy Joker, Hercules back, 1914	200	250	300
Jack Daniels, oversize nostalgia pack, square corners, metal box, 1972	5	12	20
Jeffries Championship, W.P. Jeffries Co., Pittsburgh, boxing photos, 1909	600	1000	1500
Johnson's Gulf Service, nude with hatbox, early 1950s	10	14	18
Kem Double Deck, Kem Playing Card Co., Poughkeepsie, NY, plastic cards, 1935	10	20	30
Laugh-In, Stancraft, MN., TV's Rowan and Martin and wisecracks, 1969	25	37	50
Le Florentin, Philibert, France, provocative designs, 1955	100	175	250
Maxfield Parrish, Parrish designed several for Edison Mazda, depending on condition and illus., 1930–40	100	350	600

Coca-Cola advertising decks. —Photo courtesy Collectors Auction Service.

	LOW	AVG.	HIGH
Medieval, New York Consolidated Card Co., Art Nouveau King, Queen, and Jack, 1897	450	1025	1600
Movie Souvenir, Moriarty, NY, different movie star on each card, Charlie Chaplin Joker, 1916	85	115	150
M.V. Card, superb advertising and transformation pack for Murphy Varnish, 1883	1000	2250	3500
Nile Fortune Telling	16	30	42
O'Callaghan City of Chicago, w/ booklet, 1930	100	165	225
Pan-American 1901 Exposition, Aluminum Mfg. Co., Wisc. Alum. pack and case, Buffalo Joker	800	1250	2000
Pep Boys Pinochle, 48 cards and extra card, Manny, Moe, and Jack on backs	20	32	45
Picturesque Canada, photo scenes on cards for Canadian Pacific Railway, several versions, 1900–10	25	85	150
Royal Caribbean, blue, anchors and ships	10	12	15
Royal Revelers, anti-prohibition, double deck, Mr. Bluenose Joker, Merry Cards, 1932	100	200	300
Seminole Wars, J.Y. Humphries, Philadelphia, 1819	2000	9000	16,000
Stag Party Pack, suggestive cartoons on slightly oversizd cards, 1953	20	30	40
Standard 52-Card Pack, Hunt, England, one-way courts, 1850	125	235	350
Steamboats, depending on maker, Joker, prices pre-1910 only	50	175	300
Triplicate Playing Cards, Andrew Dougherty, tiny cards as corner indices, 1869–76	150	325	500
Union Playing Cards, American Card Co., Benjamin Hitchcock, new patriotic suits, 1862	700	1050	1400
Union Playing Cards, American Card Co., Benjamin Hitchcock, new patriotic suits, w/ background, 1862	450	675	900
United Airlines, "Fly the Friendly Skies," aqua	7	10	12
Vanity Fair, U.S. Playing Card Co., first transormation pack, 1895	225	455	700
Votes for Women, Woman Suffrage Publishing Co., NY, promotes women's vote, 1910	250	400	550
W.C. Fields, movie shots on each card, cheating booklet, 1971	10	20	30
World's Fair Souvenir, 1893 Colombian Expostion	150	225	300

Hard-A-Port Tobacco Insert Cards, c1890.

Premiums

The excitement of getting a prize or an extra gift is a temptation for consumers. Combining this with a child's favorite radio, comic book or television hero creates a powerful inducement to purchase. Premiums gained momentum in the radio days of the Great Depression. Cereal, soap and other companies hosted programs; in turn radio Orphan Annie, Captain Midnight, the Lone Ranger and others promoted the host's product. When television replaced radio, many programs made the switch as well. These personalities induced young viewers with mail-in offers for membership packages, decoder rings, books, badges and toys. Other premiums were included with the package and occasionally offered at the store.

Collectors actively seek these items. They collect a range of items basing their collection on characters or types of items like decoders or rings. In recent years astounding prices have been paid for rare premium rings. Collectors are also seeking newer premiums from the 1960s and 1970s. Quisp and Quake items are currently very popular. The presence of original packaging and instructional materials increases the prices of premiums, so don't throw them away. Premiums are still used as sales inducements, mainly by the cereal industry. Prices below are for items in excellent to near mint condition. Each entry contains the character who promoted the product, a brief description of the premium, the date of issue and the company who made the product.

For further reading see *Hake's Price Guide to Character Toys, 2nd Edition* by Ted Hake, Gemstone Publishing, Timonium, MD, 1998, distributed by Avon Books and *Overstreet Premium Ring Price Guide, Third Edition* by Robert M. Overstreet, Gemstone Publishing, Timonium, MD, 1997.

	LOW	HIGH
Admiral Byrd, Map of 2nd Antarctic Expedition, stiff cardboard, General Foods, 1933	$70	$100
Archie, plastic head bobber w/ spring, Post Cereals, 1969	8	15
Big Boy, club button, litho, Big Boy Restaurants, 1960s	7	12
Blondie, Comic Togs button, fashion manuf., 1947	40	60
Bobby Benson, code rule, cardboard, Hecker-H-O, 1935	100	150
Bozo, peanut butter glass (1 of 5), 1965	8	12
Buck Rogers Ring of Saturn ring, Post, 1930s	525	825
Buck Rogers, Wilma pendant, Cream of Wheat, 1930s	80	120
Cap'N Crunch, button, Quaker, 1965	20	30
Cap'N Crunch, figural bank, Quaker, 1966	80	100
Cap'N Crunch, figural ring, Quaker, 1963	225	325
Cap'N Crunch, Jean Lefoot figural bank, Quaker, 1966	70	90
Cap'N Crunch Oath of Allegiance, Quaker, 1964	35	45
Cap'N Crunch, Sea Cycle, Quaker, 1965	25	45
Cap'N Crunch, Ship Shake, Quaker, 1968	25	45
Captain Marvel, pinback button, Comic, 1940s	45	65
Captain Marvel, Rocket Raider compass ring, Comic, 1946	2000	3000
Captain Midnight, decoder, 1957	300	350
Captain Midnight, membership card, 1939	60	80
Captain Midnight, Mirro-Flash Code-O-Graph, Ovaltine, 1946	180	220
Captain Midnight, mug, Ovaltine, 1940s	50	70
Captain Midnight, Mystic Sun God ring, Ovaltine, 1947	1600	3000
Captain Midnight, Secret Squadron decoder badge, 1955	180	240
Captain Midnight, Secret Squadron membership manual, Ovaltine, 1941	100	170
Captain Midnight, shake-up mug, Ovaltine, 1947	100	170
Captain Video, flying saucer ring, w/ 2 saucers, Powerhouse, 1950s	800	1200
Captain Video, Mystocoder instruction folder, TV, 1950s	100	150
Captain Video, photo ring, Powerhouse, 1950s	200	300
Charlie McCarthy, diecut cardboard figure, Chase and Sanborn, 1938	80	120

Captain Tim Healy, Ivory Stamp Club album (front and back covers), 72 pages, 1934, Ivory Soap, $30–$50. —Photo courtesy Ray Morykan Auctions.

	LOW	HIGH
Charlie McCarthy, spoon, Chase and Sanborn, 1938	30	40
Crackle, rubber head ring, Rice Crispies, 1950s	300	400
Death Valley Days, booklet, Story of Death Valley, 24 pages, Borax, 1931	35	45
Dick Tracy, pocket flashlight, Quaker Oats, 1939	100	150
Dizzy Dean, Winners Club membership pin, Post Cereal, 1930s	60	90
Droopy Dog, popping head figure, General Mills, 1960	30	40
Eddie Cantor, trick cards and instructions, Pobeco Toothpaste, 1935	30	40
Fibber McGee and Molly, cast photo, Johnson Wax, 1940s	25	35
Flash, flash pinback button, Comic, 1943	1000	2000
Flash Gordon, movie serial button, Theater, 1930s	400	600
Frank Buck, Ivory initial ring, Ivory Soap, 1939	300	400
Funny Face, Chug-A-Lug mug, Funny Face, 1960s	15	20
Funny Face, walkers, Funny Face, 1960s	80	100
Green Hornet, seal ring, General Mills, 1966	18	22
Green Hornet, secret compartment glow-in-the-dark ring, General Mills, 1947	900	1200
Hopalong Cassidy, Savings Club folder, Savings and Loan, 1950s	40	60
Howdy Doody, pinback button, TV, 1950s	40	70
Junior Detective, Junior Detective Corps captain badge, Post Toasties, 1933	40	60
Linus the Lionhearted, stuffed doll, Post, 1965	40	60
Lone Ranger, blackout kit, 1943	150	200
Lone Ranger, membership badge, Silver-Cup Bread, 1935	60	90
Lone Ranger, movie film ring w/ film, Cheerios, 1948	150	200
Lone Ranger, secret compartment ring, 2 photos, Kix, 1945	600	900
Lone Ranger, secret compartment ring, 1 photo, Kix, 1945	350	450
Lone Ranger, silver bullet/compass, Cheerios, 1947	50	70
Lone Ranger, six-shooter gun ring, Kix, 1947	100	150
Lone Wolf, manual, 32 pages, Wrigley Gum, 1932	100	150
Mandrake the Magician, figural membership button, Taystee Bread, 1934	100	150
Mary Poppins, chimney toy, Kellogg's, 1964	80	100
Melvin Purvis, badge, Post Toasties, 1936	60	90
Melvin Purvis, Sacred Scarab ring, Post, 1937	1000	1500
Orphan Annie, 6 diecut cardboard shadowettes, 1938	90	140
Orphan Annie, pin, Ovaltine, 1934	50	70
Orphan Annie, pin, Ovaltine, 1935	50	70

	LOW	HIGH
Orphan Annie puzzle, Ovaltine, 1933	60	80
Orphan Annie, Secret Guard magnifying ring, 1940s	2200	3200
Orphan Annie Secret Society manual, Ovaltine, 1940	200	300
Orphan Annie, shake-up mug #1, full figure, 1931	50	70
Orphan Annie, shake-up mug #2, bust figure, Ovaltine, 1935	50	70
Orphan Annie, shake-up mug #3, Annie dancing, Ovaltine, 1938	80	120
Orphan Annie, shake-up mug #4, jumping rope, Ovaltine, 1939	80	120
Orphan Annie, sunburst decoder pin, Ovaltine, 1937	80	100
Pop, rubber head ring, Rice Crispies, 1950s	300	500
Quake, Earth Digger car, Quaker, 1965	150	200
Quaker, figural ring, Quaker, 1966	400	600
Quisp, friendship ring, Quaker, 1966	1000	1500
Quisp, meteorite ring, Quaker, 1960s	300	400
Quisp, unicycler, Quaker, 1969	80	100
Rootie Kazootie, club button, 1950s	30	40
Rootie Kazootie, Lucky Spot Seal ring, 1950s	350	650
Roy Rogers, badge/whistle, Quaker, 1950	80	100
Roy Rogers, branding iron ring, black cap, Quaker, 1948	180	220
Roy Rogers, figural mug, plastic, Quaker, 1950	35	55
Roy Rogers, postcard, Quaker, 1949	20	30
Roy Rogers, two 45 rpm record set, 1950s	80	100
Sekatary Hawkins, membership card, oath on back, Ralston, 1932	30	50
Sgt. Preston, celluloid membership button, Quaker, 1950s	800	1600
Sgt. Preston, totem pole set, Quaker, 1950s	70	90
Shadow, black stone crocodile ring, Carey Salt, 1947	700	1000
Shadow, blue coal glow-in-the-dark ring, Blue Coal, 1941	400	600
Shadow, matchbook, Blue Coal, 1930s	80	100
Sky King, Detectowriter, Peter Pan, 1950	90	130
Sky King, microscope, Peter Pan, 1947	100	150
Sky King, Navaho treasure ring, Peter Pan, 1950	180	220
Sky King, secret signal scope, Peter Pan, 1947	100	150
Sky King, Teleblinker ring, TV, 1940s	150	200
Smokey Bear, soaky bottle, Colgate, 1965	15	22
Snap, rubber head ring, Rice Crispies, 1950s	200	250
Superman Tim, membership button, 1950	45	65
Ted Williams, figural ring w/ ball on wire, Nabisco, 1948	800	1000
Tom Mix, badge, Ralston, 1945	70	90
Tom Mix, bandanna, Ralston, 1933	80	100
Tom Mix, book, *Trail of the Terrible Six,* Ralston, 1935	25	35
Tom Mix, brass compass magnifier, Ralston, 1940	90	130
Tom Mix, ID bracelet, Ralston, 1947	90	110
Tom Mix, illustrated manual, 24 pages, Ralston, 1933	50	70
Tom Mix, paper face mask of Tom, 1930s	200	400
Tom Mix, six-gun decoder, Ralston, 1941	90	110
Tom Mix, Straight Shooter bangle bracelet, Ralston, 1930s	80	100
Tom Mix, telephone set, Ralston, 1938	100	150
Trix, rabbit mug and bowl, General Mills, 1963	30	40
Winnie the Pooh, plastic spoon hanger, Nabisco, 1965	15	20
Wizard of Oz, Ozma, The Little Wizard Book, Jell-O, 1933	60	90
Woody Woodpecker, cup and log cereal bowl, Kellogg's, 1965	40	60
Woody Woodpecker, plastic cup, Kellogg's, 1965	10	15
Yogi Bear, Yogi Bear for President button, 1964	25	45

Robots and Space Toys

The word robot is derived from "robata" for forced labor. Robot first appeared in the 1921 play *R.U.R.* by Czechoslovakian playwright Karl Capek. It was not until the futuristic 1950s that robots really hit their stride, when toy robots and spacecraft started to appear. Although some were made in the United States (by firms such as Marx, Remco and Ideal) and Germany, the majority were produced in Japan. Friction drives and keywind mechanisms were employed but battery power increased the complexity of the toy. With batteries, metal monsters and spaceships could twirl, spin, light up, roll backwards, change directions and perform a multitude of other tricks. Collectors call this "action" and it attracts them to these toys.

Most of the toys listed below are Japanese lithographed tinplate with battery power and were produced in the 1950s and 1960s. We have noted when the predominant material is something other than tinplate and when a toy is friction or keywind, otherwise assume that it is battery operated. The abbreviation *rc* refers to remote control.

When collecting these toys beware of condition; make sure there are no missing parts, including remote controls, battery boxes or antennas. Make sure there is no restoration; battery boxes should be checked closely. Never leave a battery in a toy; it can leak and cause damage. The prices below are for mint without box (MNB) and mint in the box (MIB) examples. Rust, scratches and restoration will lower these prices.

In recent years astronomical prices achieved for rare items (over $25,000 at auction for a Robby Space Patrol car) have encouraged people to create new robots such as the Robby Space Patrol, Mr. Atomic and the Rosko Astronauts. Some of these toys are incredible reproductions of the original toy, right down to the box. Other robots are old style new products. Be sure of what you are buying. Robots are listed either by the name that appears on the original box or the name coined by collectors. Different robots often have the same or similar names. To clarify things, we have listed reference numbers after the name. The B# refers to *Robot–Robots et autres Fusees d'vant la lune,* Pierre Boogaerts, Futuropolis, Paris, 1978. The K# refers to *Robots, Tin Toy Dreams,* Teruhisa Kitahara, Chronicle Books, CA, 1985.

	MNB	MIB
Acrobat, K#119, blue, yellow, and red plastic, 10" h	$100–$150	$250–$350
Action Planet Robot, B#292, keywind Robby-style, black and red, w/ sparking mechanism, Yoshiya, 9" h	180–220	300–500
Answer Game Machine, K#105, multicolor w/ buttons for calculations, Ichida, 14" h	600–800	900–1500
Apollo 11 Eagle Lunar Module, B#68, w/ 7 automatic actions, Daishin, for Mego, 8" h	80–140	220–320
Apollo 11 Moon Rocket, friction, Ashai, 14" h	40–60	90–130
Astro Captain, B#210, keywind, Mego, 6" h	70–90	150–220
Astronaut w/ Child's Head, K#65, blue, similar to the red Cragstan Astronaut, Daiya, 12" h	700–900	1000–1500
Atom Boat, B#124, friction, Chinese, 10" l	80–120	200–250
Atomic Robot Man, K#81, keywind, boiler plate style, litho w/ diecast hands	400–600	700–1300
Atomic Rocket, B#92, push-lever action, w/ side fins displaying Saturn and star motif, Masudaya, 6" l	150–200	300–400
Attacking Martian, B#191, rotomatic, w/ guns in hinged door chest, 12" h	150–200	300–350
Battery Operated Tractor, similar to K#112, red and black w/ 1200 plaque on battery case, Nomura, 7" l	400–600	700–900
Big Loo Moon Robot, Marx, 38" h	600–800	1000–1500
Blink-A-Gear Robot, B#7, black w/ transparent chest panel housing rotating gears, Taiyo, 14" h	500–700	900–1300
Blue Rosko Astronaut, B#230, Rosko Toys, 13" h	900–1300	1500–2200

Left to right: Answer Game Machine (K#105); Gear Robot (K#50); Mr. Atomic (K#114).

	MNB	MIB
Bulldozer w/ Robot Operator, similar to B#144, silver robot on blue and red dozer, 9" l	200–300	500–700
Busy Cart Robot, B#269, black and yellow w/ hardhat and wheelbarrow, Horikawa, 12" h	700–900	1000–1500
Capsule 7, B#188, w/ rotating astronaut, Masudaya, 10" l	60–90	120–180
Chime Trooper, K#137, keywind, boy astronaut plays music, Aoshin, 9.5" h	1200–1500	2000–3000
Circus 8 Car, B#154, friction, clown robot driving Circus 8 Mercedes, Ashai, 8" l	600–900	1200–1600
Colonel Hap Hazard, B#61, astronaut in white NASA spacesuit w/ whirling copter blade, Marx, 11" h	800–1000	1200–1800
Cragstan X-07 Space Surveillant, B#108, oval-shaped flying saucer w/ astronaut pilot under bubble dome, Masudaya, 9" l	70–90	150–200
Cragstan's Mr. Robot, K#25, red body, litho chest panel, swiveling domed head, Yonezawa, 11" h	450–650	800–900
Dino Robot, K#97, robot head folds down to reveal roaring dinosaur, Horikawa, 11" h	500–700	900–1400
Driving Robot, K#74, keywind, robot-driven auto swing, 6" h	300–500	600–900
Dux Astroman, Western Germany, green plastic astroman w/ radar antenna over clear dome, white head w/ red features, rock crushing action, rc, 14" h	1200–1500	2000–3000
Earth Man, K#144, tan astronaut, silver helmet, sounding and blinking gun, rc, Nomura, 9" h	700–900	1200–1800
Engine Robot, B#2, keywind, sparks and gears in chest window panel, 9" h	180–220	300–400
Engine Robot, B#213, gray w/ whirling gears in see–through chest panel, Horikawa, 9" h	100–150	200–300
Fighting Space Man, B#159, chest panel w/ swiveling gun and litho circuitry, Horikawa, 12" h	100–150	200–300
Fighting Space Man, B#159, yellow w/ domed astronaut's head, Horikawa, 12" h	200–250	300–400
Firebird Space Patrol, K#57, similar to Sonicon Rocket, finished in green and red, Masudaya, 14" l	300–400	500–700

Left to right: Television Spaceman (B#217); Dino Robot (K#97); Mighty Robot (K#23); Mighty 8 Robot. —Photo courtesy James D. Julia.

	MNB	MIB
Flying Jeep, circular vehicle on wheels, KKS, 3" h	70–90	120–180
Forbidden Planet Robby the Robot Talking Figure, hard plastic, Masudaya, c1980s, 15" h	90–140	180–230
Forklift Robot, B#270, yellow w/ red cap, plastic forklift and crate, Horikawa, 11.5" h	1000–1500	1800–2400
Friendship 7-Space Capsule, B#95, friction, interior floating astronaut, Horikawa, 9" l	50–70	100–140
Gear Robot, K#50, chest window gear display and speed control switch on head, 11" h	120–180	250–350
Great Garloo, green plastic, Marx, c1961, 18" h	250–350	500–700
Hi-Bouncer Moon Scout, K#63, silver astronaut w/ copter blade, shoots balls from chest, rc, Marx Toys, 12" h	1000–1500	2000–3000
High Wheel Robot, K#32, blue w/ red feet, see-through chest panel, moving gears, rc, Yoshiya, 9" h	400–500	700–1100
Hysterical Robot, K#128, plastic, laughs and grins, 13" h	100–150	250–350
Interplanetary Space Fighter, tinplate vehicle w/ retractable side fins, Nomura, 12" l	200–300	400–500
Jumping Rocket, B#251, keywind, robot rocket w/ feet, 6" l	100–150	250–350
King Jet Racer, B#119, friction, light blue, bubble dome w/ driver, 12" l	200–300	500–700
Krome Dome, K#131, multicolor plastic w/ clam-shaped head and accordion torso, Yonezawa, 10" h	60–80	120–180
Laughing Robot, plastic, clown head, 14" h	150–180	200–300
Lavender Robot, K#28, a.k.a. Nonstop Robot, lavender w/ lithographed machinery panels and gauges, masudaya, 14" h	3000–4500	5000–8000
Lighted Space Vehicle, B#226, blue car w/ domed cockpit, astronaut, and floating ball action, Masydaya, 9" l	90–140	200–300
Man Made Satellite, B#109, litho base w/ signal missile, Mars, Earth w/ satellite, Hoku, 7" l	200–250	400–600
Man in Space, tinplate and celluloid astronaut, rc, Alps	100–200	600–900
Mars King or Tank Robot, K#133, w/ side-mounted tracks and TV screen in chest, Horikawa, 9" h	150–200	300–400
Martian Supersensitive Radar Patrol, friction, Jeep, 9" l	700–900	1400–2000

	MNB	MIB
Space Car, B#40, robot driver and floating ball, Yonezawa, 8" l	1000–1500	2200–3200
Space Chick, B#271, keywind, Yone, 3" h	80–120	150–200
Space Dog, K#106, keywind, silver w/ spark window, Yoshiya, 6.5" l	500–600	800–1000
Space Dog, K#106, friction, red w/ spark window, Yoshiya, 6.5" l	500–600	800–1000
Space Explorer, K#104, gray, initially square, raises to reveal head, arms, and 3-D TV screen, Yonezawa, 12" h open size	500–700	800–1400
Space Fighter Rocket Car, B#183, friction, blue, red, and yellow w/ 2 pilots and sparking mechanism, 18.5" l	700–1000	1200–3000
Space Giant, B#13, saucer, gray and red w/ domed cockpit (largest flying saucer toy), 12" dia	700–900	1200–1500
Space Giant Robot, K#118, charcoal w/ red accents, pop-out guns, Horikawa, 16" h	100–150	200–300
Space Guard MS-61, B#257, space tank w/ dual spring-loaded rockets, rc, Masudaya, 9.5" l	180–220	300–400
Space Patrol, B#239, helmeted driver w/ firing gun, 9" h	100–150	200–350
Space Patrol Car, B#82, astronaut driver w/ lighting fun, Nomura, 9.5" h	200–300	400–600
Space Patrol X-11, B#206, green w/ hinged door cockpit, Yonezawa, 8.5" l	40–60	70–90
Space Sight Seeing Bus, B#285, V-shaped astro bus, domed cockpit w/ lithographed pilots and passengers, 13" l	150–200	500–700
Space Tank, B#227, bubble dome w/ radar shield and astronaut pilot, Masudaya, 8" l	70–90	180–220
Space Trip, B#121, racing game similar to Terre a la Lune, Masudaya, 19" l	200–250	400–600
Space Whale, K Yesterday of Toys #85, keywind, space blue w/ Saturn motif, Yoshiya, 8" l	500–700	1000–1500
Spaceman, B#175, astronaut in silver suit w/ red leggings, white helmet w/ head lamp, flashlight, and gun, rc, 8.5" h	700–1000	1200–1600
Spaceship X-11, B#161, saucer w/ 2 tinplate pilots and floating spaceman, Masudaya, 8" dia	50–65	80–120
Sparky Robot, K#84, keywind, silver and red, 6" h	180–240	350–500
Star Strider Robot, red and gray, guns in hinged chest, Horikawa, 11" h	100–150	200–250
Strolling Space Station, keywind, Yone, 3.5" dia	50–80	120–180
Swinging Baby Robot, K#72, mechanical tot in keywind swing, Yonezawa, 6" h	200–300	400–600
Target Robot, B#278, a.k.a. Shooting Game Robot, purple w/ red target on chest, w/ darts, Masudaya, 14" h,	4000–5500	8000–15,000
Television Robot, K#52, robot head, double loop antenna, TV in chest, Horikawa, 12" h	100–150	200–250
Television Spaceman, B#196, keywind, TV screen chest, Alps, 6" h	80–100	150–220
Television Spaceman, B#217, gray, plastic legs, TV screen chest, Alps, 10" h	300–500	600–900
Terra Lune, B#120, keywind race to the moon toy, Technofix, German, c1947, 18" l	500–700	800–1200
Tetsujin 28-GO, K#218, keywind, purple armor, moveable arms, Nomura, 10" h	400–600	700–900
Thor Delta 54, B#141, friction, connected capsule, Daiya, 12" h	80–100	150–200
Train Robot, K Yesterday of Toys #28, a.k.a. Sonic Robot, red and black, w/ siren, Masudaya, 14" h	2500–4000	6000–9000
Traveling Sam the Peace Corps Man, keywind, stars and stripes litho body w/ global wheels and flapping jaw, Sy Toy, 7" h	120–160	250–400
Tremendous Mike, K#36, keywind, gray w/ red arms and bolt-headed shoulders, Aoshin, 10" h	700–900	1200–1800

Left to right: King Jet Racer (B#119); X-5 Space Vehicle; Space Patrol Car (B#82). —Photo courtesy Sotheby's.

	MNB	MIB
Twirly Whirly Rocket Ride, K#165, 2 rockets orbiting tripod base, Alps, 12" h	200–300	500–800
Two-Stage Earth Satellite, B#54, tinplate rocket w/ crankwind base, Linemar, 9" l	180–220	300–500
Two-Stage Rocket Launching Pad, B#102, technician at control panel screen, w/ silo and 2 rockets, Nomura, 7.5" h	300–400	500–800
U.N. Planet Cruiser 751, B#106, light-up rotary engine, 10" l	180–220	300–400
UFO X-5 Flying Saucer, Masudaya, 7" dia	50–70	80–120
Ultra Man, K#197, gray and green, removable mask, Bull Mark, 13" h	300–400	500–750
Ultra Man Leo, K#200, keywind, red body, green vinyl head, Bull Mark, 9" h	400–600	700–900
Unit 5 Area Radiation Tester Vehicle, B#107, Sears exclusive, 19.5" l	200–300	400–600
Universe Car, B#189, blue w/ plastic fins and light–up bubble dome, Chinese, 10" l	80–120	150–200
Uran, K#188, keywind, tinplate body w/ vinyl head (Uran is the younger sister of Tetsuwan Atom), Nomura/Bandai, 8.5" h	500–700	800–1100
V-2 Space Tank, K#159, Robby-style robot driver, Yoshiya, 6.5" l	60–80	100–150
Voyage a la Lune, friction, rocket ship on perforated steel band, Gunthermann, 7" l	180–220	300–400
Wheel-A-Gear Robot, K#31, similar to Blink-A-Gear Robot, belt-driven gears, retractable antenna on back, Taiyo, 14" h	1000–1500	1800–2200
Wind-Up Moon Astronaut, B#179, red w/ blue helmet, gun in right hand, Daiya, 9" h	700–900	1800–2200
Winkie, keywind, gray tinplate w/ red feet, 3-D winking eyes, meter on chest, Yonezawa, 9" h	450–550	700–900
Winner-23, B#185, jet-style vehicle, domed cockpit, 6" l	80–120	200–300
Wizard of Oz Tin Man Robot, silver and blue plastic, Remco, 21" h	80–140	180–220
X-5 Space Vehicle, litho light blue and red tank-form vehicle w/ rotating antenna and astronaut gunner on rotating emplacement, 9" l	400	600
X-9 Space Robot Car, K#58, robot-driven green car w/ bubble dome w/ pop-up balls, Masudaya, 7" l	1200–1800	2000–3000
X-25 Robot, keywind, round human head and oversized glasses, Daiya, 7" h	80–120	180–220
X-70 Space Robot, K#121, petals open to TV camera and screen, 12" h	800–1200	1500–200
X-80 Planet Explorer, B#96, saucer w/ light-up central dome, 8" dia	40–60	70–90

Schoenhut

Albert Schoenhut began production of the Humpty & Dumpty Circus at his Philadelphia toy company in 1903. Advertised as "The World's Most Popular Toy," the animals and people are valued today for their lively representations and charm.

Our consultant for this area is Judith Lile (she is listed at the back of this book).

In the following listings the designation *NA* means that the animal was not produced in that style. Collectors look for pieces whose condition is as close to original as possible; some paint or fabric wear and missing ears or tails are considered minor flaws, but repaints, touch-ups or replaced clothing affect the prices more significantly.

Cracker-Jack Clown from Humpty & Dumpty Circus, $743 at auction. —Photo courtesy Gene Harris Antique Auction Center.

Animals

	PAINTED EYES			GLASS EYES			REDUCED SIZE		
	Fair	Good	Exc.	Fair	Good	Exc.	Fair	Good	Exc.
Alligator	$200	$300	$375	$350	$500	$650	—	NA	—
Buffalo, carved mane	200	300	400	600	900	1400	$250	$325	$400
Buffalo, cloth mane	—	NA	—	450	575	650	—	NA	—
Bulldog	400	600	750	700	1100	1600	—	NA	—
Burro	200	300	350	300	375	450	—	NA	—
Camel, 1 hump	275	325	400	350	475	600	—	NA	—
Camel, 2 humps	200	300	375	900	1300	1600	225	325	400
Cat	800	1100	1500	1500	2000	2500	—	NA	—
Cow	300	400	500	400	650	850	—	NA	—
Deer	300	500	700	600	900	1200	—	NA	—
Donkey	75	100	125	100	150	200	60	80	100
Elephant	95	150	175	125	200	275	75	100	125
Gazelle	1000	1200	1500	1200	1800	2400	—	NA	—
Giraffe	275	350	500	400	500	600	275	350	425
Goose	275	375	500	—	NA	—	—	NA	—
Gorilla	2000	2800	3400	—	NA	—	—	NA	—
Hippopotamus	275	350	450	350	500	600	300	350	400
Horse, brown	125	200	250	225	325	400	75	125	150
Horse, white	150	200	275	225	325	400	75	125	150
Hyena	1100	1500	1800	1800	2800	3800	—	NA	—

Left: Full size and reduced size Ring Masters and Lady Circus Riders (some redressed), painted eye buffalo w/ carved mane, glass eye bulldog, and painted eye lion w/ carved mane.

Right: Clown w/ 2-part face, Trapeze Acrobat w/ bisque head, Bareback Rider w/ bisque head, Lion Tamer w/ bisque head, (some redressed); Polar Bear w/ painted eyes, Ostrich with painted eyes, and Black Bear w/ glass eyes.

Left: Ring Master w/ bisque head, Bareback Rider w/ bisque head, Ring Master w/ bisque head, Negro Dude w/ 2-part face, (some redressed); reduced size Donkey w/ painted eyes, and reduced size Elephant w/ painted eyes.

—Photos courtesy Gene Harris Antique Auction Center.

Painted Eye Animals: Deer, Leopard, Giraffe, and Lion w/ carved mane. —Photo courtesy Gene Harris Antique Auction Center.

	PAINTED EYES			GLASS EYES			REDUCED SIZE		
	Fair	Good	Exc.	Fair	Good	Exc.	Fair	Good	Exc.
Kangaroo	600	750	900	800	1100	1300	—	NA	—
Leopard	275	375	450	400	550	700	250	300	350
Lion, carved mane	225	300	400	600	1000	1400	250	300	350
Lion, cloth mane	—	NA	—	400	550	650	—	NA	—
Monkey	300	400	500	—	NA	—	—	NA	—
Ostrich	275	375	500	400	550	750	300	450	500
Pig	250	325	375	325	425	500	300	450	500
Polar Bear	550	700	900	700	1000	1300	—	NA	—
Poodle, carved mane	150	200	250	600	900	1200	300	400	450
Poodle, cloth mane	—	NA	—	200	275	350	—	NA	—
Rabbit	500	650	800	2000	3000	3500	—	NA	—
Rhinocerous	250	350	450	325	500	650	250	350	425
Sea Lion	400	550	750	600	900	1300	—	NA	—
Sheep	300	400	600	450	600	750	—	NA	—
Tiger	275	375	450	400	550	700	200	275	325
Wolf	1000	1500	1800	1800	2500	3500	—	NA	—
Zebra	225	300	400	400	550	700	225	325	425

People

	1-PART HEAD			BISQUE HEAD			REDUCED SIZE		
	Fair	Good	Exc.	Fair	Good	Exc.	Fair	Good	Exc.
Chinaman	$300	$450	$600	—	NA	—	—	NA	—
Clown	75	100	150	—	NA	—	$75	$110	$135
Gent Acrobat	—	NA	—	$300	$450	$600	—	NA	—
Hobo	200	300	400	—	NA	—	325	400	450
Lady Acrobat	300	400	450	300	450	550	—	NA	—
Lady Circus Rider	225	300	350	275	375	450	175	225	275
Lion Tamer	300	450	600	300	450	600	—	NA	—
Negro Dude	325	400	500	—	NA	—	375	450	500
Ring Master	300	375	450	350	425	550	175	225	275

Star Trek Memorabilia

Star Trek first appeared on NBC on September 8, 1966 but lasted only three seasons. When NBC canceled it, enraged fans bombarded the network with over one million letters of protest. Ironically, the show became even more popular in syndication. Reruns spurred the production of books, pins, fanzines and toys. "Trekkie" fan clubs and conventions evolved. Speculation regarding the series' return was surpassed only by rumors of a Beatles reunion.

Star Trek: The Motion Picture spawned a lot of material, but the 1979 film was a disappointment. Less material was produced for *Star Trek II: The Wrath of Khan.* That film re-established *Star Trek* and it has been followed by five movies and several new TV shows. The films and programs have created a new generation of fans and collectors.

The prices below are based on items in excellent or mint condition. Since the same items can be bought at a variety of locations at different prices, we devised a range system. The low range (MNP) covers complete, near mint to mint items without the package. The higher range (MIP) reflects the prices of complete, near mint to mint items in near mint to mint original packaging. Prices below are for complete like-new items. Prices of scratched, chipped or altered items are not included.

Abbreviation: Regarding manufacturers, *M*–Mego, *G*–Galoob, *E*–Ertl, *R*–Remco, *Ry*–Rayline, *ID*–Ideal and *B*–Bradley. To conserve space we have shortened some words. After the manufacturer we also list the production the item was based on: *TVS*–the original TV series, *NGTV–The Next Generation* TV show, *STMP–Star Trek: The Motion Picture* (Star Trek I), *STIII–Star Trek III: The Search for Spock* and *FF–The Final Frontier.* Most items in this section are action figures and toys followed by a small group of books. Years listed are approximate.

For more information see *House of Collectibles Price Guide to Star Trek Collectibles, Fourth Edition* by Sue Cornwell and Mike Kott, House of Collectibles, NY, 1996; *Greenberg's Guide to Star Trek Collectibles, Volumes I–III* by Chris Gentry and Sally Gibson-Downs; and *Toy Shop* magazine listed in the front of this book.

Action Figures and Toys

	MAKER	PROD.	YEAR	MNP	MIP
Andorian, 8"	M	TVS	1974	$180–$220	$400–$500
Antican, 3.75"	G	NGTV	1988	20–30	45–65
Arcturian, 3.75"	M	STMP	1979	60–90	120–180
Arcturian, 12"	M	STMP	1979	40–50	70–100
Betelgeusian, 3.75"	M	STMP	1979	70–100	180–220
Cheron, 8"	M	TVS	1974	60–90	120–180
Com. Bridge, 3.75"	M	STMP	1979	50–80	100–150
Data, blue/green face, 3.75"	G	NGTV	1988	50–70	90–150
Data, flesh face, 3.75"	G	NGTV	1988	10–12	20–30
Data, spot face, 3.75"	G	NGTV	1988	12–14	20–30
Decker, 3.75"	M	STMP	1979	8–12	18–24
Decker, 12"	M	STMP	1979	50–70	90–140
Dr. McCoy, 3.75"	M	STMP	1979	10–14	20–30
Dr. McCoy, 8"	M	TVS	1974	25–40	60–75
Enterprise Bridge, 8" fig.	M	TVS	1974	80–120	200–250
Ferengi, 3.75"	G	NGTV	1988	20–30	50–60
Ferengi Fighter Vehicle, 3.75"	G	NGTV	1989	15–25	35–60
Galileo Craft, 3.75"	G	NGTV	1988	18–22	35–55
Gorn, 8"	M	TVS	1974	80–100	180–220
Ilia, 3.75"	M	STMP	1979	5–8	14–18
Ilia, 12"	M	STMP	1979	25–35	50–75

	MAKER	PROD.	YEAR	MNP	MIP
Kirk, 3.75"	E	ST III	1984	6–9	18–24
Kirk, 3.75"	M	STMP	1979	8–12	20–30
Kirk, 7"	G	FF	1989	15–18	30–40
Kirk, 8"	M	TVS	1974	18–22	40–50
Kirk, 12"	M	STMP	1979	40–50	80–100
Klaa, 7"	G	FF	1989	15–20	30–40
Klingon, 3.75"	M	STMP	1979	70–90	150–200
Klingon, 8"	M	TVS	1974	20–25	40–50
Klingon, 12"	M	STMP	1979	50–60	120–160
Kruge and Dog, 3.75"	E	ST III	1984	8–10	30–40
La Forge, 3.75"	G	NGTV	1988	3–5	9–12
Lt. Uhura, 8"	M	TVS	1974	30–40	90–120
McCoy, 7"	G	FF	1989	15–20	35–40
Megarite, 3.75"	M	STMP	1979	90–120	150–200
Mis. Gam. VI, 8"	M	TVS	1976	250–350	500–700
Mugato, 8"	M	TVS	1974	125–175	250–350
Neptunian, 8"	M	TVS	1974	80–100	140–220
Picard, 3.75"	G	NGTV	1988	5–7	12–15
Q, 3.75"	G	NGTV	1988	25–35	60–80
Rigellian, 3.75"	M	STMP	1979	70–100	140–180
Riker, 3.75"	G	NGTV	1988	3–4	10–12
Romulan, 8"	M	TVS	1974	250–350	500–700
Scotty, 3.75"	E	ST III	1984	7–9	18–22
Scotty, 3.75"	M	STMP	1979	9–12	18–24
Scotty, 8"	M	TVS	1974	30–40	60–80
Selay, 3.75"	G	NGTV	1988	20–30	50–75
Spock, 3.75"	E	ST III	1984	9–12	20–30
Spock, 3.75"	M	STMP	1979	10–15	25–30
Spock, 7"	G	FF	1989	10–15	25–35
Spock, 8"	M	TVS	1974	20–25	45–60
Spock, 12"	M	STMP	1979	30–40	60–90
Sybok, 7"	G	FF	1989	10–15	25–35
Talosian, 8"	M	TVS	1974	120–160	250–350
The Keeper, 8"	M	TVS	1974	80–100	170–220
Worf, 3.75"	G	NGTV	1988	3–5	8–12
Yar, 3.75"	G	NGTV	1988	8–12	15–25
Zaranite, 3.75"	M	STMP	1979	70–100	120–160

Books

	LOW	HIGH
Adobe of Life, Corey, 1982, pbk.	$4	$6
Best of Trek, 1974–91, based on mag., 16 dif., #1–#16 pbks., ea.	3	5
Chekov's Enterprise, W. Koenig, 1980, pbk.	15	20
Come and Be With Me, L. Nimoy, 1978, pbk.	18	22
Covenant of the Crown, Weinstein, 1981, hrdcov.	8	12
Death's Angel, K. Sky, 1981, pbk.	12	18
Making of Star Trek II, Asherman, 1982, pbk.	14	18
Star Trek Maps, an intro. to navigation, Jeff Maynard, 1980	70	90
Starfleet Medical Manual, Palestine, Ballantine, 1977	15	20
Coloring Book, 1968	20	30

Left: Vulcan Ears, 20th anniversary promotional giveaway, Pocket Books, 1986, $20.

Right: Board Game, Star Trek The Next Generation Interactive VCR Board Game, Decipher Inc., ©1993, $20–$25.

Miscellaneous

	LOW	HIGH
Astro Walkie Talkie, 1967, Remco Industries, pr.	$70	$140
Audio Cassette, Star Trek episode tapes, Startone Recordings, 50-minute versions, 1983,	7	9
Blueprint, Star Fleet communicator, 1986, Nova Productions	5	7
Board Game, Star Trek 3-D Game, 1968, Dimensional Industries Corp.	30	50
Bumper Sticker, 1984, Lincoln Enterprises	3	5
Cap, *U.S.S. Enterprise* insignia, 1980, Thinging Cap Co., no trim	8	12
Clock, ASA Incorporated, kitchen clock depicting *U.S.S. Enterprise*	60	90
Model, *U.S.S. Enterprise* Spaceship, AMT, 1966, 10" x 15" box	300	500
Paper Doll, Saalfield book #C2272, activity book, punch-out, stand-up dolls, Kirk, Spock, McCoy, Uhura and Sulu, 1975	50	75
Phaser, Remco, 1975	40	80
Phaser Battle Game, Mego	250	450
Phaser Rocket Gun, 1974, Lonestar Products Ltd., in box	30	50
Photo Pin, Langley Associates, photo only, 1976, 2.25" dia	5	7
Spock Head Mask, Don Post Studios, 1980	60	90
Star Fleet Communications Newsletter, Star Trek fan club, 1968	10	15
Star Trek Board Game, Ideal, 1966	80	120
Tracer Pistol, Rayline, 1966	60	120
Tricorder, Mego, 1976	70	160
Vulcan Ears, Franco, 1975	80	120
Watch, Spock, Bradley, 1979	25	50

Star Wars Memorabilia

Star Wars burst onto movie screens in 1977. Stunning special effects made it an instant success. Two equally successful sequels followed, *The Empire Strikes Back* (ESB) in 1980 and *Return of the Jedi* (ROTJ) in 1983. *Star Wars* not only revolutionized special effects, it also introduced a smaller sized action figure. Although sizes vary they are generally 3.75" or smaller. Most of the following toys are the 3.75" figures and the vehicles made for them. Kenner made the figures and most of the toys listed below.

Dating carded *Star Wars* figures is relatively easy. The back of each card pictures each figure in the product line; as the line grows so do the number of illustrations. The original 12 figures are referred to as 12 backs. Packaging is more important in *Star Wars* items than any other area. The same figure on a *Star Wars* (SW) card is worth more than on an ESB or ROTJ card and an ESB carded figure is worth more than an ROTJ carded figure. Power of the Force (POTF), produced in 1985, is a series of figures that usually includes a collector coin. These figures are generally more valuable than ROTJ or ESB. The other factor affecting price is condition. The first price quoted (MINT) is for mint complete figures. The other range is for mint items on mint cards (MOC). Many times figures came with weapons or clothing. Loose figures are devalued if they are lacking this original equipment. Because Kenner marketed *Star Wars* toys worldwide, there is an incredible range of packaging variations.

The demand for toys and *Star Wars* products continues. The sharpest increases are for early small figures, produced for the first movie, in mint condition on mint cards. Another area that has seen significant increases is the large figure category. For more information see *House of Collectibles Price Guide to Star Wars Collectibles, Fourth Edition* by Sue Cornwell and Mike Kott, House of Collectibles, NY, 1997 and *The Galaxy's Greatest Star Wars Collectibles Price Guide, 1999 Edition* by Stuart W. Wells III, Antique Trader Books, Norfolk, VA, 1998.

	SERIES	MINT	MOC
A Wing Pilot	POTF	$10–$15	$60–$80
Admiral Ackbar	ROTJ	4–6	18–24
Amanaman	POTF	20–25	90–130
AT-AT	—	50–70	160–220
AT-AT Commander	ESB	6–8	35–45
AT-AT Driver	ESB	6–8	35–45
AT-ST Driver	ROTJ	4–5	15–20
B-Wing Figher	ROTJ	25–35	70–90
B-Wing Pilot	ROTJ	5–7	15–20
Barada	POTF	8–12	80–100
Ben Kenobi, large fig.	—	90–110	220–300
Ben (Obi-Wan) Kenobi	ESB	8–10	50–70
Ben (Obi-Wan) Kenobi	POTF	8–10	70–80
Ben (Obi-Wan) Kenobi	ROTJ	8–10	30–35
Ben (Obi-Wan) Kenobi	SW 12 back	8–10	150–200
Ben (Obi-Wan) Kenobi	SW 20/21 back	8–10	90–110
Bespin Security Guard, black	ESB	5–7	35–45
Bespin Security Guard, white	ESB	6–8	40–50
Bib Fortuna	ROTJ	5–7	18–24
Biker Scout	ROTJ	4–6	18–22
Blue Snaggletooth, Sears	SW 20/21 back	90–120	—
Boba Fett, large fig.	—	100–150	300–400
Boba Fett, working Rocket Launcher	SW (mail–in)	30–50	350–550
Bossk Bounty Hunter	ESB	8–10	50–65
C-3PO	POTF	8–10	50–70
C-3PO	ROTJ	8–10	25–30
C-3PO	SW 12 back	8–10	100–135

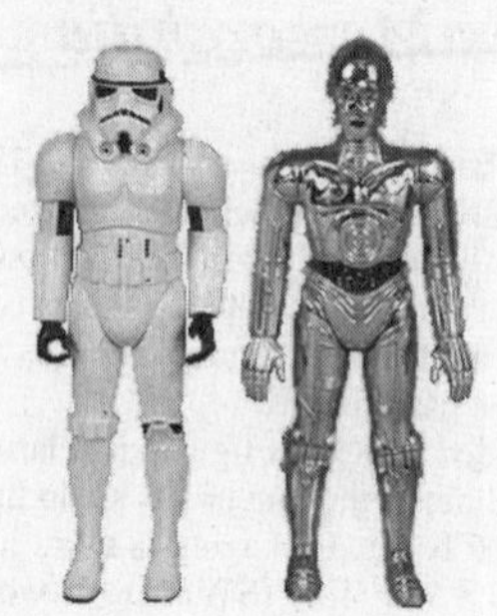

Above, left to right: Admiral Ackbar Figure, Return of the Jedi, $18–$24; Storm Trooper and C-3PO Action Figures, $7–$10 each.

Left: Lude Skywalker's Snowspeeder Model, The Empire Strikes Back, c1980, $30–$50.

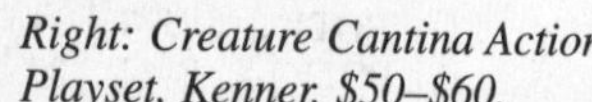

Right: Creature Cantina Action Playset, Kenner, $50–$60.

Left: Electronic Millennium Falcon Play Set, Kenner, 1996, $20–$40.

	SERIES	MINT	MOC
C-3PO	SW 20/21 back	8–10	70–90
C-3PO, large fig.	SW	50–75	120–180
C-3PO, removable limbs	ESB	8–10	40–55
C-3PO Bust Case, gold chrome	—	50–65	120–150
Cantina Adventure Set, Sears	SW	90–130	350–500
Chewbacca	ESB	8–10	50–70
Chewbacca	POTF	8–10	70–90
Chewbacca	ROTJ	8–10	25–35
Chewbacca	SW 12 back	8–10	100–170
Chewbacca	SW 20/21 back	8–10	60–90
Chewbacca, large fig.	—	50–65	120–150
Chewbacca Bandoleer Strap	ROTJ	3–4	12–18
Chief Chirpa	ROTJ	5–7	18–24
Cloud Car Pilot	ESB	5–7	35–45
Creature Cantina	SW	30–50	90–110
Darth Vader	ESB	8–10	50–70
Darth Vader	POTF	8–10	70–90
Darth Vader	ROTJ	8–10	30–40
Darth Vader	SW 12 back	8–10	150–200
Darth Vader	SW 20/21 back	8–10	70–90
Darth Vader, large fig.	—	60–80	150–200
Darth Vader Bust Case, plastic	—	18–22	40–50
Darth Vader TIE Fighter	SW	25–35	80–110
Darth Vader 2-Part Mask	—	50–60	60–70
Death Squad Commander	ESB	8–10	70–80
Death Squad Commander	ROTJ	8–10	50–60
Death Squad Commander	SW 12 back	8–10	120–180
Death Squad Commander	SW 10/21 back	8–10	90–120
Death Star Droid	SW 20/21 back	8–10	100–130
Death Star Playset	SW	60–70	150–190
Dengar	ESB	6–8	40–50
Desert Sail Skiff	ESB	5–7	18–24
Droid Factory	SW	25–35	80–120
Early Bird, 4 figs. in mailing box	SW	80–100	400–500
Early Bird Kit	SW	80–100	400–500
8D8	ROTJ	5–7	18–24
Emperor's Royal Guard	ROTJ	4–5	22–26
Endor Forest Ranger Vehicle	ESB	7–9	20–30
EV-9D9	POTF	12–18	90–110
Ewok Assault Catapult	ROTJ	7–9	20–30
Ewok Combat Glider 8	ESB	7–9	20–30
Ewok Village	ROTJ	30–40	70–90
4-Lom	ESB	6–8	70–90
FX-7 Medical Droid	ESB	6–8	50–60
Gamorrean Guard	ROTJ	4–6	18–22
General Madine	ROTJ	4–6	18–22
Greedo	SW 20/21 back	8–10	90–110
Hammerhead	SW 20/21 back	8–10	90–120
Han Solo	ESB	10–14	150–200
Han Solo	POTF	10–14	90–120
Han Solo	ROTJ	10–14	20–30
Han Solo	SW 12 back	10–14	300–500
Han Solo	SW 20/21 back	10–14	200–300
Han Solo, Bespin outfit	ESB	8–10	60–70

	SERIES	MINT	MOC
Han Solo, Hoth outfit	ESB	10–12	45–65
Han Solo, large fig.	—	120–180	350–500
Han Solo, trench coat	ROTJ	8–10	30–40
Han Solo in Carbonite Chamber	POTF	50–70	180–220
Ice Planet Hoth Playset	ESB	35–45	80–120
IG-88, large fig.	—	200–250	400–500
IG-88 Bounty Hunter	ESB	6–8	45–55
Imperial Commander	ESB	5–7	30–40
Imperial Gunner	POTF	18–22	80–100
Imperial Shuttle	ROTJ	40–60	150–200
Imperial Stormtrooper, Hoth battle gear	ESB	7–9	18–22
Imperial TIE Fighter Pilot	ESB	5–7	55–785
Imperial TIE Fighter Vehicle	SW	25–35	80–110
Imperial Troop Transporter	SW	25–30	90–120
Jabba the Hutt Throne	ROTJ	10–12	35–45
Jawa, cloth cape	ESB	10–12	70–90
Jawa, cloth cape	POTF	10–12	50–60
Jawa, cloth cape	ROTJ	10–12	30–40
Jawa, cloth cape	SW 12 back	10–12	100–150
Jawa, cloth cape	SW 20/21 back	10–12	80–90
Jawa, large fig.	—	60–80	175–225
Jawa, plastic cape	SW 12 back	150–250	600–900
Klaatu	ROTJ	5–7	15–20
Klaatu, Skiff Guard outfit	ROTJ	4–6	18–22
Lando Calrissian	ESB	8–10	35–45
Lando Calrissian, General Pilot	POTF	18–22	70–90
Lando Calrissian, Skiff Guard disguise	ROTJ	6–8	18–24
Landspeeder	SW	20–30	70–90
Laser Rifle Case	ROTJ	15–20	40–60
Lobot	ESB	6–8	35–45
Logray	ROTJ	10–14	25–35
Luke Skywalker	ESB	10–14	50–70
Luke Skywalker	ESB	10–14	50–70
Luke Skywalker	SW 12 back	10–14	200–300
Luke Skywalker	SW 20/21 back	10–14	150–200
Luke Skywalker, battle poncho	POTF	18–22	80–100
Luke Skywalker, Bespin fatigues	ESB	8–10	90–110
Luke Skywalker, Hoth battle gear	ESB	8–10	60–80
Luke Skywalker, Jedi knight outfit	ROTJ	10–15	60–80
Luke Skywalker, large fig.	—	90–120	200–300
Luke Skywalker, Stormtrooper outfit	POTF	50–70	200–300
Luke Skywalker X-Wing Pilot	SW 20/21 back	10–14	100–130
Lumar	POTF	8–12	30–40
Millennium Falcon Spaceship	SW	60–80	150–220
Nien Nunb	ROTJ	4–6	18–24
Nikto	ROTJ	4–6	18–22
Paploo	POTF	8–12	30–40
Patrol Dewback Playset	SW	15–20	50–70
Power Droid	SW 20/21 back	8–10	90–110
Princess Leia	ESB	10–14	180–220
Princess Leia	SW 12 back	10–14	200–300
Princess Leia	SW 10/21 back	8–10	220–260
Princess Leia, Bespin gown	ESB	15–20	60–80
Princess Leia, Boushh disguise	ROTJ	10–15	40–50

	SERIES	MINT	MOC
Princess Leia, combat poncho	ROTJ	10–12	30–40
Princess Leia, Hoth outfit	ESB	10–12	45–60
Princess Leia, large fig.	—	90–120	200–300
Prune Face	ROTJ	5–7	15–20
R2-D2	ESB	8–10	40–60
R2-D2	ROTJ	8–10	25–30
R2-D2	SW 12 back	10–14	90–120
R2-D2	SW 20/21 back	10–14	70–90
R2-D2, large fig.	—	50–60	120–160
R2-D2, pop-up lightsaber	POTF	25–35	120–160
R2-D2, sensorscope	ESB	8–10	40–50
R5-D4	SW 20/21 back	8–10	80–100
Ranco Keeper	ROTJ	5–7	15–20
Rancor Monster	ROTJ	10–15	35–45
Rebel Armored Snowspeeder, vehicle	ESB	30–40	80–100
Rebel Commander	ESB	5–7	30–40
Rebel Commando	ROTJ	5–7	18–22
Rebel Soldier, Hoth battle gear	ESB	6–8	40–50
Rebel Transport	ESB	25–35	80–100
Romba	POTF	8–12	30–40
Sand People, Tusken Raider	ESB	9–12	70–80
Sand People, Tusken Raider	ROTJ	9–12	45–60
Sand People, Tusken Raider	SW 12 back	9–12	140–200
Sand People, Tusken Raider	SW 20/21 back	9–12	90–130
Scout Walker	ESB	20–25	60–90
Slave 1	ESB	30–40	80–120
Snaggletooth	SW 20/21 back	8–10	90–110
Speeder Bike	ROTJ	7–9	20–30
Squid Head	ROTJ	7–9	18–22
Stormtrooper	ESB	7–9	50–60
Stormtrooper	POTF	7–9	50–60
Stormtrooper	ROTJ	7–9	100–125
Stormtrooper	SW 12 back	7–9	150–190
Stormtrooper	SW 20/21 back	7–9	60–80
Stormtrooper, large fig.	—	60–80	200–250
Sy Snootles and the Rebo Band	ROTJ	20–30	50–80
Tauntaun, solid belly	ESB	10–15	25–35
Tauntaun, split belly	ESB	12–18	40–50
Teebo	ROTJ	4–6	18–22
The Emperor	ROTJ	8–10	25–30
Twin-Pod Cloud Car	ESB	20–25	60–90
2-1B	ESB	6–8	50–70
Ugnaught	ESB	6–8	50–60
Walrus Man	SW 20/21 back	8–10	90–110
Warok	POTF	8–12	30–40
Weequay	ROTJ	4–6	18–22
Wicket W. Warrick	ROTJ	5–7	18–22
X-Wing Fighter, battle damage	SW	25–35	90–110
X-Wing Fighter Vehicle	SW	25–35	90–110
Y-Wing Fighter	ROTJ	30–40	80–100
Yak Face	POTF	90–130	300–400
Yoda	ESB	6–8	45–55
Yoda Handpuppet	—	18–22	30–40
Zuckuss	ESB	6–8	40–55

Steiff

	AUCTION	RETAIL Low	RETAIL High
Bear on Wheels, tan mohair, shoe button eyes, iron frame, c1908, 18" l	$173	$200	$400
Dachshund, black and brown wool, fully jointed, black shoe button eyes, emb. nose, mouth, and claws, c1930, 18" l	345	500	750
Dog on Wheels, off-white and tan shepherd, ear button, glass eyes (1 missing), emb. nose and mouth, cast-iron wheels, c1910, 8" l	173	200	400
Fox, mohair, fully jointed, excelsior stuffing, glass eyes, emb. nose, mouth, and claws, c1913, 5.5" h, 10.25" l	432	600	800
Lamb Pull Toy, curly wool coat, excelsior stuffing, felt face, ears, and legs, glass eyes, ear button, metal frame and wheels, c1913, 11.125" h, 12.5" l	1610	2000	2500
Mickey Mouse, velveteen, applied leatherette eyes, painted features, red shorts, yellow gloves, ginger shoes, 1930s, 7" h	1150	1500	2000
Rabbit, velveteen, ear button, cream w/ rust markings, black bead eyes, 1908, 5" h	345	500	750
Rabbit, blonde mohair, excelsior stuffing, fully jointed, pink glass eyes, c1913, 12" h	805	1200	1500
Sitting Dog, yellow mohair, glass eyes, black emb. nose, mouth, and claws, 1913, 5.5" h	173	200	400
Squirrel, blonde mohair, fully jointed, excelsior stuffing, black steel eyes w/ felt backing, emb. nose, mouth, and claws, 1920, 7.5" h	403	600	820
Teddy Bear, golden mohair, fully jointed, excelsior stuffing, blank ear button, black steel eyes, black emb. nose, mouth, and claws, felt pads, 1905-09, 14" h	1380	2000	2600
Teddy Bear, golden mohair, fully jointed, excelsior stuffing, black steel eyes, brown emb. nose, mouth, and claws, felt pads, c1905, 16" h	1955	3000	4000
Teddy Bear, light yellow mohair, fully jointed, excelsior stuffing, ear button, "Heins" glass eyes, black emb. nose, mouth, and claws, 1920s, 24" h	2760	4000	5500
Wire-Haired Fox Terrier on Wheels, mohair plush, glass eyes, ear button, steel frame and wheels, 20.75" h, 21" l	457	625	950

Left: Dutch Girl, center face seam, black steel eyes, light brown hair, c1913, 13.75" h, $1150 at auction.

Right: Teddy Bear, golden mohair, fully jointed, excelsior stuffing, black steel eyes, black emb. nose, mouth, and claws, felt pads, ear button, growler, c1905, 17" h, $2990 at auction.

—Photos courtesy Skinner, Inc., Boston, MA.

Tonka Toys

Tonka toys became the post-war symbol of the well-crafted American toy. In an industry turning increasingly to plastic and smaller sizes, Tonka's large, light, pressed steel vehicles ruled sandbox construction sites. The firm began as Mound Metal Works in 1946. The Tonka name came with the move to Minnetonka, Minnesota.

Since children used the vehicles for heavy duty projects and often left them outside (moms often banished the heavy toys from the house), the condition of Tonka toys is often poor. In the following listing we give two price ranges: excellent (EXC) for toys with some light wear but no significant rust or major paint loss and near mint (NM) for toys with only traces of wear and in excellent original boxes. Keep in mind that collectors often pay a hefty premium for mint in mint box examples. Such toys may bring more than prices quoted below. Rusty, damaged pieces will bring signifcantly less than those in excellent or better condition.

For further information we recommend *Collectors Guide to Tonka Trucks, 1947–63* by Don and Barb DeSalle, L–W Book Sales, Gas City, IN and *Collecting Toys: Identification and Value Guide, No. 8* by Richard O'Brien, Krause Publications, Iola, WI, 1997.

	EXC.	NM
Allied Van Lines #400, 1953	$90–$110	$200–$300
Big Mike State Hi-Way Dept. Truck #45, orange w/ V-shape plow, 1958	250–350	500–750
Car Carrier #840, yellow w/ 3 cars, 1963	200–300	400–500
Carnation Milk Delivery Van #750, 1955	150–200	320–380
Carry-All Tractor Trailer #120, red cab, blue trailer, 1949	100–120	180–220
Carry-All Tractor Trailer #120, blue cab, blue trailer w/ #50 Steam Shovel, 1949	200–250	320–440
Carry-All Tractor w/ Crane and Clam #170 and #150, yellow and green, 1949	200–250	300–400
Cement Truck #120, red and white, 1960	200–250	300–400
Clipper Boat and Trailer #AC360, 1960	80–120	200–250
Crane and Clam #150, yellow and black, 1947	90–140	200–300
Crane and Clam w/ Tracks #150, yellow and black, 1949	80–120	200–250
Dump Truck #180, red and green, 1949	100–150	200–250
Dump Truck, red cab, green box, 1955	70–90	160–210
Dire Truck, Hydraulic Aerial Ladder, red w/ #5 and TFD decals, 1957	200–230	300–400
Gasoline Truck #33, red, 1958	250–400	600–800
Grain Hauler #550, semi, red cab w/ aluminum box, 1952	90–150	200–250
Green Giant Tractor Trailer Transport #650, white w/ Green Giant decals, 1953	120–180	250–350
Green Giant Utility Truck #175, white w/ Green Giant decals and solid rubber tires, 1953	120–160	280–320
Hydraulic Dump Truck, brown, 1957	200–300	400–600
Jeep Wrecker #375, white, w/ winch and plow, 1964	200–300	400–600
Livestock Semi #500, red, 1952	80–140	190–240
Log Hauler #575, red cab, 1953	90–130	200–250
Minute Maid Box Van #750, w/ dual rear wheels, 1955	250–350	400–600
Pickup Truck #02, bronze, 1960	60–90	120–180
Pickup Truck #02, dard blue, 1956	100–150	200–300
Pickup Truck #02, dark blue, 1958	60–90	120–180
Pickup Truck #530, w/ camper, 1963	100–150	220–280
Pickup Truck Sportsman #05, dark blue w/ cap, 1958	90–130	180–220
Power Lift Truck and Trailer #200, 1948	120–160	200–250
Rescue Van #105, 1960–61	100–150	300–400
Road Grader #600, 1953	50–70	90–110

	EXC.	NM
Sanitary System Truck #140, rounded back, 1960	250–300	400–500
Sanitary Stystem Truck #B203, square back, w/ bins and scoop, 1959	300–400	500–700
Ser-vi-Car #201, 3-wheel cart, white	60–80	100–130
Star-Kist Tuna Box Van #725, 1954	250–350	420–620
State Hi-Way Dept. Dump Truck, orange, 1957	90–120	200–250
State Hi-Way Dept. Dump Truck, orange w/ side dump, 1957	90–130	200–300
Steam Shovel #100, red and black w/ tracks, 1949	80–130	200–250
Steam Shovel #100, red and black, wheels, 1947	80–130	200–250
Steam Shovel #50, red and blue, 1949	80–120	180–220
Steel Carrier Tractor Trailer #145, orange or yellow cab w/ green box, 1950	100–130	200–250
Suburban Pumper #46 Fire Truck, red w/ #5 decal and fire hydrant, 1957	200–250	300–400
Tonka Air Express Box Van and "Piggyback" Trailer, 1959	180–220	350–450
Tonka Farms Stock Rack Truck, 1957	200–250	350–400
Tonka Marine Service #41, blue semi w/ 4 boats, 1959	250–350	450–550
Tonka Service Van #103, 1961	80–130	200–250
Tonka Tanker, 1960	150–200	350–450
Tonka Toy Transport Tractor Trailer #140, red, box features opening doors, 1949	200–250	300–400
Utility Truck #175, green cab w/ yellow body, 1950	80–130	180–220
Wrecker Truck #250, 1953	100–150	220–280

Toy and Miniature Soldiers

The soldiers in the following section are lead. Of the various producers of toys and miniature soldiers, we chose Britains, Mignot and Courtenay.

In 1893 William Britain, founder of a London toy firm, and his sons developed hollow-cast lead toy soldiers. They were cheaper to produce and ship than earlier solid figures. They were packaged in distinctive red boxes with elaborate labels. They established 54mm (2.125") as a standard size, and by the early 1900s were outproducing their German and French competitors. Britains production reached a peak between the two world wars and in the 1950s. Pre-World War II sets usually command a premium price and are listed as pre-war in the descriptions below. Production of hollow-cast lead figures ceased in 1966. The company now produces a new line of metal toy soldiers and plastic figures. Because Britains improved designs and updated uniforms over the years, there can be many variations of the same set. For further information see *The Art of the Toy Soldier,* Henry I. Kurtz and Burtt R. Ehrlich, Abbeville Press, NY, 1987 and *Collecting Foreign-Made Toy Soldiers: Identification and Value Guide,* Richard O'Brien, Krause Publications, Iola, WI, 1997.

Three French toy makers founded C.B.G. Mignot in the 1820s. The firm is known for fine quality 55mm toy soldiers representing the French army, with special emphasis on the Napoleonic Wars and World War I. Although still in existence, production is limited, and figures are made for collectors rather than children. The sets listed below were made in the 1970s and 1980s. Dates following descriptions refer to the period of the unit represented rather than the year of production.

Although Richard Courtenay began by producing a line of toy figures in the 1920s, he is best known for his line of high quality, miniature medieval knights, produced from 1938 to 1963. These spectacular figures are now highly sought by connoisseur collectors. The figures represent knights of the 100 Years War, specifically, the Battle of Poitiers (1356). Courtenay assigned numerical designations according to the position of the knight, e.g. a knight lunging with battle ax is position 7. We have listed position numbers in the descriptions below. Courtenay signed many of his figures but not all. An unsigned figure will bring approximately 20% less than the prices listed. For further information see *Heraldic Miniature Knights* by Peter Greenhill, Guild of Master Craftsmen, East Sussex, 1991.

We list two price ranges for Britains and Mignot sets: one for excellent unboxed sets, the second for excellent to near mint condition sets in the original boxes. Courtenay figures are listed with one range for excellent to near mint condition, no box. Set numbers and the number of figures are included for Britains. Prices are based primarily on recent auction results.

Our consultant for this section is Henry Kurtz, co-author of *The Art of the Toy Soldier* and president of Henry Kurtz Limited, an auction house specializing in toy and miniature soldiers. He is listed in the back of this book.

Britains

	# FIGS.	SET #	UNBOXED	BOXED
11th Hussars, pre-war	5	12	$200–$250	$300–$400
16th/5th Lancers, pre-war	5	33	125–150	225–275
1st King George V's Own Gurkha Rifles	8	197	100–125	150–200
3rd Hussars	5	13	300–350	500–600
4.5" Anti-Aircraft Gun	—	1522	200–250	300–400
4th/7th Dragoon Guards, pre-war	5	127	300–350	500–600
6th Dragoon Guards, pre-war	15	106	300–350	500–600
7th Bengal Infantry, pre-war	8	1342	250–350	600–700
9th Queen's Royal Lancers, pre-war	5	24	150–175	250–300
Arabs of the Desert on Foot, camels, horses	11	224	200–250	300–400
Argyll and Sutherland Highlanders, pre-war	8	15	125–150	200–250
Armoured Car	—	1321	250–350	400–500
Band of the Life Guards in State Dress	12	101	300–400	400–500

Britains, top to bottom: 4th Bombay Grenadiers, No. 68, c1932, $300–$400; Royal Marines, No. 35, c1934, $150–$200; Argentine Cavalry, No. 217, post-war, $300–$400.

	# FIGS.	SET #	UNBOXED	BOXED
Band of the Royal Air Force	12	2116	400–500	700–900
Band of the Royal Berkshire Regiment	25	2093	300–1000	1000–1500
Band of the Royal Marines	12	1291	200–300	400–500
Bikanir Camel Corps, pre-war	3	123	250–350	450–550
Black Watch	6	11	80–100	150–175
Black Watch, pre-war	8	11	125–150	200–250
British Infantry	8	195	80–100	150–175
British Infantry in Tropical Dress	8	1924	200–250	400–500
British Territorial Infantry	8	1537	300–350	400–500
Cameronians	7	1913	700–900	1000–1500
Changing of the Guard	83	1555	600–800	1000–1500
Chinese Infantry	8	241	200–250	350–450
Coldstream Guards	8	2082	90–120	150–200
Coldstream Guards, 3 positions	24	90	450–550	600–800
Colour Party of the Black Watch	6	2111	350–450	500–700
Danish Life Guard	7	2019	200–250	350–450
Drum and Fife Band of the Line	17	321	400–600	800–1200
Drums and Fifes of the Welch Guards	12	2108	500–700	900–1200
Duke of Connaught's Own Lancers	5	66	100–125	150–200
Egyptian Camel Corps	3	48	150–175	200–300
Egyptian Cavalry	5	115	125–150	175–225
Fire Fighters of the Royal Air Force	8	1758	400–500	700–900
French Foreign Legion in Action	8	2095	200–250	350–450
French Infantry of the Line, pre-war	8	141	200–250	300–400
Gentlemen at Arms	9	2149	500–700	1000–1200
Gordon Highlanders	6	77	80–100	150–175
Gov. General's Horse Guards of Canada	5	1631	125–150	175–225
Greek Evzones	8	196	90–120	150–175
Grenadier Guards	8	312	90–120	150–200
Her Majesty's State Coach	10	1470	200–300	350–450
Indian Army Serivce Corps	8	1893	120–140	175–225
Italian Cavalry	5	165	400–500	800–1000
Italian Infantry	8	166	250–300	400–500
Japanese Infantry, pre-war	8	134	400–500	700–900
Knight w/ Mace, mounted, Agincourt	1	1569	90–120	150–175
Knight w/ Sword, mounted, Agincourt	1	1660	110–130	150–175
Knights of Agincourt on Foot	4	1664	125–150	200–250
Life Guards	5	400	100–125	150–200
Mexican Infantry (Rurales), pre-war	8	186	300–350	500–700
Mounted Band of the Royal Scots Greys	7	1720	250–350	500–600
Mountain Gun of the Royal Artillery	12	28	200–250	300–400
New Zealand Infantry	8	1542	100–125	175–225
Papal Swiss Guards	9	2022	150–175	250–300
Pipe Band of the Black Watch	20	2109	600–800	1000–1200
Prussian Hussars	5	153	200–300	350–450
Regiment Louw Wepener	8	1900	400–500	800–1000
Rodeo Set	12	2043	200–300	400–500
Royal Company of Archers	13	2079	200–300	400–500
Royal Engineers Pontoon Sect. Rev. Order	7	203	500–600	800–1000
Royal Horse Artillery at the Gallop	13	39	300–400	400–600
Royal Marine Light Infantry	8	97	500–600	900–1200
Royal Marines	7	2071	90–120	150–200
Royal Marines in Tropical Dress	8	1619	500–700	900–1200
Royal Navy Landing Party	11	79	200–250	300–400

Above, left to right: Bikanir Camel Corps, No. 123, c1920; Japanese Infantry, No. 134, 1906, charging; Royal Marines, No. 2071, troop, 1958; Russian Infantry, No. 133, officer, 1908.

Below, left to right: Royal Navy Landing Party w/ Gun, No. 79, 1953; Gordon Highlanders, No. 77, 1933; Royal Welsh Fusiliers, No. 74, 1955; Grenadier Guards, No. 312, troop, c1953.

	# FIGS.	SET #	UNBOXED	BOXED
Royal Scots Greys, pre-war	5	32	125–150	200–250
Royal Welsh Fusiliers	8	74	80–100	150–200
Russian Infantry	8	133	175–225	300–400
Seaforth Highlanders	17	2062	300–350	500–600
Somersetshire Light Infantry	8	17	125–150	200–250
South Australian Lancers	5	49	350–450	700–900
Standard Bearer, mounted, Agincourt	1	1662	100–125	150–175
State Open Road Landau	10	9402	300–350	400–450
U.S. Cavalry	8	228	90–120	150–175
U.S. Marine Corps Ban in Summer Dress	25	2112	1000–1500	2000–2500
U.S. Marine Corps Color Guard	4	2101	150–200	200–300
U.S. Military Band "The Snowdrops"	12	1301	300–400	500–700
U.S. Navy Blue Jackets, pre-war	8	230	125–150	200–250
Uruguayan Cavalry	4	220	100–125	200–250
Venezuelan Infantry	15	2105	175–225	300–350

	# FIGS.	SET #	UNBOXED	BOXED
Waterloo Period Line Infantry, 1815	9	1518	150–200	200–300
West India Regiment	9	19	200–300	400–500
West Point Cadets	8	299	90–120	150–175
Yeomen of the Guard	9	1257	125–150	200–250
Zulu Warriors of Africa	8	147	100–125	150–200

Courtenay

	SINGLE FIG.
Boy Prince Philip "Le Hardi," position 21	$300–$350
Erle of Armagnac, position Z-5	350–450
Erle of Rochechouaret, position 12	350–450
Fallen Knight, Sieur de la Rosay, position 13	350–450
French Knight Matthew de Rouvray, position 7	350–450
King John of France, position 3	350–450
Lord de Chargny, position 6	600–800
Lord de la Warr, position 15	300–350
Pierre, Sieur de Loigny, position 15	600–800
Sieur de Basentian, position 14	300–400
Sieur John de Landis, position Z-2	300–400
Sir Bartholomew Burghursh, position H-1	500–700
Sir John de Clinton, position H-2	600–800
Sir John Treffrey, position X-2	350–450
Sir Nele Loring, K.G., position H-6	700–900
Sir Thomas Warenhale, position H-3	600–800
Sir William Thorne, position 16	300–400

Mignot Set #228, Garde Imperiale de Russe, at the trot w/ standard bearer and bugler, c1950, $345 at auction. —Photo courtesy Wm. Doyle Galleries.

Mignot

	FIG. #	UNBOXED	BOXED
Departmental Guard of Paris (1810)	12	$175–$225	$200–$300
English First Life Guards (1815)	6	125–150	200–250
French Napoleonic Marines of the Guard	12	150–175	200–250
Israeli Infantry in Action	12	200–250	250–350
Legion of the North (1806)	12	175–225	200–250
Monaco Royal Guards	12	175–225	200–300
Mounted Band of the Polish Lancers (1810)	11	400–500	700–900
Vistula Legion (1808)	12	150–175	250–300

Trolls

Do you have trolls? You may have them or remember them from the mid-1960s to the early 1970s. Although trolls have existed in folklore for hundreds of years, the trolls we are addressing trace their roots to the late 1950s in Denmark, when Thomas Dam made a troll for his daughter. By the mid-1960s Dam produced and exported the dolls with crazy hair and scrunched-up faces. They were a sensation which, in turn, created a troll-collecting frenzy and competition for Dam from Scandia House (they later joined forces) and Uneeda Doll Company, who called their trolls "Wishniks." There were also lower-quality imitators. The following listing focuses on Dam and Wishniks. In the 1990s another wave of troll mania hit, introducing trolls to a younger generation. After their burst of success, the Dam toys were not available in the United States for many years. They are now marketed here as Norfins. Wishniks never really left the scene, with its company repackaging and releasing trolls over the years. Dam Trolls were the standard of the troll world, just as their successors, Norfins, are today. The troll market also boasts Russ Trolls, Magic Trolls and Treasure Trolls, and again a host of lower-quality imitators.

The following are just a few of the thousands of trolls produced. Since trolls are still manufactured and identification is an art rather than a science, do some research. Compare new and old, high quality and cheap imitators. The Dam Animals, some of the most widely sought trolls, were recast from the original molds by Norfin in 1990. They were limited to a run of 500, sold for $50 and comprise the large horse, the large cow, the large elephant and the lion. Since the edition was so limited, it probably will have little or no effect on the price of the originals. Dam Trolls may bear a variety of "Dam" markings, and Wishniks may bear the double horseshoe mark or "Uneeda Wishnik" or "Uneeda Dolls."

The prices below are based on items in excellent to mint condition with original clothing, accessories and tags. Packaging is not as important as in other areas but it always adds value and desirability. Permanent marks and stains on the trolls themselves, as well as damaged hair and clothes, adversely affect value. Clothing and accessories are an important factor in determining value. Many times trolls are redressed or missing part of their original ensemble. Replacement clothes may add some value to an otherwise undressed troll, but crisp, bright original clothes with original accessories demand the highest values. The following descriptions list what is currently known as outfits and accessories for the specific troll.

For further information refer to *Trolls: Identification and Price Guide* by Debra Clark, Hobby House, Cumberland, MD, 1993 and *Collector's Guide to Trolls* by Pat Peterson, Collector Books, Paducah, KY, 1995. See also the newsletter *Troll Monthly*, 216 Washington St., Canton, MA 02021.

	LOW	HIGH
Astronaut, w/ helmet and spacesuit, Dam, 7" h	$60	$90
Black Girl, Dam, 12" h	300	425
Book, *It's a Dam Dam World*, by Hal Goodman and Larry Klein	10	15
Boy Bank, wearing raincoat, pants, and cap, Dam, 7" h	40	70
Boy Bank, purple and white outfit, Dam, 7" h	35	45
Car, log-shaped, Irwin	70	100
Cow, limited edition, Dam, 7" h	60	80
Cow, small, Dam, 3" h	30	50
Cow, w/ bell, Dam, 6" h	120	200
Cowboy, w guns and hat, Wishnik, 5.5" h	12	18
Cowboy Bank, w/ hat, 6-shooters, kerchief, shirt, and pants, Dam, 7" h	50	70
Doctor, 2-pc. uniform w/ hat and stethoscope, Dam, 3" h	15	25
Donkey, Dam, 3" h	30	40
Donkey, w/ jointed head, Dam, 9" h	120	200
Double-Nik, 2-headed troll, Wishnik, 4" h	50	70
Elephant, blue, w/ cap, bow tie, and saddle blanket, Japan, 4" h	22	32
Elephant, Dam, 3" h	34	42

	LOW	HIGH
Elephant, Dam, 6" h	140	220
Giraffe, Dam, 11.5" h	90	149
Girl Bank, wearing raincoat w/ pants and cap, Dam, 7" h	40	70
Girl Bank, purple and white outfit, Dam, 7" h	35	45
Here Comes the Judge "Laugh-In" Troll, printed black smock, Wishnik, 6" h	40	50
Horse, Dam, 3" h	30	55
Hula-Nik, w/ skirt, Wishnik, 5" h	25	35
Hunt-Nik, w/ rifle, pants, and checkered flannel shirt, Wishnik, 3" h	25	35
Iggy-Normous, in caveman outfit w/ tag, Dam, 12" h	100	160
Iggy-Normous, in sailor costume w/ tag, Dam, 12" h	120	190
Indian Girl Bank, w/ headband, feather, belt, and wrap, Dam, 7" h	50	70
Lamp, 5.5" troll on wooden base, Wishnik, 18" h	80	100
Lion, Dam, 5" h	80	120
Monkey, R. Shekter, 3.5" h	25	35
Mouse, Dam, 5" h	60	85
Nurse, wearing uniform, hat, and shoes, Scandia House, 3" h	15	25
Outa Sight, Groovies series, w/ rhinestone eyes and outfits printed w/ various sayings, Wishnik, 3" h	18	25
Pirate Boy Bank, w/ striped shirt, 1 earring, pants, belt, and eyepatch, Dam, 7" h	50	75
Pirate Girl Bank, striped shirt, 2 earrings, pants, belt, vest, and hat, Dam, 7"	50	75
Playboy Bunny, including tail, tie, ears, and cuffs, Dam, 5.5" h	40	50
Playboy Bunny, including tail, tie, ears, and cuffs, Scandia House, 3" h	20	30
Rock-Nik, black and red outfit w/ attached guitar, Hong Kong, 6" h	20	30
Santa, Dam, 12" h	175	225
Sock-It-To-Me, large white eyes, dressed in smock w/ "Laugh-In" slogans, Wishnik, 6" h	50	60
Superman, w/ man of steel costume w/ cape, Wishnik, 5.5" h	50	70
Tartan Girl, Dam, 12" h	125	175
Troll Cave Carrying Case, Standard Plastics, 9.5" h	30	40
Troll 2/ Tail and Jointed Head, Dam, 6.5" h	150	220
Turtle, molded green shell, Dam, 3" h	175	225
Viking, w/ molded plsatic hat, 1-pc. outfit w/ belt and red wrist tag, Dam, 6.5" h	120	160

Viewmaster

Visitors to the 1939 World's Fair were treated to many spectacular new inventions, including the Viewmaster, which was introduced there by Sawyer. The invention of Harry Gruber, Viewmaster produced reels for the war effort. Pre-1945 single reels were either dark blue with a gold sticker or blue and tan. These early reels command a premium price among collectors. After the war, Sawyer did numerous travel site and National Parks reels. In 1952 they purchased their competitor, Tru-Vue, thereby acquiring the licensing rights to Disney productions. Some of the most sought after reel packs are those depicting classic TV shows and cartoons from the 1950s and 1960s. There is a lot of cross-over collecting from the television memorabilia field. The firm stopped selling three-packs in 1980 but are still in business. Having been owned by five different companies, including Sawyer and GAF, they are now owned by Tyco. Collectors love the frozen-time aspect of Viewmaster, this century's stereoscope.

The prices below are based on items in near mint to mint condition, which means no damage to the reels or package, including all flaps (4). If the package states that instructions were enclosed they should be present. Blister packs should display virtually no signs of wear. We removed "The" from several titles in order to make the listings easier to use. All those listed are three-packs except those that specify *1R* (one reel), or *BP* (Blister pack). Dates are approximate and the number of each pack is listed after the date.

Viewmaster Assortment.

	LOW	HIGH
Abe Lincoln's New Salem and Springfield, Ill. 1950, 298	$4	$6
Adirondack Mountains, N.Y., SP-9028	4	6
Airplanes of the World, B773	20	30
Albuquerque, N. Mex. 1948, SP-9036	4	6
Arches National Monument, Utah, 1950, SP-9048	4	6
Aztec Ruins National Monument, N. Mex., 288	2	4
Bambi, B400	9	13
Baseball Stars of the Major Leagues I, w/ booklet, 725	20	30
Baseball Stars of the Major Leagues II, w/ booklet, 726	20	30
Baseball Stars of the Major Leagues III, w/ booklet, 727	20	30
Batman, B492	30	45
Battlefields of World War II, Normandy, 1420	4	6
Beautiful Caverns of Luray, Va., 194	4	6
Bedknobs and Broomsticks (Disney), B366	13	20
Beep, Beep, The Road Runner, B538	9	13
Bellingrath Gardens, Mobile, 1952, SP-9064	4	6
Bern, 2003	3	5
Black Hills, S. Dak., A486	5	8
Blondie and Dagwood, B537	17	25
Boys Town Nebr. 1951, SP-9062	4	6
Buenos Aires I, 656	3	5
Bugs Bunny, B531	17	25
Buildings and Swiss Guards, Vatican State, 2722	2	4
Bullfight in Spain, w/ booklet, 720	9	13
Bullwinkle, B515	20	30
Busch Gardens, Tampa, A988	5	7
By the Zuider Zee, 1900	3	5
Canada, A090	9	13
Carlo Collodi's Pinocchio, B311	4	6
Carlsbad Caverns National Park, 252	3	5
Carlsbad Caverns II National Park, A377	3	5
Casper the Friendly Ghost, B533	20	30
Cave of the Winds, Colo., 234	4	6
Charlie Brown's Summer Fun, B548	9	13
Charros, Costumes and Dances of Mexico, 524	5	8
Chicago, Ill., 333	4	6
Christmas Story, B383	20	30
Circus Hall of Fame, A995	20	30
Colorful Ozarks, 372	4	6
Conquest of Space-Astronauts, B681	20	30
Coronation of Queen Elizabeth II June 2, 1953, 405	6	9
Coronation of Queen Elizabeth II June 2, 1953, 406	6	9
Coronation of Queen Elizabeth II June 2, 1953, 407	6	9
Cypress Gardens and Bok Tower, 164	2	4
Daniel Boone, B479	20	30
Denver and Denver Mtn. Parks, 246	3	5
Dioramas, Mesa Verde National Park, Col., 226	2	4
Disney on Parade, B517	17	25
Dr. Shrinker, H2	5	8
Edison Institute, Greenfield Village, 85	20	30
Edison Institute Museum, 84	8	12
Emergency, B597	13	20
England, B156	13	20
Eskimos, 309	3	5

	LOW	HIGH
Exploring the Universe Astronomy, B687	25	40
Fiddler on the Roof, B390	34	50
Fire Fighters in Action, w/ booklet, 710	17	25
Flying Nun, B495	60	90
Forging a Nation 1787-1886,m B811	9	13
Franconia Notch, Lost River, White Mountains, 260	9	13
Garden of the Gods, 51	3	5
Gene Autry and His Wonder Horse "Champion," 950	9	13
Geneva Switzerland, 1947, 2020	2	4
Gettysburg National Military Monument II, 348	9	13
Ghost Town, Knott's Berry Farm, Buena Park, SP-9038	4	6
Glacier National Park, Mountain Trip IV, SP-49	4	6
Golidlocks, B317	6	9
Grand Canyon National Park, South Rim, A361	9	13
Grand Coulee Dam, 196	2	4
Grand Teton National Park, 41	2	4
Grand Teton National Park, A307	9	13
Great Barrier Reef, Queensland, 5010	3	5
Great Smoky Mountains National Park, Tenn., 336	9	13
Great Smoky Mountains National Park, Tenn., 337	3	5
Greece, B205	4	6
Guatemala City, 551	4	6
Havana, Cuba I, 572	9	13
Hawaii, The 50th State, A120	9	13
Historic Philadelphia and Valley Forge, Pa., 351	2	4
Historical Philadelphia, A635	13	19
History of Flight, B685	9	13
Home of Santa's Workshop, North Pole, 1951, SP-9058	4	6
Hong Kong Colony, 4810	2	4
Honolulu, 63	4	6
Hopalong Cassidy (William Boyd) and "Topper," 955	9	13
Howe Caverns I, N.Y., SP-9021	4	6
Huckleberry Finn, B343	14	25
Huckleberry Hound, B512	50	75
Hunters of the Forests, B722	35	50
In Darkest Africa, B095	25	40
Inauguration of President Dwight D. Eisenhower, 400	12	20
Indian Tribal Ceremonial, Gallup, N. Mex., 286	4	6
Interior of George Washington's Mount Vernon Home, SP-9057	4	6
Interlaken Region I, 2009	3	5
Iowa, The Hawkeye State, 249	3	5
Island of Bermuda, 595	9	13
Island of Hawaii, 66	4	6
Island of Oahu, 64	4	6
It's a Bird Charlie Brown, B556	13	19
Jasper National Park I, 316	3	5
Jerusalem, The Old City, w/ booklet, 4000	6	9
Joshua Tree National Monument, Calif, SP-9056	4	6
Kansas, The Wheat State, 365	2	4
Kauai, The Garden Isle, SP-72	13	19
Killarney, 1301	2	4
King's Canyon National Park, Grant Grove, 118	2	4
Landmarks of American History, B814	45	65
Las Vegas, Nev., SP-9044	9	13

	LOW	HIGH
Las Vegas, A159	13	20
Lassie, Look Homeward, B480	17	25
Lincoln Heritage Trail, A390	9	13
Lincolnland, Springfield-New Salem, A557	20	30
London I England, 1947, 1001	2	4
London II England, 1947, 1002	2	4
London III England, 1003	9	13
Lookout Mountain, Chattanooga, Tenn., 338	2	4
Los Angeles, Calif., 221	3	5
Lost in Space, B482	85	125
Mackinac Island and Vicinity, Michigan, 248	3	5
Maharaja's Festival, Mysore, 4302	5	8
Mammoth Cave, A846	3	5
Mammoth Cave National Park, 339	5	8
Mammoth Cave National Park, 340	9	13
Mardi Gras, New Orleans, La., 332	4	6
Marine Studios, St. Augustine, 166	2	4
Martha's Vineyard Island, Mass., SP-9051	4	6
Mary Poppins (Disney), B376	26	38
Matterhorn and Zermatt, Switzerland, 1948, 2001	2	4
Meramec Caverns, A451	9	13
Mesa Verde National Park, 227	2	4
Mexico City I, 501	3	5
Mickey Mouse, B528	20	30
Mickey Mouse in Clock Cleaners, B551	9	13
Mighty Mouse, B526	13	20
Miss America Beauty Pageant, Atlantic City, 1954, 155	20	30
Mod Squad, B478	20	30
Monterey Peninsula, Calif., 184	2	4
Monticello, A827	5	8
Montreal, Quebec, Canada, 380	3	5
Monument Valley, Ariz. and Utah, 174	2	4
Mormon Temple, Tabernacle and Grounds, 122	9	14
Mount Hood, Oreg., 212	4	6
Mount Sunapee State Park, N.H., 270	4	6
Mount Washington and Cog Road, N.H., SP-9019	3	5
Mt. Fuji and Rural Scenes, 4872	4	6
Mt. McKinley National Park, 306	2	4
Museum of Science and Industry, Chicago, Ill., A552	20	30
Museums and Galleries, Vatican State, 2723	2	4
Nanny and the Professor, B573	34	50
Nassau, Bahamas, 597	2	4
Navajo Indians, N. Mex. and Ariz., 175	4	6
New England Covered Bridges and Fall Foliage, A611	9	13
New Orleans, La., 331	2	4
Niagara Falls, Ont., Canada, 375	3	5
Oklahoma, The Sooner State, 370	3	5
Old Castile, 1701	3	5
Old Covered Bridges, New England, SP-9020	9	13
Old Delhi, 4306	6	9
Old Sturbridge Village, Sturbridge, Ma., 281	6	9
Ottawa, Ont., Canada, 378	3	5
Overseas Highway and Key, 162	2	4
Painted Desert, 177	3	5

	LOW	HIGH
Palace of Versailles, 1410	2	4
Pan American's 747, B747	20	30
Panama City I, 530	3	5
Paricutin Volcano, 510	9	13
Paris I France, 1401	2	4
Paris II France, 1402	2	4
Park of the Red Rocks, 53	3	5
Petrified Forest, 176	2	4
Philadelphia, Pa., 350	2	4
Phoenix, Ariz., SP-180	4	6
Pike's Peak, 245	3	5
Pike's Peak, A321	4	6
Popeye, B516	13	19
Poseidon Adventure, B391	26	38
Prehistoric Animals, B619	13	29
Quebec City I, 383	2	4
Quebec City Canada II, 384	3	5
Race Horse of the Bluegrass Country, Ky., 342	3	5
Redwood Highway, Calif., 112	9	13
Revolutionary War, B810	9	13
Rio De Janeiro, Brazil, 670	2	4
Robin Hood (Disney), B342	6	9
Rockefeller Center, Empire State Building, 1858	4	6
Rocky Mountain National Park, 102	2	4
Romantic Seville, 1700	3	5
Roosevelt's Little White House, Ga., 343	2	4
Rowan and Martin's Laugh-In, B497	26	38
Roy Rogers, King of the Cowboys, and "Trigger," 945	9	13
Rudolf the Red-Nosed Reindeer Shines Again, B870	13	19
San Antonio, Tex., 328	2	4
San Diego, Calif., 1953, SP-9039	4	6
San Juan Capistrano Mission, Calif., SP-189	9	13
Sanctuary of Our Sorrowful Mother, SP-9013	2	4
Santa Catalina, 201	2	4
Santa Fe, N. Mex., 1948, SP-282	4	6
Santiago, 641	3	5
Secret Squirrel and Atom Ant, B535	34	50
Sequoia and Kings Canyon National Park, A174	4	6
Seven Wonders of the World, B901	9	13
Shenandoah National Park, Skyline Drive, 261	3	5
Shenandoah National Park, Skyline Drive, 262	9	13
Sigmond and the Sea Monsters, B595	13	19
Silver Springs, A962	9	13
Snoopy and the Red Baron, B544	9	13
St. Augustine, Ostrich, Alligator Farm, 160	2	4
St. Louis, Missouri, 1951, SP-9059	4	6
St. Peter's Basilica, Vatican State, 2721	2	4
St. Petersburg, SP-9037	4	6
Star Trek: "Mr. Spock's Time Trek" (cartoon), B555	17	25
Steve Canyon in "Crisis At Big Thunder," B582	26	38
Sun Valley, Idaho Summer Variant, SP-207	4	6
Sunken Gardens, St. Petersburg, A992	13	19
Sydney, New South Wales, 5001	9	13
Timberline Lodge and Mount Hood, SP-9023	4	6

Adventures of Tarzan, "Tarzan Rescues Cheta," 975, $9–$13.

	LOW	HIGH
Timberline Lodge and Mt. Hood, Oreg., 211	4	6
Tipperary, 1302	2	4
Tokyo, 4871	4	6
Top Cat, B513	17	25
Toronto and Vicinity, Ont., 376	3	5
Tucson, Ariz., SP-179	9	13
Tulip Time in Holland, Mich., 1952, SP-9071	4	6
Twin Cities and Southern Minnesota, 1952, SP-9072	4	6
Two Mouseketeers/Tom and Jerry, B511	13	19
U.S. Spaceport, John F. Kennedy Space Center, B662	13	19
United Nations, A651	13	19
United States Naval Academy, Annapolis, Md., 139	3	5
Vancouver, British Columbia, Stanley Park, 311	2	4
Vermont State, North Section, 272	2	4
Victoria and Vicinity, B.C., 313	2	4
Victoria Falls, 3100	3	5
Walt Disney Presents Jungle Book, Rudyard Kipling, B363	17	25
Walt Disney Presents Sword in the Stone, B316	9	13
Walt Disney Presents TheAristocats, B365	9	13
Waltons, B596	13	19
War Between the States, B790	26	38
Washington, D.C., 136	3	5
Washington, D.C., 137	2	4
Westward Expansion, B812	13	19
Wild Animals of the World, B614	9	13
Wild Flowers, Rocky Mountain Region, 276	4	6
Windmill Land, South Holland, 1901	3	5
Wisconsin Dells, A526	9	13
Wizard of Oz, B361	13	19
Woody Woodpecker in "The Pony Express Ride," 820	2	4
Yellowstone National Park, 126	2	4
Yellowstone National Park, 127	2	4
Yosemite National Park, 131	2	4
Yosemite National Park, 132	2	4
Zorro, B469	38	56
Zuni and Navajo Indian Crafts and Arts, 294	4	6

Transportation Collectibles

Automobiles

The antique car market is coming back. Cars from the 1960s and early 1970s show increased prices even for ordinary models. Flashy cars from the late 1950s are extremely popular, especially those with big fins. However, the cars of the 1980s, even the high end models, have yet to see a return on investment for their buyers.

The cars listed in this section are divided into six categories: A) salvageable only for parts, B) restorable, C) working order, but deteriorated, D) very good, drivable original or good amateur restoration, E) fine, well-restored or well-maintained original with minimal wear, and F) excellent, professional quality restoration or perfect original.

For further information see *The Official Price Guide to Collector Cars, Eighth Edition* by Robert H. Balderson, House of Collectibles, New York, 1996, and *The Standard Guide to Cars and Prices, 10th Edition,* edited by James T. Lenzke and Ken Buttolph, Krause Publications, Iola, WI, 1997.

Audi

	A	B	C	D	E	F
1972, 100LS, sedan	$200	$600	$1000	$2200	$4000	$6000
1973, Fox sedan	175	400	850	1500	3000	4500
1976, 100LS, sedan	250	650	1000	2500	4200	6000
1981, 5000, sedan	250	650	1000	2250	4000	5700
1984, 4000, sedan	200	500	900	2000	3500	5000

Bentley

	A	B	C	D	E	F
1947, Sedan	$1000	$3000	$5000	$10,000	$20,000	$27,000
1950, Sedan	1000	3000	5000	10,000	20,000	27,000
1952, Grayber, coupe	1600	5000	8000	17,000	30,000	42,000
1953, Frankdale Saloon	1200	3500	6000	12,000	20,000	30,000
1967, James Young	1800	5800	9500	20,000	34,000	50,000
1971, Touring Car	1200	3800	6500	14,000	24,000	35,000
1980, Corniche	2000	6000	10,000	20,000	35,000	50,000

BMW

	A	B	C	D	E	F
1953, 501 Sedan	$400	$1200	$2000	$4000	$7000	$9500
1960, 501 Sedan	400	1200	2000	4000	7000	10,000
1965, 3200CS Coupe	700	2000	3500	7000	12,000	15,000
1976, Bavaria	400	800	1300	2500	5500	8000
1982, 521E Sedan	500	1500	2500	5000	8000	12,000

Buick

	A	B	C	D	E	F
1919, Sedan	$650	$2000	$3200	$6500	$10,000	$14,500
1921, Sedan	450	1300	2200	4200	8000	10,000
1923, Sedan	450	850	1600	2600	6200	7900
1924, Sedan	550	1300	2200	4300	7400	9500
1926, Sedan	550	1300	2300	4300	6500	11,000
1928, Sedan	550	1500	2700	4400	8000	11,500
1932, Sedan	800	2100	3200	6300	11,500	16,500

	A	B	C	D	E	F
1934, Sedan	750	1850	3100	4600	9300	12,500
1936, Limited Series Sedan	725	2250	3750	7500	12,400	18,500
1938, Limited Series Sedan	850	2600	4200	8300	14,500	21,000
1940, Limited Series Sedan	1100	2700	4750	10,500	16,750	25,000
1942, Century	550	1550	2750	5400	9500	13,500
1946, Roadmaster Convertible	1000	3500	6000	12,000	20,000	30,000
1950, Roadmaster Convertible	1000	3000	5000	10,000	18,000	25,000
1953, Roadmaster Convertible	1000	3000	5000	10,000	18,000	25,000
1955, Roadmaster Sedan	450	1250	2200	4400	7500	11,000
1957, Convertible	1000	3200	5000	10,000	18,000	25,000
1959, Sedan	450	750	1250	2600	4200	6600
1961, Sedan	225	650	1100	2200	4200	6600
1963, Sedan	200	600	1000	2200	4000	6300
1965, Sedan	200	500	900	2000	3500	5200
1967, Sedan	150	350	750	1500	3000	4200
1969, Sedan	150	300	700	1200	2500	4000
1971, Skylark	125	250	700	1200	2300	3500
1973, Electra	150	400	750	1400	3100	4700
1974, Electra	150	400	750	1500	3000	4200
1975, Regal	125	200	650	1100	2400	3400
1976, Skylark	125	250	700	1200	2500	3500
1977, Century	125	250	700	1200	2500	3600
1978, Riviera	200	600	1000	2000	4000	6000
1979, LeSabre	150	300	750	1400	3000	4000
1983, Skylark	200	350	750	1500	3000	4200
1985, LeSabre	225	650	1000	2200	4200	5700
1986, Somerset	235	525	850	2000	3500	5300

Cadillac

	A	B	C	D	E	F
1903, Model "A"	$1400	$4200	$7500	$15,000	$25,000	$35,000
1907, Model "G"	1250	3700	6200	12,000	20,000	30,000
1912, Model 30	1500	4500	8000	16,000	26,000	38,000

Cadillac, 1962, Fleetwood 75, Series 6700, $19,516 at auction. —Photo courtesy Auction Team Breker.

	A	B	C	D	E	F
1918, Type 57	1300	4200	7500	13,000	23,000	38,000
1927, Fleetwood	1700	5500	9500	18,000	33,000	45,000
1930, Series 353, sedan	1700	5500	9000	18,000	32,000	46,000
1935, Fisher Body	2200	6300	10,500	19,000	33,000	48,000
1940, Series 62, convertible	2100	7250	11,400	22,500	38,500	55,000
1948, Sedan	900	2700	4300	8750	15,500	22,000
1954, Series 75	1100	3600	5750	11,500	21,000	29,000
1960, DeVille, sedan	625	1850	3100	6200	10,500	16,000
1963, El Dorado	1000	3000	5000	10,000	17,500	25,000
1968, Calais	400	1000	1500	3000	6000	9500
1973, DeVille	325	750	1100	2300	4400	6500
1977, Fleetwood	350	700	1200	2300	4700	6700
1980, Seville	350	700	1100	2400	4700	6500
1985, DeVille	225	750	1100	2500	4750	7000

Chevrolet

1913, Classic	$1200	$3500	$6000	$12,000	$20,000	$30,000
1918, Series "D"	850	2600	4300	8500	15,000	22,000
1927, Model "AA," sedan	350	750	1250	2400	5000	7000
1931, Model "AE," sedan	500	1500	2500	5000	9000	13,000
1934, Master Coupe	400	1200	2000	4000	7000	10,000
1937, Master Sedan	450	1000	1600	3300	6300	9000
1939, Master 85, station wagon	900	2700	4500	9000	16,000	23,000
1942, Fleetwood	500	1000	1700	3600	6500	9500
1946, Stylemaster	350	850	1500	3100	6000	8500
1951, Styleline Special	350	800	1300	2600	5500	7700
1955, Bel Air, sedan	400	1300	2300	4500	8000	11,000
1958, Biscayne	225	600	1000	2300	4200	6300
1961, Impala, sedan	250	700	1250	2500	4500	6500
1966, Chevelle	175	400	750	1600	3200	4500
1969, Impala, station wagon	175	350	750	1500	3000	4000
1970, Camaro	500	1500	3000	5000	8500	12,000

Chevrolet, 1955, Bel Air, sedan. —Photo courtesy Kruse International.

	A	B	C	D	E	F
1974, Nova	175	300	750	1400	2800	4000
1977, Monza	150	250	700	1200	2500	3500
1981, Citation	150	250	700	1200	2500	3500
1985, Celebrity	175	450	750	1500	3000	4000

Chrysler

	A	B	C	D	E	F
1925, Town Car	$500	$1600	$2750	$5100	$9250	$13,500
1928, Series 62, sedan	350	800	1450	2750	5600	8300
1931, Series 77, coupe	550	1750	2800	5750	10,000	15,000
1933, Royal Sedan	550	1600	2750	5600	9500	14,000
1939, New Yorker	550	1700	3000	5800	10,000	14,500
1942, Saratoga, coupe	400	1300	2200	4500	8000	12,500
1953, New Yorker	400	1000	1700	3000	6000	10,000
1957, LeBaron	500	1600	2700	5500	10,000	14,000
1960, Saratoga, sedan	200	600	1000	2500	4000	6000
1964, Newport, sedan	150	275	750	1200	2750	4000
1968, New Yorker	250	600	1000	2000	4000	5500
1972, Imperial	250	600	1000	2200	4200	6200
1977, LeBaron	175	300	700	1300	2800	4300
1981, Newport	175	400	750	1600	3000	4700
1985, Laser	175	400	750	1600	3000	4600

Corvette

	A	B	C	D	E	F
1955, Convertible	$1200	$4500	$7500	$15,000	$25,000	$37,000
1963, Sport Coupe	1000	3000	5000	10,000	20,000	26,000
1972, Convertible	700	2000	3000	7500	13,000	18,000
1986, Corvette	500	1600	2600	5500	9000	14,000

Datsun

	A	B	C	D	E	F
1969, Sedan	$150	$200	$600	$1000	$2000	$3000
1976, 280Z, coupe	300	700	1100	2200	4500	6500

Desoto

	A	B	C	D	E	F
1930, Model "CK" Coupe	$450	$1000	$1750	$3700	$6750	$9700
1934, Airflow	450	1250	2000	4500	7500	11,000
1940, S7 Deluxe	350	800	1250	2500	5000	7500
1946, S11, sedan	200	700	1200	2400	4500	6500
1953, Powermaster 6	300	700	1200	2400	4700	7000
1958, Firesweep, sedan	200	600	1000	2300	4000	5700
1960, Adventurer, sedan	200	600	1000	2000	3700	5500

Dodge

	A	B	C	D	E	F
1917, Coupe	$400	$950	$1750	$3250	$6500	$9500
1923, Sedan	250	550	950	2100	3600	5200
1934, Convertible	1200	3500	6000	12,500	22,000	31,000
1939, Coupe	450	1000	1600	3500	6500	9000
1946, Coupe	350	800	1300	2500	5500	8300
1953, Coronet	350	750	1200	2500	5000	7500
1957, Royal Sedan	250	600	1000	2500	4000	6000
1960, Seneca	250	550	1000	2200	3750	5750

	A	B	C	D	E	F
1955, Convertible	$1200	$4500	$7500	$15,000	$25,000	$37,000
1963, Polara Sedan	200	500	900	2000	3500	5000
1966, Monoco	250	600	1000	2200	4000	5500
1969, Monoco	175	400	800	1800	3500	4750
1973, Colt	150	250	600	1000	2200	3500
1976, Crestwood	150	300	700	1200	2500	4000
1980, Diplomat	175	300	700	1200	2600	4000
1984, Aries	175	350	750	1500	3100	4200
1986, Lancer	225	500	1000	2000	3500	5200

Ford

	A	B	C	D	E	F
1909, Model "T"	$750	$2200	$4000	$8000	$13,500	$21,000
1914, Model "T"	500	1500	2700	5250	9500	15,500
1926, Model "T," coupe	400	800	1400	2750	6500	8000
1930, Model "A," station wagon	600	1800	3000	6000	10,000	14,500
1935, Model 48, sedan	500	1100	1700	3500	6500	10,000
1939, Model 922, coupe	400	1300	2300	4500	8000	11,000
1942, Model 21A, sedan	400	800	1200	2750	5300	7500
1952, Sedan	225	500	850	2000	4000	5500
1956, Mainline	250	600	1000	2200	4000	6000
1958, Thunderbird, convertible	1000	3000	5500	12,000	20,000	30,000
1964, Sprint	400	1300	2300	4600	8000	11,000
1967, Futura	200	500	800	2000	3500	5000
1970, Cobra	600	2200	3500	7000	12,000	18,000
1972, Maverick	150	300	700	1200	2500	4500
1974, LTD	150	350	750	1300	2700	4500
1978, Thunderbird	250	650	1000	2000	4000	6000
1982, Escort	150	300	700	1200	2600	3800
1985, Tempo	125	250	700	1200	2500	3500

Ford, 1930, Model "A" Phaeton, $27,880 at auction. —Photo courtesy Auction Team Breker.

Hudson

	A	B	C	D	E	F
1911, Model 33	$1000	$3000	$5000	$10,000	$18,000	$25,000
1915, Sedan	700	2000	3500	7000	12,000	17,500
1920, Coupe	450	1100	1700	3700	7000	10,000
1924, Sedan	350	800	1500	2850	6100	8200
1928, Coupe	450	1500	2500	5000	9200	12,500
1931, Sedan	500	1000	1700	3500	6500	10,000
1934, Challenger, coupe	350	750	1300	2500	5500	8000
1937, Custom 6, sedan	350	750	1200	2400	5000	7000
1939, Big Boy	600	1750	3000	6000	10,000	15,000
1942, Traveller	400	1000	1700	3500	6500	9000
1950, Pacemaker, sedan	500	1250	2100	4000	7000	10,000
1953, Hornet, sedan	400	1250	2100	4000	7000	10,000
1957, Sedan	450	1250	2100	4000	7000	10,000

Lincoln

	A	B	C	D	E	F
1920, Sedan	$1300	$4500	$7500	$15,000	$25,000	$35,000
1923, Towncar	2000	5000	9000	17,500	31,000	46,000
1929, Town, sedan	1250	4000	6200	12,500	24,000	35,000
1932, Model "KB," sedan	1500	4700	7500	15,000	25,000	37,500
1936, Zephyr	900	3000	5000	10,000	18,000	25,000
1939, Series "K," sedan	1500	5000	8000	15,000	27,000	38,000
1942, Zephyr, sedan	500	1600	2700	5500	9500	14,000
1950, Cosmopolitan, sedan	425	1350	2250	4500	8000	11,000
1956, Capri, sedan	500	1500	2500	5000	9000	13,000
1960, Premier, sedan	500	1000	1700	3500	6500	10,000
1965, Lincoln Continental, sedan	400	800	1500	3000	6000	8500
1967, Lincoln Continental, sedan	400	800	1500	3000	6000	8500
1970, Contenental Mark III	500	1500	2500	5000	8500	12,500
1975, Mark IV	500	1000	1700	3500	6500	9000
1980, Versailles	200	600	900	2000	4000	6000
1983, Towncar	350	700	1200	2400	5000	7000

Mercury

	A	B	C	D	E	F
1940, Sedan	$500	$1000	$1700	$3500	$6500	$9500
1942, Coupe	400	1300	2200	4500	8000	11,000
1946, Sedan	350	800	1500	3000	6000	8500
1951, Mercury, convertible	750	2500	4000	8000	14,000	20,000
1955, Montclaire, sedan	350	900	1500	3000	6000	8500
1957, Monterey, sedan	300	700	1200	2400	4500	6500
1959, Parklane, convertible	900	2500	4000	8500	14,000	22,000
1961, Meteor 600	200	500	900	2000	3700	5500
1962, Comet	200	600	1000	2200	4000	5500
1964, Comet, sedan	200	500	900	2000	3500	5000
1970, Marquis	150	400	750	1500	3000	4500
1974, Cougar	200	600	1000	2300	4000	5700
1975, Bobcat	125	250	700	1200	2600	3700
1977, Marquis	150	300	750	1400	3000	4200
1979, Zephyr	150	300	700	1200	2500	3700
1981, Grand Marquis	200	500	900	2000	3400	5000

Nash

	A	B	C	D	E	F
1918, Sedan	$500	$1000	$1700	$3500	$6750	$10,000
1920, Coupe	400	900	1750	3200	6500	9500
1922, Sedan	350	750	1250	2600	5250	7500
1925, Light 6, sedan	225	500	1000	2400	4500	6000
1928, Standard, sedan	350	750	1200	2400	5000	7500
1930, Single, coupe	350	700	1300	2750	5000	8000
1933, Ambassador, coupe	500	1500	2500	5000	9000	12,500
1935, Lafayette	350	750	1300	2500	5000	7000
1937, Ambassador, sedan	350	750	1200	2300	5000	6500
1940, Ambassador, coupe	350	750	1400	2700	5500	8500
1942, Ambassador 600, sedan	350	700	1200	2400	5000	7000
1946, 600	200	500	900	2000	3500	5000
1949, 600 Custom	200	600	1000	2200	4000	6000
1952, Statesman, sedan	200	600	1000	2300	4000	6000
1955, Rambler	200	600	1000	2200	4000	6000
1957, Rambler	200	600	1000	2000	3700	6000

Oldsmobile

	A	B	C	D	E	F
1905, Touring Car	$1200	$4000	$6500	$13,000	$23,000	$35,000
1912, Defender	1350	4200	7500	14,500	25,000	35,000
1915, Model 42	1100	3250	5000	11,000	18,000	26,000
1917, Model 45	1100	3250	5000	11,000	20,000	27,000
1920, Model 37-B	400	1300	2300	4500	8250	12,500
1923, Model 43-A, sedan	500	1200	1800	4000	7250	10,000
1926, Coupe	350	900	1500	3000	6000	9000
1929, Sedan	400	800	1500	3000	6000	8500
1931, Model F-31	500	1500	2500	5000	8000	12,000
1934, Model F-34	400	1000	1700	3500	6500	9500
1938, Model F-38	450	1000	1600	3400	6000	9000
1940, Series 70	400	1000	1600	3500	6500	9000
1942, Station Wagon	1000	3000	5500	12,000	20,000	30,000
1946, Special Series, convertible	800	2500	4000	8500	15,000	21,000
1949, Futuramic 76, sedan	200	600	1000	2000	4000	6000
1953, Classic, convertible	1000	3500	6000	12,000	20,000	30,000
1956, Series 98, sedan	400	1300	2200	4500	7500	10,000
1959, Series 88, sedan	400	750	1300	2500	5000	8000
1961, Dynamic 88	300	700	1000	2200	4200	6000
1963, Jetfire	350	1000	1600	3300	6000	9000
1965, Cutlass	350	800	1200	2500	5000	8000
1967, Vista Cruiser	200	600	1000	2000	3700	5500
1969, Delta 88	350	750	1200	2500	5000	7000
1971, Dleta 98	200	500	900	1800	3600	5000
1973, Cutlass	175	300	700	1200	2700	4000
1976, Omega	150	200	650	1200	2400	3500
1981, Delta 98	200	500	900	2000	3500	5000
1983, Cutlass	150	450	750	1700	3300	5000

Packard, 1931, Model 833, coupe. —Photo courtesy Kruse International.

Packard

	A	B	C	D	E	F
1904, Model "L"	$2500	$7500	$13,500	$26,000	$46,000	$66,000
1912, Model "NE"	1500	4500	7000	15,000	25,000	37,500
1915, Model 5-48	2000	6000	10,500	19,000	32,000	45,000
1921, Single 6	1200	4000	7000	12,000	21,000	35,000
1924, Single 8, sedan	1100	3300	6000	11,000	20,000	30,000
1928, Standard, coupe	1100	3000	5000	10,000	17,000	25,000
1931, Model 833, coupe	2000	7000	11,000	23,000	40,000	57,000
1932, Model 900, sedan	1000	3500	6000	11,000	20,000	30,000
1933, Model 10005, sedan	2000	6000	10,000	20,000	40,000	55,000
1935, Series 1204, coupe	2000	7000	11,000	23,000	40,000	57,000
1937, Model 120-C, sedan	1000	3500	6000	12,000	20,000	30,000
1939, Model 1801, convertible	2000	5000	10,000	18,000	31,000	45,000
1942, Series 2001	700	2200	3600	7500	13,000	20,000
1946, Clipper	500	1500	2500	5000	9000	14,000
1949, Super Eight, sedan	1000	2000	4000	7000	13,000	20,000
1953, Patrician	700	2000	3500	7000	12,000	18,000
1956, Caribbean	1200	4000	6000	11,000	18,000	27,000

Pierce-Arrow

	A	B	C	D	E	F
1903, One Cylinder	$1250	$4100	$6750	$12,500	$25,000	$36,000
1906, Great Arrow	3000	8000	13,000	30,000	50,000	70,000
1909, Model 40	2000	6000	10,000	20,000	34,000	50,000
1913, Model 66A	3000	10,000	16,000	30,000	50,000	75,000
1919, Model 48-B-5	2500	8000	13,000	27,000	44,000	62,000
1923, Model 38, sedan	1200	4000	6500	13,000	24,000	35,000
1926, Model 33, touring car	2000	7000	12,000	23,000	39,000	54,000
1929, Model 126	3000	9000	15,000	30,000	47,000	67,000
1933, Model 1236	1700	5000	9000	18,000	30,000	45,000
1936, Salon 12	2000	5000	9000	18,000	30,000	42,000
1938, Pierce-Arrow 8	1500	4000	7000	15,000	25,000	40,000

Plymouth

	A	B	C	D	E	F
1928, Model "Q," sedan	$350	$800	$1500	$3000	$6000	$8500
1933, PC, coupe	400	1000	1600	3300	6000	9000
1937, Roadking	300	700	1200	2500	4500	6500
1940, P9 Roadking	300	700	1200	2300	4500	7000
1946, P15 Deluxe, sedan	225	600	1000	2200	4000	5700
1949, Deluxe	300	800	1200	2500	5000	8000
1952, Cambridge	300	700	1300	2500	5000	7500
1955, Plaza	200	700	1200	2500	4500	6200
1959, Suburban	225	500	900	2000	3700	5500
1966, Valiant	225	400	800	1500	3000	4500
1971, Regent Wagon	175	300	700	1300	2700	4000
1974, Fury	175	250	700	1200	3000	4000
1976, Volare	175	300	750	1500	3000	4000
1978, Arrow	175	300	700	1200	2500	3750
1981, Reliant	175	300	700	1300	2600	3800

Pontiac

	A	B	C	D	E	F
1926, Model 6-27	$400	$1000	$1550	$3100	$6250	$9500
1932, Model 302, sedan	400	1300	2200	4300	7500	11,000
1936, Silver Streak, sedan	400	750	1250	2500	5000	7000
1939, Special Series, coupe	400	1000	1600	3200	6000	9000
1941, Torpedo	350	800	1400	2600	5500	8000
1949, Chieftain	300	700	1200	2400	4800	7000
1953, Chieftain	400	900	1500	2500	5000	8000
1957, Chieftain	300	700	1200	2500	5000	7000
1960, Safari	200	700	1100	2300	4500	6500
1963, Catalina	300	700	1000	2300	4000	6500
1966, GTO	500	1500	3000	5000	10,000	15,000
1968, Tempest	300	700	1000	2000	3700	6000
1972, Bonneville	200	500	800	1700	3200	4800
1975, LeMans	100	200	700	1200	2400	3500
1978, Sunbird	100	200	600	1100	2200	3000
1980, Phoenix	150	300	700	1200	2700	4000
1984, Parisienne	150	450	800	1800	3300	5000

Studebaker

	A	B	C	D	E	F
1905, Model 9502	$1000	$3000	$5000	$10,000	$18,500	$27,500
1914, Model 1 SC	900	2700	4500	9000	16,000	23,000
1923, Model EK, coupe	525	1200	2100	4250	7500	11,000
1927, Commander, coupe	525	1150	1850	3500	7500	11,000
1930, Dictator, sedan	500	1000	1700	3500	6500	11,000
1933, Commander, coupe	600	2000	3000	6000	11,000	16,000
1936, President 8, sedan	400	1300	2200	4300	7500	12,000
1939, Model "G," sedan	350	750	1200	2400	5000	7300
1942, Commander Skyway	500	1500	2500	5000	9000	13,000
1947, Champion, sedan	200	600	1000	2300	4400	6500
1951, Champion Deluxe	300	650	1200	2500	4500	6500
1956, Champion	150	400	750	1750	3350	4750
1959, Lark Regal	200	600	900	200	3500	5500
1965, Daytona	200	500	900	2000	3750	5600

Aviation

Aviation memorabilia ranges from the era of early flight—in balloons, bi-planes and airships—through the period of early scheduled commercial transcontinental Clipper flight and World War II combat flight, to the present day of commercial jets and space exploration. As with other commercial enterprises, those offering service to the public distinguished their particular operations by the type and design of objects used in passenger service, such as dining china and silver, in-flight giveaways and flight badges and uniforms. These items, together with passenger timetables, promotional photographs of aircraft, early calendars, airport-related objects (e.g., ashstands with metal aircraft figures, restaurant and earlier souvenir china), and crash fragments are highly collectible. Our consultants for this area are Christopher Wolfe and Scott Townsend of Townsend, Wolfe & Company; they are listed in the back of this book.

Left to right: Pilot Wings, Continental Airlines, gold, 1990, $20; Stewardess' Jacket Wings, "PAA Stewardess," single wing, gold, 1945, $85.

	LOW	AVG.	HIGH
Ashtray, Lufthansa, 1 cigarette well, twice side mkd. in blue w/ yellow logo, 3" top dia, 1.5" deep	$8	$10	$12
Ashtray, Pan American, 3 cigarette wells, white glass, side mkd. "PAN AM" 3 times around outside, 4.375" top dia, 1.375" h	18	22	25
Beverage Glass, National Airlines, Sun King side logo	10	14	18
Blanket, TWA passenger service, 1960s	25	30	40
Calendar, TWA, monthly photos, w/ wartime route suspensions, 1943	30	40	50
Cap, junior flight captain, TWA, c1965	15	20	25
Casserole Dish, Piedmont Airlines, back mkd. in china mold, white/ivory	4	7	10
Cigar Box, La Guardia Airport, cedar w/ silver printing, 8" x 5.25" x 2"	65	70	75
Coaster, Delta Airlines, multicolor printed metal, c1960	4	5	6
Coffee Cup, American Airlines "airlite," side mkd. w/ logo and random star pattern in blue, Syracuse, late 1940s/early 1950s, 5 oz.	40	45	55
Coffee Cup, Braniff, china, ftd., square handle, broad black stripe, back stamped, 4" h, 2" top dia	18	20	22
Coffee Cup, Branif, plastic, ftd., square handle, broad black stripe, back stamped, 4" h, 2" top dia	10	12	14
Coffee Cup and Saucer, Newark Airport profile w/ DC-3, 1944	55	75	85
Coffee Cup and Saucer, United Airlines, silver logo on white china, c1970	25	35	45
Coffee Mug, Northeast Airlines "Yellowbird"	15	25	35
Coffeepot, TWA, silver plate, large size, side mkd. logo, c1960	55	75	100

	LOW	AVG.	HIGH
Cordial Glass, United Airlines, stemmed, side logo, c1960	10	15	20
Creamer, Western Airlines, individual size	8	10	15
Cup and Saucer, TWA "Royal Ambassador," solid red stripe w/ gold crest	10	15	20
Demitasse Cup and Saucer, Army Air Corps, wing logo side mark on cup, top mark on saucer, Syracuse	25	30	35
Demitasse Cup and Saucer, Pan Am, PAA/wing side logo	100	125	150
Dinner Plate, President Eisenhower, on front: "DDE" w/ colored flowers, gold; reverse includes; "The Presidential Plane/Columbine/ May 1956," Syracuse	375	425	500
Food Warmer, American Airlines, silver plate w/ wood handle, c1950	40	55	65
Glassware, Chicago & Southern Air Lines, side mkd. w/ name and airplane in green enamel, 8 oz., 4.75" h	25	30	35
Glassware, Eastern Air Lines, "Fly Eastern's New Silver Falcon/ World's Most Advanced Twin Engine Airliner" and "complements of Eddie Rickenbacker" on back, red, white, and blue enamel, Libbey, 9 oz., 4.75" h	20	23	26
Juice Cup, United Airlines, light blue plastic, side logo, 1935–1960s	4	8	12
Knife, dinner, American Airlines "Flagship," c1935	20	25	35
Letter Opener, souvenir of airship "Akron," Duralum, late 1920s	70	85	100
Miniature Liquor Bottle, North Central Airlines, full and w/ tax stamp, c1968	20	25	30
Miniature Liquor Bottle Series, KLM, Dutch buildings, w/ blue detailing, unopened and w/ tax stamp, Delft, 1970s, price each	30	40	50
Model, travel agent's, TWA Constellation, metal, c1953	1200	1500	2000
Plate, "Cal Aero Academy," name at top is part of a stylized plane, red, white, blue, and black on beige china, Tepco, late 1940s/early 1950s, 10"	35	40	42
Plate, oval, Eastern Airlines, white w/ silver pinstripe, 9.375" l, 6.5" w	10	14	16
Playing Cards, Piedmont Airlines, 1984	4	6	10
Playing Cards, TWA Collector Series, 1966	6	10	14
Playing Cards, TWA Stratoliner, c1940	100	150	175
Postcard, "Graf Zeppelin," unused, 1936	20	30	45
Salad Dish, Delta Airlines, white w/ red and blue side logo, ABCO	3	5	7
Service Plate, Air America (C.I.A.), platinum logo, Noritake, c1970s, 10.525" dia	100	150	175
Service Plate, National Aviation Club, top logo, legend on reverse, 10.525" dia	25	35	45
Shot Glass, Southern Airways, 10th year anniversary	40	50	60
Souvenir Mug, Lufthansa, side mkd.	10	15	18
Souvenir Plate, O'Hare Airport, pictures terminal and plane, pierced side border, 1950s	35	38	40
Teapot, Northwest Airlines, silver plate	55	70	90
Timetable, American Airlines, c1950	12	16	20
Timetable, Continental Airlines, c1935	35	40	50
Timetable, Eastern Airlines, 1948	10	15	20
Timetable, Pan American Airways, 1937	25	35	45
Timetable, TWA, c1946	12	17	20

Bicycles

Bicycles fall into four categories. Running machines, known as hobby-horses, the precursor to the bicycle, were introduced in 1817 and do not have pedals. The addition of cranks and pedals to the front driving wheel in the early 1860s created the first bicycle, generally known as the velocipede or boneshaker. Enlarging the front driving wheel for greater speed created the high wheel bicycle (c. 1870–1892). The rear wheel size was reduced to save weight and facilitate mounting the machine. As these bicycles were quite dangerous to ride, safer versions called high wheel safeties were developed. High wheel tricycles fall into this category and became quite popular in the 1880s. Finally, the bicycle with chain drive to the rear wheel was introduced in 1885, and began entering the market around 1888. These were called, quite simply, safeties. The addition of pneumatic tires in the early 1890s led to the "golden age" of the bicycle. In the 1920s, bicycles began assuming a motorized look, with tanks and balloon tires. In the 1930s they became streamlined. Balloon-tire bicycles are known as Classic bicycles.

As with automobiles, prices for bicycles vary widely depending on model, year and condition. This is particularly true with balloon-tire bicycles. Therefore, the prices below only represent a general average, though in each case values represent machines that are complete with original parts. Girls' models usually fetch a lower price than boys' bicycles, being that men are usually doing the buying! Also note that the following listing is in chronological order, according to the year each type of bicycle was introduced.

High Wheel Bicycle, c1879.

	LOW	AVG.	HIGH
Running Machine (Hobby-Horse), 1818 and later	$7000	$15,000	$25,000
Velocipede (Boneshaker), c1869	2500	5000	10,000
Velocipede Tricycle, c1869	6000	9000	12,000
Child's Velocipede Tricycle, c1869–75	1000	1500	1800
Child's Velocipede Horse Tricycle, c1869	1500	2000	3000
High Wheel Bicycle, c1879	3500	5500	6500
High Wheel Bicycle, c1883–91	2500	4000	5000
High Wheel Safety, c1880–90; Star	6000	7500	9000
High Wheel Safety, c1880–90; Eagle, Facile, Kangaroo, Xtraordinary, etc.	8500	12,000	14,000
Child's High Wheeler, c1885	1800	2500	3500
High Wheel Tricycle, c1885	8000	14,000	16,000
Child's High Wheeler Tricycle, c1885	4500	5500	6500
Tandem/Sociable Adult Tricycle, c1885	8000	14,000	16,000

	LOW	AVG.	HIGH
Solid Tire Safety, often w/ spring forks, c1888–92	4000	5500	11,500
Pneumatic Safety, standard model, c1896	250	550	750
Pneumatic Safety, unusual model, c1896	250	550	750
Pneumatic Safety, tandem, c1896	1200	1800	2400
Chainless Bicycle, c1900	800	1200	1600
Safety, c1910	150	300	450

Balloon-Tire Bicycles (Classic), after 1920

Bowden Spacelander	$4000	$6000	$8000
Character Bikes: Donald Duck, Hopalong Cassidy, etc.	1500	2500	4000
Schwinn Aerocycle, Elgin Bluebird, Roadmaster	6000	8000	10,000
Schwinn Black Phantom	800	2000	3500
Schwinn Stinng Ray	100	350	850
Silver King	500	1500	3000

Above: 1936 Silver King, $1700 at auction.

Left: 1950 Western Flyer, $666 at auction. —Photo courtesy Collectors Auction Services.

Railroad Memorabilia

Before airplanes and the interstate highway system, railroads crisscrossed the United States. The building of the transcontinental railroad in the post-Civil War era ignited the growth of heavy industry; with the establishment of regular shipping routes for agricultural and industrial products, mail and passenger service, and uniform time zones, the United States was on its way toward becoming the nation as we know it today.

Collectors of railroad memorabilia may concentrate on lines that once ran through their hometowns or region. This fosters regional differences of what people collect and how much they pay for items. Other collectors concentrate on a topic, or type of item, regardless of region. The following prices are for items in excellent condition.

Beware of items with no identifying marks or provenance. Some railroads used stock china patterns, with or without custom top or back marks. If special markings are documented to a railroad, authentic pieces are most often required to have these markings. Some railroad china patterns have been reproduced, but not all are clearly and permanently labeled as such. "Fantasy pieces" are china patterns never made for any railroad but which are produced with actual railroad logos and colors. These are often produced in smaller, less common shapes, such as butter pats, teapots, and mustard pots. Be particularly wary of overglaze decoration, as the manufacturers of originals ordinarily applied all but metallic coloring under the glaze. If the glaze over an important part of a piece is more yellowed than the glaze overall, it could indicate applied fraudulent additions.

Fake glass signs purportedly used in railroad stations recently appeared on the market, as well as expertly manufactured, fraudulent badges. Very small rubber stamps with a railroad logo, which may or may not be authentic, have been offered for sale, and could of course have been illegitimately used. Finally, beware of items with interchangeable parts. Lanterns, in particular, have appeared as marriages of fraudulent intent.

Our consultants for this area are Christopher Wolfe and Scott Townsend of Townsend, Wolfe & company; they are listed in the back of this book.

Badge, Penn Central RR Police Sergeant, Ohio jurisdiction, lacquered brass, 1969–76, $40–$50.

	LOW	AVG.	HIGH
Badge, conductor's hat badge, New York Central	$30	$40	$50
Badge, conductor's cap badge, Missouri Pacific RR, copper color	125	150	160
Badge, Penn Central RR Police	40	45	50
Badge, Philadelphia & Reading RR Railway Police, round w/ cut-out star	50	65	80
Badge, porter's hat badge, Illinois Central	105	125	135
Blanket, Pullman, full size, top mkd. "Pullman" and "S-20" in center, wool	85	100	125

Above: Mug, New York Central, brown on cream ground, stamp mark, Shenango, $30.

Left: Dinner Napkin, Chessie logo, paper, blue on white, 1960, 4" x 8.5" folded size, $10.

	LOW	AVG.	HIGH
Bowl, grapefruit, Alaska RR, logo Mt. McKinley, Shenango, 6.5" dia	210	260	300
Bread Tray, Pere Marquette, silver plate, oval, side and back mkd., Wallace, 8.5" l	135	160	180
Brochure, Colorado Midland RR, 12 panels w/ map, 1897	90	100	110
Bud Vase, Great Northern, silver plate, side and back mkd., International Silver, 1948, 6.75" h	160	200	225
Butter Pat, Atlantic Coast Line, "Flora of the South," back mkd., 3.5"	85	100	110
Butter Pat, Boston & Albany, silver plate, back mkd., Reed & Barton, 3.875" dia	45	55	65
Butter Pat, Pullman, Indian Tree pattern, single center flower, top mkd. "Pullman," 3.375" dia	95	105	115
Calendar, Great Northern, Glacier National Park, 1932	25	35	45
Calendar, Pennsylvania RR, "Dynamic Progress," complete pad, 1955	65	80	90
Celery Tray, Erie RR, Susquehana pattern, top and back mkd., 10" l	125	150	170
Cereal Bowl, Amtrak, National pattern, no marking, Mayer, 6.5" dia	10	12	15
Champagne Goblet, Chicago, Milwaukee, St. Paul & Pacific, side logo, 3.525" h	55	65	80
Chocolate Pot, Atchison, Topeka & Santa Fe, California Poppy pattern, no back mark	90	120	140
Chocolate Pot, Atchison, Topeka & Santa Fe, California Poppy pattern, Santa Fe back mark	250	325	375
Coffee Cup and Saucer, Canadian National, side and back mkd., Syracuse	25	40	50
Coffee Cup and Saucer, Union Pacific RR, Challenger pattern, Syracuse	70	85	95
Coffeepot, Chicago, Minneapolis & St. Paul, silver plate, back mkd., International Silver, 1 pint, c1910	175	210	230
Cup and Saucer, Pennsylvania Railroad, Mountain Laurel pattern, no back stamp, Shenango, 6 oz. cup	25	30	35
Demitasse Cup and Saucer, Baltimore & Ohio, blue Centenary pattern, Lamberton	70	90	115

	LOW	AVG.	HIGH
Dinner Plate, C&O, Chessie pattern, Syracuse, 9.875" dia	180	210	250
Dinner Plate, Pullman, Calumet pattern, name in black w/ pinstripes, OP Co. 9.75"	150	175	210
Divided Plate, Fred harvey's orange "FH" monogram in circle at top, Southwest pattern, 3 sections, Liberty, 10.5" dia	120	140	180
Egg Cup, double, Missouri Pacific, Eagle pattern, side logo, Syracuse	75	85	100
Fingerbowl, Pennsylvania RR, silver plate, pierced sides, side and back mkd., International Silver	125	150	165
Fingerbowl w/ Attached Liner, Long Island Rail Raod, silver plate, backstamped, International Silver, 1928	150	175	200
Fork, dinner, Grand Trunk, Westfield pattern, top mkd.	24	30	36
Fork, Gulf, Mobile & Ohio, Broadway pattern top mkd.	20	25	30
Glassware, Pennsylvania Railroad, pair of roly poly glasses, side mkd. in red and white enamel, 4 oz., 2.25" h, 2.5" top dia	15	25	35
High Ball Glass, Long Island Railroad, "Dashing Commuter" side mark, 14 oz.	20	25	35
Ladle, cream, New York Central, Century pattern, back mkd.	20	23	27
Lantern, Chicago, Cleveland, Cincinnati & St. Louis, Handlan clear cast globe	80	90	100
Luggage Rack, Pullman, brass, no stamp, c1910s–20s, 41" l, 9.5" h	165	185	220
Medal, B&O, "One Hundred Years/Safety Strength Speed" w/ locomotive and mythological figure on obverse, B&O's "Tom Thumb" on reverse, bronze, 2.75" dia	65	70	75
Menu, dinner, Great Northern, 1932	15	20	25
Oiler, New York Central, long spout, emb. mark	20	30	40
Pass, Canadian Northern, 1904	30	35	40
Pass, Central RR of New Jersey, 1892	45	50	55
Pass, Kansas City, Ft. Scott & Memphis RR, 1900	30	35	40
Pass, Lehigh Valley RR, ornate, 1889	50	55	60
Pass, New York, Chicago & St. Louis, 1927	7	10	15
Pass, Rio Grande Southern RR, 1944	10	12	15
Pass Wabash RR, 1894	20	25	30
Plate, B&O, Centenary pattern, deep blue pictorial design covering most of plate, backstamped, Scammel Lamberton, 8.375" dia	65	68	75
Plate, Chicago, Milwaukee, St. Paul & Pacific, Traveler pattern, oval, pink w/ flying geese w/ black detailing, backstamped, Syracuse, 8" l	45	60	75
Plate, Southern Pacific, Prairie Mountain Wild Flowers pattern, multicolroed flowers in groups around rim, backstamped w/ flower names and railroad name, Syracuse, 7.5" dia	50	55	65
Plate, Union Pacific, "Winged Streamliner," top and back mkd., Syracuse, 6.5" dia	25	35	40
Platter, Lehigh Valley Traction Co., Liberty Bell logo, oval, 13.5" l	500	650	775
Platter, Pullman, Indian Tree pattern w/ center design, Buffalo, 8.25" l	75	85	100
Playing Cards, Florida East Coast, diesel through orange grove, boxed	25	30	35
Salt and Pepper Shakers, Cleveland Terminal souvenirs, white metal, w/ medallions attached, c1950s	25	28	30
Sauce Dish, B&O, Capitol pattern, oval, top mkd. w/ Capitol dome in gold and gold stripe, Shenango, 6.25" l, 4.25" w	55	60	65
Service Plate, Missouri Pacific, center diesel w/ state capitals on border, back mkd. Syracuse, 1949–61	245	270	325
Soup Plate, New York Central, Vanderbilt pattern, gold pinstripe, green and orange geometric border, back mkd., Buffalo, 9.25" dia	85	100	115
Spoon, bouillon, Union Pacific, Westfield pattern, International Silver	20	24	27
Spoon, grapefruit, Southern RR, Century pattern, International Silver	21	24	30

	LOW	AVG.	HIGH
Spoon, iced tea, Erie RR, Grecian pattern, top mkd., International Silver	23	28	33
Stock Certificate, Colorado Midland, preferred stock, 1898	55	65	75
Stock Certificate, Western Maryland RR, 1917	16	23	28
Sugar Bowl, cov., Chicago & Eastern Illinois, silver plate, Reed & Barton, 1946, 8 oz.	150	185	215
Sugar Tongs, Atlantic Coast Line, Cromwell pattern, side mkd., International Silver	85	951	110
Tablecloth, California Zephyr, name spelled in center, cotton, 43" x 52"	35	40	50
Teapot, Amtrak, National pattern, Hall	10	15	20
Teapot, Michigan Central, silver plate, back mkd., Reed & Barton, c1917, 7 oz	195	225	265
Thermos, Pullman, silver-colored, side mkd., 9" h	50	75	85
Timetable, Ann Arbor RR and SS lines, w/ fold-out map, 1923	60	65	70
Timetable, Central New England RR, broadside, 1915, 16" x 23"	50	55	60
Timetable, Nashville, Chattanooga & St. Louis, ornate, 34 pages, 1914	35	40	50
Timetable, Reading RR, Philadelphia-Atlantic city, broadside, 1913, 22" x 14"	40	60	75
Timetable, Southern Pacific, Sunset Route, w/ map, 20 pages, 1891	60	65	70
Timetable, Wabash RR, Winter 1905	20	25	30
Tip Tray, Canadian Intercolonial Railway, litho w/ moose logo, 5.5" dia	225	260	275
Tureen, cov., B&O, individual size, silver plate, backstamped, Reed & Barton, 7.5" l	165	175	185
Tureen, cov., w/ attached liner, Chicago, Cincinnati, Chicago & St. Louis, silver plate, back mkd., Reed & Barton, c1910, 1 pint	235	265	285
Vest, Pullman, blue wool, all large and small brass buttons intact	45	50	55
Water Glass, Union Pacific, white frosted band, 4.25" h	12	15	20

Watches

Fine watches contain a varying number of jewels, usually synthetic ruby which is second in hardness only to diamond, within the movement mechanism to reduce friction and wear. They improve the accuracy of the watch and generally increase its value.

We abbreviate "jewel" as "j" (e.g., 17j means 17 jewels). American pocket watch movements are described in standard sizes (abbreviated as "s" in this book), ranging from popular sizes including 16s (1.7"), 12s (1.566"), 10s (1.5"), 0s (1.166") and 000s (1.1").

For purposes of simplicity we have given three value levels. Low: rough, serviceable, but needs repair or restoration. These watches are priced as needing a minimum of $100 in parts or repair. You must decide whether the cost to repair outweighs any possible profit. Average: normal to extended wear depending on age. Minor cost for parts or repair. High: in fine condition with minimum of wear, needing only possible cosmetic touch-ups.

Numerous fakes are circulating on the open market including 24j examples of Illinois and Rockford watches as well as original Rolex and Piaget movements in bogus cases. As always, it pays to do your homework prior to any purchase. If it looks too good to be true, it probably is.

Our consultant for this section is Brett O'Connor, G.G., of Christie's Jewelry Dept. For further information, see *Complete Guide to Watches, Eighteenth Edition* by Cooksey Shugart, Tom Engle and Richard E. Gilbert, Cooksey Shugart Publications, Cleveland, TN, 1998.

Pocket Watches

	LOW	AVG.	HIGH
American, 18s, Wm. Ellory, M#1857	$50	$100	$150
American, 18s, Paragon, 15j	100	150	200
American, 16s, Premier, 9-17j	50	75	100
American, 16s, Riverside, 15-19j	50	100	150
American, 16s, Riverside Maximus, 16j	400	500	600
American, 16s, Royal, 15-17j	50	100	150
American, 0s, Royal, 16j	75	100	125
American, 0s, Seaside, 7-15j	100	150	200
Ansonia Sesqui-Centennial	250	300	350
Aurora Watch Co., 18s, 7-11j	100	150	200
Aurora Watch Co., 18s, 15j	200	300	400
California Watch Co., 18s, 11-15j	1000	1500	2000
Dudley Watch Co., Masons, 14s	3000	4000	5000
Dudley Watch Co., Masons, 12s	1500	2000	2500
Elgin, 18s, Father Time, 21j	150	175	200
Elgin, 18s, Overland, 17j	100	150	200
E.H. Flint, 18s, 4-7j, 18k	4000	5000	6000
Fredonia, 18s, 7-16j	150	250	350
Jonas G. Hall, 18s, 15j	1500	2000	2500
Hamilton, 18s, 15-21j	150	250	350
Hamilton, 16s, 16-17j	200	300	400
Hamilton, 12s, 17-19j	50	100	150
Hampden Watch Co., 16s, 7-15j	50	100	150
Hampden Watch Co., 000s, 7-15j	100	150	200
E. Howard & Co., N size (18), I-VIII, 15j	1000	2000	3000
E. Howard Watch Co., 12s series 6-8	200	300	400
Illinois Watch Co., 18s, Allegheny, 11j	`50	100	150
Illinois Watch Co., 18s, Bunn, 15j	500	750	100
Illinois Watch Co., 18s, Bunn Special, 21j	150	200	250
Illinois Watch Co., 18s, Columbia, 11j	75	125	175

Left to right: E. Howard & Co., #301286, subsidiary seconds dial, chased and engraved case, 18k yellow gold, $920 at auction; English, goldtone floral engraved dial, subsidiary seconds dial, key wind, 9k rose gold, $259 at auction. —Photos courtesy Skinner, Inc., Boston, MA.

	LOW	AVG.	HIGH
Illinois Watch Co., 18s, Currier, 11j	75	125	175
Illinois Watch Co., 18s, Montgomery Ward, 17j	150	175	200
Illinois Watch Co., 18s, The National, 11j	75	100	125
Illinois Watch Co., 18s, Time King, 17-21j	150	225	300
Illinois Watch Co., 16s, Ariston, 11-15j	50	85	125
Illinois Watch Co., 16s, Ariston, 17-19j	150	225	300
Illinois Watch Co., 16s, Ariston, 23j	500	750	1000
Illinois Watch Co., 16s, Ben Franklin, 17-21j	300	450	600
Illinois Watch Co., 16s, Burlington, 15-17j	75	125	175
Illinois Watch Co., 16s, Dispatcher, 19j	50	100	150
Illinois Watch Co., 16s, Getty model, 17-21j	100	150	200
Illinois Watch Co., 16s, Lakeshore, 17j	100	150	200
Illinois Watch Co., 16s, Railroad King, 17j	200	250	300
Illinois Watch Co., 16s, Sangamo, 21j	150	200	250
Illinois Watch Co., 16s, Santa Fe Special, 17j	150	200	250
Illinois Watch Co., 14s, 7-21j	50	100	150
Illinois Watch Co., 4s, 7-15j	50	85	125
Illinois Watch Co., 0s, 201-204, 11-17j	75	115	150
Ingersoll, Dollar type, Buck	50	85	125
Ingersoll, Dollar type, Climax	40	60	75
Ingersoll, Dollar type, Colby	20	30	40
Ingersoll, Dollar type, Crown	20	30	40
Ingersoll, Dollar type, Defiance	30	45	60
Ingersoll, Dollar type, Ensign	30	40	50
Ingersoll, Dollar type, Escort	20	30	40
Ingersoll, Dollar type, Gotham	15	25	35
Ingersoll, Dollar type, Kelton	15	20	25
Ingersoll, Dollar type, Major	10	155	20
Ingersoll, Dollar type, Patrol	40	50	60

Left to right: Patek, Philippe & Co., 19s, 21j, 14k gold, c1910, $2070 at auction; E. Howard & Co., R.N. Lockwood case, "N" size, 14k yellow gold, $600–$800. —Photos courtesy Skinner, Inc., Boston, MA.

	LOW	AVG.	HIGH
Ingersoll, Dollar type, Radiolite	30	40	50
Ingersoll, Dollar type, Saturday Post	150	200	250
Ingersoll, Dollar type, Solar	25	40	50
Ingersoll, Dollar type, Trump	40	50	60
Ingersoll, Dollar type, Uncle Sam	40	50	60
Ingersoll, Dollar type, Winner	20	30	40
E. Ingraham Co., Autocrat	15	20	25
E. Ingraham Co., Baltimore	10	15	20
E. Ingraham Co., Century	25	30	35
E. Ingraham Co., Clipper	20	30	40
E. Ingraham Co., Cub	15	20	25
E. Ingraham Co., Dot	15	20	25
E. Ingraham Co., Laddie	20	30	40
E. Ingraham Co., Overland	30	40	50
E. Ingraham Co., Pilot	30	45	60
E. Ingraham Co., Rex	15	20	25
E. Ingraham Co., St. Regis	15	20	25
E. Ingraham Co., Sturdy	10	15	20
E. Ingraham Co., Top Notch	40	50	60
E. Ingraham Co., Trail Blazer	150	200	250
E. Ingraham Co., Viceroy	20	30	40
E. Ingraham Co., Zep	150	200	250
Kelly Watch Co., 16s, aluminum	50	100	150
Keystone Standard Watch Co., 18s, 7-15j	75	125	175
Knickerbocker Watch Co., 6-18s	50	75	100
Lancaster, 18s, Comet	150	175	200
Lancaster, Ben Franklin	250	300	350
Lancaster, Malvern	50	75	100
Lancaster, Radnor	100	150	200

Left to right: Hunter Case, porcelain dial, engraved case, key, 18k yellow gold, crack to dial, $345 at auction; Gruen, #96516, chased and engraved case depicting a griffin, 14k yellow gold, $920 at auction. —Photos courtesy Skinner, Inc., Boston, MA.

	LOW	AVG.	HIGH
Lancaster, Sidney	100	125	150
Melrose Watch Co., 18s, 7-15j	250	350	450
New England Watch Co., Alden	40	50	60
New England Watch Co., Columbian	20	25	30
New England Watch Co., Putnam	70	85	100
New England Watch Co., Tuxedo	20	30	40
Otay Watch Co., 15j	1200	1600	2000
Peoria Watch Co., 18s, 15j	200	300	400
Philadelphia Watch Co., 18s, 11j	150	200	250
Rockford, 18s, Dome model	150	200	250
Rockford, 18s, Ramsey, 11-15j	100	125	150
Rockford, 18s, 7j	50	100	150
Rockford, 18s, 13j	100	150	200
Rockford, 18s, #835	100	150	200
Rockford, 18s, #950	2000	3000	4000
Rockford, 16s, Peerless	75	100	125
Rockford, 16s, Prince of Wales	300	450	600
Rockford, 16s, 7j	100	150	200
Rockford, 16s, Winnebago	150	225	300
Rockford, 16s, #102	150	175	200
San Jose Watch Co., 16s	1500	2000	2500
Seth Thomas, 18s, Century	50	100	150
Seth Thomas, 18s, Eagle Series	50	100	150
Seth Thomas, 18s, Edgemere	50	100	150
Seth Thomas, 18s, Keywind	200	300	400
Seth Thomas, 18s, Maidenlane, 17-24j	1000	1500	2000
Seth Thomas, 18s, Henry Molineux	500	1000	1500
Seth Thomas, 18s, #33-#201	50	100	150
Seth Thomas, 18s, #245	1000	1250	1500
Seth Thomas, 18s, #281-382	150	200	250
Seth Thomas, 16s, Centennial	50	75	100
Seth Thomas, 16s, Locust	50	100	150
Seth Thomas, 16s, Republic	50	65	75

Left to right: Tiffany & Co., International Watch Co. movement, #102444, 17j, 14k yellow gold, $500–$700; M.T. Stauffer, chrono., minute register, 2 subsidiary dials, 15j, 14k yellow gold, sgd. "Schwob Freres," $500–$700. —Photos courtesy Skinner, Inc., Boston, MA.

	LOW	AVG.	HIGH
Seth Thomas, 16s, #25-336	50	100	150
Seth Thomas, 12s, Republic	50	60	70
Seth Thomas, 12s, #25-328	50	75	100
Seth Thomas, 0s, 7-17j	50	100	150
South Bend, 18s, 15j	100	150	200
South Bend, 18s, Studebaker	200	300	400
South Bend, 18s, #309	75	100	125
South Bend, 18s, #333	100	125	150
South Bend, 18s, #344	300	400	500
South Bend, 18s, #355	1000	1250	1500
South Bend, 16s, 7-9j	50	100	150
South Bend, 16s, #207	50	100	150
South Bend, 16s, #211	50	100	150
South Bend, 16s, #280	100	125	150
South Bend, 16s, #290	200	250	300
South Bend, 16s, #294	300	400	500
South Bend, 12s, Chesterfield	50	100	150
South Bend, 12s, #407	30	45	60
South Bend, 12s, #419	150	175	200
Trenton Watch Co., 18s, "M" #3-5	50	100	150
Trenton Watch Co., 16s, "M" #1-3	50	85	125
Trenton Watch Co., 12s, Fortuna	50	60	70
Trenton Watch Co., 6s, 7-15j	40	50	60
Trenton Watch Co., 0s, 7-15j	50	60	70
U.S. Watch Co., 18s, Wm. Alexander	200	300	400
U.S. Watch Co., 18s, F. Atherton, 15-17j	250	350	450
U.S. Watch Co., 18s, F. Atherton, 19j	600	900	1200
U.S. Watch Co., 18s, S.M. Beard	250	350	450
U.S. Watch Co., 18s, G. Channing	250	350	450
U.S. Watch Co., 18s, J.W. Deacon	200	300	400
U.S. Watch Co., 18s, Fellows	400	500	600
U.S. Watch Co., 18s, Asa Fuller	200	300	400
U.S. Watch Co., 18s, North Star	300	400	500

Left to right: Chas. E. Jacot, hunter case, nickel jeweled movement, monogrammed case, 18k gold, $800–$1000; J. Alfred Jurgensen, Copenhagen, #785, hunter case, jeweled movement, elaborate monogramming, 18k gold, $3002 at auction. —Photos courtesy Skinner, Inc., Boston, MA.

	LOW	AVG.	HIGH
U.S. Watch Co., 18s, Penna. RR	2500	3000	3500
U.S. Watch Co., 18s, H. Randel	250	350	450
U.S. Watch Co., 18s, Edwin Rollo	200	300	400
U.S. Watch Co., 18s, Rural NY	200	300	400
U.S. Watch Co., 18s, F. Stratton	250	350	450
U.S. Watch Co., 18s, I.H. Wright	200	300	400
U.S. Watch Co., 16s, 15-19j	500	750	1000
U.S. Watch Co., 14s, 7-15j	250	350	450
U.S. Watch Co., 10s, 11-15j	100	200	300
Waterbury Watch Co., Series B-E	200	250	300
Waterbury Watch Co., Series G-H	200	375	350
Waterbury Watch Co., Series I-Z	75	115	150
Waterbury Watch Co., Oxford	50	75	100
Westclox, Boy Proof	40	50	60
Westclox, Bull's-eye	15	20	25
Westclox, Country Gentleman	40	50	60
Westclox, Dax	10	15	20
Westclox, Everbrite	20	25	30
Westclox, Explorer	200	250	300
Westclox, Ideal	30	40	50
Westclox, Mark IV	40	50	60
Westclox, Maxim	30	40	50
Westclox, Mustang	40	50	60
Westclox, Smile	25	40	50

Wrist Watches

	LOW	AVG.	HIGH
American Waltham, 15j, protective grill, c1907	$1300	$1450	$1600
American Waltham, 17j, Cromwell	80	105	130
American Waltham, 17j, curvex	200	450	700
American Waltham, 17j, Oberlin	80	105	130
American Waltham, 17j, Stanhope	75	100	125
American Waltham, 17j, w/ hackset, stainless steel	50	65	75
American Waltham, 21j, Albright	100	125	150
American Waltham, 21j, Sheraton	125	150	175
Angelus, 17j, 14k, 1943	400	500	600
Angelus, 17j, 18k, c1943	750	950	1150
Angelus, 17j, gold-filled, c1943	150	200	250
Angelus, 27j, quarter repeater, stainless steel	2700	2950	3200
Aramis, 15j, self-winding, stainless steel, c1933	600	750	900
Arbu, 17j, double chronog., stainless steel	200	300	400
Arbu, 17j, triple date, moon phase, 18k	800	1000	1200
Aristo, 17j, chronog., stainless steel	100	165	225
ARSA, 15-17j, moon phase, 18k	900	1050	1200
ARSA, 15-17j, moon phase, stainless steel	300	350	400
Asprey, 15j, duo-dial, 18k	1500	1850	2200
Asprey, 16-17j, 9k	200	350	500
Audemars Piguet, 17-36j, modern	1200	2600	4000
Autorist, 15j, lug action	400	900	1400
Ball W. Co., 25j	375	440	500
Baume and Mercier, 17-18j, 14k or stainless steel	400	550	700
Baume and Mercier, 17-18j, 18k, triple chronog.	1200	1900	2600
Benrus, 15j, 14k or gold-filled, c1950	100	175	250
Benrus, 15j, date, stainless steel, c1948	50	60	70
Benrus, 15-18j, mystery diamond dial, 18k	500	600	700
Breguet, 17j, silver dial, Finn model, 18k	1200	1400	1600
Breguet, 21j, skeletonized, 18k, c&b	7000	7500	8000
Breitling, 17j, chronog., Chronomat, 18k, gold-filled	300	400	500
Breitling, 17j, chronog., Chronomat, 18k, stainless steel	250	350	450
Breitling, 17j, chronog., Navitimer, 18k	3000	3300	3600
Breitling, 17j, chronog., Navitimer, 18k, stainless steel	500	600	700
Bueche-Girod, 17j	600	700	800
Bulova, Accutron "Spaceview," 14k	400	550	700
Bulova, Accutron "Spaceview," 18k	600	700	800
Bulova, Accutron "Spaceview," stainless steel	100	175	250
Bulova, 17j, duo-dial, stainless steel, c1935	300	350	400
Bulova, 17j, fancy bezel, 14k or gold-filled	100	200	300
Bulova, diamond dial, rect., late 1930/early 1940s	200	275	350
Cartier 21, quartz, gold-plated, large	175	500	800
Cartier American Tank, mechanical, large, 18k	1700	2800	4200
Cartier Cougar, stainless steel, 32mm	350	650	1200
Cartier Diablo, quartz, 18k, large	1000	2000	3200
Cartier Tank, gold-plated, large	200	350	550
Cartier Tank, quartz, 18k, large	800	1500	2000
Chevrolet, 6j, in form of car radiator, silver, c1927	400	500	600
Clebar, 17j, chronog., stainless steel	75	85	100
Concord, 17j, 14k	125	150	175
Cortebort, 15-17j, gold-filled or stainless steel	50	75	100
Cortebort, 17j, "sport," triple date, moon phase, 18k	1000	1200	1400

Left to right: Cartier, Vermeil Tank, $288; Rolex, Oyster Perpetual Day-Date, 18k yellow gold, $690; Piaget, diamond frame, 2.24 cts., 18k yellow gold, $2530; Movado, Moonphase Triple Calendar, 14k yellow gold, $2875; Longines, Lindbergh Hour Angle, 18k yellow gold, $2000–$3000; Rolex, Cellini, 18k yellow gold, $1610. —Photos courtesy Skinner, Inc., Boston, MA.

	LOW	AVG.	HIGH
Corum, 17j, in form of Rolls Royce car radiator, 18k	1800	2000	2200
Corum, 17-21j, 18k	400	650	900
Croton, 17j, diamond bezel, 14k	700	800	900
Cyma, 17j, 14k	175	215	250
Cyma, 17j, 18k	200	250	300
Cyma, 17j, stainless steel	65	75	85
Daynite, 7j, 8-day movement, stainless steel	250	325	400
Dome, 25j, tirple dates, 18k	500	600	700
Doxa, 17j, center sec., w/ or wo/ chronog., 14k or stainless steel	100	200	300
Doxa, 17j, chronog., triple date, 18k	500	600	700
E. Gubelin, 19j, 18k	400	500	600
E. Gubelin, 25j, triple date	3500	4500	5500
Ebel, 17j, slide open to wind, silver	200	250	300
Ebel, 17j-18j, chronog.	400	525	650
Ebel, 21j, chronog., perpetual calendar, 18k	7000	8000	9000
Eberhard, 17j, chronog., stainless steel	400	500	600
Eberhard, 17j, tele-tachymeter, 18k, c1930	2600	3100	3600
Eberhard, 18j, split sec., chronog., 3 reg., 18k	7000	9000	11,000
Electra W. Co., 17j, chronog., silver	500	600	700
Elgin, 7j, gold-filled	60	130	200
Elgin, 7j, "Official Boy Scout Model," stainless steel	50	65	85
Elgin, 7j, stainless steel	50	65	80
Elgin, 15j, "Official Boy Scout Model," stainless steel	100	140	175
Elgin, 15j, round dial, aux. sec., silver	150	185	225
Elgin, 15-17j, rect., gold-filled	100	120	140
Elgin, 17j, rect., 14k	200	275	350
Elgin, 17-21j, Lord, stepped case, fancy bezel, gold-filled	100	120	140
Enicar, 17j, stainless steel	30	40	50
Eska, 17j, enamel dial, 18k	3100	3600	4100

Left to right: Universal, Geneve, Uni-Compax, 2-dial, chronog., 18k yellow gold, $978; Bulgari, quartz movement, 18k yellow gold, $1800–$2200; Rolex, Oyster Perpetual, 14k yellow gold, $805; Swiss movement, domed bezel, 18k yellow gold, $920; Rolex, Oyster Perpetual, stainless steel, $1035. —Photos courtesy Skinner, Inc., Boston, MA.

	LOW	AVG.	HIGH
Evans, 17j, chronog., 2 reg., 18k, c1940	300	400	500
Gallet, 15j, atutowind, stainless steel	50	75	100
Gallet, 17j	200	300	400
Geneve, 15j, dual dial	300	350	400
Girard-Perragaux, 39j	300	350	400
Glycine, 17-18j	100	150	200
Grouen, 17j, autowind	300	400	500
Grouen, 17j, curvex	200	300	400
Grouen, 17j, double dial	500	600	700
Hamilton, Altair	500	600	700
Hamilton, Bolton	100	150	200
Hamilton, Brock	100	150	200
Hamilton, Dunkirk	300	400	500
Hamilton, Essex	100	150	200
Hamilton, Lee	100	150	200
Hamilton, Midas	300	350	400
Hamilton, Otis, reversible	1200	1500	1800
Hamilton, Perry	100	125	150
Hamilton, Vantage	150	200	250
Hamilton, Ventura	1000	1500	2000
Hamilton, Victor II	150	200	250
Hamilton, Winthrop	200	250	300
Hamilton, Yorktown	150	175	200
Hampton, 15j	75	125	175
Helbros, 17j	200	250	300
Hydepark, 17j, flip top	450	550	650
Illinois, 17j, Aviator	150	200	250
Illinois, Chieftain	300	400	500
Illinois, Console	300	400	500

Top to bottom: Chalet, Retro, 14k gold, $850–$950; Movado, #2038, dual dial, platinum, $690. —Photos courtesy Skinner, Inc., Boston, MA.

	LOW	AVG.	HIGH
Illinois, Jolly Roger	200	250	300
Illinois, Major	200	250	300
Illinois, Picadilly	500	600	700
Illinois, Pilot	150	200	250
Illinois, Speedway	200	250	300
Ingraham, 7j, Wristfit	5	10	15
Ingersoll, grill cover	50	60	70
Ingersoll, Radiolite dial	10	20	30
International, 17j, 18k	850	1050	1250
International, 36j, Da Vinci	6500	8000	9500
Kurth, 17j, Certina	30	40	50
Le Coultre, 17j	400	500	600
Le Coultre, 17j, Astronomic	1800	2300	2800
Le Coultre, 17j, Futurematic	700	1000	1200
Le Coultre, 17j, Reverso, 18k	6500	8000	9500
Le Coultre, 17j, Reverso, stainless steel	2000	2500	3000
Lemania, 17j, chronog., 18k	600	750	900
Lemania, 17j, stainless steel	50	60	70
Longines, 17j, chronog.	500	1000	1500
Longines, 17j, diamond dial, 14k	400	500	600
Longines, 17j, flared	400	600	800
Longines, 17j, Lindberg, nickel	6000	7500	9000
Meylan, 27j, chronog.	800	1000	1200
Mido, 15j, car radiator	2000	2500	3000
Mido, 17j, chronog.	500	600	700
Mido, 17j, multifort	150	200	250
Minerva, 17j, autowind	70	85	100
Minerva, 17j, chronog., stainless steel	200	300	400
Monarch, 7j	50	75	100
Movado, 15j	400	500	600
Movado, 15j, Jump Hour, manual wind, 14k yellow gold, 1930s	3200	3800	4200
Movado, 17j, polypan, elongated	1500	2000	2500
Movado, Calendarmeto (center opening)	600	750	900
National, 17j	50	100	150
New Haven, 7j	10	15	20
Omega, 17j	300	400	500

	LOW	AVG.	HIGH
Omega, 17j, Flightmaster	6000	7000	8000
Omega, 17j, Seamaster, 14k	1500	2000	2500
Omega, 17j, Seamster, stainless steel	800	1000	1200
Orvin, 17j	70	80	90
P. Ditisheim, 17j, "Solvil," diamond dial, platinum	700	1150	1600
Patek Philippe, Ellipse, 18j, 18k yellow gold, c1969	1500	1700	1900
Patek Philippe, rect., platinum, 18j, c1920	2500	2800	3200
Patek Philippe, round, fancy lugs, 18j, c1954	6500	7200	8000
Piaget, 18j	400	550	700
Piaget, 18j, $20 gold piece	2200	2500	2800
Piaget, round stepped bezel automatic, 18k yellow gold, c1960s	350	500	750
Record, 17j, 4-dial chronog.	5000	6000	7000
Roamer, 17-23j	30	45	60
Rolex, 17j, Daytona, 18k	10,000	12,500	15,000
Rolex, 17j, Daytona, stainless steel	5000	5500	6000
Rolex, 17j, Prince, dual dial, 18k	6200	8000	9500
Rolex, 17j, Prince, dual dial, silver	3000	4000	5000
Rolex, 17j, Prince, dual dial, stainless steel	2000	3000	4000
Rolex, 26j, GMT-master	4000	5000	6000
Rolex, 26j, Milgauss, stainless	400	500	600
Rolex, 26j, Presidential, diamond dial	5000	7000	9000
Rolex, 26j, Submariner, 18k	6000	7500	9000
Rolex, 26j, Submariner, stainless steel	1000	1500	2000
Rolex Air King, oyster, perpetual calendar, stainless steel	600	1100	1400
Rolex Thunderbird, oyster, perpetual calendar, date juste, 18k	8000	8500	9000
Rolex Yachtmaster, 18k	8300	10,500	13,000
Tiffany, 15-21j	1000	1250	1500
Tiffany, 26j, repeater, automaton	8000	10,000	12,000
U. Nardin, 17j, chronog.	2500	3500	4500
U. Nardin, 29j, Astrolabium	6500	8000	9500
Universal, 17j, chronog., 18k	2000	3000	4000
Universal, 17j, chronog., stainless steel	400	600	800
Vacheron, 17j, triple date	5000	7000	9000
Vacheron, 18j, 18k	2200	3200	4200
Vacheron & Constantin Bombe, 16j, 14k yellow gold	2200	2600	3000
Zenith, 17j, chronog., 18k	1000	1250	1500
Zenith, 36j, stainless steel	500	600	700

Swatch Watches

Swatch™ watches appeared out of nowhere (Switzerland) to become an instant hot collectible. Their brightly colored flashy plastic dials are seen on chic and trendy (and other) wrists around the world. Original bands are a must! Although occasionally showing up at auction, they're more often found on the Internet.

	LOW	AVG.	HIGH
Adam, Peter Gabriel Musics II, 1996	$50	$60	$70
Anne Libowitz, 1996	60	70	80
Aquachrono in a Can, USA, 1994	150	200	250
Artist Set, 6 watches, Fall 95, 1995	350	400	450
Artist Set, 6 watches, Fall 96, 1996	350	400	450
Artist Set, 6 watches, Spring 96, 1996	350	400	450
Artist Set, 6 watches, Spring 97, 1997	350	400	450
Beach Virgin	50	60	80
Big Blue, Aquachrono, 1994	125	150	175
Boggie Mood	50	60	80
Bottone, 1991	140	170	200
Breakdance, Gents, 1985	600	800	1000
C'era Una Volta, Boston, 1993	150	200	250
Cancun	20	30	40
Chandelier, 1992	150	200	250
Cinema 100, set of 3 watches, 1995	450	500	550
Coco Noir, 1989	150	200	250
Color Wheel	30	40	50
Coloured Love	110	150	190
Cool Fred	20	30	40
Crash!!	50	65	80
Crazy Eight, Japan, 1993	150	200	250
Crush, sgd. M. Giacon, 1991	125	150	175
Crystal Surprise, 1994	100	140	180
Despiste, 1995	80	95	110
Elements, 3 watches, Japan, 1997	225	250	275
En Vauge	40	55	70
Encantador, 1990	225	250	275
Engineer	70	90	110
Europe in Concert, w/ CD, 1993	125	150	175
Fandango, Italy, 1994	225	250	275
First	60	85	110
Fitz N' Zip, sgd. by Kenny Scharf, 1995	60	70	80
Floral Story, Japan, 1994	150	200	250
For Your Heart Only, boxed	60	85	110
Golden Jelly, 1991	190	250	310
Gulp!!, sgd. M. Giacon, 1991	90	100	110
Hocus Pocus, 1991	320	420	530
Hot Stuff, 1995	50	60	70
Jungle Tangle, France, limited edition of 65, 1997	125	150	175
Lady and the Mirror, Japan, 1997	125	150	175
Leaf, 1994	80	100	120
Light Tree, sgd. M. Brown, 1996	190	250	310
London, GBR pkg., 1994	100	125	150
Looka, 1996	100	120	140
Lots of Dots, 1992	110	140	180

Neospeed, Flumotions, 1988, $290.

	LOW	AVG.	HIGH
Magic Spell, 1995	150	175	200
Masquerade, USA, 1993	40	50	60
Meooow	60	80	100
Michael Johnson, Goldmedal chrono, 1996	70	80	90
Mille Pattes, K. Haring, 1985	1000	1200	1400
Monster Time, sgd. by Kenny Scharf	50	60	80
Olympia Set, 9 watches, 1994	325	375	425
Olympia Set, 9 watches, 1995	375	425	475
Olympic Press Gala, w/ 5 color loops, 1996	90	110	130
Olympic Venue, w/ 12 oclor loops, 1996	70	80	90
Oracolo, 1050 made, 1996	150	200	250
Oracolo, Halloween, 1996	40	50	60
Oracolo, Italy, 715 made, 1996	350	400	450
Orb, 1993	225	250	275
Passport, Space People and Enjoy It, 1992	100	125	150
Photoshooting	60	80	100
Pizza Box, USA, 1994	100	120	140
Point of View, 1995	100	125	150
Pompadour, 1988	350	400	450
Putti, cigar box, 1992	80	110	140
Ravenna	70	95	120
Roi Soleil, 1993	200	250	300
Romeo and Juliet, 1996	40	50	60
Sailor's Joy, Germany, 1993	80	100	120
Scribble, 1993	80	100	120
Sea-Monsta, 1995	100	125	150
Serpent, K. Haring, 1985	1000	1200	1400
Sex-Teaze	70	95	120
Sir Limelight	230	300	380
Smila, 1996	150	200	250
Soupe De Poisson, 1993	60	70	80
Spark Vessel	50	60	80
St. Moritz, Switzerland pkg., 1994	90	110	130
Stalefish, sgd. J. Vigon, 1991	100	125	150
Step by Step Kit-Presentation Box, 1994	225	250	275
Time Cut Chronometer, 1500 made 1996	500	600	700
Time to Reflect, 1995	120	150	180
Top Class	20	30	40
Tresor Magique, 1993	1750	2000	2250
Unlimited, 1995	80	90	100
Veruschka, special pkg.	70	90	110
Weightless, sgd. R. McGuire, 1996	100	125	150
Windwatch, blue, Lucerne Auction, 1993	225	250	275

Weathervanes

The most valued weathervanes are those handmade of sheet copper before 1850. These are quite rare. In the nineteenth and early twentieth centuries factory workers made weathervanes of copper hammered in iron molds. Important makers include Cushing and White of Waltham, Massachusetts, and the J. Howard Company of East Bridgewater, Massachusetts. Many reproductions have been made from original molds.

Values listed below are for fine examples at auction (A), semiantique reproductions (S–R) and retail (R).

Left: Locomotive, sheet metal, 19th C, $7700 at auction. —Photo courtesy James D. Julia.

Above, left to right: Horse and Sulky, molded gilt copper, attributed to J.W. Fiske & Co., 19th C, 45.25" l, $28,750 at auction; Cow, molded gilt copper, attributed to Harris and Co., Boston, late 19th C, 33" l, $23,000 at auction. —Photos courtesy Skinner, Inc., Boston, MA.

	A	S–R	R
Black-Hawk Horse, Cushing, full-bodied, orig. gilding, 33" l	$7000	—	$13,000
Black-Hawk Horse, gold leaf, 25" l	1300	—	3000
Cockerel, primitive sheet iron, 20" l	700	—	—
Cow, cast iron and copper, full-bodied, 27" l	3000	$1000	8000
Flying Eagle, A.L. Jewell, full-bodied, orig. gold leaf, 19" l	4250	—	9000
Hambeltonian Horse, W.A. Snow and Co., copper, 26" l	1000	550	2900
Horse, copper, full-bodied, late 19th C, 26" l	1000	550	2700
Horse, J. Howard, copper, gilt, mid 19th C, 20" l	6000	1500	16,000
Horse, Rochester Ironworks, cast iron, mid 19th C, 36" w	9000	1500	24,000
Horse and Rider, red painted sheet iron, 19th C, 52" l	1000	450	2700
Indian Archer, Berks Co., PA, painted sheet iron, c1880, 25" h	850	450	2300
Jockey and Running Horse, copper, full-bodied, 29" l	3250	1750	8000
Jockey and Running Horse, J.W. Fiske, #515, copper, 30" l	3600	1700	9000
Jumping Horse, 28" l	1600	—	5000
Mountain Boy, copper and gilt, mounted on stand, 38" h	1000	550	2700

	A	S–R	R
Peafowl, copper, full-bodied, old patina, 29" h	4250	1000	11,400
Peafowl, gilt copper, full-bodied, 18" h	1250	650	3300
Pig, L.W. Cushing, gilt copper, full-bodied, c1883, 36" w	16,500	1500	44,00
Prancing Horse, A.L. Jewell, gold leaf, 40" l	11,000	—	20,000
Quill-Form, copper, 36" l	1700	935	4500
Quill Pen, J.W. Fiske, c1880, 54" l	4000	—	9500
Rooster, American, sheet copper, 25" h	1800	—	5500
Rooster, carved wood, gray paint, 12" h	750	400	2000
Rooster, cast iron, 23" h	1500	825	4250
Rooster, J. Howard, c1890, 24" l	4000	—	9500
Rooster, J. Howard, zinc cast, full-bodied, 27" l	5400	—	12,000
Rooster, molded copper, full-bodied, 22" h	1500	800	4000
Rooster, molded copper, painted highlights, full-bodied, 23" h	1500	800	4000
Rooster, primitve w/ flat tail, 27" l	1900	—	5500
Running Horse, American, copper, full-bodied, orig. green patina, 31" l	2800	—	7000
Running Horse, American, copper w/ zinc head, full-bodied, 42" l	3750	—	10,000
Running Horse, gilt copper, green patina, 31" l	2900	1600	7500
Running Horse, in verde antique, 44" l	2100		6000
Running Horse, J. Harris and Son, copper, full-bodied, 28" l	850	470	2200
Sailing Ship, Washburn, c1920, 36" l	1800		4800
Schooner, metal sails and rigging, painted, c1910, 35" l	400	220	1000
Setter, Washburn, gilded, full-bodied, 33" l	7000		13,000
Steer, molded copper and cast iron, 29" l	1300	715	3500

Assortment of Weather Vanes. —Photo courtesy Skinner, Inc., Boston, MA.

Woodenware

While many types of wood items are highly sought-after collectibles, this section lists miscellaneous wooden items including tools and kitchen utensils. Wooden utensils are most commonly made of maple. Other woods used include cedar, pine, hickory, ash and oak. Prices vary depending on item and type of wood.

	LOW	AVG.	HIGH
Apple Peeler, wooden gears, c1880, 8" l	$350	$450	$550
Apple Peeler, wooden w/ iron gears, c1900, 7" x 14"	60	75	90
Bandbox, oval, plain, 7" l	160	200	250
Bandbox, oval, painted, 9" l	250	500	750
Barrel, staved, 4 wooden bands, 14" x 25"	100	150	200
Black Powder Shovel, 19th C, 35" l	210	290	370
Blanket Clothespins, early 19th C, 6" h	30	50	60
Boot Jack, plain, c1780	30	40	50
Bowl, burl, 6" dia	400	500	600
Broom, oak splint, 19th C	160	220	280
Bucket, cov., mincemeat, concave, 11" dia	200	215	230
Bucket, sap, 9.5" dia	310	345	380
Bucket, cov., sugar, loop handles, flat handle, c1890, 5" dia	380	405	430
Bucket, tin cov., walnut, "S" shaped legs, 17" dia	350	370	390
Bucket Carrier, 40" l	100	140	180
Butcher's Block, hardwood	200	400	600
Butter Churn, 18th C, 19.5" h	400	550	700
Butter Churn, cylinder type, white cedar, 1 gallon	160	175	190
Butter Chrun, staved, dasher, 4 gallon	480	565	650
Butter Churn, windmill paddles, side turn handle, 15" h	450	500	550
Candlestick, walnut, c1760, 6" dia	600	700	800
Canteen, 18th C, 11.5" dia	240	330	420
Card Case, Tunbridge ware, c1790	300	400	500
Clothes Wringer, crank, handle, and roller	40	50	60
Coaster, oak, English, c1810, 4" dia	250	300	350
Coffee Grinder, box type, 19th C	170	210	250
Coffee Grinder, carved handle	130	170	210
Coffee Grinder, lap type, cherry, handled	220	240	260
Coffee Grinder, lap type, cherry box, brass fittings, crank	200	245	290
Coffee Mill, hand crank, iron blade, storage box	130	150	170
Colander, circ., c1700s	600	700	800
Cookie Board, 4 different molded designs, 6" l	50	70	90
Cookie Board, walnut, carved geometric design, 9" l	45	70	105
Cookie Board, walnut, carved pattern, 8" l	140	165	190
Croupier's Paddle, 36" l	90	120	150
Cutting Board, chestnut, c1800, 19" l	120	170	210
Grain Shovel	570	640	710
Juicer, hinged, wood and ceramic, 9" l	60	80	100
Juicer, on stand, 14" x 9"	240	270	300
Juicer, short handle, ridged press, 10" l	50	60	70
Keg, staved construction, 19th C, 9.75" h, 6.25" dia	160	220	280
Knitting Needles, ball finials, 18th C, 13.5" l	280	390	490
Mangle, chip carved, 18th C	720	990	1260
Masher, ash, 18th C, 14.5" l	130	180	230
Mortar and Pestle, mahogany, 18th C, 7.5" h mortar	280	390	490
Mortar and Pestle, miniature, 19th C, 1.75" h	120	170	210

	LOW	AVG.	HIGH
Noodle Board, round w/ paddle handle, 24" l	180	205	230
Noodle Roller, maple, perforated crank, c1840, 21" l	10	115	220
Nutcracker, c1750, 10" l	400	460	520
Nutcracker, bear's head, c1880, 9" l	140	175	210
Nutcracker, wood w/ iron presses, c1650, 5.5" l	730	805	880
Pantry Box, oval, finger tongue construction, 7" l	280	390	490
Pantry Box, round, carved handle, 7.5" dia	180	250	320
Pastry Wheel, late 18th C, 9.5" l	120	170	210
Pipe Case, for clay pipe, c1750, 10.25" l	240	330	410
Porringer, carved from single piece of wood, 18th C, 4.5" dia	160	220	270
Queen Bee Box, 19th C, 4.5" h	150	210	260
Rum Keg, 18th C, 5" h	120	170	210
Scoop, burlwood, 18th C, 10" l	200	280	350
Spice Box, sliding panel top, dovetailed, orig. paint, c1800, 11" x 8.25"	380	530	670
Spice Box, urn form, c1800, 6.5" h	160	220	270
Tape Loom, dated 1776, 27" l	680	940	1190
Toddy Stick, early 19th C	40	70	100
Toddy Stick, pestle-style, hand carved, turned wood	20	30	40
Wash Bowl, chestnut, c1790	280	350	420
Whisk Broom, Fuller Brush Company, 8" l	90	115	140
Wool Comb, carved handle, 13" l	30	50	70
Writing Board, tombstone-form, 18th C, 21" l	220	310	390
Yarn Winder, box-type, spindle suspended on spike over box, 18" h	70	90	110

Left: Candle Drying Rack, PA, $375 at auction.

Right, top to bottom: Chip-Carved Butter Molds, $175–$200 each; Burl Bowl, hand-carved, probably Iroquois, 18th C, $2200 at auction.

—Photos courtesy Aston Macek.

Zippo Lighters

The first Zippos appeared in 1932. One of the most active areas in this market is the "Vietnam Zippos." American G.I.s used these lighters during the Vietnam War. Although made in Bradford, Connecticut, G.I.s commissioned a variety of decorations ranging from the patriotic to the absurd. In some cases they decorated the lighters themselves. There are two types of reproductions in this area: old, undecorated lighters sometimes acquire a new decoration; other reproductions are entirely new, made in Asia.

For further information on collectible lighters see *Collecting Cigarette Lighters, Volumes I and II* by Neil S. Wood, L–W Book Sales, Gas City, IN.

Sinclair Gasoline adv., debossed metal, 2.25" h, $105 at auction. —Photo courtesy Collectors Auction Services.

	LOW	HIGH
Advertisement, applied, 1960	$30	$40
Advertisement, applied, 1990	25	35
Advertisement, stamped, 1948	30	40
Advertisement, stamped, 1962	25	35
Ambassador Scotch, slim, 1968	30	40
American Mission, Athens, Greece, 1963	60	90
Benj C. Betner Co., 1950	70	100
Black Leather-Wrapped, 1950	225	350
Bush-Gorbi, 1990	80	125
Cain's Quality Foods, 1950	70	100
Chicago Heights Steel Co., 1958	70	100
Crawford Furniture, 1958	60	90
Green Leather-Wrapped, 1950	275	400
Linen Supply Roamer, 1952	70	100
Lumbermen's Wholesale Service, 1958	70	100
Lynn Welding and Tool Service, 1958	70	100
Masonic Emblem, applied, 1985	18	25
Nat'l Electric Products, 1950	80	125
Omsteel Products, 1958	70	100
Op Art, enamel decoration, 1993	12	18
Owen Zippo, 1958	70	100
Ozan Lumber Co., 1958	70	100
Rotary Int'l, 1944	135	200
Silver, impressed, 1935	200	270
Silver, plain, 1952	20	25
Silver Tartan, diamonds and mgr., 1977	15	20
Texas Dental Ass'n., 1952	70	100
Textured Metal, 1993	20	25
The George W. King Printing Co., Baltimore, 1958	60	90
U.S. Marines Medallion, applied, 1954	50	70

Auction Houses

The following auctioneers and auction companies generously supply Rinker Enterprises, Inc., with copies of their auction lists, press releases, catalogs and illustrations, and prices realized. Those heading the list also supplied numerous photographs for this edition of *The Official Price Guide to Antiques & Collectibles.*

AUCTION HOUSES & PHOTO CREDITS

Aston Macek
154 Market Street
Pittston, PA 18640
(717) 654-3090

Auction Team Köln, Breker – Die Spezialisten
Postfach 50 11 19
D-50971 Köln, Germany
Tel: 0221/38 70 49; Fax: 0221/37 48 78
Jane Herz, International Rep US
(941) 925-0385; Fax: (941) 925-0487

Bill Bertoia Auctions
1881 Spring Road
Vineland, NJ 08361
(609) 692-1881; Fax: (609) 692-8697
e mail: bba@ccnj.net
web: http://bba.ccnj.net.com

Butterfield, Butterfield & Dunning's
755 Church Road
Elgin, IL 60123
(847) 741-3483; Fax: (847) 741-3589
web: http://www.butterfields.com

Collectors Auction Services
RR 2, Box 431 Oakwood Road
Oil City, PA 16301
(814) 677-6070; Fax: (814) 677-6166

William Doyle Galleries, Inc.
175 East 87th Street
New York, NY 10128
(212) 427-2730; Fax: (212) 369-0892
web: www.doylegalleries.com

Fink's Off the Wall Auction
108 East 7th Street
Lansdale, PA 19446
(215) 855-9732; Fax: (215) 855-6325
web: http://www/finksauctions.com
e mail: lansbeer@finksauction.com

Garth's Auction, Inc.
2690 Stratford Road, PO Box 369
Delaware, OH 43015
(614) 362-4771; Fax: (614) 363-1064

Glass–Works Auctions
PO Box 180
East Greenville, PA 18041
(215) 679-5849; Fax: (215) 679-3068
web: http://www.glswrk-auction.com

Gene Harris Antique Auction Center, Inc.
203 South 18th Avenue
Marshalltown, IA 50158
(515) 752-0600; Fax: (515) 753-0226
e mail: ghaac@marshallnet.com

Michael Ivankovich Antiques, Inc.
PO Box 2458
Doylestown, PA 18901
(215) 345-6094; Fax: (215) 345-6692
e mail: wnutting@comcat.com

Jackson's Auctioneers & Appraisers
2229 Lincoln Street
Cedar Falls, IA 50613
(319) 277-2256; Fax: (319) 277-1252
web: http://jacksonauction.com

James D. Julia, Inc.
PO Box 830
Fairfield, ME 04937
(207) 453-7125; Fax: (207) 453-2502

Gary Kirsner Auctions
PO Box 8807
Coral Springs, FL 33075
(954) 344-9856; Fax: (954) 344-4421

Kruse International
PO Box 190
Auburn, IN 46706
(800) 968-4444; Fax: (219) 925-5467

Lang's Sporting Collectables, Inc.
31R Turtle Cove
Raymond, ME 04071
(207) 655-4265

Wm Morford
RD 2
Cazenovia, NY 13035
(315) 662-7625; Fax: (315) 662-3570
e mail: morf2bid@aol.com

Ray Morykan Auctions
1368 Spring Valley Road
Bethlehem, PA 18015
(610) 838-6634
e mail: dmorykan@enter.net

Gary Metz's Muddy River Trading Co.
263 Key Lakewood Drive
Moneta, VA 24121
(540) 721-2091; Fax: (540) 721-1782

Past Tyme Pleasures
101 First Street, Suite 404
Los Altos, CA 94022
(510) 484-4488; Fax: (510) 484-2551

Poster Mail Auction Co.
PO Box 133
Waterford, VA 20197
(703) 684-3656; Fax: (540) 882-4765

David Rago Auctions, Inc.
333 North Main Street
Lambertville, NJ 08530
(609) 397-9374; Fax: (609) 397-9377

Skinner, Inc.
Bolton Gallery
357 Main Street
Bolton, MA 01740
(978) 779-6241; Fax: (978) 350-5429
web: www.skinnerinc.com

York Town Auction, Inc.
1625 Haviland Road
York, PA 17404
(717) 751-0211; Fax: (717) 767-7729

AUCTION HOUSES

Action Toys
PO Box 102
Holtsville, NY 11742
(516) 563-9113; Fax: (516) 563-9182

Sanford Alderfer Auction Co., Inc.
501 Fairgrounds Road, PO Box 640
Hatfield, PA 19440
(215) 393-3000
e mail: auction@alderfercompany.com
web: http://www.alderfercompany.com

American Social History and Social Movements
4025 Saline Street
Pittsburgh, PA 15217
(412) 421-5230; Fax: (412) 421-0903

Arthur Auctioneering
RD 2, Box 155
Hughesville, PA 17737
(800) ARTHUR 3

Butterfield & Butterfield
220 San Bruno Avenue
San Francisco, CA 94103
(415) 861-7500; Fax: (415) 861-8951
web: http://www.butterfields.com

Butterfield & Butterfield
7601 Sunset Boulevard
Los Angeles, CA 90046
(213) 850-7500; Fax: (213) 850-5843
web: http://www.butterfields.com

Cards From Grandma's Trunk
The Millards
PO Box 404
Northport, IN 49670
(616) 386-5351

Christie's
502 Park Avenue at 59th Street
New York, NY 10022
(212) 546-1000; Fax: (212) 980-8163
web: http://www.christies.com

Christie's East
219 East 67th Street
New York, NY 10021
(212) 606-0400; Fax: (212) 737-6076
web: http://www.christies.com

Christmas Morning
1806 Royal Lane
Dallas, TX 75229-3126
(972) 506-8362; Fax: (972) 506-7821

Cobb's Doll Auctions
1909 Harrison Road
Johnstown, OH 43031-9539
(740) 964-0444; Fax: (740) 927-7701

Collector's Sales and Service
PO Box 4037
Middletown, RI 02842
(401) 849-5012; Fax: (401) 846-6156
web: www.antiquechina.com
e mail: collectors@antiquechina.com

Copake Auction
Box H, 226 Route 7A
Copake, NY 12516
(518) 329-1142; Fax: (518) 329-3369

Dawson's
128 American Road
Morris Plains, NJ 07950
(973) 984-6900; Fax: (973) 984-6956
web: http://idt.net/-dawson1
e mail: dawson1@idt.net

Dixie Sporting Collectibles
1206 Rama Road
Charlotte, NC 28211
(704) 364-2900; Fax: (704) 364-2322
web: http://www.sportauction.com
e mail: gun1898@aol.com

Dunbars Gallery
76 Haven Street
Milford, MA 01757
(508) 634-8697; Fax: (508) 634-8698
e mail: dunbar2bid@aol.com

Early Auction Co.
Roger and Steve Early
123 Main Street
Milford, OH 45150
(513) 831-4833; Fax: (513) 831-1441

Etude Tajan
37, Rue de Mathurins
75008 Paris, France
Tel: 1-53-30-30-30; Fax: 1-53-30-30-31
web: http://www.tajan.com
e mail: tajan@worldnet.fr

Ken Farmer Auctions & Estates, LLC
105A Harrison Street
Radford, VA 24141
(540) 639-0939; Fax: (540) 639-1759
web: http://kenfarmer.com

Flomaton Antique Auction
277 Old Highway 31
Flomaton, AL 36441

Frank's Antiques
Box 516
Hilliard, FL 32046
(904) 845-2870; Fax: (904) 845-4000

Frasher's Doll Auctions, Inc.
Route 1, Box 142
Oak Grove, MO 64075
(816) 625-3786; Fax: (816) 625-6079

Greenberg Auctions
7566 Main Street
Sykesville, MD 21784
(401) 795-7447

Marc Grobman
94 Paterson Road
Fanwood, NJ 07023-1056
(908) 322-4176
web: mgrobman@worldnet.att.net

Gypsyfoot Enterprises, Inc.
PO Box 5833
Helena, MT 59604
(406) 449-8076; Fax: (406) 443-8514
e mail: gypsyfoot@aol.com

Hakes' Americana and Collectibles
PO Box 1444
York, PA 17405
(717) 848-1333; Fax: (717) 852-0344

Norman C. Heckler & Co.
Bradford Corner Road
Woodstock Valley, CT 06282
(860) 974-1634; Fax: (860) 974-2003

The Holidays Auction
4027 Brooks Hill Road
Brooks, KY 40109
(502) 955-9238; Fax: (502) 957-5027

Horst Auction Center
50 Durlach Road
Ephrata, PA 17522
(717) 859-1331

Charles E. Kirtley
PO Box 2273
Elizabeth City, NC 27906
(919) 335-1262; Fax: (919) 335-4441
e mail: ckirtley@erols.com

Henry Kurtz, Ltd.
163 Amsterdam Avenue, Suite 136
New York, NY 10023
(212) 642-5904; Fax: (212) 874-6018

Los Angeles Modern Auctions
PO Box 462006
Los Angeles, CA 90046
(213) 845-9456; Fax: (213) 845-9601
web: http://www.lamodern.com
e mail: peter@lamodern.com

Howard Lowery
3812 West Magnolia Boulevard
Burbank, CA 91505
(818) 972-9080; Fax: (818) 972-3910

Mad Mike
Michael Lerner
32862 Springside Lane
Solon, OH 44139
(216) 349-3776

Majolica Auctions
Michael G. Strawser
200 North Main, PO Box 332
Wolcottville, IN 46795
(219) 854-2859; Fax: (219) 854-3979

Manion's International Auction House, Inc.
PO Box 12214
Kansas City, KS 66112
(913) 299-6692; Fax: (913) 299-6792
web: www.manions.com
e mail: collecting@manions.com

Ted Maurer, Auctioneer
1003 Brookwood Drive
Pottstown, PA 19464
(610) 323-1573
web: www.maurerail.com

New England Absentee Auctions
16 Sixth Street
Stamford, CT 06905
(203) 975-9055; Fax: (203) 323-6407
e mail: neaauction@aol.com

New England Auction Gallery
Box 2273
West Peabody, MA 01960
(508) 535-3140; Fax: (508) 535-7522
web: http://www.oldtoys.com

Norton Auctioneers of Michigan, Inc.
Pearl at Monroe
Colwater, MI 49036-1967
(517) 279-9063; Fax: (517) 279-9191
e mail: nortonsold@juno.com

Nostalgia Publications, Inc.
21 South Lake Drive
Hackensack, NJ 07601
(201) 488-4536

Richard Opfer Auctioneers, Inc.
1919 Greenspring Drive
Timonium, MD 21093
(410) 252-5035; Fax: (410) 252-5863

Ron Oser Enterprises
PO Box 101
Huntingdon Valley, PA 19006
(215) 947-6575; Fax: (215) 938-7348
web: members.aol.com/ronoserent

Pacific Book Auction Galleries
139 Townsend Street, 4th Floor
San Francisco, CA 94108
(415) 989-2665; Fax: (415) 989-1664
web: www.nbn.com/pba; e mail: pba@slip.net

Pettigrew Auction Co.
1645 South Tejon Street
Colorado Springs, CO 80906
(719) 633-7963; Fax: (719) 633-5035

Phillips Ltd.
406 East 79th Street
New York, NY 10021
(800) 825-2781; Fax: (212) 570-2207
web: http://www.phillips-auctions.com

Postcards International
PO Box 5398
Hamden, CT 06518
(203) 248-6621; Fax: (203) 248-6628
web: csmonline.com/postcardsint/
e mail: postcrdint@aol.com

Provenance
PO Box 3487
Wallington, NJ 07057
(201) 779-8785; Fax: (212) 741-8756

Lloyd Ralston Gallery
109 Glover Avenue
Norwalk, CT 06850
(203) 845-0033; Fax: (203) 845-0366

Red Baron's
6450 Roswell Road
Atlanta, GA 30328
(404) 252-3770; Fax: (404) 257-0268
e mail: rbarons@onramp.net

Remmey Galleries
30 Maple Street
Summit, NJ 07901
(908) 273-5055; Fax: (908) 273-0171
e mail: remmeyauctiongalleries@worldnet.att.net

L. H. Selman Ltd.
761 Chestnut Street
Santa Cruz, CA 95060
(800) 538-0766; Fax: (408) 427-0111
web: http://paperweight.com
e mail: selman@paperweight.com

Slater's Americana
1535 North Tacoma Avenue, Suite 24
Indianapolis, IN 46220
(317) 257-0863; Fax: (317) 254-9167

R. M. Smythe & Co., Inc.
26 Broadway, Suite 271
New York, NY 10004-1701
(800) 622-1880; Fax: (212) 908-4047

Steffen's Historical Militaria
PO Box 280
Newport, KY 41072
(606) 431-4499

Susanin's
Gallery 228 Merchandise Mart
Chicago, IL 60654
(312) 832-9800; Fax: (312) 832-9311
web: http://www.theauction.com

Theriault's
PO Box 151
Annapolis, MD 21404
Fax: (410) 224-2515

Tiques Auction
RRI Box 49B
Old Bridge, J 08857
(732) 721-0221; Fax: (732) 721-0127
web: www.tiques.com
e mail: tiquesauc@aol.com

Tool Shop Auctions
Tony Murland
78 High Street
Needham Market, Suffolk
1P6 8AW England
Tel: 01449 722992; Fax: 01449 722683
web: http://www/toolshop.demon.co.uk
e mail: tony@toolshop.demon.co.uk

Toy Scouts
137 Casterton Avenue
Akron, OH 44303
(330) 836-0668; Fax: (330) 869-8668

James A. Vanek
7031 NE Irving Street
Portland, OR 97213; (503) 257-8009

Victorian Images
PO Box 284
Marlton, NJ 08053
(609) 953-7711; Fax: (609) 953-7768

Tom Witte's Antiques
PO Box 399, Front Street West
Mattawan, MI 49071
(616) 668-4161; Fax: (616) 668-5363

If you would like to be included on this list, write or phone Rinker Enterprises at 5093 Vera Cruz Road, Emmaus, PA 18049; (610) 965-1122.

BOARD OF COLLECTORS

Howard Brenner
106 Woodgate Terrace
Rochester, NY 14625

David Galt
Games and Names
302 West 78th Street
New York, NY 10024
(212) 769-2514

Jim Glaab's Collector's Showcase
78 Genesee Street
Greene, NY 13778
(607) 656-8805

Rebecca Greason
Rebecca of SunnyBook Farm
PO Box 209
Hershey, PA 17033-0209
(717) 533-3039

Jack Herbert
267½ West 11th Street
New York, NY 10014
(212) 989-5175

Marcia Hersey
PO Box 976
Ansonia Station
New York, NY 10023-0976

Henry Kurtz
163 Amsterdam Avenue
Suite 136
New York, NY 10023
(212) 642-5904

Judith Lile Antiques
346 Valleybrook Drive
Lancaster, PA 17601
(717) 569-8175

Gaston and Joan Majeune
Toys in the Attic
167 Phelps Avenue
Englewood, NJ 07631
(201) 568-6745

Matrix Quality Antique Dolls
PO Box 1410
New York, NY 10023
(212) 787-7279

Bill Mugrage
3819 190th Place S.W.
Lynnwood, WA 98036
(425) 774-9849

Brett O'Connor
Christie's Los Angeles
Jewelry Department
360 North Camden Drive
Beverly Hills, CA 90210

Adam G. Perl
Pastimes Antiques
Dewitt Bldg.
Ithaca, NY 14850
(607) 277-3457
aperl@lightlink.com

Sy Schreckinger
PO Box 104
East Rockaway, NY 11518
(516) 536-4154

Steven and Leon Weiss
Gemini Antiques
PO Box 1732
Bridgehampton, NY 11932
(516) 537-4565

Jim and Kaye Whitaker
Eclectic Antiques
PO Box 475
Lynnwood, WA 98046

Christopher Wolfe and Scott Townsend
Townsend, Wolfe & Company
PO Box 158
Coopersburg, PA 18036
(610) 282-4831

INDEX

EDITORIAL STAFF

Rinker Enterprises, Inc.

Harry L. Rinker
President

Dena C. George
Associate Editor

Dana N. Morykan
Senior Editor

Kathy Williamson
Associate Editor

Nancy Butt
Librarian

Virginia Reinbold
Controller

Richard Schmeltzle
Support Staff